138-452 ✓
200-219 ✓
438-452 ✓

ENTERTAINMENT LAW

CASES AND MATERIALS ON FILM, TELEVISION, AND MUSIC

By

Sherri L. Burr
Professor of Law,
University of New Mexico School of Law

William D. Henslee
Associate Professor of Law,
Florida A & M University College of Law

AMERICAN CASEBOOK SERIES®

WEST

Mat #40260929

American Casebook Series and West Group are trademarks
registered in the U.S. Patent and Trademark Office.

© 2004 West, a Thomson business
    610 Opperman Drive
    P.O. Box 64526
    St. Paul, MN 55164–0526
    1–800–328–9352
Printed in the United States of America
ISBN 0–314–15395–0

*TEXT IS PRINTED ON 10% POST
CONSUMER RECYCLED PAPER*

Sherri Burr dedicates this book to her friend Jami, who tirelessly pursues her quest for knowledge about the entertainment industry while fighting a debilitating illness, and her nephew in hopes that his music career will never falter along the lines of cases in this book.

Bill Henslee dedicates this book to Margaret, Heather, and William, Jr. for their love and support.

*

Preface

Film, television, and music are the core entertainment businesses to the majority of entertainment lawyers in Los Angeles, New York, Nashville, and in other cities and towns across the country. This book is divided into three parts and can be used to teach the survey course in Entertainment Law, or separated into a specialty seminar on film, television or music. The sections are roughly parallel in their coverage with modifications made for each specialty area.

Throughout this text, you will find references to copyright law, trademark law, contract law, torts, constitutional law, employment law, labor law, criminal law, family law, property law, business organizations, tax law, bankruptcy law, antitrust law, agency law, immigration law, and professional responsibility. Each section of the book begins with an industry overview.

We hope you enjoy reading and studying this book as much as we took pleasure in researching and writing it.

Editorial Note

In editing the cases and articles, we omitted some footnotes and references to the record without indication. Any remaining footnotes retain their original footnote number. We indicate textual deletions with asterisks.

Citations in the preparatory and note material, as well as some citations in the cases have been slightly altered to conform to the 17th edition of *The Bluebook: A Uniform System of Citation* (2000), with the exceptions of films, which is often italicized in the text as opposed to using large and small capitalization. When referring to scripts and treatments, however, we indicate them in quote marks, such as the treatment "King for a Day."

Sherri Burr wrote and edited chapters 1–6, 9–10, 12–13, 19, and contributed interviews and notes to the reality TV portion of chapter 7 and to the symphony orchestra portion of Chapter 14. William Henslee wrote and edited chapters 8–9, 14–18, 20, and most of chapter 7 including the introductory explanation.

*

Acknowledgements

The process of researching, writing, editing and preparing this book for publication could not have been accomplished without the assistance of numerous friends, colleagues, students, former students, staff, and associates. While it is impossible to identify all of them and still maintain this as a single-volume work, some deserve special recognition.

We would like to thank the following busy industry experts who submitted material or allowed us to interview them: Diane Bloom, Greg Brooker, Harold Brown, Johnnie Cochran, Charles Cohen, Max Evans, Chris Eyre, Stephen Frears, John Frey, Guillermo Figueroa, Walon Green, Bob Guiney, Rex Heinke, Matt Jackson, Carl Mazzacone, Shirley MacLaine, Bertram McCann, Duncan North, Don Ohlmeyer, Michelle Carswell Pritchard, Jim Rogers, Wayne Rosso, Howard Suber, Ted Turner, Marc Vlessing, Fee Waybill, Jessica Weisel, Samuel Wong, and Frank Zuniga.

Sherri Burr would like to thank her colleague Chuck DuMars, former UNM Law School students Ana Andzic-Tomlinson and Willow Parks for their research and analytical skills, and Joseph Blecha of the University of New Mexico Law School for his assistance in transcribing and word processing some of the material found in these pages. She also thanks UNM Law School staff Elodie Collins and Cindy Nee for their photocopying assistance, and the following UNM Law School staff and students for their proof-reading and cite-checking assistance: Paul Bossert, Katie Curry, Catherine Begaye, Shelby Bradley, Eileen Cohen, Janet Cox, Rachel Gudgel, Matthew Ingram, Barbara Jacques, Barbara Lah, Lorraine Lester, Marcos Martinez, Michelle Rigual, Jared Slade, Krista Smith, Sherri Thomas, Ron Wheeler, and Emily Williams.

Bill Henslee would like to thank his research assistants who helped assemble materials for this book. At Florida A&M, he thanks: Terrie L. Tressler, Jamie Roberto, James Brey, Eileen Gongora, Christine E. Sago, Avie Meshbesher Croce. At Pepperdine, he thanks: Wendy Lau, Tambry Bradford, Ann Kim, Rachael Godfrey, Michael Reardon, Eric Griffin, A. Ian Keasler, Dana Glasser, and Jennifer Lewis Kokes. And he sends special thanks to faculty secretaries Doranne Riggio at Florida A&M and Candice Warren at Pepperdine.

Moreover, Burr acknowledges the support of UNM Law School Dean Scarnecchia who announced in August 2003 that Burr had been awarded UNM's Friedman award, in part to recognize her work on this book.

We appreciate the contributions of all these individuals to the book and apologize to anyone we may have inadvertently left out. Any errors you find are ours.

*

Permissions

The following authors, publishers, organizations, and publications have granted permission to reprint copyrighted material:

American Family Physician

> Karl E. Miller, *Children's Behavior Correlates with Television Viewing*, 7, No. 3 AMERICAN FAMILY PHYSICIAN 593–4 (Feb. 1, 2003). Reprinted with Permission from American Family Physician granted in February 2004.

Burr, Sherri

> S. Burr, *A Critical Assessment of Reid's Work for Hire Framework and its Potential Impact on the Market Place for Scholarly Works*, 24 JOHN MARSHALL L. REV. 119 (1990), © 1990 by Sherri Burr.
>
> S. Burr, *An Actresses' View of Lawyers*, Author Interview with Actress Shirley MacLaine, © 2004 by Sherri Burr.
>
> S. Burr, *Classical Music: Striving for 'Undemocratic Oneness'*, Author Interviews with Conductors Guillermo Figueroa and Samuel Wong, © 2004 by Sherri Burr.
>
> S. Burr, *Client Expectations*, Author Interview with Screenwriter Duncan North, © 2004 by Sherri Burr.
>
> S. Burr, *Copyright Issues and Documentary Filmmaking*, Author Interview with Documentary Filmmaker Diane Bloom, © 2003 by Sherri Burr.
>
> S. Burr, *Editing for Reality TV*, Author Interview with Television Editor Craig Serling, © 2003 by Sherri Burr.
>
> S. Burr, *Making Native Films*, Author Interview with Director Chris Eyre, © 2004 by Sherri Burr.
>
> S. Burr, *Picking Representation*, Author Interview with Author/Screenwriter Max Evans, © 2004 by Sherri Burr.
>
> S. Burr, *The Piracy Gap: Protecting Intellectual Property in an Era of Artistic Creativity and Technological Change*, 33 WILLAMETTE L.R. 245, 248–250 (Winter 1997), © 1997 by Sherri Burr.
>
> S. Burr, *Screenwriter Credits*, Author Interview with Screenwriter Greg Brooker, © 2003 by Sherri Burr.
>
> S. Burr, *Television & Societal Effects: An Analysis of Media Images of African-Americans in Historical Context*, 4 J. GENDER, RACE & JUST., 159 (2001), © 2001 by Sherri Burr.

W. Henslee, *Making the Band*, Author Interview with Lou Pearlman, Copyright © 2003 by William Henslee.

Journal of Broadcasting & Electronic Media

Robert D. McIlwraith, *"I'm addicted to television": the personality, imagination, and TV watching patterns of self-identified TV addicts*, 42, No. 3 JOURNAL OF BROADCASTING & ELECTRONIC MEDIA, at 371 (Summer 1998). Reprinted with Permission from the Journal of Broadcasting & Electronic Media granted in February 2004.

Journal of Consumer Affairs

Hae-Kyong Bang and Bonnie B. Reece, *Minorities in Children's Television Commercials: New, Improved, and Stereotyped, American Council on Consumer Interests*, 37, No. 1 JOURNAL OF CONSUMER AFFAIRS 42 (June 22, 2003). Reprinted with Permission from the journal granted in February 2004.

Judge, Shawn K., and the Ohio Journal of Dispute Resolution

Shawn K. Judge, *Giving Credit Where Credit is Due?: The Unusual Use of Arbitration in Determining Screenwriting Credits*, 13 OHIO ST. J. ON DISP. RESOL. 221 (1997). Reprinted with Permission from the author and the journal granted in February 2004.

Los Angeles Times

Claudia Eller & James Bates, *Talent Agents About to Demand Bigger Piece of Pie*, L. A. TIMES, Oct. 31, 2000. Reprinted with Permission from the Los Angles Times granted in February 2004.

Amy Wallace, *Hollywood Agents Lose the Throne; Personal managers are the rising moguls as they greatly expand their roles and some stars shun agencies altogether. Lack of state regulation is seen as big advantage*, L. A. TIMES, Dec. 11, 1998. Reprinted with Permission from the Los Angles Times granted in February 2004.

Patrick Goldstein, *The Big Picture: Another Suitor for Filmmakers*, LOS ANGELES TIMES, Sept. 30, 2003, at Calendar, Part 5, Page 1. Reprinted with Permission from the Los Angeles Times granted in February 2004.

Mazzocone, Carl

Producing Boxing Helena, Copyright © 2004 by Carl Mazzocone.

Monthly Review Foundation

>   Buhle, Paul, *ALTING McCARTHYISM: THE STAMLER CASE IN HISTORY; civil rights case involving professor Jeremiah Stamler*, MONTHLY REVIEW FOUNDATION, INC., No. 5, Vol. 51; Pg. 44, Oct. 1, 1999. Reprinted with Permission from the Monthly Review Foundation granted in February 2004.

New York Times

>   Simon Romero, *Coming Soon to a Screen Near You: New Mexico*, N.Y. TIMES, Jan. 26, 2004, at C1. Reprinted with Permission from the New York Times granted in March 2004.

>   Jim Rendon, *Unions Aim to Share in the Success of Reality TV*, N.Y. TIMES, Jan. 25, 2004, at Business. P. 4. Reprinted with Permission from the New York Times granted in March 2004.

Ted Turner

>   Ted Turner, *Monopoly or Democracy?*, WASHINGTON POST, May 30, 2003. Reprinted with Permission from Mr. Turner granted in February 2004.

Variety

>   John Brodie, *Poaching Piques Percenters; Agents get ugly over A-list defectors,* VARIETY, Oct. 24, 1994—Oct. 30, 1994, at 1. Reprinted with Permission from Variety, Inc. granted in February 2004.

>   Dan Cox, *Legal Eagles Invade 10 Percenter's Nest*, VARIETY, Apr. 4–10, 1994. Reprinted with Permission from Variety, Inc. granted in February 2004.

>   Peter Bart, *Living on Credit,* VARIETY, INSIDE MOVIES (Sept. 19, 1994—Sept. 25, 1994). Reprinted with Permission from Variety, Inc. granted in February 2004.

VNU Business Media

>   Bill Dunlap, *Coping with Budget Blues: Film Offices Prove Their Worth*, SHOOT MAGAZINE, January 24, 2003. Reprinted with Permission from VNU Business Media granted in March 2004.

Washington Post

>   Sharon Waxman, *Location, Location; Hollywood Loses Films to Cheaper Climes*, WASHINGTON POST, June 25, 1999. Reprinted

with Permission from the Washington Post granted in March 2004.

Williams, Gary, and the Journal of Gender, Race and Justice

Gary Williams, *"Don't Try to Adjust Your Television—I'm Black": Ruminations on the Recurrent Controversy over the Whiteness of TV*, 4 J. GENDER RACE & JUST. 99 (2001). Reprinted with Permission of the author and the journal granted in February 2004.

*

Summary of Contents

*

Table of Contents

Table of Cases

The principal cases are in bold type. Cases cited or discussed in the text are roman type. References are to pages. Cases cited in principal cases and within other quoted materials are not included.

ENTERTAINMENT LAW

CASES AND MATERIALS ON FILM, TELEVISION, AND MUSIC

*

Part I

FILM LAW

Chapter 1

THE FILM PROCESS: FROM IDEA TO THE BIG SCREEN

A. INTRODUCTION

In his book *Making Movies*, director Sidney Lumet describes film-making as "a complex technical and emotional process. It's art. It's cinema. It's heartbreaking and it's fun." SIDNEY LUMET, MAKING MOVIES at x (1995). For anyone who saw *The Player* (Fine Line Features, 1992) starring Tim Robbins, you know that the film process begins with a pitch. Agents, managers, actors, and producers routinely make brief presentations on their projects to people in a position to provide resources or ultimately "green-light" the film. Green-light is an industry term referring to the ability of someone with power to give the final approval to send the movie into production.

Typically producers will be accorded three minutes to pitch their ideas and writers will receive 45 minutes. The writer is expected to outline the story, including the beginning, middle and end. He should be able to provide character and story arcs, indicating how both the main character and the overall plot will develop. Immediately following the pitch meeting, while a writer might turn over the entire script if there is sufficient interest, a producer will prepare or submit a treatment. A treatment can range from a page or two to several dozen pages. The treatment provides an overview of the film, including plotlines, essential characters, sometimes locations and settings, and what it would take to make the movie work. The purpose of the treatment is to give the reader a sense of how this project might develop on screen.

This pre-production process also involves preparing and submitting scripts, hiring talent (actors and directors) and the production crew, scouting locations, and obtaining financing. With all aspects of pre-production settled, the film moves into the production phase during which principal photography commences and the movie is shot.

Post-production encompasses editing and putting together all the pieces of the film, including dialogue and soundtracks. Sidney Lumet, the director of over 40 films including *12 Angry Men*, *The Verdict*, and

2

Serpico, describes the mix, in which filmmakers put all the sound tracks together to make the final sound track of the movie, as the only dull part of moviemaking. The last stage is to color balance the film and produce the answer print, which will be used to print the film shown in theaters. We highly recommend Lumet's *Making Movies*, as it is a delightful review of the filmmaking process complete with amusing anecdotes.

Section B illustrates legal issues that arise during this initial phase of the production process when people submit an idea, either by an oral pitch or a written treatment, to those that can turn it into a feature film. The *Blaustein* case involves a situation where the idea was submitted orally and no contract was signed. In *Buchwald* the idea was submitted in a written treatment and a contract was signed. Section B also includes an interview with screenwriter Walon Green (*The Wild Bunch, Dinosaur,* and *The Hi–Lo Country*) and discusses the problems of creating a script based on an already delineated character and submitting material directly to a studio.

B. IDEA SUBMISSION: PITCHES & TREATMENTS

BLAUSTEIN v. BURTON

California Court of Appeals, 1970.
9 Cal.App.3d 161, 88 Cal.Rptr. 319.

FRAMPTON, Judge.

* * * Plaintiff, on November 14, 1967, filed his complaint against the defendants Richard Burton, Elizabeth Taylor Burton, Franco Zeffirelli, and Does I through X, wherein he sought damages for (1) breach of contract, (2) unjust enrichment, (3) breach of confidential relationship and (4) services rendered and benefits conferred. Answer to the complaint was filed by the Burtons on January 16, 1968, and no other defendant was served or appeared in the action. * * *

Appellant, in his deposition, testified that he had been in the motion picture business since 1935. After serving as a reader, a story editor, the head of a story department, and an editorial supervisor, he became a producer of motion picture films in 1949. * * * The functions of a producer of a motion picture are to (1) generate the enthusiasm of the various creative elements as well as to bring them together; (2) search out viable locations which would be proper for the artistic side of the production and would be proper from the logistic physical production side; (3) create a budget that would be acceptable from the physical point of view as well as satisfactory from the point of view of implementing the requirements of the script; (4) make arrangements with foreign government where the photography would take place; (5) supervise the execution of the script, the implementation of it onto film; (6) supervise the editing of all the production work down through the dubbing process and the release printing process, at least through the answer print process with Technicolor in this case; (7) the obligation of consulting with the United Artists people on advertising and publicity; (8) arrange casting;

(9) engage the interests of the kind of star or stars that they (the United Artists' people) would find sufficiently attractive to justify an investment; and (10) develop the interest of a proper director.

During 1964, appellant conceived an idea consisting of a number of constituent elements including the following: (a) the idea of producing a motion picture based upon William Shakespeare's play *The Taming of the Shrew*; (b) the idea of casting respondents Richard Burton and Elizabeth Taylor Burton as the stars of this motion picture; (c) the idea of using as the director of the motion picture Franco Zeffirelli, a stage director, who at that time had never directed a motion picture and who was relatively unknown in the United States; (d) the idea of eliminating from the film version of the play the so-called "frame" (i.e., the play within a play device which Shakespeare employed), and beginning the film with the main body of the story; (e) the idea of including in the film version the two key scenes (i.e., the wedding scene and the wedding night scene) which in Shakespeare's play occur offstage and are merely described by a character on stage; (f) the idea of filming the picture in Italy, in the actual Italian settings described by Shakespeare. * * *

[The appellant spoke to Hugh French, the agent for Richard Burton, about his ideas and was later introduced to Burton. Appellant also disclosed his ideas directly to Richard Burton and Elizabeth Taylor, and to Mr. Zeffirelli at separate meetings. Toward the end of a meeting with the Burtons on June 20, 1964, Mr. Burton stated, "Well, let's plan to go ahead now. Elizabeth and I would like to do this. We think Zeffirelli is a good idea. We will accept him." On December 30, 1964, appellant met with the Burtons attorney Martin Gang and learned that his position in the project was in jeopardy. At this time, Mr. Gang and Mickey Rudin, a partner in Gang's law firm, advised appellant that he had no legal rights in the project and should simply accept that.]

Thereafter, a motion picture based upon William Shakespeare's play *The Taming of the Shrew* was produced and exhibited commencing in or about March 1967. The motion picture stars respondents Richard Burton and Elizabeth Taylor Burton, and is directed by Franco Zeffirelli. The motion picture was financed and distributed by Columbia Pictures Corporation, although at the time of taking Mr. Gang's deposition (March 26, 1968), the formal contract between Columbia and the respondents remained to be completed. Mr. Rudin has represented Mr. and Mrs. Burton in the negotiations with Columbia. The motion picture as completed utilizes the following ideas disclosed by appellant to respondents: (1) It is based upon the Shakespearean play *The Taming of the Shrew*; (2) it stars Elizabeth Taylor Burton and Richard Burton in the roles of Katherine and Petruchio, respectively; (3) the director is Franco Zeffirelli; (4) it eliminates the "frame," i.e., the play within a play device found in the original Shakespearean play, and begins with the main body of the story; and (5) it includes an enactment of the two key scenes previously referred to by appellant which in Shakespeare's play occur off-stage.

In addition, the film was photographed in Italy, although not in the actual locales in Italy described by Shakespeare.

Respondents have paid no monies to appellant, nor have they accorded him any screen or advertising credit. * * * Appellant urges that (1) there are triable issues of fact as to whether a contract was entered into between appellant and respondents pursuant to which appellant is entitled to compensation by reason of respondents' utilization of the idea disclosed to them by appellant; (2) there are triable issues of fact as to whether appellant is entitled to recover from respondents under quasi-contract for services rendered and benefits conferred, and (3) there are triable issues of fact as to whether appellant is entitled to recover from respondents for breach of a confidential relationship. * * *

The rights of an idea discloser to recover damages from an idea recipient under an express or implied contract to pay for the idea in event the idea recipient uses such idea after disclosure is discussed in *Desny v. Wilder*, 46 Cal.2d 715, 731–739, 299 P.2d 257, as follows:

"The Law Pertaining to Ideas. Generally speaking, ideas are as free as the air and as speech and the senses, and as potent or weak, interesting or drab, as the experiences, philosophies, vocabularies, and other variables of speaker and listener may combine to produce, to portray, or to comprehend. But there can be circumstances when neither air nor ideas may be acquired without cost. * * *

" * * * As Mr. Justice Traynor stated in his dissenting opinion in *Stanley v. Columbia Broadcasting System*, 35 Cal.2d 653, 674, 221 P.2d 73, 23 A.L.R.2d 216 (1950): 'The policy that precludes protection of an abstract idea by copyright does not prevent its protection by contract. Even though an idea is not property subject to exclusive ownership, its disclosure may be of substantial benefit to the person to whom it is disclosed. That disclosure may therefore be consideration for a promise to pay ... Even though the idea disclosed may be "widely known and generally understood" * * *, it may be protected by an express contract providing that it will be paid for regardless of its lack of novelty." * * *

"Whether the resulting 'contract' * * * is classified as express (as may be fictionized by the law's objective test) or as implied-in-fact (as also may be fictionized by the law) or whether in the same or slightly differing circumstances an obligation shall be 'implied' and denominated 'quasi contractual' because it is strong-armed by the law from nonconsensual acts and intents, is probably important in California—and for the purposes of resolving the problems now before us—principally as an aid to understanding the significance of rulings and discussions in authorities from other jurisdictions. Here, our terminology and the situations for application of the pertinent rules are simplified by codification.

"Our Civil Code declares that (§ 1619) 'A contract is either express or implied'; (§ 1620) 'An express contract is one, the terms of which are stated in words' and (§ 1621) 'An implied contract is one, the existence and terms of which are manifested by conduct.' The same code further provides that (§ 1584) '[T]he acceptance of the consideration offered with a proposal, is an acceptance of the proposal'; (§ 1589) 'A voluntary acceptance of the benefit of a transaction is equivalent to a consent to all the obligations arising from it, so far as the facts are known, or ought to be known, to the persons accepting'; (§ 1605) 'Any benefit conferred ... upon the promisor, by any other person, to which the promisor is not lawfully entitled ... is a good consideration for a promise'; and (§ 1606) '[A] moral obligation originating in some benefit conferred upon the promisor ... is also a good consideration for a promise, to an extent corresponding with the extent of the obligation, but no further or otherwise.' * * *

"From what has been shown respecting the law of ideas and of contracts we conclude that conveyance of an idea can constitute valuable consideration and can be bargained for before it is disclosed to the proposed purchaser, but once it is conveyed, i.e. disclosed to him and he has grasped it, it is henceforth his own and he may work with it and use it as he sees fit. In the field of entertainment the producer may properly and validly agree that he will pay for the service of conveying to him ideas which are valuable and which he can put to profitable use. Furthermore, where an idea has been conveyed with the expectation by the purveyor that compensation will be paid if the idea is used, there is no reason why the producer who has been the beneficiary of the conveyance of such an idea, and who finds if valuable and is profiting by it, may not then for the first time, although he is not at that time under any legal obligation so to do, promise to pay a reasonable compensation for that idea—that is, for the past service of furnishing it to him—and thus create a valid obligation." * * *

It is held that "... if a producer obligates himself to pay for the disclosure of an idea, whether it is for protectible or unprotectible material, in return for a disclosure thereof he should be compelled to hold to his promise. * * * There is nothing unreasonable in the assumption that a producer would obligate himself to pay for the disclosure of an idea which he would otherwise be legally free to use, but which in fact, he would be unable to use but for the disclosure." * * *

We are of the opinion that appellant's idea of the filming of Shakespeare's play *The Taming of the Shrew* is one which may be protected by contract. * * *

Express or implied contracts both are based upon the intention of the parties and are distinguishable only in the manifestation of assent. * * * The making of an agreement may be inferred by proof of conduct as well as by proof of the use of words. (12 Cal.Jur.2d, Contracts, § 4, p. 186.) * * * Whether or not the appellant and respondents here, by their oral declarations and conduct, as shown by the depositions and affidavits, entered into a contract whereby respondents agreed to compensate appellant in the event respondents used appellant's idea, is a question of fact which may not be properly resolved in a summary judgment proceeding, but must be resolved upon a trial of the issue. * * *

If the trial court should find that the condition under which appellant disclosed his idea, and the condition which was impliedly agreed to by respondents was "that in the event defendants used my ideas and went foreword with production of a film version of The Taming of the Shrew, I would be engaged as producer of the film at my then going rate and receive the usual screen and advertising credits as such producer, or I would receive the monetary equivalent of such compensation and credit," then appellant would not have a right to actually participate as the producer, but would only have the obligation so to do as a condition of his right to payment. But as long as he was prepared to render such services, respondents remained obligated to pay the monetary equivalent of what he would have received had he, in fact, rendered such services, even if respondents elected not to use his services. Respondents' obligation to pay is triggered not by the use of appellant's services as a producer, but rather by their use of appellant's idea. * * *

[handwritten margin note: obligation triggered by use of idea]

Under the rules governing the granting of a summary judgment, the foregoing declaration on the part of appellant, made in opposition to the motion for summary judgment, is sufficient to raise a triable issue of fact as to whether the disclosure of his idea to respondents was made in confidence, and was accepted by respondents upon the understanding that they would not use it without the consent of appellant. * * * The judgment is reversed.

Notes

1. During their first marriage to each other, Elizabeth Taylor and Richard Burton searched for film projects that they could do together. They began their initial affair while filming *Cleopatra* in 1962, when Taylor was the world's highest paid actress receiving $1 million per picture plus a percentage of the gross receipts. They married on March 15, 1964 only to divorce on June 26, 1974. When they remarried on October 10, 1975, Burton became husbands number five and six of Taylor's eventual eight spouses. Burton died in 1984. Taylor has maintained a sense of humor as she has aged. She was asked at the 2001 Taos Talking Pictures Festival, where she received the Maverick Award, "If you had to do it all over again, what would you have done differently?" She replied, "Marry a few more times." *See* Sherri Burr, *We all swoon as Elizabeth schmoozes and Elvis Smooches*, Albuquerque Tribune, April 12, 2001, at C.1.

2. The Law of Ideas falls between the middle ground of offering no legal protection and offering full legal protection under copyright law. The Law of Ideas affords the creator the right to obtain compensation from those who benefit directly from his idea. However, by restricting free use of ideas, does the Law of Ideas delay societal benefits in the creative process? *See* Note, *The Legal Protection of Ideas: Is it Really a Good Idea?*, 18 William Mitchell L. Rev. 134 (1992).

3. The Law of Ideas is considered a small subsection of intellectual property law that requires state protection to be actionable for theft. Unlike copyright law and patent law, which Congress is constitutionally bound to protect, *see* Art. 1, Section 8, Clause 8 of the U.S. Constitution, a plaintiff can only protect an idea if the state permits under its property and contract laws. Note the discussion in *Blaustein* about whether an express or implied contract had been created between the parties and compare what happened between Blaustein and the Burtons with the interaction between Art Buchwald and Paramount in the following case.

BUCHWALD v. PARAMOUNT PICTURES

Superior Court of California, 1990.
13 U.S.P.Q.2d (BNA) 1497.
(most citations omitted)

SCHNEIDER, Judge.

In early 1982 Art Buchwald (Buchwald), an internationally renowned writer and humorist, prepared an eight page screen treatment entitled "It's a Crude, Crude World." Buchwald testified that he wrote this treatment by himself without the help from anyone. The inspiration of the principal character came from Buchwald's observance of a state visit by the Shah of Iran. Alain Bernheim (Bernheim), a close friend of Buchwald and co-plaintiff in this action, or Louis Malle, a prominent film director, suggested that the principal character be made a black man.

In March 1982 Buchwald sent his treatment to Bernheim. Bernheim registered the treatment with the Writers Guild of America.

Subsequently, Bernheim suggested to Buchwald that the latter reduce his eight page treatment to a shorter version, which Buchwald did. The shorter treatment is basically a condensed version of the eight page treatment, except for the ending.

In late 1982, Bernheim met with Jeff Katzenberg (Katzenberg), the head of motion picture production at Paramount Pictures Corporation (Paramount), for the purpose of "pitching" Buchwald's story to Paramount for development into a movie starring Eddie Murphy. Murphy was then under contract to Paramount. In fact, Bernheim apparently retyped Buchwald's three page treatment and inserted Eddie Murphy's name after the name of the emperor. Katzenberg read Buchwald's treatment and had a high regard for the concept as a movie. Katzenberg described Buchwald's treatment as "a succinct, smart, straightforward idea with a lot of potential to it."

In late 1982 and early 1983 Paramount was extremely anxious to develop a project for Eddie Murphy. Buchwald's treatment, the title of which had by this time been changed to "King for a Day" by Paramount, was a project in which Paramount was interested. In fact, in January 1983 Paramount registered the title "King for a Day" with the MPAA. Bernheim and Katzenberg remained in communication and a search for a writer began. During this period of time, there was no doubt Paramount considered "King for a Day" a possible project for Eddie Murphy.

In fact, Paramount's creative executives loved Buchwald's story and concept and thought it would be a terrific vehicle for Eddie Murphy. Paramount envisioned Murphy playing at least two roles in Buchwald's story.

On February 24, 1983, Paramount and Bernheim entered into an agreement pursuant to which Bernheim was to produce and be entitled to certain payments if Paramount entered into an agreement with Buchwald acquiring Buchwald's story idea. After the Bernheim–Paramount agreement was executed, the search for a writer for "King for a Day" continued. On March 22, 1983, Buchwald and Paramount entered into an agreement pursuant to which Paramount purchased the rights to Buchwald's story and concept entitled "King for a Day." According to Paramount creative executive David Kirkpatrick (Kirkpatrick), in his ten years at Paramount, Buchwald's treatment was the only one optioned by Paramount. Paramount did, of course, frequently option screenplays.

On March 28, 1983, Kirkpatrick and Ricardo Mestres (Mestres), another Paramount creative executive, sent a memorandum to Jeff Katzenberg. In this memorandum it was indicated that a search for a writer for "King for a Day" was continuing. The same memorandum indicated that the project was being developed for Eddie Murphy "based on Art Buchwald." On the same day "King for a Day" was listed as a project "potentially committed or active in development." On April 2, 1983, in a handwritten note, Katzenberg indicated to Kirkpatrick and Mestres that he wanted a "full court press" on the "King for a Day" project. Several persons, including Buchwald himself, were being considered as potential screenplay writers. Other persons were under consideration as possible directors.

In the spring of 1983, Kirkpatrick met at the Ma Maison Restaurant with Eddie Murphy and others to discuss various potential movie development projects for Murphy. Katzenberg was present, as was Robert Wachs (Wachs), one of Murphy's managers. During this dinner meeting, ten or twelve potential movie projects were discussed. The Paramount executives went through the ten or twelve projects with Murphy and talked basically about characters or people involved. One of the stories that was discussed was Buchwald's "King For A Day." Murphy was positively responsive to the "King For A Day" presentation. At the same meeting Murphy indicated that he liked playing the African character in "Trading Places."

On March 23, 1983, Kirkpatrick sent a status report to Wachs, in which Wachs was advised that Paramount was still searching for a writer for the potential Eddie Murphy project "King for a Day." Katzenberg testified that he spoke regularly with Wachs during 1983, both in person and on the telephone. They discussed projects that were in development for Murphy at Paramount. Katzenberg had similar conversations with Murphy's other manager, Richie Tiankin. On June 6, 1983, Kirkpatrick sent Wachs a short outline of Buchwald's "King For A Day."

On July 9, 1983, a meeting was held at Paramount's office. Present were Kirkpatrick, Katzenberg, Mestres, Bernheim and Tad Murphy who ultimately wrote the first screenplay for "King for a Day." After receiving a synopsis of Buchwald's treatment, Katzenberg suggested a number of changes. These changes included making the Eddie Murphy character more likable, having the Murphy character change in a cultural, rather than financial way, and having Murphy play a number of different roles. On June 13, 1983, Kirkpatrick reported that the first draft of "King For A Day" was due on July 22, 1983. Four days later, in a memorandum, "King For A Day" was described as the "Art Buchwald idea" that Paramount was "now developing for Murphy." In late June the "Eddie Murphy picture" "King For A Day" was described as a possible project for direction by John Landis. On July 1, 1983, Kirkpatrick wrote a letter to Landis which was accompanied by a description of a number of projects that were being proffered by Paramount for consideration by Landis. The description for "King For a Day" stated in pertinent part:

> "KING FOR A DAY is high-style political satire inspired by Art Buchwald. The movie is intended for Eddie Murphy, who is familiar with the idea and likes it very much. If necessary, however, I believe anyone of several comedy stars would be excellent in the role. The writer is Tad Murphy, who has proven in another project that he has a terrific sense for Eddie Murphy's style. We expect a first draft in about four weeks."

In a memorandum dated July 12, 1983, the budget for "King For a Day" was estimated to be in the ten to twelve million dollar range by Mestres and Kirkpatrick. In late July 1983, an agreement was reached between Paramount and Tad Murphy, pursuant to which the latter was hired to do the first screenplay for "King for a Day."

In August 1983, "King for a Day" was still being considered by Paramount as a possible project for Landis. As of August 19, 1983, it was anticipated by Kirkpatrick that Tad Murphy's first draft would be ready on September 2, 1983. This date was later changed to September 23, 1983. In mid September 1983 the budget for "King for a Day" was still estimated at ten million dollars. The date for submission of the first draft of "King for a Day" was later extended to September 30, 1983. At this time "King for a Day" was still identified among "potential Eddie Murphy projects."

On September 30, 1983, Tad Murphy submitted his first draft of "King For a Day." The script was not well received by Paramount, Bernheim or, apparently, anyone else. As a result, the search for a writer for "King for a Day" continued. In the meantime, Paramount paid $2500 to Buchwald to extend its option on "King for a Day."

In late October 1983 the search for a writer focused on the French writer and director, Francis Veber. At the same time, "King for a Day" was still being thought of by Paramount as a possible project for John Landis. Additionally, Paramount was still referring to "King For a Day" as a high-style political satire inspired by Art Buchwald. On December 6,

1983, Kirkpatrick reported that Paramount was negotiating with Veber to write the script for "King For A Day" and that the deal might close that day. A copy of this memorandum was sent to Wachs, Murphy's manager. In December, Paramount indicated that a screenplay draft was expected by March 16, 1984, and that "King for a Day" was targeted for release in the summer of 1984. On December 8, 1983, Wachs was sent a review of one of Veber's movies. On December 12, 1983, Katzenberg sent a letter to Brandon Tartikoff, President of NBC Entertainment. In this letter, "King for a Day" was identified as a "priority development" that "Eddie Murphy will star in."

On January 4, 1984, Kirkpatrick reported that negotiations with Veber were still ongoing with respect to "King for a Day"—a potential Eddie Murphy project. A copy of this report was sent to Wachs and Murphy's agent, Hildy Gottlieb. On January 17, 1984, "King for a Day" was still listed as an "active" project. Negotiations with Veber were still ongoing as of January 23, 1984. On January 24, 1984, Katzenberg was notified that the title "King for a Day" had been cleared for use by Paramount. In late January, Paramount's financial agreement with Bernheim was amended. At the same time it was again reported that the deal with Veber was nearly closed. On February 14, 1984, it was reported at Paramount that a draft for "King For A Day" was due to be submitted by Veber by May 30, 1984. In a February 17, 1984, memorandum relating to "Eddie Murphy projects," "King for a Day" was described as a "political satire inspired by Art Buchwald" that was an excellent candidate for release in summer 1985.

Sometime in 1984, Veber went to Washington, D.C., where he was shown around the ghetto by Bernheim and Buchwald.

On March 20, 1984, Paramount exercised its second option on Buchwald's work.

In a memorandum dated May 14, 1983, Katzenberg informed Frank Mancuso, the head of Paramount, that "King for a Day" was one of the top three projects under development for Eddie Murphy at the time. Katzenberg stated: "Francis Veber, who is set to direct, will deliver his script [on "King For A Day"] mid-June. This is an excellent idea, and the marriage of Murphy and Veber could be something very special."

On June 20, 1984, Kirkpatrick reported to Katzenberg that Veber's script should be ready by mid-August and that Veber would like "to shoot in the spring."[2] Wachs is shown as receiving a copy of this memorandum.

On July 30, 1984, Katzenberg informed Kirkpatrick that Paramount should obtain a one-year extension on its option from Buchwald "for cheap money."

On August 1, 1984, Bernheim reported to Katzenberg that Veber had read his script to him (Bernheim) and that Bernheim was very

2. Veber was paid $300,000 by Paramount to write the script for "King For a Day." This was a large sum of money for such a script. (RT 148–149)

impressed. Bernheim stated that Veber had "captured" Buchwald's idea and that "Eddie is, I believe, in for a treat."

In a memorandum dated August 3, 1984, Darlene Chan of Paramount reported "King For A Day" was scheduled for a summer 1985 release. On August 15, 1984, the Paramount–Buchwald agreement was amended to provide for a third option.

On October 1, 1984, Katzenberg was informed by Michael Besman, a member of Paramount's creative group, that Veber had "unofficially submitted the first draft of his screenplay." Besman reported that the "feeling was that the material was good, but it was hard to digest because of the format of the script."

On October 3, 1984, Katzenberg informed Mancuso that Kirkpatrick had read the first third of Veber's screenplay, that Veber was coming to America the end of November and that there was a deal in place for Veber to direct "King for a Day."

On October 10, 1984, Bernheim wrote Mancuso and informed him that he (Bernheim) had "been working with Francis Veber on our Eddie Murphy project (King for a Day)." Bernheim stated that he hoped Veber would arrive in Los Angeles by the end of November with the completed script.

On October 16, 1984, Paramount exercised its third option on Buchwald's work. On October 19, 1984, Ned Tanen, who by this time had taken over as President of Paramount, authorized payment of an additional $10,000 to Bernheim by reason of the latter's efforts in holding the "King for a Day" project together.

In mid-November Veber's first draft screenplay was submitted.

On January 1, 1985, Kirkpatrick directed a memorandum to Eddie Murphy's agents and managers—Gottlieb, Tiankin and Wachs. "King For a Day" was identified as one of the two strong development projects that would be "coming down the pike at the end of the month." In his memorandum Kirkpatrick reported that Veber was unhappy with his first script and wanted to revise it before it was shown to "Eddie's people." Veber produced his revised draft in January 1985. On February 1, 1985, it was reported that May 1, 1985, was the final date for Paramount to exercise its option on "King for a Day." On the same date Bernheim wrote Tanen and inquired whether "Eddie [was] still interested in the basic Buchwald premise." Bernheim noted that he had been told that "Eddie and his associates were very high on the idea."

On February 7, 1985, Bernheim again wrote Tanen. Bernheim indicated he had had a recent telephone conversation with Kirkpatrick in which the latter hung up on him. Bernheim also referred to the fact that they were "on the verge of signing a new writer (John See)."

On February 20, 1985, Richard Fowkes of Paramount reported that a deal had been made with the writing team of Mierson and Krikes to do a rewrite on "King for a Day." However, one week later it was reported that the deal with Mierson and Krikes "has been aborted."

On March 6, 1985, Kirkpatrick sent a copy of the "King for a Day" script to Wachs, with copies to Gottlieb and Tamara Rawitt (of Eddie Murphy Productions). Wachs received the script and read at least part of it.

On March 29, 1985, Bernheim was informed that Paramount was abandoning "King for a Day." On April 18, 1985, Paramount confirmed that "King for a Day" was "in turnaround."[3] On April 3, 1985, Virginia Briggs of Paramount confirmed that "King for a Day" had been abandoned as of March 29, 1985. "King for a Day" was described as: "First draft screenplay by Tab Murphy; first draft and set of revisions by Francis Veber; both based upon original story and concept by Art Buchwald." However, on May 5, 1985, in a report identifying the "state of potential Eddie Murphy projects," "King for a Day" was listed as one of the "projects in abeyance/on hold." This memorandum was sent to Wachs, Tiankin, Rawitt and Gottlieb.

On August 14, 1985, a "cover"[4] was written for the title "Ambassador At Large." The person who prepared this cover likened "Ambassador At Large" to a story that Paramount had optioned from Art Buchwald.

After Paramount abandoned "King for a Day," Bernheim became interested in finding another production company for the project. He was informed that Paramount had invested in excess of $418,000 in developing "King for a Day." Although Bernheim attempted to purchase an option on the screenplay from Paramount, he was unsuccessful.

In May 1986, Buchwald optioned his treatment "King for a Day" to Warner Brothers. Bernheim also entered into an agreement with Warner Brothers on the same project.

In the summer of 1987, Paramount began the development process of a property called "The Quest," which was reported to be based upon a story by Eddie Murphy. The director selected for this project was John Landis. Barry Blaustein and David Scheffield were chosen to collaborate on the screenplay with Eddie Murphy and Arsenio Hall. The shooting script for "Coming To America," the subsequent title for "The Quest," is dated October 21, 1987. In the meantime, Warner Brothers was still involved in developing the Buchwald treatment. A script entitled "King Jomo" by Allen Katz was ready in revised form in November 1987.

In early November 1987, after Bernheim learned that Paramount was going to begin shooting a movie in which Eddie Murphy was to play a black prince who comes to America to find a wife, Bernheim and Tanen met for lunch. Tanen became angry when Bernheim suggested that Paramount's movie was based on a character close to the one suggested by Buchwald. Tanen insisted Paramount's film had nothing to do with Buchwald's story.

---

3. The term "turnaround" means that a producer is given the right to "take the project, call it his own, and try to set it up at another studio or third party financing."

4. A "cover" is a document in which the story is broken down, synopsized and explained. This document permits a reader to obtain a quick understanding of the story being synopsized.

In January 1988, Warner Brothers cancelled the "King For A Day" project. Warner Brothers executive Bruce Berman made it clear that the cancellation was due, at least in part, to Warner's discovery of the fact that Paramount was shooting *Coming to America* starring Eddie Murphy.

When *Coming to America* was released, the screenplay credit was given to Sheffield and Blaustein and Eddie Murphy received the story credit.

On June 29, 1988, Michael Batagglia of Paramount reported on *Coming to America* field publicity and promotions. One of the promotions was the use of a "King for a Day" concept, where a prize winner was afforded the opportunity to go on a shopping spree.

DISCUSSION

Introduction

At the outset the Court desires to indicate what this case is and is not about. It is *not* about whether Art Buchwald or Eddie Murphy is more creative. It is clear to the Court that each of these men is a creative genius in his own field and each is an uniquely American institution. This case is also *not* about whether Eddie Murphy made substantial contributions to the film "Coming to America." The Court is convinced he did. Finally, this case is *not* about whether Eddie Murphy "stole" Art Buchwald's concept "King for a Day." Rather, this case is primarily a breach of contract case between Buchwald and Paramount (not Murphy) which must be decided by reference to the agreement between the parties and the rules of contract construction, as well as the principals of law enunciated in the applicable legal authorities.

The Contract Between Buchwald and Paramount

As indicated, the starting point for the analysis of this case is the contract between Buchwald and Paramount. Pursuant to this agreement Buchwald transferred to Paramount "the sole and exclusive motion picture and other rights" to the "original story and concept written by Art Buchwald ... tentatively entitled "KING FOR A DAY", also known as "It's a Crude, Crude World" (which material, as defined in said Standard Terms is hereinafter called the 'Work')." In the agreement Buchwald warranted "[t]hat the Work is original with Author; that neither the Work nor any part thereof are taken from or based upon any other material or any motion picture. . . ." As is pertinent to the present case, the agreement provided that:

> 'Work' means the aforementioned Material and includes all prior, present and future versions, adaptations and translations thereof (whether written by Author or by others), its theme, story, plot, characters and their names, its title or titles and subtitles, if any, . . . and each and every part of all thereof. " 'Work' does not include the material referred to in paragraph 2(f) above, written or prepared by Purchaser or under Purchaser's Authority." (*Id.* at 15)

Finally, the agreement entitled Buchwald to certain "contingent consideration" "[f]or the first theatrical motion picture (the 'Picture'): If, but only if, a feature length theatrical motion picture shall be produced *based upon* Author's Work." (Emphasis added.)

The Meaning of "Based Upon"

Since the agreement provided Buchwald was entitled to payment only if Paramount produced "a feature length theatrical motion picture" "based upon Author's Work," the threshold inquiry in this case is what is meant by the term "based upon." Because the term is not defined in the contract, it was the Court's hope that the term had a specific meaning in the entertainment industry and that the experts who testified would so indicate. Unfortunately, there was as little agreement among the experts concerning the meaning of this term as there was between plaintiffs and Paramount concerning whether *Coming to America* is based upon Buchwald's treatment. For example, David Kirkpatrick testified that his understanding of "based upon," as used in the entertainment industry, is that "there exists some underlying antecedents that triggered the realization of the story in a screenplay." Kirkpatrick amplified his answer to state that "based upon" has two aspects—"the studio or production company had purchased or had access to [the author's work]. And two, that the antecedents were of a significant story nature to claim a based upon credit." In other words, Kirkpatrick opined that a movie is based upon a writer's work if it "was created out of significant elements from the underlying materials." By significant elements, Kirkpatrick meant "that there were character similarities, story similarities as it relates to the Act One, to (sic) Two, Three structure."

Helene Hahn, a Paramount attorney, testified (by way of deposition) that, in her opinion, "based upon" meant that the "screenplay of the motion picture had been derived from and incorporated the elements of author's work as herein defined." Alexandra Denman, another Paramount attorney, testified (by way of deposition) that "based upon" meant that the screenplay was written "with the elements of Mr. Buchwald's story, I mean the specific elements of the story, which is the work."

David Rintels, a writer, testified (by way of deposition) that "based upon" means "intent." Mr. Rintels further testified: "Before you get into plot you'll be able to see, just because you've been doing it for 30 years yourself, or I'll be able to see that—if I think that there is a similarity in spirit over—regardless of details, I think that's a factor, for something to be based on."

Edmond H. North, another writer, testified (by way of deposition) that he believed the focus in making the "based upon" determination should be whether there is an overriding similarity to plot, theme and characters. Lynn Roth, another writer, defined "based upon" as meaning "something came from something else." Miss Roth conceded that "because we're dealing with so many kinds of material, you could not put

"based on" = basic theme

into a specific or as neat a definition as you can other credits in the industry, because we are dealing with, as I said before, different things. ..." In determining whether one work came from an earlier work, according to Miss Roth, one looks at the essence of the material, i.e., "the basic theme" but not plot, characters and motivation because these relate to the "development of the project," not its theme (i.e., nucleus).

Since the Court found the testimony of the entertainment experts, both individually and collectively, to be of little value with respect to the "based upon" issue, the Court turned to the appellate decisions of this State for guidance. Fortunately, that guidance existed. Indeed, as will be discussed more fully below, the Court believes these decisions provide a road map through the "based upon" mine field. * * *

Based upon the authorities discussed above and the provisions of the contract involved in this case, the Court concludes that *Coming to America* is a movie that was "based upon" Buchwald's treatment "King for a Day."[10] Bearing in mind the unlimited access ... [proved] in this case and the rule that the stronger the access the less striking and numerous the similarities need be, ... [the Court concludes that Paramount has] appropriated and used a qualitatively important part of plaintiff's material in such a way that features discernible in * * * [Paramount's] work are substantially similar thereto. * * * [11]

Finally, the Court wishes again to emphasize that its decision is in no way intended to disparage the creative talent of Eddie Murphy. It was Paramount and not Murphy who prepared the agreement in question. It is Paramount and not Murphy that obligated itself to compensate Buchwald if any material element of Buchwald's treatment was utilized in or inspired a film produced by Paramount. *Coming to America* is no less the product of Eddie Murphy's creativity because of the Court's decision than it was before this decision was rendered.

The Issue of the Originality of Buchwald's Treatment

As indicated, in the agreement between Buchwald and Paramount, the former sold to Paramount his "original story and concept" and warranted that his work was original and not taken from or based upon any other material or motion picture. During the trial, Paramount was permitted to introduce into evidence a movie made in the 1950's by Charlie Chaplin entitled "A King in New York." Although the Court understood it to be Paramount's position during trial that Buchwald's treatment was not original in that it was based upon "A King in New York," it appears that this position was abandoned by Paramount during

10. The Court wishes to add that to the extent there is an ambiguity with respect to interpreting the "based upon" provision of the contract, that ambiguity must be resolved against Paramount as the drafter of the agreement. (Civ.Code § 1654; Glenn v. Bacon, 86 Cal.App. 58 (1927).

11. The statement by Judge Learned Hand in *Fred Fisher, Inc. v. Dillingham*, 298 F. 145 (1924) is appropriate to quote at this point. Judge Hand stated: "Everything registers somewhere in our memories, and no one can tell what may evoke it." Eddie Murphy, with commendable candor, admitted as much when he testified (by way of deposition) that he did not know "what triggers my subconscious."

oral argument. Paramount's present position, as the Court understands it, is that if the Court concludes *Coming to America* is based upon Buchwald's treatment, it must similarly conclude that Buchwald's treatment is based upon "A King in New York" since the same degree of similarity exists between Buchwald's treatment and each of the two movies. The Court does not agree.

It is true that Buchwald testified that he saw "A King in New York" in Paris in the 1950's and wrote a column concerning his review of the movie after seeing it. Besides these facts, there is not a scintilla of evidence that Buchwald's treatment was in any way based on "A King in New York." Indeed Buchwald testified that his treatment was an original document and that he could not remember anything about the Chaplin movie. Moreover, the Court has viewed "A King in New York." Besides the fact that this movie involves a king who comes to America, there is not the slightest resemblance between "A King in New York" and "King for a Day." In Chaplin's movie the king is an elderly Caucasian who is already married and deposed by the time he comes to America. Although he loses his fortune, he spends the entire movie living in luxury at the Ritz Hotel. Moreover, and most significantly, the movie is a satirical look at the McCarthy era and the American mentality during that period of time.

In sum, to the extent Paramount still intends to advance the argument, the Court rejects the contention that Buchwald's treatment was not original and that it was in any way based upon "A King in New York." Stated another way, while plaintiffs have proved by a preponderance that *Coming to America* is "based upon" "King for a Day," plaintiffs have also proved by a preponderance of the evidence that "King for a Day" is not "based upon" "A King in New York." * * *

Notes

1. The *Buchwald* case represents a rare win for the outsider. What factors do you think caused the court to rule in Buchwald's favor? Do you think it made a difference that Buchwald enjoyed a measure of fame himself as an author and newspaper columnist? According to Joy Horowitz, the *Buchwald* case amounted to an induction to "the world of idea theft in Hollywood, a subterranean zone where the mudslinging is rampant, the desparation factor is acute, and the charges and countercharges of ethical misconduct are about as common as the lineup of BMW's and Mercedes in a studio parking lot." *See* Joy Horowitz, *Hollywood Law: Whose Idea is it, Anyway?* N.Y. Times, March 15, 1992, at H.1.

2. Art Buchwald was fortunate that he had a contract with Paramount. Note that the court spends a fair amount of time talking about the meaning of "based upon" in the industry. Is this meaning significantly different from the Standard English or legal dictionary definition? The challenge for entertainment lawyers is to make sure they understand the meanings that are peculiar to the entertainment business. In his book *Fatal Substraction: How Hollywood Really Does Business*, Buchwald's lawyer Pierce O'Donnell

indicates that based on his initial reading of Buchwald's contract, he expected a recovery in the millions. They were both in for a rude awakening. For a discussion of what happened in the second and third phases of the case, see Chapter 5, Part B on net compensation.

3. Since the Law of Ideas is derived from common law, each state is free to independently develop its own doctrine. New York, for example, required for several decades that an idea be novel and original before a property interest can be inferred. *See* Downey v. General Foods Corp., 31 N.Y.2d 56, 334 N.Y.S.2d 874, 286 N.E.2d 257 (1972) ("Lack of novelty in an idea is fatal to any cause of action for its unlawful use."). In 2000, the New York Court of Appeals abrogated the requirement that an idea had to be novel in order to be protected in *Nadel v. Play–By–Play Toys & Novelties, Inc.*, 208 F.3d 368 (2d Cir. 2000). The court held that in a contracts claim, the idea does not have to be original or novel, the idea only needs to be novel to the buyer. Prior New York law had had an adverse effect on the pitching of ideas in New York as producers became more comfortable that California state law would more effectively protect their ideas from theft. California, on the other hand, will protect an idea if it was disclosed as part of a confidential relationship. *See* Peter Swarth, *The Law of Ideas: New York and California are More than 3,000 Miles Apart*, 13 Hastings Comm/Ent L.J. 115 (1989).

4. Having the court decide that *Coming to America* was based on his idea produced an unintended consequence for Buchwald. In *Beal v. Paramount Pictures, Eddie Murphy, and Art Buchwald*, 806 F.Supp. 963 (N.D. Ga. 1992), Aveda King Beal claimed that all the defendants, including Buchwald, infringed the copyright in her book called "The Arab Heart" when they produced *Coming to America*. The court noted that the book and the movie do contain some resemblance as both involve a foreign prince coming to the United States. However, it concluded, "[T]he very general similarities in theme between the two works are not copyrightable." The court decided that the likeness between the two works are "scenes a faire," which are "incidents or plot that ordinarily result from a common theme or setting and such scenes a faire are not protectible under the copyright laws." *Id*.

5. The *Buchwald* case inadvertently illustrates how Hollywood treats screenwriters. While screenwriters and script doctors are well paid, they are paid for their draft and then excused from the production process. One of the issues involved in the 2002 Writers Guild negotiations was professional respect: The writers wanted to be welcomed on the set and invited to premiers.

Sherri Burr
The Law of Ideas from a Screenwriter's Viewpoint:
Author Interview With Walon Green

Copyright © 2003 by Sherri Burr.

[At the Santa Fe, NM, Film Festival on December 6, 2003, screenwriter Walon Green discussed his filmmaking career with author Sherri Burr.

Green began writing for the silver screen in the 1960s. His first Oscar nomination came in 1969 for *The Wild Bunch*, a Sam Peckinpah directed Western. By 2003, he had received credit for writing 13 feature films, including the 1998 *Hi-Lo Country* starring Woody Harrelson and the 1982 *The Border* starring Jack Nicholson. He has also written and produced several television series including *Hill Street Blues*, *ER*, and *Law and Order*. In 1971, his *Hellstrom Chronicles* won the Oscar for Best Documentary.]

"The first obligation a writer has is to make sure he's not going to be sued, that he didn't steal the idea from someone. He has to sign a contract to that effect. Agents tell you to give the contract to a lawyer. Some people don't give it to a lawyer and they end up in trouble. They wait to find a lawyer when they haven't been paid. By then it may be too late.

"Writers can recoup on the backend [net profits], but they need a lawyer's help to negotiate the definition of profits. If the definition is not well defined, the studio has an easier time cheating the writer.

"Hollywood writers were ecstatic when Art Buchwald won. Finally someone had the courage to take on the studio system. After all this time, I still get ripped off. I've only seen honest back-end profits on one project, *Hellstrom Chronicles*. With *Hellstrom Chronicles*, I was close to the people who did the film and no one cheated anyone. *Dinosaur*, however, made over $400 million at the box office and I've never seen one penny of my 2–1/2% net gross. *Law and Order* has been one of the most popular television series for the last two seasons and the producers claim it is in the hole to the tune of $40 million.

"To obtain backend profits on my projects, I'd have to hire a forensic accountant. The cost of hiring the accountant and an attorney would probably exceed what the accountant found. Lawyers can help keep you from getting sued, but they can't prevent you from getting screwed.

"Studios know what they are doing is wrong, but they gamble that if they cheat everyone, only a few will actually sue so they can get away with not paying back-end profits. Studios are not unlike car companies who think it's cheaper to let a particular car model explode than to fix the engine for everyone.

"I was once sued by a studio that wanted to break a contract and not pay the last part of my fee. The studio claimed that I was in breach for not delivering a script in time. I was in Europe during a strike and didn't return right away. The studio offered to drop the suit in return for my not requesting the final $60,000 payment. I settled and later found out that they brought the suit just to keep from making the final payment.

"The Writers Guild is a mixed blessing for writers. The WGA performs legal services that writers cannot afford to do on their own. The contract that the WGA has with the studios allows them to decide things like credit arbitration. I've arbitrated four times and lost once. Only three of my 13 credited films went through arbitration. Arbitration can occur in strange ways. I'm adapting a book now that has been through three prior screenplay adaptations. While I haven't seen the prior adaptations, it's possible that we will all have similar scenes since we are working from the book. This is the kind of situation that could easily end in arbitration to determine who is entitled to the credit for writing the film."

Notes

1. What are some of the ways that individual lawyers might improve the treatment of screenwriters? Can you think of some perks that individual lawyers might seek to write into their screenwriters' contracts?

2. In considering the following case, note how the material was presented to Sylvester Stallone.

ANDERSON v. SYLVESTER STALLONE

United States District Court, Central District of California, 1989.
1989 WL 206431.
(some citations omitted)

KELLER, U.S. District Judge.

* * * The movies *Rocky* I, II, and III were extremely successful motion pictures. Sylvester Stallone wrote each script and played the role of Rocky Balboa, the dominant character in each of the movies. In May of 1982, while on a promotional tour for the movie *Rocky III*, Stallone informed members of the press of his ideas for Rocky IV. Although Stallone's description of his ideas would vary slightly in each of the press conferences, he would generally describe his ideas as follows:

> I'd do it [Rocky IV] if Rocky himself could step out a bit. Maybe tackle world problems. So what would happen, say, if Russia allowed her boxers to enter the professional ranks? Say Rocky is the United States' representative and the White House wants him to fight with the Russians before the Olympics. It's in Russia with everything against him. It's a giant stadium in Moscow and everything is Russian Red. It's a fight of astounding proportions with 50 monitors sent to 50 countries. It's the World Cup—a war between 2 countries.

Waco Tribune Herald, May 28, 1982; Section D, pg. 1.

In June of 1982, after viewing the movie *Rocky III*, Timothy Anderson wrote a thirty-one page treatment entitled "Rocky IV" that he hoped would be used by Stallone and MGM Registered TM UA Communications Co. (hereinafter "MGM") as a sequel to *Rocky III*. The treatment incorporated the characters created by Stallone in his prior movies and cited Stallone as a co-author.

In October of 1982, Mr. Anderson met with Art Linkletter, who was a member of MGM's board of directors. Mr. Linkletter set up a meeting on October 11, 1982, between Mr. Anderson and Mr. Fields, who was president of MGM at the time. Mr. Linkletter was also present at this October 11, 1982 meeting. During the meeting, the parties discussed the possibility that plaintiff's treatment would be used by defendants as the script or Rocky IV. At the suggestion of Mr. Fields, the plaintiff, who is a lawyer and was accompanied by a lawyer at the meeting, signed a release that purported to relieve MGM from liability stemming from use of the treatment. Plaintiff alleges that Mr. Fields told him and his attorney that "if they [MGM & Stallone] use his stuff [Anderson's treatment] it will be big money, big bucks for Tim." * * *

On April 22, 1984, Anderson's attorney wrote MGM requesting compensation for the alleged use of his treatment in the forthcoming Rocky IV movie. On July 12, 1984, Stallone described his plans for the Rocky IV script on the *Today Show* before a national television audience. Anderson, in his deposition, states that his parents and friends called him to tell him that Stallone was telling "his story" on television. * * *In a diary entry of July 12, 1984, Anderson noted that Stallone "explained my story" on national television. * * *

Stallone completed his Rocky IV script in October of 1984. Rocky IV was released in November of 1985. The complaint in this action was filed on January 29, 1987.

CONCLUSIONS OF LAW

[The court concluded that it could not rule as a matter of law that Anderson's contract claims were barred by the statute of limitations; however Anderson's breach of confidence claim was barred by the statute of limitations.] * * *

In Count Twelve of his complaint, Anderson claims that the defendants committed a breach of confidence by revealing the contents of his script. In *Davies v. Krasna*, 121 Cal. Rptr. 705 (1975), the California Supreme Court set forth the requirements for a breach of confidence claim. The Court held that "an action for breach of confidence ... arises whenever an idea, offered and received in confidence is later disclosed without permission." *Id.* at 710. Davies also held that a breach of confidence claim is governed by the two year statute of limitation period set forth in Cal. Civ. Proc. Code § 339. *Id.* at 711.

It is uncontroverted that on July 12, 1984, Stallone described ideas for a Rocky IV script on the *Today Show* before a national television audience. This interview included a description by Stallone of the East/West confrontation theme for Rocky IV. In his deposition, Anderson claims that Stallone was revealing "his story" on national television. On July 12, 1984, Anderson also noted in his diary that Stallone had explained his story. Stallone did not have Anderson's permission to disclose the ideas in Anderson's treatment. If, as Anderson alleges, Stallone did take Anderson's ideas, the breach of confidence occurred on July 12, 1984. This action was filed in January of 1987. The breach of confidence claim was not filed within the two year statute of limitations and is time barred.

Plaintiff argues that the statute should not begin to run until the release of *Rocky IV* since he suffered no appreciable harm until that time. This argument was considered and rejected in *Davies*. There, in an analogous fact situation, the court held that a disclosure of ideas would destroy marketability of a story and cause actual damage to an author and would immediately trigger the running of the statute of limitations. *Davies*, 121 Cal. Rptr. 711–12. The same impact on marketability occurred here. Anderson's ideas for an East/West boxing confrontation were revealed to millions of people on July 12, 1984. His ideas then entered the public domain and could be used and developed by others without payment to him. If his allegations are true, he suffered an injury the moment his ideas were disclosed without permission. * * *

Plaintiff also argues that even if the marketability of his ideas was impacted on July 12, 1984, the amount of damages he suffered was too uncertain to warrant the running of the statute of limitations. The court in *Davies* explicitly held, contrary to plaintiff's contentions here, "neither uncertainty as to the amount of damages nor difficulty in proving damages tolls the period of limitations". 121 Cal. Rptr. at 713. The holding in *Davies* also comports with common sense, as "adoption of a certainty" requirement for the running of a statute would create chaos as courts attempted to determine on what date a plaintiff knew or should have known the extent of his damages. Anderson's action accrued at the moment of disclosure on July 12, 1984, and there are no facts before this Court that warrant tolling of the statute. Thus, Anderson's breach of confidence claim is time barred. * * *

IV.   DEFENDANTS ARE ENTITLED TO SUMMARY JUDGMENT ON ANDERSON'S COPYRIGHT INFRINGEMENT CLAIMS

This Court finds that the defendants are entitled to summary judgment on plaintiff's copyright infringement claims on two separate grounds. First, Anderson's treatment is an infringing work that is not entitled to copyright protection. Second, *Rocky IV* is not substantially similar to Anderson's treatment, and no reasonable jury could find that *Rocky IV* is a picturization of Anderson's script. * * *

The *Rocky* characters are one of the most highly delineated group of characters in modern American cinema. The physical and emotional characteristics of Rocky Balboa and the other characters were set forth in tremendous detail in the three *Rocky* movies before Anderson appropriated the characters for his treatment. The interrelationships and development of Rocky, Adrian, Apollo Creed, Clubber Lang, and Paulie are central to all three movies. Rocky Balboa is such a highly delineated character that his name is the title of all four of the *Rocky* movies and his character has become identified with specific character traits ranging from his speaking mannerisms to his physical characteristics. This Court has no difficulty ruling as a matter of law that the *Rocky* characters are delineated so extensively that they are protected from bodily appropriation when taken as a group and transposed into a sequel by another author. Plaintiff has not and cannot put before this Court any evidence to rebut the defendants' showing that *Rocky* characters are so highly delineated that they warrant copyright protection.

* * * This Court also finds that the *Rocky* characters were so highly developed and central to the three movies made before Anderson's treatment that they "constituted the story being told." All three Rocky movies focused on the development and relationships of the various characters. The movies did not revolve around intricate plots or story lines. Instead, the focus of these movies was the development of the *Rocky* characters. The same evidence which supports the finding of delineation above is so extensive that it also warrants a finding that the *Rocky* characters—Rocky, Adrian, Apollo Creed, Clubber Lang, and Paulie—"constituted the story being told" in the first three Rocky movies.

* * * Stallone owns the copyrights for the first three Rocky movies. Under 17 U.S.C. § 106(2), he has the exclusive right to prepare derivative works based on these copyrighted works. This Court has determined that Anderson's treatment is an unauthorized derivative work. Thus, Anderson has infringed upon Stallone's copyright. *See* 17 U.S.C. § 501(a).

Notes

1. The outcome of this case was the reverse of what Anderson sought when he initiated the lawsuit. Instead of a ruling that Stallone stole Anderson's work, the court decided that Anderson was the thief. Thus, one lesson from this case is that writers should beware of composing treatments based on already created fictional characters. For a more substantial discussion of treatments and the film process please see the following books by Micheal Halperin, *Writing the Killer Treatment: Selling Your Story Without a Script* (2002), and Kenneth Atchity & Chi–Li Wong, *Writing Treatments that Sell: How to Create and Market Your Story Ideas to the Motion Picture and TV Industry* (2003).

2. Brian Devine maintains, "[I]dea submission claims continue to be a prominent source of Hollywood litigation, and many of the legal issues involved remain unsettled." *Free As The Air: Rethinking The Law Of Story Ideas,* 24 HASTINGS COMM. & ENT. L.J. 355, (1998). Since most cases settle, resulting in relatively few judicial opinions, the law is far from fixed. Debates continue as to what a plaintiff must show to establish formation of an implied-in-fact contract and what is required to prove "use" of an idea. These topics require a consideration of the rule and their broader social implications. What do you think should be the policy behind idea submission? Should the law protect ideas? Do ideas have value independently or only if they are explored by the right person, like a Steven Spielberg?

BARRY J. SPINELLO v. AMBLIN ENTERTAINMENT CO.

California Court of Appeals, 1994.
29 Cal.App.4th 1390, 34 Cal.Rptr.2d 695.

VOGEL, Judge.

Barry J. Spinello sued Amblin Entertainment, Universal City Studios, Inc., and Steven Spielberg for damages, alleging they had appropriated his ideas and were using them for a new movie. Relying on a written agreement which included an arbitration clause, the defendants moved to compel arbitration. The motion was denied and the defendants appeal. We reverse and remand with directions to grant the motion.

BACKGROUND

In April 1988, Spinello (a self-described motion picture producer, writer and director with more than 20 years' experience in "the industry") discussed his script, "Adrian and the Toy People," with Deborah Jelin Newmyer, an Amblin executive. Newmyer told Spinello he could have his agent submit the script and, in November 1988, Spinello's agent mailed a copy to Newmyer. By that time, Newmyer was away on maternity leave and the script was reviewed by another executive, Bettina Viviano. By letter dated January 9, 1989, Viviano returned the script to Spinello, explaining Amblin wasn't interested in it.

In early 1990, Spinello met Alan Davio, one of Spielberg's cameramen. Spinello told Davio about "Adrian and the Toy People" and showed Davio some photographs he had used to illustrate animated portions of his script. From Davio's "body language" and "face," Spinello concluded that (a) Davio liked the photographs and (b) Davio thought Spielberg would be interested in seeing the photographs.

Thus encouraged, on February 6, 1990, Spinello submitted his script to Spielberg at Amblin, explaining in a cover letter that Davio "thought you might be interested in seeing [my] photos" but neglecting to mention that Amblin had previously rejected his script. The script was referred to Newmyer (who had returned from maternity leave) and Newmyer, in turn, wrote to Spinello, explaining that Amblin would review his script only if he signed and returned Amblin's standard submission agreement.

Spinello did not talk to Newmyer or anyone else at Amblin. Instead, he contacted his literary agent, Barry Salomon, and discussed the submission agreement with him (and may have sent him a copy). Salomon told Spinello to sign the agreement, which he said was "standard," and to submit the script. On March 20, 1990, Spinello signed and dated the agreement and, on March 26, sent it to Amblin with a copy of his script. * * * It is this agreement which contains the arbitration clause. * * *

By letter dated April 24, 1990, Newmyer returned Spinello's script, rejecting it on behalf of Amblin. Both before and after his two submissions to Amblin, Spinello submitted copies of the same script to about seventy other studios and producers.

In April 1992, *Daily Variety* announced that Amblin and Universal had purchased a script from Gavin Scott, a British screenwriter, entitled "Small Soldiers," a "fantasy adventure about a young boy's . . . escapades with an army of toy soldiers who come to life." Based solely on this article, Spinello concluded "Small Soldiers" was based on his idea. He therefore sued Amblin, Spielberg and Universal in the Los Angeles Superior Court, alleging breach of contract and a variety of tort theories (intentional interference with prospective economic advantage, conversion, breach of an implied covenant of good faith and fair dealing, breach of confidence and fraud), all based on the same claim—that the defendants had unlawfully used "Spinello's novel script and ideas for a possible major motion picture." * * *

In October 1992, Amblin removed the action to federal district court, contending the conversion claim was a disguised copyright infringement action over which the federal court had exclusive jurisdiction. Upon arrival in federal court, Amblin moved to compel arbitration. The federal district court denied the motion without prejudice and, in February 1993, dismissed the conversion claim and remanded the action back to the Los Angeles Superior Court.

Amblin answered and moved to compel arbitration. The trial court denied the motion, finding the arbitration clause was both "procedurally and substantively unconscionable" and thus unenforceable. Amblin, Spielberg and Universal (henceforth referred to collectively as Amblin) appeal.

DISCUSSION

* * * [T]he appropriate question in this case is whether the agreement between Spinello and Amblin was a contract of adhesion. Clearly, it was not. Spinello had the opportunity to negotiate and simply failed to do so. When the agreement was submitted to him, he could have asked his agent to request deletion or modification or limitation of the arbitration provision, or he could have done so himself. As he admits, however, he did not do so. Spinello was not a novice—he had about 20 years' experience in the entertainment industry and he was represented by a literary agent. If we accept as true Spinello's statement that he understood the cameraman's response to suggest Amblin would be interested, it follows logically that Spinello believed he had a valuable property and, therefore, a basis for negotiation.

And as Spinello also admits, he had the opportunity to go elsewhere and, in fact, did so—he submitted his script to approximately 70 other producers (at least several of whom did not require execution of submission agreements)—a consideration which shows that this was not an adhesion contract under *Madden* [Madden v. Kaiser Foundation, 17 Cal. 3d 699, 131 Cal.Rptr. 882, 552 P.2d 1178 (1976)] or, if the rule applied, an unconscionable contract under *Dean Witter* [Dean Witter Reynolds v. Superior Court, 211 Cal.App.3d 758, 259 Cal.Rptr. 789 (1989).

III.

In defense of the trial court's order, Spinello contends Amblin's failure to require execution of a submission agreement the first time the script was submitted means there is no arbitration provision covering Amblin's initial review of Spinello's script and that, since it cannot now be determined when Amblin stole his ideas, none of Spinello's claims are subject to the arbitration clause. We disagree.

At the time of the second submission (1990), Spinello (who obviously knew he had submitted the same script to Amblin in 1988) agreed that "any dispute" arising out of the agreement, specifically including Amblin's determination that it had the right to use material containing features or elements similar or identical to those contained in Spinello's script, would be submitted to arbitration and that, except as so provided, Spinello released Amblin from any and all claims that might arise in relation to the submitted material. By signing this agreement, Spinello clearly and unequivocally agreed to arbitrate all disputes about this script, without limitation to the 1990 submission.

Moreover, the Amblin executive Spinello dealt with in 1990 (Newmyer) was not the same person he dealt with in 1988 (Viviano). Spinello nevertheless failed to mention that the 1988 review had been pursued by Viviano without a submission agreement, an omission which weighs heavily against Spinello's current effort to avoid his agreement by reliance on the earlier submission. In our view, his signature on the 1990 agreement was tantamount to a waiver of any different rights he might have had based on the unconditional acceptance of the script in 1988.

Finally, no inequity results from this interpretation. As mentioned in the submission agreement and noted by experts in the field, "[m]otion picture production companies, agents and others in the entertainment industry receive vast numbers of stories, treatments, screenplays and so forth for consideration for development. Out of a tremendous volume of materials, a relatively few projects are selected for development and even fewer are ultimately produced. There are serious concerns for the recipients in accepting unsolicited (and even solicited) material, in particular regarding the originality and ownership of the material, as well as regarding potential copying claims, especially if it should turn out that the production company has a similar project of its own already in development. For these reasons, production companies will usually refuse to accept material unless it is represented by an agent. Even when material is accepted, either directly or through an agent, production companies may require the owner to sign a submission release to provide certain protections for the production company." KENOFF & ROSENBERG, ENTERTAINMENT INDUSTRY CONTRACTS: NEGOTIATING AND DRAFTING GUIDE § 2.02, pp. 2–3 (1994). Under these circumstances, the arbitration agreement (and our interpretation of it to cover both submissions) is patently fair to all parties. * * *

DISPOSITION

The order is reversed and the matter is remanded to the trial court with directions to grant Amblin's motion to compel arbitration of all claims raised by Spinello. Amblin is awarded its costs of appeal.

Notes

1. While Spinello argued that the contract he signed was one of adhesion, given his experience in the business, should he have forseen that some companies would expect him to sign such an agreement? Companies do so to forestall what happened here: if the studio has something in production, they do not want another person to claim later that studio stole his idea.

2. How do Hollywood production companies protect themselves from potential charges of idea theft? Often a Hollywood production company, studio, agency or management conglomerate imposes rules on receiving material from outsiders. If the unsolicited material is sent through the mail, they will return it unopened. If they opened it, they return it with a statement that unsolicited material cannot be accepted unless it comes through an authorized agent.

If the person blurts out the idea in person, s/he may lose all rights and power over idea unless there is a confidential relationship with the recipient indicating that payment might be expected. Some companies will accept an idea, but only after a person signs a waiver disclaiming ownership or releasing them from liability, or after a person signs a waiver agreeing to accept compensation at the studio's discretion.

Can you think of other precautions a studio might take to reduce the chance that someone will later charge it with idea theft?

MANN v. COLUMBIA PICTURES, WARREN BEATTY AND ROBERT TOWNE

California Court of Appeal, 1992.
128 Cal.App.3d 628, 180 Cal.Rptr. 522.

STEPHENS, Acting Presiding Justice.

Plaintiff and appellant, Bernice Mann, appeals from a judgment notwithstanding the verdict and conditional grant of a new trial. The trial court granted the motions of defendants and respondents, Columbia Pictures Industries, Inc. ("Columbia"), Warren Beatty, and Robert Towne, after a jury awarded plaintiff a verdict in the sum of $185,000. * * *

Mann seeks to recover the reasonable value of ideas embodied in a 29–page written format, entitled "Women Plus," which she allegedly submitted for Columbia's consideration as the basis for a motion picture.

Plaintiff contends that her outline was accepted by Columbia, and used by defendants in the motion picture production *Shampoo*. * * *

From her experience as a beauty salon employee, Mann wrote descriptions of various characters and scenes evolving from a salon scenario. She prepared the outline as a possible framework for a motion picture. Mann titled the completed compilation "Women Plus," and registered her work with the Writers Guild of America on October 15, 1969.

Florence Klase, Mann's personal friend, had a neighbor, Evelyn Light, who knew Harry Caplan. Klase informed plaintiff that Caplan "was an important man at Columbia." As a favor to Mann, Klase agreed to deliver "Women Plus" and "Two Weeks," plaintiff's other work, to Light. Light was to submit the two writings to Caplan. Caplan assured Light that a Columbia "reader" would review plaintiff's works and determine if either could be the basis for a motion picture. * * *

Uncontradicted testimony establishes that plaintiff never met or conversed with Caplan prior to trial. Mann never imposed any conditions on the submission of her works to Caplan. Plaintiff was pleased with the opportunity to have a "reader" review her efforts. * * * Caplan did not open plaintiff's envelope to inspect its contents. He submitted the envelope to a "reader" in the same condition in which he received it from Light. As a personal favor to Light, Caplan delivered on his assurance that a "reader" would review Mann's efforts. But he submitted plaintiff's envelope to Gary Crutcher, a story editor at Filmmakers. Caplan testified that he never submitted the envelope or its contents to any "reader" employed by Columbia. * * *

Crutcher read material strictly for Filmmakers. He had no relationship with Columbia, nor did he summarize any material for that studio, during his employment at Filmmakers. Filmmakers did not have the right to use the files in Columbia's story department. Furthermore, Crutcher had no association with the production of *Shampoo*. Uncontroverted testimony shows that Crutcher never met or spoke with either defendant Beatty or defendant Towne prior to this litigation. * * *

In February, 1975, the motion picture *Shampoo* was released theatrically. Plaintiff and her husband viewed *Shampoo* in a local theatre that same month. They recognized several similarities between the motion picture and "Women Plus." Plaintiff determined that Columbia retained her submission of "Women Plus" and used the treatment in the production of *Shampoo*. Shortly thereafter, plaintiff engaged Charles Rubin, an attorney, to determine whether legal action was available. Rubin conducted the initial investigation of the alleged "Columbia connection." However, Mann later enlisted the services of her current counsel, who filed plaintiff's complaint on January 13, 1976.

At trial, plaintiff and her husband both testified as to similarities they perceived between "Women Plus" and the motion picture *Shampoo*. In addition, plaintiff introduced a chart into evidence for the jury's consideration. This chart presented a detailed comparison of several similarities between plaintiff's treatment and a written transcription of the scenes and dialogue in *Shampoo*.[2] The jury also viewed the motion picture *Shampoo*. Richard Lanham, defendants' expert analyst of literary works, compared "Women Plus," the written transcription of *Shampoo*, and defendant Towne's 1970 written screenplay. Professor Lanham described "overall similarities" between plaintiff's outline and the motion picture.[3] * * *

overall similarities

Columbia entered a written agreement to finance the production of *Shampoo* in February, 1974. The filming of *Shampoo* began in late March, 1974. Defendant Towne, a screenwriter, testified that he was still working on the "shooting script" for *Shampoo* before the filming started. Towne also stated that he changed the script several times during the "shooting" of the motion picture. The screenwriter indicated that he never read "Women Plus," and has "never been anywhere near" Columbia's story department.

Defendant Beatty collaborated with Towne on the *Shampoo* script and its subsequent changes during filming. Beatty testified that he had never seen "Women Plus" before the trial. He also indicated that he was never inside the story department at Columbia. According to Beatty, no Columbia representative ever showed him another person's treatment or screenplay filed in the company's story department. * * *

The analytical framework for the case at bar is shaped by the answers to two questions. Desny v. Wilder, 46 Cal.2d 715, 744, 299 P.2d 257 (1956). First, did Mann submit "Women Plus" to defendants for sale? The trial record shows no evidence, nor does plaintiff even allege, that her treatment was ever submitted to either defendant Beatty or defendant Towne. Mann alleges, however, that "Women Plus" was submitted to defendant Columbia through either Caplan or Crutcher. The alleged access of Towne and Beatty to the treatment is contingent upon its purported presence in Columbia's story files. Therefore, the asserted contractual obligation exists, if at all, only between Mann and Columbia. Donahue v. Ziv Television Programs, Inc., 245 Cal.App.2d 593, 607–608, 54 Cal.Rptr. 130 (1966).

The existence of that contractual obligation is also dependent upon the answer to the second question. Did Columbia, knowing that "Women Plus" was offered to it for sale, accept and use that treatment, or any part thereof, in the motion picture *Shampoo*? Since there was no express agreement in this case, Mann must show Columbia's implied promise to pay for the alleged use of her ideas. Desny v. Wilder, 46 Cal.2d 715, 738, 299 P.2d 257.

2. The parallel comparison listed ten areas of similarity between "Women Plus" and *Shampoo*, ranging from the characters and story line to a review of various scenes.

3. Professor Lanham referred to the beauty salon setting, two homosexual hairdressers, a hairdresser's sexual exploits, a mother-daughter competition involving sexual accusations, a shampoo girl, and the interruption of a hairdresser while he is working on a woman involved in a political gathering that evening. Lanham conceded that each of these features appeared in both "Women Plus" and *Shampoo*.

For this court to find that Mann and Columbia entered an implied in fact contract, plaintiff must demonstrate that she clearly conditioned her offer of "Women Plus" upon an obligation to pay for it, or its ideas, if used by Columbia; and Columbia, knowing the condition before it knew the ideas, voluntarily accepted their disclosure (necessarily on the specified basis) and found them valuable and used them, * * * Columbia's implied promise, if it is to be found, must be based on circumstances which were known to the studio at and preceding the time the ideas were allegedly disclosed to it. Columbia must have voluntarily accepted "Women Plus" with knowledge of the conditions of tender. * * *

In this case, Mann must prove Columbia's conduct from which defendant's promise may be implied. * * * The trial court properly instructed the jurors on Mann's burden, and the preceding prerequisites for finding an implied in fact contract.

The submission of "Women Plus" to Columbia is not only a requirement for the contractual obligation alleged herein, but it is also the basis for plaintiff's argument that defendants Beatty and Towne had access to her treatment. For purposes of this discussion, the court assumes that "Women Plus" remained enclosed in the envelope transferred from plaintiff to Florence Klase, Evelyn Light, and Harry Caplan. Caplan was a Filmmakers production manager when he received plaintiff's envelope from Light. Mann concedes that the submission of the envelope was not conditioned on its delivery to Columbia. Caplan transferred the envelope to a colleague, Gary Crutcher, who was a story editor at Filmmakers. There is no substantial evidence in the trial record that either Caplan or Crutcher acted for Columbia in accepting Mann's submission.

Mann stresses that the jury viewed the motion picture *Shampoo*. The jurors also examined plaintiff's chart comparison of several similarities between "Women Plus" and *Shampoo*. Mann also emphasizes the script changes made while filming *Shampoo*, and Columbia's willingness to review something Towne had read and offer comments before filming the motion picture. Plaintiff concludes that the foregoing is substantial evidence for the jury's determination that "Women Plus" was submitted to Columbia. Mann also asserts that the jury reasonably inferred the access of Towne and Beatty to her treatment, and their use of her ideas in filming *Shampoo*.

Similarity, access, and use present questions of fact for the jury. Kurlan v. Columbia Broadcasting System, 40 Cal.2d 799, 810, 256 P.2d 962 (1953). One of the jury's functions in this action was to determine whether such similarity existed between *Shampoo* and "Women Plus" as to suggest defendants' use of ideas originating with plaintiff. Stanley v. Columbia Broadcasting System, 35 Cal.2d 653, 660, 221 P.2d 73 (1950). * * *

The jury's determination of similarity between "Women Plus" and *Shampoo* was substantially supported by the jurors' examination of plaintiff's chart comparison and view of the motion picture. But any similarities between the two works in this case are without legal significance. The jury may have inferred defendants' access and use of "Women Plus" from its comparison with *Shampoo*. This inference, however, was rebutted by clear, positive and uncontradicted evidence. * * * Caplan, Crutcher, Beatty, and Towne all testified that the first two men had no contact with the two defendants before this litigation. Their testimony in this regard was not even challenged by plaintiff. More importantly, neither [Columbia employees] Merzbach, Snell, nor Nagy was impeached or contradicted in testifying that Columbia's story files contained no record that Mann's "Women Plus" was ever submitted to the studio. The preceding testimony constitutes a clear and positive rebuttal of the inference of access and use raised by the similarities between the two works herein. * * *

The "independent effort" of Towne and Beatty in developing the *Shampoo* script provides Columbia with a complete defense against the contractual obligation alleged herein. * * * The defense is established in this case because the inference of access and use was rebutted. Since there was neither a submission of "Women Plus" to Columbia, nor any contact between the screenplay authors and the people alleged to have possessed plaintiff's treatment, there is no substantial evidence to support the jury verdict.

The action of the trial court in granting judgment notwithstanding the verdict was correct. * * * We affirm the order of the trial court granting judgment notwithstanding the verdict. In view of our holding, it is not necessary to discuss the trial court's conditional grant of a new trial, or the other points argued by the parties herein.

The judgment is affirmed.

Notes

1. Can you legally rely on what friends tell you? This case illustrates the problem of using a chain of friends to get a story idea submitted to a film studio. Mann gave the envelope containing her treatment to her friend Florence Klase, who gave it to her neighbor, Evelyn Light, who gave it to Harry Caplan, who gave it to Gary Crutcher, who worked at Filmmakers not Columbia. Mann had no direct contact with Caplan, Crutcher, or anyone from Columbia, yet assumed that Columbia must have received her treatment because her friend told her she would get it to Columbia, and then *Shampoo* was released and was similar to her treatment. Similarities between a film and someone's idea are irrelevant if there is no connection between the parties because each can independently create the same idea. Mann lost because she could not prove that Columbia had even received her treatment, let alone used it.

2. Warren Beatty is the younger brother of actress Shirley MacLaine, whose compensation case appears in Chapter 5. As of 2004, Beatty has starred in 21 films including his debut role as Bud Stamper in the 1961 *Splendor in the Grass*, the character of Clyde Barrow in the 1967 *Bonnie and Clyde*, and the legendary mobster Bugsy Siegel in the 1991 *Bugsy*. Beatty

has also produced nine films, written seven and directed four. While many of his films became huge hits, Beatty also bears responsibility for the 1987 box office disaster *Ishtar,* which cost $55 million while taking in a domestic box office gross of $12.7 million, and the 2001 *Town & Country,* whose budget was $85 million and domestic gross yield was $6.7 million.

Beatty won an Academy Award for best director for the 1981 film *Reds.* In 2000, he received the Academy's Irving G. Thalberg Memorial Award given to producers whose bodies of work reflect a consistently high quality of motion picture production. He is the only person to be twice nominated for Academy Awards for producer, director, writer, and actor on a film. *See generally* http://movies.yahoo.com/shop?d=hc & id=1800020836 & cf=movies & intl=us and http://www.oscars.org/press/pressreleases/2000/00.01.19.a.html.

END 8.25

Chapter 2

COPYRIGHT PROTECTION OF FILMS

Under Article 1, Section 8, Clause 8 of the U.S. Constitution, "The Congress shall have the Power ... to Promote the Progress of Science and useful Arts, by securing for limited Times to Authors and Inventors the exclusive Right to their respective Writings and Discoveries." Congress first implemented this provision with the Copyright Act of 1790, which modeled England's Statute of Anne, 8 Anne, c.19 (1709). By implementing the Statute of Anne, England produced a breakthrough against piracy that arose after the invention of the first printing press in 1450 by German Johannes Gutenberg and the second 26 years later by Englishman William Claxton.

Prior to the invention of these printing presses, monks and scribners copied books by hand, averaging a book a year. With this slow process of producing books, authors worried little about others stealing their work. Indeed, the book that was reproduced most often was "The Bible." The printing press revolutionized the manufacture of books, permitting mass reproduction and theft of original work.

The Statute of Anne gave authors 14 years of protection for their work, after which it fell into the public domain. The U.S. Copyright Act of 1790 gave authors an initial 14 years of protection with the option to renew for an additional 14 years. While Congress initially protected only books, charts, and maps, it has expanded coverage of new forms of art and technology as they have been invented. Congress began protecting photographs in 1865, motion pictures in 1912, sound recordings in 1972, and computer disks in 1976.

The term of years has expanded as well from the initial maximum of 28 years to the current lifetime of the author plus 70 years or a flat 95 years if the work is owned by a legal entity like a corporation. There are three requirements for an item to be copyrightable. It must possess all the following:

1. Copyrightable subject matter
2. Fixation in a tangible medium of expression
   a. physical rendering of the work

      b.   material object

      c.   paper

      d.   magnetic tape

      e.   marble block

   3. Work must originate with the author:

      Copyright claimant must not have copied the work from someone else.

The second two requirements have yielded far fewer lawsuits and confusion than the first, which is discussed in Section A of this chapter. Motion pictures, television shows, and music are obviously fixed in a tangible medium of expression. They are physical and can be touched and handled. Theaters show movies from reels and buyers can purchase them in DVD or VHS formats. Television shows are also played from tapes or digital format in studios, or downloaded from a satellite feed. Music can be physically rendered in sheet music, on tapes, or CDs.

The requirement that the work originate with the author produces some disputes particularly when an allegation of plagiarism surfaces. In bringing an action for theft, the plaintiff is claiming that the defendant's work originated with the plaintiff. Originality can have a dual meaning when it comes to derivative works. The courts ask whether the newcomer contributed anything new or novel to the first work. This issue arose in the case of *Gracen v. Bradford Exchange*, 698 F.2d 300 (7th Cir. 1983), which is reviewed in Section A below.

Section A also discusses the thorny issue of what qualifies for copyright protection. Section B provides an overview of the formalities required to protect copyrighted work. Section C explores moral rights and the colorization of films. Section D analyzes copyright infringement issues and Section E probes the amorphous fair use problem and how to use another person's copyrighted work without having to pay compensation.

A. COPYRIGHTABLE SUBJECT MATTER

Under 17 U.S.C. § 102:

   (a) Copyright protection subsists, in accordance with this title, in original works of authorship fixed in any tangible medium of expression, now known or later developed, from which they can be perceived, reproduced, or otherwise communicated, either directly or with the aid of a machine or device. Works of authorship include the following categories:

     (1) literary works;

     (2) musical works, including any accompanying words;

     (3) dramatic works, including any accompanying music;

     (4) pantomimes and choreographic works;

    (5) pictorial, graphic, and sculptural works;

    (6) motion pictures and other audiovisual works;

    (7) sound recordings; and

    (8) architectural works.

    (b) In no case does copyright protection for an original work of authorship extend to any idea, procedure, process, system, method of operation, concept, principle, or discovery, regardless of the form in which it is described, explained, illustrated, or embodied in such work.

The following two cases in this section discuss what constitutes an original creative work and the circumstances under which a second work based on the original work can be prepared. The second work is often referred to as a derivative work, in that it derives its origin in part from a first work. The *Bleistein* case is one of the seminal cases in this area, although it refers to another form of entertainment, namely artwork of a circus family.

BLEISTEIN v. DONALDSON LITHOGRAPHING CO.

United States Supreme Court, 1903.
188 U.S. 239, 23 S.Ct. 298, 47 L.Ed. 460.

Mr. Justice HOLMES delivered the opinion of the court.

    This case comes here from the United States circuit court of appeals for the sixth circuit by writ of error. * * * The alleged infringements consisted in the copying in reduced form of three chromolithographs prepared by employees of the plaintiffs for advertisements of a circus owned by one Wallace. Each of the three contained a portrait of Wallace in the corner, and lettering bearing some slight relation to the scheme of decoration, indicating the subject of the design and the fact that the reality was to be seen at the circus. One of the designs was of an ordinary ballet, one of a number of men and women, described as the Stirk family, performing on bicycles, and one of groups of men and women whitened to represent statues. The circuit court directed a verdict for the defendant on the ground that the chromolithographs were not within the protection of the copyright law, and this ruling was sustained by the circuit court of appeals. * * *

    There was evidence warranting the inference that the designs belonged to the plaintiffs, they having been produced by persons employed and paid by the plaintiffs in their establishment to make those very things. * * * It fairly might be found, also, that the copyrights were taken out in the proper names. One of them was taken out in the name of the Courier Company and the other two in the name of the Courier Lithographing Company. The former was the name of an unincorporated joint-stock association formed under the laws of New York (Laws of 1894, chap. 235), and made up of the plaintiffs, the other a trade variant on that name. * * *

Finally, there was evidence that the pictures were copyrighted before publication. There may be a question whether the use by the defendant for Wallace was not lawful within the terms of the contract with Wallace, or a more general one as to what rights the plaintiff reserved. But we cannot pass upon these questions as matter of law; they will be for the jury when the case is tried again, and therefore we come at once to the ground of decision in the courts below. That ground was not found in any variance between pleading and proof, such as was put forward in argument, but in the nature and purpose of the designs.

We shall do no more than mention the suggestion that painting and engraving, unless for a mechanical end, are not among the useful arts, the progress of which Congress is empowered by the Constitution to promote. The Constitution does not limit the useful to that which satisfies immediate bodily needs. * * * It is obvious also that the plaintiff's case is not affected by the fact, if it be one, that the pictures represent actual groups,—visible things. They seem from the testimony to have been composed from hints or description, not from sight of a performance. But even if they had been drawn from the life, that fact would not deprive them of protection. The opposite proposition would mean that a portrait by Velasquez or Whistler was common property because others might try their hand on the same face. Others are free to copy the original. They are not free to copy the copy. * * * The copy is the personal reaction of an individual upon nature. Personality always contains something unique. It expresses its singularity even in handwriting, and a very modest grade of art has in it something irreducible, which is one man's alone. That something he may copyright unless there is a restriction in the words of the act.

If there is a restriction it is not to be found in the limited pretensions of these particular works. The least pretentious picture has more originality in it than directories and the like, which may be copyrighted. * * * The amount of training required for humbler efforts than those before us is well indicated by Ruskin. 'If any young person, after being taught what is, in polite circles, called 'drawing,' will try to copy the commonest piece of real *work*,—suppose a lithograph on the title page of a new opera air, or a woodcut in the cheapest illustrated newspaper of the day,—they will find themselves entirely beaten.' Elements of Drawing, first ed. 3. There is no reason to doubt that these prints in their *ensemble* and in all their details, in their design and particular combinations of figures, lines, and colors, are the original work of the plaintiffs' designer. If it be necessary, there is express testimony to that effect. It would be pressing the defendant's right to the verge, if not beyond, to leave the question of originality to the jury upon the evidence in this case, as was done in *Hegeman* v. *Springer*, 49 C. C. A. 86, 110 Fed. 374.

We assume that the construction of Rev. Stat. § 4952 (U. S. Comp. Stat. 1901, p. 3406), allowing a copyright to the 'author, designer, or proprietor ... of any engraving, cut, print ... [or] chromo' is affected by the act of 1874 (18 Stat. at L. 78, 79, chap. 301, § 3, U. S. Comp. Stat. 1901, p. 3412). That section provides that, 'in the construction of this act, the words 'engraving,' 'cut,' and 'print' shall be applied only to pictorial illustrations or works connected with the fine arts.' We see no reason for taking the words 'connected with the fine arts' as qualifying anything except the word 'works,' but it would not change our decision if we should assume further that they also qualified 'pictorial illustrations,' as the defendant contends.

These chromolithographs are 'pictorial illustrations.' The word 'illustrations' does not mean that they must illustrate the text of a book, and that the etchings of Rembrandt or Müller's engraving of the Madonna di San Sisto could not be protected today if any man were able to produce them. Again, the act, however construed, does not mean that ordinary posters are not good enough to be considered within its scope. The antithesis to 'illustrations or works connected with the fine arts' is not works of little merit or of humble degree, or illustrations addressed to the less educated classes; it is 'prints or labels designed to be used for any other articles of manufacture.' Certainly works are not the less connected with the fine arts because their pictorial quality attracts the crowd, and therefore gives them a real use,—if use means to increase trade and to help to make money. A picture is none the less a picture, and none the less a subject of copyright, that it is used for an advertisement. And if pictures may be used to advertise soap, or the theatre, or monthly magazines, as they are, they may be used to advertise a circus. Of course, the ballet is as legitimate a subject for illustration as any other. A rule cannot be laid down that would excommunicate the paintings of Degas.

Finally, the special adaptation of these pictures to the advertisement of the Wallace shows does not prevent a copyright. That may be a circumstance for the jury to consider in determining the extent of Mr. Wallace's rights, but it is not a bar. Moreover, on the evidence, such prints are used by less pretentious exhibitions when those for whom they were prepared have given them up.

It would be a dangerous undertaking for persons trained only to the law to constitute themselves final judges of the worth of pictorial illustrations, outside of the narrowest and most obvious limits. At the one extreme, some works of genius would be sure to miss appreciation. Their very novelty would make them repulsive until the public had learned the new language in which their author spoke. It may be more than doubted, for instance, whether the etchings of Goya or the paintings of Manet would have been sure of protection when seen for the first time. At the other end, copyright would be denied to pictures which appealed to a public less educated than the judge. Yet if they command the interest of any public, they have a commercial value,—it would be bold to say that they have not an aesthetic and educational value,—and the taste of any public is not to be treated with contempt. It is an ultimate fact for the moment, whatever may be our hopes for a change. That these pictures had their worth and their success is sufficiently shown by the desire to reproduce them without regard to the plaintiffs' rights. * * * We are of [the] opinion that there was evidence that the plaintiffs have rights entitled to the protection of the law.

The judgment of the Circuit Court of Appeals is reversed; the judgment of the Circuit Court is also reversed and the cause remanded to that court with directions to set aside the verdict and grant a new trial.

MR. JUSTICE HARLAN, dissenting.

Judges Lurton, Day, and Severens, of the circuit court of appeals, concurred in affirming the judgment of the district court. Their views were thus expressed in an opinion delivered by Judge Lurton: 'What we hold is this: * * * We are unable to discover anything useful or meritorious in the design copyrighted by the plaintiffs in error other than as an advertisement of acts to be done or exhibited to the public in Wallace's show. No evidence, aside from the deductions which are to be drawn from the prints themselves, was offered to show that these designs had any original artistic qualities. The jury could not reasonably have found merit or value aside from the purely business object of advertising a show, and the instruction to find for the defendant was not error. Many other points have been urged as justifying the result reached in the court below. We find it unnecessary to express any opinion upon them, in view of the conclusion already announced. The judgment must be affirmed.' * * *

I entirely concur in these views, and therefore dissent from the opinion and judgment of this court. The clause of the Constitution giving Congress power to promote the progress of science and useful arts, by securing for limited terms to authors and inventors the exclusive right to their respective works and discoveries, does not, as I think, embrace a mere advertisement of a circus.

Notes

1. Justices Holmes & Harlan ably debate whether chromolithographs, which fall somewhere between an original painting and a poster on an art scale, are entitled to copyright protection. Central to their debate is the question, "what constitutes art?" What is your definition of art? To what extent are films considered art? Do you think Justice Holmes is correct when he admonishes, "It would be a dangerous undertaking for persons trained only to the law to constitute themselves final judges of the worth of pictorial illustrations, outside of the narrowest and most obvious limits?" For more discussion of the legal definitions of art, see Chapter 1 of DUBOFF, BURR, & MURRAY, ART LAW: CASES & MATERIALS (2004).

2. Is Justice Holmes' admonition also true for films? What one person might consider an exceptional film, could another person easily dismiss as unworthy of the $2.25 cost of a film in Buenas Aires. When worldwide film prices range from a low for $2.25 to a high of $19.00 in London, do filmmakers have a responsibility to deliver art to the viewing public? *See* Robert Mackey, *A World of Ticket Prices*, N.Y. TIMES, Jan.22, 2004, at Sec. 2, P. 8.

3. As you review the following case, consider whether Judge Posner is in effect ignoring Justice Holmes' admonition, although he paraphrases it?

GRACEN v. BRADFORD EXCHANGE

United States Court of Appeals, Seventh Circuit, 1983.
698 F.2d 300.

POSNER, Circuit Judge.

This appeal brings up to us questions of some novelty, at least in this circuit, regarding implied copyright licenses and the required originality for copyrighting a derivative work.

In 1939 MGM produced and copyrighted the movie "The Wizard of Oz." The central character in the movie, Dorothy, was played by Judy Garland. The copyright was renewed by MGM in 1966 and is conceded, at least for purposes of this case, to be valid and in effect today. In 1976 MGM licensed Bradford Exchange to use characters and scenes from the movie in a series of collectors' plates. Bradford invited several artists to submit paintings of Dorothy as played by Judy Garland, with the understanding that the artist who submitted the best painting would be offered a contract for the entire series. Bradford supplied each artist with photographs from the movie and with instructions for the painting that included the following: "We do want *your* interpretation of these images, but your interpretation must evoke all the warm feeling the people have for the film and its actors. So, *your* Judy/Dorothy must be very recognizable as everybody's Judy/Dorothy."

Jorie Gracen, an employee in Bradford's order-processing department, was permitted to join the competition. From photographs and her recollections of the movie (which she had seen several times) she made a painting of Dorothy as played by Judy Garland; Figure 1 at the end of this opinion is a reproduction of a photograph of Miss Gracen's painting (an inadequate one, because the original is in color). Bradford exhibited it along with the other contestants' paintings in a shopping center. The passersby liked Miss Gracen's the best, and Bradford pronounced her the winner of the competition and offered her a contract to do the series, as well as paying her, as apparently it paid each of the other contestants, $200. But she did not like the contract terms and refused to sign, and Bradford turned to another artist, James Auckland, who had not been one of the original contestants. He signed a contract to do the series and Bradford gave him Miss Gracen's painting to help him in doing his painting of Dorothy. The record does not indicate who has her painting now.

Gracen's counsel describes Auckland's painting of Dorothy as a "piratical copy" of her painting. Bradford could easily have refuted this charge, if it is false, by attaching to its motion for summary judgment a photograph of its Dorothy plate, but it did not, and for purposes of this appeal we must assume that the plate is a copy of Miss Gracen's painting. This is not an absurd supposition. Bradford, at least at first, was rapturous about Miss Gracen's painting of Dorothy. It called Miss Gracen "a true prodigy." It said that hers "was the one painting that conveyed the essence of Judy's character in the film ... the painting that left everybody saying, 'That's Judy in Oz.'" Auckland's deposition states that Bradford gave him her painting with directions to "clean it up," which he understood to mean: do the same thing but make it "a little more professional."

Miss Gracen also made five drawings of other characters in the movie, for example the Scarecrow as played by Ray Bolger. Auckland's affidavit states without contradiction that he had not seen any of the drawings when he made his paintings of those characters. Pictures of the plates that were made from his paintings are attached to the motion for summary judgment filed by MGM and Bradford, but there is no picture of his Dorothy plate, lending some support to the charge that it is a "piratical copy." But apparently the other plates are not copies at all.

Auckland completed the series, and the plates were manufactured and sold. But Miss Gracen meanwhile had obtained copyright registrations on her painting and drawings, and in 1978 she brought this action for copyright infringement against MGM, Bradford, Auckland, and the manufacturer of the plates. MGM and Bradford counterclaimed, alleging among other things that Miss Gracen had infringed the copyright on the movie by showing her drawings and a photograph of her painting to people whom she was soliciting for artistic commissions.

The district court granted summary judgment against Miss Gracen on both the main claim and the counterclaim. It held that she could not copyright her painting and drawings because they were not original and that she had infringed MGM's copyright. The court entered judgment for $1500 on the counterclaim. Neither the judgment nor the opinion accompanying it refers to the noncopyright claims in the counterclaim, thus inviting the question whether that judgment is final and hence appealable under 28 U.S.C. § 1291. But this is not a serious problem, because the judgment purports to dispose of "their [MGM's and Bradford's] counterclaims" and both sides have treated it as disposing of the counterclaim in its entirety. The noncopyright claims must therefore be regarded as having been either dismissed or abandoned.

The briefs and argument in this court follow the district court in treating the principal question as whether Miss Gracen's painting and drawings are sufficiently original to be copyrightable as derivative works under 17 U.S.C. § 103. But this emphasis may be misplaced. The question of the copyrightability of a derivative work ("a work based upon one or more preexisting works, such as a[n] ... art reproduction ... or any other form in which a work may be recast, transformed, or adapted," 17 U.S.C. § 101) usually arises in connection with something either made by the owner (or a licensee) of the copyright on the underlying work, as in *Durham Industries, Inc. v. Tomy Corp.*, 630 F.2d 905, 909 (2d Cir.1980), or derived from an underlying work that is in the public domain, as in *L. Batlin & Son, Inc. v. Snyder*, 536 F.2d 486, 491–92 (2d

Cir.1976) (en banc). At issue in such a case is not the right to copy the underlying work but whether there is enough difference between the derivative and the underlying work to satisfy the statutory requirement of originality, see 17 U.S.C. § 102(a), and thus make the derivative work copyrightable. Since the copyright owner's bundle of exclusive rights includes the right "to prepare derivative works based upon the copyrighted work," 17 U.S.C. § 106(2), even if Miss Gracen's painting and drawings had enough originality to be copyrightable as derivative works *she* could not copyright them unless she had authority to use copyrighted materials from the movie. "[P]rotection for a work employing preexisting material in which copyright subsists does not extend to any part of the work in which such material has been used unlawfully." 17 U.S.C. § 103(a).

Miss Gracen does not claim that she painted the 16–year-old Judy Garland who appeared in "The Wizard of Oz" in 1939 from life or from photographs taken from the movie, or that her painting is not of Judy Garland but is an imaginative conception of the character Dorothy. The painting was based on the movie, both as independently recollected by Miss Gracen and as frozen in the still photographs that Bradford supplied her. As with any painting there was an admixture of the painter's creativity—how much we shall consider later—but that it is a painting of Judy Garland as she appears in photographs from the movie (such as the photograph reproduced at the end of this opinion as Figure 2), and is therefore a derivative work, is beyond question. The same is true of the drawings.

Therefore, if Miss Gracen had no authority to make derivative works from the movie, she could not copyright the painting and drawings, and she infringed MGM's copyright by displaying them publicly. But obviously she had *some* authority, having been invited by Bradford to make a painting of Dorothy based on the movie. And although Bradford was not expressly authorized to sublicense the copyright in this way, there can be no serious doubt of its authority to do so. Thus the question is not whether Miss Gracen was licensed to make a derivative work but whether she was also licensed to exhibit the painting and to copyright it.

Bradford made no written agreement with the contestants for the disposition of their paintings. It could have required each contestant to give it full rights as consideration for $200 and a shot at a potentially lucrative contract, but it did not do so, not in writing anyway, and though it argues that it "bought" Miss Gracen's painting of Dorothy for $200 we find no evidence to support this characterization of the transaction. Miss Gracen testified in her deposition that Foster, who was in charge of the contest, said he would return the painting to her; and we must ask what he thought she would do with the painting when she got it back, if they failed to come to terms. Destroy it? Keep it in a closet till MGM's copyright expired? Bradford, in promising Miss Gracen (as for purposes of this appeal we must assume it did) that she could keep the painting, must have known she would exhibit it to advance her career as an artist. And while Bradford's license from MGM may not have authorized it to make any such promise, Bradford may have had apparent authority to do so and that is all that would be necessary to give Miss Gracen (who presumably knew nothing of the terms of the license) the right to exhibit her painting. *See* Seavey, Handbook of the Law of Agency 125–28 (1964). We do not say she actually had the right, but only that there is a genuine issue of material fact concerning the scope of her implied license to make a derivative work.

It is less likely that Miss Gracen was entitled to exhibit, or even to make, the drawings. Their making was no part of the contest. Yet she testified that Foster told her to make the drawings to improve her chances of winning, and this testimony was not contradicted or inherently incredible. If she was authorized to make the drawings maybe she was also authorized—or reasonably believed she was authorized—to exhibit them, at least if she did not come to terms with Bradford.

The grant of summary judgment on the counterclaim was therefore erroneous—assuming an oral nonexclusive copyright license is enforceable. Nimmer describes this as the law both before and after the Copyright Act was revised in 1976, *see* 3 Nimmer on Copyright § § 10.03[A]-[B] at pp. 10–36 to 10–37 and nn. 17, 22, 23 (1982), and though support for this conclusion is sparse, and there is some contrary authority, *see Douglas Int'l Corp. v. Baker,* 335 F.Supp. 282, 285 (S.D.N.Y.1971), we think Nimmer is right. This case shows why. MGM and Bradford do not even argue that Bradford had no authority to permit Miss Gracen to *make* a derivative work, though nothing in the license to Bradford purports to authorize sublicensing. They thus tacitly acknowledge the impracticality of requiring written licenses in all circumstances; and we do not see how it can be argued that only the existence and not the scope of a license can be proved by parol evidence.

This disposes of the counterclaim, but we have still to consider Miss Gracen's claim that she had valid copyrights which the defendants infringed. The initial issue is again the scope of her implied license from Bradford. Even if she was authorized to exhibit her derivative works, she may not have been authorized to copyright them. Bradford was licensed to use MGM's copyright in its series of collectors' plates but not to copyright the derivative works thus created. A copyright owner is naturally reluctant to authorize a licensee to take out copyrights on derivative works—copyrights that might impede him in making his own derivative works or in licensing others to do so. And it would have made no more sense for Bradford, the licensee, to arm Miss Gracen, its sublicensee, with a weapon—the right to copyright her derivative works—that she could use to interfere with Bradford's efforts to get another artist to do the plates if it could not cut a deal with her. The affidavits submitted with the motions for summary judgment deny that Miss Gracen was authorized to copyright derivative works based on the movie and are not contradicted on this point. (In contrast, they do not deny that she was authorized to exhibit her painting of Dorothy.)

We are reluctant to stop here, though, and uphold the dismissal of the complaint on the basis of an issue of fact that the district judge did not address, and that we therefore may have got wrong, so we shall go on and consider his ground for dismissal of the complaint—that Miss Gracen's painting and drawings are not original enough to be copyrightable.

Miss Gracen reminds us that judges can make fools of themselves pronouncing on aesthetic matters. But artistic originality is not the same thing as the legal concept of originality in the Copyright Act. Artistic originality indeed might inhere in a detail, a nuance, a shading too small to be apprehended by a judge. A contemporary school of art known as "Super Realism" attempts with some success to make paintings that are indistinguishable to the eye from color photographs. *See* Super Realism: A Critical Anthology (Battcock ed. 1975). These paintings command high prices; buyers must find something original in them. Much Northern European painting of the Renaissance is meticulously representational, see, e.g., Gombrich, The Story of Art 178–80 (13th ed. 1978), and therefore in a sense—but not an aesthetic sense—less "original" than Cubism or Abstract Expressionism. A portrait is not unoriginal for being a good likeness.

But especially as applied to derivative works, the concept of originality in copyright law has as one would expect a legal rather than aesthetic function—to prevent overlapping claims. *See L. Batlin & Son, Inc. v. Snyder, supra,* 536 F.2d at 491–92. Suppose Artist A produces a reproduction of the Mona Lisa, a painting in the public domain, which differs slightly from the original. B also makes a reproduction of the Mona Lisa. A, who has copyrighted his derivative work, sues B for infringement. B's defense is that he was copying the original, not A's reproduction. But if the difference between the original and A's reproduction is slight, the difference between A's and B's reproductions will also be slight, so that if B had access to A's reproductions the trier of fact will be hard-pressed to decide whether B was copying A or copying the Mona Lisa itself. Miss Gracen's drawings illustrate the problem. They are very similar both to the photographs from the movie and to the plates designed by Auckland. Auckland's affidavit establishes that he did not copy or even see her drawings. But suppose he had seen them. Then it would be very hard to determine whether he had been copying the movie stills, as he was authorized to do, or copying her drawings.

The painting of Dorothy presents a harder question. A comparison of Figures 1 and 2 reveals perceptible differences. A painting (except, perhaps, one by a member of the Super Realist school mentioned earlier) is never identical to the subject painted, whether the subject is a photograph, a still life, a landscape, or a model, because most painters cannot and do not want to achieve a photographic likeness of their subject. Nevertheless, if the differences between Miss Gracen's painting of Dorothy and the photograph of Judy Garland as Dorothy were sufficient to make the painting original in the eyes of the law, then a painting by an Auckland also striving, as per his commission, to produce something "very recognizable as everybody's Judy/Dorothy" would look like the Gracen painting, to which he had access; and it would be difficult for the trier of fact to decide whether Auckland had copied her painting or the original movie stills. True, the background in Miss Gracen's painting differs from that in Figure 2, but it is drawn from the movie set. We do not consider a picture created by superimposing one copyrighted photographic image on another to be "original"—always bearing in mind that the purpose of the term in copyright law is not to guide aesthetic judgments but to assure a sufficiently gross difference between the underlying and the derivative work to avoid entangling subsequent artists depicting the underlying work in copyright problems.

We are speaking, however, only of the requirement of originality in derivative works. If a painter paints from life, no court is going to hold that his painting is not copyrightable because it is an exact photographic likeness. If that were the rule photographs could not be copyrighted—the photographs of Judy Garland in "The Wizard of Oz," for example—but of course they can be, 1 Nimmer on Copyright § 2.08[E] (1982). The requirement of originality is significant chiefly in connection with derivative works, where if interpreted too liberally it would paradoxically inhibit rather than promote the creation of such works by giving the first creator a considerable power to interfere with the creation of subsequent derivative works from the same underlying work.

Justice Holmes' famous opinion in *Bleistein v. Donaldson Lithographing Co.,* 188 U.S. 239 (1903), heavily relied on by Miss Gracen, is thus not in point. The issue was whether lithographs of a circus were copyrightable under a statute (no longer in force) that confined copyright to works "connected with the fine arts." Holmes' opinion is a warning against using aesthetic criteria to answer the question. If Miss Gracen had painted Judy Garland from life, her painting would be copyrightable even if we thought it *kitsch;* but a derivative work must be substantially different from the underlying work to be copyrightable. This is the test of *L. Batlin & Son, Inc. v. Snyder, supra,* 536 F.2d at 491, a decision of the Second Circuit—the nation's premier copyright court—sitting en banc. Earlier Second Circuit cases discussed in *Batlin* that suggest a more liberal test must be considered superseded.

We agree with the district court that under the test of *Batlin* Miss Gracen's painting, whatever its artistic merit, is not an original derivative work within the meaning of the Copyright Act. Admittedly this is a harder case than *Durham Industries, Inc. v. Tomy Corp., supra,* heavily relied on by the defendants. The underlying works in that case were Mickey Mouse and other Walt Disney cartoon characters, and the derivative works were plastic reproductions of them. Since the cartoon characters are extremely simple drawings, the reproductions were exact, differing only in the medium. The plastic Mickey and its cartoon original look more alike than Judy Garland's Dorothy and Miss Gracen's painting. But we do not think the difference is enough to allow her to copyright her painting even if, as we very much doubt, she was authorized by Bradford to do so.

The judgment dismissing the complaint is therefore affirmed. The judgment on the counterclaim is vacated and the case remanded for further proceedings consistent with this opinion. No costs in this court.

Notes

1. As you review the following two pictures, ask yourself whether there is a difference between artistic originality and legal originality? Figure 1 replicates a photograph of the Gracen painting. Figure 2 replicates a photograph of Judy Garland from a movie still from the *Wizard of Oz*.

2. Given that a derivative work is derived from another work, is Posner creating an unrealistic standard by requiring that "a derivative work must be substantially different form the underlying work to be copyrightable"? Should the originality requirement for derivative works be more or less stringent?

The Gracen Painting

Figure 1

A Photograph From *The Wizard of Oz*

Figure 2

B. COPYRIGHT FORMALITIES

The following section discusses the formalities required to secure copyright protection of your work.

1. COPYRIGHT NOTICE, DEPOSIT AND REGISTRATION

To give notice to the world that you are protecting your copyright requires the following:

> Copyright or ©, name and year. For example, this book initially contained the following notice: © Copyright 2003 by Sherri Burr and William Henslee.

After Congress passed the Berne Implementation Act amendments to the U.S. Copyright Law, copyright notice is optional. Your work is protected automatically whether you place a notice on it or not. There is an incentive to continue to apply notice to your work: you eliminate the innocent infringer defense, or someone claiming that they used your work not knowing that someone claimed a copyright to the work.

Similarly, registering the work by filling out the copyright forms, paying the applicable fee, and depositing two copies of the best edition of the work is also optional. The forms to register the work can be found at www.loc.gov/copyright. You click on performing arts to find the appropriate form for motion pictures.

Registration remains a prerequisite before you can initiate a suit in U.S. courts. Registration is considered prima facie evidence that you own the work.

Depositing two copies of the best edition of the work (i.e. two DVDs or VHS copies) is no longer a prerequisite to suit, but fines may be imposed if the Library of Congress requests the work and you decline to send it. The fines are often the equivalent of what it would cost the Library of Congress to purchase two copies of the work.

2. DURATION OF COPYRIGHT

Copyright endures for a limited number of years depending on who the author is and when the work was first copyrighted. These details can be found in 17 U.S.C. § 302 et seq.:

§ 302. Duration of copyright: Works created on or after January 1, 1978

(a) In General.—Copyright in a work created on or after January 1, 1978, subsists from its creation and, except as provided by the following subsections, endures for a term consisting of the life of the author and 70 years after the author's death.

(b) Joint Works.—In the case of a joint work prepared by two or more authors who did not work for hire, the copyright endures for a term consisting of the life of the last surviving author and 70 years after such last surviving author's death.

(c) Anonymous Works, Pseudonymous Works, and Works Made for Hire.—In the case of an anonymous work, a pseudonymous work, or a work made for hire, the copyright endures for a term of 95 years from the year of its first publication, or a term of 120 years from the year of its creation, whichever expires first. * * *

In October 1998, Congress passed and President Clinton signed into law The Sonny Bono Copyright Term Extension Act, which retroactively extended the duration of protection from life of the author plus 50 years to life of the author plus 70 years. Additionally, the law extended the term for works of corporate authorship and works first published before January 1, 1978 from the prior 75 years to 95 years. The law's provisions applied to works under copyright on the date of its implementation. An exception permits libraries, archives, and non-profit educational institutions to treat copyrighted works in their last twenty years of protection as if they were in the public domain for non-commercial purposes, under certain limited conditions.

The extension was challenged in the case of *Eldred v. Ashcroft,* 537 U.S. 186, 123 S.Ct. 769, 154 L.Ed.2d 683 (2003), as preventing a number of works, beginning with those published in 1923, from entering the public domain in 1998 and subsequent years as would have occurred under the previous law. Books, films and other materials, which the plaintiffs had been prepared to republish or restore, were now unavailable due to copyright restrictions.

The lead petitioner, Eric Eldred, a noncommercial Internet publisher of public domain texts and derivative works, was joined by a group of commercial and non-commercial interests who rely on the public domain for their work. Among the petitioners were Dover Publications, a commercial publisher of paperback books; Luck's Music Library, Inc. and Edwin F. Kalmus & Co., Inc., publishers of orchestral sheet music; and a large number of *amici curiae* including the Free Software Foundation, the American Association of Law Libraries, and the College Art Association.

The Supreme Court rejected the petitioners' challenges to the Copyright Term Extension Act, finding that "Congress acted within its authority and did not transgress constitutional limitations." *Eldred v. Ashcroft,* 537 U.S. 186, 123 S.Ct. 769, 154 L.Ed.2d 683 (2003).

C. COPYRIGHT OWNERSHIP AND TRANSFER

Film is a collaborative medium with many creative people contributing to the final product. On any given film, the following supply their talent: writers, actors, directors, producers, set designers, wardrobe designers, make-up artists, camera operators, editors, soundtrack composers, stunt performers, special effects supervisors, animators, and lighting designers. Without copyright ownership defined by contracts, customs and statutes, anyone from the above list could claim authorship of the film and inhibit its exploitation. The work for hire doctrine resolves problems concerning authorship and copyright ownership. The following is an example of what can go wrong when copyright issues are not settled before the commencement of the filmmaking process.

Sherri Burr
Copyright Issues and Documentary Filmmaking:
Author Interview With Diane Bloom

Copyright © 2003 by Sherri Burr.

[On December 7, 2003, author Sherri Burr sat down at the 2003 Santa Fe Film Festival with Diane Bloom, who screened *An Unlikely Friendship*, a 34–minute film about a relationship that developed between a black woman activist and the leader of the Durham, North Carolina, Ku

Klux Klan. Bloom possesses a MPH (masters of public health) degree and a PhD in psychology. This was her first venture into the filmmaking process.]

"I read about a friendship between a black woman and a Klansman in Osha Grey Davidson's book "The Best of Enemies" and thought the story should be told in their own words before they died. I wasn't thinking about any legal issues, but I learned my lesson.

I loved the story and decided to apply for a grant from the University of North Carolina two days before the application was due. I stayed up all night to write the proposal and was happy when I received $5000, which was enough to hire a photographer and an editor. I didn't know anything about work for hire agreements.

By the end everyone was claiming the copyright. The interviewer claimed copyright. The University of North Carolina claimed copyright because they gave us the money. The person who agreed to loan me the editing equipment left me in the lurch, but he claimed copyright. I had to hire a lawyer who told me that the interviewer and the University weren't entitled to copyright. Eventually they backed down.

The irony is that we worked on a film about peace and reconciliation and no one was talking to each other in the end. We screened the film to 300 people at the University of North Carolina. We received a standing ovation, but I went home and cried my eyes out.

I was an accidental filmmaker (it wasn't my living and I wasn't trained in it) and the film was unexpectedly successful. I originally thought it would play one night and basically sit on the shelf from then on. If that had happened, the legal work wouldn't have been necessary. My problems started because it was successful! Yet I still would not have predicted the turf-grabs, because in documentaries, there is usually NO money to be made!!

After the fact, I spent a lot of my own money on hiring a lawyer. If it ever makes royalties, one editor and the person who contributed the editing equipment want to receive royalties. It was terrible new equipment that crashed due to a faulty hard drive. I lost three months worth of work, but the guy still wants royalties. I learned that everyone always over estimates their contribution to the entire work.

All the fights drained my creativity. I wanted to dive in and tell the story. I didn't even know I needed release agreements from the interviewees. I had to go back and get them after the filming was done. It was detail work that I didn't even think about. If I had to do it all over again, I would hire a lawyer at the beginning. I could have saved myself a lot of grief."

Note

1. If a filmmaker like Diane Bloom came to see you in your law office, what would be your advice to her before she began the filmmaking process?

As you read the following article and cases in this section, think about what you might do to assist someone like Bloom?

1. WORK FOR HIRE

Sherri Burr
A Critical Assessment of Reid's Work for Hire Framework and its Potential Impact on the Market Place for Scholarly Works

24 John Marshall L. Rev. 119 (1990).
Copyright © 1990 by Sherri Burr [footnotes omitted.]

* * * In most instances, the person who actually creates the work is considered the author of the copyright. There is a limited exception to this general rule that was initially created judicially, then was codified into law in the 1909 Act, and was expanded upon in the 1976 Act. In the 1976 Act, the exception provides that "[i]n the case of work made for hire, the employer or other person for whom the work was prepared is considered the author for purposes of this title, and, unless the parties have expressly agreed otherwise in a written instrument signed by them, owns all of the rights comprised in the copyright. Classifying a work as "made for hire" determines not only the initial ownership of its copyright, but also the copyright duration, the owner's renewal rights with respect to works published before January 1, 1978, the owner's termination rights, and sometimes whether the work is copyrightable at all.

As defined in § 101, a work made for hire is:

(1) a work prepared by an employee within the scope of his or her employment; or

(2) a work specially ordered or commissioned for use as a contribution to a collective work, as a part of a motion picture or other audiovisual work, as a translation, as a supplementary work, as a compilation, as an instructional text, as a test, as answer material for a test, or as an atlas, if the parties expressly agree in a written instrument signed by them that the work shall be considered a work made for hire.

The plain language of § 101 indicates that a "work made for hire" arises from status, and can only be prepared by either an employee or a person who was specially commissioned or ordered to prepare the work. If the work is prepared by an employee, the resulting work must be within the scope of his or her employment to qualify as a "work made for hire" under subsection (1). If the work is prepared on special order or commission, then the resulting work must be within one of the nine enumerated categories to qualify as a "work made for hire" under subsection (2). While no written instrument is required in the case of an employee work, a written instrument is required in the case of a work prepared on special order or commission to make it a "work made for hire."

This requirement of a writing for specially ordered works under subsection (2) means that the creator of that type of work must consciously—assuming the contract is read—give up the copyright to the work that he or she would normally have as the creator of the work. By contrast, with employee works produced within the scope of employment under subsection (1), the act presumes the employer to be the author and requires an express written instrument signed by both parties for the employee to retain any of the rights comprised in the copyright. * * *

Notes

1. In the film industry, contributions to motion pictures fall under subsection 2. Although screenwriters, for example, will be given credit for writing the film and can copyright the script individually, once they sell the script, their work becomes incorporated into the film and is considered a work made for hire. The studio or production company will copyright the film in their name.

2. Oral agreements can lead to misunderstandings as to who owns the copyright. In the fall of 1985, Community for Creative Non–Violence (CCNV), a Washington, D.C. organization dedicated to eliminating homelessness, entered into an oral agreement with James Earl Reid to produce a statue to dramatize the plight of the homeless for display at a 1985 Christmas pageant in Washington, D.C. The parties agreed that CCNV would cover the cost of the materials and assistants and that Reid would donate his services. Similar to documentary filmmaker Diane Bloom's situation, neither party discussed copyright ownership. Subsequently, a dispute erupted over copyright and CCNV claimed that Reid was an employee under the work for hire doctrine. The Supreme Court decided that the relationship was not a work for hire and remanded to determine whether it was a joint work. *Community for Creative Non–Violence v. James Earl Reid*, 490 U.S. 730, 109 S.Ct. 2166, 104 L.Ed.2d 811 (1989). For a more thorough discussion of this case, *see* Sherri Burr, *A Critical Assessment of Reid's Work for Hire Framework and Its Impact on the Marketplace for Scholarly Works*, 24 JOHN MARSHALL L. REV. 119, 125–142 (1990).

2. JOINT WORKS AND JOINT OWNERSHIP

The Copyright Act provisions on works made for hire and joint works apply to motion pictures and music, as they are collaborative art forms. In the case of joint works, often two or more people may contribute to the creative output. Others sometimes feel their collaboration is worthy of author credit.

JEFRI AALMUHAMMED v. SPIKE LEE

United States Court of Appeals, Ninth Circuit, 2000.
202 F.3d 1227.

KLEINFELD, Circuit Judge.

This is a copyright case involving a claim of coauthorship of the movie *Malcolm X.* We reject the "joint work" claim but remand for further proceedings. * * *

I. FACTS

In 1991, Warner Brothers contracted with Spike Lee and his production companies to make the movie *Malcolm X,* to be based on the book, *The Autobiography of Malcolm X.* Lee co-wrote the screenplay, directed, and co-produced the movie, which starred Denzel Washington as Malcolm X. Washington asked Jefri Aalmuhammed to assist him in his preparation for the starring role because Aalmuhammed knew a great deal about Malcolm X and Islam. Aalmuhammed, a devout Muslim, was particularly knowledgeable about the life of Malcolm X, having previously written, directed, and produced a documentary film about Malcolm X.

Aalmuhammed joined Washington on the movie set. The movie was filmed in the New York metropolitan area and Egypt. Aalmuhammed presented evidence that his involvement in making the movie was very extensive. He reviewed the shooting script for Spike Lee and Denzel Washington and suggested extensive script revisions. Some of his script revisions were included in the released version of the film; others were filmed but not included in the released version. Most of the revisions Aalmuhammed made were to ensure the religious and historical accuracy and authenticity of scenes depicting Malcolm X's religious conversion and pilgrimage to Mecca.

Aalmuhammed submitted evidence that he directed Denzel Washington and other actors while on the set, created at least two entire scenes with new characters, translated Arabic into English for subtitles, supplied his own voice for voice-overs, selected the proper prayers and religious practices for the characters, and edited parts of the movie during post production. Washington testified in his deposition that Aalmuhammed's contribution to the movie was "great" because he "helped to rewrite, to make more authentic." Once production ended, Aalmuhammed met with numerous Islamic organizations to persuade them that the movie was an accurate depiction of Malcolm X's life.

Aalmuhammed never had a written contract with Warner Brothers, Lee, or Lee's production companies, but he expected Lee to compensate him for his work. He did not intend to work and bear his expenses in New York and Egypt gratuitously. Aalmuhammed ultimately received a check for $25,000 from Lee, which he cashed, and a check for $100,000 from Washington, which he did not cash.

During the summer before *Malcolm X*'s November 1992 release, Aalmuhammed asked for a writing credit as a co-writer of the film, but was turned down. When the film was released, it credited Aalmuhammed only as an "Islamic Technical Consultant," far down the list. In November 1995, Aalmuhammed applied for a copyright with the U.S. Copyright Office, claiming he was a co-creator, co-writer, and co-director of the movie. The Copyright Office issued him a "Certificate of Registration," but advised him in a letter that his "claims conflict with previous registrations" of the film.

On November 17, 1995, Aalmuhammed filed a complaint against Spike Lee, his production companies, and Warner Brothers, (collectively "Lee"), as well as Largo International, N.V., and Largo Entertainment, Inc. (collectively "Largo"), and Victor Company of Japan and JVC Entertainment, Inc. (collectively "Victor"). The suit sought declaratory relief and an accounting under the Copyright Act. In addition, the complaint alleged breach of implied contract, quantum meruit, and unjust enrichment, and federal (Lanham Act) and state unfair competition claims. The district court dismissed some of the claims under Rule 12(b)(6) and the rest on summary judgment.

II. ANALYSIS

A. Copyright claim

Aalmuhammed claimed that the movie *Malcolm X* was a "joint work" of which he was an author, thus making him a co-owner of the copyright. He sought a declaratory judgment to that effect, and an accounting for profits. He is not claiming copyright merely in what he wrote or contributed, but rather in the whole work, as a co-author of a "joint work." The district court granted defendants summary judgment against Mr. Aalmuhammed's copyright claims. We review de novo.

Defendants argue that Aalmuhammed's claim that he is one of the authors of a joint work is barred by the applicable statute of limitations. A claim of authorship of a joint work must be brought within three years of when it accrues. Because creation rather than infringement is the gravamen of an authorship claim, the claim accrues on account of creation, not subsequent infringement, and is barred three years from "plain and express repudiation" of authorship.

The movie credits plainly and expressly repudiated authorship, by listing Aalmuhammed far below the more prominent names, as an "Islamic technical consultant." That repudiation, though, was less than three years before the lawsuit was filed. The record leaves open a genuine issue of fact as to whether authorship was repudiated before that. Aalmuhammed testified in his deposition that he discussed with an executive producer at Warner Brothers his claim to credit as one of the screenwriters more than three years before he filed suit. Defendants argue that this discussion was an express repudiation that bars the claim. It was not. Aalmuhammed testified that the producer told him "there is nothing I can do for you," but "[h]e said we would discuss it further at some point." A trier of fact could construe that communication as leaving the question of authorship open for further discussion. That leaves a genuine issue of fact as to whether the claim is barred by limitations, so we must determine whether there is a genuine issue of fact as to whether Aalmuhammed was an author of a "joint work."

Aalmuhammed argues that he established a genuine issue of fact as to whether he was an author of a "joint work," *Malcolm X.* The Copyright Act does not define "author," but it does define "joint work":

> A "joint work" is a work prepared by two or more authors with the intention that their contributions be merged into inseparable or interdependent parts of a unitary whole.

* * * The statutory language establishes that for a work to be a "joint work" there must be (1) a copyrightable work, (2) two or more "authors," and (3) the authors must intend their contributions be merged into inseparable or interdependent parts of a unitary whole. A "joint work" in this circuit "requires each author to make an independently copyrightable contribution" to the disputed work. [*Richardson v. United States,* 526 U.S. 813, 119 S.Ct. 1707, 143 L.Ed.2d 985 (1999)] *Malcolm X* is a copyrightable work, and it is undisputed that the movie was intended by everyone involved with it to be a unitary whole. It is also undisputed that Aalmuhammed made substantial and valuable contributions to the movie, including technical help, such as speaking Arabic to the persons in charge of the mosque in Egypt, scholarly and creative help, such as teaching the actors how to pray properly as Muslims, and script changes to add verisimilitude to the religious aspects of the movie. Speaking Arabic to persons in charge of the mosque, however, does not result in a copyrightable contribution to the motion picture. Coaching of actors, to be copyrightable, must be turned into an expression in a form subject to copyright. The same may be said for many of Aalmuhammed's other activities. Aalmuhammed has, however, submitted evidence that he rewrote several specific passages of dialogue that appeared in *Malcolm X,* and that he wrote scenes relating to Malcolm X's Hajj pilgrimage that were enacted in the movie. If Aalmuhammed's evidence is accepted, as it must be on summary judgment, these items would have been independently copyrightable. Aalmuhammed, therefore, has presented a genuine issue of fact as to whether he made a copyrightable contribution. All persons involved intended that Aalmuhammed's contributions would be merged into interdependent parts of the movie as a unitary whole. Aalmuhammed maintains that he has shown a genuine issue of fact for each element of a "joint work."

But there is another element to a "joint work." A "joint work" includes "two or more authors." Aalmuhammed established that he contributed substantially to the film, but not that he was one of its "authors." We hold that authorship is required under the statutory definition of a joint work, and that authorship is not the same thing as making a valuable and copyrightable contribution. We recognize that a contributor of an expression may be deemed to be the "author" of that expression for purposes of determining whether it is independently copyrightable. The issue we deal with is a different and larger one: is the contributor an author of the joint work within the meaning of 17 U.S.C. § 101.

By statutory definition, a "joint work" requires "two or more authors." The word "author" is taken from the traditional activity of one person sitting at a desk with a pen and writing something for publication. It is relatively easy to apply the word "author" to a novel. * * * But as the number of contributors grows and the work itself becomes less the product of one or two individuals who create it without much help, the word is harder to apply.

Who, in the absence of contract, can be considered an author of a movie? The word is traditionally used to mean the originator or the person who causes something to come into being, or even the first cause, as when Chaucer refers to the "Author of Nature." For a movie, that might be the producer who raises the money. Eisenstein thought the author of a movie was the editor. The "auteur" theory suggests that it might be the director, at least if the director is able to impose his artistic judgments on the film. Traditionally, by analogy to books, the author was regarded as the person who writes the screenplay, but often a movie reflects the work of many screenwriters. Grenier suggests that the person with creative control tends to be the person in whose name the money is raised, perhaps a star, perhaps the director, perhaps the producer, with control gravitating to the star as the financial investment in scenes already shot grows. Where the visual aspect of the movie is especially important, the chief cinematographer might be regarded as the author. And for, say, a Disney animated movie like "The Jungle Book," it might perhaps be the animators and the composers of the music.

The Supreme Court dealt with the problem of defining "author" in new media in *Burrow-Giles Lithographic Co. v. Sarony* [*111 U.S. 53, 61, 4 S.Ct. 279, 28 L.Ed. 349 (1884)*]. The question there was, who is the author of a photograph: the person who sets it up and snaps the shutter, or the person who makes the lithograph from it. Oscar Wilde, the person whose picture was at issue, doubtless offered some creative advice as well. The Court decided that the photographer was the author, quoting various English authorities: "the person who has superintended the arrangement, who has actually formed the picture by putting the persons in position, and arranging the place where the people are to be—the man who is the effective cause of that"; " 'author' involves originating, making, producing, as the inventive or master mind, the thing which is to be protected"; "the man who really represents, creates, or gives effect to the idea, fancy, or imagination." [*Id.* at 61, 4 S.Ct. 279 (quoting Nottage v. Jackson, 11 Q.B.D. 627 (1883).] The Court said that an "author," in the sense that the Founding Fathers used the term in the Constitution [Art. 1, § 8, cl. 8] was " 'he to whom anything owes its origin; originator; maker; one who completes a work of science or literature.' " [Burrow–Giles, 111 U.S. at 58, 4 S.Ct. 279 (quoting Worcester)].

Answering a different question, what is a copyrightable "work," as opposed to who is the "author," the Supreme Court held in *Feist Publications* [499 U.S. 340, 345 (1991)] that "some minimal level of creativity" or "originality" suffices. But that measure of a "work" would be too broad and indeterminate to be useful if applied to determine who are "authors" of a movie. So many people might qualify as an "author" if the question were limited to whether they made a substantial creative contribution that that test would not distinguish one from another. Everyone from the producer and director to casting director, costumer, hairstylist, and "best boy" gets listed in the movie credits because all of their creative contributions really do matter. It is striking in *Malcolm X* how much the person who controlled the hue of the lighting contributed, yet no one would use the word "author" to denote that individual's relationship to the movie. A creative contribution does not suffice to establish authorship of the movie.

* * * *Burrow-Giles* [111 U.S. 53, 58 (1883)] defines author as the person to whom the work owes its origin and who superintended the whole work, the "master mind." In a movie this definition, in the absence of a contract to the contrary, would generally limit authorship to someone at the top of the screen credits, sometimes the producer, sometimes the director, possibly the star, or the screenwriter—someone who has artistic control. After all, in *Burrow-Giles* the lithographer made a substantial copyrightable creative contribution, and so did the person who posed, Oscar Wilde, but the Court held that the photographer was the author. [*Id.* at 61.] * * *

Aalmuhammed did not at any time have superintendence of the work. Warner Brothers and Spike Lee controlled it. Aalmuhammed was not the person "who has actually formed the picture by putting the persons in position, and arranging the place...." Spike Lee was, so far as we can tell from the record. Aalmuhammed, like Larson's dramaturg, could make extremely helpful recommendations, but Spike Lee was not bound to accept any of them, and the work would not benefit in the slightest unless Spike Lee chose to accept them. Aalmuhammed lacked control over the work, and absence of control is strong evidence of the absence of co-authorship.

Also, neither Aalmuhammed, nor Spike Lee, nor Warner Brothers, made any objective manifestations of an intent to be coauthors. Warner Brothers required Spike Lee to sign a "work for hire" agreement, so that even Lee would not be a co-author and co-owner with Warner Brothers. It would be illogical to conclude that Warner Brothers, while not wanting to permit Lee to own the copyright, intended to share ownership with individuals like Aalmuhammed who worked under Lee's control, especially ones who at the time had made known no claim to the role of co-author. No one, including Aalmuhammed, made any indication to anyone prior to litigation that Aalmuhammed was intended to be a co-author and co-owner.

Aalmuhammed offered no evidence that he was the "inventive or master mind" of the movie. He was the author of another less widely known documentary about Malcolm X, but was not the master of this one. What Aalmuhammed's evidence showed, and all it showed, was that, subject to Spike Lee's authority to accept them, he made very valuable contributions to the movie. That is not enough for co-authorship of a joint work.

The Constitution establishes the social policy that our construction of the statutory term "authors" carries out. The Founding Fathers gave Congress the power to give authors copyrights in order "[t]o promote the progress of Science and useful arts." Progress would be retarded rather than promoted, if an author could not consult with others and adopt their useful suggestions without sacrificing sole ownership of the work. Too open a definition of author would compel authors to insulate themselves and maintain ignorance of the contributions others might make. Spike Lee could not consult a scholarly Muslim to make a movie about a religious conversion to Islam, and the arts would be the poorer for that.

The broader construction that Aalmuhammed proposes would extend joint authorship to many "overreaching contributors," like the dramaturg in *Thomson* [147 F.3d at 200 (internal quotations omitted)] and deny sole authors "exclusive authorship status simply because another person render[ed] some form of assistance." [*Id.* At 202] Claim jumping by research assistants, editors, and former spouses, lovers and friends would endanger authors who talked with people about what they were doing, if creative copyrightable contribution were all that authorship required.

Aalmuhammed also argues that issuance of a copyright registration certificate to him establishes a prima facie case for ownership. A prima facie case could not in any event prevent summary judgment in the presence of all the evidence rebutting his claim of ownership. "The presumptive validity of the certificate may be rebutted and defeated on summary judgment." [*S.O.S., Inc. v. Payday, Inc.*, 886 F.2d 1081, 1086 (9th Cir.1989)] The Copyright Office stated in its response to Aalmuhammed's application for copyright (during the pendency of this litigation) that his claims "conflict with previous registration claims," and therefore the Copyright Office had "several questions" for him. One of the questions dealt with the "intent" of "other authors," i.e., Warner Brothers. The evidence discussed above establishes without genuine issue that the answers to these questions were that Warner Brothers did not intend to share ownership with Aalmuhammed.

Because the record before the district court established no genuine issue of fact as to Aalmuhammed's co-authorship of *Malcolm X* as a joint work, the district court correctly granted summary judgment dismissing his claims for declaratory judgment and an accounting resting on co-authorship. * * *

AFFIRMED in part, REVERSED and REMANDED in part.

Notes

1. How much of a contribution does it take to become worthy of joint authorship? Note that in documentary filmmaker Diane Bloom's situation,

the interviewer, the university that provided a grant, and the person who loaned the editing equipment that broke claimed copyright. Make a list of Aalmuhammed's contributions. How do they compare to drafting an entire script or directing an entire movie? Part of Aalmuhammed's problem is that he sought something that even Spike Lee did not have—the right to claim authorship or ownership of the movie. That right resided in the studio. If Aalmuhammed simply wanted credit as a screenwriter, he should have brought the dispute to the Writers Guild. For more information on the Guild, see Chapter 3 on "Film Representation: Agents, Managers, Lawyers, and Unions."

2.   Part of Aalmuhammed's difficulty may stem from the fact that he is claiming authorship over a highly regarded film director. By 2004, Spike Lee had directed 19 films, acted in 18, and written 11. He received Academy Award nominations for best original screenplay for the 1989 film *Do the Right Thing* and for best documentary for the 1997 feature documentary *4 Little Girls. See* http://movies.yahoo.com/shop?d=hc & cf=gen & id=1800019419 & intl=us. Despite their best efforts, judges and juries are likely to consider the underlying question of who is more creative: Aalmuhammed, who they have never heard of before or Spike Lee, whose movies they have seen?

3.   Aalmuhammed was not as fortunate as James Earl Reid, whose dispute with the Community for Creative Non–Violence was mentioned earlier in this chapter. On remand, the parties entered into a consent decree under which Reid was confirmed as the sole author of the statue Third World America and CCNV was declared the sole owner of the original copy of Third World America. *See* Community for Creative Non–Violence v. Reid, 1991 WL 415523 (D.D.C. Jan. 7, 1991). The parties agreed that Reid would be the sole owner of all rights with respect to three-dimensional reproductions and CCNV and Reid would co-own the rights to two-dimensional reproductions. Both parties could exercise their rights without obtaining permission from the other.

3. ASSIGNMENT RIGHTS

The rights of authorship include the ability to assign your work to another. The following case addresses how assignment rights can conflict with renewal terms.

STEWART v. ABEND

United States Supreme Court, 1990.
495 U.S. 207, 110 S.Ct. 1750, 109 L.Ed.2d 184.

Justice O'CONNOR delivered the opinion of the Court.

The author of a pre-existing work may assign to another the right to use it in a derivative work. In this case the author of a pre-existing work agreed to assign the rights in his renewal copyright term to the owner of a derivative work, but died before the commencement of the renewal period. The question presented is whether the owner of the derivative work infringed the rights of the successor owner of the pre-existing work by continued distribution and publication of the derivative work during the renewal term of the pre-existing work.

I

Cornell Woolrich authored the story "It Had to Be Murder," which was first published in February 1942 in Dime Detective Magazine. The magazine's publisher, Popular Publications, Inc., obtained the rights to magazine publication of the story and Woolrich retained all other rights. Popular Publications obtained a blanket copyright for the issue of Dime Detective Magazine in which "It Had to Be Murder" was published.

The Copyright Act of 1909, 35 Stat. 1075, 17 U.S.C. § 1 *et seq.* (1976 ed.) (1909 Act), provided authors a 28–year initial term of copyright protection plus a 28–year renewal term. See 17 U.S.C. § 24 (1976 ed.). In 1945, Woolrich agreed to assign the rights to make motion picture versions of six of his stories, including "It Had to Be Murder," to B.G. De Sylva Productions for $9,250. He also agreed to renew the copyrights in the stories at the appropriate time and to assign the same motion picture rights to De Sylva Productions for the 28–year renewal term. In 1953, actor Jimmy Stewart and director Alfred Hitchcock formed a production company, Patron, Inc., which obtained the motion picture rights in "It Had to Be Murder" from De Sylva's successors in interest for $10,000.

In 1954, Patron, Inc., along with Paramount Pictures, produced and distributed *Rear Window,* the motion picture version of Woolrich's story "It Had to Be Murder." Woolrich died in 1968 before he could obtain the rights in the renewal term for petitioners as promised and without a surviving spouse or child. He left his property to a trust administered by his executor, Chase Manhattan Bank, for the benefit of Columbia University. On December 29, 1969, Chase Manhattan Bank renewed the copyright in the "It Had to Be Murder" story pursuant to 17 U.S.C. § 24 (1976 ed.). Chase Manhattan assigned the renewal rights to respondent Abend for $650 plus 10% of all proceeds from exploitation of the story.

Rear Window was broadcast on the ABC television network in 1971. Respondent then notified petitioners Hitchcock (now represented by cotrustees of his will), Stewart, and MCA Inc., the owners of the *Rear Window* motion picture and renewal rights in the motion picture, that he owned the renewal rights in the copyright and that their distribution of the motion picture without his permission infringed his copyright in the story. Hitchcock, Stewart, and MCA nonetheless entered into a second license with ABC to rebroadcast the motion picture. In 1974, respondent filed suit against these same petitioners, and others, in the United States District Court for the Southern District of New York, alleging copyright infringement. Respondent dismissed his complaint in return for $25,000.

Three years later, the United States Court of Appeals for the Second Circuit decided *Rohauer v. Killiam Shows, Inc.,* 551 F.2d 484, cert. denied, 431 U.S. 949 (1977), in which it held that the owner of the copyright in a derivative work ... may continue to use the existing derivative work according to the original grant from the author of the pre-existing work even if the grant of rights in the pre-existing work lapsed. 551 F.2d, at 494. Several years later, apparently in reliance on *Rohauer,* petitioners re-released the motion picture in a variety of media, including new 35 and 16 millimeter prints for theatrical exhibition in the United States, videocassettes, and videodiscs. They also publicly exhibited the motion picture in theaters, over cable television, and through videodisc and videocassette rentals and sales.

Respondent then brought the instant suit in the United States District Court for the Central District of California against Hitchcock, Stewart, MCA, and Universal Film Exchanges, a subsidiary of MCA and the distributor of the motion picture. Respondent's complaint alleges that the re-release of the motion picture infringes his copyright in the story because petitioners' right to use the story during the renewal term lapsed when Woolrich died before he could register for the renewal term and transfer his renewal rights to them. Respondent also contends that petitioners have interfered with his rights in the renewal term of the story in other ways. He alleges that he sought to contract with Home Box Office (HBO) to produce a play and television version of the story, but that petitioners wrote to him and HBO stating that neither he nor HBO could use either the title, *Rear Window* or "It Had to Be Murder." Respondent also alleges that petitioners further interfered with the renewal copyright in the story by attempting to sell the right to make a television sequel and that the re-release of the original motion picture itself interfered with his ability to produce other derivative works.

Petitioners filed motions for summary judgment, one based on the decision in *Rohauer, supra,* and the other based on alleged defects in the story's copyright. Respondent moved for summary judgment on the ground that petitioners' use of the motion picture constituted copyright infringement. Petitioners responded with a third motion for summary judgment based on a "fair use" defense. The District Court granted petitioners' motions for summary judgment based on *Rohauer* and the fair use defense and denied respondent's motion for summary judgment, as well as petitioners' motion for summary judgment alleging defects in the story's copyright. Respondent appealed to the United States Court of Appeals for the Ninth Circuit and petitioners cross-appealed.

The Court of Appeals reversed, holding that respondent's copyright in the renewal term of the story was not defective, *Abend v. MCA, Inc.,* 863 F.2d 1465, 1472 (1988). The issue before the court, therefore, was whether petitioners were entitled to distribute and exhibit the motion picture without respondent's permission despite respondent's valid copyright in the pre-existing story. Relying on the renewal provision of the 1909 Act, 17 U.S.C. § 24 (1976 ed.), respondent argued before the Court of Appeals that because he obtained from Chase Manhattan Bank, the statutory successor, the renewal right free and clear of any purported assignments of any interest in the renewal copyright, petitioners' distribution and publication of *Rear Window* without authorization infringed his renewal copyright. Petitioners responded that they had the right to continue to exploit *Rear Window* during the 28–year renewal period because Woolrich had agreed to assign to petitioners' predecessor in interest the motion picture rights in the story for the renewal period.

Petitioners also relied, as did the District Court, on the decision in *Rohauer v. Killiam Shows, Inc., supra.* In *Rohauer,* the Court of Appeals for the Second Circuit held that statutory successors to the renewal copyright in a pre-existing work under § 24 could not "depriv[e] the proprietor of the derivative copyright of a right . . . to use so much of the underlying copyrighted work as already has been embodied in the copyrighted derivative work, as a matter of copyright law." *Id.,* at 492. The Court of Appeals in the instant case rejected this reasoning, concluding that even if the pre-existing work had been incorporated into a derivative work, use of the pre-existing work was infringing unless the owner of the derivative work held a valid grant of rights in the renewal term.

* * * We granted certiorari to resolve the conflict between the decision in *Rohauer, supra,* and the decision below. 493 U.S. 807 (1989). Petitioners do not challenge the Court of Appeals' determination that respondent's copyright in the renewal term is valid, and we express no opinion regarding the Court of Appeals' decision on this point.

II

A

Petitioners would have us read into the Copyright Act a limitation on the statutorily created rights of the owner of an underlying work. They argue in essence that the rights of the owner of the copyright in the derivative use of the pre-existing work are extinguished once it is incorporated into the derivative work, assuming the author of the pre-existing work has agreed to assign his renewal rights. Because we find no support for such a curtailment of rights in either the 1909 Act or the 1976 Act, or in the legislative history of either, we affirm the judgment of the Court of Appeals.

Petitioners and *amicus* Register of Copyrights assert, as the Court of Appeals assumed, that § 23 of the 1909 Act, and the case law interpreting that provision, directly control the disposition of this case. Respondent counters that the provisions of the 1976 Act control, but that the 1976 Act reenacted § 24 in § 304 and, therefore, the language and judicial interpretation of § 24 are relevant to our consideration of this case. Under either theory, we must look to the language of and case law interpreting § 24.

The right of renewal found in § 24 provides authors a second opportunity to obtain remuneration for their works. Section 24 provides:

"[T]he author of [a copyrighted] work, if still living, or the widow, widower, or children of the author, if the author be not living, or if such author, widow, widower, or children be not living, then the author's executors, or in the absence of a will, his next of kin shall be entitled to a renewal and extension of the copyright in such work for a further term of twenty-eight years when application for such renewal and extension shall have been made to the copyright office and duly registered therein within one year prior to the expiration of the original term of copyright." 17 U.S.C. § 24 (1976 ed.)

Since the earliest copyright statute in this country, the copyright term of ownership has been split between an original term and a renewal term. Originally, the renewal was intended merely to serve as an extension of the original term; at the end of the original term, the renewal could be effected and claimed by the author, if living, or by the author's executors, administrators, or assigns. See Copyright Act of May 31, 1790, ch. XV, § 1, 1 Stat. 124. In 1831, Congress altered the provision so that the author could assign his contingent interest in the renewal term, but could not, through his assignment, divest the rights of his widow or children in the renewal term. See Copyright Act of February 3, 1831, ch. XVI, 4 Stat. 436; see also G. Curtis, Law of Copyright 235 1847). The 1831 renewal provisions created "an entirely new policy, completely dissevering the title, breaking up the continuance . . . and vesting an absolutely new title eo nomine in the persons designated." White–Smith Music Publishing Co. v. Goff, 187 F. 247, 250 (1st Cir. 1911). In this way, Congress attempted to give the author a second chance to control and benefit from his work. Congress also intended to secure to the author's family the opportunity to exploit the work if the author died before he could register for the renewal term. * * *

In its debates leading up to the Copyright Act of 1909, Congress elaborated upon the policy underlying a system comprised of an original term and a completely separate renewal term. See *G. Ricordi & Co. v. Paramount Pictures, Inc.,* 189 F.2d 469, 471 (2nd Cir.) (the renewal right "creates a new estate, and the . . . cases which have dealt with the subject assert that the new estate is clear of all rights, interests or licenses granted under the original copyright"), cert. denied, 342 U.S. 849 (1951). "It not infrequently happens that the author sells his copyright outright to a publisher for a comparatively small sum." H.R.Rep. No. 2222, 60th Cong., 2d Sess., 14 (1909). The renewal term permits the author, originally in a poor bargaining position, to renegotiate the terms of the grant once the value of the work has been tested. "[U]nlike real property and other forms of personal property, [a copyright] is by its very nature incapable of accurate monetary evaluation prior to its exploitation." 2 M. Nimmer & D. Nimmer, Nimmer on Copyright § 9.02, p. 9–23 (1989) (hereinafter Nimmer). "If the work proves to be a great success and lives beyond the term of twenty-eight years, . . . it should be the exclusive right of the author to take the renewal term, and the law should be framed . . . so that [the author] could not be deprived of that right." H.R.Rep. No. 2222, *supra,* at 14. With these purposes in mind, Congress enacted the renewal provision of the Copyright Act of 1909, 17 U.S.C. § 24 (1976 ed.). With respect to works in their original or renewal term as of January 1, 1978, Congress retained the two-term system of copyright protection in the 1976 Act. See 17 U.S.C. § § 304(a) and (b) (1988 ed.) (incorporating language of 17 U.S.C. § 24 (1976 ed.)).

Applying these principles in *Miller Music Corp. v. Charles N. Daniels, Inc.,* 362 U.S. 373 (1960), this Court held that when an author dies before the renewal period arrives, his executor is entitled to the renewal rights, even though the author previously assigned his renewal rights to another party. "An assignment by an author of his renewal rights made before the original copyright expires is valid against the world, if the author is alive at the commencement of the renewal period. *[Fred] Fisher Co. v. [M.] Witmark & Sons,* 318 U.S. 643, so holds." *Id.,* 362 U.S., at 375. If the author dies before that time, the "next of kin obtain the renewal copyright free of any claim founded upon an assignment made by the author in his lifetime. These results follow not because the author's assignment is invalid but because he had only an expectancy to assign; and his death, prior to the renewal period, terminates his interest in the renewal which by § 24 vests in the named classes." *Id.* The legislative history of the 1909 Act echoes this view: "The right of renewal is contingent. It does not vest until the end [of the original term]. If [the author] is alive at the time of renewal, then the original contract may pass it, but his widow or children or other persons entitled would not be bound by that contract." 5 Legislative History of the 1909 Copyright Act, Part K, p. 77 (E. Brylawski & A. Goldman eds. 1976) (statement of Mr. Hale). Thus, the renewal provisions were intended to give the author a second chance to obtain fair remuneration for his creative efforts and to provide the author's family a "new estate" if the author died before the renewal period arrived.

An author holds a bundle of exclusive rights in the copyrighted work, among them the right to copy and the right to incorporate the work into derivative works. By assigning the renewal copyright in the work without limitation, as in *Miller Music,* the author assigns all of these rights. After *Miller Music,* if the author dies before the commencement of the renewal period, the assignee holds nothing. If the assignee of all of the renewal rights holds nothing upon the death of the assignor before arrival of the renewal period, then, *a fortiori,* the assignee of a portion of the renewal rights, *e.g.,* the right to produce a derivative work, must also hold nothing. See also Brief for Register of Copyrights as *Amicus Curiae* 22 ("[A]ny assignment of renewal rights made during the original term is void if the author dies before the renewal period"). Therefore, if the author dies before the renewal period, then the assignee may continue to use the original work only if the author's successor transfers the renewal rights to the assignee. This is the rule adopted by the Court of Appeals below and advocated by the Register of Copyrights. * * * Application of this rule to this case should end the inquiry. Woolrich died before the commencement of the renewal period in the story, and, therefore, petitioners hold only an unfulfilled expectancy. Petitioners have been "deprived of nothing. Like all purchasers of contingent interests, [they took] subject to the possibility that the contingency may not occur." *Miller Music, supra,* 362 U.S., at 378, 80 S.Ct., at 796. * * *

For the foregoing reasons, the judgment of the Court of Appeals is affirmed, and the case is remanded for further proceedings consistent with this opinion.

Notes

1. The assignment in *Stewart v. Abend* was given under the 1909 Copyright Act when the copyright lasted for an initial term of 28 years and could be renewed for another 28 years. Under the 1976 Act, as amended, copyright now endures for the lifetime of the owner plus 70 years for individual owners and a flat 95–year term for corporate, work made for hire, anonymous and pseudonymous owners. Under 17 U.S.C. § 201 (d)(1), ownership of copyright may be transferred in whole or in part. Any transfer of copyright, other than a work made for hire, may be terminated under conditions set forth in 17 U.S.C. § 203 (a) (e) "at any time during a period of five years beginning at the end of thirty-five years from the date of execution of the grant." To effectuate termination, the author or certain heirs (spouse, children, grandchildren) or executor (including administrator, personal representative or trustee) must "serve advance notice in writing" stating the effective date of termination. 17 U.S.C. § 203 (4).

2. A derivative work like the one at issue in *Stewart v. Abend*, which was granted before its termination, may continue to be utilized under the terms of the grant after its termination, but no further derivative works can be prepared under the grant. 17 U.S.C. § 203(b)(1).

4. MORAL RIGHTS & COLORIZATION

The concept of moral rights originated in France where they are known as *droit moral* and include the following:

1. Right to Create, prohibiting the completion of a work from being judicially mandated;

2. Right of Disclosure, permitting the author to determine when to make work public;

3. Right to Withdraw Work after it has been Disclosed, a limited right that applies only to publishing contractors and requires the author to indemnify publisher for losses;

4. Right of Name Attribution (or Authorship), permitting the author to be recognized as author of created work, to publish as anonymous or pseudonymous, to prevent work from being attributed to another, and to prevent name from being used on works not created, or distorted;

5. Right of Integrity, permitting the author to prevent alterations, distortions or destruction of his work; and

6. Right of Protection from Excessive Criticism, permits the author to publish a reply to unjustified criticism.

granted to authors in European Nations

NOT ADOPTED

By

Congress in The US,

US—
Right
of
Authorship

The United States officially recognizes the Right of Authorship and the Right of Integrity in 17 U.S.C. § 106A, but only gives these rights to visual artists. *See, e.g.,* Sherri Burr, *Introducing Art Law,* 37 COPYRIGHT WORLD 22, 24 (Feb. 1994). The entertainment industry has looked to other aspects of U.S. law for protection. For example, the "Right to Create" can be found in the prohibition against specifically enforcing personal service contracts. The Right of Disclosure relates to the Copyright Act's grant of the right to copy under 17 U.S.C. § 106. Entertainers who seek "The Right of Protection from Excessive Criticism" may find it in U.S. libel law.

As for protection against distortions, sometimes entertainers have found relief under 15 U.S.C. § 1125 of the Lanham Act, which prohibits false designation of origin and false description. *See e.g., Gilliam v. ABC,* 538 F.2d 14 (2d Cir. 1979), which is discussed in Chapter 9, Television Contracts. When John Huston's heirs sought to prohibit his *Asphalt Jungle* from being colorized by Turner Broadcasting Corporation, they found moral rights relief in France. Below is the French court's decision in the case.

TURNER ENTERTAINMENT v. HUSTON

Court of Appeal of Versailles [France], 1994.
16 Ent. L. Rptr. 10:3 (1995).

M. THAVAUD, President.

* * * After due deliberation by the same magistrates of the Court of Appeal, in accordance with the law, the following judgment was pronounced:

I

1. The cinematographic work entitled "ASPHALT JUNGLE" was produced in 1950 in the UNITED STATES by the METRO GOLDWYN MAYER (MGM) company, a division of LOEW'S Inc. The film was shot in black and white by the late John HUSTON, a movie director of American nationality, at the time bound by a contract of employment to LOEW'S Inc. and co-author of the screenplay with Ben MADDOW, bound to the same company by a contract as a salaried writer.

2. On 2nd May 1950, LOEW'S Inc. obtained from the U.S. COPYRIGHT OFFICE a certificate of registration of its rights to the film. This registration was duly renewed in 1977. On 26th September 1986 the benefit of this registration was transferred to the TURNER ENTERTAINMENT Co. by virtue of a merger with MGM, including transfer of the ownership of MGM's movie library and connected rights.

3. The TURNER company had the movie colorized, an operation which on 20th June 1988 resulted in registration of a copyright application, and it enabled the Fifth French Television Channel (LA CINQ) to announce that it would broadcast this colorized version at 8:30 p.m. on 26th June 1988.

4.   The broadcast was objected to by John HUSTON's heirs, Angelica, Daniel and Walter HUSTON, who were subsequently joined by Mr Ben MADDOW, the Societe des Auteurs et Compositeurs Dramatiques (SACD), the Societe des Realisateurs de Films (SRF), the Syndicat Frangais des Artistes Interpretes (SFA), the Federation Europeenne des Relisateurs de l'Audiovisuel (FERA), the Syndicat Frangais des Realisateurs de Television CGT and the Syndicat National des Techniciens de la Production Cinematographique et de Television. They opposed the broadcast because they deemed it a violation of the author's moral right, aggravated in their opinion by the fact that John HUSTON had opposed colorization of his works during his life.

5.   The dispute thus arising with LA CINQ and the TURNER ENTERTAINMENT Co. (TEC) resulted in FRANCE in the following decisions:

> [The court noted that the Court of Appeal of PARIS suspended the broadcast of the colorized film as being likely to cause unacceptable and irreparable damage on 25th June 1988. The Court of First Instance of PARIS on 23rd November 1988 affirmed this decision. On July 8, 1989, however the Court of Appeal of PARIS, appealed to by the TURNER company, judged] that the author of the film entitled 'ASPHALT JUNGLE' is the TURNER company and that, the heirs of John HUSTON as well as Ben MADDOW have no moral right to this work shot in black and white; Notes that the colorized version of the said film is an adaptation, under U.S. law, for which the TURNER company obtained a registration certificate on 20th June 1988; States that the principle of colorization could not be criticized by the heirs of John HUSTON and by Ben MADDOW, even if they could claim a moral right to the black and white film; Accordingly, reversing the judgment, Dismisses the claims of the heirs of John HUSTON and Ben MADDOW and judges admissible but unfounded the interventions of the six legal entities supporting their claims; Authorizes the Fifth Channel to broadcast the colorized version of the film entitled 'ASPHALT JUNGLE', formally recognizing the cognizance petitioned for."

The judgment further provided for various warning notices intended for television viewers, with respect to the possibility of using the color control device and respect for the memory of John HUSTON.

In reversing the judgment against which the appeal was brought, the Court of Appeal of PARIS settled the conflict of laws in favor of U.S. law, the law of the first publication of the work having, according to said court, granted the status of author solely to LOEW's, which cannot be defeated by the BERNE Convention, effective from 1st March 1989, which is an instrument to harmonize relations between the member countries and is not competent to affect acquired rights or the effect of contracts between producer and director. Moreover, it dismissed the exception according to which the French conception of international law was violated and held that the copyright granted to the "derivative work'' transferred in 1988 to the TURNER company made it impossible for Messrs and Mrs HUSTON and Mr MADDOW to raise it if they had a moral right to claim.

6.   Messrs and Mrs HUSTON and Mr MADDOW and the intervenors appealed against this judgment of the Court of Appeal of PARIS to the Cour de Cassation.

In a ruling dated 28th May 1991, the Supreme Court reversed and cancelled every provision of the judgment of the Court of Appeal for violation of Section 1.2 of Law 64–689 of 8th July 1964 and Section 6 of the Law of 11th March 1957, stating: "According to the first of these texts, the integrity of a literary or art work cannot be affected in FRANCE, regardless of the State in whose territory the said work was made public for the first time. The person who is its author, by its creation alone, enjoys the moral right stipulated in his favor by the second of the aforesaid texts; these are laws of mandatory application."

[The court then discussed the arguments of the Turner Entertainment Company and Mr. & Mrs. Huston as follows:]

III

* * * 3. The TURNER company first opposes to Messrs and Mrs HUSTON and Mr MADDOW and the intervenors that U.S. law should be applied to determine who has the status of the film's author; it designates the producer, i.e. LOEW's Inc., which obtained the copyright on 2nd May 1950 and whose rights, renewed on 2nd May 1977, were transferred to the TURNER company; the action of Messrs and Mrs HUSTON and Mr MADDOW to protect rights which they have not acquired is therefore not admissible.

4.   But the judges in first instance correctly stressed the "very different conceptions" of U.S. and French laws, the first focusing exclusively on the protection of economic rights without referring to the creative act underlying the inalienable moral right recognized by French law, viz. Section 6 of the Law of 11th March 1957, at the time applicable, which provides that "the author enjoys the right to respect for his name, his status, his work—this right is attached to his person—it is perpetual, inalienable and imprescribable—it is transmitted after death to the author's heirs".

John HUSTON and Ben MADDOW, of whom it is not disputed that the first is the co-author of the screenplay and the director of the film entitled "ASPHALT JUNGLE" and the second the co-author of the same film, as already referred to under (I–1), are in fact its authors, having created it, and whereas they are therefore, in the meaning of the aforesaid law, vested with the corresponding moral right, which is part of public law and therefore mandatorily protected.

5.   Section 1 of Law No 64–689 of 8th July 1964 on the application of the principle of reciprocity with respect to copyright provides as follows:

Subject to the provisions of the international conventions to which FRANCE is a party, in the event that it is noted, after consultation of the Minister of Foreign Affairs, that a State does not provide adequate and effective protection for works disclosed for the first time in FRANCE, irrespective of the form thereof, works disclosed for the first time in the territory of the said State shall not benefit from the copyright protection recognized by French law. However, the integrity or authorship of such works may not be violated. In the case provided for in paragraph 1 heretofore, royalties shall be paid to organizations of general interest designated by decree.

The defect in protection thus likely to affect the foreign work on the conditions governing reciprocity, as laid out in paragraph 1, can only concern its economic aspects, i.e. the patrimonial rights attached thereto, in that it is limited by the general mandatory rule providing for respect of an author's moral right as proclaimed without reservation in paragraph 2.

6. It follows that the moral rights attached to the person of the creators of the work entitled "ASPHALT JUNGLE" could not be transferred and, therefore, the judges in first instance correctly ruled that Messrs and Mrs HUSTON and Ben MADDOW were entitled to claim recognition and protection thereof in FRANCE.

7. However, the TURNER company, which it is not disputed is the holder of the author's economic rights, maintains that these rights include the right to adapt the work and therefore to colorize the film entitled "ASPHALT JUNGLE", arguing that it cannot be maintained that this denatures the work; Me PIERREL, ex-officio, follows the same argument, submitting that the colorized version of the film is merely an adaptation of the original black-and-white version which is left intact and is therefore not affected.

8. However, "colorization" is a technique based on the use of computer and laser and it makes it possible, after transferring the original black-and-white tape onto a videographic media, to give color to a film which did not originally have color; the application of this process is in no event to be considered an adaptation, defined as "an original work both in its expression and in its composition", even if it borrows formal elements from the pre-existing work; colorization, far from meeting these criteria, in fact merely consists in modifying the work by adding an element thus far not part of the creator's aesthetic conception.

9. The judges in first instance in the present case have precisely pointed out that the aesthetic conception which earned John HUSTON his great fame is based on the interplay of black and white, which enabled him to create an atmosphere according to which he directed the actor and selected the backdrops; moreover, he expressed himself clearly about his film entitled "The Maltese Falcon" when stating, "I wanted to shoot it in black and white like a sculptor chooses to work in clay, to pour his work in bronze, to sculpt in marble".

In 1950, while color film technique was already widespread and another option was available, the film entitled "ASPHALT JUNGLE" was shot in black and white, following a deliberate aesthetic choice, according to a process which its authors considered best suited to the character of the work.

10.   Therefore, the film's colorization without authorization and control by the authors or their heirs amounted to violation of the creative activity of its makers, even if it should satisfy the expectations of a certain public for commercially obvious reasons; the use of this process without the agreement of Messrs and Mrs HUSTON and Ben MADDOW infringed the moral right of the authors as mandatorily protected under French law; Messrs and Mrs HUSTON and Ben MAD-DOW have therefore good grounds to petition the court for reparation of their prejudice at the hands of the TURNER company, and they will therefore be allotted FRF 400,000 by way of damages and costs for the damage done; moreover, the judges in first instance correctly recognized their right to demand that LA CINQ SA be forbidden to broadcast the modified version of the film entitled "ASPHALT JUNGLE".

11.   It is constant that, contrary to the act required by the Court of First Instance, LA CINQ SA broadcast the colorized version of the film entitled "ASPHALT JUNGLE" further to a judgment by the Court of Appeal of PARIS, quashed by the Cour de Cassation on the conditions reiterated under (I–5); this broadcasting is also a direct and definite violation of the moral right whose protection was demanded by Messrs and Mrs HUSTON and Ben MADDOW, who are also wellfounded to demand reparation on this head; the Court has the elements needed to allot them the sum of FRF 200,000 by reversing the referred judgment on the pronounced cognizance.

12.   Me PIERREL, ex-officio as court-appointed liquidator of LA CINQ SA, loses his case and will bear the costs; therefore, his claim under Section 700 of the New Code of Civil Procedure is inadmissible.

Equity does not justify the claim lodged ex-officio by Me LAFONT under this Section.

On the other hand, the same consideration of equity prompts the allotment, in application of the said Section 700 of the New Code of Civil Procedure, of FRF 60,000 to Messrs and Mrs HUSTON and Ben MAD-DOW and FRF 2,000 each to SRF, SFA, FERA, Syndicat Francais des Realisateurs de Television CGT and Syndicat National des Techniciens de la Production Cinematographique et de Television.

On These Grounds

The Court, judging publicly, after hearing all parties and in last instance as Court of Remand; Pursuant to the closing order pronounced on 17th February 1994;

* * * 4. CONFIRMS the judgment pronounced on 23rd November 1988 by the Court of First Instance of PARIS, subject to the cognizance

and the provisions dismissing application of Section 700 of the New Code of Civil Procedure in favor of Messrs and Mrs HUSTON and Ben MADDOW and the secondary intervenors;

Judging again and adding:

5. STATES that the colorization of the film entitled "ASPHALT JUNGLE" by the TURNER ENTERTAINMENT Co. and its broadcasting by LA CINQ SA in this version, contrary to the will of the authors or their heirs, has violated their moral right;

6. ORDERS the TURNER ENTERTAINMENT Co. to pay Messrs and Mrs HUSTON and Ben MADDOW FOUR HUNDRED THOUSAND FRENCH FRANCS (FRF 400,000) by way of damages and costs;

7. ORDERS Maitre PIERREL, ex-officio as court-appointed liquidator of Societe d'Exploitation de la Cinquieme Chaine (LA CINQ SA) to pay them TWO HUNDRED THOUSAND FRENCH FRANCS (FRF 200,000) in damages and costs; * * *

9. ORDERS it jointly and severally with the TURNER ENTERTAINMENT Co. to pay Messrs and Mrs HUSTON and Ben MADDOW SIXTY THOUSAND FRENCH FRANCS (FRF 60,000) under the same Section 700 of the New Code of Civil Procedure and to pay TWO THOUSAND (FRF 2,000) to each of the intervenors referred to under (2), except SACD, which has lodged no claim in this respect;

10. ORDERS it further, jointly and severally with the TURNER ENTERTAINMENT Co., to bear the full cost of the appeal and authorizes SCP JULLIEN–LECHARNY–ROL and SCP LISSARRAGUE & DUPUIS, avoues, to collect the said costs directly under Section 699 of the New Code of Civil Procedure.

THIS JUDGMENT WAS PRONOUNCED AND SIGNED BY: Mr THAVAUD, President. * * *

Note

1. The following law review articles explore the colorization issue in elaborate detail: Craig A. Wagner, *Motion Picture Colorization, Authenticity, and The Elusive Moral Right*, 64 N.Y.U. L. Rev. 628 (1989); Anne Marie Cook, *The Colorization of Black and White Films: An Example of the Lack of Substantive Protection for Art in the United States*, 63 Notre Dame L. Rev. 309 (1988); and Anna S. White, *The Colorization Dispute: Moral Rights Theory as a Means of Judicial & Legislative Reform*, 38 Emory L.J. 237 (1989).

D. COPYRIGHT INFRINGEMENT & REMEDIES

The prior section discussed issues related to copyright ownership. Once declared an owner, the copyright holder is entitled to the following exclusive rights under Section 106 of the U.S. Copyright Act, subject to the limitations found in section 107 through 121:

(1) to reproduce the copyrighted work in copies or phonorecords;

(2) to prepare derivative works based on the copyrighted work;

(3) to distribute copies or phonorecords of the copyrighted work to the public by sale or other transfer of ownership, or by rental, lease or lending;

(4) in the case of literary, musical, dramatic, and choreographic works, pantomimes, and motion pictures and other audiovisual works, to perform the copyrighted work publicly;

(5) in the case of literary, musical, dramatic, and choreographic works, pantomimes, and pictorial, graphic, or sculptural works, including the individual images of a motion picture or other audiovisual work, to display the copyrighted work publicly; and

(6) in the case of sound recordings, to perform the copyrighted work publicly by means of a digital audio transmission.

17 U.S.C. § 106. Section 501(a) provides, "Anyone who violates any of the exclusive rights of the copyright owner ... is an infringer of the copyright or right of the author, as the case may be." 17 U.S.C. § 501.

To prove copyright infringement, the plaintiff must establish (1) that he or she owns the copyrighted work; and (2) that the defendant copied the work or took another exclusive right of the plaintiff. To determine whether a defendant has infringed a plaintiff's copyright, courts use words such as theft or plagiarism to refer to the unauthorized taking of one party's work by another. The plaintiff may offer either direct or circumstantial evidence to prove the unauthorized taking. Circumstantial evidence most often consists of showing that the defendant had access to the copyrighted work and that there exists a substantial similarity of ideas and expression between the plaintiff's and defendant's works.

Once the plaintiff has put forth his prima facie case, the burden then shifts to the defendant to refute the evidence that he stole the plaintiff's work. The defendant can offer proof of independent creation (he or she created his or her own work), that he only took noncopyrightable items from the plaintiff; or that the use was somehow authorized, such as making a fair use of the plaintiff's work.

MGM v. AMERICAN HONDA MOTOR CO., INC.

United States District Court, Central District of California, 1995.
900 F.Supp. 1287.

KENYON, District Judge.

* * * This case arises out of Plaintiffs Metro–Goldwyn–Mayer's and Danjaq's claim that Defendants American Honda Motor Co. and its advertising agency Rubin Postaer and Associates violated Plaintiffs' "copyrights to sixteen James Bond films and the exclusive intellectual property rights to the James Bond character and the James Bond films" through Defendants' recent commercial for its Honda del Sol automobile.

Premiering last October 1994, Defendants' "Escape" commercial features a young, well-dressed couple in a Honda del Sol being chased by a high-tech helicopter. A grotesque villain with metal-encased arms jumps out of the helicopter onto the car's roof, threatening harm. With a flirtatious turn to his companion, the male driver deftly releases the Honda's detachable roof (which Defendants claim is the main feature allegedly highlighted by the commercial), sending the villain into space and effecting the couple's speedy get-away.

Plaintiffs move to enjoin Defendants' commercial pending a final trial on the merits, and Defendants move for summary judgment.

II. FACTUAL BACKGROUND

In 1992, Honda's advertising agency Rubin Postaer came up with a new concept to sell the Honda del Sol convertible with its detachable rooftop. For what was to become the commercial at issue, Rubin Postaer vice-president Gary Yoshida claims that he was initially inspired by the climax scene in *Aliens*, wherein the alien is ejected from a spaceship still clinging onto the spacecraft's door. From there, Yoshida and coworker Robert Coburn began working on the storyboards for the "Escape" commercial. As the concept evolved into the helicopter chase scene, it acquired various project names, one of which was "James Bob," which Yoshida understood to be a play on words for James Bond. In addition, David Spyra, Honda's National Advertising Manager, testified the same way, gingerly agreeing that he understood "James Bob to be a pun on the name James Bond."

While the commercial was initially approved by Honda in May 1992, it was put on hold because of financing difficulties. Actual production for the commercial did not begin until after July 8, 1994, when Honda reapproved the concept. Defendants claim that, after the initial May 1992 approval, they abandoned the "James Bob" concept, whiting out "James" from the title on the commercial's storyboards because of the implied reference to "James Bond." However, Plaintiffs dispute this assertion, pointing to the fact that when casting began on the project in the summer of 1994, the casting director specifically sent requests to talent agencies for "James Bond"-type actors and actresses to star in what conceptually could be "the next James Bond film."

With the assistance of the same special effects team that worked on Arnold Schwarzenegger's *True Lies*, Defendants proceeded to create a sixty-and thirty-second version of the Honda del Sol commercial at issue: a fast-paced helicopter chase scene featuring a suave hero and an attractive heroine, as well as a menacing and grotesque villain.

The commercial first aired on October 24, 1994, but was apparently still not cleared for major network airing as late as December 21, 1994. Plaintiffs first viewed the film during the weekend of December 17 and 18, 1994; they demanded that Defendants pull the commercial off the air on December 22; Defendants refused on December 23; and Plaintiffs filed this action on December 30, 1994. After a brief telephone conference with this Court on January 4, 1995, the Court allowed Plaintiffs to conduct expedited discovery in this matter.

On January 15, 1995, in an effort to accommodate Plaintiffs' demands without purportedly conceding liability, Defendants changed their commercial by: (1) altering the protagonists' accents from British to American; and (2) by changing the music to make it less like the horn-driven James Bond theme. This version of the commercial was shown during the Super Bowl, allegedly the most widely viewed TV event of the year.

Plaintiffs filed the instant motion for preliminary injunction on January 23, 1995, and Defendants filed their summary judgment motion on February 21, 1995.

III. *LEGAL ANALYSIS*

* * * A claim for copyright infringement requires that the plaintiff prove (1) its ownership of the copyright in a particular work, and (2) the defendant's copying of a substantial, legally protectable portion of such work. Pasillas v. McDonald's Corp., 927 F.2d 440, 442 (9th Cir. 1991). "An author can claim to 'own' only an original manner of expressing ideas or an original arrangement of facts." Cooling Systems and Flexibles, Inc. v. Stuart Radiator, Inc., 777 F.2d 485, 491 (9th Cir. 1985). The plaintiff need only show that the defendant copied the protectable portion of its work to establish a prima facie case of infringement.

a. *Plaintiffs' Ownership of the Copyrights*

Plaintiffs claim that the Honda commercial: (1) "infringes [P]laintiffs' copyrights in the James Bond films by intentionally copying numerous specific scenes from the films;" and (2) "independently infringes [P]laintiffs' copyright in the James Bond character as expressed and delineated in those films."

Neither side disputes that Plaintiffs own registered copyrights to each of the sixteen films which Plaintiffs claim "define and delineate the James Bond character." However, Defendants argue that because Plaintiffs have not shown that they own the copyright to the James Bond character in particular, Plaintiffs cannot prevail. * * * Specifically, Defendants claim that James Bond has appeared in two films in which Plaintiffs hold no copyright—*Casino Royale* and *Never Say Never Again*—and therefore, Plaintiffs cannot have exclusive rights to the James Bond character.

It appears that Defendants misconstrue Plaintiffs' claim. First, Plaintiffs do not allege that Defendants have violated Plaintiffs' copyright in the James Bond character itself, but rather in the James Bond character as expressed and delineated in Plaintiffs' sixteen films. To the extent that copyright law only protects original expression, not ideas, Plaintiffs' argument is that the James Bond character as developed in the sixteen films is the copyrighted work at issue, not the James Bond character generally. * * * Second, there is sufficient authority for the proposition that a plaintiff who holds copyrights in a film series acquires copyright protection as well for the expression of any significant characters portrayed therein. * * * And third, the *Sam Spade* case, [216 F.2d 945, 949–50], on which Defendants' rely, is distinguishable on its facts because *Sam Spade* dealt specifically with the transfer of rights from author to film producer rather than the copyrightability of a character as developed and expressed in a series of films.

Accordingly, Plaintiffs will likely satisfy the "ownership" prong of the test. * * *

b. What Elements Of Plaintiffs' Work Are Protectable Under Copyright Law

Plaintiffs contend that Defendants' commercial infringes in two independent ways: (1) by reflecting specific scenes from the 16 films; and (2) by the male protagonist's possessing James Bond's unique character traits as developed in the films.

Defendants respond that Plaintiffs are simply trying to gain a monopoly over the "action/spy/police hero" genre which is contrary to the purposes of copyright law. Specifically, Defendants argue that the allegedly infringed elements identified by Plaintiffs are not protectable because: (1) the helicopter chase scene in the Honda commercial is a common theme that naturally flows from most action genre films, and the woman and villain in the film are but stock characters that are not protectable; and (2) under the Ninth Circuit's Sam Spade decision, the James Bond character does not constitute the "story being told," but is rather an unprotected dramatic character.

(1) Whether Film Scenes Are Copyrightable

In their opening brief, Plaintiffs contend that each of their sixteen films contains distinctive scenes that together comprise the classic James Bond adventure: "a high-thrill chase of the ultra-cool British charmer and his beautiful and alarming sidekick by a grotesque villain in which the hero escapes through wit aided by high-tech gadgetry." * * * Defendants argue that these elements are naturally found in any action film and are therefore unprotected "scenes-a-faire."[5]

Both sides provide expert testimony to support their claims that such scenes are distinctive or generic, and both sides question the qualifications—and hence, the testimony—of the others' experts. Indeed, there is a notable difference in the backgrounds of the parties' experts. Plaintiffs' impressive array of James Bond experts includes: (1) Lee Pfeiffer, a writer and James Bond expert whose 1992 book is entitled "The Incredible World of 007"—he has appeared on many radio and television programs as a James Bond expert; (2) Richard B. Jewell, a

---

5. Situations, incidents, or events that naturally flow from a common theme, or setting or basic plot premise are "scenes-a-faire." See, e.g., Nichols v. Universal Pictures Corp., 45 F.2d 119, 121 (2d Cir.1930), cert. denied, 282 U.S. 902, 51 S.Ct. 216, 75 L.Ed. 795 (1931); 3 M. & D. Nimmer, Nimmer on Copyright, § 13.03[B][4], at 13–80– 82 (1994) (discussing scenes-a-faire doctrine). * * *

professor at the USC School of Cinema-Television who recently taught a course on James Bond films in the Spring of 1994; (3) Mark Cerulli, a writer/producer at HBO who has written articles and film reviews of many of the Bond films; (4) Drew Casper, a professor and film historian at the USC School of Cinema–Television; and (5) Irwin Coster, president of Coster Music Research Enterprises, Inc. Defendants' less-impressive expert list includes: (1) Arnold Margolin, a writer and producer, who considers himself to be "conversant with the genre to which James Bond and his films belong," because he has been a fan of Bond films since 1959 and has written several screenplays in the "spy film" genre; and (2) Hal Needham, a movie director responsible for the "Cannonball Run" and "Smokey and the Bandit" comedy film series.

Plaintiffs' experts describe in a fair amount of detail how James Bond films are the source of a genre rather than imitators of a broad "action/spy film" genre as Defendants contend. Specifically, film historian Casper explains how the James Bond films represented a fresh and novel approach because they "hybridize[d] the spy thriller with the genres of adventure, comedy (particularly, social satire and slapstick), and fantasy. This amalgam ... was also a departure from the series' literary source, namely writer Ian Fleming's novels." Casper also states: "I also believe that this distinct melange of genres, which was also seminal ... created a protagonist, antagonist, sexual consort, type of mission, type of exotic setting, type of mood, type of dialogue, type of music, etc. that was not there in the subtype of the spy thriller films of that ilk hitherto." In addition, Professor Jewell and Lee Pfeiffer describe the aforementioned elements in more detail and how these are in essence copied by the Honda commercial.

Based on Plaintiffs' experts' greater familiarity with the James Bond films, as well as a review of Plaintiffs' James Bond montage and defense expert Needham's video montage of the "action/spy" genre films, it is clear that James Bond films are unique in their expression of the spy thriller idea. A filmmaker could produce a helicopter chase scene in practically an indefinite number of ways, but only James Bond films bring the various elements Casper describes together in a unique and original way.

Thus, the Court believes that Plaintiffs will likely succeed on their claim that their expression of the action film sequences in the James Bond films is copyrightable as a matter of law.[8]

(2) Whether James Bond Character Is Copyrightable

The law in the Ninth Circuit is unclear as to when visually-depicted characters such as James Bond can be afforded copyright protection. In the landmark *Sam Spade* case, *Warner Bros.*, 216 F.2d at 950, the Ninth Circuit held that the literary character Sam Spade was not copyrightable because he did not constitute "the story being told." The court opined: "It is conceivable that the character really constitutes the story being

8. Of course, these film sequences would be only "scenes-a-faire" without James Bond. It is Bond that makes a James Bond film as the following section bears out.

told, but if the character is only the chessman in the game of telling the story he is not within the area of the protection afforded by the copyright." Id.

Two subsequent Ninth Circuit decisions have cast doubt on the continued viability of the Sam Spade holding as applied to graphic characters. In *Walt Disney Productions v. Air Pirates*, 581 F.2d 751, 755 (9th Cir.1978), *cert. denied*, 439 U.S. 1132 (1979), the circuit panel held that several Disney comic book characters were protected by copyright. In acknowledging the *Sam Spade* opinion, the court reasoned that because "comic book characters * * * are distinguishable from literary characters, the [*Sam Spade*] language does not preclude protection of Disney's characters." Id. The *Air Pirates* decision may be viewed as either: (1) following *Sam Spade* by implicitly holding that Disney's graphic characters constituted the story being told; or (2) applying a less stringent test for the protectability of graphic characters. * * * One rationale for adopting the second view is that, "[a]s a practical matter, a graphically depicted character is much more likely than a literary character to be fleshed out in sufficient detail so as to warrant copyright protection." Anderson, 1989 WL 206431, at *7. However, as one district court warned, "this fact does not warrant the creation of separate analytical paradigms for protection of characters in the two mediums." Id.

A second Ninth Circuit opinion issued in 1988 did little to clarify *Air Pirates'* impact on the Sam Spade test. In *Olson v. National Broadcasting Co.*, 855 F.2d 1446, 1451–52 n. 6 (9th Cir.1988), the court cited with approval the Sam Spade "story being told" test and declined to characterize this language as dicta. Later in the opinion, the court cited the *Air Pirates* decision along with Second Circuit precedent,[9] recognizing that "cases subsequent to [the Sam Spade decision] have allowed copyright protection for characters who are especially distinctive." Id. at 1452. Olson also noted that "copyright protection may be afforded to characters visually depicted in a television series or in a movie." Id. However, later in the opinion, the court distanced itself from the character delineation test applied by these other cases, referring to it as "the more lenient standard adopted elsewhere." Id.

There have been no Ninth Circuit cases on the protectability of visually-depicted characters since Olson, and therefore, it behooves this Court to analyze James Bond's status under the Sam Spade/Olson/Ninth Circuit "story being told" test, as well as under the Air Pirates/Second Circuit "character delineation" test.

Predictably, Plaintiffs claim that under either test, James Bond's character as developed in the sixteen films is sufficiently unique and

9. The Second Circuit has adopted an alternate test for determining whether dramatic characters are protectable under copyright law. In the landmark case of Nichols, 45 F.2d at 121, the court held that copyright protection is granted to a character if it is developed with enough specificity so as to constitute protectable expression. This has been viewed to be a less stringent standard than Sam Spade's "story being told" test.

deserves copyright protection, just as Judge Keller ruled that Rocky and his cohorts were sufficiently unique. *See Anderson*, 1989 WL 206431, at *7–8. Plaintiffs point to various character traits that are specific to Bond—i.e. his cold-bloodedness; his overt sexuality; his love of martinis "shaken, not stirred;" his marksmanship; his "license to kill" and use of guns; his physical strength; his sophistication—some of which, Plaintiffs' claim, appear in the Honda commercial's hero.

On the other hand, Defendants assert that, like Sam Spade, James Bond is not the "story being told," but instead "has changed enormously from film to film, from actor to actor, and from year to year." Moreover, Defendants contend that even if Bond's character is sufficiently delineated, there is so little character development in the Honda commercial's hero that Plaintiffs cannot claim that Defendants copied more than the broader outlines of Bond's personality. * * *

Reviewing the evidence and arguments, the Court believes that James Bond is more like Rocky than Sam Spade—in essence, that James Bond is a copyrightable character under either the Sam Spade "story being told test" or the Second Circuit's "character delineation" test. Like Rocky,[10] Sherlock Holmes, Tarzan, and Superman,[11] James Bond has certain character traits that have been developed over time through the sixteen films in which he appears. Contrary to Defendants' assertions, because many actors can play Bond is a testament to the fact that Bond is a unique character whose specific qualities remain constant despite the change in actors. *See* Pfeiffer and Lisa, The Incredible World of 007, at 8 ("[Despite the different actors who have played the part] James Bond is like an old reliable friend."). Indeed, audiences do not watch Tarzan, Superman, Sherlock Holmes, or James Bond for the story, they watch these films to see their heroes at work. A James Bond film without James Bond is not a James Bond film. Moreover, as discussed more specifically below, the Honda Man's character, from his appearance to his grace under pressure, is substantially similar to Plaintiffs' Bond.

Accordingly, the Court concludes that Plaintiffs will probably succeed on their claim that James Bond is a copyrightable character under either the "story being told" or the "character delineation" test.

c. *Defendants' Alleged Infringement*

After identifying the scope of Plaintiffs' copyrightable work, the Court must focus on whether Defendants copied Plaintiffs' work. Since direct evidence of actual copying is typically unavailable, the plaintiff may demonstrate copying circumstantially by showing: (1) that the defendant had access to the plaintiff's work, and (2) that the defendant's work is *substantially similar* to the plaintiff's. Shaw v. Lindheim, 919 F.2d 1353, 1356 (9th Cir.1990).

10. See *Anderson*, 1989 WL 206431, at *7 (discussing copyrightability of Rocky characters).

11. See *Warner Bros. Inc. v. American Broadcasting Cos.*, 654 F.2d 204, 208–09 (2d Cir. 1981) (comparing Superman and the "Greatest American Hero" character and concluding that they are not substantially similar).

(1) Access

To demonstrate access, the plaintiff must show that the defendant had "an opportunity to view or to copy plaintiff's work." Sid & Marty Krofft Television Productions, Inc. v. McDonald's Corp., 562 F.2d 1157, 1172 (9th Cir.1977). Access may not be inferred through mere "speculation or conjecture." Ferguson v. National Broadcasting Co., 584 F.2d 111, 113 (5th Cir.1978). There must be a reasonable possibility to view plaintiff's work, not just a bare possibility. *See* Meta–Film Associates, Inc. v. MCA, Inc., 586 F.Supp. 1346, 1355 (C.D.Cal.1984).

In this case, Plaintiffs contend that Defendants conceded access during the telephone conference with the Court on January 4, 1995. Defendants raise access as an issue, arguing that the inventor of the Honda commercial, Gary Yoshida, states in his declaration that he has never watched more than a few minutes of any one James Bond film, and that he got the idea for the commercial from the climax scene in *Aliens.*

The Court notes that: (1) Yoshida's admission that he has at least viewed portions of the James Bond films on television; (2) the "Honda man's" having been referred to as "James Bob"; and (3) the casting director's desire to cast "James Bond"-type actors and actresses, are factors sufficient to establish Defendants' access to Plaintiffs' work. Moreover, the sheer worldwide popularity and distribution of the Bond films allows the Court to indulge a presumption of access. *See, e.g.,* Warner Bros. Inc., 654 F.2d at 208 (holding that access to Superman character assumed based on character's worldwide popularity).

Thus, the Court concludes that Plaintiffs will probably succeed on their claim that Defendants had access to Plaintiffs' work.

(2) Substantial Similarity Test

The Ninth Circuit has established a two-part process for determining "substantial similarity" by applying both the "extrinsic" and "intrinsic" tests. Krofft, 562 F.2d at 1164–65. "The [Krofft] test permits a finding of infringement only if a plaintiff proves both substantial similarity of general ideas under the 'extrinsic test' and substantial similarity of the protectable expression of those ideas under the 'intrinsic test.' " Shaw, 919 F.2d at 1356 (emphasis in original). This "idea-expression" dichotomy is particularly elusive to courts and the substantial similarity test necessarily involves decisions made on a case-by-case basis. * * *

(a) Extrinsic Test

The "extrinsic" test compares specific, objective criteria of two works on the basis of an analytic dissection of the following elements of each work—plot, theme, dialogue, mood, setting, pace, characters, and sequence of events. * * * Evidence is usually supplied by expert testimony comparing the works at issue. Because the extrinsic test relies on objective analytical criteria, "this question may often be decided as a matter of law." * * *

Here, both Plaintiffs' and Defendants' experts go through specific analyses of the similarities in ideas between the James Bond films and the Honda commercial. Plaintiffs contend that the commercial illegally copies specific protected portions of the James Bond films and the James Bond character itself. Defendants claim that the commercial depicts a generic action scene with a generic hero, all of which is not protected by copyright. Alternatively, Defendants argue that they did not copy a substantial portion of any one James Bond work to be liable for infringement as a matter of law.

Viewing Plaintiffs' and Defendants' videotapes and examining the experts' statements, Plaintiffs will likely prevail on this issue because there is substantial similarity between the specific protected elements of the James Bond films and the Honda commercial: (1) the theme, plot, and sequence both involve the idea of a handsome hero who, along with a beautiful woman, lead a grotesque villain on a high-speed chase, the male appears calm and unruffled, there are hints of romance between the male and female, and the protagonists escape with the aid of intelligence and gadgetry; (2) the settings both involve the idea of a high-speed chase with the villain in hot pursuit; (3) the mood and pace of both works are fast-paced and involve hi-tech effects, with loud, exciting horn music in the background; (4) both the James Bond and Honda commercial dialogues are laced with dry wit and subtle humor; (5) the characters of Bond and the Honda man are very similar in the way they look and act—both heroes are young, tuxedo-clad, British-looking men with beautiful women in tow and grotesque villains close at hand; moreover, both men exude uncanny calm under pressure, exhibit a dry sense of humor and wit, and are attracted to, and are attractive to, their female companions.

In addition, several specific aspects of the Honda commercial appear to have been lifted from the James Bond films:

(1) In "The Spy Who Loved Me," James Bond is in a white sports car, a beautiful woman passenger at his side, driving away down a deserted road from some almost deadly adventure, when he is suddenly attacked by a chasing helicopter whose bullets he narrowly avoids by skillfully weaving the car down the road at high speed. At the beginning of the Honda commercial, the Honda man turns to his companion and says, "That wasn't so bad"; to which the woman replies, "Well, I wouldn't congratulate yourself quite yet"—implying that they had just escaped some prior danger. Suddenly, a helicopter appears from out of nowhere and the adventure begins.

(2) In "Dr. No.," the villain has metal hands. In the Honda commercial, the villain uses his metal-encased hands to cling onto the roof of the car after he jumps onto it.

(3) In "Goldfinger," Bond's sports car has a roof which Bond can cause to detach with the flick of a lever. In the Honda commer-

cial, the Honda del Sol has a detachable roof which the Honda man uses to eject the villain.

(4) In "Moonraker," the villainous henchman, Jaws, sporting a broad grin revealing metallic teeth and wearing a pair of oversized goggles, jumps out of an airplane. In the Honda commercial, the villain, wearing similar goggles and revealing metallic teeth, jumps out of a helicopter.

(5) In "The Spy Who Loved Me," Jaws assaults a vehicle in which Bond and his female sidekick are trying to make their escape. In the Honda commercial, the villain jumps onto the roof of the Honda del Sol and scrapes at the roof, attempting to hold on and possibly get inside the vehicle.

(6) In "You Only Live Twice," a chasing helicopter drops a magnetic line down to snag a speeding car. In the Honda commercial, the villain is dropped down to the moving car and is suspended from the helicopter by a cable.[13]

In sum, the extrinsic ideas that are inherent parts of the James Bond films appear to be substantially similar to those in the Honda commercial.

(b) Intrinsic Test

The "intrinsic" test asks whether the "total concept and feel" of the two works is also substantially similar. Litchfield v. Spielberg, 736 F.2d 1352, 1357 (9th Cir. 1984), *cert. denied*, 470 U.S. 1052 (1985). This is a subjective test that requires a determination of whether the ordinary reasonable audience could recognize the Defendants' commercial as a picturization of Plaintiffs' copyrighted work. * * *

Because this is a subjective determination, the comparison during the intrinsic test is left for the trier of fact. This would involve showing the Honda commercial to the members of the jury so that they may compare the same with the sixteen Bond films at issue. Viewing the evidence, it appears likely that the average viewer would immediately think of James Bond when viewing the Honda commercial, even with the subtle changes in accent and music.

As in this Court's Jaws opinion, *Universal*, 543 F.Supp. at 1141, the Court finds that Defendants' attempt to characterize all of the alleged similarities between the works as scenes-a-faire to be unavailing. There are many ways to express a helicopter chase scene, but only Plaintiffs' Bond films would do it the way the Honda commercial did with these very similar characters, music, pace, and mood. Plaintiffs are therefore likely to prevail on the "intrinsic test."

---

13. . . . Plaintiffs identify a seventh similarity that is less compelling, but nonetheless interesting: In "Diamonds Are Forever," Sean Connery, playing James Bond, wears a toupee to cover his, by then, balding pate, a fact widely reported in the media and repeated in the Bond literature. In the Honda commercial, once the car's roof flies off flinging the villain into the air, the woman remarks, "Don't you just love the wind through your hair?," to which the man replies, "What I have left."

(3) Independent Creation

After the plaintiff has satisfied both the "access" and "substantial similarity" prongs of the test, the burden then shifts to the defendant to show that the defendant's work was not a copy but rather was independently created. Kamar Int'l, Inc. v. Russ Berrie and Co., 657 F.2d 1059, 1062 (9th Cir.1981).

Defendants claim that their commercial was independently created, as evidenced from the Yoshida declaration stating that he was inspired not by James Bond, but by *Aliens*. Moreover, Defendants claim that their intent is irrelevant in determining whether their commercial infringes or not.

Plaintiffs raise two points in response: (1) there is other evidence before the Court to suggest that Honda never abandoned the idea of using James Bond as the basis for its commercial—for example, the casting director's notes, Yoshida's reference in his deposition to the Honda Man as "James," etc.; and (2) this evidence of intent is relevant to counter Defendants' claim of independent creation * * *.

For the reasons discussed above, Defendants' evidence is neither very strong nor credible; it is highly unlikely that Defendants will be able to show that they created their commercial separate and apart from the James Bond concept. Accordingly, Plaintiffs should prevail on this issue.

Notes

1. For a thorough discussion on the protection of fictional characters, *see* Leslie A. Kurtz, *The Independent Legal Lives of Fictional Characters*, 1986 Wisc. L. Rev. 429 (1986).

2. Have you ever seen a product in a Bond film and wanted to purchase it? If so, you are not alone. Producers and advertisers count on your interest and that of others. In a typical James Bond film, the character will drive a fancy new car, wear an exclusive watch, or utilize other merchandize. Producers sell product placements in their films to generate additional revenue to offset costs in their production budget. As CNN reported, "Bond has evolved from a suave, English superspy to a flashy, moving billboard for global advertisers such as BMW, Omega watches, Martinin vodka—even construction machinery manufacturer Caterpillar. All those products are prominently featured in the * * * Bond film, *The World is not Enough.* * * * The Bond attraction is such that companies have been building entire advertising campaigns around products featured in the movie. BMW has made its Bond car an integral part of its marketing strategy, for instance." *See* CNN, *From Omega to Caterpillar, companies covet 007's cachet*, (Nov. 22, 1999) *at* http://www.cnn.com/SHOWBIZ/Movies/9911/22/bond.gadgets/.

NICHOLS v. UNIVERSAL PICTURES CORP.

United States Court of Appeals, Second Circuit, 1930.
45 F.2d 119.

L. HAND, Circuit Judge.

The plaintiff is the author of a play, 'Abie's Irish Rose,' which it may be assumed was properly copyrighted under section five, subdivision (d), of the Copyright Act, 17 USCA § 5(d). The defendant produced publicly a motion picture play, *The Cohens and The Kellys*, which the plaintiff alleges was taken from it. As we think the defendant's play too unlike the plaintiff's to be an infringement, we may assume, arguendo, that in some details the defendant used the plaintiff's play, as will subsequently appear, though we do not so decide. It therefore becomes necessary to give an outline of the two plays.

'Abie's Irish Rose' presents a Jewish family living in prosperous circumstances in New York. The father, a widower, is in business as a merchant, in which his son and only child helps him. The boy has philandered with young women, who to his father's great disgust have always been Gentiles, for he is obsessed with a passion that his daughter-in-law shall be an orthodox Jewess. When the play opens the son, who has been courting a young Irish Catholic girl, has already married her secretly before a Protestant minister, and is concerned to soften the blow for his father, by securing a favorable impression of his bride, while concealing her faith and race. To accomplish this he introduces her to his father at his home as a Jewess, and lets it appear that he is interested in her, though he conceals the marriage. The girl somewhat reluctantly falls in with the plan; the father takes the bait, becomes infatuated with the girl, concludes that they must marry, and assumes that of course they will, if he so decides. He calls in a rabbi, and prepares for the wedding according to the Jewish rite.

Meanwhile the girl's father, also a widower, who lives in California, and is as intense in his own religious antagonism as the Jew, has been called to New York, supposing that his daughter is to marry an Irishman and a Catholic. Accompanied by a priest, he arrives at the house at the moment when the marriage is being celebrated, but too late to prevent it and the two fathers, each infuriated by the proposed union of his child to a heretic, fall into unseemly and grotesque antics. The priest and the rabbi become friendly, exchange trite sentiments about religion, and agree that the match is good. Apparently out of abundant caution, the priest celebrates the marriage for a third time, while the girl's father is inveigled away. The second act closes with each father, still outraged, seeking to find some way by which the union, thus trebly insured, may be dissolved.

The last act takes place about a year later, the young couple having meanwhile been abjured by each father, and left to their own resources. They have had twins, a boy and a girl, but their fathers know no more than that a child has been born. At Christmas each, led by his craving to see his grandchild, goes separately to the young folks' home, where they encounter each other, each laden with gifts, one for a boy, the other for a girl. After some slapstick comedy, depending upon the insistence of each that he is right about the sex of the grandchild, they become reconciled when they learn the truth, and that each child is to bear the given name of a grandparent. The curtain falls as the fathers are exchanging amenities, and the Jew giving evidence of an abatement in the strictness of his orthodoxy.

The Cohens and The Kellys presents two families, Jewish and Irish, living side by side in the poorer quarters of New York in a state of perpetual enmity. The wives in both cases are still living, and share in the mutual animosity, as do two small sons, and even the respective dogs. The Jews have a daughter, the Irish a son; the Jewish father is in the clothing business; the Irishman is a policeman. The children are in love with each other, and secretly marry, apparently after the play opens. The Jew, being in great financial straits, learns from a lawyer that he has fallen heir to a large fortune from a great-aunt, and moves into a great house, fitted luxuriously. Here he and his family live in vulgar ostentation, and here the Irish boy seeks out his Jewish bride, and is chased away by the angry father. The Jew then abuses the Irishman over the telephone, and both become hysterically excited. The extremity of his feelings make the Jew sick, so that he must go to Florida for a rest, just before which the daughter discloses her marriage to her mother.

On his return the Jew finds that his daughter has borne a child; at first he suspects the lawyer, but eventually learns the truth and is overcome with anger at such a low alliance. Meanwhile, the Irish family who have been forbidden to see the grandchild, go to the Jew's house, and after a violent scene between the two fathers in which the Jew disowns his daughter, who decides to go back with her husband, the Irishman takes her back with her baby to his own poor lodgings. The lawyer, who had hoped to marry the Jew's daughter, seeing his plan foiled, tells the Jew that his fortune really belongs to the Irishman, who was also related to the dead woman, but offers to conceal his knowledge, if the Jew will share the loot. This the Jew repudiates, and, leaving the astonished lawyer, walks through the rain to his enemy's house to surrender the property. He arrives in great defection, tells the truth, and abjectly turns to leave. A reconciliation ensues, the Irishman agreeing to share with him equally. The Jew shows some interest in his grandchild, though this is at most a minor motive in the reconciliation, and the curtain falls while the two are in their cups, the Jew insisting that in the firm name for the business, which they are to carry on jointly, his name shall stand first.

It is of course essential to any protection of literary property, whether at common-law or under the statute, that the right cannot be limited literally to the text, else a plagiarist would escape by immaterial variations. That has never been the law, but, as soon as literal appropriation ceases to be the test, the whole matter is necessarily at large, so that, as was recently well said by a distinguished judge, the decisions cannot help much in a new case. Fendler v. Morosco, 253 N.Y. 281, 292, 171 N.E. 56. When plays are concerned, the plagiarist may excise a separate scene * * *; or he may appropriate part of the dialogue. * * * Then the question is whether the part so taken is 'substantial,' and therefore not a 'fair use' of the copyrighted work; it is the same question arises in the case of any other copyrighted work. * * * But when the plagiarist does not take out a block in suit, but an abstract of the whole, decision is more troublesome. * * * As respects plays, the controversy chiefly centers upon the characters and sequence of incident, these being the substance.

* * * [W]e do not doubt that two plays may correspond in plot closely enough for infringement. How far that correspondence must go is another matter. Nor need we hold that the same may not be true as to the characters, quite independently of the 'plot' proper, though, as far as we know such a case has never arisen. If Twelfth Night were copyrighted, it is quite possible that a second comer might so closely imitate Sir Toby Belch or Malvolio as to infringe, but it would not be enough that for one of his characters he cast a riotous knight who kept wassail to the discomfort of the household, or a vain and foppish steward who became amorous of his mistress. * * * It follows that the less developed the characters, the less they can be copyrighted; that is the penalty an author must bear for marking them too indistinctly.

In the two plays at bar we think both as to incident and character, the defendant took no more—assuming that it took anything at all—than the law allowed. The stories are quite different. One is of a religious zealot who insists upon his child's marrying no one outside his faith; opposed by another who is in this respect just like him, and is his foil. Their difference in race is merely an obbligato to the main theme, religion. They sink their differences through grandparental pride and affection. In the other, zealotry is wholly absent; religion does not even appear. It is true that the parents are hostile to each other in part because they differ in race; but the marriage of their son to a Jew does no apparently offend the Irish family at all, and it exacerbates the existing animosity of the Jew, principally because he has become rich, when he learns it. They are reconciled through the honesty of the Jew and the generosity of the Irishman; the grandchild has nothing whatever to do with it. The only matter common to the two is a quarrel between a Jewish and an Irish father, the marriage of their children, the birth of grandchildren and a reconciliation.

If the defendant took so much from the plaintiff, it may well have been because her amazing success seemed to prove that this was a subject of enduring popularity. Even so, granting that the plaintiff's play was wholly original, and assuming that novelty is not essential to a copyright, there is no monopoly in such a background. Though the plaintiff discovered the vein, she could not keep it to herself; so defined, the theme was too generalized an abstraction from what she wrote. It was only a part of her 'ideas.'

Nor does she fare better as to her characters. It is indeed scarcely credible that she should not have been aware of those stock figures, the low comedy Jew and Irishman. The defendant has not taken from her more than their prototypes have contained for many decades. If so, obviously so to generalize her copyright, would allow her to cover what was not original with her. But we need not hold this as matter of fact, much as we might be justified. Even though we take it that she devised her figures out of her brain de novo, still the defendant was within its rights.

There are but four characters common to both plays, the lovers and the fathers. The lovers are so faintly indicated as to be no more than stage properties. They are loving and fertile; that is really all that can be said of them, and anyone else is quite within his rights if he puts loving and fertile lovers in a play of his own, wherever he gets the cue. The Plaintiff's Jew is quite unlike the defendant's. His obsession in his religion, on which depends such racial animosity as he has. He is affectionate, warm and patriarchal. None of these fit the defendant's Jew, who shows affection for his daughter only once, and who has none but the most superficial interest in his grandchild. He is tricky, ostentatious and vulgar, only by misfortune redeemed into honesty. Both are grotesque, extravagant and quarrelsome; both are fond of display; but these common qualities make up only a small part of their simple pictures, no more than any one might lift if he chose. The Irish fathers are even more unlike; the plaintiff's a mere symbol for religious fanaticism and patriarchal pride, scarcely a character at all. Neither quality appears in the defendant's, for while he goes to get his grandchild, it is rather out of a truculent determination not to be forbidden, than from pride in his progeny. For the rest he is only a grotesque hobbledehoy, used for low comedy of the most conventional sort, which any one might borrow, if he chanced not to know the exemplar.

The defendant argues that the case is controlled by my decision in *Fisher v. Dillingham*, 298 F. 145 (S.D.N.Y. 1924). Neither my brothers nor I wish to throw doubt upon the doctrine of that case, but it is not applicable here. We assume that the plaintiff's play is altogether original, even to an extent that in fact it is hard to believe. We assume further that, so far as it has been anticipated by earlier plays of which she knew nothing, that fact is immaterial. Still, as we have already said, her copyright did not cover everything that might be drawn from her play; its content went to some extent into the public domain. We have to decide how much, and while we are as aware as any one that the line, wherever it is drawn, will seem arbitrary, that is no excuse for not drawing it; it is a question such as courts must answer in nearly all cases. Whatever may be the difficulties a priori, we have no question on which side of the line this case falls. A comedy based upon conflicts between Irish and Jews, into which the marriage of their children enters, is no more susceptible of copyright than the outline of Romeo and Juliet.

The plaintiff has prepared an elaborate analysis of the two plays, showing a 'quadrangle' of the common characters, in which each is represented by the emotions which he discovers. She presents the resulting parallelism as proof of infringement, but the adjectives employed are so general as to be quite useless. Take for example the attribute of 'love' ascribed to both Jews. The plaintiff has depicted her father as deeply attached to his son, who is his hope and joy; not so, the defendant, whose father's conduct is throughout not actuated by any affection for his daughter, and who is merely once overcome for the moment by her distress when he has violently dismissed her lover. 'Anger' covers emotions aroused by quite different occasions in each case; so do 'anxiety,' 'despondency' and 'disgust.' It is unnecessary to go through the catalogue for emotions are too much colored by their causes to be a test when used so broadly. This is not the proper approach to a solution; it must be more ingenuous, more like that of a spectator, who would rely upon the complex of his impressions of each character.

We cannot approve the length of the record, which was due chiefly to the use of expert witnesses. Argument is argument whether in the box or at the bar, and its proper place is the last. The testimony of an expert upon such issues, especially his cross-examination, greatly extends the trial and contributes nothing which cannot be better heard after the evidence is all submitted. It ought not to be allowed at all; and while its admission is not a ground for reversal, it cumbers the case and tends to confusion, for the more the court is led into the intricacies of dramatic craftsmanship, the less likely it is to stand upon the firmer, if more naive, ground of its considered impressions upon its own perusal. We hope that in this class of cases such evidence may in the future be entirely excluded, and the case confined to the actual issues; that is, whether the defendant copied it, so far as the supposed infringement is identical.

The defendant, 'the prevailing party,' was entitled to a reasonable attorney's fee (section 40 of the Copyright Act (17 USCA § 40)).

Decree affirmed.

Notes

1. In *Nichols,* Judge Hand wrote, "We assume the plaintiff's play is altogether original, even to the extent it is hard to believe." Do the plaintiffs suffer from the same problem as Gracen when she tried to prove originality in a derivative work? Can you name other fictional works, besides Shakespeare's "Romeo & Juliet," that involve the theme of star-crossed lovers from families that do not get along?

2. The following case contains four stories: the true story, the play, the book and the movie. As you read *Sheldon v. Metro–Goldwyn Pictures*, 81 F.2d 49 (2d Cir. 1936), make notes about the characters, the settings, the communication details and the method of poisonings in each story, and ask yourself whether the movie come from the book, as the defendants claimed,

or from the play as the plaintiffs claimed? Both the book and play acknowledge that they are based on the original story.

SHELDON v. METRO–GOLDWYN PICTURES

United States Court of Appeals, Second Circuit, 1936.
81 F.2d 49.

L. HAND, Circuit Judge.

The suit is to enjoin the performance of the picture play, *Letty Lynton*, as an infringement of the plaintiffs' copyrighted play, 'Dishonored Lady.' The plaintiffs' title is conceded, so too the validity of the copyright; the only issue is infringement. The defendants say that they did not use the play in any way to produce the picture; the plaintiffs discredit this denial because of the negotiations between the parties for the purchase of rights in the play, and because the similarities between the two are too specific and detailed to have resulted from chance. The judge thought that, so far as the defendants had used the play, they had taken only what the law allowed, that is, those general themes, motives, or ideas in which there could be no copyright. Therefore he dismissed the bill.

An understanding of the issue involves some description of what was in the public demesne, as well as of the play and the picture. In 1857 a Scotch girl, named Madeleine Smith, living in Glasgow, was brought to trial upon an indictment in three counts; two for attempts to poison her lover, a third for poisoning him. The jury acquitted her on the first count, and brought in a verdict of 'Not Proven' on the second and third. The circumstances of the prosecution aroused much interest at the time not only in Scotland but in England; so much indeed that it became a cause celebre, and that as late as 1927 the whole proceedings were published in book form. An outline of the story so published, which became the original of the play here in suit, is as follows: The Smiths were a respectable middle-class family, able to send their daughter to a 'young ladies' boarding school'; they supposed her protected not only from any waywardness of her own, but from the wiles of seducers. In both they were mistaken, for when at the age of twenty-one she met a young Jerseyman of French blood, Emile L'Angelier, ten years older, and already the hero of many amorous adventures, she quickly succumbed and poured out her feelings in letters of the utmost ardor and indiscretion, and at times of a candor beyond the standards then, and even yet, permissible for well-nurtured young women. They wrote each other as though already married, and he assuming to dictate her conduct and even her feelings; both expected to marry, she on any terms, he with the approval of her family. Nevertheless she soon tired of him and engaged herself to a man some twenty years older who was a better match, but for whom she had no more than a friendly complaisance. L'Angelier was not, however, to be fobbed off so easily; he threatened to expose her to her father by showing her letters. She at first tried to dissuade him by appeals to their tender memories, but finding this useless and thinking herself otherwise undone, she affected a return of her former passion and invited him to visit her again. Whether he did, was the turning point of the trial; the evidence, though it really left the issue in no doubt, was too indirect to satisfy the jury, perhaps in part because of her advocate's argument that to kill him only insured the discovery of her letters. It was shown that she had several times bought or tried to buy poison,—prussic acid and arsenic,—and that twice before his death L'Angelier became violently ill, the second time on the day after her purchase. He died of arsenical poison, which the prosecution charged that she had given him in a cup of chocolate. At her trial, Madeleine being incompetent as a witness, her advocate proved an alibi by the testimony of her younger sister that early on the night of the murder as laid in the indictment, she had gone to bed with Madeleine, who had slept with her throughout the night. As to one of the attempts her betrothed swore that she had been with him at the theatre.

This was the story which the plaintiffs used to build their play. As will appear they took from it but the merest skeleton, the acquittal of a wanton young woman, who to extricate herself from an amour that stood in the way of a respectable marriage, poisoned her lover. The incidents, the characters, the mis en scene, the sequence of events, were all changed; nobody disputes that the plaintiffs were entitled to their copyright. All that they took from the story they might probably have taken, had it even been copyrighted. Their heroine is named Madeleine Cary; she lives in New York, brought up in affluence, if not in luxury; she is intelligent, voluptuous, ardent and corrupt; but, though she has had a succession of amours, she is capable of genuine affection. Her lover and victim is an Argentinian, named Moreno, who makes his living as a dancer in night-clubs. Madeleine has met him once in Europe before the play opens, has danced with him, has excited his concupiscence; he presses presents upon her. The play opens in his rooms, he and his dancing partner who is also his mistress, are together; Madeleine on the telephone recalls herself to him and says she wishes to visit him, though it is already past midnight. He disposes of his mistress by a device which does not deceive her and receives Madeleine; at once he falls to wooing her, luring her among other devices by singing a Gaucho song. He finds her facile and the curtain falls in season.

The second act is in her home, and introduces her father, a bibulous dotard, who has shot his wife's lover in the long past; Laurence Brennan, a self-made man in the fifties, untutored, self-reliant and reliable, who has had with Madeleine a relation, half paternal, half-amorous since she grew up; and Denis Farnborough, a young British labor peer, a mannekin to delight the heart of well ordered young women. Madeleine loves him; he loves Madeleine; she will give him no chance to declare himself, remembering her mottled past and his supposedly immaculate standards. She confides to Brennan, who makes clear to her the imbecility of her self-denial; she accepts this enlightenment and engages herself to her high-minded paragon after confessing vaguely her evil life and being assured that to post-war generations all such lapses are peccadillo.

In the next act Moreno, who has got wind of the engagement, comes to her house. Disposing of Farnborough, who chances to be there, she admits Moreno, acknowledges that she is to marry Farnborough, and asks him to accept the situation as the normal outcome of their intrigue. He refuses to be cast off, high words pass, he threatens to expose their relations, she raves at him, until finally he knocks her down and commands her to go to his apartment that morning as before. After he leaves full of swagger, her eye lights on a bottle of strychnine which her father uses as a drug; her fingers slowly close upon it; the audience understands that she will kill Moreno. Farnborough is at the telephone; this apparently stiffens her resolve, showing her the heights she may reach by its execution.

The scene then shifts again to Moreno's apartment; his mistress must again be put out, most unwillingly for she is aware of the situation; Madeleine comes in; she pretends once more to fell warmly, she must wheedle him for he is out of sorts after the quarrel. Meanwhile she prepares to poison him by putting the strychnine in coffee, which she asks him to make ready. But in the course of these preparations during which he sings her again his Gaucho song, what with their proximity, and this and that, her animal ardors are once more aroused and drag her, unwillingly and protesting, from her purpose. The play must therefore wait for an hour or more until, relieved of her passion, she appears from his bedroom and while breakfasting puts the strychnine in his coffee. He soon discovers what has happened and tries to telephone for help. He does succeed in getting a few words through, but she tears away the wire and fills his dying ears with her hatred and disgust. She then carefully wipes away all traces of her finger prints and manages to get away while the door is being pounded in by those who have come at his call.

The next act is again at her home on the following evening. Things are going well with her and Farnborough and her father, when a district attorney comes in, a familiar of the household, now in stern mood; Moreno's mistress and a waiter have incriminated Madeleine, and a cross has been found in Moreno's pocket, which he superstitiously took off her neck the night before. The district attorney cross-questions her, during which Farnborough several times fatuously intervenes; she is driven from point to point almost to an avowal when as a desperate plunge she says she spent the night with Brennan. Brennan is brought to the house and, catching the situation after a moment's delay, bears her out. This puts off the district attorney until seeing strychnine brought to relieve the father, his suspicions spring up again and he arrests Madeleine. The rest of the play is of no consequence here, except that it appears in the last scene that at the trial where she is acquitted, her father on the witness stand accounts for the absence of the bottle of strychnine which had been used to poison Moreno.

At about the time that this play was being written an English woman named Lowndes wrote a book called Letty Lynton, also founded on the story of Madeleine Smith. Letty Lynton lives in England; she is eighteen years old, beautiful, well-reared and intelligent, but wayward. She has had a more or less equivocal love affair with a young Scot, named McLean, who worked in her father's chemical factory, but has discarded him, apparently before their love-making had gone very far. Then she chances upon a young Swede—half English—named Ekebon, and their acquaintance quickly becomes a standardized amour, kept secret from her parents, especially her mother, who is an uncompromising moralist, and somewhat estranged from Letty anyway. She and her lover use an old barn as their place of assignation; it had been fitted up as a play house for Letty when she was a child. Like Madeleine Smith she had written her lover a series of indiscreet letters which he has kept, for though he is on pleasure bent Ekebon has a frugal mind, and means to marry his sweetheart and set himself up for life. They are betrothed and he keeps pressing her to declare it to her parents, which she means never to do. While he is away in Sweden Letty meets an unmarried peer considerably older than she, poor, but intelligent and charming; he falls in love with her and she accepts him, more because it is a good match than for any other reason, though she likes him well enough, and will make him suppose that she loves him.

Thereupon Ekebon reappears, learns of Letty's new betrothal, and threatens to disclose his own to her father, backing up his story with her letters. She must at once disown her peer and resume her engagement with him. His motive, like L'Angelier's, is ambition rather than love, though conquest is a flattery and Letty a charming morsel. His threats naturally throw Letty into dismay; she has come to loathe him and at any cost must get free, but she has no one to turn to. In her plight she thinks of her old suitor, McLean, and goes to the factory only to find him gone. He has taught her how to get access to poisons in his office and has told of their effect on human beings. At first she thinks of jumping out the window, and when she winces at that, of poisoning herself; that would be easier. So she selects arsenic which is less painful and goes away with it; it is only when she gets home that she thinks of poisoning Ekebon. Her mind is soon made up, however, and she makes an appointment with him at the barn; she has told her father, she writes, and Ekebon is to see him on Monday, but meanwhile on Sunday they will meet secretly once more. She has prepared to go on a week-end party and conceals her car near the barn. He comes; she welcomes him with a pretence of her former ardors, and tries to get back her letters. Unsuccessful in this she persuades him to drink a cup of chocolate into which she puts the arsenic. After carefully washing the pans and cups, she leaves with him, dropping him from her car near his home; he being still unaffected. On her way to her party she pretends to have broken down and by asking the help of a passing cyclist establishes an alibi. Ekebon dies at his home attended by his mistress; the letters are discovered and Letty is brought before the coroner's inquest and acquitted chiefly through the alibi, for things look very bad for her until the cyclist appears.

The defendants, who are engaged in producing speaking films on a very large scale in Hollywood, California, had seen the play and wished to get the rights. They found, however, an obstacle in an association of motion picture producers presided over by Mr. Will Hays, who thought the play obscene; not being able to overcome his objections, they returned the copy of the manuscript which they had had. That was in the spring of 1930, but in the autumn they induced the plaintiffs to get up a scenario, which they hoped might pass moral muster. Although this did not suit them after the plaintiffs prepared it, they must still have thought in the spring of 1931 that they could satisfy Mr. Hays, for they then procured an offer from the plaintiffs to sell their rights for $30,000. These negotiations also proved abortive because the play continued to be objectionable, and eventually they cried off on the bargain. Mrs. Lowndes' novel was suggested to Thalberg, one of the vice-presidents of the Metro–Goldwyn Company, in July, 1931, and again in the following November, and he bought the rights to it in December. At once he assigned the preparation of a play to Stromberg, who had read the novel in January, and thought it would make a suitable play for an actress named, Crawford, just then not employed. Stromberg chose Meehan, Tuchock and Brown to help him, the first two with the scenario, the third with the dramatic production. All these four were examined by deposition; all denied that they had used the play in any way whatever; all agreed that they had based the picture on the story of Madeleine Smith and on the novel, "Letty Lynton." All had seen the play, and Tuchock had read the manuscript, as had Thalberg, but Stromberg, Meehan and Brown swore that they had not; Stromberg's denial being however worthless, for he had originally sworn the contrary in an affidavit. They all say that work began late in November or early in December, 1931, and the picture was finished by the end of March. To meet these denials, the plaintiffs appeal to the substantial identity between passages in the picture and those parts of the play which are original with them.

The picture opens in Montevideo where Letty Lynton is recovering from her fondness for Emile Renaul. She is rich, luxurious and fatherless, her father having been killed by his mistress's husband; her mother is seared, hard, selfish, unmotherly, and Letty has left home to escape her, wandering about in search of excitement. Apparently for the good part of a year she has been carrying on a love affair with Renaul; twice before she has tried to shake loose, has gone once to Rio where she lit another flame, but each time she has weakened and been drawn back. Though not fully declared as an amour, there can be no real question as to the character of her attachment. She at length determines really to break loose, but once again her senses are too much for her and it is indicated, if not declared, that she spends the night with Renaul. Though he is left a vague figure only indistinctly associated with South America somewhere or other, the part was cast for an actor with a marked foreign accent, and it is plain that he was meant to be understood, in origin anyway, as South American, like Moreno in the play. He is violent, possessive and sensual; his power over Letty lies in his strong animal attractions. However, she escapes in the morning while he is asleep, whether from his bed or not is perhaps uncertain; and with a wax figure in the form of a loyal maid—Letty in the novel had one—boards a steamer for New York. On board she meets Darrow, a young American, the son of a rich rubber manufacturer, who is coming back from a trip to Africa. They fall in love upon the faintest provocation and become betrothed before the ship docks, three weeks after she left Montevideo. At the pier she finds Renaul who has flown up to reclaim her. She must in some way keep her two suitors apart, and she manages to dismiss Darrow and then to escape Renaul by asking him to pay her customs duties, which he does. Arrived home her mother gives her a cold welcome and refuses to concern herself with the girl's betrothal. Renaul is announced; he has read of the betrothal in the papers and is furious. He tries again to stir her sensuality by the familiar gambit, but this time he fails; she slaps his face and declares that she hates him. He commands her to come to his apartment that evening; she begs him to part with her and let her have her life; he insists on renewing their affair. She threatens to call the police; he rejoins that if so her letters will be published, and then he leaves. Desperate, she chances on a bottle of strychnine, which we are to suppose is an accouterment of every affluent household, and seizes it; the implication is of intended suicide, not murder. Then she calls Darrow, tells him that she will not leave with him that night for his parents' place in the Adirondacks as they had planned; she renews to him the pledge of her love, without him she cannot live, an intimation to the audience of her purpose to kill herself.

That evening she goes to Renaul's apartment in a hotel armed with her strychnine bottle, for use on the spot; she finds him cooling champagne, but in bad temper. His caresses which he bestows plentifully enough, again stir her disgust not her passions, but he does not believe it and assumes that she will spend the night with him. Finding that he will not return the letters, she believes herself lost and empties the strychnine into a wine glass. Again he embraces her; she vilifies him; he knocks her down; she vilifies him again. Ignorant of the poison he grasps her glass, and she, perceiving it, lets him drink. He woos her again, this time with more apparent success, for she is terrified; he sings a Gaucho song to her, the same one that has been heard at Montevideo. The poison begins to work and, at length supposing that she has meant to murder him, he reaches for the telephone; she forestalls him, but she does not tear out the wire. As he slowly dies, she stands over him and vituperates him. A waiter enters; she steps behind a curtain; he leaves thinking Renaul drunk; she comes out, wipes off all traces of her fingerprints and goes out, leaving however her rubbers which Renaul had taken from her when she entered.

Next she and Darrow are found at his parents' in the Adirondacks; while there a detective appears, arrests Letty and takes her to New York; she is charged with the murder of Renaul; Darrow goes back to New York with her. The finish is at the district attorney's office; Letty and Darrow, Letty's mother, the wax serving maid are all there. The letters appear incriminating to an elderly rather benevolent district attorney; also the customs slip and the rubbers. Letty begins to break down; she admits that she went to Renaul's room, not to kill him but to get him to release her. Darrow sees that that story will not pass, and volunteers that she came to his room at a hotel and spent the night with him. Letty confirms this and mother, till then silent, backs up their story; she had traced them to the hotel and saw the lights go out, having ineffectually tried to dissuade them. The maid still further confirms them and the district attorney, not sorry to be discomfited, though unbelieving, discharges Letty.

We are to remember that it makes no difference how far the play was anticipated by works in the public demesne which the plaintiffs did not use. The defendants appear not to recognize this, for they have filled the record with earlier instances of the same dramatic incidents and devices, as though, like a patent, a copyrighted work must be not only original, but new. That is not however the law as is obvious in the case of maps or compendia, where later works will necessarily be anticipated. At times, in discussing how much of the substance of a play the copyright protects, courts have indeed used language which seems to give countenance to the notion that, if a plot were old, it could not be copyrighted. * * * But we understand by this no more than that in its broader outline a plot is never copyrightable, for it is plain beyond peradventure that anticipation as such cannot invalidate a copyright. Borrowed the work must indeed not be, for a plagiarist is not himself pro tanto an 'author'; but if by some magic a man who had never known it were to compose anew Keats's Ode on a Grecian Urn, he would be an 'author,' and, if he copyrighted it, others might not copy that poem, though they might of course copy Keats's. Bleistein v. Donaldson Lithographing Co., 188 U.S. 239, 249 (1903). * * * But though a copyright is for this reason less vulnerable than a patent, the owner's protection is more limited, for just as he is no less an 'author' because others have preceded him, so another who follows him, is not a tort-feasor unless he pirates his work. * * * If the copyrighted work is therefore original, the public demesne is important only on the issue of infringement; that is, so far as it may break the force of the inference to be drawn from likenesses between the work and the putative piracy. If the defendant has had access to other material which would have served him as well, his disclaimer becomes more plausible.

In the case at bar there are then two questions: First, whether the defendants actually used the play; second, if so, whether theirs was a 'fair use.' The judge did not make any finding upon the first question, as we said at the outset, because he thought the defendants were in any case justified; in this following our decision in *Nichols v. Universal Pictures Corporation*, [45 F.2d 119 (2d Cir. 1930)]. The plaintiffs challenge that opinion because we said that 'copying' might at times be a 'fair use'; but it is convenient to define such a use by saying that others may 'copy' the 'theme,' or 'ideas,' or the like, of a work, though not its 'expression.' At any rate so long as it is clear what is meant, no harm is done. In the case at bar the distinction is not so important as usual, because so much of the play was borrowed from the story of Madeleine Smith, and the plaintiffs' originality is necessarily limited to the variants they introduced. Nevertheless, it is still true that their whole contribution may not be protected; for the defendants were entitled to use, not only all that had gone before, but even the plaintiffs' contribution itself, if they drew from it only the more general patterns; that is, if they kept clear of its 'expression.' We must therefore state in detail those similarities which seem to us to pass the limits of 'fair use.' Finally, in concluding as we do that the defendants used the play pro tanto, we need not charge their witnesses with perjury. With so many sources before them they might quite honestly forget what they took; nobody knows the origin of his inventions; memory and fancy merge even in adults. Yet unconscious plagiarism is actionable quite as much as deliberate. * * *

The defendants took for their mis en scene the same city and the same social class; and they chose a South American villain. The heroines had indeed to be wanton, but Letty Lynton 'tracked' Madeleine Cary more closely than that. She is overcome by passion in the first part of the picture and yields after announcing that she hates Renaul and has made up her mind to leave him. This is the same weakness as in the murder scene of the play, though transposed. Each heroine's waywardness is suggested as an inherited disposition; each has had an errant parent involved in scandal; one killed, the other becoming an outcast. Each is redeemed by a higher love. Madeleine Cary must not be misread; it is true that her lust overcomes her at the critical moment, but it does not extinguish her love for Farnborough; her body, not her soul, consents to the lapse. Moreover, her later avowal, which she knew would finally lose her her lover, is meant to show the basic rectitude of her nature. Though it does not need Darrow to cure Letty of her wanton ways, she too is redeemed by a nobler love. Neither Madeleine Smith, nor the Letty of the novel, were at all like that; they wished to shake off a clandestine intrigue to set themselves up in the world; their love as distinct from their lust, was pallid. So much for the similarity in character.

Coming to the parallelism of incident, the threat scene is carried out with almost exactly the same sequence of event and actuation; it has no prototype in either story or novel. Neither Ekebon nor L'Angelier went to his fatal interview to break up the new betrothal; he was beguiled by the pretence of a renewed affection. Moreno and Renaul each goes to his sweetheart's home to detach her from her new love; when he is there, she appeals to his better side, unsuccessfully; she abuses him, he returns the abuse and commands her to come to his rooms; she pretends to agree, expecting to finish with him one way or another. True, the assault is deferred in the picture from this scene to the next, but it is the same dramatic trick. Again, the poison in each case is found at home, and the girl talks with her betrothed just after the villain has left and again pledges him her faith. Surely the sequence of these details is pro tanto the very web of the authors' dramatic expression; and copying them is not 'fair use.'

The death scene follows the play even more closely; the girl goes to the villain's room as he directs; from the outset he is plainly to be poisoned while they are together. (The defendants deny that this is apparent in the picture, but we cannot agree. It would have been an impossible denoument on the screen for the heroine, just plighted to the hero, to kill herself in desperation, because the villain has successfully enmeshed her in their mutual past; yet the poison is surely to be used on some one.) Moreno and Renaul each tries to arouse the girl by the memory of their former love, using among other aphrodisiacs the Gaucho song; each dies while she is there, incidentally of strychnine not arsenic. In extremis each makes for the telephone and is thwarted by the girl; as he dies, she pours upon him her rage and loathing. When he is dead, she follows the same ritual to eradicate all traces of her presence, but forgets telltale bits of property. Again these details in the same sequence embody more than the 'ideas' of the play; they are its very raiment.

Finally in both play and picture in place of a trial, as in the story and the novel, there is substituted an examination by a district attorney; and this examination is again in parallel almost step by step. A parent is present; so is the lover; the girl yields progressively as the evidence accumulates; in the picture, the customs slip, the rubbers and the letters; in the play, the cross and the witnesses, brought in to confront her. She is at the breaking point when she is saved by substantially the same most unexpected alibi; a man declares that she has spent the night with him. That alibi there introduced is the turning point in each drama and alone prevents its ending in accordance with the classics canon of tragedy; i.e., fate as an inevitable consequence of past conduct, itself not evil enough to quench pity. It is the essence of the authors' expression, the very voice with which they speak.

We have often decided that a play may be pirated without using the dialogue. * * * *Dymow v. Bolton*, 11 F.2d 690; and *Nichols v. Universal Pictures Corporation*, supra, 45 F.2d 119, do not suggest otherwise. Were it not so, there could be no piracy of a pantomime, where there cannot be any dialogue; yet nobody would deny to pantomime the name of drama. Speech is only a small part of a dramatist's means of expression; he draws on all the arts and compounds his play from words and gestures and scenery and costume and from the very looks of the actors themselves. Again and again a play may lapse into pantomime at its most poignant and significant moments; a nod, a movement of the hand, a pause, may tell the audience more than words could tell. To be sure, not all this is always copyrighted, though there is no reason why it may not be, for those decisions do not forbid which hold that mere scenic tricks will not be protected. [Serrana v. Jefferson, 33 F. 347 (C.C.S.D.N.Y. 1888); Barnes v. Miner, 122 F. 480 (C.C.S.D.N.Y. 1903); Bloom et al. v. Nixon, 125 F. 977 (C.C.E.D.Pa. 1903)]. The play is the sequence of the confluents of all these means, bound together in an inseparable unity; it may often be most effectively pirated by leaving out the speech, for which a substitute can be found, which keeps the whole dramatic meaning. That as it appears to us is exactly what the defendants have done here; the dramatic significance of the scenes we have recited is the same, almost to the letter. True, much of the picture owes nothing to the play; some of it is plainly drawn from the novel; but that is entirely immaterial; it is enough that substantial parts were lifted; no plagiarist can excuse the wrong by showing how much of his work he did not pirate. We cannot avoid the conviction that, if the picture was not an infringement of the play, there can be none short of taking the dialogue.

The decree will be reversed and an injunction will go against the picture together with a decree for damages and an accounting. The plaintiffs will be awarded an attorney's fee in this court and in the court below, both to be fixed by the District Court upon the final decree.

Notes

1.   Notice in all of these cases that courts primarily analyze the facts. If a client comes to you claiming that someone stole his copyrighted work, be sure to track all the similarities between the two works and with public domain works. Who are the main and subsidiary characters? How are they similar and different? How do the scenes progress? What is the nature of the conflict? How do the two stories end?

Howard Suber, the founding chair of U.C.L.A. film school's Independent Film and Television Producers Program, is an acknowledged expert witness who has given depositions and testimony in numerous cases involving copyright and related matters for over 29 years. He prepared the following comparison of the films *Gone With The Wind* and *Casablanca*. As you read his comparisons, observe the similarities he finds between the two films.

1.   Both films involve romance set against the background of war: Rhett and Scarlett with the Civil War, Rick and Ilsa with World War II.

2.   Both films involve a love triangle: Rhett loves Scarlett who loves Ashley; Victor loves Ilsa who loves Rick.

3.   Both films have bittersweet, hopeful endings involving loss.

4.   In both films, the male lead begins the film out for himself and not committed to either side of the conflict, but each belatedly joins the cause on the side of the underdog: Rick decides to help the Free French and Rhett goes off to join the rebel lads.

5.   In both films, the female lead "offers" herself to the male lead in exchange for something: Ilsa for the letters of transmit, Scarlett for back taxes on Tara.

6.   In each film, the illicit passion between the male and female leads threatens an idealistic, seemingly guileless character who ultimately prevails (Melanie, Victor Laszlo).

7.   In both films, the male and female leads are forced to flee a city (Paris, Atlanta) which is being invaded by marauding forces (Germans, Yankees)

8. In each film, the male lead saves the life of his rival by risking his own life and deceiving authorities (Rick saves Victor from the Nazis by deceiving Major Strasser; Rhett saves Ashley from the Yankees by deceiving the Yankee Captain).

9. In each film, wisdom and solace are dispensed to one of the lead characters by a supportive but challenging Black character (Sam in Casablanca, Mammy in Gone with the Wind).

Reprinted with permission received from Howard Suber on Jan. 12, 2004.

2. As the Internet has expanded technological access to motion pictures, studios have been faced with more theft of their films. *See e.g., Studios Fume as Pirates Flood Internet With Films Technology: 'z' and other bootleggers are making first-run movies freely available via computer*, L.A. TIMES, Aug. 14, 1999, at A1. In 2003, the Motion Pictures Association of America (MPAA) launched a comprehensive international anti-piracy campaign that included trailers in movie theaters urging audiences to protect copyrights and informing them that they were hurting the jobs of carpenters and make-up artists when they download movies without paying for them. More information is available at *http://www.mpaa.org/anti-piracy*.

E.   FAIR USE

The Fair Use statute seems uncomplicated on its face, yet it has generated considerable litigation, primarily because it requires a balancing of four factors to determine whether a particular use of a copyrighted work is fair. No one can ever be absolutely certain whether he or she has used a work fairly until the use has been litigated and decided by a court. Here is the statute in its entirety:

17 U.S.C. § 107

Limitations on Exclusive Rights: Fair Use

Notwithstanding the provisions of sections 106 and 106A, the fair use of a copyrighted work, including such use by reproduction in copies or phonorecords or by any other means specified by that section, for purposes such as criticism, comment, news reporting, teaching (including multiple copies for classroom use), scholarship, or research, is not an infringement of copyright. In determining whether the use made of a work in any particular case is a fair use the factors to be considered shall include—

(1) the purpose and character of the use, including whether such use is of a commercial nature or is for nonprofit educational purposes;

(2) the nature of the copyrighted work;

(3) the amount and substantiality of the portion used in relation to the copyrighted work as a whole; and

(4) the effect of the use upon the potential market for or value of the copyrighted work.

Parodies that claim fair use of the original work are particularly problematic. Indeed, as Sherri Burr wrote in *Artistic Parody: A Theoretical Construct*, "what may be fair for one parodist may be unfair for another. Even with the same parody, the district court may consider the use fair, the court of appeals may find it unfair, and then the Supreme Court may ultimately decide it is fair." Sherri Burr, *Artistic Parody: a Theoretical Construct*, 14 CARDOZO ARTS & ENTERTAINMENT L. J. 65, 67 (1996). The following case illustrates how the fair use statute has been applied to a use of Margaret Mitchell's book "Gone With the Wind," which was turned into a major motion picture starring Vivian Leigh and Clark Gable.

SUNTRUST BANK v. HOUGHTON MIFFLIN CO.

United States Court of Appeals, Eleventh Circuit, 2001.
268 F.3d 1257.

BIRCH, Circuit Judge.

In this opinion, we decide whether publication of The Wind Done Gone ("*TWDG*"), a fictional work admittedly based on Margaret Mitchell's Gone With the Wind ("*GWTW*"), should be enjoined from publication based on alleged copyright violations. The district court granted a preliminary injunction against publication of *TWDG* because it found that Plaintiff–Appellee Suntrust Bank ("Suntrust") met the four-part test governing preliminary injunctions. We VACATE the injunction and REMAND for consideration of the remaining claims. * * *

Suntrust is the trustee of the Mitchell Trust, which holds the copyright in *GWTW*. Since its publication in 1936, *GWTW* has become one of the best-selling books in the world, second in sales only to the Bible. The Mitchell Trust has actively managed the copyright, authorizing derivative works and a variety of commercial items. It has entered into a contract authorizing, under specified conditions, a second sequel to *GWTW* to be published by St. Martin's Press. The Mitchell Trust maintains the copyright in all of the derivative works as well.

Alice Randall, the author of *TWDG*, persuasively claims that her novel is a critique of *GWTW*'s depiction of slavery and the Civil–War era American South. To this end, she appropriated the characters, plot and major scenes from *GWTW* into the first half of *TWDG*. According to Suntrust, *TWDG* "(1) explicitly refers to [*GWTW*] in its foreword; (2) copies core characters, character traits, and relationships from [*GWTW*]; (3) copies and summarizes famous scenes and other elements of the plot from [*GWTW*]; and (4) copies verbatim dialogues and descriptions from [*GWTW*]." Suntrust Bank v. Houghton Mifflin Co., 136 F.Supp.2d 1357, 1364 (N.D.Ga.2001), vacated, 252 F.3d 1165 (11th Cir. 2001). Defendant–Appellant Houghton Mifflin, the publisher of *TWDG*, does not contest the first three allegations, but nonetheless argues that there is no substantial similarity between the two works or, in the alternative, that the doctrine of fair use protects *TWDG* because it is primarily a parody of *GWTW*.

After discovering the similarities between the books, Suntrust asked Houghton Mifflin to refrain from publication or distribution of *TWDG*, but Houghton Mifflin refused the request. Subsequently, Suntrust filed an action alleging copyright infringement, violation of the Lanham Act, and deceptive trade practices, and immediately filed a motion for a temporary restraining order and a preliminary injunction.

After a hearing, the district court granted the motion, preliminarily enjoining Houghton Mifflin from "further production, display, distribution, advertising, sale, or offer for sale of" *TWDG*. Suntrust Bank, 136 F.Supp.2d at 1386. In a thorough opinion, the court found that "the defendant's publication and sale of [*TWDG* would] infringe the plaintiff's copyright interests as protected under the copyright laws." *Id*. Houghton Mifflin appealed. At oral argument, we issued an order vacating the injunction on the grounds that it was an unconstitutional prior restraint. Suntrust Bank v. Houghton Mifflin Co., 252 F.3d 1165 (11th Cir.2001). We now vacate that order and issue this more comprehensive opinion.
* * *

[The Court review the two works and concluded that *TWDG* made substantial use of *GWTW*.] *TWDG* appropriates numerous characters, settings, and plot twists from *GWTW*. For example, Scarlett O'Hara, Rhett Butler, Bonnie Butler, Melanie Wilkes, Ashley Wilkes, Gerald O'Hara, Ellen O'Hara, Mammy, Pork, Dilcey, Prissy, Belle Watling, Carreen O'Hara, Stuart and Brenton Tarleton, Jeems, Philippe, and Aunt Pittypat, all characters in *GWTW*, appear in *TWDG*. Many of these characters are renamed in *TWDG*: Scarlett becomes "Other," Rhett Butler becomes "R.B.," Pork becomes "Garlic," Prissy becomes "Miss Priss," Philippe becomes "Feleepe," Aunt Pittypat becomes "Aunt Pattypit," etc. In several instances, Randall renamed characters using Mitchell's descriptions of those characters in *GWTW*: Ashley becomes "Dreamy Gentleman," Melanie becomes "Mealy Mouth," Gerald becomes "Planter." The fictional settings from *GWTW* receive a similarly transparent renaming in *TWDG*: Tara becomes "Tata," Twelve Oaks Plantation becomes "Twelve Slaves Strong as Trees." *TWDG* copies, often in wholesale fashion, the descriptions and histories of these fictional characters and places from *GWTW*, as well as their relationships and interactions with one another. *TWDG* appropriates or otherwise explicitly references many aspects of *GWTW*'s plot as well, such as the scenes in which Scarlett kills a Union soldier and the scene in which Rhett stays in the room with his dead daughter Bonnie, burning candles. After carefully comparing the two works, we agree with the district court that, particularly in its first half, *TWDG* is largely "an encapsulation of [*GWTW*] [that] exploit[s] its copyrighted characters, story lines, and settings as the palette for the new story." Suntrust, 136 F.Supp.2d at 1367.

Houghton Mifflin argues that there is no substantial similarity between *TWDG* and *GWTW* because the retelling of the story is an inversion of *GWTW*: the characters, places, and events lifted from *GWTW* are often cast in a different light, strong characters from the original are depicted as weak (and vice-versa) in the new work, the institutions and values romanticized in *GWTW* are exposed as corrupt in *TWDG*. While we agree with Houghton Mifflin that the characters, settings, and plot taken from *GWTW* are vested with a new significance when viewed through the character of Cynara in *TWDG*, it does not change the fact that they are the very same copyrighted characters, settings, and plot.

b. Fair Use

Randall's appropriation of elements of *GWTW* in *TWDG* may nevertheless not constitute infringement of Suntrust's copyright if the taking is protected as a "fair use." * * *

Houghton Mifflin argues that *TWDG* is entitled to fair-use protection as a parody of *GWTW*. In *Campbell*, the Supreme Court held that parody, although not specifically listed in § 107, is a form of comment and criticism that may constitute a fair use of the copyrighted work being parodied. [Campbell v. Acuff–Rose Music, Inc., 510 U.S. 569, at 579]. Parody, which is directed toward a particular literary or artistic work, is distinguishable from satire, which more broadly addresses the institutions and mores of a slice of society. *Id.* at 580–81, 581 n. 15. * * * Thus, "[p]arody needs to mimic an original to make its point, and so has some claim to use the creation of its victim's ... imagination, whereas satire can stand on its own two feet and so requires justification for the very act of borrowing." *Id.* at 580–81. * * *

The fact that parody by definition must borrow elements from an existing work, however, does not mean that every parody is shielded from a claim of copyright infringement as a fair use. "The [Copyright] Act has no hint of an evidentiary preference for parodists over their victims, and no workable presumption for parody could take account of the fact that parody often shades into satire when society is lampooned through its creative artifacts, or that a work may contain both parodic and nonparodic elements." *Id.* at 581. * * *. Therefore, Houghton Mifflin's fair-use defense of parody, like any other claim of fair use, must be evaluated in light of the factors set out in § 107 and the constitutional purposes of copyright law. * * *

For purposes of our fair-use analysis, we will treat a work as a parody if its aim is to comment upon or criticize a prior work by appropriating elements of the original in creating a new artistic, as opposed to scholarly or journalistic, work. * * * Under this definition, the parodic character of *TWDG* is clear. *TWDG* is not a general commentary upon the Civil–War-era American South, but a specific criticism of and rejoinder to the depiction of slavery and the relationships between blacks and whites in *GWTW*. The fact that Randall chose to convey her criticisms of *GWTW* through a work of fiction, which she contends is a more powerful vehicle for her message than a scholarly article, does not, in and of itself, deprive *TWDG* of fair-use protection. We therefore proceed to an analysis of the four fair-use factors.

i. Purpose and Character of the Work

The first factor in the fair-use analysis, the purpose and character of the allegedly infringing work, has several facets. The first is whether *TWDG* serves a commercial purpose or nonprofit educational purpose. § 107(1). Despite whatever educational function *TWDG* may be able to lay claim to, it is undoubtedly a commercial product. * * * As the Supreme Court has stated, "[t]he crux of the profit/nonprofit distinction is not whether the sole motive of the use is monetary gain but whether the user stands to profit from exploitation of the copyrighted material without paying the customary price." Harper & Row, 471 U.S. at 562. * * * The fact that *TWDG* was published for profit is the first factor weighing against a finding of fair use. * * * However, *TWDG*'s for-profit status is strongly overshadowed and outweighed in view of its highly transformative use of *GWTW*'s copyrighted elements. "[T]he more transformative the new work, the less will be the significance of other factors, like commercialism, that may weigh against a finding of fair use." Campbell, 510 U.S. at 579. * * * "[T]he goal of copyright, to promote science and the arts, is generally furthered by the creation of transformative works." *Id*. A work's transformative value is of special import in the realm of parody, since a parody's aim is, by nature, to transform an earlier work. * * *

The issue of transformation is a double-edged sword in this case. On the one hand, the story of Cynara and her perception of the events in *TWDG* certainly adds new "expression, meaning, [and] message" to *GWTW*. From another perspective, however, *TWDG*'s success as a pure work of fiction depends heavily on copyrighted elements appropriated from *GWTW* to carry its own plot forward. * * *

Where Randall refers directly to Mitchell's plot and characters, she does so in service of her general attack on *GWTW*. In *GWTW*, Scarlett O'Hara often expresses disgust with and condescension towards blacks; in *TWDG*, Other, Scarlett's counterpart, is herself of mixed descent. In *GWTW*, Ashley Wilkes is the initial object of Scarlett's affection; in *TWDG*, he is homosexual. * * * In *GWTW*, Rhett Butler does not consort with black female characters and is portrayed as the captain of his own destiny. In *TWDG*, Cynara ends her affair with Rhett's counterpart, R., to begin a relationship with a black Congressman; R. ends up a washed out former cad. In *TWDG*, nearly every black character is given some redeeming quality—whether depth, wit, cunning, beauty, strength, or courage—that their *GWTW* analogues lacked.

* * * It is hard to imagine how Randall could have specifically criticized *GWTW* without depending heavily upon copyrighted elements of that book. A parody is a work that seeks to comment upon or criticize another work by appropriating elements of the original. "Parody needs to mimic an original to make its point, and so has some claim to use the creation of its victim's (or collective victims') imagination." Campbell, 510 U.S. at 580–81. * * * Thus, Randall has fully employed those conscripted elements from *GWTW* to make war against it. Her work,

TWDG, reflects transformative value because it "can provide social benefit, by shedding light on an earlier work, and, in the process, creating a new one." Campbell, 510 U.S. at 579. * * *

* * * In the case of *TWDG*, consideration of this factor certainly militates in favor of a finding of fair use, and, informs our analysis of the other factors, particularly the fourth, as discussed below.

ii. Nature of the Copyrighted Work

The second factor, the nature of the copyrighted work, recognizes that there is a hierarchy of copyright protection in which original, creative works are afforded greater protection than derivative works or factual compilations. *Id*. at 586. * * * *GWTW* is undoubtedly entitled to the greatest degree of protection as an original work of fiction. This factor is given little weight in parody cases, however, "since parodies almost invariably copy publicly known, expressive works." *Id*. at 586. * * *

iii. Amount and Substantiality of the Portion Used

The third fair-use factor is "the amount and substantiality of the portion used in relation to the copyrighted work as a whole." § 107(3). It is at this point that parody presents uniquely difficult problems for courts in the fair-use context, for "[p]arody's humor, or in any event its comment, necessarily springs from recognizable allusion to its object through distorted imitation. . . . When parody takes aim at a particular original work, the parody must be able to 'conjure up' at least enough of that original to make the object of its critical wit recognizable." *Id*. at 588. * * * Once enough has been taken to "conjure up" the original in the minds of the readership, any further taking must specifically serve the new work's parodic aims. [*Id*.] * * *

There are numerous instances in which *TWDG* appropriates elements of *GWTW* and then transforms them for the purpose of commentary. *TWDG* uses several of *GWTW*'s most famous lines, but vests them with a completely new significance. For example, the final lines of *GWTW*, "Tomorrow, I'll think of some way to get him back. After all, tomorrow is another day," are transformed in *TWDG* into "For all those we love for whom tomorrow will not be another day, we send the sweet prayer of resting in peace." Another such recasting is Rhett's famous quip to Scarlett as he left her in *GWTW*, "My dear, I don't give a damn." In *TWDG*, the repetition of this line (which is paraphrased) changes the reader's perception of Rhett/R.B.—and of black-white relations—because he has left Scarlett/Other for Cynara, a former slave. Another clear instance in which a memorable scene from *GWTW* is taken primarily for the purpose of parody is Gerald/Planter's acquisition of Pork/Garlic. In *GWTW*, Gerald won Pork in a card game with a man from St. Simons Island. In *TWDG*, Planter wins Garlic in a card game with a man from St. Simons Island, but Garlic, far from being the passive "chattel" in *GWTW*, is portrayed as being smarter than either white character by orchestrating the outcome of the card game and determining his own fate. There are many more such transformative uses of elements of *GWTW* in *TWDG*.

On the other hand, however, we are told that not all of *TWDG*'s takings from *GWTW* are clearly justified as commentary. We have already determined that *TWDG* is a parody, but not every parody is a fair use. Suntrust contends that *TWDG*, at least at the margins, takes more of the protected elements of *GWTW* than was necessary to serve a parodic function.

For example, in a sworn declaration to the district court, Randall stated that she needed to reference the scene from *GWTW* in which Jeems is given to the Tarleton twins as a birthday present because she considers it "perhaps the single most repellent paragraph in Margaret Mitchell's novel: a black child given to two white children as a birthday present ... as if the buying and selling of children thus had no moral significance." Clearly, such a scene is fair game for criticism. However, in this instance, Suntrust argues that *TWDG* goes beyond commentary on the occurrence itself, appropriating such nonrelevant details as the fact that the twins had red hair and were killed at Gettysburg. * * *

A use does not necessarily become infringing the moment it does more than simply conjure up another work. Rather, "[o]nce enough has been taken to assure identification, how much more is reasonable will depend, say, [1] on the extent to which the [work's] overriding purpose and character is to parody the original or, in contrast, [2] the likelihood that the parody may serve as a market substitute for the original." Campbell, 510 U.S. at 588. * * * As to the first point, it is manifest that *TWDG*'s raison d'etre is to parody *GWTW*. * * * The second point indicates that any material we suspect is "extraneous" to the parody is unlawful only if it negatively effects the potential market for or value of the original copyright. Based upon this record at this juncture, we cannot determine in any conclusive way whether " 'the quantity and value of the materials used' are reasonable in relation to the purpose of the copying." *Id.*, 510 U.S. at 586. * * *

iv. Effect on the Market Value of the Original

The final fair-use factor requires us to consider the effect that the publication of *TWDG* will have on the market for or value of Suntrust's copyright in *GWTW*, including the potential harm it may cause to the market for derivative works based on *GWTW*. * * * In addressing this factor, we must "consider not only the extent of market harm caused by the particular actions of the alleged infringer, but also whether unrestricted and widespread conduct of the sort engaged in by the defendant * * * would result in a substantially adverse impact on the potential market." *Id.* * * * More specifically, the Campbell Court continued: "[T]he only harm to derivatives that need concern us ... is the harm of market substitution. The fact that a parody may impair the market for derivative uses by the very effectiveness of its critical commentary is no more relevant under copyright that the like threat to the original market." *Id.*, 510 U.S. at 593. * * *

As for the potential market, Suntrust proffered evidence in the district court of the value of its copyright in *GWTW*. Several derivative works of *GWTW* have been authorized, including the famous movie of the same name and a book titled Scarlett: The Sequel. * * * *GWTW* and the derivative works based upon it have generated millions of dollars for the copyright holders. Suntrust has negotiated an agreement with St. Martin's Press permitting it to produce another derivative work based on *GWTW*, a privilege for which St. Martin's paid "well into seven figures." Part of this agreement was that Suntrust would not authorize any other derivative works prior to the publication of St. Martin's book.

An examination of the record, with its limited development as to relevant market harm due to the preliminary injunction status of the case, discloses that Suntrust focuses on the value of *GWTW* and its derivatives, but fails to address and offers little evidence or argument to demonstrate that *TWDG* would supplant demand for Suntrust's licensed derivatives. However, the Supreme Court and other appeals courts have made clear that, particularly in cases of parody, evidence of harm to the potential market for or value of the original copyright is crucial to a fair use determination. "[E]vidence about relevant markets" is also crucial to the fair use analysis. Campbell, 510 U.S. at 590. * * * "Evidence of substantial harm to [a derivative market] would weigh against a finding of fair use." *Id.* at 593. * * * "What is necessary is a showing by a preponderance of the evidence that some meaningful likelihood of future harm exits." Sony, 464 U.S. at 451. * * * It should also be remembered that with a work as old as *GWTW* on which the original copyright may soon expire, creation of a derivative work only serves to protect that which is original to the latter work and does not somehow extend the copyright in the copyrightable elements of the original work. * * *

In contrast, the evidence proffered in support of the fair use defense specifically and correctly focused on market substitution and demonstrates why Randall's book is unlikely to displace sales of *GWTW*. Thus, we conclude, based on the current record, that Suntrust's evidence falls far short of establishing that *TWDG* or others like it will act as market substitutes for *GWTW* or will significantly harm its derivatives. Accordingly, the fourth fair use factor weighs in favor of *TWDG*.

c.   SUMMARY OF THE MERITS

We reject the district court's conclusion that Suntrust has established its likelihood of success on the merits. To the contrary, based upon our analysis of the fair use factors we find, at this juncture, *TWDG* is entitled to a fair-use defense. * * *

We VACATE the judgment of the district court and REMAND the case for further proceedings consistent with this opinion.

Notes

1.   The film *Gone With the Wind* was made in 1939 on the then-staggering budget of $3.9 million. The film went on to win eight Oscars, including best picture and the first Academy Award for an African–America, Hattie McDaniel, who played Mammy. While *Titanic*, which earned over $1 billion in worldwide box office receipts is the highest grossing movie of all times, if the $390 million that *Gone With the Wind* earned when tickets sold for 50 cents were adjusted for inflation, some consider *Gone With The Wind* to be one of the best film investments ever made. *http://www.cri-key.com.au/business/2003/01/13–movielist.html* By one estimate, *Gone With The Wind* has earned $1.1 billion when adjusted for inflation. http://ebts.dk/adjustedusa.htm.

2.   Both the book and movie *Gone With the Wind* have inspired other parodies. In *MGM v. Showcase Atlanta Co-op. Productions*, 479 F.Supp. 351 (N.D.Ga. 1979), the plaintiffs created a musical called "Scarlet Fever" which they claimed was a parody after they were sued. The court concluded that the musical infringed MGM's copyrights in the movie and issued an injunction against production of the play.

3.   Russian readers were subject to tantalizing rip-offs of "Gone With the Wind" such as "We Call Her Scarlet," "The Secret of Scarlett O'Hara," and the "Last Love of Scarlett." *See* Alessandra Stanley, *Frankly My Dear, Russia Gives a Damn*, N.Y. TIMES, Aug. 29, 1994, at B1–2. Writer Yuliya Hilpatrik created the illegal sequels, which sold in Moscow for $2 to $3, almost twice the price of Alexandra Ripley's authorized 1991 bestseller, "Scarlet." *Id*.

4.   Fair use is a much-litigated area of copyright law. For a discussion on whether still photos can be parodied in a movie poster, *see Leibovitz v. Paramount Pictures Corp.*, 137 F.3d 109, 114 (2d Cir. 1998), where the Second Circuit found that the smirking face of actor Leslie Nielsen in an ad for *Naked Gun 2* contrasted so strikingly with the serious expression of Demi Moore in the Annie Leibovitz *Vanity Fair* cover photo that "the ad may reasonably be perceived as commenting on the seriousness, even the pretentiousness, of the original." The court ultimately concluded that a "photographer posing a well known actress in a manner that calls to mind a well known painting must expect, or at least tolerate, a parodist's deflating ridicule." For other cases applying fair use application to still photos, see *Richard Feiner & Co., Inc. v. H.R. Industries, Inc.*, 10 F.Supp.2d 310 (S.D.N.Y. 1998). *See also, Columbia Pictures Industries, Inc. v. Miramax Films Corp.*, 11 F.Supp.2d 1179 (C.D. Cal. 1998), where Miramax was enjoined from promoting its Michael Moore documentary *The Big One* in a manner that infringed on Columbia Pictures poster for *Men In Black*.

5.   Film production companies also have to be careful about how they use paintings on walls. *See Jackson v. Warner Bros. Inc.*, 993 F.Supp. 585 (E.D.Mich. 1997); *Amsinck v. Columbia Pictures Industries, Inc.*, 862 F.Supp. 1044 (S.D.N.Y. 1994). In some instances they need to receive and/or pay for permission to use the image.

Chapter 3

AGENTS, MANAGERS, LAWYERS, AND UNIONS: REPRESENTING FILM ARTISTS

———

This chapter explores the relationships between film artists and those who represent them, namely agents, managers, lawyers, and unions. Hollywood agents have become the butt of many jokes and as a group may rival lawyers in the public perception of challenged integrity. Yet, artists need agents to advance their careers as most studios and production companies will not accept and look at unsolicited manuscripts and projects sent directly from talent. The primary job of an agent is to *solicit* and *obtain employment* for their clients or material for future exploitation. California caps agents' fees at ten percent.

Managers may assist talent in picking scripts that diversify their abilities, lawyers to draft contracts, professionals to manage finances, and publicists who assist talent in selling their image. Managers may receive 5 to 25% of the talent's income. If the manager belongs to a management conglomerate, he may be responsible for several filmmakers' careers.

To work in the entertainment industry, it is helpful if the lawyer acquires knowledge about corporate and business law, tax law, labor law, intellectual property, criminal law, family law, contracts, and immigration. While many lawyers typically begin their careers at a studio on the legal side, some may move to the business side if they demonstrate sufficient skill or venture forth as screenwriters or producers. Studio lawyers are paid a salary, while law firms may charge by the hour or job. In some instances, lawyers enter into contracts to do all the talent's legal work (including contracts, divorces, adoptions, wills and criminal defense) in return for 5% of the talent's gross dollar revenue.

Unions negotiate agreements with studios and agents that provide minimum fees and working conditions for talent, which are known as minimum basic agreements. Once they become eligible to join a union such as the Screen Actors Guild, the Directors Guild, or the Writers Guild, the talent must pay membership dues. The challenge for lawyers entering the entertainment law field is to know what the unions have negotiated for their clients so that they do not waste time haggling over rights that the talent already possesses.

This chapter presents disputes that have arisen between talent and their agent, manager, lawyer, and union representatives.

A. AGENTS

William Goldman, the author of *Adventures in the Screen Trade* (1983), writes "[S]tars come and go. Only agents last forever." Agents endure because the system is set up to guarantee their survival. Film artists just starting out may find themselves caught in a Catch 22—they cannot get work without an agent, and they cannot get an agent to look at them until they can demonstrate that they have talent.

Anyone, including already licensed lawyers, seeking to become a talent agent with a conglomerate may have a tough road ahead. Typically, the big agencies like Creative Artist Agency, International Creative Management, United Talent Agency, and William Morris, hire and place recruits in the mailroom sorting the incoming correspondence and making deliveries. After succeeding in the mailroom job, they may move on to become desk and personal assistants to other agents. This apprentice rotation can take two years before the recruit becomes an assistant agent or full agent.

The rewards associated with succeeding as an agent are potentially huge with income exceeding $1 million a year, as one Los Angeles agent privately told author Sherri Burr, but the downsides are equally enormous. While Burr sat in the agent's office for a few hours observing his routine, he said that he fields over 100 calls and 125 e-mails daily. A desk assistant sits in his office to make and receive phone calls, and to do instant fact checking. Sometimes while he is on the phone with one person, he'll have the desk assistant call another agent to verify the truth of what the person on the phone is telling him. He said it is harder for others to lie to him because he has access to a wealth of knowledge. He confessed that another downside of the job is that the hours are long and he can never afford to take more than two or three days off. When he travels to nice places like the *Cannes* Film Festival, he works. This agent was also aware that no matter how much effort he contributes to building an artist's career, the artist might leave at any moment for another agent. When asked about whether a gentlemen's agreement keeps agents from poaching each other's clients, he remarked, "You steal from us; we steal from you."

For many individuals, the rewards of becoming an agent are worth the risks. Over the years, California and New York, the two main entertainment centers, have passed legislation to regulate agents. California talent agents are regulated by the California Labor Law code, a few provisions of which are reprinted below, and by the Screen Actors Guild to the extent that they represent film artists.

Cal Lab Code § 1700.4 (2003)

"Talent Agency"; "Artists"

(a) "Talent agency" means a person or corporation who engages in the occupation of procuring, offering, promising, or attempting to procure employment or engagements for an artist or artists, except that the activities of procuring, offering, or promising to procure recording contracts for an artist or artists shall not of itself subject a person or corporation to regulation and licensing under this chapter. Talent agencies may, in addition, counsel or direct artists in the development of their professional careers.

(b) "Artists" means actors and actresses rendering services on the legitimate stage and in the production of motion pictures, radio artists, musical artists, musical organizations, directors of legitimate stage, motion picture and radio productions, musical directors, writers, cinematographers, composers, lyricists, arrangers, models, and other artists and persons rendering professional services in motion picture, theatrical, radio, television and other entertainment enterprises.

Sherri Burr
The Director and the Agent:
Author Interview With Stephen Frears

Copyright © 2003 by Sherri Burr.

[At the Santa Fe, NM, Film Festival, Sherri Burr sat down with Stephen Frears on December 6 & 7, 2003, to discuss his career. Stephen Frears became interested in the stage after studying law at Cambridge University in England. Director Karel Reisz offered him his first film job as an assistant director in 1966. Frears directed his first feature *Gumshoe* in 1972. He has since directed *The Hit* starring John Hurt and Terrance Stamp, *My Beautiful Laundrette* starring Daniel Day Lewis, *Dangerous Liaisons* starring Glen Glose, John Malkovich and Michelle Pfeiffer, *Hero* staring Dustin Hoffman, *Mary Reilly* starring Julia Roberts, *The Hi–Lo Country* starring Woody Harrelson, Billy Crudup and Penelope Cruz, and *Dirty Pretty Things*, which was released in 2003. Frears was nominated for a best director Oscar for the 1990 *The Grifters* starring Angelica Huston and John Cusak]

"I got into films by mistake. I knew I was more interested in theater than law and began working on the stage after Cambridge. Then I met Karel Reisz and he offered me my first film job as an assistant director. I took on several AD jobs before getting to direct my first feature.

I get bored easily and that's why my films are all different. I look to see whether the book or screenplay seizes me, like when you fall in love. In *The Hi–Lo Country*, there was this nice little story about two men and a woman that weaves through the book. I knew nothing about westerns and had to learn everything. In London there are no prairies. It's a humbling experience when you have to learn everything.

I like to hire the best people for the role and then let them act. Penelope Cruz and her agent in Spain sent me a clip of her playing the role of Josepha in *The Hi–Lo Country*. I saw the clip and thought she'd be perfect for the role. We had fun on the set of *Hi-Lo Country*, but it was also serious business.

Dirty Pretty Things attracted me because it presented a good accent of modern London that wasn't high minded. It's a serious film, but it's also entertaining. I go out on a limb. Artists are allowed to go out on a limb as long as people will still back them.

Hero was a story about a man who did a powerful thing in spite of himself. Most heroes are created by situations. People are thrown in circumstances where they have to choose to act or not act.

My advice to creators involved in the business is to not take any money until they are sure they want to work with particular people. I was once sued by Ismail Merchant. We talked about a story and I said I would do it. He sent my agent some money before I had a chance to review the script. When I saw the script I realized it wasn't for me and I decided to back out.

My agent and I went to see a lawyer. After my lawyer heard what happened, he asked my agent to leave the room. He then said that I might have a claim against my agent for taking the money. I learned my lesson. Taking money creates a contract and expectations that you are really going to do the picture. I don't take any money until I'm absolutely certain that I want to work with the particularly people and their picture.''

Note

1. Did Stephen Frears' agent make a mistake by accepting employment for his client before the client was clear that he wanted to accept the job? As you read the following cases, note the duties of agents and clients towards each other? What are the responsibilities?

GRAMMER v. THE ARTISTS AGENCY

United States Court of Appeals, Ninth Circuit, 2002.
287 F.3d 886.

TASHIMA, Circuit Judge.

Plaintiffs Kelsey Grammer and Grammnet, Inc. (collectively, "Grammer"), and William Morris Agency, Inc., appeal a district court order confirming a Screen Actors Guild ("SAG") labor arbitration award, totaling over $2 million in unpaid commissions. Grammer argues that the arbitrators made factual findings unsupported by the record and that they exceeded their jurisdiction. We have jurisdiction under 28 U.S.C. § 1291, and we affirm the district court.

I. Factual Background

The Artists Agency ("Artists Agency") began representing Grammer in the 1980s, representation that included both Grammer's television and motion picture projects. Grammer became increasingly dissatisfied with Artists Agency in the early 1990s, as its representation had secured no motion picture projects for him and Grammer's two most significant television projects ("Cheers" and "Frasier") were not obtained through Artists Agency.

Grammer sought modification of his Artists Agency contract so that he could seek alternative representation for potential theatrical motion picture projects. After some negotiation, Grammer and Artists Agency agreed in January 1995 that, in exchange for Grammer's extending for two years his television and commercial obligations to Artists Agency (the "renewal contracts"), Artists Agency would substantially release Grammer from his theatrical motion picture obligations (the "settlement agreement") (collectively, the "1995 agreements"). The settlement agreement was executed on January 11, 1995. The renewal contracts were executed on January 17, 1995, were post-dated to commence on May 20, 1996, and expired May 20, 1998.

Artists Agency filed the renewal contracts with SAG in May 1995, but they were originally rejected. Counsel for Artists Agency contacted Joan Meyer ("Meyer"), SAG's Executive Administrator, explained the arrangement forged between Grammer and Artists Agency, and forwarded to her the settlement agreement as evidence of that arrangement.[1] Satisfied that the renewal contracts were in the best interests of Grammer, and that both sides had been competently represented by counsel, Meyer accepted the renewal contracts for filing with SAG.

In August 1996, Grammer terminated his relationship altogether with Artists Agency and, in August 1998, Grammer stopped paying commissions to Artists Agency. Grammer denied any obligations to Artists Agency, arguing that the 1995 agreements violated Rule 16(g) of the collective bargaining agreement ("CBA") among SAG, the Association of Talent Agents ("ATA"), and the National Association of Talent Representatives.[2] Grammer alleged that the 1995 agreements: (1) were post-dated so that the execution date and the commencement date did not correspond, in violation of Rule 16(g) § IV(C)(4)(a); (2) effectively spanned longer than three years as a result of this post-dating, in

---

1. The settlement agreement provided that Artists Agency was permitting Grammer to seek theatrical motion picture representation with another agency in exchange for extending his television representation commitment to Artists Agency for two years. It further states that the renewal contracts would be "deemed signed and delivered on or about May 20, 1995."

2. Rule 16(g) governs all aspects of the relationship between SAG members and "franchised" talent agents (i.e., those talent agents officially recognized by SAG). The CBA, inter alia, prohibits SAG members from dealing with non-franchised talent agents, requires that particular form contracts be used between SAG members and talent agents, dictates the manner in which SAG members and talent agents can enter into, and renegotiate, representation agreements, and limits the commission percentage that talent agents may charge SAG members.

violation of Rule 16(g) § IV(C)(4)(a); (3) were executed prior to the last third of the term of the previous contract between Grammer and Artists Agency, in violation of Rule 16(g) § IV(D)(3); and (4) were filed more than 15 days after their execution, in violation of Rule 16(g) § IV(C)(1). Any one of these violations arguably voids the renewal contracts.[3] When Artists Agency filed a statement of claim with SAG, seeking payment of the commissions allegedly due, Grammer counterclaimed, alleging that Artists Agency owed him commissions already paid pursuant to those purportedly void contracts.

A three-member arbitration panel held hearings over the course of 18 days, at which witnesses were examined and cross-examined, and documentary evidence was introduced.[4] The panel determined that the 1995 agreements were valid, that Artists Agency had enforceable rights pursuant to those 1995 agreements, that those rights entitled Artists Agency to more than $2 million in back commissions, and that Grammer's counterclaim was without merit. Specifically, the panel found that, while "[i]t is not disputed that the Settlement Agreement effected a transaction that was at variance from Rule 16(g)," Meyer had de facto granted a waiver of that variance after reviewing the settlement agreement, determining that Grammer's interests were both furthered and protected by legal counsel, and accepting the renewal contracts and settlement agreement for filing with SAG.

Grammer then filed this action for a declaration vacating the labor arbitration award. Grammer alleged that: (1) the arbitration panel did not apply the plain language of Rule 16(g), which would have rendered the 1995 agreements void and unenforceable; (2) there was no evidence in the record to support a finding that SAG had granted Artists Agency a waiver for its Rule 16(g) violations; (3) even if the 1995 agreements were valid, their execution in January 1995 voided the pre-existing agency agreement between Grammer and Artists Agency, meaning that Grammer owed Artists Agency no commissions for income derived between January 1995 and November 1996; and (4) the arbitration panel lacked jurisdiction to award Artists Agency a $36,000 commission on "consulting fees" paid to Grammer while working on the television show "Frasi-

---

3. Rule 16(g) § IV(C)(1) provides:

All contracts not in writing or not complying with these Regulations, whether as to form, filling in of blanks, execution, delivery, filing or otherwise, shall be void except as hereafter provided. The agent shall have no right under such void contract to receive any commission on a reasonable or other basis for services rendered or otherwise. * * *

4. Rule 16(g) requires that disputes between SAG members and franchised talent agents be resolved by arbitration:

All disputes and controversies of every kind and nature whatsoever between an agent and his client arising out of or in connection with or under any agency contract between the agent and his client executed prior to, on, or since July 31, 1962, as to the existence of such contract, its execution, validity, the right of either party to avoid the same on any grounds, its construction, performance, non-performance, operation, breach, continuance, or termination, shall be submitted to arbitration regardless of whether either party has terminated or purported to terminate the same.

Rule 16(g) § VI(A).

er." The district court rejected these arguments, confirmed the arbitration award, and denied Grammer's counterclaim.

II. STANDARD OF REVIEW

denovo

We review de novo the confirmation of an arbitration award. First Options, Inc. v. Kaplan, 514 U.S. 938, 947–48, 115 S.Ct. 1920, 131 L.Ed.2d 985 (1995). * * * Although we apply "ordinary, not special standards" when reviewing a trial court's confirmation of an arbitration award, First Options, 514 U.S. at 948, 115 S.Ct. 1920, we nonetheless afford labor arbitration awards "nearly unparalleled * * * deference." * * * Stead Motors v. Auto. Machinists Lodge No. 1173, 886 F.2d 1200, 1204 (9th Cir. 1989) (en banc). * * * We presume that factual findings underlying a labor arbitration award are correct, rebuttable only by a clear preponderance of the evidence. Carpenters Pension Trust Fund v. Underground Constr. Co., 31 F.3d 776, 778 (9th Cir. 1994). * * *

III. DISCUSSION

All parties agree that the 1995 agreements violate the terms of Rule 16(g). We must decide whether the arbitration panel erred in concluding that the 1995 that the arbitration panel's decision to enforce the 1995 agreements was a reasonable interpretation of the CBA; we therefore affirm the district court.

A. *Waiver of Rule 16(g) Violations*

16 g
Violations

At the very least, it is clear that the 1995 agreements were: (1) executed and set to commence on different dates, in violation of Rule 16(g) § IV(C)(4)(a); (2) executed prior to the last third of the term on the previous contract between Grammer and Artists Agency, in violation of Rule 16(g) § IV(D)(3); and (3) filed more than 15 days after their execution, in violation of Rule 16(g) § IV(C)(1). In light of these Rule 16(g) violations, the arbitration panel observed that "[i]t is not disputed that the Settlement Agreement effected a transaction that was at variance from Rule 16(g)," and the district court found that "the parties do not dispute that the various agreements at issue in the arbitration deviated from the standard regulations set forth in Rule 16(g)."

These Rule 16(g) violations, however, do not necessarily void the 1995 agreements. Grammer correctly observes that neither he nor Artists Agency ever requested a formal, written waiver from SAG. Citing Rule 16(g) § IV(J), Grammer argues that the absence of such a formal, written waiver renders the arbitration panel's determination patently inconsistent with the plain language of Rule 16(g), and it therefore should be vacated. However, although Rule 16(g) instructs that such violations void applicable contracts and that waivers of violations must be issued by SAG in writing, these ostensibly "plain" provisions must be construed in the larger context of Rule 16(g) specifically and industry practice generally. When Rule 16(g) is considered in its entirety, its text is not as "plain" as Grammer suggests. The arbitration panel characterized Rule 16(g) as "sometimes contradictory"; ample evidence supports this conclusion. Initially, Rule 16(g) is facially inconsistent when it comes to prescribing how waivers ought to be granted. For example, while § IV(J) suggests that waivers cannot be offered without SAG's written consent, § IV(C)(1) provides that "inadvertent error or oversight . . . shall be deemed waived unless the objection of invalidity is raised by the actor or SAG within 60 days." * * *

Contradictions such as these led Karen Stuart ("Stuart"), the executive director of the ATA, to testify that Rule 16(g) "is riddled with inconsistencies and that is why custom and practice become important and SAG and ATA speak almost daily because there are problems in interpreting this agreement."

Additionally, while arbitrators cannot ignore the plain wording of collectively bargained contracts, they also are "not confined to the express terms of the contract . . . [They] may also consider the industrial common law which is equally a part of the collective bargaining agreement although not expressed in it." Hawaii Teamsters, 241 F.3d at 1181 (citation and internal quotation marks omitted). * * *

There was sufficient evidence to sustain the arbitration panel's finding that SAG waived the variances between Rule 16(g) and the 1995 agreements. Meyer testified that SAG generally will accept agreements that do not strictly comport with the requirements of Rule 16(g) when there are side agreements protecting the actor and the agent. Furthermore, both Meyer and Stuart testified that SAG occasionally overlooks Rule 16(g) violations of the exact type asserted by Grammer, without the use of formal waivers. In light of this testimony, which explains the course and practice of SAG's Rule 16(g) interpretation, the arbitration panel's finding that SAG had granted a waiver by filing the renewal contracts easily meets the deferential standard of review that this court must apply.

B. Contractual Obligations Between January 1995 and May 1996

Grammer argues that even if the arbitration panel correctly held that SAG had granted waivers for the 1995 agreements' Rule 16(g) violations, when those agreements were executed in January 1995, the pre-existing agency contract between Grammer and Artists Agency[10] was automatically terminated. Because the 1995 renewal contracts did not go into effect until May 1996, Grammer argues that there was no agency contract in effect between January 1995 and May 1996, and that Artists Agency is not entitled to commissions stemming from that period. The arbitration panel rejected this argument, finding that an agency agreement was in effect between January 1995 and May 1996. The district court affirmed this conclusion as a reasonable interpretation of Rule 16(g), and we affirm this district court holding.

---

10. Grammer had signed an agency agreement with Artists Agency in 1993, covering representation for television programs, which spanned three years, from May 20, 1993, to May 19, 1996.

The thrust of Meyer's and Stuart's testimony was that Rule 16(g) merely provides a default framework to protect the interests of actors and agents and that these rules can be waived when the parties are represented by counsel and (particularly) when the agreement in question benefits the SAG member. Here, Grammer was seeking to get out of contractual obligations to Artists Agency so that he could seek theatrical motion picture representation with United Talent Agency. The 1995 agreements permitted him to do exactly that, so long as he extended his television representation obligations to Artists Agency for an additional two years.

Grammer now tries to use a technicality found in Rule 16(g) § IV(D)(3) to assert that the 1995 agreements left him altogether uncommitted to Artists Agency from January 1995 to March 1996. This purported "lapse" in Grammer's and Artist Agency's contract, however, was an eventuality clearly not contemplated by the parties when forming the 1995 agreements. In fact, Grammer's interpretation of the 1995 agreements is belied by the fact that Artists Agency represented Grammer in November 1995 during negotiations with Paramount Studios. Obviously, Artists Agency would not have represented Grammer in these negotiations had it not believed that the 1993 agency agreement was still in effect. And, by permitting Artists Agency actively to represent him and to pursue his interests during this period, Grammar clearly intended that the representation continue uninterrupted.

Given that Rule 16(g) violations can be waived by SAG when the parties are represented by counsel, when the waiver is consistent with the parties' assent, and when the waiver benefits the SAG member, it was reasonable for the arbitration panel to find that a valid agency contract existed between Grammer and Artists Agency from January 1995 to May 1996.

C. Consulting Fees

The arbitration panel awarded Artists Agency $36,000 in commissions on Grammer's consulting fees. Pointing to the absence of a "consulting" category in the CBA, Grammer argues that SAG (and by implication, the SAG arbitration panel) did not have jurisdiction to award consulting fee commissions.

The arbitration panel rejected this argument, finding that payment for consulting fees is within the scope of the renewal contracts and Rule 16(g), which provides:

> Rule 16(g) shall, commencing August 1, 1975, apply to the representation of actors by agents in connection with, or relating to, the actor's employment or professional career as an employee in the production of motion pictures made for all purposes, uses and methods of exhibition including, without limitation, motion pictures made for theatrical, commercial, industrial, educational and television use, as provided in Article XII of the Basic Contract. Except as expressly provided to the contrary herein, all provisions of these

Regulations shall apply to the representation of actors by agents in connection with their employment or professional careers as employees in television motion pictures.

Rule 16(g) § XXII (emphasis added). The arbitration panel determined that Grammer's consulting services were "in connection with" his television employment, and the district court concluded that this interpretation was reasonable.

We likewise conclude that the arbitration panel's determination was reasonable. Rule 16(g)'s language of "in connection with" is sufficiently vague to support the arbitration panel's interpretation and there is no contradictory provision that expressly precludes commissions on consulting fees. Thus, we defer to the arbitration panel and affirm its consulting fee award.

IV. CONCLUSION

For the foregoing reasons, we hold that the labor arbitration panel acted reasonably in concluding that SAG waived violations of Rule 16(g), that a representation contract existed between Grammer and Artists Agency from January 1995 to March 1996, and that an award of commissions on consulting fees was permitted under the CBA. The district court's order confirming the arbitration award is, therefore,

AFFIRMED. *AFFM'D*

Notes

1. One of the goals of the Talent Agencies Act (Lab. Code, §§ 1700–1700.47) is to prevent improper persons from becoming talent agents and to regulate such activity for the protection of the public. The Act voids contracts between an unlicensed agent and an artist. Waisbren, v. Peppercorn Productions, Inc., 41 Cal.App.4th 246, 48 Cal.Rptr.2d 437 (2d Dist. 1995).

2. By SAG rule, agents are limited to charging 10% commissions in California. The NY General Business Law, section 185, provides

"For a placement in class "C" employment [theatrical engagements] the gross fee shall not exceed, for a single engagement, ten per cent of the compensation payable to the applicant, except that for employment or engagements for orchestras and for employment or engagements in the opera and concert fields such fees shall not exceed twenty per cent of the compensation."

3. How do New York rules differ from California's? According to Professor Biederman, "A talent agent must be licensed by the Commissioner of Labor (for agents located in New York City, by the Commissioner of Consumer Affairs), * * * who investigates the applicant for character and responsibility. * * * The license fee is $200 at issuance ($400 if the agency has more than four employees) and a $5,000 bond is required. A written contract is required. * * * The Commissioner is empowered to suspend or revoke an agency license for "violat[ion] of any provision of this article or [if

the agent] is not a person of good character and responsibility." * * * *The action of the Commissioner is subject to review by the New York Supreme Court * * * in a so-called "Article 78 proceeding," in which the "substantial evidence" rule generally applicable to review of administrative decisions applies. * * * In addition, violation of the article can constitute a misdemeanor punishable by imprisonment for up to a year and/or a fine of not more than $1,000. * * * Criminal proceedings may be instituted by the Commissioner or by 'any person aggrieved by such violations.' * * * The Commissioner has no power to nullify contracts between the artist and agent, nor does the Commissioner have power to order an agent to return commissions already paid to the agent. Moreover, the Commissioner has no power to hear complaints against unlicensed agents. Aggrieved artists must pursue their remedies in the New York Supreme Court." *See* Biederman, *Agents v. Managers Revisited: What Hath Ovitz Wrought?*, 1 Vand. J. Ent. L. & Prac. 5 (Spring 1999) (footnotes omitted).

FRIEDKIN v. WALKER

New York Civil Court, 1977.
90 Misc.2d 680, 395 N.Y.S.2d 611.

COHEN, Judge.

Does article 11 of the New York State General Business Law, requiring employment agencies to be licensed, apply to a booking agent who secures lectures and engagements for a client who is a motion picture and theatrical personality? The answer is in the affirmative unless the agent is in the business of managing such a clientele and the seeking of employment is only incidentally involved.

Plaintiff is a well-known theatrical and motion picture personality whose accomplishments include direction of "The French Connection", "The Exorcist" and the production of the most recent "Oscar" presentation television program. Defendant is a well-known but unlicensed agent in the business of managing, directing and promoting lectures, talks and addresses for various personalities, including four former candidates for President and Vice-President and several United States Senators, Representatives and other newsworthy personalities. It is noted that the plaintiff is in the entertainment business as a film director and his lectures involve this medium.

Underlying this motion by plaintiff for a summary judgment are two causes of action of an amended complaint. The first seeks the return of commissions held by the defendant amounting to $4,743.32, on grounds that the contract between the parties is invalid as defendant is an unlicensed employment agency in contravention of section 172 of the General Business Law and, in any event, the fee is in excess of the amount allowed by statute.

The second cause of action seeks $2,450 as his share of fees allegedly wrongfully retained, for three lectures.

The defendant denies liability and counterclaims for lost earnings allegedly due to plaintiff's failure to keep 20 lecture engagements (of 23

[handwritten margin note: Bookings agents must be licensed unless in the business of managing such a clientele & seeking of employment is only incidentally involved.]

booked) and for irreparable injury to his reputation. Defendant admits to being unlicensed and to the retention of a portion of plaintiff's share of fees, but claims exemption from the statutory licensing requirement.

The parties executed a contract on June 13, 1972 whereby plaintiff agreed to employ defendant as his sole and exclusive agent for a stated purpose: to negotiate and secure engagements and to book, manage and arrange all his lectures, talks and addresses. Defendant had discretion as to plaintiff's gross fees and was to retain 30% of the gross receipts from any and all lectures, talks and addresses plaintiff undertook, including those generated by invitations made directly to plaintiff. Other clauses show that defendant's obligations included the billing and collection of all fees, in its own name, from any and all lectures, talks and addresses given by plaintiff. It was also agreed that defendant would seek to prevent the unauthorized use of plaintiff's name or photograph in the advertising or listing of any other bureau, manager or agent and that plaintiff would join in legal proceedings necessary to effectuate that purpose, at no expense to plaintiff. A further provision obligated plaintiff to provide photographs, press releases and brochures and permitted defendant to take certain steps at plaintiff's expense to obtain some of those materials when unavailable to plaintiff.

Section 172 of the General Business Law provides that "No person shall ... own, operate or carry on any employment agency unless such person shall have first procured a license ... in the city of New York such license shall be issued by the commissioner of consumer affairs."

Under section 171 (subd 2, par d) of the General Business Law an employment agency shall include "any theatrical employment agency".

Subdivision 8 of section 171 of the General Business Law provides in part that a theatrical employment agency is "any person ... who procures or attempts to procure employment or engagements ... or other entertainments or exhibitions or performances" and enumerates several specific types of engagements for which a theatrical engagement, defined in subdivision 9 of section 171 of the General Business Law, may be sought by a theatrical employment agency. However, subdivision 8 of section 171 of the General Business Law specifically exempts from the definition of a theatrical employment agency "the business of managing such entertainments, exhibitions or performances, or the artists or attractions constituting the same, where such business only incidentally involves the seeking of employment therefor." (Italics added.)

Section 171 (subd 2, par a) of the General Business Law defines an employment agency as "any person ... who, for a fee, procures or attempts to procure: (1) employment or engagements for persons seeking employment or engagements".

Section 190 of the General Business Law makes it a misdemeanor to violate, inter alia, the licensing requirements of section 172 of the General Business Law.

It is readily apparent that defendant is a <u>de facto employment agency whose activities require a license unless the exemption under subdivision 8 of section 171 is applicable.</u> The question whether defendant's business only incidentally involves the seeking of employment as corollary to being a personal manager of plaintiff would ordinarily be a matter of factual determination, and thus not resolved upon summary judgment * * *. It is, however, axiomatic that to defeat a motion for summary judgment, one must lay bare his proofs and present evidentiary facts rather than conclusory allegations of fact or of law * * *. Where no significant doubt is raised regarding the existence of a material and triable issue of fact, summary judgment will lie (Philips v Kantor & Co., 31 NY2d 307).

Defendant's self-serving statements that it is "a business representative" and "not an employment agency which gets job placements for a fee" and the simple denial that it acted as an employment agency when representing plaintiff will not suffice. Nor can the pleadings raise sufficient factual issues. * * *

Defendant has failed to submit evidentiary facts with any probative value specifying or describing the performance of its alleged managerial activities. Defendant submits that the contract merits exclusion from the statutory mandate. On the other hand, plaintiff submits an affidavit from his personal manager fully and clearly delineating his managerial functions and responsibilities on behalf of the plaintiff.

The instant contract cannot be characterized as one of management: it is abundantly clear upon a reading <u>that defendant's obligation is to solicit lecturing engagements for plaintiff, and that any other duties to be performed for plaintiff are incidental thereto.</u> Where ambiguities exist in a contract, they may be resolved on a motion for summary judgment (Rentways v O'Neill Milk & Cream Co., 308 NY 342; 10 NY Jur, Contracts, § 190), but the instant contract needs no resort beyond its four corners to glean its specific intent. <u>It plainly states defendant's obligation</u> to act as plaintiff's "<u>sole and exclusive agent to negotiate and secure engagements and book, manage and arrange all . . . lectures, talks and addresses.</u>" Moreover, defendant's characterization that the general contractual terms, which it drew, constitute a managerial contract cannot overcome the obvious overriding intent and purpose of the agreement and its factual setting securing the most profitable engagements for plaintiff. * * *

It is, therefore, clear that defendant's <u>primary, if not sole, obligation was to secure lecture engagements for plaintiff.</u> The fee billing and collection functions were incidental conveniences, perhaps for defendant's protection but in any event unrelated to the alleged personal management of plaintiff.

The defendant's argument that the scope of article 11 of the General Business Law is limited primarily to job placements is without merit in view of the express and unequivocal contrary statutory provisions and the cases cited herein.

Defendant is clearly an unlicensed employment agency within section 171 (subd 2, par a) of the General Business Law and the exclusionary provision of subdivision 8 of section 171 of the General Business Law is clearly inapplicable. * * * Under the foregoing, it is immaterial whether defendant is deemed a theatrical employment agency within subdivision 8 of section 171 of the General Business Law or whether the engagements pursuant to the contract may be deemed as theatrical engagements pursuant to subdivision 9 of the General Business Law. Likewise, whether the fees in accordance with the contract are within legal limits is also immaterial, as the contract is unenforceable.

It is a valid exercise of the police power of the State to regulate and license the business of conducting a private employment agency. (People ex rel. Armstrong v Warden, 183 NY 223.) This is to be distinguished from a licensing requirement for mere revenue raising purposes. (See Williston, Contracts [3d ed], § § 1766–1769; 8 Encyclopedia NY Law, Contracts, § § 2417, 2419.) A contract made in violation of such statute is unenforceable. (Carmine v Murphy, 285 NY 413; * * *).

Subdivision 1 of section 186 of the General Business Law expressly requires the return of any fees wrongfully obtained within one week after demand: "Any employment agency which collects, receives or retains a fee or other payment contrary to or in excess of the provisions of this article, shall return the fee ... within seven days after receiving a demand therefor." It would be a mere formalism to require, in consideration of the first cause of action, that a demand be a condition precedent; it is inferred from commencement of the lawsuit. * * * Moreover, the criminal penalty and civil sanctions * * * demonstrate a public policy militating against the accrual of benefits to a business being conducted in violation of a licensing requirement pursuant to the State police power. * * *

In accordance with the foregoing, plaintiff shall have judgment upon both causes of action, and the counterclaims are dismissed as they are not supported by any evidentiary matter, and dismissal is warranted.
* * *

Note

1. Besides the legal regulations requiring agents to be licensed in New York and California, should there be ethical requirements for agents? Should agents be allowed to steal each other's clients? Should poaching be considered fair business practice?

John Brodie
Poaching Piques Percenters;
Agents Get Ugly Over A-List Defectors
VARIETY, Oct. 24, 1994–Oct. 30, 1994, at 1.

Earlier this year, a prominent young talent agent got wind that two agents from International Creative Management were romancing one of the biggest stars on his roster. He jumped in his car, sped down Wilshire Boulevard, arrived at their office and demanded to see the would-be poachers.

"When I got the two of them alone in an office," says the agent, "I told them they were messing with the wrong guy. I warned them if they didn't leave my client alone, I would devote the next six months to screwing up their deals and stealing their clients. I also threatened to kill them both. I meant it . . . literally."

Such is today's cutthroat tenor of the gentleman's profession known as the agency business. Two years ago, a whirlwind round of agency mergers had talent spinning their heads as they tried to keep up with agents who were leapfrogging from office to office. Now that the business has settled down, it's the agents who are reeling—and the talent doing the shuffling.

Discharging their agents in recent months have been actors Eddie Murphy, Bill Paxton, Matt Dillon, Sean Penn, Chazz Palminteri ("Bullets Over Broadway") and Tia Carrere ("True Lies"), plus directors James Cameron, Renny Harlin, Andrew Davis and Jeremiah Chechik ("Benny and Joon"). Poaching, and client loyalty, are once again the talk of the town.

Most agents agree that poaching is on the upswing, and that it ultimately is bad for business because it distracts them from their real job: getting the right parts for their people. And studio executives worry that talent will consolidate even more into the hands of a few suppliers.

Meanwhile, many agents blame malaise at the studios for this fall's rise in client turnover; less projects getting the greenlight means less work for actors, who may blame their agents. And they lament that while competition for clients is fierce in any industry, agency poaching is particularly devastating because in many cases agents spend years nurturing a young talent—only to see him jump ship when stardom finally arrives.

Just coincidence?

Agents from ICM, the William Morris Agency and Creative Artists Agency argue that this fall's high-profile game of musical chairs is coincidence. Jeremiah Chechik's agent moved from ICM to CAA several weeks ago, so it is not surprising that he would follow suit. CAA claims that Andrew Davis came to it on its own initiative from the small agency where he was repped for over a decade. Sources at that boutique house, Becsey Wisdom Kalejian, beg to differ. Ron Howard, too, was nurtured by Larry Becsey before moving to CAA.

Agents at boutiques like the Gersh Agency say that unlike the days when Lew Wasserman, Stan Kamen and Abe Lastfogel ran ten-percenteries, today's major agencies have become increasingly predatory. They say Big Three agents are frequently violating their own in-house edicts against stealing from the smaller shops.

"With the dominant position of CAA, the agency business has become very cutthroat," says veteran ten-percenter Phil Gersh. "Instead of just stealing from each other, they will go after us as soon as we get a hot actress like Sharon Stone, or one of our directors moves from made-fors to features."

The Gersh Agency did, in fact, lose Stone to ICM around the time her career took off in "Basic Instinct," but the agency received the commission on that film. Stone, currently starring in Universal's Martin Scorsese film "Casino," is now being wooed by both CAA and ICM. The Las Vegas location of "Casino" has become a frequent-flyer hub for Tinseltown's finest handlers.

CAA, ICM and WMA agents all stress that they have policies against stealing from the smaller agencies. The big boys refrained from poaching the late John Candy from boutique APA even after his agent Marty Klein died in 1992. But some agents admit that policy is not always followed.

Plow that niche

Increasingly the boutiques are developing niche businesses as a financial survival tactic. The Gersh Agency operates a lucrative below-the-line division that reps cinematographers and other craftspeople.

Studio executives fear poaching will result in the consolidation of talent in the hands of a few. That in turn allows the major ten-percenteries to drive up prices on feature film packages. "It's not good for the buyer to have all the talent represented by two places," says one studio head.

Poaching can also hurt talent when worried agents practice what's known as "agenting defensively"—keeping clients working without being discriminating about material.

Once a poach goes down, the new agency does not immediately start earning income from its client. Often the old agency will earn commission on any existing projects it has put the star in. Also, the old shop may have a contract with several years remaining on it. In that case, the new and old shop may hammer out a split-fee arrangement.

The best timing

Births, deaths, divorces and holidays are the best times to poach—so goes an old adage of the agency game. Then there's the production malaise caused by recent management changes at Disney, Sony and Paramount. It has been tough getting projects to gel during the past couple of months—meaning that actors and directors are increasingly competing for a reduced pool of jobs. Nothing makes a client more susceptible to a poach than catching splinters on the bench.

Temptation comes in many forms, but the seducing agent usually finds a client's psychological weakness and then exploits it. Actors may be showered with scripts from a rival agency trying to get their attention. Directors and screenwriters most often fall prey to the siren song of working with big-time actors.

When Dolph Lundgren was led away from United Talent Agency to William Morris, the new agency promised the action actor that its New York office would build a theater career for the star of "Universal Soldier." While Lundgren has yet to play Hamlet at the Public Theater, a source in WMA's New York office confirms that Lundgren has read for several roles.

That weak spot

Almost any weakness will do. Many agents encourage rumors about the usual dissension that occurs at ten-percenteries—particularly those that have been through mergers and acquisitions in the past three years.

Rival agents looking to pry clients from ICM will talk about the lack of teamwork in that shop. Agents looking to poach from WMA mention the lingering tension between the firm's former Triad partners and the old-line Morris agents. Agents looking to pry clients away from UTA have been fueling rumors of a partner split. That agency, which was formed by merging three disparate boutiques two years ago, is increasingly competing with the Big Three and is viewed by many in the industry as a bridge between the boutiques and the majors.

All 10 UTA partners have in fact been having the usual give-and-take as the agency goes through growing pains, but they agreed to spend this past weekend sorting out their problems with a facilitator. Sources say they remain committed to keeping the agency together.

At some point, agents concede they have to throw their hands up. "Sometimes the client is tapped out, finished, but the client can't fire himself, so he has to fire us or the manager," says one top ten-percenter.

#Even CAA has not managed to stay above the fray. Last week, WMA picked up Sean Penn from CAA. That snag no doubt lessened The Morris Agency's disappointment over the recent loss to CAA of Chazz Palminteri, a client it built virtually from scratch, and of Bill Paxton, whose career is hot after "True Lies."

Chances are Morris will continue to gun for CAA clients. ICM recently snagged Matt Dillon from Morris and Herb Ross from CAA.

And, of course, when agents talk of poaching, they all wax nostalgic for the days when clients had loyalty. Despite the best efforts of many a Big Three agent, both Harrison Ford and Jack Nicholson have spent the majority of their careers represented by the same Mom-and-Pop operations that handled them when they were turning heads in "American Graffiti" and "Easy Rider," respectively. Ford has been with Patricia McQueeney for 25 years and Nicholson has been with Sandy Bresler for 35.

Claudia Eller & James Bates
Talent Agents About to Demand
Bigger Piece of Pie

L.A. Times, Oct. 31, 2000.

With its strike against the ad industry now settled, the Screen Actors Guild is staring another urgent problem in the face: forging a new agreement with agents. The changes under discussion could lead to a permanent realignment of Hollywood's talent representation business.

Beginning Thursday, SAG and the Assn. of Talent Agents trade group will meet for weeklong negotiations aimed at hammering out a new deal. In short, agents are asking to be able to enter new business ventures as well as to get a cut of all streams of income flowing to their clients. actors, on the other hand, want assurances that such changes will not leave them vulnerable to agent abuses.

"We can't stay in business under the rules," says ATA Executive Director Karen Stuart. "This business is going to be a graveyard business if we are not able to grow our companies." She said that in recent years, at least 10 of the ATA's smaller agencies have closed up.

SAG officials recognize that some of the rules governing agents need to be revised.

"It is a changing business and appropriate changes may be needed. But actors must continue to be protected," Leonard Chassman, the Hollywood executive director of SAG, said Monday.

For more than 60 years, SAG has "franchised" agents, authorizing its members to be represented by them as long as the agents abide by SAG's rules. These regulations govern many aspects of the agency business, including limiting agent commissions to 10% and determining contract lengths.

Agents argue that the entertainment industry has changed dramatically in recent years and that SAG's rules have become antiquated and financially restrictive, and so need to be radically altered.

The agents want to be allowed to expand their operations both by developing new businesses and by getting a cut of all the streams of revenues that flow to actors, including video and DVD sales.

Without change, they predict, more agencies will disappear, agents will further flee the ranks to become unregulated managers and, as a result, actors on the lower rungs will have a difficult time finding decent representation.

However valid those arguments, actors are reluctant to embrace radical change. They are worried that loosening the rules could result in agents becoming arms of production companies and even studios, a situation rife with conflicts of interest that could hurt actors. Unhappy with current safeguards, actors also want new rules defining the fiduciary responsibility of agents toward their clients.

At this early point, both SAG and ATA are optimistic that a new agreement recognizing their respective issues can be worked out by Nov. 8.

It doesn't hurt that SAG appreciates the formal support of agents during their six-month strike against the ad industry. ATA members refused to send their clients out for work that would violate the union's strike rules.

The parties began talking about changing the rules—the first amendments since 1975—last spring, but negotiations were put on hold until the commercial strike could be resolved. The talks resumed recently and, sources say, some progress already has been made.

There is ample evidence that the talent agency business has changed.

Over the last few years, there has been a proliferation of management outfits in Hollywood. In 1998, Michael Ovitz, co-founder of Creative Artists Agency, formed a major talent management firm, Artists Management Group, which represents actors, writers, directors, sports figures and animators.

Stuart said that in the five years she has been with ATA, "I've heard over and over again that there are agents that are leaving the business, that members of the Screen Actors Guild are being represented by representatives other than franchised agents, and what are we as agents doing in a box when it's apparent that you don't need to sign a franchise agreement to represent their membership?"

Franchise agreements were originated to establish some ground rules for the representation business, which grew out of vaudeville and radio.

Today, ATA represents more than 100 agencies, from industry giants like CAA, International Creative Management and the William Morris Agency down to tiny independent shops.

Of SAG's 98,000 active members, less than 30% work enough to have agents, according to the guild. Stuart estimates that ATA member companies represent close to 90% of all working actors.

Agents are particularly rankled by the double standard that exists between how they are forced to operate their businesses and the lack of rules governing how managers operate.

Unlike agents, managers are unregulated and not required to be licensed by the state. This gives managers the freedom to charge as much commission as they want—typically 15%, compared to the agents' capped 10%—and to produce and own programming.

Stuart says agents are not asking to raise the 10% commission they charge clients on the initial compensation of any job they book.

But they want to be able to draw commissions from all forms of payment involving the reuse of a movie or TV show, be it video and DVD sales or cable and pay TV runs. Present rules prohibit agents in

California from doing so, although in some other states such restrictions do not apply.

For some time, agents and actors have sharply disagreed over how commissions should apply to the Internet. ATA maintains that the regulations, written in 1939 and amended 25 years ago, have no jurisdiction over new media, but SAG holds the opposite position and has a proposal addressing the issue.

Agents insist that boosting their income is imperative given the increased costs associated with talent representation, including messengers, faxes, tape dubbings and other expensive client services.

"You can't make money booking and taking 10% anymore," Stuart insists.

But aren't agents, especially those at the big agencies collecting six- and seven-figure salaries, just being greedy?

Stuart insists not. "In every other business, you can raise costs as your costs rise. But we can't pass on our costs.

"If we wanted an equal playing field, we'd give up our franchise and become managers," she asserts. "We want to stay agents. We don't want to be managers. But financially, we are not going to be able to stay in business under the [existing] SAG regulations."

Note

1. The Talent Agencies Act (Lab. Code, §§ 1700–1700.47) is considered a remedial statute designed to correct abuses that have been the subject of both legislative action and judicial decision. The statute was enacted to protect artists. The question arises whether the act covers personal managers who procure employment for artists? At least once case argues that to exempt managers would create a standard so vague as to be unworkable and would undermine the purpose of the act. *See* Waisbren v. Peppercorn Productions, Inc., 41 Cal.App.4th 246, 48 Cal.Rptr.2d 437 (2d Dist. 1995) (In an action for breach of contract brought by a personal manager against his former client, an artistic production company, the trial court properly voided the parties' oral agreement because plaintiff had performed the duties of a talent agent, by procuring employment for defendant, without first obtaining the necessary license under the Talent Agencies Act (Lab. Code, §§ 1700–1700.47)). The conflict between agents and managers is an enduring one.

B. THE CONFLICT BETWEEN AGENTS & MANAGERS

WACHS v. CURRY

California Court of Appeals, 1993.
13 Cal.App.4th 616, 16 Cal.Rptr.2d 496.

JOHNSON, Judge.

The Talent Agencies Act (Lab. Code, § § 1700–1700.47)[1] requires persons who procure employment for artists in entertainment fields, such as motion pictures, television and radio, to be licensed as talent agents by the labor commissioner. The Act exempts from licensing those persons who procure only recording contracts. Plaintiffs, who are not licensed talent agents, challenge the licensing requirement on the grounds it violates their rights to due process and equal protection of the laws.

[handwritten margin note: exempt only recording K's]

The trial court held the licensing requirement is constitutional and granted the labor commissioner's motion for summary judgment. The court subsequently entered judgment against plaintiffs. We affirm.

FACTS AND PROCEEDINGS BELOW

Plaintiffs Wachs and X Management, Inc., provide personal management services to artists and entertainers. Plaintiffs entered into a written contract to provide personal management to entertainer Arsenio Hall in return for 15 percent of Hall's earnings from his activities in the entertainment industry during the term of the contract. The contract recites "You [Hall] have not retained our personal management firm under this agreement as an employment agent or a talent agent. This firm has not offered or attempted or promised to obtain employment or engagement for you and this firm is not obligated, authorized or expected to do so."

Subsequently, Hall filed a petition to determine controversy under section 1700.44 of the Act alleging Wachs had acted as an unlicensed talent agent in procuring and attempting to procure employment for him and requesting the labor commissioner order Wachs to return all moneys collected from Hall or Hall's employers in connection with any of Hall's activities in the entertainment industry. Wachs filed an answer to the petition generally denying Hall's allegations.

While Hall's petition was pending before the labor commissioner, Wachs and X Management filed the present action against the commissioner and other state officials charged with enforcing the Act. The complaint alleges the licensing provisions of the Act are unconstitutional on their face and as applied because no rational basis exists for providing an exemption from the licensing requirement to those who procure recording contracts but not for those who procure other contracts in the entertainment industry and because it cannot be determined from the language of the Act which activities require licensing as a talent agent. Wachs seeks a judgment declaring the licensing provisions of the Act unconstitutional for the reasons stated and enjoining defendants from enforcing those provisions.

On the state's motion for summary judgment the trial court determined there were no triable issues of material fact and the licensing

---

1. All future references are to the Labor Code unless otherwise noted. The Talent Agencies Act is referred to as the Act.

provisions were constitutional. The court granted the motion and subsequently entered judgment for defendants. * * * [Parts I and II omitted.]

III.   A RATIONAL BASIS EXISTS FOR EXEMPTING THOSE WHO PROCURE RECORDING CONTRACTS FROM THE LICENSING REQUIREMENTS OF THE ACT

* * * [T]he state enjoys a wide latitude in economic and social legislation. The conventional "rational relationship" test applies in cases involving occupational licensing. * * *

The Act provides, "No person shall engage in or carry on the occupation of a talent agency without first procuring a license therefor from the Labor Commissioner." (§ 1700.5, subd. (a).) The Act defines "talent agency" as a "person or corporation who engages in the occupation of procuring, offering, promising, or attempting to procure employment or engagements for an artist...." (§ 1700.4, subd. (a).) The Act, however, contains an exemption from its licensing requirement for those who procure employment in the form of recording contracts. This provision states: "the activities of procuring, offering, or promising to procure recording contracts for an artist or artists shall not of itself subject a person or corporation to regulation and licensing under this chapter." *Id.*

Plaintiffs, who are not licensed talent agents, contend the licensing *unconstitutional* provisions of the Act are unconstitutional because there is no rational basis for exempting from the licensing requirement those who engage in procuring recording contracts but not other kinds of contracts.

The provision exempting the procurement of recording contracts was added to the Act in 1982 with a sunset provision of January 1, 1986. (Stats. 1982, ch. 682, § 1, p. 2814; Stats. 1984, ch. 553, § 1, p. 2185.) At the same time, the Legislature created the California Entertainment Commission to study and recommend revisions to the Act. (Stats. 1982, ch. 682, § 4, p. 2816.) The commission, after two years of study, submitted its recommendations to the Legislature which adopted them with minor language changes. (Stats. 1986, ch. 488, p. 1804; *see* O'Brien, *Regulation of Attorneys Under California's Talent Agencies Act: A Tautological Approach to Protecting Artists* 80 CAL L. REV. 471, 493–495 (1992) [hereafter O'Brien].)

One of the issues the commission studied was whether any changes should be made to the provision exempting persons who procure recording contracts for an artist. The majority of the commission recommended this exemption should be retained in the Act. The commission gave the following reasons for its recommendation.

> "A recording contract is an employment contract of a different nature from those in common usage in the industry involving personal services. The purpose of the contract is to produce a permanent and repayable showcase of the talents of the artist. In the recording industry, many successful artists retain personal managers to act as their intermediaries, and negotiations for a recording

contract are commonly conducted by a personal manager, not a talent agent. Personal managers frequently contribute financial support for the living and business expenses of entertainers. They may act as a conduit between the artist and the recording company, offering suggestions about the use of the artist or the level of effort which the recording company is expending on behalf of the artist. . . .

However, the problems of attempting to license or otherwise regulate this activity arise from the ambiguities, intangibles and imprecisions of the activity.

The majority of the Commission concluded that the industry would be best served by resolving these ambiguities on the side of preserving the exemption of this activity from the requirements of licensure." (Rep. of the Cal. Entertainment Com. (1985) pp. 13–14.) On the commission's recommendation, the exemption for those who procure recording contracts became permanent. (Stats. 1986, ch. 488, § 2, p. 1804; O'Brien, *supra*, 80 Cal.L.Rev. at p. 495.)

We believe the report from the Legislature's own commission of experts provides a sufficiently rational basis for the exemption from the licensing requirement. Numerous decisions support the proposition persons in the same general type of business may be classified differently where their methods of operation are not identical. (Marsh & McLennan of Cal., Inc. v. City of Los Angeles, 62 Cal.App.3d 108, 121, 132 Cal.Rptr. 796 (1976), and cases cited therein.)

IV. THE LICENSING REQUIREMENTS OF THE
ACT ARE NOT VOID FOR VAGUENESS

Plaintiffs contend the term "occupation of procuring [employment]" as used in section 1700.4, subdivision (a) does not sufficiently define the conduct which requires a license. Thus, persons such as plaintiffs, who provide a variety of services to artists and entertainers, cannot determine in advance what conduct they may lawfully engage in without a license. As a result, plaintiffs operate at great financial risk because a subsequent finding by the labor commissioner they "procured" employment without a license may relieve the client of any obligation to repay funds advanced to promote the client's career and entitle the client to restitution of all fees paid the agent * * *.

Although the Act contains no criminal penalty for the unlicensed procuring of employment, the financial penalties to which the unlicensed agent is exposed are clearly sufficient to raise due process concerns. "Statutes, regardless whether criminal or civil in nature, must be sufficiently clear as to provide adequate notice of the prohibited conduct as well as to establish a standard of conduct which can be uniformly interpreted by the judiciary and administrative agencies." (Hall v. Bureau of Employment Agencies, 64 Cal.App.3d 482, 491, 138 Cal.Rptr. 725 (1976).)

In *Hall v. Bureau of Employment Agencies, supra,* 64 Cal.App.3d at
494, the court summarized the test a statute must pass to satisfy due
process:

> " '[I]f the words used may be made reasonably certain by reference
> to the common law, to the legislative history of the statute involved,
> or to the purpose of that statute, the legislation will be sustained
> ...; and a standard fixed by language which is reasonably certain,
> judged by the foregoing rules, meets the test of due process "not-
> withstanding an element of degree in the definition as to which
> estimates might differ." [Citations.]' " Further, even though all
> statutes regardless of nature must be sufficiently clear to provide
> fair notice of prohibited conduct: " 'Reasonable certainty is all that
> is required. A statute will not be held void for uncertainty if any
> reasonable and practical construction can be given its language.
> [Citation.] It will be upheld if its terms may be made reasonably
> certain by reference to other definable sources.' " [Citations omit-
> ted.]

Resort to the dictionary definitions of the words at issue and the
legislative purpose and history of the Act convinces us the statute has an
objective content from which ascertainable standards of conduct can be
fashioned.

The relevant dictionary definition of "occupation" is "the principal
business of one's life: a craft, trade, profession or other means of earning
a living." [WEBSTER'S NEW INTERNAT. DICT. 1560 (3d ed. 1981).]

The history of the Act further illuminates the legislative intent with
respect to activities requiring a talent agent's license.

Regulation of what we now refer to as talent agencies originated
with the Artists' Managers Act of 1943. (Stats. 1943, ch. 329, p. 1326.)
The Artists' Managers Act defined an artist's manager as "a person, who
engages in the occupation of advising, counseling, or directing artists in
the development or advancement of their professional careers and who
procures, offers, promises or attempts to procure employment or engagements for an artist only in connection with and as a part of the duties
and obligations of such person under a contract with such artist by
which such person contracts to render services of the nature above
mentioned to such artist." *Id.,* at § 1, p. 1326.

With the adoption of the Act (Stats. 1978, ch. 1382, p. 4575), the
Legislature made a significant change in the definition of the covered
activities. The Act provided, "A talent agency is hereby defined to be a
person or corporation who engages in the occupation of procuring,
offering, promising, or attempting to procure employment or engagements for an artist or artists. Talent agencies may, in addition, counsel
or direct artists in the development of their professional careers." *Id.,* at
§ 6, p. 4576.

Comparison of the activities regulated in the two acts shows a
marked change of emphasis from the counseling function to the employ-

ment procurement function. Under the Artists' Managers Act the focus was on persons who engaged in "the occupation of advising, counseling or directing artists" in the "development or advancement" of their careers and who engaged in procuring employment "only in connection with and as a part of" their duties as advisor and counselor. Under the Act, the focus is on persons engaged "in the occupation of procuring . . . employment or engagements for an artist. . . ." These persons "may, in addition, counsel or direct artists in the development of their profession-al careers."

We conclude from the Act's obvious purpose to protect artists seeking employment and from its legislative history, the "occupation" of procuring employment was intended to be determined according to a standard that measures the significance of the agent's employment procurement function compared to the agent's counseling function taken as a whole. If the agent's employment procurement function constitutes a significant part of the agent's business as a whole then he or she is subject to the licensing requirement of the Act even if, with respect to a particular client, procurement of employment was only an incidental part of the agent's overall duties. On the other hand, if counseling and directing the clients' careers constitutes the significant part of the agent's business then he or she is not subject to the licensing requirement of the Act, even if, with respect to a particular client, counseling and directing the client's career was only an incidental part of the agent's overall duties. What constitutes a "significant part" of the agent's business is an element of degree we need not decide in this case. (Hall v. Bureau of Employment Agencies, supra, 64 Cal.App.3d at p. 494.)

Plaintiffs' concentrate their attack on the alleged vagueness of the word "procure." They posit numerous examples of conduct which they claim have little if any relationship to the purpose of the Act but which the labor commissioner has held, or might hold, constitutes "procuring" employment. However, as we noted above, the only question before us is whether the word "procure" in the context of the Act is so lacking in objective content that it provides no standard *at all* by which to measure an agent's conduct. * * *

To "procure" means "to get possession of: obtain, acquire, to cause to happen or be done; bring about." [WEBSTER'S NEW INTERNAT. DICT., *supra,* at p. 1809].

The term "procure" in connection with employment is used in numerous California statutes. The fact none of these statutes has ever been challenged is some evidence the term is well understood.

We recognize the Legislature's failure to define the term "procure" for purposes of section 1700.4 has been criticized by several commentators. (O'Brien, *supra,* 80 CAL.L.REV. at pp. 496–499; Johnson & Lang, *The Personal Manager in the California Entertainment Industry* (1979) 52 SO.CAL.L.REV. 375, 387–388; Lane, *Fees or Famine: Could California's Personal Managers Survive Regulation?* (Winter 1990) J. OF ARTS MAN-

AGEMENT & LAW 5, 23–24.) None of these commentators have suggested, however, the term "procure" is so lacking in objective content as to render the Act facially unconstitutional.

We conclude the term "occupation of procuring [employment]" is not "so patently vague and so wholly devoid of objective meaning that it provides no standard *at all.*" Cranston v. City of Richmond, *supra,* 40 Cal.3d at p. 765; italics in original.) Whether the Act is unconstitutional as applied to plaintiffs is a question for another day.

Disposition: The judgment is affirmed.

Note

1.   What exactly are the responsibilities of an artist manager? According to the court in *Raden v. Lauri,* one is not an artist's manager unless he advises, counsels and directs artists in the development of their professional careers and also procures or attempts to procure employment for an artist in connection with and as a part of the duties under a contract. 120 Cal.App.2d 778, 262 P.2d 61 (1953). Does the latter part contradict the holding in *Wachs v. Curry? Raden v. Lauri* is discussed in more detail below in *Buchwald v. Superior Court*, 254 Cal.App.2d 347, 62 Cal.Rptr. 364 (1967), which involved the management of a professional music group known as "Jefferson Airplane," yet sheds light on management issues for film artists as well.

BUCHWALD v. SUPERIOR COURT

California Court of Appeals, 1967.
254 Cal.App.2d 347, 62 Cal.Rptr. 364.

ELKINGTON, Associate Justice.

By their 'Petition for Writ of Review (and/or, in the Alternative, a Writ of Prohibition or Mandamus)' petitioners seek review of orders of the superior court in an action commenced by them against Matthew Katz, hereinafter referred to as Katz, who is here the real party in interest. Concerned is the Artists' Managers Act which we shall hereafter refer to as the Act.

The Act comprises sections 170–1700.46 of the Labor Code. It is found in division 2, part 6 of that code, relating to 'Employment Agencies.' It requires licensing, and regulates the business, of artists' managers.[2]

The Act is a remedial statute. Statutes such as the Act are designed to correct abuses that have long been recognized and which have been the subject of both legislative action and judicial decision. * * * Such

---

2. Section 1700.4 defines artists' managers as follows: 'An artists' manager is hereby defined to be a person who engages in the occupation of advising, counseling, or directing artists in the development or advancement of their professional careers and who procures, offers, promises or attempts to procure employment or engagements for an artist only in connection with and as a part of the duties and obligations of such person under a contract with such artist by which such person contracts to render services of the nature above mentioned to such artist.'

statutes are enacted for the protection of those seeking employment. * * * They properly fall within the police power of the state * * * and their constitutionality has been repeatedly affirmed. * * *

Since the clear object of the Act is to prevent improper persons from becoming artists' managers and to regulate such activity for the protection of the public, a contract between an unlicensed artists' manager and an artist is void. * * * Contracts otherwise violative of the Act are void. * * * And as to such contracts, artists, being of the class for whose benefit the Act was passed, are not to be ordinarily considered as being in Pari delicto. * * *

Section 1700.44 of the Act, as pertinent here, provides: "In all cases of controversy arising under this chapter the parties involved shall refer the matters in dispute to the Labor Commissioner, who shall hear and determine the same, subject to an appeal within 10 days after determination, to the superior court where the same shall be heard de novo."

Petitioners constitute a professional musical group known as the 'Jefferson Airplane.' They are 'artists' as defined by section 1700.4 of the Act. Each petitioner entered into a separate and identical contract with Katz, who for a percentage of each petitioner's earnings undertook, among other things, to act as 'exclusive personal representative, advisor and manager in the entertainment field.' The contract contained a provision reading: 'It is clearly understood that you (Katz) are not an employment agent or theatrical agent, that you have not offered or attempted or promised to obtain employment or engagements for me, and you are not obligated, authorized or expected to do so.' It also provided for arbitration of any dispute thereunder in accordance with the rules of the American Arbitration Association.

A dispute arose between the petitioners and Katz in relation to the subject matter of the contract. Katz thereupon, on September 21, 1966, commenced proceedings with the arbitration association seeking to compel arbitration of the dispute.

On October 18, 1966, petitioners filed with the labor commissioner a 'Petition to Determine Controversy,' alleging among other things: 'Complainants complain that in September of 1965, defendant (Matthew Katz) acting as an artists-manager and through false and fraudulent statements and by duress, caused complainants to sign with defendant as an artists-manager; that defendant, prior to the time of signing said contracts, promised the complainants and each of them that he would procure bookings for them; that defendant thereafter procured bookings for the complainants and insisted that the complainants perform the bookings procured by him; that complainants sought to procure their own bookings, and that defendant refused them the right to procure their own bookings; that at the time that said contracts were negotiated, defendant Matthew Katz was not licensed as an artists-manager pursuant to the provisions of the California Labor Code, Section 1700.5;[3] that

---

3. Section 1700.5, as pertinent here, provides: 'No person shall engage in or carry on the occupation of an artists' manager without first procuring a license therefor from the Labor Commissioner. * * *'

the contract presented to each complainant was not submitted to the Labor Commissioner, State of California, as required under Section 1700.23;[4] that Matthew Katz has not performed in accordance with Sections 1700.24, 1700.25, 1700.26, 1700.27, 1700.28, 1700.31, 1700.32, 1700.36 and 1700.40 of the Labor Code and other provisions of the Labor Code; that Matthew Katz never rendered an accounting to the complainants for thousands of dollars received by Mr. Katz for their services; that Matthew Katz has not allowed complainants to inspect the books and records maintained by Matthew Katz with respect to fees earned by the complainants; that Matthew Katz has and continues to obtain payments intended for one or more of the above complainants and has cashed checks intended for one or more of the above complainants for his own use and benefit.'

Katz appeared and filed his answer to the petition, in which he objected to the jurisdiction of the labor commissioner and denied that he had agreed to act, or that he was or had been acting, as an artists' manager.

On October 21, 1966 while the labor commissioner proceedings were pending, petitioners filed an action against Katz in the superior court, seeking relief, among other things, that Katz be restrained from proceeding before the arbitration association.

In the superior court action Katz appeared and moved the court to order petitioners to arbitrate as provided by the contracts, and to restrain the proceedings before the labor commissioner. Petitioners opposed Katz' motion contending that a bona fide controversy existed before the labor commissioner as to whether Katz had agreed to act, and had been acting as their artists' manager, and as to the legality and validity of the contracts. They contended that the language of the contracts 'you have not offered, or attempted or promised to obtain employment or engagements for me, etc.' was but a subterfuge to conceal the fact that Katz did act, and had agreed to act, as an artists' manager. Evidence was introduced by petitioners in support of their contentions. Katz offered evidence to the contrary.

The court thereafter on January 17, 1967 made its orders denying petitioners' motion to restrain arbitration; restraining petitioners from proceeding further before the labor commissioner; and ordering them to arbitrate their dispute before the arbitration association. These orders are the subject of the instant proceedings.

Real party in interest Katz has rather clearly stated the issues to be determined in this proceeding. Our discussion will follow the contentions as presented by him. * * *

---

4. Section 1700.23, as pertinent here, provides: 'Every artists' manager shall submit to the Labor Commissioner a form or forms of contract to be utilized by such artists' manager in entering into written contracts with artists for the employment of the services of such artists' manager by such artists, and secure the approval of the Labor Commissioner thereof. * * *'

SECOND CONTENTION: The Artists' Managers Act does not give the labor commissioner jurisdiction over an artists' manager who is not licensed as such by the commissioner.

Admittedly Katz was not licensed as an artists' manager.

The Act, section 1700.3, defines 'licensee' as an 'artists' manager which holds a valid, unrevoked, and unforfeited license....' Section 1700.4 defines 'artists' manager' (see fn. 2, ante).

Certain sections, i.e., 1700.17, 1700.19, 1700.21, 1700.42, 1700.43, refer to licensee in such context that the word can reasonably apply only to a licensed artists' manager. Other sections including those which are the subject of the Petition to Determine Controversy, refer to artists' manager in such manner that they apply reasonably to both licensed and unlicensed artists' managers. The Act thus refers to and covers two classes of persons, 'licensees' who are artists' managers with valid licenses, and 'artists' managers' who may or may not be so licensed.

"It is well settled that a legislative body has the power within reasonable limitations to prescribe legal definitions of its own language, and when an act passed by it embodies a definition it is binding on the courts." Application of Monrovia Evening Post, 199 Cal. 263, 269–270, 248 P. 1017, 1020; *see also* People v. Western Air Lines, Inc., 42 Cal.2d 621, 638, 268 P.2d 723; In re Miller, 31 Cal.2d 191, 198, 187 P.2d 722. If possible, significance should be given to every word and phrase of an act in pursuance of the legislative purpose. * * *

Remedial statutes should be liberally construed to affect their objects and suppress the mischief at which they are directed. * * * It would be unreasonable to construe the Act as applying only to licensed artists' managers, thus allowing an artists' manager, by nonsubmission to the licensing provisions of the Act, to exclude himself from its restrictions and regulations enacted in the public interest. 'Statutes must be given a reasonable and common sense construction in accordance with the apparent purpose and intention of the lawmakers—one that is practical rather than technical, and that will lead to wise policy rather than to mischief or absurdity.' (45 Cal.Jur.2d, Statutes, § 116, pp. 625—626.)

We conclude that artists' managers (as defined by the Act), whether they be licensed or unlicensed, are bound and regulated by the Artists' Managers Act.

THIRD CONTENTION: By virtue of his written contract, Katz as a matter of law is not an artists' manager and therefore is not subject to the Artists' Managers Act.

The Act gives the labor commissioner jurisdiction over those who are artists' managers in fact. The petition filed with the labor commissioner alleges facts which if true indicate that the written contracts were but subterfuges and that Katz had agreed to, and did, act as an artists' manager. Clearly the Act may not be circumvented by allowing language of the written contract to control—if Katz had in fact agreed to, and had acted as an artists' manager. The form of the transaction, rather than its substance, would control.

'It is a fundamental principle of law that, in determining rights and obligations, substance prevails over form.' San Diego Federation of Teachers v. Board of Education, 216 Cal.App.2d 758, 764, 31 Cal.Rptr. 146, 149; Civ.Code, § 3528. This principle is recognized in a case Katz cites and relies upon, Pawlowski v. Woodruff, 122 Misc. 695, 203 N.Y.S. 819, 820, where the court said, 'This contract is no subterfuge to evade the General Business Law. An employment agency could not circumvent the statute by putting its contract to procure employment for an artist in the form of an agreement for management.'

The court, or as here, the labor commissioner, is free to search out illegality lying behind the form in which a transaction has been cast for the purpose of concealing such illegality. * * * 'The court will look through provisions, valid on their face, and with the aid of parol evidence, determine that the contract is actually illegal or is part of an illegal transaction.' (1 Witkin, Summary of Cal.Law, Contracts, s 157, p. 169.)

In support of his position that as a matter of law he is not an artists' manager Katz cites *Raden v. Laurie*, 120 Cal.App.2d 778, 262 P.2d 61 (1953). That case, decided in 1953, concerned the Private Employment Agencies Act, sections 1550—1650 (also found in part 2, div. 6 relating to 'Employment Agencies') which at that time regulated persons doing business as artists' managers.

Raden was employed by Laurie, an actress, as a counselor and advisor under a written contract which specified he was to receive 10 percent of Laurie's professional earnings. Among other things the contract provided: 'It is expressly agreed that . . . nothing herein contained shall be deemed to require you or authorize you to seek or obtain employment for the undersigned (Laurie).' 120 Cal.App.2d at p. 779, 262 P.2d at p. 63. Raden was not paid his 10 percent so he sued in the superior court. As to the subject matter of the complaint the superior court clearly had jurisdiction. Laurie moved for summary judgment, alleging the suit to be without merit. (Code Civ.Proc. s 437c.) She contended the contract was invalid because it was a subterfuge used by an artists' manager who had not complied with the Private Employment Agencies Act. The motion for summary judgment was granted by the superior court.

The appellate court reversed, stating as follows (at p. 782, at p. 65 of 262 P.2d): 'It would seem clear that his (Raden's) duties were intentionally limited to the rendition of services which would not require his being licensed as an artists' manager. Respondent says: 'It is the act of seeking employment, not the contract provision, which brings the legislation into play.' This might be true if the contract were a mere sham and pretext designed by plaintiff to misrepresent and conceal the true agreement of the parties and to evade the law. But there was no evidence which would have justified the court in reaching that conclusion. There was no evidence of misrepresentation, fraud or mistake as to the terms of the contract nor as to plaintiff's obligations thereunder, nor evidence that defendants did not understand and willingly accept the limitation of plaintiff's duties. . . . In the absence of any evidence that the July 30th agreement was a mere subterfuge or otherwise invalid the court was required to give effect to its clear and positive provisions. . . . Since plaintiff was employed only to counsel and advise (Laurie) and to act as her business manager in matters not related to obtaining engagements for her, he was not acting as an 'Employment Agency' as defined by § 1551, Labor Code.' (Emphasis added; pp. 782–783, p. 65 of 262 P.2d)

The inapplicability of *Raden v. Laurie* to the instant controversy is obvious. There, on a motion for summary judgment, no showing, prima facie or otherwise, was made (as regards the contract sued upon or its subject matter) that Raden had agreed to act, or had acted as an artists' manager (or employment agency). The District Court of Appeal found no evidence which would support a conclusion that the contract was a sham or pretext designed to conceal the true agreement or to evade the law. On the uncontroverted facts the court had jurisdiction over the controversy and the labor commissioner did not. In the proceedings before us a prima facie showing was made to the labor commissioner as to matters over which he had jurisdiction.

FOURTH CONTENTION: The superior court had jurisdiction over the controversy referred to the labor commissioner by petitioners. * * *

§ 1700.44

Section 1700.44 of the Act is mandatory. It provides that the parties involved, artists and artists' manager, in any controversy arising under the Act, Shall refer the matters in dispute to the commissioner.[6] * * *

We hold as to cases of controversies arising under the Artists' Managers Act that the labor commissioner has original jurisdiction to hear and determine the same to the exclusion of the superior court, subject to an appeal within 10 days after determination, to the superior court where the same shall be heard de novo. (See § 1700.44.)

* * *

SEVENTH CONTENTION: The superior court had jurisdiction to determine, as in Raden v. Laurie, supra, 120 Cal.App.2d 778, 262 P.2d 61, whether the controversy here in question fell within the Act's grant of jurisdiction to the labor commissioner.

In *Raden v. Laurie*, as previously stated, the District Court of Appeal found no evidence on a motion for summary judgment to support Laurie's contention that Raden agreed to or did act as an artists' manager. Here a prima facie showing was made to the labor commissioner that Katz had so agreed and had so acted. The labor commissioner had the power and the duty to determine, in the first instance, whether the controversy was within the Act's grant of jurisdiction. See *United*

---

6. Although the Act says "the parties involved shall refer the matters in dispute" it is sufficient if one of the parties shall submit the controversy. (See Bess v. Park, 144 Cal.App.2d 798, 805, 301 P.2d 978.)

States v. Superior Court, 19 Cal.2d 189, 195, 120 P.2d 26, 29, where the court stated: '(I)t lies within the power of the administrative agency to determine in the first instance, and before judicial relief may be obtained, whether a given controversy falls within a statutory grant of jurisdiction.'

We conclude that petitioners are entitled, by way of certiorari, to the relief sought by them. The orders of the superior court dated January 17, 1967 are annulled.

Amy Wallace
Hollywood Agents Lose the Throne;
Personal Managers Are The Rising
Moguls as They Greatly Expand
Their Roles and Some Stars Shun
Agencies Altogether. Lack of
State Regulation Is Seen as
Big Advantage

L.   A. TIMES, DEC. 11, 1998.

Pity the poor Hollywood agent.

In the '80s and early '90s, talent agents ruled the industry. Movie studios and television networks found themselves beholden to International Creative Management, the Creative Artists Agency and the time-tested William Morris Agency, the "big three" agencies that had a lock on most A-list stars. Agents made big money for both their clients and themselves, charging the TV networks, for example, huge so-called packaging fees to assemble talent for shows.

Even for the most famous actors, it was often unclear who needed whom more: agent or client?

No more. Today, some of the biggest stars don't have agents. Kevin Costner and Sharon Stone use their lawyers to close deals. Winona Ryder, though now represented by ICM, recently went for two years without an agent, letting her personal manager handle her career. Leonardo DiCaprio is represented solely by his manager. So is martial arts star Jackie Chan.

The rising Hollywood mogul is the personal manager, a position once largely seen as an indulgence by actors, and certainly not essential to success. Although the vast majority of "name" actors, directors and writers still have agents, when it comes to representing talent these days, "It's a free-for-all," said one prominent lawyer. Times are changing, and lately, so are a lot of agents—changing into managers, that is.

In recent months, more than half a dozen agents (representing actors and directors such as Chan, Alan Alda, Drew Barrymore, Macaulay Culkin, Ed Harris, Kevin Spacey, Paul Verhoeven and Vanessa Williams) have quit, packing up their Rolodexes and turning into personal managers.

When Michael Ovitz, once the most powerful talent agent in town, unveiled plans to form a management company—Artists Management Group, which began full operations this week—it only confirmed what most people in Hollywood already knew: "Agents are no longer the kings," said Frank Rose, author of the 1995 book "The Agency: William Morris and the Hidden History of Show Business."

Agents, who are licensed by the state, make their money negotiating contracts. Under long-standing agreements with Hollywood's labor unions, they may charge no more than 10% commissions and may not produce movies or television shows. Managers, by contrast, are largely unregulated. They can charge clients what they like (many take 15%) and can produce clients' projects, taking lucrative production fees as well as on-screen credits. Theoretically, they may not procure work for clients, although they may offer counsel and participate in negotiations with agents.

In recent years, managers have become commonplace not only for actors, but for directors and writers as well. Not only is the field less restrictive and potentially more lucrative than the agency world, but many managers find their services are much in demand.

"It is so hard to get a job," said one 32–year-old actress who employs both an agent and a manager. Even with featured roles in more than a half-dozen recent studio films under her belt, she said, she considers the money she pays her two representatives a necessary cost of doing business. "Basically, the more people you have on your team, who listen to what you're trying to make happen and are out there trying to get it for you, the more chance you have of success."

Moreover, this actress said, big agencies often weigh one client's interests against another's. Managers have fewer clients and are perceived to be more focused on the individual needs of each one.

"They just have that much more time in the day to look out for you," she said.

The trend of hiring teams of advisors has an impact on more than individual careers. It also affects, for better or worse, the way movies and television shows are produced.

For example, several hit TV shows count their stars' managers among their producers. Erwin More and Brian Medavoy, whose More–Medavoy Management company manages actress Jenna Elfman, are credited on her ABC sitcom, "Dharma & Greg." Brad Grey and Bernie Brillstein of Brillstein–Grey Enterprises, which represents actor David Spade, are executive producers of NBC's "Just Shoot Me."

The same goes for movies. Referring to Warren Zide, the wunderkind manager of young writers who was credited on Sony Pictures' recent action-comedy, "The Big Hit," one fellow manager quipped: "He's producing more movies than MGM!"

Because producers' fees are covered by the studio or network, managers can sometimes be paid handsomely while costing their clients nothing. This has prompted some managers to become known derisively as "cling-ons" who demand producing credits on projects simply for making their clients available.

And there are conflict-of-interest concerns. Comedian Garry Shandling recently filed a $100–million lawsuit alleging that his manager, Grey of Brillstein–Grey, failed to protect Shandling's interests while furthering his own. Grey has denied the charges, filing a countersuit.

Karen Stuart, executive director of the Assn. of Talent Agents, a 60–year-old group that represents more than 100 agencies, says these issues only become more troublesome as the ranks of managers grow. Especially in light of Ovitz's latest gambit, she said, the group has informally begun to lobby the guilds to help even up the playing field.

"We have all the regulations, but we're not getting anything in return," said Stuart, who said agents have always agreed to guilds' restrictions in return for the exclusive right to represent their members—a right agents no longer enjoy. "No business person in their right mind could possibly stay in a situation like this, and we won't."

Given the immense power—and profits—that talent agencies have enjoyed, it is hard to get too worked up about their current plight. In fact, many see it as hypocritical for agencies to cry foul, considering the TV packaging fees they reap when they deliver the top actors, directors or writers that land a series on the air. ICM, which packaged the NBC sitcom "Friends," will make an estimated $50 million off that show alone. William Morris is said to have pocketed about the same amount for packaging "Roseanne" and "Murphy Brown."

Producers say agents' packaging fees and managers' producing fees are equally abhorrent in that both drive up production costs.

"You've got an above-the-line item, a fee, for someone who is [not contributing to the creative process]. So less money is up on the screen," said Leonard Hill, a producer who is active in the Caucus for Writers, Producers and Directors, a 26–year-old group that has petitioned the state labor commissioner to hold hearings on the issue. "Agents and managers are representing their own interests over the interests of their clients."

"A producer credit should mean the person performs the function of a producer. It should not be for performing the function of a huckster," said Charles B. FitzSimons, executive director of the Producers Guild of America.

Managers, meanwhile, are also fretting. The reason: Ovitz.

One agent-turned-manager who asked not to be named said that Ovitz indirectly created the need for more managers by encouraging his agents at CAA to "poach"—to steal clients from other agencies. This manager blamed Ovitz for making the theft of clients—once a rarity—prevalent throughout the agency business. Many believe poaching has permanently damaged the agent-client relationship by removing agents' incentive to keep clients' long-term interests paramount.

"As soon as CAA became a megalith, agents' attitude was, 'Book the client [in anything] because they're going to leave you anyway.' That's when managers started really catching on," said this manager.

Another agent-turned-manager said she feared that Ovitz will "make the same ethic [for managers that] he created at CAA. As a manager, I've started thinking like a human being.... And I don't want to lose that."

Ovitz declined to comment. But a source who is aware of his unfolding business plan said the new company's goals and methods will be very different than CAA's—and from those of most management firms, as well.

MASSIVE RAID BY CAA IN '80s

William Morris' Stan Kamen was one of the most powerful agents of his time. He made a leading man out of Steve McQueen in the 1960s and was an aggressive advocate for his clients, at one point persuading Columbia Pictures to change the gender of the lead in the 1979 film "The China Syndrome" so Jane Fonda could play it.

But there were limits to what he would do to bag a client. Which is why Ovitz made him so mad. Kamen had a few rules. He never raided the clients of smaller agencies. And when he pursued another big agency's client, he thought it only sporting to let the other agent know.

According to Rose's history of the William Morris Agency, Ovitz was not so courtly. During the mid-'80s, in what became known as one of the most thorough talent raids in industry history, CAA took aim on Kamen's client list. In the fall of 1985, Fonda, Barbra Streisand, Chevy Chase, Al Pacino and Goldie Hawn began to defect to CAA. When Ovitz learned that Kamen was ill, he refrained from signing more Kamen clients as a gesture of respect. But he continued to talk to them.

"What's the matter, Mike?" Rose says Kamen cried in one phone call to Ovitz during this period. "Isn't there enough business for everybody?"

Within three months of Kamen's death, virtually his entire list had signed with CAA.

The story, which Ovitz will not comment on, is oft-repeated in Hollywood, especially lately. As the industry's trade papers provide almost daily tallies of the latest talent reps to join Ovitz's new firm, the threat of poaching is in the air.

"How is it to be an agent now?" asked longtime agent Marty Bauer. "You come home to the love of your life with a bottle of champagne and flowers. You draw a bath, do your whole seduction act. And the next morning, your three best friends call her and say, 'You'd be better off with me.' That's the life of an agent."

As a manager, by contrast, "You still have your wife the next day," he said.

Bauer was co-founder of two agencies, United Talent and the now defunct Bauer–Benedek, and he has had many high-profile clients. For years, he kept a fake shark snout in the top drawer of his desk, explaining, "I put this on when I'm making deals."

But in March, after more than 20 years, he become a manager, setting up shop in the same Beverly Hills building as several other agents-turned-managers: Carol Bodie, Lou Pitt, the partnership of Judy Hofflund and Gavin Polone, and now Ovitz.

"The greatest service an agent can do for a client is telling them to say no to a [bad] project." Bauer said, lamenting that in an atmosphere where poaching is commonplace, many agents are more likely to say yes. If a client is working, they're less likely to jump ship.

Working as an agent in this kind of culture, Bauer said, "you can't guide people's careers. And as you get older, you get tired of that."

Sitting in her office four floors above Bauer's, Hofflund agreed.

As an agent, Hofflund had 35 clients and sometimes spent half her day in staff meetings. Now, she has 13 clients (among them Kenneth Branagh, Cybill Shepherd and Laura Dern). As one of two principals in a small firm, she rarely goes to meetings.

"As an agent, oftentimes my orientation was forced to be, 'Get it done. Get it off the phone sheet. Make the offer work.' It's how you're trained. I like to think I stood back and said, 'Is this a good move?' But ... as a manager, I have more time to think," she said.

Hofflund's client Kim Basinger recently was offered a film role and wanted Hofflund's help deciding whether to take the part.

"As an agent, I might have just read the script and thought, 'Well, the director's worked with some big stars.' I wouldn't have had the time to analyze it as much," Hofflund said. Instead, over a weekend, she watched all the director's films. Ultimately, she urged Basinger to pass.

Hofflund and many other managers stress that they see themselves as complements to agents, not competitors with them.

"It's the philosophy of a team," said More of More–Medavoy, which represents David Schwimmer, Maria Bello and Chevy Chase, among others. "We don't want the agents not to be involved. We want them to be vested. And you know what? Now that they've become aware that managers are becoming a little more powerful, they are. That's to the benefit of the client."

"We have great loyalty and incredible relationships with agencies," said Medavoy, pointing to how closely he works with Schwimmer's agent, Leslie Siebert of the mid-size Gersh Agency.

"Leslie and I collaborate every single day in terms of thinking about David's career," he said of the "Friends" star. Siebert agreed.

"When you're in sync, it's the best thing in the world and the relationship can be very productive," said the agent, who also represents actor Tobey Maguire. Still, she said, enormous changes in the talent representation world may require agents to take action.

"Every meeting I'm in, it's the topic of conversation: How is [Ovitz's new venture] going to affect us?" she said, adding that she thinks the big three agencies, who represent the biggest stars, have more to fear than her shop. Her prediction about Ovitz? "He's going to attack the larger agencies with the huge stars, saying, 'What the hell do you need an agent for?' "

Belt-Tightening Spawns More Changes

Recent belt-tightening in the entertainment world has made people even fiercer, of late, about guarding their turf. The television business is contracting, with some independent production companies disappearing as the networks supply more of their own shows. Fewer runaway hits have meant smaller profits. Likewise, in the movie industry, studios are shelving projects whose budgets are too high and are making fewer films.

There have been layoffs at the major television networks and, lately, at the big talent agencies as well. ICM and William Morris are letting agents go, and year-end bonuses there have been described by some agents as anemic.

Meanwhile, Ovitz has been busy wooing managers and agents around town. Among those seeking to join him are at least three managers from a single firm, Industry Entertainment: Rick Yorn (whose clients include DiCaprio, Cameron Diaz and Claire Danes), Julie Silverman Yorn and Eli Selden (who together represent Samuel L. Jackson, Teri Hatcher and James Spader). ICM agent JoAnne Colonna is joining Ovitz as well.

In light of these defections and others (Brian Gersh, the former co-head of the William Morris Agency's motion picture talent department, recently hung out a management shingle) some say the state Legislature should move to regulate managers.

"Talent agents morph themselves into managers in order to avoid regulation," said Hill, the producer. "The fact is, managers for some time now have been growing into unregulated quasi-agents who do procure and negotiate. It's a ludicrous loophole and it's incumbent on the Legislature to close it."

Sandy Bresler, Jack Nicholson's agent and president of the Assn. of Talent Agents, says that for now, the few actors who don't have agents are merely "a dot in the ocean which has a potential to be a tidal wave." But he's keeping a keen eye on the horizon.

"Anybody would be foolish not to watch their competition," he said. * * * Within three months of Kamen's death, virtually his entire list had signed with CAA.

The story is oft-repeated in Hollywood. As the industry's trade papers provide almost daily tallies of the latest talent reps to join Ovitz's new management company, the threat of poaching is in the air.

"How is it to be an agent now?" asked long-time agent Marty Bauer. "You come home to the love of your life with a bottle of champagne and flowers. You draw a bath, do your whole seduction act. And the next morning, your three best friends call her and say, 'You'd be better off with me.' that's the life of an agent."

C. LAWYERS

Sherri Burr
Picking Representation:
Author Interview with Author/Screenwriter Max Evans

Copyright © 2004 by Sherri Burr.

In his 40–year writing career, Max Evans has penned 30 novels, three of which have been turned into the feature films; *The Rounders* (1965); *The Wheel* (1971); and *The Hi–Lo Country* (1998). In an April 2001 conversation with law students that was later rebroadcast on *ARTS TALK* on Cable Channel 27 in Albuquerque, New Mexico, Evans was asked, "What is your criteria for choosing an entertainment lawyer?"

Evans responded, "I managed to hold a friendship with Sam Peckinpah [director and writer, *The Wild Bunch* (1969); director, *The Getaway* (1972)] for 25 years because of a lawyer, Norma Fink. We call her "Big Red." I recommended Sam Peckinpah to her and he was with her several years. I recommended Slim Pickens [actor, *Dr. Strangelove* (1964); *The Getaway* (1969)] to her when his career started booming. She's still taking care of his family.

"Norma's never had a client that doesn't honor her as if she's a bishop. She's mean to me. She's mean to everybody. She's just mean. But the point of it is she's going to be mean for you. There's no way a studio can buy her out or intimidate her. She has a very powerful clientele.

"I've had one long-term lawyer and one great agent. In my lifetime, I've fired more than 20 agents. While I was working with Steve Anderson [director, *Colors* (1992); *Dead Men Can't Dance* (1997)] on a project, we compared notes and found we had fired six of the same agents.

"I don't like it when agents make out like they've read your novel when they haven't. They do it all the time."

As for how to pick great people to represent talent, Evans concluded, "It's a recommendation process."

Notes

1.   How brutal must attorneys be to attract and maintain relationships with successful clients? Max Evans implies that clients appreciate tough attorneys because they'll be ruthless on their behalf. How exactly does a

lawyer go about cultivating a "mean" reputation? Are there advantages and disadvantages to having such a reputation?

2.   Can lawyers be tough, but fair while negotiating with the studios, producers and other players in the entertainment industry?

Sherri Burr
Client Expectations
Author Interview with Screenwriter Duncan North.

Copyright © 2004 by Sherri Burr.

Duncan North co-authored the screenplay *The Tao of Steve*, which was about a plump guy who is highly successful with women. The film premiered at the 2000 Sundance Film Festival where Donal Logue was awarded a Special Jury Prize for Outstanding Performance as the lead character whose philosophy has three components: (1) Be desire-less; (2) Be excellent; and (3) Be gone.

Mary Beth Shewan, co-host of the Santa Fe radio show *Dharma: The Search for Right Livelihood*, termed the precepts, "Buddhism meets the Neanderthal man."

As a guest on *Arts Talk* (Comcast Cable Channel 27 television broadcast, 2000), North was asked what were his expectations when looking for representation. He answered, "The way in which lawyers and agents are valuable to you is (a) not to easy to explain, [and] (b) when it is explained, it's scary."

"If I were a lawyer telling someone how I could be useful to them, I would say, 'Everybody out here is going to take whatever they can and the only way to protect your interest is to have someone as vermicious as the next guy and I promise you that I will push everything right to the edge to make sure that I look after yours.' [This] is not a very spiritual thought.

"Let's just assume, let's be wacky, that you're going through your day thinking, 'I want to get closer to God.' And at the same time you want to make as much money as possible to slack off and get closer to God. Then the lawyer who is best for you is the one who will most assiduously fight for your stuff. But part of the whole getting closer to God thing is about detachment, and selflessness, and egolessness, but you don't want that in your lawyer.

"You don't want the lawyer to say, 'Look, dude, do you care about property? Let's just go along. I really like their lawyer too. And I don't want to get in a big fight. So what do you say we just let them keep all the ancillary rights.'

"That would suck! That would be counterproductive. Lawyers and agents are not your spiritual mentors. But if they are really, really good, then they make it easier for you to be that way. It's a strange balance."

Notes

1.   North indicates that clients do not want lawyers to be their best buddies. Ideally, attorneys protect the client's rights in a manner that enables the client to produce his or her best work. As you read the Dan Cox article, *Legal Eagles Invade 10 Percenter's Nest,* notice the statements that lawyers make about clients and whom they would most prefer to represent. Where is the overlap in what the two parties are seeking? What is the ideal talent/attorney relationship?

2.   What is the best way for a law student interested in entertainment law to break into the business? There are no easy answers to this question, as it is dependent on the student's educational background, experiences, and contacts in the business. The authors of this book have interviewed numerous lawyers who practice entertainment law and they recommend seeking an entertainment-related internship during law school and beginning in a law firm to develop practice experience in corporate areas while maintaining your interest in entertainment law.

3.   Besides working for law firms and studios, lawyers are fortunate in that they have many options like becoming an agent or manager for a talent person. With sufficient ambition and drive to endure the difficult apprentice programs, lawyers can become successful agents and managers.

4.   Among the challenges that lawyers face in representing clients in the entertainment industry is dealing with strong egos. Johnnie Cochran was asked on Sherri Burr's cable television show *Arts Talk* what was the most difficult aspect of being an entertainment lawyer. He replied, "Having to say no to people who are not used to having people say no to them." ARTS TALK (Comcast Channel 27 television broadcast, January 31, 2000).

Dan Cox
Legal Eagles Invade 10 Percenter's Nest

VARIETY, Apr. 4–10, 1994, at 7.

The latest joke around Hollywood: A producer goes to see a showbiz attorney and asks him what his least expensive fee is.

"A thousand dollars for three questions," the lawyer says.

"Isn't that a bit much for just three questions?" queries the producer.

"Yes," the lawyer says. "Now what's your final question?"

Lawyer-bashing, yes. But lately, more lawyers are taking percentage cuts of the clients' action rather than a flat fee. They're reading scripts, seeking out projects, searching for talent. In short, more and more they're acting like agents.

"Obviously, a substantial majority of lawyers out there work on a percentage because they think they do more than just read contracts," proclaimed one high-profile industry attorney.

The industry sea change has stirred up the legal community, with lawyers arguing both for and against the percentage deals. But the greatest fallout in the showbiz community has been indie producers, who are finding it harder to get representation for their projects.

EXCLUSIVE LIST

While actors, directors and especially writers are sizzling with earning potential for lawyers, unknown producers—and some well-known ones, too–can't get Hollywood's A-list lawyers to even open their doors.

"We are very, very selective in taking on motion picture producers," admits Ken Ziffren, whose firm Ziffren, Brittenham and Branca represents some of TV's hottest writer/producers and dealmakers, but relatively few feature producers.

"We prefer to take those who either have their own money or access to money, whether that money is for development or production."

Ziffren's lead is acknowledged if not followed by most of Tinseltown's top legal reps. While Hollywood has tightened its belt over the last five years, the legal profession has felt the squeeze. More than a handful of entertainment firms have been sunk partly because they entered into percentage partnerships with producers on films that never got off the ground.

Suddenly, the lawyers want to see the money up front. "If you have a producer who is just a producer on a percentage, chances are you'll lose money," says Alan U. Schwartz, rep for such clients as Mel Brooks, Ismail Merchant and James Ivory. "You probably shouldn't be on a percentage with just a producer."

SELECTIVE LIST

Alan Grodin, an attorney at Weissmann, Wolff, which reps Alan Pakula, Mark Rydell, Gene Wilder, Cheech Marin, boxer George Foreman and wrestler Hulk Hogan, says the firm handles producers, too, but only rarely on a percentage basis.

"You can get killed with that," Grodin says. "They might ask you to do 26 option deals for properties that don't go anywhere."

On the other hand, A-list actors can bring in $10 million per pic with all sorts of gross participation deals for merchandise and licensing. Helmers get the same treatment with back-end deals, though salaries usually top off in the $5 million to $6 million range.

NEW AFFLUENCE

Writers, too, have recently been collecting multimillion-dollar paydays on spec scripts against even more moolah once they're made.

"Anyone who works on a regular basis and who you don't have to spend a lot of time developing" is the best client, says attorney Linda Lichter.

Lichter's boutique firm of Lichter, Grossman & Nichols reps stars Johnny Depp, Mary Stuart Masterson, scribe Quentin Tarantino and helmers Joe Rubin and Kathryn Bigelow.

FINDING THE STABLE CLIENT

"If a law firm doesn't need the business, they'll only take on the most desirable clients," she adds. "It winnows out those people who don't have backing from their families or big companies."

But unlike their counterparts in film, TV writer/producers have become the golden boys for lawyers looking to strike it rich. With syndication and back-end participation, a writer/producer of a hot show like a "Roseanne," "Seinfeld" or "Cheers" can garner upwards of $100 million for a single deal.

"If you have a homerun hit TV series that has an afterlife in syndication, the numbers can be very high," says Steven Katleman, who handles many of the TV clients at Weissmann, Wolff.

Added another lawyer, whose firm reps some of the small screen's top scripters: "TV writers are great clients because they're paid a lot of money and are easy to deal with. They can certainly be lucrative because they have an extremely high upside. They generate a lot of dough."

Ziffren says his firm built itself into one of the top entertainment firms around cash-cow producers such as Steven J. Cannell, Gary David Goldberg, Brandon Tartikoff and Fred Silverman. "We're proud of the fact that we rep a number of TV writer-producers. They are the core of our talent business," he says.

Of course, not all TV shows turn into "Roseanne."

Katleman says it can be hit-or-miss for attorneys who get into the guessing game of picking future shows to farm. That's where the lawyers' duties verge on the agents' duties. Attorneys are always on the lookout for a hot young star, whether helmer, scripter or thesp.

"You can spend a lot of time and energy on something that never pans out," Katleman says. "The important thing to remember is that whatever lawyers make pales in comparison to what agents make."

True enough. Agents collect roughly 10% of some mighty hefty deals. Lawyers, at best, skim 5% off their clients' paychecks.

Some attorneys claim that producers beg them to take a percentage, or even a cut of the overall deal. A-list stars, on the other hand, often insist on paying flat fees.

Mike Adler—one of Hollywood's top wheeler-dealer attorneys whose firm Mitchell, Silberberg & Knupp reps Jack Nicholson, Norman Jewison, Jaye Davidson and Steven Soderbergh, among others—says the hourly rate has suddenly become attractive to writers, directors and actors who might have once been tied to a 5% deal.

Helmers like Steven Spielberg, who raked in a reported $200 mil on "Jurassic Park" back-end deals, often opt for the flat fee. But Spielberg's attorney, Bruce Ramer, is thought to have done well on the deal. Simply negotiating the front end of a deal like that, says one source, can often mean an easy payday of half a million dollars.

BARTER POWER

"Clients are getting more and more sophisticated," Adler says. "We're in a recessionary mode. Clients are negotiating for legal services the way we negotiate for everything in our lives."

Adler helped negotiate Jack Nicholson's reported $60 mil take on "Batman," but the lawyer refuses to comment for the record on whether he had a percentage or a flat fee.

Katleman says clients on a percentage deal often abuse the privilege, calling up the lawyers at all hours with unimportant questions. "When they're on an hourly, clients are frequently reluctant to pick up the phone and call," he says. "Sometimes you don't get the information. When you're on a percentage you're more like a partner with your client. You tend to get more information. The flipside is that if you choose wrong, you'll get people who abuse that relationship."

Schwartz, of the firm Manatt, Phelps & Phillips, says even if an attorney works on a flat fee, if he negotiates a lucrative deal, he'll see some of it in the back-end.

"There are premiums to be had," Schwartz says. "If we can put together a package for your productions, there can be a flat-fee premium over the hourly rate or maybe a finder's fee for financing. There are all sorts of variations of how these lawyers can be ethically compensated."

Schwartz, too, is reluctant to discuss his arrangements with such high-profile clients as Mel Brooks, James Ivory and Ismail Merchant. But he says once in a while it makes sense for even the most high-powered attorneys to take a chance on a nobody client.

"When I started to represent Mel Brooks, he was a crazy writer and that's all he was," says Schwartz. "We represent Michael Douglas, he's now big business. He wasn't always that way."

Notes

1. In The *Talent Agencies Act: Reconciling the Controversies Surrounding Lawyers, Managers, and Agents Participating in California's Entertainment*, 28 PEPPER. L. REV. 381 (2001), Gary E. Devlin defines the contemporary roles of the lawyer, manager, and agent participating in California's entertainment industry and introduces the dispute between managers and agents. Devlin notes that lawyers in the industry have been known to package deals, shop talent and creative material, and advise on financial matters, thereby crossing over into the definitional realms of agent and manager. At the same time, the personal manager has evolved into a powerful force, commanding up to twenty percent of an artist's gross income and obtaining production credit that result in fees from studios. Agents are thereby left to attend to the one glaring need that managers cannot fulfill due to the provisions of the Act—procuring employment for artists.

2. <u>For more information comparing agents, managers, and lawyers</u>, see Edwin F. McPherson, *The Talent Agencies Act: Time for a Change*, HASTINGS COM. AND ENTER. L. J. (COMM/ENT) (Summer, 1997).

D. LABOR UNIONS

The Screen Actors Guild (SAG), The Directors Guild of America (DGA), The Writers Guild of America (WGA), and the International Alliance of Theatrical Stage Employees (IATSE) <u>are the major unions that represent actors, directors, screenwriters, and crew respectively.</u> They negotiate minimum basic agreements with studios and producers to obtain minimum scale wages, acceptable working conditions, creative rights, and credits for their members.

SAG's Global Rule One requires, "No member shall work as a performer or make an agreement to work as a performer for any producer who has not executed a basic minimum agreement with the Guild which is in full force and effect." SAG warns members that they "lose Pension & Health benefits, residuals payments, work safety, and other protections from SAG when they work without a SAG contract." *http://www.sag.org/sagWebApp/index.jsp*. SAG also negotiates limited exhibition agreements, which, depending on the size of the production budget, permit producers to be able to defer salaries (at a production budget of less than $75,000), pay significantly lower rates ($200,000 production budget), and cover fewer number of background actors ($500,000 production budget). SCREEN ACTORS GUILD, FILM CONTRACTS DIGEST 2–6 (2003). In other words, the size of the production budget determines the minimum fees that the actors get paid. For a production budget of less than $2,000,000 effective July 1, 2003, a general background actor must receive a minimum of $115, a day performer must receive $466, and a weekly performer $1,620. *Id.* at 9–10.

The DGA negotiates working conditions and minimum salaries for directors depending on the size of the budget. From July 1, 2003 to June 30, 2004, employers were required to pay a minimum weekly salary of $8,150 for low budget films (up to $500,000), $9,263 for medium budget films ($500,000 to $1.5 million) and $12,969 for high budget films (that exceed $1.5 million). The size of the budget will also determine minimum salary scale for preparation and post-production editing time. Like SAG, the DGA announces annual awards recognizing the talent of its members. According to the DGA website, http://www.dga.org/index2.php3, only six times between 1949 and 2003 has the winner of the DGA Award not gone on to win the Best Director Oscar®.

The Writers Guild has two divisions, the Writers Guild East and the Writers Guild West, who divide the country along the Mississippi. The WGA West represents screenwriters who live west of the Mississippi. Under the contract that both Guilds negotiated in 2001, screenwriters receive a minimum of $50,100 for an original screenplay, including treatment. WRITERS GUILD, SCHEDULE OF MINIMUMS (May 2, 2003). Since the WGA represents employees, you have to be employed before you can join

& pointscript and – independently

and yet the signatories are limited to hiring only WGA members. To evade this Catch–22, new screenwriters must find someone who wants to buy their script, who is willing to sign the minimum basic agreement. In the event of a dispute over which screenwriters are entitled to credit on a film, the WGA will arbitrate the dispute and award credit. An ampersand (&) indicates two writers wrote the script as a joint work; a written "and" indicates writers who worked independently of each other.

IATSE's full name is the International Alliance of Theatrical Stage Employees, Moving Picture Technicians, Artists and Allied Crafts of the United States, Its Territories and Canada. IATSE was formed more than a century ago to represent film technicians. With a membership of over 104,000 members, IATSE boasts that it is the largest labor union in the entertainment and related industries. http://www.iatse-intl.org/about/welcome.html. On January 1, 2004, IATSE completed negotiations with companies such as Intermedia Films, Miramax Pictures, and New Line Pictures, to increase the low budget cap from $7 to 8.5 million to give producers more operating flexibility and in return the producers would improve rest periods and meal provisions. http://www.iatse-intl.org/index_html.html.

The Catch–22, which the new writer experiences, also affects the new actor. Sometimes by the time SAG confirms the member's eligibility for employment, the role may disappear.

MARQUEZ v. SCREEN ACTORS GUILD

United States Supreme Court, 1998.
525 U.S. 33, 119 S.Ct. 292, 142 L.Ed.2d 242.

O'CONNOR delivered the opinion of the Court.

Section 8(a)(3) of the National Labor Relations Act (NLRA), 49 Stat. 452, as added, 61 Stat. 140, 29 U.S.C. § 158(a)(3), permits unions and employers to negotiate an agreement that requires union "membership" as a condition of employment for all employees. We have interpreted a proviso to this language to mean that the only "membership" that a union can require is the payment of fees and dues, *NLRB v. General Motors Corp.*, 373 U.S. 734, 742, 83 S.Ct. 1453, 10 L.Ed.2d 670 (1963), and we have held that § 8(a)(3) allows unions to collect and expend funds over the objection of nonmembers only to the extent they are used for collective bargaining, contract administration, and grievance adjustment activities, *Communications Workers v. Beck*, 487 U.S. 735, 745, 762–763, 108 S.Ct. 2641, 101 L.Ed.2d 634 (1988). In this case, we must determine whether a union breaches its duty of fair representation when it negotiates a union security clause that tracks the language of § 8(a)(3) without explaining, in the agreement, this Court's interpretation of that language. We conclude that it does not. * * *

I.

A.

The language of § 8(a)(3) is at the heart of this case. In pertinent part, it provides as follows:

"It shall be an unfair labor practice for an employer—

"(3) by discrimination in regard to hire or tenure of employment ...
to encourage or discourage membership in any labor organization:
Provided, That nothing in this subchapter, or in any other statute of
the United States, shall preclude an employer from making an
agreement with a labor organization ... to require as a condition of
employment membership therein on or after the thirtieth day following the beginning of such employment or the effective date of
such agreement, whichever is the later.... Provided further, That
no employer shall justify any discrimination against an employee for
nonmembership in a labor organization ... if he has reasonable
grounds for believing that membership was denied or terminated for
reasons other than the failure of the employee to tender the periodic
dues and the initiation fees uniformly required as a condition of
acquiring or retaining membership." 29 U.S.C. § 158(a)(3).

This section is the statutory authorization for "union security clauses,"
clauses that require employees to become "member[s]" of a union as a
condition of employment. See *Communications Workers v. Beck, supra,*
at 744–745, 108 S.Ct. 2641. * * *

B

Respondent Screen Actors Guild (SAG or union) is a labor organization that represents performers in the entertainment industry. In 1994,
respondent Lakeside Productions (Lakeside) signed a collective bargaining agreement with SAG, making SAG the exclusive bargaining agent for
the performers that Lakeside hired for its productions. This agreement
contained a standard union security clause, providing that any performer
who worked under the agreement must be "a member of the Union in
good standing." Tracking the language of § 8(a)(3), the clause also
provided:

"The foregoing [section], requiring as a condition of employment
membership in the Union, shall not apply until on or after the
thirtieth day following the beginning of such employment or the
effective date of this Agreement, whichever is the later; the Union
and the Producers interpret this sentence to mean that membership
in the Union cannot be required of any performer by a Producer as a
condition of employment until thirty (30) days after his first employment as a performer in the motion picture industry.... The Producer shall not be held to have violated this paragraph if it employs a
performer who is not a member of the Union in good standing ... if
the Producer has reasonable grounds for believing that membership
in the Union was denied to such performer or such performer's
membership in the Union was terminated for reasons other than the
failure of the performer to tender the periodic dues and the initiation fee uniformly required as a condition of acquiring or retaining
membership in the Union. ..." *Id.*, at 28–29.

The present dispute arose when petitioner, a part-time actress, successfully auditioned for a one-line role in an episode of the television series, Medicine Ball, which was produced by Lakeside. Petitioner accepted the part, and pursuant to the collective bargaining agreement, Lakeside's casting director called SAG to verify that petitioner met the requirements of the union security clause. Because petitioner had previously worked in the motion picture industry for more than 30 days, the union security clause was triggered and petitioner was required to pay the union fees before she could begin working for Lakeside. There is some dispute whether the SAG representative told Lakeside's casting director that petitioner had to "join" or had to "pay" the union; regardless, petitioner understood from the casting director that she had to pay SAG before she could work for Lakeside. Petitioner called SAG's local office and learned that the fees that she would have to pay to join the union would be around $500.

Over the next few days, petitioner attempted to negotiate an agreement with SAG that would allow her to pay the union fees after she was paid for her work by Lakeside. When these negotiations failed to produce an acceptable compromise and petitioner had not paid the required fees by the day before her part was to be filmed, Lakeside hired a different actress to fill the part. At some point after Lakeside hired the new actress, SAG faxed a letter to Lakeside stating that it had no objection to petitioner working in the production. The letter was too late for petitioner; filming proceeded on schedule with the replacement actress.

Petitioner filed suit against Lakeside and SAG alleging, among other things, that SAG had breached the duty of fair representation. According to petitioner, SAG had breached its duty by negotiating and enforcing a union security clause with two basic flaws. First, the union security clause required union "membership" and the payment of full fees and dues when those terms could not be legally enforced under General Motors and Beck. Petitioner argued that the collective bargaining agreement should have contained language, in addition to the statutory language, informing her of her right not to join the union and of her right, under Beck, to pay only for the union's representational activities. Second, the union security clause contained a term that interpreted the 30–day grace period provision to begin running with any employment in the industry. According to petitioner, this interpretation of the grace period provision contravened the express language of § 8(a)(3), which requires that employees be given a 30–day grace period from the beginning of "such employment." She interprets "such employment" to require a new grace period with each employment relationship. Finally, in addition to these claims about the language of the union security clause, petitioner alleged that SAG had violated the duty of fair representation by failing to notify her truthfully about her rights under the NLRA as defined in Beck and General Motors.

The District Court granted summary judgment to the defendants on all claims, ruling first that SAG did not breach the duty of fair representation by negotiating the union security clause. The court also determined that no reasonable factfinder could conclude that SAG had attempted to enforce the union security clause beyond the lawful limits. Finally, the court ruled that petitioner's challenge to the grace period provision was actually an unfair labor practice claim, and thus it was preempted by the exclusive jurisdiction of the NLRB.

Petitioner appealed, and the Court of Appeals for the Ninth Circuit affirmed in part and reversed in part. 124 F.3d 1034 (1997). The Court of Appeals reversed the grant of summary judgment on petitioner's claim that SAG's enforcement of the union security clause breached the duty of fair representation, finding that there were genuine issues of material fact remaining to be resolved on this issue. For example, the record contains conflicting evidence on whether the union told petitioner that she had to "join" the union, or whether it told her that she had to "pay" the union. Id., at 1041. The Court of Appeals also reversed the grant of summary judgment on petitioner's claim that the union had breached the duty of fair representation by failing to notify her of her right, under Beck, to pay only the lesser "core" fees associated with the union's collective bargaining functions. The District Court had not addressed this claim, so the Court of Appeals remanded this issue for consideration. Id., at 1042–1043.

On the two issues before this Court, however, the Court of Appeals affirmed the judgment of the District Court. First, the court held that SAG had not breached the duty of fair representation merely by negotiating a union security clause that tracked the language of the NLRA. * * *

Second, the Court of Appeals affirmed the District Court's judgment that it did not have jurisdiction over petitioner's challenge to the grace period provision. * * *

We granted certiorari to resolve the conflict over the facial validity of a union security clause that tracks the language of § 8(a)(3), and to clarify the standards for defining the primary jurisdiction of the NLRB. 523 U.S. 1019, 118 S.Ct. 1298, 140 L.Ed.2d 465 (1998).

II.

A.

This case presents a narrow question: Does a union breach its duty of fair representation merely by negotiating a union security clause that tracks the language of § 8(a)(3)? To understand why this is a narrow question, it is helpful to keep in mind what issues we are not resolving in this case. First, we are not deciding whether SAG illegally enforced the union security clause to require petitioner to become a member of the union or to require her to pay dues for non-collective bargaining activities. Petitioner's complaint includes a claim that the union breached the duty of fair representation by enforcing the clause illegally, but that claim is not before us. The Court of Appeals held that there were factual disputes that precluded the grant of summary judgment on this issue, and so this claim was remanded to the District Court for further proceedings. 124 F.3d, at 1041–1042. Second, we are not deciding whether SAG breached its duty of fair representation by failing to adequately notify petitioner of her rights under *Beck* and *General Motors*. The Board has held (and SAG concedes * * *) that unions have an obligation to notify employees of their *Beck* rights. * * * The Board is currently in the process of defining the content of the notification right to give guidance to unions about what they must do to notify employees about their rights under *Beck* and *General Motors*. * * * Petitioner's suit alleges that SAG failed to notify her of her *Beck* and *General Motors* rights, but this claim, too, is not before us. The Court of Appeals remanded this claim to the District Court for reconsideration. 124 F.3d, at 1042–1043.

With this background, the question we are resolving comes into sharper focus. There is no disagreement about the substance of the union's obligations: If a union negotiates a union security clause, it must notify workers that they may satisfy the membership requirement by paying fees to support the union's representational activities, and it must enforce the clause in conformity with this notification. The only question presented by this case is whether a union breaches the duty of fair representation merely by negotiating a union security clause that uses the statutory language without expressly explaining, in the agreement, the refinements introduced by our decisions in *General Motors* and *Beck*. To rephrase the question slightly, petitioner's claim is that even if the union has an exemplary notification procedure and even if the union enforces the union security clause in perfect conformity with federal law, the mere negotiation of a union security clause that tracks the language of the NLRA breaches the duty of fair representation. We hold that it does not. * * *

In sum, on this record, the union's conduct in negotiating a union security clause that tracked the statutory language cannot be said to have been either arbitrary or in bad faith. The Court of Appeals correctly rejected petitioner's argument that, by negotiating this clause, the union breached its duty of fair representation. * * *

Accordingly, the judgment of the United States Court of Appeals for the Ninth Circuit is affirmed.

It is so ordered.

Justice KENNEDY, with whom Justice THOMAS joins, concurring. Kennedy joined the opinion of the Court and offered further observations.

Notes

1. How does an actor in Marquez's situation avoid such a conflict? Should she have confirmed her standing before she accepted the job with Lakeside Productions? Should Lakeside have been required to keep the job open until it confirmed her status? What would be the downside of such a requirement?

2. AFTRA and SAG have joined forces on a number of issues. On Oct. 28, 2003, their memberships voted jointly to approve the new three-year television and radio commercials contracts by a majority of 94% in favor to 6% against. On March 18, 2004, the two unions ratified a 1–year extension with modest increases to their basic film-TV contract with the Alliance of Motion Picture and Television Producers. The two unions have formed at least one joint website, the AFTRA–SAG Washington D.C., located at *http://www.aftrasagdcbalt.com/index.php?section=main.* The website defines the two organizations separately and invites individuals to join one or the other. On the main page it states, "Nationally, AFTRA represents more than 80,000 professional actors, news broadcasters and writers, announcers, vocalists, and others who work in the fields of television, radio, sound recordings, and industrial productions. SAG represents over 98,000 professional actors who work in film, television, industrial productions, and infomercials."

3. For more information on other Hollywood strikes that were eventually settled, see Marc Cooper, *Residual Anger: Hollywood unions on the brink*, THE NATION, April 2, 2001; and Jess Cagle, *Hollywood's writers and actors are threatening to walk. A primer on why and what it means to you*, TIME MAG., April 23, 2001, at 74.

4. Unions also negotiate health plans for their members. See Meg James & James Bates, *SAG Health Plan Targets Reel Fraud; Labor: Benefits officials investigate the fictional roles some actors claim to gain coverage*, L. A. TIMES, June 22, 2001, at Part 3; Page 1.

5. When a new television genre becomes established, unions will take notice. In Chapter 9, Television Contracts, you can read the following article on the efforts of unions to organize reality TV talent and crew: Jim Rendon, *Unions Aim to Share in the Success of Reality TV*, N.Y. TIMES, Jan. 25, 2004, at Business. P. 4.

NICK MARINO v. WGA

United States Court of Appeals, Ninth Circuit, 1993.
992 F.2d 1480.

FERNANDEZ, Circuit Judge.

Nick Marino appeals the district court's summary judgment in favor of the Writers Guild of America ("WGA"), Francis Coppola and Mario Puzo in Marino's action seeking to vacate an arbitration award. WGA, as arbitrator, awarded screenwriting credit for "Godfather III" to Coppola and Puzo, and not to Marino and his cohort, Thomas Wright. Marino contends that the arbitration procedures used to determine the screenwriting credit were fundamentally unfair. Marino also argues that WGA violated its duty of fair representation by adopting the arbitration procedures and by failing to follow those procedures. Finally, Marino challenges the district court's denial of his request to discover the identities of the arbitrators. We affirm.

[handwritten margin note: fundamentally unfair arbitration procedures]

BACKGROUND

The WGA is a labor union which was certified as the collective bargaining representative of screenwriters in the movie industry. Marino has been a WGA member since 1985. Pursuant to a collective bargaining agreement between WGA and the employers of writers in the movie industry, WGA determines which writers will receive screen credit for the writing of a screenplay. Both economic benefits and the writer's status in the industry are affected by the receipt of screen credit. Absent the rights set forth in the collective bargaining agreement, the power to allocate credits would be in the hands of the movie producers.

A portion of the collective bargaining agreement titled "Theatrical Schedule A, Theatrical Credits," sets forth the general rules of credit determination. The procedures for arbitration of credit disputes are set out in WGA's "Credits Manual." They are not part of the collective bargaining agreement, but are approved by WGA's board of directors and by vote of its membership. According to the Credits Manual, the arbitration has three phases.

What we will call the first phase is a procedure through which common factual disputes can be resolved. If there are disputes as to "authenticity, identification, sequence, authorship or completeness of any literary material to be considered" a special committee conducts "a hearing at which all participating writers may present testimony and documentary evidence." Manual, Credit Determination Procedure (CDP) § D.4. That committee's factual determination is binding and forms a part of the basis of the material that goes to those who conduct the second phase of the process.

The second phase of the process is conducted by the use of three individuals, called arbiters. Unlike the decision makers in the first phase, the arbiters do not hear oral testimony or argument. They read and cogitate. Their task is to decide who should get screen credit for the screenplay. Their names are kept confidential from the public, the participating writers, and even from one another. * * * Each arbiter makes this difficult decision on creativity in isolation and based upon written materials. Those are materials submitted by the film company and they include "all material written by participants as well as * * * source material." * * * The participating writers are encouraged to review that material and may ask that appropriate materials be added. A participating writer may also submit a position statement for the purpose of helping the arbiters in their consideration of the written materials. *Id.* Writers are encouraged to do so. Each arbiter then makes a decision and notifies the Credit Arbitration Secretary. A majority decides the question. After the arbiters have made their decision, the participating writers are informed and the third phase becomes available.

The third phase is a review procedure. Within twenty-four hours of notification of the credit determination, any of the writers involved may request a review by a Policy Review Board ("PRB"). CDP § D.5. The PRB's scope of review is limited to determining whether there has been "any serious deviation from the policy of the Guild or the procedure as set forth in this Manual." More specifically, the PRB may consider questions involving dereliction of duty on the part of the arbiters, or any of them, any use of undue influence upon the arbiters, any misinterpretation, misapplication, or violation of WGA policies, and any "[i]mportant new written material" which was, for valid reasons, not previously available. *Id.* The PRB has the authority to direct the original three arbiters to reconsider the case or to order a new proceeding. The entire arbitration process must occur within 21 business days. If it does not, the producer's own selection may become final.

x 21 days

In 1985, Marino and Wright wrote an adaptation of literary material, referred to as a treatment, for "Godfather III," which Paramount Pictures Corporation ("Paramount") purchased.

Paramount hired Marino to write a motion picture script, or screenplay, based on the treatment. Marino completed the screenplay in 1985, but Paramount chose not to produce it at that time.

In 1987, Marino wrote a second treatment and sent it to executives at a production studio owned by Coppola and related to the prior "Godfather" pictures. The production studio neither solicited nor purchased Marino's 1987 treatment. In 1989 and 1990, Coppola and Puzo co-wrote a screenplay for "Godfather III." The movie was produced and completed in 1990.

Before the movie was distributed, Marino was notified that WGA would be conducting an arbitration to determine the writing credits for "Godfather III," pursuant to the collective bargaining agreement. Accordingly, Marino, Coppola and Puzo submitted written materials and statements for the arbiters' review.... On November 5, 1990, the Arbitration Secretary informed Marino that Coppola and Puzo would receive sole writing credit. Marino requested a hearing before the PRB where he objected to the arbitration procedure. The PRB telephoned the three arbiters and presented Marino's allegations to them. The PRB discovered that one arbiter had not read Marino's 1985 treatment. That arbiter was sent the 1985 treatment for review, and the arbiter then reaffirmed the prior conclusion. In a letter dated November 21, 1990, the PRB informed Marino that a new arbitration was unnecessary and that the arbitration decision was final.

state court

Marino then filed this action in state court in which he sought to vacate the arbitration award and to obtain declaratory relief. The action was removed to district court on grounds that the proceedings were governed by a collective bargaining agreement and preempted by federal labor law. WGA moved for summary judgment as did Marino. On October 25, 1991, after a hearing, the district court granted WGA summary judgment. * * *

DISCUSSION

Marino makes a number of attacks upon the arbitration procedures in general and upon their particular application to this case. A number of those revolve around his claim that it is fundamentally unfair to keep the identities of the arbiters confidential. That has the potential, he says, for concealing bias. Moreover, the result is that he cannot appear before them or cross examine witnesses before them. As we will explain, Marino waived the right to mount this group of attacks.

He also asserts that the procedures were applied to him in an improper manner. He claims that he was refused the right to have the participating writers remain anonymous, that he was prevented from submitting what he deemed to be relevant evidence, that he was unable to see the other writers' written submissions, that the arbiters considered evidence that they should not have, and did not consider evidence that they should have.

A.   Waiver; the Anonymity Claims

Arbitration is a favored method for the resolution of disputes, particularly in the labor area. * * * It is undoubtedly true that all notions of procedural fairness cannot be jettisoned simply because the parties have agreed to arbitrate. * * * However, because arbitration is contractual, rather than imposed by law, what we have come to see as the hallmarks of judicial justice are not necessarily required in arbitral justice. * * * One reason is that arbitration can take account of unique problems. Arbitration can supply high-powered expertise to a particular and narrow area—such as deciding who should get credit for creating an imaginative work. At the same time, it can supply unique ways for avoiding the kinds of biases and pressures that judges are all too aware of. Lifetime appointments help insulate federal judges from those vices; arbitration procedures may offer other ways.

If arbitration is to work, it must not be subjected to undue judicial interference. * * * Moreover, parties must be encouraged, nay required, to raise their complaints about the arbitration during the arbitration process itself, when that is possible.

Thus, it is well settled that a party may not sit idle through an arbitration procedure and then collaterally attack that procedure on grounds not raised before the arbitrators when the result turns out to be adverse. * * * This rule even extends to questions, such as arbitrator bias, that go to the very heart of arbitral fairness. * * *

This rule applies when there is an objection to the adequacy or form of procedures used in commercial arbitration. * * * It also applies when it is claimed that a labor arbitration was not fairly conducted. * * * It is no less applicable when the claim is phrased in terms of a violation of the duty of fair representation. * * *

Here, the major thrust of Marino's objection is his assertion that WGA precluded him from ascertaining the qualifications or partiality of the arbiters. The WGA's refusal to disclose the arbiters' identity was pursuant to the procedures which we have outlined. Under the procedures, "[a]s has always been [WGA] practice, the names of the arbiters selected remain confidential." CDP § D.1. WGA's confidentiality policy is "supported by important and legitimate considerations, including the necessity that arbitrators be entirely freed from both real and perceived dangers of pressure, retaliation, and litigation." *Ferguson v. Writers*

Guild of Am., W., Inc., 226 Cal.App.3d 1382, 1391, 277 Cal.Rptr. 450 (Cal. Ct.App.1991) (upholding WGA's confidentiality policy).

The procedures allow the participating writers to strike a reasonable number of names from the list of arbiters. The list is long, and if one did not have substantial familiarity with the writing community, it may be well nigh impossible to ferret out possible bias in all of the persons on it. Still, Marino, without objection, took advantage of that opportunity. Between him and Wright, 85 names were stricken. From the remaining names on the list, three arbiters were chosen. Each potential arbiter was screened for potential bias by an arbitration coordinator.

While the notion of an anonymous judge may jar those who are used to judicial proceedings, no doubt WGA and its members understand the practical difficulties involved in having the arbiters' names disclosed. Very important people may be unhappy with a decision and may be in a good position to pressure or take revenge against the arbiters. Moreover, the WGA and its members have decided that the best arbiters will be experienced working members of the screenwriters community. The heavy responsibility of the arbiter's mantle might well be declined by hard-working writers if they knew that they could be hauled through recriminatory judicial proceedings, accused of bias, and the like. The procedures that reflected and dealt with these concerns had existed for decades. They were grounded on the collective bargaining agreement and were designed to implement its terms. Presumably they were fair. * * *

In the face of this, Marino made no objection until the arbiters had found against him. Presumably the procedure was satisfactory to him, just as it was to the other members of the WGA. That is, it was satisfactory to him until the arbiters' decision went against him.

It is important to notice that Marino's attack on the anonymity of the arbiters, and the other concomitants of that anonymity, is very much like a claim of arbitrator bias. In fact, its central proposition is that the arbiters might be biased against him but he cannot tell for sure because he does not know whom they are. Of course, he cannot know for sure whether they are biased or not because he has not had an opportunity to investigate or grill them on that issue. Nevertheless, the claim is a bias claim at root. We hold that this claim, like that of actual bias, was waived when Marino failed to protest the procedure before the arbiters were selected and performed their task. A claim of true bias can be considered and dealt with before individuals have invested their time and decided the case. So too could this claim have been taken account of. Here the individuals who were being asked to decide a knotty screen credit question with celerity and certainty could have been informed that their impartiality and qualifications were being challenged. The WGA could have taken steps to ameliorate *those* claims. Just as importantly, the prospective arbiters, once being made aware of the claims, could have decided that they did not wish to become a part of a process which is, as the Manual says, "arduous and unpleasant." Perhaps individuals who had no objection to disclosure of their names could be found. We do not know. What we do know is that this bias issue, like others, should have been raised before the arbiters acted, not after. We understand Marino's focus on what he perceives as an issue of fairness to himself. We, however, must focus on fairness to all involved, including the arbiters and all of the other union members and officers who have relied on the arbitration process for so long.

As we see it, Marino's complaint of his inability to have a face-to-face hearing before the arbiters, complete with cross-examination—issues also not raised before his loss—must fall with the anonymity claim. They are its accompaniments.

We hasten to add two additional thoughts. We recognize that it would be possible to create a procedure so palpably unfair on its face that no prior objection should be expected or required. An anonymous coin toss might be an example of that. On the record before us, that is *not* the procedure we are dealing with. While Marino focuses on the arbiters' phase of the process, he loses sight of the overall arbitration process itself. He ignores the phase one evidentiary hearing process and likewise ignores the phase three procedural review process. The former, of course, provides for all of the usual confrontation and evidentiary rights. The latter provides some assurance of procedural fairness. Marino's claim that he is not in a position to assert procedural problems because he did not appear before the arbiters is not persuasive. He did assert problems. As we will soon discuss, they were dealt with. Also, while it is true that the arbiters could have failed to consider materials or proceeded to commit other wrongs in a hidden way, that could occur despite hearings and despite knowledge of the arbiters' identities. In effect, Marino's claims in this regard do, once again, come back to the single issue of arbiter anonymity.

In a similar vein, we do not hold that every possible endemic procedural defect must be raised in advance or waived. We need not, and should not, sweep that broadly. It may often be the case that a union member should simply go through the provided procedures, especially if no objection can possibly change them. *Cf. Carr,* 904 F.2d at 1317–18. In *Carr,* for example, the plaintiffs claimed that the grievance procedures were flawed because they did not provide for discovery or representation by counsel, among other things. There we said that "at a minimum" the plaintiffs should have presented and prosecuted their claims through the contractual procedures despite their assertions of inadequacy. *Id.* 904 F.2d at 1318. We did not decide whether a failure to object to those procedures in advance would have waived the claims. Similarly, we do not now decide that question, or others like it.

B.   *Duty of Fair Representation; the Other Claims*

In addition to his assault on the heartland of the arbitration procedure—anonymity—Marino has raised a number of other claims about the handling of the "Godfather III" proceeding. He asserts that in handling this proceeding, WGA breached its duty of fair representation.

"The undoubted broad authority of the union as exclusive bargaining agent in the negotiation and administration of a collective bargaining contract is accompanied by a responsibility of equal scope, the responsibility and duty of fair representation." *Humphrey v. Moore,* 375 U.S. 335, 342, 84 S.Ct. 363, 368, 11 L.Ed.2d 370 (1964). "Unions have broad discretion to act in what they perceive to be their members' best interests. This court has construed the unfair representation doctrine in a manner designed to protect that discretion." *Moore v. Bechtel Power Corp.,* 840 F.2d 634, 636 (9th Cir.1988) (citation omitted).

This court engages in a two-step analysis to determine whether a union has breached the duty of fair representation. First, we must decide whether the alleged union misconduct "involved the union's judgment, or whether it was 'procedural or ministerial.'" Second, if the conduct was procedural or ministerial, then the plaintiff may prevail if the union's conduct was arbitrary, discriminatory, or in bad faith. However, if the conduct involved the union's judgment, then "the plaintiff may prevail only if the union's conduct was discriminatory or in bad faith." Burkevich v. Air Line Pilots Ass'n, Int'l, 894 F.2d 346, 349 (9th Cir. 1990) (citations omitted). * * *

Marino's claims raise a potpourri of fair representation issues, some of which relate to judgment and others of which are procedural in nature. All of them, he says, should result in the overturning of the arbitration award. We will consider each of them.

He begins by asserting that the whole procedure is fundamentally unfair. * * * Of course, the adoption of procedures is a matter of judgment. For the most part, this is just another iteration of his waived complaint about arbiter anonymity. Thus, it must fail. He does, however, add yet another complaint. He says he was not given an opportunity to reply to the written statements of the other participating writers because he could not see those statements. The Manual does preclude that opportunity. *See* CDP § D.4(b). However, the statements are supposed to be just that—mere statements and not evidence. We see no fundamental unfairness. When time is of the essence, as it is in credit determinations, the receipt of simultaneous briefs is not a shocking development by any means. That certainly would justify the decision not to allow replies. We are somewhat more concerned about the requirement that the statements remain confidential; replies could be denied or discouraged, without that added stricture. However, it can hardly be said that this alone makes the procedure discriminatory or in bad faith. It is simply a part of an approach to speedy decision making that the writers have long since adopted. At any rate, Marino was given a copy of the Coppola and Puzo statement during discovery in the district court proceedings. His failure to bring any actual problems to that court's attention suggests that he did not suffer prejudice to a strong interest of a kind that can justify a determination that the duty of fair representation was breached. * * *

Marino next claims that he was denied the right to have the identities of the writers remain anonymous. The Manual clearly provides that, upon request, the identities of all participating writers will be kept from the arbiters. CDP § D.3. He asserts that he demanded that right but was told by the Screen Credits Coordinator that he could not have anonymity. That, if so, would itself be a procedural violation. However, it was exactly the kind of issue that the third phase of the arbitration procedure was designed to deal with. Marino brought this problem to the attention of the PRB. That body did not ignore his claim. Rather, it appears that the PRB conducted an investigation and questioned the Arbitration Coordinator. It then determined that Marino never requested an anonymous arbitration despite many opportunities to do so over a lengthy period. The PRB examined Marino's written statements submitted to the arbiters and noticed that Marino had included his own name. There was no evidence that Marino's materials included a statement that he was submitting his name under protest. The PRB then decided that his rights were not compromised.

Although there might have been a factual dispute as to whether Marino actually requested anonymity, the fact that a dispute exists does not establish that WGA's conduct was discriminatory or in bad faith. Nor, for that matter, does it indicate that it was arbitrary. * * * In fact, it appears that the WGA considered Marino's complaint in a manner far from perfunctory. After investigating the allegation, it reached a reasoned conclusion. In sum, we see no grounds to overturn that arbitral decision. Similarly, to the extent it reflects an exercise of judgment by the WGA, we find no breach of the duty of fair representation.

Next, Marino asserts that he was prevented from submitting certain evidence that he deemed to be important—that is, his 1987 treatment. He says that he sought to have a phase one hearing on that subject but was denied it. He raised this issue before the PRB and it explained that because Marino "was not employed by a signatory company to write [the] treatment and it was not purchased or licensed by a signatory company," that treatment was not under the jurisdiction of the WGA. Given that, it said, the material could not be considered. Because those facts were admitted by Marino, there was no need to hold an evidentiary hearing regarding them.

Even if other interpretations of the collective bargaining agreement would have been plausible, there is nothing to indicate that this decision was discriminatory or made in bad faith. There is no indication that it was a recent or idiosyncratic interpretation designed for the purpose of injuring Marino. In short, the making of that decision does not show that the WGA violated its duty of fair representation.

Marino then claims that the arbiters failed to review the materials submitted to them, and reviewed materials not submitted to them. In particular, he says that the WGA should have ordered a new arbitration when it ascertained that (1) two of the arbiters did not read the literary material thoroughly, and (2) the arbiters considered the predecessor "Godfather" movies and Puzo's novel, "The Godfather." These contentions involve the exercise of the WGA's judgment, and, therefore, Marino must show that the WGA's decisions were made discriminatorily or in bad faith. *See Burkevich,* 894 F.2d at 349–50.

Two arbiters did indicate that they focused their attention mostly on the writings offered by Marino, Wright, Coppola, and Puzo, as opposed to the several other submissions from writers who were not seeking credit. They said they did so because these four were the only parties vying for screen credits. If anything, that would seem to inure to Marino's benefit. Certainly it does not establish that his work was glossed over. It is not at all apparent that he was prejudiced and he has not shown that he was. *See Moore,* 840 F.2d at 636 (union's conduct must prejudice a strong interest of the union member). Moreover, nothing in the record indicates that WGA's decision to accept the arbiters' award was discriminatory or in bad faith. *See Burkevich,* 894 F.2d at 352 (union's judgment call, even if poorly made, does not constitute breach of duty of fair representation). Marino also asserts that one arbiter at first failed to read his 1985 treatment. The PRB investigated this allegation, agreed with Marino, and corrected the problem. That does not smack of discrimination or bad faith; it tends to show that the process was working properly. *See Vaca,* 386 U.S. at 194, 87 S.Ct. at 919.

Finally, Marino states, the arbiters improperly considered *ex parte* evidence, specifically the predecessor "Godfather" movies and the book. Under the Procedures, "the Arbitration Committee bases its decision on the written scripts, including story and source material." CDP § D.3. According to WGA, "source material" includes material from the book and from the previous movies to which "Godfather III" is the sequel. Moreover, Marino made references to the predecessor movies in his own written statement. One wonders how that really could be avoided. It appears disingenuous of him to contend now that the arbiters improperly considered that material. Again, no discrimination or bad faith is shown.

C. *Discovery*

Marino argues that the district court erred by denying his discovery request that the arbiters' identities be revealed. He asserts that identification was necessary if he was to determine whether the arbiters were properly qualified and whether they were biased or partial.

The district court committed no error. As we have already held, the arbiter anonymity issue has been waived. It cannot be resurrected through the use of a discovery order. That information, under the circumstances of this case, was not relevant. *See* Fed.R.Civ.P. 26(b).

CONCLUSION

Movies are expensive creative works. Once they are ready for release their owners wish to move quickly. When the WGA wrested the unilateral power to decide screen credits from the producers, it did so at the price of an agreement that WGA itself would move quickly. The need for speed is part of the right it negotiated for on behalf of its members. That need drives the whole process; in the absence of quick determinations, it is likely that the right itself would wither away.

The procedures adopted by WGA were designed to make the difficult screen credit decision in a speedy and fair fashion. Although the three-phase arbitration procedure is not the same as the more deliberate judicial procedures that we are accustomed to, this case helps show why it cannot be. "Godfather III" was released over three years ago, and only now is the second phase of federal judicial procedures moving toward completion. That is not the fault of the parties or of the judicial system. Our procedures require time; other needs demand other procedures.

On this record, and based upon the issues properly before us for decision, we cannot say that the procedures designed for speed overwhelmed the ideal of justice.

AFFIRMED.

Notes

1. For a discussion of how the WGA determines credits, see Shawn K. Judge, *Giving Credit Where Credit is Due?: The Unusual Use of Arbitration in Determining Screenwriting Credits*, 13 OHIO ST. J. ON DISP. RESOL. 221 (1997). *See also* Dana N. Glasser, *Stranding Dorothy In Oz And Keeping The Wizard Behind The Curtain?:Writer's Guild Determination Of Screenwriting Credits Through Arbitration*, 3 PEPP. DISP. RESOL. L.J. 27. Glasser discusses the unique arbitration process employed by the WGA, holding it up to scrutiny as well as comparing it with traditional arbitration procedure. She also compares and contrasts the WGA process with the traditional arbitration model and concludes that despite its flaws, WGA arbitration efficiently and expediently meets the needs of the frenetic entertainment world, and thus appears not only here to stay, but susceptible to little change.

2. Grace Reiner, *Separation of Rights for Screen and Television Writers*, L.A. LAWYER (2001), discuses the most recent addition to the separated rights possessed by writers—the right of reacquisition, which is similar to a turnaround but with stricter requirements and different payments. She writes, "If original material (which, in the case of a reacquisition, means material that is not based on any preexisting material) has not been produced within five years, the writer has two years to buy the material back. The writer may do so as long as the material is not in active development. The writer's two-year opportunity starts five years after the completion of the original writer's services or five years after acquisition, whichever is later. To reacquire the material, the writer must pay the company the amount the writer was paid for the purchase and/or writing services. In addition, the writer must then obligate the new buyer to pay the balance of direct literary material costs plus interest. That amount is due upon commencement of principal photography. Direct literary material costs must be directly attributable to the writing, including the first writer's pension and health contributions and costs of other writers. Unlike turnarounds, however, the costs do not include overhead or other production costs." *Id.*

3. When more than one writer participates in a film, can anyone claim true ownership of the project? In the following interview, screenwriter Greg Brooker had much to say on this issue.

Sherri Burr
Screenwriter Credits:
Author Interview With Greg Brooker

[On December 7, 2003, author Sherri Burr spoke to Greg Brooker, who received a co-credit for writing *Stuart Little* with M. Night Shyamalan, at the Santa Fe, NM, Film Festival, about his screenwriting career.]

"Columbia Pictures came to me with *Stuart Little* in 1992. I worked on the screenplay for three years. The project got shelved when the Columbia exec left the studio. When she returned, the project got revived and became a different movie.

"I wrote a screenplay that was faithful to the book. The mother gives birth to the mouse in the book. We don't know how, but she comes home from the hospital with this little bundle. Once the project was revived, they decided to make it about adoption.

"In the end there were 17 writers. A lot of them were brought in to write a line or two for the animals. A lot of these writers became alienated from the process. You could say that *Stuart Little* was written by committee. After we went through the Writers Guild credit arbitration, only two writers received credit: me and M. Night Shyamalan. I was the first writer, and he was the third.

"I spent a lot of time writing my letter to the WGA explaining how I created my screenplay and what was mine. I didn't claim the whole picture because the concept changed.

"A lot of writers can make a good living writing screenplays in Hollywood, even if they [the screenplays] don't see the light of day. I kind of fell into film writing to support my poetry habit. I studied American poetry at U.C.L.A. and wanted to become a poet. I planned to go to graduate school in poetry. However, a friend sold a screenplay for a lot of money and I thought I could do that too. So I began writing in 1987 and have been making a living at it since 1988.

"I wrote scripts that peopled liked and remembered. I get a job once a year to write or re-write a script. However, I can't continue to do that forever. At my age, 39, you have to graduate to another level like writer-director to maintain your career. The reason I say at my age is because the studios love a 25–year-old male writer. They feel he'll be closer to their target audience. But they will always need someone to write the *American Beauty* type scripts. I can't remember a single 25–year-old who won the best picture Oscar.

"Writers tend to keep on the periphery of the business. You don't see a lot of writers hanging out at parties because they're home writing.

That's also why you're less likely to see the top actors at parties because they're out on sets.

"I am now working on becoming a director. I plan to use my short *Nosferatu L.A.–02* as my calling card to get directing work. My short imagines Dracula coming to live in L.A. and the loneliness he experiences.

"The legal issue I had to address on *Nosferatu* is that I wanted to use clips from a 1922 film. It's my understanding that all films created before 1923 are in the public domain. In 1922, a filmmaker named Murnau wanted to make a film from Bram Stoker's *Dracula* but his estate refused to give permission. Murnau made the film anyway but changed the title and a few other details. Stoker's estate sued, won, and required Murnau to burn all copies. Somehow one copy of the original Murnau film survived and others have since used it. Murnau's estate has gone after these people. I think it's ironic that the thief became the victim.

"I'm not too worried because I think Murnau's work is in the public domain. I use very little and am not planning to make money off of it."

Notes

1. What did the shared credit for Greg Brooker and M. Night Shyamalan look like given that Hollywood denotes using an ampersand symbol (&) when the two writers worked together and the word "and" when they did not?

2. There have been many disputes over credits on films, which will be discussed in more detail in Chapter 5. For the curious about the kind of credit process that Brooker endured, see Tad Friend, *Annals of Arbitration: Credit Grab*, THE NEW YORKER, Oct. 20, 2003, at 160–169. Friend discusses the credit arbitration for the film *The Hulk* which by a two-to-one vote ended with the following credit: "Screenplay by John Turman (writer A) and Michael France (Writer C) and James Schamus (Writer I); Story by James Shamus.

3. Who is bound by guild agreements? In Hollywood Online (1996), Allen R. Grogan and Sam C. Mandel wrote the following:

"Guild agreements are contracts. Typically, they bind guild members and producer signatories to the agreement. If a performer, director, writer or crew member is a member of a guild, the guild's work rules typically prevent that person from rendering services in the areas covered by the guild's collective bargaining agreements for anyone other than a producer signatory. Although actually becoming a member of a guild can be difficult, becoming a producer signatory typically is quite easy, and requires only that a letter of adherence and related paperwork be completed by the producer. Once the producer is a signatory to a guild agreement, he or she may hire members of that guild to provide services. The catch is that, once a signatory, a producer typically may hire solely guild members for such services, subject only to labor law restrictions. Furthermore, although the exact rules will differ with each guild agreement, most guild agreements contain cross-affiliation provisions which, in the case of an individual producer signatory, bind not only the individual but also all companies controlled by such individual and in the case of a corporate signatory, bind all subsidiaries of such entity. (Whether signatory status by a subsidiary will act to bind a corporate parent has at times been a contested issue between producers and the guilds.) Because of the possibility that non-union activities could be hampered, an online provider or producer should be very cautious about becoming a producer signatory to any entertainment guild agreement, and if signatory status is appropriate for any reason, care should be taken to select the specific entity that executes signatory documents." *Id.*

Chapter 4

CONTRACTUAL PROTECTION
OF FILMS

Contracts are the lifeblood of the film industry. Written contracts endeavor to spell out precisely what is expected of the parties involved. Oral contracts are also a staple of the industry. Some entertainers discover that they are bound by their oral agreements once another party has acted to secure financing based on the expectation that actors' words are their bonds. Whether oral or written, it is important for talent to understand the provisions of their contracts before they sign them. Insurance contracts are also important to filmmaking as they guarantee that the picture will be completed. Problems arise when actors die, such as when the singer Aaliyah perished in a plane crash, before completing her role in *The Matrix: Reloaded*. Nona Gaye, the daughter of singer Marvin Gaye, replaced Aaliyah.

In reviewing the contracts at issue in Sections A, B, & C of this chapter, ask the following: What are the crucial provisions? What is the custom prevailing in the industry? Be aware that parties may be bound by the industry custom unless they specifically change it in writing to create different expectations.

Section D provides a discussion of public financing as individual states follow Canada's lead and attempt to lure film production away from Hollywood by offering incentives that lower the cost of making films. Canada has the advantages of a favorable exchange rate and cities that resemble New York, Chicago, and Los Angeles, which makes filming there attractive to producers. States are offering tax incentives and in some instances loans and rebates to compete with Canada.

Section E concludes this chapter with the reproduction of a contract to assign copyright in a screenplay entitled "The Gambler," which was a 1999 motion picture filmed in Hungary and produced by an American with international talent and crew members.

A. PERSONAL SERVICE CONTRACTS

MAIN LINE PICTURES, INC. v. BASINGER

California Court of Appeals, 1994.
No. B077509, 1994 WL 814244.

GRIGNON, Judge.

Defendants and appellants, actress Kim Basinger and her "loan-out" corporation Mighty Wind, Inc., appeal from an $8 million judgment against them and in favor of plaintiff and respondent Main Line Pictures, Inc. in Main Line's breach of contract action relating to production of the movie "Boxing Helena." Among other contentions relating to the sufficiency of the evidence and the excessiveness of the damages, defendants assert the special verdicts were prejudicially ambiguous in that they failed to differentiate between the liability of Basinger and Mighty Wind by use of the term "and/or." Because we agree the "and/or" special verdicts require reversal, we need not reach defendants' remaining contentions. We reverse.

FACTS

In December 1990, Main Line sent a copy of the screenplay of "Boxing Helena" to Basinger. Basinger was a well known actress, having starred in many movies, including "Batman" and "9 1/2 Weeks." On December 28, 1990, Main Line's president, Carl Mazzocone wrote to Basinger through her agent Intertalent offering Basinger $500,000 plus additional deferred compensation to star in the movie.

Basinger was excited about the script and interested in playing the female lead. Barbara Dreyfus, Basinger's assistant and Mighty Wind's director of development, arranged for Basinger to meet the film's screenwriter and director, Jennifer Lynch.

Mighty Wind was Basinger's "loan-out" corporation, a company through which Basinger "loaned" her acting services. Payment for Basinger's services was made to Mighty Wind, which in turn employed and paid Basinger. On January 11, 1991, Lynch, Basinger and Dreyfus met at Mighty Wind's office. Basinger expressed an interest in the movie, which she believed would be a tremendous showcase for an actress. She also stated she felt a kinship to the role because it concerned a woman who was obsessed, a situation which was familiar to Basinger.

The screenplay contained a few nude scenes. On January 18, 1991, Basinger and Lynch met to address Basinger's concerns regarding the treatment of the nude scenes. Lynch explained in detail how she expected to film the scenes with Basinger, stating there would be no gratuitous sex scenes or frontal nudity below the waist. While the film would be sensual, it would not be explicit. The meeting lasted more than one hour and all issues involving nudity were resolved. Basinger agreed to act in the film as it had been presented to her in the script.

1/24/91
agreed
to act

On January 24, 1991, Basinger met with Intertalent and agreed to act in "Boxing Helena."

Main Line's attorney, Robert Wyman, discussed the contract's material terms with defendants' attorneys Robin Russell and Julie Philips. Mazzocone also had contract discussions with Attorney Russell. Other contract discussions took place between Attorney Wyman, Mazzocone or Lynch and Intertalent or Dreyfus.

Compensation and credit were discussed at the outset. The parties agreed Basinger would receive her usual fee of $3 million for the picture, consisting of guaranteed compensation of $600,000 plus additional deferred and contingent compensation. Basinger agreed to accept second billing behind Ed Harris, the male lead.

On February 27, 1991, Mazzocone, Attorney Wyman and Attorney Philips discussed each material term of the contract. Attorney Wyman reviewed a checklist of all terms in issue, Attorney Philips agreeing to each term as described. Following this conversation, Attorney Wyman sent Attorney Philips a "deal memo" dated February 27, 1991, setting forth the contractual terms for Basinger's performance in "Boxing Helena."[3]

deal memo

On February 28, 1991, Attorney Philips sent an annotated copy of the "deal memo" back to Attorney Wyman.

Attorney Philips's annotations requested certain changes to be included in a formal written document. For example, she wanted to change the number of days Basinger would work in post-production. On Attorney Philips's own copy of the document, she noted "[t]here is substantial nudity—KB ok with it . . . no frontal nudity—nothing graphic—more subliminal." Attorney Philips also noted that the "Loan[-]out company is Mighty Wind Productions." Mazzocone understood Mighty Wind was "Kim's production company and that's who the contract should be made with and that's where the payment [was to] be paid—to Mighty Wind." Such arrangements were standard and did not materially change the contract.

As soon as the agreement for Basinger's acting services was reached at the end of February, Main Line received authorization to use Basinger's photo to promote the movie. On February 28, 1991, Republic Pictures, a foreign distribution company, learned that Basinger had agreed to perform in the film; it began preselling the film in foreign markets with Basinger's name attached. Eventually, foreign presales for the movie with Basinger's name attached totaled $6.8 million. Main Line reasonably expected to receive approximately $3 million in domestic

---

3. The memorandum provided for "guaranteed compensation" of $600,000, "Gross deferment [compensation] payable out of first receipts of producer of $400,000[, [ ] a]djusted gross receipts . . . of $1,000,000 payable out of 35% of producer's receipts . . . [, [ ] a]djusted gross receipts deferment of $1,000,000 payable out of 25% of producer's receipts . . . and . . . [ ] [c]ontingent compensation equal to 15% of producer's receipts thereafter."

presales. The money obtained from the foreign presales would secure financing for the film.[4]

In April 1991, Main Line began preproduction activities including casting, wardrobe, special effects and model construction.

Because timing is critical, film industry contracts are frequently oral agreements based on unsigned "deal memos." Often, artists authorize their agents or lawyers to bind them. Sometimes, however, the parties also desire to memorialize the agreement in an executed written contract, commonly referred to as a "long form agreement." This written contract is usually negotiated by attorneys and contains many standard terms. Although the parties may intend their oral agreement to be binding, many subsidiary or ancillary terms may subsequently be agreed upon and incorporated into the written contract. The written agreement also enables parties to formalize their understanding in legal language. The absence of an executed written agreement does not mean there is no legally binding agreement. Basinger, for example, had entered into executed written agreements for only two of her prior films.

long form agmt.

After the oral agreement had been reached, Attorney Wyman incorporated its material terms into written documents, an "Acting Service Agreement" and a "Producer's Standard Terms and Conditions for an Actor/Actress—Loan-out." An "Inducement" was also drafted. These documents were sent to Attorney Philips on March 7, 1991. Thereafter, Attorney Wyman and Attorney Philips exchanged numerous drafts of the Acting Service Agreement and the Producer's Standard Terms and Conditions, copies of which were sent to Basinger and others. During the exchange process, many ancillary terms were revised and eventually agreed upon.

In April 1991, Basinger changed agents; she replaced Intertalent with International Creative Management (ICM). After ICM read the screenplay for "Boxing Helena," ICM concluded Basinger should not do the film.

Sometime in May of 1991, Lynch heard a rumor that Basinger was not intending to perform in the movie. Lynch telephoned Dreyfus and relayed the rumor. Dreyfus repeated the rumor to Basinger, who at the time was in the room with Dreyfus. Basinger denied the rumor and confirmed her commitment to star in the film.

On May 6, 1991, Basinger called Lynch and Mazzocone and expressed reservations about the script. Basinger stated she wanted the character to be more sympathetic. Two days later, ICM told Lynch and Mazzocone it had suggested to Basinger she not act in the film. Lynch attempted to accommodate Basinger's reservations by modifying the script. Lynch met with Basinger at Basinger's office to discuss the proposed changes.

---

4. A presale is a minimum guarantee by a distributor in a specific market to procure that distributor's rights to show the movie in a given territory. After Basinger declined to perform in "Boxing Helena," Main Line produced the movie with a lesser known actress. Without Basinger, total presales declined to $2.5 million.

On May 29, 1991, Attorney Wyman sent to Attorney Philips final execution drafts dated "February 29, 199[1]," of the Acting Service Agreement and the Producer's Standard Terms and Conditions. The cover letter stated Attorney Wyman was delivering an execution copy of the "Agreement between Main Line Pictures, Inc. and Mighty Wind Productions, Inc. f/s/o [for the services of] Kim Basinger."

The Acting Service Agreement described Main Line as "producer," Mighty Wind as "lender" and Basinger as "artist." The Agreement called for "Lender [to] cause Artist to report for the rendition of exclusive services in connection with * * * ['Boxing Helena.']" Compensation was to be paid to lender, subject to lender's and artist's full performance. The Acting Service Agreement specified artist's credit and perquisites, such as transportation and dressing facilities. It also provided for merchandising and the use of artist's likeness. The signature line called for execution by "Main Line Pictures, Inc. By Carl Mazzocone" and "Mighty Wind Productions, Inc. By Kim Basinger." There was no place for Basinger to sign as an individual. The Acting Service Agreement was never executed.

The Producer's Standard Terms and Conditions provided that Mighty Wind, "employer," agreed to "loan-out" the services of Basinger to Main Line. It provided, inter alia, that Main Line was entitled to seek equitable relief if artist breached and employer was to indemnify producer if artist made any claim for compensation. Employer warranted that it was a duly organized and bona fide corporation. No signature lines were included in this document.

There is nothing in the record to indicate whether an Inducement was sent to Attorney Philips on May 29, 1991, along with the other two documents. Moreover, there was no testimony concerning this document. The Inducement is in the nature of a personal guarantee. The unexecuted Inducement calls for Basinger's signature. It provides the following:

> Basinger is familiar with the agreement between Main Line and Mighty Wind and consents to its execution. She will look solely to Mighty Wind for payment. If Mighty Wind breaches the agreement, Main Line may join her in the action without first being required to exhaust remedies against Mighty Wind. If Mighty Wind ceases to exist, Basinger is deemed to be employed directly by Main Line.

On June 10, 1991, Main Line learned that Basinger was not going to act in "Boxing Helena."

Procedural Background

On June 21, 1991, Main Line filed a complaint naming as defendants Basinger and Mighty Wind. The complaint alleged that defendants breached an oral and a written contract to provide Basinger's acting services. The complaint contained no alter ego allegations.[5]

---

5. The complaint also alleged that ICM induced the breach of contract. The trial court granted ICM's motion for nonsuit based upon the manager's privilege. At the

During trial, the parties submitted proposed jury instructions. Defendants argued that since Mighty Wind was a corporation, it was entitled to instructions separate from Basinger. They asserted that Main Line had the burden to prove defendants were not distinct. Basinger argued that she was not a party to any contract. In opposition, Main Line argued no distinction existed between Basinger and Mighty Wind for purposes of this case. Main Line asserted that since the bargained-for services were Basinger's, if Basinger breached, then both Basinger and Mighty Wind breached. With no basis in the record, Main Line contended that Mighty Wind was simply a "tax configuration." Main Line did not assert an alter ego theory. The trial court refused to instruct the jury as requested by defendants. Basinger moved for a directed verdict, arguing that if there was any contract, it was with Mighty Wind and not her. The motion was denied.

The trial court formulated its own special verdicts based upon the earlier discussions. The special verdicts consistently referred to "Basinger and/or Mighty Wind." The trial court requested that the parties examine these special verdicts. It reminded defendants that previously the trial court had requested evidence of the separate existence of Mighty Wind and noted that the "only" evidence which made the two defendants different was that Mighty Wind was a corporation. In an offer of proof, defendants indicated they could prove Mighty Wind was a corporation. The trial court found, as a matter of law, that the jury could not find a "separation between the two." When defendants mentioned there might be due process problems in disregarding the corporation, Main Line indicated it was willing to take that risk. The trial court concluded that everything done by Mighty Wind was done by Basinger. The special verdicts prepared by the trial court did not separate Basinger from Mighty Wind. Thus, for example, Question No. 1 of the special verdicts asked, "Did Kim Basinger and/or Mighty Wind enter into an oral contract with Main Line for Ms. Basinger to perform acting services in the movie 'Boxing Helena?'" (Emphasis in original.) Question No. 2 was almost identical, except that it asked if there was a written contract. Question No. 4 inquired, "Did Ms. Basinger and/or Mighty Wind breach a contract with Main Line?" and Question No. 5 asked whether "the breach of contract by Ms. Basinger and/or Mighty Wind [was] the legal cause of damage or harm to Main Line?" The damage questions also contained the phrase "Basinger and/or Mighty Wind."

The jury concluded that "Basinger and/or Mighty Wind" had entered into both an oral and a written contract, had breached the contract and had caused damages to Main Line in the amount of $7,421,694. The jury further determined that "Basinger and/or Mighty Wind" had denied in bad faith the existence of the contract, and awarded an additional $1.5 million in damages. The jury did not award any punitive damages.

end of the trial, the trial court awarded ICM $24,203.69 in costs. Main Line has not   appealed from this judgment.

In post-trial proceedings, defendants once again argued Mighty Wind and Basinger had separate legal existence. Defendants' motions for new trial and for judgment notwithstanding the verdict were denied, except insofar as the trial court struck the $1.5 million award for bad faith denial of the contract as duplicative. Upon motion, the trial court awarded Main Line $713,522.05 in attorney's fees and costs. A $8,135,216.05 judgment was entered against Basinger and/or Mighty Wind.

Defendants appeal from the judgment.

DISCUSSION

On appeal, " '[a] verdict should be interpreted so as to uphold it and to give it the effect intended by the jury, as well as one consistent with the law and the evidence.' " All–West Design, Inc. v. Boozer, 183 Cal.App.3d 1212, 1223 (1986). However, reversal is required (Cal. Const., art VI, § 13) when a verdict is hopelessly ambiguous * * * or contains an incorrect statement of the law which probably confused and misled the jury. * * * We do not interpret the ambiguous verdict of a jury when it cannot be determined from the verdict which party the jury found to be liable. If the jury's verdict leaves open the possibility of numerous conclusions as to liability, we will not draw our own conclusions from the facts if contrary factual conclusions can be reached. The result of an ambiguous jury verdict as to liability is a failure of the jury to make a finding on a critical issue. * * * Such a failure requires reversal. * * *

The term "and/or" is inherently ambiguous. * * * It "gives rise to multiple meanings; specifically, it can mean either or it can mean both." (Dinkins v. American National Ins. Co., 92 Cal.App.3d 222, 232 (1979) * * *. Only if the options are synonymous is there no ambiguity. (*Ibid.*)

Corporations are separate legal entities, distinct from their shareholders and officers. * * * They are formed for numerous business reasons, including as a shield from liability and for tax purposes. The statutory scheme which provides for the formation of corporations affords such entities privileges of separability. * * * The liability of a corporation does not automatically attach to its shareholders, the owners of the corporation. * * * This is so even if the stock of the corporation is wholly owned by a single person. * * * Rather, a corporation sues in its own name, is sued in its own name, transacts business separate from its shareholders and enters into contracts on its own accord. By their very nature, corporations have a separate identity from their owners and corporate obligations are not obligations of the shareholders. * * * Where it appears on the face of a contract that it is entered into on behalf of the corporation "by" its agent, the corporation is liable and the agent is not. * * *

Individual professionals incorporate for a variety of reasons. * * * Such personal service corporations are entitled to the same separability of identity as are other corporations. (Cf. Laughton v. Comr. (1939) 40 B.T.A. 101 [actor].) Performers' "loan-out" companies are not sham entities. (*Ibid.*) As a general rule, the sole shareholder of a personal service corporation is not liable for the obligations of the corporation. (*Ibid.*) The applicability of this general rule to sole shareholder personal service corporations is evidenced by the fact that for public policy reasons, the Legislature has determined that certain licensed or certified professionals who do business through a professional service corporation,[6] such as physicians and attorneys, may be personally responsible for professional malpractice. (Corp. Code, § 13404.5, subd. (c).) The Legislature has recognized the separate nature of these corporations, but has determined that for some types of corporations and some types of liability, the corporate shield should not be available. No such special rules apply to the contractual obligations of an actress's "loan-out" corporation.

Typically, claimants reach shareholders for corporate debts by asserting the shareholder is the alter ego of the corporation, the corporate form should be disregarded and the corporate veil should be pierced. * * * In this case, however, Main Line expressly rejected both at trial and on appeal any reliance on an alter ego theory. Accordingly, Main Line presented no evidence on many key alter ego factors, such as the number or identity of the shareholders, directors or officers of the corporation, the extent of its capitalization or its compliance with corporate form and formalities.

We conclude the "and/or" special verdicts in this case in connection with the contractual obligations of Basinger and Mighty Wind are prejudicially ambiguous and require reversal. "And/or" as used in the special verdicts may mean Basinger only, Mighty Wind only or both Basinger and Mighty Wind. Mighty Wind is a separate corporate entity, distinct from Basinger. The record does not disclose whether Basinger is the sole shareholder of Mighty Wind or an officer or director of the corporation. In the absence of alter ego findings, Mighty Wind and Basinger are not synonymous. Unless Mighty Wind is the alter ego of Basinger, she is not liable for the corporate obligations.

Although there is substantial evidence to support findings that both Basinger and Mighty Wind entered into and breached an oral contract with Main Line, the facts do not compel only this conclusion. The jury could have concluded that the contract was entered into only with Mighty Wind. Discussions took place at Mighty Wind's offices and the parties discussed that the agreement would be between Main Line and Mighty Wind. The written, but unexecuted agreements, contemplate an agreement with the corporation only. The "deal memos" evidenced an intent that the contract be entered into with Mighty Wind. The execution copy of the Acting Service Agreement called for the corporation to enter into the agreement; the signature line specified "Mighty Wind Productions, Inc. By Kim Basinger," an agent designation. No individual signature line was provided for Basinger. The record also includes the

6. Professional service corporations are corporations engaged in rendering professional services in a single profession which may be rendered only pursuant to a license, certificate or registration. (Corp. Code, § 13401.)

separate Inducement, which was apparently to be signed by Basinger individually. However, the Inducement is a separate contract in the nature of a personal guarantee and the record contains no testimony concerning the Inducement. There is no evidence concerning the custom in the industry with regard to Inducements. Neither the Acting Service Agreement nor the Producer's Standard Terms and Conditions makes reference to the Inducement.

The jury could also have concluded that the contract was entered into only with Basinger. Basinger personally discussed the project with Lynch; she gave her agents the authority to bind her in a contract; the parties consistently referred to Basinger's performance; and the written documents always included Basinger's personal obligations.

Further, the jury could have concluded that both Basinger and Mighty Wind entered into a contract. Basinger's participation may have been on her own behalf, as well as on behalf of her corporation. The corporation may have been used by Basinger only as a tax vehicle; for purposes of this contract, she and the corporation both expected to be bound. The agreement was originally between Basinger and Main Line, and Mighty Wind may have been added as a party to the contract as an accommodation to Basinger.

The special verdicts contain no finding as to the party or parties who entered into the oral contract. The form of the special verdicts prevented the jury from performing its obligation to determine the separate existence of Mighty Wind and Basinger. On the record before us, the jury may have concluded Basinger personally entered into the contract. It also may have concluded Mighty Wind entered into the contract. In addition, the jury may have concluded that both Basinger and Mighty Wind entered into the contract. Had the jury concluded that only Mighty Wind entered into the contract, only Mighty Wind would be liable for breach of the contract. Even though the acting services were to be performed by Basinger, if the contract was only with Mighty Wind, then, when Basinger failed to perform, Main Line's remedy would be against Mighty Wind.

Although Basinger's services were key to the contract, the issue is the party or parties responsible if she fails to perform. If the contract is only with Mighty Wind, then only Mighty Wind can be liable for a breach of the contract. We cannot ascertain from the record whether the jury found that Basinger entered into the contract, Mighty Wind entered into the contract or they both entered into the contract. Thus, the jury verdicts fail to render a finding on a key factual issue, and the judgment must be reversed.

Defendants have requested that we not only reverse the judgment against them, but also order judgment entered in their behalf. They contend Main Line precipitated the ambiguity in the special verdicts, invited the error of the trial court in drafting the special verdicts and thereby waived a retrial. As a general rule, a reversal on the basis of improper special verdicts is unqualified. (Byrum v. Brand, *supra*, 219 Cal.App.3d at p. 939.) Such an unqualified reversal "puts the case 'at large,' as if no trial had ever taken place." (Ibid.) Upon filing of the remittitur, the case may be retried. Ordinarily, an unqualified reversal is warranted even where the plaintiff-respondent has to some extent invited or waived the error. * * * In certain exceptional circumstances, however, appellate courts have applied to a respondent the doctrines of waiver and invited error, which are typically applied to appellants, resulting in a reversal without a new trial. * * *

Such a result is unwarranted in this case. In Myers, we struck a punitive damage award in favor of plaintiff-respondent because no tort finding was made by the jury. The jury had rendered a decision on a contract cause of action and not a tort cause of action. Unlike Myers, however, in this case, we do not have the total absence of a finding on a severable issue. Rather, the special verdicts are ambiguous on issues which are not be severable.

DISPOSITION

The judgment is reversed. Main Line is to bear defendants' costs on appeal.

Notes

1. Personal service contracts have always raised problems, particularly when to hold someone to a contract may be considered as running afoul of the 13th Amendment to the Constitution, which prohibits slavery. Nevertheless, is an actor better off honoring a commitment than wincing on a deal? The time it would have taken to fulfill her commitment to Mainline was probably far less than what she spent defending this lawsuit.

2. After Basinger lost this lawsuit, she declared bankruptcy, forcing her to sell for $1 million the town of Braselton, Georgia, which she had acquired in 1989 for $20 million. Basinger's career, which went into a slump along with her finances after this lawsuit, was revitalized only after she took a role in a small independent film called *L.A. Confidential*. That film, which also starred the relatively unknown Russell Crowe, won her an Academy Award for best supporting actress. She eventually settled her dispute with Mainline Cinema. For more information on actress Kim Basinger, see her biographical sketch at http://www.konary.com/kim/bio.html.

3. Carl Mazzocone, the producer of *Boxing Helena*, graduated from Ithaca College's School of Communications with a degree in Cinema Studies and Business Management in 1981, and began working in television production. In 1982, he served as location manager on his first feature film, *Jaws 3–D*. Mazzocone's credits include *Starman*, *Ruthless People*, and *Dumb and Dumberer: When Harry Met Lloyd*. The following is an account of his experience producing *Boxing Helena*.

Carl Mazzocone
Producing Boxing Helena

Copyright © 2004 by Carl Mazzocone.

After graduation, I worked on seven feature films in physical production, prior to starting a production company called Main Line Pictures, Inc. in October 1987 to pursue my career as a creative producer. Our little company of five employees worked diligently to find a good screenplay and get a movie made in order to gain credibility in this industry town. It's hard when you are independent because studios and agencies want nothing to do with you. You're an unknown and untested entity. We started to build some credibility through relationships I had established while working in production and from hiring a development executive away from CBS theatrical.

Our break came when CAA's [Creative Artists Agency] young turk, Jay Maloney, a right hand to Mike Ovitz, sent us a script called *Boxing Helena* in order to find someone to finance and produce the first film of Jennifer Lynch, the daughter of David Lynch, a young writer and want-to-be director. This was very enticing because not only was *Boxing Helena* a unique script, it was well written, not commercial, an art film that would undoubtedly receive lots of attention. The fact that CAA was willing to help us cast the film was extremely valuable.

With CAA's help we approached Madonna for the lead role. She wanted to be in our little movie with one contingency. Madonna provided us with a list of the male co-stars she wanted to work with. On Madonna's short list were actors like William Hurt and Daniel Day–Lewis, to name a few. We ultimately decided not to pursue the actors on Madonna's list and sought other male actors we liked for the lead male role. Madonna dropped out of the picture when we didn't get an actor on her list. We contacted Ed Harris and got him interested in the part. We also started meeting with other actresses. When Madonna heard that Ed Harris had committed to the film, she started calling us in hope of returning to the picture. Virtually, every morning for over a week when we checked our office answering machine in our humble 1000 square-foot office, we received messages from Madonna. In one of the messages she conveyed something to the effect of: "every time I read this screenplay it's as if you (Jennifer Lynch, the writer) put a tape recorder under my bed at night." It was very enticing for an independent company to have a star like that, a music icon, wanting to be in our movie.

We negotiated a "Deal Memo" with Madonna through her CAA agent and began pre-selling the foreign rights to raise production funds to finance the movie. Main Line Pictures' investors agreed to bridge any shortfall in funds. We were off and running and the picture commenced pre-production just two years after we opened our doors for business. Three weeks into pre-production, just about four weeks away from commencement of principal photography, I got a phone call from Madonna's agent who said Madonna was dropping out of the movie. Her agent indicated that she cited a multilevel problem which she couldn't discuss with me. That was it. Nobody at CAA would talk to us and we had to shut down pre-production. Our nightmare had just begun; pre-production had cost us $300,000; we were contractually obligated to refund the money we had raised from the International sub-distributors since Madonna's failure to act in the picture was considered a default. My partner and I now needed to find a way to pay the crew and our vendors, and a way to convince Ed Harris not to leave the crumbling picture.

Two days after we were confident there was no way to resurrect Madonna's involvement in the picture, we went out to all the leading ladies in town, and we generated interest from Kim Basinger. Madonna quit in December of 1990 and we had a meeting with Kim Basinger on January 18, 1991. It was a very successful meeting. She met with Jennifer Lynch several more times, and then committed to star in *Boxing Helena*. Kim Basinger told us that we would have to wait six months since she had also committed to star in *Cool World* and in *Final Analysis* with Richard Gere. The Deal Memo we had negotiated with CAA for Madonna seemed to be worthless. The agents use this way of business as a one-way street to manipulate deals for their talent. One minute you have a deal, and the next minute you don't. In order not to get stuck like this again, I realized that we needed to have a binding agreement. I immediately pursued a long form acting service agreement with Kim Basinger's representatives. It took five months of back and forth to negotiate the long form with her lawyers and agents. On the seventh draft, all the deal points had been agreed to by her. During the time we negotiated Kim Basinger's deal, we re-sold the international rights to *Boxing Helena* at a much greater profit.

We were approximately two weeks away from principal photography and in full fledge pre-production, which includes finalizing other cast deals, building sets, purchasing wardrobe and set dressing. Our pre-production costs were approaching $1.4 million, including the pay or play offers to other actors. Out of the blue, I received a call from Kim Basinger's lawyer telling us she wasn't going to do the movie. I was informed at that time that Kim had changed agents and her new agent hated the movie and talked her out of doing the film. I immediately called Basinger's new agent at ICM, Guy McIllwayne, who informed me that when he read the script he hated it and threw the script across the room. In the trial records, he said he called Basinger on the phone and forbid her to do the movie. Then McIllwayne allegedly called Julie Phillips, Ms. Basinger's lawyer at Bloom, Dekom and asked if there was a deal in place. Ms Phillips stated that there was no deal in place, so Kim Basinger simply walked away from her commitment to star in the film.

The walls went up like lightning; all the lawyers got involved. I was never able to get through to Kim Basinger directly to try and salvage her involvement in the picture. Once again I found myself out in the cold. With no actress, the foreign financing commitments crumbled because we had negated our contractual obligations to deliver actress Kim Basinger. It was like building a house of cards in a windstorm.

Once again we had to return all of the money to the foreign financers because we were in breach of our international agreements. I found myself in the uncomfortable position now of not only owing $300,000 from Madonna's involvement, but also an additional $1.4 million to cover the pre-production expenses incurred prior to the time Basinger decided to walk away from the deal. I didn't think I could survive this. I thought for sure I would have to turn to corporate and personal bankruptcy. I just couldn't believe it—how did I get here? I couldn't believe the people in this town and how they operated.

When I was first looking for guidance, I sought advice from the successful producers I knew who unanimously suggested I seek legal action. When I talked to managers and agents about it, they said I couldn't beat an actor. Allegedly MGM had at one time sued Raquel Welch and she ended up winning. Nobody in town sues actors because once they get up on the stand they can do what comes naturally, act.

I don't like conflict; however, I also believe in justice and equality. I felt very little hesitation in this situation to pursue any avenue to level the playing field. My opponents were the most powerful agents and lawyers in town. They were all untouchable—hiding behind their walled fortresses. Main Line Pictures, Inc. filed a legal complaint seeking $5 million for breech of contract and bad faith denial against Ms. Basinger and her agency ICM. Before reaching the first day of trial we spent another million dollars in discovery.

During the first week of the trial we intently studied the jury because they held our destiny in their hands. We had a cross sampling of average Americans: a librarian, a Mobil oil worker, a mortgage broker, housewives, little old ladies and retired men. In the beginning of the trial, none of the men of the jury could take their eyes off of Kim Basinger because she is such a beautiful woman. None of the women could keep their eyes off of Alec Baldwin. We realized that in some way celebrities are the equivalent of American royalty. Luckily the trial was long enough to take the novelty of the celebrity away. Kim Basinger's own testimony dismantled her star status. At one point under direct examination from my attorney, Kim was asked, "At what time can you breach an agreement?" Ms. Basinger answered, "anytime I want to." That was a pretty unattractive answer. On one level, we (society) all realize that we all have to live by the same rules. Celebrities believe they live in a parallel universe above the law and they have been known to get away with murder. At the end, the jury found that not only did Main Line Pictures have an oral agreement, but we had the written agreement as well. The written agreement existed due to the highly negotiated long form acting service agreement that went between lawyers seven times until execution copies were created. The jury awarded us a verdict almost double what we asked for, $9.8 million, which was later reduced by the judge to $8.1 million.

I find that the legal system is much like a tree. The roots of the tree are your discovery process; the trunk of the tree is your trial; and the branches at the top of the tree are all the avenues the losing party can travel in order to avoid paying what they owe you. You've got to have financial longevity to chase down a defendant who wants to spend money in order to hide from facing their inevitable fate. So after the trial, instead of negotiating a settlement or filing a bond, Kim Basinger filed for Chapter 11 reorganization bankruptcy protection. We engaged new bankruptcy attorneys and started our new education of the rules of bankruptcy law. This cost us another million plus dollars in legal fees to reach a conclusion. It started with Kim Basinger trying to negotiate a reorganization plan in Chapter 11 and then at the eleventh hour (no pun intended) Ms. Basinger made a very calculated move to liquidation under Chapter 7. By the time she had traveled down every branch available in Chapter 7, Ms. Basinger was successful in having the verdict reversed on appeal, which may have been the best thing that could have happened to us. We were reversed based on a technicality in how the verdict form presented to the jury was phrased. Kim Basinger owns a corporation entitled, Mighty Wind Productions. Mighty Wind Productions primarily serves as a loan out company. It is kind of like a temporary tax shelter. As a loan out company, it lends Kim Basinger's acting services to a film. Therefore, studios and producers pay all compensation to Mighty Wind rather than directly to Basinger; in turn Ms Basinger avoids paying the immediate withholding of both state and federal income tax from any compensation received. She can use her gross income and pay her taxes later. This is a common procedure in Hollywood.

At trial, we believed we established that her loan out company was an alter ego corporation. We believed we successfully pierced the corporate veil. We argued that if Kim Basinger didn't perform acting services, Mighty Wind could not fulfill the agreement. How could Mighty Wind act in the movie? Still we were reversed on appeal based on one question asked the jury: "[d]id Kim Basinger and/or Mighty Wind Productions have an obligation to render services in *Boxing Helena*?" We were reversed because the Court of Appeals said the question as phrased did not afford both Kim Basinger and Mighty Wind due process because it did not distinguish between them. The jury question should have been split into two questions, one asking whether Kim Basinger had an obligation to render services in Boxing Helena and another asking the same thing about Mighty Wind.

The great thing was that everything had already been entered into evidence in the court record, so if the case needed to be retried, the other side couldn't recant their stories or testimony. Court TV had just been invented and the last place I believe Kim Basinger wanted to be was the star of Court TV. That really helped to facilitate a settlement prior to the commencement of a second trial.

The New York Times did an article on how the bankruptcy courts were being manipulated. They did is a scathing expose of Kim Basinger and how she had used bankruptcy to escape paying the judgment. They showed a picture of a town Kim Basinger owned called Brazelton, Georgia, and the fact that she pays $7,500.00 per month in pet care. The very next day, Alec Baldwin was on the tonight show with David Letterman doing damage control for Kim. Certainly I can't get on Letterman. I remember an interview Kim Basinger gave to Connie Chung. When asked about the lawsuit, Kim Basinger referred to me as "the devil." Even during the trial, I was shocked at the privileges provided to Kim Basinger by our judge. The judge allowed Ms. Basinger to use the judge's private bathroom and the judge's side entrance. We are all supposed to be equal in the eyes of the law, but star power reaches deep into this society. That's not fair and that's not right, but that's how we treat celebrities in America.

Many influential and powerful people within the entertainment industry have told me that there should be a bronze statue of me on Hollywood Boulevard for what I've done for this town. Dozens of managers, agents, and lawyers have confessed that they never had the ability to keep an actor contractually bound before the Basinger Lawsuit. Since my lawsuit, many studios, production companies and producers use my case to seek restitution from actors who have quit their movies. *Main Line Pictures vs. Kimila Basinger* is a milestone. It cost me millions in legal fees and six years of my life and it burned my career. If it is to be my only contribution to the film business, then that was my destiny. It's a shame, because I feel I have so much more to offer. In the final analysis, I did not profit from that lawsuit. My investors were paid back their money, the lawyers were paid their fees, and at the end of the day, I was left with nothing but a lesson on how Hollywood operates and my attempt to change it.

The trial had a tremendous effect on my career. The town is controlled by the three major talent agencies: ICM, William Morris, and CAA. I had sued ICM on the theory that it had had induced the breach of contract. I knew I was burning my bridges there. After the trial was over, Kim Basinger sought representation at CAA and Alec Baldwin went to the other big agency. The flow of material from the agencies to Main Line Pictures almost stopped. If you are an agency or studio, who are you going to align yourself with, a young producer who just produced his first movie or two big stars? My days at Main Line were made impossible. Since *Boxing Helena*, Main Line Pictures produced one more picture called *Body Count* starring Forest Whitaker, Ving Rhames and Linda Fiorientino. I have been surviving as a line producer. Main Line Pictures is an active corporation and still has a few writers developing pictures for it. I can't let it die. I will keep it going until the day I retire to prove that they couldn't put me out of business. I'm hoping that enough time has passed that my new round of projects will be able to reemerge me as a hot producer, with the same momentum I had when Madonna was calling us up begging to be in our picture.

Note

1. Are Basinger's lawyer and agent partially responsible for the dispute that arose between Basinger and Main Line? The agent forbade her to do the picture and the lawyer went along. Prior to this lawsuit, Basinger took an imperial actress approach to her career, believing that she could break a contract anytime she wanted to. How should lawyers, agents, and managers go about disabusing actors and actresses of similar beliefs? Would it be sufficient to hand them a copy of *Main Line Pictures v. Basinger*?

B. CONTRACTS TO PROTECT REPUTATION

PREMINGER v. COLUMBIA PICTURES

New York Supreme Court, 1966.
49 Misc.2d 363, 267 N.Y.S.2d 594.

ARTHUR G. KLEIN, Judge.

The interesting question presented for decision is the right of a *[ISSUE]* producer, in the absence of specific contractual provision, to prevent, by injunction, minor cuts in his motion picture, when shown on television, and the usual breaks for commercials.

The litigation involves the production of the motion picture *Anatomy of a Murder*.

The complaint alleges that plaintiff Preminger is a producer and director of motion pictures, including the motion picture involved; and plaintiff Carlyle Productions, Inc., a California corporation, was the owner of all rights to the picture, and Carlyle Productions, a limited New York partnership, its assignee; that Carlyle Productions, Inc., entered into a series of agreements with Columbia Pictures Corporation between 1956 and 1959, which are collectively referred to as the contract, copies of which are annexed to the complaint.

Defendant Columbia and defendant Screen Gems, Inc., its subsidiary, the complaint continues, have licensed over 100 television stations to exhibit the motion picture on television, and those license agreements purport to give the licensees the right to cut, to eliminate portions of the picture, and to interrupt the remainder of the picture for commercials and other extraneous matter. *[gives licensees the right to cut + eliminate portions of the picture]*

Unless enjoined, the complaint asserts, defendants will (a) detract from the artistic merit of *Anatomy of a Murder*; (b) damage Preminger's reputation; (c) cheapen and tend to destroy *Anatomy's* commercial value; (d) injure plaintiffs in the conduct of their business; and (e) falsely represent to the public that the film shown is Preminger's film.

It is then alleged, and not denied, that *Anatomy* is one of a very few motion pictures with a rating of AA–1; that it has been licensed in blocks of 60 to 300 pictures; and that the others are artistically and commercially inferior to *Anatomy*.

Finally it is alleged that defendants have allocated an unfairly and unreasonably low share of license fees to *Anatomy*. This allegation is denied.

All these acts are described as willful and wanton breaches of the contract with Carlyle as owner and Preminger as producer.* * *

[T]he only question before the court in this proceeding is the plaintiffs' right to a permanent injunction.

I

The plaintiffs plant themselves upon article VIII of the contract, which provides: "You [Carlyle] shall have the right to make the final cutting and editing of the Picture, but you shall in good faith consider recommendations and suggestions with respect thereto made by us [Columbia]; nevertheless, you shall have final approval thereof, provided however that notwithstanding the foregoing, in the event that cutting or re-editing is required in order to meet censorship requirements and you shall fail or refuse to comply therewith, then we shall have the right to cut and edit the Picture in order to meet censorship requirements without obligation on our part to challenge the validity of any rule, order, regulation or requirement of any national, state or local censorship authority." The import of the paragraph is that plaintiffs have the right to make the final "cutting and editing" of the picture; giving the defendants the right to make suggestions, only.

This article must be read, however, in juxtaposition with article X of the contract, which provides as follows: "The rights herein granted, without limiting the generality of the foregoing, shall include and embrace all so-called 'theatrical' as well as 'non-theatrical' rights in the Picture (as those terms are commonly understood in the motion picture industry); and shall include the right to use film of any and all gauges. You hereby give and grant to us throughout the entire world the exclusive and irrevocable right during the term herein specified to project, exhibit, reproduce, transmit and perform, and authorize and license others to project, exhibit, reproduce, transmit and perform, the picture and prints thereof by television, and in any other manner, and by any other means, method or device whatsoever, whether mechanical, electrical or otherwise, and whether now known or hereafter conceived or created."

This article, it will be noted, which contains the specific grant of television rights, makes no reference to "cutting and editing".

In these circumstances the court is inclined to the view that the right to the "final" cutting and editing, reserved to the plaintiffs, is limited to the original or theatrical production of the picture, and not to showings on television; and that as to such showings, in the absence of specific contractual provision, the parties will be deemed to have adopted the custom prevailing in the trade or industry.

This view is confirmed by the authorities and fortified by the evidence.

II

We begin with the proposition that the law is not so rigid, even in the absence of contract, as to leave a party without protection against publication of a garbled version of his work. This, as pointed out by Frank, J., concurring in *Granz v. Harris* (198 F. 2d 585, 589 [C. A. 2d, 1952] is not novel doctrine.

The court "appreciates that the failure of the community . . . to protect its gifted men of letters led to tragedies which comprise scars in the history of civilization". (Geller, J., in *Seroff v. Simon & Schuster*, 6 Misc 2d 383, 386–387 [N. Y. County, 1957], affd. 12 A D 2d 475 [1st Dept., 1960].)

And in *Granz* (*supra*) the United States Court of Appeals for the Second Circuit held that publication of a truncated version of plaintiffs' phonograph recording should be enjoined (pp. 587–588).

In the case at bar, however, the contract must serve as a guide to the intention of the parties.

A

Thus, where the parties have particularized the terms of a contract, an apparently inconsistent general statement to a different effect must yield. (*Petty v. Fidelity Union Trust Co.*, 238 App. Div. 96, 99–100 [2d Dept., 1933], affd. 262 N. Y. 690 [1933]; 1 Restatement, Contracts, § 236, subd. [c]; N. Y. Contracts Law, § 818.) Therefore, the clause in this contract, general in its terms, giving plaintiffs the right to "finally" cut and edit as to the original production of the motion picture, must yield to the specific clause with respect to television showing, which contained no such right.

B

So it is, too, that in the construction of a contract, weight will be given to the custom prevailing in the trade to which it refers. (*Smith v. Clews*, 114 N. Y. 190 [1889].)

This brings us to a review of the evidence, on which, of course, the burden of proof rests on the plaintiffs.

C

At the trial, extensive testimony was presented by both sides with respect to the normal customs prevailing in the television and motion picture industries as to the significance of the right to "final cut".

A review of the testimony demonstrates that, at least for the past 15 years, the right to interrupt the exhibition of a motion picture on television for commercial announcements and to make minor deletions to accommodate time segment requirements or to excise those portions which might be deemed, for various reasons, objectionable, has consistently been considered a normal and essential part of the exhibition of motion pictures on television.

Implicit in the grant of television rights is the privilege to cut and edit. (*Autry v. Republic Prods.*, 213 F. 2d 667, 669 [C. A. 9, 1954], cert. den. 348 U.S. 858 [1954].)

D

No proof has been adduced that this cutting and editing would be done in such a manner as to interfere with the picture's story line.

The licensing agreements provide: "Licensee shall telecast each print, as delivered by Distributor, in its entirety. However, Licensee may make such minor cuts or elimination as are necessary to conform to time segment requirements or to the orders of any duly authorized public censorship authority and may add commercial material at the places and of the lengths indicated by Distributor, but under no circumstances shall Licensee delete the copyright notice or the credits incorporated in the pictures as delivered by the Distributor, provided, however, in no event may the insertion of any commercial material adversely affect the artistic or pictorial quality of the picture or materially interfere with its continuity."

Defendants' witnesses, Lacey of WCBS, Howard of WNBC and Gilbert of WABC, testified with respect to the practices customarily prevailing throughout the television industry. Plaintiffs' witnesses did not controvert the testimony concerning the customary practices in the trade with regard to interruptions for commercials, and minor cuts. As a matter of fact, Sherwin, one of plaintiffs' witnesses, the program director of KHJ, Los Angeles, testified, as had defendants' witnesses, that his station had never purchased any motion picture without the right to make interruptions as well as minor cuts. Whether or not, in an isolated instance, a picture was exhibited with less than the customary number of commercials is not determinative of the issue. We are concerned not with what might have happened in some rare instance but instead with what was the common practice and custom at the time the parties herein signed their contract.

Thus, Villante, a vice-president of the Batten, Barton, Durstine & Osborn advertising agency, described a program known as the "Schaefer Award Theatre" which is handled by his advertising agency. This is a late show program in which feature films are shown without cuts, and with only four interruptions for commercial announcements. Villante acknowledged repeatedly that the Schaefer program was unique. In one instance, he stated, a picture called "The Nun Story" was shown on this same program without any interruptions for commercials whatsoever. He further testified that the purpose of deviating from usual industry practice in the case of this one program was not out of any concern for the rights of the producer, but rather as a public relations device to contribute to the public image of the Schaefer Company, and pursuant to agreement with said sponsor.

With respect to the expression "final cut", sufficient testimony was adduced to indicate that this phrase, as used in article VIII of the contract, relates only to a phase in the production of the picture for theatrical showing and has no relation to the interruptions and minor cuts here under discussion. Even plaintiffs' own witnesses identified the "final cutting and editing" of a picture as the last stage in its production *for theatrical exhibition*. (Emphasis supplied.)

Final cut

III

Although plaintiffs consistently refer to the practice of interrupting and making minor cuts as "mutilation", their own witnesses have conceded that the minor cuts customarily made in a television exhibition of a picture have such a minimal impact upon its over-all effect that these are rarely even noticed.

Undisputed is the fact that not a single television station has ever failed to insist upon the right to interrupt for commercials. Similarly unrefuted is defendants' proof to the effect that no station ever purchased a motion picture without reserving to itself the right to interrupt for commercials and to make minor cuts.

IV

Plaintiff Preminger admitted that when he signed the agreement for *Anatomy of a Murder*", he was aware that the practice of the television industry was to interrupt motion pictures for commercials and to make minor cuts. Aware of this practice, plaintiffs at the time the instant contract was signed nevertheless did not specifically provide for conditions other than those known to them to be prevalent in the industry.

Two contracts between Preminger and United Artists Corporation were received in evidence. These were contracts pertaining to "Man With The Golden Arm" and "The Moon Is Blue", the last two pictures produced by Preminger prior to *Anatomy of a Murder*, which he made for Columbia. In both the contract for "The Moon Is Blue" and the contract for "Man With The Golden Arm", clauses appeared which demonstrate that Preminger was aware of the prevailing practice in the television industry with respect to interrupting motion pictures for commercials and making minor cuts therein for normal television purposes. These contracts further show that when Preminger desired to prevent television distribution in the normal manner, he so provided.

In the contract between the Carlyle corporation and United Artists Corporation, dated December 20, 1954, for "Man With The Golden Arm", it was expressly provided that United Artists' right "to make such changes, additions, alterations, cuts, interpolations and eliminations as may be required for the distribution of the picture in television" should be subject to the approval of producer.

In similar fashion, the contract with United Artists Corporation with respect to "The Moon Is Blue", dated April 28, 1952, provided that United Artists' right "to make such changes, additions, alterations, cuts, interpolations, and eliminations as may be required for the distribution of the picture in television" should be "subject to the approval of Producer or its sales representative".

Both Preminger and United Artists were aware that granting the producer this right of approval was tantamount to giving him a veto power over ultimate television distribution of the film, for in other provisions of both of the above contracts it was expressly recognized that television distribution was not to take place without the producer's prior approval.

Plaintiffs' entry into the instant contract which failed to contain such a clause may be considered by the court as evidence of the parties' intention. * * *

V

Should a viewer resent the fact that the film is interrupted too often for commercials, and assuredly many do, this resentment would be directed at the station or the sponsor of the program. It is difficult to conceive how such resentment would be directed at the film's producer or director.

So standardized has the practice of interrupting films for commercials become, that guidelines have been established in the television industry as to the maximum number of commercials regarded as acceptable in a given time period. * * *

VII

The criterion for the determination of what the defendants were likely to do with respect to interrupting and cutting the subject film, in the absence of a specific contractual arrangement, was not what plaintiffs might disapprove of or dislike but, rather, what was the normal custom and practice in the industry.

The issues in the case, in the court's view, are therefore issues of law: i.e., (1) whether plaintiffs may thwart the making of minor cuts or interpolations in the absence of specific contractual provision; the court finds the answer to this question to be in the negative; and (2) whether, under this contract, in the light of the custom in the trade, plaintiffs left to the station masters the right to use their judgment and exercise their discretion, instead of plaintiffs', as to which minor cuts, eliminations, and interpolations are appropriate. In view of the variety of stations, localities, audiences, and commercials, the court answers this question in the affirmative.

The running time of the full motion picture is 161 minutes. The brochure for WABC–TV advertised the picture to potential sponsors as a 100–minute feature. The station master, however, testified, and the court credits his testimony, that this was a mistake; that it was never intended to permit any such extensive cutting. This applies as well to the asserted cutting of the picture to 53 minutes. Obviously such cuts would not be minor and indeed could well be described as mutilation. Should such "mutilation" occur in the future, plaintiffs may make application to this court for injunctive or other relief against such violation as they may be advised. (*Autry v. Republic Prods.*, 213 F. 2d 667, 669: ["We can conceive that some such cutting and editing could result in emasculating the motion pictures so they would no longer contain substantially the same motion and dynamic and dramatic qualities which it was the purpose of the artist ... to produce"]; *Granz v. Harris*, 198 F. 2d 585, *supra.*)

Conclusion

On this record, the court holds that plaintiffs have not sustained their burden of establishing their right to injunctive relief.

To the extent, therefore, that the complaint seeks an injunction, it is dismissed; but without prejudice, as heretofore indicated.

In view of the foregoing disposition, the court does not find it necessary to reach the affirmative defenses.

Judgment may be settled accordingly.

AUTRY v. REPUBLIC PRODUCTIONS

United States Court of Appeals, Ninth Circuit, 1954.
213 F.2d 667.

BONE, Circuit Judge.

injunction

Appellant brought this action for an injunction to restrain appellees from exhibiting motion pictures in connection with commercially sponsored or sustaining television broadcasts, where those motion pictures contain appearances of appellant. In its opinion below, 104 F.Supp. 918, the District Court gave judgment to appellees, holding that the contracts between appellees and appellant placed no restrictions upon appellees' use or exhibition of the motion pictures. There were five contracts executed over a period of a dozen years, but the contracts are sufficiently similar that they need not be discussed individually. The trial judge used paragraph 9 of the 1938 contract as an example. That was fair to both parties, and we shall do likewise:

> "9. The producer shall have the right to photograph and/or other-wise reproduce any and all of the acts, poses, plays and appearances of the artist * * * during each employment period, and to record for motion picture purposes the voice of the artist * * * and to repro-duce and/or transmit the same in connection with such acts, poses, plays and appearances as the producer may desire, and the producer shall own solely and exclusively all rights of every kind and charac-ter whatsoever in and to the same perpetually, including the right to use and exploit all or any part of the same in such manner as the producer may desire, and including, as well, the perpetual right to

use the name and likeness of the artist and recordations and reproductions of his voice in connection with the advertising and exploitation thereof. The artist does hereby also grant to the producer the right to make use of and to allow others to make use of his name (in addition to and other than in connection with the acts, poses, plays and appearances for the artist hereunder) for the purpose of advertising, exploiting and/or publicizing photoplays in which the artist appears, as well as the right to make use of and distribute his physical likeness and his voice for the like purpose. * * *.''

This contract, like the contracts in Republic Pictures Corp. v. Rogers, 9 Cir., 213 F.2d 662 contains the descriptive words (1) "acts, poses, plays and appearances" and (2) "name, voice, and likeness." As set forth in our opinion in the Rogers case, we interpret these two sets of words as applying to two different and distinct subject matters. The former refers to the artist's activities or appearances in a motion picture as such; the latter set of words refers to a reproduction of the name, voice or likeness of the artist apart from his activities or appearances in the former, and lacking the motion and dynamic and dramatic qualities contained in motion pictures. There are limitations placed upon appellees' use of the latter, but appellant granted for valuable consideration all rights, unrestricted to appellees in their ownership of the former.

Although appellees unquestionably have the right to cut and edit the motion pictures, and to license others to do the same, we can conceive that some such cutting and editing could result in emasculating the motion pictures so that they would no longer contain substantially the same motion and dynamic and dramatic qualities which it was the purpose of the artist's employment to produce. And although appellees unquestionably have the right to exhibit the motion pictures in connection with or for the purpose of advertising commercial products of all sorts, we can conceive that some such exhibitions could be so "doctored" as to make it appear that the artist actually endorses the products of the programs' sponsors.

The record in this case shows that the appellees proposed to license motion pictures featuring appellant, which said picture would be edited to 53 or 53 1/2 minutes each, in length, thus permitting approximately 7 minutes of advertising in an hour television program. It was this proposed use that was alleged in appellant's complaint and as to which an injunction was asked. The parties stipulated that the License Agreement through which the pictures were proposed to be exhibited, expressly prohibited " * * * any advertising * * * [or] any statements which * * * may be understood to be an endorsement of any sponsor * * * [etc.[by * * * any actor or actress appearing therein * * * or * * * that any such person is connected or associated with * * * Station or any Sponsor. * * * All advertising issued * * * relating to any picture shall give cast and due credits in the same manner * * * as such credits appear in the main title of the respective picture.''

The issue here, is whether appellees should be enjoined from cutting the appellant's performances to approximately 53 minutes, and showing them in connection with commercial advertising over television, pursuant to a License Agreement such as that above quoted. The judgment from which the appeal is taken goes farther than the printed opinion, in that it expressly permits appellees:

> " * * * to cut, edit and otherwise revise and to license others [to do likewise] * * * in any manner, to any length and for any purpose * * *."

Appellant has put in issue the breadth and sweep of this judgment. We agree with appellant that this broad language nullifies all of the clauses in the employment contracts which were introduced therein for the protection of appellant wit reference to the type and quality of photoplays in which he rendered his services. The issue tendered to the trial court was whether appellees could make use of the motion pictures in the manner proposed; the issue was not one of ascertaining what other uses could be made of them, or how far appellees might go. Because this part of the judgment goes beyond the issues presented to the trial court, we hereby disapprove of it. We simply hold that appellees should not be enjoined from cutting the appellant's performances to approximately 53 minutes, and showing them in connection with commercial advertising over television, pursuant to a License Agreement such as that above quoted.

Appellant has raised the issue of unfair competition and the possible application of the Lanham Act, Title 15 U.S.C.A. § § 1125 and 1126. Even aside from the consent which we find was given by appellant to appellees in the contracts, appellant argues that appellees might so alter or emasculate the motion pictures as to render them substantially different from the product which the artist produced. Further, that the exhibition of old pictures which depict appellant in clothes which are no longer in style, and in autos which are no longer modern, could be quite harmful to his modern reputation. As to the latter point, the consent which we have found in the contracts extends to this risk. As to the question of appellees' emasculating the pictures, we have attempted to leave that question open, to be properly presented when and if the occasion arises; we have disapproved that part of the lower court judgment which could be considered authority for such possible abuse, although our disapproval should not be taken as passing on the merits of what was there said. Appellant is not in a position to further urge unfair competition, since it is our interpretation of the contracts that appellant consented to such exhibition of the pictures as is proposed here.

As herein modified, the judgment of the trial court is affirmed.

Notes

1. Throughout the study of Entertainment Law, students will find references to the prevailing standard in the industry that industry insiders

are charged with knowing. In both of these cases, the presumption was that granting television rights included the right to edit for commercials. Should industry standard provisions be spelled out in contracts so that both parties are absolutely clear on the potential changes to their works?

2. How profitable are movie rights to talent? When singing cowboy Gene Autry died of cancer in 1998 at the age of 91, he left an estate valued at $300 million to his second wife, Jackie, the Autry Foundation and the Autry National Center in Los Angeles's Griffith Park. *Walter Scott's Personality Parade,* PARADE MAGAZINE, Oct. 19, 2003, at 2.

C. INSURANCE CONTRACTS ON FILMS

CNA INTERNATIONAL REINSURANCE CO. v. PHOENIX

Florida District Court, 1996.
678 So.2d 378.

JOANOS, Judge.

* * * The case arises from the unfortunate death of the young actor, River Phoenix, originally of Gainesville, Florida, apparently due to an overdose of illegal drugs, before completion of two films, "Dark Blood" and "Interview With the Vampire," in which he had contracted to appear. As a result of the death, the "Dark Blood" project was totally abandoned. "Interview With the Vampire" was completed with another actor replacing Phoenix. CNA and American Casualty, which are both members of the CNA group of insurance companies, had written entertainment package insurance policies covering various aspects of the two productions. After paying the policy holders, CNA and American Casualty became subrogated to the claims the insureds had against the estate.[1]

CNA attempted to state a cause of action for breach of contract against Phoenix's estate, based on an "actor loanout agreement," between Jude Nile, a corporation owned and run by Phoenix and his mother, Arlyn Phoenix, and Scala Productions. The agreement, signed by Phoenix, allegedly included a general obligation not to do anything which would deprive the parties to the agreement of its benefits. CNA further alleged that by deliberately taking illegal drugs in quantities in excess of those necessary to kill a human being, Phoenix deprived the parties of his services and breached his obligation. American Casualty also couched its complaint for declaratory judgment in terms of breach of contract based on an actor loanout agreement between Jude Nile and Geffen Pictures, which gave Geffen the right to loan Phoenix to Time Warner. In addition to the count for breach of contract, the CNA complaint contained a second count, for fraud and misrepresentation, based on an allegedly false representation in a medical certificate, allegedly signed by Phoenix, denying that Phoenix had ever used "LSD, heroin, cocaine, alcohol in excess, or any other narcotics, depressants,

1. CNA paid out over $5.7 million under its policy. American Casualty had not yet paid all claims, and sought a declaratory judgment on the coverage issue. It had paid out $15,000 of approximately $400,000 in claims.

stimulants or psychedelics whether prescribed or not prescribed by a physician.''

The estate moved to dismiss both complaints, contending there could be no cause of action for breach of contract because the personal services contracts were rendered impossible to perform due to the death. The estate further alleged that reliance on any representation in the medical certificate was unreasonable as a matter of law as of the effective dates of the policies, which it contended were in November, 1993, after the widely publicized death on October 31, 1993. After hearings, the trial court granted the motions to dismiss with prejudice.

On appeal, CNA and American Casualty contend that the defense of impossibility of performance does not apply in this case because that doctrine requires that the impossibility be fortuitous and unavoidable, and that it occur through no fault of either party. They contend that because the death occurred from an intentional, massive overdose of illegal drugs, that this is not a situation in which neither party was at fault. The trial court very clearly ruled that even if the death was a suicide (there is no indication in the record that it was) or the result of an intentional, self-inflicted act, the doctrine of impossibility of performance applied.

Appellants have candidly conceded that no case authorities exist in support of their position concerning fault in a case of impossibility due to death. Appellants ask this court to find support for their theory in the following language of the Restatement of Contracts 2d § § 261 and 262:

> § 261   Where, after a contract is made, a party's performance is made impracticable without his fault by the occurrence of an event the non-occurrence of which was a basic assumption on which the contract was made, his duty to render that performance is discharged, unless the language or the circumstances indicate the contrary.

> § 262   If the existence of a particular person is necessary for the performance of a duty, his death or such incapacity as makes performance impracticable is an event the nonoccurrence of which was a basic assumption on which the contract was made.

Appellants contend the Restatement dictates that impossibility of performance due to the destruction of one's own health is not the sort of conduct that will excuse performance, * * * and that the same reasoning should apply in a case of self-induced death. Appellants also suggest a policy basis for the ruling they advocate, arguing that in a society dealing with increasing problems created by illegal drug abuse, such conduct should not excuse the performance of the contract.

At oral argument of this case, it became apparent that any attempt to discern fault in a death case such as this one, or in a similar case, perhaps involving the use of tobacco or alcohol would create another case by case and hard to interpret rule of law. Being mindful that there are already too many of these in existence, we are not persuaded by the facts or the arguments presented to depart from the clear and unambiguous rule that death renders a personal services contract impossible to perform. See 17A Am.Jur.2d "Contracts" § 688 (1991). In such contracts, "there is an implied condition that death shall dissolve the contract." Id. With this implied condition in mind, we believe the parties to the agreements could have provided specifically for the contingency of loss due to the use of illegal drugs, as they provided for other hazardous or life threatening contingencies.[3] We affirm the trial court's ruling that the doctrine of impossibility of performance applies in this case.

We reverse the trial court's ruling that, as a matter of law, the policies were not effective until the issuance date, November 12, 1993, after Phoenix's death on October 31, 1993. The policies, as well as pertinent endorsements, clearly reflect earlier effective dates of July 23, 1993, and August 15, 1993 on their faces. Generally, the parties to a contract are competent to fix the effective date. See John A. Appleman and Jean Appleman, Insurance Law and Practice § 105 (1981). At the very least, further development of the record is in order on this issue.

AFFIRMED in part, REVERSED in part, and REMANDED for further proceedings consistent with this opinion.

OUT OF CHAOS, LTD. v. AON CORPORATION

United States Court of Appeals, Fourth Circuit, 2001.
15 Fed.Appx. 137.

PER CURIAM.

Appellant, Out of Chaos, Ltd ("OCL"), a "start up" film production company, filed a multi-count lawsuit against Appellees Aon Corporation and AON/Albert G. Ruben Insurance Services (hereinafter, jointly, "AON/AGR"), an insurance agency, and other entities not parties to this appeal, in the United States District Court for the Eastern District of Virginia, seeking substantial damages for losses OCL incurred in connection with an aborted film production. The district court granted judgment on the pleadings in favor of Appellees on OCL's claims for fraud and conversion. Subsequently, at the conclusion of discovery, the district court granted summary judgment in favor of Appellees on OCL's negligence claims. We discern no error in the district court's rulings; accordingly, we affirm.

I

Brothers James and Randall Starrett formed OCL and entered into a one million dollar contract with Discovery Communications, Inc. ("Dis-

---

3. For example, the actor loanout agreement pertaining to "Interview With the Vampire" provided:

From the date two (2) weeks before the scheduled start date of principal photography until the completion of all services required of Employee hereunder, Employee will not ride in any aircraft other than as a passenger on a scheduled flight of a United States or other major international air carrier maintaining regularly published schedules, or engage in any ultra hazardous activity without Producer's written consent in each case.

The entertainment package policies contained exclusions based on similar activities.

covery"), to film "Tournament of Shadows," a docudrama about the British explorer Sir Francis Younghusband's expedition into the mountains of central Asia.

On Discovery's recommendation, the Starretts contacted Kristi Jones, a broker with AON/AGR, to secure insurance for their undertaking, as the contract required. Jones advised the Starretts that OCL would be eligible to obtain insurance under the Discovery blanket policy with Chubb. Jones faxed to OCL a document which stated as follows: "The following brief description of motion picture and television production insurance is general in nature and is not meant to be a complete explanation of the policy terms. Specimen policies are available through our firm." The Starretts never requested specimen policies prior to paying the necessary premiums. Randy Starrett testified on deposition that he understood that the policies "cover[ed] all risk [sic] except those risks which are excepted."

In fact, AON/AGR procured coverage for that part of OCL's production of "Tournament of Shadows" that would not be based in Pakistan under a package of insurance provided by Federal Insurance Company, Vigilant Insurance Company and Pacific Indemnity Company, three companies affiliated with Chubb Corporation (hereinafter, collectively, "Chubb"). AON/AGR obtained on OCL's behalf a separate foreign policy from the Insurance Company for the State of Pennsylvania ("ICSOP") to provide workers' compensation, automobile and commercial general liability insurance for filming in Pakistan.

In her communications with the Starretts, Jones did not explain every policy exclusion. Specifically, she did not explain that there was an employee infidelity exception in the Chubb coverage. Significantly, neither of the Starretts advised Jones that OCL faced any special risk of misconduct by employees or representatives. Moreover, James Starrett specifically stated on deposition that he would not have attempted to purchase different or additional insurance had he known beforehand about the employee infidelity exclusion.

AON/AGR faxed OCL confirmation that it had bound OCL's insurance effective in June 1997. The fax transmission included a declarations page stating that all standard exclusions applied.

After it had obtained the insurance, OCL hired Pavel Lounguine to develop the screenplay and direct the film; shortly thereafter, filming began in Pakistan. Relations between Lounguine and the Starretts soon soured. By the time principal photography in Pakistan had been completed in December 1997, the project was seriously over budget. Lounguine and his editor went to Paris to process and assemble the film. In February 1998, after he had completed this work, Lounguine absconded with the computer disks containing the film assembly and announced he would no longer work for OCL.

In March 1998, Lounguine filed a lawsuit against OCL in Paris ("the French lawsuit"), and the bailiff of the French court seized the film. Discovery advised OCL that it must settle the French lawsuit and cease all production activity. By April 1998, OCL's counsel had negotiated a settlement of the French lawsuit "upon terms dictated by" Discovery. Discovery obtained possession of the film, which it retains. Pursuant to the French settlement, OCL paid $7,000 unconditionally, and it deposited an additional $45,875 in escrow. When the French lawsuit was not dismissed as required by the settlement, the French court dismissed the case. Virtually all of the escrowed settlement funds were returned to OCL. Discovery advised OCL that before OCL could regain possession of the film and complete the production, it had to pay the extra expenses the project had incurred, totaling $975,510. (J.A. 125.) OCL has not paid these extra costs and has never completed the film.

A portion of the damages OCL sought in this action allegedly resulted directly from the French lawsuit and its surrounding circumstances, while other claimed damages resulted indirectly. In particular, OCL alleged that it incurred $63,057 in defense costs in connection with the French lawsuit. According to OCL, its other damages claims against AON/AGR are rooted in (1) the "undisclosed" employee infidelity exclusion in the Chubb coverage and (2) the confusion and delay (which OCL asserts resulted in the failure of the entire production) attending AON/AGR's awkward efforts to process and deliver to the appropriate insurers OCL's claims for indemnity under the policies that AON/AGR had obtained on OCL's behalf from the various insurers. * * * In short, OCL has sought to assign as a cause of the collapse of the film project AON/AGR's acts and omissions.

Ultimately, OCL filed this suit in April 2000. OCL joined as defendants all of the insurers with whom AON/AGR had placed insurance, as well as AON/AGR. Eventually, all defendants except AON/AGR were dismissed from the lawsuit. Specifically, ICSOP settled with OCL and paid it $113,097.32. According to the uncontradicted affidavit of ICSOP's vice-president, even if ISCOP had received timely notice of the French lawsuit, ISCOP would have merely provided OCL a defense through a reasonable period (i.e., September 1998) in order to effect a reasonable settlement, which OCL had indeed achieved on its own, albeit under pressure from Discovery. Chubb also settled the claims asserted by OCL's in this action, but the terms of that settlement are not in the record. * * *

OCL's amended complaint alleged that AON/AGR committed fraud and conversion when it did not obtain the insurance it agreed to obtain and when it utilized OCL's insurance premiums for its own purposes. Under Virginia law, "a party can, in certain circumstances, show both a breach of contract and a tortious breach of duty." Richmond Metropolitan Authority v. McDevitt, Street, Bovis, Inc., 256 Va. 553, 507 S.E.2d 344, 347 (Va.1998) (internal quotations omitted). The Virginia Supreme Court further held that "the duty tortiously or negligently breached must be a common law duty, not one existing between the parties solely by virtue of the contract." *Id.* (internal quotations omitted).

A claim for "fraud in the inducement" is not foreclosed by the rule of McDevitt, Street, Bovis, Inc., 507 S.E.2d at 348 (citing Flip Mortgage Corp. v. McElhone, 841 F.2d 531 (4th Cir.1988)). To make out such a claim, the plaintiff must allege facts that demonstrate the defendant's intent (at the time the promises are made) never to abide by the terms of the contract. Id. When, as in the instant case, the allegations of fraud or conversion "are nothing more than allegation[s] of negligent performance of contractual duties," such alleged breaches of duty are not actionable in tort. *Id.* at 347.

Essentially, OCL alleged that it had a contract with AON/AGR that OCL would pay premiums and AON/AGR would secure insurance for "Tournament of Shadows." OCL alleged that AON/AGR did not secure insurance as the contract required, and made fraudulent statements and issued fraudulent documents stating that it had. In addition, OCL alleged that AON/AGR converted OCL's premiums for its own use. Each of these alleged wrongful acts arise from AON/AGR's contractual duty to OCL, i.e., to use OCL's payments to buy insurance. AON/AGR had no separate common law duty to do these things for OCL; rather, such duties inhere solely in AON/AGR's contractual undertakings.

Plainly, as the district court correctly concluded, OCL did not plead that it had been fraudulently induced to enter into the (oral) contract with AON/AGR for the procurement of insurance... Nor is there a scintilla of evidence that AON/AGR misapplied funds intended for use as premium payments. Thus, the district court properly entered judgment on the pleadings as to the claims for fraud and conversion.

We are likewise satisfied that the district court did not err in granting summary judgment to AON/AGR on OCL's negligence claims. OCL theorized that AON/AGR negligently "fail[ed] to procure [adequate] insurance" and negligently "fail[ed] to professionally process" OCL's claims for coverage. Even if AON/AGR had an independent tort duty to comply with a relevant standard of care which required, specifically, that it disclose and explain to the Starretts the employee infidelity exclusion, or to expeditiously process OCL's claims, and even if we assume that AON/AGR breached these duties, there is no genuine dispute of material fact whether OCL suffered any damages proximately caused by these ostensible breaches. It did not.

A

The district court correctly granted summary judgment to AON/ AGR on the adequacy of insurance issue because the record stands undisputed that even if James Starrett had obtained actual possession of the policy documents (as he was invited to do) and discussed with Jones, the AON/AGR broker, the employee infidelity clause in the Chubb coverage, he would not have sought substitute coverage or otherwise done anything differently. Thus, the fact that the Chubb coverage obtained by AON/AGR contained an employee infidelity exclusion was not a proximate cause of injury to OCL.

B

Similarly unavailing is OCL's contention that AON/AGR's breach of its duty to process OCL's claims in a professionally reasonable manner and to provide timely notice of loss to the respective insurance companies proximately caused injury to OCL. Even if AON/AGR had an independent duty to provide timely notice to the insurers of OCL's claims, the breach of which would give rise to a claim sounding in tort, OCL failed to generate a genuine dispute of material fact as to whether a breach of such duty caused it injury or damage.

It is undisputed that ICSOP's policy covered third party claims for personal injury or property damage, and that the French lawsuit included a claim for personal injury to Lounguine. Thus, there was a potentiality of coverage. ICSOP, though belatedly notified of the French litigation, has settled with OCL, paying recompense for the direct damages caused by the French lawsuit.... Without contradiction, ICSOP's vice-president has attested that had ICSOP known about the French lawsuit while it was pending, it would have covered OCL's defense costs only for the purpose of securing a prompt settlement of that action. OCL alleges it was forced to settle the French lawsuit because no insurance company came forward to defend it; however, the most that OCL would have obtained from ICSOP would have been assistance in settling the case. More to the point, it was Discovery that insisted that OCL cease film production and settle the French case immediately. Pursuant to the French settlement, OCL paid $7,000 unconditionally and deposited an additional $45,875 in escrow. When Lounguine failed to dismiss the French lawsuit in accordance with the terms of the settlement, virtually all of the escrowed funds were returned to OCL. As a matter of law, therefore, as the district court correctly concluded, OCL suffered no cognizable damage from the delay in ICSOP's receipt of notice of the claim.

OCL alleges that Discovery canceled production of "Tournament of Shadows" because of the French lawsuit, and that AON/AGR's failure to deliver timely notice to ICSOP of the French lawsuit was therefore the proximate cause of the damages flowing from the production cancellation. These bald allegations are unsupported by any evidence in the summary judgment record and therefore lack merit. First, as explained above, even if AON/AGR had notified ICSOP sooner, this possibility would not have altered the consequences to OCL of the seizure of the film and the institution of the French lawsuit. ICSOP, like Discovery, would have insisted on prompt settlement, which is precisely what occurred.

Second, OCL has failed to generate a factual dispute as to whether the film production was actually canceled as a result of the French lawsuit. The undisputed evidence in the record shows that, in accordance with the French settlement, the film was returned to Discovery, which retains possession of it. Discovery informed OCL that it would not allow it to complete the film until OCL paid Discovery $975,510 in cost overruns. Plainly, it is because OCL has never paid this sum to Discovery that the production was canceled.

OCL insists that the $975,510 should have been paid by Chubb or ICSOP. But there is no factual support in the record for OCL's assertion that the policies with these companies did or would have required any such payments. Accordingly, the issue of whether AON/AGR unreasonably failed to provide timely notice to the insurers of OCL's losses resulting from the cancellation of the production is immaterial to the issue that is dispositive of OCL's damages claims based on its negligence theories.

In sum, the district court correctly concluded that OCL failed to produce evidence that AON/AGR's acts or omissions were a proximate cause of OCL's damages.

AFFIRMED.

Notes

1. Do actors like Anne Heche face career risks when they reveal their inner demons in television interviews? Heche told Barbara Walters in a *20/20* interview on September 4, 2001, that she possessed a special language that allowed her to speak directly to God. She then proceeded to demonstrate the language. Heche was ostensibly on the show to promote her then new book *Call Me Crazy*.

2. Producers and studios insure actors to guarantee their performance. If an actor dies in the middle of filming, like Brandon Lee and John Candy, the insurance company covers the cost of re-shooting with a double or shutting down production.

3. What risk do actors pose to their careers when they possess a known drug and/or alcohol problem? Actors, like Robert Downey Jr., who are arrested and jailed for drug possession find that it affects insurability. Insurance companies consider actors like Downey a high risk and increase their rates accordingly. If the rates rise significantly or an actor becomes uninsurable, production companies and studios may forgo working with that actor. According to the New York Times, Downey was set to star in a Woody Allen project when producers dropped him after they "found out that there was no affordable way to resolve the cost of insuring him." The Times quotes Allen as saying, "He's a great talent, he'd just done two movies with no problem and we were crushed that the insurance company was being so difficult." Mim Udovitch, *The Sobering Life of Robert Downey Jr.*, N.Y. TIMES MAGAZINE, Oct. 19, 2003, at 35.

4. Is Allen being too hard on the insurance company when he accuses them of being difficult? After all, it is a business and no company wants to voluntarily enter into a venture that they know may flop, or would they? In May 2003, The American Lawyer published an article entitled "The Ensuing Cross–Border Conflict is that Much Messier Because of a Certain Creative Contract Provisions," discussing the efforts of producers of independent films to collect on flop insurance. The producers' films generated $1 billion-

plus in paper losses and the insurance companies refused to pay, claiming they were defrauded because of faulty Hollywood accounting methods.

5. Can anyone ever predict that a film will be a hit? The Motion Picture Association of America states, "Moviemaking is an inherently risky business. Contrary to popular belief that moviemaking is always profitable, in actuality, only one in ten films ever retrieves its investment in domestic exhibition. In fact, four out of ten movies **never** recoup the original investment. In 2000, the average major studio film cost $55 million to produce with an extra $27 million to advertise and market, a total cost of over $80 million per film." http://www.mpaa.org/anti-piracy/content.htm. It is the high cost of the industry that has caused the MPAA to adopt its anti-piracy campaign, which can be accessed at www.respectcopyrights.org.

D. PUBLIC FILM FINANCING

Film production has always been risky business. As William Goldman writes in *Adventures in the Screen Trade*, "Nobody knows anything. Not one person in the entire motion picture field *knows* for a certainty what's going to work. Every time out it's a guess—and, if you're lucky, an educated one." See WILLIAM GOLDMAN, ADVENTURES IN THE SCREEN TRADE 39 (1983) (emphasis in original).

To diminish the risk by reducing cost, many studios choose to craft films in locales that offer tax incentives, making them cheaper to produce. In the following article the, Washington Post reported on the direct impact on the U.S. economy of runaway film and television production.

Sharon Waxman
Location, Location; Hollywood Loses
Films to Cheaper Climes
WASHINGTON POST, June 26, 1999.

A new study ... estimates that the U.S. economy suffered a direct loss of $2.8 billion last year because of so-called runaway film and television production. That number is more than five times what it was in 1990, when the figure was $500 million, according to the research, conducted by the Monitor group for the Screen Actors Guild and the Directors Guild of America.

What has happened? According to the study, countries like Canada and Australia have been aggressively using tax incentives and favorable exchange rates to lure increasing numbers of big-budget, small-budget and television movie productions away from the United States. Major films like the recent release "The Matrix" are being filmed in Australia instead of Hollywood, as is the coming action sequel "Mission: Impossible II." Recent telefilms like "Dash and Lilly," "Thanks of a Grateful Nation" and "Hiroshima" were shot in Canada, though the stories were all set in the United States, and prime-time series like "The Outer

Limits," "La Femme Nikita" and "Harsh Realm" are now being made in Canada.

According to the study, of the 1,075 film and television productions released in the United States last year, 27 percent were produced abroad for economic reasons, an increase of nearly four times over 1990. Twenty-four of those productions were big-budget films—up from zero in 1990—another growing trend that has alarmed Hollywood.* * *

The bulk of "runaway" productions—about 81 percent—have been fleeing to Canada; the number of U.S.-based productions there jumped from 63 in 1990 to 232 in 1998. Government incentives to producers are hard to resist: Tax credits offered by the Canadian government and provinces usually add up to about 22 percent savings on labor costs. Australia has been following a similar model.

For studios, the economics of moving production overseas are tempting. " 'The Matrix' cost us 30 percent less than it would have if we shot in the United States," said Lorenzo di Bonaventura, the Warner Bros. president of production. "The rate of exchange is 62 cents on the dollar. Labor costs, construction materials are all lower. And they want us more. They are very embracing when we come to them." Di Bonaventura said he gained as much as $12 million in tax incentives on "The Matrix," which cost about $62 million to make.

The economic impact of this flight, according to the study, is vast. The direct loss to the American economy in 1998 from runaway production was $2.8 billion, a figure that calculated production budgets and adjusted for revenue that flowed back into the United States, such as leading actors' salaries. But the study said that when calculated with the multiplier effect—the ripple that a dollar spent here sends through the economy—the impact could be as much as $10.3 billion, affecting such diverse industries such as real estate, restaurants, clothing and hotels. The study estimated that 20,000 jobs were lost in 1998 because of runaways, everything from jobs for supporting actors to stage managers to costume designers to caterers.

For years independent movie producers have pinched pennies by shooting in Canada. Even in Hollywood, studios often choose not to shoot on their own lots because of the high cost of sound stages and production equipment, opting instead to rent cheaper raw space elsewhere or shoot on location. It is not that surprising, then, that as movie budgets have ballooned, studios have begun to invest in production facilities abroad. In October 1996 Disney bought a 12,000–square-foot studio in British Columbia for its productions. In 1997 Paramount sank $10 million in four sound stages and production space in Vancouver. In 1998 Fox Studios Australia opened its doors in Sydney. This investment by the studios has swiftly helped to compensate for Canada's initial lack of technical expertise in the movie business. * * *

Notes

1. Do runaway productions create a Catch–22 for the U.S. economy? On the one hand, jobs are lost to foreign countries, but on the other hand studios stand to increase their global revenue because they can make films cheaper.

2. As William Goldman indicated, films are a risky business. Most films fail to recover their initial production and advertising costs. Since studios receive an average of 5% annual return on their investment, would the film business be a wise use of public money? Many states are now encouraging filmmakers to produce within their environs by passing legislation that assists with the film budget. Assuming that a state may not recoup its initial investment, does it gain other advantages from filmmaking in its locale? What advice would you give to states seeking to lure film production into their environs? See Frank Rizzo, *State hopes to use new incentives to attract moviemakers*, HARTFORD COURANT, Apr. 25, 1993, at G1. The following article explores other issue, as states become suitors for Hollywood filmmakers.

Patrick Goldstein
The Big Picture: Another Suitor for Filmmakers

L.A. TIMES, Sept. 30, 2003, at Calendar, Part 5, Page 1.

Tova LAITER has fallen in love with the backers of her new comedy, "Elvis Has Left the Building," which stars Kim Basinger as a Pink Lady beauty consultant who accidentally kills several Elvis impersonators and ends up on the run from the FBI.

"I've never dealt with people so polite and professional," says Laiter, a producer who began shooting the film Sept. 15 with director Joel ("My Big Fat Greek Wedding") Zwick. "When we came to scout locations, they arranged for free hotels, restaurants and transportation. When we needed to shoot at the local convention center, we got to use it for five days—gratis."

The object of Laiter's affection isn't a scrum of German tax fund accountants or a Silicon Valley zillionaire. It's the state of New Mexico.

A growing number of states offer tax credits as a way to lure Hollywood dollars. But New Mexico actually is investing in movies—the state has established a fund of $85 million for the purpose. The money comes in the form of no-interest loans, repayable in two to five years. The state will invest as much as $7.5 million in any movie that passes muster with the New Mexico State Investment Council, as long as filmmakers agree to spend most of their shooting schedule in state and hire a crew made up of at least 60% New Mexico residents.

On top of that, New Mexico offers any film, whether financed by the state or not, a 15% tax rebate for every dollar spent locally. It also has a mentor program that offers an eye-popping 50% salary rebate for advancing the skills of crew members who are either hired for the first time or promoted to higher positions. The law also allows filmmakers to get their tax credits immediately, allowing the money to go directly into the film's production budget.

I'm not sure we've stolen any film production away from Canada yet, but we're going to try. This is a way for us to compete with them for film dollars," says Greg Kulka, the alternative investments portfolio manager for the state's investment council. For a low-budget film such as "Elvis Has Left the Building," which was put together by London-based Capitol Films, producers of the upcoming "Sylvia," starring Gwyneth Paltrow, the state's investment represents a lion's share of the movie's $11.5–million budget. But more importantly, by giving the state a big rooting interest in the film's success, it smooths over the bureaucratic hurdles that often beset filmmakers in less welcoming environs— hint, hint—such as Los Angeles.

"It makes your life easier because the state and the film commission are your partners," says Laiter. "Everything you ask for is doable. When we had our session to qualify for the loan, the governor said, 'If you have any problems, just call me.' That's a pretty nice situation, where you think to yourself, 'Well, we've had so few problems I haven't had to call the governor yet.'"

FROM POCKET TO PRODUCTION

When the western "The Missing" filmed in New Mexico this spring, Gov. Bill Richardson invited director Ron Howard, line producer Todd Hallowell and screenwriter Akiva Goldsman to dinner at the governor's mansion. "Getting a 15% tax credit on every dollar you spend in the state is a very real savings," says Hallowell. "We ended up getting millions of dollars in credits that we could put up on the screen."

It's hard not to contrast New Mexico's bold outreach program with the baby steps taken in California. The state has been staggered by a vast exodus of filmmaking dollars to Canada, which offers mountains, prairies, big cities and a lopsided exchange rate that has prompted an onslaught of runaway film production.

Unlike New Mexico's Legislature, which unanimously voted for its no-interest loan scheme, California's Assembly balked last fall at passing even the most meager of tax incentives. Things are so bad that when Gov. Gray Davis' office sent a news release last week boasting about new legislative initiatives that would protect the state's entertainment industry, all the governor could say about combating runaway film production was that the Legislature hadn't managed to kill the California Film Commission.

The news release neglected to mention what matters most to filmmakers: the Legislature's gutting of the state's much-ballyhooed Film California First program. Launched several years ago with a $15–million war chest aimed at reimbursing film companies for shooting on state property, the program got zero funding this year.

Arnold Schwarzenegger, the gubernatorial candidate with the most personal stake in this issue, was widely quoted last week saying that one of the first things he wants to do when he becomes governor "is bring the movie business back to California." It's a nice sound bite, but the candidate's track record makes it look like a dubious promise. As a $30–million movie star, Arnold has plenty of say in where his films shoot. But of the last three movies he's made, "The 6th Day" was shot in Canada and "Collateral Damage" was filmed primarily in Mexico.

California Film Commission director Karen R. Constine put the best face on things, saying the state still offers the best talent, locations, postproduction services and infrastructure. But she acknowledged that "we still have to compete in a global marketplace." Levi Strauss, America's leading bluejeans manufacturer, just closed its last U.S. factory, meaning the next pair of jeans we buy will be made by a low-paid worker far off in the Third World. My sneakers are made in China, my khakis come from Guatemala. Will America's movies someday be filmed mostly in Canada or some other low-cost tax haven?

"California is just sitting back, assuming that the business that began in California will always be there," says "Missing's" Hallowell, who heads this week to Toronto, where he and Howard will film "Cinderella Man," a boxing drama starring Russell Crowe. "It's like Pittsburgh assuming they'd always have the steel business—it isn't necessarily so.

"I'm like most film people—I want to sleep in my own bed at night. But if other states start emulating what New Mexico is doing, it could be another nail in the coffin for keeping filmmaking in Los Angeles."

New Mexico's lessons

If California ever regains the political will and the economic means to fight for its most high-profile business, it should study how New Mexico engineered its loan plan.

In years past, New Mexico was a popular location for films, especially westerns, but production fell off dramatically when Canada's seductive exchange rate reared its ugly head. New Mexico has several key advantages that allowed the state to fight back. It is a new or second home for a significant number of industry people, from gaffers and set painters to such actors as Val Kilmer, Gene Hackman and Shirley MacLaine, who has a home north of Santa Fe and is chairwoman of the state's Film Advisory Board. Having a wealth of in-state talent means New Mexico can supply film producers with nearly three full film crews; both "Elvis" and "The Missing" have crews made up of 80% local residents. But here's New Mexico's real advantage: After squirreling away tax revenue from its mining, oil and gas income, the state has a $12–billion endowment known as the Severance Tax Permanent Fund. When the state was looking for a way to woo film production, the fund provided ample capital from which to draw.

Knowing that film investing was fraught with peril, especially for inexperienced outsiders, the state hired veteran entertainment lawyer Peter Dekom to get the program up and running. Dekom came up with the idea of a guaranteed no-interest loan and helped draft the legislation that sailed through the Legislature last year. He plays a key role in reviewing loan requests, assessing the project's commercial prospects and reviewing the reliability of the film's financial backing. The state's investment is insured by a guarantee from a bank or major corporate entity; if the movie makes money, the state is a profit participant.

"Even if the movie loses money, we come out ahead," says Dekom. "For every dollar spent in New Mexico, the state is getting three or four times that back in the impact from all the jobs created—and the buying and shopping that goes on. It's a great deal for New Mexico."

Kulka says officials from several other states have called, wanting details about the program. He may be new to the movie business, but he already sounds like an old Hollywood pro. "When they ask me what the key to this deal is, my first comment is always make sure you structure it so you can get your money back, or you won't have a program for long."

Sherri Burr
The New Mexico Film Industry:
Author Interview With Frank Zuniga

Copyright © 2004 by Sherri Burr.

[On January 9, 2004, author Sherri Burr sat down with film director Frank Zuniga to discuss his new role as director of the New Mexico Film Office. Zuniga is a graduate of U.C.L.A. Film School and directed several television and feature films before becoming an administrator.]

"I started my film career in 1961 as a second unit cameraman for Disney. By 1967, I had become one of the directors of NBC's *Disney's Wonderful World of Color*. In 1979, I made the hardest career leap to become director of feature films. I was lucky because I was given the opportunity to direct *The Further Adventures of the Wilderness Family* as a sequel to *The Wilderness Family,* which came out in 1981. I'm one of the few guys who can say none of my films have ever lost money. For example, I shot *The Wilderness Family* movie for $1.42 million and it has made $50 million. My 1983 film *The Golden Seal* continues to pay me residuals.

"Before I became director of the New Mexico Film Office on January 1, 2004, I held positions as a teacher and dean of Media Arts at Columbia College Hollywood, which has no connection to New York's Columbia University. I also helped a Korean television station launch a film school to train Koreans in Hollywood techniques. I took my current position because New Mexico aims to build infrastructure for the media industries in the near future.

"We asked ourselves, 'What can New Mexico do to help producers with their bottom line?' The New Mexico legislature came up with several incentives that enable filmmakers to get their movies made. For qualified producers making a film with an anticipated rating of "R" or lower, the New Mexico Investment Council will consider investing up to $7.5 million, which may represent up to 100% of the budget. The producer must (1) shoot their film wholly or substantially in the State of New Mexico; (2) must have a distribution agreement or pre-sales plan in place; (3) 60% of the below-the-line payroll must be New Mexico residents; (4) they must have a completion bond; and (5) have a guarantor that will guarantee payment of the loan, that is a AAA company or bank. New Mexico's money is never at risk.

"We also offer a 15% tax credit on all New Mexico-based production expenses, including wages and salaries, supplies, camera and equipment rental, wardrobe rentals, and hair and make-up supplies. Companies register with the Film Office, and then apply to the Taxation and Revenue Department prior to filing a return. Under this program, if a producer spends $5 million in New Mexico and the expenditures qualify, the state will return $750,000.

"Further, we offer fee-free use of over 800 state buildings, including a 1940's era state penitentiary. When we receive a script, my office does a synopsis and a location breakdown. We suggest state buildings, like the Capital, courthouses, or museums, which can be used to shoot scenes. Through the Film Office and the Property Control Division of the General Services Department, producers can also obtain surplus property for free to use in their films.

"Additionally, we have established a "Be Our Guest" Program to encourage filmmakers to take a look at our state. This program provides up to three days of complementary lodging, car rentals, and meals to producers. Instead of paying $2000 a person to visit New Mexico, they may end up spending only $150 on drinks and snacks.

"With our workforce training program, the state will pay 50% of the salary of New Mexico interns for up to 1040 hours, which equals roughly 86 twelve-hour days of work. Thus, the more producers employ New Mexicans, the further this program will affect their bottom line. After the producers of *Around the Bend*, starring Michael Caine and Christopher Walker, wrapped production here in December 2003, they said, "Your crews are world class."

"Our goal is to keep New Mexico competitive in the changing digital environment. We plan to bring the arts and science communities together in ways that have not been done before. With worldwide video game revenue exceeding feature films, by $10.1 billion to $9.1 billion according to a recent Price Waterhouse Cooper study, we are encouraging artists to think of storytelling in new and different ways. We believe that once artists are exposed to the new technology, it becomes just another canvas, just another brush.

"Survival and success in this current competitive environment depends on how well you can think outside the box."

Notes

1. What are the advantages to filmmakers to film in a state like New Mexico? What are the disadvantages? Why are states trying to follow New Mexico's lead in the manner it has chosen to attract film production to its location? Other states, like Arizona, are decrying that New Mexico's film incentives will lead to the elimination of their state film offices. See Polly Higgins, *Meanwhile in New Mexico,* Tucson Citizen, Feb. 27, 2003, at 4A.

2. Zuniga's publicity efforts have been rewarded with favorable press across the country. The following is an article that appeared in the New York Times on the efforts of New Mexico's film office to persuade filmmakers to produce in the state.

Simon Romero
Coming Soon to a Screen Near You: New Mexico
N.Y. Times, Jan. 26, 2004, at C.1.

As many cash-short states reduce financing for their film offices, New Mexico is headed defiantly in the opposite direction. Blessed with a budget surplus, the state has started one of the nation's most aggressive film incentive programs, resulting in a flurry of projects like the somber "21 Grams" from Alejandro González Iñárritu and "The Missing," a violent tale of abduction, from Ron Howard.

The New Mexico Film Office estimates that filmmaking in the state—counting salaries, lodging, food and transportation—generated $80 million in spending in 2003, up from $8 million a year earlier. With several more projects planned this year, Frank Zúñiga, director of the film office, said, "I have every confidence that we'll have double the financial impact in 2004."

How times have changed. Jon Hendry, a Scot who arrived In New Mexico 19 years ago to work on the set of the western "Silverado" and never left, was despondent about its film industry a couple of years ago.

"I was tired of not doing anything, of being unemployed," said Mr. Hendry, the business agent for New Mexico's film technicians union. Last year, membership in his union surged to 400 from 60.

The force behind New Mexico's film boom was the creation of an $85 million fund that invests directly in film projects through no-interest loans. The money comes from New Mexico's $3.5 billion Severance Tax Permanent Fund, financed by royalties from natural gas, oil, coal and timber extraction.

The program, drafted by Peter J. Dekom, a prominent entertainment industry lawyer in Los Angeles, allows the state to lend as much as $7.5 million to help produce films. It also grants a 15 percent tax rebate on all local production costs, provided the film is made largely in New Mexico.

"Our main objective is to become a supportive satellite of Hollywood," Gov. Bill Richardson said in an interview. "We don't want to be greedy with this, but for a state with low per capita income, it's a way for us to attract a clean, environmentally friendly industry that leaves a positive impact."

Unlike many states, New Mexico has a Constitution that mandates a balanced budget, and it also has a history of reining in public spending. As a result, there was little resistance to legislation allowing the state to invest in film projects. In fact, the state's finances allowed officials to expand the authority and influence of its film commission while other states were cutting back.

Few states are as aggressive in luring film projects as New Mexico, with its no-interest loans, although several, like Louisiana and Illinois, offer similar tax incentives.

In California, the film commission was recently folded into the Department of Business, Transportation and Housing and its budget was cut nearly 60 percent. Still, a department spokesman, Patrick Dorinson, said, "Filmmaking has been a priority for the California economy and will continue to be one." He declined to comment on New Mexico's program.

According to The Hollywood Reporter, a newspaper that covers the entertainment industry, Colorado eliminated most of its film office budget last year, and the New Jersey film office was nearly shut down. In Massachusetts, the state film office was closed in 2002. Private fundraisers responded by creating a nonprofit organization, the Massachusetts Film Bureau, to promote the state as a destination for filmmakers.

"I wish we had something in the way of loans," said Robin Dawson, the bureau's executive director. "New Mexico is going to be the envy of every film commission in the country."

Elliott Lewitt, producer of "Around the Bend," a road movie about four generations of men from the same family, said the incentives saved the project about $500,000 on a budget of $6 million. The film, starring Michael Caine and Christopher Walken, was shot in 2003 in Los Lunas, N.M., south of Albuquerque, and is scheduled for release in October.

"This was a picture we wouldn't have been able to do if we couldn't recover some of the costs," Mr. Lewitt said.

New Mexico's resources have allowed it to attract projects beyond the westerns that have often used the state's rugged landscape as a backdrop. Guillermo Arriaga, the screenwriter for "21 Grams," said the experience opened his eyes to the state.

"The desert there, the open spaces, they enhanced the feeling of solitude that I was looking for," Mr. Arriaga said in a telephone interview from Mexico City. "Albuquerque, except for its downtown, felt like Mexico to me. It's certainly a place where I would do another film."

Another recently completed film, "Elvis Has Left the Building," which stars Kim Basinger as a cosmetics saleswoman who accidentally kills two Elvis impersonators, was shot in and near Albuquerque.

Still, the incentive program has not proceeded without criticism. Jonathan Wacks, an independent filmmaker and chairman of the moving image arts department at the College of Santa Fe, has warned that New Mexican directors and producers risk losing out if the program relies mainly on out-of-state projects.

"If we want a sustainable film industry in New Mexico, we need to get creative and start funding low-budget films done by New Mexicans," he said.

There is also the matter of finding enough qualified crewmembers. The state has started to subsidize training of film technicians, hoping to increase its supply of technicians, Mr. Zúñiga of the film office said.
* * *

http://www.nytimes.com/2004/01/26/business/media/26film.html?
ex=1076122805 & ei=1

Note

1.   New Mexico is using revenue from its Permanent Fund to finance its ventures into the filmmaking business. Rather than relying on the films to become hits, it structures the contracts so that a bank or other institution of sufficient financial worthiness guarantees the loan amounts. The article below suggests that instead of getting into the film business, some states are actually pulling out, viewing that the potential upside is not worth the risk in an era of tight budgeting.

Bill Dunlap
Coping With Budget Blues: Film Offices
Prove Their Worth

Shoot Magazine, January 24, 2003.

Newspaper headlines on the budget crises in almost every state are everywhere these days. The headlines are justifiably almost always about cuts in schools, prisons, police and health care. But for the motion picture, television and commercial production community, the story beneath the radar is the pressure that tight budgets are putting on state film commissions-the bodies that facilitate on-location filming, help states provide incentives to producers and, collectively, play a role in keeping production in the United States.

Film commissioners note that it's sometimes difficult to defend what they do when governors and legislatures are cutting critical public services in an effort to narrow budget gaps. Many in and out of state government see the film offices as unnecessary. Film commissioners respond by pointing out that their relatively small budgets help generate heavy in state spending by filmmakers.

"The film office is the first to be cut, even though they've constantly proven their worth in terms of the economic return on investment they've brought," says Dawn Keezer, director of the Pittsburgh Film Office, and chair of Film US, a trade group of state film commissioners that seeks to keep film work in the United States. "It seems very shortsighted to cut the budgets of people bringing money in."

The Pittsburgh Film Office, she says, brings $45 in production to the region for each dollar of its budget. Others cite ratios as high as $100 to $1. Matt Miller, president/CEO of the Association of Independent Commercial Producers (AICP), says spotmakers recognize the value of film commissions. "There's nothing more valuable in a location shoot, especially a complex one, than a film commissioner," he stresses. It plays the other way, too, he adds, with commissions earning their keep in the states. "If you take that piece out, who is going to be out there attracting what is a very lucrative, low-impact business?" he notes. "With locations all over the world competing for our shoots, it would be the equivalent of knocking out your customer service department."

So far, only a handful of state film offices have been closed. Where that's happened, stopgap measures have been put in place to provide some services. Ohio and Wisconsin offices were shut, but in the former, the state tourism office along with the nonprofit Greater Cincinnati & Northern Kentucky Film Commission and Greater Cleveland's Film Commission are picking up the slack. In Wisconsin, the director of marketing for travel and tourism has stepped in. In Massachusetts, the state film office closed, but the production community in the Boston area set up a privately funded office.

The Washington State Film Office narrowly avoided closure, and today operates with full funding. Still, commissioner Suzy Kellett says it's difficult to prove value to the state. "The national film industry understands the benefits of a film commission, the time and cost savings," she says.

"Historically, it has always been far more difficult to convince local governments that this is worthwhile and should be funded and supported and increased. Many [commissions] don't have huge budgets, but the return on the dollar is huge. In the past decade, for every dollar this office spent, the industry left one hundred dollars."

Compounding the difficulty film offices are having in protecting their budgets is the fact that, in most states, film production was off sharply in 2001 and '02. In Washington State, for example, overall production spending declined through the late '90s to $17.5 million in '99. It boomed in '00 to $50.5 million on the strength of an extraordinary 18–fold increase from '99 in TV production to $42.7 million. Spending fell in '01 to $21.3 million and was lower in '02, Kellett says, although final numbers aren't yet available. Commercial production spending was steadier, but also declined from a level of more than $12 million in '95 and '96 to $6.5 million in '00 and $3.3 million in '01.

MARKETING IDEAS

States like Arizona and Colorado, where deserts, canyons and mountains attract heavy filming in all categories, have both had their film offices cut sharply. These and other states are taking some innovative measures to maintain service to the industry. Over the last couple of years, Colorado has had its film commission budget cut three times, most recently last June, and its staff has shrunk from six full-timers to three, with two part-time staffers, according to Stephanie Two Eagles, program manager for the Colorado Film Commission. "We had to regroup," she says. "We have a new Web site with a searchable database. That helped because we're a lot more efficient for scouting. We have a lot of information online now and the production guide gets about two hundred hits a day."

The Web site was funded through a grant from a state marketing agency and Two Eagles has benefited from volunteer interns and a pro bono ad campaign from MGA Communications of Denver. Former MGA creative director Anthony Castellano continues to do creative for the commission out of his new firm, Castellano Advertising & Design, Lakewood, Colo. The Colorado Film and Video Association publishes the state's production guide and the local film community came up with $11,700 to match a state grant for a University of Colorado research project on the contribution of the film industry to the Colorado economy. The commission also has a training program in place called Colorado Camera Ready. "We've been training our communities on how to set up a local film commission since 1991," Two Eagles says. "We have over one hundred local contacts throughout the state who are trained. In times like these, our communities have really gone to bat. We give producers general information, and from there, when they decide they could work in Telluride or La Junta, we put them in touch with the local contact."

Feature filming has been slow in recent years, Two Eagles says, although low budget indies are still being shot in Colorado. "Major feature films are going to Canada," she explains. "Canada looks like us. We had a piece of About Schmidt filmed here and HBO's The Laramie Project in 2001. Commercials are strong for us; we get a lot of car shoots."

The Arizona Film Commission has seen its budget cut by about 58 percent over the last year, according to its director, Robert Detweiler. "We've done some things internally to restructure and to keep the film office going because it's been a target," he says.

Detweiler, who was in the film business himself and later helped Arizona establish its Rural Development Office, used that experience to reposition the commission. "When the previous director resigned, we put together a proposal that brought the film office under the Rural Development Office," he explains.

"That allowed us to provide some things that weren't available before," but not at the expense of urban locations, he says. "It was a bit easier to display the return on investment when we had a bit more of a focus on the smaller communities."

Detweiler notes that Gov. Jane Dee Hull has said the state is done cutting agencies. "We feel pretty good about keeping [our office's budget] where it is," he says. "We're probably not going to be able to do the marketing that everyone would love to do, but we still can do the marketing that keeps us in the game.

We're fortunate that we have a good portion of commercial work." The Arizona commission counted 134 film projects in the fiscal year (which ended on June 30, '02), including 53 commercial shoots and five features.

PUBLIC VS. PRIVATE

In Ohio, Chris Carmody, president of Greater Cleveland's Film Commission, ays the new arrangement with the Cincinnati-area office works better than the defunct Ohio Film Office. "The Ohio Office of Travel and Tourism channels all Southern Ohio requests to Cincinnati and all Northern Ohio requests to us," Carmody explains. Both film offices are nonprofit, private-sector operations, which gives them advantages over the state office, he continues. "The state office couldn't offer incentives—even something as simple as taking producers to lunch. One person could not adequately serve the eighty-eight-county area, and we found producers were often confused about where to start. And, as a public employee, the state film commissioner, by law, could not lobby the state to make government more film-friendly. Both of our organizations can. The closing of the state office has been a shot in the arm for us."

In Wisconsin, film office functions have been handed over to Sarah Klavas, director of marketing for the Wisconsin Dept. of Tourism, who says the state's location between Chicago and Minneapolis has helped to attract increased commercial production. "Marketing feature film production and television commercial production is very similar to marketing the state as a leisure travel destination," Klavas says, although she acknowledges that the office works to assist filmmakers who have decided to film in Wisconsin rather than try to attract them to the state. "We don't have an aggressive marketing posture. We're reactive," she says.

In Massachusetts, where the state shut down the film office last July, the local film community banded together to form the private Massachusetts Film Bureau, headed by Robin Dawson, who had been director of the state office. Bob Hirsch, manager of film and video lighting for Boston's High Output, helped establish the new office, which he says will perform many of the functions of the state office, and will lobby the state to reestablish the film office. "We realized we had to create a privately operated office that would serve production from out of the area and advocate for our local organization," Hirsch says.

He is optimistic that a public-private office will happen, despite a state budget crisis. "High Output supplied equipment for Mitt Romney's campaign advertising," Hirsch says, referring to the new governor of Massachusetts. "He didn't miss an opportunity when he was on a film set to approach the technicians working there and let them know that he understood the need for a state film office."

INCENTIVES

One area that may suffer as states grapple with budget shortfalls is their ability to provide any new or expanded incentives to visiting filmmakers. Most states have offered tax relief in the form of sales or hotel tax rebates, but almost all of the latter require a 30–day stay, which generally rules out commercial shoots.

"Incentives aren't something states want to look at right now," Kellett says. "We have some. I know Oregon is trying to do theirs, but this is not the climate to try to make that happen."

Only a couple of states are providing real financial incentives. The Film California First program reimburses certain film costs—such as state, local and federal employee costs and some local use fees—incurred on public land, up to $300,000 per production. Gov. Gray Davis has supported that and other incentive programs vigorously, but no state program seems secure, given the state's severe budget crisis.

New Mexico put two new incentive programs in place last year. One provides film companies with a 15 percent rebate on all direct film expenditures made in New Mexico during production, and the other allows for direct investments and low interest and interest-free loans for film projects using local people. For the latter, New Mexico recently invested $4.7 million in a feature film called Blind Horizon. The film, directed by Michael Haussman, who directs spots via bicoastal Person Films and London-based Serious Pictures, was shot in Las Vegas, N.M.

Florida and Miami–Dade County are both considering rebates on film spending, according to Jeff Peel, director of the Miami Dade Mayor's Office of Film & Entertainment, but nothing is in place yet. The Miami Dade office has doubled its marketing budget to about $225,000, Peel says, with the Visitor and Convention Bureau funneling in another $100,000. In South Florida, Peel says the year is starting out strong. "This is the height of our season right now and we're seeing a lot of activity on features and the commercials side," he notes. "And a couple of TV pilots look like they're coming here."

Peel notes that '02 was a good year for filmmaking in the area. "We had a lot of big feature films last year," he says. "We did a little over sixty-million dollars in features, over twenty-five million in TV and almost thirty-five million in commercials." Peel hopes the additional marketing dollars will help bring even more work to the area this year.

Collectively, rebates and tax incentives are believed to have an influence in curbing runaway production, and the state commissions are seeking broader federal incentives through Film US, a four-year-old association of 196 state and local film commissions. Keezer says that the organization's mission includes educating state governments about the size and importance of the film production business and the value of film commissions, and helping to keep production in the United States. "The problems U.S. film commissions are having are making us less competitive." Keezer says. "Other countries are adding more incentives to get the work."

Film US is working to reintroduce legislation in Congress that would provide a federal tax credit to filmmakers shooting stateside "Last year, we got seventy-seven congressional co-sponsors, which is huge," Keezer says. But House and Senate bills died when Congress adjourned.

As to the outlook for local production or the commissions themselves, the commissioners, in general, don't profess to have a crystal ball about the rest of '03 and years beyond. "The industry is very cyclical," Keezer says. "And I believe the ebb and flow of state economies also is cyclical, so I'm confident and hopeful that people will see the value of these film offices and rally together."

Kellett suggests the national production industry will never be what it once was, except in a few major centers. "It's gone global and it's never coming back," she says. "This year hopefully will not be as terrible as this last year was, but it's hard to predict more than three months in advance."

E. INTERNATIONAL FILM CONTRACTS

Filmmaking has become a global business, with international companies purchasing most of the Hollywood studios and Hollywood studio and production companies choosing to make more films abroad to take advantage of sets, locations, and financial incentives offered by national film offices. The December 2003 film *Cold Mountain* starring Nicole Kidman and Jude Law was shot in Romania as the director Anthony Minghella found the mountains of Romania more representative of Civil War times than the actual Cold Mountain area in North Carolina.

Charles Cohen is a screenwriter (*Ernest Goes to Jail*, 1990) who produced *The Gambler*, a 1999 film that mixes fact and fiction in telling the story of Dostoyevsky's struggles as an impoverished, gambling-addicted writer and his relationship with the stenographer hired to take dictation of his novel, "The Gambler." The story-within-a-story parallels the romance between Dostoyevsky and Anna with that of the main characters of "The Gambler." *http://www.hollywood.com/movies/detail/movie/177037*. Below is a reprint of the contract between Cohen's production company, Trendraise Company Ltd., trading as Gambler Productions, and the writer for assignment of copyright. As the producer on the movie, Cohen was in charge of securing the contracts from all the talent before principal photography could commence. Names and dollar amounts have been omitted.

CONTRACT FOR ASSIGNMENT OF COPYRIGHT IN SCREENPLAY ENTITLED "THE GAMBLER"

May 16, 1996 between Trendraise Company Ltd. and Writer.
Reprinted with Permission from Charles Cohen and Marc Vlessing.

THIS ASSIGNMENT is made on the 16th of May 1996

BETWEEN

(1) TRENDRAISE COMPANY LIMITED trading as GAMBLER PRO-DUCTIONS of 35 Camden Square, London NW1 9XA, U.K. (hereinafter called "the Company"); and

(2) WRITER co/ 123 Main Street, Santa Monica, California, 90405, U.S.A. (hereinafter called ("the writer").

PREAMBLE

A. The Writer co-wrote with Charles Cohen an original screenplay ("the Screenplay") for a full length feature film presently entitled **"THE GAMBLER"** ("the Film") which the Company intends to produce

B. By various agreements the Writer granted to the Company a sole and exclusive option to acquire the entire copyright and all other rights of whatever nature in and to the Screenplay, which option has been extended and which the Company now wishes to exercise

TERMS

1.   COPYRIGHT AND CONSENTS

1.1   The Writer hereby assigns to the Company with full title guarantee the entire copyright throughout the world and to the extent relevant by way of present assignment of future copyright for the full term (including all renewals and extensions) thereof and all other rights of whatsoever kind or nature including any so-called rental or lending rights and all satellite broadcasting and cable transmission rights throughout the world in and to the Screenplay and all other works, materials and contributions made by the writer in relation to the Screenplay and/or the Film (together "the Products") TO HOLD the same to the Company absolutely and without in any way limiting the foregoing it is expressly agreed that all material (including any and all sets poses photography sound effects literary and dramatic material writing plot dialogue and title ideas) furnished or suggested by the Writer in connection with the Film shall automatically become the absolute property of the Company which shall have the exclusive right to photography transmit record and/or reproduce the same or make any use thereof in any manner language or form it may desire. Whenever required by the Company the Writer will at the Company's expense execute and deliver further instruments confirming to the Company all such rights and property and for the purposes of United States' copyright law the products shall be considered "works made for hire" for the Company.

1.2   The writer hereby grants to the Company full and complete right to adapt change take from add to and use and treat in any way and in any language the Products and to use them or any part thereof in conjunction with the work of any other person or persons but the Company shall not be bound to make any use thereof or any part thereof. The Company shall have the exclusive right if it so desires to use and permit the use of the Writer's name and/or photography solely or otherwise in connection with the Film and the advertising exploiting and exhibiting of the same.

1.3   The Writer gives every consent under the Act or any statutory modification or re-enactment thereof for the time being in force to enable the Company to make the fullest use of the Writer's services hereunder and of the Products.

1.4   The Writer shall when required by the Company executed and so all such assignments, documents, acts and things in such form and otherwise as the Company may reasonably require for perfecting or enforcing the Assignment hereby made, for protecting the Company's interest in the Products and/or the Film or for effecting or facilitating the exercise b the Company of its powers, authorities and discretions hereby or by statute conferred on it and the Writer herby appoints the Company as her attorney-in-fact toe execute and do as aforesaid in her stead if she shall fail to do so, which power shall be coupled with and interest and be irrevocable.

2.   WRITERS WARRANTIES

The Writer hereby warrants to and undertakes with the Company that:

2.1   the Products shall be original in her and shall not infringe upon the copyright or any other third of any third party not to the best of his knowledge and belief and after making all due enquiries be defamatory.

2.2   the Writer is not now nor will be under any obligation or disability which might prevent the Writer from making this Assignment or from giving the undertakings herein contained or from fully observing and performing the terms and conditions hereof or from granting the rights and consents referred to herein;

2.3   at the expiration of this engagement the Writer shall hand over to the Company all writing manuscripts drafts photographs books plans drawings accounts papers documents and effects whatsoever prepared or made by the Writer or in his care in connection with the Products and/or the Film.

3. PAYMENT

3.1 Subject to the provisions of this Agreement herein contained and to the due compliance by the Writer with all his obligations hereunder the Company shall as inclusive remuneration and as full consideration for the Writer's entire services and for the rights granted to the Company hereunder pay to the Writer:

  3.1.1 the sum of U.S. $_____ (U.S. dollars) on or before the first day of principal photography; and

  3.1.2 a further $_____ (U.S. dollars) as a deferment and payable as a second position deferment (defined in the main finance and distribution agreements for the Film (first position deferments amounting to $_____ and payable prorate with one second position deferment of $_____ payable to _____ _____ as director of the film;

  3.1.3 further sums from time to time equal to 2.5% (two and a half per cent) of the balance of Producer's Share of Net Profits (defined as aforesaid) after payment of all deferments.

3.2 The writer hereby acknowledges that the consideration payable to her hereunder shall be full consideration for all the rights granted hereby (including but not by way of limitation rental and lending rights and any other right which may be subject to equitable remuneration in consequence of a Directive made by the European Parliament and or under the provisions of any present or future legislation adopted by any member state of the European Community in compliance with such Directive). Notwithstanding this sub-clause 3.2, nothing in this Agreement shall prevent the Writer from being entitled to receive in respect of rental and lending rights in the Film, income under collective and other agreements negotiated by recognized collection societies under the laws of any jurisdictions PROVIDED FURTHER THAT nothing herein shall imply any obligation upon the Company regarding the collection of such income.

3.3 All sums payable hereunder shall be exclusive of any Value Added Tax payable thereon which shall be paid by the Company upon presentation of a valid invoice thereof.

4. CREDIT

4.1 If the Company shall make the Film based on substantial parts of the Screenplay it shall (subject as set out below) accord the Writer credit in the words "Written by Writer & Charles Cohen and _____ _____" (subject to any determination to the contrary by the appropriate Writer's Guild), in the same size and style of type as that for and in all respects equal to the credit of the director of the Film:

  4.1.1 on all negatives and positive copies of the Film made by or to the order of the Company in a separate frame on which the name of no other person (except Charles Cohen and _____ _____) shall appear, immediately before the credit for the individual producers of the Film;

4.1.2   in all major paid advertising and publicity relating the Film issued by or under control of the Company;

4.2   The Company shall use all reasonable endeavors to ensure that the distributors of the Film accord the Writer like credit.

4.3   The provisions of this Clause shall not apply to the following group list or so-called "teaser advertising publicity or exploitation; special advertising publicity or exploitation of the Film relating to any member or members of the cast the author or other personnel concerned in its production or similar matters; any exploitation publication or fictionalization of the story screenplay or other literary or musical material upon which the Film is based or by-products of any kind (including but not limited to sheet music and sound recordings); advertising relating to the television exhibition of the film; "trailer" or other advertising on the screen or radio or television or to institutional or other advertising or publicity not relating primarily to the Film; so called "award ads" in which only the name of the recipient or nominee is mentioned; or to advertising of such nature that consent to the use of the Writer's name in connection therewith has not been granted hereunder. Nothing herein contained with respect to size of type shall apply to advertising or publicity material in narrative form.

4.4.   No casual or inadvertent failure of the company to comply with the provision of this Clause and no casual or inadvertent failure of persons other than the Company to comply with their contracts with the Company shall constitute a breach of this Agreement by the Company. The rights and remedies of the Writer in the event of such failure shall be limited to his right (if any) to recover damages in an action at law and in no event shall the Writer or any on his behalf be entitled by reason of any such failure to enjoin or restrain the distribution or exhibit of the Film.

5.   ASSSIGNABILITY

The Company shall be entitled to assign license or otherwise dispose of or deal with the benefit of this assignment and all other rights to which the Company is entitled hereunder to any person or company.

6.   PREVIOUS TERMS

This Assignment shall supersede all previous agreements, arrangements, representations and/or assignments (written, oral or implied) between the parties hereto or otherwise with respect to the Screenplay, the Producers and/or the Film.

7.   GOVERNING LAW

This Assignment shall supersede all previous agreements, arrangements, representations and/or assignments (written, oral or implied) between the parties hereto or otherwise with respect to the Screenplay, the Products and/or the Film.

AS WITNESS the hands of the parties hereto the day and year first before written.

_____ SIGNED by WRITER

_____SIGNED by MARC VLESSING for and on behalf of TRENDRAISE COMPANY LIMITED

Notes

1. Besides inserting commas and using the American version of words like "fictionalization," how might an American attorney draft this contract? Would the provisions be similar or different?

2. Chapter 5, Billing, Credit, and Compensation, will explore in detail issues such as credit and compensation that are present in this contract.

Chapter 5

STAR BILLING, CREDIT,
& COMPENSATION

During the era of silent films, studios did not indicate which actors starred in their films. According to William Goldman, if fans wanted to write actors, they sent letters to "The Butler with the Mustache" or "The Girl with the Curly Blonde Hair." ADVENTURES IN THE SCREEN TRADE 5 (1983). Viewers saw only the name of the film and production company, until the companies recognized that giving credit improved the selling of films as audience members were likely to return to see a particular actor in their next picture. Similarly, if viewers liked the writing in *Casablanca* they might rush to see *Arsenic & Old Lace* once they realized that Julius J. Epstein penned both pictures.

Currently, at the beginning and end of films, the credits roll or blink in and out on screen. "Credit" refers to the listing of the person's name next to the function he or she performed in the entertainment project. The "story by" credit indicates the person who developed the story but did not write the screenplay. That credit is denoted as "written by" and may go to one or more people. An ampersand (&) indicates two or more writers who worked together to create a joint work. The word "and" designates two or more authors who contributed to the script after the first author had finished the original script. The "script supervisor" took detailed notes (scene number, take number, camera position, & dialogue running time) during the filming, which aids the director and editor in deciding which cuts to add to the final product. Depending on the size of the project and the amount of special effects, over 100 credits may scroll across the screen at the end. While national audiences tend to depart when the credits commence, L.A. audiences often stay to the last frame, usually the copyright indicator, is shown out of deference to those who participated in the venture.

Credits have both financial and psychological consequences. Talent and crew find that their pay rises as their credit increases from "Best Boy or Girl" (first assistant electrician who adjust lighting) to "Gaffer" (chief electrician) or from "Grip" (a laborer who creates and breaks down stage sets) to "Key Grip" (the head of the crew). While pay is

220

based on contributions, it increases as reputation for producing excellent work in the industry grows. Likewise, the psychological reward comes from the acknowledgement of the person's role in project, that no matter how small the task may have been, it added value to the film.

Billing is particularly important to actors as their stature may be based on whether their name is placed before or after the title of the film. If the actor is not the star, the sooner her name appears after the star the better, unless they get the final listing (e.g. and Catherine Zeta Jones). Stars will sometimes trade pay for credit to appear in a lower budget film that showcases their talent in other genres. By augmenting their range, the star may start to receive a higher quality range of scripts. After getting his start in sexually explicit films (*The Italian Stallion)* and then becoming known for action flicks (*Rocky, Rambo,* and *Cliffhanger)*, Sylvester Stallone took less compensation for the 1997 *Copland* to play a chubby, passive sheriff driven to action in a New Jersey town full of rogue New York cops that included the Academy Award Winner Robert De Niro.

Credit and billing are linked to compensation. Above the title actors like Tom Cruise, Jim Carey, Tom Hanks, Robert Williams can make $22 million a picture, plus a cut of the box office gross. Jack Nicholson, for example, received total compensation exceeding $56 million for playing the role of The Joker the 1989 *Batman.*

The pay of stars often increases with the box office gross of their pictures. Bruce Willis, for example was paid $20 million for the 1995 *Die Hard with a Vengeance*, an increase by four times what he received for the original 1998 *Die Hard*. The former took in $365 million in worldwide box office compared to $139 million for the original film. In between, Willis starred in *Die Hard 2: Die Harder*, which earned $237,500,000. The increasing successes of these ventures enabled Willis to command higher fees.

This chapter first discusses star billing from the perspective of actors, writers, directors and producers and then explores compensation issues, which includes a delineation of net profits and pay or play contract clauses. As the next case illustrates, given the connection between future compensation and billing, stars can become quite upset if credit is not given exactly as it is negotiated for in the star's contract.

A.   STAR BILLING

With films costing and average $55 million to produce and $27 million to advertise in 2000, stars who sell over $200 million in tickets are worth their salary to many studios.

1.   THE STAR

"What is a star? Used to be an easy answer: A star was a performer who was billed above the title. But those were the days when billing meant something; now, more often than not, it's something that's doled out in lieu of a higher salary.... But in the movies, the answer to 'Who is a star?' is 'It's whoever *one* studio executive with 'go' power *thinks* is a star and will underwrite with a start date.' (A superstar is someone they'll all kill for....)''

William Goldman, Author
ADVENTURES IN THE SCREEN TRADE 11–13 (1983)

The stars for who the studios would kill changes over the decades. In 1961, the top ten box office stars were Elizabeth Taylor, Rock Hudson, Doris Day, John Wayne, Sandra Dee, Jerry Lewis, William Holden, Tony Curtis, and Elvis Presley. *Id.* at 8. By 1981, the top ten were headlined by Burt Reynolds, Clint Eastwood, Dudley Moore, Dolly Parton, Jane Fonda, Harrison Ford, Alan Alda, Bo Derek, Goldie Hawn, and Bill Murray. *Id.* at 7. In 2003, Quigley Publications rated the top box office draws as Jim Carrey, Nicole Kidman, Jack Nicholson, Tom Cruise, Julia Roberts, Johnny Depp, Russell Crowe, Tom Hanks, Will Ferrell and Renee Zellweger.

While the list may change over the decade, star billing can mean a great deal to certain actors.

SOPHIA LOREN v. SAMUEL BRONSTON PRODUCTIONS

New York Supreme Court, 1962.
32 Misc.2d 602, 224 N.Y.S.2d 959.

HOFSTADTER, Justice.

The egocentricity which appears to be indigenous to 'show business' is here manifested by the passionate insistence of a well-known motion-picture actress to have her name emblazoned on Broadway not only in the same type of the same size, but also on the same line, as that of her male lead. Such vanity—'the frail estate of human things', a 'splendid but destructive egotism', as it has variously been called—doubtless is due in measurable part to the adulation which the public showers on the denizens of the entertainment world in a profusion wholly disproportionate to the intrinsic contribution which they make to the scheme of things when seen in correct perspective. For that matter often in disproportion to any true talent, latent or apparent!

Sophia Loren, the world-famed winner of the New York Film Critics' Award as the outstanding motion picture actress of 1961, and a corporation, owning the exclusive right to her services, of which her husband, Carlo Ponti is the president and sole stockholder, as plaintiffs, have brought this action for an injunction against the producer and the distributor of the epic motion picture 'El Cid', which opened at the Warner Theatre in this city on December 14, 1961 and is being shown there to capacity houses. The owner and operator of the Warner Theatre is also a defendant in the action. The plaintiffs now move for injunctive relief during the pendency of the action substantially the same as they would obtain if successful at the trial.

Sophia Loren plays the leading female role of Chimene in 'El Cid'; the part of 'El Cid', a national hero of Spain, is taken by Charlton Heston. The plaintiffs' asserted grievance is that Miss Loren has not received the billing of which a written agreement of October 14, 1960, entitles her. This agreement provides that in all paid advertising of 'El Cid' Miss Loren is to be accorded 'second (2nd) star billing above the title, 100% the size and type of the title, on the same line, same size, same prominence as that used for Charlton Heston, who received first (1st) star billing.' The plaintiffs complain of non-compliance with the foregoing provisions, especially in the design of electrically illuminated upright signs, on which the name of Sophia Loren appears below that of Charlton Heston, and the type of their names is different and smaller than that of the title 'El Cid'. The names of the two top stars on these signs, are, however, in the same size type and there is no differentiation in prominence, except insofar as the position of one above the other may imply. Moreover, on the marquee in front of the Warner Theatre facing Broadway their names are on the same line. The defendants dispute that they are doing anything in derogation of the plaintiffs' rights; they rely on the billing clause of a later employment agreement fully complied with, which, they say, either binds the plaintiffs contractually or which, in the light of their conduct, equity and good conscience will not permit the plaintiffs now to disavow.

In view of the disposition to be made, further statement of the facts or detailed analysis of the conflicting contentions of the parties will not be fruitful. It suffices for present purposes that study of the papers persuades me that the case presents substantial issues as to the plaintiffs' ultimate rights. There is also a genuine question whether, even if the plaintiffs' claims under the billing clause of the October 14, 1960 agreement are upheld, Miss Loren is really in danger of suffering the loss of prestige and other damage attributed to its non-observance. The injunction prayed for would do far more than preserve the status quo, for the plaintiffs demand the removal of the electric signs and changes in the advertising program for the picture. Under established authority, the plaintiffs' rights at this juncture are not so clear as to warrant such an injunction and the motion therefor is denied (*Bachman v. Harrington*, 184 N.Y. 458, 77 N.E. 657; *Gilbert v. Burnside*, 6 A.D.2d 834, 835, 175 N.Y.S.2d 989, 992; *Durante v. Paramount Pictures Corp.*, Sup., 111 N.Y.S.2d 138).

However, an early trial is indicated. The case is placed at the head of the General Equity Calendar of February 19, 1962, for which date the clerk is directed to accept a note of issue on payment of his fees. Statement of readiness is dispensed with.

Notes

1. The judge likens Ms. Loren's concern that her name was not on the same level and the same type without realizing the number of lawyer hours that probably went into negotiating Ms. Loren's credit clause. While SAG

[margin handwritten note: actors can determine by the size + placement of the credit.]

negotiates a minimum credit requirement, actors can determine by contract the size and placement of the credit.

2.   Is your client likely to win when the judge begins the case, "The egocentricity which appears to be indigenous to 'show business' is here manifested by?" While there is value in having celebrity clients participate in their own trials, particularly when the person has a pleasant demeanor, the strategy can backfire should the client treat the judge with contempt or otherwise display blatant arrogance.

3.   While Sophia Loren may not have placed high in the judge's esteem, People Magazine designated her as among the *50 Most Beautiful People in the World* in 1991 and Playboy Magazine ranked #6 in its *Sex Stars of the Century*.   See   http://www.amiannoying.com/(hcup0045wmhmvn2 tcksrct55)/view.aspx?ID=3118

2.   THE WRITER

While some writers endure credit arbitrations to receive credit on a film, there may be times when they do not want to be associated with a film.

KING v. INNOVATION BOOKS

United States Court of Appeals, Second Circuit, 1992.
976 F.2d 824.

MINER, Circuit Judge.

Defendants-appellants, Allied Vision, Ltd. and New Line Cinema Corporation, appeal from an order of the United States District Court for the Southern District of New York (Motley, J.) granting a preliminary injunction in favor of plaintiff-appellee Stephen King in connection with King's claims under the Lanham Act and New York law. King, who is the author of such best-selling horror thrillers as *The Shining, Carrie* and *Salem's Lot,* contended that Allied and New Line falsely designated him as the originator of the motion picture "The Lawnmower Man," which was produced by Allied and distributed in North America by New Line. The injunction, which prohibits any use of King's name "on or in connection with" the movie, encompasses two forms of credit to which King objected: (i) a possessory credit, describing the movie as "Stephen King's The Lawnmower Man," and (ii) a "based upon" credit, representing that the movie is "based upon" a short story by King. For the reasons that follow, we affirm the district court's order to the extent that it prohibits use of the possessory credit, but reverse the order to the extent that it prohibits use of the "based upon" credit.

BACKGROUND

In 1970, King wrote a short story entitled "The Lawnmower Man" (the "Short Story"). The Short Story, published in 1975 and running about ten printed pages in length, involves Harold Parkette, a homeowner in the suburbs. Parkette begins to neglect his lawn after an incident in which the boy who usually mows his lawn mows over a cat.

By the time Parkette focuses his attention again on his overgrown lawn, the boy has gone away to college. Parkette therefore hires a new man to mow his lawn. The lawnmower man turns out to be a cleft-footed, obese and vile agent of the pagan god Pan. The lawnmower man also is able to move the lawnmower psychokinetically—that is, by sheer force of mind.

After starting the lawnmower, the lawnmower man removes his clothing and crawls after the running mower on his hands and knees, eating both grass and a mole that the mower has run over. Parkette, who is watching in horror, phones the police. Using his psychokinetic powers, however, the lawnmower man directs the lawnmower after Parkette, who is chopped up by the lawnmower's blades after being chased through his house. The Short Story ends with the discovery by the police of Parkette's entrails in the birdbath behind the home.

In 1978, King assigned to Great Fantastic Picture Corporation the motion picture and television rights for the Short Story. The assignment agreement, which provided that it was to be governed by the laws of England, allowed the assignee the "exclusive right to deal with the [Short Story] as [it] may think fit," including the rights

(i) to write film treatments [and] scripts and other dialogue versions of all descriptions of the [Short Story] and at all times to add to[,] take from [,] use[,] alter[,] adapt ... and change the [Short Story] and the title [,] characters[,] plot[,] theme[,] dialogue[,] sequences and situations thereof....

(ii) to make or produce films of all kinds ... incorporating or based upon the [Short Story] or any part or parts thereof or any adaptation thereof.

In return, King received an interest in the profits of "each" film "based upon" the Short Story.

In February 1990, Great Fantastic transferred its rights under the assignment agreement to Allied, a movie production company organized under the laws of the United Kingdom and having offices in London. In May 1990, Allied commissioned a screenplay for a feature-length film entitled "The Lawnmower Man." The screenplay was completed by August 1990, and pre-production work on the movie began in January 1991. By February 1991, Allied began to market the forthcoming movie by placing advertisements in trade magazines and journals. The picture generally was described as "Stephen King's The Lawnmower Man," and as "based upon" a short story by King. Actual filming of the movie began in May 1991. About one month later, Allied, through its United States subsidiary, licensed New Line, a domestic corporation with offices in New York and California, to distribute the movie in North America. The licensing agreement was concluded in California, and a press release announcing the distribution deal was issued from that state as well. New Line initially paid $250,000 for the distribution rights, with an additional $2.25 million to be paid thereafter.

King learned of the forthcoming movie in early October 1991, from an article in a film magazine. He then contacted Rand Holston, an agent handling King's film rights, in an attempt to gather information about the film; asked Chuck Verrill, his literary agent, to obtain a "rough cut" of the movie; and instructed Jay Kramer, his lawyer, to inform Allied that King did not like the idea of a possessory credit (a form of credit apparently portended by the article).

By letter dated October 9, 1991, Kramer advised Allied that King "d[id] not want" a possessory credit to appear on the film. Kramer also requested a copy of the movie and the tentative movie credits King was to receive. In another letter to Allied dated October 21, 1991—written after Kramer secured a copy of the movie's screenplay—Kramer advised that "we emphatically object" to the possessory credit contained in the screenplay, and noted that he had yet to receive a copy of the tentative credits.

It appears that King learned of New Line's involvement with the film in November 1991. On King's direction, Verrill contacted New Line for a copy of the film. Verrill was informed that a copy would not be available until January 1992. Verrill contacted New Line again on February 6, 1992, but this produced no copy of the film either. Kramer and Holston shortly advised New Line, in a February 18, 1992 telephone call with New Line's President of Production Sara Risher, that King was "outraged" that the movie was being described as "Stephen King's The Lawnmower Man."

In a February 28, 1992 letter, Kramer again insisted to Risher that the possessory credit was a "complete misrepresentation," and attached copies of the October 1991 letters sent to Allied. As of this time, New Line had paid the balance of the price due to Allied for purchase of the distribution rights, had expended about $7.5 million in advertising and marketing costs, and had become committed to release the movie in theaters throughout North America.

On March 3, 1992—four days or so before release of the movie in theaters—King viewed a copy of the movie in a screening arranged by Allied and New Line. The protagonist of the two hour movie is Dr. Lawrence Angelo. Experimenting with chimpanzees, Dr. Angelo develops a technology, based on computer simulation, known as "Virtual Reality," which allows a chimp to enter a three-dimensional computer environment simulating various action scenarios. Dr. Angelo hopes to adapt the technology for human use, with the ultimate goal of accelerating and improving human intelligence.

Eventually, Dr. Angelo begins experimenting with his technology on Jobe, who mows lawns in Dr. Angelo's neighborhood and is referred to as "the lawnmower man." Jobe, a normal-looking young man, is simple and possesses a childlike mentality. Dr. Angelo is able greatly to increase Jobe's intellect with Virtual Reality technology. However, the experiment spins out of control, with Jobe becoming hostile and violent as his intelligence and mental abilities become super-human. In the build-up to the movie's climax, Jobe employs his newly acquired psychokinetic powers to chase Dr. Angelo's neighbor (a man named Harold Parkette) through his house with a running lawnmower, and to kill him. The police discover the dead man's remains in the birdbath behind his home, and, in the climax of the movie, Dr. Angelo destroys Jobe.

The film and advertising seen by King contained both possessory and "based upon" credits. On the evening of March 3, after viewing the film, King wrote to Holston:

> I think *The Lawnmower Man* is really an extraordinary piece of work, at least visually, and the core of my story, such as it is, is in the movie. I think it is going to be very successful and I want to get out of the way. I want you to make clear to [the] trolls at New Line Pictures that I am unhappy with them, but I am shelving [at least for the time being] any ideas of taking out ads in the trades or trying to obtain an injunction to stop New Line from advertising or exploiting the picture. I would like to talk to you late this week or early next about doing some brief interviews which will make my lack of involvement clear, but for the time being, I am just going to step back and shut up.

In a March 23, 1992 letter, Kramer again advised Allied of King's "long standing objection" to the possessory credit, and also took note of "the apparent failure of [Allied] to inform New Line of Mr. King's objection until the movie was about to be released." However, no objection to the "based upon" credit ever was registered until May 20, 1992. From March through May 1992, New Line expended another $2.5 million in promotion and entered into certain hotel movie and television commitments, as well as home video arrangements.

King initiated the instant suit on May 28, 1992, seeking damages as well as injunctive relief. He claimed that the possessory and "based upon" credits violated section 43(a) of the Lanham Act, *see* 15 U.S.C. § 1125(a), as well as the New York common law of unfair competition and contracts, the New York General Business Law, and the New York Civil Rights Law. A motion for preliminary injunction was made on June 3, and a hearing was held on June 29.

[handwritten margin note: Lanham Act]

The district court agreed with King on all of his claims and granted the injunction on July 2, concluding that the possessory credit was false on its face, that the "based upon" credit was misleading, and that the irreparable harm element of a preliminary injunction action had been satisfied. The equitable defenses of laches, estoppel and waiver interposed by Allied and New Line were rejected.

The injunction prohibited use of King's name "on or in connection with" the motion picture, and by its terms encompassed both the possessory and "based upon" credits. The injunction applied to distribution of the film by Allied abroad as well as by New Line in North America, either in theaters or on videocassette or on television. We granted appellants' application for a stay pending this expedited appeal, but conditioned the stay upon suspension of use of the possessory credit.

At oral argument, counsel for New Line informed us that the videocassettes of the movie now in circulation contain only the "based upon" credit.

DISCUSSION

* * * As the district court observed, a party such as King seeking an injunction "must demonstrate (1) irreparable harm should the injunction not be granted, and (2) either (a) a likelihood of success on the merits, or (b) sufficiently serious questions going to the merits and a balance of hardships tipping decidedly toward [that] party...." *Resolution Trust Corp. v. Elman*, 949 F.2d 624, 626 (2d Cir.1991); *Coca-Cola Co. v. Tropicana Products, Inc.*, 690 F.2d 312, 314–15 (2d Cir.1982).

I.   Likelihood of Success on the Merits

The district court correctly noted that a false reference to the origin of a work, or a reference which, while not literally false, is misleading or likely to confuse, may form the basis of a claim under section 43(a) of the Lanham Act. *See* 15 U.S.C. § 1125(a) (1988) (prohibiting use in commerce of "any false designation of origin, false or misleading description of fact, or false or misleading representation of fact" which is "likely to cause confusion . . . or to deceive as to [ ] affiliation, connection, or association"); *Gilliam v. American Broadcasting Companies, Inc.*, 538 F.2d 14, 24–25 (2d Cir.1976).

A.   The Possessory Credit

We perceive no error in the district court's conclusion that King is likely to succeed on the merits of his objection to the possessory credit. The district court was entirely entitled to conclude, from the testimony at the preliminary injunction hearing, that a possessory credit ordinarily is given to the producer, director or writer of the film; and that the credit at a minimum refers to an individual who had some involvement in, and/or gave approval to, the screenplay or movie itself. In contrast to other films for which he has been given a possessory credit, King had no involvement in, and gave no approval of, "The Lawnmower Man" screenplay or movie.

Under the circumstances, therefore, the arguments advanced by Allied and New Line as to why the possessory credit is not false—that the other movie credits make clear that King was not the producer, director or writer of the film, and that King has in the past received a possessory credit where he merely approved in advance of the screenplay or movie—do not alter the conclusion that King is likely to succeed on his challenge to the possessory credit. Appellants also contend that King offered no evidence of public confusion in relation to the possessory credit. As will be detailed in our discussion of irreparable harm, however, there was some such evidence offered. In any event, as the district court recognized, no evidence of public confusion is required where, as is the case with the possessory credit, the attribution is false on its face. *See*

PPX Enterprises, Inc. v. Audiofidelity Enterprises, Inc., 818 F.2d 266, 272
(2d Cir.1987) (citations omitted).

B. The "Based Upon" Credit

As the district court recognized, a "based upon" credit by definition
affords more "leeway" than a possessory credit. The district court
nevertheless concluded that the "based upon" credit at issue here is
misleading and likely to cause confusion to the public, reasoning in
essence that the "climatic scene from the [S]hort [S]tory is inserted into
the film in a manner wholly unrelated to the plot of the film," and that
the credit "grossly exaggerates" the relationship between the Short
Story and the film. While particular findings of fact are subject to the
clearly erroneous standard of review, we have said that the weighing of
factors in "the ultimate determination of the likelihood of confusion is a
legal issue subject to *de novo* appellate review." *Hasbro, Inc. v. Lanard
Toys, Ltd.,* 858 F.2d 70, 75–76 (2d Cir.1988) (citations omitted) (Lanham
Act trade mark claim). We believe that in so heavily weighing the
proportion of the film attributable to the Short Story in the course of
finding the "based upon" credit to be misleading and confusing, the
district court applied a standard without sufficient support in the testimony and applicable law.

John Breglio, an attorney of the law firm of Paul, Weiss, Rifkind,
Wharton & Garrison specializing in entertainment law, testified as an
expert witness for King. Breglio opined that the term "based upon," in
the context of royalty obligations under King's assignment agreement,
was not identical to the term "based upon" in a movie credit. After
speaking of a test of "substantial similarity" between the literary work
and movie, and opining that there was not substantial similarity between the Short Story and the film, Breglio went on to state that the
industry standard for determining the meaning of a "based upon" movie
credit is very similar to that used by copyright lawyers in examining
issues of copyright infringement. Breglio further explained that this
standard involved looking "at the work as a whole and how much
protected material *from the underlying work* appears in the derivative
work." (emphasis added)

Indeed, in cases of alleged copyright infringement it has long been
appropriate to examine the quantitative and qualitative degree to which
the allegedly infringed work has been borrowed from, and not simply the
proportion of the allegedly *infringing* work that is made up of the
copyrighted material. *See Harper & Row v. Nation Enterprises,* 471 U.S.
539, 565–66, 105 S.Ct. 2218, 2233, 85 L.Ed.2d 588 (1985) (citing *Sheldon
v. Metro–Goldwyn Pictures Corp.,* 81 F.2d 49, 56 (2d Cir.) (L. Hand, *J.*),
cert. denied, 298 U.S. 669, 56 S.Ct. 835, 80 L.Ed. 1392 (1936)). Accordingly, the propriety of the "based upon" credit should have been evaluated with less emphasis on the proportion of the film attributable to the
Short Story, and with more emphasis on the proportion, in quantitative
and qualitative terms, of the Short Story appearing in the film. Where a
movie draws in material respects from a literary work, both quantitative-

ly and qualitatively, a "based upon" credit should not be viewed as misleading absent persuasive countervailing facts and circumstances. Our concern is the possibility that under the district court's apparent approach, substantially all of a literary work could be taken for use in a film and, if unrelated ideas, themes and scenes are tacked on or around the extracted work, a "based upon" credit would be deemed misleading.

In the case before us, the apparent "core" of the ten page Short Story—a scene in which a character called "the lawnmower man" uses psychokinetic powers to chase another character through his house with a running lawnmower and thereby kill him—is used in the movie. In both the movie and the Short Story, the remains of the murdered man (who is named Harold Parkette in both works) are found in the birdbath by the police; the two police officers in both works have the same names and engage in substantially similar dialogue. As King himself described it, "the core of my story, such as it is, is in the movie." The red lawnmower seen in the movie also appears to be as described in the Short Story. A brief reference to the Pan mythology of the Short Story appears in the movie as well; dialogue between Jobe and another character includes a reference to "Pan pipes of the little people in the grass."

We recognize that several important and entertaining aspects of the Short Story were not used in the film, and that conversely the film contains a number of elements not to be found in the Short Story. However, when the resemblances between the Short Story and the motion picture at issue here are considered together, they establish to our satisfaction that the movie draws in sufficiently material respects on the Short Story in both qualitative and quantitative aspects.

Nor are there any persuasive countervailing facts or circumstances in the record to lead us away from the conclusion that the "based upon" credit is proper in this case. King himself apparently was not bothered much (if at all) by the "based upon" credit, in marked contrast to his sustained and strong objections to the possessory credit, until shortly before he initiated this suit. He has not pointed us to evidence in the record of industry or public perception of, or confusion over, the "based upon" credit beyond the thoughts offered by Breglio. Professor George Stade, Vice Chairman of the English Department at Columbia University and King's other expert witness, did opine that, despite similarities, the movie was not based upon the Short Story. However, even Professor Stade indicated at one point in his testimony that "substantial" portions of the Short Story appear in the film.

In *Gilliam v. American Broadcasting Companies, Inc.*, 538 F.2d 14 (2d Cir.1976), we found a violation of section 43(a) by the ABC television network, which had aired, under license from the BBC, the "Monty Python's Flying Circus" programs of the British comedy group. Monty Python's agreement with the BBC gave the comedy group substantial control over any editing by the BBC. *See id.* at 17. However, ABC on its own substantially edited the programs it aired under the BBC license, so as to eliminate many thematically essential and humorous portions of the original programs. *See id.* at 24–25 & n. 12. King suggests, in disputing the legitimacy of the "based upon" credit, that Allied's treatment of the Short Story is analogous to ABC's editing in *Gilliam.*

However, at issue in *Gilliam* were original Monty Python programs which were edited by ABC and then rebroadcast as Monty Python's work. We specifically noted that Monty Python was being "present[ed] to the public as the creator of a work not [its] own, and [made] subject to criticism for work [it] has not done." *Id.* at 24 (quotation omitted). While *Gilliam* certainly supports the view we have taken of the possessory credit, the case is not very helpful in evaluating the accuracy of a "based upon" credit, which by definition deals with altered and derivative works.

It is undoubtedly the case that King's assignment agreement does not permit Allied to use King's name fraudulently, and we express no view as to the degree of overlap between the term "based upon" in the King assignment agreement and the term "based upon" in a theatrical credit. However, we do note that the agreement contemplates substantial alterations to the Short Story, and even obligates Allied to give King credit in the case of a film "based wholly or substantially upon" the Short Story. We think that King would have cause to complain if he were *not* afforded the "based upon" credit.

II.   IRREPARABLE HARM

As the district court observed, a presumption of irreparable harm arises in Lanham Act cases once the plaintiff establishes likelihood of success on a claim of literal falseness, as King has established with respect to the possessory credit . . . Nothing in the record persuades us that the district court erred in concluding that this presumption was not rebutted.

Appellants contend that any presumption of irreparable injury was rebutted because King delayed in seeking relief. However, the greatest conceivable delay attributable to King is about eight months: from early October 1991, when he first learned of the movie, to early June 1992, when he moved for a preliminary injunction. During that time, however, King, through his agents, contacted Allied and New Line and repeatedly objected to any use of a possessory credit, and attempted to obtain the screenplay, tentative credits and film for viewing. This is not conduct that undercuts a sense of urgency or of an imminent threat, and indeed the circumstances in this case contrast with those in which we have found a delay negating the presumption of irreparable harm.

* * *

The March 3 letter written by King to Rand Holston, in which King indicated that he was impressed by the movie and that he was "shelving" legal action, together with apparently similar remarks made by King to counsel at that time, could be viewed as countering an irreparable harm presumption. However, the district court did not accept this argument, and we are unable to find error in this under all the circumstances. While King refers in the letter to shelving action against New Line's advertising of the picture, King does not say in the letter that he is shelving action against Allied or action in relation to the credits appearing in the movie itself. Further, because of the references in the letter to "at least for the time being" and "at this time," King's reactions as of March 3 could be viewed as tentative in nature. Indeed, shortly after King's March 3 letter was written, Kramer again wrote to Allied to reiterate King's "long standing objection" to the movie's possessory credit.

Appellants also suggest that the presumption of irreparable harm, was rebutted because King himself enjoyed the movie, continues to be a popular literary figure, and was unable to specify particular financial injury. However, we have observed that the irreparable harm in cases such as this often flows not so much from some specific reduction "in fact" to an individual's name or reputation, but rather from the wrongful attribution to the individual, in the eye of the general public, of responsibility for actions over which he or she has no control. * * *

In this connection, King testified to the obvious point that his name and artistic reputation are his major assets, and offered into evidence certain unfavorable reviews of the movie. These reviews tended to discuss the movie in possessory terms and portray the work as a kind of failure on the part of King personally—persuasive evidence of the type of damage and confusion caused by the possessory credit. One reviewer, for instance, who thought the movie uninspiring, commented sarcastically: "Coming next week to a theater near you: *Stephen King's Grocery List.*" Another review began with the statement that "Steven [sic] King's latest film, *The Lawnmower Man,* continues to reinforce the impression that he and Hollywood just don't work well together."

III. LACHES

A party asserting the equitable defense of laches must establish both plaintiff's unreasonable lack of diligence under the circumstances in initiating an action, as well as prejudice from such a delay.... The district court used March 3, 1992—the date King viewed the film—as the baseline from which to evaluate the laches question in this case. The district court concluded, using this date, that a mere three month delay in bringing suit was not unreasonable, and that prejudice also was absent because appellants had entered into the great majority of their commitments in connection with the movie by March 3. According to Allied and New Line, however, King knew everything he needed to know to assert his rights by October 1991, when a copy of the screenplay (with credits) was obtained. Appellants argue, therefore, that October 1991 is the proper time from which to consider the laches question, and note that many commitments were made, and much money expended, after that time.

The issue of laches is committed to the discretion of the district court, *see Dickey v. Alcoa Steamship Co.,* 641 F.2d 81, 82 (2d Cir.1981) (citations omitted), and we see no abuse of that discretion here. King could not be certain about what the film would contain—the film credits lying at the heart of this dispute—until he actually viewed a copy of the film. Indeed, in the very same letter of October 21 in which he acknowledged having the screenplay, Kramer specifically complained that he had not yet seen the tentative film credits. Accordingly, October 1991 does not seem to us to be a useful date at which to draw a baseline. * * *

The district court also found that appellants together delayed King's viewing of the film. This finding was supported by the evidence. A January 17, 1992 letter from Peter McRae of Allied to Sandra Ruch, for example, indicated that any "approach" to King had to be "carefully considered" in light of "the potential benefits we may gain." Ruch handwrote on this letter that "[w]e don't want S King to see it [the movie] before opening date." This kind of "unclean hands" behavior confirms our belief that there was no abuse of discretion in the district court's rejection of the equitable defense of laches. * * *

CONCLUSION

The order of the district court granting a preliminary injunction is affirmed to the extent it prohibits use of the possessory credit, but reversed to the extent it prohibits use of a "based upon" credit.

Notes

1. Stephen King's suit generated comment in the trade press. In January 1993, the Entertainment Law Reporter ran the story *Distributors of "The Lawnmower Man" may state that film is "based upon" Stephen King story, but may not use possessory credit,* 14 No.8 Enter. L. Rptr. 9 (1993). Does New Line risk loss of reputation when it advertises a movie to be a Stephen King film when King says it is not?

2. Would you expect that New Line would comply with the judge's order? In August, 1994, The *Entertainment Law Reporter* discussed the May 1993 settlement agreement that incorporated a final consent degree. According to the *Entertainment Law Reporter,* "New Line agreed to take "immediate steps" to provide "paste-over" stickers or otherwise remove any references to King on videos of "The Lawnmower Man," and to provide compliance instructions to its distributors and wholesalers." Nevertheless, "Federal District Court Judge Constance Baker Motley has found that New Line delayed mailing paste-over stickers or new sleeves and that the company did not determine how many stickers or sleeves retailers actually might require. It also was found that the company did not provide adequate instructions to distributors and wholesalers concerning the corrective material. Judge Motley observed that a month after the decree was entered, "there remained in the inventories of New Line's distributors and wholesalers between 24,000 and 54,000 videocassettes packaged in offending sleeves." *New Line Cinema is held in contempt of consent order for using*

Stephen King's name in connection with videocassettes of "The Lawnmower Man," 16 No.3 Enter. L. Rptr. 4 (1994).

New Line was found in contempt of court and ordered to "pay a fine" to King in the amount of $10,000 per day until the noncompliance is cured. Judge Motley further stated that King would be entitled to any "unlawful profits" earned by New Line from sales or rentals of *The Lawnmower Man* videocassettes or laser discs during the period of noncompliance, and ordered New Line to produce a statement of such net profits. King also will be entitled to recover the attorneys' fees and costs he incurred in the matter.

3. The case hit the press again in June 1995 when New Line was again fined $10,000 per day for failing to supply corrective materials to remove Stephen King's name from *The Lawnmower Man* videos. New Line failed to notify its licensees and distributors by certified mail of the consent degree and did not follow up with the parties who failed to respond to the initial market. *See New Line Cinema must pay Stephen King $10,000 per day for failing to cure contempt of consent decree entered in dispute over "The Lawnmower Man" videocassette credits,* 17 No.1 Enter. L. Rptr. 16 (1995). Does New Line gain anything from failing to comply? Are they lazy or calculating that they will sell more tapes with Stephen King's name on the cassettes that without and the difference will offset the fines?

4. Even when Stephen King's name receives top billing with his approval, it does not guarantee success. "Steven King's Kingdom Hospital," a television series that debuted on ABC on March 3, 2004, was subjected to scathing commentary from at least one reviewer. Hal Boedeker, of the *Orlando Sentinel,* called the show "the biggest disappointment, a botch of monumental proportions." He added, " 'Kingdom Hospital' is a mess of ridiculous characters, meandering plots, baffling apparitions and inexplicable medicine.... The King portions, which should have been personal and scary, come off as simply bewildering." Hal Boedeker, *TV Review: "Stephen King's Kingdom Hospital" and "The Mystery of Natalie Wood,"* Orlando Sentinel, Feb. 29, 2004, at 4.

PARAMOUNT PRODUCTIONS v. SMITH

United States Court of Appeals, Ninth Circuit, 1937.
91 F.2d 863.

HANEY, Circuit Judge.

Breach of

Judgment was rendered for appellee in his action against appellant for breach of contract, and the latter appealed.

It is admitted by the pleadings that appellee is the sole author of a story entitled 'Cruise to Nowhere'; that appellee sold the story to appellant on April 29, 1933, for $2,500, as evidenced by a written contract containing the terms and conditions of the sale. This contract contains the following provisions:

'Second: The Author hereby grants to the Purchaser all the motion picture rights throughout the world, in and to and in connection with the said story, together with the sole and exclusive rights to use, adapt, translate, subtract from, add to and change the said

story and the title thereof in the making of motion picture photoplays and/or as a part of and/or in conjunction with any motion
picture photoplay and/or to combine the said story with any other
work, to use the said title and/or any similar title in conjunction
with motion picture photoplays based upon the said story and/or
other literary, dramatic and/or dramatico-musical [works]. * * *'

'Eighth: The Purchaser agrees to announce on the film of the
motion picture photoplays that may be produced pursuant hereto
that such motion picture photoplays are based upon or adapted from
a story written by the Author, or words to that effect.'

In paragraph 'Second,' supra, by the use of the recondite and occult
typographical jumble 'and/or,' a near approach to totality of confusion
and unintelligibility has been accomplished, but, inasmuch as the determination of this appeal is dependent upon the construction of the eighth
paragraph of the contract rather than the second, we abandon without
regret all effort to determine, by reference to its written word, the
meaning, if any there be, of the provisions of the second paragraph
aforesaid.

The complaint alleged that in 1934 appellant completed the production and thereafter exhibited generally throughout the United States a
'talking motion picture' under the title of 'We're Not Dressing,' which
'was based upon, and adapted from, said original story of plaintiff herein,
entitled 'Cruise to Nowhere' * * *'; that appellant violated the eighth
provision of the contract quoted, in that appellant 'wholly failed to
announce upon said films, or at any of the public exhibitions thereof,
that the same was either written by plaintiff, or that it was based upon,
or adapted from, a story written by' appellee. Appellant admitted production and exhibition of the picture 'We're Not Dressing,' but denied the
remainder of these allegations. * * *

Appellant says that the primary question is whether or not the
picture was based upon or adapted from appellee's story. That statement
is only partially true. Our function is to ascertain whether or not there is
any substantial evidence to sustain the verdict. Specifically, the question
presented is whether or not there is any substantial evidence to sustain
the finding of the jury that the picture 'We're Not Dressing' was based
upon or adapted from appellee's story, 'Cruise to Nowhere.'

An examination of the record discloses that the evidence was conflicting. Three of appellant's witnesses defined and distinguished between 'based upon' and 'adapted from.' There was evidence showing that
the picture produced was not based upon or adapted from appellee's
story. We are not interested in such evidence, however, but only in the
evidence of the opposite fact.

The cost sheet hereinabove discussed is some evidence of the fact
found by the jury. Correspondence between officers of appellant had
some months before filming was started indicates that appellant may
have used the story. Appellee introduced a manuscript of his story into

evidence, and read it to the jury. During the trial, the court and its attendants, the jury, appellee, and counsel for the parties saw a showing of the picture. The jury was able to make a comparison. Afterward, appellee testified, 'I saw in the picture much of the plot which I originally had in mind; much of the basic idea.' We believe this is sufficient to warrant submission of the issue to the jury, and, since the jury believed it, the verdict is supported thereby.

Finally appellant urges that there is a lack of evidence to support the award of damages, in that there was no standard by which damages could be gauged. Appellee contends that the true rule on uncertainty of damages is that the prohibition is directed against uncertainty as to cause, rather than uncertainty as to measure or extent.

We do not believe the evidence is subject to the charge of uncertainty. Appellee testified that he and another writer collaborated in writing a story and sold it without screen credit for $10,000, which the two writers divided. Appellee's story was sold for $2,500, but under a contract that required that he be given screen credit. From these figures, the jury might easily compute the advertising value of the screen credit. He also testified that he received screen credit for a play; that prior thereto his salary was $250 per week; and that afterward he received $350 per week at one time, and $500 per week for a period of two weeks, due to the screen credit he had received. That evidence is, if believed, likewise sufficient as a gauge for the measure of the damages.

Finding no error affecting the substantial rights of appellant, the judgment is affirmed.

WILBUR, Circuit Judge (dissenting).

I dissent. With reference to the question as to whether or not there was substantial evidence that the film play produced by the defendant was based upon a story written by the plaintiff entitled 'Cruise to Nowhere' and purchased by the defendant for the purpose of screen production, I am unable to agree with the conclusion of my associates. In the first place, statements contained in the books of the corporation showing that the cost of the story purchased from the plaintiff was charged against the film play produced by the defendant was clearly admissible as a declaration against interest. The same is true with reference to the press release indicating that the defendant produced a screen play based upon plaintiff's story. These admissions might be sufficiently substantial to sustain the verdict were it not for the fact that other evidence supplements and explains these admissions and deprives them of any weight. Beyond question, the defendant purchased the plaintiff's story for film reproduction and went to work to adapt it for screen reproduction. The admissions above referred to were made during the preliminary stages of screen adaptation. But the evidence shows that it was later decided that plaintiff's story was not suitable for the type of production desired at that time, and that several screen writers were employed to write the scenario for reproduction. Later, when the play was produced, they were given credit for this work, and the plaintiff was not given the credit to which he deemed himself entitled under his contract with the defendant. That the story produced was vastly different from that purchased is clear from a comparison of the two stories. It follows that the admissions of the defendant made at the time when it was the intention to use plaintiff's story became valueless in determining whether or not they did in fact use his story. I conclude, therefore, that the admissions of the defendant that the produced story 'We're Not Dressing' was based upon plaintiff's story 'Cruise to Nowhere' are without probative value in determining whether or not the plaintiff was entitled to screen credit.

The provision of the contract relating to screen credit is quoted in the main opinion, and it is unnecessary to repeat it. It is a method of advertising to the public the fact that the production they are about to witness is the result of the ingenuity, inventive genius, and literary skill of the person to whom screen credit is given. Thus it is believed other motion picture producers will seek to avail themselves of the services of the person given screen credit to produce other stories for such reproduction. It is clear that to give screen credit to a person not reasonably entitled thereto would be a fraud upon the public, while on the other hand, to deny the author his contract rights if the play produced is based upon his story would be a violation of the contract. * * *

As a matter of fact the evidence shows that the plaintiff abandoned his efforts in the moving picture line and withdrew from the field and devoted his time to writing a novel. Although he testified that he intended at some time to return to Hollywood for the purpose of engaging as an author in the moving picture industry, the testimony as to his change of occupation increases the speculative character of the jury's verdict based upon hypothetical losses due to a failure to secure contracts in the moving picture industry.

Shawn K. Judge
Giving Credit Where Credit Is Due?:
The Unusual Use of Arbitration in
Determining Screenwriting Credits

13 Ohio St. J. on Disp. Resol. 221 (1997).
Reprinted with Permission from the Author and Journal.
Footnotes omitted.

The Screenwriter and the Importance of Credits

There are two basic ways in which a screenwriter receives work. The more prominent method is to accept writing assignments, in which the screenwriter will work with a studio or production company (or both) to develop a script from a story idea; the idea need not originate with the writer. In addition, a screenwriter may be brought in to rewrite another writer's script entirely, or to "polish" various story elements, such as dialogue or plot. Such practices, termed script doctoring, can be especially lucrative; it is not uncommon for top screenwriters to doctor a script

script doctoring

for anywhere from $150,000 to $200,000 per week—with no expectation of ever receiving credit on screen.

The second method of writing for film involves the screenwriter producing a "spec script"—a script written on speculation, with no guarantee of making a sale. Sales of spec scripts often receive increased attention both in and outside the industry, with formerly unknown writers who had never made a sale suddenly receiving hundreds of thousands of dollars—sometimes more—for spec scripts. Such success has been compared to winning a screenwriting lottery. ... but the prospects of making such a sale ... and of sustaining a career after the initial sale ... do not lie in the writer's favor.

Ultimately, both methods of writing for motion pictures often depend upon one thing, credits. Amid the Hollywood atmosphere of continual risky investment and pursuit of successful material, the screenwriter occupies an interesting position. The screenwriter is the beginning of the filmmaking process, serving an integral function that is wholly indispensable. However, "(w)riters hold a unique position in the motion picture and television industries—a position of both respect and disdain.... The status of writers in the metaphoric Hollywood is merely that of another employee of the producer." ... This apparent dichotomy is an outgrowth of the paradoxical nature of the industry, where while everyone wants to produce the next successful script, everyone also wants to avoid failure—or perhaps more specifically, the industry decisionmakers want to avoid the appearance of fault. Consequently, it is not uncommon for screenwriters to be routinely closed off from the filmmaking process after the script has been delivered and any contractually-required opportunities for rewriting have been allowed by the producer, ... or to be shut out of consideration for writing assignments altogether due to a lack of perceived status....—status derived not necessarily from talent, but from credits received on past financially successful films. Such credit has been defined by one screenwriter as "the lifeblood of everyone in this industry", due to its potential impact upon a screenwriter's career "screen credit is probably the single most important factor for artists in the entertainment business.... (t)his factor determines who is "hot" and who is not; it is the basis for determining whether artists are offered subsequent assignments and their increase in compensation for those assignments." ...

The desire to avoid failure by looking to credits in making executive decisions has helped contribute to an industry mentality emphasizing "hot" screenwriters over lesser known scribes: "Whether it's to lure a star or to cover themselves in case of a flop, many studio execs today are more comfortable paying a 'name' screenwriter $1 million to write a draft than hiring a seasoned but less glitzy veteran scribe for less than half that amount." ... This mentality reflects the paranoia felt by studio executives who don't read much themselves, or who fear rocking the corporate boat.... (A) producer with a studio deal explains, "(The executives) think an expensive writer will get it right the first time. And if he doesn't, the executive has protected himself by using a pre-approved writer." ...

The pre-approved writer mentality has resulted in an inordinate amount of work allocated to those screenwriters perceived as hot writers within the industry, an estimated thirty or so individuals. While some studios actually circulate a list of acceptable hot writers for writing assignments, other studios require their executives to commit the roster to memory.

The result of such a credit-based, hit-based mentality has had a significant economic impact upon the screenwriting community. In 1995, the screen and television writers' union, the Writers Guild of America, Inc. (WGA), reported record earnings of $535.8 million by its members, with the top fifty screenwriters providing for approximately one-half of 1995's income growth. The WGA has 11,000 members, ... a membership which grew by an estimated one to two screen or television writers joining per day,... of which approximately 1680 screenwriters were employed in 1995. Yet, only the top one percent of employed writers enjoyed the extremely lucrative six to seven figure paydays, as the median income of a Guild member was a lesser $62,000. In addition to the up-front payment for drafting a script, credit on a film can produce other fiscally rewarding dividends depending upon contractual negotiations: residual payments, royalty payments, percentage of profit participation in gross receipts and percentage participation in film-related products.... Credits, then, determine perceived status within the industry, which in turn determine future work allocation and income. As a result, competition for credit has become increasingly important, and disputes requiring resolution have become commonplace, with between twenty-five to thirty percent of all films brought before the WGA resulting in Guild-conducted arbitration designed to quickly and efficiently determine to whom credit is due....

3. THE DIRECTOR

Mark Caro
The Director or the Writer:
Whose Film Is It?

CHICAGO TRIBUNE, Nov. 24, 2000.

As the opening titles of the independent film "Our Song" played during a Sundance Film Festival screening earlier this year, the familiar phrase "A film by" popped onto the screen. But instead of writer-director Jim McKay's name following, the screen filled with the names of every cast and crew member who had worked on the movie.

The crowd, composed largely of people who had taken nonmarquee jobs on this and other films, erupted in applause.

"I remember that, and I applauded it also," Sundance founder Robert Redford said recently. "I think this has gotten out of whack."

"This" is the escalating use of so-called possessory credits, the line in movie titles and ads that reads "A film by So-and-So," "A So-and-So film" or "So-and-So's 'Film Title.'"

Such billing used to be reserved for the industry's top directors, such as Frank Capra, David Lean and Alfred Hitchcock. But now the credit is taken by any director whose agent can successfully negotiate for it.

Bruce Paltrow got an above-the-title "A film by" credit for the critical and commercial dud "Duets," the only feature he has directed aside from 1982's "A Little Sex." Sally Field took a similar credit for her directorial debut, "Beautiful," an even bigger bomb. Neither of those directors received screenplay credits.

Such claims of film authorship, particularly by directors who didn't write their movies, rankle the Writers Guild of America so much that abolishing the possessory credit is one of the union's key demands in its upcoming negotiations with the studios on a new contract. That condition, plus others that try to give writers more prominent billing and creative control, could prove to be thorny in a negotiation expected to be so combative that the studios currently are rushing films into production to beat the May 1 strike deadline.

* * *

It also puts the Writers Guild on a collision course with the Directors Guild, whose current agreement with the studios, which expires in 2002, affirms a director's right to take the possessory credit.

"At a time when the two guilds should be presenting a united front to the studios on issues such as residual payments and how to deal with new technologies, the WGA is seeking to expand the power of writers at the expense of directors and the product," the Directors Guild charges in its official response to the Writers Guild's proposals, as posted on the DGA Web site (at http://www.dga.org).

"It's a big war over an apostrophe," said Cheryl Rhoden, the Writers Guild's assistant executive director.

The possessory credit dates back to cinema's earliest days, with films such as D.W. Griffith's "Birth of a Nation" (1915) or Cecil B. De Mille's "The Ten Commandments" (1923 and again in 1956), according to a summer 1998 DGA Magazine history of the credit. Until the mid–1960s, no uniform standards for possessory credits existed, so anyone theoretically could negotiate for such status.

But at the end of 1966, the Writers Guild and the Assn. of Motion Picture and Television Producers ratified an agreement that limited "A film by" credit to a filmmaker who had written the screenplay or the movie's source material. The Directors Guild was furious and talked strike.

In a cable to a DGA committee meeting, reprinted in DGA Magazine, Lean wrote, "Take my own latest case, 'David Lean's film of "Dr.

Zhivago." 'I worked one year with the writer. Unlike him, I directed not only the actors but the cameraman, set designer, costume designer, sound men, editor, composer and even the laboratory in their final print. Unlike him, I chose the actors, the technicians, the subject and him to write it. I staged it. I filmed it. It was my film of his script, which I shot when he was not there.''

* * *

A strike was averted when the studios and producers agreed to restore the director's right to negotiate individually for any credits when the Writers Guild contract expired in 1970.

"Thirty years ago, when the Writers Guild gave up a measure of control as to who received the credit, the commitment that was made by the companies was that it would be reserved for a handful of directors who had a significant body of work, like Hitchcock or Capra," Rhoden said. "Now it's proliferated to the point where someone right out of film school gets it."

The chief objection, she added, is that "the credit that says 'A film by' makes it sound like one person, a director, is responsible for the film, and it denigrates the writer. A director can't direct from a blank page. An actor can't perform from a blank page."

Kevin Smith, who has written and directed each of his four features without taking a "film by" credit, agreed.

"A film is probably the most collaborative art form there is," the filmmaker of "Clerks" and "Dogma" said. "No one person makes a movie. So taking that 'A film by' kind of leaves everybody out.

"I write and I direct, and those are the credits I take. Saying 'a film by' means that there were no grips, there was no crew, there was no producer, there was no PA production assistant that got the star to the set when you needed them."

Rod Lurie said DreamWorks initially included "A film by Rod Lurie" on its advertising for "The Contender," which he wrote and directed, until he requested that the credit be removed.

"It's simply a piece of arrogance to have it on your first or second or third work," Lurie said, though he admitted a possessory credit appeared on his 1999 debut, "Deterrence." "Even more importantly, I'm not going to be taking an authorial credit on any more of my films until the Writers Guild is satisfied with the policy of having those possessory credits on film. I feel very strongly bonded to the WGA."

But Robert Altman, who long ago achieved "A film by" stature, called the Writers Guild "full of it" for its attempts to limit directors' credits.

"The writer does the basis of the film, but it is not the film," he said. "The writer is a major, major collaborator, but the writer is not as important as the actors. Nobody's as important as the actors. The actors come in and put the script to life and make the changes in that dialogue."

Still, Altman added, "if they said you can no longer give directors that credit, that doesn't bother me at all."

Darren Aronofsky, whose "A film by" credit appears above the title of his second film, "Requiem for a Dream," defended the practice as long as the director was involved in the writing.

"I think a film is 'A film by' someone if it's written and directed by one person," he said. "I think if the writing credit is shared with the director, then it can also be 'A film by,' but if it's a director who's adapting someone else's work, then maybe there is an argument that the 'A film by' credit is overused."

The gray area is that some directors have more of a personal imprint than others. Hitchcock didn't take writing credits, yet his works rightfully belong to the genre of "Hitchcock movies." Filmmakers such as Aronofsky and Quentin Tarantino have fewer films under their belts, but their works boast a distinctive style, certainly more so than Donald Petrie, whose numerous credits include "Grumpy Old Men," "My Favorite Martian" and the upcoming "Donald Petrie film," "Miss Congeniality."

Smith conceded that "a Quentin Tarantino film" or "a Spike Lee Joint" has marketing power, although he's insisted that his own films be advertised with lines like "from the people that did 'Clerks.'"

"What really burns me is when you have guys who have made one movie and they throw their name out there, 'A film by such-and-such,'" Smith said. "What does that mean to anybody? It means nothing for marketability, so really it comes down to that director just wanting to stand out as the person who did the entire thing . . . and that's so not the case."

Despite the theory that the director is a film's auteur, Lurie contended that the writer can be "the true author of the movie. When David Mamet writes a screenplay, that's his movie; I don't care who directs it. When Tarantino wrote 'True Romance,' that's a Quentin Tarantino movie, in my opinion."

But Aronofsky said he still would tilt the scale in favor of the director.

"I think a director's involvement with a movie is a lot more significant in some cases than a writer's connection to a film," he explained. "I've only done films that I've written, but when I split it up in my own head, definitely directing is more time-consuming than writing. A director lives with a movie for three years every single day, and a writer in general is about six months of work, and some writers are even under that. I don't think it's the same sort of job."

Sherri Burr
The Independent Directors View:
Author Interviews with Film Directors Chris Eyre and
John Carlos Frey.
Copyright © 2004 by Sherri Burr.

In separate interviews, Chris Eyre (*Smoke Signals*, *Signs*) and John Carlos Frey (*The Gatekeeper*) talked about some of the issues facing directors of independent films, from credit to child labor laws, and from distribution to dealing with film commissions.

Credits are important because they serve as calling cards in Hollywood and can lead to bigger budgets for films. Eyre says, "The 'film by credit' is an important credit. Traditionally it has been a director's credit. I agree that film is such a collaborative effort, but I don't push away film credits. With Native [American] films, I know that the film wouldn't come to light if not for me. John Kilik and I were instrumental in getting our film financed. Producing credit is really important too."

Directors can also offer credit to lure others who might otherwise be too expensive for their budgets. John Frey was able to attract an award-winning Australian cinematographer because he was "dying to get a U.S. film credit." Frey says that while the man had won seven Australian Academy Awards, "none of those awards translated in the United States and studios were not willing to hire him because he was not an American citizen. He did my film for pennies on the dollar."

Both Eyre and Frey direct small budget independent pictures, which are not financed by Hollywood studios. "I've never made a Hollywood movie per se," says Eyre. "When I'm hired to direct a movie, I'd rather be hands-on from beginning to distribution. I also get involved in the screenwriting and producing aspects of filmmaking."

Says Frey, "Hollywood films are expensive to make, distribute and advertise. Each film print may cost upwards of $2000. If your film appears on 8000 screens, that is $16 million just on copies. For the *Matrix*, in addition to the $84 million the studio spent to make the film, it spent $62 million to advertise it. The studio was thus looking at nearly $200 million just to get it to the screen. They make the money back on ticket sales, video and DVD releases, product placements, merchandizing, hotel sales."

Frey shot *The Gatekeeper* in 18 days at a cost of $200,000. To shoot a film on that limited a budget requires, says Frey that "the actors work for nearly free, the crew works nearly for free, your locations get donated, your food gets donated, and you go begging, basically, to pull it off."

Frey raised the money himself, a not uncommon story for a director of an independent film. He says, "I ended up taking a second mortgage out on my house. I borrowed some money from my family, drained my savings, ran up my credit card debt, and got a rag-tag crew together."

Among his many challenges was becoming familiar with unions and child labor laws. Unions regulate a 12–hour working day for adult actors. Frey said, "Actors get overtime after 10 hours. With a 12–hour day, they must receive one full hour lunch and two half-hour breaks. Crew can work 12 hours and not get any overtime, but they have to have two one-hour lunches and two half-hour breaks. If you don't abide by that, the union can shut you down."

Since many scenes included a child actor, Frey also had to be cognizant of child labor laws, which limit the number of hours that a child can work at night. In a scene where the little boy sat in the van looking scared, he actually filmed it first while the audience will see it at the end of the sequence.

If a director needs to use animals in his film, he calls in a professional animal handler. "You can't just make a chicken do cartwheels on your own," Frey said. "But if they're just in the background and lying still, just being animals and don't have to perform any stunts, we don't need a handler."

For *The Gatekeeper*, Frey also needed a gun permit, even though his actors did not use real guns, just in case a cop drove by or came in response to a member of the public's call. He had to secure rights from the property owner whose ranch he used and to let the municipality know what his plans were. He contacted the city of San Diego's Film Commission. "The city's film commission often serves as a liaison between us and the town."

For Frey, the San Diego Film Commission ran interference with the fire department when he needed to blow up a building. He had to hire pyrotechnics to set off the explosion, a demolition team to take away the building's remains, and pay for resources for the fire department. He says, "The city had to be notified, and we had to have permits and a water truck. The fire department will not supply water. We had to supply our own."

Another legal issue facing directors involves the use of trademarked products in their films. "If you can read the product, that company is going to make you pay," says Frey. "If they want to be in your film, like when BMW introduced its new Roadster in the Bond film, then they pay you. It's big business, but that's rare in independent films."

Frey blocked out the name "Budweiser" on a beer can that sat on a table during a rape scene. "Budweiser does not want to be associated with rape. I could be sued," he said.

As directors of independent films, Frey and Eyre must distribute them differently. Both men screen at film festivals, and take advantage of the ethnic nature of their films. Eyre, whose films tell Native American stories, says, "There's a whole national Native community that supports its own, with many Native American film festivals."

Because *The Gatekeeper* focused on Mexican immigrant issues and had a strong female character role, Frey initially submitted his script to

Jennifer Lopez's production company. "I knew that Jennifer Lopez was looking for a Latino role where she could play an ethnic character and do something for her people," he said. "In my film, the female lead has a serious struggle in life, but it is not a heroic role. I submitted the script, and received notes back from her people, saying 'We think she would like it more if it was toned down a bit.' Later they said, 'How about making it more of a love story. How about writing the female role a little bigger, make her a little bit more important. After a couple of years of back and forth, they passed. She ended up making *Maid in America*."

Frey says, "I ended up making a story very close to my heart. I was born in Tijuana, Mexico. I grew up on the border. I'm a Mexican immigrant myself. The subject matter is geared to me. I didn't want to water it down. I didn't want to make it a love story."

Frey finished *The Gatekeeper* in late 2002 and traveled throughout the country from 2003–2004, screening it at film festivals and movie theaters that show independent films. His efforts were rewarded when *The Gatekeeper* won best film at the International Hispanic Film Festival, the Phoenix International Film Festival, the Temecula Valley Film Festival, the Winslow Film Festival, and The San Diego Latino Film Festival. Frey also won best director at the same Phoenix festival and best performance at the Hispanic festival. His website, http://www.gatekeeperfilm.com/, keeps potential audience members informed of when the film will screen near them.

Notes

1. John Frey's comments on the Motion Picture Association of America's ratings system can be found in Chapter 6, Movie Censorship. Further thoughts from Chris Eyre on the challenges of making Native American films can be found in Chapter 12, Television Diversity, Censorship, and Cultural Matters.

2. Given the amount of work, time, and money involved, why do independent directors make movies? Jon Moritsugu, the director of the 1999 film *Fame Whore*, says, "I have to make a movie about something that really matters to me. From the time you start to the time you finish, it can take up to five or ten years to make a movie. . . . With my movies, I have a voice in society. It gives me a chance to put a little bit of my money and all of my time and off of my friends' time and energy into a project that . . . ultimately will get out into the world and say something and will hopefully affect something." *Arts Talk* (Olelo Television broadcast, 1999). With *Fame Whore*, Moritsugu chose to depict people who seek fame at any cost. He said, "Fame is one of those things that people want and have a hard time getting. There is a naïve view that once you're famous, that everything will fall into place. Fame can be a particularly deadly drug." *Id.*

4. THE PRODUCER

TAMARIND LITHOGRAPHY WORKSHOP, INC. v. SANDERS

California Court of Appeals, 1983.
143 Cal.App.3d 571, 193 Cal.Rptr. 409.

STEPHENS, Judge.

The essence of this appeal concerns the question of whether an award of damages is an adequate remedy at law in lieu of specific performance for the breach of an agreement to give screen credits. Our saga traces its origin to March of 1969, at which time appellant, and cross-complainant below, Terry Sanders (hereinafter Sanders or appellant), agreed in writing to write, direct and produce a motion picture on the subject of lithography for respondent, Tamarind Lithography Workshop, Inc. * * *

Pursuant to the terms of the agreement, the film was shot during the summer of 1969, wherein Sanders directed the film according to an outline/treatment of his authorship, and acted as production manager by personally hiring and supervising personnel comprising the film crew. Additionally, Sanders exercised both artistic control over the mixing of the sound track and overall editing of the picture.

After completion, the film, now titled "Four Stones for Kanemitsu," was screened by Tamarind at its 10th anniversary celebration on April 28, 1970. Thereafter, a dispute arose between the parties concerning their respective rights and obligations under the original 1969 agreement. Litigation ensued and in January 1973 the matter went to trial. Prior to the entry of judgment, the parties entered into a written settlement agreement, which became the premises for the instant action. Specifically, this April 30, 1973, agreement provided that Sanders would be entitled to a screen credit entitled "A Film by Terry Sanders."

Tamarind did not comply with its expressed obligation pursuant to that agreement, in that it failed to include Sanders' screen credits in the prints it distributed. As a result a situation developed wherein Tamarind and codefendant Wayne filed suit for declaratory relief, damages due to breach of contract, emotional distress, defamation and fraud.

Sanders cross-complained, seeking damages for Tamarind's breach of contract, declaratory relief, specific performance of the contract to give Sanders screen credits, and defamation. Both causes were consolidated and brought to trial on May 31, 1977. A jury was impaneled for purposes of determining damage issues and decided that Tamarind had breached the agreement and awarded Sanders $25,000 in damages.

The remaining claims for declaratory and injunctive relief were tried by the court. The court made findings that Tamarind had sole ownership rights in the film, that "both June Wayne and Terry Sanders were each creative producers of the film, that Sanders shall have the right to modify the prints in his personal possession to include his credits." All other prayers for relief were denied.

It is the denial of appellant's request for specific performance upon which appellant predicates this appeal.

Since neither party is contesting the sufficiency of Sanders' $25,000 jury award for damages, the central issue thereupon becomes whether that award is necessarily preclusive of additional relief in the form of specific performance, i.e., that Sanders receive credit on all copies of the film. Alternately expressed, the issue is whether the jury's damage award adequately compensates Sanders, not only for injuries sustained as a result of the prior exhibitions of the film without Sanders' credits, but also for future injuries which may be incurred as a result of any future exhibitions of the film without his credit. Commensurate with our discussion below, we find that the damages awarded raise an issue that justifies a judgment for specific performance. Accordingly, we reverse the judgment of the lower court and direct it to award appellant the injunctive relief he now seeks.

Our first inquiry deals with the scope of the jury's $25,000 damage award. More specifically, we are concerned with whether or not this award compensates Sanders not only for past or preexisting injuries, but also for future injury (or injuries) as well.

Indeed, it is possible to categorize respondent's breach of promise to provide screen credits as a single failure to act from which all of Sanders' injuries were caused. However, it is also plausible that damages awarded Sanders were for harms already sustained at the date of trial, and did not contemplate injury as a result of future exhibitions of the film by respondent, without appropriate credit to Sanders.

Although this was a jury trial, there are findings of facts and conclusions of law necessitated by certain legal issues that were decided by the court. Finding of fact No. 12 states:

"By its verdict the jury concluded that Terry Sanders and the Terry Sanders Company are entitled to the sum of $25,000.00 in damages for all damages suffered by them arising from Tamarind's breach of the April 30th agreement." The exact wording of this finding was also used in conclusion of law No. 1. Sanders argues that use of the word "suffered" in the past tense is positive evidence that the jury assessed damages only for breach of the contract up to time of trial and did not award possible future damages that might be suffered if the film was subsequently exhibited without the appropriate credit. Tamarind, on the other hand, contends that the jury was instructed that if a breach occurred the award would be for *all* damages past and future arising from the breach. The jury was instructed: "For the breach of a contract, the measure of damages is the amount which will compensate the party aggrieved, for the economic loss, directly and proximately caused by the breach, or which, in the ordinary course of things, would be likely to result therefrom" and " ... economic benefits including enhancement of one's professional reputation resulting in increased earnings as a result of screen credit, if their loss is a direct and natural consequence of the breach, may be recovered for breach of an agreement that provides for screen credit. Economic benefits lost through breach of contract may be estimated, and where the plaintiff [Tamarind], by its breach of the contract, has given rise to the difficulty of proving the amount of loss of such economic benefit, it is proper to require of the defendant [Sanders] only that he show the amount of damages with reasonable certainty and to resolve uncertainty as to the amount of economic benefit against the plaintiff [Tamarind]."

The trial court agreed with Tamarind's position and refused to grant the injunction because it was satisfied that the jury had awarded Sanders all the damages he was entitled to including past and possible future damages. The record does not satisfactorily resolve the issue. However, this fact is not fatal to this appeal because, as we shall explain, specific performance as requested by Sanders will solve the problem.

The availability of the remedy of specific performance is premised upon well established requisites. These requisites include: A showing by plaintiff of (1) the inadequacy of his legal remedy; (2) an underlying contract that is both reasonable and supported by adequate consideration; (3) the existence of a mutuality of remedies; (4) contractual terms which are sufficiently definite to enable the court to know what it is to enforce; and (5) a substantial similarity of the requested performance to that promised in the contract. (See *Henderson v. Fisher* (1965) 236 Cal.App.2d 468, 473 [46 Cal.Rptr. 173], and Civ. Code, § § 3384, 3386, 3390, 3391.)

It is manifest that the legal remedies available to Sanders for harm resulting from the future exhibition of the film are inadequate as a matter of law. The primary reasons are twofold: (1) that an accurate assessment of damages would be far too difficult and require much speculation, and (2) that any future exhibitions might be deemed to be a continuous breach of contract and thereby create the danger of an untold number of lawsuits.

There is no doubt that the exhibition of a film, which is favorably received by its critics and the public at large, can result in valuable advertising or publicity for the artists responsible for that film's making. Likewise, it is unquestionable that the nonappearance of an artist's name or likeness in the form of screen credit on a successful film can result in a loss of that valuable publicity. However, whether that loss of publicity is measurable dollar wise is quite another matter.

By its very nature, public acclaim is unique and very difficult, if not sometimes impossible, to quantify in monetary terms. Indeed, courts confronted with the dilemma of estimating damages in this area have been less than uniform in their disposition of same. Nevertheless, it is clear that any award of damages for the loss of publicity is contingent upon those damages being reasonably certain, specific, and unspeculative. * * *

The varied disposition of claims for breach of promise to provide screen credits encompasses two schools of thought. On the one hand, there is the view that damages can be ascertained (to within a reasonable degree of certainty) if the trier of fact is given sufficient factual data. (See *Paramount Productions, Inc. v. Smith* (9th Cir. 1937) 91 F.2d 863, cert. den. 302 U.S. 749 [82 L.Ed. 579, 58 S.Ct. 266].) On the other hand, there is the equally strong stance that although damages resulting from a loss of screen credits might be identifiable, they are far too imponderable and ethereal to define in terms of a monetary award. (See *Poe v. Michael Todd Co.* (S.D.N.Y. 1957) 151 F.Supp. 801.) If these two views can be reconciled, it would only be by an independent examination of each case on its particular set of facts.

In *Paramount Productions, Inc. v. Smith, supra.*, 91 F.2d 863, 866–867, the court was provided with evidence from which the "... jury might easily compute the advertising value of the screen credit." (*Id.*, at p. 867.) The particular evidence presented included the earnings the plaintiff/writer received for his work on a previous film in which he did not contract for screen credits. This evidence was in turn easily compared with earnings that the writer had received for work in which screen credits were provided as contracted. Moreover, evidence of that artist's salary, prior to his receipt of credit for a play when compared with earnings received subsequent to his actually receiving credit, was "... if believed, likewise sufficient as a gauge for the measure of damages." (*Id.*, at p. 867.)

In another case dealing with a request for damages for failure to provide contracted-for screen credits, the court in *Zorich v. Petroff* (1957) 152 Cal.App.2d 806 [313 P.2d 118] demonstrated an equal awareness of the principle. The court emphasized "... that there was no evidence from which the [trial] court could have placed a value upon the screen credit to be given plaintiff as an associate producer. (Civ. Code, § 3301.)" (*Id.*, at p. 811.) Incident to this fact, the court went on to surmise that because the motion picture which was at the root of the litigation was an admitted financial failure, screen credit, if given, "... could reasonably have been regarded as a detriment to him." (*Id.*, at p. 811.)

At the other extreme, it has been held that failure to give an artist screen credit would constitute irreparable injury. In *Poe v. Michael Todd Co., supra.*, 151 F.Supp. 801, the New York district court was similarly faced with an author's claim that his contractual right to screen credit was violated. The court held: "Not only would money damages be difficult to establish, but at best they would hardly compensate for the real injury done. A writer's reputation, which would be greatly enhanced by public credit for authorship of an outstanding picture, is his stock in trade, it is clear that irreparable injury would follow the failure to give screen credit if in fact he is entitled to it." (*Id.*, at p. 803.)

[handwritten margin note: failure to give credit would constitute irreparable injury.]

Notwithstanding the seemingly inflexible observation of that court as to the compensability of a breach of promise to provide screen credits, all three cases equally demonstrate that the awarding of damages must be premised upon calculations, inferences or observations that are logical. Just how logical or reasonable those inferences are regarded serves as the determining factor. Accordingly, where the jury in the matter sub judice was fully apprised of the favorable recognition Sanders' film received from the Academy of Motion Picture Arts and Sciences, the Los Angeles International Film Festival, and public television, and further, where they were made privy to an assessment of the value of said exposure by three experts,[6] it is reasonable for the jury to award monetary damages for that ascertainable loss of publicity. However, pecuniary compensation for Sanders' future harm is not a fully adequate remedy. * * *

We return to the remaining requisites for Sanders' entitlement to specific performance. The need for our finding the contract to be reasonable and supported by adequate consideration is obviated by the jury's determination of respondent's breach of that contract. The requisite of mutuality of remedy has been satisfied in that Sanders had fully performed his obligations pursuant to the agreement (i.e., release of all claims of copyright to the film and dismissal of his then pending action against respondents). (See Civ. Code, § 3386.) Similarly, we find the terms of the agreement sufficiently definite to permit enforcement of the respondent's performance as promised.

In the present case it should be obvious that specific performance through injunctive relief can remedy the dilemma posed by the somewhat ambiguous jury verdict. The injunction disposes of the problem of future damages, in that full compliance by Tamarind moots the issue. Of course, violation of the injunction by Tamarind would raise new problems, but the court has numerous options for dealing with the situation and should choose the one best suited to the particular violation.

In conclusion, the record shows that the appellant is entitled to relief consisting of the damages recovered, and an injunction against future injury. * * *

Considering the extent of this controversy, in conjunction with our decision to reverse the judgment below, we think it in the best interests of all parties concerned for the trial court to determine what effect, if any, the agreement should have on the action. In effect, respondents' petition is tantamount to a motion to dismiss the entire action, as opposed to the mere dismissal of this appeal. It would appear that the trial court is the more appropriate forum to receive evidence and adjudicate the merits of this issue. If it were to reach a determination unfavorable to petitioners, it would be in position to grant the relief we have determined appellants are entitled to. On the other hand, a contrary determination by the trial court would still leave that court with the authority to take the action requested by petitioners.

6. Those experts all rendered opinions that publicity received by someone with the credit "A film by" for a documentary similar to appellant's, which received similar honors, could be quantified in monetary terms between $50,000 and $150,000.

The judgment denying appellants' prayer for injunctive relief is hereby reversed and the action, with the addition of this new issue, is remanded to the trial court to take appropriate action in conformity with the views expressed in this opinion, including the taking of additional evidence, oral or written, if deemed appropriate, on the motion to dismiss.

Peter Bart
Living on Credit

VARIETY, Inside Movies, (Sept. 19, 1994–Sept. 25, 1994).

I greatly admired Robert Redford's new movie, "Quiz Show," but one detail left me downright quizzical. As the interminable production credits paraded past, I asked myself why it would take 11—count 'em, 11—producers to create this movie? Did all 11 stand around on the set, advising Redford—a rather obdurate chap even under ideal conditions—how to direct a scene? Then I asked myself another question: If I were only one of 11 producers on a film, how much money would I pay to have my name removed from the credits.

When I started investigating, of course, I found my original information was incomplete. There were, in fact, 14 producers on the show, and three had indeed asked that their names be removed: Richard Goodwin, Barry Levinson and Mark Johnson.

It required several weeks to work out a viable device for listing all the credits—which would be co-producers, executive producers, "also produced by" producers and so forth. When one refused to go along with the settlement, the entire "grid" had to be painstakingly reconstructed.

The whole issue of credits has become a hot button lately. As the development process grows ever more convoluted, and development hell less hospitable, the few projects that manage to emerge all but drown in a sea of credits. Whenever a film ignites any sort of public response, a dispute promptly breaks out as to who was responsible—who really came up with the idea, who really wrote it, who produced it, etc.

When as many as 35 writers toil on a script, such as "The Flintstones," how do you really determine who supplied the creative spark?

"Quiz Show" was certainly one project that had an astonishing number of parents. There was a high-concept comedy at Disney called "One for the Money" that wasn't going anywhere. There was a TriStar project involving Levinson, Johnson and Fred Zollo, among others, that was banished into turnaround. There was a documentary involving a filmmaker named Julian Krainin. Along the way even Richard Dreyfuss and his producing partner, Judith James, joined the flotilla of producers.

Despite all these would-be captains, the ship was still going nowhere until Redford signed on. And Redford, a man who hardly needs another credit, promptly insisted on being producer plus director.

Whether they're stars or neophytes, most denizens of Hollywood today are credit-hungry. On those not infrequent occasions when a studio decides to "buy out" someone's credit—that is, pay to remove a name from a project–the buyout price often amounts to twice the original fee.

In some cases, to be sure, companies simply ignore the contracts and invent their own rules. Such was allegedly the case in a fascinating dispute that was resolved last week—a case in which the court actually attached a specific monetary value to a credit.

In the judgment of Los Angeles Superior Court judge Richard C. Hubbell, the Samuel Goldwyn Co. will be required to pay $3.3 million plus legal costs to a small British video company named Virgin Vision to cover damages involved in removing Virgin Vision's name from foreign prints of "sex, lies and videotape." Having entered into a deal with Virgin Vision covering certain foreign territories, Goldwyn acted in "willful, deliberate or in conscious disregard for the plaintiff's rights" by turning their back on Virgin Vision, said the court.

"The judgment was a much-needed reminder that the big guy can't push the little guy around," says Bill Tennant, the American who heads Virgin Vision and spent well over $1 million over four years on the lawsuit. What Goldwyn was doing, he insists, amounted to "a contemporary version of claim jumping." Goldwyn Co. naturally disagrees and plans to pursue a variety of appeals.

In arguing for substantial damages, David Held, the expert witness for Virgin Vision and a former chief of business affairs for Paramount, brought forth elaborate documentation to demonstrate that credits can be "more important than any monetary compensation" because, among other things, they serve as the basis for an artist's reputation. In disputes involving producers or writers, he pointed out, a considerable body of precedent has been established whereby the cavalier denial of credits results in doubling the financial payout. In the case of Goldwyn, invocation of the Lanham Act triggered a tripling of damages.

"The law of the jungle would prevail if not for decisions like this," insists Tennant, and he has a point. Practitioners of the "sue me" school of dealmaking have proliferated in the entertainment business—that is, commitments are made only to be ignored with the casual remark, "So sue me." The Kim Basinger case put a chill over relations between actors and producers—performers are no longer quite so glib about squirming out of a meeting with a vague "I'll do it!" Those three words can now put one in a courtroom, albeit four or five years later.

While I'm glad "the law of the jungle" has taken a setback, I nonetheless wonder whether the few real producers left in Hollywood shouldn't marshal a little jungle law of their own to sort out the credits issue. Old-timers like Hal Wallis or David O. Selznick would turn over in their graves if they could see the assortment of characters who get producer credit today. The lineup embraces brothers-in-law, development assistants, production managers, stunt doubles—whoever the stars or star directors decided to muscle onto the credit list.

The result is the sort of melange we see on "Quiz Show": a list of helpmates that turns the issue of who contributed what into one big Quiz Show.

B. COMPENSATION

The labor unions, like SAG, DGA, and the Writers Guild, negotiate minimum compensation for talent. For a modified low budget film costing less than $500,000 to produce, SAG requires producers to pay a day performer $248 and a weekly performer $864. SCREEN ACTORS GUILD, FILM CONTRACTS DIGEST 6–7 (2003). For the same low budget picture, the director must receive a weekly minimum salary of $8,150 with a guaranteed preparation period of two weeks, guaranteed shooting period of eight weeks, and guaranteed cutting allowance of one week. *http://www.dga.org/contracts.*

248 pd
864 week

Individuals are nevertheless free to bargain for even higher salaries and a percent of the profits. As their clients' esteem arises with the public, agents will obtain for them net profit participation deals. Talent can graduate to gross participation deals after they demonstrate a connection between their roles and their films' blockbuster revenues exceeding $200 million. Stars at the top of their game may also bargain for contracts that contain clauses unique to the industry like "pay or play" and "approvals," which permit stars to the final say on the hiring of the director, writer, or co-star.

1. PAY OR PLAY

SHIRLEY MACLAINE PARKER v. TWENTIETH CENTURY–FOX FILM CORP.

California Supreme Court, 1970.
3 Cal.3d 176, 89 Cal.Rptr. 737, 474 P.2d 689.

BURKE, Justice.

Defendant Twentieth Century–Fox Film Corporation appeals from a summary judgment granting to plaintiff the recovery of agreed compensation under a written contract for her services as an actress in a motion picture. As will appear [evident], we have concluded that the trial court correctly ruled in plaintiff's favor and that the judgment should be affirmed.

Plaintiff is well known as an actress, and in the contract between plaintiff and defendant is sometimes referred to as the "Artist." Under the contract, dated August 6, 1965, plaintiff was to play the female lead in defendant's contemplated production of a motion picture entitled "Bloomer Girl." The contract provided that defendant would pay plaintiff a minimum "guaranteed compensation" of $53,571.42 per week for

53,500 A week
for 14 wks

14 weeks commencing May 23, 1966, for a total of $750,000. Prior to May 1966 defendant decided not to produce the picture and by a letter dated April 4, 1966, it notified plaintiff of that decision and that it would not "comply with our obligations to you under" the written contract.

By the same letter and with the professed purpose "to avoid any damage to you," defendant instead offered to employ plaintiff as the leading actress in another film tentatively entitled "Big Country, Big Man" (hereinafter, "Big Country"). The compensation offered was identical, as were 31 of the 34 numbered provisions or articles of the original contract.[1] Unlike "Bloomer Girl," however, which was to have been a musical production, "Big Country" was a dramatic "western type" movie. "Bloomer Girl" was to have been filmed in California; "Big Country" was to be produced in Australia. Also, certain terms in the proffered contract varied from those of the original.[2] Plaintiff was given one week within which to accept; she did not and the offer lapsed. Plaintiff then commenced this action seeking recovery of the agreed guaranteed compensation.

The complaint sets forth two causes of action. The first is for money due under the contract; the second, based upon the same allegations as the first, is for damages resulting from defendant's breach of contract. Defendant in its answer admits the existence and validity of the contract, that plaintiff complied with all the conditions, covenants and promises and stood ready to complete the performance, and that defen-

---

1. Among the identical provisions was the following found in the last paragraph of Article 2 of the original contract: "We [defendant] shall not be obligated to utilize your [plaintiff's] services in or in connection with the Photoplay hereunder, our sole obligation, subject to the terms and conditions of this Agreement, being to pay you the guaranteed compensation herein provided for."

2. Article 29 of the original contract specified that plaintiff approved the director already chosen for "Bloomer Girl" and that in case he failed to act as director plaintiff was to have approval rights of any substitute director. Article 31 provided that plaintiff was to have the right of approval of the "Bloomer Girl" dance director, and Article 32 gave her the right of approval of the screenplay.

Defendant's letter of April 4 to plaintiff, which contained both defendant's notice of breach of the "Bloomer Girl" contract and offer of the lead in "Big Country," eliminated or impaired each of those rights. It read in part as follows: "The terms and conditions of our offer of employment are identical to those set forth in the 'BLOOMER GIRL' Agreement, Articles 1 through 34 and Exhibit A to the Agreement, except as follows:

"1. Article 31 of said Agreement will not be included in any contract of employment regarding 'BIG COUNTRY, BIG MAN' as it is not a musical and it thus will not need a dance director.

"2. In the 'BLOOMER GIRL' agreement, in Articles 29 and 32, you were given certain director and screenplay approvals and you had preapproved certain matters. Since there simply is insufficient time to negotiate with you regarding your choice of director and regarding the screenplay and since you already expressed an interest in performing the role in 'BIG COUNTRY, BIG MAN,' we must exclude from our offer of employment in 'BIG COUNTRY, BIG MAN' any approval rights as are contained in said Articles 29 and 32; however, we shall consult with you respecting the director to be selected to direct the photoplay and will further consult with you with respect to the screenplay and any revisions or changes therein, provided, however, that if we fail to agree ... the decision of ... [defendant] with respect to the selection of a director and to revisions and changes in the said screenplay shall be binding upon the parties to said agreement."

dant breached and "anticipatorily repudiated" the contract. It denies, however, that any money is due to plaintiff either under the contract or as a result of its breach, and pleads as an affirmative defense to both causes of action plaintiff's allegedly deliberate failure to mitigate damages, asserting that she unreasonably refused to accept its offer of the leading role in "Big Country."

Plaintiff moved for summary judgment under Code of Civil Procedure section 437c, the motion was granted, and summary judgment for $750,000 plus interest was entered in plaintiff's favor. This appeal by defendant followed. * * *

As stated, defendant's sole defense to this action which resulted from its deliberate breach of contract is that in rejecting defendant's substitute offer of employment plaintiff unreasonably refused to mitigate damages.

The general rule is that the measure of recovery by a wrongfully discharged employee is the amount of salary agreed upon for the period of service, less the amount which the employer affirmatively proves the employee has earned or with reasonable effort might have earned from other employment. * * *[4] However, before projected earnings from other employment opportunities not sought or accepted by the discharged employee can be applied in mitigation, the employer must show that the other employment was comparable, or substantially similar, to that of which the employee has been deprived; the employee's rejection of or failure to seek other available employment of a different or inferior kind may not be resorted to in order to mitigate damages. * * *

Applying the foregoing rules to the record in the present case, with all intendments in favor of the party opposing the summary judgment motion—here, defendant—it is clear that the trial court correctly ruled that plaintiff's failure to accept defendant's tendered substitute employment could not be applied in mitigation of damages because the offer of the "Big Country" lead was of employment both different and inferior, and that no factual dispute was presented on that issue. The mere circumstance that "Bloomer Girl" was to be a musical review calling upon plaintiff's talents as a dancer as well as an actress, and was to be produced in the City of Los Angeles, whereas "Big Country" was a

---

4. Although it would appear that plaintiff was not discharged by defendant in the customary sense of the term, as she was not permitted by defendant to enter upon performance of the "Bloomer Girl" contract, nevertheless the motion for summary judgment was submitted for decision upon a stipulation by the parties that "plaintiff Parker was discharged."

In the present case defendant has raised no issue of reasonableness of efforts by plaintiffs to obtain other employment; the sole issue is whether plaintiff's refusal of defendant's substitute offer of "Big Country" may be used in mitigation. Nor, if the

"Big Country" offer was of employment different or inferior when compared with the original "Bloomer Girl" employment, is there an issue as to whether or not plaintiff acted reasonably in refusing the substitute offer. Despite defendant's arguments to the contrary, no case cited or which our research has discovered holds or suggests that reasonableness is an element of a wrongfully discharged employee's option to reject, or fail to seek, different or inferior employment lest the possible earnings therefrom be charged against him in mitigation of damages ...

straight dramatic role in a "Western Type" story taking place in an opal mine in Australia, demonstrates the difference in kind between the two employments; the female lead as a dramatic actress in a western style motion picture can by no stretch of imagination be considered the equivalent of or substantially similar to the lead in a song-and-dance production.

Additionally, the substitute "Big Country" offer proposed to eliminate or impair the director and screenplay approvals accorded to plaintiff under the original "Bloomer Girl" contract (see fn. 2, *ante*), and thus constituted an offer of inferior employment. No expertise or judicial notice is required in order to hold that the deprivation or infringement of an employee's rights held under an original employment contract converts the available "other employment" relied upon by the employer to mitigate damages, into inferior employment which the employee need not seek or accept. * * *

Statements found in affidavits submitted by defendant in opposition to plaintiff's summary judgment motion, to the effect that the "Big County" offer was not of employment different from or inferior to that under the "Bloomer Girl" contract, merely repeat the allegations of defendant's answer to the complaint in this action, constitute only conclusionary assertions with respect to undisputed facts, and do not give rise to a triable factual issue so as to defeat the motion for summary judgment. * * *

In view of the determination that defendant failed to present any facts showing the existence of a factual issue with respect to its sole defense-plaintiff's rejection of its substitute employment offer in mitigation of damages-we need not consider plaintiff's further contention that for various reasons, including the provisions of the original contract set forth in footnote 1, *ante*, plaintiff was excused from attempting to mitigate damages.

The judgment is affirmed.

McCOMB, J., PETERS, J., TOBRINER, J., KAUS, J., and ROTH, J., concurred.

SULLIVAN, Acting C.J. (dissenting):

* * * I remain convinced that the relevant question in such cases is whether or not a particular contract provision is so significant that its omission creates employment of an inferior kind. This question is, of course, intimately bound up in what I consider the ultimate issue: whether or not the employee acted reasonably. This will generally involve a factual inquiry to ascertain the importance of the particular contract term and a process of weighing the absence of that term against the countervailing advantages of the alternate employment. In the typical case, this will mean that summary judgment must be withheld.

In the instant case, there was nothing properly before the trial court by which the importance of the approval rights could be ascertained, much less evaluated. Thus, in order to grant the motion for summary judgment, the trial court misused judicial notice. In upholding the summary judgment, the majority here rely upon per se rules which distort the process of determining whether or not an employee is obliged to accept particular employment in mitigation of damages.

I believe that the judgment should be reversed so that the issue of whether or not the offer of the lead role in "Big Country, Big Man" was of employment comparable to that of the lead role in "Bloomer Girl" may be determined at trial.

Notes

1. A typical "pay or play" provision will say the following:

This Agreement is on a "pay or Play" basis (as this term is understood in the UK film industry) PROVIDED THAT:

the financier(s) providing the majority of the funding for the Film and the completion guarantor bonding the Film shall have gone on risk in relation to the Film, i.e. become so legally obligated without unfulfilled conditions precedent, within 3 weeks of the date hereof;

the Artist shall mitigate the Producer's liability under this pay or play provision, whereby the liability hereunder shall be reduced to the extent that the Artist be remunerated for any services rendered to any third party during any period that would or could have constituted any part of the Rehearsal Period and/or the Shooting Period (as defined in Clause 2.2 above).

Reprinted with permission from Marc Vlessing, of Trendraise Company Limited. Do you think this clause differs substantially from the one at issue in the *Parker* case?

2. A typical contract to procure acting services will state the term of the engagement (the number of weeks for rehearsals and principal photography); the remuneration (how much the actor is to be paid and in what installments); expense payments (for transportation, housing and per diem); and the actress' services and obligations (specifying that the actress will complete the role and comply with all directions. A health provision requires the actress to indicate that she is not suffering from any physical or mental incapacity that would prevent her from rendering services. Other provisions may deal with copyright, dubbing, insurance, and force majeure. If the actress becomes incapacitated or fails to perform her services, the producer may suspend her services.

3. After reading *Parker v. Twentieth Century Fox Film Corp.*, who do you think benefits from having a "pay or play" provision written into an actor's contract, and who is burdened by such a clause? Is this necessarily true when the actor is an up-and-coming fresh face versus a mega-watt super-star? *See Parker*, 474 P.2d at 692 ("However, before projected earnings from other employment opportunities not sought or accepted by the discharged employee can be applied in mitigation, the employer must show that the other employment was comparable, or substantially similar, to that of which the employee has been deprived; the employee's rejection of or failure to seek

other available employment of a different or inferior kind may not be resorted to in order to mitigate damages.'').

4. In the early 1960s, Shirley MacLaine was one of the top-ten box office stars in Hollywood. She won two Best Actress Oscar nominations and two Golden Globe wins for *The Apartment* in 1960 and *Irma la Douce* in 1963. She was born Shirley McLean Beaty and her only marriage to producer Steve Parker ended in divorce.

Sherri Burr
An Actress' View of Lawyers:
Author Interview with Shirley MacLaine

[Shirley MacLaine has acted in over 35 feature films. She was discovered on Broadway when as an understudy she took over after the lead broke her leg. Her first film was the 1955 *The Trouble with Harry*. She won the Academy Award for Best Actress for the 1983 *Terms of Endearment*. She talked to Sherri Burr by phone on February 19, 2004.]

"Nobody likes to be involved in a lawsuit. I sued 20th Century Fox because I had turned down a year and a half of pictures to do 'Bloomer Girl.'

"Sometimes lawyers help, sometimes they don't.

"I did many pictures where I never signed a contract. That doesn't hold water any more. People's word is not as good as it used to be. I would say get the contract down and get it signed by everyone involved. I've never cared that much about billing but whatever is in the contract should be observed.

"Actresses and actors don't worry too much about the law. Their lawyers and agents do that. When actresses hire lawyers, they expect the lawyers to do everything. We usually just follow their recommendations."

Notes

1. Shirley MacLaine says that she "did many movies where [she] never signed a contract. . . . People's word is not as good as it used to be." Is that necessarily true? Explain how oral contracts can later be enforced. If there is a concern that the oral contract may not be enforceable, what options do both parties to the contract have to secure their claims?

2. MacLaine also mentions that most "actors don't worry too much about the law." As attorneys, what does her statement say about the intersection of entertainment and law? As an actor, would it be prudent to have an attorney on retainer?

3. Shirley MacLaine proved that "pay or play" clauses could be valuable entities. Actress Raquel Welch demonstrates in the following case that producers violate such contract passages at their peril.

RAQUEL WELCH v. MGM

California Supreme Court, 1988.
254 Cal.Rptr. 645.

WOODS, Justice.

This lawsuit arises from the firing of the motion picture actress Raquel Welch from her starring role in the film "Cannery Row." The jury found in favor of Welch and Raquel Welch Productions, Inc. (hereinafter sometimes collectively referred to as Welch) on counts of breach of contract, conspiracy to induce breach of contract, slander, and breach of the implied covenant of good faith and fair dealing (bad faith). Welch recovered $2 million in compensatory damages and over $8 million in punitive damages from appellants Metro–Goldwyn–Mayer Film Co. (MGM), several successor corporations to MGM (TBS Entertainment Co., Production, Inc., Lab, Inc., and Lot, Inc.), David Begelman (the president of MGM), and Michael Phillips (the producer of the film).

Welch filed a cross-appeal from the trial court's granting of summary judgment on a count of intentional infliction of emotional distress, but has abandoned the cross-appeal in her briefing.

Appellants raise numerous issues on appeal, including that (1) there is no basis for a conspiracy between Phillips and MGM because Phillips's actions were privileged as a matter of law; (2) Welch as an individual lacked standing to sue for conspiracy to induce breach of contract or bad faith because the contract for her services was between MGM and Raquel Welch Productions, Inc.; (3) the trial court should not have permitted the bad faith count to be added at the close of Welch's case-in-chief as an amendment to conform to proof; (4) the bad faith cause of action cannot stand because there was no evidence of a special relationship between Welch and MGM similar to that of an insured to an insurer, and/or because the jury was not instructed on that issue; (5) there was insufficient evidence to show either a conspiracy to induce breach of contract or a bad faith breach of contract; (6) there was insufficient evidence of slander; (7) Welch's counsel committed misconduct in his closing argument; (8) the successor corporations cannot be held liable for the wrongful acts of MGM; and (9) various errors occurred in the jury's award of compensatory and punitive damages.

We find no error, and affirm.

The evidence showed that Welch appeared in about 30 films between 1965 and 1980 and had a reputation as a strong willed professional actress who sometimes clashed with directors. She was considered a sex symbol, and the only serious dramatic role was as a roller derby queen in "Kansas City Bomber." She turned down all film offers between 1977 and 1980, concentrating during that period on a television special and a television drama about an American Indian woman, for which she served as producer as well as actress.

Prior to 1980, Michael Phillips and David Ward had collaborated on two films, one of which was the Academy Award winner, "The Sting." Over several years, Phillips and Ward developed a film package based on the John Steinbeck novellas "Cannery Row" and "Sweet Thursday." Ward wrote the screenplay and was to be the director, although he had never directed a commercial film before. Phillips was to be the producer. An actor named Nick Nolte was to portray the leading male character.

Phillips and Ward had difficulty finding financing for the film. In early 1980, the project was finally accepted by David Begelman, who had just become president of MGM. Phillips and Ward signed contracts with MGM which gave the studio the right to replace either of them if their service proved unsatisfactory.

Begelman insisted that an actress with a recognizable name be selected for the leading female character, a prostitute named Suzy. Numerous actresses were considered, among whom were Welch and Debra Winger. * * *

On October 8, 1980, Raquel Welch Productions, Inc. (RWPI), a "loan-out" company utilized by Welch for tax purposes, entered into a contract with MGM to provide Welch's services on the film. Welch was promised $250,000, with payment divided into weekly increments during filming. She agreed to participate in nine weeks of actual filming, and to be available for rehearsals and wardrobe fittings for two weeks before shooting began.

The contract included a standard "pay or play" clause, under which the studio could terminate Welch from the film at any time, but was obligated to pay her the full contract price, unless she failed to fulfill her contractual obligations. It further required that Welch be provided a fully equipped, "star-type" trailer for makeup purposes; her choice of hairdresser and makeup artist, on first call to her; and a wardrobe assistant. * * *

[After conflict on the set, Welch was fired. She sued and the jury found in her favor and awarded compensatory and punitive damages on bad faith grounds. Parts I, II, III omitted.]

IV

Appellants contend that the award on the bad faith count must be reversed because one of the essential elements of bad faith, a "special relationship" similar to the relationship between an insurance company and an insured, was lacking as a matter of law. Alternatively, they maintain that, if there was a trial issue as to the existence of a special relationship, the trial court should not have refused their requested instruction on the necessary criteria for the relationship. Welch maintains that because her contract made her an employee of MGM, a special relationship existed as a matter of law.

The record shows that the trial court gave a series of instructions based on existing law involving bad faith termination of employment contracts. (Koehrer v. Superior Court (1986) 181 Cal.App.3d 1155 [226 Cal.Rptr. 820].) The jury was told that appellants were guilty of bad faith breach of contract if they sought "to avoid all liability on a meritorious contract claim by denying that liability without probable cause and with no good faith belief in the existence of a defense, ..." The trial court refused to instruct that a prerequisite to a finding of bad faith was the existence of the factors which make the contractual relationship a special relationship as set forth in Wallis v. Superior Court (1984) 160 Cal. App.3d 1109, 1118 [207 Cal.Rptr. 123]. We must decide whether there were unique features of the employment relationship here which justify an exception to the usual rule that only bad faith and lack of probable cause need be shown in the employment context.

The employment contract for Welch's services was arrived at through careful negotiations between MGM's representatives on one side and Welch's agent and attorney on the other. In addition to compensation, the contract provided for a series of conditions negotiated on behalf of Welch, such as billing; approval of nude scenes and nude stills; effect of changes in the screenplay; effect of replacement of Nolte, Ward, or Phillips; approval, as discussed, of dressing room, hairdresser and make-up artist; a wardrobe assistant and double (actress); and no makeup call earlier than 6 a.m. The contract otherwise incorporated all of MGM's standard terms, including the "pay or play" clause, and the basic agreement of the screen actors guild. * * *

We agree with appellants that the nature of the relationship between Welch and MGM would be subject to challenge under the factors identified by Seaman's as justifying extension of bad faith principles outside the realm of insurance contracts. Indeed, the Wallis court noted in a footnote that "the characteristics of the insurance contract which give rise to an action sounding in tort are also present in most [not all] employer-employee relationships." (160 Cal.App.3d at p. 1116, fn. 2, italics added.) We have declined to apply the Seaman's-Wallis criteria to the case before us because this is a bad faith discharge case and the trial court followed well established law that no special relationship beyond the employer-employee relationship is necessary in a bad faith discharge case. Permitting distinctions to be drawn based upon perceived relative bargaining power in an employment relationship would create whole new areas of litigation in the already confused bad faith area.

V

Appellants further contend that there was insufficient evidence to establish either a conspiracy to induce breach of contract or a breach of the implied covenant of good faith and fair dealing. We disagree.

The record suggests that the defendants may have had different underlying motivations. Phillips wanted to protect himself from removal from the film, Begelman needed to protect his new position at MGM and show his strength in dealing with stars, and MGM wanted a different actress for the role. The end result was the same: a conspiracy to falsely blame Welch for the production's problems and to create a pretext for firing her which would provide a basis for not paying her under her contract. That conspiracy explained the studio's insistence on Welch's making up at the studio on Friday morning rather than the following Monday, even though she had previously had permission to make up at home, had never been late for filming, was upset by the talk of breach, and was facing her first major dialogue scene. The conspiracy and bad faith counts were further supported by: (1) the repudiation by Winger's manager and attorney of the testimony of numerous MGM witnesses regarding when the negotiations for Winger began; (2) Phillips's statements to Welch, Weinfeld and Stein on Thursday night that a breach letter was going out, even though Welch had not yet disobeyed the studio's make up order for Friday morning; (3) the failure to contact Levy before threatening the breach letter, when even MGM's expert testified that problems with a star are usually handled through her agent; (4) Phillips's and Neumann's insistence, contrary to the testimony of Weinfeld and Levy, that they were never told that Welch would use the new make up room on Monday; (5) Phillips's emphasis on Welch's refusal to meet with him over the weekend, when she had repeatedly communicated with him through Levy, and had agreed to a Monday meeting; and (6) the abrupt firing of Welch on Sunday, without waiting to see if she would fulfill her promises regarding Monday, and at a time when 98 percent of the details of Winger's contract had been agreed upon.

[Parts VI–VIII omitted.]

IX

We next consider appellants' claims of error in the awards of compensatory damages.

Appellants raise a variety of relatively minor issues regarding the wording of some of the instructions. We see no error in the instructions as a whole.

Appellants maintain that there was insufficient evidence to support an award of $1 million for loss of professional income on the bad faith count, as Welch did not have a reasonably certain future career as a serious film actress. We disagree. The lost income award was supported by the amount of money Welch had made from previous film work, the absence of film offers subsequent to "Cannery Row," the expert testimony that she would have obtained additional film roles but for the "Cannery Row" firing, and the amount of money film stars were making at the time of trial. The $1 million the jury awarded for lost income was considerably less than the $3,200,000 for which her counsel argued.

We similarly reject appellant's argument that there was insufficient evidence to support damages of $750,000 for loss of reputation on the bad faith count. Appellants ignore the difference between Welch's pre-

"Cannery Row" reputation as a somewhat difficult but professional actress and her post-"Cannery Row" reputation as a contract breaker who had been fired for cause.

Appellants also maintain that MGM cannot be liable for $300,000 of compensatory damages for slander when Begelman, who made the slanderous statement, was found liable for only $25,000 of such damages. We disagree. The jury was instructed that MGM's liability depended upon whether Begelman was speaking solely as an individual or was expressing MGM's official corporate position. The verdict shows that the jury believed that Begelman was speaking on behalf of the studio and that the statement caused more damage coming from the studio than from an individual.

Appellants further complain that the various categories of compensatory damages which were awarded on the bad faith count were duplicative of each other or duplicated the compensatory damages which were awarded on other counts.

On the bad faith count, the jury was instructed to consider: (1) lost contract benefits, including the agreed compensation and loss of value of appearing in the film; (2) loss of professional income; (3) damage to reputation; and (4) emotional distress. The jury verdict form on the bad faith count mirrored the factors in that instruction. As to the other counts, the jury was simply asked to determine the amount of compensatory damages which applied, without specification of the source of the damages.

Appellants never objected to the form of the verdicts, and never contended at the trial court level that there were duplications within the damages on the bad faith count. After the verdicts were returned, they raised some, but not all, of the contentions of duplication which they now make before us. By acquiescing in the measure of damages which was presented to the jury, appellants waived the right to raise this issue on appeal. * * * Moreover, as to those issues of duplication which the trial court was asked to consider, the record supports the trial court's determinations that the only duplication was in the $194,000 awarded both for breach of contract and conspiracy to induce breach of contract; the other damages compensated for different types of losses. The $194,000 duplication was corrected at the trial court level.

X

Finally, we consider appellants' contentions that the punitive damages are excessive or duplicative as a matter of law.

As previously indicated, the jury awarded $3,750,000 against MGM and $500,000 against Phillips as punitive damages on count II (conspiracy to induce breach of contract); $150,000 against MGM and $2,500 against Begelman as punitive damages on count III (slander); and

$3,750,000 against MGM as punitive damages against MGM on count IV (breach of the implied covenant of good faith and fair dealing.

An award of punitive damages will be found excessive on appeal only if the record shows that it was so grossly disproportionate that it resulted from passion or prejudice. * * * Among the pertinent factors are the reprehensibility of the conduct, the relationship between the amounts of compensatory and punitive damages, and the wealth of the particular defendant. * * * Great weight is given to the determination of a trial court on motion for new trial that the damages were not excessive. * * * Such a ruling was made here.

The punitive damages the jury awarded were substantially less than Welch requested. As to MGM, her counsel asked the jury for $7.5 million on the slander count and that same amount on the bad faith count. The $500,000 awarded against Phillips for bad faith was exactly what counsel requested. Counsel argued for $700,000 on the slander count, based on one dollar for each Rolling Stone subscriber.

It was stipulated below that MGM had a net worth of $215 million and Phillips of $5 million. The punitive damages thus represented 3.6 percent of MGM's net worth and 10 percent of Phillips's net worth as an individual. As to MGM, the ratio of punitive damages to compensatory damages was 2.8:1. The same ratio as to Phillips was 2.1:1.

As shown by the cases summarized in *Devlin v. Kearny Mesa AMC/Jeep/Renault, Inc., supra,* 155 Cal.App.3d 381, the size of the punitive damage awards here were not inconsistent with or disproportionate to awards which have been affirmed in the past. * * * We realize that MGM lost money on the film, and Phillips's salary for producing it was $200,000. Still, given the net worths of the defendants, their complete disregard of the likelihood that the unjustified firing would ruin Welch's film career, and the relatively high actual damages, the jury could properly conclude that appellants' conduct justified the amount of punitive damages which was awarded. * * *

The judgment is affirmed. * * *

2. NET COMPENSATION

Once Art Buchwald and his co-plaintiff Alain Bernheim won their initial lawsuit discussed in Chapter 1 to have Buchwald credited with providing the idea for *Coming to America* and Bernheim as its producer, they found themselves in the uncomfortable position of having to enforce a contract that limited them to 1.5% of net profit for Buchwald and 40% reducible to 17.5% for Bernheim. Thereafter Buchwald and Bernheim soon discovered, as others had before them, that Hollywood accounting rules never produce net profit. In the second phase of the case, Judge Schneider found Paramount's definition of net profits unconscionable. The following case represents the third chapter in the saga.

BUCHWALD v. PARAMOUNT PICTURES CORPORATION

California Superior Court, 1992.
1992 WL 1462910.

SCHNEIDER, Judge.

INTRODUCTION

In the first phase of the trial of this case, the court concluded that Paramount's highly successful film *Coming to America* was "based upon," i.e., inspired by, a concept created by humorist Art Buchwald. In the second phase of the trial the court decided, inter alia, that certain provisions of Paramount's net profit formula were unconscionable. * * * As a consequence of the court's decisions in the first two phases of this case and the June 14, 1991 Order, the third and final phase of this case was concerned with establishing the compensation to which plaintiffs Alain Bernheim and Art Buchwald are entitled.

SUMMARY OF THE EVIDENCE PRESENTED

Plaintiffs approached the issue of the contributions of Bernheim and Buchwald to the success of *Coming to America* by assuming that in 1987 Paramount had given the go-ahead for a motion picture to be made based on Buchwald's concept, and that Paramount was already committed to pay Eddie Murphy and John Landis millions of dollars in compensation, whether or not the picture was actually made. Not surprisingly, under this "gun-to-the-head" approach to fair market value, one of plaintiffs' witnesses (Jeffrey Robin) opined that Bernheim and Buchwald were entitled to combined compensation in the amount of $6.2 million.

The court rejects plaintiffs' approach to the issue of the compensation to which Bernheim and Buchwald are entitled, and specifically rejects as unfounded in fact the testimony of Mr. Robin. In rejecting this testimony, the court wishes to make it clear that it does not doubt Mr. Robin's good-faith belief in the opinion expressed by him.

Paramount, on the other hand, proffered the opinions of three experienced motion picture producers and executives, all of whom testified that Bernheim is entitled to "up-front" compensation in the range of $150,000–$200,000, and Buchwald in the range of $25,000–$65,000. All of these witnesses believe Bernheim and Buchwald are entitled to no additional contingent compensation because *Coming to America* has generated no net profits.

Paramount's economist, Benjamin Klein, utilizing a regression analysis, testified that Bernheim was entitled to compensation in the amount of $252,000. He also opined that Buchwald was entitled to compensation in the range of $22,000–$82,000.

Although the court believes Paramount's experts came closer to the mark in establishing the compensation to which plaintiffs are entitled than did plaintiffs' experts, the court is not prepared to accept the opinion of Paramount's experts in toto. Specifically, the court declines to accept in full the testimony of plaintiffs' motion picture producers and executives because, as will be discussed below, the court believes these witnesses failed to give sufficient consideration to factors which increase the compensation to which plaintiffs are entitled. The court declines to accept in full Professor Klein's analysis in part because, by his own admission, his opinion is based upon arbitrary assumptions. Moreover, the court observes that even Professor Klein was required to admit that if certain adjustments were made for provisions of the net profit formula which the court found to be unconscionable, Bernheim's compensation would increase to $347,000.

The Court's Approach to the Value of Bernheim's Services

Since the court declines to accept either plaintiffs' or defendants' evidence, is the court entitled to establish compensation within the parameters established by the evidence of the parties? Under established law, the answer to this question is clearly in the affirmative. * * * Moreover, while the court finds Paramount's evidence to be more persuasive, the court concludes that the opinions of value expressed by Paramount's experts are too low for the reason that such experts failed to ascribe sufficient value to factors which the court believes are important. It is these factors to which the court now turns.

At the outset, the court notes that under the contract entered into by Bernheim and Paramount, Bernheim was to receive $200,000 in "up-front" compensation if a movie was made based upon Buchwald's concept and, in addition, contingent compensation in the amount of 33.5 percent of net profits reducible to 17.5 percent.[2] This deal, which was negotiated at a time when the parties believed the net profit formula was valid, is better than the amount some of plaintiffs' experts believe Bernheim is presently entitled to receive. In other words, plaintiffs' experts appear to ascribe no value to the kind of deal Bernheim might have been able to negotiate had both parties known the net profit formula was invalid.

The court also believes Paramount's experts have failed, in arriving at the value of Bernheim's compensation, to give sufficient consideration to the fact that Bernheim controlled Buchwald's concept—a concept that virtually everyone who testified at trial indicated was unique[3]—and that this control enhanced the value of Bernheim's services. Similarly, although several of Paramount's experts opined that the fact Buchwald's name was associated with the project would have resulted in increased media attention, it appears to the court none of these ascribed any additional value to that fact.

2. Although the contract between the parties actually provided that Bernheim was to receive 40 percent of net profits reducible to 17.5 percent, plaintiffs have stipulated that the actual percentage should be 33.5 percent.

3. Plaintiffs' expert, Howard Suber, testified that he was aware of no other motion picture that involved a member of African royalty coming to America and becoming involved in life in the urban ghetto. * * *

Further, although the evidence revealed that Eddie Murphy and John Landis earned millions of dollars in "up-front" compensation for their respective roles in "Coming to America," and although plaintiffs' expert, Dr. Suber, testified that the twin pillars of the success of *Coming to America* were Buchwald's concept and Murphy's persona, none of Paramount's witnesses appeared to take these factors into consideration in arriving at Bernheim's compensation.[4]

Finally, and importantly, the court notes that although Paramount has earned tens of millions of dollars of gross profits from "Coming to America," none of Paramount's experts considered that fact in arriving at the compensation to be paid to Bernheim. The fact is, however, that it is entirely permissible for the court to consider the success of *Coming to America* in determining what compensation should be awarded Bernheim. * * *

Since the court has decided that the evidence of the parties sets the outside limits (i.e., the high and low) of the compensation to which Bernheim is entitled, but not the precise amount of that compensation, the question remains: To what compensation is Bernheim entitled? In reaching this decision, the court is fully mindful of the fact that its task is to produce a fair and equitable result—neither a windfall to Bernheim nor unjust enrichment for Paramount. Additionally, since the standard for an expert witness "is not mathematical exactness but only a reasonable approximation," (Sheldon v. Metro–Goldwyn Pictures Corp., 309 U.S. 390, 408, 60 S.Ct. 681, 84 L.Ed. 825 (1940), it is clear the trier of fact cannot be held to a stricter standard.

Having considered all the above, the court believes the fair and just compensation for Bernheim for his contribution to *Coming to America* is $750,000. The court observes that, given the fact it was stipulated that Paramount has earned tens of millions of dollars of gross profits from "Coming to America," the compensation awarded to Bernheim represents less than 1 percent of Paramount's gross profits (if *Coming to America* generated gross profits as high as $100 million) and less than 5 percent of Paramount's gross profits (if *Coming to America* generated gross profits as low as $20 million). In awarding compensation to Bernheim, the court has also considered the fact that *Coming to America* was the product of creative efforts by many persons other than Bernheim and Buchwald, although that film was clearly based upon Buchwald's concept and Bernheim had a significant role in the early development of that concept.

The court's decision concerning the compensation to which Bernheim is entitled is buttressed by other evidence in the record. For example, Paramount's Exhibit 901 is entitled "Data on Films Meeting Court Specified Discovery Criteria." This summary reflects that total

4. There was testimony adduced at trial that Bernheim's contribution to *Coming to America* was comparable to that of John Landis, the director. While the court seriously doubts this is true, the fact that Bernheim made a lesser contribution to *Coming to America* than Landis did not justify Paramount's experts in ascribing little value to Buchwald's concept and Bernheim's control of it.

producer compensation on five comparable films ranged between $150,000 and $4.3 million. The amount awarded to Bernheim falls within the range of total compensation paid to producers on the comparable films.[6]

The Court also finds Exhibit 157, and the testimony of Jeffrey Robin, to be somewhat helpful in arriving at the compensation to which Bernheim is entitled. Mr. Robin testified:

> "A: If one has gross participation, you're trying to determine how much net, in essence, you're giving away to third parties when you're converting gross to net. It's normal to do it at a two-to-one ratio, which is what Mr. Gelfan has done. If you look at Mr. Murphy's 15 percent of the gross, 29.5 percent of the net is approximately two times."

As the court interprets Exhibit 157 and Mr. Robin's testimony, Paramount and other studios consider 1 percent of gross profits to be the equivalent of 2 percent of net profits. In this case, Paramount's expert, David Picker, testified that Bernheim was entitled to receive contingent compensation of 10 percent of net profits reducible to 5 percent, and plaintiffs' other expert, Martin Ransohoff, testified that Bernheim was entitled to contingent compensation of 35 percent of net profits reducible to 12.5 percent. Taking the low number from each witness's testimony (Picker 5 percent and Ransohoff 12.5 percent) and utilizing the conversion factor of 1 percent of gross profits being equal to 2 percent of net profits, the result would be that 5 percent to 12 percent of net profits would be the equivalent of 2.5 percent to 6.25 percent of gross profits. Since Paramount has earned tens of millions of dollars of gross profits on "Coming to America," the range of gross profits to which Bernheim would be entitled, using these percentages and assuming a low gross profit figure of $20–million, would be $500,000 (2.5 percent of $20 million) to $1,250,000 (6.25 percent times $20 million). The amount awarded to Bernheim falls within this range.

THE COURT'S APPROACH TO THE VALUE OF BUCHWALD'S CONCEPT

If the evidence presented by the parties was less than persuasive with respect to the compensation to which Bernheim is entitled, it was even less so with respect to Buchwald. Paramount's experts did opine, however, that Buchwald was entitled to compensation in the range of $22,000 to $82,000. As indicated, Jeffrey Robin, the only one of plaintiffs' experts who ascribed a number to the compensation to which

---

6. The court is fully aware that the costs on *Coming to America* were far greater than on any of the comparable films. One of the main reasons for this is that substantial gross profit participation shares were paid to Eddie Murphy and John Landis. The court was presented, of course, with no evidence concerning the contributions made by any of the producers on the comparable films. The court has been presented, however, with evidence of a number of factors which the court believes increases the compensation to which Bernheim is entitled, which factors were not given sufficient consideration by Paramount's experts. The court has concluded, therefore, that Bernheim is entitled to the compensation awarded in this decision, notwithstanding the substantial costs on "Coming to America."

Buchwald and Bernheim were entitled, opined that the plaintiffs were entitled to combined compensation of $6.2 million.

As stated above, the court is unable to accept plaintiffs' evidence with respect to the compensation to which Bernheim and Buchwald are entitled. On the other hand, the court believes Paramount's evidence with respect to Buchwald's entitlement to compensation is even closer to the mark than was its evidence with respect to Bernheim. As was the case with Bernheim, however, the court finds that Paramount's experts failed to give sufficient consideration to factors which have caused the court to conclude Buchwald is entitled to somewhat more compensation than testified to by Paramount's experts. These factors include the uniqueness of Buchwald's concept and the effect of that concept on the success of *Coming to America*; Buchwald's stature as a nationally known humorist and the media attention that would result from a film based upon a concept created by him; and the fact that Paramount has earned tens of millions of dollars of gross profits on "Coming to America." Considering all of these factors, the court concludes Buchwald is entitled to compensation in the amount of $150,000. * * *

Notes

1.   For more information on the issue of net profits, *see* Note, *Buchwald v. Paramount Pictures Corp.* and the Future of Net Profit, 9 Cardozo Arts & Enter. L. Rev. 545 (1991).

2.   Is it a wise decision for attorneys to accept entertainment law cases on a contingent fee arrangement? In Hollywood, even when you win you may lose. In the third phase of the trial, the court awarded Buchwald compensation of $150,000 for his idea based on his entitlement to 1.5% of net profits and his partner Alain Bernheim $750,000 based on his initial entitlement to a minimum of 17.5% of net profits. Their attorney Pierce O'Donnell, a partner at the prestigious Kaye Scholer, Fierman, Hays, & Handler's Los Angeles office, ran up a $2.5 million legal bill and over $500,000 in costs to complete the three and a half year case. O'Donnell, a former Supreme Court clerk to Justice Byron White, had taken the case on a contingency fee arrangement that made Buchwald & Bernheim responsible only for the cost of the trial. In the end, O'Donnell and his team spent $3 million to reap a judgment of $900,000 for their clients. O'Donnell wrote the book *Fatal Subtraction: How Hollywood Really Does Business* (1992), detailing the inside story of *Buchwald v. Paramount Pictures*, in part to recoup some of his investment. O'Donnell left Kaye Scholer in 1996 to start his own firm, O'Donnell & Shaeffer LLP.

3.   Compensation has become a more important issue to talent as the amount of money studios make from movies. Leonardo DiCaprio earned $1.8 million plus 18% of net compensation to star in *Titanic*, which earned $600,000,000 domestically as part a global box office of around $2 billion. Like all movies, *Titanic* never earned a profit because of the studio accounting system. DiCaprio received guaranteed compensation of $20,000,000 for his next picture *The Man in the Iron Mask* released in 1998.

4.   Despite, or because of, the publicity surrounding Buchwald's case other producers became furious with their net profit deals. The *Batman* films generated the following worldwide domestic gross:

Batman	$411.2 million
Batman & Robin	$233.7 million
Batman Forever	$333.6 million
Batman Returns	$282.5 million

The *Batman* films have earned over $1 billion in box office revenues. Imagine the surprise of the producers when they failed to receive additional revenue on their net profit deals.

BATFILM PRODUCTIONS, INC. v. WARNER BROS., INC.

California Superior Court, March 14, 1994.
No. BC 051653 and No. BC 051654.

YAFFE, Superior Court Judge.

PHASE I STATEMENT OF DECISION.

The Court divided the trial of this case into two phases. Phase I consisted of a bench trial of plaintiffs' non-jury claims. Those claims primarily concern plaintiffs' "Net Profits" participation in the Batman motion pictures.

The plaintiffs are two individuals, Benjamin Melniker and Michael Uslan, and the two corporations that furnish their services, Batfilm Productions, Inc., and Franklin Enterprises, Ltd. The defendants are Warner Bros. and Polygram Pictures, Inc.

(The Court previously granted the summary judgment notion of defendants Peter Guber, Jon Peters, and the Guber–Peters Entertainment Co.) Polygram Pictures did not participate in the bench trial.

In 1979, Mr. Melniker and Mr. Uslan obtained an option on the motion picture rights to the Batman comic book characters. In November 1979, they made a deal with Casablanca Productions (Polygram's predecessor) for the development and production of a motion picture to be based on those characters (the "Casablanca Agreement"). Under the Casablanca Agreement, Mr. Melniker and Mr. Uslan were entitled to receive certain fixed and contingent compensation if a Batman motion picture were produced.

In 1981, Polygram assigned to Warner Bros. its rights and obligations under the Casablanca Agreement. In 1988, Mr. Melniker and Mr. Uslan and Warner Bros. signed a written amendment to the Casablanca Agreement (the "Warner Agreement"). Under the Warner Agreement, Mr. Melniker and Mr. Uslan were entitled to receive $300,000 in fixed compensation for Batman, plus a $100,000 "deferment" once the film generated a certain level of receipts, plus 13% of the so-called "Net Profits," as defined in an attachment to the Warner Agreement.

Warner Bros. has paid Messrs. Melniker and Uslan the $300,000 fixed fee and $100,000 deferment. Under the Warner Agreement, Warner Bros. has also paid Melniker and Uslan an additional $700,000 in fixed fees on two additional motion pictures (Batman Returns and Batman: Mask of the Phantasm). Warner Bros. will have similar financial obligations to plaintiffs on each additional Batman motion picture. Although Batman has generated more revenue than any other Warner Bros. film, it has not generated any "Net Profits" under plaintiffs' contract.

Melniker and Uslan filed suit in 1992 claiming, inter alia, they were denied their fair "Net Profits" compensation. The primary claims originally to be tried to the Court were the Tenth Cause of Action for an accounting of the revenues and expenses of Batman and the Eleventh Cause of Action for a declaration that plaintiffs' "Net Profits" definition is unconscionable and, thus, unenforceable. On the first day of trial, however, plaintiffs dismissed their accounting claims. Warner Bros. is therefore entitled to prevail on that cause of action. At the close of plaintiffs' case, Warner Bros. moved for judgment pursuant to section 631.8 of the Code of Civil Procedure. In reviewing the evidence, the Court believed that Mr. Melniker and Mr. Uslan had offered evidence to prove that the Warner Agreement was contract of adhesion that should be strictly interpreted against Warner Bros. And should not be interpreted in a way that would be contrary to plaintiffs' reasonable expectations.

But a contract of adhesion is a contract, and a contract of adhesion is not the same as an unconscionable contract, which is no contract at all. "Unconscionability" requires a far different level of proof. The plaintiffs did not prove that they are to be relieved of their contract with Warner Bros. on the ground of unconscionability.

Mr. Melniker negotiated the Warner Agreement on his and Mr. Uslan's behalf. No one is less likely to have been coerced against his will into signing a contract like the Warner Agreement than Mr. Melniker. This former general counsel and senior executive of a major motion picture studio (Metro–Goldwyn–Mayer) knew all the tricks of the trade; he knew inside and out how these contracts work, what they mean, and how they are negotiated.

Even with Mr. Melniker's knowledge and experience, plaintiffs complain that Warner Bros. knew when the parties signed the Warner Agreement in 1988 that Batman would not generate "Net Profits." Plaintiffs did not explain the relevance of this to the issue of whether their contract is unconscionable. Even if they had, however, they failed to prove that Warner Bros. knew in 1988 that Batman would not generate any "Net Profits."

At the core of plaintiffs' case is their argument that the contract was not fair to them because Warner Bros. and others earned millions of dollars on Batman and plaintiffs did not. The answer that argument is that ever since the King's Bench decided Slade's Case in 1602, right down to today, courts do not refuse to enforce contracts or remake contracts for the parties because the court or the jury thinks that the contract is not fair.

That principle is not some medieval anachronism. This society, this country, this culture operates on the basis of billions of bargains struck willingly every day by people all across the country in all walks of life. And if any one of those people could have their bargain reexamined after the fact on the ground that it was not fair or on an assertion that it was not fair, we would have a far different type of society than we have now; we would have one that none of the parties to this case would like very much.

When one talks about a motion picture and the claims of this type that are made, they all have one thing in common: the plaintiff comes in and says, "Without me, they would have had nothing, and look how they treated me." But the process of making a motion picture consists of the process of bargaining with many talented people on many different and inconsistent bases, and making bargains with them that cannot rationally be compared one to another. It would not be good for the motion picture business or for the parties to this case if any one of those people on any motion picture could come back and ask a court to remake the bargain that he made on the ground that he now asserts, after the fact and in light of the success of the picture, that he was not fairly treated in comparison with others. Whether a contract is fair is not the issue. A contract is not unconscionable simply because it is not fair. Plaintiffs claim that the Warner Agreement is unconscionable within the meaning of Civil Code section 1670.5. To be unconscionable, a contract must "shock the conscience" or, as plaintiffs alleged in paragraph 139(b) of their complaint, it must be "harsh, oppressive, and unduly one-sided."

After considering all the evidence, the Court finds that the plaintiffs have failed to prove that the Warner Agreement, taken as a whole, is unconscionable. That, however, is not the end of the inquiry that the Court must make. Under Civil Code section 1670.5, if the evidence shows that any part of a contract is unconscionable, the Court may refuse to enforce that part of the contract.

During the trial, plaintiffs claimed that eight elements of the Warner Agreement's "Net Profits" definition were unconscionable: (1) the 10% advertising overhead charge; (2) Warner Bros.' retention of any economic value of United States tax credits created by the payment of taxes in the foreign territories where Batman was distributed; (3) application of the 15% production overhead charge on participation payments to third parties; (4) application of the 15% production overhead charge on the $100,000 deferment; (5) all of the interest charges; (6) the costs charged by Pinewood Studios in England for holding sets and stages after completion of photography; (7) application of the 15% production overhead charge to the costs incurred at the Pinewood Studio lot; and (8) the inclusion in "gross receipts" of only 20% of the revenue from videocassettes, less a distribution fee. (These items, and the dollar amounts associated with them, are listed on Exhibit B9.)

In considering Warner Bros.' motion for judgment under Code of Civil Procedure section 631.8, the Court had little difficulty in rejecting seven of plaintiffs' claims. As to all of the items relating to overhead charges (Items One, Three, Four, and Seven), the Court granted Warner Bros.' motion for judgment because the plaintiffs failed to prove that historically Warner Bros.' indirect general administrative expenses for motion picture production and advertising—"overhead"—do not equal or exceed the amount charged under the "Net Profits" definition, namely, 15 percent of production costs and 10 percent of advertising expenditures. As a matter of fact, plaintiffs conceded that they could not show that the overhead charges under the "Net Profits" definition exceeded Warner Bros.' actual overhead costs, taken as a whole.

Plaintiffs argued that charging overhead on certain production costs, advertising expenses, gross participations, deferred payments, and payments paid to foreign studios was unconscionable because the administrative cost of providing those goods or services was less than the contractual 10 or 15 percent overhead surcharge. Plaintiffs did not prove that allegation. And, more important, the test is not whether Warner Bros.' overhead charge on a particular direct cost item exceeded the "actual" administrative or other indirect expenses associated with providing that one item or service to the production or advertising of a movie. As the accounting experts for both sides testified, overhead cannot be assessed with such precision. Under the circumstances, the test must be whether the production and advertising overheads charged by using the percentage allocations are, in total, unconscionably higher than Warner Bros.' actual production and advertising overhead costs on a motion picture. Plaintiffs offered no evidence to support such a finding. Plaintiffs also failed to show that the advertising costs, gross participations, deferred payments, and payments paid to foreign studios were not historically included in the pool of costs that were compared to Warner Bros.' general and administrative expenses to estimate its rate of overhead. In sum, plaintiffs simply failed to prove that any of the overhead charges are unconscionable.

The Court also granted Warner Bros.' motion for judgment as to Item Two, the foreign tax credit. According to plaintiffs, when a motion picture is distributed overseas, many countries impose a tax on the receipts generated. That tax payment gives rise to a credit that can be used under certain circumstances to offset United States income tax obligations. Plaintiffs claimed that, in calculating their "Net Profits," it is unconscionable for Warner Bros. to deduct foreign taxes as a distribution expense without adding something for the value of the foreign tax credits. The plaintiffs failed to prove, however, that Warner Bros. received any foreign tax credits on Batman, or the amounts thereof, or that Warner Bros. received any actual financial benefit from those tax credits when calculating and paying its United States tax obligations. Even if such a credit had been received, the plaintiffs failed to prove that they ever asked Warner Bros. to agree that, in computing "Net Profits," Warner Bros. would augment the gross receipts of the picture by the amount of the tax credits. No such provision is contained in plaintiffs' contract and there was no evidence that they ever expected such treatment of the tax credits. The Court also granted the motion for judgment as to Item Six, the Pinewood Studios sound stage holdover costs, because there was no evidence that the holdover charge is not properly a cost of the first Batman movie.

The Court granted the motion for judgment as to Item Eight, videocassette distribution, on the ground that Mr. Melniker knew that a 20 percent royalty was standard in the industry. He never questioned it. He never asked that it be changed. The plaintiffs did not prove that the 20 percent royalty unconscionably exceeded the actual revenues, less expenses, from videocassette distribution. They also offered no evidence that a "distribution fee" on the distribution of videocassettes was unconscionable. Nor did they prove that they could have negotiated a better deal elsewhere at the time this deal was made, in which a higher percentage of video revenue, without deduction of a distribution fee, would be credited to the picture in calculating "Net Profits."

Item Five concerned the "interest" charge on production costs. Under paragraph 2A of plaintiffs' contract, "Net Profits" become payable once the picture generates enough gross receipts to cover the specified distribution fees, distribution expenses, and production costs. Until then, under paragraphs 2A and 9 of plaintiffs' "Net Profits" definition, the production costs bear an interest charge. Under the contract, Warner Bros. reduces the interest-bearing balance of production costs with only those gross receipts that remain after deducting the distribution fees and expenses.

Plaintiffs claim that is unconscionable for Warner Bros. to not credit the interest-bearing production cost balance with all of the gross receipts of the picture. They also claim that because the distribution fee represents a source of "profit" for Warner Bros., this method of calculating interest is unconscionable because it allows Warner Bros. to charge interest on the cost of production after the picture has generated revenues in excess of that amount.

Plaintiffs did present sufficient evidence to require Warner Bros. to defend its method of computing interest under the contract. After listening to the evidence presented by Warner Bros. and the arguments of counsel, however, the Court finds that Warner Bros. met its burden of showing that the method of calculating interest provided in their contract is not unconscionable. Warner Bros. met its burden in a number of ways. Warner Bros. showed that the interest provision in the Warner Agreement is really the same provision found in the 1979 Casablanca Agreement that Warner Bros. did not have anything to do with. Plaintiffs were bound by that contract before they ever dealt with Warner Bros. They cannot complain that they were harmed by being required to abide by a similar provision with the same effect.

Warner Bros. also showed that plaintiffs would not have gotten any better deal on the calculation of interest if they had borrowed the production costs from a third party lender, had produced Batman themselves as independent producers, and had hired Warner Bros. (or presumably anybody else) just to distribute it for them. In that case, plaintiffs would not have been able to use all of the gross receipts generated by the film to repay their lender. Just as in their contract with Warner Bros., they would have been able to repay the production financier only with the gross receipts left over after the distributor retained enough to cover the distribution fees and expenses.

And, if there is a "profit" embedded within Warner Bros.' distribution fee, plaintiffs did not prove the amount of it or that it prevented the picture from showing a net profit.

All of that evidence is sufficient to overcome the plaintiffs' evidence as to the unconscionability of the method of calculating interest under their "Net Profits" contract.

Separately, plaintiffs argued that the language of their "Net Profits" contract did not permit Warner Bros. to continue charging interest once the gross receipts of the picture—prior to the deduction of distribution fees and expenses—exceed the total production costs. The duty of the Court is to find out what the parties meant by the language of their contract. If the contract is one of adhesion, the Court interprets it so that it does not defeat the reasonable expectations of the party who was forced to adhere to it. But the Court will not substitute its own interpretation of the contract if that is not what the evidence shows that the parties intended.

The Court rejects plaintiffs' argument because there was no evidence that plaintiffs ever interpreted the language of the interest provisions in the manner claimed at trial. Mr. Melniker was an old hand at motion picture agreements of this type and had negotiated other "Net Profits" contracts like this himself. He had experience with similar provisions yet he never mentioned the interest issue with anyone at Warner Bros. Plaintiffs offered no evidence that they expected Warner Bros. to compute interest in any other manner. They have thus failed to prove that the contract defeated their reasonable expectations.

Given the Court's decision in favor of Warner Bros. on plaintiffs' unconscionability claim, Warner Bros. is entitled to prevail on plaintiffs' Thirteenth Cause of Action for "unfair competition" because that claim was dependent on a finding that their "Net Profits" contract was unconscionable.

Finally, Warner Bros. is entitled to prevail on plaintiffs' Fourteenth Cause of Action arising from the exhibition of the animated Batman television series. Plaintiffs presented no evidence on this cause of action at trial.

Notes

1. The net profit sagas continue. Matt Damon and Ben Affleck, the writers and stars of the 1997 *Good Will Hunting*, found themselves in a similar position as the producers of Batman. Harvey Weinstein had invested between $15 and $20 million on *Good Will Hunting*, which returned a worldwide box office gross of $226 million worldwide, excluding network, cable, and video. Damon was paid an acting fee of $650,000, while Affleck received a little less. Weinstein eventually gave them a bonus of $500,000 each. In an interview with Peter Biskind, Affleck said, "*Good Will Hunting* had done enormously well by then, but we had gotten an accounting statement that said the movie was $50 million in the red, and it was just like, This is fucked! You had to some great accounting to hide net profits on that movie."

Affleck further indicated that he and Damon had made a Faustian bargain with Weinstein and his brother. "The exchange is," [he said,] "they'll spend money promoting the movie, they'll spend money on an Academy campaign, they'll win you an Oscar, and their reputation is they make better movies. But they're a nightmare to work with . . . So, yeah, we kind of got screwed, but when it came right down to it, it worked out great for us."

Peter Biskind, Down and Dirty Pictures (2004*), reprinted in Vanity Fair*, Feb. 2004, at 118, 166.

2. Affleck probably feels "it worked out great" because while he and Damon did not receive their financial due on *Good Will Hunting*, they did win the Oscar for best Screenplay and now command millions of dollars per picture. Both of them have also produced their share of bombs. Affleck starred in *Gigli* with his former girlfriend Jennifer Lopez, which cost $54 million to make and returned about $10 million. *Gigli* received savage reviews. http://209.157.64.200/focus/f-news/958183/posts.

Chapter 6

FILM CENSORSHIP

Films may be censored, banned, or boycotted for a number of reasons that gives offense to one group or another. Some individuals are offended by nudity, sex and violence. The Motion Picture Association of America (MPAA) has developed codes to indicate the level of sex and violence in a picture to give guidance to parents. These ratings can impact the potential domestic box office gross of the picture as fewer individuals become eligible to see pictures that have been given an "R" rating, and others will choose not to see a film that receives a "NC 17" or "X" rating.

Other individuals fault films for their depiction of women, minorities, and religion in a degrading manner. Several African–Americans called for a boycott of the 2002 film *The Barbershop*, which was produced and written by Blacks, for its negative discussion of Civil Rights icons Rosa Parks, Martin Luther King Jr., and Jesse Jackson. When Jackson and politician Al Sharpton called for a boycott, the film sold more tickets and brought out commentators, even as far away as London, to come to the movie's defense. *See* John Patterson, *Snipping Yarns: Everyone loves Barbershop—except Jesse Jackson and Al Sharpton*, THE GUARDIAN, Oct. 4, 2002, *http://film.guardian.co.uk/patterson/story/ 0,12830,907372,00. html*. Patterson said,

> What can Jesse Jackson and Al Sharpton be thinking? A film comes along, almost entirely funded and made by African–Americans, and soars to the top of the box-office charts. Buoyed by impressive reviews, it stays there for two weeks, an almost unheard of achievement for an "urban-themed" movie. And how do America's most prominent black politicians respond? With threats of a boycott. With demands that MGM, the film's distributor, cut certain scenes for the video release. With a spasm of knee-jerk responses that put them both squarely in the company of fundamentalist right-wingers like Revs Donald Wildmon, Pat Robertson and Jerry Falwell, censorious lefties like Sen Joseph Lieberman, and all those other culture-phobic assholes, be they on the left or right, who want Huckleberry Finn and Harry Potter taken from libraries and burned.

Id. As in many cases, the calls for boycotting and censoring *The Barbershop* had the opposite effect. Not only did the film sell more tickets, but also the cries led the producers to create *Barbershop 2: Back in Business,* which was released into theaters on February 6, 2004. During its first five weeks, *Barbershop 2: Back in Business* took in $61,343,779. Nevertheless Variety predicted that its final domestic box office would "approach but likely not surpass the $75.8 million generated by the 2002 original.... But substantial home entertainment revenues will make this limitation a moot point." Todd McCarthy, *Barbershop 2: Back in Business, available at* http://www.variety.com/review/ VE1117922989?categoryid=31 & cs=1.

Patterson references religious leaders, because they have called for many film boycotts. Many Catholics were upset with how their religious doctrine was portrayed in *Dogma,* which starred Matt Damon, Ben Affleck, Salma Hayak and Chris Rock. In being viewed as anti-Christian the 1999 *Dogma* was joined by the 1997 *Last Temptation of Christ.* The First Presbyterian Church of Rowlett, Texas, declared on its website, ""The Last Temptation of Christ" is idolatrous and blasphemous and attempts to bring shame upon the person of our blessed Lord and Savior Jesus Christ, Who was and continues to be holy, harmless, and undefiled." *http://www.fpcr.org/blue_banner_articles/images7.htm.*

Mel Gibson's 2004 *The Passion of Christ* became the subject of boycott calls from individuals who thought the film harsh towards Jews and anti-Semitic, even before its scheduled release date on February 25, 2004. It received support, however, from Rabbi A James Rudin, the American Jewish Committee's senior adviser on inter-religious affairs, who saw a rough cut of the film and urged Jewish leaders to use it as an example of how Christ's death has been used to stoke up anti-Semitism. *See Senior Rabbi: Don't boycott Gibson's Passion,* THE GUARDIAN, Nov. 28, 2003, *http://film.guardian.co.uk/news/story/0,12589,1095418,00.html.* After Pope John Paul II saw *The Passion of Christ,* he is reported to have said, "It is as it was." These five words became the subject of further controversy after one cardinal tried to deny then. Journalist Peggy Noonan then wrote an article in the Wall Street Journal confirming the Pope's words. Peggy Noonan, *'It Is as It Was,'* WALL STREET JOURNAL, Jan. 22, 2004, at E.1.

The Passion of Christ opened nationwide on Wednesday, February 25, to heated debate, conflicting reviews and phenomenal box office. receipts. Churches brought out entire theaters for its congregations. Movie reviewer Roger Ebert said, "This is the most violent film I have ever seen." Roger Ebert, *Movie Impressive in Depth of Feeling,* ALBUQUERQUE JOURNAL, Feb. 24, 2004, at A.3.

The Passion of Christ earned $23.6 million on opening day and $295.3 million during its first 26 days, making it the highest grossing "R" rated film ever when it surpassed *The Matrix.* Carl DiOrio, *Passion becomes highest grossing R-rated pic,* VARIETY Box Office News, Mar. 21, 2004. *The Passion of Christ* also earned $15 million in 19 territories during the weekend of March 19–21, setting industry highs in Latin American countries like Mexico, Brazil, Chile, and Peru. Don Groves, *'Passion' packs auds: Gibson pic hauls $15 mil o'seas*, VARIETY Box Office News, March 22, 2004. By April 18, 2004, *The Passion of Christ* had earned $360,761,619 in the United States.

This chapter first presents cases that address the MPAA ratings in Part A. Part B explores restrictions on political speech that have troubled the motion picture industry during the 1940s and 1950s.

A. THE RATINGS SYSTEM

Sherri Burr
The Different Ratings Standards for Trailers and Feature Films: Author Interview with Filmmaker John Carlos Frey

Copyright © 2003 by Sherri Burr.

[John Carlos Frey was an accomplished film and television actor (*The Practice, Days of Our Lives, Married With Children, JAG, Weird Science, Party of Five* and *Freaky Friday*) before venturing forth as a screenwriter and director. In 2003, he traveled the country, exhibiting and discussing his feature film *The Gatekeeper*, a film about Mexican immigrants, which he wrote, starred in, and directed. He spoke to Sherri Burr's Entertainment Law class on September 24, 2003. The following is an excerpt from that nearly two-hour class.]

"Making movies has a lot of complications, even down to dealing with the Motion Picture Association of America [MPAA] ratings. If you want your trailer, or coming attraction, to screen in all of the theaters and advertise your film, you have to make it approved by all audiences. Trailers are for advertising a film, for coming attractions. You may have seen the little tag that comes out, "approved by, for all audiences." If you have a rated R trailer, you can only screen it with rated R pictures. Filmmakers strive to have a trailer approved for all audiences so that it screens with all coming attractions.

"In *The Gatekeeper*, there's a scene where guns are raised towards the audience. It's seven frames, which is less than a second, yet it earned our first trailer an R rating. We had to take that out. The other thing was that we used music from a movie called *Unforgiven*, but the MPAA thought the music was too loud. They did not approve of the escalation in volume in the trailer. You can have as loud of a movie as you want and it won't affect the movie rating. You can blast people ears out if you want too. A lot of summer blockbusters do. But when it comes to sound on a trailer, it cannot be above a certain decibel level because that means it is going to go above and beyond somebody else's. You can't be sitting in a theater watching somebody's upcoming attraction and then the next

[handwritten: R rated trailers]

one that comes up and is ten times louder. The MPAA will not allow that.

"We had already produced the trailer, but had to go back, re-cut it and strike it again.

"Has anyone ever heard the F-word? *The Gatekeeper* is rated R and the predominate reason is because of the F-word. You can have four F-words in a movie. If you have five, it's rated R. If there's a sex scene in a film, the nudity isn't as important as the props. I'm not making a joke here; this is absolutely true. Men make the rules so women's breasts are okay. That will get you a PG rating. If you have above the waist nudity and there is thrusting motion, you can have that happen twice, and still get a PG rating. Three thrusts would make it rated R.   *Three thrusts R*

"The MPAA has criteria and is not really creative about it. A film can be very violent, you can chop a hundred people's heads off and if you don't say the F-word, it can be rated PG. Yet three men holding up a rifle towards the audience was not approved. They call it the eleven o'clock to one o'clock shot. I can be pointing the gun sideways and that would be fine. But as soon as the gun moves toward the audience between 11 o'clock and 1 o'clock, it would be rated R. The thinking behind this is that there might be kids in the audience watching the trailer, and the gun would be pointed directly at them. With a PG rating, the trailer is approved for all audiences regardless of age.

"Does that make sense? To get a rated R for a trailer is a lot different from getting an R rating for a movie. The company, the Motion Picture Association of America, is exactly the same, but it has separate criteria for trailers.

"There are no NC–17 ratings for trailers. They're either approved for all audiences or rated R. There are very few movies that are rated NC–17. If trailers were rated NC–17, then you could only show your upcoming attractions on an NC–17 film. You must make it clear, you're either rated R or for a general audience.   *GA or R trailers*

Note

1. As you read the following three cases that challenge the award of particular MPAA ratings, notice the content of the films? What earns an X rating, R rating or PG rating? Do you think these films were unfairly rated based on their content? Are American censors overly sensitive to sexual subject matter and not sensitive enough to violent matter?   *Sex only*

MIRAMAX FILMS CORP. v. M.P.A.A.
New York Supreme Court, 1990.
148 Misc.2d 1, 560 N.Y.S.2d 730.

RAMOS, Judge.

In this CPLR Article 78 proceeding petitioners Miramax Films Corp. and Pedro Almodovar challenge the "X" rating given their controversial film, "Tie Me Up! Tie Me Down!" by respondent The Motion Picture Association of America, Inc. ("MPAA"). They seek a court imposed modification of the rating from "X" to "R". The petitioners complain that the classification of "Tie Me Up! Tie Me Down!" as "X" rated runs afoul of the prohibition against arbitrary and capricious conduct (CPLR Article 78). It appears that for the first time the courts have been asked to intervene and address issues previously dealt with by film critics and the motion picture industry regarding the fairness and methodology of ratings given films by the dominant film rating organization in this country.

Traditionally, any controversy regarding the content of a motion picture focused on the issues of censorship and free speech, not on the fairness of action taken with regard to a particular film by an industry rating board.

FAIRNESS IN RATINGS ?

Censorship is an anathema to our Constitution and to this Court. The respondent which created and administers the present rating system also proclaims that it is against censorship. However, notwithstanding the denials of censorship by the respondent, the present system of rating motion pictures "G", "PG", "PG–13", "R" and "X" is an effective form of censorship. It is censorship from within the industry rather than imposed from without, but censorship nevertheless.

effective form of censorship

The repeatedly expressed concern by the MPAA that its rating system is the industry's only defense to government censorship is unwarranted in light of First Amendment guaranties. The courts of this state and of the United States have sought to articulate a standard which would reconcile the interests that conflict—the preservation of individual liberties and creative freedoms on the one hand, and the protection of legitimate public concerns such as the emotional well-being of our children, on the other. The effort has produced a balancing point, the point at which speech stops and obscenity begins. Justice Brennan stated the present view in *Roth v. United States,* 354 U.S. 476, 484, 77 S.Ct. 1304, 1 L.Ed.2d 1498 (1957):

> "All ideas having even the slightest redeeming social importance—unorthodox ideas, controversial ideas, even ideas hateful to the prevailing climate of opinion—have the full protection of the guaranties, unless excludable because they encroach upon the limited areas of more important interests. But implicit in the history of the First Amendment is the rejection of obscenity as utterly without redeeming social importance."

Roth standard ?

There is nothing inherent in the rating system that would modify or extend the *Roth* standard. The standard in *Roth* was intended to apply in cases of governmental action to suppress or to prosecute and cannot be imposed upon the MPAA as its standard.

For its part, the MPAA contends that because First Amendment issues are not at stake, its rating determination must stand unless there is overt administrative misconduct. Once there is a finding of no administrative misconduct, the argument goes, its expertise ought to be

Rating determination must stand unless there is overt administrative misconduct.

Standard —rational not arbitrary

deferred to as a legitimately authorized and duly constituted administrative body. Omitted from this analysis is the question of the reasonableness of the standard which the MPAA applies. If the MPAA is to avoid the relief sought herein then that standard must be rational, not arbitrary.

Initially, the Court notes that there is no serious dispute that the Court has the jurisdiction to review a film rating determination of the MPAA in the context of an Article 78 proceeding. As shall be further discussed herein, the standard of proof necessary for relief and the method of judicial review is very much in dispute.

Respondent MPAA is a New York not-for-profit corporation and its members are producers and distributors of motion pictures and television programs. It administers a voluntary rating system, Classification and Rating Administration ("CARA") which reviews most, if not all, popularly screened films in this country. It is clearly the most significant, to the point of exclusive, film rating system and the tremendous impact of its ratings to the economic viability of a film is undisputed.

Films are submitted to respondent for review by CARA. Films are rated and placed in one of the following categories:

"G"—General Audiences—All ages admitted.

"PG"—Parental Guidance Suggested; some material may be suitable for children.

"PG–13"—Parents strongly cautioned. Some material may be inappropriate for children under 13.

"R"—Restricted, under 17 requires accompanying parent or adult guardian (age varies in some jurisdictions).

"X"—No one under 17 admitted.

With regard to "Tie Me Up! Tie Me Down!" a seven member Board viewed the film and unanimously determined that the film should be classified with an "X" rating. The Board members individually filled out, in their usual course of operations, rating forms which detailed the basis for the "X" rating. Each of the raters found that two sexually explicit scenes warranted giving the film an "X" rating. The Board also found the visual depiction of the sex acts and language accompanying one scene to justify an "X" rating.

Petitioners were afforded an opportunity to delete or edit the objectionable scenes and declined. An appeal of the ruling was heard by the Rating Appeals Board which split down the middle on whether the film warranted an "X" rating. As a two-thirds vote of the Appeals Board is required to reverse the underlying determination, the "X" rating was upheld.

Petitioners point to no deviance from standard procedures of the MPAA in the rating of the film.

The Court notes that at any time a producer may withdraw a film from consideration by respondent and distribute the film unrated. The negative economic impact of not obtaining a satisfactory rating is clear and severe. Petitioners chose to distribute the film unrated.

The MPAA's standard for rating films was described in a memo to the Rating Board members from the Chair of CARA, Mr. Richard D. Heffner. In that memo Mr. Heffner states that the MPAA rates films "as we honestly believe most American parents will want us to". It is evident that the MPAA standard is to rate films "G" through "X" based upon the tastes of the average American parent ("AAP"). The stated purpose of the rating system is "to provide advance information to enable parents to make judgments on movies they wanted their children to see, or not to see" (Valenti, The Voluntary Movie Rating System, MPAA, 1987, p. 4). As such the MPAA rating system is clearly not designed to rate the merits of a film or even to advise adults as to which films they may wish to see.

*[margin note: Avg. American *Parent]*

The MPAA's list of cinematic no-nos is predictable: language, violence, nudity, drug use and sex. Notably absent is any sensitivity to the offenses suffered by women, minorities, the disabled and those who may not share the values of the AAP.

This court cannot avoid the notion that the standard is reasonable only if one agrees with it. This standard, *by definition,* restricts material not because it is harmful, but because it is not average fare.

[margin note: restricts b/c not average not harmful]

There is a breach between the standard for protected speech in *Roth* and material which the rating board finds acceptable that is wide indeed. Into that breach step those who would create and distribute motion pictures. The manner in which the MPAA rates all films, not just "Tie Me Up! Tie Me Down!" causes this Court to question the integrity of the present rating system.

The court notes that the initial Rating Board and the Ratings Appeals Board members have no special qualifications.

"There are no special qualification for Board membership, except one must have a shared parenthood experience, and one must love movies, must possess an intelligent maturity of judgment, and have the capacity to put himself or herself in the role of most parents and view a film as most parents might—parents trying to decide whether their younger children ought to see a specific film." Valenti, *Voluntary Movie Rating System*, MPAA, 1987, p. 5.

[margin note: to be on Ratings Board + Appeals Board]

Petitioners allege in conclusory fashion that the Board members and Ratings Appeals Board are selected and subject to the control of the major motion picture producers and distributor establishment. This Court is unable to address this issue because no attempt at offering a factual underpinning for such allegations has been made.

An even more substantial concern is the question, not addressed by the parties, of whether respondent is adequately meeting the needs of America's children in film rating. Having voluntarily taken on this responsibility there may well be the obligation to competently address the task. An often leveled criticism of the MPAA is that violence in films

violence condoned more than sexual activity

is condoned to a far greater extent than displays of sexual activity. Without professional guidance or input it may well be that the interests of children are not adequately protected or are even endangered by providing color of acceptability to extremely violent and psychologically damaging films.

Although each of the categories which the rating system uses is cloaked in terms which suggest that they are fashioned to protect America's children, the inference of concern for the welfare of children is not borne out by any scrutiny of the standard and the guidance given to the rating board members. The standard is not scientific. There are no physicians, child psychiatrists or child care professionals on the board, nor is any professional guidance sought to advise the board members regarding any relative harm to minor children. No effort is made to professionally advise the board members on the impact of a depiction of violent rape on the one hand and an act of love on the other, nor is any distinction made between levels of violence. In this regard, the Court notes the following from Mr. Heffner's December 1988 memo to Rating Board members:

> "Be concerned about violence, for American parents increasingly are ... *but* remember always how much violence seems to be accepted, perhaps even expected, in television and films."

Excerpts of Valenti's description of what the ratings indicate are probative of the relative tolerance with which violence in films is permitted related to material of a sexual nature:

> "R: 'Restricted, under 17 requires accompanying or adult guardian' (Age varies in some jurisdictions)...."

> "The language may be rough, the violence may be hard, drug use content may be included, and while explicit sex is not to be found in R-rated films, nudity and lovemaking may be involved...."

> "X: 'No one under 17 admitted'...."

> "The reason for not admitting children to X-rated films can relate to the accumulation of sexually connected language or of explicit sex, or of excessive and sadistic violence ..." (Valenti, The Voluntary Movie Rating System, MPAA, 1987, p. 8).

Thus, the MPAA rates films on a purely subjective basis of what they believe is the AAP criteria for their children. A film may be viewed by children that may contain "hard violence" and "drug use" but not "explicit sex." Only "excessive and sadistic violence" will result in an "X" rating. It may well be that the MPAA ratings are skewed towards permitting film makers huge profits pandering to the appetite for films containing "hard violence" and "drug use" while neglecting the welfare of children intended to be protected by the rating system. This Court concludes that reliance upon a non-professional rating board is misplaced and that the effort by the MPAA to encourage a more lenient policy toward violence is indefensible.

The failure of the rating system to provide a professional basis leaves only the viewing taste of the AAP, the consumers, as the standard. This standard may serve as a basis for a successful marketing strategy but may not coincide with the advice child care professionals might offer.

It may make good business sense not to ask a question if you might not like the answer, but it does render as hypocritical Mr. Heffner's claim that the *sole* rationale for the "X" rating is to avoid psychological abuse of children (December 1988 memo). The industry that profits from scenes of mass murder, dismemberment and the portrayal of war as noble and glamorous apparently has no interest in the opinions of professionals, only the opinions of its consumers.

The record also reveals that films are produced and *negotiated* to fit the ratings. After an initial "X" rating of a film whole scenes or parts thereof, are cut in order to fit within the "R" category. Contrary to our jurisprudence which protects all forms of expression, the rating system censors serious films by the force of economic pressure. The MPAA requires that American films deal with adult subjects in non-adult terms, or face an "X" rating. Films shown under the present system tend to be restricted to those fit for children under 17, as defined by the AAP.

The heart of petitioners' grievance is that an "X" rating stigmatized their film and lumped it into a category with pornographic films which none of the parties or serious critics contend should be done. Petitioners wish the Court to award an "R" rating or alternatively seek to have the Court determine that the rating system itself is patently arbitrary and capricious or without rational basis.

At its inception, the rating system denoted the various levels by the use of symbols and registered those symbols as trademarks, with the notable exception of the "X" rating. The effect of that exception (not explained in the papers submitted or during oral argument) has been to permit those who characterize themselves as pornographers to appropriate the "X" rating for their own purposes. "X rated" is now synonymous with pornography. For a film not intended for the pornography market, the rating of "X" is a stigma that relegates the film to limited advertising, distribution and income.

While it may be true that the MPAA has permitted the "X" rating to be appropriated by the pornography industry with a concomitant tainting of any film awarded an "X" rating, petitioners do not allege any bad faith or foresight in respondent's failing to register the "X" rating. While arguing in conclusory fashion that the current system works to the detriment of certain types of films and film makers, petitioners do not set forth an adequate factual basis on the papers before this Court, or oral argument, to warrant such findings.

The Court notes that it is clearly precluded in judicial review from substituting its judgment for that of the body reviewed or from considering the facts *de novo*. * * * This court is also precluded from imposing a different (professional) standard because the MPAA may not be required to do so under the First Amendment. Therefore, the burden is on petitioners to set forth facts indicating that respondent acted arbitrarily, capriciously and without rational basis in applying the standard of the AAP. This petitioners have clearly failed to do. Within the context of this rating system for parental guidance there has been no showing that the "X" rating afforded "Tie Me Up! Tie Me Down!" was without a rational basis or arbitrary and capricious. Petitioners themselves acknowledge that the film contains material that is not suitable for those under the age of eighteen and there is no dispute that the film contains language and sexually explicit scenes that parents might not wish their children to view.

As a part of this proceeding, the court has been requested to view selected scenes from "Tie Me Up! Tie Me Down!" and scenes from other films rated "R" in order to determine if the "X" rating was arbitrary. That determination this Court declines to make.

This court will not dignify the present system by rendering an opinion on so frivolous a standard as the wishes of the AAP. What is offensive is the unprofessional standard itself, not the manner in which the rating board applies it. The standard of the AAP is a marketing standard, a tool to aid in promoting films. There is no basis in the record for the Court to conclude that the MPAA does not know how to label its products for market, there is only a question as to the significance of the labeling.

At best the offering of clips of "R" rated films into evidence amounts to an argument of discriminatory enforcement of the rating standards. That over the course of more than two decades a handful of films may have been as sexually explicit as "Tie Me Up! Tie Me Down!" or arguably, in the eyes of the beholder, more explicit and unsuitable for youthful viewers and have obtained an "R" rating is not inherently arbitrary and capricious or without rational basis. To find respondent's actions of affording the "R" rating to certain films and not to "Tie Me Up! Tie Me Down!" to be wrongful, the Court believes petitioners need offer evidence of clear and intentional discrimination. * * * Petitioners have failed to do so. Merely alluding in conclusory fashion to possible vague discrimination is not sufficient. Additionally, the over-riding concern is whether respondent acted in good faith in furtherance of its own legitimate purpose. * * * Petitioners do not, other than by cursory conjecture, substantiate any basis to indicate respondent acted in bad faith or outside of its stated function in its rating of "Tie Me Up! Tie Me Down!"

There are also questions of the good faith of the petitioners in instituting this proceeding. As aforesaid, the allegations of economic prejudice and discrimination are unsubstantiated and the exploitation of the "X" rating by the petitioners in their advertising and their refusal to cooperate in the review process until after they had physical possession of the "X" certificate leads to the inference that this proceeding may be just publicity for "Tie Me Up! Tie Me Down!"

must offer clear and intentional discrimination

Petitioners, without a shred of substantiation, contend that respondent may be motivated by a prejudice towards foreign films as well as a prejudice towards independent distributors. Such allegations, in the form of conjecture and wholly conclusory in nature, will not provide a basis for relief or even an evidentiary hearing. * * * However, the court notes, and respondent should be guided accordingly, that should such discriminatory practice be substantiated in the context of an Article 78 proceeding or a plenary action by such a subject discriminated group of film makers, based upon restraint of trade or intentional interference with prospective economic advantage, there may well prove to be a basis for relief.

This court is mindful of constitutional limitations on the imposition of a governmental system of censorship. * * * The courts would thus be reluctant to tamper with a voluntary independent system of film rating. However, in view of the dominant and preemptive role played by the MPAA in the film industry there is an obligation to administer the system fairly and with a foundation that is rationally based. This proceeding has raised certain issues which need be addressed by respondent although no relief may be afforded herein. The initial problem is the need to avoid stigmatizing films of an adult nature, which ought not be seen by children, but which are clearly not pornographic. The MPAA, having acquiesced in the use of the "X" rating by the pornography industry, may well have some affirmative responsibility to avoid stigmatizing films with an "X" rating.

This court also concludes that the rating system's categories have been fashioned by the motion picture industry to create an illusion of concern for children, imposing censorship, yet all the while facilitating the marketing of exploitive and violent films with an industry seal of approval.

While the petition before this court does not adequately present a case for addressing these serious issues, it appears that the MPAA should strongly consider some changes in its methods of operations to properly perform its stated mission. Unless such concerns are meaningfully dealt with, the MPAA may find its rating system subject to viable legal challenge by those groups adversely affected herein, including organizations charged with the responsibility of protecting children.

If the MPAA chooses to rate films for the benefit of children it is its duty to do so with standards that have a rational and professional basis or to leave the task to others whose interests are not subject to the powerful economic forces at work within the industry. The respondent is strongly advised either to consider proposals for a revised rating system that permits of a professional basis for rating films or to cease the practice altogether. The petition before this Court is, however, not the appropriate vehicle to afford such relief.

Accordingly, the petition is dismissed and the relief sought denied.

BORGER BY BORGER v. BISCIGLIA

United States District Court, Eastern District of Wisconscin, 1995.
888 F.Supp. 97.

REYNOLDS, District Judge.

On August 18, 1994 sixteen-year-old Benjamin Borger ("Borger") filed this First Amendment civil rights suit (by his father, Darrell Borger), against the Kenosha School District, its superintendent, and its board of education ("School Board") because they refused to allow the movie "Schindler's List" to be shown as part of his high school curriculum. Borger now seeks summary judgment and a declaration that the defendants' decision to prevent the viewing of any R-rated film, including "Schindler's List", as part of the curriculum at his school violated Borger's and other students' rights under the First and Fourteenth Amendments. He also asks for an injunction barring the defendants from enforcing the portion of the School Board's policy prohibiting the instructional use of any film which the Motion Picture Association has rated "R". The School Board and superintendent have filed a cross motion for summary judgment. For the following reasons, the court grants the defendants' summary judgment motion, denies Borger's motions for summary judgment and for preliminary injunction, and dismisses this case.

FACTS

In early 1994, several United States History teachers at Bradford High School in Kenosha, Wisconsin, asked principal Joseph Mangi to send a memorandum to superintendent Anthony Bisciglia requesting that the school sponsor a viewing of the R-rated film, "Schindler's List," as a supplement to the educational materials available to tenth grade students. On February 11, 1994, Principal Mangi sent that letter, requesting that the teachers be allowed to take the students to a local theater to view the film during a school day. Superintendent Bisciglia rejected the request for the singular reason that "Schindler's List" has been rated "R" by the Motion Picture Association of America ("MPAA"), and was therefore banned from the curriculum by the Kenosha School District policy (section 6161.11) on the selection of instructional materials, which limits the use of rated commercial films in the classroom to those rated PG–13, PG, and G.

The School Board created policy 6161.11 in 1976 and has revised it twice since then—in 1981 and 1991. The current version of policy 6161.11 states:

> Commercial entertainment films having obvious educational value may be included when appropriate to the subject being studied.

> Commercial films that are unrated or rated PG or PG–13 shall not be shown to students in the District without advance written notice

to the parents. Such notice shall contain an accurate description of the contents of the film.

No films having a rating of R, N17, or X shall be shown to students at any school.

Thus, when determining which films may be shown in school, the School District relies on the ratings established by the voluntary movie rating system of the Motion Picture Association of America ("MPAA"). The MPAA's full-time rating board in Los Angeles decides the ratings by majority vote. According to a 1994 document put out by the MPAA and written by Jack Valenti, President and Chief Executive Officer of the MPAA, the rating board looks to the "theme, violence, language, nudity, sensuality, drug abuse, and other elements" to determine what rating to give a film.

The MPAA rating board gave "Schindler's List" an R-rating. According to the MPAA literature, an R-rating means that the movie is "restricted," and that children under 17 require an "accompanying parent or adult guardian." The literature explains, that when the rating board gives an R rating:

> In the opinion of the Rating Board, this film definitely contains some adult material. Parents are strongly urged to find out more about this film before they allow their children to accompany them.

> An R-rated film may include hard language, or tough violence, or nudity within sensual scenes, or drug abuse or other elements, or a combination of some of the above, so that parents are counseled, in advance, to take this advisory rating very seriously. Parents must find out more about an R-rated movie before they allow their teenagers to view it.

The rating board gave "Schindler's List" an "R" rating "for language, some sexuality and actuality violence."

Ben Borger attends Bradford High School and was a tenth-grader in February of 1994. Although they were not allowed to show "Schindler's List", the teachers in the 1993/94 tenth grade United States History classes at Bradford found many creative ways (including the use of other films) to teach about the Holocaust. Nonetheless, on February 22, 1994, Borger circulated a petition among the students which stated:

> We, the undersigned, students of Bradford High School ask for the Board to reconsider the decision against seeing the film Schindler's List.

Borger obtained over 400 signatures attached to this petition, which he took with him to present to the School Board meeting that very night. The School Board refused to take action on the issue, and so Borger filed this case.

Borger is now in the eleventh grade, and wants the School Board to allow the Government class teachers to show "Schindler's List".

ANALYSIS

The court must grant a motion for summary judgment if the pleadings, depositions, answers to interrogatories, admissions, and affidavits "show that there is no genuine issue as to any material fact and that the moving party is entitled to a judgment as a matter of law." Fed.R.Civ.P. 56(c). In this case, no material facts are in dispute, and the court finds that the law does not support Borger's First Amendment claim.

Students do not lose their First Amendment rights when they walk through the schoolhouse door. *Tinker v. Des Moines Indep. Community Sch. Dist.*, 393 U.S. 503, 506, 89 S.Ct. 733, 736, 21 L.Ed.2d 731 (1969). However, courts have decided that the scope of the First Amendment within the classroom must be tempered, and that the content of the curriculum is within the sound discretion of school officials, with exceptions in rare cases. So strong is this concept, that the U.S. Court of Appeals for the Seventh Circuit has proclaimed that high school students contesting the curriculum decisions of local authorities must raise issues which "cross a relatively high threshold before entering upon the field of a constitutional claim suitable for federal court litigation." *Zykan v. Warsaw Community Sch. Corp.*, 631 F.2d 1300, 1306 (7th Cir.1980) (high school administration's removal of certain books from English course and school library upheld against students' challenge). Courts should not interfere with local educational discretion unless "local authorities begin to substitute rigid and exclusive indoctrination for the mere exercise of their prerogative to make pedagogic choices regarding matters of legitimate dispute." *Id.* Only a "flagrant abuse of discretion" merits judicial intervention. *Id.*

Thus, school officials have abundant discretion to construct curriculum, and they only violate the First Amendment when they limit access to materials "for the *purpose* of restricting access to the political ideas or social perspectives discussed in them, when that action is motivated simply by the officials disapproval of the ideas involved." *Board of Ed. v. Pico*, 457 U.S. 853, 879–80, 102 S.Ct. 2799, 2814, 73 L.Ed.2d 435 (1982) (Blackmun, J. concurring). Thus, the court must consider whether or not the defendants' decision bore a reasonable relationship to a legitimate pedagogical concern. * * *

This is not a case in which the plaintiff alleges that school officials acted pursuant to political or religious beliefs. The undisputed facts establish that the superintendent and School Board decided not to allow "Schindler's List" to be shown solely because it was R-rated and banned by policy 6161.11. The defendants have presented an unrebutted "legitimate pedagogical concern"—that its students not be subjected to movies with too much violence, nudity, or "hard" language. This is a viewpoint-neutral, non-ideological reason for a facially neutral policy and a viewpoint-neutral application of that policy. Borger does not dispute that the school has a legitimate policy to try to keep harsh language, violence, and nudity out of the history or government classroom curriculum.

[handwritten margin note: only a flagrant abuse of discretion merits judicial intervention]

Nor is this a case in which a student asks that the court force the school to add a film to the curriculum. Such a case would doubtlessly fail under *Pico,* 457 U.S. at 871, 102 S.Ct. at 2810, in which Justice Brennan's plurality opinion doubted that students would be able to force the School Board to *add* new school materials even though they might be able to stop the School Board from *eliminating* materials already at school. *Id.*

Instead, this case is about whether the defendants can rely on the MPAA rating system, instead of upon their own viewing of the film, in order to exclude it from the curriculum due to language, violence, and nudity. In other words, Borger argues that the use of the MPAA ratings system is not reasonably related to the School Board's admittedly legitimate concern. The court disagrees.

It is true that a private organization's rating system cannot be used to determine whether a movie receives constitutional protection. For instance, a city cannot rely on the rating system to determine which movies are "obscene speech" and thereby less protected. * * * Neither this court nor the School Board is bound by the R-rating that "Schindler's List" received.

However, that does not mean that the School Board cannot choose to use the ratings system as a filter of films. As noted above, the Supreme Court has said that schools and classrooms are non-public forums, outside the general marketplace of expression, and school boards have more discretion to censor within that environment than do bodies governing the public sphere. *Hazelwood,* 484 U.S. 260, 108 S.Ct. 562 (school newspaper part of curriculum and therefore non-public forum, subject to censorship which is reasonably related to legitimate pedagogical concern). The grounds for school board curriculum decisions need only bear a reasonable relationship to their legitimate purpose. *Id.* The School Board has established, through literature on the MPAA, that relying on the ratings is a reasonable way of determining which movies are more likely to contain harsh language, nudity, and inappropriate material for high school students. Borger has not presented any evidence to counter this evidence. The School Board has also presented unrebutted evidence that as the ratings change, the policy gets amended or at least reconsidered. Movies with lesser ratings than "R" are dealt with on a case-by-case basis. However, "R" ratings are the threshold which the School Board has chosen as movies that will not even be considered. An R-rating indicates that reasonable people could determine that high school students should not view the film. *See Krizek,* 713 F.Supp. at 1139. That "reasonableness" is all that is necessary in a high school setting. This is a constitutional exercise of school board discretion, and the court shall not enjoin the enforcement of policy 6161.11.

IT IS THEREFORE ORDERED that Benjamin Borger's motions for summary judgment, preliminary injunction, and class certification are DENIED.

IT IS FURTHER ORDERED that the defendants' motion for summary judgment is GRANTED, and this case is DISMISSED.

MALJACK PRODUCTIONS, INC. v. MOTION PICTURE ASSOCIATION OF AMERICA

United States Court of Appeals, District of Columbia Circuit, 1995.
52 F.3d 373.

WILLIAMS, Circuit Judge.

Maljack, an independent movie and video production company, sued the industry's major trade association, the Motion Picture Association of America, for breach of contract. Maljack asserted that the Association's film-rating arm had discriminated against it because it was not a member of the Association. The district court dismissed the complaint under Fed.R.Civ.P. 12(b)(6) for failure to state a claim, holding that Maljack's assertions of discrimination—that its movie had received an "X" rating for violence, while more violent films produced by companies belonging to the Association had been given "R"s—were not adequate to allege a breach of the ratings contract. We reverse.

* * * Maljack is an Illinois corporation primarily engaged in distributing videocassettes to the home market. Its first major venture into the production of general-release films came in the mid–1980s, when it produced *Henry: Portrait of a Serial Killer,* a movie depicting, in documentary style, the life of a fictional serial murderer loosely based on a person on death row in Texas. Maljack concedes that *Henry* contains several explicit scenes of physical violence, including depictions of two rapes and several brutal murders.

The Motion Picture Association of America is a New York-incorporated trade association consisting of many of the largest American producers and distributors of television programs and motion pictures. Maljack is not a member. Among its other activities, the Association operates the Code and Rating Administration ("CARA"), located in California, which reviews movies prior to their release and evaluates their suitability for viewing by children. At the time of the events at issue, CARA rated movies either "G," "PG," "PG–13," "R," or "X"— with the exception of the last, all federally registered certification marks owned by the Association. Submission of a film to CARA is wholly voluntary, and producers are free to distribute movies without obtaining an Association rating.

In March 1988 Maljack submitted *Henry* to CARA for rating and paid a fee calibrated to the film's production costs. CARA gave *Henry* an "X" on grounds of its violence. That marked it, according to the Association's published general description of the rating, as having an "accumulation of brutal or sexually connected language, or of explicit sex or excessive and sadistic violence" that rendered it "patently an adult film." A representative of CARA explained that four sequences in the movie were particularly offensive and would have to be cut before CARA would even consider giving *Henry* an "R," the next most restrictive rating. Maljack refused to make the cuts and instead appealed the "X" rating to the Association's Classification and Rating Appeals Board. The Appeals Board affirmed the "X" rating.

In February 1989 Maljack surrendered the ratings certificate for *Henry* and chose instead to distribute the movie unrated. Maljack alleges that the picture was not as successful as it would have been if the Association had given *Henry* an "R": a substantial number of movie theaters will not show films that either are "X"-rated or lack a CARA rating altogether. Maljack maintains that the Association denied Henry an "R" rating because it was a small, independent production company that did not belong to the Association.

Maljack filed a two-count complaint against the Association in May 1990. Count I asked the court to cancel the Association's registered certification mark for the "R" rating on the grounds that the defendant applied its ratings in an illegally discriminatory fashion; the trial court dismissed this count on jurisdictional grounds, and Maljack does not appeal that ruling. Count II alleged that the Association's discrimination breached a covenant of good faith and fair dealing implied by law in CARA's agreement to rate *Henry* for a set fee. The district court also dismissed this count, holding that the complaint was devoid of non-conclusory factual allegations capable of supporting an inference that the Association had acted unfairly or in bad faith. Maljack moved to amend its complaint, but the district court denied leave to amend on the ground that the proposed amended complaint suffered from the same basic flaw.

Maljack now appeals both the dismissal of its original complaint and the denial of leave to amend. We need reach only the first issue. * * *

The parties and the district court have so far assumed that California law governs the rating agreement, and we will proceed on the same assumption. * * * Under California law, "all contracts contain an implied covenant of good faith and fair dealing [that] 'requires each contracting party to refrain from doing anything to injure the right of the other to receive the benefits of the agreement,'" San Jose Prod. Credit Ass'n v. Old Republic Life Ins. Co., 723 F.2d 700, 703 (9th Cir.1984) (quoting Egan v. Mutual of Omaha Ins. Co., 24 Cal.3d 809, 169 Cal.Rptr. 691, 695, 620 P.2d 141, 145 (1979)). A complaint alleging breach of this covenant must plead deliberate and conscious bad faith on the part of the defendant:

> [A]llegations which assert such a claim must show that the conduct of the defendant, whether or not it also constitutes a breach of a consensual contract term, demonstrates a failure or refusal to discharge contractual responsibilities, prompted not by an honest mistake, bad judgment or negligence but rather by a conscious and deliberate act, which unfairly frustrates the agreed common purposes and disappoints the reasonable expectations of the other party thereby depriving that party of the benefits of the agreement.

Careau & Co. v. Security Pacific Business Credit, Inc., 222 Cal.App.3d 1371, 272 Cal.Rptr. 387, 399–400 (1990).

If the Association deliberately gave *Henry* an "X" rating instead of an "R" because Maljack was not a member, it breached this implied covenant. The Association's assertion that Maljack "bargained to receive CARA's subjective judgment and nothing more" is inaccurate: as it stated in its complaint, Maljack reasonably expected that CARA would rate *Henry* in good faith based upon the content of the film alone and not the identity of its producer and that producer's links (or lack of links) to the Association. This expectation of fair dealing is protected under California law as if it were an explicit obligation of the contract.

The question, then, is whether the original complaint adequately alleged the sort of discrimination that would violate the implied covenant. Maljack pled the following:

- That it did not belong to the Association,

- That although *Henry* contained some violent scenes, "the scenes were neither overly explicit or gory as compared to other films produced or released by members of the [Association] and given a "R" rating by the [Association],"

- That because of the small ($1,100) rating fee paid by Maljack under CARA's production-cost-based sliding scale, CARA was aware that *Henry* was not a major-studio "big budget" film,

- That CARA gave *Henry* an "X" rating without ever explaining "why other films containing equal or greater violence and released by member companies of the [Association] had received an 'R' rating," and

- That the Association breached the covenant of good faith and fair dealing implied in the rating agreement "by rating [*Henry*] in a discriminatory manner when compared to other films it had given an 'R' rating to."

The Association objects to the conclusory tone of this last paragraph and faults Maljack for never stating explicitly that it was discriminated against because it did not belong to the Association. This is too stingy a reading of the complaint. The context makes clear the plaintiff's claim that the discrimination mentioned in the last paragraph flowed from Maljack's non-member status.

The Association's more serious objection is that the mere fact that *Henry* received an "X" while more violent films by member companies were rated "R" cannot logically support an inference that CARA acted with improper motive. It is true, as the Association points out, that the complaint would have been stronger if it had alleged that the rating criteria were biased against independent producers, or that CARA had a pattern of giving unwarranted "X" ratings to similar movies, or that the Association's member companies had a financial interest in sabotaging *Henry,* or that there was some direct communication from the Association indicating bad faith. But the absence of such confirming data does not nullify what *has* been alleged. Disparate treatment is the essence of all discrimination claims: at their core is always the assertion that the defendant has treated like cases differently on the basis of some impermissible criterion. And this is exactly what Maljack's complaint has alleged. The fact, which we must take as true, that the Association routinely assigned "R" ratings to member films more violent than *Henry* certainly suggests that it may have applied a different standard to *Henry* because of the identity of its producer. Later on, of course, at the summary judgment or trial phase of this litigation, it will not be easy for Maljack to show so skewed a ratings pattern as to support the inference necessary to meet California's quite demanding requirements for demonstrating bad faith, but federal pleading standards do not require the plaintiff to stuff its complaint with all of the details establishing the discrepancy. See Conley v. Gibson, 355 U.S. at 47–48, 78 S.Ct. at 102–03 (pointing to liberal discovery and other devices by which details of claim may be explored). This is especially true in a case where, as here, the alleged discriminator is applying rather broad and amorphous criteria (e.g., "excessive ... violence"), so that countless details may be needed to support an inference of discrimination.

The Association effectively conceded at oral argument that this method of proof—comparing treatment in an individual case to the pattern of related decisions—is meaningful in this context. When asked to consider a hypothetical case in which a children's film like *Snow White* was given an "X" rating, Association counsel acknowledged that an observer could legitimately say something was amiss: *Snow White*'s "X" would be so out of line with CARA's other decisions as to raise a compelling inference of something more than a simple judgment error or difference of opinion. Such logic is no different from that contained in Maljack's complaint. Henry the Serial Killer may be no Snow White (nor even her wicked stepmother), but the degree of difference is a question of fact, and we must now take the facts to be as Maljack alleges.

We therefore reverse the district court's order dismissing the original complaint and remand the case for further proceedings.

Notes

1. The ratings codes may be enforced differently by movie theaters. Some cinemas, for example, require parents to buy the teen a ticket for a Rated "R" flick and permit the teen to attend by herself whereas other theaters oblige the parent to purchase sufficient tickets to accompany to the teen to the movie. To avoid this problem, underage teens procure tickets for a rated "PG or PG–13" movie and sneak into the rated "R" film. Aware of this tactic, some cinemas placed guards outside the doors to the 2003 *Matrix: Reloaded* to stem the flow of teen switchers. When teens buy a ticket for one movie and swap to another, they artificially alter the accounting balance for films by inflating the revenue for the movie they purchased and deflating the income for the one they actually watched.

2. Should there be different rating standards for sexual versus violent content? Mosk, *The Jurisprudence of Ratings Symposium Part I*, 15 CARDOZO

ARTS & ENT. L.J. 135 (1997), argues that movies are "one of America's major exports and are regarded as portraying, and even having an influence on, culture, morals, and behavior." He notes that violence "is a difficult area to rate because there is an infinite number of variations in type and intensity of such violence, but generally, films with significant violence receive restricted ratings." *Id.*

3. Can ratings of one's movies impact a career? Rush & Molloy reported that according to a $10 million lawsuit "Steven Spielberg's DreamWorks SKG studio sabotaged one of its own movies so Spielberg would be sure to get a British knighthood." Producer Jerome O'Connor charged in a complaint that DreamWorks "set out to quash" his comedy "An Everlasting Piece" because director Barry Levinson wouldn't cut scenes that didn't amuse British officials. *No 'Piece,' No Justice, Says Suit,* DAILY NEWS (NEW YORK), Jan. 9, 2001.

4. In *Ashcroft v. Free Speech Coalition,* 535 U.S. 234, 122 S.Ct. 1389, 152 L.Ed.2d 403 (2002), the Supreme Court ruled that the Child Pornography Prevention Act of 1996 (CPPA), 18 U.S.C. § 2251 *et seq.,* abridges the freedom of speech, finding it overbroad and unconstitutional. The CPPA extends the federal prohibition against child pornography to sexually explicit images that appear to depict minors but were produced without using any real children. The statute prohibits, in specific circumstances, possessing or distributing these images, which may be created by using adults who look like minors or by using computer imaging.

B.   RESTRICTIONS ON POLITICAL SPEECH

LAWSON v. UNITED STATES

United States Court of Appeals, District of Columbia Circuit, 1949.
176 F.2d 49.

CLARK, Circuit Judge.

John Howard Lawson, appellant in No. 9872, and Dalton Trumbo, appellant in No. 9873, have separately appealed from two separate judgments of the District Court convicting and sentencing them for separate violations of 2 U.S.C.A. § 192, which makes it a misdemeanor to refuse to answer 'any question (of a Congressional Committee) pertinent to the question under inquiry.' On motion of appellants, the two appeals were consolidated for oral argument before this court and this opinion will dispose of both appeals.

In October of 1947, the Committee on Un–American Activities of the House of Representatives of the United States (hereinafter called 'the Committee'), then engaged in investigation of 'Communist infiltration of the motion picture industry,' scheduled public hearings in Washington, D.C. Pursuant to two validly issued subpoenas, Lawson and Trumbo, both prominent writers in the motion picture industry, appeared before a subcommittee of the Committee consisting of Chairman Thomas and Congressman McDowell and Vail. Lawson testified on October 27, 1947, and Trumbo's testimony occurred the following day. Both of appellants testified under oath. The single-count indictment against Lawson charged him with refusal to answer a question as to 'whether or not he was or had ever been a member of the Communist Party.' Trumbo's indictment, in two counts, charges that he refused to answer questions (1) as to 'whether or not he was a member of the Screen Writers Guild,' and (2) as to 'whether or not he was or had ever been a member of the Communist Party.' At the separate jury trials below neither Lawson nor Trumbo testified in his own behalf. Both trials resulted in convictions and the imposition of the maximum sentence allowed by 2 U.S.C.A. 192 of one year imprisonment and $1,000 fine. Both Lawson and Trumbo were allowed to remain on bond pending appeal. * * *

Appellants strongly urge at the outset that they are protected under specified Amendments to the Constitution from being compelled to disclose their private beliefs and associations and thus the questions asked appellants by the subcommittee were improper and the trial judge therefore erred in upholding the subcommittee's inquiry and in allowing a conviction for refusal to answer. Their argument is that the Bill of Rights protects all individuals against being compelled to disclose their private beliefs and associations regardless of what those beliefs and associations may be, that the right of privacy of an individual is absolute, and that an individual may not be punished for remaining silent as to those beliefs and associations. This is not a novel contention. It has been before this and other federal courts several times in recent years with appropriate variations to fit the facts of the particular case. It was raised in very similar form in *Barsky et al. v. United States*, 1948, 83 U.S.App. D.C. 127, 167 F.2d 214. * * *

In that case, Barsky was subpoenaed by the Committee to produce certain records of the Joint Anti–Fascist Refugee Committee, of which he was Executive Secretary. He appeared but refused to produce the documents subpoenaed. Having been indicted, along with others, for that willful failure, one of his major defenses, if not the principal one, was that the Congressional Committee lacked the power to inquire because the inquiry might disclose that Barsky and the others were believers in Communism or members of the Communist Party and that they thereby would be subjected to 'exposure' of their assertedly private political beliefs in violation of the First Amendment. This was a material issue, squarely raised as justification for the offense charged in the *Barsky* case. The point was extensively briefed and strenuously argued before this court in the *Barsky* case. It received the full consideration of all the judges sitting in that case. * * * The above-quoted portions of the majority opinion in the *Barsky* case are, therefore, the holding in that case and not in any sense dicta. That holding is controlling here in deciding appellants' foremost contention in these appeals against these appellants. We hereby reaffirm the holding of the majority opinion of this court in the *Barsky* case and adopt its reasoning as applicable to appellants in the present cases. So that there may be no mistake or misunderstanding and because the point here involved has proven to be one of constant recurrence, we expressly hold herein that the House Committee on Un-American Activities, or a properly appointed subcommittee thereof, has the power to inquire whether a witness subpoenaed by it is or is not a member of the Communist Party or a believer in Communism and that this power carries with it necessarily the power to effect criminal punishment for failure or refusal to answer that question under 2 U.S.C.A. § 192. This is equally true of the inquiry whether appellants were members of the Screen Writers' Guild, a question which only Trumbo refused to answer. To hold otherwise would indeed by holding that the power to inquire is a 'powerless power.'

We think it appropriate to quote with approval here the following language of the majority of a three-judge statutory court sitting in this jurisdiction. 'It is fully established by reiterated holdings of the Supreme Court that the right of free speech is not absolute but must yield to national interests justifiably thought to be of larger importance. The same is true of the right to remain silent. When legislating to avert what it believes to be a threat of substantive evil to national welfare, Congress may abridge either freedom. The right to be silent may be interfered with in either of two ways: as an incident to the accomplishment of a legislative purpose, Congress may require an individual to make a statement specifically prescribed by it; or it may require generally that an individual make any statement essential to avert the anticipated evil, without defining the statement.'

Lawson and Trumbo make various other attacks on the authority of the Committee, the pertinency of the questions asked and the failure to provide immunity for persons who answer the questions. We do not discuss these contentions in detail for they have all been raised and decided adversely to appellants in the prior opinions of this and other federal courts. All of these claims raise constitutional questions decided by the *Barsky* case, supra, the case of *United States v. Josephson*, the case of *Eisler v. United States*, and the case of *Dennis v. United States*. The combined rationale of these recent decisions as to this very Committee leave it no longer subject to the slightest doubt that the Committee was and is constitutionally created, that it functions under valid statute and resolution which have repeatedly and without exception been upheld as constitutional, that the 'question under inquiry' by the Committee was proper, that the power of inquiry includes power to require a witness before the Committee to disclose whether or not he is a Communist, and that failure or refusal of a witness so to disclose is properly punishable under 2 U.S.C.A. § 192. To this we need only add that these particular cases offer the best possible application of the principles of law restated above. No one can doubt in these chaotic times that the destiny of all nations hangs in balance in the current ideological struggle between communistic-thinking and democratic-thinking peoples of the world. Neither Congress nor any court is required to disregard the impact of world events, however impartially or dispassionately they view them. It is equally beyond dispute that the motion picture industry plays a critically prominent role in the molding of public opinion and that motion pictures are, or are capable of being, a potent medium of propaganda dissemination which may influence the minds of millions of

American people. This being so, it is absurd to argue, as these appellants do, that questions asked men who, by their authorship of the scripts, vitally influence the ultimate production of motion pictures seen by millions, which questions require disclosure of whether or not they are or ever have been Communists, are not pertinent questions. Indeed, it is hard to envisage how there could be any more pertinent question in these circumstances where the Committee was then investigating, pursuant to statutory authorization, 'the extent, character, and objects of un-American propaganda activities in the United States,' and 'the diffusion within the United States of subversive and un-American propaganda that is instigated from foreign countries or of a domestic origin and attacks the principle of the form of government as guaranteed by our Constitution,' and where, as was said in the *Barsky* case, Communistic ideology 'is antithetical to the principles which underlie the form of government incorporated in the Federal Constitution and guaranteed by it to the States.' * * *

There being no further contentions raised in either case which merit discussion herein, it follows that both judgments appealed from in these cases are

Affirmed.

Buhle, Paul,
Halting McCarthyism: The Stamler Case in History; Civil Rights Case Involving Professor Jeremiah Stamler

Monthly Review Foundation, Inc. No. 5, Vol. 51; Pg. 44, October 1, 1999.

* * * The now-forgotten Stamler case [Stamler v. Willis, 287 F.Supp. 734 (1968)] is a reminder of the days that followed the McCarthy era. * * * No one rang a bell to say that an era was over and the U.S. courts were open for the Bill of Rights. Instead, persistent and able lawyers, battling side by side with a renewed social (civil rights) movement, discovered that after the long night they could get things done in U.S. courts. The Stamler case achieved no less than a softening up of the House Committee on UnAmerican Activities (HUAC) for its congressional demise in 1974. * * *

The Stamler case begins properly with Stamler himself. Jeremiah Stamler was active in Chicago's progressive movements from the 1940s onward and, in college, was a close friend of Arthur Kinoy, who would later be his legal defender. He had also distinguished himself in the world of medicine. Beginning in the mid–1950s, he pioneered the thesis that diet, most especially manifested in the overabundance of cholesterol and salt, had raised the proportions of heart conditions and fatal heart attacks in the United States. By the late 1950s, closely aided by his wife, Rose Stamler, and his nutritionist-assistant, Yolanda Hall (a longtime Chicago progressive and wife of Spanish Civil War veteran Charles Hall),

Stamler gained permission to test population groups such as the employees of Chicago's power and gas company. In 1958, as his scientific work gained worldwide recognition, Stamler was named to Chicago's Board of Health as director of the new Heart Disease Control Program.

* * * In May 1965, a resilient House Committee on UnAmerican Activities—by no means as respectable as during the 1950s, but with hopes of reviving itself to quash the new waves of radicalism—held hearings in Chicago, demanding that Stamler and Yolanda Hall (among other Chicagoans) testify about their "red" pasts and connections. This was a signal that progressives and civil libertarians had seen coming.

Almost twenty years earlier, in 1947, screenwriters facing similar scrutiny insisted upon their right to employ the First Amendment and took their case to the Supreme Court. Three years later, after the replacement of two New Deal justices with appointees of Harry Truman, the Supreme Court refused to review the writers' convictions and the "Hollywood Ten" were sent to jail for contempt.

HUAC now raced along, and unfriendly witnesses (here and in other venues) fell back upon the Fifth Amendment, which provided only the limited remedy of personal non-compliance rather than calling into question the legitimacy of any congressional inquisition into personal beliefs and affiliations. * * *

Stamler and Hall immediately filed a civil suit, refusing to appear before the HUAC hearings in Chicago. They determined to test the constitutionality and legality of the House resolution which had established the Committee decades earlier, the proceedings taking place in Chicago, and the subpoenas that they had received personally. Behind them, an army of activists mobilized, and therein lies perhaps the most significant part of the story.

A unique "M.D. Defense Committee," to raise funds among doctors and professors, was set up under the imprimatur of Paul Dudley White, Dwight Eisenhower's personal physician, and a legal fund of one hundred thousand dollars raised quickly. An academic committee (including anthropologists Dell Hymes, Marvin Harris, and Oscar Lewis) set out on a parallel path, with a massive petition to Congress from scientists, clergymen, and assorted intellectuals. The Stamler Defense also managed to secure the assistance of Attorney Albert Jenner, a prominent and ostensibly conservative Chicago Republican with civil liberties leanings. Cooperation with the ACLU against the witch hunts resumed after a dismal quarter-century marked by ACLU head Morris Ernst's close liaison with secret police chief J. Edgar Hoover. New York Civil Liberties Union lawyer Jerry Gutman joined the Stamler legal team. * * *

They did so energetically, and with wide support, including that of several victims of the Hollywood Blacklist, beloved local media figures (such as Studs Terkel), and a host of artists (including Rudolf Baranik, Alexander Calder, Jules Feiffer, Harry Gottlieb, David Levine, Louis Lozowick, Larry Rivers, and Moses and Raphael Soyer, to name only a

few), who donated work to be sold at a prestigious auction in Chicago.
* * *

By now, journalists and politicians who had actually supported earlier investigations or held their tongues began to pronounce HUAC an embarrassment and an anachronism. The Washington Post, the New York Times, the Chicago Daily News, and even prominent Chicago congressmen articulated a deep desire to have the whole thing, HUAC and its attackers, simply go away. * * *

After four years of public meetings, petitions, lobbying, legal research work, and press conferences, the Seventh Circuit Court of Appeals ruled that the challenge to the Committee's constitutionality was indeed appropriate for trial. * * *

In 1974, a weakened and badly discredited HUAC was formally abolished by Congress. * * *

Robert Brent Toplin
Movie Censorship and American Culture;
Review; Book Reviews

Film Quarterly, September 22, 1998.

This informative anthology studies some of the representative cultural struggles that raised issues of censorship from the time of the earliest motion pictures to the 1990s. The authors consider controversies created by the movies' depictions of diverse subjects—sexuality, crime, religion, ethnicity, and ideology, for example—and examine the pressures that various citizens' groups brought on the motion picture industry as well as the efforts of Hollywood leaders to deal with these protests. Editor Francis G. Couvares has assembled an all-star group of contributors for the task, including a number of individuals who have been especially prominent in the recent scholarship on film and culture.

The editor provides one of the best essays in the book, a study entitled "Hollywood, Main Street, and the Church." In an insightful analysis, Couvares produces some surprises for those unfamiliar with the details of the battles over regulating movies in the 1920s and 1930s. Couvares shows, for example, that Protestants in the United States had difficulty agreeing about what they liked and disliked and what they tolerated or wanted regulated. * * * Couvares also reveals that Catholics were uncomfortable with government-centered censorship (Catholics feared state power in a predominantly Protestant society), and preferred arrangements for self-regulation of the movies—a strategy that nicely suited the interests of the film business. The editor also notes the way America's three major religious groups performed different but connected roles in Hollywood's enterprises. The industry was largely financed by Protestant bankers, operated by Jewish studio executives, and policed by Catholic bureaucrats. * * *

The other essays provide a variety of perspectives on censorship issues. Some of the studies focus tightly on one person's story, while others provide a broader picture of developments. In the studies of individuals, Charlene Regester offers an interesting look at the talented and provocative African–American filmmaker Oscar Micheaux, whose bold portrayals in nearly 50 films produced between 1918 and 1948 managed to anger both whites and blacks. Micheaux attacked the bigotry of the KKK directly as well as white squeamishness about interracial romance, but he also exposed problems in the black community, noting the color prejudice of light-skinned African Americans and the troublesome behavior of hypocritical ministers and corrupt politicians. Marybeth Hamilton observes the tremendous popularity of Mae West in the late 20s and early 30s, and argues that West excited resistance not only because of her brazen sexuality but because she challenged gender relationships, relishing sexual power and independence from male control. West's popularity slipped quickly after 1934, when censorship erased much of the sexuality and humor that had made her movies popular. * * *

The anthology carries the title "Movie Censorship and American Culture," but the material is clearly skewed toward the first part of the title. The authors concentrate their discussions on criticisms of the movies' portrayals and the efforts of Hollywood to deal with these objections, and not much attention is paid to the people and the cultures that resisted Hollywood's entertainment. A fuller discussion of the social milieu and ideas of the protesters would be helpful for understanding the conditions that fostered demands for censorship. * * *

Stephen Vaughn's essay, "Political Censorship and the Hollywood Ten," allows an interesting twist of interpretation. Like many writers on the Hollywood Ten, Vaughn expresses sympathy for the troubled writers under attack from the viciously anti-Communist House Un–American Activities Committee. Yet the information he provides about the ideas of leading Hollywood Ten members illustrates how they got into trouble in the tense period of growing disagreements with the Soviet Union. Vaughn shows that one of the Ten's most articulate members, John Howard Lawson, argued that "film is ideology" ...), and claimed that "class struggle was the driving force of history" .... Vaughn also notes that various members of the Hollywood Ten justified the Soviet Union's interventionist foreign policy, favored a Marxist orientation, described capitalism as the root of American society's troubles, traced the roots of racism to capitalism, and called American foreign policy a manifestation of Western imperialism. At the end of the essay, Vaughn says the Hollywood Ten's critique of American society won much greater public acceptance "when a new generation came of age during the 1960s and 1970s." The Ten did, indeed, win greater sympathy in later years, but that interest probably had much more to do with American society's growing discomfort with the excesses of anti-Communism than with sympathy for the ideas that Vaughn attributes to the Hollywood Ten.

Movie Censorship and American Culture displays some shortcomings common to anthologies that require authors to address large subjects in relatively brief essays. The work is, nevertheless, an informative and useful addition to the scholarship about Hollywood's relationship with diverse and often critical audiences.

Notes

1. Why does the public care about the sexual, political, racial content of films? Should producers be able to produce whatever they want and the public should just vote with its feet as to whether something is worthy of being seen or not?

2. The McCarthy era was an intense one for filmmakers. Anyone who attended a communist meeting or was married to someone who had could be subjected to being blacklisted. Lillian Hellman, whose FBI file contained 307–censored pages, wrote an interesting account of the era called *Scoundrel Time* (1976). Hellman wrote four films before being blacklisted in 1952. Subsequently, she wrote only one film, the 1966 *The Chase* starring Marlon Brando, Robert Redford, and Jane Fonda. She died in 1984.

*

Part II

TELEVISION LAW

Chapter 7

THE TELEVISION PROCESS—FROM IDEA TO THE LITTLE SCREEN

This chapter introduces the process of taking an idea and turning it into a television show. Many types of programs make up a network's program schedule. To appeal to a wide audience, each network will schedule a combination of sitcoms (situation comedies), dramas, game shows, reality shows, talk shows, news, and sports. This chapter discusses the legal issues surrounding these various types of programs as well as Court TV. The last section of this chapter discusses the tension between television news and the right to privacy.

A. FROM IDEA TO FINAL PRODUCTION

Married With Children was one of the longest running sitcoms in the history of television. The show is now enjoying its syndication run. According to Andrew Susskind, who spoke to William Henslee's Pepperdine classes on several occasions, a television producer and director who was a creative executive at Paramount Television at the time, the show was created from an idea that he had about a dysfunctional married couple. Mr. Susskind called two staff writers into his office to discuss his idea. He played tapes of Sam Kinison a woman-hating comedian and of Roseanne Barr, a man-hating comedian, and said, "Imagine if these two were married to each other." One of the writers said, "That's my life!" And the show was born. Even though both Sam Kinison and Roseanne Barr declined the opportunity to star in the program, the producers were able to find actors who could create the desired chemistry on the screen. When asked why she declined the opportunity, Roseanne Barr said that she would never work on television. *Married With Children* was successful because an A-list writer was interested in the material and could relate to the characters so that he could bring them alive. The writers got the "created by" credit and Mr. Susskind moved on to establish his own production company.

All television shows begin with an idea. The idea can come from a writer, director, producer, show-runner, or an ordinary person. If the idea comes from someone outside of the entertainment business, the idea must be communicated to someone who can take the idea and turn it into a show, usually a producer or show-runner. A show-runner is either *Show runner* a producer or a writer with a proven track record of producing television shows. The networks will only work with people with demonstrated records because the network cannot afford a half an hour or an hour of dead air time should the person not fulfill his commitment.

The pitch season for television shows is in the fall. During the pitch season, producers and show-runners pitch their ideas to the network buyers or creative executives. Networks receive thousands of pitches for new television shows each pitch season. Pitches for television shows can be very simple because the acceptance or rejection of the show will hinge on who has agreed to be the writer. Television is a writer-driven medium.

If the network accepts the pitch, it orders a pilot script. An A-list writer must author the pilot script in order for the network to accept the script. A-list writers possess time-tested track records of penning successful television shows. The writer of the pilot script receives the "created by" credit on all subsequent telecasts of the show regardless of how many seasons the show continues and long after the writer has moved on to other projects. The "created by" writer receives royalties every time a show with his or her "created by" credit, a coveted asset, is broadcast on television.

After the script has been submitted for approval, the networks will decide whether to order a pilot show. Pilots are usually shot in the spring prior to the fall season for which the show is planned. All of the actors in the pilot who are to be regulars in the program must be signed to a five-year commitment so that the network can be guaranteed that the show will have actor continuity through syndication. It typically takes 100 episodes, representing five seasons of 22 episodes per season, before a show can sustain a syndication run.

Final decisions are made in early summer so that production can begin on the show. From the thousands of pitches, the networks will order two to five new programs for the fall season. Show orders range from three, six, or 13 episodes to a full season order of 22 episodes. Getting from idea to production is an arduous, competitive process.

Once the network places an order, the production company must deliver the shows for their weekly time slot. When a network orders a show, it normally pays 80% of the production budget. This means that the production company must fund the remaining 20%. The shortfall for a show that cost approximately $1,000,000 per episode would be $200,000. A production company earns back its production deficit when the show has compiled at least 100 episodes and goes into syndication. Until that time, the company must be able to finance the deficit for 22 episodes over five years.

Networks normally get a first run plus a rerun license for its production fee. Networks do not share in the syndication revenue unless the network has an ownership interest in the program. Since the repeal of the Fin/Syn rules (the Financial/Syndication rules that prohibited the networks from owning any interest in the programs they aired) by Congress, networks have begun creating their own programs and/or demanding an ownership interest in the programs they choose to air.

Networks earn their revenue from advertisements shown in conjunction with a particular show. Advertising revenue drives the network executive's decision to keep or cancel a show. Whether a show is able to stay on the air depends on how it is received by the public. Viewership is measured by ratings and shares. The rating indicates the number of televisions tuned to a particular program out of the total number of televisions in the country. The share indicates the total number of televisions tuned to a particular program out of the televisions that are actually in use. The share is usually a larger number than the rating.

Networks aim to capture an overall large viewing audience, particularly among the most coveted age demographic, the 18–to 49–year-olds. The target demographic, which used to be 18–to 36–year-olds, has aged with the baby boomer generation. Formerly, advertisers did not believe that commercials could influence people over the age of 36, as it was rare for someone over 36, for example, to change his or her brand of toothpaste after using it for years. Unlike their parents, however, baby boomers have continued to spend money on advertised items.

The typical path of a television show that makes it into syndication is from a network to an independent television station or a cable channel. Independent television stations and cable channels buy programs in syndication to run as their primetime programs. The popularity of the program during its first run dictates the price of the program in syndication.

Monk and *Queer Eye for the Straight Guy* are two shows that have recently bucked the trend. Both shows began on cable and migrated to network television. Neither show has yet to accumulate enough episodes to go into syndication.

Comedies typically do not travel overseas. Humor tends to be more regional and national than international. Imported shows, like *Monty Python*, have had limited success with capturing an audience and are more often shown on PBS (public television). *Gilliam v. ABC, Inc.*, which is included in Chapter 9 below, demonstrates the problems the show encountered when ABC cut three 30–minute episodes to 22 minutes each to accommodate commercials and the demands of its censor.

The popularity of show genres may vary throughout the years. Westerns were once as ubiquitous as reality TV is now on network schedules. In the late 1950's there were 30 different westerns on three network channels. *See* Emily Nusbaum, *The Lone Gunman: Justice was a One–Man Job on 'Gunsmoke,' the 'Law and Order' of the 50's (and 60's and 70's)*, N.Y. TIMES, Mar. 21, 2004. *Gunsmoke*, which premiered in

1955 and ran unto 1975, was set in a raw frontier town in Kansas and featured the 6–foot–7 James Arness as Matt Dillon, the lawman who pulled "his pistol one second slower than his opponent, but with better aim." *Id.*

After a long absence, the western reappeared on television when HBO launched *Deadwood* in March 2004. *See* Ned Martel, *Resurrecting the Western to Save the Crime Drama*, N.Y. TIMES, Mar. 21, 2004. The remainder of this chapter explores the varied legal issues that different genres encounter, beginning with game shows and ending with network news.

B. GAME SHOWS

The 1950's saw the birth of quiz shows such as *Truth and Consequences* and *The $64,000 Question.* Quiz shows, like *Jeopardy!* test factual knowledge, while game shows, similar *to The Gong Show*, were based on physical stunts or gambling. These shows are popular and inexpensive to produce because of the limited number of sets and people required for production.

Eventually many game and quiz shows became synonymous as *The Price is Right* was altered to create a boisterous atmosphere to draw viewership. For more information on quiz shows and game shows, see Olaf Hoerschelmann, Quiz and Game Shows, The Museum of Broadcast Communications Web site, at http://www.museum.tv/archives/etv/Q/htmlQ/quizandgame/quizandgame.htm

MORRISON v. NBC

New York Court of Appeals, 1967.
19 N.Y.2d 453, 280 N.Y.S.2d 641, 227 N.E.2d 572.

FULD, Judge.

This case, still in the pleading stage, arose in connection with a highly popular television show which turned into a national scandal several years ago. According to the complaint, the plaintiff is a university professor who, in 1958, was induced to appear and participate as a contestant on a quiz show known as "21". The program, which was broadcast weekly, was designed to pit experts in various fields of knowledge against one another for substantial cash prizes and, at the height of its popularity, was consistently viewed by millions of people. Although the plaintiff and the public were led to believe that the quiz was conducted honestly and in good faith, without any coaching or assistance to contestants, the program was rigged, the results actually prearranged: certain contestants, other than the plaintiff, were told beforehand the questions which would be asked and the correct answers which should be given. In this manner, it was possible for the producers to control the "winners" and "losers" and to bring about tie games for the purpose of increasing the suspense for the television viewing audience. These machinations became common knowledge in the Fall of 1959, following investigations by several public bodies, including grand juries and a Special Subcommittee of the House of Representatives.

It is alleged that the exposure of the hoax caused the public to believe that all of the contestants were privy to the fraud and, as a consequence, the plaintiff claims in his first cause of action—which is the only one before us—that he "has been brought into public scorn, contempt, and obloquy; has been held up as an object of scorn, shame, and contempt; and his professional standing and reputation had been seriously and pecuniarily damaged." In addition to such general damages, of $250,000, the plaintiff asks for special damages of $7,500, arising from the denial by each of two separate foundations of his applications, originally made in October, 1959, for a fellowship in that amount. Upon the basis of his background, he says, he "had reason to believe" that one of those applications would have been granted to him were it not for the "publicity which cast doubt upon the honesty of all those who have participated in the '21' quiz show" and that, "On information and belief," it was because of this that "the foundations were led to their rejection of his applications". * * *

We do not find it necessary to decide whether the defendants' conduct was actionable. Even if we were to assume that the plaintiff could have stated a valid cause of action against them, the complaint before us would, nevertheless, have to be dismissed. In the first place, it fails to allege special damages with sufficient particularity, the plaintiff's speculations concerning the reasons for his failure to obtain a fellowship being simply not adequate for that purpose. * * *

In the case before us, the plaintiff complains, in effect, that the defendants' conduct "brought an idea" that he was dishonest "to the perception" of the general public. It follows, therefore, that his cause of action must be deemed to fall within the ambit of tortuous injury which sounds in defamation. * * *

The plaintiff specifically alleges that "in late October of 1959 . . . the full extent of the 'fixing' of the '21' quiz show became widely and publicly known." It is indisputable that, if at that time the defendants had accused the plaintiff of having knowingly been a party to the hoax, any suit against them for defamation would have been time-barred after the lapse of one year. In fact, the defendants never implicated the plaintiff in the wrongdoing at all and his reputation suffered only because the guilty were so numerous that the public, according to the complaint, came to suspect everyone and to believe no one who had been associated with the quiz show. Under these circumstances, if the plaintiff has a cause of action, he should not be permitted to sue on it beyond the period within which he could have prosecuted a claim against the defendants for having caused the identical injuries by telling falsehoods about him. Since the complaint is dated September, 1961—more than two years after the defendants' acts upon which the plaintiff bases his cause of action—the court at Special Term properly dismissed it as untimely.

The order of the Appellate Division should be reversed, without costs, the first question certified answered in the negative, the second question certified answered in the affirmative and the order of Special Term dismissing the first cause of action of the complaint reinstated.

Order of Appellate Division reversed and that of Special Term, insofar as it dismissed the first cause of action of the complaint, reinstated, without costs. First question certified answered in the negative; second question certified answered in the affirmative.

Note

1. Is it possible to draft a contract that would release television producers from liability when they lie to quiz or game show applicants and audiences? What would be the legal ramifications of such a clause?

GELBMAN v. VALLEYCREST PRODUCTIONS, LTD.

Supreme Court of New York County, New York, 2001.
189 Misc.2d 403, 732 N.Y.S.2d 528.

RAMOS, Judge.

This action involves the television game show "Who Wants to be a Millionaire" (the Game). The plaintiff, Robert Gelbman (Gelbman), commenced this action for breach of contract, and negligent and intentional infliction of severe emotional distress after being eliminated from the game for incorrectly answering a question which, according to Gelbman, was ambiguous. The defendants, Valleycrest Productions, Ltd. (Valleycrest), the Walt Disney Company (Disney) and American Broadcasting Company (ABC), have moved * * * for dismissal on the grounds that plaintiff has failed to state a cause of action, signed a release indemnifying the defendants from any suit by the plaintiff, and upon documentary evidence.

BACKGROUND

On August 18, 1999, Gelbman was a contestant on the Game. It consists of players answering a series of questions for money. The player is given a question and four possible correct answers and the player must decide which of the four possibilities he or she believes is the correct answer. Each correct answer raises the level of monetary award, i.e., the first question is worth $100, the second $200, the third $300, the fourth $500 and so on. If the player answers 15 questions correctly the prize is $1,000,000. The game ends if any question is answered incorrectly and depending on how many questions the player has answered correctly he or she may win nothing, $1,000 or $32,000. The player may stop at any time prior to answering a question incorrectly, in which case he or she wins the amount assigned to the last correctly answered question.

Gelbman answered the first nine questions correctly. The tenth question he was asked, "Beginning in January, which of the following signs of the Zodiac comes last?" The possible answers were "A) Aquarius, B) Aries, C) Leo, or D) Scorpio." Plaintiff answered (A) Aquarius, while defendants indicated that the correct answer was (D) Scorpio and Gelbman was eliminated from the game and awarded $1,000. Gelbman maintains that the question was ambiguous. Gelbman felt that the question did not clearly state whether they were asking which sign came last in the calendar year or the Zodiac year. Since the Zodiac year begins with the sign Aries, Aquarius would be that last sign. The producers of the show maintained that the question was not ambiguous and declined to change their decision despite Gelbman's complaints.

Before the show, Gelbman signed two documents, the contest release and eligibility form (release) on August 17, 1999, and the official rules (rules) on August 18, 1999, the day of the taping. Both the release and the rules expressly state that the decisions concerning all matters of the game, including questions and answers, of the producers and ABC are final. The release also holds Valleycrest and all others involved in the production of "Who Wants to be a Millionaire" harmless from "any and all claims arising out of injury and damage to [plaintiff] in any way resulting from [plaintiff's] participation in the Contest and/or Program."

Gelbman claims that by not being allowed to continue in the game after incorrectly answering an ambiguous question with two possible answers, the defendants have breached the contract and damaged Gelbman and by their actions have caused him emotional distress. The defendants allege that there is no contract, and that in the alternative no breach has occurred since the terms of the release bar the action. In addition, they allege that Gelbman's claim of emotional distress is also barred by the release and does not meet the standard for such an action.

DISCUSSION

* * * The defendants assert that there was no contract. However, the traditional elements of a contract—offer, acceptance and consideration—have been sufficiently pleaded. The defendants offer potential contestants on their show a chance to win large sums of money in return for their appearance on the show. In addition, the defendants provide round trip air fare to New York, free lodging and a per diem allowance. Gelbman accepted this offer by applying to be a contestant and successfully fulfilling all the screening requirements. Undoubtedly, Gelbman received consideration having an objective value. Defendants received some value as well. Without contestants there is no show, and therefore it is arguably consideration. The plaintiff has sufficiently demonstrated a contract for purposes of this motion.

Plaintiff has failed to specify what terms of the agreement were breached. Essentially, he alleges that the defendants breached the contract by asking, in the course of the contest, a question that was "ambiguous and misleading." However, both the release and the rules contain clauses in which defendants reserve final judgment in all matters concerning the contest. The release states, "VCP's and ABC Broadcast Standards and Practices decisions on all discretionary matters (including the playing of the game and all decisions relative thereto) shall be final." The rules state, "By entering, each player accepts and agrees to be bound by these rule[s] and by the decisions of ABC Broadcast Standards and Practices and Valleycrest Productions, Ltd. which are final and binding on all matters relating to all aspects of the game, *including questions and answers.*" * * *

Generally, courts have upheld contract clauses reserving final judgment of the rules and results of a contest to the producers of the contest. * * * Further, the possibility of two correct answers to a question does not invalidate a clause reserving final judgment to the producers of a contest. In *Furgiele v Disabled Am. Veterans Serv. Found.*, 116 F.Supp. 375 (S.D.N.Y. 1952), a contestant in a word puzzle game alleged that the producers of the contest had failed to follow their own rules in not accepting his alternate answers to the puzzle in question which would have, if allowed, been the high score. As in the instant case, the contest rules included a clause stating that, "Each contestant ... agrees to be bound by the rules and instructions and in any event with the decisions of the DAV Service Foundation and/or its committee on awards on any of the matters affecting the contest." *Id.* at 376 (internal quotation marks omitted). The court declined to consider whether the plaintiff's answers were a correct alternative answer. "The whole matter comes down to this. Plaintiff is dissatisfied with defendant's solution of the puzzles. On that issue in accord with the contract between the parties, plaintiff may not succeed." *Id.* Having a question with two possible answers is not a breach of any provision of the contract that plaintiff signed. In fact, the plaintiff's main complaint seeks to penalize the defendants for enforcing an express provision of the contract which gives them sole discretion to decide which is the correct answer. * * *

Plaintiff argues that the defendants have acted in bad faith by propounding an unfair contest question with two correct answers, and failing to judge the answers impartially, rationally and nonarbitrarily. * * * Plaintiff has stated in his complaint and affidavit that both his and the defendants' answers were correct. Therefore, the point of contention is that the plaintiff disagrees with the defendants' answer and, as stated above, that is not a breach of the contract that the plaintiff signed.

Plaintiff further alleges that the contract itself was one of adhesion and therefore inherently unfair. Adhesion is found where the party seeking to enforce the contract used high pressure tactics or deceptive language in the contract, where there is inequality of bargaining power between the parties and the contract inflicts substantive unfairness on the weaker party. *Matter of Ball (SFX Broad.)*, 236 A.D. 2d 158, 161 (3d Dept. 1997). * * * Plaintiff contends that the contract was unfair because he was not given a complete set of the rules to sign until just before the taping began. He claims that there were initially three pages missing, including the page with the clause reserving final judgment on answers and questions to the defendants, and that when pointed out to the producers of the show, the producers explained that they forgot to copy the backside of the pages and subsequently provided them, telling contestants, including plaintiff, to sign the papers immediately or they would be replaced.

Because of this, plaintiff claims that he did not have time to read the rules before the contest due to the high pressure tactics of the defendants. However, the clause reserving final judgment to the defendants is contained in both the rules and the release. The plaintiff signed the release the day before the contest. At the very top of the release is the caption, "DO NOT SIGN THIS UNTIL YOU HAVE READ IT." In addition, the release contains the language, "I have been given ample opportunity to read, and have carefully read, this entire Agreement." Plaintiff cannot claim, in the face of this documentary evidence, that he did not have the opportunity to read the clause in the contract reserving the right of final judgment to the defendants. Therefore, he cannot claim that said term was not within reasonable expectation.

There is no reasonable argument that the contract was oppressive, unconscionable or contrary to public policy. Plaintiff was given free round trip tickets for two to New York, free travel and accommodations during his stay, a per diem spending allowance and the opportunity to win vast sums of money (of which he won $1,000) and all the plaintiff was to give in return was to appear on the show (which is something he clearly wanted to do).

As for the claims for emotional distress, they are entirely without merit. Plaintiff has made no showing that a disagreement over the answer to a game show question and disqualifying the plaintiff from moving on in the show even begins to approach the rigorous and difficult to satisfy requirement of "extreme and outrageous conduct," which must be to such a degree as to go beyond all possible bounds of decency. *Howell v. New York Post Co.*, 81 N.Y. 2d 115, 122 (1993). * * * Accordingly, it is ordered that the defendant's motion is granted and the action is dismissed in its entirety.

WINSTON v. NBC

California Court of Appeals, 1991.
231 Cal.App.3d 540, 282 Cal.Rptr. 498.

DANIELSON, Judge.

* * * FACTUAL AND PROCEDURAL STATEMENT

On June 25, 1985, Winston filed an action against NBC arising from the latter's refusal to pay Winston the cash he won while a contestant on NBC's game show Sale of the Century. The verified complaint pleaded seven causes of action, respectively, for breach of oral contract, fraud, negligent misrepresentation, intentional infliction of emotional distress, invasion of privacy (appropriation of Winston's name and likeness), invasion of privacy (false light), and invasion of privacy (commercial appropriation. . . .) * * *

In sum, NBC argued that the undisputed facts showed that Winston forfeited any right to his "winnings" on the game show because of his fraudulent misrepresentations regarding his eligibility to appear on the show Sale of the Century, and that pursuant to the contract between them NBC had the unqualified right to use his name and likeness in advertising the show and to broadcast those episodes in which he appeared.

Based on the following facts NBC argued that Winston was not eligible to appear on the NBC game show Sale of the Century on November 10, 11, and 13, 1983, and, thus, was disqualified from receiving the prizes he had won on those dates on the show.

Pursuant to NBC's rules, the maximum number of audience participation or game shows, NBC or otherwise, a person was allowed to be on was three in that person's lifetime. To enforce that rule the written contract between NBC and each prospective contestant of a game show provided that the contestant understood that NBC reserved the right to require him or her to forfeit all prizes credited to the contestant if any of the representations made in the contract by him or her "are false whether by intention, inadvertence, or mistake. . . . whether or not the program on which [the contestant] appear[s] is broadcast."

In his written contract with NBC Winston expressly represented on November 10, 11, and 13, 1983, that he had been on two NBC shows: Split Second in 1973 and 3 For The Money in 1975. He failed to disclose the fact that he had also been on the show Double Dare in 1977.

NBC asserted that Winston was not excused from disclosing that fact by virtue of his letter to NBC dated September 15, 1983, requesting NBC not to count his appearance on 3 For The Money in determining his eligibility to appear on Sale of the Century. In that letter Winston claimed that his appearance on 3 For The Money should not be counted because of irregularities in its taping.

NBC responded by letter dated October 7, 1983 (Harper letter). In that letter NBC informed Winston that due to the time lapse of eight years since that show had been aired, NBC was unable to investigate the circumstances surrounding the asserted irregularities but felt that had there been any substantive errors at the taping they would have been corrected. * * *

NBC argued that the above facts showed that NBC did not by its letter dated October 7, 1983, approve of or give Winston permission to be a contestant on Sale of the Century since it had cautioned Winston that he was not eligible if he had been a contestant since his appearance on 3 For The Money in 1975 and at that time NBC did not know of Winston's appearance on Double Dare in 1977.

As for Winston's claims concerning the use of his name, likeness, and the broadcast of his appearances on Sale of the Century, NBC asserted that it had no obligation to pay defendant for such uses and broadcasts. Pursuant to his contract Winston specifically agreed that NBC "shall have unlimited and perpetual rights worldwide in all media covering everything that [Winston] say[s] and do[es] on the program," that "[t]he photographs, tapes, movies, and recordings of everything [he said] or [did] on the program will be owned by [NBC] to do with as [it wishes] at any time in the future," and that NBC "may use [Winston's] name, photographs, recordings and biographical information for advertising or publicizing the program." * * *

In an April 4, 1984, letter Marshall informed Winston that after its investigation NBC found no merit to his claim that his appearance on 3 For The Money should be considered a "non-appearance" and that NBC's decision to declare Winston ineligible to receive his prizes from Sale of the Century "still stands." * * * In its supplemental papers dated August 11, 1987, NBC argued that NBC did not learn about Winston's ineligibility, i.e., he had been on three prior game shows, until after all seven segments of the Sale of the Century had been taped. * * *

On November 10, 1983, all contestants were briefed on NBC game show rules, including the one that they were only allowed to appear on a total of three game shows and if they violated any NBC rule, they would not get any prizes they might win. At that time Winston signed the contestant agreement.

Although he was not picked as a contestant on that date, he returned on November 11 at which time the contestants were again briefed as to the NBC rules and Winston signed the agreement a second time. Winston appeared as a contestant that day.

When Winston returned on November 13, 1983, all contestants were briefed about the rules and Winston again signed the agreement before taping began. After his appearances were taped, Winston retired from the show as a champion.

During the next week Sullivan received a call from someone who identified himself as "Robert Jackson" (Jackson) and told Sullivan that Winston was ineligible to appear on the Sale of the Century, because he had already appeared on three prior game shows, Split Second, 3 For The Money, and Double Dare. * * * Sullivan then called CBS which checked its records and told Sullivan, a day or two around Thanksgiving 1983, that a Raymond Winston, Social Security number 573–88–7275 had been a contestant on Double Dare. That Social Security number is the same as Winston had put on his NBC records.

Sullivan stated that NBC was faced with a difficult dilemma. On one hand NBC was faced with a violation of its eligibility rules and on the other it had seven shows " 'in the can' " ready to air.

In his declaration Joseph E. Bures, a vice-president of NBC, stated that "had NBC not aired the seven shows on which Winston was a contestant, it would have cost NBC $137,410 and, since the shows would not have been broadcast, NBC could not obtain advertising revenues to offset those costs. In short, Winston's violation of NBC's rules would have cost NBC $137,410." * * *

DISCUSSION

I. No Issues of Material Fact Exist Regarding Estoppel

* * * Based on our review of the record we conclude Winston's contentions are patently meritless. We find, as a matter of law, that there are no triable issues of fact which would preclude NBC from enforcing its forfeiture provision in Winston's contract based on a theory of estoppel or waiver. * * * We further find that, as a matter of law, there is no question about the nature of the document that Winston signed. A plain reading of the contents of that document reveals that within its four corners is an agreement by Winston that if he failed to disclose a material fact, such as the names of prior audience participation or game shows, NBC or otherwise, on which he had appeared and the years in which he appeared, he would then forfeit any prizes he won on the show. * * *

The judgment is affirmed.

Notes

1. Why do you think game shows have rules on the number of times that a contestant can appear? What is the advantage to the game shows to ban a contestant for life after being on three different shows?

2. Most games shows run five times a week. Game shows can tape ten episodes over a two-day period, thus producing an efficient two weeks of programming. This format is economical for production companies considering the low cost for high ratings.

3. A game show is an idea or concept, but cases have found that copyright is not available to protect the method of playing a game. When two shows appear to have similar formats, it is difficult to prove copyright infringement without evidence that someone stole elements or questions from another game. The name of a game show can be protected under trademark law. MATHEW BENDER, ENTERTAINMENT INDUSTRY CONTRACTS: ACQUISITION OF RIGHTS. Ch. 3–63A Entertainment Industry Contracts § 63A.01.

4. Is there any limit to the types of niche television networks that can be created? In 2004, David Hawk plans to launch the Casino and Gaming Television Network as a digital cable and satellite channel with shows such as *Winning Hand* (poker experts offering game tips) and *Dusk 'Til Dawn* (tours of ultimate gambling habitats like Las Vegas and Monaco). Hawk cites research conducted by the American Gambling Association that 50 million Americans made more than 300 million visits to casinos in 2002 as an indication that the public would watch gambling on television. *See* Lynn Elber, *TV Channel Bets on Gambling Fans*, ALBUQUERQUE JOURNAL, Oct. 28, 2003, at C9.

C. REALITY TELEVISION

Reality television is a recent phenomenon that has captured the interest of the viewing public. Americans tune in to watch shows like *Survivor, The Bachelor*, and *Married by America* to observe participants compete for love and money. Indeed, one reality show called *For Love or Money* aired during the summer of 2003. *The Apprentice* starring real estate developer Donald Trump premiered in January 2004. Its 16 contestants vied to receive a $250,000 job running one of Trump's companies. Audience participation version of these shows ask the public to call in to decide who should be voted off of a musical competition show (*American Idol*) or selected to become the husband of a particular female who comes with a potential $1,000,000 dowry (*Cupid*). Other programs, like *Extreme Makeover* and *Queer Eye for the Straight Guy*, alter the appearance of volunteer participants.

High ratings and low costs for shows like the original *Joe Millionaire*, which drew in 40 million viewers for its final episode on February 17, 2003, keep these shows on the air. While network producers are attracted to these shows for the enormous potential profits generated from not having to pay professional actors, the public tunes in to watch ordinary people practice the seven deadly sins of envy, sloth, greed, lust, gluttony, pride, and wrath.

Sherri Burr
Editing for Reality Television:
Author Interview with Craig Serling

Copyright © 2003 by Sherri Burr.

[Craig Serling received his A.B. Degree from Rochester Institute of Technology and a M.F.A. from the American Film Institute. He edited the first four seasons of the television show *Survivor*, two seasons of *The Amazing Race*, and several other shows for a total of over 500 hours shown on television. Sherri Burr interviewed Serling on December 7, 2003, at the Santa Fe Film Festival in New Mexico.]

"Education gives you the tools to practice your craft as a filmmaker. I started out editing low budget documentaries. Docs are editorial intense. I discovered that I could make a pretty good living editing other people's work. I fell into the commercial side when my friend who was the director of *Survivor* hired me.

"Editing reality television poses different challenges. The shooting ratio for feature films is approximately 30 to 1; for every 30 minutes of film you shoot you know that 29 minutes will not be shown and only one minute will end up on the screen. For reality television, the shooting ratio is 200 to 300 minutes of raw footage for every one minute that gets shown. This allows you the flexibility to create in postproduction story elements that work.

"In reality TV, we film everything before we start the editing process. There are a fleet of people in postproduction who log in everything and we go from there. Both producers and editors decide the story line. Like in all drama, reality TV needs story arc and character development. Some people think of reality people and discard it, yet I've edited episodes of reality television where 25 million people watched. At the Santa Fe Film Festival, maybe 40 people will see my short *Jam*. People watch reality TV because they are drawn into a story they can relate to.

"I try to avoid legal issues at all cost. The biggest legal issue on reality television is that ordinary people sign contracts that allow the producer to portray them in any way the producer sees fit. They relinquish all rights by agreeing to appear on a reality television show. My advice to people is to not go on a reality television show. People go on a reality TV show because they want to be famous. After the show is up and they've experienced their 15 minutes of fame, they find that they are just an ordinary Joe."

SEG, INC. v. STILLMAN

California Court of Appeals, 2003.
2003 WL 21197133.

CROSKEY, Judge.

* * * FACTUAL AND PROCEDURAL BACKGROUND

* * * In December 1999, Stillman applied to be a contestant on a new television "reality" show that was being produced for CBS by SEG. The name of the new show was "Survivor" and it involved 16 contestants who would be "marooned" on a remote island in the South China Sea, divided into two "tribes," required to engage in multiple contests between the tribes and then, on a regular periodic basis, asked to vote on which member to evict from the tribe. A majority vote of the then existing members of the tribe that had lost the most recent contest with the other tribe would be sufficient to evict a member of that tribe. This process would go on over several weeks until there was only one surviving contestant who would win $1 million. All of these activities would be recorded by television cameras for broadcast by CBS during the period May to August 2000. * * *

In January and February of 2000, Stillman went through an extended screening process that included multiple personal interviews in San Francisco and Los Angeles and medical and psychological testing. As a part of her application process, Stillman entered into several written agreements including an Applicant Agreement. In that agreement, Stillman promised not to disclose, without SEG's consent, any information concerning the show and its production.[3] The record leaves little doubt that Stillman was aware of and understood this obligation.[4]

After being accepted as one of the 16 contestants, Stillman, along with the others, traveled to Malaysia in March of 2000. She was assigned to the tribe designated "Tagi." The Survivor series was shot over a 39–day period (for later broadcast on CBS from May 31, 2000 to August 23, 2000). Every three days during the shooting, one of the two tribes (i.e., the one that had lost the most recent immunity challenge contest) was required to vote to evict one of its members. The first contest was lost by the Tagi tribe and participant Sonja Christopher was voted off. This left Tagi with seven members, including Stillman. Tagi won the second contest, but lost the third. As a result, on the 9th day of shooting, the Tagi tribe was again required to vote off another member. The tribe voted 5–2 to evict Stillman.

According to her declaration, * * * Stillman states that she was informed on August 23, 2000 and again in October 2000, by another Tagi tribe member, Dirk Been, that he and one other member (Sean Kenniff) had been told by the show's executive producer, Mark Burnett (an officer of SEG), to vote to evict Stillman. As a result of these conversations, Stillman came to believe that the producer had manipulated the votes of at least two of the members of the Tagi tribe. It was her view that such actions were not only unfair, and contrary to the free competition theme of the "Survivor" show, but also constituted a violation of federal laws prohibiting the "rigging" of game shows. During October 2000, Stillman had exchanged written and oral conversations with one Peter Lance who was then in the process of researching a book about the "Survivor" show

3. In section 19 of that agreement, clearly entitled "Confidentiality and Life Story Rights," it was provided, in relevant part:

"I understand any appearance I may make on the Series is strictly for the purpose of participating in the Series as a contestant. Except as specifically provided herein or as otherwise authorized by Producer and/or CBS, I will not myself, and I will not authorize others to, publicize, advertise or promote my appearance on the Series, receive or generate any monetary advantage from my appearance on the Series, or use or disclose to any party any information or trade secrets obtained or learned as a result of my participation in the Series, including without limitation any information concerning or relating to the Series, the contestants, the events contained in the Series or the outcome of the Series, for a period from the date of this agreement until three (3) years after the initial broadcast of the last episode of the Series. Without limiting the foregoing, I acknowledge that the initial broadcast of the episodes in which I may participate will occur, if at all, after the contest is completed and that any information re-

vealed or disclosed prior to broadcast will cause irreparable harm to Producer and CBS. In that connection, I specifically agree that any information regarding the elimination of contestants and the selection of any winner is to be held in strict confidence by me and cannot be disclosed by me to any third parties.... I agree that disclosure by me in violation of the foregoing shall constitute and be treated as a material breach of this agreement which will cause irreparable harm to Producer and/or CBS and will cause substantial damage in excess of $5,000,000, entitling Producer to seek, among other things, (a) injunctive relief, without posting any bond, to prevent and/or cure any breach of threatened breach of this paragraph by me, (b) return or recovery of the value of any prize received or to be received in connection with the Series, (c) recovery or disgorgement of the monies or other consideration received in connection with such disclosure, if any, and (d) recovery of Producer's attorneys' fees incurred to enforce this paragraph."

4. At the time she signed the Applicant Agreement, Stillman was a practicing lawyer. * * * She negotiated certain modifications to the Applicant Agreement. Finally, the agreement itself provided (just above

(later published in November 2000 under the title "Stingray").[5] In these exchanges, she discussed this information with him.

Thereafter, Stillman hired an attorney who sent a demand letter to CBS and Mark Burnett in which Stillman's concerns about how the "Survivor" show had been manipulated were discussed. * * * After her complaint was filed, Stillman distributed copies to three newspapers and she is informed that the media put the pleading on the internet. She admits that she thereafter spoke to media outlets, but she claims that she did so only after CBS issued a statement calling her lawsuit frivolous. On February 20, 2001, SEG filed this action against Stillman in the Los Angeles Superior Court. * * *

SEG's complaint alleges that Stillman applied to be a contestant on the "Survivor" show and agreed, in writing, as a part of the application process, that she would not use or disclose any information or trade secrets learned as a result of her participation in the show. SEG alleged that Stillman breached that agreement and disclosed information and trade secrets to a writer (Peter Lance) knowing that he intended to write a book about the program. SEG's defamation claim is based on allegations that (1) Stillman orally and in writing stated that SEG and its officers and employees rigged the outcome of the program by coaching and manipulating the participants voting choices, (2) Lance published his book and included the falsehoods by Stillman and (3) Stillman repeated these falsehoods in numerous public appearances beginning February 5, 2001. * * *

On June 26, 2001, the trial court * * * granted Stillman's motion for reconsideration. * * * The court then analyzed the evidentiary showing made by SEG and concluded, as it had in its original order, that SEG had provided a prima facie showing supporting its defamation claim, but had not provided any evidence supporting either the breach of contract or breach of the implied covenant causes of action. The alleged disclosures made by Stillman, that SEG claimed constituted contract violations, all related to the "rigging" or manipulation of the outcome of the show. These were, at most, disclosures of discreditable facts and, as such, could not provide a legal basis for any claim of breach. * * *

DISCUSSION

* * * There Was Not Sufficient Evidence to Establish a
Prima Facie Case for Breach of Either an Express
Contract or an Implied Covenant

* * * The protectible information and trade secrets that the Applicant Agreement sought to protect could not, as a matter of law, include the manipulation of the results of the show. * * * [If Stillman disclosed

---

her signature) that Stillman (1) had had ample opportunity to read the agreement and had done so, (2) fully understood its provisions and (3) had reviewed them with her own legal counsel prior to signing.

5. For example, she is quoted in Lance's book as stating (in an e-mail addressed to him explaining why CBS would not object

to her sale of several pictures she took during the filming of the show): "Boo hoo, CBS. If they go after me, I have info that establishes a nice federal offense they wouldn't want disclosed and could undermine SII." In his book, Lance states that she later explained what she meant by repeating the information she had received from Dirk Been.

anything, it was information which the terms of the agreement could not legally protect.] * * * Given this state of the law, it is clear that there was no evidence of disclosure of any information that was lawfully protected by the Applicant Agreement. * * *

SEG Did Produce Sufficient Evidence to Establish
a Prima Facie Case for Defamation

* * * All of Stillman's written and oral statements, which she does not dispute, accused Mark Burnett (and thus SEG) of manipulating the outcome of a contestant game show and that such manipulation resulted in her being ousted as a contestant. If false and unprivileged, these statements are defamatory per se. * * * As a result, SEG was under no obligation to prove that it suffered any damages. Having presented evidence that supports a conclusion of per se defamation, proof of special damages is *not* required. * * *

The record reflects that SEG presented evidence that Stillman had engaged in outright fabrications and made disparaging statements with the "knowledge that [they were] false or with a reckless disregard" for the truth. *Reader's Digest Assn. v. Superior Court, supra,* 37 Cal. 3d at p. 246. Support for the claim of deliberate fabrication and utter falsity of Stillman's hearsay accusations is set forth in the declarations of Mark Burnett and the other show participants, particularly the four (4) participants, Sean Kenniff, Richard Hatch, Rudy Boesch and Susan Hawk—whose votes resulted in Stillman's ouster. All four of these individuals confirmed that their votes against Stillman were the result of their own determination that Stillman should be the next one ousted from the island, and *not* the result of any manipulation or influence by anyone involved in the production of the show.

Such evidence is sufficient to support an inference that she knowingly and deliberately fabricated false statements of fact in her effort to defame SEG and the Survivor show. Such deliberate fabrications are in turn sufficient, standing alone, to support an inference of actual malice. *Eastwood v. Nat'l Enquirer, Inc.,* 123 F.3d 1249, 1256 (9th Cir. 1997) ["intentional [falsehood] satisfies the 'actual malice' standard"]. * * *

DISPOSITION

The order of the trial court of June 26, 2001, is affirmed. Each party shall bear its own costs on appeal.

Sherri Burr
The Benefits and Burdens of Reality TV:
Author Interview with The Bachelor's
Bob Guiney and band member
Matt Jackson

Copyright © 2004 by Sherri Burr.

People go on reality television shows for many reasons. Some seek fame, fortune, or both. Others may chase fifteen minutes in the limelight to prove they are somebody. For Bob Guiney, it was about his music.

Guiney became a hit with women around the country when he was featured on four episodes of *The Bachelorette* in January and February 2003. He was cut by Trista Rehn during the episode when she had to pare the field of suitors from six to four. She told Guiney, "If I could give out a fifth rose, hands down I would pick you."

While Guiney failed to win Rehn's heart on *The Bachelorette*, his appearance as the affable guy telling fat jokes and break dancing resonated with millions of American women. They called and e-mailed the producers of the ABC television show demanding that he be selected as the next star of *The Bachelor*. The producers pursued him for two months.

"I didn't want to do *The Bachelor*," says Guiney in an interview after the Bob Guiney band performed a 45–minute set at Ned's in Albuquerque, NM, on February 17, 2004. "Oprah convinced me to do it."

Guiney cites his friendship with Oprah as the biggest benefit to come out of his appearance on *The Bachelorette*. He was invited to attend her 50th birthday bash. He says that the biggest downside that came from his starring on *The Bachelor* was, "I got sued. It sucks."

And Syndicated Productions (ASP), a division of Telepictures Productions that makes *The Bachelor/Bachelorette* series for ABC, sued Guiney in December 2003 claiming that he violated an exclusivity clause in his TV contract that barred him from promoting other products without the producer's permission. In seeking a temporary restraining order against Guiney, ASP claimed that he and Wind-up Records expected to make a "windfall profit at ASP's expense, thereby diluting the value of Mr. Guiney's public image, and tarnishing the series' goodwill and public esteem."

"Fortunately, I won the first round in court," he says. "The judge saw it my way. I had made three albums before appearing on the show, and they [the producers] agreed to allow me to sing on the show. Besides, they let one bachelor [Aaron] promote his restaurant and another [Andrew] promote his winery on the show. They should either try to shut us all down or none of us."

Guiney says that in December 2003 he ran into an ABC executive on the streets of New York who thanked him for being on the show. "He talked about how I helped with ratings and made them all this money. I finally said to him, 'Stop suing me'."

Guiney says that he's hired lawyers to defend the lawsuit because of Oprah's encouragement. "She urged me to fight for what I believe in."

Guiney began singing as part of a group calling itself "Fat Amy" in 1992 as a college student at Michigan State University. Fellow band member Matt Jackson says, "We began as a bar band, playing whatever gigs we could get."

Jackson says that he was the instigation behind the band's recent name change to "Bob Guiney." "I'm in advertising," says Jackson. "After Bob's appearance on *The Bachelorette*, I urged him to change the name. We had to explain "Fat Amy" but we wouldn't have to explain "Bob Guiney." Bob was against the name change. The TV shows never changed him. He's still the same guy. He preferred to keep our group name."

Guiney confirmed that he preferred to keep their original name. "I'm a group kind of guy."

His being on the two shows led record companies to pursue Guiney and his band. They decided to contract with Wind–Up Records as both their publishing and recording company, together with a separate merchandising company.

"When you get to this level," says Jackson, "You can no longer do it all. Bob and I used to be our own booking agent and manager. Now we have to hire a team to push us. We have to look to attorneys for guidance. At a certain level, you can't handle it all."

For the Bob Guiney band, that level came when Wind–Up Records decided to promote them. In February 2004, the band toured radio stations to get them to play their records. "It used to be the stations played 60 or 70 records throughout the day," says Jackson. "Now they play 17–19 records all day long. We're trying to get in that mix so that people are hearing our songs and wanting to go buy our CDs."

Guiney confesses that he would prefer people to hear the music first, rather than respond to his name. "I want them to have an organic response to the music," he says.

The line grows long after the show at Neds in Albuquerque as women seek 60 seconds with Guiney for an autograph or just to gab. "I feel like I know you," one woman says as she gives him a hug.

Guiney encourages people not to pose the three most common questions. "People often ask me, 'Which came first: the music or the TV show?'" he says. "Anyone willing to do a little bit of homework will know that it was the music. I also get asked, 'Why did I not choose Kelly Jo and why did I dump Estella?' I sometimes wish I could just record the answers. I felt Kelly Jo and I would make great friends. I chose Estella because we had a lot in common and she was easy to talk to. What people don't realize is that Estella and I dated for six weeks while I was also dating 24 of her friends. We were then apart for four months. They put us back together again and expected us to be in love. It just doesn't work that way."

Band member Jackson says, "We are trying to get as far away from *The Bachelor* as we can. We don't want anything to do with roses."

After all the encounters with adoring fans and their personal questions, Guiney acknowledges that he can't complain about the loss of privacy. "I did this to myself."

Notes

1. Are reality TV stars caught in a double bind if they try to use their sudden fame to further another career? On the one hand, women come out

to hear Bob Guiney play his music and they buy his CDs because they saw him on television. On the other hand, while he and his band members would prefer these women to be enchanted by their music, the women are enticed because they liked *Bachelor* Bob.

2. If you were representing Guiney in his lawsuit, what would be some of your arguments to support his contention that he should be allowed to promote his band? Does ABC suffer from an assumption of the risk problem from knowing that he was a singer before his appearance on *The Bachelorette* and agreeing to let him sing on *The Bachelor*? Does ABC continue to benefit from Guiney's growing fame? If he becomes even more renowned as a musician, does that potentially increase the popularity of *The Bachelor*?

3. Reality TV stars may be paid for their appearances. Guiney told Sherri Burr that Trista Rehn received $10,000 total for both the *Bachelor* and the *Bachelorette*. Rehn and Ryan Sutter were subsequently paid $1 million to wed on television. Guiney said he negotiated for a higher payment than $10,000 because he was taking time away from his job as a mortgage banker. According to *Newsweek*, Donald Trump was paid $100,000 per episode for *The Apprentice*, which proved a top 10 hit for NBC on Thursday evenings in the Spring of 2004. For the next edition of the show, he told *Newsweek* he would get paid "a lot more." Keith Naughton and Marc Peyser, *The World According to* Trump, NEWSWEEK MAGAZINE, March 1, 2004.

4. How do the doctors, lawyers, accountants, teachers, and airline pilots manage to take several weeks off from their day jobs to film or appear live on a reality TV show? Because *Survivor* requires 39 days of filming, casting director Lynne Spillman says that one third of its participants quit their jobs to participate. Spillman told *Newsweek*, "The people who apply are at a crossroads." *The lure of shows like 'Apprentice' is a headache for bosses*, NEWSWEEK MAGAZINE, March 1, 2004. *Newsweek* also reported that investment banker Kwame Jackson quit Goldman Sachs to appear on *The Apprentice*, attorney Alex Michel quit Boston Consulting Group to star in the initial *Bachelor*, and Randi Coy was forced to leave her teaching job after taking too much time off to star in *My Big Fat Obnoxious Fiancé*. Michel said, "Anyone who'd take a two-month leave is putting their career progress at risk." *Id.* Nevertheless, some individuals, like *The Bachelorette's* Trista Rehn or *Survivor's* Richard Hatch, have found a pot of gold at the end of the reality TV rainbow.

SEELIG v. INFINITY BROADCASTING CORP.

California Court of Appeals, 2002.
97 Cal.App.4th 798, 119 Cal.Rptr.2d 108.

SIMONS, Judge.

Reality television and talk radio are two of the more popular cultural phenomena of the new century. In the first, real people often compete for a prize under the most unrealistic, often demeaning conditions. In the second, a host discusses topics of current interest with live guests and call-in audience members. These discussions often, though not always, include generous portions of insult and invective. Given these programming themes, it was inevitable that a participant in a reality television competition would be insulted by a talk-radio host and sue for defamation. * * *

BACKGROUND

Plaintiff participated as one of 50 contestants in the television program *Who Wants to Marry a Multimillionaire* (Fox Network, Feb. 15, 2000) (hereafter the Show). In this program, women contestants competed for the right to marry a wealthy stranger. In addition to the marriage, complete with a prenuptial agreement, the bride received a $35,000 wedding ring and a new car. Plaintiff was not chosen to marry the putative multimillionaire, nor even selected as one of the five finalists, though she did appear briefly as a contestant in a portion of the television broadcast. During her time on air, she stated only her name, that she was from San Francisco, and that she worked in sales at KFRC, a San Francisco radio station. Her total participation in the television broadcast lasted less than one minute. Though plaintiff was not paid for her participation in the Show, she received the cost of the trip to Las Vegas and some gifts.

The taping of the Show occurred before its airing on February 15, 2000, with all taping involving plaintiff being completed prior to February 1, 2000. To plaintiff's knowledge, her name and likeness were neither aired nor made public in any way by the producers of the Show before the television broadcast.

Defendant Uzette Salazar (Uzette) contacted plaintiff on or about February 1, 2000, and asked if she would participate in a discussion regarding the Show on KLLC's "Sarah and Vinnie" morning radio program. Plaintiff declined. She informed Uzette that she competed in the contest only as a personal experience, and that she did not wish to be interviewed on their radio program because she did not want to bring attention to herself or to chance being ridiculed or subjected to public humiliation. She also told Uzette that she was contractually prohibited from entering into any type of publicity concerning the Show.

On February 15, 2000, during the radio program, but before the Show was televised, the following colloquy occurred between Sarah Clark (Sarah) and Vincent Crackhorn (Vinnie), KLLC's morning broadcast co-host, along with Uzette, the radio program's on-air producer:

"VINNIE: . . . and what is this, the *Marry A Millionaire* show?

"SARAH: *Who Wants to Marry a Millionaire*?

"VINNIE: Right.

"SARAH: It's on tonight. Two hour long thing. Fifty chicks are gonna fight it out for the top five spots and then they all put on uh wedding gowns and somebody gets married at the end.

"VINNIE: Right. And we have uh, a local loser on the, on the prog—

"SARAH: m, uh hum—

"VINNIE: from what I heard.

"UZETTE: (Laughter.)

"VINNIE: Now uh, this is, this is crackin me up because I'm not, and I'm not saying any names—

"UZETTE: I know.

"VINNIE: Whatever.

"UZETTE: Go ahead.

"VINNIE: But uh, this person apparently we were gonna have her on the show to see what her bucket's all about, why she wants to marry some random guy—

"SARAH: Right.

"VINNIE: and she wouldn't come on without like, what—you tell me.

"UZETTE: She wanted like some written consent that we weren't going to bag on her, and uh, she, she's just not, I don't think she's a real fan.

"VINNIE: Chicken butt!

"UZETTE: She actually works at another station—

"SARAH: Oh really!

"VINNIE: Chicken butt!

"UZETTE: and I found out more dirt about this girl, since we're not saying her name. She actually is the ex-wife of someone who works at our sister station down the hall. And uh yeh, he just says what a big skank she is. * * *

After the radio program, but before the airing of the Show, plaintiff received numerous telephone calls from individuals, business associates, and personal friends, stating that they were aware she had been humili-ated on the broadcast. Plaintiff became extremely upset and angry with her ex-husband because she thought he had made the statements about her until he assured her he had not. Plaintiff's ex-husband was never asked if he thought plaintiff was a "skank" and he never stated to anyone connected with KLLC that his ex-wife was a skank. The state-ment Uzette attributed to him was false, and Uzette later apologized to him for stating he had called plaintiff a big skank.

As a result of the radio broadcast, plaintiff filed a complaint against defendants alleging causes of action for: (1) slander per se; (2) slander; (3) invasion of privacy; (4) negligent hiring, retention and supervision of employees; (5) and intentional infliction of emotional distress. * * *

II. Plaintiff's Complaint Falls Within the Purview of the Anti–SLAPP Statute

* * * The offending comments arose in the context of an on-air discussion between the talk-radio co-host and their on-air producer

about a television show of significant interest to the public and the media. This program was a derivative of *Who Wants to Be a Millionaire*, which had proven successful in generating viewership and advertising revenue. Before and after its network broadcast, *Who Wants to Marry a Multimillionaire* generated considerable debate within the media on what its advent signified about the condition of American society. One concern focused on the sort of person willing to meet and marry a complete stranger on national television in exchange for the notoriety and financial rewards associated with the Show and the presumed millionaire lifestyle to be furnished by the groom. By having chosen to participate as a contestant in the Show, plaintiff voluntarily subjected herself to inevitable scrutiny and potential ridicule by the public and the media. * * *

III. *It Is Unlikely Plaintiff Will Prevail on Her Claim*

* * * To ascertain whether the statements in question are provably false factual assertions, courts consider the " 'totality of the circumstances.' " *Rudnick v. McMillan,* 25 Cal. App. 4th 1183, 1191 (1994). " 'First, the language of the statement is examined. For words to be defamatory, they must be understood in a defamatory sense.... Next, the context in which the statement was made must be considered.... This contextual analysis demands that the courts look at the nature and full content of the communication and to the knowledge and understanding of the audience to whom the publication was directed.' " * * *

Here, plaintiff complains about several derogatory comments made concerning her on the radio broadcast. Vinnie referred to plaintiff once as a "local loser" and three times as a "chicken butt," while Uzette falsely claimed that plaintiff's ex-husband had said she was a "big skank." A few seconds later, Uzette qualified her remark by noting that her source had been a "jilted ex-husband, [and w]hat does he know." Thus, the key question before this court is whether these statements, examined in context, can reasonably be understood to state actual facts about plaintiff that are provably false. We conclude that none of the statements constitute actionable statements of fact. * * *

The phrase big skank is not actionable because it is too vague to be capable of being proven true or false. Attributing the comment to a specific source, plaintiff's ex-husband, does not alter that conclusion. The word skank is a derogatory slang term of recent vintage that has no generally recognized meaning. * * * Indeed, plaintiff provided no accepted dictionary definition for the term skank to the trial court and, instead, only proffered a declaration from her ex-husband stating his understanding of the term skank as referring to "a woman of loose morals." Plaintiff has cited no reported decision in California or elsewhere that has held the term skank constitutes actionable defamation, nor has our own research revealed any such decision. * * *

In summary, we conclude that none of the comments regarding plaintiff are actionable, because no finder of fact could reasonably

interpret the comments as stating provable facts about her. As such, the motion to strike should have been granted. Since all of plaintiff's causes of action arise from and depend upon her claims of defamation, the motion to strike should have been granted as to her entire complaint.
* * *

Notes

1. Which of the seven deadly sins are at issue in these cases? Should reality television shows come with a warning, *Participant Beware*?

2. Reality shows often require the participants to sign agreements releasing producers from liabilities. What are some of the liabilities that producers would seek to be released from? What are some of the potential dangers to participating on a show like *Survivor*, *The Bachelor* or *Who Wants to Marry a Millionaire*? After *Who Wants to Marry a Millionaire* aired, the press revealed that Rick Rockwell, the so-called millionaire, was one on paper only and that a prior girlfriend had taken out a restraining order against him. After the newlyweds returned from their honeymoon, they immediately split up. Darva Conger, the putative bride, later posed for *Playboy Magazine* to "get her privacy back." Is privacy something that a reality TV participant/*Playboy* centerfold can reclaim? Note that after she posed for *Playboy*, Conger ceased to be a news topic.

3. Is reality TV taking over the networks? With two-dozen major network shows during the summer of 2003—twice as many as during the summer of 2002, *Vanity Fair* said they are "dominating the prime–time lineup. Whether reality TV tanks or triumphs from overexposure remains to be seen." *Vanity Fair* also proclaimed David Darnell, Fox's executive vice president of specials and alternative programming, a "king of reality TV." Darnell oversaw *Celebrity Boxing* (in which minor stars engage in slugfests), *American Idol*, *The Simple Life* (with Paris Hilton and Nicole Richie), *Who Wants to Marry a Millionaire*, and *Joe Millionaire*. Mike Fleiss, who sometimes works with Darnell and produced ABC's *The Bachelor*, *The Bachelorette*, *Are You Hot*, and *The Will,* was dubbed the other king of reality TV. See Mark Seals, *Reality Kings,* Vanity Fair, July 2003.

Given the variety of shows that Darnell and Fox have produced, is there no limit to what aspect of human nature that could become the subject of reality television?

4. Can anyone create a reality TV show? As an exercise, write a treatment to create a reality show. Treatments are usually one page long and they give a title, a short overview of the concept, the participants, the location, and the logistics of what it would take to make the show work. For more information about treatments, see Michael Atchity's *Writing Treatments that Sell* (1988).

5. Can reality TV be used to advertise a corporate conglomerate? Donald Trump's competitors accused him of doing just that by starring in *The Apprentice*. Peter Hauspurg, chairman of Eastern Consolidated Properties, called the show "a watershed in self-promotion, coldly and carefully designed as a business strategy to achieve millions in free publicity." Charles Bagli, *Due Diligence on the Donald*, N.Y. TIMES, Sunday, Jan. 25, 2004.

6. Will reality TV shows lead to shorter seasons and the elimination of traditional mid-September to mid-May schedule with sweeps months in November, February, and May? In a *New York Times* article, Bill Carter wrote that "[i]nstead of the typical 22–episode seasons that viewers have become accustomed to, the networks are also planning a greater number of short term programs, including reality shows and even scripted dramas. And they will be offered in bursts of 8 or 10 or 13 episodes in consecutive weeks.... The lone holdout is CBS, which is committed to a traditional structure of 22 or so episodes in a season, followed by a summer of mostly repeats." Bill Carter, *Shorter Seasons? No Sweeps? TV Networks Rethink the Rules*, N. Y. Times, Feb. 8, 2004, at P–1.

What prompted Mr. Carter's article was the decision of NBC to place *The Apprentice* starring Donald Trump in its coveted Thursday night line-up in the Spring of 2004 and then to announce plans to bring it back in the same time slot in the Fall of 2004. "All of the old rules are going," said Jeff Zucker, the president of NBC Entertainment to Carter. "If you play by the old rules, you will be left behind." *Id.* Over 28 million Americans watched *The Apprentice* final on April 15, 2004, making it the top-rated show the week of April 12–18, according to Nielsen Media Research.

D. COURT TV

Court TV is reality television for lawyers. Court TV has demystified the courtroom process and made armchair lawyers out of the masses. Major trials can transform counsel into a media star. The result of cameras in the courtroom is considered in the cases and article that follow.

KAVANAU v. COURTROOM TELEVISION NETWORK

United States District Court, Southern District of New York, 1992.
1992 WL 197430.

PATTERSON, Judge.

* * * I.   Plaintiffs' Concept: "The Crime
and Justice Network"

Plaintiff Ted Kavanau is a New Jersey resident who has worked for over 30 years in network, local, and cable television. In the 1980s, Kavanau was employed by Cable News Network ("CNN"). He alleges that during his employment at CNN, he created the concept and format for a 24–hour cable television service with a mainstay of live broadcast of trials throughout the United States. He presented that concept to CNN's Ted Turner, but CNN declined to pursue the idea.

Shortly thereafter, Kavanau became Vice–President (News and Information) at MCA Broadcasting ("MCA"), the entity which owns WWOR–TV in Secaucus, New Jersey. Kavanau presented his concept to Larry Fraiberg, an MCA Division President, in a 12–page memo dated April 9, 1988. The memo proposed a cable television service called "Crime Net" which would focus on crime and justice related issues. The proposed format contemplated live and taped coverage of trials from different parts of the country. Kavanau envisioned: Not unlike ABC's WIDE WORLD OF SPORTS, we would be able to pick and choose between the ongoing trials, switching from one to another, based on the level of activity and interest generated by each trial at any particular time.

In his April 9, 1988 memo, Kavanau also suggested ideas for filler material, including: crime news, a program on fugitives, debate segments, a talk show, and interviews with prisoners and law enforcement officers.

Fraiberg supported Kavanau's idea and edited his April 9, 1988 memo. * * * Fraiberg forwarded the April 19, 1988 memo to Sid Sheinberg, then the President of MCA in Los Angeles. MCA ultimately decided, however, not to pursue the project.

Kavanau continued his attempts to market his idea by incorporating Plaintiff Crime Net, Inc. as a New Jersey corporation. Kavanau spent from April to July 1988 preparing a 60–page presentation of his concept entitled "Concept and Business Plan—CRIME AND JUSTICE NETWORK" (the "CJN Plan").

The CJN Plan described a 24–hour cable television network called "The Crime and Justice Network" ("CJN"). Kavanau envisioned CJN to be a two tiered network: one tier consisting of coverage of trials, and one tier consisting of coverage of crime.

Trial coverage would consist of broadcasts of four trials around the country. Four satellite uplink production unit trucks would travel around the country with cameras and editing facilities to tape the trials for broadcast. Senior producers at CJN's home base would be "switching between four available trials, picking highlight moments for live broadcast, not unlike ABC's Wide World of Sports switching between major sporting events." Throughout the day, producers would create highlight packages to update viewers on the day's programs. In addition to coverage of trials, the production units would travel to Washington, D.C. to cover major crime or corruption hearings. Affidavit of Peter Low, sworn to on March 6, 1992.

CJN's coverage of crime would consist of a "a regularly scheduled 24–hour cycle of crime news and crime-related programming." The CJN Plan proposed seven such programs:

* Crime News regularly scheduled hour and half-hour programs of crime news.

* Fugitive—a half-hour program detailing what happened during a crime and identifying the criminal being sought.

* At Issue—a talk show hosted by a conservative prosecutor and a liberal defense attorney discussing a crime-related or similar theme.

* Wanting Out—15 minute programs depicting prisoners claiming innocence or who say they have been punished enough and should be paroled.

* Our Nation's Finest—five minute segments honoring a law enforcement officer.

* Inside Advice—five minute segments taped inside prisons across the country which show daily life inside a prison and in which prisoners tell what led to their incarcerations.

* Your Personal Safety—two minute vignettes aimed at women and children in which experts give advice about personal safety.

The CJN Plan also included "one possible schedule of programming" for CJN, Kavanau's resume, and a financial presentation.

II. PLAINTIFFS' CONTACTS WITH DEFENDANTS

MCA's Fraiberg sent Kavanau's April 19, 1988 memo to Defendant Robert Pittman, then the president of Quantum Media, an entity affiliated with MCA. On or about June 23, 1988, Pittman and Kavanau met to discuss Kavanau's idea. Kavanau claims that he advised Pittman that he was in the process of developing a more detailed presentation of his concept, and that he was presenting not just an idea, but a complete product and total concept. Kavanau claims that Pittman expressed interest in the concept and even discussed the terms of a potential offer.

Kavanau and Pittman met a second time, and Kavanau delivered several copies of his completed CJN Plan. Pittman admits having received and reviewed the CJN Plan. After their second meeting, however, the parties did not communicate further.

In late September or October 1988, Kavanau met with Defendant Peter Low, then vice president of programming at Defendant Cablevision Systems Corporation ("Cablevision"). Cablevision is a Delaware corporation with its principal place of business in Woodbury, New York. Through its subsidiary Rainbow Programming Holdings, Inc. ("Rainbow"), Cablevision is involved in creating and developing original programming networks for cable television systems.

The purpose of the meeting was for Kavanau to present the CJN Plan to Low. Prior to discussing his idea, Kavanau required Low to sign a "Confidential Information Agreement," whereby Low agreed not to disclose information about Kavanau's "crime story related television concept." Kavanau then presented his CJN idea and gave Low a copy of the CJN Plan. After the meeting, the parties had no further communication.

III. COURT TV

In early 1989, Pittman ended his relationship with MCA and became a consultant to Warner Communications Inc. ("Warner"). Warner, a Delaware corporation, is a wholly owned subsidiary of Time Warner, Inc., also a Delaware corporation.

In March 1989, Warner announced its intention to acquire a majority interest in American Lawyer Media, L.P. ("ALM"), a partnership with its principal place of business in New York City. ALM is a publisher of legal periodicals, and Defendant Steven Brill is ALM's founder, president, and chief executive officer. The transaction closed in June 1989. Thereafter, Pittman worked with Brill on developing a 24–hour courtroom cable television channel. The plans for the project, entitled "The American Courtroom Network," were publicly announced in January 1990.

Meanwhile, Rainbow, cablevision's subsidiary, was also involved in the development of a 24–hour courtroom cable television channel called "In Court." Plaintiffs claim that In Court was developed by Cablevision and Defendant NBC Cablevision, Inc. ("NBCC"), a Delaware corporation with its principal place of business in New York City.

Plaintiffs allege that Time Warner and ALM were competing with Cablevision and NBCC to determine which would be the first to air, The American Courtroom Network or In Court. Ultimately, however, the two entities merged and formed Defendant "Courtroom Television Network" ("Court TV").

Court TV is a joint venture among four companies: TW Courtroom Inc., an indirect wholly owned subsidiary of Time Warner Inc.; Liberty Court, Inc., an indirect subsidiary of Liberty Media Corporation, a cable television company; In Court Holding Corporation, an indirect subsidiary of Cablevision; and NBC Cable Courtroom Holding, Inc., an individual subsidiary of National Broadcasting Company. ALM, a partnership between Time Warner Inc. and Brill, manages and holds a contingent interest in Court TV.

Court TV is a national satellite cable television network devoted to televising judicial and legislative proceedings and related programming. On an average day, Court TV broadcasts nine hours of live or taped coverage of trials or other courtroom proceedings. * * *

IV. PLAINTIFFS' CLAIMS

Plaintiffs charge that The American Courtroom Network, In Court, and Court TV all result from the Defendants' misappropriation of Kavanau's idea and the CJN Plan. * * *

I. THE NOVELTY OF KAVANAU'S IDEA

Defendants argue that even assuming that they used Kavanau's idea in developing Court TV, they are entitled to summary judgment on all of Plaintiffs' claims because, as a matter of law, Kavanau's idea was not novel. * * *

A. *Pre-existing Proposals for a Courtroom Cable Network*

Plaintiffs argue that Kavanau's idea was novel because no cable television network devoted to the broadcast of judicial proceedings and related programming existed prior to the formulation of his idea. * * * Defendants claim that a courtroom cable network had been proposed well before Kavanau came up with his idea for CJN. * * * Defendants also note that in 1982, Philadelphia attorney Malcolm J. Berkowitz

Novel
ided(?)

proposed "a cable television network to be entirely devoted to the legal system and the judicial process to be known as 'CABLE COURTS NETWORK.'" Berkowitz proposed: live and taped television of actual trials from the lowest traffic court to the highest trial courts in all of the States, as well as live and taped presentations of appellate arguments ranging from the United States Supreme Court to the intermediate courts of appeals in the various States as well as the Federal Courts.

Berkowitz envisioned the broadcast of other law-related programming, including interviews with people connected to the judicial process, rating states with regard to their disposition of cases, and rating the performance of attorneys and judges. In 1982, Mr. Berkowitz sent his proposal to various television entities, including Warner Amex Communications, Inc. and Time, Inc. Video Group, but he received no responses expressing interest.

Defendants thus show that as early as 1982, a definitive proposal for a 24–hour cable television network devoted to the broadcast of courtroom proceedings and law-related programming was in circulation in the television industry. Although Kavanau's proposal was more developed and more definitive than pre-existing plans such as Berkowitz's, and thus in a layman's sense it may have been new or novel, it was not the first such idea and therefore it cannot meet the test of novelty under New York law. Accordingly, as a matter of law, Kavanau's idea for a courtroom cable television network is not protectible and cannot form the basis for any claims for relief.

B. Kavanau's Use of Existing Television Elements

Kavanau's assertion of novelty must also be rejected because the CJN Plan is a mere compilation of elements which were already in use in the television industry at the time Kavanau developed his idea. While the embodiment of elements long in use does not of itself negate the novelty of an idea, a protectable idea must: show genuine novelty and invention, and not merely clever or useful adaptation of existing knowledge. Improvement of standard technique or quality, the judicious use of existing means, or the mixture of known ingredients in somewhat different proportions—all the variations on a basic theme—partake more of the nature of elaboration and renovation than innovation. * * *

Kavanau identifies five substantive elements in his plan for CJN: (1) a 24–hour cable television network; (2) devoted to the nationwide broadcast of live crime-related trials and taped highlight segments; (3) the use of satellite uplink technology to permit switching between four trials in the style of ABC's "Wide World of Sports;" (4) a substructure of crime-related programming; and (5) the use of a host or anchorman at a central studio. * * *

What Kavanau proposed was therefore a mere compilation of and expansion on existing television elements to fill a single 24–hour cable television network. This fails to satisfy the test for novelty under New York law. "The concept of novelty under New York law is that special protection is afforded only to truly innovative ideas while allowing the free use of ideas that are 'merely clever or useful adaptations of existing knowledge.' '' While the success of court TV suggests that Kavanau's idea for CJN was indeed clever and useful, the derivative nature of his idea demonstrates its lack of novelty under New York law. * * *

Here, the Court has determined that Kavanau's idea for a courtroom cable television network was not novel because (1) similar proposals were in circulation at least as early as 1982, and (2) his idea was essentially derivative in nature. Thus, Kavanau's idea lacked novelty from the very instant it was conceived. It does not become novel simply because it is similar to the Defendants' program, and because the Defendants, in "media hype" and in self-promotional claims, have asserted that their program is unique, exciting, not derivative, or a breakthrough. * * *

Accordingly, Plaintiff's reliance on Defendants' promotional statements is misplaced because those statements cannot show the novelty of his idea.

II. SIMILARITY OF KAVANAU'S CONCEPT AND COURT TV

Because the Court finds as a matter of law that Plaintiff's idea for CJN was not novel, the issue of the similarity between CJN and Court TV need not be addressed.

CONCLUSION

Defendants' motion for summary judgment is granted.

IT IS SO ORDERED.

KULIK PHOTOGRAPHY v. COCHRAN

United States District Court, Eastern District of Virginia, 1997.
975 F.Supp. 812.

MEMORANDUM OPINION

CACHERIS, Chief Judge.

This matter is before the Court on Defendants Johnnie L. Cochran, Jr. and F. Lee Bailey's Motion to Dismiss. As grounds for the Motion, Defendants assert Lack of Personal Jurisdiction, Insufficiency of Process, Improper Venue, and Failure to State a Claim.

Plaintiff Kulik Photography ("Kulik") alleges in its Complaint that the Defendants violated the copyrights laws of the United States by using a photograph belonging to, and copyrighted by, the Plaintiff. The Defendants used the photograph in a courtroom in California as part of their defense of O.J. Simpson. The Plaintiff contends that this case is properly brought because the Defendants ignored warnings about the copyrighted nature of the photograph and used the photograph knowing that it would be displayed, via television, to the Commonwealth of Virginia. * * *

The foundation on which the Plaintiff builds the remainder of his argument is that Cochran and Bailey were responsible for the televising of the copyrighted photograph into this District. Plaintiff contends that "Court TV was merely the instrument of infringement. 'But for' the acts of Cochran and Bailey no infringement would have occurred."

The Court cannot accept that argument. Assuming for purposes of this Motion that the Defendants did violate the copyright laws, the offensive activity transpired in California. * * * In this case, even assuming that the Defendants knew that their actions would be televised, the television stations were not agents of, nor were under the control of, the Defendants. * * *

Because no personal jurisdiction exists and the venue is improper, the Court need not consider the other bases asserted. However, the Court does believe that the Defendants have accurately argued that the action at issue would be privileged because it transpired during the course of a judicial proceeding. In many instances, otherwise actionable conduct is not a proper basis for suit because it transpired during a lawsuit. * * *

The Court also finds the Defendants' "fair use" argument to be persuasive. The statute itself states that "news reporting" is a legally recognized "fair use." 17 U.S.C. § 107. Plaintiff failed to address this argument in its Opposition, and ignored the fact that Court TV had a legal right to provide television news coverage of the trial in California to the rest of the country. Accordingly, the only action to have transpired in Virginia (the televising of the trial) was a legal and proper "fair use."

The Court makes one final note about the Plaintiff's argument that the Defendants acted improperly in using a copyrighted photograph without permission. The photograph at issue had already been admitted into evidence by the presiding trial judge, and the Defendants were representing a client who faced two murder charges. This Court cannot agree that the Defendants did anything wrong in using an item of evidence already accepted into the case during their closing argument. To permit otherwise would permit the copyright laws to trump the constitutional rights of a criminal defendant.

The Court notes that these Defendants should not be required to face trial on these claims anywhere. The Court does not believe that a transfer of this case serves the interests of justice. A more appropriate result is dismissal. Accordingly, this Court grants the Defendants' Motion and orders this case dismissed with prejudice. * * *

CAMERAS IN THE COURTROOM
IN THE O.J. SIMPSON CASE
By Michelle Carswell Pritchard.*

It has been called the trial of the century. Television documentaries and biographies, books, Internet sites, and editorials are still being

---

* Michelle C. Pritchard is an Associate Attorney at the Law Firm of Byrd, Byrd, Ervin, Whisnant & McMahon, P.A. since 1999. She was a law clerk to the Honorable Lance A. Ito during the case *People v. Orenthal James Simpson.*

generated by the Simpson case and its legacy. Other cases have received widespread media attention, but for whatever reasons, (probably a mixture of social climate, racial attitudes, and the public's always insatiable need for information on the misfortunes and woes of the celebrity) this case led the prime time news on most major broadcast stations every night for the majority of the year and a half in which it took to take the case from arrest to jury selection to verdict. Information about the case ran on the front page of most major newspapers for the duration as well. This extent of coverage rivals and exceeds interest in wars the nation has fought and scandals involving top government officials. Every detail, no matter how trivial, no matter how weak or unreliable the source, was the object of every journalist's obsession. Erroneous information and speculation ran rampant.

The immense media frenzy already surrounding the case was one of the reasons that the Trial Judge, Lance A. Ito, decided to allow the trial to be televised. He had reservations that the speculation that was going on in the media would overshadow the facts of the case. However, in the end he decided that the speculation would continue outside his courtroom and was beyond his control. (The Hollywood Reporter, November 8, 1994). Better, he reasoned, that the public be able to see and hear firsthand what was being said and done rather than get tainted or incorrect information from the media. Many legal commentators have voiced their opinions that cameras do not belong in the courtroom. However, this opinion has always been stated with the benefit of hindsight, something it is easy to forget no one had at the time this case began, including Judge Ito.

Court T.V. and CNN had already begun their steady climb up the ratings ladder, but this case catapulted both to a new level of respect within the cable television community. As a law clerk for Judge Ito, I know that the Judge received many letters from retired and disabled people, housewives, and anyone else who had access to daytime television stating that they watched the trial religiously and had given up their soap opera addictions to watch the real soap opera unfolding before their eyes.

From the day the story broke that the former wife of football legend O.J. Simpson had been found brutally murdered, and that O.J. was a suspect, the media knew they had a goldmine. Their only concern was would they be granted access to the court proceedings? The media was represented in the hearing before the court by Kelli Sager, an attorney who represented more than a dozen media clients and attorneys from the ACLU, among others, all of whom argued vigorously for television to be allowed, quoting the First Amendment and free speech concerns. In the end, the media's argument carried the day and the court ruled that the court proceedings could be televised with a ten second delay to weed out information not to be released to the public.

The negative arguments for cameras not being allowed in the courtroom have been repeated numerous times, but consist largely of the following: 1) Television coverage made the attorneys, witnesses, and court staff, etc., pander to the cameras and act in ways they would not have if cameras were not present. 2) Televising the trial made it last longer than it would have otherwise. 3) The coverage affected the decorum of the courtroom. 4) The televised court proceedings stirred up the public's interest to epic proportions that would not have existed otherwise. 5) The camera's presence affected the outcome of the verdict.

The court had no hand in the decision to move the case from the Santa Monica courthouse to the Downtown courthouse, where it fell to the downtown judges to handle. That decision was made by the District Attorney's Office. In addition, the District Attorney's Office requested that the jury be sequestered to shield them from prejudicial publicity. Judge Ito was selected as the most qualified judge to hear the case. Many of the attorneys for both the prosecution and defense had been in front of Judge Ito before, and they knew his style, which consisted of letting the lawyers try their case without undue interference from the court. As the trial got under way, the attorneys appeared to take advantage of his style, but by then, if the court made major changes in the way it handled the case mid-trial, it was sure there would be reports of the court trying to help one side or the other or adding to the alleged cover-up.

The case was so much at the forefront of the media spotlight, that everybody everywhere wanted to be involved. There were many peripheral issues that had to be addressed by the Court. As the case proceeded, attorneys on both sides and the Court were inundated daily by reports of juror misconduct, new witnesses, alleged conspiracies, and new evidence. The publicity of the case inevitably brought out additional potential witnesses for both sides who were looking for their fifteen minutes of fame.

At the same time, it appeared that several witnesses were reluctant to take the stand due to the nationwide media and television coverage. Football player and former friend of O.J. Simpson, Marcus Allen, indicated that he did not wish to be called as a character witness in the trial. Evidently, O.J. Simpson was not the only person concerned about his or her public image.

Two members of the Mafia, brothers Craig and Larry Fiato, testified to remarks that detective Phillip Vanatter had allegedly spoken in their presence. The only problem was that the two men were in the witness protection program. The United States Department of Justice ordered that their testimony must not be televised. Another potential key witness, the maid for O.J. Simpson's neighbor, Rosa Lopez, clearly did not wish to be called as a witness about what she saw or heard that night. She went into hiding at her daughter's residence and wanted to go back home to El Salvador without having to testify. Because she was a potential key witness in the case, the Court stopped the court proceedings and held four (4) days of televised testimony outside the presence of the jury so that if she indeed left the country at least her testimony would be preserved by video.

Several potential witnesses were not called at the trial due to credibility problems. Since this was *the* news story, media outlets were offering money to get people to sell their story. If they succumbed before they were called as witnesses, a decision had to be made to determine if they still had enough credibility to be believed as witnesses. For example, Jill Shively testified at the grand jury proceedings about having seen O.J. Simpson during the relevant time period driving at a location between the two crime scenes. She sold her story to the tabloids and was never called by the prosecution as a witness at trial. The defense was affected as well. Defense witness Mary Ann Gerchas stated she had seen four Hispanic males running away from the crime scene. She also sold her story to a tabloid. It was later determined that she had a criminal record and was known for trying to place herself in the middle of high-profile cases.

The trial was stalled often while reports that appeared to be credible were investigated. Many of these items would probably not have surfaced in a lower profile case. I am of the opinion that the problem would have existed even if the proceedings weren't televised, but perhaps to a lesser degree. Obviously, the trial lengthened every time one of these reports was investigated. Reports of juror misconduct took up huge amounts of time. As more and more jurors were dismissed and the Court was told of discord among the remainder, the Court felt the pressure of trying to get the case to the jury without a mistrial. The case had already become the most expensive trial in California's history. A retrial would be devastating to the Los Angeles coffers, not to mention the collective uneasiness present in the city.

Since the defendant had exercised his right to a speedy trial, proceedings got under way quickly. Normally cases are not heard this quickly. Due to the time frame, investigation and discovery were still going on during the trial. A facsimile machine was placed in the courtroom for the use of the prosecution and defense attorneys. More than once information and questions were faxed to the attorneys in the courtroom by others working on the case, during the actual testimony of witnesses. This certainly would not have been possible if the proceedings were not televised because the people working outside the courtroom would not have been able to hear the trial as it occurred.

The positive effects of televising the trial deserve to be looked at in weighing whether or not cameras should have been allowed in this case. The racial and social tensions of the city had not fully quieted down after the riots sparked by the Rodney King verdicts in 1992. The protection of the city was always a constant concern for the Court. No one knew how close the city was to more riots breaking out. The city had been crippled financially by the riots, and was only now beginning to recover. Reports of more police cover-ups and police misconduct would likely fuel social tensions. If the proceedings were televised, at least the people could see the facts for themselves instead of listening to a second hand version of what had taken place.

The tapes that surfaced during the trial in which Detective Mark Fuhrman was interviewed by aspiring screenwriter Laura Hart–McKinney were filled with racial epithets and explosive stories of police misconduct and cover-ups in the Los Angeles Police Department. Again, no one knew if the racial tensions would boil over again into more civil unrest. Judge Lance Ito had to make the difficult decision about which examples of racial slurs and police misconduct, if any, to allow as evidence in the trial. Not only did he have a difficult legal decision to make, he was mindful of the many social concerns that existed as well. Again the tabloids had somehow gotten copies of the tapes and/or transcripts, and were already broadcasting these to the public at large before the Court even issued its ruling.

Later in the civil trial held in Santa Monica, where the victims' families sued O.J. Simpson for the wrongful deaths of their loved ones, presiding Judge Fujusaki would have the benefit of hindsight, and the trial and error learning process undergone by his colleague, Judge Lance A. Ito, on his decision on whether or not to televise the civil proceedings.

So, with those thoughts in mind, was it a good idea to televise the case of the *State of California vs. Orenthal James Simpson*? In my mind, that is an easy question to answer. At the time the decision was made, the public would probably not have stood for any other decision. Proof of this reared its ugly head when the Court stopped media coverage for a portion of Prosecutor Marcia Clarke's closing argument when portions of the notes Mr. Simpson was writing on his legal pad to his attorneys were accidentally shown for several seconds by the cameras. The court had threatened to stop media coverage earlier in the case when the camera caught a momentary glimpse of an alternate juror while panning the courtroom. But this time, the court pulled the plug and ceased television coverage for several minutes. Most headlines regarding the situation used one common word . . . panic, describing the momentary blackout of coverage. Some things in the world are bigger than a single person, and laying the blame for a trial that did not showcase the highlights of American jurisprudence at the feet of Judge Lance Ito was, is, and continues to be unfair. As a clerk for him from January 1995 until mid-October 1995, I can honestly say I have met few people like him and I admire him greatly. He did the job that was asked of him and he did it well. I remember him saying that he was asked by someone if he had it all to do over again, would he do it? His response was, if I knew then what I know now, I would have run down the hall the other way.[1]

1. Judge Ito has given only one print interview after the case to college senior, Gayle Gomer, from Cal–State Northridge. (See Los Angeles Times, October 25, 1995, p.B3). He, unlike many of the other members of the prosecution and defense team, has not written a book or profited from this case in any way. His law clerks and legal research attorney were privy to information that most others were not, including most in-chambers proceedings. However, I think it speaks to the integrity of the Judge and his clerks that no one connected to him has tried to profit from this case. Other criti-

Did televising the case affect the jury's decision in this case? In my opinion, no. The jury was going to hear the message the defense was sending of alleged cover-ups and misconduct by law enforcement and the district attorney's office, in the presence of cameras or not. End of story. For better or worse, the public saw the criminal justice system in an unnatural and rare environment. Few people realize that most everyday trials don't go like this, but then again, most trials don't include a sports legend and television and movie actor and the alleged brutal murder of his ex-wife and her friend. Most cases end in plea bargains, and the few cases that are tried normally have defendants which must have public defenders appointed because they cannot afford the prospect of a lengthy trial. This is true in all fifty states. Cameras in the courtroom, belied somewhat by the backlash of this case, still take up much of Court T.V.'s daytime spots. The public wants the information, and as we all know, what the public wants, the public gets. And who is to say that the public is wrong. We are the public after all.

Note

1. After reading the cases and the article by Michelle Carswell Pritchard, should cameras be allowed in the courtroom?

E. SPORTS

Sports are an institution on television. Professional and amateur sports have long been the staple of Saturday and Sunday afternoon television. Sports then moved into prime time television with *Monday Night Football*, the Olympics, ice skating, and various other special sporting events. ESPN was the first all-sports network launched to satisfy the need for sports programming twenty-four hours a day. Networks spend billions of dollars to obtain the rights to broadcast college and professional football, college and professional basketball, baseball, golf, and NASCAR racing. Sports programming typically delivers a younger male demographic to advertisers.

With the tremendous popularity in reality TV, television stations dedicated to adrenaline junkies have been introduced. One of these networks is called the Extreme Sports Channel. This channel offers 24–hour coverage of surfing, snowboarding, in-line skating and even mountain biking. The channel broadcasts through a worldwide satellite network. Though the network initially broadcast only in Europe in 1999, the channel has expanded to nine countries. The channel will begin Internet broadcast at *http://www.extreme.com*. Extreme Television goes

cisms were that Judge Ito made special provisions for reporters and famous people by inviting them back to his chambers during the trial. For the record, when any of the court staff had family or friends observe the trial, he always invited the guests back and spoke to them in his chambers. He spent no more time or effort speaking to Larry King, than he did my grandmother from a small town in North Carolina. Judge Lance Ito is still doing criminal trials in Department 110 of the Los Angeles Criminal Courts Building.

24 Hours, *PR Newswire,* at http://www.thessn.com/snow_5_2.html (May 1, 2003).

The WWF SMACKDOWN! wrestling has become increasingly popular among sport enthusiasts of all ages, including children. For a few years in the late 1990s, wrestling beat Monday Night Football in the ratings and in key demographic categories. Popularity has created some unintended problems. The World Wrestling Federation Entertainment, Inc., sued for defamation when attorneys tried to use a "wrestling defense" for an accidental killing in *World Wrestling Federation Entertainment, Inc. v. Bozell.*

WORLD WRESTLING FEDERATION ENTERTAINMENT, INC. v. BOZELL

United District Court, Southern District of New York, 2001.
142 F.Supp.2d 514.

CHIN, District Judge.

On January 25, 2001, in a Florida criminal court, fourteen year-old Lionel Tate was convicted of first-degree murder in the death of a six year-old girl. During the proceedings, Tate's attorney argued the "wrestling defense"—the boy was an avid fan of professional wrestling who was simply mimicking wrestling moves he had seen on television when he accidentally killed the girl. The defense was rejected. Lionel Tate was found guilty and sentenced to life in prison.

This death and the deaths of three other children prompted defendants in this case—self-proclaimed media "monitors," their executives, and Lionel Tate's attorney—to publicly attack plaintiff World Wrestling Federation Entertainment, Inc. (the "WWFE") and its highly successful wrestling programs, including the television show WWF SMACKDOWN! Defendants publicly blamed the WWFE and WWF SMACKDOWN! for the deaths of the four children. * * *

Here, the WWFE alleges, with specificity, that defendants made statements that were false and defamatory, that were made with malice, and that were made for commercial purposes—raising money and self-promotion. Assuming, as I must, that the allegations of the Amended Complaint are true for purposes of this motion, I conclude that the WWFE has stated claims upon which relief can be granted. Accordingly, and for the reasons set forth below, defendants' motions to dismiss the Amended Complaint are denied in all respects.

BACKGROUND

A. The Parties

The WWFE is a media and entertainment company. It markets products under the popular and successful World Wrestling Federation (the "WWF") brand. It began airing a television program entitled WWF SMACKDOWN! on August 26, 1999.

Defendant Media Research Center (the "MRC") is a non-profit corporation that purportedly seeks to "bring political balance to the nation's news media and responsibility to the entertainment media." In 1995, the MRC established defendant Parents Television Council (the "PTC") as its entertainment division. The PTC's stated purpose is to monitor television programming and to denounce what it considers inappropriate programs. * * *

Defendant James Lewis is a defense attorney, residing in Florida. Lewis was defense counsel for fourteen year-old Lionel Tate in his criminal trial for the 1999 death of six-year-old Tiffany Eunick. During the criminal proceedings, Lewis argued that Tate was "simply ... replicating what he saw being done by Sting, Hulk Hogan or The Rock, familiar names to wrestling aficionados." Between September 1999 and May 2000, Lewis appeared on a number of television and radio programs, including "Dateline," "Leeza," MSNBC, Court TV, and CBS Radio, to discuss the Lionel Tate case and his defense. On March 9, 2001, after having been found guilty of murder in the first degree, Lionel Tate was sentenced to life in prison.

B. The PTC's Campaign Against the WWFE

In the summer of 1999, the PTC defendants began a campaign attacking the WWFE and WWF SMACKDOWN!, for what they perceived as the excessive violence and inappropriateness of plaintiff's programming. The stated goal of the PTC's campaign was to "educate" its members and the WWFE's sponsors and advertisers to the purported fact that the WWFE and WWF SMACKDOWN! caused or was responsible for the deaths of four children.

As part of its campaign to "educate" its members, the PTC engaged in the following: sending "Action Alerts" and "Urgent Grams" via the Internet; sending letters; publishing articles on its Internet website and in the "PTC Insider," its newsletter; having Bozell write about the WWFE in his nationally syndicated column; and sending fundraising videotapes that focused on the WWFE and its products. With respect to "educating" the WWFE's corporate advertisers and sponsors, the PTC's campaign included: sending the corporations letters and videotapes; urging the PTC members to contact the corporations directly; speaking at the shareholders' meeting of the corporations; sending letters to politicians (the United States armed forces are advertisers); and advertising in newspapers.

C. The Allegedly Defamatory Statements

Within these many communications, defendants made allegedly false and defamatory statements about the WWFE and its products. These statements fall into two categories: (1) statements asserting that the WWFE (and its programs, including WWF SMACKDOWN!) "caused and/or is responsible for the deaths of four particular children"; and (2) statements misrepresenting the number of corporate sponsors and advertisers who have "pulled" or "withdrawn" their support of WWF SMACKDOWN! (collectively, the "defamatory statements"). * * *

The WWFE contends that the statements in the first category are false because neither it nor any of its programs was responsible for the deaths of any of the four children.

An example of the second category is the following statement made by Honig to shareholders of ConAgra, another sponsor of WWF SMACK-DOWN!: I am here to ask you: Does ConAgra plan to continue sponsoring WWF Smackdown! Or, will you decide, as have nearly 40 other major U.S. corporations, to make what is a socially and corporately responsible decision and stop sponsoring this trash?

The WWFE contends that the statements in the second category are false because it was not true that "nearly 40" major corporations had decided to withdraw their advertisements from WWF SMACKDOWN!

Lewis is alleged to have "echoed" the other defendants' "falsehood that WWFE was responsible for four children's deaths" on various television talk shows, including shows produced and broadcast in New York, when he purportedly knew the statements were false. * * *

I.   The First Amendment

* * * Specifically, drawing all reasonable inferences in favor of the WWFE, I must determine whether the Amended Complaint sufficiently alleges that defendants' statements were false, defamatory, and made with "actual malice"—with knowledge that the statements were false or with reckless disregard of whether they were false. * * *

Thus, the First Amendment issues raise four areas for consideration: (a) whether defendants' statements constitute commercial or noncommercial speech; (b) whether the statements were false; (c) whether the statements were defamatory; and (d) whether the statements were made with malice.

A.   Commercial Speech

1.   Applicable Law

* * * Three factors are to be considered in determining whether speech is commercial: "(i) whether the communication is an advertisement, (ii) whether the communication refers to a specific product or service, and (iii) whether the speaker has an economic motivation for the speech."

2.   Application

Applying these principles to the Amended Complaint, I hold that the WWFE has sufficiently alleged that defendants' statements constitute commercial speech for purposes of defendants' motions to dismiss. * * * PTC's statements do more than merely propose commercial transactions, as the PTC attacks the extent to which the WWFE, and the entertainment industry as a whole, exposes children to violence. * * *

Second, defendants also allegedly used the attacks on the WWFE to champion themselves and to raise the profile of the PTC. " * * * The combination of these characteristics—the goals of making money and self-promotion—support the WWFE's allegation that defendants' speech is commercial, notwithstanding the fact that their speech discusses public issues. *Cf. Bolger,* 463 U.S. at 67–68 (finding that informational pamphlets were commercial speech even though they contained discussions of "important public issues"). * * *

B. Falsity

Throughout its Amended Complaint, the WWFE asserts that defendants' allegedly defamatory statements are false. For example, the Amended Complaint alleges that defendants repeatedly made statements alleging that four children were killed by other children who were emulating wrestling moves they learned by watching programs such as WWF SMACKDOWN! The Amended Complaint alleges that these statements were false because the children were not emulating wrestling moves, and WWF SMACKDOWN! did not begin to air until after three of the incidents had occurred. The Amended Complaint alleges, in the case of Lionel Tate, that he never stated that he was emulating wrestling moves and that in fact he had told police he was playing "tag." * * * The Amended Complaint sufficiently alleges falsity.

C. Defamatory Meaning

* * * Here, the Amended Complaint alleges statements that are reasonably susceptible of defamatory meaning. A reasonable fact-finder could conclude that defendants' statements blaming the WWFE for the deaths of at least four children exposed the WWFE to shame and disgrace. Many of defendants' statements were even more explicit, outrightly accusing the WWFE of engaging in conduct that was "criminal" and "criminally irresponsible." * * * These statements were surely damaging to the WWFE's reputation. The Amended Complaint sufficiently alleges defamatory meaning.

D. Malice

To prove actual malice, a plaintiff must prove that the defendant "had a subjective awareness of either falsity or probable falsity of the defamatory statement, or acted with reckless disregard of its truth or falsity." *Celle,* 209 F.3d at 182 (quoting *New York Times,* 376 U.S. at 280). * * * Throughout the Amended Complaint, the WWFE alleges that defendants knew that their statements were false and that they uttered them with malice. * * * Actual malice "typically" will be inferred from "objective facts," *Bose Corp. v. Consumers Union of United States, Inc.,* 692 F.2d 189, 196 (1st Cir. 1982), and here the Amended Complaint alleges objective facts from which one can reasonably infer both New York Times malice as well as common law malice—that defendants acted with spite, ill will, hatred, or the intent to inflict harm. The death of the 6–year-old girl in the Lionel Tate case occurred on July 28, 1999, and the death of the 3–year-old boy in North Dallas occurred even earlier, on May 27, 1999. Yet, defendants attributed the deaths of these two children to the show, even though WWF SMACKDOWN! did not air until August 26, 1999. Moreover, defendants used words like "criminal," "criminally irresponsible," and "evil." Then, in an effort to persuade advertisers not to advertise on WWF SMACKDOWN!, defendants publicly stated that as many as 40 major corporations had already withdrawn their sponsorship when that apparently was not true. A reasonable fact-finder could certainly infer reckless disregard for the truth and/or spite, ill will, and an intent to harm from these and other objective facts.

In short, the WWFE has sufficiently alleged that defendants' statements were false, defamatory, and made with actual malice. *See Church of Scientology Int'l v. Behar*, 238 F.3d 168, 173 (2d Cir. 2001) (noting that resolution of "falsity and actual malice inquiries typically requires discovery" and, therefore, should not be resolved at pleadings stage). In addition, the WWFE has sufficiently alleged that defendants' speech should be classified as commercial speech that is not entitled to heightened constitutional protection. Against this background, I now separately address each of the WWFE's claims. * * *

III. DEFENDANT LEWIS

In his motion to dismiss the Amended Complaint, defendant Lewis raises two arguments that relate solely to him, and which require separate consideration. First, Lewis asserts that this Court lacks personal jurisdiction over him; he argues that he is a Florida resident who has no contacts with the Southern District of New York, and that New York's long-arm statute does not apply here because the WWFE's claims are grounded in defamation, which is beyond the statute's reach. Second, Lewis asserts that his allegedly defamatory statements are shielded by the judicial proceedings privilege; he argues that he made the statements concerning the WWFE in the context of his representation of Lionel Tate. Both arguments fail. * * *

CONCLUSION

The PTC defendants' motion to dismiss the Amended Complaint is denied in all respects. Lewis's motion to dismiss the Amended Complaint is also denied in all respects. * * *

SO ORDERED.

Notes

1. On January 27, 2004, Lionel Tate was released from his life-without-parole sentence in a Florida prison. For articles on his release, see the Juvenile Law Center website, *available at* http://www.jlc.org/tate.htm.

2. While there is an assumption of risk for extreme sports participants, should the television production companies be held liable for injuries sustained during production?

F. TALK SHOWS

Late night talk shows have been a television staple since the beginning of broadcast television. Talk shows changed significantly in the 1980's with the introduction of daytime talk shows like Phil Donahue, Oprah Winfrey, Sally Jessy Raphael, and Geraldo Rivera. The *Phil Donahue Show* was taped in Chicago from 1974–1985, but the show moved to New York City from 1985–1996. For more information on talk shows, see *Biography Online Database,* (2003) *at* http://search.biography.com/print_record.pl?id=23305. For additional information on talk shows see, Charles Coletta, *St. James Encyclopedia of Pop Culture*, (2002), *at* http://www.findarticles.com/g1epc/bio/2419200326/p1/article.jhtml.

In 1984, Oprah Winfrey, a former TV anchor, moved to Chicago to host WLS–TV's morning talk show, *AM Chicago*. This show received high ratings and then became *The Oprah Winfrey Show*. This show became the top-rated talk show for 14 television seasons. See "Her Life," at http://www.oprah.com/about/ostory/about_ostory_herjourney.jhtml (2003). Winfrey plans to end the show after the 2005–06 season to mark the 20th anniversary of the show's debut in national syndication.

Geraldo Miguel Rivera also set a record as the first Hispanic to have a nationally syndicated talk show. The *Geraldo* show debuted in 1987. Rivera earned his law degree from the University of Pennsylvania Law School and a journalism degree from Columbia University. Nicolás Kanellos, *Geraldo Rivera*, St. James Encyclopedia of Pop Culture (2002) *at* http://www.findarticles.com/g1epc/bio/2419201013/p1/article.jhtml.

The *Geraldo* show opened the doors to other controversial talk shows such as *The Jerry Springer Show, Jenny Jones,* and *The Ricki Lake Show*. Though Jerry Springer experienced a surge of popularity in the mid–1990s, his popularity has not endured. The ratings have declined over the last several years. Springer considered running for a Senate seat, which would have led to the demise of *The Jerry Springer Show*. Belinda Halter, "Is Jerry Springer preparing to bail out?," About. Com Web site *(March 23, 2003) at h*ttp://talkshows.about.com/cs/jenny-jones/a/demisejj_2.htm

Other talk shows have experienced ratings slumps. *Jenny Jones* was be cancelled at the end of the 2003 season after having received some of the lowest ratings for syndicated talk shows. *The Ricki Lake Show* may be next. Belinda Halter, *The Demise of "Jenny Jones," About.Com Web site (March 23, 2003) at http://talkshows.about.com/cs/jenny-jones/a/demisejj.htm*. The lawsuits that these shows have generated have also not endeared them to sponsors.

CAMPOVERDE v. SONY PICTURES ENTERTAINMENT

United States District Court, Southern District of New York, 2002.
2002 WL 31163804.

MEMORANDUM AND ORDER

PRESKA, District J.

Plaintiffs Juan Campoverde ("Campoverde") and his attorney, Susan Chana Lask ("Lask"), filed their complaint in this Court based on diversity jurisdiction against defendants Sony Pictures Entertainment ("SPE") and Columbia Tristar Television Distribution ("CTTD") on August 20, 2001, alleging eight causes of action: breach of contract, false imprisonment, fraud, assault and battery, intentional infliction of emotional distress, negligence, negligence per se, and negligent infliction of emotional distress. Pursuant to the Affirmation of Susan Chana Lask, dated January 10, 2002, plaintiffs withdrew their claim for negligence per se. Defendants now move to dismiss the seven remaining claims under Fed.R.Civ.P. 12(b)(6) for failure to state a claim upon which relief can be granted. For the reasons set forth below, the motion is granted with respect to plaintiffs' claims for fraud, intentional infliction of emotional distress, negligence, and negligent infliction of emotional distress. Defendants' motion is denied with respect to the remaining claims for breach of contract, false imprisonment, and assault and battery.

BACKGROUND

All of the following facts are taken from plaintiffs' complaint. Because this is a motion to dismiss for failure to state a claim, I accept the factual allegations in plaintiffs' complaint as true.

In December 2000, Lask represented Campoverde in an adoption proceeding that attracted "worldwide media attention," and as a result, both plaintiffs appeared on several television shows, in various newspapers, and on the radio. On or about December 23, 2000, Barbara Weinberg ("Weinberg"), a senior producer for The Ricki Lake Show (the "Show"), called Lask to invite her and Campoverde to appear on the Show. Lask declined because the case was in litigation and "being on a talk show was not in her client's best interests at that time." Plaintiff requested that Weinberg not call her again but from December 23, 2000 to about January 3, 2001, Weinberg called Lask "at all hours throughout plaintiff LASK's work day and insisted she would produce a show sympathetic to plaintiff CAMPOVERDI's case, that the show would be newsworthy and it would help other father's [sic] who lost their children like plaintiff CAMPOVERDE."

On January 3, 2001, Weinberg offered, on behalf of SPE and CTTD, to provide: (1) on the day of the taping, travel arrangements to and from the set of the Show by defendants' car service; (2) an overnight stay at The South Gate Towers (the "Hotel") in New York City on the night of the taping; (3) $60.00 in cash to each plaintiff for time and expenses, a check to Lask for $775.00, and a check to Campoverde for $250.00, all of which would be paid on the day of the taping; and (4) that Lask's contact information, specifically, her office phone number, would be placed in chyron during the show so that viewers could contact her. On or about January 3, 2001, Campoverde spoke to Weinberg and indicated that he would not appear on the Show without Lask, and Weinberg responded by "assur[ing] plaintiff CAMPOVERDE that his appearance and case would be treated sympathetically and they would respect his attorney's presence on the show." Later that day, Lask spoke to Weinberg, explained that plaintiffs' time was valuable and that the taping would take up a day of work for each, and Weinberg promised that defendants would provide the items listed as (1) through (4) above. As a result, plaintiffs arranged to appear at the Show on January 11, 2001 for the taping and took that day off from work.

Between January 3, 2001 and January 8, 2001, Lask received several phone calls from Weinberg's assistants, who requested the plaintiffs' addresses and "other personal information." Lask was "annoyed by the constant calls from Weinberg's office" because it interrupted her work schedule. One of the assistants called Lask several times and asked for her social security number, which Lask refused to give. Lask requested that the assistant stop calling her to ask for the social security number, and the assistant agreed not to ask for the number again. On or about January 6, 2001, Lask called Weinberg and told her that Weinberg's staff was "harassing her by demanding her social security number," and Weinberg "assured plaintiff LASK they did not need her social security number and the requests would stop."

Also on January 6, 2001, Weinberg "agreed to execute a contract specifying the terms agreed upon to appear on the show [items (1)–(4) above], and return it the same day she received it from plaintiff LASK." On January 8, 2001, Lask wrote and faxed a one page document labeled "Facsimile Cover Sheet" to Weinberg, which Weinberg did not return "despite calls from plaintiff LASK from January 8 through January 11, 2001."

On January 11, 2001, the day of the taping, Weinberg called Lask and "insisted that a car was ready to pick her up and LASK had to get in the car," but Lask refused because Weinberg had not signed and returned the faxed document. Weinberg then signed and faxed it back to Lask on the same day, and the document "confirm[ed]" that: plaintiffs would appear at the studios on January 11, 2001, for taping; the car service would pick up Campoverde at his address in New York and Lask at her address in New Jersey at 2:15; after the taping, which would end no later than 6:00 p.m., the car service would take plaintiffs back to the Hotel and defendants would provide a car service voucher to take plaintiffs back to their respective addresses in New York and New Jersey; Campoverde's compensation would be based on his pay stubs and proof of tips, up to $250.00, Lask would receive $775.00 and each plaintiff would receive $60.00 for meals based on "standard sag scale," and all payments were to be received upon plaintiffs' arrival on the set; Ricki Lake would announce Lask's name and office phone number during the show, which would also be displayed in chyron during the show; and finally, that defendants acknowledge that none of the guests at the January 11 taping "know [Campoverde] or had any relationship with him in any way and that they are complete strangers to him."

At about 2:00 p.m. on January 11, 2001, defendants' car service picked Lask up at her residence in New Jersey and dropped her off at the Hotel so that she could drop off her "files, clothes and other personal and expensive items." The Hotel, however, had no reservations for either of the plaintiffs. Lask called Weinberg and her assistants, the problem subsequently was resolved, and Lask left her property in the hotel room.

Lask arrived at the television studio at about 3:30 p.m. and was brought to a small waiting room with no windows, no phone and one door to exit from, where Campoverde and his friend, Paul Guerero ("Guerero"), were waiting. Weinberg then arrived with two ten-page contracts, which she "demanded" that the plaintiffs execute before appearing on the show. Lask refused, stating that she was "not there to work by reviewing ten page contracts," that there was already an agreement in place pursuant to the faxed January 11, 2001 document, that the new contracts stated different, objectionable terms and did not state the terms of payment, and "all of this was a complete surprise." Lask specifically objected to the fact that the ten-page contract included a general release clause that released defendants from any negligence and defamation, in addition to the provisions stating that the Show could discuss anything of a personal nature regarding plaintiffs' appearance and that the contract was complete and "there were no other agreements."

Weinberg "insisted" that the contracts be signed before anything else could occur, left the room, and Lask crossed out the objectionable terms and inserted language reflecting that set forth in the January 11, 2001 faxed document. Weinberg returned, "became very angry that the contracts were not signed," and left to show the contracts to her superiors. An assistant entered the room at that point and tried to convince plaintiffs to sign the contracts. When plaintiffs refused, the assistant indicated that "it would not be a problem" and asked Lask to follow her to the make-up room down the hall. Defendants' employees escorted Lask to the make-up room where another female was waiting.

In the make-up room, another assistant entered with an AFTRA (the union for television actors) wage agreement and "demanded" that Lask execute the agreement and give them her social security number before she received any money from the defendants. Lask refused, stating that the AFTRA agreement did not apply to her, she was supposed to have been paid upon her arrival, and, pursuant to her prior telephone conversations with Weinberg's assistant, she did not have to give her social security number. Another assistant entered and insisted that Lask sign the AFTRA agreement, and the "make-up person also joined in with the intimidation tactics and told plaintiff LASK she should just sign the AFTRA contracts." Plaintiff felt "intimidated, threatened, embarrassed, upset and humiliated," "told the employees she felt uncomfortable and wanted to leave," but the "employees told plaintiff LASK that she better sign the AFTRA agreement and give them her social security number or else noone [sic] gets paid."

Meanwhile, Weinberg and two assistants re-entered the waiting room and tried to "convince and intimidate" Campoverde by stating that he did not have to follow Lask's advice and that he should sign the contracts. Campoverde refused and "demanded to see his attorney." Weinberg also presented Campoverde with an AFTRA agreement, stating that he should sign it and the ten-page contracts because his attorney had already signed them. Campoverde refused to sign, asked to see Lask, and Weinberg left the room, closing the door behind her. Campoverde and Guerero opened the door and "saw about 8 employees, most of [whom] were male, surrounding the door and preventing their exit."

At around 4:00 p.m., an assistant escorted Lask from the make-up room to "another smaller room" where she was told to give her social security number to a "fact checker." Lask "was now surrounded by three female employees of defendants, including the female Fact Checker, who insisted plaintiff LASK had to give them her social security number. Plaintiff LASK asked to leave and they would not let her leave." The employees then phoned defendants' attorney in California and told Lask to speak to her. Lask "explained to that attorney that she felt uncomfortable and was being intimidated to sign AFTRA contracts and defendants' own contracts that did not apply," and she "told the attorney she just wanted to leave." The attorney "insisted that plaintiff LASK sign the agreements and give them her social security number." Lask then saw Weinberg in the hallway and stated that "she wanted to leave the set that moment with her client, plaintiff CAMPOVERDE, because she felt uncomfortable about their mistreatment on the set and the fact that defendants were trying to coerce and pressure them" into signing the AFTRA agreements and other contracts. Weinberg "assured" Lask that she would take care of the situation and led her back into the waiting room where Campoverde and Guerero were.

At the waiting room Lask saw "a large crowd of defendants' employees in front of the door which was now shut and two very large men standing guard there," which caused Lask to "vocalize her distress." Lask insisted that she wanted to leave but she was "ushered into the waiting room and the door was shut behind her." Plaintiffs decided to open the door and ask to leave. Lask opened the door and two men were standing guard, one of whom told her to "shut the door and keep it shut because he was security." Plaintiffs demanded to know his name, why they could not leave, and that an executive producer be sent over, but the guard laughed, "told plaintiffs they had no right to ask any questions" and slammed the door shut.

Lask tried to call the police on her cell phone but received no signal. She then "suffered a panic attack wherein she could not breathe and

became dizzy from the fear" that she was "trapped." Campoverde also
became "extremely distressed" and "very nervous and upset." Fifteen
minutes later, Weinberg entered the room, "came in contact with
plaintiff LASK with her hand by pushing plaintiff LASK aside," and told
Campoverde that he should sign the contracts and appear on the Show.
Lask told Weinberg not to speak to her client, and Weinberg then
"became more abusive, hostile and belligerent towards" Lask. When
Campoverde refused to disregard his attorney's advice "Weinberg became furious, left the waiting room, shut the door behind her and never
returned." Lask then opened the door and saw a "larger crowd of
employees" standing by the door, in addition to the two guards.

At about 5:00 p.m., the guards opened the door and told plaintiffs to
follow them. Lask asked where they were going but the guards did not
answer. Plaintiffs stated that they wanted to call the police and the
guards laughed. The guards then "moved abruptly and in a threatening
manner towards the plaintiffs, forcing plaintiffs to walk backwards."
Lask "demanded" that plaintiffs be paid pursuant to the faxed document
and that they be provided with transportation back to the Hotel and to
their homes. Plaintiffs saw Weinberg in the hallway and asked her for
help, but Weinberg "yelled, 'You don't deserve anything, get them out of
here.'" When Lask "demanded to know about her property at the
Hotel," Weinberg laughed and stated that she had "no rights to anything." The guards "continued to back plaintiffs and Paul Guerrero out
of the studio and into the street" and slammed the studio door.

Plaintiffs then ran to the Hotel, where they were told that the
reservation had been canceled by defendants' employees. They gathered
their property and walked to a friend's apartment twenty blocks away,
who loaned them approximately $90.00 in cab fare to return to their
residences in New York and New Jersey.

On January 12, 2001, because she was "still extremely distressed,"
Lask called Connie Best at AFTRA and explained what had happened.
Best told Lask that because plaintiffs were not AFTRA members, defendants had no right to make them sign such an agreement, and that
plaintiffs' report of defendants' misconduct would be noted in their files
and followed up on when plaintiff filed a formal report. On about July
18, 2001, defendants' attorney Joel Grossman called Lask and told her
that defendants had insisted on an AFTRA agreement because they were
going to pay plaintiffs using AFTRA monies. Lask informed Grossman
that defendants were committing a fraud because they knew that plaintiffs were not a part of, and did not want to be a part of, AFTRA.

Plaintiffs filed a complaint in this Court on August 20, 2001, which
defendants now move to dismiss for failure to state a claim.

DISCUSSION

I. Relevant Legal Standard

When deciding a motion to dismiss under Rule 12(b)(6), I must
accept as true all well-pleaded factual allegations of the complaint and

draw all inferences in favor of the pleader. * * * In order to avoid dismissal, plaintiffs must do more than plead mere "[c]onclusory allegations or legal conclusions masquerading as factual conclusions." * * * Dismissal is proper only when "it appears beyond doubt that the plaintiff can prove no set of facts in support of his claim which would entitle him to relief." * * *

II. Breach of Contract

Defendants argue that plaintiffs' breach of contract claim should be dismissed because there is no valid, binding contract between the parties and, even if a contract did exist, plaintiffs failed to perform. Plaintiffs maintain that the facsimile cover sheet constitutes a final and binding contract between the parties and that Weinberg's presentation of the ten-page contract at the studio therefore was an attempt to modify the original contract, which required plaintiffs' consent.

To form a contract under New York law (which the parties do not dispute applies here), there must be an offer, acceptance, and consideration, in addition to a showing of a meeting of the minds, which demonstrates the parties' mutual assent and mutual intent to be bound. * * * Each element of the claim need not be pled separately; the "essential elements to pleading a breach of contract under New York law are the making of an agreement, performance by the plaintiff, breach by the defendant, and damages suffered by the plaintiff." * * *

Defendants first argue that, in this case, there is no consideration because the cover sheet only contains plaintiffs' terms and does not provide for any benefit to defendants. Consideration can be "either benefit to promisor or loss or detriment to promisee ... It can also be understood as a bargained for exchange." * * * The cover sheet states, however, that plaintiffs "will appear at [defendants'] studios for a taping on 1/11/01" and then provides for, *inter alia,* payment from the defendants. Moreover, plaintiffs specifically allege in their complaint that they rearranged their work schedules to appear on the Show, that they requested compensation for the day they would have to take off from work, and that "Weinberg agreed to execute a contract specifying the terms agreed upon to appear on the show," As such, I find that plaintiffs' promise to appear on the Show adequately alleges consideration.

Defendants also argue that there was no "meeting of the minds" or mutual assent here. According to the defendants, the facsimile cover sheet did not create a binding contract because "where the parties contemplate further negotiations and the execution of a formal instrument, a preliminary agreement does not create a binding contract." * * * Defendants argue that the parties continued negotiations when Weinberg presented the ten-page contracts at the studios. On the other hand, plaintiffs allege that this was an attempt to modify an already existing contract. * * *

To determine whether, and to what extent, the parties intended to be bound, I must look to "the words and deeds [of the parties] which constitute objective signs in a given set of circumstances." *Winston v. Mediafare Entm't Corp.*, 777 F.2d 78, 80 (2d Cir.1986) (alteration in original) (quoting *R.G. Group*, 751 F.2d at 74). Defendants point out that the facsimile cover sheet does not contain the word "agreement," does not state that it is binding, leaves terms open regarding editorial rights and a general release of liability, and that agreements of this type, i.e., for a guest appearance on a television show, are normally the subject of a formal contract. However, the complaint alleges that Weinberg agreed to execute a "contract specifying the terms agreed upon to appear on the show" and to return it the same day. As late as the morning of the taping, Lask alleges that she refused to appear on the Show because Weinberg had not signed and returned the cover sheet. When Weinberg returned the document, she signed it without any notations or further limitations, and it included the date and time, price, and time of payment, among other things. In addition, defendants partially performed the alleged agreement set forth in the cover sheet when they sent a car to pick up plaintiffs at their residences on January 11, 2001. "Aside from unilateral contracts, partial performance is an unmistakable signal that one party believes there is a contract; and the party who accepts performance signals, by that act, that it also understands a contract to be in effect." *Id.* at 75–76. As such, plaintiffs have sufficiently alleged that the cover sheet was a contract between the parties.

In addition, defendants argue that plaintiffs cannot state a claim for breach of contract because they did not perform. The cover sheet states that plaintiffs would appear at the studio on January 11, 2001 for the Show's taping, which they did. Plaintiffs allege that the defendants breached their agreement to pay plaintiffs when they arrived, and otherwise prevented plaintiffs from performing by demanding that plaintiffs sign a new contract and by "mistreating, threatening, and harassing" plaintiffs. These allegations sufficiently assert that performance was excused. Accordingly, accepting all of the facts in plaintiffs' complaint as true, I find that plaintiffs have sufficiently stated a claim for breach of contract.

III. False Imprisonment

Under New York law, to establish a claim for false imprisonment, plaintiffs must show that (1) defendants intended to confine them; (2) plaintiffs were conscious of the confinement; (3) plaintiffs did not consent to the confinement; and (4) the confinement was not otherwise privileged. * * * "A false imprisonment claim requires a prima facie showing of actual confinement or threatening conduct," and the unlawful detention can be for any length of time. * * *

Plaintiffs need not show that they physically attempted to leave, * * * and plaintiffs are "not required to incur the risk of personal violence by resisting until it actually is used." * * * Moreover, "[d]efendant exercises the requisite complete dominion over plaintiff when the plaintiff submits to an apprehension of force reasonably understood from the defendant's conduct." * * * In *Farina v. Saratoga Harness Racing Ass'n,* which defendants cite, plaintiff voluntarily accompanied defendant's employees to "clear himself of any implication of criminality," 20 A.D.2d 750, 246 N.Y.S.2d 960, 961 (3d Dep't 1964), which is not the case here. Defendants also cite to *Lee* for support, where security personnel from plaintiff's employer called plaintiff into a meeting and interrogated him for about five hours regarding his alleged misconduct. 1998 WL 107119, at *2–3. The court found that "[s]ummoning an employee into an interview in familiar surroundings in the employer's office does not indicate an intent to confine," *id.* at *5, but the facts in the instant case clearly are distinguishable.

At this stage of the litigation I must draw all inferences in plaintiffs' favor, and I therefore cannot find that plaintiffs can prove no set of facts in support of their false imprisonment claim. Accordingly, defendants' motion to dismiss the second cause of action is denied.

IV. Fraud

Defendants allege that plaintiffs' third cause of action should be dismissed because it improperly restates the breach of contract claim. When a complaint alleges both breach of contract and fraud, to maintain the fraud action, plaintiffs "must either: (i) demonstrate a legal duty separate from the duty to perform under the contract; or (ii) demonstrate a fraudulent misrepresentation collateral or extraneous to the contract; or (iii) seek special damages that are caused by the misrepresentation and unrecoverable as contract damages." * * * Defendants argue that plaintiffs have failed to allege any of these elements. * * *

I find that plaintiffs have failed to allege facts in their complaint sufficient to state a claim for fraud because the alleged misrepresentations here are "inextricably linked with the contract." * * *

Accordingly, defendants' motion to dismiss the fraud claim is granted.

V. Assault and Battery

An assault is "an intentional placing of another person in fear of imminent harmful or offensive conduct." * * * In addition, "words not accompanied by circumstances inducing a reasonable apprehension of bodily harm, such as movements of drawing back a fist, aiming a blow, or the show of a weapon, do not constitute an assault." * * * A battery is "an intentional wrongful physical contact with another person without consent. * * *

Defendants argue that plaintiffs fail to allege a claim for assault because their alleged fear was "nebulous" and they did not plead a reasonable apprehension of harmful contact. Moreover, plaintiffs argue, Lask's acts of demanding compensation and confronting defendants' employees are "hardly [those] of a person who fears for her personal safety."

Plaintiffs allege that defendants' employees "in a threatening manner, intentionally came towards plaintiffs several times, causing plaintiffs to walk backwards in consequence of which created fear and apprehension thereof." Accepting these allegations as true and drawing all inferences in plaintiffs' favor, as I must do on a 12(b)(6) motion to dismiss, I find that plaintiffs have sufficiently stated a claim for assault. They have alleged that defendants' employees physically moved toward them threateningly, causing plaintiffs to retreat because they were in fear of imminent harm. In addition, a plaintiff is "not deprived of an action merely because of being too courageous to be frightened or intimidated." * * * At this early point in the litigation, I cannot find that plaintiffs can prove no set of facts in support of their assault claim. * * *

In a cause of action for battery, "the required intent is merely that the defendant intentionally made bodily contact and that the intended contact was itself offensive or without consent." * * * The test is what an "ordinary person not unduly sensitive" would find offensive. * * * However, "the slightest unlawful touching of the person of another is sufficient" to show a battery because "the law cannot draw the line between different degrees of violence and therefore totally prohibits the first and lowest stage." * * *

Plaintiff Lask alone alleges a claim for battery in the instant case, stating, "Weinberg touched plaintiff LASK by shoving plaintiff LASK aside, intentionally coming in contact with LASK to come between LASK and her client ... causing a battery upon plaintiff LASK, and push[ing] her aside during one of Weinberg's outbursts in the waiting room." In the complaint Lask also alleges that Weinberg "came in contact with plaintiff LASK with her hand by pushing plaintiff LASK aside." Defendants argue that "[b]rushing someone aside to speak to another" does not constitute battery. Defendants cite to *Zgraggen v. Wilsey,* where the court held as a matter of law that the contact was not offensive and indicated that lack of plaintiff's consent, while an element to consider, is not conclusive in determining whether the defendant's contact was offensive. 200 A.D.2d 818, 819, 606 N.Y.S.2d 444 (3d Dep't 1994).

I find, however, that plaintiffs have sufficiently stated a claim for battery against plaintiff Lask because Lask alleged that Weinberg deliberately touched her and that the contact was offensive and unwelcome. * * * Plaintiff Lask did not allege that Weinberg "brushed her aside" to speak to someone else, as defendants state, but she instead characterized Weinberg's action as a "push" and "shove." *Cf. Lucas v. South Nassau Cmtys. Hosp.,* 54 F.Supp.2d 141, 151 (E.D.N.Y.1998) * * *

Accordingly, defendants' motion to dismiss plaintiffs' assault and battery claim is denied.

VI. *Intentional Infliction of Emotional Distress*

Plaintiffs must demonstrate four elements to establish a claim for the tort of intentional infliction of emotional distress ("IIED"): (1) that the defendants engaged in extreme and outrageous conduct; (2) that the defendants intended to cause severe emotional distress; (3) that the defendants' conduct caused the plaintiffs severe emotional distress; and (4) that the plaintiffs suffered severe emotional distress. * * * New York courts have imposed a very high threshold for intentional infliction of emotional distress claims, requiring that the conduct must be so outrageous and extreme "as to go beyond all possible bounds of decency, and to be regarded as atrocious, and utterly intolerable in a civilized community." * * *

Defendants argue that plaintiffs have failed to allege extreme and outrageous behavior sufficient to state a claim for intentional infliction of emotional distress. In the complaint, plaintiffs allege that defendants' employees became "abusive" and "threatening," separated plaintiffs to intimidate them into signing a new contract, "kept plaintiffs behind a shut and guarded door" and refused to let them leave, and threw plaintiffs out onto the street, the combination of which, plaintiffs argue, constitutes extreme and outrageous behavior. In support of their position, plaintiffs cite to *Bower v. Weisman,* 639 F.Supp. 532 (S.D.N.Y. 1986) and *Kaminski v. United Postal Service,* 120 A.D.2d 409, 501 N.Y.S.2d 871 (1st Dep't 1986). * * *

While the facts of *Kaminski* are more similar to plaintiffs' case than *Bower,* I find that the facts as alleged here do not rise to the extreme and outrageous level required by *Kaminski* and other New York cases. In the complaint, plaintiffs repeatedly allege that defendants were insistent, demanding, and tried to "convince," "intimidate," "coerce," and "pressure" them into signing the contracts, but such allegations do not constitute outrageous conduct—particularly in the talk show environment at issue. * * *

Here, the basis for plaintiffs' intentional infliction of emotional distress claim may be remedied through their assault and battery and false imprisonment claims. Accordingly, defendants' motion to dismiss is granted, and plaintiffs' fifth cause of action for intentional infliction of emotional distress is dismissed.

VII. *Negligence and Negligent Infliction of Emotional Distress*

To establish a claim for negligence, plaintiffs must show 1) that defendants owed a duty to plaintiff, 2) a breach of that duty, and 3) that plaintiffs suffered injury as a result of that breach. * * * Plaintiffs allege that, as invitees of the defendants, defendants owed a duty of reasonable care to "prevent any harm upon plaintiffs while on their premises, ... including emotional distress, insult, annoyance or mistreatment." Plaintiffs also allege that it was reasonably foreseeable that they would suffer emotional harm and distress when defendants harassed and intimidated, verbally abused, imprisoned, and ultimately "threw plaintiffs out onto the street."

Because plaintiffs were business invitees, defendants owed them a duty to "maintain [their] property in a reasonably safe condition." * * *

Here, however, plaintiffs do not allege that they suffered any physical injuries as a result of their visit to the Show. In fact, in their memorandum of law in opposition to the defendants' motion to dismiss, plaintiffs allege that their complaint states a "valid cause of action for negligence in inflicting severe mental and emotional distress." As such, plaintiffs' claim for negligence is encompassed by their claim for negligent infliction of emotional distress.

Plaintiffs have failed to state a claim for negligent infliction of emotional distress ("NIED"). First, plaintiffs must allege conduct that "was so outrageous and extreme as to support a claim for emotional distress," which is the same standard used in intentional infliction of emotional distress cases. * * * As previously discussed, I find that plaintiffs failed to allege such extreme and outrageous conduct. * * *

Accordingly, defendants' motion to dismiss the causes of action for negligence and NIED is granted.

CONCLUSION

For the reasons set forth above, plaintiffs' claims for fraud (third cause of action), intentional infliction of emotional distress (fifth cause of action), negligence (sixth cause of action), and negligent infliction of emotional distress (eighth cause of action) are dismissed for failure to state a claim upon which relief can be granted. Defendants' motion to dismiss the remaining claims, for breach of contract (first cause of action), false imprisonment (second cause of action), and assault and battery (fourth cause of action) is denied. * * *

SO ORDERED

Note

1. Some talk shows have turned out to be hazardous to the health of guests. The *Jenny Jones* show was sued by the survivors of a guest killed by another guest after the airing of a segment on July 24, 2000. This case will be discussed in detail in the final chapter of this book, 'The Devil Media Made Me Do It.'

G. SITCOMS

Sitcom is short for Situation Comedy, a television genre that is usually aired in half hour segments. Sitcoms depict "normal" human activities in a humorous way. *Ozzie and Harriet* introduced the viewing public to the family sitcom. The genre has evolved as a reflection of social changes in the United States. *Sanford and Son* and *The Jeffersons* introduced minorities to the genre. *All in the Family* broke new ground with its handling of bigotry and prejudice. The sitcom has long been a vehicle for shaping the social consciousness of America. You could call it, "lessons learned while laughing."

In the 1990s, one of the most popular TV shows was *Seinfeld*, the show about nothing. By 1993, this TV series was one of the top shows and won the Emmy for best comedy series. In 1999, the show aired its final episode of unusual characters and odd events around New York City. *The Unofficial Jerry Seinfeld Fan Site*, Bio, *at* http://www.jerryseinfeld.com/

As one of the most popular TV series of the 1990s, there was a lawsuit that challenged the originality of one of the characters, George Costanza, in *Costanza v. Seinfeld*.

COSTANZA v. SEINFELD

Supreme Court, New York County, New York, 1999.
181 Misc.2d 562, 693 N.Y.S.2d 897.

TOMPKINS, Judge.

A person is seeking an enormous sum of money for claims that the New York State courts have rejected for decades. This could be the plot for an episode in a situation comedy. Instead, it is the case brought by plaintiff Michael Costanza who is suing the comedian, Jerry Seinfeld, Larry David (who was the cocreator of the television program Seinfeld), the National Broadcasting Company, Inc. and the production companies for $100 million. He is seeking relief for violation of New York's Civil Rights Law §§ 50 and 51, being cast in a false light, invasion of privacy and defamation.

PLAINTIFF'S CONTENTIONS

The substantive assertions of the complaint are that the defendants used the name and likeness of plaintiff Michael Costanza without his permission, that they invaded his privacy, that he was portrayed in a negative, humiliating light and that he was defamed by defendant Larry David when reports were published by a spokesman that plaintiff Michael Costanza had a tenuous connection and was a "flagrant opportunist" seeking to cash in when the hyperbole of the Seinfeld program's final episode was at its peak. Plaintiff Michael Costanza asserts that the fictional character of George Costanza in the television program Seinfeld is based upon him. In the show, George Costanza is a long-time friend of the lead character, Jerry Seinfeld. He is constantly having problems with poor employment situations, disastrous romantic relationships, conflicts with his parents and general self-absorption.

These aspects are part of the comedic interplay with Jerry Seinfeld and the other actors that lead to the great success of the television show Seinfeld. Plaintiff Michael Costanza points to various similarities between himself and the character George Costanza to bolster his claim that his name and likeness are being appropriated. He claims that, like him, George Costanza is short, fat, bald, that he knew Jerry Seinfeld from college purportedly as the character George Costanza did and they both came from Queens. Plaintiff Michael Costanza asserts that the self-centered nature and unreliability of the character George Costanza are attributed to him and this humiliates him.

FALSE LIGHT AND PRIVACY

* * * In New York State, there is no common-law right to privacy (*see, Freihofer v Hearst Corp.*, at 140) and any relief must be sought under the statute (Civil Rights Law §§ 50, 51).

CIVIL RIGHTS LAW §§ 50, 51

The court now turns to the assertion that plaintiff Michael Costanza's name and likeness are being appropriated without his written consent. This claim faces several separate obstacles. First, defendants assert that plaintiff Michael Costanza has waived any claim by appearing on the show. The statute clearly provides that written consent is necessary for use of a person's name or likeness (*see, Kane v. Orange County Publs.*, 232 A.D.2d 526 [2d Dept. 1996]). However, defendants note the limited nature of the relief provided by Civil Rights Law §§ 50 and 51. It extends only to the use of a name or likeness for trade or advertising (*see, Freihofer v Hearst Corp.*, at 140). The sort of commercial exploitation prohibited and compensable if violated is solicitation for patronage (*see, Delan v CBS, Inc.*, 91 A.D.2d 255 [2d Dept. 1983]). In a case similar to this lawsuit involving the play "Six Degrees of Separation," it was held that "works of fiction and satire do not fall within the narrow scope of the statutory phrases 'advertising' and 'trade' " (*Hampton v Guare*, 195 A.D.2d 366 [1st Dept. 1993]). The Seinfeld television program was a fictional comedic presentation. It does not fall within the scope of trade or advertising (*see, Freihofer v. Hearst Corp., supra; Hampton v. Guare, supra*).

Plaintiff Michael Costanza's claim for violation of Civil Rights Law §§ 50 and 51 must be dismissed. * * *

DEFAMATION

Plaintiff Michael Costanza's final claim involves the reports that defendant Larry David or individuals on his behalf stated that he was a "flagrant opportunist who barely knew Jerry (Seinfeld) less than a year." An exhibit to the defendants' moving papers is a copy of a book by plaintiff Michael Costanza entitled "The Real Seinfeld." The book was published at the time of the final episode of the show Seinfeld. The use of the phrase "flagrant opportunist" in the context of the circumstances under which it was uttered is a statement of opinion (*see, Shinn v Williamson*, 225 A.D.2d 605 [2d Dept. 1996]). This claim of defamation is also dismissed. * * *

Essentially, plaintiff was informed that his case was based on nothing. While a program about nothing can be successful, a lawsuit must have more substance. The court awards sanctions in the sum of $2,500 each against plaintiff Michael Costanza and his attorney.

Note

A copy of this decision has been faxed to counsel for plaintiff Michael Costanza and defendants. The court will not entertain any application for reargument, review or stay and any such relief should be sought through the appellate process.

1. Television series are based on books, scripts, developed treatments, and ideas. A production company will option rights for a certain period of time needed to sell the property to a network, syndicator, cable program service, or group of television stations. Only one in ten properties optioned ever become a pilot; then only one in ten pilots becomes a series. The time of the initial option period will be from six months to two years. The option fee could vary from a few hundred dollars to $25,000. A production company needs to be able to make and distribute TV episodes. The company also may want international television rights, international home video rights, rights to produce merchandise and books, and the option to do spin-off series. The production company may also request interactive rights. * * * The interactive rights include exploitation on CD–ROM, similar interactive digital formats, and computer on-line rights. Mathew Bender, *Part III TELEVISION: Chapter 62 LITERARY RIGHTS—OPTION AND PURCHASE* (2003).

H. TELEVISION NEWS

Network news is highly competitive. Local news lead-ins can help or hurt the network program. Local news is as competitive as the network news that follows. Ratings are closely watched and the programs are adjusted to improve the ratings. Networks employ anchors who viewers feel comfortable inviting into their homes on a nightly basis. Trusted anchors and reporters build a following that influences people to watch the same news channel on a daily basis. A strong news program gives the network an opportunity to advertise its upcoming programs and can boost the ratings for the evening.

1. EMPLOYMENT AND AGE DISCRIMINATION

Don Henley wrote about "that bubble headed bleach blond that comes on at five," in his hit song *Dirty Laundry*. Local and network news channels regularly choose their on-air personalities for their looks. KABC in Los Angeles has had a history of employing former Miss America contestants (and winners) as anchors. Christine Lund was the KABC anchor that Don Henley was referring to in his song. Because of the desire of news directors to deliver the most aesthetically appealing programming, young, good-looking anchors and reporters are preferred over their older counterparts. The desire to keep a news program fresh and young has created litigation.

MINSHALL v. McGRAW HILL BROADCASTING COMPANY, INC.

United States Court of Appeals, Tenth Circuit, 2003.
323 F.3d 1273.

MURPHY, Circuit Judge.

I. INTRODUCTION

David Minshall ("Minshall") filed this suit against his former employer, McGraw–Hill Broadcasting Company ("McGraw–Hill"), alleging that McGraw–Hill unlawfully discriminated against him on the basis of age in violation of the Age Discrimination in Employment Act ("ADEA"), 29 U.S.C. §§ 621–634, and Colo. Rev. Stat. §§ 24–34–401 to–406. Minshall also alleged a claim for intentional infliction of emotional distress. * * *

After a trial on the merits of Minshall's discrimination claims, a jury returned a verdict in his favor finding that McGraw–Hill discriminated against him on the basis of age. Answering special interrogatories, the jury also found that McGraw–Hill's conduct was willful. The jury awarded Minshall back pay in the amount of $212,326.00 and found that the award of back pay should not be reduced by any failure to mitigate damages. * * * In a post-trial order, the district court awarded Minshall front pay in the amount of $137,500.00. The court also awarded $212,326.00 in liquidated damages and $153,958.00 in attorney's fees. * * *

McGraw–Hill appeals the district court's denial of its motions for JMOL, new trial, and to alter or amend the judgment. Exercising jurisdiction pursuant to 28 U.S.C. § 1291, this court affirms the judgment.

II. BACKGROUND

McGraw–Hill does business as KMGH–TV ("KMGH") in Denver, Colorado. Minshall worked as an on-air investigative reporter with KMGH from 1980 until KMGH decided not to renew his contract on March 10, 1997. At the time KMGH decided not to renew his contract, Minshall was over 50 years old.

At trial, evidence was introduced that in 1995, Minshall violated an agreement to protect the anonymity of a source by allowing a document to be aired showing the source's name. McGraw–Hill introduced evidence that Minshall appeared visibly intoxicated while accepting an award for a series on drunk driving at a 1995 Emmy Awards ceremony. Minshall testified that he apologized for his conduct at the Emmy Awards ceremony and admitted that he was partially at fault for the disclosure of the source's identity. KMGH did not threaten to terminate Minshall over either of these incidents.

In April 1996, KMGH hired Melissa Klinzing ("Klinzing") as News Director. To promote KMGH's news programs and boost ratings, Klinzing initiated a news format known as "Real Life, Real News." Klinzing designed "Real Life, Real News" with the intention of reaching a younger demographic than that which historically watched KMGH news programs. To achieve this goal, the cosmetic look of the news programs was altered. Klinzing considered the physical appearances of the on-air anchors and reporters in making changes to the overall appearance of the news programs.

Under Klinzing's direction, anchors Ernie Bjorkman ("Bjorkman") and Bertha Lynn ("Lynn"), individuals over the age of 40, were removed from the ten o'clock nightly news and replaced by anchor Natalie Pujo ("Pujo") who was between 20 and 30 years old. Both Bjorkman and Lynn testified that they believed they were removed from the ten o'clock nightly news because of their age. Ron Allen ("Allen"), a weatherman at KMGH over the age of 40, testified that he was also given increasingly less favorable job assignments at KMGH. At trial, Minshall also introduced evidence of several age-related statements made by Klinzing in reference to the news format, Minshall, and other on-air news personalities who were over the age of 40. McGraw–Hill, however, presented evidence that reporters Bill Clarke ("Clarke") and Paul Reinertson ("Reinertson"), who were over 40 years old, received no less on-air time after Klinzing was employed at KMGH.

Minshall's contract was set to expire in August 1996. Executive Producer Kathleen Sullivan ("Sullivan") testified that she recommended Klinzing not renew his employment. McGraw–Hill presented evidence that Minshall submitted several stories late and submitted a report during a ratings period that was unacceptable. Clarke, a reporter and news anchor, testified that Minshall's scripts were easily recognized for being incomplete and for containing factual errors.

Anchors Bjorkman and Lynn, however, testified that they were of the opinion that Minshall was a good reporter. Lynn testified that his scripts were no worse than other reporters. Allen testified that Minshall was a motivated and tenacious reporter. Minshall testified that, prior to Klinzing's employment, he had never been informed that his script writing or punctuality was a problem.

Klinzing renewed Minshall's contract for six months in August 1996. She, however, wrote Minshall a detailed memorandum summarizing her expectations for his improvement. Klinzing wrote, "At the end of the 6 months, if you're performing up to expected levels, we'll talk about a new contract." By letter, Minshall accepted the conditions of the August 1996 memorandum and the six-month contract.

McGraw–Hill presented evidence that, after accepting the six-month contract, Minshall sometimes failed to attend morning staff meetings, failed to suggest ideas for new stories, and finished assignments immediately before deadlines. * * *

At the end of the six-month contract, Klinzing recommended that Minshall's contract not be renewed. On March 10, 1997, KMGH decided not to renew his contract. KMGH instructed Klinzing not to interview anyone under the age of 40 to replace Minshall.

After KMGH decided not to renew his contract, Minshall chose not to search for employment as an investigative reporter outside of Denver because he did not want to relocate his family. Minshall, however, made telephone calls and sent letters to other television stations in Denver. After failing to obtain employment as an investigative reporter, he attempted to secure employment in public relations. A few months later, Minshall was hired by BVP Media to teach media training. At BVP Media, he earned approximately $70,000 in salary and benefits. Minshall, however, quit this job after approximately one year to work as a self-employed media trainer.

III. Discussion * * *

1. Age Discrimination Claims

McGraw–Hill argues that Minshall failed to present sufficient evidence to establish that it discriminated against him on the basis of age when deciding not to renew his contract. *See Fallis v. Kerr–McGee Corp.,* 944 F.2d 743, 744 (10th Cir.1991) (holding that after a full trial on the merits of plaintiff's discrimination claim, the remaining "single overarching issue [is] whether plaintiff adduced sufficient evidence to warrant a jury's determination that adverse employment action was taken against him on the basis of age"). After reviewing the record as a whole, this court is satisfied that Minshall offered sufficient evidence on which the jury could reasonably conclude McGraw–Hill's decision not to renew his contract was impermissibly based on his age. * * *

Allen testified that Klinzing told him not to "wear a tie" and to "try to go with a younger look." Allen also testified that Klinzing said she didn't care if older people were watching television and that she was disgusted when she saw "an old fart" on television without a shirt. Minshall testified that Klinzing constantly talked to him about "a younger presentation, a more youthful presentation," and that she wanted "sexier stories" that would appeal to a younger audience. Minshall and Lynn both testified that Klinzing asked them about their ages. Scott Sobel, a former reporter and anchor at KMGH, testified that Klinzing said Allen was "too fucking old" for the news format. Finally, Minshall introduced evidence that Klinzing said, in reference to her father, "old people should die." * * *

McGraw–Hill also argues that the statements attributed to Klinzing were stray comments and constitute an insufficient basis from which to draw an inference of age discrimination. * * * Because Minshall presented evidence that Klinzing's decision not to renew his contract was motivated by her desire to reduce the presence of on-air reporters over 40 years old under the news format, however, there was a nexus between Klinzing's statement regarding Allen and her decision not to renew

Minshall's contract. Further, Klinzing's statements regarding older people watching or being broadcast on television were not stray comments. Klinzing testified that she considered the physical appearance of the on-air reporters in making changes to the overall appearance of the news program. As stated above, there was a nexus between Klinzing's statements made regarding the news format and her decision not to renew Minshall's contract. Similarly, there was a nexus between these statements and the decision not to renew Minshall's contract. * * * Viewing the record as a whole, this court is satisfied that the jury reasonably concluded that KMGH unlawfully discriminated against Minshall on the basis of age when it decided not to renew his contract. * * *

IV. CONCLUSION

For the foregoing reasons, this court affirms the district court's denial of McGraw–Hill's motions for JMOL, new trial, and to alter or amend the judgment for front pay and back pay.

Note

1. For Hollywood's take on television news, watch the movies *Network* and *Broadcast News*. Watch *Network* first.

2. TELEVISION NEWS VERSUS THE RIGHT TO PRIVACY

The struggle between the first amendment and the right to privacy has been litigated many times. The tension is exacerbated by the blurring line between news and entertainment. Reality shows that focus on "newsworthy" tragedy strain the definition of news. The public seems to have an insatiable appetite for personal disaster stories, as long the story involves someone else. The need to preserve personal dignity versus the public's need to know make the decisions difficult. As the case law on the subject evolves, a line is developing; not a bright line, but a line nevertheless.

MILLER v. NBC

California Court of Appeals, 1986.
187 Cal.App.3d 1463, 232 Cal.Rptr. 668.

HANSON, Judge.

* * * The events giving rise to this action occurred on the night of October 30, 1979, when an NBC television camera crew entered the apartment of Dave and Brownie Miller in Los Angeles, without their consent, to film the activities of Los Angeles Fire Department paramedics called to the Miller home to administer life-saving techniques to Dave Miller, who had suffered a heart attack in his bedroom. The NBC television camera crew not only filmed the paramedics' attempts to assist Miller, but NBC used the film on its nightly news without obtaining anyone's consent. In addition, after it had received complaints from both Brownie Miller and her daughter, Marlene Miller Belloni, NBC later

used portions of the film in a commercial advertising an NBC "mini-documentary" about the paramedics' work.

The paramedics were unable to successfully resuscitate Dave Miller; he died that October evening at Mount Sinai Hospital. His widow, Brownie, and daughter, Marlene (hereinafter, sometimes plaintiffs or plaintiff wife and plaintiff daughter), brought suit against defendants National Broadcasting Company (NBC), doing business as KNBC, a Los Angeles television station, Ruben Norte (Norte), a producer employed by NBC, and the City of Los Angeles (City) for damages, alleging trespass, invasion of privacy, and infliction of emotional distress against all defendants. After considerable discovery and amendment of pleadings, the trial court granted defendants' motion for summary judgment. Plaintiffs appeal. We affirm in part and reverse in part. * * * *On June 20, 1985*, the superior court denied plaintiffs' motion for a new trial. * * *

THE SCENARIO

Defendant Norte, an NBC news field producer in charge of new stories and projects, was assigned a minidocumentary on fire department paramedics and their work. The mini-documentary was to run during the five weekdays for two weeks, airing for five minutes at the end of the 6 p.m. news, and about half that time on the 11 p.m. news. The first week concerned the paramedics' work generally. The second week focused on the administering of CPR by a paramedic team. * * *

Norte contacted Tony De Domenico, the Los Angeles City Fire Department medical representative, and discussed the feasibility of having a film crew accompany a unit of paramedics, and was advised that it would be acceptable with the City. (Norte in his deposition testified that he did not discuss with De Domenico or anyone else a requirement of getting permission from any of the persons whose home the film crew would enter.) Norte testified that "My intent was to film and document whatever their work was and whatever it happened to be when we filmed." He told the paramedics' media representative, Brown, that he wanted to film something "dramatic." He personally accompanied his film crew, consisting of a cameraman and a soundman, and between 10 and 15 times entered private residences with the film crew while filming with the paramedics. He testified that about half of the time someone asked what they were doing, that he always responded, and that no one objected. Norte also testified that it was standard practice in the television industry to secure consent before entering someone's home to film, but that he had not considered the necessity for such permission when accompanying the paramedics on their rounds.

Turning specifically to the instant case, Norte testified that his crew was with the paramedic unit which was responding to a call that Mr. Miller had suffered an apparent coronary. Before proceeding to the Miller home, the paramedic unit had responded to at least four other calls, including an overdose case and an automobile accident. Norte rode in back of the paramedics' ambulance with Stan Riley (carrying a film-tape recorder) and John Parson (carrying a camera). When they arrived at the Miller home, all three NBC personnel immediately followed the two paramedics into the apartment and the bedroom, where they filmed the paramedics performing CPR on Dave Miller. At no time did Norte or any other NBC employee seek or obtain consent to follow the paramedic team into the residence. The cameraman and soundman left with the paramedics, who placed the heart attack victim on a gurney and took him to Mount Sinai Hospital, where he subsequently died.

Although Norte later learned that the coronary victim had died, he did not attempt to ascertain the exact location of the filming or the identity of the deceased's relatives. He did not believe that was necessary, because "there was no identity made of the victim verbally or visually [on film]." Norte, while supervising the editing of the film, did observe a tattoo on the victim's arm, but it showed for a "couple of frames, couple of seconds" and he stated that he "would be surprised if anybody could identify him from the film that was aired."

While Norte conceded it was normal procedure to get permission to enter a house, because of the emergency situation "there was no one to ask."

Norte testified that to his knowledge the only time the footage was shown containing this heart attack victim was on the 6 p.m. news on November 19 and a shorter (cut down) version on the 11 p.m. news. He was not aware that some footage was used as a lead commercial for the following week's series on CPR.

Norte received a telephone call on November 19 after the 6 p.m. news from a woman who said she thought the person in the film was her father, who had passed away recently. Norte told her he was sorry to hear her father passed away. Following the telephone call, he did nothing to ascertain the identity of the victim, but did review the film footage and concluded that it did not show enough of the person that he could be identified.

Plaintiff wife's deposition was taken under oath on September 22, 1983, and she testified substantially as follows: that on October 30, 1979, she and her husband Dave Miller resided in apartment 3, 8211 Blackburn; that at about 10 p.m. on that date, Dave Miller collapsed onto the bedroom floor; and that she screamed and a neighbor came and called the paramedics. Although aware that the paramedics arrived and were administering CPR to her husband, she was completely unaware that the NBC filming unit had arrived and left with them. A police officer who had arrived escorted her to another room while the paramedics were working on her husband. She at no time asked anyone to leave the apartment and no one asked her permission to film the paramedics.

Plaintiff Miller saw the film of her husband and the paramedics weeks after his death; at 10:30 a.m., while she was "flipping" channels looking for a "soap opera" to watch, suddenly the film was shown. She screamed and turned the television off. That was the only time she saw the film.

Plaintiff Miller also received telephone calls from friends who had seen the sequence; the calls upset her. She called Norte only once and said: "What nerve did you have to come into my home and invade my privacy and do the things that you did to disturb my whole household." Norte's answer was, "I am sorry. I am very sorry." She "told him what nerve he had to come in and to do what he did. He was—my husband was a very private person. He would never have liked anything like that to have been on television." Norte's answer was, "I'm sorry. I'm very sorry." * * *

ISSUES

In addition to identification of causes of action, a principle issue in this litigation is the extent to which the First Amendment to the United States Constitution and article I, section 2 of the California Constitution (hereinafter collectively referred to as First Amendment rights, on occasion) protect newsgathering of this kind from civil liability.

DISCUSSION

I.   *Trespass: Plaintiff Wife's First Cause of Action*

Plaintiff wife has alleged, and it is undisputed, that defendants made an unauthorized entry into her apartment on October 30, 1979. Common law defined such entry as a trespass. "The essence of the cause of action for trespass is an 'unauthorized entry' onto the land of another. Such invasions are characterized as intentional torts, regardless of the actor's motivation." * * * Under California law, the "consequences" flowing from an intentional tort such as a trespass may include emotional distress either accompanied by a physical injury to the person or to the land. *See, e.g., Acadia, California, Ltd.* v. *Herbert,* 54 Cal. 2d 328, 337–38 (1960). * * *

In the case at bench, the "consequences" would include plaintiff wife's anguish, i.e., her emotional distress when NBC broadcast her husband's dying moments. Thus, pursuant to common law principles accepted in California law, plaintiff wife has stated a cause of action for trespass unless First Amendment rights preclude it. * * *

II.   *Invasion of Privacy—Plaintiff Wife's Second Cause of Action*

Plaintiff wife has alleged in her complaint a trespass which also constituted the tort of intrusion, one of a group of torts which comprise privacy invasion. * * * The case at bench involves the first category of privacy rights, the right to be secure from *intrusion.* Restatement Second of Torts, section 652B declares that "[one] who intentionally intrudes, physically or otherwise, upon the solitude or seclusion of another or his private affairs or concerns, is subject to liability to the other for invasion of his privacy, *if the intrusion would be highly offensive to a reasonable person.*" (Italics added.) * * *

Here, reasonable people could construe the lack of restraint and sensitivity NBC producer Norte and his crew displayed as a cavalier disregard for ordinary citizens' rights of privacy, or, as an indication that they considered such rights of no particular importance.

In our view, reasonable people could regard the NBC camera crew's intrusion into Dave Miller's bedroom at a time of vulnerability and confusion occasioned by his seizure as "highly offensive" conduct, thus meeting the limitation on a privacy cause of action Restatement of Torts, section 652B imposes. * * * In the instant case, the NBC camera crew, the uninvited media guests, not only invaded the Millers' bedroom without Dave Miller's consent, they also invaded the home and privacy of his plaintiff wife, Brownie Miller, referred to by Norte in his deposition as "a woman in the hallway." Not only was the "woman in the hallway" Dave Miller's wife, the hallway was a part of her home, a place where NBC had no right to be without her consent. * * *

III. *Plaintiff Wife's Cause of Action for the Intentional Infliction of Emotional Distress*

Plaintiff wife seeks redress for the intentional infliction of emotional distress by defendants. "The elements of a prima facie case for the tort of intentional infliction of emotional distress were summarized in *Cervantez* v. *J.C. Penney Co.* (1979) 24 Cal.3d 579, 593, * * * as follows: '(1) extreme and outrageous conduct by the defendant with the intention of causing, or reckless disregard [for] the probability of causing, emotional distress; (2) the plaintiff's suffering severe or extreme emotional distress; and (3) actual and proximate causation of the emotional distress by the defendant's outrageous conduct.'" *Davidson* v. *City of Westminster,* 32 Cal. 3d 197, 209 (1982). * * *

The key to analysis of the facts before us was the trespass committed by the NBC camera crew in crossing the threshold of a private residence without, apparently, even a moment's hesitation. The record contains no evidence that crew members, including the producer, Norte, had any specific malicious or evil purpose. Here, the record discloses that the NBC camera crew apparently devoted little or no thought whatsoever to its obvious transgression. * * *

With respect to plaintiff wife's cause of action, we leave it to a reasonable jury whether the defendants' conduct was "outrageous." Not only was her home invaded without her consent, but the last moments of her dying husband's life were filmed and broadcast to the world without any regard for the subsequent protestations of both plaintiffs to the defendants. Again, the defendants' lack of response to these protestations suggests an alarming absence of sensitivity and civility. * * *

It is immaterial that in defendants' judgment (expressed by Norte in his deposition testimony) that upon review of the film in question, the body of Dave Miller was not identifiable *by the average viewer*. Plaintiff wife was not an average viewer, a member of the general viewing public;

the film depicted her house and her husband, and that fact was known to her.

She has stated a cause of action for the intentional infliction of emotional distress unless precluded by the defense of First Amendment privilege. * * *

V. Constitutional Rights

Defendants have vigorously defended against liability in the instant case, relying, in addition to *Flynn*, on two propositions: (1) that by calling for the paramedics, the Millers impliedly consented to the entry of the NBC camera crew and (2) plaintiff wife's cause of action was precluded by NBC's constitutionally recognized and protected First Amendment right to gather news.

The first proposition is devoid of merit. One seeking emergency medical attention does not thereby "open the door" for persons without any clearly identifiable and justifiable official reason who may wish to enter the premises where the medical aid is being administered. In *Dietemann v. Time, Inc., supra*, 449 F.2d 245, the court held that news gatherers cannot immunize their conduct by purporting to act jointly with public officials such as the police or paramedics. The clear line of demarcation between the public interest served by public officials and that served by private business must not be obscured.

The second argument, however, merits discussion. As a preliminary matter, we note that conceptually speaking, as noted First Amendment scholar Melville R. Nimmer has stated, with respect to the Prosser categories of privacy rights, both "intrusion" and "appropriation" may be "put to one side.... Intrusion does not raise first amendment difficulties since its perpetration does not involve speech or other expression. It occurs by virtue of the physical or mechanical observation of the private affairs of another, and not by the publication of such observations. The appropriation form of privacy invasion probably also does not raise first amendment problems, although here speech and other expression is involved." Nimmer, *The Right to Speak From Times to Time: First Amendment Theory Applied to Libel and Misapplied to Privacy*, 56 Cal. L. Rev. 935, 957 (1968). * * *

We assume, for the purpose of discussion here, that public education about paramedics, as well as about the use of cardio-pulmonary resuscitation (CPR) as a life-saving technique almost anyone might either need or be called upon to administer to another, qualifies as "news."

The First Amendment of the United States Constitution declares that "Congress shall make no law ... abridging the freedom of speech, or of the press...." The protection afforded the disseminators of the news, be they reporters, broadcasters or television newspersons, has been perceived throughout our history as of the utmost importance in maintaining a free society. The protection extends not only to prohibit direct state action, but must be considered when any private citizen seeks to impose civil liability for invasion of privacy by the press or media through access to state courts. *New York Times Co.* v. *Sullivan*, 376 U.S. 254 (1964). * * *

Where the United States Supreme Court has addressed the problem of providing adequate constitutional protection for newsgathering, however, it has been careful to point out that the protection is limited, rather than absolute. *Branzburg*, for example, cited with approval the statement that " '[the] publisher of a newspaper has no special immunity from the application of general laws. He has no special privilege to invade the rights and liberties of others.' *Associated Press* v. *NLRB*, 301 U.S. 103, 132–133 (1937)." * * *

Nicholson notes that the protection extended for newsgathering does not mandate "that the press and its representatives are immune from liability for crimes and torts committed in news gathering activities simply because the ultimate goal is to obtain publishable material...." *Nicholson* v. *McClatchy Newspapers*, 177 Cal. App. 3d 509, 518.

We conclude, in the case before us, that the obligation not to make unauthorized entry into the private premises of individuals like the Millers does not place an impermissible burden on news gatherers, nor is it likely to have a chilling effect on the exercise of First Amendment rights. * * * Others besides the media have rights, and those rights prevail when they are considered in the context of the events at the Miller home on October 30, 1979.

In summary, we hold that plaintiff wife, Brownie Miller, has stated three causes of action against defendants and that since there are triable issues of material fact, the trial court erred in awarding summary judgment to defendants as to plaintiff wife, Brownie Miller. * * * The judgment as to plaintiff Miller's causes of action is reversed. * * * Plaintiff Miller is to recover her costs.

Notes

1. Mickey Dora was a famous surfer in the 1950s in Malibu Beach, California. Dora sued Frontline Video, Inc., for common law and statutory appropriation of name or likeness in *Dora v. Frontline Video, Inc.*, 15 Cal.App.4th 536, 18 Cal.Rptr.2d 790 (2d Dist.1993). The appeals court affirmed the ruling in favor of Frontline Video. In 1987, Frontline Video was making a documentary called "The Legends of Malibu." This documentary featured video footage of Dora surfing simultaneously with an audio interview and some photographs. Dora said he did not approve the use of these materials for the documentary. However, the court ruled the program had public interest and the footage was voluntarily taken while he was at the beach, a public place where he waived his privacy rights. Therefore, Frontline Video did not need Dora's permission to include his name, likeness, and voice in the documentary.

2. For an excellent piece on the tension between the right to privacy and the first amendment, see David A. Elder, Neville L. Johnson & Brian A. Rishwain, *Establishing Constitutional Malice for Defamation and Priva-*

cy/False Light Claims When Hidden Cameras and Deception Are Used by the News Gatherer, 22 Loy. Ent. L.R. 327 (No. 2, 2001–2002).

END 9.1

Chapter 8

TELEVISION IDEAS & COPYRIGHT PROTECTION

A. IDEA PROTECTION

Ideas are the lifeblood of Hollywood. As discussed in Chapter 7, every show on television begins with someone's idea. Ideas can range from adapting a novel for a show, to remaking an old show, to a completely new and novel concept. Because an idea cannot be copyrighted, protecting an idea can be a difficult proposition. Ideas are typically in the public domain, free for anyone to use. The more general the idea, the more difficult it is to protect. Detailed ideas are more likely to be protected from use by another, but there is no guarantee. With copyright protection generally unavailable, ideas have to be protected by using a contracts theory. Ideas can be protected when they are presented in a pitch meeting with a creative executive. The more formal the pitch meeting, the more likely the courts will imply a contract to force the company that used the idea to compensate the idea originator.

MURRAY v. NBC

United States Court of Appeals, Second Circuit, 1988.
844 F.2d 988.

ALTIMARI, Circuit Judge.

It was almost a generation ago that a young comedian named Bill Cosby became the first black entertainer to star in a dramatic network television series. That program, *I Spy*, earned Cosby national recognition as an actor, including three Emmy Awards (1966, 1967 and 1968) for best performance in a dramatic series, and critical acclaim for the portrayal of a character without regard to the actor's race. Although keenly aware of the significance of his achievement in breaking the color line on network television, Cosby set his sights then on "accomplish[ing] something more significant for the Negro on TV." In an interview in 1965, he envisioned a different approach to the situation comedy genre made popular by *The Dick Van Dyke Show*. The *Daily News* described Cosby's "dream" series as not unlike other situation comedies. There'll

373

be the usual humorous exchanges between husband and wife.... Warmth and domestic cheerfulness will pervade the entire program.

Everything on the screen will be familiar to TV viewers. But this series will be radically different. Everyone in it will be a Negro. * * * "I'm interested in proving there's no difference between people," [explained Cosby]. "My series would take place in a middle-income Negro neighborhood. People who really don't know Negroes would find on this show that they're just like everyone else."

Nearly twenty years later, on September 20, 1984, Cosby's dream for a "color-blind" family series materialized with the premier of *The Cosby Show*—a situation comedy about a family known as the Huxtables. Bill Cosby stars in the leading role as Heathcliff ("Cliff") Huxtable together with his TV wife Clair and their five children.

Plaintiff-appellant Hwesu Murray, an employee of defendant-appellee ("NBC"), claims in the instant case that in 1980, four years prior to the premier of *The Cosby Show* on NBC's television network, he proposed to NBC a "new" idea for a half-hour situation comedy starring Bill Cosby. In a written proposal submitted to NBC, Murray described his series called "Father's Day" as "wholesome ... entertainment" which will focus upon the family life of a Black American family.... The leading character will be the father, ... a devoted family man and a compassionate, proud, authority figure. * * *

On this appeal from an order of the United States District Court for the Southern District of New York (*Cedarbaum, J.*) granting defendants-appellees' motion for summary judgment, we are asked to determine whether, under New York law, plaintiff has a legally protectible interest in his idea which he maintains was used by NBC in developing *The Cosby Show*. Because we agree with the district court's conclusion that, under New York law, lack of novelty in an idea precludes plaintiff from maintaining a cause of action to prevent its unauthorized use, we affirm the district court's order granting summary judgment and dismissing the complaint.

BACKGROUND

Plaintiff Hwesu S. Murray has been employed in the television industry for the past ten years. Murray holds a Bachelor of Arts degree in English and graduate degrees in broadcast journalism and law. In 1979, defendant-appellee NBC hired Murray as a Unit Manager and financial analyst in its sports division. A year later, plaintiff contacted an NBC official outside of NBC Sports about some "extracurricular" ideas he had for future television programs, and the official apparently instructed him to submit his proposals in writing. Soon thereafter, in June 1980, plaintiff submitted five written proposals, one of which was entitled "Father's Day." Murray allegedly informed NBC that if it were interested in any of the proposals, he expected to be named executive producer and to receive appropriate credit and compensation as the creator of the eventual program. Plaintiff also allegedly told NBC that his ideas were being submitted in confidence.

Murray's proposal for "Father's Day" is the subject matter of this action. The NBC official who originally had requested it encouraged Murray to "flesh out" his proposal and submit it to Josh Kane, then an NBC vice-president and a top official with NBC Entertainment, the division of NBC responsible for network television programming. Plaintiff thereupon submitted to Kane an expanded proposal for "Father's Day." In a two-page memorandum dated November 1, 1980, Murray first suggested that Bill Cosby play the part of the father. At that time, plaintiff also made several other casting suggestions, including roles for a working spouse and five children, and again indicated that the proposed series would "combine humor with serious situations in a manner similar to that of the old *Dick Van Dyke Show*" but "with a Black perspective." * * * NBC apparently decided not to pursue Murray's proposal. On November 21, 1980, Kane returned the "Father's Day" submission to plaintiff and informed him that "we are not interested in pursuing [its] development at this time."

Four years later, in the fall of 1984, *The Cosby Show* premiered on NBC. *The Cosby Show* is a half-hour weekly situation comedy series about everyday life in an upper middle-class black family in New York City. The father, played by Bill Cosby, is a physician, and the mother is a lawyer. In its first season, *The Cosby Show* soared to the top of the Nielsen ratings and has become one of the most popular programs in television history. * * *

Less than a month after viewing the premier, plaintiff wrote to NBC to advise it that *The Cosby Show* had been derived from his idea for "Father's Day." In January 1985, NBC responded through its Law Department, stating its position that " 'Father's Day' played absolutely no role in the development of 'The Cosby Show' . . . [since m]uch of the substance and style of 'The Cosby Show' is an outgrowth of the humor and style developed by Bill Cosby throughout his career." NBC further maintained that *The Cosby Show* was developed and produced by The Carsey–Werner Company ("Carsey–Werner"), an independent production company and the executive producers of the series.

In his complaint, plaintiff claimed that *The Cosby Show's* portrayal of a strong black family in a nonstereotypical manner is the essence of "Father's Day," and "it is that portrayal of Black middle-class life that originated with plaintiff." Murray also alleged that Josh Kane showed plaintiff's "Father's Day" proposal to his superiors at NBC, including defendant-appellee Brandon Tartikoff, President of NBC Entertainment. Tartikoff, together with Cosby and Carsey–Werner, have been credited with the creation and development of *The Cosby Show*. Plaintiff maintains that NBC and Tartikoff deliberately deceived plaintiff into believing that NBC had no interest in "Father's Day" and then proceeded to develop and eventually produce plaintiff's idea as *The Cosby Show*. * * *

In a decision dated July 15, 1987, 671 F.Supp. 236 (S.D.N.Y.), the district court considered whether plaintiff's idea was "property" that could be subject to legal protection. Since the parties agreed that New York law applied to plaintiff's claims, the district court proceeded to analyze defendants' motion for summary judgment in light of the New York Court of Appeals decision in *Downey v. General Foods Corp.*, 31 N.Y.2d 56 (1972). * * * The district court, therefore, determined that the "sole issue" before it was the novelty of plaintiff's "Father's Day" proposal, and accordingly assumed, for purposes of defendants' motion, that defendants in fact used plaintiff's idea in the development of *The Cosby Show*. * * *

In focusing on the novelty of plaintiff's proposal, the district court determined that Murray's idea was not subject to legal protection from unauthorized use because "Father's Day" merely combined two ideas which had been circulating in the industry for a number of years—namely, the family situation comedy, which was a standard formula, and the casting of black actors in non-stereotypical roles.

The district court found that, to the extent "Father's Day," in Murray's words, "may well resemble 'Father Knows Best' and 'The Dick Van Dyke Show,'" it could not be considered novel. In addition, the portrayal of a black family in nonstereotypical roles, according to the court, precluded a finding of novelty because 1) the television networks already had cast some black actors, including Bill Cosby himself, e.g., *I Spy* (1965–68), *The Bill Cosby Show* (1969–71), and *Fat Albert and the Cosby Kids* (1972–79), in such roles, and 2) the idea of combining the family situation comedy theme with an all-black cast already had been suggested publicly by Bill Cosby some twenty years before the creation of *The Cosby Show*. The district court also determined that Murray's casting of Bill Cosby in the lead role in "Father's Day" was no mere coincidence. Rather, it was "further evidence that Cosby is connected—even in plaintiff's mind—with the concept that plaintiff seeks to monopolize." * * *

As the district court recognized, the dispositive issue in this case is whether plaintiff's idea is entitled to legal protection. Plaintiff points to "unique"—"even revolutionary"—aspects of his "Father's Day" proposal that he claims demonstrate "genuine novelty and invention." * * * Murray claims that the novelty of his idea subsequently was confirmed by the media and the viewing public which instantly recognized the "unique" and "revolutionary" portrayal of a black family on *The Cosby Show*.

We certainly do not dispute the fact that the portrayal of a nonstereotypical black family on television was indeed a breakthrough. Nevertheless, that breakthrough represents the achievement of what many black Americans, including Bill Cosby and plaintiff himself, have recognized for many years—namely, the need for a more positive, fair and realistic portrayal of blacks on television. While NBC's decision to broadcast *The Cosby Show* unquestionably was innovative in the sense that an intact, nonstereotypical black family had never been portrayed on television before, the mere fact that such a decision had not been made before does not necessarily mean that the idea for the program is itself novel. *See Educational Sales Programs*, 317 N.Y.S.2d at 843 ("not every 'good idea' is a legally protectible idea"). * * *

Appellant would have us believe that by interpreting New York law as we do, we are in effect condoning the theft of ideas. On the contrary, ideas that reflect "genuine novelty and invention" are fully protected against unauthorized use. *Educational Sales Programs*, 317 N.Y.S.2d at 844. But those ideas that are not novel "are in the public domain and may freely be used by anyone with impunity." *Ed Graham Productions*, 347 N.Y.S.2d at 769. Since such non-novel ideas are not protectible as property, they cannot be stolen.

In assessing whether an idea is in the public domain, the central issue is the uniqueness of the creation. Murray insists that there is at least a question of fact as to the novelty of "Father's Day" because *The Cosby Show* is indisputably unique. * * *

We disagree. The Carsey–Werner contract contemplates a fully-produced television series. The contract refers to, *inter alia*, the program format, titles, set designs, theme music, stories, scripts, and art work as well as to the "program idea." Taken together, these elements no doubt would be considered original and therefore protectible as property. On the other hand, we think it equally apparent that the mere idea for a situation comedy about a nonstereotypical black family—whether that idea is in the hands of Murray, Carsey–Werner, NBC, or anyone else—is not novel and thus may be used with impunity. * * * Consequently, we find that New York law requires that an idea be original or novel in order for it to be protected as property. *See Downey*, 334 N.Y.S.2d at 877. Since, as has already been shown, plaintiff's proposal for "Father's Day" was lacking in novelty and originality, we conclude that the district court correctly granted defendants' motion for summary judgment. * * *

Having determined that plaintiff's idea is not property under New York law, we turn now to a consideration of the district court's dismissal of the various claims in the complaint.

A. *State law claims*

"[W]hen one submits an idea to another, no promise to pay for its use may be implied, and no asserted agreement enforced, if the elements of novelty and originality are absent. . . ." *Downey*, 334 N.Y.S.2d at 877. As the district court recognized, non-novel ideas do not constitute property. As a result, there can be no cause of action for unauthorized use of Murray's proposal since it was not unlawful for defendants to use a non-novel idea. We conclude therefore that the district court properly dismissed plaintiff's state law claims for breach of implied contract, misappropriation, conversion, and unjust enrichment. * * *

Similarly, plaintiff's fraud claim also fails since, as the district court recognized, plaintiff "cannot be defrauded of property that he does not

handwritten note (left margin): fraud must show injury as proximate result of alleged fraudulent conduct.

fraud
must show
injury as
proximate
result of
alleged fraudulent
conduct.

Body:

own." Essential to a cause of action for fraud is a showing of injury as the proximate result of the alleged fraudulent conduct. * * * Because plaintiff's idea for "Father's Day" was in the public domain when NBC allegedly used it in the creation of *The Cosby Show*, Murray suffered no injury. His cause of action for fraud thus was properly dismissed. * * *

CONCLUSION

Our review of New York intellectual property law leads us to the inescapable conclusion that the district court did not err in deciding that there was no material issue of fact as to the novelty of plaintiff's proposal. In our judgment, the basic premise underlying the concept of novelty under New York law is that special protection is afforded only to truly innovative ideas while allowing the free use of ideas that are "merely clever or useful adaptation[s] of existing knowledge." *Educational Sales Programs*, 317 N.Y.S.2d at 844. In this case, the record indicates that plaintiff's idea for a situation comedy featuring the nonstereotypical portrayal of a black family simply was not uniquely plaintiff's creation. Accordingly, we affirm the district court's order granting summary judgment and dismissing the complaint.

Affirmed.

PRATT, Circuit Judge, dissenting.

Today this court holds that the idea underlying what may well be the most successful situation comedy in television history was, in 1980, so unoriginal and so entrenched in the public domain that, as a matter of law, it did not constitute intellectual property protected under New York law. Because I am convinced that the novelty issue in this case presents a factual question subject to further discovery and ultimate scrutiny by a trier of fact, I respectfully dissent. * * *

I agree with the majority that there is some evidence that Murray's idea was not novel. But clearly, there is also evidence indicating novelty. Initially, there is the admission by NBC, in its agreement with Carsey–Werner, that the television series is "unique, intellectual property." Although NBC argues, and the majority agrees, that this clause refers to a "fully-produced television series", and not Murray's program idea, such analysis ignores two important facts.

First, the "unique, intellectual property" language is found in the remedies section of the development agreement. This section gives NBC the right to prevent the loss of its "unique, intellectual property" should Carsey–Werner fail to perform. However, if Carsey–Werner does not perform—that is, if it subsequently refuses to develop the television series—the only "unique, intellectual property" to be protected is the program's underlying idea. In other words, from the outset NBC wanted to make certain that if its relationship with Carsey–Werner faltered, the novel idea it had given Carsey–Werner would be protected from disclosure. And because, for purposes of this appeal, we must assume that NBC got its idea from Murray, the Carsey–Werner development agreement, at a minimum, constitutes admissible evidence that Murray's idea was unique, thus making the novelty determination a question of fact. *See Anderson v. Liberty Lobby, Inc.*, 477 U.S. 242 (1986).

That the "unique, intellectual property" mentioned in the agreement refers to Murray's basic idea underlying the series rather than a fully-produced series, also finds support in the second fact the majority ignores. The definition section of the development agreement specifically defines this "property", not, as the majority contends, as "titles, set designs, theme music, stories, scripts, and art work"—indeed, these are separately defined in the agreement as the "elements" to be developed by Carsey–Werner—but rather, the development agreement defines the actual "property" exclusively to be the "story, literary property, program idea, and/or program format *which form(s) the basis*" for the television series. This provision provides additional evidence that it was Murray's underlying idea, not the developed elements of the series as a whole, which NBC desired to protect as unique and novel property. * * * In short, there is substantial evidence, both within and independent of the Carsey–Werner development agreement, which directly conflicts with the majority's holding that, as a matter of law, Murray's idea was not novel. * * *

The majority's decision prematurely denies Murray a fair opportunity to establish his right to participate in the enormous wealth generated by *The Cosby Show*. Accordingly, I would reverse the district court judgment and remand the case for further consideration.

Notes

1. *Murray* is no longer the law in New York. In *Nadel v. Play–By–Play Toys & Novelties, Inc.*, 208 F.3d 368 (2d Cir. 2000), the Court of Appeals abrogated the requirement that an idea had to be novel in order to be protected. The court held that in a contract claim, the idea does not have to be original or novel, the idea only needs to be novel to the listener or buyer. *Murray* had had an adverse effect on the pitching of ideas in New York as producers became more comfortable that California state law would more effectively protect their ideas from theft.

2. The submission of an idea to a network can be risky business. In *Eaton v. N.B.C.*, 972 F.Supp. 1019 (E.D. Va. 1997), Wendy C. Eaton had an idea for a TV series called *Genuine Gypsy* about a female mechanic. In 1992, she wrote a script for the pilot and the full treatment package for the series set in an auto garage in Virginia. She sent the script to NBC in 1994 and claimed her work was used to develop the show *Brotherly Love* starring Joey Lawrence. However, NBC claimed they did not see the script because it was discarded as a "fringe submission," which is a submission turned in by an agent who is not known in the industry. NBC further asserted the shows were not "substantially similar." *Brotherly Love* featured a boy who decides to stay with his step-brothers at the family auto garage after claiming his inheritance. The show ran only for the 1995 season on NBC. The court ruled Eaton did not prove that NBC had access to the script and that the two were substantially similar. Though the shows had a similar setting with female mechanics, they differed in plots. The settings were both in auto garages, but

copyright law does "not protect *scenes a faire*," which are events that occur after choosing a particular setting. The court ruled that Eaton did not prove the shows were similar enough to prove copyright infringement and granted summary judgment for NBC.

3. Laurie and Jerome Metcalf thought of the idea for an inner-city hospital drama after reading newspaper articles about the Army training surgeons at inner-city hospitals in preparation for combat. They pitched the idea to CBS and television producer Steven Bochco in 1992, but were rejected. A similar show then was broadcast in 2000 called *The City of Angels*. This show was written by Bochco about an inner-city hospital in Los Angeles and involved primarily black characters. The couple then sued for copyright infringement in *Metcalf v. Bochco*, 294 F.3d 1069 (9th Cir. 2002). The trial court ruled that even though Bochco had access to the screenplay, the works were not substantially similar. Also, testimony indicated that Bochco read and liked the couple's script. The appeals court reversed the ruling because the settings and plot were similar.

4. Ernest Olson claimed that NBC stole his idea when creating the popular TV show *The A–Team*. Olson claimed copyright infringement for his treatment and screenplay for a pilot called *Cargo* in *Olson v. NBC*, 855 F.2d 1446 (9th Cir. 1988). *Cargo* had Vietnam veterans who worked as corrupt drug enforcement agents and their adventures around the world. *The A–Team* also had Vietnam veterans who escaped from prison after being forced to rob a bank. Both were action-adventure series depicting Vietnam vets, but the plot and settings were different. Olson did not show substantial similarity between the two series. The appeals court affirmed the district court's finding that both series were not substantially similar in idea or protectible expression.

5. Idea protection is handled differently in each state. Following the *Nadel* case (above in note 1), New York's law moved closer to California's law on the protection of ideas. When looking at the two jurisdictions, the individual who comes up with an idea for a show still receives better protection in California. In California, consideration and mutual assent are needed, while novelty and concreteness do not have to be shown. Furthermore, California courts find the act of disclosing the idea to be adequate consideration for an implied contract if there is no express contract. In New York, *Nadel* will now allow ideas to be protected under a contracts theory if the idea is new and novel to the buyer. The best way to solve a dispute in either state is to have a written contract. Do you see an advantage to either jurisdiction?

B. COPYRIGHT OWNERSHIP AND TRANSFER

1. PERFORMANCE RIGHTS

Performance rights in television programs are covered in the licensing agreement between the production company and the network or cable company broadcasting the program. The typical first-run license allows for the program to be broadcast once in its regularly scheduled time slot and once again as a rerun in the summer. Additional broadcasts can be negotiated for additional fees. Cable and satellite issues are covered in more detail in Chapter 13 on Satellite and Cable Television.

2. WORK FOR HIRE VS. JOINT WORKS

Whether a program is a work for hire or a joint work is critical for purposes of ownership and control. If a project is a work for hire, the party producing the project is typically considered the author and copyright owner. If the project is a joint work, both parties are considered the joint authors and both parties own the copyrights in the project. As always, a good contract that addresses all of the possibilities before the project begins is the best way to avoid having to resolve the dispute in the courtroom.

QUINTANILLA v. TEXAS TELEVISION, INC.

United States Court of Appeals, Fifth Circuit, 1998.
139 F.3d 494.

REAVLEY, Circuit Judge.

This is a copyright case. The father of the popular singer, Selena, sued a television station for infringement of his rights in a videotape of a concert that was made by the station. The district court granted summary judgment for the defendant television station. Because the proof will not support plaintiffs' claim to sole ownership of the videotape, we affirm.

BACKGROUND

Appellant Abraham Quintanilla, Jr. (Quintanilla) is the father of Selena Quintanilla Perez (Selena). Selena led a Tejano band named Selena y Los Dinos (the band). Quintanilla was the manager and owner of the band.

On February 7, 1993, the band performed a live concert at the Memorial Coliseum in Corpus Christi. By agreement between Quintanilla and Jay Sanchez, a director for appellee Texas Television, Inc. d/b/a KIII–TV (KIII), the concert was recorded on videotape by KIII personnel. Prior to the concert, Sanchez sent Quintanilla a note stating: "Thank you for allowing us to videotape the concert tomorrow night.... As per our agreement, we will use the video on the Domingo Show and other news shows. In turn, we will provide you with a master copy on 3/4 to use for promotional purposes." Later, Sanchez sent videotapes of the concert to Quintanilla, with a note stating: "As we agreed, enclosed please find copies of the concert for your use. In exchange, we will use the footage on the Domingo Show."

Appellants contend that after the concert, songwriters (the Songwriters) whose compositions had been performed at the concert obtained copyright registrations for the songs with the United States Copyright Office, and Quintanilla obtained a copyright registration for the videotape. The parties do not dispute that Quintanilla acted as agent for the Songwriters in entering into the agreement with KIII.

After Selena's death, KIII aired portions of the videotape on its programs, including a March 31, 1996, "Selena Special" on the anniversary of her death. Quintanilla and the Songwriters brought this suit against KIII, alleging copyright infringement and state law claims. Quintanilla claimed that he is the exclusive owner of the copyright to the videotape and that KIII received only a limited nonexclusive license to use the concert footage on a single KIII entertainment show, The Domingo Show. In addition to claims under the Copyright Act, the complaint asserted state law claims under the court's supplemental jurisdiction, including claims for breach of contract, misappropriation of name or likeness, fraud, deceptive trade practices, and negligent misrepresentation.

The district court granted summary judgment in favor of KIII on the copyright claims, and dismissed the remaining state law claims without prejudice.

DISCUSSION

* * * We conclude that the district court properly granted summary judgment on the federal copyright claims.

A. Work Made for Hire Doctrine

Quintanilla argues that he is the exclusive owner of the copyright in the videotape because the videotape was a work made for hire, and KIII's efforts in making the videotape fall within that doctrine. As the Supreme Court explained in *Community for Creative Non–Violence v. Reid*, the Copyright Act "provides that copyright ownership 'vests initially in the author or authors of the work,' " and the author is generally the party "who actually creates the work, that is, the person who translates an idea into a fixed, tangible expression entitled to copyright protection." [490 U.S. 730, 737.]

The Act provides differently for works made for hire, where "the employer or other person for whom the work was prepared is considered the author" and owns the copyright, absent an agreement between the parties to the contrary. The Act defines two sets of circumstances in which a work is made for hire:

A "work made for hire" is—(1) a work prepared by an employee within the scope of his or her employment; or (2) a work specially ordered or commissioned for use as ... a part of a motion picture or other audiovisual work ... if the parties expressly agree in a written instrument signed by them that the work shall be considered a work made for hire.

Quintanilla produced no written instrument where the parties expressly agreed "that the work shall be considered a work made for hire" as required by the second subsection of the definition.

Quintanilla therefore can prevail on his work for hire theory only if the KIII personnel sent to videotape the concert were his "employees" under the first subsection of the definition. * * * Looking to the factors named in *Reid*, KIII established as a matter of law that the personnel it sent to videotape the concert were not employees of Quintanilla. * * * Quintanilla offered evidence that he selected the forum, controlled the lighting and stage setup for the concert, and was the overall producer of the concert. KIII counters that it controlled the creation of the videotape. While Quintanilla told Sanchez where he wanted the two fixed and roving cameras located and told members of the camera crew when certain parts of the concert were coming up so they could get good images, the evidence shows that KIII had ultimate control over the creation of the videotape. KIII sent a seven-member crew to film the event. It provided four cameras all linked to a "Live Eye" truck where Sanchez worked during the concert. Sanchez, an experienced director, decided which of the four images streaming into the truck simultaneously would be used. Sanchez communicated with the KIII cameramen by microphone and directed them to focus on certain images or to set up certain camera angles or shots throughout the concert. He testified that while Quintanilla made suggestions about camera placement, the final decision was his. Quintanilla had no authority over the editing of the tapes done after the concert. Quintanilla conceded that "I don't know anything about that [camera] equipment," and that, with reference to the camera truck, "I don't know anything about how those things work."

In short, Quintanilla had control over the concert, but did not control the manner in which KIII taped the event. He may have made useful suggestions to the camera crew, about such things as when the lighting was about to change, but Sanchez had ultimate authority to tell the camera crew what to do. KIII had sole discretion to decide which of four simultaneous camera shots to record, and how the tape would be edited. On similar facts, we held that a television station had not created a work for hire in *Easter Seal Soc. for Crippled Children and Adults of Louisiana, Inc. v. Playboy Enter* [815 F.2d 323 (5th Cir.1987)]. In *Easter Seal*, entertainer Ronnie Kole, acting on behalf of the Easter Seal Society, contracted with television station WYES to videotape a staged parade and musical jam session. WYES recorded the live performances on videotape, and its unit director Beyer controlled the videotaping by supervising all unit employees, "making the final aesthetic and technical decisions about the deployment of six video cameras and sound equipment." [*Id.* at 324.] Although Kole told Beyer in advance about musical arrangements "so that Beyer ... could position his camera operators and tape appropriate shots of each band member," [*Id.*] and made suggestions about certain camera angles, we held that the Society's copyright claim failed because WYES was an independent contractor under the Copyright Act. [*Id.* at 336.]

Considering all the factors discussed above, we agree with the district court that KIII established as a matter of law that the personnel it supplied to videotape the concert were not employees of Quintanilla.

B.   Joint Ownership

* * * Under the Copyright Act, a "joint work" is "a work prepared by two or more authors with the intention that their contributions be merged into inseparable or interdependent parts of a unitary whole."

We agree with the district court that appellants did not plead a federal cause of action based on a theory of joint copyright ownership. "It is widely recognized that '[a] co-owner of a copyright must account to other co-owners for any profits he earns from the licensing or use of the copyright. . . . '" * * * "A co-owner of a copyright cannot be liable to another co-owner for infringement of the copyright." Further, the complaint throughout argued that plaintiffs' copyright interests were exclusive, inconsistent with a theory of joint ownership.

We also hold that the district court did not abuse its discretion in denying Quintanilla leave to amend to add a joint ownership claim. This suit was filed in February of 1997. At a May 8, 1997 pretrial hearing, counsel for appellants was equivocal as to whether he was asserting a claim of joint ownership. Later, the court again asked counsel what his cause of action was, to which counsel stated that it was based on sole ownership of the copyright by Quintanilla. Counsel also stated that he did not want to add any new causes of action, although the court repeatedly stated its view that the complaint did not assert a claim based on joint ownership. KIII filed its summary judgment motion on May 28, after fairly extensive discovery that included the depositions of Quintanilla, Sanchez, and KIII's general manager. On June 20, plaintiffs sought leave to amend to add a joint ownership claim as to Quintanilla, which the court denied. * * * Given the circumstances described above, we cannot say that the district court abused its discretion in denying leave to amend.

C.   Transfer of Copyright

Quintanilla argues that KIII's copyright interest in the videotape was transferred to him. We agree with the district court that Quintanilla never pleaded such a theory. Further, a transfer of copyright ownership "is not valid unless an instrument of conveyance, or a note or memorandum of the transfer, is in writing and signed by the owner of the rights conveyed or such owner's duly authorized agent." Quintanilla produced no writing mentioning KIII's copyright interests in the videotape or purporting to convey such interests to Quintanilla. Even as to their oral understandings, Quintanilla and Sanchez both testified that there was no discussion of who would own the copyright to the videotape.

D.   The Songwriters

The Songwriters argue that they asserted a copyright infringement claim independent of the claim that the videotape was a work made for hire. Perhaps the complaint asserted a claim that KIII had exceeded its limited license to use a derivative work of the Songwriters. The complaint alleged that Quintanilla, on his own behalf and on behalf of the Songwriters, negotiated an agreement whereby KIII would have a limited nonexclusive license to play the videotape of the concert on the Domingo Show only, and that KIII exceeded the scope of the license. While not using the term "derivative work," the complaint alleged that the concert videotape "was based entirely on pre-existing works," including the Songwriters' compositions, and that KIII infringed on the copyrights in their compositions.

A derivative work "is a work based upon one or more preexisting works, such as a ... musical arrangement ... or any other form in which a work may be recast, transformed, or adapted." Even if the videotape qualifies as an independent work of authorship entitled to copyright protection, it might also be a derivative work based in part on the underlying copyrighted songs performed at the concert. * * *

In contrast to co-owners of a joint work, who as explained above cannot sue each other for copyright infringement, the owner of a copyright can sometimes sue a party licensed to create a derivative work for copyright infringement. If a songwriter grants a limited license restricting the use of a videotape of a concert in which the songwriter's copyrighted composition is performed, breach of the license agreement might constitute copyright infringement, particularly where, as alleged here, the breach was material.

However, to prevail on a copyright infringement claim the plaintiff must prove that he owned a copyright and that the defendant impermissibly copied or otherwise infringed upon the copyright. Plaintiffs offered no summary judgment proof that the songwriters were the current owners of copyrights in the songs that were performed at the concert. Further, the Copyright Act provides that "no action for infringement of the copyright in any work shall be instituted until registration of the copyright claim has been made in accordance with this title." The Songwriters offered no summary judgment proof of copyright registration in the underlying songs. The only copyright registration in the record is Quintanilla's registration for the copyright to the videotape.

AFFIRMED.

C. COPYRIGHT INFRINGEMENT & REMEDIES

Anyone who owns a copyright can sue for infringement of any one of the bundle of rights. Courts can issue temporary and permanent injunctions to stop further copyright infringement. Another remedy is the impoundment or destruction of copies allegedly in violation of the copyright, including masters, tapes, and film negatives. The infringer can be required to pay damages incurred and profits made as a result of the infringement. Statutory damages are available to copyright owners who have complied with the statutory requirements of the Copyright

Act. *Copyright Law of the United States of America and Related Laws Contained in Title 17 of the United States Code*, Circular 92, Copyright Law—Chapter 5, Copyright Office, *at* http://www.copyright.gov/title17/92chap5.html.

SID & MARTY KROFFT TELEVISION PROD., INC. v. McDONALD'S CORP.

United States Court of Appeals, Ninth Circuit, 1977.
562 F.2d 1157.

CARTER, Circuit Judge.

This is a copyright infringement action. Plaintiffs Sid and Marty Krofft Television Productions, Inc., and Sid and Marty Krofft Productions, Inc. were awarded $50,000.00 in their action against defendants McDonald's Corporation and Needham, Harper & Steers, Inc. Defendants were found to have infringed plaintiffs' "H. R. Pufnstuf" children's television show by the production of their "McDonaldland" television commercials. * * *

We believe that the district court's finding of infringement was not clearly erroneous, and see no merit to defendants' first amendment claims. We find, however, that the district court was in error in awarding damages. We therefore affirm in part, reverse in part, and remand for further proceedings.

Facts

In 1968, Sid and Marty Krofft were approached by the NBC television network to create a children's television program for exhibition on Saturday morning. The Kroffts spent the next year creating the H.R. Pufnstuf television show, which was introduced on NBC in September 1969. The series included several fanciful costumed characters, as well as a boy named Jimmy, who lived in a fantasyland called "Living Island," which was inhabited by moving trees and talking books. The television series became extremely popular and generated a line of H. R. Pufnstuf products and endorsements.

In early 1970, Marty Krofft, the President of both Krofft Television and Krofft Productions and producer of the show, was contacted by an executive from Needham, Harper & Steers, Inc., an advertising agency. He was told that Needham was attempting to get the advertising account of McDonald's hamburger restaurant chain and wanted to base a proposed campaign to McDonald's on the H. R. Pufnstuf characters. The executive wanted to know whether the Kroffts would be interested in working with Needham on a project of this type.

Needham and the Kroffts were in contact by telephone six or seven more times. By a letter dated August 31, 1970, Needham stated it was going forward with the idea of a McDonaldland advertising campaign based on the H. R. Pufnstuf series. It acknowledged the need to pay the Kroffts a fee for preparing artistic designs and engineering plans. Shortly thereafter, Marty Krofft telephoned Needham only to be told that the advertising campaign had been cancelled.

In fact, Needham had already been awarded McDonald's advertising account and was proceeding with the McDonaldland project. Former employees of the Kroffts were hired to design and construct the costumes and sets for McDonaldland. Needham also hired the same voice expert who supplied all of the voices for the Pufnstuf characters to supply some of the voices for the McDonaldland characters. In January 1971, the first of the McDonaldland commercials was broadcast on network television. They continue to be broadcast.

Prior to the advent of the McDonaldland advertising campaign, plaintiffs had licensed the use of the H. R. Pufnstuf characters and elements to the manufacturers of toys, games, lunch boxes, and comic books. In addition, the H. R. Pufnstuf characters were featured in Kellogg's cereal commercials and used by the Ice Capades. After the McDonaldland campaign, which included the distribution of toys and games, plaintiffs were unable to obtain new licensing arrangements or extend existing ones. In the case of the Ice Capades, the H. R. Pufnstuf characters were actually replaced by the McDonaldland characters.

Plaintiffs filed suit in September 1971. The complaint alleged, *inter alia,* that the McDonaldland advertising campaign infringed the copyrighted H. R. Pufnstuf television episodes as well as various copyrighted articles of Pufnstuf merchandise. * * *

The three week jury trial began on November 27, 1973. The jurors were shown for their consideration on the question of infringement: (1) two H. R. Pufnstuf television episodes; (2) various items of H. R. Pufnstuf merchandise, such as toys, games, and comic books; (3) several 30 and 60 second McDonaldland television commercials; and (4) various items of McDonaldland merchandise distributed by McDonald's, such as toys and puzzles. The jury was instructed that it was not to consider defendants' *profits* in determining damages, but could consider the *value of use* by the defendants of plaintiffs' work.

A verdict in favor of plaintiffs was returned and damages of $50,000.00 assessed. After the verdict, the parties briefed the question of whether plaintiffs were entitled to additional monetary recovery in the form of profits or statutory "in lieu" damages. The district court denied plaintiffs' claim for such relief. The court found that these matters were properly for the jury to consider so that it would not exercise its discretion in hearing further evidence. These appeals followed.

I. Infringement

Proof of Infringement

It has often been said that in order to establish copyright infringement a plaintiff must prove ownership of the copyright and "copying" by the defendant. *See, e.g., Reyher v. Children's Television Workshop,* 533 F.2d 87, 90 (2 Cir. 1976); *Universal Athletic Sales Co. v. Salkeld,* 511

F.2d 904, 907 (3 Cir. 1975); 2 M. Nimmer on Copyright § 141 at 610–11 (1976) (hereinafter "Nimmer"). "Copying," in turn, is said to be shown by circumstantial evidence of access to the copyrighted work and substantial similarity between the copyrighted work and defendant's work. *Reyher v. Children's Television Workshop, supra,* 533 F.2d at 90; 2 Nimmer § 141.2 at 613. But an analysis of the cases suggests that these statements frequently serve merely as boilerplate to copyright opinions. * * *

Clearly the scope of copyright protection does not go this far. A limiting principle is needed. This is provided by the classic distinction between an "idea" and the "expression" of that idea. It is an axiom of copyright law that the protection granted to a copyrighted work extends only to the particular expression of the idea and never to the idea itself. *Mazer v. Stein,* 347 U.S. 201, 217–18 (1954); *Baker v. Selden,* 101 U.S. 99, 102–03 (1879). This principle attempts to reconcile two competing social interests: rewarding an individual's creativity and effort while at the same time permitting the nation to enjoy the benefits and progress from use of the same subject matter.

The real task in a copyright infringement action, then, is to determine whether there has been copying of the expression of an idea rather than just the idea itself. "No one infringes, unless he descends so far into what is concrete [in a work] as to invade.... [its] expression." *Nat'l Comics Publ'n v. Fawcett Publ'n,* 191 F.2d 594, 600 (2 Cir. 1951). Only this expression may be protected and only it may be infringed.

The difficulty comes in attempting to distill the unprotected idea from the protected expression. No court or commentator in making this search has been able to improve upon Judge Learned Hand's famous "abstractions test" articulated in *Nichols v. Universal Pictures Corp.,* 45 F.2d 119 (2nd Cir. 1930), *cert. denied,* 282 U.S. 902, 51 S. Ct. 216, 75 L. Ed. 795 (1931): "Upon any work, and especially upon a play, a great number of patterns of increasing generality will fit equally well, as more and more of the incident is left out. The last may perhaps be no more than the most general statement of what the play is about, and at times might consist of only its title; but there is a point in this series of abstractions where they are no longer protected, since otherwise the playwright could prevent the use of his 'ideas,' to which, apart from their expression, his property is never extended." 45 F.2d at 121. * * *

The test for infringement therefore has been given a new dimension. There must be ownership of the copyright and access to the copyrighted work. But there also must be substantial similarity not only of the general ideas but of the expressions of those ideas as well. Thus two steps in the analytic process are implied by the requirement of substantial similarity. * * * The test for similarity of ideas is still a factual one, to be decided by the trier of fact.

We shall call this the "extrinsic test." It is extrinsic because it depends not on the responses of the trier of fact, but on specific criteria which can be listed and analyzed. Such criteria include the type of artwork involved, the materials used, the subject matter, and the setting for the subject. Since it is an extrinsic test, analytic dissection and expert testimony are appropriate. Moreover, this question may often be decided as a matter of law. * * *

The test to be applied in determining whether there is substantial similarity in expressions shall be labeled an intrinsic one—depending on the response of the ordinary reasonable person. * * * It is intrinsic because it does not depend on the type of external criteria and analysis which marks the extrinsic test. As this court stated in *Twentieth Century–Fox Film Corp. v. Stonesifer,* 140 F.2d 579, 582 (9 Cir. 1944): "The two works involved in this appeal should be considered and tested, not hypercritically or with meticulous scrutiny, but by the observations and impressions of the average reasonable reader and spectator." * * * This same type of bifurcated test was announced in *Arnstein v. Porter,* 154 F.2d 464, 468–69 (2 Cir. 1946), *cert. denied,* 330 U.S. 851 (1947). The court there identified two separate elements essential to a plaintiff's suit for infringement: copying and unlawful appropriation. Under the *Arnstein* doctrine, the distinction is significant because of the different tests involved.

"The trier of fact must determine whether the similarities are sufficient to prove copying. On this issue, analysis ('dissection') is relevant, and the testimony of experts may be received to aid the trier of facts. * * * If copying is established, then only does there arise the second issue, that of illicit copying (unlawful appropriation). On that issue.... the test is the response of the ordinary lay hearer; accordingly, on that issue, 'dissection' and expert testimony are irrelevant." 154 F.2d at 468.

We believe that the court in *Arnstein* was alluding to the idea-expression dichotomy which we make explicit today. When the court in *Arnstein* refers to "copying" which is not itself an infringement, it must be suggesting copying merely of the work's idea, which is not protected by the copyright. To constitute an infringement, the copying must reach the point of "unlawful appropriation," or the copying of the protected expression itself. We analyze this distinction in terms both of the elements involved—idea and expression—and of the tests to be used—extrinsic and intrinsic—in an effort to clarify the issues involved.

copying must equal unlawful appropriation

The Tests Applied

In the context of this case, the distinction between these tests is important. Defendants do not dispute the fact that they copied the idea of plaintiffs' Pufnstuf television series—basically a fantasyland filled with diverse and fanciful characters in action. They argue, however, that the expressions of this idea are too dissimilar for there to be an infringement. They come to this conclusion by dissecting the constituent parts of the Pufnstuf series—characters, setting, and plot—and pointing out the dissimilarities between these parts and those of the McDonald-land commercials.

This approach ignores the idea-expression dichotomy alluded to in *Arnstein* and analyzed today. * * * Analytic dissection, as defendants have done, is therefore improper.

Defendants contest the continued viability of *Arnstein.* * * * But the case's tests for infringement have consistently been approved by this court. *See, e.g., Goodson–Todman Enter., Inc. v. Kellogg Co.,* 513 F.2d 913, 914 (9th Cir. 1975); *Overman v. Loesser,* 205 F.2d 521, 523 (9th Cir. 1953). They have also been accepted by other courts. *See, e.g., Universal Athletic Sales Co. v. Salkeld, supra,* 511 F.2d at 907; *Scott v. WKJG, Inc.,* 376 F.2d 467, 469 (7th Cir. 1967). We believe *Arnstein* is still good law. * * *

The present case demands an even more intrinsic determination because both plaintiffs' and defendants' works are directed to an audience of children. This raises the particular factual issue of the impact of the respective works upon the minds and imaginations of young people. * * * The H. R. Pufnstuf series became the most popular children's show on Saturday morning television. This success led several manufacturers of children's goods to use the Pufnstuf characters. It is not surprising, then, that McDonald's hoped to duplicate this peculiar appeal to children in its commercials. It was in recognition of the subjective and unpredictable nature of children's responses that defendants opted to recreate the H. R. Pufnstuf format rather than use an original and unproven approach.

Defendants would have this court ignore that intrinsic quality which they recognized to embark on an extrinsic analysis of the two works. For example, in discussing the principal characters—Pufnstuf and Mayor McCheese—defendants point out: " 'Pufnstuf' wears what can only be described as a yellow and green dragon suit with a blue cummerbund from which hangs a medal which says 'mayor'. 'McCheese' wears a version of pink formal dress—'tails'—with knicker trousers. He has a typical diplomat's sash on which is written 'mayor', the 'M' consisting of the McDonald's trademark of an 'M' made of golden arches."

So not only do defendants remove the characters from the setting, but dissect further to analyze the clothing, colors, features, and mannerisms of each character. We do not believe that the ordinary reasonable person, let alone a child, viewing these works will even notice that Pufnstuf is wearing a cummerbund while Mayor McCheese is wearing a diplomat's sash. * * *

We have viewed representative samples of both the H. R. Pufnstuf show and McDonaldland commercials. It is clear to us that defendants' works are substantially similar to plaintiffs'. They have captured the "total concept and feel" of the Pufnstuf show. *Roth Greeting Cards v. United Card Co.,* 429 F.2d 1106, 1110 (9th Cir. 1970). We would so conclude even if we were sitting as the triers of fact. There is no doubt that the findings of the jury in this case are not clearly erroneous.

Unity of Idea and Expression

* * * There is no special standard of similarity required in the case of "things." Nor is any such standard suggested by any of the cases cited by defendants. For example, in *Monogram Models, Inc. v. Industro Motive Corp.*, 492 F.2d 1281, 1284 (6th Cir. 1974), the issue was one of copyright infringement of scale model airplane kits. Defendant admitted copying, but argued lack of substantial copying. The court affirmed a jury finding of infringement, citing the ordinary reasonable observer test. *Id.* at 1286. *See also Williams v. Kaag Mfr., Inc., supra,* 338 F.2d at 951 (cowboy statuettes); *Day-Brite Lighting, Inc. v. Sta–Brite Fluorescent Mfr. Co.,* 308 F.2d 377, 380 (5th Cir. 1962) (catalogue).

No standard more demanding than that of substantial similarity should be imposed here. This is not a case where the idea is indistinguishable as a matter of law from the expression of that idea. *See Goodson–Todman Enter., Inc. v. Kellogg Co., supra,* 513 F.2d at 914. The expression inherent in the H. R. Pufnstuf series differs markedly from its relatively simple idea. The characters each have developed personalities and particular ways of interacting with one another and their environment. The physical setting also has several unique features.

Lest we fall prey to defendants' invitation to dissect the works, however, we should remember that it is the *combination* of many different elements which may command copyright protection because of its particular subjective quality. *Reyher v. Children's Television Workshop, Inc., supra,* 533 F.2d at 91–92; *Ideal Toy Corp. v. Sayco Doll Corp.,* 302 F.2d 623, 624 (2nd Cir. 1962). As the court said in *Malkin v. Dubinsky,* 146 F.Supp. 111, 114 (S.D.N.Y. 1956): "While any one similarity taken by itself seems trivial, I cannot say at this time that it would be improper for a jury to find that the over-all impact and effect indicate substantial appropriation." The same is true here. * * *

Access

In addition to substantial similarity, a plaintiff must show access in order to prove infringement. *Reyher v. Children's Television Workshop, supra,* 533 F.2d at 90; 2 Nimmer § 141.2 at 613. Access is proven when the plaintiff shows that the defendant had an opportunity to view or to copy plaintiff's work. *Arrow Novelty Co. v. Enco Nat'l Corp.,* 393 F.Supp. 157, 160 (S.D.N.Y.), *aff'd,* 515 F.2d 504 (2nd Cir. 1975); *Universal Athletic Sales Co. v. Salkeld,* 340 F.Supp. 899, 901 (W.D. Pa. 1972). In this case, there is no dispute as to defendants' access to plaintiffs' work. Indeed, defendants were engaged in negotiations with plaintiffs for licensing of the works even while preparing the McDonaldland commercials. * * *

In this case, representatives of Needham actually visited the Kroffts' headquarters in Los Angeles to discuss the engineering and design work necessary to produce the McDonaldland commercials. They did this *after* they had been awarded the contract by McDonald's and apparently with no intention to work with the Kroffts. We believe that this degree of access justifies a lower standard of proof to show substantial similarity. Since the subjective test applies, it is impossible to quantify this standard. But there is no question it is met here.

II. DAMAGES

Awarding Damages

* * * The jury assessed damages of $50,000 against defendants in this case. Subsequent to the return of the verdict, counsel for both sides, at the district court's request, briefed the question of whether plaintiffs were entitled to additional monetary recovery either in the form of profits or statutory "in lieu" damages. After considering this question, the district court concluded that plaintiffs were not entitled to any additional recovery and denied plaintiffs' motion for an accounting of profits by defendants. * * *

The judgment of the district court *[on infringement]* is affirmed. The McDonald's commercials in general use the same ideas as the H.R. PufnStuf series, and the commercials are sufficiently similar so that a jury applying an extrinsic test could find infringement. This is especially true here since there was evidence of access. * * *

William Hensler

Copyright Issues from an Expert Witness:
An Interview with Howard Suber

(2006) *by William Hensler*

"I had my first experience as an expert witness in 1973, when Mel Nimmer, my colleague on the UCLA faculty, brought me into a copyright suit involving *The Exorcist*. During more than three decades of working in this area, I've been involved about equally on the side of plaintiffs and defendants.

"Plaintiffs go overboard in listing substantial similarities, perhaps because they or their lawyers assume that the more you throw against the wall, the more chance you have that some of it will stick. But this often leads to overreaching. For example, in one case, the plaintiffs made a point of the fact that, in their screenplay, a character is smoking in the very first scene, and the same thing occurs in the defendant's film. So what?

"The first principle when doing a structural analysis is to ask, 'What would happen if you removed this element from the work? Would it fundamentally *change* the nature of the work as a whole?' If the answer is no, then it really isn't important to the work. If you ask with regard to the smoking example I cited above, 'What would happen if *neither* character was smoking?' the answer was: nothing. So, whether or not someone is smoking is not important, one way or the other, to *either* work.

"Mel Nimmer, in his famous treatise on copyright, makes the point that it doesn't matter how dissimilar two works are; what matters are the things that are similar. For example, the plaintiffs in a suit I was involved with listed literally hundreds of similarities between their work and the plaintiffs, but they neglected to reveal to the court the fact that their work was a murder mystery farce in which a 30–year-old virgin who wanted to be a nun was involved in twelve attempts at murder, while the defendants' work was anything *but* a farce, and it had no murders, no nuns, and no virgins. When you remove things from their context you often misrepresent what is being expressed. The most consistent mistake I see in copyright cases is the presentation of side-by-side lists of abstract similarities that fail to take into account the context and function of the elements being compared.

"Another thing I think is often confused in copyright cases is the distinction between 'substantial similarities' and 'striking similarities.' In practice, 'substantial' just means, 'a lot.' But 'striking,' doesn't refer to quantity, it refers to a *quality* of the similarity. Most often, 'striking' means that the element being analyzed is so unusual, either in itself or in the way it is juxtaposed with other elements that it is highly unlikely that another creator would come upon the same element or juxtaposition with other elements.

" 'Striking similarities' are often treated as the 'smoking gun' copyright cases, but it's that what you're claiming is *really* striking. In one of my cases, the plaintiffs pointed out that in their work a Polish character utters the toast, 'Nastrovia,' and in the defendants' work a *Russian* character utters the same Polish toast. The plaintiffs claimed that the fact that the defendant used the *same* toast—and made the "mistake" of putting it in the mouth of a Russian—was a smoking gun that *proved* the defendant had copied from the plaintiff. I responded that there was one problem with the plaintiffs' striking similarity: Russian and Polish are both Slavic languages, and 'Nastrovia' is a toast used in *both* languages. So, their similarity just made them look foolish. One moral of this story is: do your homework. Equally important is to ask the inelegant question, 'So what?' If *neither* character in the two works had used the hackneyed toast, 'Nastrovia,' would either work have been significantly different? Was 'Nastrovia' *important* to either work?

"The plaintiffs claimed in one of my cases that one of the themes of both their work and the plaintiffs was, 'To thine own self be true.' I responded by asking in what works was the theme, 'To thine own self be *false*?' The plaintiff, in essence, was complaining, 'You stole my cliché!' Although the 9th Circuit Court lists 'theme' as one of the elements that can be compared and dissected in copyright cases, I have never seen anyone—including myself—prove anything *significant* by analyzing theme, probably because, by definition, a theme *is* an abstraction.

"People with little knowledge of the 2,500 year history of western drama often think that there are a myriad number of ways for a story to develop, and if they see that someone else's story develops in ways that are similar to their own, they may conclude that the other person stole their stuff. Theft of copyrighted material does occur, of course. But it is important to consider whether similarities occur because that's the way others have told similar stories, because there aren't that many different ways for the story to develop—or because the 'similarities' are stated at a level of abstraction that ignores the concrete objective *expression* of the two works.

"In copyright, you first have to determine where idea leaves off and expression begins. Then, I would argue, it is equally important to determine what in the expression is *important* to the nature and structure each work. Only when you have accomplished *both* tasks have you done a meaningful analysis of the works in dispute."

[handwritten in margin: is the expression important to the nature + structure of each work]

Note

1. Copyright infringement must occur in the United States to enable protection from infringers. However, is it a copyright infringement when the programming is transmitted via satellite? The satellite transmission of unlicensed footage abroad is discussed below in *Los Angeles News Service v. Reuters Television Inc.*

LOS ANGELES NEWS SERVICE v. REUTERS TELEVISION, INC.

United States Court of Appeals, Ninth Circuit, 1998.
149 F.3d 987.

SCHWARZER, Senior District Judge.

On this appeal we must decide whether, under the Copyright Act, a plaintiff may recover actual damages accruing from the unauthorized exploitation abroad of copyrighted work infringed in the United States; whether defendants' exploitation of the work was protected as fair use; and whether the district court erred in its award of statutory damages.

BACKGROUND

Los Angeles News (LANS) is an independent news organization which produces video and audio tape recordings of newsworthy events and licenses them for profit. During the April 1992 riots following the Rodney King verdict, LANS covered the events at Florence Avenue and Normandie Boulevard in Los Angeles from its helicopter, producing two videotapes: "The Beating of Reginald Denny" and "Beating of Man in White Panel Truck" (the works). LANS copyrighted these works and licensed them to National Broadcasting Company, Inc. (NBC), which used them on the *Today* show with the logo of KCOP, a Los Angeles station not affiliated with NBC, superimposed (known in the trade as the downstream). Under the agreement, LANS retained ownership of the works and the right to license them.

The Reuters defendants (Reuters Television International, Ltd., Reuters America Holdings, Inc., and Reuters America, Inc., collectively

Reuters) are television news agencies that gather and provide audiovisual and other news material to their subscribers for an annual fee. Visnews International (USA), Ltd. (Visnews), a joint venture of Reuters Television Limited, NBC and the British Broadcasting Company, had a news supply agreement with NBC News Overseas. When NBC broadcast the *Today* show featuring the LANS footage to its affiliates, it simultaneously transmitted the show via fiber link to Visnews in New York. Visnews made a videotape copy of the works as broadcast and transmitted it to subscribers in Europe and Africa. It also transmitted copies of the videotape to the New York office of the European Broadcasting Union (EBU), which in turn made a videotape copy and transmitted it via satellite to Reuters' London branch, which provided copies to its subscribers.

LANS brought this action for copyright infringement against the Reuters defendants and Visnews. Defendants moved for summary judgment on several grounds. So far as relevant to this appeal, they contended that (1) extraterritorial infringement does not violate American copyright law, (2) the fair use doctrine precludes a finding of infringement, and (3) LANS had no evidence of actual damage. The district court granted defendants' motion with respect to extraterritorial infringement and the claim for actual damages. It denied the motion with respect to the fair use defense and entered partial summary judgment for LANS determining that the defense did not shield defendants' actions. Following a bench trial on the remaining issues, the district court found that Visnews had infringed by making one copy of each videotape and contributing to the making by EBU of one copy of each tape, LANS failed to prove the infringement was willful, and defendants failed to prove that it was innocent. The court entered judgment for LANS for $60,000 in statutory damages based on the four domestic infringements by Visnews. In a subsequent order, the court denied LANS's and Reuters' applications for costs and attorney's fees.

LANS appeals from the ruling barring extraterritorial damages and defendants cross-appeal from the ruling denying the fair use defense and from the damage award. Both appeal from the order denying attorney's fees and costs. We have jurisdiction pursuant to 28 U.S.C. § 1291.

DISCUSSION

I.   Extraterritorial Damages

It is settled that the Copyright Act does not apply extraterritorially. *Subafilms, Ltd. v. MGM–Pathe Communications Co.*, 24 F.3d 1088, 1094 (9th Cir. 1994) (en banc). For the Act to apply, "at least one alleged infringement must be completed entirely within the United States." *Allarcom Pay Television Ltd. v. General Instrument Corp.*, 69 F.3d 381, 387 (9th Cir. 1995). The district court found that "any damages arising extraterritorially are the result of extraterritorial infringement." *Reuters I*, 942 F.Supp. at 1269. Relying on *Allarcom*, the court held that "the transmissions from Visnews and [EBU] did not violate the Copyright

Act.... Therefore, Defendants are not liable ... for damages arising extraterritorially." *Id.* at 1269. * * *

The district court's ruling was premised on the assumption that LANS's claim was based on the transmissions from Visnews and EBU to Reuters. However, it also held that Visnews completed acts of infringement in the United States when it copied the works in New York and then transmitted them to EBU which also copied them in New York. Each act of copying constituted a completed act of infringement. *See* 17 U.S.C. § 106(1). It was only after these domestic acts of infringement had been completed that Visnews and EBU transmitted the works abroad. * * *

The issue before us—which the *Subafilms* court did not resolve—is whether LANS "may recover damages for international distribution of the [works] based on the theory that an act of direct infringement, in the form of a reproduction of the ... [works], took place in the United States." *Subafilms*, 24 F.3d 1088 at 1099; *see also id.* at 1094. While this circuit has not heretofore addressed the issue, the Second Circuit has done so in a line of cases beginning with *Sheldon v. Metro–Goldwyn Pictures Corp.*, 106 F.2d 45, 52 (2d Cir. 1939), *aff'd*, 309 U.S. 390 (1940). In *Sheldon* the court held, in an opinion by Judge Learned Hand, that plaintiff could recover the profits from exhibiting a motion picture abroad where the infringing copy had been made in the United States. As Judge Hand explained: The [copyrighted film] negatives were "records" from which the work could be "reproduced", and it was a tort to make them in this country. The plaintiffs acquired an equitable interest in them as soon as they were made, which attached to any profits from their exploitation, whether in the form of money remitted to the United States, or of increase in the value of shares of foreign companies held by the defendants. We need not decide whether the law of those countries where the negatives were exploited, recognized the plaintiffs' equitable interest; we can assume arguendo that it did not, for, as soon as any of the profits so realized took the form of property whose situs was in the United States, our law seized upon them and impressed them with a constructive trust, whatever their form. 106 F.2d at 52. * * * Recovery of damages arising from overseas infringing uses was allowed because the predicate act of infringement occurring within the United States enabled further reproduction abroad.

LANS urges us to adopt the Second Circuit's rule because the unauthorized copying of its works in the United States enabled further exploitation abroad. While the extraterritorial damages resulted from Reuters's overseas dissemination of the works received by satellite transmissions from Visnews and EBU, those transmissions were made possible by the infringing acts of copying in New York. The satellite transmissions, thus, were merely a means of shipping the unlicensed footage abroad for further dissemination.

The *Subafilms* court's concerns are inapplicable to the present case. The Second Circuit rule would not permit application of American law to "acts of infringement that take place entirely abroad." *Subafilms*, 24 F.3d at 1098. Nor would a copyright holder be entitled to recover extraterritorial damages unless the damages flowed from extraterritorial exploitation of an infringing act that occurred in the United States. * * * We therefore hold that LANS is entitled to recover damages flowing from exploitation abroad of the domestic acts of infringement committed by defendants. * * *

III.   Statutory Damages

Because we reverse the district court's ruling on extraterritorial damages and affirm its ruling on the fair use defense, we must remand for a new trial on actual damages. Accordingly, we conditionally vacate the award of statutory damages. LANS retains the right, however, to make an election before final judgment to recover statutory damages instead of actual damages and profits. 17 U.S.C. § 504(c)(1). Should LANS elect statutory damages, the district court should reinstate its prior award. Against that eventuality, we will address defendants' cross-appeal challenging the statutory damages award.

A.   Innocent Infringement

The district court found that defendants did not sustain their burden of proving that they were not aware and had no reason to believe that their acts constituted an infringement of copyright, and thus were not entitled to the reduction in statutory damages under § 504(c)(2). Whether the defendants' infringement was innocent is a factual determination which we review for clear error. *See Frank Music Corp. v. Metro–Goldwyn–Mayer, Inc.*, 772 F.2d 505, 515 (9th Cir. 1985).

1.   LANS's works were embedded in a licensed work

Defendants contend first that they had "no practicable alternative but to copy those portions of [LANS's] works which were embedded in a licensed work." But practicability is not a proxy for innocence. The argument does not sustain the burden of proving that Visnews "was not aware and had no reason to believe that [its] acts constituted an infringement." *See* 17 U.S.C. § 504(c)(2).

2.   Defendants' awareness of limitations on use

* * * The court also found, however, that it can be inferred that whoever at Visnews and EBU made the copies of the *Today* show knew that the feed contained "a downstream that credited KCOP for the production." *Reuters II*, 942 F.Supp. 1275 at 1280. The downstream indicates that the portion of tape belongs to someone other than NBC and "could indicate that there were in fact restrictions on any further use of the copyrighted works, and lead a reasonable person to inquire whether copying the feed would infringe a copyright held by KCOP or by another." *Id.*

Defendants have the burden of proving that the infringement was innocent. *See* 17 U.S.C. § 504(c)(2). The district court's finding that they failed to meet their burden is not clearly erroneous.

B.   Even Assuming No Innocent Infringement, the Award Was Excessive

Defendants argue, in the alternative, that the award was excessive because LANS licensed the works to the networks and others for lesser amounts and had even established a liquidated damage figure of $10,000 for *un*authorized use of the works. * * *

The court found that although LANS charged the networks only $3,500 for the licenses, these licenses carried numerous restrictions and were of limited duration. Later licenses with various restrictions and durations brought from $5,000 to $6,500. LANS secured a total of $250,000 to $300,000 in license fees for the Reginald Denny tape and less for the other tape. LANS would have charged $250,000 for an unlimited domestic license for the works. The court also took into account the public benefit from such works and the need to encourage their creation. To this end, LANS "must be allowed to profit from them, without concern that expediency, exigent circumstances or the very nature of the fast-breaking news-gathering business will deprive [it] of potential profits from those works." *Reuters II*, 942 F.Supp. at 1283.

The district court "is in a better position than are we to determine appropriate damages." *Harris*, 734 F.2d at 1335; *Peer Int'l Corp.*, 909 F.2d at 1337. Its determination of the amount of statutory damages was not clearly erroneous. * * *

IV.   Denial of Attorney Fees

The district court denied the applications for attorney's fees, concluding that "both parties prevailed on significant issues in the case and thus neither can be viewed to be *the* prevailing party." (Emphasis in the original.) Because we reverse the district court's ruling on extraterritorial damages and remand for a trial on actual damages, we must vacate the attorney's fees order without prejudice, of course, to further proceedings following trial.

LANS requests attorney's fees on appeal pursuant to 17 U.S.C. § 505. We conclude that fees are warranted inasmuch as it served the purposes of the Copyright Act for LANS to establish its right to extraterritorial damages and to defend its favorable ruling below on fair use. *Fantasy, Inc. v. Fogerty*, 94 F.3d 553, 561 (9th Cir. 1996). We award LANS its costs and attorney's fees on appeal, the amount to be determined by the district court on remand.

CONCLUSION

The district court's judgment is affirmed in part and reversed in part. We AFFIRM the court's ruling barring the fair use defense. We REVERSE the ruling barring the claim for extraterritorial damages and REMAND for a trial on actual damages, with directions that if LANS elects to recover actual damages, the award of statutory damages be vacated. If LANS elects to recover statutory damages, the present award shall stand. The ruling denying attorney's fees and costs is VACATED without prejudice to further proceedings upon entry of judgment. We award LANS its attorney's fees and costs on appeal, the amount of attorney's fees to be determined by the district court on remand.

Notes

1. Paramount Pictures, which owned the copyright in the *Star Trek* TV series and movies, sued Carol Publishing Group publishing a book that allegedly infringed their copyrights in *Paramount Pictures Corp. v. Carol Publishing Group,* 11 F.Supp.2d 329 (S.D.N.Y. 1998). Sam Ramer wrote the 1997 "Joy of Trek: How to Enhance Your Relations with a STAR TREK Fan" using quotes taken from the series. Paramount alerted Carol Publishing that the book infringed its copyright and to stop publication, but Carol Publishing refused. The court ruled the book was substantially similar to the Star Trek Properties, thus infringing the copyright. Ramer claimed the use of the material was fair use, "criticism, comment, news reporting, teaching, scholarship, or research." However, the court decided his extensive use of copyrighted material was not used for these purposes and not fair use. Carol Publishing was enjoined from publishing and distributing the book.

2. Gail Brewer–Giorgio is the writer of books that claim that singer Elvis Presley did not die in 1977. She documented sightings of Elvis around Kalamazoo, Mich. She also allegedly received a telephone call from Presley about 11 years after his death. *Gail Brewer–Giorgio*, Fortune City, *at* http://members.fortunecity.com/sivlenoramoran/gail.htm. She based popular TV specials on her copyrighted books. There was a dispute about the second TV special in *Brewer-Giorgio v. Producers Video, Inc.*, 216 F.3d 1281 (11th Cir. 2000). Brewer–Giorgio claims Elvis is still alive and has written a book called "The Elvis Files." Producer's Video received the rights to use information in her book to make a television program called "The Elvis Files." She wrote the special and was on the show. A sequel was made called "The Elvis Conspiracy," but Brewer–Giorgio could not agree about payments from the original special. She refused to participate in the sequel and would not approve the show. However, the sequel was broadcast anyway in 1992 with her name and part of the first show replayed. At the end, the show's host indicated that Elvis died on August 16, 1977. She filed for copyright infringement in 1995, just three days before the statute of limitations ran out. The court ruled the lawsuit was barred because she had not registered the copyright in the scripts before the tolling of the statute of limitations and affirmed the ruling for the defendants.

D. FAIR USE

The 1976 Copyright Act allows "fair use" of items that are copyrighted to make new works for a number of purposes including educational uses and for personal use. Authors can take others' work to make their own derivative work; people can reproduce works for their own uses, such as entertainment; educators and others can copy for "teaching, scholarship, or learning." Four factors must be used to analyze whether a particular use is a fair use, including: a) use of the work, because if it is for a commercial purpose then it uses the copyright; b) establish the type of work to see if it is "a creative work, a compilation, or a derivative work;" c) the proportion of the work used; d) the effect on the work's market as a result of its use. *Regents Guide to Understanding Copyright & Educational Fair Use,* Board of Regents of the University System of Georgia, *at* http://www.usg.edu/admin/legal/copyright/.

PACIFIC & SOUTHERN CO. v. DUNCAN

United States Court of Appeals, Eleventh Circuit, 1984.
744 F.2d 1490.

JOHNSON, Circuit Judge.

Pacific and Southern Company, the owner of a television station, charges that Carol Duncan, d/b/a TV News Clips, has infringed its copyright by videotaping its news broadcasts and selling the tapes to the subjects of the news reports. We hold that the appellant has violated the copyright laws because her activities do not constitute "fair use" of the material. We also conclude that the television station is entitled to a permanent injunction preventing the appellant from continuing to infringe its copyright. Accordingly, we affirm in part and reverse in part.

I. FACTS

Pacific and Southern Company does business as WXIA–TV, a television station in Atlanta, Georgia. It broadcasts four local news programs each day and places a notice of copyright at the end of each newscast. A program consists of self-contained news stories originating outside the studio and linked together by live commentary from the anchor persons, along with weather reports and shorter news reports originating from the studio itself. WXIA records the entire program on videotape and audiotape. It retains a written transcript of the program for a year and the audiotape for an indefinite period of time; it also maintains videotape copies of all the news stories taped before broadcast and stories originating live from a location outside the studio. The station erases the videotape of the entire program after seven days, a practice that destroys any record of the visual element of segments of the show broadcast live from within the studio.

WXIA does not currently market videotape copies of its news stories. Nevertheless, some people ask the station for a chance to view a tape at the station or to purchase a copy for personal use. WXIA has always honored requests to view tapes and usually allows persons to buy the tapes they want. The revenue from tape sales is a small portion of WXIA's total profits.

Carol Duncan operates a business known as TV News Clips, a commercial enterprise belonging to a nationwide association of news clipping organizations. TV News Clips videotapes television news programs, identifies the persons and organizations covered by the news reports, and tries to sell them copies of the relevant portion of the newscast. It does not seek the permission of WXIA or any other broadcaster before selling the tapes, nor does it place a notice of copyright on the tapes. A label on each tape does say, however, that it is "for personal use only not for rebroadcast." TV News Clips erases all tapes after one month.

This case began when TV News Clips sold a copy of a news feature to Floyd Junior College, the subject of a story aired by WXIA on March 11, 1981. WXIA obtained the tape purchased by Floyd Junior College, registered its copyright, and brought this action to obtain damages for the infringement of its copyright and an injunction preventing unauthorized copying and sales of its news program. The district court, 572 F.Supp. 1186, found that the news feature was protected by the copyright laws and that TV News Clips had not made "fair use" of the material. It rejected the fair use defense without reaching the four factors listed in 17 U.S.C.A. § 107 (1977), because TV News Clips had not met its threshold burden of showing that its activity served a purpose such as "criticism, comment, news reporting, teaching ... scholarship, or research," categories listed in the preamble to Section 107. Yet despite finding that TV News Clips had clearly violated WXIA's copyright, the district court denied the request for an injunction for three reasons. First, the sales did not seriously threaten WXIA's creativity, so an injunction would not significantly further the main objective of the copyright laws, fostering creativity. Second, the court feared that an injunction would threaten First Amendment values served by the increased public availability of the news made possible by TV News Clips. Finally, the court found that WXIA had abandoned its copyright on several portions of the newscasts; it declined to formulate a decree that would distinguish between the abandoned and unabandoned portions.

II. "Fair Use" Defense to Statutory Liability

The news feature broadcast by WXIA undoubtedly falls within the protection of the copyright laws. The editorial judgment used to present effectively the events covered by the broadcast made it an "original" work of authorship, *Wainwright Sec., Inc. v. Wall St. Transcript Corp.*, 558 F.2d 91, 95 (2d Cir.1977), *cert. denied*, 434 U.S. 1014 (1978), and the feature became "fixed" in a tangible medium when it was recorded at the time of transmission. Thus, it met the requirements of 17 U.S.C.A. § 102 (1977). The fact that the infringing tape is the only exact copy of the transmission still in existence does not nullify the copyright. The statute requires only that the original work be "fixed" for a period of "more than transitory duration," not for the entire term of the copyright. 17 U.S.C.A. §§ 101, 102 (1977).

A copyright grants to the owner several exclusive rights, including the right to reproduce the copyrighted work and to distribute copies to the public. The courts have, however, developed over the years the concept of "fair use" to describe some limited and useful forms of copying and distribution that are tolerated as exceptions to copyright protection. The 1976 Copyright Act codified this judicial doctrine at 17 U.S.C.A. § 107 (1977) without significantly altering it. The statute divides into a "preamble" and a list of factors to consider during the search for fair use: The fair use of a copyrighted work, including such use by reproduction in copies ... for purposes such as criticism, comment, news reporting, teaching (including multiple copies for classroom use), scholarship, or research, is not an infringement of copyright. In determining whether the use made of a work in any particular case is a fair use the factors to be considered shall include—(1) the purpose and character of the use, including whether such use is of a commercial nature or is for nonprofit educational purposes; (2) the nature of the copyrighted work; (3) the amount and substantiality of the portion used in relation to the copyrighted work as a whole; and (4) the effect of the use upon the potential market for or value of the copyrighted work. 17 U.S.C.A. § 107 (1977).

* * * We agree with TV News Clips that the district court should have considered the four factors set out in the statute. The statute uses mandatory language to the effect that in a fair use determination, the "factors to be considered *shall* include" (emphasis added) the four listed. The preamble merely illustrates the sorts of uses likely to qualify as fair uses under the four listed factors. * * *

The district court resolved all the issues of fact necessary for us to conclude as a matter of law that TV News Clips' activities do not qualify as a fair use of the copyrighted work. *See Triangle Publ'n, Inc. v. Knight–Ridder Newspapers, Inc.*, 626 F.2d 1171, 1175 (5th Cir.1980) (analyzing usage under the four statutory factors where district court had made findings under an erroneous view of controlling legal principles).

The purpose and character of TV News Clips' use of WXIA's work heavily influences our decision in this case. TV News Clips copies and distributes the broadcast for unabashedly commercial reasons despite the fact that its customers buy the tapes for personal use. The district court characterized TV News Clips as a "full-fledged commercial operation." 572 F.Supp. at 1189. TV News Clips denies that its activities have a commercial purpose; instead, it says that its purpose is "private news reporting," meant to provide the public with a record of news reports. Of course, every commercial exchange of goods and services involves both the giving of the good or service and the taking of the purchase price. The fact that TV News Clips focuses on the giving rather than the taking cannot hide the fact that profit is its primary motive for making the exchange. * * *

We also note that TV News Clips' use is neither productive nor creative in any way. It does not analyze the broadcast or improve it at all. Indeed, WXIA expressed concern over the technical inferiority of the tapes. TV News Clips only copies and sells. As the uses listed in the preamble to Section 107 indicate, fair uses are those that contribute in some way to the public welfare. * * * The unproductive nature of TV News Clips' use affects the balance in this case.

The fourth fair use factor, the effect on the potential market for the work, is closely related to the first. By examining the effect of a use, a reviewing court can measure the success of the original purpose and single out those purposes that most directly threaten the incentives for creativity which the copyright tries to protect. Some commercial purposes, for example, might not threaten the incentives because the user profits from an activity that the owner could not possibly take advantage of. But in this case, TV News Clips uses the broadcasts for a purpose that WXIA might use for its own benefit. The fact that WXIA does not actively market copies of the news programs does not matter, for Section 107 looks to the "potential market" in analyzing the effects of an alleged infringement. Copyrights protect owners who immediately market a work no more stringently than owners who delay before entering the market. TV News Clips sells a significant number of copies that WXIA could itself sell if it so desired; therefore, TV News Clips competes with WXIA in a potential market and thereby injures the television station. This evidence is reinforced by a presumption established in *Sony* that a commercial use naturally produces harmful effects. 104 S. Ct. at 793. The actual harmful effect, along with the presumption, undermines any fair use defense.

The third factor directs our attention to the amount and substantiality of the portion used in relation to the copyrighted work as a whole. The Floyd Junior College story stands alone as a coherent narrative, and WXIA saves it as a distinct unit for future reference apart from the rest of the March 11 broadcast. The Register of Copyrights issued a certificate of copyright for the Floyd Junior College segment and for the entire broadcast. Moreover, the district court found that WXIA had properly registered the story and the whole broadcast. We agree with the district court that the feature stands alone as a copyrighted work in this case. Hence, TV News Clips copied an entire work. And even if the story could not stand independent of the entire newscast, we could not ignore the fact that TV News Clips tapes virtually all of the broadcast on a daily basis. By bringing a suit for injunctive relief as well as damages, WXIA is challenging the entire practice of copying and selling news stories, not just the sale of the Floyd Junior College story. Because TV News Clips uses virtually all of a copyrighted work, the fair use defense drifts even further out of its reach. *See Marcus v. Rowley*, 695 F.2d 1171 (9th Cir. 1983).

Finally, the second factor calls on us to analyze the nature of the copyrighted work. This is the only factor that arguably works in favor of TV News Clips. The importance to society of the news could affect the definition of a fair use for a number of reasons. But the courts should also take care not to discourage authors from addressing important topics for fear of losing their copyright protections. The necessarily limited impact of this second factor, along with the commercial and unproductive purpose of the use, the injury to the potential market, and the substantial amount of copying, leads us to conclude that TV News Clips has not made fair use of the protected work. * * *

III. CONSTITUTIONAL LIMITS ON STATUTORY LIABILITY

The appellant claims that even if its fair use defense fails, the First Amendment protects its activity. WXIA, when it enforces the copyright, allegedly violates the First Amendment in two different ways. First, it destroys and suppresses evidence of possible use in a defamation action against itself, and second, it denies the public its right of access to broadcast material. An effort to discourage defamation suits might be an abuse of the copyright laws and a violation of the First Amendment, but that possibility is entirely imaginary in this case. As for the right of public access, we acknowledge that the public has a limited interest in "making television broadcasting more available." 104 S. Ct. at 795. This public interest might be threatened if WXIA absolutely refused to allow the public to view recordings or scripts of its broadcasts. But as the Supreme Court made clear in *Sony*, the public interest in broadcast availability does not protect every activity that exposes more viewers to a broadcast. Furthermore, TV News Clips only increases access in a limited way by selling to a small group of customers, some of whom would buy a tape from WXIA anyway. Because the public already has access to this material and TV News Clips does not offer any access that WXIA could not provide, TV News Clips' activities fall well beyond whatever protections might be available to further this public access interest. The First Amendment does not conflict with WXIA's effort to enforce its copyright in this case.

Finally, TV News Clips argues that every copyright must further the ends of the Copyright Clause of the Constitution. WXIA's copyright, TV News Clips says, does not further those ends and should not be enforced, because WXIA systematically destroys its broadcast videotapes and deprives the public of the benefits of its creative efforts. We agree that the Constitution allows Congress to create copyright laws only if they benefit society as a whole rather than authors alone. That is what the Congress has done. But this does not mean that every copyright holder must offer benefits to society, for the copyright is an incentive rather than a command. * * *

WXIA provides complete access for seven days and permanent access to everything except the visual images broadcast live from within the studio. The public benefits from this creative work; therefore, enforcing the copyright statute in this case does not violate the Copyright Clause.

IV. REMEDY

WXIA has proven that TV News Clips infringed its copyright. The district court found that TV News Clips had regularly copied the newscast and sold the tapes, and would continue to do so. Unless it can obtain an injunction, WXIA can only enforce its copyrights against TV News Clips by finding out which stories have been copied and sold, registering those stories, and bringing many different infringement actions against TV News Clips. Each infringement action would yield a rather small damage recovery. This is a classic case, then, of a past infringement and a substantial likelihood of future infringements which would normally entitle the copyright holder to a permanent injunction against the infringer pursuant to 17 U.S.C.A. § 502(a) (1977). *See Milene Music, Inc. v. Gotauco*, 551 F.Supp. 1288 (D.R.I. 1982); 3 *Nimmer on Copyright* § 13.05[B] (1983). The question is whether the district court abused its discretion in refusing to issue the injunction. Because none of the three grounds relied upon by the court for denying injunctive relief is legally sufficient to support the decision, we hold that the court did abuse its discretion. * * *

Finally, the district court found injunctive relief inappropriate because WXIA regularly abandons the copyright on a portion of its program when it erases the videotape of the entire broadcast. Certainly the erasure shows that WXIA did not desire to distribute post-broadcast copies of parts of the program. Failure to distribute a work does not mean, however, that an owner intends to allow others to use the work, and it is questionable whether WXIA had such an intent. Destroying the only known copy of a work would seem to be the best way to assure that it will not be used by another. Still, we do not say that destruction of the only copy of a work can never establish intent to abandon. We defer to the trial court's factual finding that WXIA intended to abandon portions of its program. * * * Thus, the trial court relied on irrelevant and insufficient grounds in its refusal to grant injunctive relief. It correctly found that TV News Clips had infringed the copyright of WXIA but abused its discretion by refusing to grant injunctive relief. Accordingly, the judgment is AFFIRMED IN PART, REVERSED IN PART, and REMANDED for further proceedings consistent with this opinion.

RINGGOLD v. BLACK ENTERTAINMENT TELEVISION, INC.

United States Court of Appeals, Second Circuit, 1997.
126 F.3d 70.

NEWMAN, Circuit Judge.

* * * Background

1. *The copyrighted work*. Faith Ringgold is a successful contemporary artist who created, and owns the copyright in, a work of art entitled "Church Picnic Story Quilt" (sometimes hereafter called "Church Picnic" or "the story quilt"). "Church Picnic" is an example of a new form of artistic expression that Ringgold has created. She calls the form a "story quilt design." These designs consist of a painting, a handwritten text, and quilting fabric, all three of which Ringgold unites to communicate parables. The painting is a silk screen on silk quilt. "Church Picnic" is an example of this unusual art form, conveying aspects of the African–American experience in the early 1900's. The painting component of the work depicts a Sunday school picnic held by the Freedom Baptist Church

in Atlanta, Georgia, in 1909. Above and below the painting are twelve numbered panels containing a text written in the idiomatic African–American dialect of the era. * * *

Although Ringgold has retained all rights in the copyright in "Church Picnic," the work itself is owned by the High Museum of Art (the "High Museum") in Atlanta, Georgia. Since 1988 the High Museum has held a non-exclusive license to reproduce "Church Picnic" as a poster (" 'Church Picnic' poster" or "the poster"), and to sell those reproductions. The "Church Picnic" poster sells for $20.00 a copy and was not produced as a limited edition. Thousands of copies of the poster have been sold since 1988. Although the license to reproduce poster copies of "Church Picnic" has terminated, copies of the poster remain available for sale.

Below the portion of the poster that displays "Church Picnic" are several identifying words. "High Museum of Art" appears in letters 1 1/4 inches high. Below these words is the phrase "Faith Ringgold, Church Picnic Story Quilt, 1988, gift of Don and Jill Childress" in letters 1/8 inch high. Below this line, in smaller type, appears "Courtesy Bernice Steinbaum Galley, New York City. Poster 1988 High Museum of Art, Atlanta."

2. *The alleged infringing use.* HBO Independent Productions, a division of HBO, produced "ROC," a television "sitcom" series concerning a middle-class African–American family living in Baltimore. Some time prior to 1992, HBO Independent Productions produced an episode of ROC in which a "Church Picnic" poster, presumably sold by the High Museum, was used as part of the set decoration.

The title character of "ROC" lives with his wife, Eleanor, his adult brother, Joey, and his father. In the episode in question, Roc pressures Joey, a jazz trumpeter, into giving trumpet lessons to some children in the church congregation, so that Joey, a perpetually unemployed gambler, can earn money to repay a debt he owes to Roc. After the children have taken some lessons, the minister of the church suggests that they give a recital in the newly-remodeled church hall. A five-minute scene of the recital concludes the episode. The "Church Picnic" poster was used as a wall-hanging in the church hall. * * *

In the scene, at least a portion of the poster is shown a total of nine times. In some of those instances, the poster is at the center of the screen, although nothing in the dialogue, action, or camera work particularly calls the viewer's attention to the poster. The nine sequences in which a portion of the poster is visible range in duration from 1.86 to 4.16 seconds. The aggregate duration of all nine sequences is 26.75 seconds. We describe these sequences in more detail below.

The copy of the poster used in the episode was framed without the identifying wording that appears beneath the artwork. As framed, the poster includes a notice of copyright, but the type is too small to be discernible to a television viewer.

A broadcast television network first televised the episode in 1992, and in October 1994 BET aired the episode for the first time on cable television. In January 1995, Ringgold happened to watch the episode on BET (apparently a repeat showing), and at that time became aware of the defendants' use of the poster as part of the set decoration.

3. *District Court proceedings.* Ringgold sued the defendants, alleging infringement of her copyright in "Church Picnic Story Quilt," in violation of 17 U.S.C. § 106 (1994), because of the unauthorized use of the poster as part of the set decoration for the episode of "ROC." The complaint also alleged common law unfair competition and a violation of New York's statute protecting artistic authorship rights. *See* N.Y. Arts & Cult. Aff. Law § 14.03 (McKinney Supp. 1995). * * * The District Court denied the plaintiff's motion for a preliminary injunction, granted defendants' motion for summary judgment, and dismissed the complaint. Apparently accepting, or at least assuming, that the plaintiff had sufficiently alleged a claim of copyright infringement, Judge Martin rejected her infringement claim on the ground that undisputed facts established the defendants' fair use defense. * * *

DISCUSSION

The Copyright Act grants certain exclusive rights to the owner of a copyright, see 17 U.S.C. § 106 (1994), including the right to make and distribute copies and derivative works based on the copyrighted work, and the right to display the copyrighted work publicly, id. § 106(1)-(3), (5). In the absence of defenses, these exclusive rights normally give a copyright owner the right to seek royalties from others who wish to use the copyrighted work. See Am. Geophysical Union v. Texaco, Inc., 60 F.3d 913, 929 (2d Cir. 1994, as amended, July 17, 1995) ("American Geophysical"); see also DC Comics, Inc. v. Reel Fantasy, Inc., 696 F.2d 24, 28 (2d Cir. 1982) (noting that one benefit of owning a copyright is the right to license its use for a fee). Ringgold contends that the defendants violated this licensing right by using the "Church Picnic" poster to decorate the set of their sitcom without her authorization.

The case law provides little illumination concerning claims that copyright in a visual work has been infringed by including it within another visual work. * * * HBO and BET defend their use of the poster on two separate, though related grounds: (a) that their use of the poster was *de minimis*, and (b) that, as Judge Martin ruled, their use of the poster was a permissible "fair use," see 17 U.S.C. § 107.

I.   *De minimis*

A.   *The de minimis Concept in Copyright Law*

The legal maxim "*de minimis non curat lex*" (sometimes rendered, "the law does not concern itself with trifles") insulates from liability those who cause insignificant violations of the rights of others. In the context of copyright law, the concept of de minimis has significance in three respects, which, though related, should be considered separately.

First, *de minimis* in the copyright context can mean what it means in most legal contexts: a technical violation of a right so trivial that the law will not impose legal consequences. * * * In *Knickerbocker Toy Co. v. Azrak–Hamway Int'l, Inc.,* 668 F.2d 699, 703 (2d Cir. 1982), we relied on the *de minimis* doctrine to reject a toy manufacturer's claim based on a photograph of its product in an office copy of a display card of a competitor's product where the display card was never used. *See id.* at 702.

Second, *de minimis* can mean that copying has occurred to such a trivial extent as to fall below the quantitative threshold of substantial similarity, which is always a required element of actionable copying. *See* Nimmer § 13.03[A], at 13–27. * * * In the pending case, there is no dispute about copying as a factual matter: the "Church Picnic" poster itself, not some poster that was similar in some respects to it, was displayed on the set of defendants' television program. What defendants dispute when they assert that their use of the poster was *de minimis* is whether the admitted copying occurred to an extent sufficient to constitute actionable copying, i.e., infringement. That requires "substantial similarity" in the sense of actionable copying, and it is that sense of the phrase to which the concept of *de minimis* is relevant. * * *

In cases involving visual works, like the pending one, the quantitative component of substantial similarity also concerns the observability of the copied work—the length of time the copied work is observable in the allegedly infringing work and such factors as focus, lighting, camera angles, and prominence. Thus, as in this case, a copyrighted work might be copied as a factual matter, yet a serious dispute might remain as to whether the copying that occurred was actionable. Since "substantial similarity," properly understood, includes a quantitative component, it becomes apparent why the concept of de minimis is relevant to a defendant's contention that an indisputably copied work has not been infringed. * * *

Third, *de minimis* might be considered relevant to the defense of fair use. One of the statutory factors to be assessed in making the fair use determination is "the amount and substantiality of the portion used in relation to the copyrighted work as a whole," 17 U.S.C. § 107(3) (emphasis added). * * * The third fair use factor concerns a quantitative continuum. Like all the fair use factors, it has no precise threshold below which the factor is accorded decisive significance. If the amount copied is very slight in relation to the work as a whole, the third factor might strongly favor the alleged infringer, but that will not always be the case. *See, e.g., Iowa State Univ. Research Found., Inc.* v. *Am. Broad. Co., Inc.,* 621 F.2d 57, 59, 61–62 (2d Cir. 1980) (television program's copying of portions of copyrighted film, including an eight second segment). More important, the fair use defense involves a careful examination of many factors, often confronting courts with a perplexing task. If the allegedly infringing work makes such a quantitatively insubstantial use of the copyrighted work as to fall below the threshold required for actionable copying, it makes more sense to reject the claim on that basis and find no infringement, rather than undertake an elaborate fair use analysis in order to uphold a defense.

B. The de minimis Concept Applied to Defendants' Copying

* * * The parties differ, at least in emphasis, as to the observability of what was copied. Our own inspection of a tape of the program reveals that some aspects of observability are not fairly in dispute. In the longest segment, between 4 and 5 seconds, nearly all of the poster, at least 80 percent, is visible. The camera is positioned to the right of about eight members of the audience seated on the left side of the center aisle (facing the stage), and the poster is on the wall immediately to the left of the end of the rows of two or three spectators. * * *

Since the camera focuses precisely on the members of the audience, the poster, hung to their left, is not in perfect focus, but it is so close to them that the poster is plainly observable, even though not in exact focus. An observer can see that what is hung is some form of artwork, depicting a group of African–American adults and children with a pond in the background. The brevity of the segment and the lack of perfect focus preclude identification of the details of the work, but the two-dimensional aspect of the figures and the bold colors are seen in sufficient clarity to suggest a work somewhat in the style of Grandma Moses. Only the painting portion of the poster is observable; the text material and the bordering quilting cannot be discerned.

All the other segments are of lesser duration and/or contain smaller and less distinct portions of the poster. However, their repetitive effect somewhat reinforces the visual effect of the observable four-to-five-second segment just described.

A helpful analogy in determining whether the purpose and duration of the segments should be regarded as de minimis is the regulation issued by the Librarian of Congress providing for royalties to be paid by public broadcasting entities for the use of published pictorial and visual works. See 37 C.F.R. § 253.8 (1996) (implementing 17 U.S.C. § 118(b)). The Librarian appoints the Register of Copyrights, who serves as the director of the Copyright Office. See 17 U.S.C. § 701. The Librarian's regulation distinguishes between a "featured" and a "background" display, setting a higher royalty rate for the former. Id. § 253.8(b)(1)(i)(A), (B). Obviously the Librarian has concluded that use of a copyrighted visual work even as "background" in a television program normally requires payment of a license fee. Moreover, the Librarian has defined a "featured" display as "a full-screen or substantially full screen display for more than three seconds," id. § 253.8(b)(2), and a "background" display as "any display less than full-screen or substantially full-screen, or full-screen for three seconds or less," id. If defendants' program were to be shown on public television, plaintiff would appear to be entitled to a "background" license fee for a "less than full-screen" display. * * *

The painting component of the poster is recognizable as a painting, and with sufficient observable detail for the "average lay observer," see

Rogers v. Koons, 960 F.2d 301, 307 (2d Cir. 1992) (internal quotation omitted), to discern African–Americans in Ringgold's colorful, virtually two-dimensional style. The de minimis threshold for actionable copying of protected expression has been crossed.

II.   Fair Use

* * * In reviewing the grant of summary judgment, we note preliminarily that the District Court gave no explicit consideration to whether the defendants' use was within any of the categories that the preamble to section 107 identifies as illustrative of a fair use, or even whether it was similar to such categories. Though the listed categories—criticism, comment, news reporting, teaching, scholarship, and research, see 17 U.S.C. § 107—have an " 'illustrative and not limitative' " function, *see Campbell v. Acuff–Rose Music, Inc.*, 510 U.S. 569, 577 (1994) (quoting 17 U.S.C. § 101), and the four factors should be considered even if a challenged use is not within any of these categories, *see Pacific and S. Co. v. Duncan*, 744 F.2d 1490, 1495 (11th Cir. 1984), the illustrative nature of the categories should not be ignored. As the Supreme Court's recent and significant fair use opinion in Campbell observes, "The enquiry [concerning the first fair use factor] may be guided by the examples given in the preamble to § 107, looking to whether the use is for criticism, or comment, or news reporting, and the like. . . ." *Campbell*, 510 U.S. at 578–79.

1.   *First factor.* Considering the first fair use factor with the preamble illustrations as a "guide[]," id., we observe that the defendants' use of Ringgold's work to decorate the set for their television episode is not remotely similar to any of the listed categories. * * * The defendants have used Ringgold's work for precisely a central purpose for which it was created—to be decorative. Even if the thematic significance of the poster and its relevance to the ROC episode are not discernible, the decorative effect is plainly evident. * * *

In considering whether a visual work has been "supplanted" by its use in a movie or a television program, care must be taken not to draw too close an analogy to copying of written works. When all or a substantial portion of text that contains protectible expression is included in another work, solely to convey the original text to the reader without adding any comment or criticism, the second work may be said to have supplanted the original because a reader of the second work has little reason to buy a copy of the original. Although some books and other writings are profitably reread, their basic market is the one-time reader. By contrast, visual works are created, and sold or licensed, usually for repetitive viewing. Thus, the fact that the episode of ROC does not supplant the need or desire of a television viewer to see and appreciate the poster (or the original) again and again does not mean that the defendants' use is of a "purpose and character" that favors fair use. Indeed, unauthorized displays of a visual work might often increase viewers' desire to see the work again. Nevertheless, where, as here, the purpose of the challenged use is, at a minimum, the same decorative purpose for which the poster is sold, the defendants' use has indeed "superseded the objects" of the original, *see Folsom*, 9 F. Cas. at *348* (emphasis added), and does not favor fair use. * * *

2. *Second factor*. The District Court accepted the plaintiff's contention that the second fair use factor weighs in her favor because of the creative nature of her work.

3. *Third factor*. Though we have earlier noted that the de minimis concept is inappropriate for a fair use analysis, since a copying that is de minimis incurs no liability, without the need for an elaborate fair use inquiry, the third fair use factor obliges a court to consider the amount and substantiality of the portion used, whenever that portion crosses the de minimis threshold for actionable copying. The District Court properly considered the brevity of the intervals in which the poster was observable and the fact that in some segments only a portion of the poster and the nearly full view was not in precise focus. Our own viewing of the episode would incline us to weight the third factor less strongly toward the defendants than did Judge Martin, but we are not the fact-finders, and the fact-finding pertinent to each fair use factor, under proper legal standards, is for the District Court, although the ultimate conclusion is a mixed question of law and fact, *Harper & Row*, 471 U.S. at 560, subject to de novo review, *New Era Publ'n Int'l, ApS*, 904 F.2d 152, 155 (2d Cir. 1990). * * *

4. *Fourth factor*. The fourth fair use factor is "the effect of the use upon the potential market for or value of the copyrighted work." 17 U.S.C. § 107(4) (emphasis added). "It requires courts to consider not only the extent of market harm caused by the alleged infringer, but also 'whether unrestricted and widespread conduct of the sort engaged in by the defendant ... would result in substantially adverse impact on the potential market for the original.' " *Campbell*, 510 U.S. at 590 (quoting Nimmer § 13.05[A][4] (at 13–187 in 1997 edition)). Ringgold contends that there is a potential market for licensing her story quilts, and stated in an affidavit that in 1995 she earned $31,500 from licensing her various artworks and that she is often asked to license her work for films and television. Specifically, she avers that in 1992 she was asked to license use of the "Church Picnic" poster by the producers of another TV sitcom and declined because of an inadequate price and inadequate artist's credit. * * * We have endeavored to avoid the vice of circularity by considering "only traditional, reasonable, or likely to be developed markets" when considering a challenged use upon a potential market. Ringgold's affidavit clearly raises a triable issue of fact concerning a market for licensing her work as set decoration. She is not alleging simply loss of the revenue she would have earned from a compensated copying; she is alleging an "exploitation of the copyrighted material without paying the customary price." *SeeHarper & Row*, 471 U.S. at 562 (emphasis added). * * *

Ringgold is not required to show a decline in the number of licensing requests for the "Church Picnic" poster since the ROC episode was aired. The fourth factor will favor her if she can show a "traditional, reasonable, or likely to be developed" market for licensing her work as set decoration. Certainly "unrestricted and widespread conduct of the sort engaged in by the defendants ... would result in substantially adverse impact on the potential market for [licensing of] the original." *Campbell*, 510 U.S. at 590 (internal quotation omitted). Particularly in view of what Ringgold has averred and is prepared to prove, the record on the fourth fair use factor is inadequate to permit summary judgment for the defendants. * * *

Conclusion

For all of these reasons, plaintiff's copyright infringement claim must be returned to the District Court to afford an opportunity for further development of the record and a sensitive aggregate assessment by the fact-finder of the fair use factors in light of the applicable legal principles. Upon remand, the Court should give renewed consideration to plaintiff's claim under the New York Artists' Authorship Rights Act. However, because Ringgold has not challenged the dismissal of her preempted unfair competition claim, we affirm the District Court's dismissal of that claim.

The judgment of the District Court is reversed, and the case is remanded.

Notes

1. In *Sony Corp. of America v. Universal City Studios, Inc.*, 464 U.S. 417, 104 S.Ct. 774, 78 L.Ed.2d 574 (1984), the Supreme Court decided that the Sony Betamax did not infringe on the copyright holders rights to control the reproduction of their works. The Court loosely used the fair use test to determine that because the Betamax was capable of a non-infringing use, it was a fair use for consumers to tape shows broadcast over the air.

2. The first videocassette recorder (VCR) for home use was the ½-inch Betamax which was made by Sony beginning in 1975. Sony gambled that consumers would pay more for high quality reproduction. In 1976, JVC developed the VHS format. VHS offered lower quality reproduction, but it cost less than the Betamax. In a very short number of years, VHS captured the market and the Betamax and Beta tapes were phased out. Association of Moving Image Archivists, *at* http://www.amianet.org/11_Information/11g_VidPres/history.html.

Chapter 9

TELEVISION CONTRACTS

Contracts are important to every aspect of television production, from the idea stage to the final exhibition and licensing of material for distribution on videotapes. As in film, TV contracts may be oral or written. If oral, the question becomes whether there was sufficient agreement among the parties to form a contract. Even when there are written pages available, the parties must clearly intend their words to form a contract.

oral

This chapter explores a variety of issues related to television agreements. Part A addresses issues of contract formation. Part B presents cases where there is clearly an express contract and the question arises whether there has been a breach of the parties' intention as manifested in written form. Part C concludes this chapter by presenting situations where labor unions seek to enforce contracts entered into by their members.

The following article discusses some of the pitfalls that writers encounter in selling their work to Hollywood producers and studios.

Sherri Burr
The Writer's Journey of Selling to Hollywood:
Conversations with Tony Hillerman and
Alicia Valdés-Rodriguez

Copyright © 2004 by Sherri Burr.

Selling to Hollywood producers and studios has generated varied experiences for authors. Tony Hillerman, 78, began writing in high school and never quit. When he spoke to the Southwest Writers group on October 4, 2003, he described "writing as a hard way to make a living." He encouraged writers to "go into it because it's an incredible habit, . . . but leave out the parts the readers skip. Don't write to earn money. If you want to get rich, buy oil leases."

Hillerman's debut novel, "The Blessing Way," received 101 rejection slips before being picked up by Harper & Row, now HarperCollins, and published in 1980. Hillerman has had several of his 16 books set on the Navajo reservation optioned to become feature films and television movies. In 1993, *The Dark Wind* was turned into a feature film, starring Lou Diamond Phillips as Officer Jim Chee, which went straight to video after it failed to win a distribution deal.

Hillerman advises writers that when they receive Hollywood option money, "Tear open the envelope and run out and cash the check immediately. The writer's role in movies is to listen and nod." Over the years, Hollywood executives have suggested changing the location of Hillerman's novels from the Navajo Reservation to Santa Fe, and scriptwriters have resurrected his dead characters. One executive even inquired as to whether Leaphorn, the main protagonist, had to be Navajo.

Eventually, Robert Redford optioned the rights to "Skinwalkers" and other novels and became the executive producer of a PBS series based on Hillerman's books, which began airing in 2002. Redford hired feature film director Chris Eyre [*Smoke Signals*, *Signs*] to direct two of the films in the series. Hillerman advises writers that they have to be prepared for changes. "A good short story makes the best movies," he says.

Like Hillerman, Alicia Valdés-Rodriguez, 36, began writing as a teenager. In 2003, she sold her first novel "The Dirty Girls Social Club" to St. Martins Press for $475,000. Before good fortune struck, potential agents requested Valdés-Rodriguez craft her Hispanic characters as "more ethnic," with "more struggles." One agent asked her, "Can you take your lawyer character and make her a maid."

Valdés-Rodriguez resisted such reform efforts and when "The Dirty Girls Social Club" was published in 2003, the press proclaimed her "The Latina Terry McMillan" and "The Latina Amy Tan." Columbia Pictures paid $40,000 to option her book to become a feature film starring Jennifer Lopez. A script was written. Then *Gigli* premiered and flopped.

"Nobody wants to touch Jennifer Lopez after *Gigli*," Valdés-Rodriguez told the Southwest Writers group on March 6, 2004. "It's unfair. Male actors can have stinker after stinker and still get paid more money for their pictures. Jennifer Lopez had one bomb and everything gets shelved."

After Columbia Pictures gave up, Valdés-Rodriguez decided she would write the screenplay herself and take it to Salma Hayek's production company. She also said that NBC has given her a contract to write a TV pilot. After penning six drafts, the most common response was, "It's not street enough."

Notes

1. A typical agreement to option literary property will specify the name of the author, the title of the property, the compensation, the option period, and the credit. If the picture has the same title as the book, the credit may read, "Based on 'The Dark Wind' by Tony Hillerman," or "Based on the book 'The Dirty Girls Social Club' by Alicia Valdés-Rodriguez." The filmography of the picture or television show will credit the author as "Source

Writer." A complete contract can be found in SIMENSKY, SELZ ET. AL, ENTERTAIN-MENT LAW: DOCUMENTARY SUPP. 2nd Ed. 585–591 (1999).

2.   What are some of the other contract clauses that authors might seek in option contracts? John Grisham, one of the most successful authors to have material converted to the large screen, <u>retains script, director and actor approvals</u>. *See* John Grisham Interview (National Public Radio broadcast, May 23, 1997), *available at* http://www.law5000.com/clr/3_INTERVIEW.htm. After Oliver Stone directed *Natural Born Killers*, which two young people repeatedly viewed before embarking on a killing spree that claimed one of Grisham's friends, <u>Grisham reportedly refuses to permit Stone to direct or Woody Harrelson to act in films from his books.</u> In *Byers v. Edmondson*, 826 So.2d 551 (La. Ct. App. 2002), the judge affirmed a lower court decision dismissing Stone from the lawsuit filed by plaintiffs claiming that *Natural Born Killers* incited two people to injure them. The case is reprinted in Chapter 20, The Devil Media Made Me Do It.

A.   CONTRACT CREATION

PANIZZA v. MATTEL

United States District Court, Southern District of New York, 2003.
2003 WL 22251317.

DANIELS, Judge.

This action was commenced in the Supreme Court of the State of New York, New York County. Defendant removed the case to this Court claiming that <u>plaintiff's state claim was within the subject matter of federal copyright law.</u> Defendant is now moving to dismiss the complaint, pursuant to Fed. R.Civ.P. 12(b), on the grounds of copyright preemption. Plaintiff is cross-moving, pursuant to 28 U.S.C. § 1447(c), for an order remanding the case to the Supreme Court of the State of New York, and for costs associated with the removal and the remand proceedings. Plaintiff's motion for remand and costs is denied. Defendant's motion to dismiss is granted.

Plaintiff is seeking damages for breach of a quasi-contract. The amended complaint alleges that <u>between 1993 and 1994, plaintiff provided certain ideas for two computer programs, to The Learning Company ("TLC") on a confidential basis.</u> These ideas were allegedly accompanied by written and graphic materials, including a videotape of how the program would appear once fully developed. Plaintiff claims that the <u>ideas were presented with the understanding that if TLC was interested in the program, it would underwrite further development of the programs and enter into an agreement with plaintiff whereby TLC would manufacture and sell the programs and compensate her on a royalty basis.</u> TLC declined plaintiff's proposal. Thereafter, TLC was acquired by the defendant. Plaintiff alleges that beginning in September of 1999, defendant manufactured and sold a computer program under the name "Sesame Street Music Maker" which program incorporated many of the ideas and materials she had presented to TLC.

Plaintiff contends that in November of 2000, defendant filed declaratory judgment actions in both the United States District Court for the Central District of California and in the California Superior Court for the County of Los Angles, each seeking a declaration that defendant had not violated any of plaintiff's rights in connection with its "Sesame Street Music Maker." Plaintiff litigated those actions pro se. She claims that in the California federal action, the parties entered into a stipulation dismissing the action after plaintiff signed a declaration.

The declaration reads as follows:

[M]y claim for recovery from Mattel does not arise under any federal right or claim of recovery. I acknowledge that I do not have any claim against Mattel with regard to its "Sesame Street Music Maker" that is for any form of patent infringement, copyright infringement, trade dress infringement or trademark infringement, and I agree that I will not assert such a claim.

Plaintiff now argues that her present action is premised on the unjust enrichment defendant obtained by its unauthorized use of her ideas and materials. Since ideas are not copyrightable, she argues that the action cannot be preempted by copyright law. She further argues that even if her graphic materials could be construed as copyrightable, the complaint does not state that they were incorporated into the defendant's product.

Any civil action that could have originally been filed in federal court may be removed from state court to federal court by a defendant. 28 U.S.C. § 1441(a); Caterpillar Inc. v. Williams, 482 U.S. 386, 392, 107 S.Ct. 2425, 96 L.Ed.2d 318 (1987). The burden of proof rest upon the defendant to demonstrate that the case is properly before the federal court. United Food & Commercial Workers Union v. Centermark Properties Meriden Square, Inc., 30 F.3d 298, 301 (2d Cir.1994). * * *

Since both parties are New York residents, federal question jurisdiction is necessary to afford this Court jurisdiction. 28 U.S.C. § § 1331, 1332. * * * District courts have exclusive jurisdiction over any civil action arising under any Act of Congress relating to copyrights. 28 U.S.C. § 1338(a); see also 17 U.S.C. § 301(a). The federal copyright laws will preempt a state law claim where: (1) "the subject matter of the state-law right falls within the subject matter of the copyright laws;" and (2) "the state-law right asserted is equivalent to the exclusive rights protected by federal copyright law." Kregos v. Associated Press, 3 F.3d 656, 666 (2d Cir.1993) (citing Harper & Row, Publishing, Inc. v. Nation Enterprises, 723 F.2d 195, 200 (2d Cir.1983), rev'd on other grounds 471 U.S. 539, 105 S.Ct. 2218, 85 L.Ed.2d 588 (1985)).

Plaintiff describes her work as ideas for computer programs and related materials, rather than the actual programs themselves or a physical component thereof. Subdivision (b) of 17 U.S.C 102 precludes copyright protection for any idea or concept irrespective of the form in which it is described, explained, illustrated or embodied in such work. The copyright laws protect only the particular expression of an idea and never the idea in and of itself. Eden Toys, Inc. v. Marshall Field & Co.,

Copyright - only protects expression of ideas - not the idea itself

675 F.2d 498, 500 (2d Cir.1982); Reyher v. Children's Television Workshop, 533 F.2d 87, 90 (2d Cir.1976). "[T]he legislative history [of 17 U.S.C § 102(b)] explicitly states that copyright protects computer programs only 'to the extent that they incorporate authorship in programmer's expression of original ideas, as distinguished from the ideas themselves." 'Computer Associates, Int. v. Altai, Inc., 982 F.2d 693, 703 (2d Cir.1992) (quoting H.R.Rep. No. 1476, 94th Cong., 2d Sess. 54, reprinted in 1976 U.S.C.C.A.N. 5659, 5667)). Nevertheless, the preemptive reach of the Copyright Act encompasses state law claims concerning uncopyrightable material. * * * Thus, for purposes of preemption, the Copyright Act applies with equal force to ideas. Katz Dochrermann & Epstein, Inc. v. Home Box Office, 1999 WL 179603, *3 (S.D.N.Y. Mar.31, 1999). * * *

Additionally with respect to the written and graphic materials, including the videotape, they are copyrightable as they are original works of authorship fixed in a tangible medium of expression that include graphic, as well as audiovisual works. 17 U.S.C. § 102(a)(1)(5), (6). Notwithstanding plaintiff's contention to the contrary, the complaint unequivocally states that defendant's computer "program incorporated many of ... the materials which Plaintiff had presented to TLC." Accordingly, the subject matter prong of the test is satisfied here with respect to both the plaintiff's ideas and materials.

Turning to the second prong, referred to as the general scope requirement, courts rely on the extra element test. "[I]f an extra element is 'required instead of or in addition to the acts of reproduction, performance, distribution or display, in order to constitute a state-created cause of action, then the right does not lie within the general scope of copyright, and there is no preemption." 'Computer Associates Int., 982 F.2d at 716 (quoting 1 Nimmer § 1.01[B], at 1–14–15). A state law claim will not be preempted by federal copyright law if the extra element changes the "nature of the action so that it is quantitatively different from a copyright infringement claim." Computer Associates Int., 982 F.2d at 716 (quoting Mayer v. Josiah Wedgwood & Sons, Ltd., 601 F.Supp. 1523, 1535 (S.D.N.Y.1985)).

Plaintiff's action is for breach of a quasi-contract based upon an unjust enrichment theory. The unjust enrichment solely concerns the benefit defendant allegedly received by using plaintiff's ideas and related materials without her permission or authorization to do so. "The overwhelming majority of courts in this circuit have held that an unjust enrichment claim based upon the copying of subject matter within the scope of the Copyright Act is preempted." Boyle, 1998 WL 690816, at *5–6; see also, Cooper v. Sony Records, Int., 2001 WL 1223492, *4–5 (S.D.N.Y.2001). There is no element pled by plaintiff in her complaint to quantitatively differentiate it from those areas protected by federal copyright law. Thus, removal of the action to federal court was proper as plaintiff's state common law claim is preempted by the Copyright Act.

To state a cause of action for infringement, plaintiff must allege ownership of the copyright and the copying by the defendant. Reyher, 533 F.2d at 90 (citations omitted). Plaintiff does not own a copyright for her ideas and materials. As plaintiff herself admitted in her prior declaration, she has no claim against defendant "in any form" for copyright infringement, and will not assert such a claim. Although the nature of plaintiff's claim is preempted by federal copyright law, plaintiff has failed to plead a cognizable cause of action for copyright infringement. Hence, dismissal is warranted.

Accordingly, plaintiff's motions to remand and for costs are denied. Defendant's motion to dismiss the complaint is hereby granted.

Notes

1. The plaintiff in *Panizza v. Mattel* confronted the same issue encountered by plaintiffs in Chapter 1: How do you enforce the use of an idea without an express contract? Like film plaintiffs before her, she sought to have the law imply a quasi contract because she gave the ideas in confidence. In doing so, she found herself in a bind once the defendants removed the case to federal court, which required a federal question when the two parties are from the same court. She properly brought the idea case in state court, but once it was removed to federal court, she would have been better served if she had alleged copyright infringement. She proved once again the difficulty of bringing an idea case based on quasi contract theory.

2. Can letters constitute a contract between two parties? In the following case, the plaintiffs had written down their expectations, but were their letters sufficient to form a contract?

BURR v. AMERICAN NATIONAL THEATRE & ACADEMY

Supreme Court, New York County, New York, Special Term, Part III, 1951.
103 N.Y.S.2d 589.

WALTER, Justice.

[Eugene Burr and Ben Bodec sued the American National Theatre and Academy, C. Lawton Campbell and Vinton Freedly for breach of contract and for other relief.] Defendants move to dismiss the complaint as insufficient upon its face.

For a first cause of action, plaintiffs allege: By letters dated May 15, 1950, the corporate defendant authorized plaintiffs to offer to prospective sponsors on its behalf a proposed television program of which the corporate defendant was to be credited as producer and plaintiffs coproducers, and agreed that plaintiffs should receive $1,000 per show. Plaintiffs procured a named corporation to sponsor a series of programs in accordance with said agreement. The corporate defendant, however, in violation of its contract with plaintiffs, refused to permit the presentation of television programs under the sponsorship of the corporation procured by plaintiffs, and plaintiffs thereby were caused great damage.

Defendants contend that the complaint is insufficient because the letters do not constitute a contract because the authority granted to plaintiffs to procure a sponsor is not exclusive and plaintiffs did not agree to procure or endeavor to procure a sponsor. But even if it be true that by the letters plaintiffs did not agree to do anything, I think the conclusion that, therefore, the complaint is insufficient is untenable. The grant of the authority to procure a sponsor, whether exclusive or not, was at least an offer to pay the agreed $1,000 per show if plaintiffs procured a sponsor, and according to the allegations of the complaint plaintiffs accepted the offer by actually procuring the sponsor, and defendant's offer thereby became a binding promise. It was not necessary that plaintiffs should give a verbal promise in advance to procure a sponsor or use their best efforts to procure one. Defendant asked, not for a promise but for an act, the procurement of a sponsor, and a valid contract resulted when plaintiffs performed that act, even if they had not promised to do the act. * * *

Whether or not the corporate defendant could have withdrawn its offer by revoking plaintiffs' authority before they procured a sponsor need not be considered, because nothing upon the face of the complaint suggests that defendant ever attempted to withdraw its offer. Withdrawing its offer and refusing to produce the shows are two entirely different and unrelated things. * * *

Defendants further contend that the complaint is insufficient because it does not allege that plaintiffs procured a sponsor ready, able and willing to sponsor the program pursuant to the agreement annexed to the complaint.

I think that rests upon a misconstruction of the language of the complaint. What the complaint says in that regard is that the corporation which plaintiffs procured was ready, willing and able to sponsor said program pursuant to the terms of said agreement and in all ways consistent with established custom and usage in the broadcasting and television industry fully to comply with the terms and conditions set forth in said agreement. Defendants' counsel read that as meaning that the corporation which plaintiffs procured was willing to sponsor the program, not in accordance with the agreement, but only in accordance with some unspecified customs and usages by which defendant never agreed to be bound. I read it as meaning that the corporation was willing to sponsor the program in accordance with the agreement, and that as to all the details not specified in the agreement it would abide by established custom and usage in the broadcasting and television industry; and the letters at least imply that that is what the parties intended and agreed to do.

One of the letters states that it is of course understood that no written contract can be consummated with any sponsor except upon the prior approval of the corporate defendant's board of directors; and defendants further contend that the complaint is insufficient because it does not allege the consummation of such written contract or such approval by the board of directors. That seems to me a gross and patent failure to understand the essence and meaning of the complaint. If plaintiffs procured a sponsor ready, able and willing to sponsor the program, it was the duty of the board of directors to approve and of the corporate defendant to execute a written contract, and if they failed or refused to do so, that was a breach on defendant's part, not a failure of performance by plaintiffs. Plaintiffs performed their part of the contract if and when they produced such sponsor, and neither the corporate defendant nor its board of directors could defeat plaintiffs' right to the agreed compensation, or to the damages flowing from a breach of the contract by defendant, by then refusing to contract with the sponsor and exhibiting the program. The case in that respect is exactly analogous to one where a real estate broker procures a purchaser and thereby becomes entitled to his commission and is not deprived of that right by his employer's refusal to consummate a sale to the purchaser the broker has produced.

I conclude, therefore, that the first cause of action is sufficient on its face to state a cause of action against the corporate defendant.

I do not see, however, that it states any cause of action against either of the individual defendants. It states nothing against defendant Freedley, and the only thing it states with respect to defendant Campbell is that he represented and warranted that he was authorized to make the agreement on behalf of the corporate defendant. There is no allegation that he was not so authorized.

The first cause of action is, therefore, dismissed as to the individual defendants, but as to the corporate defendant the motion to dismiss it is denied. The dismissal of that cause of action as to the individual defendants makes paragraphs Tenth and Eleventh of the complaint immaterial, and those paragraphs consequently are stricken out. * * *

The motion is accordingly granted to the extent of dismissing the second and fourth causes of action and of dismissing the first cause of action as to defendants Campbell and Freedley, and in other respects is denied.

B.　EXPRESS CONTRACTS

In the following series of cases, the parties clearly possessed a valid contract. Questions arise when interpreting the words expressed in the agreement. The courts are concerned with whether specific provisions have been breached.

GIRL FRIENDS PRODUCTIONS, INC. v. ABC

United States District Court, Southern District of New York, 2000.
2000 WL 1505978.

RAKOFF, District Judge.

On this summary judgment motion, the pertinent facts, either undisputed or, where disputed, taken most favorably to plaintiffs, are as follows.

Around November 1993, plaintiff Sandra Furton Gabriel, a television producer and program developer, conceived the idea for a daytime talk show to be called *Girl Friends,* which would feature three non-celebrity female co-hosts, of differing ethnicities and born in different decades, who would discuss controversial issues among themselves and with guests and audience members. Ms. Gabriel and a colleague, Frank Dudley (not a party to this suit), then formed Girl Friends Productions, Inc. ("GFP"), the co-plaintiff here. On August 11, 1994, GFP entered into a contract with defendant Greengrass Productions, Inc. ("Greengrass"), a subsidiary of defendant ABC, Inc. ("ABC"), which in turn is a subsidiary of defendant American Broadcast Companies, Inc. n1 Pursuant to the contract, Greengrass agreed to fund production of a three-program "pilot" version of *Girl Friends,* in exchange for obtaining all copyrights to the pilot and the exclusive right to option the *Girl Friends* series for one year following delivery of the pilot. The contract provided that if Greengrass exercised the option, plaintiffs would receive additional compensation, and that if Greengrass did not exercise the option, plaintiffs had a year thereafter in which to license the pilot from Greengrass in order to market it to other networks.

The View

1 yr to license the pilot

The pilot was duly delivered in September, 1994. After reviewing it, Greengrass elected not to exercise the option, which therefore expired in September 1995. Plaintiffs similarly did not attempt to license the pilot during the subsequent licensing period expiring September 1995.

Nearly two years later, in August 1997, ABC began to broadcast a talk show entitled *The View* that featured defendant Barbara Walters and four other female hosts of varying ages and that was produced (beginning in April 1997) by Ms. Walters's production company, defendant Barwall Productions, Inc. ("Barwall"). Claiming that *The View* is based on and substantially similar to *Girl Friends,* plaintiffs brought suit alleging breach of contract by the ABC defendants; violation by all defendants of § 43(a) of the Lanham Act, 15 U.S.C. § 1125(a), which prohibits false designation of origin and false description; breach by the ABC defendants of an implied covenant of good faith and fair dealing; abuse by the ABC defendants of their contractual relationship with plaintiffs; unfair competition by all defendants; tortious interference with contract by defendants Barwall and Walters; tortious interference by all defendants with plaintiffs' economic opportunity; and recovery on a theory of quantum meruit from all defendants. Following discovery, defendants brought the instant motion for summary judgment on all claims.

Plaintiffs' contract claim derives from paragraph 22 of the contract, which specifies certain "contingent compensation" that plaintiffs are to receive "in the event [Greengrass] actually produces a Series based on the Pilot [of *Girl Friends*]." The parties offer differing interpretations of

K says contingent compensation if produce a series based on girl friends pilot

[handwritten margin note: What does "Based on" mean.]

what is meant by "based on," deriving, in turn, from their different views of the extent to which this provision is narrowed by the contract's conveyance of all relevant copyrights from plaintiffs to Greengrass. But the Court need not enter this thicket, for on any reasonable interpretation of "based on," *The View* is not based on *Girl Friends*, for several reasons.

First, the essence of what distinguishes *Girl Friends* from other female-hosted talk shows, according to Ms. Gabriel herself, is that the hosts are neither celebrities nor professional television personalities and are thus able, by their very lack of media experience, to convey an air of authenticity and immediacy. In Ms. Gabriel's words, the hosts of *Girl Friends* "were not journalists, they were not actors or actresses with a script ... they had to speak from the heart and they had to be truthful about it. That's what really set this show above and beyond anything else that was out there." Id. In stark contrast, *The View* is hosted by celebrities and professional television personalities. For example, of the original five hosts of *The View*, at least four were recognizable and established media figures, including Barbara Walters, acknowledged by Ms. Gabriel to be "one of the most recognizable TV personalities on the planet," Meredith Vieira, a former CBS news anchor and reporter and contributing reporter for CBS's *60 Minutes* and ABC's *Turning Point*; Star Jones, the former host of *Jones and Jury* and legal correspondent for *Inside Edition*; and Joy Behar, a stand-up comedian and the host of the Lifetime Television network's *Queens*. (The fifth was Debbie Matenopoulos, a younger and less established television correspondent.

[handwritten margin note: celeb guest spots]

Second, and similarly, the *Girl Friends* pilot, in furtherance of its concept of "authenticity," did not include celebrities as guests. By contrast, *The View* was specifically designed to attract celebrities for guest spots on the show, and through the presence of Ms. Walters, succeeded in so doing.

Third, the three *Girl Friends* hosts were chosen not only so as to be from different age decades but also so as to be from visibly different races or ethnicities. Indeed, plaintiffs' own marketing documents described the show as follows: "*Girl Friends* is a daily, hour-long show with three female co-hosts: an Hispanic in her Twenties, an African-American in her Thirties; and a White female in her Forties. Their age and ethnic differences will ignite conflict, inspire compassion and help to bridge the age and ethnic gaps with humor and explosive debates." In contrast, the five hosts of *The View*—four Caucasians and one African-American in the initial line-up—were neither especially ethnically or racially diverse nor selected with a goal of such diversity. [In his deposition, one of *The View* producers said,] "we were looking for ... a group of people that had tremendous chemistry. If we can get somebody with a specific ethnicity, that was great. If we didn't, it was fine. We ended up in the end with four white women [and one African-American woman]. I mean we didn't end up with the rainbow coalition here." While, with five hosts, The View did cover a broad spectrum of ages, and while there is evidence that representation of different "generations" was originally intended, there is no evidence that this familiar idea was derived from *Girl Friends*. Moreover, the decision to have five hosts on *The View* meant that no individual host served as an overt representative of a particular decade in the way contemplated by *Girl Friends*.

Fourth, whereas the *Girl Friends* design provided that each episode would be devoted to a single, long-range topic, *The View* devotes each episode to multiple short-range topics. This difference both derives from, and in turn impacts on, differing production methods. Thus, *Girl Friends* was designed for "stacked" production, i.e. taping of several episodes in a row for serial broadcast at later dates, thereby precluding use of time-sensitive material. By contrast, *The View* was designed for, and is produced on, a "day and date" basis, i.e., broadcast live or with the slight delay necessary to accommodate different time zones, and with an emphasis on time-sensitive material such as news events and current films. Similarly, whereas each episode of *Girl Friends* is devoted to a single topic, such as "Nice Girls Do What?," "I Love You, But Hate Your Job," and "How Do You Fix a Friendship? And When Not To!," *The View* is a multi-topic show, offering a variety of gossip and opinion, news of the day, current issues, and celebrity "spots" as part of any given show. Plaintiffs' own expert conceded these differences were significant.

In short, the undisputed differences between *Girl Friends* and *The View* are so obvious and major as to preclude any reasonable juror from rationally concluding that the latter was based on the former under any reasonable interpretation of "based on."

Moreover, even if there existed more substantial similarities between the two shows than is the case, defendants have also established to a summary judgment standard the fact that they independently created *The View*, thus negating any inference that might otherwise be drawn that *The View* was "based on" *Girl Friends* in the sense of copying. Ms. Walters testified that for nearly ten years before she "pitched" the show to ABC, she had been interested in doing an updated version of a 1960s talk show featuring several women of differing viewpoints and ages discussing topics of the day (central features of *The View*). Three of Ms. Walters's colleagues testified that she had spoken to them about this idea prior to 1993 (when Ms. Gabriel first conceived *Girl Friends*). Furthermore, when, in 1996, ABC solicited from Barwall program ideas for a daytime program featuring Ms. Walters, Ms. Walters and her colleagues submitted a proposal for the show that later became *The View* that read as follows: "Four savvy and funny female friends [in addition to Ms. Walters] from different generations sit with a famous guest and discuss everything under the sun. They open a newspaper . . . recall a movie . . . discuss hot topics . . . everybody joins in." Ms. Walters testified that both before and after this proposal was made, no one at ABC mentioned *Girl Friends* to her, that she did not know of the show's existence at that time, and that to date she has never seen the pilot.

Plaintiffs' only evidence that arguably challenges the foregoing evidence of independent creation consists of certain notes taken at an

ABC program development meeting held in early 1997, which plaintiffs contend show a link between *The View* and *Girl Friends* because, in one page of the notes, *Everybody's a Critic* (the original name for Barbara Walters's proposal) is written above the word "Girlfriends" (capitalization in the original), and in another page, the word "girlfriends" is written next to "B. Walters." Based on these snippets, plaintiffs argue that a reasonable juror could infer that the personnel at the meeting were discussing altering *Everybody's A Critic* to make it more similar to (and therefore "based on") *Girl Friends*.

[margin note: speculative inference]

This, however, is far too extended and speculative an inference to avoid summary judgment. * * * Even putting aside the very real possibility that the term "girlfriends" (with or without a capital "G") was simply being used to describe Ms. Walters's own prior concept of a show involving "four savvy and funny female friends," and hypothesizing instead that the show *Girl Friends* was being discussed at the meeting, the mere possibility that both shows were being discussed offers no reason to infer that a transformation of the Barbara Walters show into a show more closely resembling *Girl Friends* was being undertaken—and nothing in the notes or other evidence supports this further leap.

Accordingly, summary judgment must be granted to defendants on plaintiffs' breach of contract claim. For similar reasons, plaintiffs' other claims must likewise be dismissed. Thus, plaintiffs' claim of false designation of origin and false description, in violation of § 43(a) of the Lanham Act, 15 U.S.C. § 1125(a), fails because of the lack of substantial similarity between *Girl Friends* and *The View*. * * * Similarly, the lack of similarity between the two shows and the uncontroverted evidence of independent creation are fatal barriers to plaintiffs' claims for breach of implied covenant of good faith and fair dealing, abuse of contractual relationship, unfair competition, tortious interference with contract, and tortious interference with economic opportunity. Finally, plaintiffs' claim in quantum merit is also precluded by the fact that the dispute is governed by the terms of the express contract between the parties. * * *

[margin note: there is a lack of substantial similarity btw GF & The View. independent creation evidence]

Accordingly, for the foregoing reasons, defendants' motion for summary judgment dismissing plaintiffs' claims is granted in its entirety.

WEXLEY v. KTTV, INC.

United States District Court, Central District of California, 1952.
108 F.Supp. 558.

BYRNE, District Judge.

The plaintiff is the author and copyright owner of a play entitled 'The Last Mile'. On July 21, 1931, he entered into a written agreement with defendants' assignors, whereby rights to deal in motion picture versions of the play were transferred to defendants' assignors. On November 25, 1950, the defendants caused to be broadcast over television station KTTV a motion picture film of the play. Plaintiff claims infringement of his copyright and damages resulting therefrom.

[margin note: The Last Mile – author & copyright owner; written agmt.]

The sole issue in the case is whether the contract of July 21, 1931, ~~ISSUE~~ transferred to the purchaser the right to televise a motion picture produced under the provisions of the contract.

The pertinent provisions of the contract read as follows:

'Third: The owners hereby sell, assign, transfer, set over convey and grant unto the purchaser, its successors, representatives and assigns throughout the world forever the complete, entire and exclusive motion picture rights in and to the said dramatic composition, including but not in limitation all motion picture rights as said rights presently exist, are conceived and understood and as said rights may at any time hereafter exist, be conceived and/or understood in and to the said dramatic composition, its title, plot and theme, including but not in limitation the sole and exclusive right throughout the world to make, produce, adapt, sell, lease, license, sublicense, exhibit, exploit, perform, transmit and otherwise generally deal in motion picture versions of the said dramatic composition and the title thereof in any manner and method now or any time hereafter ever known or made available, * * *.

'Eleventh: The owners hereby reserve for their use, as their interests may appear, all rights not hereby granted to the purchaser, including among other rights but not by way of limitation thereof, production rights on the spoken stage with living actors, publication rights and television rights unaccompanied by a visual representation of the play, the right to transmit or otherwise make audible and visible performances of the said play direct from living actors in a place other than that in which the actors are physically present. The owners hereby agree, however, not to exercise the right to produce and render visible and audible such performances direct from said living actors not appearing in the immediate presence of their audience within the period of fifteen (15) years from the date hereof. The owners agree, however, that when they shall determine to sell the television rights, they will give the purchaser the right to acquire such rights at the then market value of the same, meaning thereby that the purchaser shall have the right to purchase upon any bona fide offer the owners may determine to accept, there being, however, no obligation upon the owners to sell such right at any time for any price.'

It will be observed that the owners grant ' * * * the sole and exclusive right throughout the world to make * * * exhibit, * * * motion picture versions of the said dramatic composition * * * in any manner and method now or any time hereafter ever known or made available * * *.' Television, being a presently known method of exhibiting motion pictures, the right to televise motion pictures is granted unless a limitation or reservation is expressly and clearly imposed.

We now turn to the reservation clause. There are four specific classes of rights reserved, (a) production rights on the spoken stage with living actors, (b) publication rights, (c) television rights unaccompanied *reservations*

by a visual representation of the play, (d) the right to transmit or otherwise make available and visible performances of the said play, direct from living actors in a place other than that in which the actors are physically present.

There is no dispute regarding (a),(b), or (d). The plaintiff concedes that (d) encompasses only 'live action television' and does not include the exhibition of a motion picture on television; but, says the plaintiff, the right to exhibit motion pictures on television is reserved in (c) because a motion picture is not a visual representation of the play. The weakness of the plaintiff's case is disclosed by this contention. That a motion picture of a play exhibited on television is a visual representation of the play cannot be open to question. Every picture, whether motion or otherwise, is a visual representation of the thing it depicts. The use of the word 'unaccompanied' in the phrase 'television rights unaccompanied by a visual representation of the play' specifically excludes the televising of motion pictures from the television rights reserved by the grantors.

Just what uses of television were foreseeable in 1931 is open to conjecture, but conceivably the parties could have contemplated recitals of the play without the picture. That would be an audible representation unaccompanied by a visual representation of the play. We do know that the right to present a visual representation of the play was not reserved under (c) because the parties so stated in unequivocal words. The only right to transmit a visible representation of the play by television which was reserved was the right to transmit 'live television' as spelled out in (d).

It is significant that, of all of the rights reserved by the grantor, only the right to transmit 'live television' was restricted. The grantor could not exercise his right to transmit 'live television' until the expiration of fifteen years from the date of the agreement. The apparent purpose of this restriction was to protect the grantees' motion picture rights from 'live television' competition for a period of fifteen years.

If we were to disregard the plain import of the term, 'visual representation of the play', and accept the plaintiff's contention that the right to televise motion pictures was reserved under (c), it would lead to an incongruous result. It would mean that the parties intended to protect the grantee from the competition of 'live television' for a period of fifteen years, but placed no restriction on the grantor's right to televise motion pictures. How illogical it would be to believe that the parties intended the grantor to have the immediate right to exhibit pictures on television while restricting the less competitive 'live television' for fifteen years.

The obvious reason for applying the fifteen year restriction 'to live television' only, was because it was considered the most serious competition to the exhibition of motion pictures. If it were intended to leave in the grantor the right to exhibit motion pictures on television, the parties unquestionably would have applied the fifteen year restriction to such right. Because the television rights reserved in (c) were in the nature of radio broadcasts unaccompanied by a picture, is precisely why the fifteen year restriction was not attached.

The plaintiff contends that because the grantors warrant that they are the owners of the television rights as well as the motion picture rights and agree 'that when they shall determine to sell the television rights, they will give the purchaser the right to acquire such rights', it was their intention to reserve all television rights. The fallacy of this reasoning is apparent. The television rights which were reserved and which they agreed to make available to the purchaser when they determined to sell, were the television rights they spelled out in the reservations clause, viz.: 'live television' and television rights unaccompanied by a visual representation of the play. If it were the intention to reserve all television rights, the parties would have so stated and would not have limited the reservation to television rights unaccompanied by a visual representation of the play. It is quite obvious that the reason television rights accompanied by a visual representation of the play were not reserved was because such a reservation would conflict with the right granted the purchaser to exhibit motion pictures in 'any manner or method now or any time hereafter ever known or made available.'

Judgment will be for the defendant. * * *

GILLIAM v. ABC

United States Court of Appeals, Second Circuit, 1976.
538 F.2d 14.

LUMBARD, Circuit Judge.

Plaintiffs, a group of British writers and performers known as "Monty Python,"[1] appeal from a denial by Judge Lasker in the Southern District of a preliminary injunction to restrain the American Broadcasting Company (ABC) from broadcasting edited versions of three separate programs originally written and performed by Monty Python for broadcast by the British Broadcasting Corporation (BBC). We agree with Judge Lasker that the appellants have demonstrated that the excising done for ABC impairs the integrity of the original work. We further find that the countervailing injuries that Judge Lasker found might have accrued to ABC as a result of an injunction at a prior date no longer exist. We therefore direct the issuance of a preliminary injunction by the district court.

[handwritten margin note: denial of prelim injunction]

Since its formation in 1969, the Monty Python group has gained popularity primarily through its thirty-minute television programs created for BBC as part of a comedy series entitled "Monty Python's Flying Circus." In accordance with an agreement between Monty Python and BBC, the group writes and delivers to BBC scripts for use in the television series. This scriptwriters' agreement recites in great detail the procedure to be followed when any alterations are to be made in the

---

1. Appellant Gilliam is an American citizen residing in England.

script prior to recording of the program.[2] The essence of this section of the agreement is that, while BBC retains final authority to make changes, appellants or their representatives exercise optimum control over the scripts consistent with BBC's authority and only minor changes may be made without prior consultation with the writers. Nothing in the scriptwriters' agreement entitles BBC to alter a program once it has been recorded. The agreement further provides that, subject to the terms therein, the group retains all rights in the script.

Under the agreement, BBC may license the transmission of recordings of the television programs in any overseas territory. The series has been broadcast in this country primarily on non-commercial public broadcasting television stations, although several of the programs have been broadcast on commercial stations in Texas and Nevada. In each instance, the thirty-minute programs have been broadcast as originally recorded and broadcast in England in their entirety and without commercial interruption.

In October 1973, Time–Life Films acquired the right to distribute in the United States certain BBC television programs, including the Monty Python series. Time–Life was permitted to edit the programs only "for insertion of commercials, applicable censorship or governmental ... rules and regulations, and National Association of Broadcasters and time segment requirements." No similar clause was included in the scriptwriters' agreement between appellants and BBC. Prior to this time, ABC had sought to acquire the right to broadcast excerpts from various Monty Python programs in the spring of 1975, but the group rejected the proposal for such a disjoined format. Thereafter, in July 1975, ABC agreed with Time–Life to broadcast two ninety-minute specials each

2. The Agreement provides:

V. When script alterations are necessary it is the intention of the BBC to make every effort to inform and to reach agreement with the Writer. Whenever practicable any necessary alterations (other than minor alterations) shall be made by the Writer. Nevertheless the BBC shall at all times have the right to make (a) minor alterations and (b) such other alterations as in its opinion are necessary in order to avoid involving the BBC in legal action or bringing the BBC into disrepute. Any decision under (b) shall be made at a level not below that of Head of Department. It is however agreed that after a script has been accepted by the BBC alterations will not be made by the BBC under (b) above unless (i) the Writer, if available when the BBC requires the alterations to be made, has been asked to agree to them but is not willing to do so and (ii) the Writer has had, if he so requests and if the BBC agrees that time permits if rehearsals and

recording are to proceed as planned, an opportunity to be represented by the Writers' Guild of Great Britain (or if he is not a member of the Guild by his agent) at a meeting with the BBC to be held within at most 48 hours of the request (excluding weekends). If in such circumstances there is no agreement about the alterations then the final decision shall rest with the BBC. Apart from the right to make alterations under (a) and (b) above the BBC shall not without the consent of the Writer or his agent (which consent shall not be unreasonably withheld) make any structural alterations as opposed to minor alterations to the script, provided that such consent shall not be necessary in any case where the Writer is for any reason not immediately available for consultation at the time which in the BBC's opinion is the deadline from the production point of view for such alterations to be made if rehearsals and recording are to proceed as planned.

comprising three thirty-minute Monty Python programs that had not previously been shown in this country.

Correspondence between representatives of BBC and Monty Python reveals that these parties assumed that ABC would broadcast each of the Monty Python programs "in its entirety." On September 5, 1975, however, the group's British representative inquired of BBC how ABC planned to show the programs in their entirety if approximately 24 minutes of each 90 minute program were to be devoted to commercials. BBC replied on September 12, "we can only reassure you that ABC have decided to run the programmes 'back to back,' and that there is a firm undertaking not to segment them."

ABC broadcast the first of the specials on October 3, 1975. Appellants did not see a tape of the program until late November and were allegedly "appalled" at the discontinuity and "mutilation" that had resulted from the editing done by Time–Life for ABC. Twenty-four minutes of the original 90 minutes of recording had been omitted. Some of the editing had been done in order to make time for commercials; other material had been edited, according to ABC, because the original programs contained offensive or obscene matter.

In early December, Monty Python learned that ABC planned to broadcast the second special on December 26, 1975. The parties began negotiations concerning editing of that program and a delay of the broadcast until Monty Python could view it. These negotiations were futile, however, and on December 15 the group filed this action to enjoin the broadcast and for damages. Following an evidentiary hearing, Judge Lasker found that "the plaintiffs have established an impairment of the integrity of their work" which "caused the film or program ... to lose its iconoclastic verve."

According to Judge Lasker, "the damage that has been caused to the plaintiffs is irreparable by its nature." Nevertheless, the judge denied the motion for the preliminary injunction on the grounds that it was unclear who owned the copyright in the programs produced by BBC from the scripts written by Monty Python; that there was a question of whether Time–Life and BBC were indispensable parties to the litigation; that ABC would suffer significant financial loss if it were enjoined a week before the scheduled broadcast; and that Monty Python had displayed a "somewhat disturbing casualness" in their pursuance of the matter.

Judge Lasker granted Monty Python's request for more limited relief by requiring ABC to broadcast a disclaimer during the December 26 special to the effect that the group dissociated itself from the program because of the editing. A panel of this court, however, granted a stay of that order until this appeal could be heard and permitted ABC to broadcast, at the beginning of the special, only the legend that the program had been edited by ABC. We heard argument on April 13 and, at that time, enjoined ABC from any further broadcast of edited Monty Python programs pending the decision of the court.

I

In determining the availability of injunctive relief at this early stage of the proceedings, Judge Lasker properly considered the harm that would inure to the plaintiffs if the injunction were denied, the harm that defendant would suffer if the injunction were granted, and the likelihood that plaintiffs would ultimately succeed on the merits. * * * We direct the issuance of a preliminary injunction because we find that all these factors weigh in favor of appellants.

There is nothing clearly erroneous in Judge Lasker's conclusion that any injury suffered by appellants as a result of the broadcast of edited versions of their programs was irreparable by its nature. ABC presented the appellants with their first opportunity for broadcast to a nationwide network audience in this country. If ABC adversely misrepresented the quality of Monty Python's work, it is likely that many members of the audience, many of whom, by defendant's admission, were previously unfamiliar with appellants, would not become loyal followers of Monty Python productions. The subsequent injury to appellants' theatrical reputation would imperil their ability to attract the large audience necessary to the success of their venture. Such an injury to professional reputation cannot be measured in monetary terms or recompensed by other relief. * * *

In contrast to the harm that Monty Python would suffer by a denial of the preliminary injunction, Judge Lasker found that ABC's relationship with its affiliates would be impaired by a grant of an injunction within a week of the scheduled December 26 broadcast. The court also found that ABC and its affiliates had advertised the program and had included it in listings of forthcoming television programs that were distributed to the public. Thus a last minute cancellation of the December 26 program, Judge Lasker concluded, would injure defendant financially and in its reputation with the public and its advertisers.

However valid these considerations may have been when the issue before the court was whether a preliminary injunction should immediately precede the broadcast, any injury to ABC is presently more speculative. No rebroadcast of the edited specials has been scheduled and no advertising costs have been incurred for the immediate future. Thus there is no danger that defendant's relations with affiliates or the public will suffer irreparably if subsequent broadcasts of the programs are enjoined pending a disposition of the issues.

We then reach the question whether there is a likelihood that appellants will succeed on the merits. In concluding that there is a likelihood of infringement here, we rely especially on the fact that the editing was substantial, i.e., approximately 27 per cent of the original program was omitted, and the editing contravened contractual provisions that limited the right to edit Monty Python material. It should be emphasized that our discussion of these matters refers only to such facts as have been developed upon the hearing for a preliminary injunction.

Modified or contrary findings may become appropriate after a plenary trial.

Judge Lasker denied the preliminary injunction in part because he was unsure of the ownership of the copyright in the recorded program. Appellants first contend that the question of ownership is irrelevant because the recorded program was merely a derivative work taken from the script in which they hold the uncontested copyright. Thus, even if BBC owned the copyright in the recorded program, its use of that work would be limited by the license granted to BBC by Monty Python for use of the underlying script. We agree.

Section 7 of the Copyright Law, 17 U.S.C. s 7, provides in part that "adaptations, arrangements, dramatizations . . . or other versions of . . . copyrighted works when produced with the consent of the proprietor of the copyright in such works . . . shall be regarded as new works subject to copyright. . . ." Manifestly, the recorded program falls into this category as a dramatization of the script, and thus the program was itself entitled to copyright protection. However, section 7 limits the copyright protection of the derivative work, as works adapted from previously existing scripts have become known, to the novel additions made to the underlying work, * * * and the derivative work does not affect the "force or validity" of the copyright in the matter from which it is derived. * * * Thus, any ownership by BBC of the copyright in the recorded program would not affect the scope or ownership of the copyright in the underlying script.

[handwritten margin note: new works new copyright]

Since the copyright in the underlying script survives intact despite the incorporation of that work into a derivative work, one who uses the script, even with the permission of the proprietor of the derivative work, may infringe the underlying copyright. * * *

If the proprietor of the derivative work is licensed by the proprietor of the copyright in the underlying work to vend or distribute the derivative work to third parties, those parties will, of course, suffer no liability for their use of the underlying work consistent with the license to the proprietor of the derivative work. Obviously, it was just this type of arrangement that was contemplated in this instance. The scriptwriters' agreement between Monty Python and BBC specifically permitted the latter to license the transmission of the recordings made by BBC to distributors such as Time–Life for broadcast in overseas territories.

One who obtains permission to use a copyrighted script in the production of a derivative work, however, may not exceed the specific purpose for which permission was granted. Most of the decisions that have reached this conclusion have dealt with the improper extension of the underlying work into media or time, i.e., duration of the license, not covered by the grant of permission to the derivative work proprietor. * * * Appellants herein do not claim that the broadcast by ABC violated media or time restrictions contained in the license of the script to BBC. Rather, they claim that revisions in the script, and ultimately in the program, could be made only after consultation with Monty Python, and

[handwritten margin note: permission — still cannot exceed the specific purpose for which permission was granted]

that ABC's broadcast of a program edited after recording and without consultation with Monty Python exceeded the scope of any license that BBC was entitled to grant.

The rationale for finding infringement when a licensee exceeds time or media restrictions on his license the need to allow the proprietor of the underlying copyright to control the method in which his work is presented to the public applies equally to the situation in which a licensee makes an unauthorized use of the underlying work by publishing it in a truncated version. Whether intended to allow greater economic exploitation of the work, as in the media and time cases, or to ensure that the copyright proprietor retains a veto power over revisions desired for the derivative work, the ability of the copyright holder to control his work remains paramount in our copyright law. We find, therefore, that unauthorized editing of the underlying work, if proven, would constitute an infringement of the copyright in that work similar to any other use of a work that exceeded the license granted by the proprietor of the copyright.

If the broadcast of an edited version of the Monty Python program infringed the group's copyright in the script, ABC may obtain no solace from the fact that editing was permitted in the agreements between BBC and Time–Life or Time–Life and ABC. BBC was not entitled to make unilateral changes in the script and was not specifically empowered to alter the recordings once made; Monty Python, moreover, had reserved to itself any rights not granted to BBC. Since a grantor may not convey greater rights than it owns, BBC's permission to allow Time–Life, and hence ABC, to edit appears to have been a nullity.

* * * Our resolution of these technical arguments serves to reinforce our initial inclination that the copyright law should be used to recognize the important role of the artist in our society and the need to encourage production and dissemination of artistic works by providing adequate legal protection for one who submits his work to the public. See Mazer v. Stein, 347 U.S. 201, 74 S.Ct. 460, 98 L.Ed. 630 (1954). We therefore conclude that there is a substantial likelihood that, after a full trial, appellants will succeed in proving infringement of their copyright by ABC's broadcast of edited versions of Monty Python programs. In reaching this conclusion, however, we need not accept appellants' assertion that any editing whatsoever would constitute infringement. Courts have recognized that licensees are entitled to some small degree of latitude in arranging the licensed work for presentation to the public in a manner consistent with the licensee's style or standards. * * * That privilege, however, does not extend to the degree of editing that occurred here especially in light of contractual provisions that limited the right to edit Monty Python material.

II.

It also seems likely that appellants will succeed on the theory that, regardless of the right ABC had to broadcast an edited program, the cuts made constituted an actionable mutilation of Monty Python's work. This cause of action, which seeks redress for deformation of an artist's work, finds its roots in the continental concept of droit moral, or moral right, which may generally be summarized as including the right of the artist to have his work attributed to him in the form in which he created it. See 1 M. Nimmer, supra, at s 110.1.

American copyright law, as presently written, does not recognize moral rights or provide a cause of action for their violation, since the law seeks to vindicate the economic, rather than the personal, rights of authors. Nevertheless, the economic incentive for artistic and intellectual creation that serves as the foundation for American copyright law, * * * cannot be reconciled with the inability of artists to obtain relief for mutilation or misrepresentation of their work to the public on which the artists are financially dependent. Thus courts have long granted relief for misrepresentation of an artist's work by relying on theories outside the statutory law of copyright, such as contract law. * * * Although such decisions are clothed in terms of proprietary right in one's creation, they also properly vindicate the author's personal right to prevent the presentation of his work to the public in a distorted form. * * *

Here, the appellants claim that the editing done for ABC mutilated the original work and that consequently the broadcast of those programs as the creation of Monty Python violated the Lanham Act s 43(a), 15 U.S.C. s 1125(a). This statute, the federal counterpart to state unfair competition laws, has been invoked to prevent misrepresentations that may injure plaintiff's business or personal reputation, even where no registered trademark is concerned. * * * It is sufficient to violate the Act that a representation of a product, although technically true, creates a false impression of the product's origin. * * *

During the hearing on the preliminary injunction, Judge Lasker viewed the edited version of the Monty Python program broadcast on December 26 and the original, unedited version. After hearing argument of this appeal, this panel also viewed and compared the two versions. We find that the truncated version at times omitted the climax of the skits to which appellants' rare brand of humor was leading and at other times deleted essential elements in the schematic development of a story line.[12] We therefore agree with Judge Lasker's conclusion that the edited version broadcast by ABC impaired the integrity of appellants' work and represented to the public as the product of appellants what was actually a mere caricature of their talents. We believe that a valid cause of action for such distortion exists and that therefore a preliminary injunction

12. A single example will illustrate the extent of distortion engendered by the editing. In one skit, an upper class English family is engaged in a discussion of the tonal quality of certain words as "woody" or "tinny." The father soon begins to suggest certain words with sexual connotations as either "woody" or "tinny," whereupon the mother fetches a bucket of water and pours it over his head. The skit continues from this point. The ABC edit eliminates this middle sequence so that the father is comfortably dressed at one moment and, in the next moment, is shown in a soaked condition without any explanation for the change in his appearance.

may issue to prevent repetition of the broadcast prior to final determination of the issues.[13]

[Part III, which reaches the conclusion that the appellants are not guilty of laches, omitted.]

For these reasons we direct that the district court issue the preliminary injunction sought by the appellants.

Note

1.   Do you think having appellants from a foreign country can influence the outcome in a U.S. court? *Gilliam* is notable for holding that ABC was bound by the contract that BBC signed with Monty Python and for finding that ABC violated Monty Python's rights when it edited the television programs for broadcast on network television. Chapter 4 on film contracts presented two cases *Preminger v. Columbia Pictures*, 49 Misc.2d 363, 267 N.Y.S.2d 594 (Sup. Ct. 1966), and *Autry v. Republic Productions*, 213 F.2d 667 (9th Cir. 1954), where both parties were unable to keep television networks from editing and cutting their work. In both instances, the court held that the American plaintiffs were bound by industry standards, which required that granting television rights indicated the right to cut and edit for television. Since Monty Python was a British production, they were not held to such a standard. For more discussion on problems of enforcing cases in international forums, see Chapter 20 on Globalization of the Entertainment Industry.

ROY EXPORT CO. OF VADUZ v. CBS

United States District Court, Southern District of New York, 1980.
503 F.Supp. 1137.

LASKER, District Judge.

Columbia Broadcasting System, Inc. ("CBS") moves for a judgment notwithstanding the verdict, or, in the alternative, for a new trial, pursuant to Rule 50(b), Fed.R.Civ.Pr., following a three week trial in which the jury found that CBS had infringed plaintiffs' statutory and common law copyrights and had unfairly competed with plaintiffs.[1] * * *

---

13. Judge Gurfein's concurring opinion suggests that since the gravamen of a complaint under the Lanham Act is that the origin of goods has been falsely described, a legend disclaiming Monty Python's approval of the edited version would preclude violation of that Act. We are doubtful that a few words could erase the indelible impression that is made by a television broadcast, especially since *The Viewer* has no means of comparing the truncated version with the complete work in order to determine for himself the talents of plaintiffs. Furthermore, a disclaimer such as the one originally suggested by Judge Lasker in the exigencies of an impending broadcast last December would go unnoticed by viewers who tuned into the broadcast a few minutes after it began.

We therefore conclude that Judge Gurfein's proposal that the district court could find some form of disclaimer would be sufficient might not provide appropriate relief.

1. The jury awarded plaintiffs $7,280 in damages for statutory copyright infringement, $1 in compensatory and $300,000 in punitive damages on the common law copyright infringement and $300,000 in compensatory and $110,000 in punitive damages on the unfair competition claim.

I. BACKGROUND

The works at issue in this case are Charlie Chaplin films and derivative works. The plaintiffs own the copyrights in, and various distribution rights to, the six motion pictures relevant to this case.[3] * * * Each film was written, produced, directed by and starred Charlie Chaplin.

[handwritten margin note: PI – copyrights distribution Rights]

Between 1956 and 1971, Roy Export acquired from Chaplin and his corporation the sole and exclusive ownership of the copyrights in the Chaplin films. Black, Inc. owns the sole and exclusive worldwide distribution rights until 1986. De Dam acquired from Black, Inc. the exclusive United States television rights to the films until 1986 and the exclusive United States theatrical rights. rbc Films has held licenses for United States non-theatrical distribution rights for the Chaplin films since 1973 and, since 1975 has held exclusive licenses for United States non-theatrical distribution rights for "The Gentleman Tramp." Bert Schneider and Mo Rothman had at all relevant times authority to act on behalf of Black, Inc. and De Dam in authorizing use of the Chaplin films.

In 1972, the Academy of Motion Picture Arts and Sciences ("AMPAS") approached Schneider with the possibility of persuading Chaplin to return to the United States for the first time in twenty years to receive a special award from AMPAS during the 1972 nationally televised Academy Awards presentation. In connection with Chaplin's appearance on the Academy Awards show, AMPAS requested that Schneider supervise the preparation of a tribute to Chaplin consisting of highlights from the Chaplin films. Schneider enlisted the aid of the noted director, Peter Bogdanovitch, who in turn recommended that Richard Pattersen be used for film editing. They selected particular scenes, planned the particular sequence and timing, and produced a 13 minute film consisting of highlights from the Chaplin films. After showing it to Chaplin, a scene was added. This film (the "Compilation") was then played on the 1972 Academy Awards telecast. As Schneider testified, the understanding with AMPAS was that the Compilation was to be used on the Academy Awards broadcast only, and that AMPAS had no right to use it again. The Compilation is the subject of plaintiffs' common law copyright infringement claim.

[handwritten margin note: TRIBUTE FILM 13 minutes]

In 1974, by virtue of various agreements entered into between plaintiffs and others, plaintiffs agreed to produce a film biography of Chaplin. Schneider acted as producer of this film, which was completed in 1975 and entitled "The Gentleman Tramp." Many of the same highlights of Chaplin's films which had been included in the Compilation were included in "The Gentleman Tramp," Roy Export having authorized their use. Two versions of "The Gentleman Tramp" were prepared, one designed for American television as a 90 minute special, the other for foreign theatrical exhibition. Roy Export owns the copyrights to "The Gentleman Tramp."

3. The films are "The Kid," "The Gold Rush," "The Circus," "City Lights," "Modern Times," and "The Great Dictator." ("The Chaplin films").

In 1973, CBS had begun work on its own retrospective program about Chaplin for use at the time of Chaplin's death. CBS soon learned of plaintiffs' copyrights on the Chaplin films and plaintiffs' plans to produce their own retrospective biography ("The Gentleman Tramp"). CBS repeatedly requested permission to use excerpts from the Chaplin films, but plaintiffs refused, explaining that they themselves were producing the "definitive" Chaplin biography. Nevertheless, CBS prepared a "rough cut" which included two scenes from copyrighted films which CBS had obtained in 1972 for use on its "60 Minutes" program.

In 1976, rbc Films sent CBS a print of "The Gentleman Tramp" in an attempt to sell CBS a license for the film. CBS screened the film but did not purchase the license. In December, 1977, rbc made another unsuccessful attempt to sell the license for "The Gentleman Tramp" to CBS.

On December 25, 1977, Charlie Chaplin died. Russell Bensley, director of the CBS Special Events Unit, attempted to contact Schneider and Rothman to see if they had changed their minds and would grant CBS permission to use excerpts. The same day, CBS obtained from NBC a copy of the Compilation which had been shown on the Academy Awards broadcast. Although CBS was unable to reach Schneider or Rothman, it decided to proceed with a retrospective. At that time, CBS had two possible versions available for broadcast, one the "rough cut" consisting primarily of public domain footage, the other a new version which incorporated, with minor editions, the Compilation as well as other copyrighted material. Richard Salant, the President of CBS News, made the final decision to use the latter version, 40% of which consisted of plaintiffs' copyrighted films. That show was broadcast on December 26, 1977, between 11:30 P.M. and Midnight (EST).

The CBS broadcast has given rise to this suit. The jury concluded that CBS' use of the Chaplin films (consisting of CBS' use of the eleven scenes contained in the Compilation, and two other copyrighted excerpts) constituted an infringement of plaintiffs statutory copyright in the films themselves, CBS' use of the Compilation constituted an infringement of plaintiffs' common law copyright, and CBS' conduct constituted unfair competition with plaintiffs' Chaplin retrospective, "The Gentleman Tramp."

[Parts II–V omitted.]

VI.   THE PRIOR AUTHORIZATION DEFENSE

CBS claims that plaintiffs' representatives had authorized it to use excerpts from "Modern Times" and "City Lights" and that such authorization presented no issue of fact, thus the statutory copyright infringement claims with respect to these two films should not have been submitted to the jury. CBS bases its argument on a March, 1972 letter agreement between CBS and Columbia Pictures (the United States theatrical distributors for the Chaplin films at that time) which granted CBS "in perpetuity, the irrevocable, non-exclusive right to use and exploit the footage as part of the above captioned broadcast, or any expanded, abridged or changed version thereof, in any manner and in any media whatsoever throughout the world.''

CBS concedes that ''the above captioned broadcast'' referred to the ''60 Minutes'' program. It maintains, however, that the contractual language, by permitting ''changed versions'' of the ''60 Minutes'' broadcast, unambiguously authorized CBS to use the footage in question in its obituary tribute, ''Chaplin.'' However, as plaintiffs contend, ''60 Minutes'' was a weekly prime time program with a regular cast and format; ''Chaplin'' was a special, one-time, late night obituary. The jury could have reasonably concluded that ''Chaplin'' was not an ''expanded, abridged or changed version'' of ''60 Minutes.'' And, since the contractual language was ambiguous, the trial judge was correct in admitting parol evidence with respect to the parties' intent and in allowing the trier of fact to resolve the question. * * *

CBS also argues that Columbia and Classic Films (the United States theatrical distributor after Columbia which granted CBS a similar license) had authority to grant CBS a license ''in perpetuity'' to use the film clips on television. However, as plaintiffs point out, under their distribution agreements Columbia and Classic Films were only theatrical distributors; their right to license the use of excerpts on television was limited to promotional broadcasts ''in connection with exhibition for theatrical broadcasts.'' The jury could reasonably have concluded that Columbia and Classic Films had no authority to license CBS' use of the films in connection with its obituary tribute. CBS points to no evidence that its use of the two films was ''in connection with'' any theatrical exhibition of the films at the time Chaplin died. Whatever controversy may exist with respect to the right of a copyright owner or distributor to convey his copyright interests through perpetual licenses, compare Rohauer v. Killiam Shows, Inc., 551 F.2d 484 (2d Cir.), cert. denied, 431 U.S. 949, 97 S.Ct. 2666, 53 L.Ed.2d 266 (1977) with 1 Nimmer on Copyright, s 3.07(A), it is axiomatic that no one can convey more than his own interest in a work. See Gilliam v. American Broadcasting Companies, 538 F.2d 14 (2d Cir. 1976).

Finally, the Columbia license pertained to specific footage from ''City Lights'' and ''Modern Times.'' CBS, in its obituary special, used additional film clips from the two films besides those purportedly licensed. * * *

In sum, CBS' motion for a judgment notwithstanding the verdict and for a new trial is denied, plaintiffs' motion for an award of attorneys fees is denied and plaintiffs' motion for an additional award under 17 U.S.C. s 101(b) is granted in the amount of $5,000. * * *

END

10.13

C. TELEVISION CONTRACTS AND LABOR RELATIONS

One of the duties of labor unions is to assist members as they seek to enforce their contracts. The following case and notes address present situations where the labor unions have sought to enforce agreements that their members have made.

DIRECTORS GUILD OF AMERICA v. MILLENNIUM TELEVISION NETWORK

United States District Court, Central District of California, 2001.
2001 WL 1744609.

MATZ, District Judge.

* * * This matter is before the Court pursuant to Plaintiffs' Motion for Summary Judgment. Plaintiffs, a group of directors and their collective bargaining representative, the Directors Guild of America, Inc. ("DGA"), have sued Defendant Millennium Television Network ("Millennium") to confirm an arbitrator's award against Millennium. Plaintiffs have also sued Defendants Frontier Insurance Company ("Frontier") and NAC Reinsurance Corporation ("NAC") for breach of payment bond. In their summary judgment motion, Plaintiffs argue Frontier and NAC are liable for the arbitration award obtained by Plaintiffs against Defendant Millennium Television Network ("Millennium").[1] The arbitration award was based on Millennium's failure to pay Plaintiffs pursuant to several individual contracts that obligated the plaintiffs to perform work for a television broadcast ("Telecast") scheduled for New Year's Eve 1999. The Telecast was ultimately canceled by Millennium before the plaintiffs performed any work on the program. The source of Frontier's and NAC's potential liability is a bond executed between Millennium and Frontier and NAC on May 20, 1999. The bond makes both NAC and Frontier liable as co-sureties to "any and all persons, companies, or corporations who perform work or labor on" the "Millennium World Broadcast" scheduled for December 31, 1999.

In opposition, Defendant NAC argues the express terms of the bond do not encompass the plaintiffs' arbitration award against Millennium.[2] NAC contends the bond only covers payment for those "who perform work or labor on" the Telecast. As a result, NAC argues, the bond does not cover Plaintiffs' arbitration award because it was based on work never actually performed due to the cancellation of the Telecast. In addition, NAC argues that it is not bound by the arbitration award

---

1. Millennium is no longer in existence and has not paid the amounts due the plaintiffs as a result of the arbitration award.

2. Defendant Frontier is now subject to an Order of Rehabilitation issued by the Supreme Court of New York. The order stays all actions involving Frontier as of October 10, 2001. For this reason, the opposition was filed solely on behalf of Defendant NAC.

obtained by the plaintiffs against Millenium, and that Plaintiffs failed to mitigate their damages following the cancellation of the telecast.

Because the Court finds that the plaintiffs' "performed work" or "labored on" the Telecast, the express terms of the bond encompass the amounts owed the plaintiffs by Millennium. As a result, the Court grants Plaintiffs' Motion for Summary Judgment.

FACTS

The relevant facts are not significantly disputed by the parties. Plaintiffs are directors retained by Millennium to work on its planned live broadcast scheduled for December 31, 1999. To obtain the necessary capital for the broadcast, Millennium's backers required it to obtain a performance and payment bond. On May 20, 1999, Millennium executed Payment Bond no. 143698 with Defendants Frontier and NAC. The Bond states that Millennium, Frontier, and NAC are "jointly and severally held and firmly bound, unto any and all persons, companies, or corporations who perform work or labor on . . . the event or services hereinafter mentioned, in the sum or Ten Million and no/100 Dollars." The Bond further states that, "If said Principal [Millennium] shall fail to pay for any . . . work or labor done thereon of any kind, the said Co–Surety, Frontier Insurance Company and NAC Reinsurance Corporation, will pay the same amount . . . and this bond shall inure to the benefit of any and all persons, companies, and corporations entitled to file claims . . ."

Due to a variety of unspecified factors, Millennium's Telecast scheduled for December 31, 1999 was cancelled on or about December 23, 1999. The cancellation occurred prior to the time Plaintiffs were scheduled to work to the Telecast. Since that time, Millennium has failed to pay Plaintiffs any compensation due under the terms of their contracts.

Pursuant to the applicable collective bargaining agreements between the plaintiffs and Millennium, all disputes regarding compensation are subject to arbitration. Pursuant to these agreements (labeled by Plaintiffs as the "Basic Agreement" and "Freelance Live and Tape Television Agreement" ("FLTTA")), the DGA filed a claim against Millennium for the monies owed the individual plaintiffs. On October 23, 2000, the arbitration hearing on the matter was held. Millennium did not appear at the arbitration. The arbitrator held that Millennium owed each individual Plaintiff a specific amount in compensation and pension/health contributions. The total amount owed by Millennium to Plaintiffs was $64,846.13 in compensation and $14,864.65 in pension/health contributions. The arbitrator also held that late charges of 1.5% per month would accrue on the compensation owed from January 4, 2000 until the obligations were paid in full. In addition, late charges of 1% per month or liquidated damages of 20%, whichever is greater, would accrue on the pension/health payments until paid in full.

Because Millennium failed to pay any amount due under the arbitration award, DGA made a written demand for the amount on Co–Sureties

Frontier and NAC on November 9, 2000. Both Frontier and NAC continue to refuse to pay the amounts owed by Millennium. On May 14, 2001, a default was entered by the Court Clerk against Millennium in this action. * * *

DISCUSSION

I. The Terms of the Bond Determine the Liability of NAC

Both sides fundamentally agree that whether NAC is liable for the amount owed the plaintiffs by Millennium is determined by the terms of the bond executed between NAC and Millennium. The plaintiffs do not argue that the arbitration award against Millennium is automatically binding against NAC as surety. Furthermore, Plaintiffs do not contend that the terms of the bond incorporate those of the collective bargaining agreement that governed the dispute between Plaintiffs and Millennium. In addition, other than arguing that two individual plaintiffs failed to mitigate their damages (infra), NAC's opposition does not question the findings of the arbitrator as to Millennium's liability to the plaintiffs. As a result, the Court finds that the express terms of the bond executed between Millennium and NAC will determine whether NAC is liable for the arbitration award against Millennium.

A. The Terms of the Bond

The bond executed between Millennium and NAC on May 20, 1999 binds NAC as Co–Surety unto any and all persons, companies, or corporations who perform work or labor on ... the event or services hereinafter mentioned, in the sum of Ten Million and no/100 dollars ... " (In addition, the bond states,

> "THE CONDITIONS OF THIS OBLIGATION ARE SUCH THAT, WHEREAS, the above bounden Principal [Millennium] has a Production Agreement for airing the 24–hour 'Millennium World Broadcast,' on or about December 31, 1999 (hereinafter called the Telecast). NOW, THEREFORE, if the said Principal, shall fail to pay for any materials, provisions, provender or other supplies or for the use of implements or equipment, used or to be used, in, upon, for, or about, the production of said Telecast or for any work or labor done thereon of any kind, the said Co–Surety, Frontier Insurance Company and NAC Reinsurance Corporation, will pay the same amount not exceeding the sum named upon this bond, and this bond shall inure to the benefit of any and all persons, companies, and corporations entitled to file claims under which the said contract, subcontract or purchase order was awarded to claimant for the Telecast as aforesaid by the Principal."

B. The Terms of the Bond Encompass the Plaintiffs' Arbitration Award

Plaintiffs argue that NAC is liable for the arbitration award against Millennium because the express terms of the bond require NAC to pay for "any work or labor done thereon [the Telecast] of any kind ..."

Plaintiffs acknowledge that the Telecast was canceled before they were required to begin work. However, Plaintiffs argue that, for directors, the work "performed" or labor "done" consists not only of the performance of certain services on a particular day, but also the act of refraining from performing work for anyone else during the period of the contract. Plaintiffs contend that this is defined as the "pay or play" principle.[3]

According to Plaintiffs, the "pay or play" principle reflects a bilateral promise between the employee and the employer that is integral to the entertainment industry. For the employer, the "pay or play" principle requires the employer to honor its promise to pay the agreed salary for the term of the guaranteed period whether or not the program or film is actually produced. In exchange, the employee-director is required to remain available for the scheduled dates by foregoing other employment options. As a result, Plaintiffs argue, despite the fact that the Telecast was cancelled before filming began, the terms of the bond nonetheless encompass the arbitration award because it was based on the concept that the plaintiffs "performed" work on the Telecast.

In opposition, NAC argues that it is not liable for the arbitration award against Millennium because the express terms of the bond obligate NAC to pay only those persons or companies who "perform work or labor on" the Telecast. Due to the cancellation of the Telecast, NAC argues, Plaintiffs did not perform any work or labor on the production of the Telecast. Furthermore, NAC contends that because the bond itself does not mention the "pay or play" arrangements between Plaintiffs and Millennium, such terms should not be read into the bond to hold NAC liable for the arbitration award against Millennium.

The defendant is correct in stating that a surety cannot be held beyond the express terms of the contract. United States Leasing Corp. v. DuPont, 69 Cal. 2d 275, 284, 444 P.2d 65, 70 Cal. Rptr. 393 (1968). However, it is also clear that a surety contract is to be interpreted by the same rules used in construing other contracts, "with a view towards effectuating the purposes for which the contract was designed." Id. For this reason, the question of whether Plaintiffs' arbitration award was based on "labor done" or "work performed" will be considered in light of the purposes of the surety contract between Millennium and NAC.

California courts have recognized in other contexts that employees in "pay or play" contracts perform labor even when their services are never required by the employer. Payne v. Pathe Studios, Inc., 6 Cal. App. 2d 136, 141, 44 P.2d 598 (1935) (finding that an actress had performed her duties under an employment contract despite the fact that she was never required to work by the defendant motion picture company); Garfein v. Garfein, 16 Cal. App. 3d 155, 93 Cal. Rptr. 714 (1971) (holding that payments to an actress under a "pay or play" contract were

---

3. Plaintiffs have produced substantial evidence that the "pay or play" principle is the customary nature of work in the entertainment industry. Both the applicable collective bargaining agreement (the "Basic Agreement") and the FTTLA incorporate "pay or play" principles. In addition, Millennium specifically agreed to be bound by the terms of the Basic Agreement in a document dated September 28, 1999.

"earnings" despite the fact that the actress was not required to appear in any motion pictures). In *Garfein,* a divorce case, the California Court of Appeal rejected the husband's argument that several payments made to his former wife/actress under "pay or play" contracts were not "earnings" because she never appeared in the motion pictures for which she was compensated. Garfein, 16 Cal. App. 3d at 159. In so doing, the court held that the wife "earned" her agreed compensation by refraining from performing for anyone except the employer during the period of the contract. Id.

Under the reasoning of *Payne* and *Garfein,* the Court finds the Plaintiffs' arbitration award was based on "labor done" or "work performed" on the Telecast, and NAC is therefore liable under the terms of the surety agreement for the amount of the award. This finding is supported by the broad language of the bond, which requires NAC to answer for any "work or labor done . . . of any kind" on the Telecast. In addition, interpreting the surety agreement between Millennium and NAC to encompass the plaintiffs' arbitration award furthers the purpose of the bond. There can be no doubt that the bond was secured by Millennium to ensure Millennium's performance on its obligations regarding the Telecast. That is, in fact, the essence of a surety agreement. To hold that the bond would not protect the plaintiffs because Millennium cancelled the Telecast would eliminate that purpose. In addition, such a result would produce a definition of "work performed" and "labor done" that would be contrary to the holdings of both *Payne* and *Garfein,* and ignore the nature of work in the entertainment industry. As a result, the Court finds the terms of the surety agreement between Millennium and NAC encompass the amounts owed the plaintiffs as a result of their arbitration award against Millennium.

II. *Plaintiffs Were Not Required to Mitigate Their Damages.*

In opposition to summary judgment, Defendant NAC argues that two individual Plaintiffs, Christine Clark Bradley and James Tanker, failed to mitigate their damages because they did not make reasonably diligent efforts to seek other employment after the cancellation of the Telecast on or about December 23, 1999. In addition, NAC contends that Plaintiff Allan Kartun did locate other work following the cancellation of the Telecast for which he was paid $1,800.00. Defendants argue that the failure of these defendants to mitigate damages, and the success of Mr. Kartun in mitigating his damages, indicate the plaintiffs are not entitled to recover their full arbitration award against Millennium.

NAC's argument is misguided. California law is clear that employees in pay or play arrangements who sue on the contract to recover the agreed upon compensation are not required to mitigate damages. Payne, 6 Cal. App. 2d at 142 (1935). In *Payne,* the California Court of Appeal addressed the issue of mitigation of damages where an actress contracted with the defendant motion picture company to act in an upcoming film. *Id.* at 138. The contract, which required the actress to work for four weeks in exchange for $5,000.00, included an additional clause that provided for the actress to be paid the $5,000.00 even if her services were ultimately not required. *Id*. The actress's services were never required, and her assignee sued to recover the $5,000.00. *Id*. In response to the motion picture company's argument that the actress had failed to mitigate her damages, the California Court of Appeal held that the doctrine of mitigation of damages has no place in an action on the contract itself for the agreed compensation. *Id*. at 142. In addition, the court held that mitigation of damages was not required in cases of contracts of hire that did not require "all or the greater portion of the time of the party employed," or which did not "preclude the party from undertaking and being engaged in the performance contemporaneously of other contracts." *Id*.

The holding of the California Court of Appeal in *Payne* directly addresses the issue of mitigation of damages in this context. The plaintiffs have produced evidence that Millennium agreed to be bound by the terms of the Basic Agreement. The Basic Agreement specifically provides that the employee be paid the agreed compensation even where the employer ultimately does not require his or her services. As a result, the plaintiffs' contract with Millennium incorporated nearly identical provisions to those at issue in *Payne*. Therefore, Plaintiffs were under no obligation to mitigate damages in an action against Millennium to recover the compensation owed them under their contracts.

CONCLUSION

For the foregoing reasons, and good cause appearing therefor, the Court hereby GRANTS Plaintiffs' Motion for Summary Judgment. The terms of the bond executed by Millennium and NAC encompass the amounts owed the plaintiffs pursuant to their arbitration award against Millennium.

Note

1. Are arbitration awards sacrosanct? In *Directors Guild of America v. Millennium Television*, the plaintiffs successfully sought to enforce an arbitration award. In contrast, the plaintiffs in *Metromedia, Inc. v. Local 819, Intern. Alliance of Theatrical Stage Employees, AFL-CIO*, 1980 WL 2164 (1980), were displeased with the outcome of the arbitration and sought to vacate the award that held that disciplinarian action can include demotion.

METROMEDIA v. LOCAL 819

United States District Court, District of Columbia, 1980.
1980 WL 2164.

GASCH, District Judge.

* * * In this action brought pursuant to § 301 of the Labor Management Relations Act, 29 U.S.C. § 185, plaintiff Metromedia, Inc. (Metromedia) seeks to vacate an arbitration award. Plaintiff alleges that

the arbitrator exceeded his powers by ignoring bargaining history and the practice of the parties under the collective bargaining agreement, by modifying the agreement, and by substituting his judgment for the business judgment of plaintiff. Defendant, Local 819, International Alliance of Theatrical Stage Employees (Local 819) has counterclaimed, seeking enforcement of the award.

Before the Court are the parties' cross-motions for summary judgment. For purposes of these cross-motions, the parties have submitted a joint stipulation of facts and exhibits.

BACKGROUND

Plaintiff Metromedia owns and operates WTTG–TV in Washington, D.C. Defendant Local 819 has been the certified collective bargaining agent of television broadcasting engineers employed by Metromedia at WTTG since 1956.

In 1973, Metromedia and Local 819 entered into a collective bargaining agreement covering three categories of employees-senior technicians, technical directors, and technicians. That agreement terminated on May 31, 1976, and a subsequent agreement was executed on June 1, 1976 covering the same provisions. Article XX of both agreements provides for arbitration of disputes.

On August 25, 1975, Walter Anderson, a member of Local 819 and a 25–year employee at WTTG–TV, was demoted from technical director to technician for disciplinary reasons. The demotion was effective September 4, 1975. Local 819 thereafter contended that the demotion violated provisions of the collective bargaining agreement, including section 17.01 governing discharge or discipline for cause. Following exhaustion of the grievance procedure, the union requested that a final determination of the dispute be made through arbitration. A Demand for Arbitration was finally made on September 4, 1977, and the dispute was submitted for arbitration to William D. Boetticher pursuant to the provisions of Article XX.

[Reinstatement Ordered]

The dispute was tried before the arbitrator in five separate sessions between July 25 and October 16, 1978. On January 23, 1979, the arbitrator issued his Decision and Award, which ordered Anderson reinstated to his position as technical director but held that he was not entitled to any back pay adjustment for the period that he was demoted. Plaintiff's motion for reconsideration was denied.

In his decision, the arbitrator found a deterioration in Anderson's job performance since about 1973, noting various reported instances of Anderson's failure to perform his job duties adequately. Based on Anderson's work history, he concluded that "disciplinary action was justified as of August 27, 1975." He also concluded that "such action could have included discharge, as it was apparent Anderson did not perform his duties as a technical director."

The arbitrator held, however, that under the terms of the collective bargaining agreement, such disciplinary action could not include demotion:

> Having found that disciplinary action was justified, the issue to be decided is whether such discipline could include demotion. The collective bargaining agreement has no management rights clause, and is silent as to the right to demote. The Union takes the position, and has supported it with some authorities, that when the contract does not retain the right to demote, the Employer contracts away such right as such an action affects the seniority rights of the employee involved and other employees in the same category. I find these authorities to be persuasive. Under the contract, seniority is a substantial benefit covering protection from layoff, promotion, and screen credits. These seniority benefits are lost upon demotion. If discipline is the desired result, a progressive system of warnings, suspensions, and eventual discharge is more appropriate as employee rights are not destroyed permanently. Hence, the demotion of Walter Anderson violated the seniority provisions of the contract and he is entitled to be reinstated to that position. I find it unnecessary to decide the other issues raised by the Union.

In denying Metromedia's motion for reconsideration, the arbitrator elaborated on his conclusion that the demotion for disciplinary reasons violated Anderson's seniority rights. With respect to promotion, the arbitrator stated that section 15.01 of the agreement provides that seniority shall be a factor to be considered in promotions, and that a demoted employee becomes displaced on the seniority ladder. With respect to screen credits, he stated that screen credit rights are accorded the two senior employees (the senior technician and the technical director) under section 21.00, and thus that an employee demoted from technical director to technician loses that contractual right to screen credits. Finally, with respect to layoffs, he noted that Anderson was personally immune from layoff by virtue of being listed in section 17.08 of the agreement, but concluded that where the employer uses demotion rather than discharge as a disciplinary device it affects the seniority rights of employees in the bargaining unit other than the demoted employee.

Following the denial of its motion for reconsideration, Metromedia filed this action seeking to vacate the arbitrator's award, and Local 819 counterclaimed for enforcement of the award.

DISCUSSION

A.

Jurisdiction to review arbitration awards arising from collective bargaining agreements is founded on § 301 of the Labor Management Relations Act, 29 U.S.C. § 185. Review of an arbitrator's award under § 301 is, however, narrowly circumscribed. The reluctance to set aside an award is based on the strong federal policy of settling labor disputes by arbitration. * * *

In *United Steelworkers v. Enterprise Wheel & Car Corp.,* 363 U.S. 593, 596–97 (1960), the Supreme Court defined the scope of review of an arbitration award under a collective bargaining agreement:

> The refusal of courts to review the merits of an arbitration award is the proper approach to arbitration under collective bargaining agreements. The federal policy of settling labor disputes by arbitration would be undermined if courts had the final say on the merits of the awards.

> When an arbitrator is commissioned to interpret and apply the collective bargaining agreement, he is to bring his informed judgment to bear in order to reach a fair solution of a problem.

> ... Nevertheless, an arbitrator is confined to interpretation and application of the collective bargaining agreement; he does not sit to dispense his own brand of industrial justice. He may of course look for guidance from many sources, yet his award is legitimate only so long as it draws its essence from the collective bargaining agreement. When the arbitrator's words manifest an infidelity to this obligation, courts have no choice but to refuse enforcement of the award.

In establishing this standard, the Court emphasized that a reviewing court cannot set aside an arbitral award premised on the arbitrator's construction of a collective bargaining agreement merely because the court disagrees with that construction:

> ... the question of interpretation of the collective bargaining agreement is a question for the arbitrator. It is the arbitrator's construction which was bargained for; and so far as the arbitrator's decision concerns construction of the contract, the courts have no business overruling him because their interpretation of the contract is different from his. *Id.* at 599. * * *

The issue in any particular case is whether the arbitrator's award "draws its essence from the collective bargaining agreement" or whether his words "manifest an infidelity to [that] obligation." To be legitimate, the award must be based on a consideration of the collective bargaining agreement, which includes the written contract as well as the "industrial common law," i.e. the practices of the industry and the shop, *United Steelworkers v. Warrior & Gulf Navigation Co.,* 363 U.S. 574, 581–82 (1960). To establish that an award fails to "draw its essence from the collective bargaining agreement," a plaintiff must, however, show more than a mere misconstruction of the contract.

Courts have generally held that an award fails to draw its essence from the collective bargaining agreement only if the award is contrary to an express provision of the written contract or if it cannot be derived in any rational way from the agreement. * * * If, on the other hand, the arbitrator interprets and applies the collective bargaining agreement and his award has its basis in the agreement, the arbitrator's decision on the merits is final. Moreover, "arbitrators have no obligation to the court to give their reasons for an award," since it is the award rather than the specific reasoning employed that must be reviewed. * * *

B.

In challenging the award in this case, plaintiff's principal argument is that the arbitrator erred in concluding that demotion had an effect on seniority rights in the areas of promotion, screen credits, and protection from layoff. Plaintiff contends that the arbitrator's conclusion is refuted by the express language of the contract—in particular section 14.01, which appears to measure seniority without regard to an employee's job classification.

Plaintiff's argument must be rejected. First, as the Court noted above, it is the award rather than the specific reasoning that is reviewed. Here, the award itself does not run counter to any express provision of the contract; as the arbitrator observed, the agreement is silent on the right to demote. Second, plaintiff unsuccessfully presented the same basic argument to the arbitrator on a motion for reconsideration and, in affirming his prior decision and award, the arbitrator explained how his challenged conclusion flowed from his interpretations of several other contract provisions—provisions which he appeared to interpret independently of section 14.01. Moreover, the arbitrator also relied, in his initial decision, on the fact that the agreement contained no management rights clause and did not expressly retain the right to demote.

[*No Basis to Vacate*]

Applying the principles of *Enterprise Wheel* and its progeny to the case at bar, it is plain that plaintiff has shown no basis for vacating the award. The arbitrator clearly focused on the provisions of the collective bargaining agreement in resolving the grievance, and his decision is based upon an interpretation of those provisions. Plaintiff, moreover, can point to no express language in the contract requiring a result contrary to the award, nor can the Court conclude that there is no rational way to derive the arbitrator's interpretation from the agreement. * * * That the Court might easily reach a contrary result concerning plaintiff's right to demote, were it to construe the collective bargaining agreement, is immaterial. The parties bargained for the arbitrator's construction, and because his award clearly drew its essence from the agreement, it must be enforced.

CONCLUSION

For the reasons stated above, the Court denies plaintiff's motion for summary judgment and grants defendant's motion for summary judgment.

Notes

1. All of the labor unions have been sued for antitrust violations. In *HBO v. Directors Guild of America, Inc.*, 531 F.Supp. 578 (S.D.N.Y. 1982), the DGA conceded that it had engaged in activities that violate the antitrust laws, but that its activities were exempt from antitrust laws. It argued that "its combinations with freelance directors, individually and through loan-out companies, with producer-directors, and with director-packagers are protected by the 'statutory' exemption afforded unilateral labor activity." The court agreed, holding that HBO "failed to establish any proper ground for enjoining the Guild's activities."

2. In certain instances, talent has preferred to bring a class action against the television networks rather than seek the protection of a particular guild. On January 16, 2003, Judge Charles McCoy Jr. dismissed *Cecile Alch v. Time Warner Entertainment*, which was brought by more than 175 writers alleging "that television networks, Hollywood studios and talent agencies discriminate against writers over the age of 40." *See* Meg James, Judge Dismisses TV Writers Suit, L.A. Times, Jan. 22, 2003, at Business Pt. 3, Pg. 2. The writers claimed that they had been "gray-listed" by networks pursuing young viewers. Judge McCoy said that "the writers could not successfully argue that an industry wide pattern existed without first proving individual violations." *Id.*

3. As the television industry changes, unions spring into action. The following article discuss the effort of several unions to organize the reality TV genre that took the networks by storm in the 2000s, moving from stepchild to full partner on the nightly schedule.

Jim Rendon
Unions Aim to Share in the Success of Reality TV
N.Y. Times, Jan. 25, 2004, at Business. P. 4.

REALITY television shows like "Fear Factor," "Big Brother" and "The Bachelor" have crossed over from sideshow entertainment to network television's main event. But their success has caught the attention of more than advertisers and disgusted critics. Hollywood's unions are showing an interest, too.

The International Alliance of Theatrical Stage Employees, which includes the International Cinematographers Guild and the Motion Picture Editors Guild, is trying to unionize reality shows that are shown by the networks, as well as gritty documentary-style cable shows like "Trauma: Life in the ER." Arguing that those who work on unscripted programs should receive health insurance, pensions, overtime pay and other benefits, the alliance has unionized "Big Brother," which is produced by Endemol USA, a unit of Telefónica S.A, and is in negotiations with "Blind Date" and "Fifth Wheel," produced by Renegade 83.

Reality shows, many of which originated in Europe and on cable channels in the United States, have traditionally been made by nonunion production companies. Now that reality shows are broadcast on the big networks, unions say their workers should get the same pay and benefits that go to unionized workers of other network shows.

If the unions are successful, some people in the industry say, there may be less eating of crickets and fewer tear-filled rejections broadcast into America's living rooms. If the producers have to pay overtime and union wages, and to make contributions to health and pension programs, the shows will be more expensive to produce. That could make them less appealing to the networks, which have come to rely on reality shows as bargains for their prime-time schedules.

Like unsuccessful strategists on "Survivor," producers of reality shows may wind up being voted off their island. "We are the bastard children of television," said Eric Schotz, president and chief executive of LMNO Productions, which has produced shows like "Man vs. Beast" and "Celebrity Boot Camp." "I find it fairly humorous that now, all of a sudden, the unions are showing up."

The recent ratings success and the lucrative advertising revenue of reality programming is part of the genre's appeal to unions, said Tris Carpenter, a national organizer with the Motion Picture Editors Guild, I.A.T.S.E. Local 700. "These shows are not paying actors, except for a host," he said. "They are made for less money but are still aired on the network, and that success is not getting passed on to everyone who makes the show happen."

Wages for reality shows, on average, are not in line with those of scripted programming. Workers on the reality shows are generally free-lancers who rarely receive benefits like health insurance or pensions, Mr. Carpenter said. Many work on a single show and then move on. Jobs can be as short as three or four months.

While an hour of prime-time reality programming for a major network costs about $700,000 to produce, the average scripted drama can cost $1 million to $2 million an hour.

LOW costs initially drew networks to reality programming, said Jerry Katzman, the director of industry relations in the department of film, television and digital media at the University of California, Los Angeles, and the former president of the William Morris Agency. While he was at the agency, it helped bring programs like "Big Brother" from Europe. "These programs helped the networks balance out the high cost of producing scripted programming," Mr. Katzman said.

The production differences between reality programs and scripted shows have attracted some unions and befuddled others. A scripted show tends to have a large production staff that includes camera operators, highly paid scriptwriters and union actors. Reality programming, on the other hand, uses contestants who are nominally paid—except for the prize winners—and, usually, small production crews. Most of the work occurs after the cameras are put away.

Jay Renfroe, a partner in Renegade 83, said that on a reality show, production crews may shoot for only a few weeks, but that post-production takes nine weeks or more. Writers do not play much of a role. "Reality TV is really written in post-production," Mr. Renfroe said. "The storytellers are the producers and the editors."

Mr. Renfroe said a reality show could employ 12 editors at a time. That is because producers do not know during filming who will be voted out of the house, or which contestant will get the final rose and win the guy. They end up shooting hundreds of hours of tape so they have everything they may need. All that tape is then dumped on the editors and producers, who determine what stories to weed out.

The editors' union wants to organize the production companies of reality programming because they employ so many editors, which as a group are crucial to the programs' creation, Mr. Carpenter said.

The Writers Guild of America is also working to unionize reality TV, said Paul Naurocki, assistant executive director of the guild, and has had some success. Although reality shows do not use traditional scripts, someone writes the host introductions and voice-overs, he said. Union members write a variety of programs, from dramas and sitcoms to game-shows.

JUST because there are no polished scripts like those in a drama like "The West Wing" does not mean that reality writers should be treated differently than writers on other shows, Mr. Naurocki said.

"Every hour of television competes with every other hour of television," he said. "If the nonunion stuff is done on the cheap, then it undercuts the standards established in dramatic programming."

And to the extent that there are writers, they are not treated like writers on other shows. Unionized writers receive residual checks, for example, when their shows are syndicated. Without union writers on the reality shows, no one gets a residual check if a program is rebroadcast.

A few reality shows have gone into syndication. Renegade 83 recently sold the first three seasons of "Blind Date" to Spike TV, but no one will receive a residual check for reruns, Mr. Renfroe said.

Organizing is also a challenge when a show's staff members rotate every few months, Mr. Carpenter said. The unions need to work quickly. In most instances they do not go through the National Labor Relations Board for official elections because, he said, the show may be done before a vote takes place. While every case is different, Mr. Carpenter said that in many instances, if the union manages to sign up a majority of employees on a show, it can approach the production company and negotiate for a contract without going through the N.L.R.B.

When a show is unionized, the I.A.T.S.E. negotiates a contract for all of the different skills it represents, from camera operators to make up artists.

The editors' union does not draw the line at unscripted network programming. In 2001, it organized New York Times Television, which produces documentary-style programs for the Discovery Channel and other cable networks. Mr. Carpenter said that these documentary-style programs are produced in much the same way as shows like "Big Brother." And editors on these shows have many of the same concerns.

David Kirchner, now an assistant editor on feature films who worked at Times Television in 2001 and helped bring in the union, said that the work environment had improved with the payment of overtime and provision of unemployment insurance and health benefits.

But not everyone is persuaded that unionizing will bring benefits. For a freelance cinematographer to gain union benefits like health coverage, members must put in 600 hours of work a year on unionized shows, a tall order for someone who works mostly on nonunion reality shows.

Brian Gaetke, a cinematographer on "Fear Factor," which is among the shows that the cinematographers' union is trying to organize, said that he had not yet been contacted by the union. But he said he had little interest in joining, particularly if he had to pay the large upfront fee, which for that union can be as high as $10,000.

"They want an exorbitant amount of money to join and offer nothing to compensate for it," Mr. Gaetke said.

The cinematographers' union did not return phone calls seeking comment, and the I.A.T.S.E. declined to comment.

To encourage people like him to join, unions are in some cases waiving the initiation fees. That was enough to persuade a camera operator on a network reality show, who spoke on condition of anonymity. The camera operator figured that joining the union would lead to work on feature films, where union membership is often required.

Most people who work in reality programming move from one show to another every three or four months. If they are union members and work on union shows, they are also allowed to work on nonunion shows, at nonunion pay. Some say that advertising their union affiliation could alienate potential employers.

"I am a bit scared about certain employers knowing that I'm in the union," the camera operator said. "I don't want people to think that I'm a troublemaker."

For some workers, salary is not a big motivator. On a scripted network show, union editors earn $2,800 a week or more, Mr. Carpenter said. On a popular reality show, they earn $2,500 or more a week.

Mr. Gaetke says that he has been happy with the nonunion work environment on "Fear Factor." He said the show paid better and in a more timely manner than many others on which he works.

Such employee satisfaction may be an obstacle for organizers. But they are also looking to organize cable shows, the bulk of reality programming, where the budgets, margins and salaries are much smaller.

Mr. Katzman cautioned that because the economics of cable television were different, inflating production costs with union salaries and benefits could be disastrous. "Cable is niche programming," he said, adding that if the cost of development rose, cable channels might find original shows less affordable.

It's an argument that Mr. Carpenter hears often, and one that he cannot say is totally without merit. But so far, he said, unionized companies that produce reality shows have been able to continue operating. And the union will continue its work.

"Cable is no different for us," he said. "Shows are crossing over. Just because it is on cable today doesn't mean it's not going to be on a network tomorrow."

http://www.nytimes.com/2004/01/25/business/yourmoney/25union.html? ex=1076123006 & ei=1 & en=9396954d599ffc3b

Notes

1. Should participants be paid on reality TV shows? Isn't the exposure sufficient reward? Several individuals have leapt into television and movie production after appearing on a reality TV show and winning. Stars of *American Idol* have received record contracts, touring gigs, and movie deals. The first *Joe Millionaire* star, Evan Marriott, received a contract to star in a television game show. Trista Rehn found true love on *The Bachelorette*, married her chosen hunk Ryan Sutter on television, and received a $1,000,000 dowry from ABC.

For more information about this topic, see Sherri Burr's interview with *The Bachelor's* Bob Guiney and the accompanying notes in Chapter 7, The Television Process.

2. Is there a stronger argument for urging writers, editors, and directors to become part of a guild? The question is will they gain more from increased benefits and defined minimum contracts than they might lose from having to pay initiation fees to participate in a labor union?

Chapter 10

TELEVISION CREDITS AND COMPENSATION

Credits and compensation are as important to television stars as they are to film talent. They can be intricately related because where someone is billed in the television project determines his importance to the project and therefore affects his future compensation. Similar to film, compensation can take many forms including upfront payments and profit participation. Stars of certain stature will bargain to include "pay or play" provisions that require the producers to compensate them even when the project is cancelled.

The following cases and notes discuss these credit and compensation issues, which are important for lawyers to understand as they seek to successfully represent television stars or talent with TV projects.

A. TV CREDITS

SMITHERS v. MGM STUDIOS

California Court of Appeals, 1983.
139 Cal.App.3d 643, 189 Cal.Rptr. 20.

NELSON, Associate Justice.

Metro–Goldwyn–Mayer Studios, Inc. (MGM), Harris Katleman (Katleman), and Bernard Weitzman (Weitzman) appeal from the judgment (as well as from the denial of a motion for judgment notwithstanding the verdict) in this action by William Smithers (Smithers). A cross-appeal from the trial court's remittitur of punitive damages was filed by Smithers.

Smithers sued MGM, Katleman and Weitzman for breach of contract, tortious breach of contract (covenant of good faith and fair dealing), and fraud. The jury returned its verdict as follows:

1. For Smithers against MGM, damages in the sum of $500,000, for breach of contract (count I);

2. For Smithers against MGM, for tortious breach of contract (covenant of good faith and fair dealing), damages in the sum of $300,000 (count II);

3. For Smithers against MGM, Katleman and Weitzman for fraud damages of $200,000 (count III);

4. For Smithers against MGM, punitive damages of $2 million (count IV).

The trial judge denied the motions of MGM, Katleman and Weitzman for judgment notwithstanding the verdict, and for new trial on Smithers' acceptance of reduction of damage for fraud (count III) from $200,000 to $1, and punitive damages from $2 million to $1 million. MGM, Katleman, and Weitzman appeal. Smithers cross-appeals.

Beginning in January 1976, MGM produced a television series entitled "Executive Suite." Harris Katleman was president of MGM Television and Bernard Weitzman was vice president of MGM in charge of Business Affairs. MGM hired an independent casting agency, the Melnick/Holstra Agency, to hire actors for the "Executive Suite" series. Through the Melnick/Holstra Agency, MGM negotiated with Smithers' agent, the William Morris Agency, to cast Smithers in the role of Anderson Galt in the series.

William Smithers is a professional actor of more than 30 years' experience. He has appeared in motion pictures, theater, and radio productions, and has been a regular or cast member in several television series. For approximately 11 years he has been billed as a "guest star," usually with his name and possibly his picture appearing alone on the screen. Appellants concede, as was established by numerous witnesses, that Smithers is a highly regarded actor.

In the course of negotiations between Smithers' agent and the casting agency, the casting director offered a provision known as a "Most-Favored-Nations" billing arrangement. This provision ultimately read as follows:

"Except for the parts of DON WALLING, HELEN WALLING, and HOWARD RUTLEDGE, this deal is on a Most Favored Nations basis, i.e., if any other performer receives greater compensation than Artist, Artist shall receive that compensation.

"Additionally, no other performer shall receive more prominent billing or a better billing provision than Artist (except with respect to where his name is placed alphabetically on the crawl)."

This Most-Favored-Nations provision was offered by the casting director for MGM since Smithers was being offered a lower than usual compensation rate. Further, MGM by this provision could "get some good people to work for reasonably low money and to not have to take up a great deal of space in the main titles." Because of the provision, and in hopes of an improved role, Smithers accepted the role. An interim agreement, called the Outline Deal Memo, was signed by the casting director for MGM and Smithers' agent setting forth the above, being binding pending the execution of a long form contract. Smithers' understanding was that he would get billing at the end of the show, name alphabetically, but that only three other actors would be given more prominent billing at the front of the show.

At a screening of the pilot film, Smithers saw that there were *four* actors with "up-front" billing, instead of the agreed upon three actors. The casting agency had employed another actor for the series during the filming of the pilot film, and had given him "star billing." Smithers saw that his billing remained the same, but preferred to wait until he was in a better bargaining position to complain. Ultimately, ten or eleven actors were given "up-front" billing, while Smithers' end-of-show-name-only billing remained the same.

When the series "Executive Suite" was sold to the CBS network, Smithers' contract provided that he would perform in at least seven of the thirteen episodes. He actually performed in ten of the episodes. Beginning in September 1976, the program was broadcast over the CBS television network. Owing to poor ratings, MGM decided to make several changes, including the "story line" and the billing of the actors. After being informed of these changes, Smithers complained that his billing was not in conformity with the most-favored-nations provision. Upon perusal by Smithers and his agency, it was discovered that the provision had been changed in the long-form contract (which was then—November 1976—still unsigned). The change would allow any number of actors to be billed more prominently than Smithers. MGM's attorney in charge of drafting the contracts testified concerning the change: "There were only two plausible explanations. Either I made a mistake or someone told me to do it," and "Generally somebody who had more authority than I told me to change it."

In mid-December Smithers was told that his role was to be written out of the series. In late December of 1976, Smithers' agent was told that the most-favored-nations provision had been a mistake, and that Smithers should waive the provision. Upon Smithers' refusal to agree to the change, Katleman told Smithers' agent, "... if he didn't, that he (Katleman) would be hard pressed to use Mr. Smithers again on any shows that he (Katleman) was involved with, and that if he (Katleman) were to tell this to Bud Grant, who was then the head of CBS for programing, if he (Katleman) were to tell him (Grant) this, that he (Katleman) was certain he (Grant) would go along as well with not using Mr. Smithers." This threat was reported to Smithers, who ultimately again refused to go along with the change. MGM then went ahead and changed Smithers to an end-of-show billing, however, on a separate card from the rest of the end-of-show billing.

The testimony was considerable on the importance of billing to an actor. Several witnesses testified that billing reflects the actor's stature in the industry, and affects his negotiations for roles, since it reflects what his status and compensation has been in the past. Billing reflects recognition by the producer and the public of the actor's importance or "star quality," and in turn affects the actor's compensation in present and future roles.

ISSUES ON MGM's APPEAL

MGM contends that Smithers was not entitled to proceed on a theory of a tortious breach of an implied covenant of good faith and fair dealing (tortious breach of contract); that damages for breach of contract were not shown, but if shown, were speculative, uncertain, and excessive; that there was no evidence of fraud, but if there were, damages should not have been allowed for emotional distress on that theory, so that no basis exists for punitive damages, which were also excessive; and that the trial court erred in refusing to give certain instructions. Our approach is, as always, to determine whether substantial evidence supports the judgment in the trial court, viewing that evidence in the light most favorable to respondent.

A.   Tortious Breach of Duty of Good Faith and Fair Dealing

The jury found that Katleman issued what amounted to a threat to blacklist Smithers and to encourage others to blacklist him also unless he would forgo his contractual rights. The question is whether the act gave rise to an action in tort. Prior to trial, Judge Cole ruled that such conduct, if proved, fit "to a T" the definition enunciated in *Sawyer v. Bank of America*, 83 Cal.App.3d 135, 139, 145 Cal.Rptr. 623 (1978): "[T]he tort of breaching an implied covenant of good faith and fair dealing consists in bad faith action, extraneous to the contract, with the motive intentionally to frustrate the obligee's enjoyment of contract rights." This developing, and confusing, area of the law has had much discussion. *See* Loudenback and Jurika, *Standards for Limiting the Tort of Bad Faith Breach of Contract*, 16 U.S.F.L.Rev. 187 (1982). * * * MGM takes the position that the rule is clearly established; however, it has an applicability limited to insurance cases or contracts of adhesions, citing *Silberg v. California Life Ins. Co.*, 11 Cal.3d 452, 521 P.2d 1103 (1974); *Wagner v. Benson*, 101 Cal.App.3d 27, 161 Cal.Rptr. 516 (1980); and dictum in *Glendale Fed. Sav. & Loan Assn. v. Marina View Heights Dev. Co.*, 66 Cal.App.3d 101, 135, fn. 8, 135 Cal.Rptr. 802 (1977). Smithers refers us to dictum in *Tameny v. Atlantic Richfield Co.*, 27 Cal.3d 167, 179, fn. 12, 164 Cal.Rptr. 839, 610 P.2d 1330 (1980) and the holding in *Cleary v. American Airlines*, 111 Cal.App.3d 443, 168 Cal.Rptr. 722 (1980), both wrongful discharge cases. *Cleary* noted that the doctrine was first formulated in insurance cases, but applies to all contracts.

The trial judge, on the motion for judgment notwithstanding the verdict, found the evidence on the issue sufficient, and we agree. Further, it is clear that the threat was extraneous to the contract, not only intending to bludgeon Smithers into foregoing his contractual rights but also threatening action directly affecting the practice of his art and damaging to his future earning power. * * * We agree with Judge Cole that such bad faith conduct fits the *Sawyer* definition. The jury's verdict is supported by substantial evidence.

B.   Breach of Contract

MGM concedes that its contract with Smithers was breached, but takes the position that damages arising from such breach were speculative and incapable of ascertainment. Damages for breach of contract must, of course, be clearly ascertainable as to their nature and origin. (Civ.Code § 3301.) However, it is clear that one who wilfully breaches the contract bears the risk as to the uncertainty or the difficulty of computing the amount of damages. Donahue v. United Artists Corp., 2 Cal.App.3d 794, 804, 83 Cal.Rptr. 131 (1969). A number of witnesses established the relationship between billing and the actor's future negotiations for compensation. The jury could reasonably conclude from the evidence that Smithers suffered an economic loss by reason of MGM's failure to live up to its agreement. Although witnesses were unable to estimate with precision how much Smithers had lost or how much he would earn in future years, the jury was provided a reasonable basis upon which to calculate damages. That fulfills the requirement of Civil Code section 3301. Distribu–Dor, Inc. v. Karadanis, 11 Cal.App.3d 463, 470, 90 Cal.Rptr. 231 (1970).

C.   Fraud

The evidence, viewed most favorably for Smithers, adequately showed that MGM, based upon later actions of its agents, had no intention of living up to its most-favored-nations provision, which was offered to induce Smithers to accept a lower than usual compensation rate. The evidence is further sufficient to sustain the jury's determination that Smithers relied upon the promise when he entered the contract. MGM's main point here is that damages were improperly allowed for emotional distress based upon a fraud theory. That contention is answered by Crisci v. Security Ins. Co., 66 Cal.2d 425, 433, 58 Cal.Rptr. 13, 426 P.2d 173 (1967); Gruenberg v. Aetna Ins. Co., 9 Cal.3d 566, 580, 108 Cal.Rptr. 480, 510 P.2d 1032 (1973); Restatement, Torts, 2d, Sect. 46, Comment b. MGM cites O'Neil v. Spillane, 45 Cal.App.3d 147, 119 Cal.Rptr. 245 (1975). That case is clearly inapposite here, involving fraud in the conveyance of real property invoking section 3343 of the Civil Code. Here the jury, based upon substantial evidence, determined that actual damage had been suffered by Smithers as a result of MGM's fraud and deceit. Following precedent, as we must, that determination will be upheld.

Smithers' Cross Appeal

Two basic contentions are urged by Smithers: The trial court should not have found the damages awarded under the fraud theory to be duplicative, and the punitive damages award should not have been reduced. Smithers, therefore, would have us reinstate the jury's verdict in its entirety.

Since the trial court, on a motion to reduce damages, sits as an independent trier of fact, we are required to accord to its order respecting damages the same deference as is given to juries' verdicts on appeal.

Therefore every presumption is in favor of the correctness of that order, in the absence of an abuse of discretion. * * *

I

The trial court, reviewing the evidence, concluded that the damages awarded on the fraud theory duplicated those found on the theories of breach of contract and tortious breach of the covenant of good faith and fair dealing. One may have many theories, but one recovery. The trial court's order respecting the duplication of damages reviewed the evidence, noting the overlapping and interweaving of the facts as they supported the various theories, concluded that such interdependence warranted essentially one recovery. That independent judgment was fully justified by the evidence, since, indeed, the summation of Smithers' counsel (though that is not dispositive) wove this very tapestry of facts for the jury. The trial court's exercise of discretion in this regard was sound. * * *

II

Concerning the reduction of punitive damages, we again accord the presumption of correctness to the trial court's order. * * * Here the trial court found punitive damages to be justified, and the record supports that conclusion. The trial court's judgment as to the gravity of MGM's acts, the amount of damages awarded, and MGM's wealth rests on substantial evidence. Reducing damages to a nominal amount on the fraud theory created a facial disproportion between that nominal amount and the punitive damages before and after such reduction. That, however, is of no consequence. * * *

Smithers' real contention is that the trial court, in contrast to its specifications as required by Code of Civil Procedure section 657 on the reduction of damages for emotional distress, did not meet those requirements concerning the reduction of punitive damages. Specification is adequate, according to *Neal*, when "it makes reference to those aspects of the trial proceedings which, in the trial court's view, improperly led the jury to inflate its award." [21 Cal.3d 910] 932, 148 Cal.Rptr. 389, 582 P.2d 980. The trial court noted that such damages were "justifiable," and that the evidence "fully supported the conclusion that the conduct of the defendants was 'extreme and outrageous.'" Fairly read, the specification notes that MGM's threat was neither carried out nor communicated to CBS, and apparently did not cause economic loss, although it caused emotional distress. Then the trial court found $1 million in punitive damages to be more reasonable than $2 million. We cannot say that the punitive damages, as ultimately awarded, did not bear a reasonable relation to the actual damages as we have affirmed them.

We therefore affirm the judgment on the appeal and on the cross-appeal. Neither party shall recover costs on appeal.

LUSTER ENTERPRISES, INC. v. JACOBS

United States District Court, Southern District of New York, 1967.
278 F.Supp. 73.

CROAKE, District Judge.

This is a motion for a temporary restraining order brought on by an Order to Show Cause. The plaintiffs, Luster Enterprises, Inc., and Helen Winston ask this court for an injunction restraining the defendants Arthur Jacobs, APJAC Productions, Inc., and their agents and assigns from producing, distributing, showing, exhibiting, advertising in the mass communications media, including but not limited to newspapers, radio, television and billboards or causing the production, distribution, showing or exhibition, etc., of any motion picture film or photoplay based on the 'Doctor Doolittle' stories for any commercial purpose unless suitable credit is given to Helen Winston. As it is claimed that Helen Winston was the architect of the present screen play, the suitable credit suggested is to take the form of an acknowledgment 'Conceived by Helen Winston.'

The present application flows from the plaintiffs' amended complaint where it is alleged in substance that the named defendants and Twentieth Century Fox Film Corp. (FOX) have plagiarized and intend to present the plaintiffs' screen play without the permission and without recognizing the contribution of Helen Winston. The plaintiffs in their amended complaint seek damages of $4,500,000.

$4.5M damages sought

Rule 65, Fed.R.Civ.P., enunciates the applicable standards for the relief requested in this case. It is a restrictive rule. It requires among other things that a showing be made that if an injunction is not granted, irreparable harm will result. * * * In considering whether to issue a preliminary injunction, the court must consider the relative importance of the rights asserted, the acts sought to be enjoined, the irreparable nature of the injury allegedly flowing from denial of preliminary relief, probability of ultimate success or failure of the suit and balancing of damages and convenience generally. * * *

In this particular case we find the determinative aspect is the nature of the irreparable harm claimed. The plaintiff, Helen Winston, states that if a preliminary injunction is not issued by this court she will suffer irreparable injury. Dealing with the substance of this claim, we find it to be without merit. Helen Winston is apparently a successful and talented screen play author. If a screen credit is improperly denied her by the defendants she has an action in damages. One of the forgotten functions of the damage remedy is to apprise members of the community of the rights which the court has adjudicated in the plaintiffs' favor. If the plaintiffs prevail in this action the attendant publicity and the subsequent damage award will make Helen Winston whole within her professional community. Outside of this small professional community, screen credits have little or no significance and any resulting harm by failure to include her name in the credits will be minimal.

On the other hand, if this court grants the preliminary injunction, FOX will be required to include Helen Winston's name in the screen credits or forego its plans to premiere the film in early December. In short, as FOX has engaged in extensive advertising with this December date in mind it would in effect be forced to include Helen Winston's name in the screen credits. As Justice Telesford noted in his opinion directed to essentially the same issues (see Luster Enterprises, Inc. v. Twentieth Century Fox Film Corp., No. 16114/1967 (Sup.Ct.New York, Oct. 18, 1967)) ' * * * such credit * * * (would) be but the first step in the building of a claim for damages.' On balance, then, in weighing the equities, we find that if the preliminary injunction issues, the plaintiffs will have in fact been granted a large part of the relief requested in advance of any trial on the merits and will be in a superior position to press their damage claims. See Dino De Laurentiis Cinematografia v. D–150, Inc., 258 F.Supp. 459, 464 (S.D.N.Y.1966). If this court grants the requested preliminary injunction, it will not be preserving the status quo but will be tipping the scales of justice in favor of the plaintiff.

Finally, the plaintiffs were aware for some time that there was a dispute as to ownership of the literary property of the screen play because they commenced their action in this court in July of 1966. It was certainly within their power to put the case in issue before this time. The plaintiffs state that the reason it took over one year from the filing of the original complaint until the service of the answer was primarily that the defendants delayed answering the complaint. We note that the time to answer was extended by stipulation ten times. From this it appears that the plaintiffs were not anxious for a speedy determination of the issues now presented.

By its determination of this motion the court implies no view on the merits of plaintiffs' action for damages. The decision is only a reflection of this court's belief that the injunctive remedy should be reserved for those urgent matters which require immediate relief.

One other matter remains to be considered. Defendants have moved to dismiss this action pursuant to Rule 12(b)(6), Fed.R.Civ.P., on the ground that neither of the plaintiffs in this action has legal title to or beneficial ownership of the literary property involved. If this is true, the complaint fails to state a claim upon which relief can be granted. See Hoffman v. Santly–Joy, Inc., 51 F.Supp. 778 (S.D.N.Y.1943); Manning v. Miller Music Corp., 174 F.Supp. 192 (S.D.N.Y.1959). The court feels that it has insufficient information to determine the precise relationship between the parties who are before it and those who are not with regard to rights in this material. Accordingly, the motion to dismiss is denied as is the application for a preliminary injunction. So ordered.

Note

1. Compare and contrast these cases discussing credits in the television industry with those in Chapter 5 addressing credits in the film industry. Are actors and writers in the film industry better off than those in the television industry?

B. TV COMPENSATION

As in film, compensation in the television industry generates a myriad of issues. The following cases explore issues involved with pay or play, net compensation, and merchandizing and product placement.

1. PAY OR PLAY

THIS IS ME, INC. v. TAYLOR

United States Court of Appeals, Second Circuit, 1998.
157 F.3d 139.

JACOBS, Circuit Judge.

Actress Cicely Tyson, through her personal services corporation, plaintiff-appellant This Is Me, Inc., agreed to undertake the lead role in a Broadway production of "The Corn is Green" and in a contemplated taping of the production for television, and sues to recover unpaid fees for her services. Several contracts are arguably in issue; some are standard Actors' Equity (sometimes "Equity") form contracts, others are not; all are signed by and on behalf of various persons and entities as producers. At issue is the unpaid portion of a so-called "pay or play" guarantee of $750,000 payable if (as happened) the show closed before Tyson earned $750,000 in salary. Among the sufficiency of evidence issues are (i) whether the various contracts are sufficiently interrelated that they may be read together; (ii) whether the contractual phrase "a contract made in relation to the Play" includes a contract governing the videotaping; and (iii) who is bound in respect of the $750,000 pay or play guarantee.   *ISSUE*

Elizabeth Taylor, the actress, and Zev Bufman, the Broadway producer, formed a theater group to produce live performances of plays on the legitimate stage and video and television versions of the same plays. They chose "The Corn is Green" as their second production, and cast Cicely Tyson in the lead role. The play soon closed, and the video was never made.

This Is Me, the corporation through which Ms. Tyson provides her services, sued Taylor and Bufman (and Zev Bufman Entertainment, Inc.) under the pay or play guarantee. Plaintiff's arguments convinced the jury, which found Taylor and Bufman personally liable. The district court, however, issued judgment as a matter of law in favor of defendants on the grounds that the individual defendants were not signatories to the only contract that contained the guarantee, and that Tyson's arguments linking Taylor and Bufman to that undertaking are barred by the parol evidence rule.

We conclude that there was sufficient evidence from which the jury could find liability, and we therefore reverse. That evidence consists of the underlying and well-disclosed purpose of the enterprise to produce

the play on stage as well as on videotape, the drafting history of the
contracts, the contemporaneity of the undertakings, the cross-referencing between and among the contracts, and the background undertakings
of the Actors' Equity rules, accepted by all the parties, that bind the
individual signatories (as producers), as well as any partnership or
venture controlled by them, to employment contracts.

BACKGROUND

Following a prior collaboration as producer and actor, Zev Bufman
and Elizabeth Taylor decided to "put a theater group together" to
produce plays on Broadway. They agreed generally that Bufman "would
take care of the business end of it" and Taylor "would take care of the
artistic end of it," specifically by "trying to get people to participate and
become involved in the group."

Taylor and Bufman entered into a letter of intent providing that: (i)
"all profits and losses will be shared equally between us;" (ii) the
primary purpose of the Group was "the production of legitimate stage
plays and television/film versions of such plays;" (iii) the Group would
"produce three (3) plays each year;" (iv) it would be "of the essence at
this time that we do not consider any play unless we are able to acquire
or have an option to acquire the rights to televise such productions;" and
(v) Taylor and Bufman would "be co-producers of every project" and
would "each consult with the other with respect to all major decisions."
Taylor testified that upon receiving the letter of intent, she scratched
out the word "losses" on her copy before signing; she maintains that
therefore she is not responsible for any losses. The letter of intent
contemplated a more formal contract and the formation of a "new
corporation" to carry out the venture, but neither eventuality came to
pass.

For the Group's second project—a live production and videotape of
Emlyn Williams's play, "The Corn is Green"—Bufman and Taylor
decided to seek Cicely Tyson's services to star in the play. Taylor took
the lead in recruiting Tyson, with whom she had worked before. In
several phone calls and a lunch meeting, Taylor played a key role in
reconciling creative differences between Tyson and the author of the
play regarding whether use of the original screenplay would be appropriate. Throughout these discussions, Taylor referred to Bufman as her
partner and noted that they were in this "50–50."

Tyson agreed to appear in the live theater production and the
videotape production of "The Corn is Green," and exacted the $750,000
"pay or play" guarantee. The guarantee reflected that Tyson, who was
at the height of her career, would have to turn down other opportunities
in film, television, and stage, and commit nearly a year to "The Corn is
Green."

An initial contract—later superseded—addressed all the undertakings concerning the stage and videotape performances of the play. This
contract (hereinafter the "superseded contract") was dated December 9,

1982, and was executed by Cicely Tyson on behalf of This Is Me and by Zev Bufman on behalf of Zev Bufman Entertainment, Inc. Ms. Tyson also signed an inducement letter to bind herself personally, which is addressed to "Zev Bufman Entertainment, Inc. d/b/a The Elizabeth Theatre Group." The obligations of the superseded contract were afterward bifurcated and expressed in two new contracts executed contemporaneously in August 1983, which provided that they were to be read together to constitute the entire agreement covering This Is Me's services in "The Corn is Green."

The first of these contracts was a standard Actors' Equity document, a run of the play contract that guaranteed Tyson's weekly salary for the Broadway run, without guaranteeing the length of the run. The producer listed on this contract was an entity called "The Corn Company" and the individual signatory was Zev Bufman.

The second of these contracts related to the video production, and contained the pay or play guarantee in the amount of the difference between $750,000 and salary paid under the run of the play contract (the "video contract"). This contract was between Zev Bufman Entertainment, Inc. and This Is Me.

Two further undertakings are potentially implicated as well, both of which arise from the efforts of Actors' Equity to protect its members from defaulting producers: It is conceded that the relationship between the actors and the producers in this production was governed by the Actors' Equity Association Agreement and Rules Governing Employment Under the Production Contract (the "Equity Agreement and Rules"). Bufman testified that "in order to put on a play in an Equity playhouse," he "had to abide by the collective bargaining agreement."

The "Security Agreement" (also an industry standard agreement), signed by Zev Bufman, requires the producer to "promptly pay to the Actors any and all sums due," including sums due under employment agreements "made in relation to the Play," and defines "producer" broadly to "include the individual, firm, partnership or corporation or any combination thereof producing or controlling the production of said Play."

After out-of-town tryouts, "The Corn is Green" had a short run on Broadway, and its closing was unlamented by the critics. The video was never made, and Ms. Tyson received only the weekly salary payments made under the run of the play agreement.

Later, Tyson commenced an arbitration against Bufman, Taylor and Zev Bufman Entertainment, Inc. She won an award of $607,078.86 against Zev Bufman Entertainment, Inc., and at the behest of the individual defendants, agreed to permanently stay the arbitration as against Bufman and Taylor (preserving, however, the right of This Is Me to pursue claims against Bufman and Taylor in court).

The present action followed. The jury found that both Taylor and Bufman were liable to Tyson for "the unpaid balance of the $750,000 she was to receive for performing in the Corn is Green," but the district court granted judgment as a matter of law dismissing the complaint on the grounds that (1) only the video agreement contained the pay or play guarantee; (2) that agreement unambiguously bound only Zev Bufman Entertainment, Inc.; and (3) the Security Agreement could not be "reasonably read to require anything more than the payments due under the Run-of-the Play [sic] Contract that it was designed to secure." This Is Me appealed; for the reasons that follow, we reverse.

DISCUSSION

[Part I, which stated the procedural posture of this case permits the court to reviews a grant of judgment as a matter of law de novo, omitted.]

II.

Under New York law, all writings forming part of a single transaction are to be read together. *See* Gordon v. Vincent Youmans, Inc., 358 F.2d 261, 263 (2d Cir. 1965) ("It is both good sense and good law that these closely integrated and nearly contemporaneous documents be construed together.") (internal quotation marks omitted). * * *

The district court properly instructed the jury on this principle:

> New York law requires that all writings which form part of a single transaction and are designed to effectuate the same purpose be read together, even though they were executed on different dates and were not all between the same parties. It is for you to determine whether the Actors' Equity run of the play contract, the Actors' Equity security agreement and the contractual obligation to pay This Is Me $750,000 were each intended to be binding on all the same parties, and were intended to impose the same obligations on each of the parties, even though they were set forth in different documents.

We conclude that there was sufficient evidence—the drafting history and chronology, the cross-referencing of the agreements, the integral nature of the undertakings for the stage and video performance, the relationships among the producing parties and entities, and the background assumptions furnished by the Equity rules—for the jury, as properly instructed, to find that Taylor and Bufman were personally liable on the pay or play guarantee. That conclusion requires a further look at the terms of the various contracts, and their cross-referencing of each other.

A.   The Superseded Contract

The original contract for Tyson's services in the production, a letter agreement dated December 9, 1982 between This Is Me and Zev Bufman Entertainment, Inc., provided that Tyson would perform in the stage production and that a performance of that stage production would be videotaped. Zev Bufman Entertainment, Inc. undertook to pay salary for the run of the play, but not less than $750,000, installments of which would be paid at specified intervals "whether or not the Artist is actually performing":

> We guaranty to "pay or play" to [This Is Me] for the services of [Tyson], the total sum of Seven Hundred Fifty Thousand ($750,000) Dollars plus Actors Equity Minimum Rehearsal Salary during the period of rehearsals. . . .

This document also provided that the parties would enter into a standard Actors' Equity Association run of the play contract, but that the pay or play obligation would supersede the run of the play agreement "notwithstanding any provisions therein to the contrary."

This original agreement was split into two superseding agreements, one concerned with the stage performances and undertaking to pay weekly salary for the run of the play, the other concerned with the video performance and undertaking the pay or play guarantee. Conflicting evidence was offered to explain this drafting history, but the jury was free to credit testimony that the producers wanted to keep the pay or play guarantee out of the run of the play contract that would be filed with Actors' Equity in order to reduce the bond required under the Equity rules.

B. The Run of the Play Contract

The run of the play contract was signed by Tyson on behalf of This Is Me and by Bufman on behalf of The Corn Company as "producer," a word left undefined by the contract, except that in Paragraph 9 the binding effect is said to reach the individual signatory as well as persons for whom the signatory acts:

> Individual signature required. The Producer agrees that execution of this Contract binds not only the producing company, but the individual signator to this Contract as well as any person under whose authority this Contract is executed.

The jury could find that Zev Bufman was personally bound because he affixed his signature, and that Taylor was bound because Bufman acted on her authority.

The run of the play contract incorporates by reference the Actors' Equity agreement and rules, and recites that they are the essence of the contractual relationship between the parties, that they set forth the minimum conditions under which the actor may work for the producer, and that they may not be waived or modified without Equity's written consent. It is therefore significant that Paragraph 7 of the Equity rules extends the binding effect of contracts beyond their signatories:

> All contracts of employment signed pursuant to these Rules are binding not only upon the signers on the face thereof, but upon any and all corporations, co-partnerships, enterprises and/or groups which said signers or each of them directs, controls, or is interested in, and are hereby agreed to be adopted as their contract by each of them.

By virtue of that clause, the run of the play contract is unquestionably binding upon Taylor and Bufman as producers, but that fact is of limited import, because the pay or play guarantee that this suit seeks to enforce does not appear in the run of the play contract. For reasons stated later in this opinion, however, there was sufficient evidence from which the jury could find that the video agreement, which contains the pay or play guarantee, cross-references the run of the play contract, which in turn incorporates the Equity rules. The interlocking nature of the agreements and the Equity rules is further confirmed by the fact that the Equity agreement and rules prohibit the videotaping of any production in which members of Equity are employed without the express permission of Equity and without adhering to the terms and conditions established by Equity.

C. The Video Contract

The video contract, signed on behalf of Zev Bufman Entertainment, Inc., guarantees payment to This Is Me of the difference between $750,000 and the salary paid pursuant to the run of the play contract. The contract recites that it constitutes the parties' "full and binding agreement with respect to . . . our proposed film and/or video recording of 'The Corn is Green,'" and that it is "intended to be executed concurrently with a 'Run of the Play' Actors Equity Association contract with respect to the Artist's services in a live stage production of the play."

D. Actors' Equity Security Agreement

The standard form Security Agreement, entered into between Actors' Equity Association and The Corn Company (Zev Bufman as signatory), provides for the posting of security and undertakes in other ways as well to ensure that actors receive payment for their services. "The subject of the agreement" is the "Play," a defined term that in this instance "is the theatrical production known as 'THE CORN IS GREEN.'" The Security Agreement requires that the "producer" pay the actor all sums due under any "individual employment agreement," independent of the obligation to deposit security.

That provision is reinforced and broadened elsewhere in the agreement by language that extends the payment guarantee to other employment contracts made with the actors "in connection with said Play" or "in relation to the Play," and imposes the payment obligation on the signatory as well as the entity named as producer, and also on any partnership or other entity that is party to an individual employment agreement. * * *

III.

Although as finders of fact we might have read the contracts as Judge Martin did, we do not believe this reading is the only one permitted by the evidence. Considering all the circumstances, we believe that (A) the several agreements should be read together, and that (B), when they are so read in the light of all the evidence, they are capable of sustaining the jury's conclusion that Bufman and Taylor were bound by the $750,000 guarantee set forth in the video contract.

A

The various agreements in this case all relate to a single transaction: Ms. Tyson's services as an actor in the production of "The Corn is Green." The videotaped and live performances were components of a single project, as defendants Bufman and Taylor intended from the outset: the letter of intent forming the Elizabeth Theatre Group indicated that it was of the essence of the venture to obtain video and/or television rights to each play that it intended to produce. The agreements with Tyson—the run of the play contract and the video contract—were executed more or less concurrently, and the video contract expressly states that the two contracts were intended to be executed together. The lawyer for Zev Bufman Entertainment, Inc. conceded in a letter that the run of the play contract and the video contract were intended to be read together to define the parties' relationship. The jury was justified under New York law in reading the contracts together, in light of the other evidence.

B.

When the contracts are read together in light of the other evidence, there are two entirely sufficient analyses that can support the jury verdict against Taylor and Bufman.

First, the video contract (which contains the $750,000 guarantee) cross-references the run of the play contract, which in turn expressly incorporates the Actors' Equity rules. And the run of the play contract, which does not say that it constitutes the parties' full and binding agreement, can be read to incorporate the video contract without contradicting its own express terms. Paragraph 9 of the run of the play contract provides that an individual who signs it in a representative capacity is also bound, and Paragraph 7 of the Equity rules extends the binding power of any employment agreement still further to any partnership or enterprise directed by the signatory. Thus the jury could have concluded that Zev Bufman's signature on the video contract on behalf of Zev Bufman Entertainment, Inc. also bound: (i) himself and (ii) the Elizabeth Theatre Group, an enterprise in which he was a partner. The jury could then further have assessed individual liability against Taylor as derivative of the Elizabeth Theatre Group's liability, because there was evidence (including Taylor's own statements to Tyson) from which the jury could conclude that Ms. Taylor was a partner in the Elizabeth Theatre Group.

Alternatively, the jury could have relied on the Security Agreement (read in conjunction with the run of the play contract and video contract). The Security Agreement provides that it applies to all "individual employment contracts," and defines such contracts as "any agreement of employment heretofore or hereafter entered into between an

Actor and the Guarantor or Producer in relation to the Play." The pertinent inquiry under this theory is whether evidence was presented from which the jury reasonably could conclude: (i) that the video contract, in addition to the run of the play contract, was an agreement "in relation to the Play;" and (ii) that Taylor and Bufman fit the definition of producers. * * * Sufficient evidence existed to support a jury verdict on this theory. * * * [T]he jury was free to find that Bufman and Taylor were producers, and that the video contract was an employment agreement made in relation to the play.

IV.

Taylor and Bufman belatedly contend that Tyson should be relegated to the Equity grievance procedures and that her failure to exhaust those procedures bars her from reliance on the Equity contracts. Defendants waited far too long to raise this as a defense; moreover, Ms. Tyson did initiate arbitration against these defendants but stipulated to a permanent stay of the arbitration (reserving to This Is Me the right to pursue claims against Ms. Taylor and Mr. Bufman) when they suggested she seek execution of the award she had already received against the corporate defendant (a company that Bufman, at least, knew lacked assets to satisfy the judgment).

CONCLUSION

The judgment of the district court is reversed, and the jury's verdict reinstated.

2. NET COMPENSATION

YERKOVICH v. MCA

United States Court of Appeals, Ninth Circuit, 2000.
211 F.3d 1276.

BEFORE: WIGGINS, RYMER, and FISHER, Circuit Judges.

MEMORANDUM OPINION.

Anthony Yerkovich appeals the district court's grant of summary judgment in favor of MCA, Inc. and Universal City Studios, Inc. (hereinafter collectively "Universal"). This suit stems from an individual services contract between Yerkovich and Universal ("the Agreement") pursuant to which Yerkovich wrote a pilot teleplay that Universal subsequently produced as the television show Miami Vice. Yerkovich granted Universal rights to Miami Vice in return for up-front compensation and a percentage of the net profits that Universal received from exploiting the show. Yerkovich alleged that Universal breached the Agreement by failing properly to account for net profits. Yerkovich also alleged various state and federal claims.

The district court granted summary judgment on Yerkovich's Third claim for breach of contract. It found that even accepting Yerkovich's interpretation of the Agreement, there was insufficient admissible evidence showing that Yerkovich was entitled to additional money under the Agreement. After conducting an extensive review of the evidence in the record, we agree with the district court's conclusion.

On appeal, Yerkovich argues he was unable to present sufficient evidence to defeat summary judgment because he was improperly denied relevant discovery. After a careful review of the record, including the magistrate judge's discovery rulings and the hearings before the district court regarding reconsideration of those rulings, we find that Yerkovich's failure to obtain the evidence he sought was attributable in large part to his own delay and litigation strategies, and in any event the district court did not abuse its discretion.

We conclude that Yerkovich has waived the issue of whether the district court erred in denying his motion for reconsideration of the summary judgment order. Yerkovich raised this issue in his "Statement of the Issues," but he did not address it further in his brief. *See* McLain v. Calderon, 134 F.3d 1383, 1384 n.2 (9th Cir. 1998), cert. denied, 525 U.S. 942, 119 S. Ct. 364, 142 L. Ed. 2d 301 (1998).

With respect to Yerkovich's claims for breach of contract, copyright infringement, and declaratory relief, the district court properly found that the Agreement assigned all of Yerkovich's rights to Universal. The district court also properly held that Yerkovich's claim that the assignment of rights provision was unconscionable was barred by the statute of limitations.

As for Yerkovich's breach of fiduciary duty claim, the district court correctly concluded that fiduciary relationships do not normally arise from arms-length business transactions. *See* Order of Nov. 28, 1996, at 18 (citing Henry v. Associated Indemnity Corp., 217 Cal. App. 3d 1405, 1419, 266 Cal. Rptr. 578 (1990)). In addition, the Agreement expressly disclaims the creation of a fiduciary relationship.

Regarding Yerkovich's breach of implied covenant of good faith and fair dealing claim, the district court correctly found that California law clearly precludes tort recovery for noninsurance contract breach of the implied covenant of good faith and fair dealing. *See, e.g.,* Freeman & Mills, Inc. v. Belcher Oil Co., 11 Cal. 4th 85, 900 P.2d 669, 679–80 (Cal. 1995). In addition, Yerkovich's claim cannot survive as a contract claim. Under California law, such an implied covenant cannot be read into a contract if it directly conflicts with the express language of the contract, unless such a covenant is necessary to keep the contract from becoming an illusory agreement. *See* Third Story Music, Inc. v. Waits, 41 Cal. App. 4th 798, 48 Cal. Rptr. 2d 747, 753 (Cal. Ct. App. 1995). The Agreement included guaranteed compensation to Yerkovich, so it is not illusory.
* * *

Finally, Yerkovich seeks review of the district court's 12(b)(6) dismissal of his claim seeking a declaratory judgment that the "arbitrability arbitration" has no bearing on this case. Because all of Yerkovich's

substantive claims were properly dismissed, this claim is moot. * * *
AFFIRMED.

Notes

1. Even had Yerkovich survived dismissal of his lawsuit, what is the likelihood that his contract granting him a percentage of net profits would have yielded him any revenue? *See* Chapter 5, Star Billing, Credit and Compensation. In an author interview with screenwriter and teleplay writer Walon Green in Chapter 1, he said they he would need to hire a "forensic accountant" to receive payout on his net profit deals, even though he wrote for some of the most successful television shows in the 1990s and 2000s. The bottom line to many Hollywood writers and stars is that net profit deals in both television and film are not worth the paper on which they are printed.

2. With any popular TV show, there are people who will try to profit from its fame. The producer of the series wanted an injunction to stop the production of T-shirts depicting cartoon drawings of the main characters in *Universal City Studios, Inc. v. T–Shirt Gallery, Ltd.*, 634 F.Supp. 1468 (S.D.N.Y. 1986). Universal City Studios produced and held the copyright for the 1984 *Miami Vice* television show. The merchandising section of Universal sells licenses to make products based on the series. The T–Shirt Gallery makes five types of "Miami Mice" T–Shirts and holds copyrights for the drawings. The shirts have two mice who wear sunglasses and outfits that resemble the *Miami Vice* main characters. Also, the characters' clothing and surroundings are in pastel colors, which are displayed on the TV show. The T–Shirt Gallery sought the merchandising rights for "Miami Mice" as an "animated parody of Miami Vice." Universal sued for copyright infringement and wanted an injunction to stop the production of the shirts. However, the Court ruled the shirts were not substantially similar to the TV series because they had a different look and feel. Additionally, the shirts acted as a parody of the series. Universal did not show irreparable injury and denied the request for an injunction stopping the production.

More information on television merchandizing and product placement is discussed in the cases and notes below.

3. TELEVISION MERCHANDIZING AND PRODUCT PLACEMENT

Merchandising has become an important source of revenue for program producers to supplement the production budget for their programs. Producers often license the use of trademark names on posters, toys, key chains, plush toys, clothing, bed sheets, towels, food products, books, video games, and magazines. In short, anything else the public may desire will be considered for merchandising opportunities.

Product placement is a corollary to merchandising. Product placement is part of every show's budget. The producer will seek remuneration from companies for including their products in the show. If the company is unable to pay, the producer may barter and take samples of the product in exchange for its inclusion in the show. Product placement is an important source for cost defrayal, if not advertising income.

REY v. LAFFERTY

United States Court of Appeals, First Circuit, 1993.
990 F.2d 1379.

SELYA, Circuit Judge.

Margret Rey, who owns the copyright to the "Curious George" children's books, challenges an award of damages to Lafferty Harwood & Partners ("LHP") for Rey's withholding of approval of various ancillary products utilizing the "Curious George" character under their 1983 licensing agreement. LHP appeals the district court order awarding Rey damages and future royalties on certain other "Curious George" products. We affirm in part and reverse in part.

I

BACKGROUND

"Curious George" is an imaginary monkey whose antics are chronicled in seven books, written by Margret and H.A. Rey, which have entertained readers since the 1940's. A mischievous personality consistently lands Curious George in amusing scrapes and predicaments. The more recent "monkey business"—leading to the present litigation—began in 1977 when Margret Rey granted Milktrain Productions an option to produce and televise 104 animated "Curious George" film episodes. The option agreement was contingent on Milktrain's obtaining financing for the film project, and adverted to a potential agreement to license "ancillary products," based on the "Curious George" character, once the 104 film episodes had been completed. * * *

C. The Ancillary Products Agreement

Production of the 104 TV episodes was completed in 1982. On January 3, 1983, an Ancillary Products Agreement (or "APA") was signed by Rey and LHP, granting [Canadian investment firm] LHP a general right to license "Curious George" in spin-off ("ancillary") products for a renewable term of five years. The APA defined "ancillary products" as: All tangible goods ... excluding books, films, tapes, records, or video productions.... However, for stories already owned by [LHP] and which have been produced as 104 episodes under the license granted in the January, 1978 agreement and the November 5, 1979 revision of that agreement, [LHP] shall have the right to produce books, films, tapes, records and video productions of these episodes under this Agreement, subject to [Rey's] prior approval ... which prior approval shall not be unreasonably withheld.

In return for these rights, Rey was to receive one-third of the royalties on the licensed products, with certain minimum annual payments guaranteed. Rey retained the right to disapprove any product, and to propose changes which would make a disapproved product acceptable

[handwritten margin notes: "K dispute prior approval", "⅓ royalties"]

to her. The APA provided, inter alia, that Rey's approval would not be withheld "unreasonably."

D. The Houghton Mifflin Contract

Following the execution of the Ancillary Products Agreement ["APA"], LHP assigned its licensing rights to a new subsidiary, Curgeo Enterprises, which turned its attention to licensing the "Curious George" character in various product forms. On March 27, 1984, Curgeo executed a contract with Houghton Mifflin Company to publish the 104 television film episodes in the form of a children's book series. The contract provided that Houghton Mifflin would publish at least four books, with illustrations drawn directly from the film negatives, in each year from 1984 through 1987; the contract was renewable for an additional five-year term if LHP and Rey agreed to extend the APA beyond 1987. Pursuant to the contract, Houghton Mifflin published four books each year from 1984 through 1987.

In 1987, LHP notified Houghton Mifflin that it had declined to extend the APA, but that Curgeo had "entered into a new operating agreement which permits us to continue to act in the capacity in which we have been acting for the last five years. . . . You are free to pick up your option to renew." In response, Houghton Mifflin extended its contract for the additional five-year term, publishing an additional four books in 1988 and again in 1989. It ceased publication of the book series in 1990, when Rey advised that the APA had been cancelled.

E. Other Product Licenses

Curgeo moved aggressively to license the "Curious George" character in other product areas as well. Beginning in 1983, the "Curious George" TV episodes were licensed to Sony Corporation, which transferred the images from the television film negatives to videotape. * * *

In 1983, Curgeo licensed "Curious George" to Eden Toys Inc., which proposed to market a "Curious George" plush toy. In the beginning, Rey rejected Eden's proposed designs for the toy, but Eden eventually proposed several versions which were acceptable to Rey. The plush toy was marketed from 1983 to 1990, but experienced poor sales and generated less revenue than expected. Eden blamed the poor market performance on Rey's alterations to Eden's original design proposals.

In 1987, Curgeo received a commitment from Sears, Roebuck to market "Curious George" pajamas through the Sears catalog. The Sears pajama project promised high returns, but catalog deadlines necessitated immediate approval of a product design. Glen Konkle, Curgeo's agent, brought Rey a prototype pajama and a flat paper sketch of "Curious George" which had been proposed as the basis for the final pattern. Rey rejected the proposal, complaining that the pajama material was "hard, ugly [and] bright yellow," and that the sketch of "Curious George" was "plump" and "not recognizable." The catalog deadline passed and the pajama manufacturers withdrew their bids. In addition, Beach Paper

Products, which had orally agreed to license "Curious George" for a line of paper novelties, withdrew its offer after learning that "Curious George" products would not receive exposure in the Sears catalog.

In 1988, Curgeo licensed "Curious George" to DLM Inc., which intended to use the "Curious George" character in a trilogy of educational software. Rey approved the software in principle, and production began in July 1988. In August 1988, however, DLM withdrew its plans to complete the "trilogy" after Rey telephoned DLM's project director and harshly criticized the design of the first software product and the accompanying manual developed by DLM.

F. The Ancillary Products Agreement Renewal

Due in part to these product rejections, LHP earned less money than it anticipated from ancillary products. When the APA came up for renewal in January 1988, LHP declined to exercise its option for an additional five-year term. Instead, the parties agreed to renew on a month-to-month basis, terminable by either party on one month's notice. Rey's royalty rate was increased to 50% (effective January 3, 1988), but with no guaranteed minimum payment. On April 10, 1989, Rey terminated the APA. LHP responded by advising that Curgeo would "continue to administer those licenses which [remained] outstanding and report to you from time to time accordingly." LHP thereupon continued to market the Sony videos and to publish the television films in book form under the Houghton Mifflin agreements.

G. "Curious George" Goes to Court

On February 8, 1991, Rey filed suit against Lafferty, Curgeo and LHP, in connection with LHP's continuing, allegedly unauthorized production of the Houghton Mifflin books and Sony videos. * * * After a four-day bench trial, the district court found for Rey on her claims for breach of contract, ruling that the book and video licenses were governed by the APA and that Rey was entitled to recover $256,327 in royalties. The court found for LHP on several LHP counterclaims, however, holding that Rey unreasonably had withheld approval of, inter alia, the Sears pajamas, the DLM software, and Eden's original plush toy design. LHP was awarded $317,000, representing lost profits and consequential damages resulting from Rey's rejection of these products.

II

Discussion * * *

1. The Houghton Mifflin Books.

The Ancillary Products Agreement provided, inter alia, that for stories already owned by [LHP] ... which have been produced as 104 episodes under the license granted in the January, 1978 agreement and the November 5, 1979 revision of that agreement, [LHP] shall have the right to produce books, films, tapes, records and video productions of these episodes under this Agreement, subject to [Rey's] prior approval. . . . (Emphasis added.) Throughout the document the term "this Agreement," utilizing the capital letter "A", refers to the APA. Thus, the plain language of the operative provision clearly contemplates that the APA was to govern the licensing of any books and "video productions" arising from the 104 films. *See Barilaro v. Consol. Rail Corp.*, 876 F.2d 260, 265 n.10 (1st Cir. 1989). * * *

In the present case, we find no "clear error" in the district court's determination that the parties contemplated separate (though related) transactions for film rights and financing. * * * Most importantly, the written and circumstantial indicia sharply contradict any suggestion of a meeting of the minds relating to the licensing of ancillary products. Rey did not participate in negotiating the RMA ["Revised Milktrain Agreement"], did not sign it, was never made a party to its terms, and expressly refused, during the RRL ["Revised Rey License"] negotiations, to license "Curious George" for the "ancillary" purposes now urged by LHP. * * * Moreover, the 1979 Private Placement Memorandum prepared by LHP acknowledges Rey's nonacceptance by attaching the RRL as an exhibit and noting that ancillary product rights "have yet to be negotiated" with Rey. * * * Thus, the district court did not err in finding that LHP's withholding of the Houghton Mifflin book royalties was wrongful, and we affirm its ruling on this point.

    2. *The Sony Videos.* * * *

    a. *"New Uses" and Copyright Law.*

For purposes of the present appeal, we accept the uncontested district court finding that the relevant video technology "was not in existence at the time that the rights" were granted under the RRL in January 1979. Consequently, it must be inferred that the parties did not specifically contemplate television "viewing" of the "Curious George" films in videocassette form at the time the RRL was signed. Such absence of specific intent typifies cases which address "new uses" of licensed materials, i.e., novel technological developments which generate unforeseen applications for a previously licensed work. * * * Under the "preferred" method, *see* 3 Nimmer at 10–85, recently cited with approval in *SAPC, Inc.* v. *Lotus Dev. Corp.*, 921 F.2d 360, 363 (1st Cir. 1990), the court will conclude, absent contrary indicia of the parties' intent, that "the licensee may properly pursue any uses which may reasonably be said to fall within the medium as described in the license." 3 Nimmer at 10–86. Under this interpretive method, the courts will presume that at least the possibility of nonspecific "new uses" was foreseeable by the contracting parties at the time the licensing agreement was drafted; accordingly, the burden and risk of drafting licenses whose language anticipates the possibility of any particular "new use" are apportioned equally between licensor and licensee. * * * An alternative interpretive method is to assume that a license of rights in a given medium (e.g., 'motion picture rights') includes only such uses as fall within the unambiguous core meaning of the term . . . and excludes any uses which lie within the ambiguous penumbra (e.g., exhibition of motion picture film on television). Thus any rights not expressly (in this case meaning unambiguously) granted are reserved. * * *

b. *Video Technology as "New Use".*

These fine-tuned interpretive methods have led to divergent results in cases considering the extension of television rights to new video forms. Thus, for example, in *Rooney v. Columbia Pictures Indus., Inc.,* 538 F.Supp. 211 (S.D.N.Y.), aff'd, 714 F.2d 117 (2d Cir. 1982), cert. denied, 460 U.S. 1084 (1983), the court determined that a series of contracts granting motion picture distributors a general license to exhibit plaintiffs' films "by any present or future methods or means" and "by any means now known or unknown" fairly encompassed the right to distribute the films by means of later-developed video technology. * * *

Though videocassettes may be exhibited by using a television monitor, it does not follow that, for copyright purposes, playing videocassettes constitutes "exhibition by television." ... Television requires an intermediary network, station, or cable to send the television signals into consumers' homes. * * * Most recently, in *Tele-Pac, Inc. v. Grainger,* 570 N.Y.S.2d 521, appeal dismissed, 588 N.E.2d 99 (1991), the court held (one judge dissenting) that a license to distribute certain motion pictures "for broadcasting by television or any other similar device now known or hereafter to be made known" did not encompass the videocassette film rights. * * *

c. *Video Rights and the RRL.*

Although the question is extremely close, under the interpretive methodology outlined above we conclude that the RRL's grant of rights to the 104 film episodes "for television viewing" did not encompass the right to distribute the "Curious George" films in videocassette form.

First, unlike the contracts in *Rooney* and *Lucasfilm,* the RRL contained no general grant of rights in technologies yet to be developed, and no explicit reference to "future methods" of exhibition. *Compare Lucasfilm,* 566 F.Supp. at 227; *Rooney,* 538 F.Supp. at 228. Rather, the RRL appears to contemplate a comparatively limited and particular grant of rights, encompassing only the 104 film episodes and leaving future uses of "Curious George" to later negotiation in the ancillary products agreement. Although the RRL conversely contains no "specific limiting language," *compare Cohen,* 845 F.2d at 853, we believe such limitation is reasonably inferable from the situation of the parties and the "general tenor of the section" in which the "television viewing" rights were granted.

Second, as properly noted in *Cohen,* "television viewing" and "videocassette viewing" are not coextensive terms. Even though videocassettes may be, and often are, viewed by means of VCRs on home television screens, * * * still, as the Ninth Circuit pointed out, a "standard television set capable of receiving television signals" is not strictly required for videocassette viewing. *Cohen,* 845 F.2d at 854. "It is only necessary to have a monitor capable of displaying the material on the magnetized tape." *Id.* Indeed, a number of non-television monitors recently marketed in the United States permit videocassette viewing on computer screens, flat-panel displays, and the like. Thus, we find insufficient reliable indicia of a contrary mutual intent on the part of Rey and LHP to warrant disturbing the district court's implicit determination that the language of the RRL is not "broad enough to cover the new use." *Bartsch*, 391 F.2d at 155.

Finally, any lingering concerns about the correctness of the district court's interpretation are dispelled by the evidence that the RRL (including its "television viewing" clause) was drafted and proposed by LHP, a professional investment firm accustomed to licensing agreements. Rey, an elderly woman, does not appear to have participated in its drafting, and, indeed, does not appear to have been represented by counsel during the larger part of the transaction. Under these circumstances, ... ambiguities in the drafting instrument are traditionally construed against the licensor and the drafter. * * * Accordingly, as the Sony videocassette sales were not encompassed by the RRL, but governed exclusively by the APA, we find no conflict between the terms of the documents, and we affirm the award of royalties to Rey under the APA.

B. The "Junk Products" Counterclaim

We next turn to the LHP counterclaim that Rey breached the APA by "wrongfully withholding" approval of ancillary products she considered "junky." The district court agreed with LHP, holding that [The Ancillary Products Agreement] clearly contemplated the exploitation of Curious George.... Based on the testimony of Ms. Stoebenau and Mr. Konkle, I find that means that there may be produced with the character, junk products, junky products.... Plaintiff [had] the right ... to insist on ... an honest and good depiction of the character. She did not have the right to disapprove the quality of the product.... She had [the] right to disapprove an incorrect, improper, bad depiction of Curious George. * * *

The court further found: Although Mrs. Rey unquestionably approved many products, I find that she improperly disapproved the Sears project for the reasons just outlined; that she was unreasonable with respect to the Eden project, and that she was so rude to Ms. Craighead as to abort the second and perhaps later trilogies of the software. * * * After careful consideration, we must agree with Rey that the district court misapplied the APA.

The product-approval procedure under the APA required that: LHP will submit product or other information sufficient to describe the product to you for prior approval. When a product is submitted ... we will wait two weeks before proceeding. If we do not receive any disapproval of the product from you within two weeks we are entitled to presume that you approve of the product. If you do disapprove of any product, you will, if feasible, suggest such changes to LHP as may render the product acceptable to you, or, if you cannot make such feasible suggestions, you may refuse to approve the product. Product approval will not be unreasonably withheld. * * *

Even though the APA's product approval clause did not preclude Rey from rejecting products based on their "junky" quality, it did obligate her to act "reasonably" in doing so. The duty to act "reasonably," like a duty to employ "best efforts," or to act in "good faith," is not reducible to "a fixed formula [, and] varies with the facts and the field of law involved." *See Triple–A Baseball Club*, 832 F.2d at 225 (discussing contractual "best efforts" clause). * * *

unreasonable

We think the APA's proscription of "unreasonable" product disapproval required, at a minimum, that Rey articulate some material reason, subjective or otherwise, for disapproving a product. That is to say, Rey could not withhold product approval without ascribing a reason, nor for reasons immaterial to the "Curious George" mark, its proposed use or commercial potential, or unrelated to Rey's artistic and reputational identification with the mark and ancillary products. Moreover, assuming there existed some material ground for withholding product approval, it would need to be communicated, consistent with contractual specifications, "within a reasonable time and in a reasonable manner, i.e., in a manner which makes it possible for [the licensee] to rework the [product] in order to meet ... approval." *See Zim*, 573 F.2d at 1324. Finally, the reason for withholding product approval could not be so preclusive as to frustrate the fundamental contractual assumptions on which the APA was formed. * * *

The district court supportably found that Rey approved "many products," including the original film series, the Houghton Mifflin books, the Sony videocassettes, the first series of DLM software, and the Eden plush toys (as modified). In addition, Rey testified, without contradiction, that she had approved "children's sweatshirts, film strips, earmuffs and school bags for children ... buttons, children's books ... paper doll books[,] wrist watch, alarm clocks, wall clocks, footwear, little tennis shoes for children, ... beach slippers, ..." After reviewing the record, we are convinced that Rey did not utilize objectively unreasonable criteria for approving products under the APA. We turn to the particular product rejections challenged on appeal.

1. The Sears Pajamas.

The district court ruled that Rey acted unreasonably by basing her disapproval of the Sears project on the "junky" quality of the pajama material which would bear "Curious George's" likeness. As we have stated, * * * the basis for the district court's finding of "unreasonableness" was insufficient as a matter of law. Rey did not unreasonably withhold approval of the Sears pajama project as unbefitting the "Curious George" image protected by her copyright, because the grounds for withholding approval were reasonably related to the integrity and commercial value of her artistic creation. *See Clifford Ross*, 710 F.Supp. at 520.

2. *The Beach Paper Products.*

Our conclusion that Rey reasonably rejected the Sears project disposes of LHP's claim for damages relating to the Beach paper products as well. Rey never saw, much less "disapproved," the Beach paper products: as the undisputed evidence shows, Beach withdrew its proposal when the Sears project fell through; it never reached agreement with LHP or presented any product to Rey for approval. Therefore, LHP's claimed right to recover potential profits from the Beach project could be justified, if at all, only as consequential damages resulting from a wrongful rejection of the Sears project. As the Sears project was not wrongfully rejected under the terms of the APA, LHP is not entitled to consequential damages related to Beach's anticipated profits. *See, e.g., Ryan v. Royal Ins. Co.,* 916 F.2d 731, 744 (1st Cir. 1990) ("unless appellants can demonstrate that [appellee] breached a duty owed to them.... consequential damages will not lie").

3. *The Eden Plush Toys.*

The district court ruled that Rey acted unreasonably with respect to the Eden plush toys project, but the court did not state whether its ruling was based on Rey's objections to the "junky" nature of the proposed product, or some other ground. We conclude, nonetheless, that remand is unnecessary in the present circumstances, *see Produits Nestle,* 982 F.2d 633 at 640–41 ("when a trial court misperceives and misapplies the law, remand may or may not be essential"), since LHP did not present sufficient evidence to enable a finding that Rey's actions with respect to Eden were "unreasonable." *See id.* at 642 (quoting *Dedham Water Co. v. Cumberland Farms Dairy, Inc.,* 972 F.2d 453, 463 (1st Cir. 1992)). * * *

The evidence before the district court clearly showed that Rey imposed a demanding aesthetic standard for the design of the Eden Toys doll. Eden's frustration at Rey's meticulous immersion in the details of toy design may indeed be understandable, the more so perhaps because of the irascible terms in which Rey appears to have chosen to couch her product criticisms on occasion. Even viewing the evidence as a whole in the light most flattering to LHP, however, we cannot conclude that her proposed changes were unrelated to her legitimate artistic concerns or to her desire to protect the aesthetic integrity of the "Curious George" image. * * * Since Rey's objections to Eden's original toy design were based on criteria reasonably related to her legitimate artistic and aesthetic concerns about the proposed ancillary product, and were communicated in a time and manner which would permit Eden to conform the product, we conclude that Rey's rejection of Eden's product designs was not "unreasonable."

4. *The DLM Software.*

Finally, we consider whether Rey's alleged rudeness to Donna Craighead, the DLM project manager, amounted to an "unreasonable withholding of approval" of the DLM software project in violation of the APA. We conclude that it did not. As all parties agree, the licensing arrangement between DLM and LHP covered only the first installment in the proposed DLM software trilogy, the first installment was approved by Rey prior to her telephone conversation with Craighead, and DLM continued to manufacture and market the first-installment software even after Rey's intemperate remarks. Given the fact that Rey's statements led to no curtailment in the production or sale of the licensed software, we are unable to discern any relevant respect in which Rey's statements to Craighead could be considered a "rejection" of the product for which LHP had issued its license to DLM. * * *

Conclusion

Under the APA, Rey is entitled to recover the royalties wrongly withheld on the Houghton Mifflin books and Sony videos; and we affirm the district court rulings respecting these claims. The APA likewise entitled Rey to withhold approval of licensed ancillary products on reasonable grounds; thus, LHP was not entitled to recover damages for Rey's reasonable exercise of her right to withhold approval of the Sears pajama project, the Beach paper products, the Eden Toys project, or the DLM software. Accordingly, the damages awards to LHP are vacated.

Affirmed in part, reversed in part; costs are awarded to Rey.

Note

1. Children have loved the adventures of Curious George in his many children's books since the character's debut in 1941. Hans Augusto Rey and Margret Elisabeth Waldstein, writers of the books, married and lived in Paris during the 1930's. Hans produced a newspaper cartoon about a giraffe and was asked to make more, which resulted in *Raffy and the Nine Monkeys* (*Cecily G. and the Nine Monkeys* in English), which introduced Curious George.

The Reys, both Jewish, needed to leave Europe before Adolf Hitler stormed their city. Hans made two bicycles, and on June 14, 1940, they fled on their bikes before they could be captured. They took a few items, including five manuscripts, including *Curious George*. The couple rode four days until they hit the border of France and Spain and sold their items for enough money to take the train to Lisbon. They fled to Brazil and then to New York City. Houghton Mifflin published the book in 1941, and more than 25 million copies of the books have been sold. The story has never been out of print. *About H.A. and Margaret Rey, Curious About George,* Houghton Mifflin Books for Children's Curious George Web site, *at* http://www.houghtonmifflinbooks.com/features/cgsite/abouthaandmargretrey.shtml.

GEISEL v. POYNTER PRODS. INC.

United States District Court, Southern District of New York, 1968.
295 F.Supp. 331.

HERLANDS, District Judge.

Can an artist who sells his signed cartoon to a magazine validly object to the magazine's making and selling a doll which is truthfully advertised as based upon the cartoon? This, capsulated, poses the critical issue herein.

THE COMPLAINT

Plaintiff, Theodor Seuss Geisel, is the world-famous artist and author, whose nom de plume is "Dr. Seuss." In a complaint against the four defendants, filed March 8, 1968, plaintiff charged that the defendants manufactured and were advertising and selling dolls "derived from" certain material which plaintiff "prepared for publication" for the now defunct Liberty Magazine in 1932 and which was published in that magazine from June to December 1932; that, although plaintiff had nothing to do with the design or manufacture of the dolls, they were being advertised and sold as "Dr. Seuss" creations; and that the dolls are "tasteless, unattractive and of an inferior quality".

On the basis of these and other allegations, plaintiff requested compensatory and punitive damages as well as an injunction enjoining defendants from using the name "Dr. Seuss" in any manner without plaintiff's consent, or in connection with any product not designed or approved by plaintiff. * * *

THE PRELIMINARY INJUNCTION

An order to show cause for a preliminary injunction was signed on March 8, 1968. On March 12, this Court heard argument on that motion, issued a temporary restraining order (which, in substance, restrained defendants from using the name "Dr. Seuss" in any manner in connection with any doll, toy or other product), and granted the parties leave to conduct discovery and to submit further papers.

On April 9, 1968, this Court concluded that there was a reasonable probability of plaintiff's success upon the trial of the Lanham Act (first) cause of action and issued a preliminary injunction restraining defendants as follows:

> "The defendants, their officers, agents, servants, employees and all persons acting under their control and each of them are hereby enjoined and restrained pendente lite from committing any of the following acts in connection with the manufacturing, displaying, advertising, distributing, selling or offering for sale of any doll, toy or other similar product: A. Representing that defendants' doll, toy or other similar product has been created, designed, produced, approved or authorized by plaintiff; B. Describing defendants' doll, toy or other similar product as having been created, designed, produced, approved or authorized by plaintiff; or C. Representing, describing or designating plaintiff as the originator, creator, designer, or producer of defendants' doll, toy or other similar products."
> * * *

THE 1932 AGREEMENT

At the trial, a substantial amount of the evidence concerned the nature of the 1932 agreement between plaintiff and Liberty Publishing

Corporation (hereafter Liberty Magazine). Plaintiff contends that the evidence proves that plaintiff assigned to Liberty Magazine the title to the cartoons with their accompanying text . . . "with the understanding that Liberty would copyright this work as part of the entire issue of the magazines in which they appeared. It was understood, however, that while Liberty had the complete rights to publish these works in one issue of Liberty Magazine, Liberty held all other rights to this work (including the right to renew the copyright and the right to make other uses of the work) in trust for plaintiff." * * *

Certain facts relating to the 1932 transaction have been stipulated as not in dispute. The parties agree that, in 1932, plaintiff " * * * prepared and sold to Liberty Magazine material which was published in weekly issues of Liberty Magazine during the months of June through December 1932"; that the material consisted of a series of twenty-three "cartoon essays" and that "each work [consisted of a page which] contained at least three cartoons and each cartoon contained several animal creations"; * * * and that plaintiff received $300 for each work. * * *

There is also no dispute that the issues of Liberty Magazine in which the cartoons appeared were copyrighted by Liberty Magazine as entire issues. Each issue contained the required notice of copyright; and Certificates of Copyright Registration were secured by Liberty Magazine. It is also agreed that "[no] separate copyright was obtained * * * " by the plaintiff upon the cartoons. * * *

Ben Wasson, who did not appear as a witness, represented plaintiff in the negotiations with Liberty Magazine. In so doing, Wasson acted as an employee of the Leland Hayward Agency. Although Hayward did not personally handle the transaction, he recalls that he had one conversation with Fulton Oursler, then editor-in-chief of Liberty Magazine. Oursler stated that plaintiff was "popular" and that his work was "very suitable" for Liberty Magazine. Hayward could not remember anything else said at that or any other time relating to the negotiations. To the best of his recollection, there was no formal written contract executed in connection with this transaction. * * * From this and other evidence, the Court infers that the works which plaintiff sold to Liberty Magazine were not in existence at the time the contract was entered into; instead, they were created at Liberty Magazine's request.

The $300 payments were made by check to the Leland Hayward Agency, which deducted its commission as agent and then remitted the balance to plaintiff.

Nothing was expressly said by either side during the negotiations regarding the scope of rights that Liberty Magazine obtained by the purchase of the material. Plaintiff denies that the words "all rights" or "complete rights" were used by either side during the negotiations.

This evidence demonstrates that plaintiff agreed to prepare cartoons for publication in Liberty Magazine; that the cartoons were published; that plaintiff received $300 a page; that the only copyright upon this material was in the name of Liberty Publishing Company; and that plaintiff did not *expressly* reserve any rights in the cartoons. * * * In this case, there was no *express* agreement that Liberty Magazine would hold the copyright in trust for plaintiff or that plaintiff reserved any rights in the cartoons. * * *

Hence, at least prima facie, Liberty Magazine owned the copyright in 1932 and defendant Liberty Library Corporation presently owns the renewed copyright without reservation. * * *

Mr. Cerf has been a *book* publisher since 1925 and has himself written books as well as articles for periodicals. Plaintiff's books are published by the firm of which Cerf is chairman of the board; and, in fact, plaintiff is the president of a division of that firm. * * *

Mr. Dworkin, a retired attorney and accountant, was an adviser or "righthand man" to the head of Macfadden Publications, a magazine publisher, which purchased Liberty Magazine in 1931. Dworkin was associated with Macfadden Publications from 1919 until 1961. * * *

On the basis of the great weight of the credible evidence, the Court finds that during the relevant period it was the custom and usage in the magazine trade for the magazine to obtain a copyright upon the entire contents of the magazine. However, the author or artist *could* also obtain a separate copyright upon his particular work, as plaintiff did with respect to a "Quick, Henry the Flit" cartoon-advertisement which appeared in Liberty Magazine in 1931. * * *

Mr. Cerf testified that, if nothing was said with respect to the scope of rights purchased, the term "always" implied in the agreement provided for the sale of "one-shot publication"—publication in one issue of the magazine—and return of the copyright thereafter upon the request of the author. He stated that the term "all rights" meant this understanding.

Mr. Cerf indicated that the basis of his knowledge of this custom or understanding was the "minimal" amount paid to plaintiff for the cartoons. He also testified that, if an author-artist received anything less than $1,000 a page in 1932 for his work, it meant that only one-time magazine rights were sold.

Although the price paid may be a circumstance probative of the scope of rights purchased by Liberty Magazine in 1932, the clear preponderance of the credible evidence demonstrates that the price of $300 per page in 1932 was a ... "reasonable price for that particular year" in view of the near "panic" caused by the depression. * * * But, Mr. Hayward repeatedly stated that "all rights" did not mean "all" and that "complete rights" did not mean "complete"; rather, that these terms had a limited meaning. According to Mr. Hayward, "complete rights" in the magazine trade meant ... "the complete right to publish that particular piece of material in a single issue ... or, in the case of serial rights, to publish parts of the material in several or more issues...." * * * Mr. Hayward further asserted that, after publication, the custom provided that the magazine . . . "would *always* assign the copyright to anyone the author requested". The magazine was thus the "custodian of the copyright". He added that he had *never* heard of a magazine sharing the revenues gained on the material after the assignment back.

If believed in its entirety, the evidence adduced in behalf of plaintiff would prove that in 1932 custom or usage in the magazine trade implied in fact in the Geisel–Liberty Magazine agreement that (a) each cartoon could be used only in a single insertion in the magazine; that (b) thereafter the copyright was held in trust for plaintiff and would be reassigned to him at his request; and that (c) the term "all rights" or "complete rights," which was understood to mean (a) and/or (b), was "implicit" in the agreement.

Meyer Dworkin, called as a witness for defendants, testified that he did not recall, and, in fact, there "categorically" never was, any custom or understanding in 1932 whereby an author . . . "would reserve impliedly all rights except the right to have the magazine publish in that issue the particular work of art". On the contrary, the custom was that "where the author said nothing and sold the manuscript to the company, the company would receive all rights. . . ." He stated that this custom was understood by Liberty Magazine, Mcfadden Publications *and by the authors* who dealt with them. Mr. Dworkin defined "complete rights" as "all rights, full rights" with no residual rights in anyone else. * * *

Alden Norton convincingly testified that, although every story purchased by a magazine was individually bargained for, . . . "if you sold me a story and you didn't ask for anything, you sold me all rights and it would say so on the check." He also testified that, if there were no written or oral agreement and no legend on the check and the author or artist simply delivered the work to a magazine and was paid $300 a page, the custom and usage in 1932 provided that "[unless] otherwise specified, [the author granted] all rights". Mr. Norton rejected the assertion that, if nothing was said, only first publication rights were acquired by the magazine. He testified that, if all rights were not acquired, there were specific negotiations—i.e., something *was said*—and a lower price would be paid for the material.

Mr. Norton's testimony indicates that the words "all rights" were a recognized term in the magazine trade in 1932. But he rejected plaintiff's contention that custom or usage gave these words a specialized meaning. As he said, "all rights" meant literally all rights—i.e., . . . "dramatic, movie, television, skywriting on Mars, anything you want to say . . . everything". He also said that where "all rights" were purchased, the author . . . "retained absolutely nothing". * * *

On the basis of the clear preponderance of the credible evidence, the Court finds that the custom and usage in 1932 in the magazine trade implied in fact in the Geisel–Liberty Magazine agreement a provision whereby all rights or complete rights were assigned to Liberty Magazine. * * *

The terms "all rights" and "complete rights," when understood according to their plain meaning, signify a totality of rights, including the right of reproduction or common law copyright and the right to secure statutory copyright without qualification. * * * Although corroboration for defendants' position—that all or complete rights were purchased by Liberty Magazine in 1932—is not necessary, corroboration is provided by Liberty's "permanent purchase record cards." Some of these cards were introduced into evidence by defendants. Each card specifies, among other things, the author's name, the title, the price paid, the date of purchase and date of publication, the "character" of the material (e.g. article, cartoon, etc.) and the rights purchased. There is a separate card corresponding to each page of plaintiff's cartoons which appeared in Liberty Magazine. Each of these cards relating to the Geisel–Liberty transaction expressly states that "complete" rights were purchased.

The Court finds and concludes that these cards are admissible under the Federal Business Records Act, 28 U.S.C. § 1732 (1964) because manifestly they were made in regular course of Liberty Magazine's business and it was the regular course of such business to make such cards and the entries thereon. Meyer Dworkin testified extensively as to the regularity of these business practices at Liberty Magazine. The Court finds his detailed testimony regarding Liberty's practices to be credible and reliable. * * *

Dworkin also testified that the same recital of rights which appeared on Liberty Magazine's cards was rubberstamped as a legend on the check sent to the author or his agent. * * * The permanent purchase record cards also circumstantially support defendants' position that complete rights or all rights had their literal meaning. Some of the cards indicated "complete" rights; another "complete, except book"; others stated first and second North American serial rights; and some included broadcast rights together with serial rights. * * * The ineluctable conclusion is that, when Liberty Magazine bought the cartoons in question from plaintiff, it purchased all rights, including the common law copyright and the right to secure statutory copyright without reservation of any rights in plaintiff.

Absent a reservation of the common law copyright or other rights, the copyright and all other rights pass with an absolute and unconditional sale. See *Pushman v. New York Graphic Soc'y*, 287 N.Y. 302, 307–308, 39 N.E.2d 249 (1942) (painting); *Dam v. Kirk La Shelle Co.*, 175 F. 902, 904 (2nd Cir. 1910) (magazine story); *Best Medium Publ'g Co. v. Nat'l Insider*, 259 F.Supp. 433, 434, 439 (N.D.Ill.1966), aff'd, 385 F.2d 384, 386 (7th Cir. 1967), cert. denied, 390 U.S. 955, (1968) (story in weekly newspaper). * * * Regardless of the formulation, the evidence in the present case convincingly establishes only one conclusion: all rights (including the common law copyright) in the cartoons were transferred to Liberty without any equitable or other rights reserved to plaintiff. * * *

THE DOLLS

Having decided that Liberty Magazine acquired *all* rights to the cartoons published in 1932, the Court now considers and determines what rights defendants have to make the dolls and to what extent, if any, defendants may use the name "Dr. Seuss" in connection therewith. * * * On September 1, 1949, Lorraine Lester entered into an option agreement with Liberty Magazine, Inc. which, as amended on March 13, 1950, permitted her, upon certain conditions to exploit short story material which had appeared in Liberty Magazine during the period 1924 to 1949 for use in connection with radio, television and motion pictures. The exclusive license agreement provided in part: ...

> "2. We shall make available for your inspection all short stories which have been published by Liberty. With respect to any stories selected by you of which we own all rights, your use thereof may commence immediately. As to any other stories selected by you, we will endeavor at your request to obtain all rights which may be required, but in no event will you be licensed to use them hereunder until we have authorized such use."

On September 20, 1949, Miss Lester signed an agreement assigning the option agreement to Lester–Fields Productions, Inc., a company in which she was a principal.

In 1950, Miss Lester learned from Osborne B. Bond, the publisher of Liberty Magazine, that Liberty planned to cease publication. She thereupon entered into negotiations on behalf of Lester–Fields Productions, Inc. to acquire the magazine's "copyright library". On August 10, 1950, Miss Lester received a letter from Liberty accepting her prior oral offer to purchase the "rights to all material contained in the Library of Liberty Magazine, Inc. from May 10, 1924 to July, 1950, inclusive. ..."

> Thereafter, on September 8, 1950 Lester–Fields and Liberty Magazine, Inc. entered into an agreement terminating the 1949 option agreement with Miss Lester and providing in part as follows: ...

> "3. Liberty hereby sells, assigns and transfers to Lester any and all right, title or interest it may have in or to any and all of the stories and articles which have been published in Liberty Magazine from May 1924 to July 1950 inclusive, provided, however, that Liberty makes no representation as to the extent of its right, title or interest in and to such stories and articles."

The material referred to in that agreement included short stories, articles, cartoons and crossword puzzles which had appeared weekly in Liberty Magazine over a period of 26 years. Approximately 17,000 literary properties were included. Lester–Fields also bought Liberty Magazine's permanent purchase record cards and checks covering the period of 1943 to 1950.

On October 5, 1950, Lester–Fields assigned this agreement to George Lessner, Lorraine Lester, Robert Fields and Samuel H. Evans. Fields subsequently assigned his interest to the others. Thereafter, on

November 10, 1964, this agreement [Pltf.Ex. 9] was assigned to Liberty Library Corporation. Thus, defendant Liberty Library Corporation is successor to all the literary assets of Liberty Publishing Corporation, publisher of Liberty Magazine in 1932.

In August 1964 Mr. Robert Whiteman called on Miss Lester in connection with film production. In the course of their conversation, he saw the 90 bound volumes of Liberty Magazine on her shelves; and, after discussion, suggested that he could help her make money by exploiting the literary properties contained in those magazine. Thereafter, Whiteman entered into an agreement with Liberty Library, whereby Whiteman represented Liberty "on an exclusive basis" in exploiting the material from defendant Liberty Magazine.

Commencing in 1964, defendant Liberty embarked on a program of actively exploiting the material which had appeared in Liberty Magazine from 1924 to 1950. In the course of selecting material for sale or licensing, Whiteman came upon plaintiff's cartoons in the 1932 issues of Liberty Magazine. Whiteman checked the Liberty record cards and secured a copyright search on that material. After receiving expressions of interest in the cartoons, "as a matter of courtesy," Whiteman contacted Random House which referred him to plaintiff's agent, Mrs. Phyllis Jackson of Ashley Famous Agency. Whiteman showed her copies of the cartoons and of the copyright search and offered plaintiff the opportunity either to join with Liberty in exploiting the material or to repurchase the rights in the works. Whiteman agreed to keep her informed regarding any offers which he received with respect to the material. Subsequently, Whiteman informed her by letter of December 15, 1964, that he had received an offer for reprint rights to the material.

Prior to the letter of December 15th, Mrs. Jackson contacted plaintiff who rejected defendant Liberty's offer. After the December 15th letter, Mrs. Jackson wrote to plaintiff advising him to have his attorney write to defendant Liberty in an effort to prevent exploitation of the cartoon material. Thereafter, plaintiff's California attorney, Frank Kockritz, Esq., sent a telegram to defendant Liberty advising it that plaintiff did not recognize Liberty's rights in the cartoons and reserving the right to institute a lawsuit.

After receiving the telegram, Whiteman consulted his attorneys and, on May 14, 1965, completed a transaction with Universal Publishing and Distributing Corporation. The agreement provided for licensing Universal to publish a paperback book of the Liberty "Dr. Seuss" cartoons. Universal subsequently wrote to plaintiff on June 6, 1966 asking plaintiff to retitle and revise his cartoons. Plaintiff rejected the proposal; Mrs. Jackson informed Universal; and plaintiff's attorney, Mr. Kockritz, sent a protest letter to Universal. However, Universal went ahead and published a paperback entitled "Dr. Seuss' Lost World Revisited".

After publication, defendant Liberty again offered to sell its rights in the cartoons back to plaintiff. This final offer of defendant Liberty to sell its rights in the cartoons back to plaintiff was suggested by Arthur F.

Abelman, Esq., who had previously discussed the matter with plaintiff's agent, Mrs. Jackson.

Finally, in 1967, Whiteman undertook to sell merchandising rights to the cartoons. Whiteman, who was experienced in licensing and merchandising items, including toys, decided to grant a license to manufacture dolls based on the cartoons. Whiteman licensed defendant Poynter Products, Inc. because he had had successful dealings with Donald B. Poynter in the past and he considered Poynter to be ... "a man of tremendous capabilities in the field of molding, sculpture, art, taste...." The licensing agreement was executed (on September 8, 1967), after Poynter had been shown the cartoons and informed of plaintiff's objection to the publication of the paperback book.

Donald B. Poynter was and is an experienced designer and manufacturer of toys, novelties and gift items, including items made for children. He had previously designed a variety of items based upon works of well known artists. He had also produced puppets; "premiums," such as T-shirts and tags, given away by sponsors of children's radio and television shows; theatrical sets; and advertising artistic layouts for a large toy manufacturer.

In view of the protest telegram from plaintiff's attorney in 1964, Whiteman decided to submit everything done with respect to the dolls to Mr. Abelman. In fact, all meetings between Whiteman and Poynter took place in Mr. Abelman's office. In November 1967, Whiteman and Poynter came to Mr. Abelman's office to discuss design of the dolls. Poynter brought with him a hand sculptured styrofoam and papier-mache model of one of the cartoon "characters" which he had prepared from "rough" sketches. Mr. Abelman found the prototype doll to be "reasonable acceptable and a faithful reproduction" and Whiteman agreed.

At the meeting in November, 1967, Mr. Abelman also advised Poynter ... "that under no circumstances should he consult any book written by Dr. Seuss, watch any television program by Dr. Seuss or use any material of Dr. Seuss outside the Liberty drawings in preparing the drawings for his dolls, and I told him that when he watched those drawings he should look at them very carefully, reproduce them as close as he possibly could, taking into account the fact that you are moving from a two-dimensional medium of paper and publishing into the three-dimensional medium of dolls". In fact, the Court finds that Poynter used the cartoons *only* as they appeared in Liberty Magazine or in the paperback book in the preparation and design of the dolls.

After the meeting, Poynter prepared additional models and then went to Japan for six weeks to work on the dolls and choose a manufacturer. By letter dated January 12, 1968, Poynter authorized the manufacture in Japan of a set of twelve small vinyl toy dolls designed from some of the creatures which appeared in the 1932 cartoons. * * * The dolls which were ultimately manufactured and sold consist of six different vinyl figures, each of which comes in two different colors. At an earlier stage, Poynter made and rejected a stuffed doll version of the figures. * * *

Prior to March 12, 1968 (when the Court entered a temporary restraining order in this matter), defendants offered and sold the dolls using the name "Dr. Seuss" in the following ways:

  1. It was engraved in very small letters on the vinyl bottom of each doll with the statement: "From Original Illustrations of Dr. Seuss Copyright 1932 Liberty Library Corporation Copyright Renewed Copyright 1966 Poynter Products Inc., Cincinnati, Ohio Made in Japan." This was done pursuant to the suggestion of defendants' counsel.

  2. A round hang tag tied around the neck of each doll stated, on one side: "From the Wonderful World of Dr. Seuss—an original Merry Menagerie"; and, on the other side: "This is my (you name it) from Dr. Seuss' Merry Menagerie." Mr. Abelman approved this tag.

* * * From March 12, 1968, when a temporary restraining order was entered in this action, until April 9, 1968, when a preliminary injunction was entered, defendants did not ship any of the dolls for sale. After the preliminary injunction was entered, defendants again began to offer the dolls for sale accompanied by revised labels and sales materials using the name "Dr. Seuss" in the following manner: a. The hang tag tied around the neck of each doll stated, on one side: "Wacky Merry Menagerie Everybody loves 'em"; and, on the other side: "Toys Created, Designed & Produced Exclusively by Don Poynter MERRY MENAGERIE Based on Liberty Magazine Illustrations by Dr. Seuss"; * * *

The name "Dr. Seuss" and the name "Don Poynter" were in the same size and style of type. The base section of the carton contained no mention of Dr. Seuss.... c. The revised handbill read: "MERRY MENAGERIE. Toys Designed, Created & Produced Exclusively by Don Poynter Based on Liberty Magazine Illustrations by Dr. Seuss."

The name "Don Poynter" and the name "Dr. Seuss" were in the same size and style of type. In regular-size type in the handbill appeared the following copy: "These lovable, huggable little creatures are from original illustrations by the celebrated author-illustrator Dr. Seuss. These early drawings were featured in the famous Liberty Magazine. Now, from these drawings Don Poynter, the inventor of 'The Thing', has created, designed and produced the newest, cutest, most charming 'merry menagerie' to 'hit' the market in many years."

EXTENT OF DEFENDANTS' RIGHTS TO MAKE THE DOLLS
AND TO USE THE NAME "DR. SEUSS"

As the owner of a copyright on the two-dimensional cartoons, defendant Liberty Library has the right to make three-dimensional figures or dolls therefrom or to license another (e.g., defendant Poynter Products) to do so. * * * More specifically, in this case the owner of the copyrighted two-dimensional cartoons has the right to make three-dimensional figures from the cartoons. * * *

The Court denies costs to either party. * * *

Notes

1. One of the most popular TV shows of all time was the 1950's hit *I Love Lucy*. In 1957, *Lucy* was watched faithfully in about 10 million out of 15 million homes. This record-breaking show also became the original TV merchandising giant. Sponsor Philip Morris cigarettes paid the show $30,000 a week, which within five years increased to $350,000 for each episode. However, the show also profited from merchandise including "Lucy blouses and Desi smoking jackets, to full-fledged living-room and bedroom sets patterned after the show's set, complete with 'Lucy' linoleum." The show lives on in syndication on television and through the "Lucy" merchandise. Kyle Pope, *Farewell, "Seinfeld": When TV History Goes Into Reruns*, WALL STREET J., May 7, 1998, available *at* http://members.aol.com/iluvlucys-num1fan/Articles/article11.html

2. Castle Rock Entertainment sued Carol Publishing Group for an alleged copyright infringement in the production of a *Seinfeld* trivia book in *Castle Rock Entm't v. Carol Publ'g Group*, 150 F.3d 132 (2d Cir. 1998). The defendant published the book that tested viewers' knowledge of events from the series about four single friends in New York. *The SAT* book had questions based on 84 episodes, with 40 questions having direct quotes from the series. The series name was on the front and back of the book, and pictures of the characters were included. Castle Rock did not approve of the publication and sued defendants for alleged copyright infringement in 1994. The district court ruled that Carol Publishing had infringed the copyright and awarded $403,000 to Castle Rock. Also, the court stopped further publishing the book and ordered the destruction of other copies. The appeals court affirmed the ruling for Castle Rock that the book infringed the show's copyright and was not deemed fair use.

3. The owner of the copyright to the dinosaur characters in "Barney and Friends" sued a costume shop owner who was renting costumes of the protected characters in *Lyons P'ship, L.P. v. Holmes*, 34 Fed. Appx. 229 (7th Cir. 2002). The district court ruled that the shop owner had infringed Lyons' copyright for "Barney" and "Baby Bop" and awarded statutory damages of $22,500 for each character, $55,543 in attorney's fees, and $2,100 in costs. The shop owner appealed and denied owning the questionable costumes. The appeals court condemned the defendant's dishonesty during discovery requests and affirmed the district court's ruling.

4. After the O.J. Simpson double murder trial, there were many products produced based on the media spectacle. One such item was the disputed *The Cat NOT in the Hat! A Parody by Dr. Juice*, which was based on *The Cat in the Hat* by Dr. Seuss. This alleged copyright and trademark infringement was discussed in *Dr. Seuss Enter., L.P. v. Penguin Books USA, Inc.*, 109 F.3d 1394 (9th Cir. 1997). The district court issued an injunction barring the publication of the book, which included rhymes about the trial, because of copyright infringement for the Dr. Seuss book. Dr. Seuss Enter-

prises owns the copyright to *The Cat in the Hat*, which was initially published in 1957. The appeals court affirmed the district court's ruling for a preliminary injunction barring the publication and distribution of the book. For an academic review of the subject, *see* Tyler T. Ochoa, *Dr. Seuss, The Juice and Fair Use: How the Grinch Silenced a Parody,* 45 J.C.P.S. 546 (1998).

Chapter 11

RIGHT OF PUBLICITY OF TELE-
VISION CELEBRITIES

The right of publicity is a valuable property right for those who are able to exploit it. The right of publicity is an offshoot from the right of privacy with some significant differences. Unlike the right of privacy, the right of publicity survives death and is descendible. This is an important right that can provide significant income streams for the heirs of celebrities. Policing the use of one's name or likeness can be a difficult task with the multitude of possible unauthorized uses and media for exploitation. The Internet has exacerbated the problem for celebrities who seek to limit their exposure to maximize the value of their right of publicity.

A. RIGHT OF PUBLICITY AS PROPERTY INTEREST

MARITOTE v. DESILU PRODUCTIONS, INC.

United States Court of Appeals, Seventh Circuit, 1965.
345 F.2d 418.

SCHNACKENBERG, Circuit Judge.

This action is maintained by Mafalda Maritote, Administratrix of the estate of Alphonse (Al) Capone, deceased, Mae Capone, his widow, and Albert Capone, his son, plaintiffs, against Desilu Productions, Inc., a California corporation, Columbia Broadcasting System, Inc., a New York corporation, and Westinghouse Electric Corporation, a Pennsylvania corporation, defendants.

Maritote claimed a property right to recover for unjust enrichment arising out of an alleged appropriation by defendants of the 'name, likeness and personality' of Al Capone. Mae Capone and Albert Capone asserted a claim for invasion of their privacy, arising out of the identical acts of defendants. There was also a prayer for an injunction.

Sustaining defendants' contention that no cause of action was stated, the district court dismissed plaintiffs' third amended and supplemental complaint and plaintiffs' case. Plaintiffs have appealed.

This is a diversity action and the law of Illinois applies. Most prominently emphasized by plaintiffs in argument is the assertion by the widow and the son of Al Capone, deceased, of an invasion of their right of privacy by defendants, resulting from the latter's 'commercial exploitation' of decedent in commercially televised fictional broadcasts after his death. Plaintiffs do not claim that they were referred to or shown in any of said broadcasts.

From these controlling facts we turn to the Illinois law. In *Bradley v. Cowles Magazines, Inc.*, 26 Ill. App. 2d 331, at 333, 168 N.E.2d 64, at 65 (1960), the court said: 'The legal question before us is, shall the right of privacy be extended to provide damages for the anguish of a mother, caused by a publication concerning the murder of her son, although she herself was not featured or substantially publicized. The articles purport to give an account of the murder as related to a b reporter by the two men who were accused and were acquitted. * * *' (Emphasis added.) The court held that the right of privacy of plaintiff should not be extended to cover the asserted claim, although in that case plaintiff was referred to at least once in the alleged offensive publication.

In *Bradley*, Justice Schwartz, 26 Ill. App. 2d at 336, 168 N.E.2d at 66, relied on *Metter v. Los Angeles Examiner*, 95 P.2d 491 (Cal. 1939), saying: * * * The court also held that a right of action for the invasion of the right of privacy was purely personal, and that the plaintiff must prove invasion of his own right of privacy before he can recover. * * *

The same reasoning appears in *Kelly v. Johnson Publishing Co.*, 325 P.2d 659 (1958), where the surviving sisters of a deceased boxer sued for invasion of their right of privacy by an article published by defendant. The article referred to the deceased brother as 'a dope-sodden derelict'. The court, at 662 of 325 P.2d, stated, 'The authorities appear to be uniform that the right of privacy cannot be asserted by anyone other than him whose privacy is invaded. The publication did not invade plaintiffs' privacy in any respect. * * *'

We hold that these authorities justified the action of the district court and, in so holding, we reject as irrelevant the contention that plaintiff Albert Capone, son of Al Capone, claimed special damages.

In counts I, II, III and IV, the administratrix of Capone's estate relies on an alleged appropriation of decedent's name, likeness and personality in the telecasting of events in his life. Recovery is sought for unjust enrichment of defendants at expense of plaintiff.

Plaintiffs have been misled by their own quotation of the court's language in *Eick v. Perk Dog Food Co.*, 106 N.E.2d 742, 745, including the following: ' * * * Relying on property rights, courts have * * * given damages for mental suffering caused by tampering with corpses of deceased relatives, * * *.' However, the Illinois court was there considering the nature of damages recoverable by those having property rights in the bodies of deceased relatives. It was not then discussing whether such right did exist.

Undoubtedly the next of kin have a right of burial of the body of a deceased person and for an invasion of that right courts will grant relief. But that right is not involved or claimed by plaintiffs here; they rely on the law pertaining to their claimed right of privacy. Accordingly, we hold that what plaintiffs call the 'dead body cases' do not apply in the case at bar.

While on July 6, 1962, by an amendment to the complaint, the widow and son were added as new parties, we agree with the district court that all of the relief sought by the several plaintiffs is essentially for a claimed invasion of a right of privacy.

Al Capone died in January, 1947. The telecasts here involved were made on April 20 and 27 and October 15 and 23, 1959 and thereafter. We here deal with claimed invasions of privacy occurring over 12 1/2 years after Capone died. It is anomalous to speak of the privacy of a deceased person. The telecasts did not mention any plaintiff here and hence the privacy of no plaintiff was invaded by defendants. As Shakespeare said, 'the evil that men do lives after them * * *.' What a man does while alive becomes a part of history which survives his death. Comment, fictionalization and even distortion of a dead man's career do not invade the privacy of his offspring, relatives or friends, if they are not even mentioned therein. If the law is to be otherwise, it should be attained by legislative enactments, as, according to plaintiffs' brief, has been done in Virginia, Utah and Oklahoma. This court has and makes no pretense to having any lawmaking power. We are fully occupied in interpreting the law and applying it.

After the filing in this court of the record on appeal, plaintiffs filed two motions asking us to take judicial notice of what they described as television showings of motion pictures of the subject matter of the initial complaint herein. There appearing to be no basis for thus extending the record on appeal, we reject said motions.

All arguments made by plaintiffs have been considered, even though not expressly mentioned herein. We find no error committed below.

For these reasons, the order of the district court from which this appeal was taken is affirmed. [Case dismissed in favor of Defendants.]

DUFFY, Circuit Judge (concurring in the result). * * *

In 1959, Desilu Productions, Inc. (Desilu) sold to Columbia Broadcasting System a two-part drama called 'The Untouchables.' This was a dramatization of certain wholly fictional events supposed to have happened during the lifetime of Capone. The scenes and incidents pertaining to Capone were pure invention and were the product of the imagination of the script writers. The commercial exploitation of the name 'Capone' succeeded so well that Desilu produced for broadcast on the American Broadcasting Company a weekly series also entitled 'The Untouchables.'

This weekly broadcast continued for the period of five years. Throughout the series, the name 'Capone' was used and, at times, his purported likeness.

Desi Arnaz was president of Desilu. He had been a boyhood friend of Sonny who pleaded with him to refrain from proceeding with the production of 'The Untouchables.' Arnaz refused to discuss the matter with Sonny. Apparently the profit motive outweighed any concern about injury to innocent people.

Another full-scale exploitation of the name, likeness and personality of Al Capone was created by Desilu in an episode called 'The Big Train.' This purportedly portrayed a plot by Capone to escape while being transferred from Atlanta prison to Alcatraz. This whole incident was completely fictitious. Nothing like it as far as Al Capone was concerned ever occurred. In fact, a public protest of this broadcast was made to the Federal Communications Commission by James V. Bennett, Director of the Federal Bureau of Prisons.

Plaintiffs argue that the magnitude of the commercial exploitation of the name, likeness and personality of Capone by Desilu makes this a case of first impression. Plaintiffs point out that Desilu depicted more than one hundred fictitious murders, machine gunnings, beatings and other crimes of violence which were falsely attributed to Al Capone, and that for approximately six years, the widow and son were mentally tortured week after week.

The defendants have been profiting, not from Al Capone's life of crime, but from the commercial exploitation of publicity values inherent in his name, likeness and personality as portrayed in the telecasting of a series of wholly fictional crimes.

I think the right of privacy of Mae Capone and Sonny Capone was invaded by Desilu and other defendants whose conduct as hereinbefore described is, in my mind, reprehensible. Their fictitious products overstepped the bounds of decency. But the question is—do the widow and son have a claim for invasion of privacy under Illinois law?

Several of the cases relied on by defendants and, to some extent, in the majority opinion, deal with a specific crime or crimes which had been committed and which were a matter of public record. These cases should be distinguished from the situation where wholly fictitious crimes were depicted as exploiting the name of Capone.

However, in this diversity case, we must decide whether Illinois courts would hold that a remedy exists under Illinois law for the violation of the privacy of the widow and son of Capone. I conclude they would not. I must, therefore, concur in the result reached by the majority.

Notes

1. In *McFarland v. Miller,* 14 F.3d 912 (3d Cir. 1994), a movie actor in the "Our Gang' movie series and "Little Rascals" television series brought an action against a restaurant that possessed a name identical to a movie character played by actor. The district court granted summary judgment to the defendants. During pendency of the appeal, the plaintiff died and his personal representative was substituted in his place. The court of appeals held that: "McFarland's action to prevent unauthorized use of the name "Spanky MacFarland" survived his death and passed to his personal representative." *Id.*

2. In *Elvis Presley Enterprises, Inc. v. Capece,* 950 F.Supp. 783 (S.D.Tex. 1996) the trial court held the name "The Velvet Elvis" did not create likelihood of confusion as to "Elvis" trademarks, but did violate Presley's right of publicity in the nightclub's advertising. The appeals court reversed holding infringement can be based upon confusion that creates initial consumer interest, even though no actual sale is finally completed as a result of the confusion. *See Elvis Presley Enterprises, Inc. v. Capece,* 141 F.3d 188 (5th Cir. 1998).

3. In *Zacchini v. Scripps–Howard Broadcasting Co.,* 433 U.S. 562 (1977), a performer in a 'human cannonball' act brought an action against a television broadcasting company to recover damages allegedly suffered when, against his wishes, the broadcasting company videotaped his entire performance and played the videotape on a television news program. The Ohio Court of Appeals and the Ohio Supreme Court rendered judgment for the broadcasting company on the grounds that it was constitutionally privileged to include matters of public interest in its newscasts which otherwise would be protected by the right of publicity. The United States Supreme Court reversed, holding that although the State of Ohio might privilege the press, the First and Fourteenth Amendments did not require it to do so.

WENDT v. HOST INTERNATIONAL, INC.

United States Court of Appeals, Ninth Circuit, 1997.
125 F.3d 806.

FLETCHER, Circuit Judge.

Actors George Wendt and John Ratzenberger appeal the district court's grant of summary judgment in favor of Host International, Inc. ("Host") and applicant in intervention Paramount Pictures Corporation ("Paramount"), dismissing their action for violations of the Lanham Act, 15 U.S.C. § 1125(a), and California's statutory and common law right of publicity. We reverse.

I. OVERVIEW

Wendt and Ratzenberger argue that the district court erred in dismissing their action because they have raised issues of material fact as to whether Host violated their trademark and publicity rights by creating animatronic robotic figures (the "robots") based upon their likenesses without their permission and placing these robots in airport bars modeled upon the set from the television show Cheers. They also appeal the district court's orders excluding appellants' survey evidence, barring presentation of expert testimony, and awarding Host and Paramount attorney's fees. We have jurisdiction, 28 U.S.C. § 1291, and we reverse and remand for trial.

II. PROCEDURAL HISTORY

In *Wendt v. Host,* 1995 U.S. App. LEXIS 5464, 1995 WL 115571 (9th Cir. 1995) ("*Wendt I*"), we reversed the first grant of summary judgment in this action and remanded. We held that appellants' state law causes of action were not preempted by federal copyright law and that disputed issues of material fact precluded summary judgment because the district court's comparison of photographs of appellants Wendt and Ratzenberger with photographs of the animatronic figures was not sufficient to resolve their claims under Cal. Civ. Code § 3344: The question here is whether the three dimensional animatronic figures are sufficiently similar to plaintiffs to constitute their likenesses. Based on the limited record before us, it cannot be said as a matter of law that the figures are so dissimilar from plaintiffs that no reasonable trier of fact could find them to be 'likenesses.' That question must be determined by a comparison of the actual, three-dimensional entities. 1995 U.S. App. LEXIS 5464, *6, 1995 WL 115571 at *2.

We concluded that this comparison must be decided without reference to the context in which the image appears. *Id.* (citing *White v. Samsung Elec. Am., Inc.,* 971 F.2d 1395, 1397 (9th Cir. 1992), *cert. denied.,* 508 U.S. 951 (1993)). We found that there were disputed issues of material fact concerning the appellants' common law right of publicity claims because the similarity between appellants' physical characteristics and those of the robots is disputed. 1995 WL 115571 at *3. Finally, we held that the appellants' claims for unfair competition under § 43(a) of the Lanham Act, 15 U.S.C. § 1125(a), require the application of a "well settled eight factor test" to determine whether Host's conduct has created a likelihood of confusion as to whether appellants were endorsing Host's product. *Id.*

Upon remand, the district court granted summary judgment for a second time after an in-court inspection of the robots. It held that it could not "find, by viewing both the robotics and the live persons of Mr. Wendt and Mr. Ratzenberger, that there is any similarity at all ... except that one of the robots, like one of the plaintiffs, is heavier than the other ... The facial features are totally different." The district court then awarded attorney's fees to Host and Paramount pursuant to Cal. Civ. Code § 3344.

Appellants argue that despite the district court's comparison of the animatronic figures and the appellants, dismissal was inappropriate because material issues of fact remain as to the degree to which the animatronic figures appropriate the appellants' likenesses. Appellants claim that the district court erred in determining that the robots were not likenesses of the appellants because the "likeness" need not be identical or photographic. Further, they argue that the likeness determination is an issue for the jury to decide in this case. We agree.

III. ANALYSIS

We review a grant of summary judgment de novo. We must determine, viewing the evidence in the light most favorable to the nonmoving party, whether there are any genuine issues of material fact, and whether the district court correctly applied the relevant substantive law. * * *

A. *The Statutory Right of Publicity*

California Civil Code § 3344 provides in relevant part: any person who knowingly uses another's name, voice, signature, photograph, or likeness, in any manner, . . . for purposes of advertising or selling, . . . without such person's prior consent . . . shall be liable for any damages sustained by the person or persons injured as a result thereof.

In *White,* 971 F.2d at 1397, we ruled that a robot with mechanical features was not a "likeness" under § 3344. However, we specifically held open the possibility that a manikin molded to Vanna White's precise features, or one that was a caricature or bore an impressionistic resemblance to White might become a likeness for statutory purposes. *Id.* The degree to which these robots resemble, caricature, or bear an impressionistic resemblance to appellants is therefore clearly material to a claim of violation of Cal. Civ. Code § 3344. Summary judgment would have been appropriate upon remand only if *no* genuine issues of material fact concerning that degree of resemblance were raised by appellants. Fed. R. Civ. P. 56.

Despite the district court's assertions that no reasonable jury could find that the robots are "similar in any manner whatsoever to Plaintiffs," we respectfully disagree. Without making any judgment about the ultimate similarity of the figures to the appellants, we conclude from our own inspection of the robots that material facts exist that might cause a reasonable jury to find them sufficiently "like" the appellants to violate Cal. Civ. Code § 3344.

We reject appellees' assertion that *Fleet v. CBS,* 50 Cal. App. 4th 1911 (Cal. Ct. App. 1996) is new controlling authority that requires us to revisit the determination on first appeal that appellants' § 3344 claims are not preempted by federal copyright law. *Wendt I,* 1995 WL 115571, at *1. *Fleet* is not controlling new authority on the preemption issue. It holds that an actor may not bring an action for misappropriation under Cal. Civ. Code § 3344 when the *only* claimed exploitation occurred through the distribution of the actor's performance in a copyrighted movie. 58 Cal. Rptr. 2d at 651 ("Appellants may choose to call their claims misappropriation of right to publicity, but if all they are seeking is to prevent a party from exhibiting a copyrighted work they are making a claim equivalent to an exclusive right within the general scope of copyright.") (internal quotations omitted).

Appellants here are not seeking to prevent Paramount from exhibiting its copyrighted work in the Cheers series. As we stated in *Wendt I*, their "claims are not preempted by the federal copyright statute so long as they 'contain elements, such as the invasion of personal rights . . . that are different in kind from copyright infringement.' " *Wendt I*, 1995 WL 115571 at *1. * * * The *Fleet* court acknowledged that it simply found a fact-specific exception to the general rule that "as a general proposition section 3344 is intended to protect rights which cannot be copyrighted." *Fleet*, 58 Cal. Rptr. 2d at 649.

Appellants' claims are not preempted by federal copyright law. Issues of material fact exist concerning the degree to which the robots are like the appellants. We reverse the grant of summary judgment on the claim under Cal. Civ. Code § 3344.

B. Common–Law Right of Publicity

California recognizes a common law right of privacy that includes protection against appropriation for the defendant's advantage of the plaintiff's name or likeness, *Eastwood v. Super. Ct. for Los Angeles County*, 149 Cal. App. 3d 409 (Cal. Ct. App. 1983). The right to be protected against such appropriations is also referred to as the "right of publicity." *Id.* A common law cause of action for appropriation of name or likeness may be pleaded by alleging 1) the defendant's use of the plaintiff's identity; 2) the appropriation of plaintiff's name or likeness to defendant's advantage, commercially or otherwise; 3) lack of consent; and 4) resulting injury. *Id.* (citing Prosser, Law of Torts § 117 804–07 (4th ed. 1971)).

The so-called right of publicity means in essence that the reaction of the public to name and likeness, which may be fortuitous or which may be managed and planned, endows the name and likeness of the person involved with commercially exploitable opportunities. The protection of name and likeness from unwarranted intrusion or exploitation is the heart of the law of privacy. *Lugosi v. Universal Pictures*, 603 P.2d 425, 431 (1979).

We have held that this common-law right of publicity protects more than the knowing use of a plaintiff's name or likeness for commercial purposes that is protected by Cal. Civ. Code § 3344. It also protects against appropriations of the plaintiff's identity by other means. *See White*, 971 F.2d at 1398 ("[a] rule which says that the right of publicity can be infringed only through the use of nine different methods of appropriating identity merely challenges the clever advertising strategist to come up with the tenth."). * * *

Appellees argue that the figures appropriate only the identities of the characters Norm and Cliff, to which Paramount owns the copyrights, and not the identities of Wendt and Ratzenberger, who merely portrayed those characters on television and retain no licensing rights to them.

They argue that appellants may not claim an appropriation of identity by relying upon indicia, such as the Cheers Bar set, that are the property of, or licensee of, a copyright owner. *Sinatra v. Goodyear Tire & Rubber Co.*, 435 F.2d 711, 716 (9th Cir. 1970).

Appellants freely concede that they retain no rights to the characters Norm and Cliff; they argue that the figures, named "Bob" and "Hank," are not related to Paramount's copyright of the creative elements of the characters Norm and Cliff. They argue that it is the physical likeness to Wendt and Ratzenberger, not Paramount's characters, that has commercial value to Host.

While it is true that appellants' fame arose in large part through their participation in Cheers, an actor or actress does not lose the right to control the commercial exploitation of his or her likeness by portraying a fictional character. *Lugosi*, 603 P.2d at 431. Appellants have raised genuine issues of material fact concerning the degree to which the figures look like them. Because they have done so, appellants have also raised triable issues of fact as to whether or not appellees sought to appropriate their likenesses for their own advantage and whether they succeeded in doing so. *See Midler*, 849 F.2d at 463. The ultimate issue for the jury to decide is whether the defendants are commercially exploiting the likeness of the figures to Wendt and Ratzenberger intending to engender profits to their enterprises. * * * We therefore reverse the grant of summary judgment on the common law right of publicity claim.

C. Unfair Competition

Section 43(a) of the Lanham Act (15 U.S.C. § 1125(a)) prohibits, *inter alia*, the use of any symbol or device which is likely to deceive consumers as to the association, sponsorship, or approval of goods or services by another person. The appellants' claim is for false endorsement—that by using an imitation of their unique physical characteristics, Host misrepresented their association with and endorsement of the Cheers bars concept.

In *Waits*, 978 F.2d at 1110, we held such a claim actionable under § 43(a): [a] false endorsement claim based on the unauthorized use of a celebrity's identity . . . alleges the misuse of a trademark, i.e., a symbol or device such as a visual likeness, vocal imitation, or other uniquely distinguishing characteristic, which is likely to confuse consumers as to the plaintiff's sponsorship or approval of the product.

In *Wendt I* we held that appellants would have a claim if "Host's conduct had created a likelihood of confusion as to whether plaintiffs were endorsing Host's product." 1995 WL 115571 at *3. In order to determine whether or not such confusion is likely to occur, we referred to a "well settled eight factor test" to be applied to celebrity endorsement cases, *Newton v. Thomason*, 22 F.3d 1455, 1462 (9th Cir. 1994). This test requires the consideration of: 1) the strength of the plaintiff's mark; 2) relatedness of the goods; 3) similarity of the marks; 4) evidence

test cont

of actual confusion; 5) marketing channels used; 6) likely degree of purchaser care; 7) defendant's intent in selecting the mark; 8) likelihood of expansion of the product lines. *Id.* at 1462. * * *

In *Wendt I* we concluded that one of the primary factors of this test was the 'similarity of the marks' and because there was a disputed issue of material fact as to that issue, summary judgment was inappropriate on this claim.

On remand, however, the district court simply compared the robots with the appellants in the courtroom and awarded judgment because there was "no similarity at all." The district court erred in failing independently to analyze any of the other relevant factors to determine whether or not there was a likelihood of confusion *to consumers* as to whether appellants sponsored, approved of, or were otherwise associated with the Cheers bars.

The Lanham Act's 'likelihood of confusion' standard is predominantly factual in nature. Summary judgment is inappropriate when a jury could reasonably conclude that most of the factors weigh in a plaintiff's favor. * * *

Application of these factors indicates that the district court erred in rejecting appellants' Lanham Act claim at the summary judgment stage because a jury could reasonably conclude that most of the factors weigh in appellants' favor. Wendt and Ratzenberger were principal players on Cheers, a popular television show. They are clearly well-known among the target customers of Host's Cheers bars. For the purposes of this analysis, a jury could reasonably conclude that their mark is strong.

For the same reason, their 'goods' (their skill and fame as actors) are obviously related to Host's 'goods' (the products sold in the Cheers bars and the bars themselves) even if they are not strictly competitive. The issue is whether a consumer would be confused as to Wendt and Ratzenberger's association with or sponsorship of Host's bars. *See White,* 971 F.2d at 1400 ("In cases concerning confusion over celebrity endorsement, the plaintiff's 'goods' concern the reasons for or source of the plaintiff's fame.") The source of their fame and the Host bars are identical: the Cheers television series. A jury could conclude that this factor weighs in appellants' favor because it would be reasonable for a customer to be confused as to the nature of Wendt and Ratzenberger's association with Host's Cheers bars and the goods sold there.

The third factor, the similarity of the marks, is the primary issue in dispute. Because appellants have raised triable issues of material fact concerning the degree to which the robots resemble the appellants, a reasonable jury might find that this factor weighs in appellants' favor. Under the Lanham Act, in camera inspection is not sufficient; the district court must view the marks "as they appear in the marketplace." *E & J Gallo Winery v. Gallo Cattle Co.,* 967 F.2d 1280, 1291 (9th Cir. 1992).

Appellants presented evidence of actual confusion, the fourth factor. Both Ratzenberger and Wendt stated in their declarations that they have been approached by members of the public who commented on the similarity between the appellants and the robots at the Cheers airport bars: "The usual comment is some variation on 'Hey George, I just had a drink with you in Kansas City.'" They also submitted evidence of consumer confusion to the district court prior to summary judgment in the form of survey evidence. The court rejected this evidence as "not a good survey." For reasons detailed below, this evidence should not have been excluded. Sufficient evidence exists by which a reasonable jury might infer actual consumer confusion.

The fifth factor, marketing channels used, weighs in the appellants' favor. The allegation is that Host is appropriating appellants' likenesses because the target audience of the Cheers bars are customers who are fans of the television series. Such a similarity in marketing channels suggests that there is at least a likelihood of consumer confusion.

The sixth factor, likely degree of purchaser care, weighs in favor of appellants as well. Consumers are not likely to be particularly careful in determining who endorses or is affiliated with an airport bar in which they might purchase only a single beverage. They will be even less likely to scrutinize the source of the animatronic figures which are not for sale, but are used instead to attract patrons to the bars. This low degree of care makes confusion of sponsorship likely. See *White*, 971 F.2d at 1400 ("consumers are not likely to be particularly careful in determining who endorses VCR's, making confusion as to their endorsement more likely.")

The seventh factor is defendant's intent in selecting the mark. Appellants have alleged facts that could give rise to an inference that Host intended to confuse customers as to Wendt and Ratzenberger's sponsorship or endorsement of the Cheers bars by creating robots with their physical characteristics. See *AMF, Inc. v. Sleekcraft Boats*, 599 F.2d 341, 354 (9th Cir. 1979) ("When the alleged infringer knowingly adopts a mark similar to another's, reviewing courts presume that the defendant can accomplish his purpose: that is, that the public will be deceived." In their opposition to summary judgment appellants submitted evidence that Host intentionally designed the animatronic figures to resemble Wendt and Ratzenberger and that it recognized from the outset that the value of the association with Wendt and Ratzenberger themselves was "a major drawing card of the Cheers concept." After being advised that appellants would not agree to the use of their likenesses, Host altered the robots cosmetically, named them "Hank" and "Bob," and refused to recast them into a "friendly neighborhood couple," as they were advised to do by Paramount. Based on this evidence, an inference can be raised that Host intended to exploit the appellants' celebrity by confusion as to the similarity between the figures and the appellants.

We have found that the eighth factor, likelihood of expansion of the product lines, "does not appear apposite to a celebrity endorsement case," *White*, 971 F.2d at 1401. Here, however, Ratzenberger has offered evidence that he would like to appear in advertisements for beer and has declined offers from small breweries in order to be available to a large brewery. "Inasmuch as a trademark owner is afforded greater protection against competing goods, a 'strong possibility' that either party may expand his business to compete with the other will weigh in favor of finding that the present use is infringing." *Sleekcraft*, 599 F.2d at 354 (citing Restatement of Torts § 731(b)). This factor therefore weighs in appellants' favor as the potential exists that in the future Ratzenberger's endorsement of other beers would be confused with his alleged endorsement of the beers sold at Host's bars.

A reasonable jury could conclude that most of the factors weigh in appellants' favor and that Host's alleged conduct creates at least the likelihood of consumer confusion. Whether appellants' Lanham Act claim should succeed, of course, is a matter for the jury. Accordingly, we reverse the dismissal of the unfair competition claim and remand.

[handwritten margin note: Host's conduct creates the likelihood of consumer confusion]

D. *Exclusion of Survey Evidence*

In their opposition to Paramount's summary judgment motion, appellants offered into evidence the results of a consumer survey taken in the vicinity of the Cheers bars at the Cleveland and Kansas City airports. The district court refused to admit the evidence, saying that the evidence was "not a good survey."

As the record stood, the refusal was an abuse of discretion. In trademark cases, surveys are to be admitted as long as they are conducted according to accepted principles and are relevant. *E & J Gallo Winery*, 967 F.2d at 1280; *see also Prudential Ins. Co. of Am. v. Gibraltar Fin. Corp.*, 694 F.2d 1150, 1156 (9th Cir. 1982). Challenges to survey methodology go to the weight given the survey, not its admissibility. *Prudential Ins.*, 694 F.2d at 1156. However, because of the paucity of the record, upon remand, the parties should have the opportunity respectively to lay a foundation for the admission of the survey or to challenge the adequacy of the foundation.

E. *Exclusion of Expert Testimony*

Prior to the first appeal in this case the district court issued a Preclusion Order barring the introduction of expert testimony as a sanction against appellants' former counsel for failure to disclose damage evidence and for being late disclosing experts. Upon remand, the district court denied appellants' request that it vacate its order.

The initial Preclusion Order was issued on August 9, 1993 as a sanction against appellants' former counsel. At that time, counsel's failure to comply with discovery rules potentially prejudiced Host and Paramount's ability to prepare adequately for trial. Today, that is not so. Both parties now have ample opportunity to begin the expert disclosure procedure anew.

Wanderer v. Johnston, 910 F.2d 652, 656 (9th Cir. 1990), requires us to determine whether a sanction is proper under a five-factor test analyzing: 1) the public's interest in expeditious resolution of litigation; 2) the court's need to manage its docket; 3) the risk of prejudice to the defendants; 4) the public policy favoring disposition of cases on their merits; 5) the availability of less drastic sanctions. We conclude that under this test, the Preclusion Order is no longer proper. Less drastic sanctions are available and the defendants are no longer prejudiced by the actions of appellants' former counsel. We grant appellants' request to vacate the Preclusion Order upon remand. However, the district court, may, in its discretion, impose reasonable monetary sanctions upon appellants' former counsel for failure to comply with discovery rules.

F.   Attorney's Fees

Because we reverse the grant of summary judgment under Cal. Civ. Code § 3344, we reverse the grant of attorney's fees to Host and Paramount and deny their requests for attorney's fees on appeal.

IV.   CONCLUSION

The grant of summary judgment is reversed and the case is remanded to the district court for trial. The admission of the survey evidence should be reconsidered at trial. The Preclusion Order is vacated and appropriate sanctions other than preclusion may be considered. The grant of attorney's fees is reversed.

REVERSED and REMANDED.

Notes

1.   In the appeal following the decision above, the court denied the defendant's request for a rehearing and denied the request for a rehearing en banc. Judge Kozinski wrote the dissenting opinion in *Wendt v. Host International, Inc.,* 197 F.3d 1284 (9th Cir. 1999). Judge Kozinski discussed the difference between the this case and the *White v. Samsung Electronics,* 971 F.2d 1395 (9th Cir. 1992) case, found later in the text, by pointing out that in the *White* case, the defendant's did not have a license from the copyright owners of Wheel of Fortune whereas in the *Wendt* case, Paramount issued a license for Host to use its copyrighted material in the creation of the theme bar.

2.   In *Motschenbacher v. R.J. Reynolds Tobacco Co.,* 498 F.2d 821 (9th Cir. 1974), the defendants altered a photograph of the plaintiff's car by changing the numbers on all racing cars depicted, transforming plaintiff's number "11" into "71," and they added the word "Winston." The appellate court found that while the "likeness" of the plaintiff is unrecognizable, the distinctive decorations appearing on the car where not. The markings were not only peculiar to the plaintiff's cars but they caused some persons to think the car in question was plaintiff's and to infer that the person driving the car was the plaintiff.

B. SPORTS STARS

Exploiting an athlete's right of publicity has become a significant source of income for athletes during their active playing days and into retirement. Andre Agassi, Tiger Woods, Venus and Serena Williams, Wayne Gretsky, Anna Kournikova and Michael Jordan are athletes who made or make more money from their endorsement contracts than from playing their respective sports. High profile athletes can supplement their income by taking advantage of their celebrity and endorsing memorabilia, goods, and services. In order to protect the value of their right of privacy, athletes have had to sue to prevent unauthorized uses.

ABDUL–JABBAR v. GENERAL MOTORS CORPORATION

United States Court of Appeals, Ninth Circuit, 1996.
85 F.3d 407.

NELSON, Circuit Judge.

Former basketball star Kareem Abdul–Jabbar appeals the district court's summary judgment in favor of General Motors Corporation ("GMC") and its advertising agency, Leo Burnett Co., in his action alleging violations of the Lanham Act, 15 U.S.C. § 1125(a), and California's statutory and common law right of publicity. Abdul–Jabbar argues that GMC violated his trademark and publicity rights by using his former name, Lew Alcindor, without his consent, in a television commercial aired during the 1993 NCAA men's basketball tournament. The district court based its judgment on all causes of action largely on its findings that Abdul–Jabbar had abandoned the name "Lew Alcindor," and that GMC's use of the name could not be construed as an endorsement of its product by Abdul–Jabbar. Having jurisdiction pursuant to 28 U.S.C. § 1291, we reverse and remand for trial.

FACTS AND PROCEDURAL HISTORY

This dispute concerns a GMC television commercial aired during the 1993 NCAA men's basketball tournament. The record includes a videotape of the spot, which plays as follows: A disembodied voice asks, "How 'bout some trivia?" This question is followed by the appearance of a screen bearing the printed words, "You're Talking to the Champ." The voice then asks, "Who holds the record for being voted the most outstanding player of this tournament?" In the screen appear the printed words, "Lew Alcindor, UCLA, '67, '68, '69." Next, the voice asks, "Has any car made the 'Consumer Digest's Best Buy' list more than once? [and responds:] The Oldsmobile Eighty–Eight has." A seven-second film clip of the automobile, with its price, follows. During the clip, the voice says, "In fact, it's made that list three years in a row. And now you can get this Eighty–Eight special edition for just $18,995." At the end of the clip, a message appears in print on the screen: "A Definite First Round Pick," accompanied by the voice saying, "it's your money." A final printed message appears: "Demand Better, 88 by Oldsmobile."

The following facts are undisputed. Kareem Abdul–Jabbar was named Ferdinand Lewis ("Lew") Alcindor at birth, and played basketball under that name throughout his college career and into his early years in the National Basketball Association ("NBA"). While in college, he converted to Islam and began to use the Muslim name "Kareem Abdul–Jabbar" among friends. Several years later, in 1971, he opted to record the name "Kareem Abdul–Jabbar" under an Illinois name recordation statute, and thereafter played basketball and endorsed products under that name. He has not used the name "Lew Alcindor" for commercial purposes in over ten years.

GMC did not obtain Abdul–Jabbar's consent, nor did it pay him, to use his former name in the commercial described above. When Abdul–Jabbar complained to GMC about the commercial, the company promptly withdrew the ad. The ad aired about five or six times in March 1993 prior to its withdrawal. The parties dispute whether Abdul–Jabbar abandoned the name Lew Alcindor and whether the ad could be construed as an endorsement by Abdul–Jabbar of the 88 Oldsmobile.

Abdul–Jabbar brought suit in federal district court in May 1993, alleging claims under the Lanham Act and California's statutory and common law rights of publicity. The district court held a hearing on March 14, 1994. During the hearing, incorporated by reference into the order of summary judgment, the district court announced its "tentative finding that plaintiff has abandoned the name Lew Alcindor, and has abandoned the right to protect that name, and the right to assert any other rights that flow from his having had that name at one time in the past." This finding forms the basis for the district court's decision to grant summary judgment in favor of GMC on both the Lanham Act and the state law causes of action. Abdul–Jabbar timely appealed.

ANALYSIS * * *

I

The Lanham Act

"[A]n express purpose of the Lanham Act is to protect commercial parties against unfair competition." *Waits v. Frito–Lay, Inc.,* 978 F.2d 1093, 1108 (9th Cir. 1992). In *Waits,* we held as a matter of first impression that false endorsement claims are properly cognizable under section 43(a), 15 U.S.C. § 1125(a), of the Lanham Act. *Id.* at 1107. "Section 43(a) [as amended in 1988] ... expressly prohibits, *inter alia,* the use of any symbol or device which is likely to deceive consumers as to the association, sponsorship, or approval of goods or services by another person." *Id.* Accordingly, we held actionable: [a] false endorsement claim based on the unauthorized use of a celebrity's identity ... [which] alleges the misuse of a trademark, i.e., a symbol or device such as a visual likeness, vocal imitation, or other uniquely distinguishing characteristic, which is likely to confuse consumers as to the plaintiff's sponsorship or approval of the product. *Id.* at 1110. Abdul–Jabbar contends that GMC's unauthorized use of his birth name, Lew Alcindor, was likely to confuse consumers as to his endorsement of the Olds 88, and thus violates the Lanham Act.

GMC offers two defenses in response to this claim: 1) Abdul–Jabbar lost his rights to the name Lew Alcindor when he "abandoned" it; and 2) GMC's use of the name Lew Alcindor was a nominative fair use which is not subject to the protection of the Lanham Act. The district court held both defenses applicable.

a) Abandonment under the Lanham Act

While the district court found that there was no dispute as to GMC's failure to seek or obtain Abdul–Jabbar's consent to use his former name in its commercial, and that "on its face, the Lanham Act applies," it held that GMC was entitled to summary judgment on the basis of its finding that Abdul–Jabbar had abandoned his former name through nonuse under the Lanham Act. Title 15 U.S.C. § 1127 (1992) provides in pertinent part: A mark shall be deemed to be "abandoned" when either of the following occurs:

> (1) When its use has been discontinued with intent not to resume such use. Intent not to resume may be inferred from circumstances. Nonuse for two consecutive years shall be prima facie evidence of abandonment. "Use" of a mark means the bona fide use of that mark made in the ordinary course of trade, and not merely to reserve a right in a mark.

> (2) When any course of conduct of the owner, including acts of omission as well as commission, causes the mark to become . . . generic. . . .

[handwritten margin note: abandoned mark]

Once created, a prima facie case of abandonment may be rebutted by showing valid reasons for nonuse or lack of intent to abandon the mark. * * * Because Abdul–Jabbar acknowledged that he had not used the name Lew Alcindor in over ten years, and because the district court found that plaintiff's proffered religious reasons for nonuse were not applicable, the court held that Abdul–Jabbar had in effect abandoned the name.

Trademark law withdraws its protection from a mark that has become generic and deems it available for general use. Given that the primary cost of recognizing property rights in trademarks is the removal of words from (or perhaps non-entrance into) our language, . . . the holder of a trademark will be denied protection if it is (or becomes) generic, i.e., if it does not relate exclusively to the trademark owner's product. *New Kids on the Block v. News America Pub., Inc.,* 971 F.2d 302, 306 (9th Cir. 1992). Similarly, the law ceases to protect the owner of an abandoned mark. Rather than countenancing the "removal" or retirement of the abandoned mark from commercial speech, trademark law allows it to be used by another. Accordingly, courts have held that an unused mark may not be held in abeyance by its original owner. *See, e.g., La Societe Anonyme des Parfums Le Galion v. Jean Patou, Inc.,* 495 F.2d 1265, 1272 (2d Cir. 1974).

While the Lanham Act has been applied to cases alleging appropriation of a celebrity's identity, the abandonment defense has never to our knowledge been applied to a person's name or identity. We decline to stretch the federal law of trademark to encompass such a defense. One's birth name is an integral part of one's identity; it is not bestowed for commercial purposes, nor is it "kept alive" through commercial use. A proper name thus cannot be deemed "abandoned" throughout its possessor's life, despite his failure to use it, or continue to use it, commercially.

In other words, an individual's given name, unlike a trademark, has a life and a significance quite apart from the commercial realm. Use or nonuse of the name for commercial purposes does not dispel that significance. An individual's decision to use a name other than the birth name—whether the decision rests on religious, marital, or other personal considerations—does not therefore imply intent to set aside the birth name, or the identity associated with that name.

While the issue of whether GMC's use of the name Lew Alcindor constituted an endorsement of its product is far from clear, we hold that GMC cannot rely on abandonment as a defense to Abdul–Jabbar's Lanham Act claim.

b) Lanham Act "fair use" doctrine

The district court cited the "fair use" defense, 15 U.S.C. § 1115(b)(4), as an alternative ground for dismissal of plaintiff's Lanham Act claim. We discussed this defense in *New Kids,* where we held that the use by two newspapers of the "New Kids" name to conduct phone-in polls measuring the group's popularity was a nominative or non-trademark "fair use" of the name not subject to protection under the Lanham Act. 971 F.2d at 306–09.

"Trademark law recognizes a defense where the mark is used only 'to describe the goods or services of [a] party, or their geographic origin.'" *Id.* at 306; (quoting 15 U.S.C. § 1115(b)(4)). We cited the example of a Volkswagen repair shop which used the name "Volkswagen" in the sign advertising its business. *Volkswagenwerk Aktiengesellschaft v. Church,* 411 F.2d 350, 352 (9th Cir. 1969). There, we had recognized that it " 'would be difficult, if not impossible, ... to avoid altogether the use of the word "Volkswagen" or its abbreviation "VW" ... [to] signify appellant's cars.' ... Therefore, his use of the Volkswagen trademark was not an infringing use." 971 F.2d at 307 (quoting *Volkswagenwerk Aktiengesellschaft v. Church,* 411 F.2d 350, 352 (9th Cir. 1969)).

We explained that "cases like these are best understood as involving a non-trademark use of a mark—a use to which the infringement laws simply do not apply." *Id.*

[W]e may generalize a class of cases where the use of the trademark does not attempt to capitalize on consumer confusion or to appropriate the cachet of one product for a different one. Such *nominative use* of a mark—where the only word reasonably available to describe a particular thing is pressed into service—lies outside the strictures of trademark law: Because it does not implicate the source-identification function that is the purpose of the trademark, it does not constitute unfair competition; such use is fair because it does not imply sponsorship or endorsement by the trademark holder. 971 F.2d at 307–08.

New Kids was not the classic fair use case because the New Kids trademark was being used not to describe the defendant's own product (newspapers), but to describe the plaintiff's product (rock band). *Id.* at 308. However, we held that in such cases, a commercial user is nevertheless entitled to the nominative fair use defense if it meets three requirements:

> First, the product or service in question must be one not readily identifiable without use of the trademark; second, only so much of the mark or marks may be used as is reasonably necessary to identify the product or service; and third, the user must do nothing that would, in conjunction with the mark, suggest sponsorship or endorsement by the trademark holder. *Id.* (footnotes omitted). Because 1) the New Kids rock band could not be referenced without using its name; and 2) the newspapers used the name only to the extent necessary to identify them; and 3) nothing in the newspaper announcements implied sponsorship or endorsement by the New Kids, we held that the papers were entitled to the nominative fair use defense.

Id. at 308–10.

The district court here found that GMC met the three *New Kids* requirements as a matter of law. We conclude, however, that there was a genuine issue of fact as to the third requirement, implied endorsement or sponsorship. Like the newspapers in *New Kids*, General Motors could not refer to plaintiff without using his name, and it used no more than was necessary to refer to him. Also, analogously to the newspapers in *New Kids* asking their readers which New Kid was the best, sexiest, etc., the defendant was selling something, newspapers or cars, different from the product the plaintiff was selling, and their products could not be confused.

The distinction between this case and *New Kids* is that use of celebrity endorsements in television commercials is so well established by commercial custom that a jury might find an implied endorsement in General Motors' use of the celebrity's name in a commercial, which would not inhere in a newspaper poll. Newspapers and magazines commonly use celebrities' names and photographs without making endorsement contracts, so the public does not infer an endorsement agreement from the use. Many people may assume that when a celebrity's name is used in a television commercial, the celebrity endorses the product advertised. Likelihood of confusion as to endorsement is therefore a question for the jury. *White v. Samsung Elec. Am., Inc.*, 971 F.2d 1395, 1400–01 (9th Cir. 1992) (holding that use of a robot dressed and posed like Vanna White next to a "Wheel of Fortune" set raised sufficient question of fact as to endorsement under the Lanham Act to preclude summary judgment), *cert. denied,* 508 U.S. 951 (1993).

Had GMC limited itself to the "trivia" portion of its ad, GMC could likely defend the reference to Lew Alcindor as a nominative fair use. But by using Alcindor's record to make a claim for its car—like the basketball star, the Olds 88 won an "award" three years in a row, and like the star, the car is a "champ" and a "first round pick"—GMC has arguably attempted to "appropriate the cachet of one product for another," if not also to "capitalize on consumer confusion." *New Kids,* 971 F.2d at 308. We therefore hold that there is a question of fact as to whether GMC is entitled to a fair use defense.

c) Abdul-Jabbar's Lanham Act claim

In considering celebrities' claims of violation under the Lanham Act, we have considered the following factors to determine whether a plaintiff has raised a genuine issue of material fact as to likelihood of confusion over endorsement: "(1) strength of the plaintiff's mark; (2) relatedness of the goods; (3) similarity of the marks; (4) evidence of actual confusion; (5) marketing channels used; (6) likely degree of purchaser care; (7) defendant's intent in selecting the mark." *White,* 971 F.2d at 1400.

The parties dispute the applicability of the factors. GMC concedes that the fifth factor, marketing channels, favors Abdul–Jabbar, but contests the rest. Because a jury could reasonably conclude that most of the factors weigh in plaintiff's favor, we hold that the question of whether Abdul–Jabbar's Lanham Act claim should succeed is a question for the jury.

II

State law claims: Common Law and Statutory Rights of Privacy

"California has long recognized a common law right of privacy ... [which includes protection against] appropriation, for the defendant's advantage, of the plaintiff's name or likeness." *Eastwood v. Superior Court for Los Angeles County,* 149 Cal. App. 3d 409 (Cal. App. 1983) (citations omitted). The right to be protected against such appropriations is also referred to as the "right of publicity," 198 Cal. Rptr. at 347.

The so-called right of publicity means in essence that the reaction of the public to name and likeness, which may be fortuitous or which may be managed and planned, endows the name and likeness of the person involved with commercially exploitable opportunities. The protection of name and likeness from unwarranted intrusion or exploitation is the heart of the law of privacy. *Lugosi v. Universal Pictures,* 603 P.2d 425, 431 (Cal. 1979).

As set out in *Eastwood,* a common law cause of action for appropriation of name or likeness may be pleaded by alleging "(1) the defendant's use of plaintiff's identity; (2) the appropriation of plaintiff's name or likeness to defendant's advantage, commercially or otherwise; (3) lack of consent; and (4) resulting injury." 198 Cal. Rptr. at 347.

We recently clarified in *White* that "the 'name or likeness' formulation referred to in *Eastwood* originated not as an element of the right of publicity cause of action, but as a description of the types of cases in which the cause of action had been recognized." 971 F.2d at 1397. Accordingly, we held that California's common law "right of publicity is not limited to the appropriation of name or likeness." *Id.* at 1398. The key issue is appropriation of the plaintiff's *identity.*

It is not important *how* the defendant has appropriated the plaintiff's identity, but *whether* the defendant has done so.... A rule which says that the right of publicity can be infringed only through the use of nine different methods of appropriating identity merely challenges the clever advertising strategist to come up with the tenth. *Id.* (internal citations omitted).

California's common law cause of action is complemented legislatively by Civil Code section 3344. As the *Eastwood* court explained, the statute is best understood as "complementing," rather than enacting, the common law cause of action, because the two are not identical. 198 Cal. Rptr. at 346. Section 3344(a) provides in pertinent part: Any person who knowingly uses another's name, voice, signature, photograph, or likeness, in any manner, on or in products, merchandise, or goods, or for purchases of advertising or selling, or soliciting purchases of, products, merchandise, goods or services, without such person's prior consent ... shall be liable for any damages sustained by the person ... injured as a result thereof. Cal. Civil Code § 3344(a) (1971).

In addition to the common law elements, the statute requires two further allegations: 1) knowing use; and 2) a "direct connection ... between the use and the commercial purpose." 198 Cal. Rptr. at 347 (quotations omitted). Furthermore, unlike the common law cause of action, section 3344 is apparently limited to commercial appropriations. As the *Eastwood* court pointed out, however, "California law has not imposed any requirement that the unauthorized use or publication of a person's name or picture be suggestive of an endorsement or association with the injured person." *Id.* at 347. This caveat apparently applies to both the common law and statutory causes of action. *See id.* at 348 ("the appearance of an 'endorsement' is not the *sine qua non* of a claim for commercial appropriation.").

We have construed the statute's protection of "name, voice, signature, photograph, or likeness" more narrowly than the common law's protection of "identity." *See, e.g., White,* 971 F.2d at 1397 (holding plaintiff stated a cause of action under common law but not under section 3344 where likeness in question was robot impersonating celebrity); *Midler v. Ford Motor Co.,* 849 F.2d 460, 463 (9th Cir. 1988) (holding common law but not statutory cause of action applicable to appropriation of singer's voice by voice-impersonator).

The district court ruled that GMC was entitled to summary judgment on both the statutory and common law causes of action. The court reasoned that section 3344 did not apply because: 1) Abdul–Jabbar had abandoned his former name; and 2) GMC did not "use" plaintiff's name because Abdul–Jabbar "did not [at the time of the ad] and does not have the name used." While the court found that GMC knowingly used the name Lew Alcindor for commercial purposes without obtaining plaintiff's consent, it concluded that GMC had not used *plaintiff's* name because he no longer bore that name.

The district court found that Abdul–Jabbar abandoned the name Lew Alcindor when he legally recorded his present name in 1971. The court acknowledged that "we have no case law in California that abandonment is a defense [to § 3344], but as I would construe the law, it surely must be." The court further found, "regardless of abandonment," that because Abdul–Jabbar no longer uses the name Lew Alcindor, "there has been no use of plaintiff's name." Extrapolating from our holdings in *White* and *Midler* that, under section 3344, "use must be of actual voice or actual likeness," the court concluded that "the actual name must be used in a name case, and . . . our case does not involve the use of plaintiff's actual name."

The court dismissed the common law cause of action on similar grounds. The court referred to and distinguished *Carson v. Here's Johnny Portable Toilets, Inc.*, 698 F.2d 831 (6th Cir. 1983) (holding distributor's use of the phrase "Here's Johnny" actionable under Michigan common law, *see id.* at 837) and *Ali v. Playgirl, Inc.*, 447 F.Supp. 723 (S.D.N.Y. 1978) (holding magazine's publication of drawing of nude black man labeled "the greatest" entitled plaintiff to preliminary injunctive relief for violations of New York statutory and common law right of publicity, *see id.* at 728), on the grounds that "one cannot say that Lew Alcindor equals Kareem Abdul–Jabbar in anywhere near the same sense that 'Here's Johnny' equals Johnny Carson . . . or the way 'the greatest' equaled Mohammed Ali, when [those cases were] tried." The court described the "essence" of the holdings in *Carson* and *Ali* to be "that the sobriquet or nickname must be in the most common present use so that it clearly identifies the person seeking recovery" and opined without reviewing any of the California cases that "[*Carson* and *Ali*] might well come out the same under California common [law]."

We have frequently held that California's common law right of publicity protects celebrities from appropriations of their *identity* not strictly definable as "name or picture." *Motschenbacher v. R.J. Reynolds Tobacco Co.*, 498 F.2d 821, 827 (9th Cir. 1974) (use of famous race car driver's well-known race car in televised cigarette ad sufficed to constitute an appropriation of his identity); *Midler*, 849 F.2d at 463 (use of sound-alike voice in radio ad supported a cause of action under California's common law right of publicity, though not under section 3344); *Waits*, 978 F.2d at 1098 (same); *White*, 971 F.2d at 1397–99 (use of robot dressed and posed like Vanna White next to a "Wheel of Fortune" set sufficiently identified her to state a cause of action under California common, but not statutory, law).

Neither the cases cited by the district court, nor the cases listed above stand for the proposition that the reference must be "in common, present use" under the statute or under California common law. Rather, they stand for the proposition that "identity" is a more flexible proposition and thus more permissive than the statutory "laundry list" of particular means of appropriation. *White,* 971 F.2d at 1398; *see also Carson,* 698 F.2d at 835 ("All that is required [under Michigan's common law right of publicity] is that the name clearly identify the wronged person.").

The district court's "common, present use" analysis appears to be a variation on its abandonment theme (*e.g.,* Abdul–Jabbar can only sue for use of his present name, because he has abandoned his former name). Abdul–Jabbar argues that abandonment cannot be a defense to appropriation because the right of publicity protects not only a celebrity's "sole right to exploit" his identity, *White,* 971 F.2d at 1399, but also his decision not to use his name or identity for commercial purposes. *See, e.g., Waits,* 978 F.2d 1093 (applying right of publicity protection to singer with moral and aesthetic objections to advertising). We agree.

Abdul–Jabbar cites *Price v. Hal Roach Studios, Inc.,* 400 F.Supp. 836, 846 (S.D.N.Y. 1975), wherein the court dismissed as "nonsensical" defendants' argument that Laurel and Hardy's failure to use their caricatures and imitations between 1940 and 1954 constituted abandonment: "It cannot be possible for Laurel and Hardy to lose rights in their own names and likenesses through 'non-use.' " *Id.* at 846 (citing New York statutory law protecting persons from commercial exploitation by others and case) and *see id.* at n.15 (citing *Grant v. Esquire,* 367 F.Supp. 876, 880 (S.D.N.Y. 1973), for the proposition that nonuse of commercial value of name and likeness does not preclude against violation by others). We find this argument persuasive.

We hold that Abdul–Jabbar has alleged sufficient facts to state a claim under both California common law and section 3344. The statute's reference to "name or likeness" is not limited to present or current use. To the extent GMC's use of the plaintiff's birth name attracted television viewers' attention, GMC gained a commercial advantage. *See East-wood,* 198 Cal. Rptr. at 349 ("The first step toward selling a product or service is to attract the consumers' attention."). Whether or not Lew Alcindor "equals" Kareem Abdul–Jabbar in the sense that " 'Here's Johnny' equaled Johnny Carson," or " 'the greatest' equaled Mohammed Ali"—or the glamorously dressed robot equaled Vanna White—is a question for the jury. *See Waits,* 978 F.2d at 1102 (observing that a celebrity's renown is relative and "adequately reflected in the amount of damages recoverable").

As to injury, the district court opined that any "loss injury" was "de minimis," though it explicitly declined to rely on this in granting GMC summary judgment. *White* does not explicitly discuss injury, but notes that "the law protects the celebrity's sole right to exploit the value" of her fame. 971 F.2d at 1399. Abdul–Jabbar alleges, and submits evidence to show, that he was injured economically because the ad will make it difficult for him to endorse other automobiles, and emotionally because people may be led to believe he has abandoned his current name and assume he has renounced his religion. These allegations suffice to support his action. Injury to a plaintiff's right of publicity is not limited to present or future economic loss, but "may induce humiliation, embarrassment, and mental distress." *Waits,* 978 F.2d at 1103 (quotations omitted).

GMC makes a final argument that its use of the name Lew Alcindor was "incidental" and therefore not actionable, citing *Namath v. Sports Illustrated,* 363 N.Y.S.2d 276 (1975), for the proposition that "newsworthy" items are privileged under right of publicity laws. The district court correctly rejected this line of reasoning as irrelevant. The *Namath* court held that Sports Illustrated was entitled under the First Amendment to use its own news stories to promote sales of its magazine. 363 N.Y.S.2d at 279–80.

A recent California case, *Montana v. San Jose Mercury News, Inc.,* 34 Cal. App. 4th 790 (1995), reaches a similar conclusion. The California Court of Appeal denied football star Joe Montana's claim that a newspaper's use of his image, taken from its Super Bowl cover story and sold in poster form, violated his section 3344 and common law right of publicity, holding that: 1) the posters represented newsworthy events, and 2) a newspaper has a constitutional right to promote itself by reproducing its news stories. 40 Cal. Rptr. 2d at 641–42. As the court noted, section 3344(d) provides that no prior consent is required for use of a "name, voice, signature, photograph, or likeness in connection with any news, public affairs, or sports broadcast or account, or any political campaign." Cal. Civ. Code § 3344; *Montana,* 40 Cal. Rptr. 2d at 640.

While Lew Alcindor's basketball record may be said to be "newsworthy," its use is not automatically privileged. GMC used the information in the context of an automobile advertisement, not in a news or sports account. Hence GMC is not protected by section 3344(d).

For the reasons set out above, we reverse the judgment of the district court and remand for trial on the claims alleging violation of the California common law right of publicity and section 3344, as well as the claims alleging violation of the Lanham Act.

REVERSED and REMANDED.

Note

1. In *Chattanoga Mfg., Inc. v. Nike, Inc.,* 301 F.3d 789 (7th Cir. 2002), Chattanooga filed suit seeking damages and injunctive relief, alleging that Nike's use of the term "Jordan" constituted infringement and unfair competition under the Lanham Act. The appeals court concluded that the district court did not err in finding that Nike was prejudiced by an unreasonable delay in bringing the action and that Michael Jordan could not be held liable in his personal capacity.

ETW CORPORATION v. JIREH PUBLISHING, INC.

United States Court of Appeals, Sixth Circuit, 2003.
332 F.3d 915.

GRAHAM, District Judge.

Plaintiff–Appellant ETW Corporation ("ETW") is the licensing agent of Eldrick "Tiger" Woods ("Woods"), one of the world's most famous professional golfers. Woods, chairman of the board of ETW, has assigned to it the exclusive right to exploit his name, image, likeness, and signature, and all other publicity rights. ETW owns a United States trademark registration for the mark "TIGER WOODS" (Registration No. 2,194,381) for use in connection with "art prints, calendars, mounted photographs, notebooks, pencils, pens, posters, trading cards, and unmounted photographs."

Defendant–Appellee Jireh Publishing, Inc. ("Jireh") of Tuscaloosa, Alabama, is the publisher of artwork created by Rick Rush ("Rush"). Rush, who refers to himself as "America's sports artist," has created paintings of famous figures in sports and famous sports events. A few examples include Michael Jordan, Mark McGuire, Coach Paul "Bear" Bryant, the Pebble Beach Golf Tournament, and the America's Cup Yacht Race. Jireh has produced and successfully marketed limited edition art prints made from Rush's paintings.

In 1998, Rush created a painting entitled *The Masters of Augusta*, which commemorates Wood's victory at the Masters Tournament in Augusta, Georgia, in 1997. At that event, Woods became the youngest player ever to win the Masters Tournament, while setting a 72–hole record for the tournament and a record 12–stroke margin of victory. In the foreground of Rush's painting are three views of Woods in different poses. In the center, he is completing the swing of a golf club, and on each side he is crouching, lining up and/or observing the progress of a putt. To the left of Woods is his caddy, Mike "Fluff" Cowan, and to his right is his final round partner's caddy. Behind these figures is the Augusta National Clubhouse. In a blue background behind the clubhouse are likenesses of famous golfers of the past looking down on Woods. These include Arnold Palmer, Sam Snead, Ben Hogan, Walter Hagen, Bobby Jones, and Jack Nicklaus. Behind them is the Masters leader board.

The limited edition prints distributed by Jireh consist of an image of Rush's painting which includes Rush's signature at the bottom right hand corner. Beneath the image of the painting, in block letters, is its title, "The Masters Of Augusta." Beneath the title, in block letters of equal height, is the artist's name, "Rick Rush," and beneath the artist's name, in smaller upper and lower case letters, is the legend "Painting America Through Sports."

As sold by Jireh, the limited edition prints are enclosed in a white envelope, accompanied with literature which includes a large photograph of Rush, a description of his art, and a narrative description of the subject painting. On the front of the envelope, Rush's name appears in block letters inside a rectangle, which includes the legend "Painting America Through Sports." Along the bottom is a large reproduction of Rush's signature two inches high and ten inches long. On the back of the envelope, under the flap, are the words "Masters of Augusta" in letters that are three-eights of an inch high, and "Tiger Woods" in letters that are one-fourth of an inch high. Woods's name also appears in the narrative description of the painting where he is mentioned twice in twenty-eight lines of text. The text also includes references to the six other famous golfers depicted in the background of the painting as well as the two caddies. Jireh published and marketed two hundred and fifty 22 1/2 "x 30" serigraphs and five thousand 9" x 11" lithographs of *The Masters of Augusta* at an issuing price of $700 for the serigraphs and $100 for the lithographs.

ETW filed suit against Jireh on June 26, 1998, in the United States District Court for the Northern District of Ohio, alleging trademark infringement in violation of the Lanham Act, 15 U.S.C. § 1114; dilution of the mark under the Lanham Act, 15 U.S.C. § 1125(c); unfair competition and false advertising under the Lanham Act, 15 U.S.C. § 1125(a); unfair competition and deceptive trade practices under Ohio Revised Code § 4165.01; unfair competition and trademark infringement under Ohio common law; and violation of Woods's right of publicity under Ohio common law. Jireh counterclaimed, seeking a declaratory judgment that Rush's art prints are protected by the First Amendment and do not violate the Lanham Act. Both parties moved for summary judgment. The district court granted Jireh's motion for summary judgment and dismissed the case. *See ETW Corp. v. Jireh Pub., Inc.*, 99 F.Supp.2d 829 (N.D. Ohio 2000). ETW timely perfected an appeal to this court. * * *

II.

TRADEMARK CLAIMS BASED ON THE UNAUTHORIZED USE OF THE REGISTERED TRADEMARK "TIGER WOODS"

ETW claims that the prints of Rush's work constitute the unauthorized use of a registered trademark in violation of the Lanham Act, 15 U.S.C. § 1114, and Ohio law. Because trademark claims under Ohio law follow the same analysis as those under the Lanham Act, our discussion of the federal trademark claims will therefore encompass the state trademark claims as well. *Rock & Roll Hall of Fame & Museum, Inc. v. Gentile Prods.*, 134 F.3d 749, 754 (6th Cir. 1998) (citing *Daddy's Junky Music Stores, Inc. v. Big Daddy's Family Music Ctr.*, 109 F.3d 275, 288 (6th Cir. 1997)).

ETW claims that Jireh infringed the registered mark "Tiger Woods" by including these words in marketing materials which accompanied the prints of Rush's painting. The words "Tiger Woods" do not appear on the face of the prints, nor are they included in the title of the painting. The words "Tiger Woods" do appear under the flap of the envelopes which contain the prints, and Woods is mentioned twice in the narrative which accompanies the prints.

The Lanham Act provides a defense to an infringement claim where the use of the mark "is a use, otherwise than as a mark, ... which is descriptive of and used fairly and in good faith only to describe the goods ... of such party[.]" 15 U.S.C. § 1115(b)(4); *see San Francisco Arts and Athletics, Inc. v. U.S. Olympic Comm.*, 483 U.S. 522, 565 (1987); *Herman Miller, Inc. v. Palazzetti Imports and Exports, Inc.*, 270 F.3d 298, 319 (6th Cir. 2001) ("Under the doctrine of 'fair use,' the holder of a trademark *cannot* prevent others from using the word that forms the trademark in its *primary* or *descriptive* sense.") (emphasis in the original); *Car-Freshner Corp. v. S.C. Johnson & Son, Inc.*, 70 F.3d 267, 270 (2nd Cir. 1995) ("Fair use permits others to use a protected mark to describe aspects of their own goods[.]"). In evaluating a defendant's fair use defense, a court must consider whether defendant has used the mark: (1) in its descriptive sense; and (2) in good faith. *Victoria's Secret Stores v. Artco Equip. Co.,*, 194 F.Supp.2d 704, 724 (S.D. Ohio 2002); *see also Cairns v. Franklin Mint Co.*, 292 F.3d 1139, 1151 (9th Cir. 2002).

A celebrity's name may be used in the title of an artistic work so long as there is some artistic relevance. *See Rogers v. Grimaldi*, 875 F.2d 994, 997 (2nd Cir. 1989); *New York Racing Ass'n v. Perlmutter Publ'g, Inc.*, No. 95–CV–994, 1996 WL 465298 at *4 (N.D.N.Y. July 19, 1996) (finding the use of a registered mark on the title of a painting protected by the First Amendment). The use of Woods's name on the back of the envelope containing the print and in the narrative description of the print are purely descriptive and there is nothing to indicate that they were used other than in good faith. The prints, the envelopes which contain them, and the narrative materials which accompany them clearly identify Rush as the source of the print. Woods is mentioned only to describe the content of the print. * * *

III.

TRADEMARK CLAIMS UNDER 15 U.S.C. § 1125(A) BASED ON THE UNAUTHORIZED USE OF THE LIKENESS OF TIGER WOODS

Section 43(a) of the Lanham Act, 15 U.S.C. § 1125(a), provides "a right of action to persons engaged in interstate and foreign commerce, against deceptive and misleading use of words, names, symbols, or devices, or any combination thereof, which have been adopted by a ... merchant to identify his goods and distinguish them from those manufactured by others[.]" *Federal-Mogul–Bower Bearings, Inc. v. Azoff*, 313 F.2d 405, 408 (6th Cir. 1963); *see also Frisch's Restaurant, Inc. v. Shoney's, Inc.*, 759 F.2d 1261, 1264 (6th Cir. 1985); *Frisch's Restaurants, Inc. v. Elby's Big Boy of Steubenville, Inc.*, 670 F.2d 642, 647 (6th Cir.), *cert. denied*, 459 U.S. 916, 74 L. Ed. 2d 182, 103 S. Ct. 231 (1982).

ETW has registered Woods's name as a trademark, but it has not registered any image or likeness of Woods. Nevertheless, ETW claims to have trademark rights in Woods's image and likeness. Section 43 (a) of the Lanham Act provides a federal cause of action for infringement of an unregistered trademark which affords such marks essentially the same protection as those that are registered. *See Two Pesos, Inc. v. Taco Cabana, Inc.*, 505 U.S. 763, 768 (1992) ("It is common ground that § 43(a) protects qualifying unregistered trademarks and that the general principles qualifying a mark for registration under § 2 of the Lanham Act are for the most part applicable in determining whether an unregistered mark is entitled to protection under § 43(a).").

The Lanham Act defines a trademark as including "any word, name, symbol, or device, or any combination thereof" used by a person "to identify and distinguish his or her goods ... from those manufactured or sold by others and to indicate the source of the goods, even if that source is unknown." 15 U.S.C. § 1127. The essence of a trademark is a designation in the form of a distinguishing name, symbol or device which is used to identify a person's goods and distinguish them from the goods of another. *See Taco Cabana*, 505 U.S. at 768 ("In order to be [protected], a mark must be capable of distinguishing the [owner's] goods from those of others."). Not every word, name, symbol or device qualifies as a protectable mark; rather, it must be proven that it performs the job of identification, *i.e.*, to identify one source and to distinguish it from other sources. If it does not do this, then it is not protectable as a trademark. *See* J. Thomas McCarthy, McCarthy on Trademarks and Unfair Competition, § 3:1 (2002).

"[A] trademark, unlike a copyright or patent, is not a 'right in gross' that enables a holder to enjoin all reproductions." *Boston Athletic Ass'n v. Sullivan*, 867 F.2d 22, 35 (1st Cir. 1989) (citing *Univ. of Notre Dame du Lac v. J.C. Gourmet Food Imports Co.*, 703 F.2d 1372, 1374 (Fed. Cir. 1983)).

Here, ETW claims protection under the Lanham Act for any and all images of Tiger Woods. This is an untenable claim. ETW asks us, in effect, to constitute Woods himself as a walking, talking trademark. Images and likenesses of Woods are not protectable as a trademark because they do not perform the trademark function of designation. They do not distinguish and identify the source of goods. They cannot function as a trademark because there are undoubtedly thousands of images and likenesses of Woods taken by countless photographers, and drawn, sketched, or painted by numerous artists, which have been published in many forms of media, and sold and distributed throughout the world. No reasonable person could believe that merely because these photographs or paintings contain Woods's likeness or image, they all originated with Woods.

We hold that, as a general rule, a person's image or likeness cannot function as a trademark. Our conclusion is supported by the decisions of other courts which have addressed this issue. In *Pirone v. MacMillan, Inc.*, 894 F.2d 579 (2nd Cir. 1990), the Second Circuit rejected a trademark claim asserted by the daughters of baseball legend Babe Ruth. The plaintiffs objected to the use of Ruth's likeness in three photographs which appeared in a calendar published by the defendant. The court rejected their claim, holding that "a photograph of a human being, unlike a portrait of a fanciful cartoon character, is not inherently 'distinctive' in the trademark sense of tending to indicate origin." *Id.* at 583. The court noted that Ruth "was one of the most photographed men of his generation, a larger than life hero to millions and an historical figure[.]" *Id.* The Second Circuit Court concluded that a consumer could not reasonably believe that Ruth sponsored the calendar: An ordinarily prudent purchaser would have no difficulty discerning that these photos are merely the subject matter of the calendar and do not in any way indicate sponsorship. No reasonable jury could find a likelihood of confusion. *Id.* at 585. The court observed that "under some circumstances, a photograph of a person may be a valid trademark—if, for example, a particular photograph was consistently used on specific goods." *Id.* at 583. The court rejected plaintiffs' assertion of trademark rights in every photograph of Ruth * * *

Here, ETW does not claim that a particular photograph of Woods has been consistently used on specific goods. Instead, ETW's claim is identical to that of the plaintiffs in *Pirone*, a sweeping claim to trademark rights in every photograph and image of Woods. Woods, like Ruth, is one of the most photographed sports figures of his generation, but this alone does not suffice to create a trademark claim. * * *

IV.

Lanham Act Unfair Competition and False Endorsement Claims, Ohio Right to Privacy Claims, and the First Amendment Defense

[Parts A, B, & C omitted.] * * *

D.   *Right of Publicity Claim*

ETW claims that Jireh's publication and marketing of prints of Rush's painting violates Woods's right of publicity. The right of publicity is an intellectual property right of recent origin which has been defined as the inherent right of every human being to control the commercial use of his or her identity. *See* McCarthy on Publicity and Privacy, § 1:3. The right of publicity is a creature of state law and its violation gives rise to a cause of action for the commercial tort of unfair competition. *Id.*

The right of publicity is, somewhat paradoxically, an outgrowth of the right of privacy. *See* McCarthy on Publicity and Privacy, § 1:4. A cause of action for violation of the right was first recognized in *Haelan Laboratories, Inc. v. Topps Chewing Gum, Inc.*, 202 F.2d 866 (2nd Cir. 1953), where the Second Circuit held that New York's common law protected a baseball player's right in the publicity value of his photograph, and in the process coined the phrase "right of publicity" as the name of this right.

The Ohio Supreme Court recognized the right of publicity in 1976 in *Zacchini v. Scripps–Howard Broadcasting Co.*, 351 N.E.2d 454 (1976). In *Zacchini*, which involved the videotaping and subsequent rebroadcast on a television news program of plaintiff's human cannonball act, the Ohio Supreme Court held that Zacchini's right of publicity was trumped by the First Amendment. On appeal, the Supreme Court of the United States reversed, holding that the First Amendment did not insulate defendant from liability for violating Zacchini's state law right of publicity where defendant published the plaintiff's entire act. *See Zacchini v. Scripps–Howard Broadcasting Co.*, 433 U.S. 562 (1977). *Zacchini* is the only United States Supreme Court decision on the right of publicity.

* * *

When the Ohio Supreme Court recognized the right of publicity, it relied heavily on the Restatement (Second) of Torts, § 652. *See Zacchini*, 47 Ohio St. 2d at 230. The court quoted the entire text of § 652(c) of the Restatement, as well as comments a., b., c. and d. The Restatement originally treated the right of publicity as a branch of the right of privacy and included it in a chapter entitled "Invasion of Privacy." In 1995, the American Law Institute transferred its exposition of the right of publicity to the Restatement (Third) of Unfair Competition, Chapter 4, § 46, in a chapter entitled "Appropriation of Trade Values." The current version of the Restatement (Third) of Unfair Competition defines the right of publicity as follows: Appropriation of the Commercial Value of a Person's Identity: The Right of Publicity.

One who appropriates the commercial value of a person's identity by using without consent the person's name, likeness, or other indicia of identity for purposes of trade is subject to liability for the relief appropriate under the rules stated in §§ 48 and 49. *Id.*

In § 46, Comment c, *Rationale for Protection*, the authors of the Restatement suggest that courts may justifiably be reluctant to adopt a broad construction of the right. The rationales underlying recognition of a right of publicity are generally less compelling than those that justify rights in trademarks or trade secrets. The commercial value of a person's identity often results from success in endeavors such as entertainment or sports that offer their own substantial rewards. Any additional incentive attributable to the right of publicity may have only marginal significance. In other cases the commercial value acquired by a person's identity is largely fortuitous or otherwise unrelated to any investment made by the individual, thus diminishing the weight of the property and unjust enrichment rationales for protection. In addition, the public interest in avoiding false suggestions of endorsement or sponsorship can be pursued through the cause of action for deceptive marketing. Thus, courts may be properly reluctant to adopt a broad construction of the publicity right. See § 47.

In § 47, Comment c, the authors of the Restatement note, "The right of publicity as recognized by statute and common law is fundamentally constrained by the public and constitutional interest in freedom of expression." In the same comment, the authors state that "the use of a person's identity primarily for the purpose of communicating information or expressing ideas is not generally actionable as a violation of the person's right of publicity." Various examples are given, including the use of the person's name or likeness in news reporting in newspapers and magazines. The Restatement recognizes that this limitation on the right is not confined to news reporting but extends to use in "entertainment and other creative works, including both fiction and non-fiction." *Id.* The authors list examples of protected uses of a celebrity's identity, likeness or image, including unauthorized print or broadcast biographies and novels, plays or motion pictures. *Id.* According to the Restatement, such uses are not protected, however, if the name or likeness is used solely to attract attention to a work that is not related to the identified person, and the privilege may be lost if the work contains substantial falsifications. *Id.*

We believe the courts of Ohio would follow the principles of the Restatement in defining the limits of the right of publicity. The Ohio Supreme Court's decision in *Zacchini* suggests that Ohio is inclined to give substantial weight to the public interest in freedom of expression when balancing it against the personal and proprietary interests recognized by the right of publicity. This suggestion is reinforced by the decision in *Vinci.* * * *

We conclude that in deciding whether the sale of Rush's prints violate Woods's right of publicity; we will look to the Ohio case law and the Restatement (Third) of Unfair Competition. In deciding where the line should be drawn between Woods's intellectual property rights and the First Amendment, we find ourselves in agreement with the dissenting judges in *White*, the Tenth Circuit's decision in *Cardtoons*, and the Ninth Circuit's decision in *Hoffman*, and we will follow them in determining whether Rush's work is protected by the First Amendment. Finally, we believe that the transformative elements test adopted by the Supreme Court of California in *Comedy III Productions*, will assist us in determining where the proper balance lies between the First Amendment and Woods's intellectual property rights. We turn now to a further examination of Rush's work and its subject.

E.   Application of the Law to the Evidence in this Case

The evidence in the record reveals that Rush's work consists of much more than a mere literal likeness of Woods. It is a panorama of Woods's victory at the 1997 Masters Tournament, with all of the trappings of that tournament in full view, including the Augusta clubhouse, the leader board, images of Woods's caddy, and his final round partner's caddy. These elements in themselves are sufficient to bring Rush's work within the protection of the First Amendment. The Masters Tournament is probably the world's most famous golf tournament and Woods's victory in the 1997 tournament was a historic event in the world of sports. A piece of art that portrays a historic sporting event communicates and celebrates the value our culture attaches to such events. It would be ironic indeed if the presence of the image of the victorious athlete would deny the work First Amendment protection. Furthermore, Rush's work includes not only images of Woods and the two caddies, but also carefully crafted likenesses of six past winners of the Masters Tournament: Arnold Palmer, Sam Snead, Ben Hogan, Walter Hagen, Bobby Jones, and Jack Nicklaus, a veritable pantheon of golf's greats. Rush's work conveys the message that Woods himself will someday join that revered group.

Turning first to ETW's Lanham Act false endorsement claim, we agree with the courts that hold that the Lanham Act should be applied, to artistic works only where the public interest in avoiding confusion outweighs the public interest in free expression. The *Rogers* test is helpful in striking that balance in the instant case. We find that the presence of Woods's image in Rush's painting *The Masters Of Augusta* does have artistic relevance to the underlying work and that it does not explicitly mislead as to the source of the work. We believe that the principles followed in *Cardtoons*, *Hoffman* and *Comedy III* are also relevant in determining whether the Lanham Act applies to Rush's work, and we find that it does not.

We find, like the court in *Rogers*, that plaintiff's survey evidence, even if its validity is assumed, indicates at most that some members of the public would draw the incorrect inference that Woods had some connection with Rush's print. The risk of misunderstanding, not engendered by any explicit indication on the face of the print, is so outweighed by the interest in artistic expression as to preclude application of the Act. We disagree with the dissent's suggestion that a jury must decide where the balance should be struck and where the boundaries should be drawn between the rights conferred by the Lanham Act and the protections of the First Amendment.

In regard to the Ohio law right of publicity claim, we conclude that Ohio would construe its right of publicity as suggested in the Restatement (Third) of Unfair Competition, Chapter 4, Section 47, Comment d., which articulates a rule analogous to the rule of fair use in copyright law. Under this rule, the substantiality and market effect of the use of the celebrity's image is analyzed in light of the informational and creative content of the defendant's use. Applying this rule, we conclude that Rush's work has substantial informational and creative content which outweighs any adverse effect on ETW's market and that Rush's work does not violate Woods's right of publicity.

We further find that Rush's work is expression which is entitled to the full protection of the First Amendment and not the more limited protection afforded to commercial speech. When we balance the magnitude of the speech restriction against the interest in protecting Woods's intellectual property right, we encounter precisely the same considerations weighed by the Tenth Circuit in *Cardtoons*. These include consideration of the fact that through their pervasive presence in the media, sports and entertainment celebrities have come to symbolize certain ideas and values in our society and have become a valuable means of expression in our culture. As the Tenth Circuit observed "celebrities . . .

are an important element of the shared communicative resources of our cultural domain." *Cardtoons*, 95 F.3d at 972.

In balancing these interests against Woods's right of publicity, we note that Woods, like most sports and entertainment celebrities with commercially valuable identities, engages in an activity, professional golf, that in itself generates a significant amount of income which is unrelated to his right of publicity. Even in the absence of his right of publicity, he would still be able to reap substantial financial rewards from authorized appearances and endorsements. It is not at all clear that the appearance of Woods's likeness in artwork prints which display one of his major achievements will reduce the commercial value of his likeness.

While the right of publicity allows celebrities like Woods to enjoy the fruits of their labors, here Rush has added a significant creative component of his own to Woods's identity. Permitting Woods's right of publicity to trump Rush's right of freedom of expression would extinguish Rush's right to profit from his creative enterprise.

After balancing the societal and personal interests embodied in the First Amendment against Woods's property rights, we conclude that the effect of limiting Woods's right of publicity in this case is negligible and significantly outweighed by society's interest in freedom of artistic expression.

Finally, applying the transformative effects test adopted by the Supreme Court of California in *Comedy III*, we find that Rush's work does contain significant transformative elements which make it especially worthy of First Amendment protection and also less likely to interfere with the economic interest protected by Woods' right of publicity. Unlike the unadorned, nearly photographic reproduction of the faces of The Three Stooges in *Comedy III*, Rush's work does not capitalize solely on a literal depiction of Woods. Rather, Rush's work consists of a collage of images in addition to Woods's image which are combined to describe, in artistic form, a historic event in sports history and to convey a message about the significance of Woods's achievement in that event. Because Rush's work has substantial transformative elements, it is entitled to the full protection of the First Amendment. In this case, we find that Woods's right of publicity must yield to the First Amendment.

V.

CONCLUSION

In accordance with the foregoing, the judgment of the District Court granting summary judgment to Jireh Publishing is affirmed.

Notes

1. In *Comedy III Productions, Inc. v. Gary Saderup, Inc.*, 25 Cal.4th 387, 106 Cal.Rptr.2d 126, 21 P.3d 797 (2001), the registered owner of all rights in former three-man comedy act sought damages and lithographs and T-shirts bearing a likeness of comedy act reproduced from charcoal drawing.

The California Supreme Court held that when an artist is faced with a right of publicity challenge to his or her work, he or she may raise as affirmative defense that the work is protected by the First Amendment inasmuch as it contains significant transformative elements or that the value of the work does not derive primarily from the celebrity's fame." *Id.*

2. National Basketball Association player Yao Ming sued Coca–Cola's Chinese subsidiary, accusing it of using his picture without permission on commemorative bottles sold in his hometown of Shanghai. Coke says it has the right to show groups of at least three members of the Chinese national team under a sponsorship agreement. Yao also requested an apology published in Chinese media and compensation of 1 Yuan (12 cents) for "spiritual and economic losses," . . . http://www.cbsnews.com/stories/2003/05/27/entertainment/main555582.shtml

C. TELEVISION CELEBRITIES

The Vanna White case expands the right of publicity beyond the previous limits of name and likeness. Even though it has been discussed in the cases above, the opinion that follows is the case that caused the revolutionary expansion of the right of privacy.

WHITE v. SAMSUNG ELECTRONICS AMERICA, INC.

United States Court of Appeals, Ninth Circuit, 1992.
971 F.2d 1395.

GOODWIN, Senior Circuit Judge.

This case involves a promotional "fame and fortune" dispute. In running a particular advertisement without Vanna White's permission, defendants Samsung Electronics America, Inc. (Samsung) and David Deutsch Associates, Inc. (Deutsch) attempted to capitalize on White's fame to enhance their fortune. White sued, alleging infringement of various intellectual property rights, but the district court granted summary judgment in favor of the defendants. We affirm in part, reverse in part, and remand.

Plaintiff Vanna White is the hostess of "Wheel of Fortune," one of the most popular game shows in television history. An estimated forty million people watch the program daily. Capitalizing on the fame which her participation in the show has bestowed on her, White markets her identity to various advertisers.

The dispute in this case arose out of a series of advertisements prepared for Samsung by Deutsch. The series ran in at least half a dozen publications with widespread, and in some cases national, circulation. Each of the advertisements in the series followed the same theme. Each depicted a current item from popular culture and a Samsung electronic product. Each was set in the twenty-first century and conveyed the message that the Samsung product would still be in use by that time. By hypothesizing outrageous future outcomes for the cultural items, the ads created humorous effects. For example, one lampooned current popular notions of an unhealthy diet by depicting a raw steak with the caption: "Revealed to be health food. 2010 A.D." Another depicted irreverent "news"-show host Morton Downey Jr. in front of an American flag with the caption: "Presidential candidate. 2008 A.D."

The advertisement which prompted the current dispute was for Samsung video-cassette recorders (VCRs). The ad depicted a robot, dressed in a wig, gown, and jewelry which Deutsch consciously selected to resemble White's hair and dress. The robot was posed next to a game board which is instantly recognizable as the Wheel of Fortune game show set, in a stance for which White is famous. The caption of the ad read: "Longest-running game show. 2012 A.D." Defendants referred to the ad as the "Vanna White" ad. Unlike the other celebrities used in the campaign, White neither consented to the ads nor was she paid.

Following the circulation of the robot ad, White sued Samsung and Deutsch in federal district court under: (1) California Civil Code § 3344; (2) the California common law right of publicity; and (3) § 43(a) of the Lanham Act, 15 U.S.C. § 1125(a). The district court granted summary judgment against White on each of her claims. White now appeals.

I.

SECTION 3344

White first argues that the district court erred in rejecting her claim under section 3344. Section 3344(a) provides, in pertinent part, that "any person who knowingly uses another's name, voice, signature, photograph, or likeness, in any manner, . . . for purposes of advertising or selling, . . . without such person's prior consent . . . shall be liable for any damages sustained by the person or persons injured as a result thereof."

White argues that the Samsung advertisement used her "likeness" in contravention of section 3344. In *Midler v. Ford Motor Co.*, 849 F.2d 460 (9th Cir. 1988), this court rejected Bette Midler's section 3344 claim concerning a Ford television commercial in which a Midler "sound-alike" sang a song which Midler had made famous. In rejecting Midler's claim, this court noted that "the defendants did not use Midler's name or anything else whose use is prohibited by the statute. The voice they used was [another person's], not hers. The term 'likeness' refers to a visual image not a vocal imitation." *Id.* at 463.

In this case, Samsung and Deutsch used a robot with mechanical features, and not, for example, a manikin molded to White's precise features. Without deciding for all purposes when a caricature or impressionistic resemblance might become a "likeness," we agree with the district court that the robot at issue here was not White's "likeness" within the meaning of section 3344. Accordingly, we affirm the court's dismissal of White's section 3344 claim.

II.

Right of Publicity

White next argues that the district court erred in granting summary judgment to defendants on White's common law right of publicity claim. In *Eastwood v. Superior Court,* 149 Cal. App. 3d 409 (1983), the California court of appeal stated that the common law right of publicity cause of action "may be pleaded by alleging (1) the defendant's use of the plaintiff's identity; (2) the appropriation of plaintiff's name or likeness to defendant's advantage, commercially or otherwise; (3) lack of consent; and (4) resulting injury." *Id.* at 417 (citing Prosser, Law of Torts (4th ed. 1971) § 117, pp. 804–807). The district court dismissed White's claim for failure to satisfy *Eastwood*'s second prong, reasoning that defendants had not appropriated White's "name or likeness" with their robot ad. We agree that the robot ad did not make use of White's name or likeness. However, the common law right of publicity is not so confined.

The *Eastwood* court did not hold that the right of publicity cause of action could be pleaded only by alleging an appropriation of name or likeness. *Eastwood* involved an unauthorized use of photographs of Clint Eastwood and of his name. Accordingly, the *Eastwood* court had no occasion to consider the extent beyond the use of name or likeness to which the right of publicity reaches. That court held only that the right of publicity cause of action "may be" pleaded by alleging, *inter alia,* appropriation of name or likeness, not that the action may be pleaded *only* in those terms.

The "name or likeness" formulation referred to in *Eastwood* originated not as an element of the right of publicity cause of action, but as a description of the types of cases in which the cause of action had been recognized. The source of this formulation is Prosser, *Privacy,* 48 Cal. L. Rev. 383, 401–07 (1960), one of the earliest and most enduring articulations of the common law right of publicity cause of action. In looking at the case law to that point, Prosser recognized that right of publicity cases involved one of two basic factual scenarios: name appropriation, and picture or other likeness appropriation. *Id.* at 401–02, nn.156–57.

Even though Prosser focused on appropriations of name or likeness in discussing the right of publicity, he noted that "it is not impossible that there might be appropriation of the plaintiff's identity, as by impersonation, without the use of either his name or his likeness, and that this would be an invasion of his right of privacy." *Id.* at 401. At the time Prosser wrote, he noted however, that "no such case appears to have arisen." *Id.*

Since Prosser's early formulation, the case law has borne out his insight that the right of publicity is not limited to the appropriation of name or likeness. In *Motschenbacher v. R.J. Reynolds Tobacco Co.,* 498 F.2d 821 (9th Cir. 1974), the defendant had used a photograph of the plaintiff's race car in a television commercial. Although the plaintiff appeared driving the car in the photograph, his features were not visible.

Even though the defendant had not appropriated the plaintiff's name or likeness, this court held that plaintiff's California right of publicity claim should reach the jury.

In *Midler,* this court held that, even though the defendants had not used Midler's name or likeness, Midler had stated a claim for violation of her California common law right of publicity because "the defendants . . . for their own profit in selling their product did appropriate part of her identity" by using a Midler sound-alike. *Id.* at 463–64.

In *Carson v. Here's Johnny Portable Toilets, Inc.,* 698 F.2d 831 (6th Cir. 1983), the defendant had marketed portable toilets under the brand name "Here's Johnny"—Johnny Carson's signature "Tonight Show" introduction—without Carson's permission. The district court had dismissed Carson's Michigan common law right of publicity claim because the defendants had not used Carson's "name or likeness." *Id.* at 835. In reversing the district court, the sixth circuit found "the district court's conception of the right of publicity . . . too narrow" and held that the right was implicated because the defendant had appropriated Carson's identity by using, *inter alia,* the phrase "Here's Johnny." *Id.* at 835–37.

These cases teach not only that the common law right of publicity reaches means of appropriation other than name or likeness, but that the specific means of appropriation are relevant only for determining whether the defendant has in fact appropriated the plaintiff's identity. The right of publicity does not require that appropriations of identity be accomplished through particular means to be actionable. It is noteworthy that the *Midler* and *Carson* defendants not only avoided using the plaintiff's name or likeness, but they also avoided appropriating the celebrity's voice, signature, and photograph. The photograph in *Motschenbacher* did include the plaintiff, but because the plaintiff was not visible the driver could have been an actor or dummy and the analysis in the case would have been the same.

Although the defendants in these cases avoided the most obvious means of appropriating the plaintiffs' identities, each of their actions directly implicated the commercial interests which the right of publicity is designed to protect. As the *Carson* court explained: [t]he right of publicity has developed to protect the commercial interest of celebrities in their identities. The theory of the right is that a celebrity's identity can be valuable in the promotion of products, and the celebrity has an interest that may be protected from the unauthorized commercial exploitation of that identity. . . . If the celebrity's identity is commercially exploited, there has been an invasion of his right whether or not his "name or likeness" is used. *Carson,* 698 F.2d at 835.

It is not important *how* the defendant has appropriated the plaintiff's identity, but *whether* the defendant has done so. *Motschenbacher, Midler,* and *Carson* teach the impossibility of treating the right of publicity as guarding only against a laundry list of specific means of appropriating identity. A rule which says that the right of publicity can be infringed only through the use of nine different methods of appropriating identity merely challenges the clever advertising strategist to come up with the tenth.

Indeed, if we treated the means of appropriation as dispositive in our analysis of the right of publicity, we would not only weaken the right but effectively eviscerate it. The right would fail to protect those plaintiffs most in need of its protection. Advertisers use celebrities to promote their products. The more popular the celebrity, the greater the number of people who recognize her, and the greater the visibility for the product. The identities of the most popular celebrities are not only the most attractive for advertisers, but also the easiest to evoke without resorting to obvious means such as name, likeness, or voice.

Consider a hypothetical advertisement which depicts a mechanical robot with male features, an African–American complexion, and a bald head. The robot is wearing black hightop Air Jordan basketball sneakers, and a red basketball uniform with black trim, baggy shorts, and the number 23 (though not revealing "Bulls" or "Jordan" lettering). The ad depicts the robot dunking a basketball one-handed, stiff-armed, legs extended like open scissors, and tongue hanging out. Now envision that this ad is run on television during professional basketball games. Considered individually, the robot's physical attributes, its dress, and its stance tell us little. Taken together, they lead to the only conclusion that any sports viewer who has registered a discernible pulse in the past five years would reach: the ad is about Michael Jordan.

Viewed separately, the individual aspects of the advertisement in the present case say little. Viewed together, they leave little doubt about the celebrity the ad is meant to depict. The female-shaped robot is wearing a long gown, blond wig, and large jewelry. Vanna White dresses exactly like this at times, but so do many other women. The robot is in the process of turning a block letter on a game-board. Vanna White dresses like this while turning letters on a game-board but perhaps similarly attired Scrabble-playing women do this as well. The robot is standing on what looks to be the Wheel of Fortune game show set. Vanna White dresses like this, turns letters, and does this on the Wheel of Fortune game show. She is the only one. Indeed, defendants themselves referred to their ad as the "Vanna White" ad. We are not surprised.

Television and other media create marketable celebrity identity value. Considerable energy and ingenuity are expended by those who have achieved celebrity value to exploit it for profit. The law protects the celebrity's sole right to exploit this value whether the celebrity has achieved her fame out of rare ability, dumb luck, or a combination thereof. We decline Samsung and Deutch's invitation to permit the evisceration of the common law right of publicity through means as facile as those in this case. Because White has alleged facts showing that Samsung and Deutsch had appropriated her identity, the district court erred by rejecting, on summary judgment, White's common law right of publicity claim. * * * [Part III omitted.]

IV.

THE PARODY DEFENSE

In defense, defendants cite a number of cases for the proposition that their robot ad constituted protected speech. The only cases they cite which are even remotely relevant to this case are *Hustler Magazine v. Falwell,* 485 U.S. 46 (1988) and *L.L. Bean, Inc. v. Drake Publishers, Inc.,* 811 F.2d 26 (1st Cir. 1987). Those cases involved parodies of advertisements run for the purpose of poking fun at Jerry Falwell and L.L. Bean, respectively. This case involves a true advertisement run for the purpose of selling Samsung VCRs. The ad's spoof of Vanna White and Wheel of Fortune is subservient and only tangentially related to the ad's primary message: "buy Samsung VCRs." Defendants' parody arguments are better addressed to non-commercial parodies. The difference between a "parody" and a "knock-off" is the difference between fun and profit.

V.

CONCLUSION

In remanding this case, we hold only that White has pleaded claims which can go to the jury for its decision.

AFFIRMED IN PART, REVERSED IN PART, and REMANDED.

Notes

1. After reading the *White* and *Wendt* cases, how is a copyright holder supposed to license the use of a show without violating the right of publicity of one or more of the actors?

2. In *Ali v. Playgirl, Inc.,* 447 F.Supp. 723 (S.D.N.Y. 1978), Muhammad Ali sued Playgirl magazine under the New York "right of privacy" statute and also alleged a violation of his common law right of publicity. The magazine published a drawing of a nude, black male sitting on a stool in a corner of a boxing ring with hands taped and arms outstretched on the ropes. The district court concluded that Ali's right of publicity was invaded because the drawing sufficiently identified him in spite of the fact that the drawing was captioned "Mystery Man." The district court found that the identification of Ali was made certain because of an accompanying verse that identified the figure as "The Greatest."

3. What affect does a television star's felony conviction have on her series? After Martha Stewart was found guilty of obstructing justice and other crimes on March 5, 2004, Viacom announced that it was pulling her show, *Martha Stewart Living,* from its CBS and UPN stations. The show, which had been on the air since 1991, had been shown in 139 media markets on various stations, covering 85% of the country. *See 'Martha Stewart Living' Cut from CBS, UPN,* ASSOCIATED PRESS, Mar. 8, 2004.

According to Television Week, Stewart's contract "contains a standard morals clause that voids the contract in cases such as this [a felony conviction." Chris Pursell and Jay Sherman, *Stewart's 'Living' Likely Dead,*

TELEVISION WEEK *available at* http://www.tvweek.com/ topstorys/030804stewart.html

Stewart, a one-time billionaire, saved $45,000 by selling stock in ImClone Systems on the eve of an adverse ruling for its cancer drug after receiving notification that ImClone's founder was dumping his stock. Daniel Kadlek, *Not a Good Thing for Martha*, TIME MAGAZINE. Mar.15, 2004.

D. TELEVISION COMMERCIALS AND ADVERTISING

Some celebrities have an aversion to lending their name to promote products in commercials and advertisements. They protect their reputations by avoiding association with commercial enterprises. These celebrities display disdain for the crass commercialism exhibited by some of their more market-friendly peers who appear in commercials and advertisements. Whether it is a secret professional jealousy of their product hawking peers or an altruistic belief that doing advertisements is bad for a career, some celebrities refuse to allow their identities to be tied to a commercial product. Having to do commercials is thought by some to be a desperate attempt to get any kind of work to extend a floundering career or one in its twilight.

BOOTH v. COLGATE–PALMOLIVE COMPANY

United States District Court, Southern District of New York, 1973.
362 F.Supp. 343.

BONSAL, District Judge.

Plaintiff, Shirley Booth, instituted this action on March 2, 1971, against defendants Colgate–Palmolive Company ("Colgate") and Ted Bates & Co., Inc. ("Bates") to recover as compensatory and exemplary damages the sum of $4,000,000, which she claims she sustained by reason of the defendants' unfair competition and defamation. Her complaint alleges three causes of action: (1) under the New York State common law of unfair competition; (2) under the Lanham Trade–Mark Act (15 U.S.C. § 1125(a); and (3) under the New York State law of defamation. Jurisdiction is asserted on the grounds of diversity of citizenship. 28 U.S.C. § 1332.

Defendants move for summary judgment pursuant to Rule 56(b) of the Federal Rules of Civil Procedure on the grounds that there is no genuine issue as to any material fact and that the defendants are entitled to judgment dismissing the complaint as a matter of law.

Plaintiff Shirley Booth is a well-known comedy and dramatic actress who has performed on the legitimate stage, in motion pictures, and on television. From 1961 to 1966, she played the title role of "Hazel" in a popular television comedy series broadcast weekly from 1961 to 1965 by the NBC television network and from 1965 to 1966 by the CBS television network. The series was based on the adventures of a copyrighted cartoon character named Hazel, with the permission of Ted Key, the character's creator and copyright holder, who was given credit during the broadcasts. Since 1967, television and audio tape recordings of the series have been presented throughout the United States and in other countries.

Defendant Bates is an advertising agency which produced radio and television commercials promoting Colgate's laundry detergent "Burst". These commercials, first broadcast on January 16, 1971, used the name and likeness of the copyrighted cartoon character Hazel pursuant to a written license agreement with Key, the creator and copyright holder, dated June 22, 1970. The voice of Hazel in the commercials was performed by Ruth Holden. Neither she nor the plaintiff was named or identified during the commercials.

The parties agree that New York law applies to plaintiff's first and third causes of action.

I

First Cause of Action: *Unfair Competition under New York Law*

Plaintiff relies on three arguments to support her first cause of action under the New York State common law of unfair competition. Plaintiff's first argument is that star performers such as herself have a property right in their performances, which property right permits the protection of those performances against both direct misappropriation, such as for example the unauthorized tape recording of a vocal performance, as well as against indirect misappropriation, such as the imitation of a performer's timing, inflection, tone, or general performing style. Plaintiff, Shirley Booth, has devoted many years to training as an actress and has attained stardom. She contends that she endowed the role of Hazel with her own unique and creative artistic interpretation, and that the "modern liberalized and considerably expanded doctrines of the New York law of unfair competition" protect her against imitation of her voice in defendants' commercials.

For the purposes of their motion, defendants concede that "Ruth Holden's voice as used in the Burst commercials constituted an 'imitation' of the 'normal speaking voice' . . . of Shirley Booth as plaintiff used it and it was heard in the 'Hazel' situation comedy series." Defendants contend, however, that imitation of a voice without more does not give rise to a cause of action for unfair competition.

Plaintiff relies on *Metropolitan Opera Association, Inc. v. Wagner-Nichols Recorder Corp.*, 101 N.Y.S. 2d 483 (Sup. Ct. 1950), aff'd, 107 N.Y.S. 2d 795 (1st Dept. 1951), as indicating the liberalized doctrines of unfair competition in New York. In that case, the court recognized the right to the exclusive use of one's own name and reputation. The court went on to say that the law also protects "the creative element in intellectual productions—that is, the form or sequence of expression, the new combination of colors, sounds or words presented by the production." 101 N.Y.S. 2d at 494. Plaintiff also cites *Lennon v. Pulsebeat*

News, Inc., 143 U.S.P.Q. 309 (Sup. Ct. N.Y. 1964); *Columbia Broadcasting System, Inc. v. Documentaries Unlimited, Inc.*, 248 N.Y.S. 2d 809 (Sup. Ct. 1964); and *Dior v. Milton*, 155 N.Y.S. 2d 443 (Sup. Ct.), aff'd, 156 N.Y.S. 2d 996 (1st Dept. 1956).

These cases, however, are not controlling here. *Metropolitan Opera, Columbia Broadcasting*, and *Lennon* involved direct misappropriation, not imitation. In *Metropolitan Opera*, for instance, the plaintiff was an opera company which had sold to a recording company the exclusive right to make and sell phonograph records of its operatic performances. The plaintiff had also sold to a radio broadcasting company the exclusive right to broadcast its opera performances. The defendants recorded these broadcasts and used their master recordings to make phonograph records of plaintiff's performances, which defendants then sold to the public.

The court granted the injunction sought by plaintiff and denied the defendants' motion to dismiss the complaint on the basis that the rights plaintiff had granted to the broadcasting company and to the recording company were contractual, exclusive rights and that defendants' conduct constituted a direct misappropriation of plaintiff's property rights. Similarly, in *Dior*, which involved the copying of plaintiff's fashion designs, the court emphasized the fact that the defendants had been permitted to see the designs on the express condition that they would not make or divulge any reproduction of any of the designs. Here, in contrast, there was neither use of an actual recording of plaintiff's voice in defendants' commercials nor any express condition to viewers of the Hazel television series analogous to that set forth in *Dior*.

Moreover, the argument that New York law protects a performer from imitators is undercut by the Supreme Court decisions in *Sears, Roebuck & Co. v. Stiffel Co.*, 376 U.S. 225 (1964), and *Compco Corp. v. Day–Brite Lighting, Inc.*, 376 U.S. 234 (1964). *Sears* and *Compco*, both involving invalid design patents, held that the states are preempted from protecting, under state unfair competition law, designs that Congress has not chosen to protect by means of the federal patent laws. The Court's reasoning, however, was not based upon peculiarities of patent law. Rather, the Court spoke in broad and general terms about the purpose of patent and copyright laws and about the need for national uniformity: "[B]ecause of the federal patent laws a State may not, when the article is unpatented and *uncopyrighted*, prohibit the copying of the article itself or award damages for such copying." 376 U.S. at 232–233. (Emphasis added.) Again emphasizing the "strong federal policy favoring free competition in ideas which do not merit patent protection," the Court reaffirmed *Sears* and *Compco* in *Lear, Inc. v. Adkins*, 395 U.S. 653, 656 (1969).

The latest Supreme Court decision, *Goldstein v. California*, 412 U.S. 546 (1973) involved "record" or "tape piracy," meaning "the unauthorized duplication of recordings of performances by major musical artists." 93 S. Ct. at 2306. In *Goldstein*, the Court upheld a California statute which made it a criminal offense to "pirate" recordings produced by others. The Court, however, reaffirmed its decisions in *Sears* and *Compco*, which had dealt with copying or imitation, and pointed out that the California statute at issue placed no restraint on the "use of an idea or concept; rather, petitioners and other individuals remain free to record the same compositions in precisely the same manner and with the same personnel as appeared on the original recording." 93 S. Ct. at 2317.

The Court of Appeals for the Ninth Circuit had occasion, before *Goldstein*, to assess the effect of *Sears* and *Compco* on the common law of unfair competition in Sinatra v. Goodyear Tire and Rubber Co., 435 F.2d 711 (9th Cir.), cert. denied, 402 U.S. 906 (1970). That case presented a factual situation similar to that presented here. The plaintiff in that case was a professional entertainer and had made a popular recording of a copyrighted song entitled "These Boots Are Made For Walking." Defendants were a tire manufacturer and an advertising company, which had conceived of an advertising campaign using as its theme the phrase "Wide Boots" as a descriptive term for defendant's tires. Radio and television commercials were made which featured a female singer, who was not identified in the commercials, singing "These Boots Are Made For Walking" under license from the copyright holder. Defendants admitted for purposes of the motion that the vocal rendition was an imitation of plaintiff's recorded performance of the song in question. The district court granted summary judgment for defendants, and the Court of Appeals, citing *Sears* and *Compco*, affirmed on the grounds that imitation alone does not give rise to a cause of action.

In *Columbia Broadcasting System, Inc. v. DeCosta*, 377 F.2d 315 (1st Cir. 1967), the Court of Appeals for the First Circuit refused to grant protection, in the absence of federal copyright protection, to the character "Paladin" and his "Have Gun, Will Travel" motif, which had been created by the plaintiff. Citing *Sears* and *Compco*, the Court of Appeals held that the federal policy of allowing free access to copy whatever the federal patent and copyright laws leave in the public domain prevailed over the plaintiff's interest in his creations.

Moreover, there are persuasive reasons of public policy for refusing to recognize a performer's right of protection against imitators. The policing of a performance or the creation of a performer in playing a role would present very difficult, if not impossible, problems of supervision for a court of equity. In addition, the recognition of a performer's right in a copyrighted work would impose undue restraints on the potential market of the copyright proprietor since a prospective licensee would have to gain permission from each of possibly many performers who might have rights in the underlying work before he could safely use it. Such a right could also conflict with the Constitutional policy of permitting exclusive use of patented and copyrighted works for only a limited period of time.

Finally, the vesting of a monopoly in the performer and the prevention of others from imitating his postures, gestures, voices, sounds, or mannerisms may impede, rather than "promote the Progress of ... useful Arts." U.S. Const., art. I, § 8. See *Sinatra, supra* at 717–718 of 435 F.2d; *DeCosta, supra* at 320 of 377 F.2d; Comment, The Twilight Zone: Meanderings in the Area of Performers' Rights, 9 U.C.L.A. L. Rev. 819 (1962).

For the foregoing reasons, the court finds that the imitation by defendants of plaintiff's voice without more, does not constitute unfair competition under New York law.

Plaintiff's second theory to support her claim of unfair competition is that the defendants infringed plaintiff's "rights of publicity" in her name, appearance, likeness, signature, or personality, for which she cites *Haelan Laboratories, Inc. v. Topps Chewing Gum, Inc.*, 202 F.2d 866 (2d Cir.), cert. denied 346 U.S. 816 (1953). *See also Cepeda v. Swift and Company*, 415 F.2d 1205 (8th Cir. 1969); *Ettore v. Philco Television Broadcasting Corp.*, 229 F.2d 481 (3d Cir. 1956); *Negri v. Schering Corp.*, 333 F.Supp. 101 (S.D.N.Y. 1971); *Uhlaender v. Henricksen*, 316 F.Supp. 1277 (D. Minn. 1970).

Under these cases, however, the plaintiff must show that her name or a likeness was used by defendants. Since the commercials in issue here are anonymous and do not use plaintiff's name or likeness in any way to identify her as the source of the voice of Hazel, this court finds that plaintiff cannot show an infringement of her rights to publicity.

Plaintiff's third theory to support her claim of unfair competition is based on her contention that the Hazel television series has been so closely connected with the voice she used in playing the part of Hazel that her voice has acquired a "secondary meaning." She contends that defendants, by "concealing the identity of the performer who imitated [her] voice," were attempting to deceive the public into thinking that the plaintiff endorsed Burst, in effect that defendants' acts constituted the tort of "freeride" unfair competition under New York law. Plaintiff argues that defendants used two "clues" to plaintiff's identity in the commercials in order to bolster the association of Colgate's laundry detergent with Shirley Booth in the mind of the public: 1) the references of the anonymous performer in the commercials to herself as "Hazel," and 2) the word "Burst" itself as a "quickly recognizable symbol of the limitless 'bursts' of energy" with which Shirley Booth portrayed the television series character.

As authority for her argument, plaintiff cites *Vaudable v. Montmartre, Inc.*, 193 N.Y.S. 2d 332 (Sup. Ct. 1959), where the court enjoined defendants from copying in their New York restaurant the name, coloring, lettering, and decor of plaintiff's well-known "Maxim's" restaurant in Paris. Plaintiff also cites *Flexitized, Inc. v. National Flexitized Corp.*, 214 F.Supp. 664 (S.D.N.Y. 1963), aff'd in part and rev'd in part, 335 F.2d 774 (2d Cir. 1964), in which the district court enjoined the defendants from using the word "Flexitized" in connection with the sales of their flexible garment stays, which products were sold in competition with those of the plaintiffs.

In *Flexitized*, the Court of Appeals held that the then recently-decided cases of *Sears* and *Compco* did not permit States, under the guise of regulating unfair competition, to grant what would be, in effect, patent protection. 335 F.2d at 781, n. 4. As the Supreme Court declared in *Sears*, the "mere inability of the public to tell two identical articles apart is not enough to support ... an award of damages for copying that which the federal patent laws [or the federal copyright laws] permit to be copied." 376 U.S. at 232. The Court of Appeals, however, in *Flexitized* distinguished *Sears* and *Compco* on the grounds that those cases permitted states to protect businesses in the use of their trademarks, labels, or distinctive dress in the packaging of goods so as to prevent others, by imitating such markings, from misleading purchasers as to the source of the goods. 335 F.2d at 781, n. 4.

In the present case, the plaintiff has not shown either that what she seeks to protect from imitation—her voice—functions as a trademark or trade name entitling it to protection, or that her voice was ever used in connection with any product or service in competition with a product or service of defendants. Moreover, in contrast to the cases cited by the plaintiff, in the present case defendants had a right to use the name and character of Hazel pursuant to the license agreement. And the name of its product, Burst, which name has been a registered trademark of Colgate's since 1956, cannot be said to identify or refer to the plaintiff. Accordingly, the strong federal policy emphasized in *Sears* and *Compco* permitting imitation prevails here over plaintiff's interest in protecting whatever secondary meaning may be attached to her voice as that of the television series' Hazel.

From the foregoing, it is evident that plaintiff's complaint does not state a cause of action for unfair competition under any of the three theories advanced.

II

SECOND CAUSE OF ACTION: *Unfair Competition under the Lanham Act*

Section 43(a) of the Lanham Trade–Mark Act (15 U.S.C. § 1125(a)) provides that:

"Any person who shall ... use in connection with any goods or services ... a false designation of origin, or any false description or representation, including words or other symbols tending falsely to describe or represent the same, and shall cause such goods or services to enter into commerce ... shall be liable to a civil action by any person doing business in the locality falsely indicated as that of origin or in the region in which said locality is situated, or by any person who believes that he is or is likely to be damaged by the use of any such false description or representation."

Plaintiff contends that defendants concealed from those who saw and heard defendants' commercials the origin of Hazel's voice, with the result that the public was deceived into thinking that the plaintiff endorsed Colgate's product Burst. It is evident, however, that for the reasons set forth above, this alleged cause of action is also insufficient to entitle the plaintiff to relief. There is no indication that plaintiff used her voice in connection with any "goods or services," nor that her voice alone can serve as a trademark or trade name, nor that plaintiff and defendants were in competition, nor even that the defendants used any description or made any representation to identify her, apart from the use of the Hazel cartoon character, for which they had permission from its copyright holder. * * *

III

THIRD CAUSE OF ACTION: *Defamation under New York Law*

Plaintiff contends that the defendants' commercials constitute a libel per se inasmuch as they deceive the public into thinking that "of necessity, Shirley Booth has been reduced to using and selling her talents for anonymous radio and television commercials and advertising announcements, and that her talents have deteriorated and are less valuable."

Plaintiff cites *Lahr v. Adell Chemical Co.*, 300 F.2d 256 (1st Cir. 1962), as indicating that the anonymous imitation of a professional entertainer's voice in a commercial may constitute defamation. In *Lahr*, the plaintiff, a professional entertainer with a unique style of vocal comic delivery, brought an action against a corporation which had used in its television commercials the anonymous services of another actor who specialized in imitating the vocal sounds of the plaintiff. The district court dismissed the complaint, but the Court of Appeals reversed, holding that "[a] charge that an entertainer has stooped to perform below his class may be found to damage his reputation." 300 F.2d at 258.

Lahr, however, cited Massachusetts law in support of its holding. Under New York law, plaintiff must show that the allegedly defamatory statement is both defamatory on its face and defamatory as to plaintiff. Without such a showing, the plaintiff must plead and prove special damages to recover. *Hinsdale v. Orange County Publications, Inc.*, 17 N.Y. 2d 284 (1966). The commercials she contends are libelous do not refer to her nor mention her name. Even if it could be found that, due to a "secondary meaning," the public would associate her either with the cartoon character Hazel or merely with the name "Hazel," it cannot be said that performing the "voice over" in television and radio commercials would have a tendency directly to injure plaintiff in her business, profession, or trade. *Cole Fischer Rogow, Inc. v. Carl Ally, Inc.*, 288 N.Y.S. 2d 556 (1st Dept. 1968). There is no allegation that the voice was performed in an inferior manner in the commercials. A star performer's endorsement of a commercial product is a common occurrence and does not indicate either a diminution of professional reputation or a loss of professional talent, though plaintiff herself might prefer to avoid such engagements. Accordingly, plaintiff's cause of action based on the theory that defendants' commercials constitute libel per se is not tenable.

For the foregoing reasons, defendants' motion for summary judgment dismissing the complaint is granted. Settle judgment on notice.

MIDLER v. FORD MOTOR COMPANY

United States Court of Appeals, Ninth Circuit, 1988.
849 F.2d 460.

NOONAN, Circuit Judge.

This case centers on the protectibility of the voice of a celebrated chanteuse from commercial exploitation without her consent. Ford Motor Company and its advertising agency, Young & Rubicon, Inc., in 1985 advertised the Ford Lincoln Mercury with a series of nineteen 30 or 60 second television commercials in what the agency called "The Yuppie Campaign." The aim was to make an emotional connection with Yuppies, bringing back memories of when they were in college. Different popular songs of the seventies were sung on each commercial. The agency tried to get "the original people," that is, the singers who had popularized the songs, to sing them. Failing in that endeavor in ten cases the agency had the songs sung by "sound alikes." Bette Midler, the plaintiff and appellant here, was done by a sound alike.

Midler is a nationally known actress and singer. She won a Grammy as early as 1973 as the Best New Artist of that year. Records made by her since then have gone Platinum and Gold. She was nominated in 1979 for an Academy award for Best Female Actress in *The Rose*, in which she portrayed a pop singer. *Newsweek* in its June 30, 1986 issue described her as an "outrageously original singer/comedian." *Time* hailed her in its March 2, 1987 issue as "a legend" and "the most dynamic and poignant singer-actress of her time."

When Young & Rubicon was preparing the Yuppie Campaign it presented the commercial to its client by playing an edited version of Midler singing "Do You Want To Dance," taken from the 1973 Midler album, "The Divine Miss M." After the client accepted the idea and form of the commercial, the agency contacted Midler's manager, Jerry Edelstein. The conversation went as follows: "Hello, I am Craig Hazen from Young and Rubicon. I am calling you to find out if Bette Midler would be interested in doing ... ? Edelstein: "Is it a commercial?" "Yes." "We are not interested."

Undeterred, Young & Rubicon sought out Ula Hedwig whom it knew to have been one of "the Harlettes" a backup singer for Midler for ten years. Hedwig was told by Young & Rubicon that "they wanted someone who could sound like Bette Midler's recording of [Do You Want To Dance]." She was asked to make a "demo" tape of the song if she was interested. She made an *a capella* demo and got the job.

At the direction of Young & Rubicon, Hedwig then made a record for the commercial. The Midler record of "Do You Want To Dance" was first played to her. She was told to "sound as much as possible like the Bette

Midler record," leaving out only a few "aahs" unsuitable for the commercial. Hedwig imitated Midler to the best of her ability.

After the commercial was aired Midler was told by "a number of people" that it "sounded exactly" like her record of "Do You Want To Dance." Hedwig was told by "many personal friends" that they thought it was Midler singing the commercial. Ken Fritz, a personal manager in the entertainment business not associated with Midler, declares by affidavit that he heard the commercial on more than one occasion and thought Midler was doing the singing.

Neither the name nor the picture of Midler was used in the commercial; Young & Rubicon had a license from the copyright holder to use the song. At issue in this case is only the protection of Midler's voice. The district court described the defendants' conduct as that "of the average thief." They decided, "If we can't buy it, we'll take it." The court nonetheless believed there was no legal principle preventing imitation of Midler's voice and so gave summary judgment for the defendants. Midler appeals.

The First Amendment protects much of what the media do in the reproduction of likenesses or sounds. A primary value is freedom of speech and press. *Time, Inc. v. Hill*, 385 U.S. 374, 388 (1967). The purpose of the media's use of a person's identity is central. If the purpose is "informative or cultural" the use is immune; "if it serves no such function but merely exploits the individual portrayed, immunity will not be granted." Felcher and Rubin, "Privacy, Publicity and the Portrayal of Real People by the Media," 88 Yale L.J. 1577, 1596 (1979). Moreover, federal copyright law preempts much of the area. "Mere imitation of a recorded performance would not constitute a copyright infringement even where one performer deliberately sets out to simulate another's performance as exactly as possible." Notes of Committee on the Judiciary, 17 U.S.C.A. § 114(b). It is in the context of these First Amendment and federal copyright distinctions that we address the present appeal.

Nancy Sinatra once sued Goodyear Tire and Rubber Company on the basis of an advertising campaign by Young & Rubicon featuring "These Boots Are Made For Walkin'," a song closely identified with her; the female singers of the commercial were alleged to have imitated her voice and style and to have dressed and looked like her. The basis of Nancy Sinatra's complaint was unfair competition; she claimed that the song and the arrangement had acquired "a secondary meaning" which, under California law, was protectible. This court noted that the defendants "had paid a very substantial sum to the copyright proprietor to obtain the license for the use of the song and all of its arrangements." To give Sinatra damages for their use of the song would clash with federal copyright law. Summary judgment for the defendants was affirmed. *Sinatra v. Goodyear Tire & Rubber Co.*, 435 F.2d 711, 717–718 (9th Cir. 1970), *cert. denied*, 402 U.S. 906 (1971). If Midler were claiming a secondary meaning to "Do You Want To Dance" or seeking to prevent the defendants from using that song, she would fail like Sinatra. But that is not this case. Midler does not seek damages for Ford's use of "Do You Want To Dance," and thus her claim is not preempted by federal copyright law. Copyright protects "original works of authorship fixed in any tangible medium of expression." 17 U.S.C. § 102(a). A voice is not copyrightable. The sounds are not "fixed." What is put forward as protectible here is more personal than any work of authorship. * * *

California Civil Code section 3344 is also of no aid to Midler. The statute affords damages to a person injured by another who uses the person's "name, voice, signature, photograph or likeness, in any manner." The defendants did not use Midler's name or anything else whose use is prohibited by the statute. The voice they used was Hedwig's, not hers. The term "likeness" refers to a visual image not a vocal imitation. The statute, however, does not preclude Midler from pursuing any cause of action she may have at common law; the statute itself implies that such common law causes of action do exist because it says its remedies are merely "cumulative." *Id.* § 3344(g).

The companion statute protecting the use of a deceased person's name, voice, signature, photograph or likeness states that the rights it recognizes are "property rights." *Id.* § 990(b). By analogy the common law rights are also property rights. Appropriation of such common law rights is a tort in California. *Motschenbacher v. R.J. Reynolds Tobacco Co.*, 498 F.2d 821 (9th Cir. 1974). In that case what the defendants used in their television commercial for Winston cigarettes was a photograph of a famous professional racing driver's racing car. The number of the car was changed and a wing-like device known as a "spoiler" was attached to the car; the car's features of white pinpointing, an oval medallion, and solid red coloring were retained. The driver, Lothar Motschenbacher, was in the car but his features were not visible. Some persons, viewing the commercial, correctly inferred that the car was his and that he was in the car and was therefore endorsing the product. The defendants were held to have invaded a "proprietary interest" of Motschenbacher in his own identity. *Id.* at 825.

Midler's case is different from Motschenbacher's. He and his car were physically used by the tobacco company's ad; he made part of his living out of giving commercial endorsements. But, as Judge Koelsch expressed it in *Motschenbacher*, California will recognize an injury from "an appropriation of the attributes of one's identity." *Id.* at 824. It was irrelevant that Motschenbacher could not be identified in the ad. The ad suggested that it was he. The ad did so by emphasizing signs or symbols associated with him. In the same way the defendants here used an imitation to convey the impression that Midler was singing for them.

Why did the defendants ask Midler to sing if her voice was not of value to them? Why did they studiously acquire the services of a sound-alike and instruct her to imitate Midler if Midler's voice was not of value to them? What they sought was an attribute of Midler's identity. Its value was what the market would have paid for Midler to have sung the commercial in person.

A voice is more distinctive and more personal than the automobile accouterments protected in *Motschenbacher*. A voice is as distinctive and personal as a face. The human voice is one of the most palpable ways identity is manifested. We are all aware that a friend is at once known by a few words on the phone. At a philosophical level it has been observed that with the sound of a voice, "the other stands before me." D. Ihde, *Listening and Voice* 77 (1976). *A fortiori*, these observations hold true of singing, especially singing by a singer of renown. The singer manifests herself in the song. To impersonate her voice is to pirate her identity. *See* W. Keeton, D. Dobbs, R. Keeton, D. Owen, *Prosser & Keeton on Torts* 852 (5th ed. 1984).

We need not and do not go so far as to hold that every imitation of a voice to advertise merchandise is actionable. We hold only that when a distinctive voice of a professional singer is widely known and is deliberately imitated in order to sell a product, the sellers have appropriated what is not theirs and have committed a tort in California. Midler has made a showing, sufficient to defeat summary judgment, that the defendants here for their own profit in selling their product did appropriate part of her identity.

REVERSED AND REMANDED FOR TRIAL.

Notes

1. Was Young & Rubicon's mistake that they asked Bette Midler to sing the song and were refused, or would they have lost the suit even if they had never contacted Ms. Midler's manager?

2. If you represent someone who sounds like a singer who is already famous, what advice would you give him or her about developing his or her talent and the chances of becoming famous?

3. The *Midler* principal was upheld in *Waits v. Frito–Lay, Inc.*, 978 F.2d 1093 (9th Cir. 1992). Tom Waits is a professional singer, songwriter, and actor. Waits has a raspy, gravelly singing voice, described by one fan as "like how you'd sound if you drank a quart of bourbon, smoked a pack of cigarettes and swallowed a pack of razor blades. . . . Late at night. After not sleeping for three days." Waits sued the snack food manufacturer and its advertising agency for voice misappropriation and false endorsement following the broadcast of a radio commercial for SalsaRio Doritos which featured a vocal performance imitating Waits' raspy singing voice. The court ruled in favor of Waits but that attorney's fees were improperly awarded because they were duplicative. The ruling was affirmed in all other respects. *Waits v. Frito–Lay, Inc.*, 978 F.2d 1093 (9th Cir.1992).

Chapter 12

DIVERSITY, CENSORSHIP, AND CULTURAL MATTERS

No one remembers that D.W. Griffith directed over 500 films in a 5–year period (in those days movies were short)[1], but they do remember that he was responsible for *Birth of a Nation*, which has been routinely pilloried as perhaps the most racist piece of entertainment ever produced. *Birth of a Nation* hit a nerve. For creative types, immortality comes from going to the creative edge and leaping. Sometimes they fly, other times they may fall flat on their speech.

The challenge for the United States entertainment industry is to balance the needs of artists, like Griffith, to fly off the creative edge against the needs of a multi-cultural and pluralistic society to get along and respect differences. This chapter explores the efforts to diversify television, the various attempts to censor the small screen, and concludes with a discussion of the cultural impact of the medium.

A. DIVERSITY IN THE TELEVISION MEDIA

METRO BROADCASTING, INC. v. FCC

United States Supreme Court, 1990.
497 U.S. 547, 110 S.Ct. 2997, 111 L.Ed.2d 445.

Footnotes omitted or renumbered

Mr. Justice BRENNAN delivered the opinion of the Court.

The issue in these cases, consolidated for decision today, is whether certain minority preference policies of the Federal Communications Commission violate the equal protection component of the Fifth Amendment. The policies in question are (1) a program awarding an enhancement for minority ownership in comparative proceedings for new licenses, and (2) the minority "distress sale" program, which permits a limited category of existing radio and television broadcast stations to be trans-

---

1. Goldman, *Adventures in the Screen Trade* 4 (Warner Books: 1983).

ferred only to minority-controlled firms. We hold that these policies do not violate equal protection principles.

I.

A.

The policies before us today can best be understood by reference to the history of federal efforts to promote minority participation in the broadcasting industry.[1] In the Communications Act of 1934, 48 Stat. 1064, as amended, Congress assigned to the Federal Communications Commission (FCC or Commission) exclusive authority to grant licenses, based on "public convenience, interest, or necessity," to persons wishing to construct and operate radio and television broadcast stations in the United States. See 47 U. S. C. §§ 151, 301, 303, 307, 309 (1982 ed.). Although for the past two decades minorities have constituted at least one-fifth of the United States population, during this time relatively few members of minority groups have held broadcast licenses. In 1971, minorities owned only 10 of the approximately 7,500 radio stations in the country and none of the more than 1,000 television stations, * * * in 1978, minorities owned less than 1 percent of the Nation's radio and television stations, * * * and in 1986, they owned just 2.1 percent of the more than 11,000 radio and television stations in the United States. * * * Moreover, these statistics fail to reflect the fact that, as late entrants who often have been able to obtain only the less valuable stations, many minority broadcasters serve geographically limited markets with relatively small audiences. * * *

The Commission has recognized that *The View*ing and listening public suffers when minorities are underrepresented among owners of television and radio stations:

"Acute underrepresentation of minorities among the owners of broadcast properties is troublesome because it is the licensee who is ultimately responsible for identifying and serving the needs and interests of his or her audience. Unless minorities are encouraged to enter the mainstream of the commercial broadcasting business, a substantial portion of our citizenry will remain underserved and the larger, non-minority audience will be deprived of *The View*s of minorities." Task Force Report 1.

The Commission has therefore worked to encourage minority participation in the broadcast industry. The FCC began by formulating rules to prohibit licensees from discriminating against minorities in employment. The FCC explained that "broadcasting is an important mass media form which, because it makes use of the airwaves belonging to the

1. The FCC has defined the term "minority" to include "those of Black, Hispanic Surnamed, American Eskimo, Aleut, American Indian and Asiatic American extraction." Statement of Policy on Minority Ownership of Broadcasting Facilities, 68 F. C. C. 2d 979, 980, n. 8 (1978). See also Commission Policy

Regarding Advancement of Minority Ownership in Broadcasting, 92 F. C. C. 2d 849, 849, n. 1 (1982), citing 47 U. S. C. § 309(i)(3)(C) (1982 ed.).

public, must obtain a Federal license under a public interest standard and must operate in the public interest in order to obtain periodic renewals of that license." * * * Regulations dealing with employment practices were justified as necessary to enable the FCC to satisfy its obligation under the Communications Act of 1934 to promote diversity of programming. * * * The United States Department of Justice, for example, contended that equal employment opportunity in the broadcast industry could " 'contribute significantly toward reducing and ending discrimination in other industries' " because of the " 'enormous impact which television and radio have upon American life.' " * * *

Initially, the FCC did not consider minority status as a factor in licensing decisions, maintaining as a matter of Commission policy that no preference to minority ownership was warranted where the record in a particular case did not give assurances that the owner's race likely would affect the content of the station's broadcast service to the public. * * * The Court of Appeals for the District of Columbia Circuit, however, rejected the Commission's position that an "assurance of superior community service attributable to.... Black ownership and participation" was required before a preference could be awarded. * * *

In April 1977, the FCC conducted a conference on minority ownership policies, at which participants testified that minority preferences were justified as a means of increasing diversity of broadcast viewpoint. * * * Building on the results of the conference, the recommendations of the task force, the decisions of the Court of Appeals for the District of Columbia Circuit, and a petition proposing several minority ownership policies filed with the Commission in January 1978 by the Office of Telecommunications Policy (then part of the Executive Office of the President) and the Department of Commerce, the FCC adopted in May 1978 its *Statement of Policy on Minority Ownership of Broadcasting Facilities*, 68 F. C. C. 2d 979. After recounting its past efforts to expand broadcast diversity, the FCC concluded:

> "[W]e are compelled to observe that *The View*s of racial minorities continue to be inadequately represented in the broadcast media. This situation is detrimental not only to the minority audience but to all of the viewing and listening public. Adequate representation of minority viewpoints in programming serves not only the needs and interests of the minority community but also enriches and educates the non-minority audience. It enhances the diversified programming which is a key objective not only of the Communications Act of 1934 but also of the First Amendment." Id., at 980–981 (footnotes omitted).

Describing its actions as only "first steps," id., at 984, the FCC outlined two elements of a minority ownership policy.

First, the Commission pledged to consider minority ownership as one factor in comparative proceedings for new licenses. When the Commission compares mutually exclusive applications for new radio or television broadcast stations, it looks principally at six factors: diversification of control of mass media communications, full-time participation in station operation by owners (commonly referred to as the "integration" of ownership and management), proposed program service, past broadcast record, efficient use of the frequency, and the character of the applicants. * * * In the Policy Statement on Minority Ownership, the FCC announced that minority ownership and participations in management would be considered in a comparative hearing as a "plus" to be weighed together with all other relevant factors. See *WPIX, Inc.*, 68 F. C. C. 2d 381, 411–412 (1978). The "plus" is awarded only to the extent that a minority owner actively participates in the day-to-day management of the station.

Second, the FCC outlined a plan to increase minority opportunities to receive reassigned and transferred licenses through the so-called "distress sale" policy. See 68 F.C.C.2d, at 983. As a general rule, a licensee whose qualifications to hold a broadcast license come into question may not assign or transfer that license until the FCC has resolved its doubts in a noncomparative hearing. The distress sale policy is an exception to that practice, allowing a broadcaster whose license has been designated for a revocation hearing, or whose renewal application has been designated for hearing, to assign the license to an FCC-approved minority enterprise. See ibid.; *Commission Policy Regarding the Advancement of Minority Ownership in Broadcasting*, 92 F.C.C.2d 849, 851 (1982). The assignee must meet the FCC's basic qualifications, and the minority ownership must exceed 50 percent or be controlling.[3] The buyer must purchase the license before the start of the revocation or renewal hearing, and the price must not exceed 75 percent of fair market value. These two Commission minority ownership policies are at issue today. * * *

B.

1.

In [case] No. 89–453, petitioner Metro Broadcasting, Inc. (Metro), challenges the Commission's policy awarding preferences to minority owners in comparative licensing proceedings. Several applicants, including Metro and Rainbow Broadcasting (Rainbow), were involved in a comparative proceeding to select among three mutually exclusive proposals to construct and operate a new UHF television station in the Orlando, Florida, metropolitan area. After an evidentiary hearing, an Administrative Law Judge (ALJ) granted Metro's application. *Metro Broadcasting, Inc.*, 96 F.C.C.2d 1073 (1983). The ALJ disqualified Rainbow from consideration because of "misrepresentations" in its application. Id., at 1087. On review of the ALJ's decision, however, the Commission's Review Board disagreed with the ALJ's finding regarding

---

3. In 1982, the FCC determined that a limited partnership could qualify as a minority enterprise if the general partner is a member of a minority group who holds at least a 20 percent interest and who will exercise "complete control over a station's affairs." 92 F. C. C. 2d, at 855.

Rainbow's candor and concluded that Rainbow was qualified. Metro Broadcasting, Inc., 99 F.C.C.2d 688 (1984).

The Board proceeded to consider Rainbow's comparative showing and found it superior to Metro's. In so doing, the Review Board awarded Rainbow a substantial enhancement on the ground that it was 90 percent Hispanic owned, whereas Metro had only one minority partner who owned 19.8 percent of the enterprise. The Review Board found that Rainbow's minority credit outweighed Metro's local residence and civic participation advantage. Id., at 704. The Commission denied review of the Board's decision largely without discussion, stating merely that it "agree[d] with the Board's resolution of this case." No. 85–558 (Oct. 18, 1985), p. 2, App. to Pet. For Cert. in No. 89–453, p. 61a.

Metro sought review of the Commission's order in the United States Court of Appeals for the District of Columbia Circuit, but the appeal's disposition was delayed; at the Commission's request, the court granted a remand of the record for further consideration in light of a separate ongoing inquiry at the Commission regarding the validity of its minority and female ownership policies, including the minority enhancement credit. See Notice of Inquiry on Racial, Ethnic or Gender Classifications, 1 F.C.C.Rcd 1315 (1986) (Docket 86–484). The Commission determined that the outcome in the licensing proceeding between Rainbow and Metro might depend on whatever the Commission concluded in its general evaluation of minority ownership policies, and accordingly it held the licensing proceeding in abeyance pending further developments in the Docket 86–484 review. See Metro Broadcasting, Inc., 2 F.C.C.Rcd. 1474, 1475 (1987).

Prior to the Commission's completion of its Docket 86–484 inquiry, however, Congress enacted and the President signed into law the FCC appropriations legislation for fiscal year 1988. The measure prohibited the Commission from spending any appropriated funds to examine or change its minority ownership policies. Complying with this directive, the Commission closed its Docket 86–484 inquiry. See Reexamination of Racial, Ethnic or Gender Classifications, Order, 3 F.C.C.Rcd. 766 (1988). The FCC also reaffirmed its grant of the license in this case to Rainbow Broadcasting. See Metro Broadcasting, Inc., 3 F.C.C.Rcd. 866 (1988).

The case returned to the Court of Appeals, and a divided panel affirmed the Commission's order awarding the license to Rainbow. The court concluded that its decision was controlled by prior Circuit precedent and noted that the Commission's action was supported by " 'highly relevant congressional action that showed clear recognition of the extreme underrepresentation of minorities and their perspectives in the broadcast mass media.' " * * * After petitions for rehearing and suggestions for rehearing en banc were denied, we granted certiorari. 493 U.S. 1017 (1990).

2

The dispute in [case] No. 89–700 emerged from a series of attempts by Faith Center, Inc., the licensee of a Hartford, Connecticut, television station, to execute a minority distress sale. In December 1980, the FCC designated for a hearing Faith Center's application for renewal of its license. * * * In February 1981, Faith Center filed with the FCC a petition for special relief seeking permission to transfer its license under the distress sale policy. The Commission granted the request, * * * but the proposed sale was not completed, apparently due to the purchaser's inability to obtain adequate financing. In September 1983, the Commission granted a second request by Faith Center to pursue a distress sale to another minority-controlled buyer. The FCC rejected objections to the distress sale raised by Alan Shurberg, who at that time was acting in his individual capacity.[10] * * * This second distress sale also was not consummated, apparently because of similar financial difficulties on the buyer's part.

In December 1983, respondent Shurberg Broadcasting of Hartford, Inc. (Shurberg), applied to the Commission for a permit to build a television station in Hartford. The application was mutually exclusive with Faith Cener's renewal application, then still pending. In June 1984, Faith Center again sought the FCC's approval for a distress sale, requesting permission to sell the station to Astroline Communications Company Limited Partnership (Astroline), a minority applicant. Shurberg opposed the sale to Astroline on a number of grounds, including that the FCC's distress sale program violated Shurberg's right to equal protection. Shurberg therefore urged the Commission to deny the distress sale request and to schedule a comparative hearing to examine the application Shurberg had tendered alongside Faith Center's renewal request. In December 1984, the FCC approved Faith Center's petition for permission to assign its broadcast license to Astroline pursuant to the distress sale policy. * * * The FCC rejected Shurberg's equal protection challenge to the policy as "without merit." * * *

Shurberg appealed the Commission's order to the United States Court of Appeals for the District of Columbia Circuit, but disposition of the appeal was delayed pending completion of the Commission's Docket 86–484 inquiry into the minority ownership policies. * * * After Congress enacted and the President signed into law the appropriations legislation prohibiting the FCC from continuing the Docket 86–484 proceeding, see supra, at 560, the Commission reaffirmed its order granting Faith Center's request to assign its Hartford license to Astroline pursuant to the minority distress sale policy.

A divided Court of Appeals invalidated the Commission's minority distress sale policy. *Shurberg Broadcasting of Hartford, Inc. v. FCC*, 278 U.S. App. D. C. 24, 876 F. 2d 902 (1989). In a per curiam opinion, the panel majority held that the policy "unconstitutionally deprives Alan Shurberg and Shurberg Broadcasting of their equal protection rights under the Fifth Amendment because the program is not narrowly

---

10. Mr. Shurberg is the sole owner of Shurberg Broadcasting of Hartford,Inc., re-   spondent in No. 89–700.

tailored to remedy past discrimination or to promote programming diversity" and that "the program unduly burdens Shurberg, an innocent nonminority, and is not reasonably related to the interests it seeks to vindicate." *Id.*, at 24–25, 876 F. 2d, at 902–903. Petitions for rehearing and suggestions for rehearing en banc were denied, and we granted certiorari. 493 U.S. 1018 (1990).

II

It is of overriding significance in these cases that the FCC's minority ownership programs have been specifically approved—indeed, mandated—by Congress. In *Fullilove v. Klutznick*, 448 U.S. 448 (1980), Chief Justice Burger, writing for himself and two other Justices, observed that although "[a] program that employs racial or ethnic criteria . . . calls for close examination," when a program employing a benign racial classification is adopted by an administrative agency at the explicit direction of Congress, we are "bound to approach our task with appropriate deference to the Congress, a co-equal branch charged by the Constitution with the power to 'provide for the . . . general Welfare of the United States' and 'to enforce, by appropriate legislation,' the equal protection guarantees of the Fourteenth Amendment." Id., at 472 * * * We explained that deference was appropriate in light of Congress' institutional competence as the National Legislature, * * * as well as Congress' powers under the Commerce Clause, * * * 7 the Spending Clause, * * * and the Civil War Amendments. * * *

A majority of the Court in *Fullilove* did not apply strict scrutiny to the race-based Classification at issue. Three Members inquired "whether the objectives of th[e] legislation are within the power of Congress" and "whether the limited use of racial and ethnic criteria . . . is a constitutionally permissible means for achieving the congressional objectives." *Id.*, at 473 (opinion of Burger, C. J.) (emphasis in original). Three other Members would have upheld benign racial classifications that "serve important governmental objectives and are substantially related to achievement of those objectives." *Id.*, at 519 (MARSHALL, J., concurring in judgment). We apply that standard today. We hold that benign race conscious measures mandated by Congress[12]—even if those measures are not "remedial" in the sense of being designed to compensate victims of past governmental or societal discrimination—are constitutionally per-

---

12. We fail to understand how JUSTICE KENNEDY can pretend that examples of "benign" race-conscious measures include South African apartheid, the "separate-but-equal" law at issue in Plessy v. Ferguson, 163 U.S. 537 (1896), and the internment of American citizens of Japanese ancestry upheld in Korematsu v. United States, 323 U.S. 214 (1944). We are confident that an "examination of the legislative scheme and its history," . . . will separate benign measures from other types of racial classifications. . . . The concept of benign race-conscious measures—even those

with at least some nonremedial purposes— is as old as the Fourteenth Amendment. For example, the Freedman's Bureau Acts authorized the provision of land, education, medical care, and other assistance to Afro-Americans. See, e. g., Cong. Globe, 39th Cong., 1st Sess., 630 (1866) (statement of Rep. Hubbard) ("I think that the nation will be a great gainer by encouraging the policy of the Freedman's Bureau, in the cultivation of its wild lands, in the increased wealth which industry brings and in the restoration of law and order in the insurgent States")....

missible to the extent that they serve important governmental objectives within the power of Congress and are substantially related to achievement of those objectives.

* * * We hold that the FCC minority ownership policies pass muster under the test we announce today. First, we find that they serve the important governmental objective of broadcast diversity. Second, we conclude that they are substantially related to the achievement of that objective.

A

Congress found that "the effects of past inequities stemming from racial and ethnic discrimination have resulted in a severe underrepresentation of minorities in the media of mass communications." H.R. Conf. Rep. No. 97–765, p. 43 (1982). Congress and the Commission do not justify the minority ownership policies strictly as remedies for victims of this discrimination, however. Rather, Congress and the FCC have selected the minority ownership policies primarily to promote programming diversity, and they urge that such diversity is an important governmental objective that can serve as a constitutional basis for the preference policies. We agree.

We have long recognized that "[b]ecause of the scarcity of [electromagnetic] frequencies, the Government is permitted to put restraints on licensees in favor of others whose views should be expressed on this unique medium." *Red Lion Broadcasting Co. v. FCC*, 395 U.S. 367, 390 (1969). The Government's role in distributing the limited number of broadcast licenses is not merely that of a "traffic officer," *National Broadcasting Co. v. United States*, 319 U.S. 190, 215 (1943); rather, it is axiomatic that broadcasting may be regulated in light of the rights of the viewing and listening audience and that "the widest possible dissemination of information from diverse and antagonistic sources is essential to the welfare of the public." *Associated Press v. United States*, 326 U.S. 1, 20 (1945). Safeguarding the public's right to receive a diversity of views and information over the airwaves is therefore an integral component of the FCC's mission. We have observed that " 'the "public interest" standard necessarily invites reference to First Amendment principles,' " *FCC v. National Citizens Committee for Broadcasting*, 436 U.S. 775, 795 (1978), quoting Columbia Broadcasting System, Inc. v. Democratic National Committee, 412 U.S. 94, 122 (1973), and that the Communications Act of 1934 has designated broadcasters as "fiduciaries for the public." *FCC v. League of Women Voters of Cal.*, 468 U.S. 364, 377 (1984).

> "[T]he people as a whole retain their interest in free speech by radio[and other forms of broadcast] and their collective right to have the medium function consistently with the ends and purposes of the First Amendment," and "[i]t is the right of the viewers and listeners, not the right of the broadcasters, which is paramount." Red Lion, supra, at 390. "Congress may ... seek to assure that the public receives through this medium a balanced presentation of

information on issues of public importance that otherwise might not be addressed if control of the medium were left entirely in the hands of those who own and operate broadcasting stations." *League of Women Voters, supra*, at 377.

Against this background, we conclude that the interest in enhancing broadcast diversity is, at the very least, an important governmental objective and is therefore a sufficient basis for the Commission's minority ownership policies. Just as a "diverse student body" contributing to a " 'robust exchange of ideas' " is a "constitutionally permissible goal" on which a race-conscious university admissions program may be predicated, *Regents of University of California v. Bakke*, 438 U.S. 265, 311–313 (1978) (opinion of Powell, J.), the diversity of views and information on the airwaves serves important First Amendment values. Cf. Wygant v. Jackson Board of Education, 476 U.S. 267, 314–315 (1986) (STEVENS, J., dissenting). The benefits of such diversity are not limited to the members of minority groups who gain access to the broadcasting industry by virtue of the ownership policies; rather, the benefits redound to all members of the viewing and listening audience. As Congress found, "the American public will benefit by having access to a wider diversity of information sources." H.R. Conf. Rep. No. 97–765, supra, at 45. * * *

B

We also find that the minority ownership policies are substantially related to the achievement of the Government's interest. One component of this inquiry concerns the relationship between expanded minority ownership and greater broadcast diversity; both the FCC and Congress have determined that such a relationship exists. Although we do not " 'defer' to the judgment of the Congress and the Commission on a constitutional question," and would not "hesitate to invoke the Constitution should we determine that the Commission has not fulfilled its task with appropriate sensitivity" to equal protection principles, *Columbia Broadcasting System, Inc. v. Democratic National Committee*, 412 U.S., at 103, we must pay close attention to the expertise of the Commission and the factfinding of Congress when analyzing the nexus between minority ownership and programming diversity. With respect to this "complex" empirical question, ibid., we are required to give "great weight to the decisions of Congress and the experience of the Commission." Id., at 102. * * *

Congress also has made clear its view that the minority ownership policies advance the goal of diverse programming. In recent years, Congress has specifically required the Commission, through appropriations legislation, to maintain the minority ownership policies without alteration. * * *

The judgment that there is a link between expanded minority ownership and broadcast diversity does not rest on impermissible stereotyping. Congressional policy does not assume that in every case minority ownership and management will lead to more minority-oriented programming or to the expression of a discrete "minority viewpoint" on the airwaves. Neither does it pretend that all programming that appeals to minority audiences can be labeled "minority programming" or that programming that might be described as "minority" does not appeal to nonminorities. Rather, both Congress and the FCC maintain simply that expanded minority ownership of broadcast outlets will, in the aggregate, result in greater broadcast diversity. A broadcasting industry with representative minority participation will produce more variation and diversity than will one whose ownership is drawn from a single racially and ethnically homogeneous group. The predictive judgment about the overall result of minority entry into broadcasting is not a rigid assumption about how minority owners will behave in every case but rather is akin to Justice Powell's conclusion in Bakke that greater admission of minorities would contribute, on average, "to the 'robust exchange of ideas.' " 438 U.S., at 313. To be sure, there is no ironclad guarantee that each minority owner will contribute to diversity. But neither was there an assurance in Bakke that minority students would interact with nonminority students or that the particular minority students admitted would have typical or distinct "minority" viewpoints. See id., at 312 (opinion of Powell, J.) (noting only that educational excellence is "widely believed to be promoted by a diverse student body") (emphasis added); id., at 313, n. 48 (" 'In the nature of things, it is hard to know how, and when, and even if, this informal "learning through diversity" actually occurs' ") (citation omitted).

Although all station owners are guided to some extent by market demand in their programming decisions, Congress and the Commission have determined that there may be important differences between the broadcasting practices of minority owners and those of their nonminority counterparts. This judgment—and the conclusion that there is a nexus between minority ownership and broadcasting diversity—is corroborated by a host of empirical evidence.[31] Evidence suggests that an owner's

---

31. For example, the CRS analyzed data from some 8,720 FCC-licensed radio and television stations and found a strong correlation between minority ownership and diversity of programming. See CRS, Minority Broadcast Station Ownership and Broadcast Programming: Is There a Nexus? (June 29, 1988). While only 20 percent of stations with no Afro–American ownership responded that they attempted to direct programming at Afro–American audiences, 65 percent of stations with Afro–American ownership reported that they did so. See id., at 13. Only 10 percent of stations without Hispanic ownership stated that they targeted programming at Hispanic audiences, while 59 percent of stations with Hispanic owners said they did. See id., at 13, 15. The CRS concluded: "[A]n argument can be made that FCC policies that enhanced minority ... station ownership may have resulted in more minority and other audience targeted programming. To the degree that increasing minority programming across audience markets is considered adding to programming diversity, then, based on the FCC survey data, an argument can be made that the FCC preference policies contributed, in turn, to programming diversity." Id., at cover page.

Other surveys support the FCC's determination that there is a nexus between ownership and programming. A University of Wisconsin study found that Afro–American-owned, Afro–American-oriented radio stations have more diverse playlists than white-owned, Afro–American-oriented stations. See J. Jeter, A Comparative Analysis of the Programming Practices of Black–Owned Black–Oriented Radio Stations and White–Owned Black–Oriented Radio Stations 130, 139 (1981) (University of Wisconsin–Madison). See also M. Spitzer, Justify-

minority status influences the selection of topics for news coverage and the presentation of editorial viewpoint, especially on matters of particular concern to minorities. "[M]inority ownership does appear to have specific impact on the presentation of minority" images in local news," inasmuch as minority-owned stations tend to devote more news time to topics of minority interest and to avoid racial and ethnic stereotypes in portraying minorities.[33] In addition, studies show that a minority owner is more likely to employ minorities in managerial and other important roles where they can have an impact on station policies.[34] If the FCC's equal employment policies "ensure that . . . licensees' programming fairly reflects the tastes and viewpoints of minority groups," *NAACP v. FPC*, 425 U.S., at 670, n. 7, it is difficult to deny that minority-owned stations that follow such employment policies on their own will also contribute to diversity. While we are under no illusion that members of a particular minority group share some cohesive, collective viewpoint, we believe it a legitimate inference for Congress and the Commission to draw that as more minorities gain ownership and policymaking roles in the media, varying perspectives will be more fairly represented on the

ing Minority Preferences in Broadcasting, California Institute of Technology Working Paper No. 718, pp. 19–29 (March 1990) (explaining why minority status of owner might affect programming behavior).

33. For example, a University of Massachusetts at Boston survey of 3,000 local Boston news stories found a statistically significant difference in the treatment of events, depending on the race of ownership. See K. Johnson, Media Images of Boston's Black Community 16–29 (Jan. 28, 1987) (William Monroe Trotter Institute). A comparison between an Afro–American-owned television station and a white-owned station in Detroit concluded that "the overall mix of topic and location coverage between the two stations is statistically different, and with its higher use of blacks in newsmaker roles and its higher coverage of issues of racial significance, [the Afro–American-owned station's] content does represent a different perspective on news than [that of the white-owned station]." M. Fife, The Impact of Minority Ownership On Broadcast Program Content: A Case Study of WGPR–TV's Local News Content, Report to the National Association of Broadcasters, Office of Research and Planning 45 (Sept. 1979). See also R. Wolseley, The Black Press, U.S.A. 3–4, 11 (2d ed. 1990) (documenting importance of minority ownership).

34. Afro–American-owned radio stations, for example, have hired Afro–Americans in top management and other important job categories at far higher rates than have white-owned stations, even those with Afro–American-oriented formats. The same has been true of Hispanic hiring at Hispan-

ic-owned stations, compared to Anglo-owned stations with Spanish-language formats. See Honig, Relationships Among EEO, Program Service, and Minority Ownership in Broadcast Regulation, in Proceedings from the Tenth Annual Telecommunications Policy Research Conference 88–89 (O. Gandy, P. Espinoza, & J. Ordover eds. 1983). As of September 1986, half of the 14 Afro–American or Hispanic general managers at TV stations in the United States worked at minority-owned or controlled stations. See National Association of Broadcasters, Minority Broadcasting Facts 9–10, 55–57 (Sept. 1986). In 1981, 13 of the 15 Spanish-language radio stations in the United States owned by Hispanics also had a majority of Hispanics in management positions, while only a third of Anglo-owned, Spanish-language stations had a majority of Hispanic managers, and 42 percent of the Anglo-owned Spanish-language stations had no Hispanic managers at all. See Schement & Singleton, The Onus of Minority Ownership: FCC Policy and Spanish–Language Radio, 31 J. Communication 78, 80–81 (1981). See generally Johnson, supra, at 5 ("Many observers agree that the single largest reason for the networks' poor coverage of racial news is related to the racial makeup of the networks' own staffs"); Wimmer, supra n. 2, at 426–427 ("[M]inority-owned broadcast outlets tend to hire more minority employees. . . . A policy of minority ownership could, over time, lead to a growth in minority employment, which has been shown to produce minority-responsive programming") (footnotes omitted).

airwaves. The policies are thus a product of " 'analysis' " rather than a " 'stereotyped reaction' " based on " '[h]abit.' " Fullilove, 448 U.S., at 534, n. 4 (STEVENS, J., dissenting) (citation omitted). * * *

D

We find that the minority ownership policies are in other relevant respects substantially related to the goal of promoting broadcast diversity. First, the Commission adopted and Congress endorsed minority ownership preferences only after long study and painstaking consideration of all available alternatives. See *Fullilove*, 448 U.S., at 463–467 (opinion of Burger, C. J.); id., at 511 (Powell, J., concurring). For many years, the FCC attempted to encourage diversity of programming content without consideration of the race of station owners. * * *

[T]he Commission established minority ownership preferences only after long experience demonstrated that race-neutral means could not produce adequate broadcasting diversity. The FCC did not act precipitately in devising the programs we uphold today; to the contrary, the Commission undertook thorough evaluations of its policies three times—in 1960, 1971, and 1978—before adopting the minority ownership programs. In endorsing the minority ownership preferences, Congress agreed with the Commission's assessment that race-neutral alternatives had failed to achieve the necessary programming diversity.

Moreover, the considered nature of the Commission's judgment in selecting the particular minority ownership policies at issue today is illustrated by the fact that the Commission has rejected other types of minority preferences. For example, the Commission has studied but refused to implement the more expansive alternative of setting aside certain frequencies for minority broadcasters. * * * In addition, in a ruling released the day after it adopted the comparative hearing credit and the distress sale preference, the FCC declined to adopt a plan to require 45-day advance public notice before a station could be sold, which had been advocated on the ground that it would ensure minorities a chance to bid on stations that might otherwise be sold to industry insiders without ever coming on the market. See 43 Fed. Reg. 24560 (1978). Soon afterward, the Commission rejected other minority ownership proposals advanced by the Office of Telecommunications Policy and the Department of Commerce that sought to revise the FCC's time brokerage, multiple ownership, and other policies. * * *

The minority ownership policies, furthermore, are aimed directly at the barriers that minorities face in entering the broadcasting industry. The Commission's task force identified as key factors hampering the growth of minority ownership a lack of adequate financing, paucity of information regarding license availability, and broadcast inexperience. * * * The Commission assigned a preference to minority status in the comparative licensing proceeding, reasoning that such an enhancement might help to compensate for a dearth of broadcasting experience. Most license acquisitions, however, are by necessity purchases of existing stations, because only a limited number of new stations are available, and those are often in less desirable markets or on less profitable portions of spectrum, such as the UHF band.[46] Congress and the FCC therefore found a need for the minority distress sale policy, which helps to overcome the problem of inadequate access to capital by lowering the sale price and the problem of lack of information by providing existing licensees with an incentive to seek out minority buyers. The Commission's choice of minority ownership policies thus addressed the very factors it had isolated as being responsible for minority underrepresentation in the broadcast industry.

The minority ownership policies are "appropriately limited in extent and duration, and subject to reassessment and reevaluation by the Congress prior to any extension or reenactment." Fullilove, 448 U.S., at 489 (opinion of Burger, C. J.) (footnote omitted). Although it has underscored emphatically its support for the minority ownership policies, Congress has manifested that support through a series of appropriations Acts of finite duration, thereby ensuring future reevaluations of the need for the minority ownership program as the number of minority broadcasters increases. In addition, Congress has continued to hold hearings on the subject of minority ownership. The FCC has noted with respect to the minority preferences contained in the lottery statute, 47 U. S. C. § 309(i)(3)(A) (1982 ed.), that Congress instructed the Commission to "report annually on the effect of the preference system and whether it is serving the purposes intended. Congress will be able to further tailor the program based on that information, and may eliminate the preferences when appropriate." *Amendment of Commission's Rules to Allow Selection from Among Certain Competing Applications Using Random Selection or Lotteries Instead of Comparative Hearings*, 93 F. C. C. 2d 952, 974 (1983). Furthermore, there is provision for administrative and judicial review of all Commission decisions, which guarantees both that the minority ownership policies are applied correctly in individual cases, and that there will be frequent opportunities to revisit the merits of those policies. Congress and the Commission have adopted a policy of minority ownership not as an end in itself, but rather as a means of achieving greater programming diversity. Such a goal carries its own natural limit, for there will be no need for further minority preferences once sufficient diversity has been achieved. The FCC's plan, like the Harvard admissions program discussed in Bakke, contains the seed of its own termination. * * *

---

46. As of mid–1973, licenses for 66.6 percent of the commercial television stations—and 91.4 percent of the VHF stations—that existed in mid–1989 had already been awarded. Sixty-eight and one-half percent of the AM and FM radio station licenses authorized by the FCC as of mid–1989 had already been issued by mid–1973, including 85 percent of the AM stations. See ... Honig, The FCC and Its Fluctuating Commitment to Minority Ownership of Broadcast Facilities, 27 How. L. J. 859, 875, n. 87 (1984) (reporting 1980 statistics that Afro–Americans "tended to own the least desirable AM properties"—those with the lowest power and highest frequencies, and hence those with the smallest areas of coverage).

Finally, we do not believe that the minority ownership policies at issue impose impermissible burdens on nonminorities.[11] Although the nonminority challengers in these cases concede that they have not suffered the loss of an already-awarded broadcast license, they claim that they have been handicapped in their ability to obtain one in the first instance. But just as we have determined that "[a]s part of this Nation's dedication to eradicating racial discrimination, innocent persons may be called upon to bear some of the burden of the remedy," Wygant, 476 U.S., at 280–281 (opinion of Powell, J.), we similarly find that a congressionally mandated, benign, race-conscious program that is substantially related to the achievement of an important governmental interest is consistent with equal protection principles so long as it does not impose undue burdens on nonminorities. Cf. Fullilove, 448 U.S., at 484. * * *

In the context of broadcasting licenses, the burden on nonminorities is slight. The FCC's responsibility is to grant licenses in the "public interest, convenience, or necessity," 47 U. S. C. §§ 307, 309 (1982 ed.), and the limited number of frequencies on the electromagnetic spectrum means that "[n]o one has a First Amendment right to a license." *Red Lion*, 395 U.S., at 389. Applicants have no settled expectation that their applications will be granted without consideration of public interest factors such as minority ownership. Award of a preference in a comparative hearing or transfer of a station in a distress sale thus contravenes "no legitimate firmly rooted expectation[s]" of competing applicants. * * *

Respondent Shurberg insists that because the minority distress sale policy operates to exclude nonminority firms completely from consideration in the transfer of certain stations, it is a greater burden than the comparative hearing preference for minorities, which is simply a "plus" factor considered together with other characteristics of the applicants. * * * We disagree that the distress sale policy imposes an undue burden on nonminorities. By its terms, the policy may be invoked at the Commission's discretion only with respect to a small fraction of broadcast licenses—those designated for revocation or renewal hearings to examine basic qualification issues—and only when the licensee chooses to sell out at a distress price rather than to go through with the hearing. The distress sale policy is not a quota or fixed quantity set-aside. Indeed, the nonminority firm exercises control over whether a distress sale will ever occur at all, because the policy operates only where the qualifications of an existing licensee to continue broadcasting have been designated for hearing and no other applications for the station in question have been filed with the Commission at the time of the designation. See Clarification of Distress Sale Policy, 44 Radio Reg. 2d (P & F) 479 (1978).

11. Minority broadcasters, both those who obtain their licenses by means of the minority ownership policies and those who do not, are not stigmatized as inferior by the Commission's programs. Audiences do not know a broadcaster's race and have no reason to speculate about how he or she obtained a license; each broadcaster is judged on the merits of his or her programming. Furthermore, minority licensees must satisfy otherwise applicable FCC qualifications requirements. Cf. Fullilove, supra, at 521 (MARSHALL, J., concurring in judgment).

Thus, a nonminority can prevent the distress sale procedures from ever being invoked by filing a competing application in a timely manner.

In practice, distress sales have represented a tiny fraction—less than 0.4 percent—of all broadcast sales since 1979. * * * There have been only 38 distress sales since the policy was commenced in 1978. * * * This means that, on average, only about 0.2 percent of renewal applications filed each year have resulted in distress sales since the policy was commenced in 1978. See 54 FCC Ann. Rep. 33 (1988). Nonminority firms are free to compete for the vast remainder of license opportunities available in a market that contains over 11,000 broadcast properties. Nonminorities can apply for a new station, buy an existing station, file a competing application against a renewal application of an existing station, or seek financial participation in enterprises that qualify for distress sale treatment. * * * The burden on nonminority firms is at least as "relatively light" as that created by the program at issue in Fullilove, which set aside for minorities 10 percent of federal funds granted for local public works projects. 448 U.S., at 484. * * *

III

The Commission's minority ownership policies bear the imprimatur of longstanding congressional support and direction and are substantially related to the achievement of the important governmental objective of broadcast diversity. The judgment in No. 89–453 is affirmed, the judgment in No. 89–700 is reversed, and the cases are remanded for proceedings consistent with this opinion. * * *

JUSTICE STEVENS, concurring.

Today the Court squarely rejects the proposition that a governmental decision that rests on a racial classification is never permissible except as a remedy for a past wrong. Ante, at 564–565. I endorse this focus on the future benefit, rather than the remedial justification, of such decisions.

I remain convinced, of course, that racial or ethnic characteristics provide a relevant basis for disparate treatment only in extremely rare situations and that it is therefore "especially important that the reasons for any such classification be clearly identified and unquestionably legitimate." Fullilove v. Klutznick, 448 U.S. 448, 534–535 (1980) (dissenting opinion). The Court's opinion explains how both elements of that standard are satisfied. Specifically, the reason for the classification—the recognized interest in broadcast diversity—is clearly identified and does not imply any judgment concerning the abilities of owners of different races or the merits of different kinds of programming. Neither the favored nor the disfavored class is stigmatized in any way. In addition, the Court demonstrates that these cases fall within the extremely narrow category of governmental decisions for which racial or ethnic heritage may provide a rational basis for differential treatment. The public interest in broadcast diversity—like the interest in an integrated police force, diversity in the composition of a public school faculty or diversity in the student body of a professional school—is in my view unquestionably legitimate.

Therefore, I join both the opinion and the judgment of the Court.

Notes

1. In *Adarand Constructors v. Pena*, 515 U.S. 200, 115 S.Ct. 2097, 132 L.Ed.2d 158 (1995), a divided court, with Justice O'Connor writing for the majority, concluded that all racial classifications, imposed by whatever federal, state or local government actor, must be analyzed by a reviewing court under strict scrutiny. 115 S.Ct. at 2105–2114. The court thus specifically overruled *Metro Broadcasting*'s decision to apply the intermediate standard of scrutiny in assessing the constitutionality of federal race-based action. The Court criticized *Metro Broadcasting*'s failure to explain when "a racial classification should be deemed 'benign'." 515 U.S. at 225. *Adarand Constructors* involved a subcontractor suing because he was not awarded the guardrail portion of a federal highway contract. He challenged a federal program designed to provide highway contracts to disadvantage business enterprises. In both *Adarand* and *Metro Broadcasting*, the Court was presented with Congressional attempts at remediation of past discrimination and encouraging diversity, while not affecting the rights of nonminorities. Can Congress do both? Or must Congress make a choice? What societal values are at stake?

2. The following article discusses the commotion that erupted when the networks announced that their 1999 season would include have no shows with major minority characters.

Professor Gary Williams
"Don't Try to Adjust Your Television—I'm Black": Ruminations on the Recurrent Controversy over the Whiteness of TV

4 J. Gender Race & Just. 99 (2001).
All footnotes omitted.

When the television networks announced their lineups for the fall 1999 season, the print media noted a striking phenomenon: of the twenty-six new shows announced by the networks, not one featured a lead character who was African American, Asian American, Native American, or Latino. Moreover, the new series sported virtually no supporting characters of color. Reacting to this news, one studio executive commented, "It's an awfully white world on television." * * *
[Parts I & II omitted]

III. THE LACK OF FACES OF COLOR ON TELEVISION AND IN TELEVISION: DOES IT REALLY MATTER?

The statistical underrepresentation of people of color in front of and behind the camera is indisputable. The question protestors of all colors must answer at this point is, "So what?" Given that people of color are underrepresented, and at times misrepresented, on television comedies and dramas, why should we care? Do the dramas and comedies we see on television really make any difference in issues of social justice? Can the paucity of color in the entertainment lineups of network television be linked, in any persuasive way, to the problems of racial harmony we face today? Is it plausible that California voters' willingness to pass Proposition 187 was, in part, attributable to the way Spanish-speaking people are portrayed on the small screen? Can we plausibly link the widespread societal acceptance of racial profiling to the constant portrayal of black males as hustlers, drug dealers, and criminals?

The United States Commission on Civil Rights began to explore these questions with its 1977 report, acknowledging that "relatively little is known about the ways in which the stereotyped images of men and women and of whites and nonwhites affect viewers' beliefs, attitudes, and behavior." The Commission did note one study that concluded white children who had little or no contact with African Americans were most likely to believe that portrayals of black people on television were realistic. The Commission revisited the question of the impact of racial stereotypes in television in 1979, when it published "Window Dressing on the Set: An Update." In a section entitled "The Effect of the Portrayal of Minorities and Women on Children," the Commission discussed children's perceptions of people of color on television. The Commission noted a study which found that children's perceptions of the appropriateness of certain occupations for minorities may be influenced by television, and that the portrayal of people of color in comic roles may have a deleterious effect on children's attitudes.

More recently, the federal government again manifested its belief that television shows are a major influence on people's behavior. In 1997, Congress approved a one-billion-dollar anti-drug advertising campaign. Under this campaign, the networks had to agree to sell advertising time to the government at half price, essentially granting the government advertising time worth two billion dollars. The White House Office of National Drug Policy subsequently created a program whereby the government gave up some of the advertising time it had purchased in exchange for getting anti-drug messages included in specific shows.

* * *

[IV. B]

1. *Enhancing Diversity Behind the Camera*

As previously discussed, the statistics documenting underrepresentation of people of color in the ranks of writers, directors, producers, and executives are very strong. This kind of statistical evidence could be used to support a prima facie showing of discrimination under the disparate treatment branch of employment discrimination law.

In International Brotherhood of Teamsters v. United States, the Supreme Court stated that statistics can prove strong enough to support a prima facie showing of discrimination:

> Our cases make it unmistakably clear that "statistical analyses have served and will continue to serve an important role" in cases in which the existence of discrimination is a disputed issue.... We have repeatedly approved the use of statistical proof, where it reached proportions comparable to those in this case, to establish a prima facie case of racial discrimination in jury selection cases.... Statistics are equally competent in proving employment discrimination.

Similarly, the statistics documenting the racial disparity in the television industry may be strong enough to prove prima facie case. However, once a prima facie case is made, the burden shifts to the employer to articulate a legitimate, nondiscriminatory business reason for the disparity. Even if the employer is not successful in doing so, they may still escape liability based on the "business necessity" defense.

2. Enhancing Diversity in Front of the Camera by Attacking Racial Disparities in Casting

By and large, the courts and the Equal Employment Opportunity Commission (EEOC) have not directly addressed the legal questions raised by racial disparities in casting. However, on its face, Title VII seems to provide an available remedy for actors of color who are unfairly excluded from television roles. Plaintiffs could potentially rely on either the disparate treatment or disparate impact theories of discrimination under Title VII. Given the nature of casting calls, the easiest approach may be the disparate treatment route. The major problem with this approach is not the prima facie case, which should be fairly easy to establish, but the possibility that the employer could argue a bona fide occupational qualification (BFOQ).

The BFOQ defense to disparate treatment is narrow, and notably does not include an exception for race. Despite the fact that there is no such exception, there is controversy in the entertainment community over race-specific casting. In addition, there is evidence that the legislature and the EEOC might support a race-based BFOQ in limited situations, including acting. This kind of argument would raise some serious questions about the nature of the entertainment industry, raising complicated questions about the rights of writers, producers, and directors to express themselves, and the rights of actors to find employment. Currently, however, no such defense exists.

In addition to the possible disparate treatment claims actor-plaintiffs may bring, actor-plaintiffs could rely upon the statistical disparities in the entertainment industry to show that the hiring practices of the television industry have a disparate impact on actors of color. The employer could, however, respond by stating that casting a certain race in a certain role is a business necessity and thus escape liability. The business necessity defense raises some of the same issues present in the BFOQ defense. The business necessity defense has the added benefit for plaintiffs of not being a complete defense to liability. However, it has the additional burden of being legitimately influenced by customer preferences.

Part of the reason there are no clear answers on this issue is that no cases squarely address the topic. Writers who have examined the issue of racial casting have advanced two plausible explanations for the absence of legal challenges to the disparities that have been documented. One argument is that people who are excluded from television and other entertainment industry jobs do not bring discrimination claims because they believe television, movies, and the arts in general are immune from discrimination law. A second view asserts that affected artists view casting decisions as matters of artistic freedom that are protected by the First Amendment and therefore immune to legal scrutiny for discrimination.

C.   Of Boycotts and "Brownouts"

In response to the lack of characters of color in fall television lineups, several organizations of color called for boycotts or "brownouts." Historically, the boycott has occasionally been an effective weapon against racism, discrimination and social injustice. The D.W. Griffith movie, Birth of A Nation, glorifies the Ku Klux Klan and demonizes African Americans. In 1915, when its racist content became known, W.E.B. DuBois and the fledgling NAACP mounted protests, calling for boycotts and censorship of the film across the United States. Those efforts enjoyed immediate success in Pasadena, California and Wilmington, Delaware, where showing of the film was blocked. In Chicago, the board of censors temporarily banned the film. In New York, the NAACP successfully lobbied the censorship board into ordering the removal of some scenes. Later, when the film was reissued with a soundtrack, the NAACP convinced the governor of Massachusetts to ban its showing. During the 1960s, boycotts were effectively used in combating segregation in the South. In the 1970s and 1980s, Cesar Chavez and the United Farmworkers Union used boycotts to educate the public about the deplorable working conditions for farm workers, and to promote the workers' right to organize. This movement initially succeeded in California, which in 1975 enacted the Agricultural Labor Relations Act. That victory was later duplicated in Arizona, Idaho and Kansas.

More recently, consumer boycotts by people of color helped convince the Disney Company to first apologize, and then settle litigation involving a promotion by one of its radio stations giving away "Black Hoes," a double entendre intended to evoke images of Black whores. Similarly, in 1999, two African American radio show hosts organized a successful boycott and write-in campaign against CompUSA, which allegedly refused to advertise on radio stations owned by or aimed at African Americans.

D. The Protests and Brownouts over the Fall 1999 Lineup

In this era of media mega-corporations and rampant consumerism, will boycotts and brownouts influence the major networks to diversify? It is questionable whether a well-organized boycott would have a significant impact on these multinational corporations. Another question is whether people who want networks to change their programming would heed a call to turn off their televisions.

After the controversy over the fall 1999 lineup erupted, a coalition of groups representing people of color called for a "brownout" during the week of September 12. When the brownout was announced, Texas state representative Ciro Rodriguez expressed fear it would be ineffective. One student at Howard University, a historically black institution, was skeptical of the impact the brownout would have: "I don't think the boycott will make that big a difference, as long as there are enough white people watching." Another student, while expressing optimism that the boycott would be successful in bringing attention to the issue, stated he would not actively participate in the boycott.

It appears Representative Rodriguez's fears were well founded. The call for a brownout was widely reported in the press and publicized on the Internet. The press reported that the campaign provoked little concern among industry executives, and Nielsen Media Research reported no significant decline in ratings during the targeted week.

In terms of lending credibility to the idea of a boycott or brownout of television, part of the problem is the level of penetration television has made, at least in the African American community. While the average American household watches television approximately fifty hours per week, African American households average seventy hours per week. Also, by some measures, African Americans are, per capita, America's biggest consumers.

Happily, television network executives reacted favorably to public and private pressure. After several rounds of discussion with a coalition of advocacy groups, each major network agreed to a wide range of reforms aimed at improving diversity at both ends of the camera. NBC, for example, agreed to place at least one writer of color on each of its second-year series, to initiate a minority hiring program, and to seek out and hire qualified directors of color. ABC agreed "to foster minority representation at all levels ... through grants, existing internship programs and by more aggressively identifying whether minority candidates have been considered in the job interview process," and by tying management bonuses to management's performance in these areas. Thus it appears that, despite the daunting economic power of the networks and the seeming apathy of population segments toward boycotts and brownouts, these tools do retain the power to persuade and cajole the networks into at least paying lip service to the principle of diversity.

V. Conclusion

The protests and negotiations over the past year have resulted in some tangible gains. There was an increase in the number of roles for

African American actors in the fall 2000 television series lineup. Asian Americans and Latinos, however, remained largely invisible. The networks have also promised to address the absence of people of color in the creative process by training more writers and producers, and by actively seeking to employ writers and producers of color already established in the business.

These mixed results are encouraging. Certainly, the consciousness of the entertainment industry has been raised regarding the importance of diversity on both sides of the camera. The question now is, Where should people of color go from here?

First, monitoring and constant vigilance over the agreements with networks are an absolute necessity. Turnover in the management suites of television networks means that promises made by today's executives can quickly be forgotten by tomorrow's replacements. The emphasis on profit makes vigilance even more important. The statements of some within the industry make clear that while the goal of diversity is "socially desirable," networks will pursue it only in the context of programs that are successful in generating revenue for the networks. If today's City of Angels struggles in the ratings or tomorrow's new program, featuring an actor of color in a prominent and serious role, fails, the networks may abandon the pursuit of diversity. So advocacy groups must insist that producers and writers of color and shows with minority themes be given the same chance to fail and "try again" that networks extend to others shows and artists.

Second, groups should explore the options of filing litigation under Title VII and pursuing administrative action before the FCC, should networks fail to live up to the promises made in those agreements. The employment statistics for actors, writers and producers of color in the television industry present a ready-made prima facie showing of employment discrimination under Title VII. Statistics on the hiring practices of broadcast licensees should become more complete and readily available in light of the FCC regulations requiring extensive record-keeping. The explanations offered publicly by television's present executives, writers, and directors for their failure to create more roles for people of color would not provide satisfactory defenses to charges of unlawful employment discrimination. The threat of action under Title VII, if the networks do not correct current conditions, should create adequate leverage for securing more diversity.

The FCC insists that diversity of viewpoint is a valid objective of its broadcast licensing regulation. This allows advocates of color to threaten to challenge network licenses in order to ensure compliance with the promises made in fall 2000. Resorting to the FCC for relief by relying upon its equal opportunity regulations has two benefits. First, the FCC is unquestionably a more receptive audience for claims of racial discrimination than the federal judiciary, given the latter's current makeup. Second, pursuit of administrative remedies will likely require fewer financial and legal resources on the part of advocacy organizations.

Finally, public pressure on the networks must be maintained. Because of concerns over reputation, television networks seem especially responsive to public criticism on issues of diversity. As this past year's episode has demonstrated, a concerted public campaign demanding greater diversity does yield positive results. To ensure the effectiveness of public campaigns for diversity on and in television, advocates of color must formulate and clearly articulate persuasive objectives. The limited objective of securing more employment for actors, writers, directors, and producers of color is certainly legitimate and laudable. That goal is not, however, the kind of incentive necessary to convince people to turn off their television sets and limit their spending.

The campaign for diversity must focus on the societal impact of television's portrayal of people of color, or its lack thereof. Advocates must emphasize how ubiquitous television is, and how the images it projects shape the attitudes of all members of society. Advocates must never lose sight of the importance of a presence behind the camera and in all facets of the creative process, for these form the foundations upon which the images and concepts that flicker across the small screen are formed. When people of color gain access to the board rooms and studios where television's images are dreamed up and produced, those images and concepts are bound to become more diverse, and the messages transmitted about people of color will be, as a whole, more positive.

To have maximum effectiveness, a grassroots campaign for diversity in television must secure commitments from substantial majorities of the affected communities. If advocates of color can convince half of their constituents to turn off WB programs until they become less stereotypical, or to refuse to visit Disneyland or Disney World until ABC lives up to its promise to diversify its programs and creative management staffs, people of color will transmit a powerful message to network executives. Unless that message is communicated to television's decision makers, the saga of 1999 is destined to repeat itself.

Notes

1. A good exercise is to look up the Nielsen ratings for the most recent week at the following website: *http://www.nielsenmedia.com*. Compare the overall top 10 ratings with the top 10 shows for African–American and Hispanic viewers. Do African–American and Hispanic viewers share any shows in common with the overall top 10 ratings, which are dominated by the viewing preferences of Caucasians? During the week of 1/12/04–1/18/04, only two primetime shows (FOX NFC Championships and CSI) were among the top ten for African–Americans and for whites. All of the top ten primetime TV programs among Hispanics were on Univision. *Id.*

2. Are gays portrayed in a positive or negative light and with the frequency that represents their presence in the U.S. population? A decade after Ellen's debut as the first major gay character, some archconservatives began to complain "TV has gone 'gay, gay, gay'." See Steve Johnson, *Gays on TV: hardly a trend*, L.A. Times, Aug. 12, 2003. These conservatives cite

examples such as *Queer Eye for the Straight Guy*, *Will & Grace*, and *Six Feet Under*. *Will & Grace*, however, is the only show that is a network hit. The other two appear on cable. *Id*. See also Joanne Ostrow, *TV, real life converge in America's gay moment*, Denver Post, Aug. 14, 2003, at F.1.; and Brian Lowry, *TV Networks in Love with Gay Characters*, L.A. Times, Sept. 1, 2003 at D.5 ("As Hollywood winds down its gay, gay summer—dominated in media circles by Bravo's ubiquitous makeover series" Queer Eye for the Straight Guy"—the debate began shifting from tonnage to quality and whether TV's latest infatuation benefits the gay community or simply exploits it.").

In January 2004, Showtime aired another show aimed at gays called *The L Word*. Cox News Service said,

> Showtime's serial about beautiful lesbians living in equal parts lust and angst in Hollywood. Like "Queer as Folk," the male gay drama on Showtime, "The L Word" is sure to be surrounded by buzz and controversy. The new series has almost as much sex (some of it explicit) and nudity as its male counterpart, but it's less raunchy. The pilot episode focuses on two stories: the stirring of lesbian feelings in one young woman and the struggle to start a family by two women whose long-term relationship needs rekindling.

http/www.news-journalonline.com/NewsJournalOnline/Entertainment/Television/

3.   Have Native Americans have been overtly stereotyped? Consider the characters of Wind–In–His–Hair in *Dances With Wolves*, Chief Bromden in *One Flew Over the Cuckoo's Nest*, and Tonto in *The Lone Ranger*? Are these roles ripe for change? Two Native American filmmakers have been breaking new ground attempting to change those perceptions. Both Sherman Alexie (director of *The Business of Fancy Dancing*, writer of *Smoke Signals*) and Chris Eyre (director of *Skins* and *Smoke Signals*) attempt to show a different side of Native America. In the following interview with Chris Eyre, he explains his perception of his role as a Native American filmmaker.

Sherri Burr.
Making Native Films:
Author Interview with Director Chris Eyre.

© 2004 by Sherri Burr.

[As a graduate student at New York University Film School, Chris Eyre won the Haig Manoogian, Warner Brothers, and Martin Scorsese Post Production Awards, and the first place Mobil Award at NYU's First Run Film Festival. In 1995, he received the prestigious Rockefeller Foundation Intercultural Film Fellowship and was selected to attend Sundance Institute's Screenwriters, Producers and Filmmakers Labs. Eyre directed the 1998 *Smoke Signals*, which won the Filmmakers Trophy at the Sundance Film Festival and was the first movie by an American Indian director to be nationally released. He also directed the feature film *Skins*, which was distributed nationwide in 2002. His television credits include *Skinwalkers* and *A Thief of Time*, shown on

PBS in 2002 and 2004 respectively. Sherri Burr interviewed him by telephone from his home in South Dakota on Monday, February 2, 2004.]

"I have an AA in television directing, a BFA in media from the University of Arizona, and a MFA from New York University. I got into filmmaking through photography. I was always drawn to still images. I consider myself to be an artist and a filmmaker, rather than a director. The difference is that I want to be involved in every aspect of the portrayal of a certain story, from the writing and producing, to doing everything it takes to get the film made. We worked on *Smoke Signals* for three years before we got it financed. I started working on the screenplay before Sherman Alexie took it over.

"I've never made a Hollywood movie per se. When I'm hired to direct a movie, I'd rather be hands-on from beginning to distribution. I also get involved in the screenwriting and producing aspects of filmmaking, which doesn't stop with exhibition at major festivals. There's a whole national Native community that supports its own, with many Native American film festivals.

"There's a large difference between Native American people and Indian country. Indian country is comprised of the people who are the backbone of who we are. My stories seek to tell their perspectives. There is a lack of representation of Indian people in the mainstream media. I think Native American people get portrayed sometimes, or I should say the politically correct romanticism of what Indians should be. However, the media doesn't portray the average Joes of Indian country who are not romantic. Instead, they live ordinary lives with ordinary problems, like the alienation between the father and the son in Smoke Signals.

"When I told the New York Times in 2002, 'The only thing that has been more detrimental to Indians than religion has been John Ford movies,' I meant the context for Indians in movies happened way before John Ford. John Ford was the point person for 30 years of Native filmmaking. He always used Indians as the antagonist in his story lines and as a people who didn't have a culture. Not once did he ever investigate or get to the reasoning behind their culture. He also kept Indian people in the period of the Indian wars. Yet he was making his films some 50 to 70 years after the Indian wars. It was almost as if Indians were never allowed to grow out of that period when Indian people were regarded as savages, uncontrollable or romanticized. John Ford perpetuated those characters. The only thing more damaging to Indian people than religion was probably cinema.

"I'm not so interested in portraying positive images of Indians as I am in depicting accurate images. I'm not saying let's have a good clean image. Rather, it's about empathizing and knowing the people you are portraying. I'm not making my people noble, holier than thou people. We are human beings.

"Indians are a hyper-paradox when it comes to media. There are lots of images, but they are not necessarily accurate. Stereotypes are stereotypes because they are true. You have to challenge yourself as an artist and that means not following the rhythms of everybody else's political correctness. If you get upset at stereotypes, it's because they are hitting too close to home.

"I portray a chronic alcoholic, because I'm him. I take responsibility for this character who is a part of my community. It's not about correctness, its about responsibility. In Skins, it's about the undying love that two brothers have for each other regardless of one brother's affliction. One is a chronic alcoholic; the other is a police officer. They are oceans apart. At one point, Mogie Yellow Lodge [the alcoholic brother] yells out, 'You rat fucker, I love this woman.' He's holding a t-shirt with a picture of Madonna with the words 'Like a Virgin.' He's buried in his Madonna t-shirt. Of course, we had to get permission to use that image and we thanked her in the credits.

"Rudy Yellow Lodge [the police officer brother] has a beer in the movie but it doesn't make him an alcoholic. He loves his brother. He honors his brother's memory with care. The movie is [ultimately] about love for a family member.

"I tried to challenge myself. I also wanted to deconstruct romantic images of Indians. The funniest part of Skins is that these are the exact tribe of people portrayed in Dances with Wolves. If Jonathan Dunbar (Kevin Costner's character) had had any effect, these people would be doing better, in reality they are the poorest of all Americans. We were hoping that *Skins* would catch on, but it's not really a movie that people in Iowa would want to see.

"Major television networks put together diversity divisions, but no one has called me about my services as a director or called my agent. I'm the only Native American director who Robert Redford has hired twice. My agent is at CAA. It comes down to protocols.

"It's not difficult being a Native American director; it's difficult for anyone. It's harder for women than it is for anyone. Jane Campion [*The Piano, In the Cut*] is wonderful. Martha Coolidge [*Valley Girl, Rambling Rose*] is great. Barbara Streisand [*The Mirror Has Two Faces, The Prince of Tides, Yentl*] has not made a movie in 10 years, but she doesn't have to make a living directing. The male to female percentage of working directors is about 9:1. It's hard for women to get their foot in the door. You can make a movie, but it doesn't mean that you're going to be working as a filmmaker let alone as a director."

Notes

1. Is Chris Eyre's work intended for a Native American audience only? In *Smoke Signals*, Thomas Builds-the-Fire, through his stories, employs various references that are likely only recognizable by Native Americans. The perception that certain films are meant for a certain ethnic audience is

not new. Spike Lee (*Jungle Fever, Malcolm X*) is often stereotyped as a Black movie maker, which is not so much a reference to his own ethnicity as it is a reference to his perceived intended audience. If Eyre is labeled the new Spike Lee, what message is the public conveying to the film making industry about the work of directors of color? Should people of color support filmmakers of color?

2.   In his interview, Chris Eyre says that he wants to portray Native American people as they *really* are. In his film *Skins*, Mogie Yellow Lodge is an unemployed, chronic alcoholic, living on the Rosebud Sioux Reservation. Is Eyre merely confirming the stereotype? Should filmmakers of color be more sensitive to the images they are creating and selling? In the alternative, are enterprising filmmakers of color just wising up and capitalizing on already identifiable and easily marketable stereotypes? If Anglo filmmakers and filmmakers of color create and sell the same stereotyped image, how can change be accomplished?

3.   At the center of the diversity question is an economic one. Should producers and networks be permitted to generate whatever programming advertisers are willing to sponsor? Does the United States, for example, have an interest in creating a diverse society? How should that interest be balanced against the economic interest of producers and networks? Should the fact that children watch more television and their accompanying commercials than adults and form their opinions of other groups based on television images impact the economic interests of producers and networks?

Hae-Kyong Bang and Bonnie B. Reece
Minorities in Children's Television Commercials: New, Improved, and Stereotyped

American Council on Consumer Interests.
37 No. 1 Journal of Consumer Affairs 42
(June 22, 2003).
[citations and tables omitted].

Mass media is one means by which consumers learn how to behave as consumers. Consumers' beliefs about minorities as consumers are also influenced by mass media, and the impact is likely highest among young children. A content analysis of 813 commercials in children's television programming reveals that while Caucasians continue to be the predominant models in terms of numbers and in the types of roles they play, the numerical representation of minorities, especially Blacks, has improved. However, the study found that minorities are more likely than Caucasians to have minor roles and to be portrayed in certain product categories, settings, and relationships. * * *

Advertising bombards children in America. The average child in the U.S. may see more than 20,000 commercials per year in addition to some television programs that are actually hour-long commercials for toys and games (Murray and Lonnborg 1995). American children aged 2 through 11 watch television for 19 hours and 40 minutes per week (Nielsen Media Research 2000). Watching television is what children do most when they are not sleeping, and, more significantly, they often watch unaccompanied by adults. Thus, although other socialization agents such as schools, peers, or parents influence children's cognitive development, television, including commercials, has become an important part of the socialization process. . . .

By transmitting selective images and ideas, television commercials not only teach young consumers to buy and consume certain products, but they also teach children to accept certain beliefs and values. Thus, what children think of various ethnic minorities such as Blacks, Hispanics, or Asian Americans is often influenced by what they see on television programs and advertising . . . According to social learning theory, people learn certain beliefs and behaviors based on their observation of other people's behaviors. . . . Thus, if a television commercial shows a bright Black student being praised for outstanding academic performance after he or she eats a Carnation breakfast bar, young viewers, particularly children of color, may believe that they can perform as well as the model in the ad if they have the breakfast bar.

Likewise, cultivation theory suggests that constant exposures to a specific image of an object can lead to distorted beliefs about the object. . . . Thus, if children are repeatedly exposed to certain portrayals of an ethnic group, they may develop corresponding beliefs about the group. For instance, if children consistently see Asian Americans playing roles of technicians or mathematicians on television, they may learn to believe that Asian Americans are smart people. . . . This impact can be even greater if the children live without much meaningful contact with ethnic groups other than their own. . . .

The idea that youngsters view television as more than an entertainment vehicle is supported by a recent national poll reported by Children Now, a nonpartisan national children's advocacy group. This organization monitors media content to bring attention to issues such as diversity or violence portrayed in the media. In 1998, Children Now surveyed 1,200 children aged 10 to 17, with equal representation of the four largest ethnic groups—Caucasians, Blacks, Hispanics, and Asian Americans. According to the poll results, children overwhelmingly felt that it was important for them to see people of their own race on television because it sends a message that they matter. Not surprisingly this belief was expressed even more strongly by children of color (82% of Blacks, 79% of Asian Americans, and 78% of Hispanics compared to 67% of Caucasians). At the same time, children of all races indicated a belief that minority groups were more likely to be negatively portrayed than Caucasians. Additionally, 71% of children indicated that, when a boss is portrayed in the workplace on television, the boss is usually a Caucasian.

The survey also reported that children value diversity and want to see it on television. This demand seems justified since nearly three-quarters of them reported that some of their "best friends" were of different races, and that they would like to see more realistic portrayals of their lives on television, including showing more people of all races interacting with one another. These reactions suggest that advertising that fails to adequately reflect reality in terms of ethnic representation and its growing integration into the mainstream culture may alienate young consumers of all ethnic backgrounds, who perceive them to be unfair, out of touch, outdated, or not relevant to them. * * *

The purpose of the present study is to examine the existing state of affairs in terms of portrayals of Blacks, Hispanics, and Asian Americans in children's advertising in mainstream television reaching broad audiences. In doing so, the study will assess whether the portrayals lend themselves to cultivating a positive image of minority children as consumers and members of society, both among the minority group and the majority. The following aspects of portrayals are examined: minority representation in numbers, prominence, and age; single group representation; and representation by product type, setting, and relationships depicted in the ad. Although the present study is cross-sectional in nature, comparisons can be made between current minority portrayals and those reported in the past, particularly with regard to minorities neglected in prior studies due to their low representation (e.g., Asian Americans and Hispanics).... The study contributes to the literature by examining new aspects of portrayals of minorities in children's advertising in addition to updating data on representation of minority groups. Mainstream television was chosen for two reasons. First, mainstream English-speaking television tends to reflect mainstream culture, which tends to influence children of all ethnic backgrounds. Second, despite the growing influence of ethnic media on minorities, mainstream television is still the medium most widely and commonly shared by children of all ethnicities. * * *

HYPOTHESES

Representation, Prominence, and Single Group Ethnicities

Minority representation is assessed by using the proportionality criterion in this study. The proportionality criterion compares the representation of a group in advertising to its proportion of the actual population (Taylor and Stern 1997; Wilkes and Valencia 1989). In order to demonstrate an adequate level of representation, the proportions of different ethnic groups featured in advertising should match those in the population. According to the U.S. Census Bureau, the proportions of the overall U.S. population for Blacks, Hispanics, and Asian Americans in 1997 were 12.7%, 11%, and 3.7% respectively. When it comes to the U.S. children, minorities account for a somewhat higher proportion of the population, with 67.4% Caucasians, followed by Blacks at 14.8%, Hispanics at 13.2%, and Asian Americans at 3.6% in 1995, a number that has risen slightly in subsequent years (Statistical Abstract of the United States 2000). While many past studies reported figures well below proportionality, more recent studies have reported an improvement in advertising targeting the general population (Taylor and Stern 1997). It will be important to see whether a similar trend has also taken place in recent children's advertising in which minorities had been underrepresented in the past. * * *

METHOD

DATA COLLECTION

A sample of advertisements directed to children was collected in the following manner. Using TV Guide, we first identified programming labeled as "children" or "cartoon." We also used Nielsen data to identify time periods when children ages two to eleven make up a larger share of the TV audience than they represent in the U.S. population as a whole. The time periods and networks identified through these two processes included Saturday a.m. on ABC, CBS, Fox, Nickelodeon, and WB; Sunday a.m. on UPN; weekday a.m. on Fox; and weekday afternoons on Fox and Nickelodeon.

We then videotaped one sample of each network's time block, for a total of 42.5 hours of programming. Taping was spread out over several weeks in order to minimize the amount of duplication among commercials, a problem we had noted in some preliminary viewing. Taping occurred during February and March of 1997 so the data set would not be affected by unusual amounts of toy advertising that might take place during the fourth quarter of the year.

The final data set included 875 commercials, including local advertisements and public service announcements. Network and local station promotional announcements were excluded. Approximately 93% of the commercials (N=813) included models, and this number was used as a starting point for our analyses. Individual commercials were the primary unit of analysis to facilitate comparisons with prior studies and because commercials represent the "viewing unit" for the audience. * * *

RESULTS

*Representation, Prominence and Single Group
Presence of Ethnic Minorities*

A total of 813 commercials showed models.... [O]ut of these 813 commercials included in the sample, 99.0% of the ads (N = 805) showed models that were identified as Caucasian. Black models appeared in 50.9% of the ads, followed by Asian Americans who were depicted in 9.2% of the ads, and by Hispanic models who were seen in 8.7% of the ads. These figures can be compared with either U.S. Census data for the general population (i.e., 12.7% for Blacks, 11% for Hispanics, and 3.7% for Asian Americans in the general population) or for the children's population (i.e., 14.8% for Blacks, 13.2% Hispanics, and 3.6% Asian Americans).

In terms of the number of ads in which they are represented, using the proportionality criterion, Blacks and Asian Americans were overrepresented and Hispanics were somewhat underrepresented. These findings show a noticeable increase in Black representation, but also in non-

Black minority representation, compared to Greenberg and Brand's 1993 study that found little non-Black minority presence in children's television advertising. The data also represent an increase for Blacks compared with Taylor and Stern's 1997 study of prime-time advertising and comparable figures for Hispanics and Asian Americans. On this basis, there was support for Hypothesis 1–A with the exception of Hispanics.

Proportionality was also calculated using the number of models rather than the number of ads. Based on the frequency distributions for each ethnic group, there were 4,557 models in the sampled commercials. There were significant differences between the observed distributions and those that might be expected if the U.S. Census proportions were applied to the total (Chi-square = 4044.16, df = 3, p < .001). Using this approach (i.e., counting the number of models, not commercials), Caucasians and Blacks were overrepresented while Hispanics and Asian Americans were underrepresented.

Regardless of numbers, a more critical issue may be whether different ethnic groups exhibit different levels of prominence when they appear in children's television advertising. For instance, Blacks were well represented, but did they appear in major roles or background roles? The results showed that Caucasians were found to be featured in major roles more frequently than any other ethnic group (Chi-square = 59.64, df 6, p < .001). As Table 1–B shows, 92.4% of the ads showing any Caucasian model showed them in major roles while the comparable figures for Black and Asian American models were 79.2% and 86.7% respectively. Hispanic models were least likely to be featured in major roles (71.8% of the ads showing Hispanics). Conversely, proportions for minor and background roles demonstrate higher minority representations. When Hispanic models appeared in the ads, 23.9% of the time they were shown in minor roles, whereas the proportion of Caucasian models set in minor roles was lowest at only 6.5%, followed by Asian Americans at 13.3% and Blacks at 17.4%. Thus, in terms of prominence, minorities were shown with less prominence than Caucasians in general, and Hispanic models were least likely to be shown in major roles but most likely to be shown in minor or background roles. Thus, Hypothesis 1–B was supported.

Despite the growing desire for diversity, members in an individual ethnic group tend to interact among themselves (Allen 1998). Of all ads included in the study, almost a half of the ads (48.5%) showed single ethnic groups, featuring Caucasians predominantly. As Table 1–C shows, 47.5% of all the ads included in the sample showed only Caucasians. Blacks appeared as a single group in 1.0% of the ads, while Hispanics and Asian Americans never appeared as a single group featured in children's television advertising. This suggests that, although children of all ethnic backgrounds are exposed to proportionately more minorities portrayed in children's advertising, all children including minority children are exposed to a single Caucasian group almost half of the time. Meanwhile Black, Hispanic or Asian American children never or almost never saw their own ethnic members as a single group in these ads. This finding is consistent with a prior study that examined mainstream magazine ads (Bowen and Schmid 1997). Thus, Hypothesis 1–C was supported.

Product Type by Ethnic Minorities [omitted] * * *

DISCUSSION

The findings of our study suggest that, in terms of the simple presence of minorities, the symbolic world portrayed in children's television advertising appears to be highly diverse with considerable minority representation. Blacks and Asian Americans, in particular, appeared in more commercials than might be expected given their numbers in the general population. This finding is consistent with those of recent content analyses of prime-time advertising (Taylor and Stern 1997) and mainstream magazine advertising (Taylor and Bang 1997). It should be noted that the low representation of Hispanics might be partly due to coding difficulties previously noted in the method section. Although many Hispanics can be easily identified based on appearance or other information provided in an ad, some Hispanics can be perceived to be Caucasians, or some other ethnic group, especially by non-Hispanic members of society. According to 1995 Census data, about 11% of Caucasians indicated that they were of Hispanic origin after identifying themselves as Caucasians. The equivalent numbers for Blacks and Asian Americans were 4.6% and 6.0% (Statistical Abstract of the U.S. 2000). Despite this issue, the study found that minorities in general were portrayed in more children's television commercials than was the case in studies conducted over the past few decades.

In spite of improved representation, the study showed that some problematic patterns persist. These patterns may affect minority consumers' views of their role in society. First, certain aspects of quantitative representation remain an issue. For instance, when the number of models was analyzed, only Blacks were over represented among minority groups. Likewise, when it came to single ethnic group representation, the study found that minorities were still seldom shown without a Caucasian model in the ad, while Caucasians were much more frequently shown as a single ethnic group. As Seiter (1990) pointed out, it is easy to pick out models of color because they rarely appear, but harder to see their absence in all-Caucasian commercials. If children learn to behave in a certain way by watching other people behave, as social learning theory suggests, children of color in particular may not have as many opportunities to learn about interaction within their group. Similarly Caucasian children may learn to believe that other ethnic groups are just like them, and thus fail to respect differences that exist among other ethnic groups. Although fair portrayals of minorities in a single group may not be an individual advertiser's communication priority, advertisers should recognize the portrayals' unintended social impact on children's perception by recognizing different ethnic groups as a single entity in an otherwise predominantly Caucasian world. A general example of recognizing an ethnic group is news coverage of Kwanzaa celebrations: it is a recognition of the Black heritage directed to the Black population because society pays respect to their distinctive culture even though it may not be necessarily personally shared by other non-Black groups. This kind of recognition can communicate to all members of the society that our culture values and celebrates its diversity. However, these types of images remain rare in advertising.

A second problem was found in the continued stereotyping of certain minorities portrayed in children's television advertising. Some current portrayals of minorities with a clear association with certain product categories may perpetuate stereotypes. For instance, our study found that Blacks were still more likely to be featured in food commercials than any other ethnic group, while simultaneously being the least likely to be featured in toy commercials. This striking association with the food category was not found with any other ethnic groups. Cultivation theory suggests that this kind of continued stereotyping can unduly influence children's beliefs about certain minorities. The underrepresentation of Black children in toy commercials may cultivate a belief that Black children are not "mainstream" enough to appear in all types of commercials.

Similar to the findings by product category, the study found that Blacks and Asian Americans were less likely than Caucasians to be shown in a home setting or in family relationships. Again, cultivation theory suggests that the absence of portrayals in these settings may contribute to a stereotype that many Black people do not have strong family ties or that many Asian American parents are too busy at their workplace to have family time at home.

The study also found that while children and teenagers accounted for the majority of the models of all ethnic groups, which was expected for children's advertising, Caucasian adult representation was much higher than the minority adult representation. This may lead to a perception that minority children are left unsupervised much more readily than Caucasian children, and that the absence of adults in minority children's life is quite widespread. Thus, in the context of minority children being exposed to the persuasive communications of advertisers, skewed portrayals may have a negative impact on consumers perceptions of other groups as consumers as well as members of society at large.

Conclusion

The findings have implications for children, both as consumers and members of society at large. Children reported that television is a major learning source (Children Now 1998; Greenberg and Atkin 1982). The frequency with which Caucasians appear, and the prominence of their roles, may reinforce the perception that Caucasians are more important than others just because they are the majority. This can have a negative impact on minority children since the importance of their existence in this world is reduced in the world of television (Powell 1982), therefore potentially harming the child's self-perception. Some prior research emphasizes this concern since studies have shown that Black children were more likely to perceive what they see in advertising as being truthful (Donohue 1975; Meyer, Donohue and Henke 1978). A negative impact may also be extended to majority children in some way because their perceived self-importance may be unduly inflated in the world of television. Therefore if a child repeatedly sees a model of his or her ethnic group playing a minor role or major role, it can lead to somewhat unrealistic self-perception. Although earlier research on minority portrayals was focused on Blacks due to the lack of presence of other minorities, similar implications can be made for other minorities (Powell 1982). Although minority consumers, particularly young ones born and growing up in the U.S., are known to move back and forth between their own culture and the mainstream culture (MarketResearch.com 2000), the Wall Street Journal (Wynter 1999) reported that many young minority consumers are going back to their roots and rediscovering the value of their ethnic identity. Thus, conscious efforts should be made to portray all ethnic groups fairly and in a non-stereotypical manner so that minority groups are seen as valued consumers well integrated into the society.

One limitation of the study involves the fact that only one medium is used—mainstream television. With much diversity found in the current media landscape, more diversity in minority portrayals can be expected. A future study should examine minority and Caucasian portrayals in ethnic media to see whether there are quantitative and qualitative differences between ethnic media and mainstream media. While society continues a discourse on race relationship and has high expectations for the generation growing up in a more diverse and open society, it is important to recognize that media content including advertising can contribute to better socialization of young consumers by adequately portraying all ethnic groups without resorting to stereotypical portrayals of certain ethnic groups.

Note

1.   The Bang & Reece study presents evidence that Blacks and Asians are statistically over-represented in commercials, yet the images they portray are not always positive. This begs the question: Were Blacks, for example, better off during the 1999–2000 television season when no new Black characters were added to network TV lineup than they are being over-represented in television commercials but the images are negative? Is no representation better than negative representation?

B.   CENSORSHIP IN TELEVISION

Another major question that arises concerning television images is whether television should be required to portray shows that do not offend the sensitivities of the American populace. Toward that end, numerous private and public institutions and individuals have tried to regulate what can and cannot be seen in American living rooms.

A furor erupted after Janet Jackson and Justin Timberlake performed a song and dance routine for the Feb. 1, 2004, Super Bowl halftime show. At the end of the routine, Timberlake sang the lyrics, "I gotta have you naked by the end of this song," as he tore off part of Jackson's top and exposed her bejeweled right breast for about a second. The performance had consequences for both singers. Jackson was reportedly dropped from starring in an ABC television movie based on the life of Lena Horne after Horne refused to cooperate with the production as long as Jackson remained in the role. *See* Lawrence Van Gelder, *Art Briefing*, N.Y. TIMES, Feb. 26, 2004. Timberlake cancelled his commitment to co-host ABC's *Motown 45* special with Lionel Richie after a coalition of African–American organizations protested the Timberlake connection. *Id.*

Hundreds of thousands of Americans contacted the FCC to protest the breast exposure, leading the U.S. Senate Commerce Committee to consider a measure aimed at cracking down on indecent television and radio broadcasts. The Senate contemplated increasing fines tenfold to $275,000 per indecency violation–up to a maximum of $3 million. Reuters, *Senate Panel to Consider New Indecency Bill—McCain*, N.Y. TIMES, Mar. 2, 2004. The House Energy and Commerce Committee mulled over an amendment to require the FCC to hold hearings on whether to revoke a broadcaster's license after three indecency violations. *Id.*

The following case discusses the efforts of the FCC to require cable operators to block or fully scramble programming primarily dedicated to sexually oriented programming.

UNITED STATES v. PLAYBOY ENTERTAINMENT GROUP

United States Supreme Court, 2000.
529 U.S. 803, 120 S.Ct. 1878, 146 L.Ed.2d 865.

Justice KENNEDY delivered the opinion of the Court.

This case presents a challenge to § 505 of the Telecommunications Act of 1996, Pub.L. 104–104, 110 Stat. 136, 47 U.S.C. § 561 (1994 ed., Supp. III). Section 505 requires cable television operators who provide channels "primarily dedicated to sexually-oriented programming" either to "fully scramble or otherwise fully block" those channels or to limit their transmission to hours when children are unlikely to be viewing, set by administrative regulation as the time between 10 p.m. and 6 a.m. U.S.C. § 561(a) (1994 ed., Supp. III); 47 CFR § 76.227 (1999). Even before enactment of the statute, signal scrambling was already in use. Cable operators used scrambling in the regular course of business, so that only paying customers had access to certain programs. Scrambling could be imprecise, however; and either or both audio and visual portions of the scrambled programs might be heard or seen, a phenomenon known as "signal bleed." The purpose of § 505 is to shield children from hearing or seeing images resulting from signal bleed.

To comply with the statute, the majority of cable operators adopted the second, or "time channeling," approach. The effect of the widespread adoption of time channeling was to eliminate altogether the transmission of the targeted programming outside the safe harbor period in affected cable service areas. In other words, for two-thirds of the day no household in those service areas could receive the programming, whether or not the household or the viewer wanted to do so.

Appellee Playboy Entertainment Group, Inc., challenged the statute as unnecessarily restrictive content-based legislation violative of the First Amendment. After a trial, a three-judge District Court concluded that a regime in which viewers could order signal blocking on a household-by-household basis presented an effective, less restrictive alternative to § 505. 30 F.Supp.2d 702, 719 (D.Del.1998). Finding no error in this conclusion, we affirm.

I

Playboy Entertainment Group owns and prepares programs for adult television networks, including Playboy Television and Spice. Playboy transmits its programming to cable television operators, who retransmit it to their subscribers, either through monthly subscriptions to premium channels or on a so-called "pay-per-view" basis. Cable operators transmit Playboy's signal, like other premium channel signals, in scrambled form. The operators then provide paying subscribers with an "addressable converter," a box placed on the home television set. The converter permits the viewer to see and hear the descrambled signal. It is conceded that almost all of Playboy's programming consists of sexually explicit material as defined by the statute.

The statute was enacted because not all scrambling technology is perfect. Analog cable television systems may use either "RF" or "baseband" scrambling systems, which may not prevent signal bleed, so discernible pictures may appear from time to time on the scrambled screen. Furthermore, the listener might hear the audio portion of the program.

These imperfections are not inevitable. The problem is that at present it appears not to be economical to convert simpler RF or baseband scrambling systems to alternative scrambling technologies on a systemwide scale. Digital technology may one day provide another solution, as it presents no bleed problem at all. Indeed, digital systems are projected to become the technology of choice, which would eliminate the signal bleed problem. Digital technology is not yet in widespread use, however. With imperfect scrambling, viewers who have not paid to receive Playboy's channels may happen across discernible images of a sexually explicit nature. How many viewers, how discernible the scene or sound, and how often this may occur are at issue in this case.

Section 505 was enacted to address the signal bleed phenomenon. As noted, the statute and its implementing regulations require cable operators either to scramble a sexually explicit channel in full or to limit the channel's programming to the hours between 10 p.m. and 6 a.m. 47 U.S.C. § 561 (1994 ed., Supp. III); 47 CFR § 76.227 (1999). Section 505 was added by floor amendment, without significant debate, to the Telecommunications Act of 1996 (Act), a major legislative effort designed "to reduce regulation and encourage 'the rapid deployment of new telecommunications technologies.' " * * *

On March 7, 1996, Playboy obtained a temporary restraining order (TRO) enjoining the enforcement of § 505. 918 F.Supp. 813 (D.Del. 1996), and brought this suit in a three-judge District Court pursuant to § 561 of the Act, 110 Stat. 142, note following 47 U.S.C. § 223 (1994 ed., Supp. III). Playboy sought a declaration that § 505 violates the Constitution and an injunction prohibiting the law's enforcement. The District Court denied Playboy a preliminary injunction, 945 F.Supp. 772 (D.Del. 1996), and we summarily affirmed, 520 U.S. 1141, 117 S.Ct. 1309, 137 L.Ed.2d 473 (1997). The TRO was lifted, and the Federal Communications Commission announced it would begin enforcing § 505 on May 18, 1997. *In re Implementation of Section 505 of the Telecommunications Act of 1996*, 12 FCC Rcd. 5212, 5214 (1997).

When the statute became operative, most cable operators had "no practical choice but to curtail [the targeted] programming during the [regulated] sixteen hours or risk the penalties imposed ... if any audio or video signal bleed occur[red] during [those] times." 30 F.Supp.2d, at 711. The majority of operators—"in one survey, 69%"—complied with § 505 by time channeling the targeted programmers. Ibid. Since "30 to 50% of all adult programming is viewed by households prior to 10 p.m.," the result was a significant restriction of communication, with a corresponding reduction in Playboy's revenues. *Ibid.*

In March 1998, the District Court held a full trial and concluded that § 505 violates the First Amendment. *Id.*, at 702. The District Court observed that § 505 imposed a content-based restriction on speech. *Id.*, at 714–715. It agreed that the interests the statute advanced were compelling but concluded the Government might further those interests in less restrictive ways. *Id.*, at 717–720. One plausible, less restrictive alternative could be found in another section of the Act: § 504, which requires a cable operator, "[u]pon request by a cable service subscriber ... without charge, [to] fully scramble or otherwise fully block" any channel the subscriber does not wish to receive. 110 Stat. 136, 47 U.S.C. § 560 (1994 ed., Supp. III). As long as subscribers knew about this opportunity, the court reasoned, § 504 would provide as much protection against unwanted programming as would § 505. 30 F.Supp.2d, at 718–720. At the same time, § 504 was content neutral and would be less restrictive of Playboy's First Amendment rights. *Ibid.*

The court described what "adequate notice" would include, suggesting "[operators] should communicate to their subscribers the information that certain channels broadcast sexually-oriented programming; that signal bleed may appear; that children may view signal bleed without their parents' knowledge or permission; that channel blocking devices ... are available free of charge ...; and that a request for a free device ... can be made by a telephone call to the [operator]." *Id.*, at 719. * * *

The District Court concluded that § 504 so supplemented would be an effective, less restrictive alternative to § 505, and consequently declared § 505 unconstitutional and enjoined its enforcement. *Id.*, at 719–720. The court also required Playboy to insist on these notice provisions in its contracts with cable operators. *Ibid.*

The United States filed a direct appeal in this Court pursuant to § 561. The District Court thereafter dismissed for lack of jurisdiction two post-trial motions filed by the Government. App. to Juris. Statement 91a–92a. We noted probable jurisdiction, 527 U.S. 1021, 119 S.Ct. 2365, 144 L.Ed.2d 769 (1999), and now affirm.

II

Two essential points should be understood concerning the speech at issue here. First, we shall assume that many adults themselves would find the material highly offensive; and when we consider the further circumstance that the material comes unwanted into homes where children might see or hear it against parental wishes or consent, there are legitimate reasons for regulating it. Second, all parties bring the case to us on the premise that Playboy's programming has First Amendment protection. As this case has been litigated, it is not alleged to be obscene; adults have a constitutional right to view it; the Government disclaims any interest in preventing children from seeing or hearing it with the consent of their parents; and Playboy has concomitant rights under the First Amendment to transmit it. These points are undisputed.

The speech in question is defined by its content; and the statute which seeks to restrict it is content based. Section 505 applies only to channels primarily dedicated to "sexually explicit adult programming or other programming that is indecent." The statute is unconcerned with signal bleed from any other channels. See 945 F.Supp., at 785 ("[Section 505] does not apply when signal bleed occurs on other premium channel networks, like HBO or the Disney Channel"). The overriding justification for the regulation is concern for the effect of the subject matter on young viewers. Section 505 is not " 'justified without reference to the content of the regulated speech.' " * * * It "focuses only on the content of the speech and the direct impact that speech has on its listeners." * * * This is the essence of content-based regulation.

Not only does § 505 single out particular programming content for regulation, it also singles out particular programmers. The speech in question was not thought by Congress to be so harmful that all channels were subject to restriction. Instead, the statutory disability applies only to channels "primarily dedicated to sexually-oriented programming." 47

U.S.C. § 561(a) (1994 ed., Supp. III). One sponsor of the measure even identified appellee by name. See 141 Cong. Rec. 15587 (1995) (statement of Sen. Feinstein) (noting the statute would apply to channels "such as the Playboy and Spice channels"). Laws designed or intended to suppress or restrict the expression of specific speakers contradict basic First Amendment principles. Section 505 limited Playboy's market as a penalty for its programming choice, though other channels capable of transmitting like material are altogether exempt.

The effect of the federal statute on the protected speech is now apparent. It is evident that the only reasonable way for a substantial number of cable operators to comply with the letter of § 505 is to time channel, which silences the protected speech for two-thirds of the day in every home in a cable service area, regardless of the presence or likely presence of children or of the wishes of the viewers. According to the District Court, "30 to 50% of all adult programming is viewed by households prior to 10 p.m.," when the safe-harbor period begins. 30 F.Supp.2d, at 711. To prohibit this much speech is a significant restriction of communication between speakers and willing adult listeners, communication which enjoys First Amendment protection. It is of no moment that the statute does not impose a complete prohibition. The distinction between laws burdening and laws banning speech is but a matter of degree. The Government's content-based burdens must satisfy the same rigorous scrutiny as its content-based bans.

Since § 505 is a content-based speech restriction, it can stand only if it satisfies strict scrutiny. *Sable Communications of Cal., Inc. v. FCC,* 492 U.S. 115, 126, 109 S.Ct. 2829, 106 L.Ed.2d 93 (1989). If a statute regulates speech based on its content, it must be narrowly tailored to promote a compelling Government interest. *Ibid.* If a less restrictive alternative would serve the Government's purpose, the legislature must use that alternative. *Reno,* 521 U.S., at 874, 117 S.Ct. 2329. * * * To do otherwise would be to restrict speech without an adequate justification, a course the First Amendment does not permit. * * *

The statute now before us burdens speech because of its content; it must receive strict scrutiny.

There is, moreover, a key difference between cable television and the broadcasting media, which is the point on which this case turns: Cable systems have the capacity to block unwanted channels on a household-by-household basis. The option to block reduces the likelihood, so concerning to the Court in *Pacifica, supra,* at 744, 98 S.Ct. 3026, that traditional First Amendment scrutiny would deprive the Government of all authority to address this sort of problem. The corollary, of course, is that targeted blocking enables the Government to support parental authority without affecting the First Amendment interests of speakers and willing listeners—listeners for whom, if the speech is unpopular or indecent, the privacy of their own homes may be the optimal place of receipt. Simply put, targeted blocking is less restrictive than banning, and the Government cannot ban speech if targeted blocking is a feasible and effective means of furthering its compelling interests. This is not to say that the absence of an effective blocking mechanism will in all cases suffice to support a law restricting the speech in question; but if a less restrictive means is available for the Government to achieve its goals, the Government must use it. * * *

Basic speech principles are at stake in this case. When the purpose and design of a statute is to regulate speech by reason of its content, special consideration or latitude is not accorded to the Government merely because the law can somehow be described as a burden rather than outright suppression. We cannot be influenced, moreover, by the perception that the regulation in question is not a major one because the speech is not very important. The history of the law of free expression is one of vindication in cases involving speech that many citizens may find shabby, offensive, or even ugly. It follows that all content-based restrictions on speech must give us more than a moment's pause. If television broadcasts can expose children to the real risk of harmful exposure to indecent materials, even in their own home and without parental consent, there is a problem the Government can address. It must do so, however, in a way consistent with First Amendment principles. Here the Government has not met the burden the First Amendment imposes.

The Government has failed to show that § 505 is the least restrictive means for addressing a real problem; and the District Court did not err in holding the statute violative of the First Amendment. In light of our ruling, it is unnecessary to address the second question presented: whether the District Court was divested of jurisdiction to consider the Government's postjudgment motions after the Government filed a notice of appeal in this Court. The judgment of the District Court is affirmed. * * *

Justice BREYER, with whom THE CHIEF JUSTICE, Justice O'CONNOR, and Justice SCALIA join, dissenting.

* * * Unlike the majority, I believe the record makes clear that § 504's opt-out is not a similarly effective alternative. Section 504 (opt-out) and § 505 (opt-in) work differently in order to achieve very different legislative objectives. Section 504 842 gives parents the power to tell cable operators to keep any channel out of their home. Section 505 does more. Unless parents explicitly consent, it inhibits the transmission of adult cable channels to children whose parents may be unaware of what they are watching, whose parents cannot easily supervise television viewing habits, whose parents do not know of their § 504 "opt-out" rights, or whose parents are simply unavailable at critical times. In this respect, § 505 serves the same interests as the laws that deny children access to adult cabarets or X-rated movies. E.g., Del.Code Ann., Tit. 11, § 1365(i)(2) (1995); D.C.Code Ann. § 22–2001(b)(1)(B) (1996). These laws, and § 505, all act in the absence of direct parental supervision. * * *

By definition, § 504 does nothing at all to further the compelling interest I have just described. How then is it a similarly effective § 505 alternative?

The record, moreover, sets forth empirical evidence showing that the two laws are not equivalent with respect to the Government's objectives. As the majority observes, during the 14 months the Government was enjoined from enforcing § 505, "fewer than 0.5% of cable subscribers requested full blocking" under § 504. Ante, at 1888. The majority describes this public reaction as "a collective yawn," ibid., adding that the Government failed to prove that the "yawn" reflected anything other than the lack of a serious signal bleed problem or a lack of notice which better information about § 504 might cure. The record excludes the first possibility—at least in respect to exposure, as discussed above. See supra, at 1900–1901. And I doubt that the public, though it may well consider the viewing habits of adults a matter of personal choice, would "yawn" when the exposure in question concerns young children, the absence of parental consent, and the sexually explicit material here at issue. See ante, at 1896–1897 (SCALIA, J., dissenting).

Neither is the record neutral in respect to the curative power of better notice. Section 504's opt-out right works only when parents (1) become aware of their § 504 rights, (2) discover that their children are watching sexually explicit signal "bleed," (3) reach their cable operator and ask that it block the sending of its signal to their home, (4) await installation of an individual blocking device, and, perhaps (5) (where the block fails or the channel number changes) make a new request. Better notice of § 504 rights does little to help parents discover their children's viewing habits (step 2). And it does nothing at all in respect to steps 3 through 5. Yet the record contains considerable evidence that those problems matter, i.e., evidence of endlessly delayed phone call responses, faulty installations, blocking failures, and other mishaps, leaving those steps as significant § 504 obstacles. See, e.g., Deposition of J. Cavalier in Civ. Action No. 96–94, pp. 17–18 (D.Del., Dec. 5, 1997) ("It's like calling any utilities; you sit there, and you wait and wait on the phone. . . . [It took] [t]hree weeks, numerous phone calls. . . . [E]very time I call Cox Cable . . . I get different stories"); Telephonic Deposition of M. Bennett, id., at 10–11 (D.Del., Dec. 9, 1997) ("After two [failed installations,] no, I don't recall calling them again. I just said well, I guess this is something I'm going to have to live with"). * * *

Of course, it is logically possible that "better notice" will bring about near perfect parental knowledge (of what children watch and § 504 opt-out rights), that cable operators will respond rapidly to blocking requests, and that still 94% of all informed parents will decided not to have adult channels blocked for free. But the probability that this remote possibility will occur is neither a "draw" nor a "tie." Ante, at 1889. And that fact is sufficient for the Government to have met its burden of proof.

All these considerations show that § 504's opt-out, even with the Court's plan for "better notice," is not similarly effective in achieving the legitimate goals that the statute was enacted to serve. * * *

Notes

indecency

1. The Federal Communications Commission makes a distinction between broadcasting obscene programming, which is not protected by the First Amendment and prohibited at all times, and broadcasting of indecent programming, which is limited to certain hours. The FCC defines indecency as "language or material that, in context, depicts or describes, in terms patently offensive as measured by contemporary community broadcast standards for the broadcast medium, sexual or excretory organs or activities." The FCC can revoke a station's license, impose monetary fines, or issue warnings for violations of its rules. Individuals may file complaints with the FCC's Enforcement Bureau, Investigations and Hearings Division, 445 12th Street, S.W., Room 3–B443, Washington, DC 20554.

2. Do television writers lose creative opportunities to censorship? In 1979, the Writers Guild of America, West, Inc. (Writers Guild), and Tandem Productions, Inc. (Tandem) instituted actions against the Federal Communications Commission (FCC) and its Commissioners Wiley, Hooks, Lee, Quello, Reid, Robinson, and Washburn, the three major television networks (ABC, CBS, and NBC), and the National Association of Broadcasters (NAB) to challenge the adoption of the so-called "family viewing policy" as an amendment to the NAB Television Code. The Writers Guild plaintiffs sought declaratory and injunctive relief against the government defendants for violations of the First Amendment, the Administrative Procedure Act, and section 326 of the Federal Communications Act, and against the private defendants on both First Amendment and antitrust grounds. Writers Guild of America v. ABC, 609 F.2d 355 (9th Cir. 1979).

3. Does society gain when parents can limit the viewing habits of their children? In Europe, for example, sexually explicit images are available on television during evening viewing hours. Europeans have argued that Americans are two uptight about sex. Are they right? Does placing television limits on sex feed into their perceptions of Americans?

4. In one category—the weight of Americans—Europeans view television as unrepresentative of reality. A Dutchman visiting Montana in 1997 told Professor Burr that his friends warned him not to think Americas will look like they do on TV. "They're all fat," his friends warned him. While the word "all" may indicate an exaggeration, some studies, as revealed in section C of this chapter, indicate that television may have an impact on individual weight gain and help explain why 2/3rds of all Americans are considered overweight.

WESTMORELAND v. CBS

United States Court of Appeals, Second Circuit, 1984.
752 F.2d 16.

OAKES, Circuit Judge.

This case presents the novel question whether a cable news network has a right to televise a federal trial and the public a right to view that trial—where the court is adjudicating a civil action, where both parties have consented to the presence of television cameras in the courtroom under the close supervision of a willing court, but where a facially applicable court rule prohibits the presence of such cameras. The rule is backed by a canon of the Code of Judicial Conduct for United States Judges and supported by resolutions, recommendations, and reports of the Judicial Conference of the United States. It was adopted by the federal district court in which the trial in question is taking place, pursuant to the statutory and rulemaking power the district court holds to determine the conduct of trial procedure within its courtrooms.

The challenge we address, however, is directed to the rule as applied to a particular trial, *Westmoreland v. CBS, Inc.*, 82 Civ. 7913 (S.D.N.Y. filed Nov. 30, 1982) (Leval, J.). The appellants argue that, given the extraordinary nature of the *Westmoreland* trial, the application of a general rule prohibiting television coverage of that trial is both beyond the court's powers and in violation of the First Amendment rights of the television network and the public. Moreover, the facts that frame the *Westmoreland* trial are asserted to be of particular importance, because the substantive issues in *Westmoreland* implicitly mirror the institutional tensions raised before this court—in *Westmoreland*, one party seeks redress of injury flowing from statements asserting that the Government withheld information from the public in order to insulate the Government from public scrutiny; while the other party, seeking to defend the integrity of those statements, implicitly defends the integrity of the medium through which those statements were made. Be this as it may, assuming arguendo that *Westmoreland* presents the paradigm case for televising a federal trial, we nevertheless affirm, for the reasons we state below.

FACTS

The trial of *Westmoreland v. CBS, Inc.* commenced before the United States District Court for the Southern District of New York, Pierre N. Leval, Judge, on October 9, 1984, in a courtroom that, we assume on judicial notice, accommodates no more than 150 seats, 80 of which have been set aside for the news media. We assume that the appellant, Cable News Network, Inc., correctly describes the case in noting "the pervasive and historical import of its issues, the prevalence of television in its facts and law, and the unanimous desire of the participants to disseminate the entire trial to all who would observe." We also assume, as put forth by the district court, that among the questions at issue in the trial will be whether the high United States military command in Vietnam willfully distorted intelligence data to substantiate optimistic reports on the progress of the war and whether one of the nation's most important sources of news and commentary subsequently engaged in defamation of a public figure. These issues are no doubt of considerable, if not, as the district court believes, the "highest" national importance.

We further assume the truth of CNN's assertion that the guidelines it proposed to the district court on a one-case experimental basis follow the guidelines of some forty-one states that now permit, in one form or another, audiovisual coverage of court proceedings, trial, appellate, or both. We may therefore assume that those guidelines have been reasonably tested in the state courts and are narrowly tailored to achieve unobtrusive distribution of audiovisual coverage. Thus, CNN's initial petition to the district court for permission to distribute comprehensive coverage of the Westmoreland trial reflects a conscientious broadcaster taking appropriate steps to join an important issue in the courts.

In a carefully reasoned opinion and order, Judge Leval felt that, for various reasons summarized in the margin, CNN's petition "should be granted." Nevertheless, he denied the application on September 19, 1984, because "the rules of the Judicial Conference and of this court are to the contrary," and because he believed that the rule was not subject to waiver. 596 F.Supp. 1166. On September 27, 1984, CNN filed a motion for reconsideration, based on the argument that the reasoning underlying the court's previous denial of CNN's petition constituted an authoritative finding that the general factual premises underlying Canon 3 A(7) of the Canons of Judicial Conduct for United States Courts (hereinafter Canon 3 A(7)) and Local General Rule 7 of the Southern District of New York do not apply to the circumstances of this case. The motion for reconsideration was denied by Judge Leval on September 28, 1984.

Meanwhile, on September 19, 1984, CNN had petitioned the Board of Judges of the Southern District for a waiver of General Rule 7. We will treat, as the parties have treated, a letter of October 1, 1984, signed by Chief Judge Constance Baker Motley, stating that "it was the view of the Board of Judges that Local Rule 7 should not be waived," as a denial of that petition.

This appeal is by CNN from the opinion and order of Judge Leval dated September 19, 1984, denying the initial petition to distribute coverage, from the denial of CNN's motion for reconsideration dated September 28, 1984, and from the determination of the Board of Judges denying CNN's petition for waiver of General Rule 7 on October 1, 1984. CNN initially filed a petition for a writ of mandamus with this court; but on the basis that such a writ may not be used in lieu of an appeal, the petition was denied by a panel consisting of Judges Kaufman, Pierce, and Winter.

DISCUSSION

Appealability

The circuits have expressed some disagreement concerning the proper avenue for appellate review of district court orders limiting media access to judicial proceedings. *See United States v. Chagra*, 701 F.2d 354, 359–60 (5th Cir.1983). Recently, this court followed the Third Circuit's approach of allowing media intervenors to appeal orders limiting courtroom access under the collateral order doctrine of *Cohen v. Beneficial Industrial Loan Corp.*, 337 U.S. 541, 69 S.Ct. 1221, 93 L.Ed. 1528 (1949), because such an order is a final disposition by the district court collateral to the rights asserted in the main action and posing a risk of irreparable harm while involving a serious and unsettled question of law. *See In re Herald Co.*, 734 F.2d 93, 96 (2d Cir.1984). Like the *Herald* panel, we find that the district court "in effect permitted [the press] to intervene in the pending . . . case, at least for the purpose of objecting to closure of the courtroom." Id. * * * We thus treat the orders of the district court and the determination of the Board of Judges as appealable.

CNN's Ultra Vires Argument

CNN argues that General Rule 7 is unauthorized as applied to this case, because 28 U.S.C. § 2072, the ultimate statutory authority for the provision, prohibits the adoption of rules that "abridge, enlarge or modify substantive rights," and the application of General Rule 7 violates that prohibition in this particular case by abridging the First Amendment rights of CNN and the public.

The salient feature of this ultra vires argument is its dependence upon the existence of a substantive right under the First Amendment to television camera access to a federal trial. CNN does not argue against the authority of the judiciary to adopt general rules prescribing the conduct of courtroom proceedings. It instead argues that in this particular case, the First Amendment abridgement resulting from the implementation of General Rule 7 renders its application here ultra vires. The constitutional issues emerge as determinative of CNN's claims in this case, and to those issues we now proceed.

The Constitutional Right to Obtain Waiver of General
Rule 7 in the Westmoreland Trial

As an initial matter, we address the First Amendment claims of the press but quickly fold them, given the circumstances of this case, into the First Amendment claims of the public, for CNN's status as a member of the press does not entitle it to claim a First Amendment right to televise federal trials. As Chief Justice Warren observed in *Estes v. Texas*, 381 U.S. 532, 585–86, 85 S.Ct. 1628, 1654, 14 L.Ed.2d 543 (1965) (concurring opinion), "On entering [the courtroom], where the lives, liberty and property of people are in jeopardy, television representatives have only the rights of the general public, namely, to be present to observe the proceedings, and thereafter, if they choose, to report them."

Similarly, in Justice Harlan's critically important concurring opinion in Estes, he said that "there is no constitutional requirement that television be allowed in the courtroom." Id. 381 U.S. at 587, 85 S.Ct. at 1662. * * * Although *Chandler v. Florida* held that Estes does not stand as a ban on state experimentation with evolving television technology, it nevertheless did not endow the media with substantive rights qua media. Cf. Nixon v. Warner Communications, Inc., 435 U.S. 589, 610, 98 S.Ct. 1306, 1318, 55 L.Ed.2d 570 (1978). * * *

Two premises underlie CNN's constitutional claim that the public possesses a First Amendment right to television camera access to this particular trial. The first is that, in the adjudication of the claims in Westmoreland, the trial serves as a public forum. The second is that the opportunity for all members of the public to see and hear the trial as it occurs is protected by the First Amendment.

The public forum premise in CNN's constitutional argument is itself predicated upon the view that trials have always been "public" in the broad sense that the courtroom is such a paradigmatic platform for public communication "that every citizen should be able to satisfy himself with his own eyes as to the mode in which a public duty is performed." *Gannett Co. v. DePasquale*, 443 U.S. 368, 429 n. 10, 99 S.Ct. 2898, 2931 n. 10, 61 L.Ed. 608 (1979). * * * The litigation involved here is said to serve as a constitutionally protected "form of political expression." *NAACP v. Button*, 371 U.S. 415, 429, 83 S.Ct. 328, 336, 9 L.Ed.2d 405 (1963). It is suggested that the federal courtroom in this case is even more clearly a public forum for the parties to the litigation than was the criminal trial at issue in *Richmond Newspapers, Inc. v. Virginia*, 448 U.S. 555, 100 S.Ct. 2814, 65 L.Ed.2d 973 (1980), where the Supreme Court upheld a First Amendment right of the public and press to observe a criminal trial over the protest of the accused. * * * However this may be, it has never been suggested that there is a link between the First Amendment interest that a litigant has in his trial as a "form of expression" and the right that the public may have to view that expression on television. Whatever public forum interest may exist in litigation, that interest is clearly a speaker's interest, not an interest in access to the courtroom. Because the ability of neither General Westmoreland nor CBS to express views at trial is altered by the presence or absence of television cameras, CNN's public forum argument is, by itself, inapposite. CNN's constitutional argument rests on its second premise.

The second premise in CNN's constitutional argument is the proposition that the public's opportunity to see and hear a trial is protected by the First Amendment. We, of course, agree that the public (in this instance, the putative viewers) has First Amendment interests that are independent of the First Amendment interests of speakers (in this instance, the parties to the trial). * * * It may also be true that the public's right to receive information may not be vitiated by appeals to the availability of alternative means for receipt of the information. * * * No case, however, has held that the public has a right to televised trials.

The cases referred to us by CNN involve orders closing the courtroom to members of the press and public. None involve orders permitting such access while not permitting television cameras in the courtroom. There is, to be sure, an abundance of support in the cases for a constitutionally grounded public right of access to the courtroom. In *Richmond Newspapers*, 448 U.S. at 580 n. 17, 100 S.Ct. at 2829 n. 17. Chief Justice Burger, speaking for himself and for Justices White and Stevens, stated that "[w]hether the public has a right to attend trials in civil cases is a question not raised by this case, but we note that historically both civil and criminal trials have been presumptively open." Justice Brennan, in his concurring opinion, *id*. 448 U.S. at 596–97, 100 S.Ct. at 2838, stated that publicizing trial proceedings aids accurate factfinding and furthers the public purposes of trials. Justice Stewart, concurring, stated that "the First and Fourteenth Amendments clearly give the press and the public a right of access to trials themselves, civil as well as criminal." *Id*. at 599. * * * As pointed out in *Globe Newspaper Co. v. Superior Court*, 457 U.S. 596, 603, 102 S.Ct. 2613, 2618, 73 L.Ed.2d 248 (1982), the decision in *Richmond Newspapers* "firmly established for the first time that the press and general public have a constitutional right of access to criminal trials . . . seven Justices recogniz[ing] that this right of access is embodied in the First Amendment." Underlying that First Amendment right of access "is the common understanding that 'a major purpose of that Amendment was to protect the free discussion of governmental affairs,' Mills v. Alabama, 384 U.S. 214, 218. * * *

Furthermore, we agree with the Third Circuit in *Publicker Industries, supra*, that the First Amendment does secure to the public and to the press a right of access to civil proceedings in accordance with the dicta of the Justices in Richmond Newspapers, because public access to civil trials "enhances the quality and safeguards the integrity of the factfinding process," *Globe Newspaper*, 457 U.S. at 606, 102 S.Ct. at 2620, "fosters an appearance of fairness," id., and heightens "public respect for the judicial process," id., while permitting "the public to participate in and serve as a check upon the judicial process—an essential component in our structure of self government," id. We may submit to all of this, and yet not submit to CNN's argument, because these cases articulate a right to attend trials, not a right to view them on a television screen. * * *

CNN argues that because a courtroom is so small that not every person who wishes to attend can be accommodated or can even arrange to be physically present, the public's rights are wholly diluted. The public may read about the trial from the printed transcript or a newspaper account only after some delay, or it may receive radio or television reports similarly filtered through a reporter, with no opportunity to hear and observe directly the trial in process. The public, CNN argues, is relegated by the operation of the rule to "qualitatively inferior, stale and wooden interpretations of what occurred."

There is a long leap, however, between a public right under the First Amendment to attend trials and a public right under the First Amendment to see a given trial televised. It is a leap that is not supported by history. It is a leap that we are not yet prepared to take. It is a leap that many federal judges and, indeed, apparently the judges of the Southern District of New York, one of the most eminent district courts in the United States, oppose. CNN's argument, of course, is not that such a right is absolute, but rather that it is qualified, arising in a case presumably of public importance, with willing parties, a willing trial court, and guidelines so that the evils of television coverage contemplated by General Rule 7 or by the recent statement of the Ad Hoc Committee of the Judicial Conference of the United States on the subject do not in fact occur.

There may indeed come a time when the "experimentation," *Chandler v. Florida*, 449 U.S. at 574, 101 S.Ct. at 809, with television coverage establishes that the concerns with expenditure of judicial time on administration and oversight of broadcasting; the necessity of sequestering juries so that they will not look at the television program of the trial itself; the difficulty in empaneling an impartial jury in the case of a retrial; the necessity of larger jury panels or increased use of marshals; the psychological effects on witnesses, jurors, lawyers, and judges; and related considerations of "solemnity," "dignity," and the like are considered secondary or basically irrelevant as impediments to the search for truth when a given case is televised. At such a time the presumption may well be that all trials should be televised, or televisable, at least where the parties agree. Before that time arrives, it is possible that on an experimental or individual basis the federal courts or a particular federal district court—we speak here of a court, as opposed to an individual judge thereof—may seek, subject to any higher authority, of course, to permit televising in individual cases. But until that time, we certainly cannot say that a given district court lacks the power to prohibit all televising of trials within the district, across the board, because the public interest in television access to the courtroom does not now lie within the First Amendment. Instead, our point is that until the First Amendment expands to include television access to the courtroom as a protected interest, television coverage of federal trials is a right created by consent of the judiciary, which has always had control over the courtrooms, a consent which the federal courts, including the Southern District of New York, have not given.

Judgment in accordance with opinion.

Notes

1.   How far should the public's right to know extend when it comes to trials of public figures and celebrities? In *Campus Communications, Inc. v. Earnhardt*, 821 So.2d 388 (Fla. App. 2002), Judge Sawaya held that Campus Communications had a constitutional right to to view and copy the autopsy photographs of race car driver R. Dale Earnhardt who became involved in a

fatal crash during the Daytona 500 race on February 18, 2001 and died on the same date. Does the public *need* to see Earnhardt's autopsy photos?

2.   In a celebrity trial, courts have held that there is a strong presumption of access to court documents including the right to videotape. When journalists sought to videotape the deposition of Prince Rogers Nelson, better known to music fans as Prince or The Artist Formerly Known As Prince, the court required that (1) the parties select the videographer jointly; (2) only the original videotape could be made; (3) a mutually agreeable nonparty (the "Custodian") would attend the deposition and take custody of each video cassette as soon as it is recorded; and (4) the Custodian would submit to the jurisdiction of the Court for purposes of enforcing the provision of the order directed to the Custodian. Paisley Park Enterprises, Inc. v. Uptown Productions, 54 F.Supp.2d 347 (S.D.N.Y. Jun. 29, 1999). Prince was concerned that the parties would use the videotape for economic advantages.

C. TELEVISION AND ITS AFFECT ON CULTURE

In addition to affecting how individuals perceive members of groups and gender issues, television can have a profound impact on individuals. People have claimed that television has made them fat, lethargic, and sometimes pathological. Cases have been brought blaming television for people's injuries and studies have been conducted to determine the direct impact of television on people's lives. In the following case, a family claimed that watching two much television made their son homicidal.

ZAMORA v. CBS

United States District Court, Southern District of Florida, 1979.
480 F.Supp. 199.

HOEVELER, District Judge.

Ronny Zamora, a minor, together with his father and mother sued the National Broadcasting Company, Columbia Broadcasting System and American Broadcasting Company for damages. Diversity and requisite amount are asserted as the bases for jurisdiction. In brief, the plaintiffs alleged that Ronny Zamora, from the age of five years (he was age 15 when this action was filed) has become involuntarily addicted to and "completely subliminally intoxicated" by the extensive viewing of television violence offered by the three defendants. The defendants are charged with breaching their duty to plaintiffs by failing to use ordinary care to prevent Ronny Zamora from being "impermissibly stimulated, incited and instigated" to duplicate the atrocities he viewed on television. The minor plaintiff, it is further charged, developed a sociopathic personality, became desensitized to violent behavior and became a danger to himself and others.

On June 4, 1977, in Miami Beach, Florida, Ronny Zamora shot and killed his 83 year old neighbor, Elinor Haggart. The complaint does not allege the circumstances under which the shooting took place. We must conclude from the complaint (as was a well-publicized fact) that young Zamara was convicted of charges growing out of the killing. The complaint further alleges that he has been deprived of his liberty and imprisoned; has become a sociopathic personality and cannot lead a normal life. The complaint also alleges that both parents have sustained certain losses for which they make claim. There is no allegation that any particular program incited young Zamora to the action in question or that his viewing of one network was more or less frequent than his viewing of others. Neither is there any allegation as to when in the ten-year span referred to the suggested duty (and consequent failure to respond) applied to any one or all of the defendants, nor whether the minor plaintiff's conduct was the product of pre-duty exposure or post-duty influence.

The defendants moved to dismiss the complaint contending variously that to permit the claims as stated would abridge their first amendment rights; that no duty of the type alleged exists by statute or otherwise and that in any event, the complaint wholly fails to set forth a legal or factual basis to support the charge of proximate cause. The Court agrees with these positions. The complaint was dismissed by separate order giving the plaintiffs leave to amend. The plaintiffs have elected not to amend. By the terms of the Court's prior order, this order becomes the final judgment of the Court.

I. Has a Cause of Action Been Stated?

The parties agree that the determination of whether the allegations in the complaint set forth a claim cognizable by the Courts, is essentially one of law. Due to the novel basis for the claim, there is little precedent within which to seek other than general instruction.

Prosser and Wade in their work, Cases and Materials on Torts, 5th Edition (1971), p. 150 state:

> "Negligence is the word used to describe the conduct of the defendant. But a cause of action for negligence requires more than such conduct. There must be a duty, and there must be consequences. The traditional formula for the elements necessary to such a cause of action include the following:
>
> 1. A duty, which is an obligation Recognized by law, requiring the actor to conform to a certain standard of conduct, for the protection of others against unreasonable risks. (Emphasis supplied)
>
> 2. A failure to conform to the standard required. This is commonly called the breach of duty. These two elements go to make up what the courts usually have called negligence; but the term frequently is applied to the second alone. Thus, it may be said that the defendant was negligent but is not liable because he was under no duty to the plaintiff not to be ..."

Essentially, the plaintiffs claim the defendants breached a duty they owed Ronny Zamora. That duty, it is suggested, was generally to avoid making "violent" shows available for voluntary consumption by him and his parents. Plaintiffs do not suggest defendants breached a statutory duty. No supporting case or common law basis (other than the most general) is asserted as the underpinning for the claim. Yet, this Court is asked to determine, as a matter of law, that the allegations in the complaint are sufficient to create a cause of action against the defendants. The questions of duty and proximate cause are, initially at least, questions of law and here, "(I)t becomes essentially a question of whether the policy of the law will extend the responsibility for the conduct to the consequences which have in fact occurred." Prosser Law of Torts, Section 42 at 244–45 (4th Ed.1971).

Is there or should there be here "an obligation, recognized by the law requiring the actor to conform to a certain standard of conduct ..." Simon v. Tampa Electric Co., 202 So.2d 209, 213 (Fla. 2nd DCA 1967). As there is no such obligation (as demanded by plaintiffs) presently articulated in the law, the merit the legal validity of the claim must be examined. In so doing, a consideration of the commentary of Harper and James "Law of Torts" Vol. 2 (1956), p. 1132, Section 20.4 is appropriate.

> "It should be noted at this point that many courts and legal writers have stressed the fact that policy considerations underlie the doctrine of proximate cause. Of course, they do, but the policies actually involved often fail to get explicit treatment. One consideration which is common to all cases under any system is the practical need to draw the line somewhere so that liability will not crush those on whom it is put. Even under comprehensive social insurance for all vicissitudes to the body there would have to be limits on the kinds of injuries to be compensated (many kinds like worry loss of enjoyment, prestige, etc., probably would not be) and on the amount of compensation."

and from p. 1133

> "another policy consideration which pervades all the cases is the need to work out rules which are feasible to administer and yield a workable degree of certainty."

Such considerations, no doubt, fathered the common law doctrine applied in Florida, that negligence unconnected with physical injury will not provide the basis (the legal "cause") for mental or emotional injuries, Kirksey v. Jernigan, (Fla.1950) 45 So.2d 188; Ellington v. United States, (M.D.Fla.) 404 F.Supp. 1165, except in limited circumstances; ... the concept that the nature of the claims presented in Ultramares Corp. v. Touche, 255 N.Y. 170, 174 N.E. 441 (1931) would cause exposure to the actor of "indeterminate" classes, amounts and times, and the statement of the 5th Circuit in DeBardeleben Marine Corp. v. United States, 451 F.2d 140, 148 (5th Cir. 1971):

> "(T)he usual publishers of newspapers, treatises, and maps lack the financial resources to compensate an indeterminate class who might read their work. Potential liability would have a staggering deterrent effect on potential purveyors of printed material."

Of interest also is the holding and language of Yuhas v. Mudge, 129 N.J.Super. 207, 322 A.2d 824 (1974) where the plaintiff was injured by a product advertised in defendant's magazine.

> "To impose the suggested broad legal duty upon publishers of nationally circulated magazines, newspapers and other publications, would not only be impractical and unrealistic, but would have a staggering adverse effect on the commercial world and our economic system. For the law to permit such exposure to those in the publishing business who in good faith accept paid advertisements for a myriad of products would open the doors 'to a liability in an indeterminate amount for an indeterminate time to an indeterminate class.' " Id. at 825.

The complex of weaknesses presented by plaintiffs' complaint join in requiring dismissal. The generality which gives rise to defendants' purely procedural attack also requires the finding that the plaintiffs seek the imposition of a duty (a standard of care) which has no valid basis and would be against public policy. A recognition of the "cause" claimed by the plaintiffs would provide no recognizable standard for the television industry to follow. The impositions pregnant in such a standard are awesome to consider. Here the three major networks are charged with anticipating the minor's alleged voracious intake of violence on a voluntary basis; his parents' apparent acquiescence in this course, presumably without recognition of any problem and finally that young Zamora would respond with a criminal act of the type in question. Again, wholly apart from additional procedural problems which should be noted, the question is appropriate; how and why should the Court create such a wide expansion in the law of torts in Florida? * * *

The clear answer is that such expansion is not warranted. Indeed, this Court lacks the legal and institutional capacity to identify isolated depictions of violence, let alone the ability to set the standard for media dissemination of items containing "violence" in one form or the other. Airway dissemination is, and to some extent, should be regulated, but not on the basis or by the procedure suggested by the plaintiffs.

It bears repeating that the plaintiffs have elected not to amend, perhaps because no more adequate statement of their claims could be presented. Stripped of conclusory language, the standard demanded is so devoid of guidance and so lacking in a showing of legal cause that the complaint must be dismissed. * * *

II.   THE FIRST AMENDMENT

The freedom of one is often the concern of another. It has been so and shall be as the nation grows. Indeed, the complexity of our developing society has spawned collisions of these concerns and freedoms much more frequently than in past years. Understandably, the "freedom" amendments have, in more recent decades been the subject of regular review and decision. * * *

The plaintiffs here seek, in fact, some kind of pervasive judicial restriction upon the three defendants incident to a determination of the violation of a heretofore undefined duty. The defects in the complaint have already been discussed. The point here, of course, is that improper judicial limitation of first amendment rights is as offensive as unwarranted legislative incursion into that area. New York Times v. Sullivan, supra.

It was the judgment of the authors of the Constitution that society's best interests would be served by free expression, not limited by punishment or other sanction; and this concept has consistently been reflected in relevant judicial development except with respect to certain narrowly limited classes of speech. Those areas which are not afforded constitutional protection involve "the lewd and obscene, the profane, the libelous and the insulting or 'fighting' words. . . ." Chaplinsky v. New Hampshire, 315 U.S. 568, 572, 62 S.Ct. 766, 769, 86 L.Ed. 1031 (1942). None of these exceptions would appear to apply here. Rather, the plaintiffs complain of Ronny Zamora's continuing exposure to "violence," and his alleged response to it. The complaint does not suggest that the event in question was a reaction to any specific program of an inflammatory nature; or that the minor plaintiff was "incited" or goaded into unlawful behavior by a particular call to action. Rather, it is asserted that at some point (unspecified in any way) he became captive to the violence he viewed and turned to unlawful conduct. * * *

Television is "press," and while moving pictures, like newspapers and radio, are included in the press whose freedom is guaranteed by the First Amendment," it is nonetheless the right of the viewers and listeners, not the right of the broadcasters, which is paramount; it is the right of the public to receive suitable access to social, political, esthetic, moral and other ideas and experiences which is crucial, and that right may not be abridged either by Congress or the F.C.C." * * *

Clearly one of the principal interests of the viewing public is to receive a variety of programs. While a discussion of access and its suitability is not entirely on point here, it is appropriate to note that the right of the public to have broad access to programming and the right of the broadcaster to disseminate should not be inhibited by those members of the public who are particularly sensitive, or insensitive. It is of further interest that for over 40 years the administration of the "Radio Act" and its successor the "Communications Act" has called for a sensitive development and balancing of the rights of the public and broadcasters. In that period, the machinery has been created by which those rights (within legislative and constitutional limits) have been protected. In passing, it is worth noting, perhaps for no more than moral or argumentative support to this Court's position, that the F.C.C. has not acted, as to these defendants in the programming area in question. * * *

Reduced to basics, the plaintiffs ask the Court to determine that unspecified "violence" projected periodically over television (presumably in any form) can provide the support for a claim for damages where a susceptible minor has viewed such violence and where he has reacted unlawfully. Indeed, it is implicit in the plaintiffs' demand for a new duty standard, that such a claim should exist for an untoward reaction on the part of any "susceptible" person. The imposition of such a generally undefined and undefinable duty would be an unconstitutional exercise by this Court in any event. To permit such a claim by the person committing the act, as well as his parents, presents an A Fortiori situation which would, as suggested above, give birth to a legal morass through which broadcasting would have difficulty finding its way.

At the risk of overdeveloping the apparent, I suggest that the liability sought for by plaintiffs would place broadcasters in jeopardy for televising Hamlet, Julius Caesar, Grimm's Fairy Tales; more contemporary offerings such as All Quiet On The Western Front, and even The Holocaust, and indeed would render John Wayne a risk not acceptable to any but the boldest broadcasters.

Further, the imposition of the duty claimed would discriminate among television productions on the basis of content and not on the basis of any of the first amendment limitations referred to above. The works of creative artists and entertainers must be protected. The First Amendment casts a "heavy burden" on those who seek to censor. The plaintiffs' complaint wholly fails to allege any specific broadcasting conduct which is unprotected because it incited young Zamora to commit the crime in question. * * *

In almost all television dramas which depict some violence, the "goods" win and the "bads" lose. Without question, television programming presents problems and the study of these continues. One day, medical or other sciences with or without the cooperation of programmers may convince the F.C.C. or the Courts that the delicate balance of First Amendment rights should be altered to permit some additional limitations in programming. The complaint before the Court in no way justifies such a pursuit. Upon the election of the plaintiffs not to amend, the complaint is dismissed with prejudice and judgment shall be entered for defendants.

Karl E. Miller
Children's Behavior Correlates with Television Viewing

67, No. 3 American Family Physician 593–4 (Feb. 1, 2003).

Children learn and develop skills by observing and experiencing the world around them. In the United States, the average child watches about three hours of television per day. Children have difficulty separating reality from fantasy when watching television. In addition, television provides children with a distorted image of the world. Multiple studies have evaluated the impact of television viewing on the behavior of children. However, none of the studies has involved the use of the Child Behavior Checklist. Özmert and colleagues used the Child Behavior

Checklist to determine the impact of television viewing on competency and problem behavior in school aged children.

The study was performed at two primary schools that were randomly selected from a city school system. One school was in a low-income district and the other was in a high-income district. The subjects were second-and third-grade students enrolled in these schools. The subjects' parents were asked to complete a questionnaire and the Child Behavior Checklist. The questionnaire sought information about the time the child spent watching television versus the time spent engaging in other daily activities. To evaluate the accuracy of parent-reported television viewing time, 10 percent of the group were randomly selected, and the parents were asked to complete a seven-day diary of television viewing. The results were compared with the parents' reports. The participants were divided into three groups based on television viewing time: group 1 watched television for two hours or less per day; group 2, for two to four hours per day; and group 3, for more than four hours per day.

The results of the questionnaire showed a mean daily television viewing time of 2.5 hours. Overall viewing time had a negative relationship with social and school achievement scores. Other scores that were negatively affected by increased television viewing time included withdrawal, social problems, thought problems, attention problems, delinquent behavior, aggressive behavior, and externalization. The total problem scores on the Child Behavior Checklist were higher in group 3, indicating more problems in this group than in children who watched less television per day.

The authors conclude that the more time children spend watching television per day, the more likely they are to have behavior problems, according to the Child Behavior Checklist. This negative effect on behavior occurs regardless of program content. The authors reinforce the American Academy of Pediatrics' recommendation that parents limit their children's television viewing time to two hours or less per day.

Robert D. McIlwraith
"I'm Addicted to Television":
The Personality, Imagination, and TV Watching Patterns of Self-identified TV Addicts

42, no.3 Journal of Broadcasting & Electronic Media, at 371 (Summer 1998).

The term "television addiction" first appeared in the popular press (e.g., Winn, 1977) bolstered only by anecdotal evidence, but it gained widespread acceptance among parents, educators, and journalists (Milkman & Sunderwirth, 1987; Winn, 1987). Comparing reports in the popular literature about TV addiction with the psychiatric criteria for addictions contained in the American Psychiatric Association's Diagnostic and Statistical Manual of Mental Disorders (DSM–IV, 1994), Kubey suggested that the behaviors people described in these popular accounts paralleled five of the seven DSM–IV criteria used for diagnosing substance dependence: television consumed large amounts of their time; they watched TV longer or more often than they intended; they made repeated unsuccessful efforts to cut down their TV watching; they withdrew from or gave up important social, family, or occupational activities in order to watch television; and they reported "withdrawal"-like symptoms of subjective discomfort when deprived of TV (Kubey, 1996). Although television dependence is not recognized as a mental disorder by the DSM–IV, Kubey argued that television addiction as described in the popular literature has similarities to pathological gambling, the only purely behavioral addiction or dependence disorder not involving use of a psychoactive substance which appears in DSM–IV (American Psychiatric Association, 1994). * * *

Television addiction is widely believed to exist. Smith (1986) reported that 65% of respondents surveyed believed TV was addictive. McIlwraith (1990) reported that 70% of a sample of university students believed television was addictive. This belief is certainly widespread among educators and parents concerned about literacy (Winn, 1987), and it appears that social policy regarding television may be strongly influenced by a popular belief for which there is nearly no empirical support. Unlike the question of TV violence effects, which has been exhaustively researched, there have been very few studies of TV addiction. To date, there are no data to tell us whether television addiction exists as a clinical phenomenon or whether it is simply a colloquial shorthand expression of ambivalent feelings about the television medium (Alexander, 1990). * * *

Research on Television Addiction

Kubey and Csikszentmihalyi (1990) studied television use in the natural environment using the Experience Sampling Method, asking people to record their activities and thoughts when paged at random intervals during a normal day. They found that while watching television, respondents reported high levels of relaxation and very low levels of effort relative to all other daily activities. Watching TV as a quick and easy means of relaxing is probably the most common use and a function it serves at some time or another for everyone. Kubey (1986) found that very heavy TV viewers were people who tended to ruminate and feel bad when they were faced with nothing to do or when they were alone. He concluded that television watching was negatively reinforced by escape from stress and negative rumination that would otherwise occur during idle time for these individuals (Kubey, 1986; Kubey, Larson, & Csikszentmihalyi, 1996; McIlwraith, Smith Jacobvitz, Kubey, & Alexander, 1991). The Experience Sampling Method studies have provided an interesting framework for understanding how TV meets viewers' needs and conceptualizing television addiction; however, Kubey has not specifically conducted any ESM studies of the daily behavior and moods of self-identified TV addicts.

In the first empirical study of television addiction, Smith (1986) collected anecdotal reports of behaviors of self-identified TV addicts from the popular literature on this topic and cast them in questionnaire format. Items included in her TV Addiction Scale related to watching too much television, the sedative function of television, subjective sense of being out of control, lack of selectivity in programs watched, unsuccessful attempts to quit, guilt about TV watching, and withdrawal symptoms. Most respondents rated these behaviors as highly uncharacteristic of themselves. The few who endorsed some of these behaviors did not tend to endorse many others; that is, the behaviors reported in the popular literature as characteristic of TV addicts did not seem to hold together as a syndrome (Smith, 1986). Only 11 of 491 respondents (2.2%) indicated that they thought they were addicted to television, and although they did report watching very large amounts of television, they did not endorse very many of the addictive behaviors. The small sample of self-identified TV addicts did not differ in any demographic characteristics from the rest of the sample.

In a subsequent reanalysis of some of Smith's data, Anderson, Collins, Schmitt, and Smith Jacobvitz (1996) reported that the amount of reported recent stress in the lives of respondents was significantly associated with reported TV addiction for women in the sample but not for men. This suggested that the perception of being addicted to television might be a result of frequent recourse to TV watching as a way of coping with stress.

McIlwraith (1990) reported a study of university students, in which he argued that the small number of self-labelled TV addicts found by Smith (1986) might be due to the manner in which the question about television addiction was embedded in a question about amount of television viewed:

"(1) I avoid watching TV.

(2) I watch TV very rarely.

(3) I watch TV now and then.

(4) I watch TV every day.

(5) I am addicted to TV." (Smith, 1986).

When McIlwraith asked the question separately ("I am addicted to television."), he found that one-eighth (12:5%) of the sample of university students responded "Agree" or "Strongly Agree" (McIlwraith, 1990). An alternative hypothesis, not addressed by McIlwraith's (1990) study, was that university students were possibly more willing to label themselves TV addicts than were the members of the more heterogeneous community sample surveyed by Smith (1986).

McIlwraith's (1990) research contrasted self-labelled TV addicts with the rest of the sample of respondents on the TV Addiction Scale (Smith, 1986), measures of personality style (Eysenck Personality Inventory), imagination (Short Imaginal Processes Inventory), and a variety of questions about how they used television (TV Use Styles Inventory).

Respondents who applied the label of TV addict to themselves scored significantly higher on the TV Addiction Scale, and the two methods of assessing TV addiction correlated +.60. This contrasted with Smith's finding that the two ways of assessing TV addiction used in her study correlated only +.26 (Smith, 1986). McIlwraith also found that self-labelled TV addicts were significantly more likely to report boredom, distractibility, and poor attentional control on the Short Imaginal Processes Inventory (SIPI) (Huba, Singer, Aneshens el, & Antrobus, 1982) but were no different from other viewers in reported positive-constructive daydreaming. Self-labelled TV addicts also were significantly more likely to report that they watched TV to be distracted from things that were bothering them when in some negative mood state and to fill time when bored. Scores on Smith's Television Addiction Scale were modestly positively correlated with the Introversion and Neuroticism scales of the EPI and with the Poor Attentional Control and Guilt-and-Fear-of-Failure Daydreams scales of the SIPI. Scores on the Television Addiction Scale were significantly positively correlated with reports of television watching for distraction from negative moods.

The general picture that emerged from the results of the McIlwraith (1990) study was that students who labelled themselves TV addicts were more generally unhappy, anxious, and withdrawn than other viewers and used television watching to distract themselves from negative moods, worries and fears, and from boredom. * * *

Notes

1.   Do people turn on the television because of boredom and loneliness, or does television viewing make people more susceptible to boredom and loneliness? This is the chicken/egg question that Robert Kubey and Mihaly Csikszentimahl posed in the February 2002 edition of *Scientific American*. They concluded that "the former is generally the case, but it is not a simple case of either/or." Their studies (using an electroencephalograph, or EEG) found that people watching television "showed less mental stimulation, as measured by alpha brain-wave production, during viewing than during reading." Further they found, "[T]he sense of relaxation ends when the set is turned off, but the feelings of passivity and lowered alertness continued."

2.   Are you a light (2 hours or less per day), medium (3 hours) or heavy (4 hours or more per day) user of television? What impact has watching television had on your life? Some individuals believe that television keeps them more informed about current events in the world. Others believe that watching television causes them stress because of the focus on negative events in the news. An interesting individual study is to watch a television news broadcast for a day (22 minutes in a 30 minute time slot) or for a week and count how many stories are positive (about contributions to local and world community) and how many are negative (about crime, wars, and humankind's inhumanity)? Then ask yourself, does watching television news add value to people's lives?

3.   There have been several other studies that indicate that watching television has a negative impact on students' homework. *See* J.M. Wober,

Text in a texture of television: children's homework experience, 18, no. 1 Journal of Educational Television 23 (1992). *See also* Carolyn M. Orange, *Child Sacrifice: Black America's Price of Paying the Media Piper*, 30:2 Journal of Black Studies 294 (2000); Donald T. Searls et. al., *The Relationship of Students' Reading Skills to TV Watching, Leisure Time Reading, and Homework*, 29:2 Journal of Reading 158–62 (1983); and Paul Van den Broek, *The role of television viewing in the development of reading comprehension*, U.S. Dept. of Education, Office of Educational Research and Improvement, Educational Resources Information Center (2001).

4.   Ultimately, do individuals bear responsibility for their own lives? No matter how much television they watch, can they still choose to adopt non-racist, non-sexist, non-homophobic attitudes? If it is true that television is, indeed, making them feel lethargic and slowing their metabolism, can they still exercise the option to turn off the electronic drug, as some commentators have called television? In Chapter 20 *The Devil Media Made Me Do It*, we explore in more detail claims that the media has made individuals commit extraordinary acts of violence.

Chapter 13

CABLE AND SATELLITE TELEVISION

When television was invented in the 1920s, the first set "consisted of a small screen (anywhere from three to twelve inches wide diagonally) inside a box, with limited programming. The audience was tiny given that radio was then the most important form of entertainment and economically, due to the Depression and World War II, relatively few people could afford to buy a television." Sherri Burr, *Television and Societal Affects: An Analysis of Media Images of African–Americans in Historical Context*, 4 J. OF GENDER RACE & JUSTICE 1, n.2 (2001). Cable television came along two decades later in 1948.

Cable television was originally christened Community Antenna Television or CATV. According to the K–State Telecom website, cable was invented by John Walson, an appliance owner who had difficulty selling television sets in rural areas because of poor reception. To solve the problem of limited signals, Walson put an antenna on top of a large utility pole and installed it on the top of a nearby Pennsylvania mountain. As television signals were received and transported to his store, Walson sold many more sets. http://www.telecom.ksu.edu/cable/history.html. From those humble beginnings, cable television grew into a successful fee-paid business with 60 million subscribers.

Home Box Office (HBO), which was introduced in 1972, became the first service to transmit its programming via satellite in 1976. Over thirty years and ten channels later, HBO is arguably the world's most successful pay service with more than 11.5 million viewers. In 1980s, a satellite system cost approximately $10,000, dropping to $3,000 by 1985, to set up with free programming. http://www.bestsatellitetvsystem.com/aboutsatellitetv.html. Currently consumers receive offers in the mail or on the telephone offering the system for free accompanied by an agreement to continue paying a monthly fee.

The creation of cable and satellite TV has brought growing pains for the industry as channels find themselves bound by the new rules that the FCC and states specifically created to regulate cable TV and long-standing copyright rules.

A. CABLE TV

1. CABLE TELEVISION AND COPYRIGHT INFRINGEMENT

CABLE VISION, INC. v. KUTV, INC.

United States Court of Appeals, Ninth Circuit, 1964.
335 F.2d 348.

KOELSCH, Circuit Judge.

In response to an antitrust action brought against it, KLIX–TV, appellees here, filed the counterclaim which is the subject of this appeal. Claiming exclusive rights by virtue of contract to the first run of its affiliated network television programs, it asserted that under Idaho law the activities of community antenna operators, appellants here, constituted tortious interference with those contractual rights and unfair competition in that the community antenna receives identical programs broadcast by other and distant stations and distributes them for profit simultaneously with the KLIX airings.

An extended trial was had. The district judge rendered his decision by a written opinion reported in 211 F.Supp. 47 (D.C.Ida.1962). As a preliminary issue and before reaching the merits the District Court concluded that Congress had not pre-empted the adjustment of property rights in the communication field by passage of the Communications Act of 1934. We agree.

On the merits, the District Court granted relief on the alternative grounds that the activities of the antenna service constituted unfair competition and interference with contract under Idaho law. It noted the absence of state statute or relevant decision of the Idaho Supreme Court but nevertheless concluded that Idaho would recognize as part of its common law, claims for contract interference like those asserted by appellees. Additionally the court declared that appellants were guilty of both torts and issued an order based upon both grounds for the issuance of an appropriate injunction to preserve and make effective appellees' exclusive first-run rights to its affiliate network programs as against these appellants (but not against non-commercial individual antenna owners).

Before reaching its conclusion the court dealt at length with communications policy. Although it expressly recognized that Federal Communications policy was ' * * * not determinative of the issues of the present case * * *' (Cable Vision, Inc., v. KUTV, Inc., 211 F.Supp. 47, 55 (D.C.Ida.1962)), the court deemed it relevant. The court noted that Congress had as yet refused to extend F.C.C. regulation to the community antenna practice complained of despite specific proposals to the contrary. Nonetheless, the court found Congressional sanction for the result reached because Congress had not sought to ' * * * abridge or alter the remedies now existing in the common law or by statute. (Sec. 414).'

After the appeal was taken and the matter had been submitted, the Supreme Court decided the companion cases of Sears, Roebuck & Co. v. Stiffel Co., 376 U.S. 225, 84 S.Ct. 784, 11 L.Ed.2d 661 (1964), and Compco Corporation v. Day–Brite Lighting, Inc., 376 U.S. 234, 84 S.Ct. 779, 11 L.Ed.2d 669 (1964). On the suggestion of counsel for appellants that those decisions settled issues of law relevant to this case and were dispositive of this appeal, we vacated the order of submission and called for supplemental briefs. We also requested that the case of R.C.A. Mfg. Co. v. Whiteman, 114 4 F.2d 86 (2d Cir. 1940), cert. den. 311 U.S. 712, 61 S.Ct. 393, 85 L.Ed. 463, be evaluated to determine if it had new significance in view of the holdings in Sears and Compco. Supplemental briefs have now been filed and the case stands finally submitted.

II

At the outset, we note and emphasize that the trial court reached its conclusion ' * * * without regard to and apart from any question of copyright ownership of particular program content,' Cable Vision, Inc., v. KUTV, Inc. supra, 211 F.Supp. at 58. It held, * * * as a matter of common law under the doctrines of tortious interference with contractual rights, and under the doctrine of unfair competition as well, that one who contractually acquires, either expressly or impliedly by reference to a general industry wide custom, the exclusive right to the first call of entertainment programs, is entitled to protection of that valuable economic right, not only against the grantor, but also against acts of third persons which tortiously and unfairly prevent exploitation of the right or diminish its value.' Ibid.

The unexamined premise in the holding and the cases cited in support of it is that common-law theories of recovery may be asserted to redeem what are in essence copyright interests. As we read Sears and Compco, however, only actions for copyright infringement or such common-law actions as are consistent with the primary right of public access to all in the public domain will lie.

In Compco, the court emphasized that the federal policy found in Art. I, § 8, Cl. 8 of the Constitution and in the implementing federal statutes is to allow ' * * * free access to copy whatever the federal patent and copyright laws leave in the public domain.' The public domain was broadly delineated in Sears: that which is either not copyrighted, not copyrightable or on which the copyright has expired is in the public domain. * * * Thus when an article is unprotected by a patent or copyright, state law may not forbid a person not the originator to merely copy and commercially exploit that article, for such a law would enable the originator to accomplish with the left hand of state authority what he was unable to accomplish with the right hand bearing the authority of the primary federal interest. No state intrusion of the federal field is permissible unless the law of the state meshes in purpose and effect with the announced objectives of federal copyright law. A limited ambit of operation is accorded state law but it may be exercised only insofar as consistent with the paramount federal interest. Accordingly, the Supreme Court expressly mentioned the state common-law action of unfair competition with the element of 'palming off,' an element Mr. Justice Holmes, concurring in International News Service v. Associated Press, referred to as ' * * * an infusion of fraud * * * necessary to turn a flavor into a poison * * * ' so as to permit ' * * * a remedy from the law * * * without legislation * * * ' as surviving its decision. And state courts have subsequently decided that a state action based upon common-law copyright also survives. * * *

III

Applying Sears and Compco's composite thesis to the case at hand, we view it as dispositive of appellees' two grounds for relief. Save for the limited protection accorded the creator of literary and intellectual works under the Copyright Act or its exceptions—and here appellees concede they are not asserting a claim for copyright infringement—anyone may freely and with impunity avail himself of such works to any extent he may desire and for any purpose whatever subject only to the qualification that he does not steal good will, or, perhaps more accurately stated, deceive others in thinking the creations represent his own work.

Here the District Court enjoined activity that lacked the element of palming off. It is incontrovertible that all broadcasts are received and distributed by the community antenna without any modification of program content; therefore no question of 'implied misrepresentation' by failing to give the originator proper credit, a misrepresentation present in International News Service v. Associated Press, supra, 248 U.S. 215, 39 S.Ct. 68 (1918), is involved in this case. We are clear that there is lacking that taint 'necessary to turn a flavor into a poison' justifying judicial relief without Congressional authorization. To the extent, then, that the District Court holding extended a new protectible interest beyond what the copyright laws confer, it ' * * * interfered with the federal policy * * * of allowing free access to copy whatever the federal patent and copyright laws leave in the public domain.' This same principle likewise applies to appellees' claim of contract interference. Parties by the mere expedient of an exclusive contract can not 'bootstrap' into existence rights from subject matter which at their source lie in the public domain. * * * To allow these appellees relief on an alternative ground not substantially differing in gravamen from other relief foreclosed in operative effect by the Supreme Court's explicit holding would be to enshrine form at the expense of substance.

In sum,

'The general rule of law,' says Mr. Justice Brandeis (International News Service v. Associated Press, supra, 248 U.S. at 250, 39 S.Ct. 68), 'is, that the noblest of human productions—knowledge, truths ascertained, conceptions, and ideas—become after voluntary communications to others, free as the air to common use.' The Constitution and Congress have made some exceptions to this general rule, by the patent and copyright laws. They have rewarded inventors and authors for their creativeness by granting them monopolies for a limited time and under carefully fixed conditions. The courts will be creating new and perpetual monopolies of their own if they enjoin non-passing-off appropriation of unpatented and uncopyrighted material. This they are properly reluctant to do. They may want to stop a particular defendant but if so they ought to stop everybody. * * *

IV

It could be contended, however, that the community antenna is misappropriating, 'reaping where it has not sown,' and therefore this court should protect a 'quasi property right' of the kind involved in International News Service v. Associated Press, supra, 248 U.S. 215, 39 S.Ct. 68 (1918). But that case, oft held by the Second Circuit as applicable only to its special facts is readily distinguishable. International News involved news which for practical reasons is not subject to copyright. Here, on the other hand, much of the material is copyrighted. International News involved an 'implied misrepresentation'; here, as we have already seen, there is none. Perhaps most significant for purposes of bringing an action, International News involved an action brought by the originator; here the action is brought by and exclusive licensee. In short, few of the considerations impelling the result in International News are present here. On the other hand, many reasons militating against such a result are.

True, the activities of the community antenna could be described as ' * * * inconsistent with a finer sense of propriety * * * ' But to grant appellees relief without Congressional authorization on other grounds not consistent with the copyright act is, in effect, to recognize a new protectible interest. To quote from Justice Brandeis, dissenting:

> 'Such taking and gainful use of a product of another which, for reasons of public policy, the law has refused to endow with the attributes of property, does not become unlawful because the product happens to have been taken from a rival and is used in competition with him.' * * * 'The unwritten law possesses capacity for growth; and has often satisfied new demands for justice by invoking analogies or by expanding a rule or principle. This process has been in the main wisely applied and should not be discontinued. Where the problem is relatively simple, as it is apt to be when private interests only are involved, it generally proves adequate. But with the increasing complexity of society, the public interest tends to become omnipresent; and the problems presented by new demands for justice cease to be simple. Then the creation or recognition by courts of a new private right may work serious injury to the general public, unless the boundaries of the right are definitely established and wisely guarded.'

More important, however, is another consideration urged by Justice Brandeis:

'Courts are ill-equipped to make the investigations which should precede a determination of the limitations which should be set upon any property right in news or of the circumstances under which news gathered by a private agency should be deemed affected with a public interest. Courts would be powerless to prescribe the detailed regulations essential to full enjoyment of the rights conferred or to introduce the machinery required for enforcement of such regulations. Considerations such as these should lead us to decline to establish a new rule of law in the effort to redress a newly disclosed wrong, although the propriety of some remedy appears to be clear.'

Grant that the conclusion reached by the District Court would appear to be consistent with the National Communications policy as formulated by the F.C.C. But as the District Court recognized, F.C.C. policy is ' * * * not determinative of the issues of the present case * * * ' And it should be emphasized that it is Congress and those whom it delegates who are charged with regulation in the public interest. Congress may, after weighing the competing interests involved, find it to be good policy to grant an additional remedy. But the courts are not charged by our constitutional system as arbiters of good policy. That function is reserved to Congress. In short, while it makes an appealing picture to see courts and administrative agencies hand in hand redeeming national communications policy, the fact remains that it is not the proper function of courts to do so. * * *

The judgment is vacated and the cause is remanded to the District Court to permit appellees to amend their counterclaim if they are able.

Note

1. HBO was one of the first cable channels to create original programming. It has suffered the same growing pains as other creators of original programming.

WILLIS v. HBO

U.S. District Court, Southern District of New York, 2001.
2001 WL 1352916, 60 U.S.P.Q.2d 1916.

MARTIN, Judge.

Many people would consider the phrase "sleazy talent agent" to be redundant. While this is no doubt as unfair a stereotype as is the "sleazy lawyer," no one could reasonably claim a copyright in the concept of a sleazy talent agent. The question presented here is what degree of detail must an author add to such a well-recognized stock character in order to obtain copyright protection.

In this case, Plaintiff prepared an outline for a television situation comedy—known in the trade as a "treatment"—that proposed a series to be called "Schmoozers" "that lampoons the lives of two smarmy 'east coast' Agents concurrently laughing at the 'show-bizzification' of everyday discourse in mainstream America." Plaintiff's Treatment somehow found its way into the files of an employee of Defendant HBO, which sometime thereafter produced a popular series entitled "Arli$$," whose central character is a smarmy west coast sports agent. * * *

DISCUSSION

To establish her claim of copyright infringement Plaintiff must establish that Defendant had access to her copyrighted work and that substantial similarities exist as to protectible material in the two works. *Walker v. Time Life Films, Inc.*, 784 F.2d 44, 48 (2d Cir. 1986); *Reyher v. Children's Television Workshop*, 533 F.2d 87, 90 (2d Cir. 1976). Although Defendant offers substantial evidence that the creators of Arli$$ never had access to Plaintiff's work, the existence of a copy of Plaintiff's Schmoozers Treatment in HBO's files creates an issue of fact that precludes summary judgment on that issue. Thus, the question that remains is whether the "protectible expression in [the plaintiff's work] is substantially similar to the equivalent portions of [the defendant's work]." *Cooling Systems & Flexibles, Inc. v. Stuart Radiator, Inc.*, 777 F.2d 485, 493 (9th Cir. 1985). *See Hoehling v. Universal City Studios, Inc.*, 618 F.2d 972, 977 (2d Cir. 1980).

In order to determine the extent to which Arli$$ employed copyrightable elements of the Schmoozers Treatment, the Court read the Treatment and Plaintiff's expert's report and viewed the first five episodes of Arli$$ and a videotape prepared by Plaintiff which compared specific portions of the Treatment with segments from various Arli$$ episodes. * * *

On the basis of this review, the Court concludes that summary judgment is appropriate because comparison of the two works at issue shows that the only similarities between them relate to non-copyrightable elements. *See generally Ring v. Estee Lauder, Inc.*, 874 F.2d 109 (2d Cir. 1989).

The problem with Plaintiff's claim and her "expert's" report is that, to the extent that there are similarities, they are found either in stock characters, or themes that are common to the talent agency business, or to situation comedies in general or in trivial detail that are not essential to either series. Plaintiff's arguments also ignore the significant differences between the two series and strain to find similarities where none exist.

As Judge Scheindlin observed in *Hogan v. DC Comics*, 48 F.Supp.2d 298, 310 (S.D.N.Y. 1999): A stock character or basic character type . . . is not entitled to copyright protection. *Robinson v. Viacom Int'l, Inc.*, 93 Civ. 2539, 1995 WL 417076, at *9 (S.D.N.Y. Jan. 4, 1995); *Sinicola v. Warner Bros.*, 948 F.Supp. 1176, 1185 (E.D.N.Y. 1996). * * * Plaintiff argues, however, that Arli$$ copied more than her theme and misappropriated her use of a male side-kick, a female assistant and an African American character with a business background. The concept of a male sidekick and female assistant is not new. * * * The interplay of male and female characters in television sitcoms was essential to the comedy of Sid Caesar, Dick Van Dyke, Jackie Gleason and Lucille Ball. None of the creators of these television classics would have thought of suing the others for copyright infringement.

Plaintiff argues that the personality traits, physical characteristics and personal histories of the Schmoozers characters and their interaction in the series are so similar to those of the Arli$$ characters that they establish an infringement of her work. While some similarities do exist, there are significant differences between the two sets of characters and the overall concept of the two shows. * * *

Despite the substantial differences between the characters in the two shows and their locales, Plaintiff, with the aid of her expert, attempts to demonstrate that the similarities between the characters in Schmoozers and the cast of Arli$$ are substantial enough to establish copyright infringement. While there are some similarities between Arliss Michaels and Tym Barker—they both wear gold-rimmed glasses and designer suits, and are utterly amoral in their approach to their businesses—these characteristics of Plaintiff's Tym Barker are not inherently distinctive.

Arliss Michaels and Tym Barker are not the same character; they are both stereotypes of the amoral talent agent. The most that could be said is that the Arliss character embodies "the broader outlines" of Tym Barker. *Hogan*, 48 F.Supp.2d at 310. However, this is not a protectible element of Plaintiff's work. * * *

Plaintiff's attempt to pull isolated segments out of the fifty-nine Arli$$ episodes to prove copying of her creative work is equally unsuccessful. It is not surprising that in this substantial number of episodes there are instances where themes outlined in the Schmoozers Treatment are found present in a show about a sports agent. As Judge Haight observed in *CK Comp. v. Burger King Corp.*, 1994 WL 533253, at *4 (S.D.N.Y. Sept. 30, 1994): 'The essence of infringement lies in taking not a general theme, but its particular expression through similarities of treatment, details, scenes, events and characterization.' *Reyher*, 533 F.2d at 91. 'The law will not grant an author a monopoly over the unparticularized expression of an idea at such a level of abstraction or generality as unduly to inhibit independent creation by others.' *Gund, Inc. v. Smile Int'l, Inc.*, 691 F.Supp. 642, 644 (S.D.N.Y. 1988), aff'd mem., 872 F.2d 1021 (2d Cir. 1989). Consistent with these principles, copyright law does not protect stock characters, incidents or settings that are as a practical matter indispensable or standard in the treatment of a given topic. *Hoehling v. Universal City Studios, Inc.*, 618 F.2d 972, 979 (2d Cir.), cert. denied, 449 U.S. 841 (1980).

Plaintiff also argues that two dramatic devices used in Arli$$ were copied from Schmoozers: 1) a character who talks directly to the audience, and 2) celebrities appearing as themselves. There is nothing novel about either of these devices. Ancient Greek tragedy employed a chorus that spoke to the audience and this device is far from unique in modern theater, film and television. Celebrities have appeared as themselves in numerous films and television shows and it is not surprising that someone creating a series about a talent agent would think it appropriate to have actual celebrities appearing as clients. Thus, even if HBO copied these devices from Plaintiff's Treatment there is no copyright violation. * * *

In sum, Plaintiff has failed to show that protectible portions of her Treatment were substantially reproduced in the Arli$$ series. Thus, even if we accept her assumption that the creators of Arli$$ had her Schmoozers Treatment and copied all of the similar ideas that may be found in the two works, Plaintiff cannot prevail.

For the foregoing reasons, Defendant's motion for summary judgment is granted and the complaint is dismissed.

WILLIS v. HBO

U.S. Court of Appeals, Second Circuit, 2003.
57 Fed. Appx. 902.

STRAUB, KATZMANN, and RAGGI, Circuit Judges.

Summary Order

Plaintiff–Appellant Patricia Willis appeals from a judgment of the United States District Court for the Southern District of New York (John S. Martin, Jr., *Judge*) granting summary judgment in favor of Defendant–Appellee Home Box Office ("HBO"). We affirm for substantially the reasons stated by the District Court in its opinion and order of November 5, 2001.

In her complaint, Willis alleges that the HBO television series *Arli$$* infringes on her copyrighted outline for a proposed television series entitled *Schmoozers*. It is true that both works are situation comedies that feature a money-driven talent agent as their primary character, and that satirize the American entertainment industry as being wholly populated by self-absorbed, morally-depraved individuals. It is also true that both works surround the primary character with a supporting cast comprised of a hapless, male sidekick and an intelligent, female assistant. We agree with the District Court, however, that such similarities are based on stereotypical characters and stock themes, and thus any copying by the defendant related to non-copyrightable aspects of Willis' work. *See Walker v. Time Life Films, Inc.*, 784 F.2d 44, 48 (2d Cir.1986) ("[A] district court may determine noninfringement as a matter of law on a motion for summary judgment . . . when the similarity concerns only noncopyrightable elements of plaintiff's work. . . .").

Willis argues that, apart from individual aspects of *Schmoozers*, the "total concept and feel" of the two works are substantially similar. We reject that assertion because we do not think that any reasonable trier of fact could so conclude. As already pointed out, the generalized similarities between *Arli$$* and *Schmoozers* relate to unoriginal elements of

Willis' work. More importantly, the distinctive "total concept and feel" of *Arli$$* is shaped primarily by its use of a dramatic device in which each episode of the series is presented as a narrated reading of a chapter from the main character's autobiography. This enables *Arli$$* to take comedic advantage of the sharp contrast between the main character's overblown and self-reverential view of an event in his life—which the audience learns throughout the episode by means of somber voiceover from that character—and the chaotic, immoral manner in which the event actually transpired. In *Schmoozers,* by contrast, the comedic foil to the main character is not the main character himself but a supporting character who occasionally relates direct criticism of her boss's actions to the audience. *Cf. Williams v. Crichton,* 84 F.3d 581 (2d Cir.1996) (distinguishing total concept and feel of book with movie).

Willis also contends that the District Court erred in dismissing her claims under New York law because "[a] state claim based upon an implied-in-fact obligation to compensate a plaintiff for use of an idea is not preempted...." While there is some support for the general principle that an implied-in-fact contract claim is not preempted by federal copyright law, *see Whitfield v. Lear,* 751 F.2d 90, 92–93 (2d Cir.1984) (applying California law); *Wrench LLC v. Taco Bell Corp.,* 256 F.3d 446, 455–59 (6th Cir.2001) (applying Michigan law); *Katz Dochrermann & Epstein, Inc. v. Home Box Office,* 97 Civ. 7763(TPG), 1999 WL 179603, at *4–*5 (S.D.N.Y. Mar. 31, 1999) (applying New York law), Willis' complaint does not actually plead an implied-in-fact contract claim, nor does it even set forth facts that would arguably support such a claim. As we observed in *Nadel v. Play–By–Play Toys & Novelties, Inc.,* 208 F.3d 368 (2d Cir.2000), a recent case involving implied-in-fact contracts under New York law:

> Of course, the mere disclosure of an ... idea to a defendant ... will not automatically entitle a plaintiff to compensation upon the defendant's subsequent use of the idea. An implied-in-fact contract requires such elements as consideration, mutual assent, legal capacity and legal subject matter.... The element of mutual assent ... must be inferred from the facts and circumstances of each case, including such factors as the specific conduct of the parties, industry custom, and course of dealing.

Id. at 376 n. 5 (internal quotation marks and citations omitted). Willis' complaint contains nothing from which "a court may justifiably infer that the promise [to pay Willis for subsequent use of her ideas] would have been explicitly made [by HBO], had attention been drawn to it." *Id.*

We also note that when HBO pressed the preemption point before the District Court as part of its overall motion for summary judgment, Willis made no arguments at all in opposition to preemption, let alone that her complaint impliedly alleged a contract claim against HBO. *See Singleton v. Wulff,* 428 U.S. 106, 120, 96 S.Ct. 2868, 49 L.Ed.2d 826 (1976) ("It is the general rule, of course, that a federal appellate court does not consider an issue not passed upon below.").

The judgment of the District Court is hereby AFFIRMED.

Notes

1. In 2004, HBO still listed Arli$$ among its original series. http://www.hbo.com/ Its most popular series that spring were *The Sopranos, Six Feet Under*, and *Sex in the City*. HBO also reinvented the western with *Deadwood* which primiered on March 21, 2004.

2. Another cable service called Showtime aired its first program on July 1, 1976, called "Celebration," with performers Rod Stewart, Pink Floyd, and ABBA in concert. Showtime was offered via satellite in 1978. Viacom International bought 50 percent interest in Showtime and then created Showtime/The Movie Channel Inc. in 1983. In 1985, Viacom became the only owner of the network. Showtime/The Movie Channel Inc. became Showtime Networks Inc. in 1988. *See 25 memorable moments in Showtime's 25–year history,* VARIETY (June 7, 2001), available *at http://www.variety.com/index.asp?layout=story & articleid=VR1117801025 & categoryid=1013 & cs=1.*

In 2004, Showtime's most controversial show was *The L Word*, a drama about lesbians and their love relationships. *The L Word* bears some resemblance to HBO's popular *Sex and the City*. Indeed Showtime advertised its show with the phrase, "same sex. different city." *http://www.sho.com/site/lword/home.do*

2. FCC'S REGULATION OF CABLE TELEVISION

The Federal Communications Commission (FCC) is the governmental body established to regulate the radio and television airways, generating conflict with states and the entities that it regulations.

CAPITAL CITIES CABLE, INC. v. CRISP

United States Supreme Court, 1984.
467 U.S. 691, 104 S.Ct. 2694, 81 L.Ed.2d 580.

Mr. Justice BRENNAN delivered the opinion of the Court.

The question presented in this case is whether Oklahoma may require cable television operators in that State to delete all advertisements for alcoholic beverages contained in the out-of-state signals that they retransmit by cable to their subscribers. Petitioners contend that Oklahoma's requirement abridges their rights under the First and Fourteenth Amendments and is pre-empted by federal law. Because we conclude that this state regulation is preempted, we reverse the judgment of the Court of Appeals for the Tenth Circuit and do not reach the First Amendment question.

I

Since 1959, it has been lawful to sell and consume alcoholic beverages in Oklahoma. The State Constitution, however, as well as implementing statutes, prohibits the advertising of such beverages, except by means of strictly regulated on-premises signs.[1] For several years, pursuant to this authority, Oklahoma has prohibited television broadcasting stations in the State from broadcasting alcoholic beverage commercials as part of their locally produced programming and has required these stations to block out all such advertising carried on national network programming. See Oklahoma Alcoholic Beverage Control Board v. Heublein Wines, Int'l, 566 P.2d 1158, 1160 (Okla.1977). At the same time, the Oklahoma Attorney General has ruled—principally because of the practical difficulties of enforcement—that the ban does not apply to alcoholic beverage advertisements appearing in newspapers, magazines, and other publications printed outside Oklahoma but sold and distributed in the State. Consequently, out-of-state publications may be delivered to Oklahoma subscribers and sold at retail outlets within the State, even though they contain advertisements for alcoholic beverages. Until 1980, Oklahoma applied a similar policy to cable television operators who were permitted to retransmit out-of-state signals containing alcoholic beverage commercials to their subscribers. In March of that year, however, the Oklahoma Attorney General issued an opinion in which he concluded that the retransmission of out-of-state alcoholic beverage commercials by cable television systems operating in the State would be considered a violation of the advertising ban. 11 Op.Okla.Atty.Gen. No. 79–334, p. 550 (Mar. 19, 1980). Respondent Crisp, Director of the Oklahoma Alcoholic Beverage Control Board, thereafter warned Oklahoma cable operators, including petitioners, that they would be criminally prosecuted if they continued to carry such out-of-state advertisements over their systems.

Petitioners, operators of several cable television systems in Oklahoma, filed this suit in March 1981 in the United States District Court for the Western District of Oklahoma, seeking declaratory and injunctive relief. They alleged that the Oklahoma policy violated the Commerce and Supremacy Clauses, the First and Fourteenth Amendments, and the Equal Protection Clause of the Fourteenth Amendment. Following an evidentiary hearing, the District Court granted petitioners a preliminary injunction and subsequently entered summary judgment and a permanent injunction in December 1981. In granting that relief, the District Court found that petitioners regularly carried out-of-state signals containing wine advertisements, that they were prohibited by federal law from altering or modifying these signals, and that "no feasible way" existed for petitioners to delete the wine advertisements.

Addressing petitioners' First Amendment claim, the District Court applied the test set forth in Central Hudson Gas & Electric Corp. v. Public Service Comm'n of N.Y., 447 U.S. 557, 100 S.Ct. 2343, 65 L.Ed.2d 341 (1980), and concluded that Oklahoma's advertising ban was an

---

1. The Oklahoma Constitution provides in pertinent part:

"It shall be unlawful for any person, firm or corporation to advertise the sale of alcoholic beverage within the State of Oklahoma, except one sign at the retail outlet bearing the words 'Retail Alcoholic

Liquor Store.'" Art. XXVII, § 5. The Oklahoma Alcoholic Beverage Control Act similarly prohibits advertising "any alcoholic beverages or the sale of same" except by on-premises signs which must conform to specified size limitations. Okla.Stat., Tit. 37, § 516 (1981).

unconstitutional restriction on the cable operators' right to engage in protected commercial speech. * * * On appeal, the Court of Appeals for the Tenth Circuit reversed, holding that, while the wine commercials at issue were protected by the First Amendment, the state ban was a valid restriction on commercial speech. Oklahoma Telecasters Assn. v. Crisp, 699 F.2d 490 (1983). Although the Court of Appeals noted that "Federal Communication[s] Commission regulations and federal copyright law prohibit cable operators from altering or modifying the television signals, including advertisements, they relay to subscribers," the court did not discuss the question whether application of the Oklahoma law to these cable operators was pre-empted by the federal regulations. Id., at 492.

While petitioners' petition for certiorari was pending, a brief was filed for Federal Communications Commission as amicus curiae in which it was contended that the Oklahoma ban on the retransmission of out-of-state signals by cable operators significantly interfered with the existing federal regulatory framework established to promote cable broadcasting. In granting certiorari, therefore, we ordered the parties, in addition to the questions presented by the petitioners concerning commercial speech, to brief and argue the question whether the State's regulation of liquor advertising, as applied to out-of-state broadcast signals, is valid in light of existing federal regulation of cable broadcasting. 464 U.S. 813, 104 S.Ct. 66, 78 L.Ed.2d 81 (1983).

Although we do not ordinarily consider questions not specifically passed upon by the lower court, see California v. Taylor, 353 U.S. 553, 557, n. 2, 77 S.Ct. 1037, 1040, n. 2, 1 L.Ed.2d 1034 (1957), this rule is not inflexible, particularly in cases coming, as this one does, from the federal courts. * * * Here, the conflict between Oklahoma and federal law was plainly raised in petitioners' complaint, it was acknowledged by both the District Court and the Court of Appeals, the District Court made findings on all factual issues necessary to resolve this question, and the parties have briefed and argued the question pursuant to our order. Under these circumstances, we see no reason to refrain from addressing the question whether the Oklahoma ban as applied here so conflicts with the federal regulatory framework that it is pre-empted.

II

Petitioners and the FCC contend that the federal regulatory scheme for cable television systems administered by the Commission is intended to pre-empt any state regulation of the signals carried by cable system operators. Respondent apparently concedes that enforcement of the Oklahoma statute in this case conflicts with federal law, but argues that because the State's advertising ban was adopted pursuant to the broad powers to regulate the transportation and importation of intoxicating liquor reserved to the States by the Twenty-first Amendment, the statute should prevail notwithstanding the conflict with federal law.[5] As

5. Section 2 of the Twenty-first Amendment provides: "The transportation or im- portation into any State, Territory, or possession of the United States for delivery or

in California Retail Liquor Dealers Assn. v. Midcal Aluminum, Inc., 445 U.S. 97, 100 S.Ct. 937, 63 L.Ed.2d 233 (1980), where we held that a California wine-pricing program violated the Sherman Act notwithstanding the State's reliance upon the Twenty-first Amendment in establishing that system, we turn first before assessing the impact of the Twenty-first Amendment to consider whether the Oklahoma statute does in fact conflict with federal law. See id., at 106–114, 100 S.Ct., at 943–947.

Our consideration of that question is guided by familiar and well-established principles. Under the Supremacy Clause, U.S. Const., Art. VI, cl. 2, the enforcement of a state regulation may be pre-empted by federal law in several circumstances: first, when Congress, in enacting a federal statute, has expressed a clear intent to pre-empt state law, Jones v. Rath Packing Co., 430 U.S. 519, 525, 97 S.Ct. 1305, 1309, 51 L.Ed.2d 604 (1977); second, when it is clear, despite the absence of explicit preemptive language, that Congress has intended, by legislating comprehensively, to occupy an entire field of regulation and has thereby "left no room for the States to supplement" federal law, Rice v. Santa Fe Elevator Corp., 331 U.S. 218, 230, 67 S.Ct. 1146, 1152, 91 L.Ed. 1447 (1947); and, finally, when compliance with both state and federal law is impossible, Florida Lime & Avocado Growers, Inc. v. Paul, 373 U.S. 132, 142–143, 83 S.Ct. 1210, 1217–1218, 10 L.Ed.2d 248 (1963), or when the state law "stands as an obstacle to the accomplishment and execution of the full purposes and objectives of Congress." Hines v. Davidowitz, 312 U.S. 52, 67, 61 S.Ct. 399, 404, 85 L.Ed. 581 (1941). * * *

The power delegated to the FCC plainly comprises authority to regulate the signals carried by cable television systems. In United States v. Southwestern Cable Co., 392 U.S. 157, 88 S.Ct. 1994, 20 L.Ed.2d 1001 (1968), the Court found that the Commission had been given "broad responsibilities" to regulate all aspects of interstate communication by wire or radio by virtue of § 2(a) of the Communications Act of 1934, 47 U.S.C. § 152(a), and that this comprehensive authority included power to regulate cable communications systems. 392 U.S., at 177–178, 88 S.Ct., at 2005–2006. We have since explained that the Commission's authority extends to all regulatory actions "necessary to ensure the achievement of the Commission's statutory responsibilities." FCC v. Midwest Video Corp., 440 U.S. 689, 706, 99 S.Ct. 1435, 1444, 59 L.Ed.2d 692 (1979). * * * Therefore, if the FCC has resolved to pre-empt an area of cable television regulation and if this determination "represents a reasonable accommodation of conflicting policies" that are within the agency's domain, United States v. Shimer, supra, 367 U.S., at 383, 81 S.Ct., at 1560, we must conclude that all conflicting state regulations have been precluded.

A

In contrast to commercial television broadcasters, which transmit video signals to their audience free of charge and derive their income

use therein of intoxicating liquors, in violation of the laws thereof, is hereby prohibited."

principally from advertising revenues, cable television systems generally operate on the basis of a wholly different entrepreneurial principle. In return for service fees paid by subscribers, cable operators provide their customers with a variety of broadcast and nonbroadcast signals obtained from several sources. Typically, these sources include over-the-air broadcast signals picked up by a master antenna from local and nearby television broadcasting stations, broadcast signals from distant television stations imported by means of communications satellites, and nonbroadcast signals that are not originated by television broadcasting stations, but are instead transmitted specifically for cable systems by satellite or microwave relay. Over the past 20 years, pursuant to its delegated authority under the Communications Act, the FCC has unambiguously expressed its intent to pre-empt any state or local regulation of this entire array of signals carried by cable television systems.

The Commission began its regulation of cable communication in the 1960's. At that time, it was chiefly concerned that unlimited importation of distant broadcast signals into the service areas of local television broadcasting stations might, through competition, "destroy or seriously degrade the service offered by a television broadcaster," and thereby cause a significant reduction in service to households not served by cable systems. Rules re Microwave–Served CATV, 38 F.C.C. 683, 700 (1965). In order to contain this potential effect, the Commission promulgated rules requiring cable systems to carry the signals of all local stations in their areas, to avoid duplication of the programs of local television stations carried on the system during the same day that such programs were broadcast by the local stations, and to limit their importation of distant broadcast signals into the service areas of the local television broadcasting stations. CATV, 2 F.C.C.2d 725, 745–746, 781–782 (1966). It was with respect to that initial assertion of jurisdiction over cable signal carriage that we confirmed the FCC's general authority under the Communications Act to regulate cable television systems. United States v. Southwestern Cable Co., supra, 392 U.S., at 172–178, 88 S.Ct., at 2002–2005.

The Commission further refined and modified these rules governing the carriage of broadcast signals by cable systems in 1972. Cable Television Report and Order, 36 F.C.C.2d 143, on reconsideration, 36 F.C.C.2d 326 (1972), aff'd sub nom. American Civil Liberties Union v. FCC, 523 F.2d 1344 (CA9 1975). In marking the boundaries of its jurisdiction, the FCC determined that, in contrast to its regulatory scheme for television broadcasting stations, it would not adopt a system of direct federal licensing for cable systems. Instead, the Commission announced a program of "deliberately structured dualism" in which state and local authorities were given responsibility for granting franchises to cable operators within their communities and for overseeing such local incidents of cable operations as delineating franchise areas, regulating the construction of cable facilities, and maintaining rights of way. Cable Television Report and Order, 36 F.C.C.2d, at 207. At the same time, the Commission retained exclusive jurisdiction over all operational aspects of cable communication, including signal carriage and technical standards. See id., at 170–176. * * *

The Commission has also made clear that its exclusive jurisdiction extends to cable systems' carriage of specialized, nonbroadcast signals—a service commonly described as "pay cable." Id., at 199–200.[9]

* * * Accordingly, to the extent it has been invoked to control the distant broadcast and nonbroadcast signals imported by cable operators, the Oklahoma advertising ban plainly reaches beyond the regulatory authority reserved to local authorities by the Commission's rules, and trespasses into the exclusive domain of the FCC. To be sure, Oklahoma may, under current Commission rules, regulate such local aspects of cable systems as franchisee selection and construction oversight, see, e.g., Duplicative and Excessive Over-Regulation–CATV, 54 F.C.C.2d 855, 863 (1975), but, by requiring cable television operators to delete commercial advertising contained in signals carried pursuant to federal authority, the State has clearly exceeded that limited jurisdiction and interfered with a regulatory area that the Commission has explicitly pre-empted. * * *

III

Respondent contends that even if the Oklahoma advertising ban is invalid under normal pre-emption analysis, the fact that the ban was adopted pursuant to the Twenty-first Amendment rescues the statute from pre-emption. A similar claim was advanced in California Retail Liquor Dealers Assn. v. Midcal Aluminum, Inc., 445 U.S. 97, 100 S.Ct. 937, 63 L.Ed.2d 233 (1980). In that case, after finding that a California wine-pricing program violated the Sherman Act, we considered whether § 2 of the Twenty-first Amendment, which reserves to the States certain power to regulate traffic in liquor, "permits California to countermand the congressional policy—adopted under the commerce power—in favor of competition." 445 U.S., at 106, 100 S.Ct., at 944. Here, we must likewise consider whether § 2 permits Oklahoma to override the federal policy, as expressed in FCC rulings and regulations, in favor of promoting the widespread development of cable communication.

9. The Commission explained its initial decision to pre-empt this area as follows:

"After considerable study of the emerging cable industry and its prospects for introducing new and innovative communications services, we have concluded that, at this time, there should be no regulation of rates for such services at all by any governmental level. Attempting to impose rate regulation on specialized services that have not yet developed would not only be premature but would in all likelihood have a chilling effect on the anticipated development." 46 F.C.C.2d, at 199–200.

More recently, the Commission has noted that it "has deliberately pre-empted state regulation of non-basic program offerings, both non-broadcast programs and broadcast programs delivered to distant markets by satellite. While the nature of that non-basic offering was (and still is) developing, the preemptive intent, and the reasons for that preemption, are clear and discernible. Today, the degree of diversity in satellite-delivered program services reflects the wisdom of freeing cable systems from burdensome state and local regulation in this area." Community Cable TV, Inc., FCC 83–525, p. 13 (released Nov. 15, 1983).

The States enjoy broad power under § 2 of the Twenty-first Amendment to regulate the importation and use of intoxicating liquor within their borders. Ziffrin, Inc. v. Reeves, 308 U.S. 132, 60 S.Ct. 163, 84 L.Ed. 128 (1939). At the same time, our prior cases have made clear that the Amendment does not license the States to ignore their obligations under other provisions of the Constitution. * * * Indeed, "[t]his Court's decisions ... have confirmed that the Amendment primarily created an exception to the normal operation of the Commerce Clause." Craig v. Boren, 429 U.S. 190, 206, 97 S.Ct. 451, 461, 50 L.Ed.2d 397 (1976). Thus, as the Court explained in Hostetter v. Idlewild Bon Voyage Liquor Corp., 377 U.S. 324, 84 S.Ct. 1293, 12 L.Ed.2d 350 (1964), § 2 reserves to the States power to impose burdens on interstate commerce in intoxicating liquor that, absent the Amendment, would clearly be invalid under the Commerce Clause. Id., at 330, 84 S.Ct., at 1296; State Board of Equalization v. Young's Market Co., 299 U.S. 59, 62–63, 57 S.Ct. 77, 78–79, 81 L.Ed. 38 (1936). We have cautioned, however, that "[t]o draw a conclusion ... that the Twenty-first Amendment has somehow operated to 'repeal' the Commerce Clause wherever regulation of intoxicating liquors is concerned would ... be an absurd over-simplification." Hostetter, supra, 377 U.S., at 331–332, 84 S.Ct., at 1298. Notwithstanding the Amendment's broad grant of power to the States, therefore, the Federal Government plainly retains authority under the Commerce Clause to regulate even interstate commerce in liquor. Ibid. * * *.

In rejecting the claim that the Twenty-first Amendment ousted the Federal Government of all jurisdiction over interstate traffic in liquor, we have held that when a State has not attempted directly to regulate the sale or use of liquor within its borders—the core § 2 power—a conflicting exercise of federal authority may prevail. In Hostetter, for example, the Court found that in-state sales of intoxicating liquor intended to be used only in foreign countries could be made under the supervision of the Federal Bureau of Customs, despite contrary state law, because the state regulation was not aimed at preventing unlawful use of alcoholic beverages within the State, but rather was designed "totally to prevent transactions carried on under the aegis of a law passed by Congress in the exercise of its explicit power under the Constitution to regulate commerce with foreign nations." 377 U.S., at 333–334, 84 S.Ct., at 1299. Similarly, in Midcal Aluminum, supra, we found that "the Twenty-first Amendment provides no shelter for the violation of the Sherman Act caused by the State's wine pricing program," because the State's interest in promoting temperance through the program was not substantial and was therefore clearly outweighed by the important federal objectives of the Sherman Act. 445 U.S., at 113–114, 100 S.Ct., at 947–948. * * *

There can be little doubt that the comprehensive regulations developed over the past 20 years by the FCC to govern signal carriage by cable television systems reflect an important and substantial federal interest.

In crafting this regulatory scheme, the Commission has attempted to strike a balance between protecting noncable households from loss of regular television broadcasting service due to competition from cable systems and ensuring that the substantial benefits provided by cable of increased and diversified programming are secured for the maximum number of viewers. See, e.g., CATV Syndicated Program Exclusivity Rules, 79 F.C.C.2d, at 744–746. To accomplish this regulatory goal, the Commission has deemed it necessary to assert exclusive jurisdiction over signal carriage by cable systems. In the Commission's view, uniform national communications policy with respect to cable systems would be undermined if state and local governments were permitted to regulate in piecemeal fashion the signals carried by cable operators pursuant to federal authority. See Community Cable TV, Inc., FCC 83–525, pp. 12–13; (released Nov. 15, 1983); Cable Television, 46 F.C.C.2d, at 178. * * *

IV

We conclude that the application of Oklahoma's alcoholic beverage advertising ban to out-of-state signals carried by cable operators in that State is pre-empted by federal law and that the Twenty-first Amendment does not save the regulation from pre-emption. The judgment of the Court of Appeals is Reversed.

Notes

1. Can a city force a cable television station to abandon one of its channels designated for public educational and governmental use ("PEG") in exchange for a Fox news program? In *Time Warner Cable of New York City v. City of New York*, 943 F.Supp. 1357 (S.D.N.Y. 1996), Judge Cote found that "The City has engaged in a pattern of conduct with the purpose of compelling Time Warner to alter its constitutionally-protected editorial decision not to carry Fox News. The City's actions violate longstanding First Amendment principles that are the foundation of our democracy." Judge Cote was affirmed in *Time Warner Cable of New York City v. Bloomberg L.P.*, 118 F.3d 917 (2nd Cir. 1997). For more information on cable systems and the first amendment, *see also* Lutzker, *The 1992 Cable Act and the first amendment: what must, must not, and may be* carried, 12 Cardozo Arts & Ent L.J. 467, 1994; and Saylor, *Programming access and other competition regulations of the new cable television law and the Primestar decrees: a guided tour through the maze*, 2 Cardozo Arts & Ent L.J. 321, 1994.

2. Congress passed *The Cable Communications Policy Act of 1984*, 47 U.S.C. §§ 521 *et seq.* (the "Cable Act"), to stabilize federal regulation of the cable television industry by addressing issues that had vexed the Federal Communications Commission for many years. For further study, *see* Wadlow and Wellstein, *The Changing Regulatory Terrain of Cable Television*, 35 Cath U L Rev 705 (Spring 1986).

TURNER v. FCC

United States Supreme Court, 1997.
520 U.S. 180, 117 S.Ct. 1174, 137 L.Ed.2d 369.

Justice KENNEDY delivered the opinion of the Court, except as to a portion of Part II–A–1. * * *

Sections 4 and 5 of the Cable Television Consumer Protection and Competition Act of 1992 require cable television systems to dedicate some of their channels to local broadcast television stations. Earlier in this case, we held the so-called "must-carry" provisions to be content-neutral restrictions on speech, subject to intermediate First Amendment scrutiny under *United States v. O'Brien*, 391 U.S. 367, 377, 88 S.Ct. 1673, 1679, 20 L.Ed.2d 672 (1968). A plurality of the Court considered the record as then developed insufficient to determine whether the provisions were narrowly tailored to further important governmental interests, and we remanded the case to the District Court for the District of Columbia for additional factfinding.

On appeal from the District Court's grant of summary judgment for appellees, the case now presents the two questions left open during the first appeal: First, whether the record as it now stands supports Congress' predictive judgment that the must-carry provisions further important governmental interests; and second, whether the provisions do not burden substantially more speech than necessary to further those interests. We answer both questions in the affirmative, and conclude the must-carry provisions are consistent with the First Amendment. * * *

On our earlier review, we were constrained by the state of the record to assessing the importance of the Government's asserted interests when "viewed in the abstract," *Turner*, 512 U.S., at 663, 114 S.Ct., at 2469–2470. The expanded record now permits us to consider whether the must-carry provisions were designed to address a real harm, and whether those provisions will alleviate it in a material way. *Id.*, at 663–664, 114 S.Ct., at 2469–2470. We turn first to the harm or risk which prompted Congress to act. The Government's assertion that "the economic health of local broadcasting is in genuine jeopardy and in need of the protections afforded by must-carry," *id.*, at 664–665, 114 S.Ct., at 2470, rests on two component propositions: First, "significant numbers of broadcast stations will be refused carriage on cable systems" absent must-carry, *id.*, at 666, 114 S.Ct., at 2471. Second, "the broadcast stations denied carriage will either deteriorate to a substantial degree or fail altogether." *Ibid*.

In reviewing the constitutionality of a statute, "courts must accord substantial deference to the predictive judgments of Congress." Id., at 665, 114 S.Ct., at 2471. Our sole obligation is "to assure that, in formulating its judgments, Congress has drawn reasonable inferences based on substantial evidence." Id., at 666, 114 S.Ct. 2471. As noted in the first appeal, substantiality is to be measured in this context by a standard more deferential than we accord to judgments of an administrative agency. See id., at 666–667, 114 S.Ct., at 2471–2472; id., at 670, n. 1, 114 S.Ct., at 2473, n. 1 (STEVENS, J., concurring in part and concurring in judgment). We owe Congress' findings deference in part because the institution "is far better equipped than the judiciary to 'amass and evaluate the vast amounts of data' bearing upon" legislative questions. Turner, supra, at 665–666, 114 S.Ct., at 2470–2471 (plurality opinion) (quoting Walters v. National Assn. of Radiation Survivors, 473 U.S. 305, 331, n. 12, 105 S.Ct. 3180, 3194, n. 12, 87 L.Ed.2d 220 (1985)). * * *

We have no difficulty in finding a substantial basis to support Congress' conclusion that a real threat justified enactment of the must-carry provisions. We examine first the evidence before Congress and then the further evidence presented to the District Court on remand to supplement the congressional determination.

As to the evidence before Congress, there was specific support for its conclusion that cable operators had considerable and growing market power over local video programming markets. Cable served at least 60 percent of American households in 1992, see Cable Act § 2(a)(3), and evidence indicated cable market penetration was projected to grow beyond 70 percent. * * * As Congress noted, § 2(a)(2), cable operators possess a local monopoly over cable households. Only one percent of communities are served by more than one cable system. * * * Even in communities with two or more cable systems, in the typical case each system has a local monopoly over its subscribers. * * * Cable operators thus exercise "control over most (if not all) of the television programming that is channeled into the subscriber's home [and] can thus silence the voice of competing speakers with a mere flick of the switch." Turner, 512 U.S., at 656, 114 S.Ct., at 2466.

Evidence indicated the structure of the cable industry would give cable operators increasing ability and incentive to drop local broadcast stations from their systems, or reposition them to a less-viewed channel. Horizontal concentration was increasing as a small number of multiple system operators (MSO's) acquired large numbers of cable systems nationwide. § 2(a)(4). The trend was accelerating, giving the MSO's increasing market power. In 1985, the 10 largest MSO's controlled cable systems serving slightly less than 42 percent of all cable subscribers; by 1989, the figure was nearly 54 percent. * * *

Vertical integration in the industry also was increasing. As Congress was aware, many MSO's owned or had affiliation agreements with cable programmers. § 2(a)(5); Senate Report, at 24–29. Evidence indicated that before 1984 cable operators had equity interests in 38 percent of cable programming networks. In the late 1980's, 64 percent of new cable programmers were held in vertical ownership. * * * Congress concluded that "vertical integration gives cable operators the incentive and ability to favor their affiliated programming services," § 2(a)(5); Senate Report, at 25 a conclusion that even Judge Williams' dissent conceded to be reasonable. See 910 F.Supp., at 775. Extensive testimony indicated that cable operators would have an incentive to drop local broadcasters and to favor affiliated programmers. * * *

In addition, evidence before Congress, supplemented on remand, indicated that cable systems would have incentives to drop local broadcasters in favor of other programmers less likely to compete with them for audience and advertisers. Independent local broadcasters tend to be the closest substitutes for cable programs, because their programming tends to be similar, and because both primarily target the same type of advertiser: those interested in cheaper (and more frequent) ad spots than are typically available on network affiliates. * * * The ability of broadcast stations to compete for advertising is greatly increased by cable carriage, which increases viewership substantially. * * * With expanded viewership, broadcast presents a more competitive medium for television advertising. Empirical studies indicate that cable-carried broadcasters so enhance competition for advertising that even modest increases in the numbers of broadcast stations carried on cable are correlated with significant decreases in advertising revenue to cable systems. * * * Empirical evidence also indicates that demand for premium cable services (such as pay-per-view) is reduced when a cable system carries more independent broadcasters. * * * Thus, operators stand to benefit by dropping broadcast stations.

Cable systems also have more systemic reasons for seeking to disadvantage broadcast stations: Simply stated, cable has little interest in assisting, through carriage, a competing medium of communication. As one cable-industry executive put it, " 'our job is to promote cable television, not broadcast television.' " * * * The incentive to subscribe to cable is lower in markets with many over-the-air viewing options. * * * Evidence adduced on remand indicated cable systems have little incentive to carry, and a significant incentive to drop, broadcast stations that will only be strengthened by access to the 60 percent of the television market that cable typically controls. Congress could therefore reasonably conclude that cable systems would drop broadcasters in favor of programmers—even unaffiliated ones—less likely to compete with them audience and advertisers. The cap on carriage of affiliates included in the Cable Act, 47 U.S.C. § 533(f)(1)(B); 47 CFR § 76.504 (1995), and relied on by the dissent, post, at 1210, 1216, is of limited utility in protecting broadcasters. * * *

Additional evidence developed on remand supports the reasonableness of Congress' predictive judgment. Approximately 11 percent of local broadcasters were not carried on the typical cable system in 1989. * * * The figure had grown to even more significant proportions by 1992. According to one of appellants' own experts, between 19 and 31 percent of all local broadcast stations, including network affiliates, were not carried by the typical cable system. Based on the same data, another expert concluded that 47 percent of local independent commercial stations, and 36 percent of noncommercial stations, were not carried by the typical cable system. The rate of noncarriage was even higher for new stations. Appellees introduced evidence drawn from an empirical study concluding the 1988 FCC survey substantially underestimated the actual number of drops, and the noncarriage problem grew steadily worse during the period without must-carry. By the time the Cable Act was passed, 1,261 broadcast stations had been dropped for at least one year, in a total of 7,945 incidents. * * *

The evidence on remand also indicated that the growth of cable systems' market power proceeded apace. The trend toward greater horizontal concentration continued, driven by "[e]nhanced growth prospects for advertising sales." Paul Kagan Assocs., Inc., Cable TV Advertising 1 (Sept. 30, 1994) (App.301). By 1994, the 10 largest MSO's controlled 63 percent of cable systems. * * * MSO's began to gain control of as many cable systems in a given market as they could, in a trend known as "clustering." Cable systems looked increasingly to advertising (and especially local advertising) for revenue growth. * * * The vertical integration of the cable industry also continued, so by 1994, MSO's serving about 70 percent of the Nation's cable subscribers held equity interests in cable programmers. * * * The FTC study the dissent cites, post, at 1211, takes a skeptical view of the potential for cable systems to engage in anticompetitive behavior, but concedes the risk of anticompetitive carriage denials is "most plausible" when "the cable system's franchise area is large relative to the local area served by the affected broadcast station," and when "a system's penetration rate is both high and relatively unresponsive to the system's carriage decisions." That describes "precisely what is happening" as large cable operators expand their control over individual markets through clustering. As they do so, they are better able to sell their own reach to potential advertisers, and to limit the access of broadcast competitors by denying them access to all or substantially all the cable homes in the market area.

This is not a case in which we are called upon to give our best judgment as to the likely economic consequences of certain financial arrangements or business structures, or to assess competing economic theories and predictive judgments, as we would in a case arising, say, under the antitrust laws. "Statutes frequently require courts to make policy judgments. The Sherman Act, for example, requires courts to delve deeply into the theory of economic organization." * * * The issue before us is whether, given conflicting views of the probable development of the television industry, Congress had substantial evidence for making the judgment that it did. We need not put our imprimatur on Congress' economic theory in order to validate the reasonableness of its judgment.

2

The harm Congress feared was that stations dropped or denied carriage would be at a "serious risk of financial difficulty," 512 U.S., at 667, 114 S.Ct., at 2472, and would "deteriorate to a substantial degree or fail altogether," id., at 666, 114 S.Ct., at 2471. Congress had before it substantial evidence to support its conclusion. Congress was advised the viability of a broadcast station depends to a material extent on its ability to secure cable carriage. One broadcast industry executive explained it this way:

> Simply put, a television station's audience size directly translates into revenue—large audiences attract larger revenues, through the sale of advertising time. If a station is not carried on cable, and thereby loses a substantial portion of its audience, it will lose revenue. With less revenue, the station can not serve its community as well. The station will have less money to invest in equipment and programming. The attractiveness of its programming will lessen, as will its audience. Revenues will continue to decline, and the cycle will repeat." Hearing on Competitive Issues, at 526–527 (statement of Gary Chapman) (App.1600).

* * * Empirical research in the record before Congress confirmed the " 'direct correlation [between] size in audience and station [advertising] revenues,' " and that viewership was in turn heavily dependent on cable carriage. * * *

Another study prepared by a large MSO in 1993 concluded that "[w]ith cable penetration now exceeding 70% in many markets, the ability of a broadcast television station to easily reach its audience through cable television is crucial." The study acknowledged that even in a market with significantly below-average cable penetration, "[t]he loss of cable carriage could cause a significant decrease in a station's ratings and a resulting loss in advertising revenues." For an average market "the impact would be even greater." The study determined that for a popular station in a major television market, even modest reductions in carriage could result in sizeable reductions in revenue. A 5 percent reduction in cable viewers, for example, would result in a $1.48 million reduction in gross revenue for the station.

To be sure, the record also contains evidence to support a contrary conclusion. Appellants (and the dissent in the District Court) make much of the fact that the number of broadcast stations and their advertising revenue continued to grow during the period without must-carry, albeit at a diminished rate. Evidence introduced on remand indicated that only 31 broadcast stations actually went dark during the period without must-carry (one of which failed after a tornado destroyed its transmitter), and during the same period some 263 new stations signed on the air. New evidence appellants produced on remand indicates the average cable system voluntarily carried local broadcast stations accounting for about 97 percent of television ratings in noncable households. * * *

Despite the considerable evidence before Congress and adduced on remand indicating that the significant numbers of broadcast stations are at risk, the dissent believes yet more is required before Congress could act. It demands more information about which of the dropped broadcast stations still qualify for mandatory carriage, about the broadcast markets in which adverse decisions take place, and about the features of the markets in which bankrupt broadcast stations were located prior to their demise. The level of detail in factfinding required by the dissent would be an improper burden for courts to impose on the Legislative Branch. That amount of detail is as unreasonable in the legislative context as it is constitutionally unwarranted. "Congress is not obligated, when enacting its statutes, to make a record of the type that an administrative agency or court does to accommodate judicial review." Turner, supra, at 666, 114 S.Ct., at 2471 (plurality opinion).

We think it apparent must-carry serves the Government's interests "in a direct and effective way." *Ward*, 491 U.S., at 800, 109 S.Ct., at 2759. Must-carry ensures that a number of local broadcasters retain cable carriage, with the concomitant audience access and advertising revenues needed to support a multiplicity of stations. * * *

III

Judgments about how competing economic interests are to be reconciled in the complex and fast-changing field of television are for Congress to make. Those judgments "cannot be ignored or undervalued simply because [appellants] cas[t] [their] claims under the umbrella of the First Amendment." *Columbia Broadcasting v. Democratic National Committee*, 412 U.S., at 103, 93 S.Ct., at 2087. Appellants' challenges to must-carry reflect little more than disagreement over the level of protection broadcast stations are to be afforded and how protection is to be attained. We cannot displace Congress' judgment respecting content-neutral regulations with our own, so long as its policy is grounded on reasonable factual findings supported by evidence that is substantial for a legislative determination. Those requirements were met in this case, and in these circumstances the First Amendment requires nothing more. The judgment of the District Court is affirmed.

Justice O'CONNOR, with whom Justice SCALIA, Justice THOMAS, and Justice GINSBURG join, dissenting.

In sustaining the must-carry provisions of the Cable Television Protection and Competition Act of 1992 (Cable Act), Pub.L. 102–385, § § 4–5, 106 Stat. 1460, against a First Amendment challenge by cable system operators and cable programmers, the Court errs in two crucial respects. First, the Court disregards one of the principal defenses of the statute urged by appellees on remand: that it serves a substantial interest in preserving "diverse," "quality" programming that is "responsive" to the needs of the local community. The course of this litigation on remand and the proffered defense strongly reinforce my view that the Court adopted the wrong analytic framework in the prior phase of this case. See *Turner Broadcasting System, Inc. v. FCC*, 512 U.S. 622, 643–651, 114 S.Ct. 2445, 2460–2464, 129 L.Ed.2d 497 (1994) (Turner); id., at 675–680, 114 S.Ct., at 2475–2478 (O'CONNOR, J., concurring in part and dissenting in part). Second, the Court misapplies the "intermediate scrutiny" framework it adopts. Although we owe deference to Congress' predictive judgments and its evaluation of complex economic questions, we have an independent duty to identify with care the Government interests supporting the scheme, to inquire into the reasonableness of congressional findings regarding its necessity, and to examine the fit between its goals and its consequences. * * * The Court fails to discharge its duty here. * * *

In sustaining the must-carry provisions of the Cable Act, the Court ignores the main justification of the statute urged by appellees and subjects restrictions on expressive activity to an inappropriately lenient level of scrutiny. The principal opinion then misapplies the analytic framework it chooses, exhibiting an extraordinary and unwarranted deference for congressional judgments, a profound fear of delving into complex economic matters, and a willingness to substitute untested assumptions for evidence. In light of gaps in logic and evidence, it is improper to conclude, at the summary judgment stage, that the must-carry scheme serves a significant governmental interest "in a direct and effective way." *Ward*, 491 U.S., at 800, 109 S.Ct., at 2759. Moreover, because the undisputed facts demonstrate that the must-carry scheme is plainly not narrowly tailored to serving the only governmental interest the principal opinion fully explains and embraces—preventing anticompetitive behavior—appellants are entitled to summary judgment in their favor. * * *

Note

1.   In recent years, the FCC began relaxing the regulations governing ownership of stations and programming, which has allowed a consolidation of media ownership. The article and notes below are designed to introduce you to the perceived problems with consolidated ownership of the nation's media outlets.

Ted Turner
Monopoly or Democracy?
WASHINGTON POST, May 30, 2003, Final Ed.

[T]he Federal Communications Commission (FCC) [was] expected to adopt dramatic rule changes [to] extend the market dominance of the five media corporations that control most of what Americans read, see and hear. I am a major shareholder in the largest of those five corporations, yet, speaking only for myself, and not for AOL Time Warner, I oppose these rules. They * * * stifle debate, inhibit new ideas and shut out smaller businesses trying to compete. If these rules had been in place in 1970, it would have been virtually impossible for me to start Turner Broadcasting or, 10 years later, to launch CNN. * * *

If a young media entrepreneur were trying to get started today under these proposed rules, he or she wouldn't be able to buy a UHF station, as I did. They're all bought up. But even if someone did manage to buy a TV station, that wouldn't be enough. To compete, you have to have good programming and good distribution. Today both are owned by conglomerates that keep the best for themselves and leave the worst for you, if they sell anything to you at all. It's hard to compete when your suppliers are owned by your competitors. We bought MGM, and we later sold Turner Broadcasting to Time Warner, because we had little choice. The big were getting bigger. The small were disappearing. We had to gain access to programming to survive.

Many other independent media companies were swallowed up for the same reason—because they didn't have everything they needed under their own roof, and their competitors did. The climate after [the] FCC decision will encourage even more consolidation and be even more inhospitable to smaller businesses.

Why should the country care? When you lose small businesses, you lose big ideas. People who own their own businesses are their own bosses. They are independent thinkers. They know they can't compete by imitating the big guys; they have to innovate. So they are less obsessed with earnings than they are with ideas. They're willing to take risks. When, on my initiative, Turner Communications (now Turner Broadcasting) bought its first TV station, which at the time was losing $50,000 a month, my board strongly objected. When TBS bought its second station, which was in even worse shape than the first, our accountant quit in protest.

Large media corporations are far more profit-focused and risk-averse. They sometimes confuse short-term profits and long-term value. They kill local programming because it's expensive, and they push national programming because it's cheap, even if it runs counter to local interests and community values. For a corporation to launch a new idea, you have to get the backing of executives who are obsessed with quarterly earnings and afraid of being fired for an idea that fails. They often prefer to sit on the sidelines waiting to buy the businesses or imitate the models of the risk-takers who succeed. (Two large media corporations turned down my invitation to invest in the launch of CNN.)

That's an understandable approach for a corporation, but for a society, it's like over fishing the oceans. When the smaller businesses are gone, where will the new ideas come from? Nor does this trend bode well for new ideas in our democracy, ideas that come only from diverse news and vigorous reporting. Under the new rules, there will be more consolidation and more news sharing. That means laying off reporters or, in other words, downsizing the workforce that helps us see our problems and makes us think about solutions. Even more troubling are the warning signs that large media corporations, with massive market power could abuse that power by slanting news coverage in ways that serve their political or financial interests. There is always the danger that news organizations can push positive stories to gain friends in government, or unleash negative stories on artists, activists or politicians who cross them, or tell their audiences only the news that confirms entrenched views. But the danger is greater when there are no competitors to air the side of the story the corporation wants to ignore.

Naturally, corporations say they would never suppress speech. That may be true. But it's not their intentions that matter. It's their capabilities. * * *

Our democracy needs a broader dialogue. As Justice Hugo Black wrote in a 1945 opinion: "The First Amendment rests on the assumption that the widest possible dissemination of information from diverse and antagonistic sources is essential to the welfare of the public." Safeguarding the welfare of the public cannot be the first concern of large publicly traded media companies. Their job is to seek profits. But if the government writes the rules in a certain way, companies will seek profits in a way that serves the public interest. * * *

Notes

1. Does deregulation lead to less programming by independent producers and more network ownership of shows? Bill Carter and Jim Rutenberg presented the following facts in the *New York Times*: (1) The four networks had a stake in 67% of the programs in the 2003 fall prime time schedule, up from 32% in the fall of 1992; and (2) For the 2003 fall prime time schedule, only 2% came from independent producers, down from 30% in 1992. Bill Carter and Jim Rutenberg, *Deregulating the Media: Opponents; Show's Creators Say Television Will Suffer in New Climate,* N.Y. Times, June 3, 2003, at C1. Only viewers can decide if the decline of independent production has led to prime-time blandness.

2. Do FCC officials have a cozy relationship with the telecommunications and broadcasting industries they regulate? The Center for Public Integrity examined the travel records of FCC employees and found, according a 2003 *New York Times* article, "over the last eight years, commissioners and staff members have taken 2,500 trips costing $2.8 million that were 'primarily' paid for by members of the telecommunications and broadcast industries." Bob Hebert, *Cozy With the F.C.C.*, N.Y. Times, June 5, 2003, at A35. "The top destination was Las Vegas, with 330 trips. Second was New Orleans, with 173 trips. And third was New York, with 102 trips. Other 'popular' destinations were London (98 Trips), San Francisco, Palm Springs, Buenos Aires and Beijing." *Id.*

3. Will the concentration of media ownership lead to more or less diverse programming? Chapter 12 explored the lack of diverse programming on network television. ABC is owned by Capital Cities, which is owned by Disney, a conglomerate that also owns the following channels: The Disney Channel, Toon Disney, ESPN and its related channels, Classic Sports Network, A&E Television, The History Channel, Lifetime Television. With some of these channels, Disney shares ownership with other corporations like the Hearst Co. and GE. In addition to its joint ventures with Disney, GE whose holdings include ownership of MSNBC, CSNBC, and the History Channel, owns NBC. VIACOM owns CBS, Showtime, MTV, VH1, and Nickelodeon.

4. This concentration of ownership gives networks options when controversy greets a planned program. After a conservative furor erupted over CBS's plans to show a miniseries called *The Reagans*, CBS shunted the series over to Showtime, where only viewers who subscribed to the cable

television channel saw it. http://www.cnn.com/2003/SHOWBIZ/TV/11/ 04/cbs.reagans.ap/

B.   SATELLITE TV

SATELLITE BROADCASTING & COMMUNICATIONS ASS'N v. F.C.C.

United States Court of Appeals, Fourth Circuit, 2001.
275 F.3d 337.

MICHAEL, Circuit Judge.

Direct broadcast satellite (DBS) service has recently joined cable and broadcast television as a major force in the market for delivering television programming to consumers. In these consolidated cases, representatives of the satellite industry raise various constitutional challenges to Congress's efforts to regulate competition in that market through the Satellite Home Viewer Improvement Act of 1999 (SHVIA). Pub.L. No. 106–113, 113 Stat. 1501A–523. In addition, petitioners from the broadcast industry argue that one provision (the "a la carte rule") of the FCC's order implementing SHVIA must be struck down as an unreasonable interpretation of the statute.[1] By enacting SHVIA, Congress sought to promote competition between the satellite and cable industries by creating a statutory copyright license that allows satellite carriers to carry the signals of local broadcast television stations without obtaining authorization from the holders of copyrights in the individual programs aired by those stations. The Act also imposes a "carry one, carry all" rule, which was designed to "preserve free television for those not served by satellite or cable and to promote widespread dissemination of information from a multiplicity of sources." H.R. Conf. Rep. No. 106–464, at 101 (1999) (SHVIA Conference Report). The rule, which is scheduled to take effect on January 1, 2002, will require satellite carriers that choose to take advantage of the statutory copyright license by carrying one broadcast station in a local market to carry all requesting stations within that market. We hold, as did the district court, that the carry one, carry all rule does not violate either the First Amendment or the other constitutional provisions cited by the satellite carriers. We also hold that the FCC's a la carte rule, which allows satellite carriers to offer local broadcast stations to their subscribers either individually or as part of a single package, is not arbitrary, capricious, or contrary to law. *See* 5 U.S.C. § 706(2)(A).

---

1. The parties in these cases fall into three groups, according to their interests regarding SHVIA: satellite industry representatives (or the "satellite carriers"), including the Satellite Broadcasting and Communications Association (SBCA), DirecTV, Inc., EchoStar Communications Corp., and Dish, Ltd., a wholly owned subsidiary of EchoStar doing business as DISH Network; broadcast representatives (or the "broadcasters"), including the National Association of Broadcasters (NAB), Paxson Communications Corp., and the Public Broadcasting Service (PBS); and the United States, essentially the Federal Communications Commission (FCC).

I.

A.

Nearly all consumers receive their television programming through one of three delivery systems: broadcast television, cable, or satellite. Broadcast television stations transmit electromagnetic signals over the air, and these signals can be captured by any receiving television antenna within range. Twenty percent of American television households rely exclusively on broadcast stations for their television programming. Viewers pay no fee to receive broadcast signals. Instead, broadcast stations are supported by advertisers who pay for air time at rates determined by the audience sizes for particular programs. The most popular broadcast stations are affiliated with one of the four major television networks (ABC, CBS, NBC, and Fox). The major network affiliates compete for viewers and advertisers with various independent broadcasters, including independent commercial stations, noncommercial stations, and affiliates of emerging networks (UPN, WB, and PAX).[2]

The broadcasters' principal competitors in the television programming delivery market are the cable and satellite industries. Cable and satellite companies now serve around 80 percent of America's television households. Unlike broadcasters, their primary source of revenue is subscription fees. Cable television distributes its signals to subscribers over a local network of wires. It has for many years been the leading provider of television programming to American homes. Roughly 67 percent of television households currently subscribe to cable. Although cable subscribers must pay for the right to receive cable signals, they receive better picture quality and a wider variety of programming options than do television viewers who rely on antennas. Today, 84 percent of cable systems offer their subscribers at least 30 channels, including national non-broadcast channels (such as ESPN, MTV, CNN, and The Weather Channel) and regional non-broadcast channels (such as the New England Sports Channel). Cable operators also retransmit the signals of local broadcast stations to their subscribers.

Providers of DBS (direct broadcast satellite) service deliver television programming by uplinking signals to satellites orbiting in space and then beaming those signals to receiving dishes connected to subscribers' television sets. In the 1980s satellite dishes were 6 to 10 feet in diameter, and satellite carriers primarily served customers in rural areas. During the 1990s satellite carriers such as EchoStar and DirecTV developed much smaller dishes and began to compete with cable for subscribers in urban and suburban areas. Today, satellite carriers provide service in each of the nation's 210 television markets and serve about 13 percent of television households.[3]

---

2. For ease of reference, we will often describe the class of broadcast stations that includes commercial independents, noncommercial stations, and emerging network affiliates as "independent" broadcast stations.

3. Our figures about the market shares of broadcast television, cable, and satellite are drawn from In the Matter of Annual Assessment of Status of Competition in Market for Delivery of Video Programming,

Whereas cable systems deliver their signals to subscribers over local wire networks, satellite is primarily a national service. The satellites currently used by DBS providers occupy one of three positions in the Earth's orbit (called full CONUS slots) that allow the satellites to transmit a single beam covering the entire continental United States. The beam from a full CONUS satellite contains multiple frequencies, and compression technology enables multiple television channels to be carried on each frequency. The FCC licenses the use of 32 frequencies at each orbital slot; thus, there are 96 total frequencies that satellite carriers can use to reach satellite subscribers across the United States. Currently, 50 of these frequencies are licensed to EchoStar and 46 to DirecTV. Using their current compression ratios, EchoStar and DirecTV each have the ability to carry between 450 and 500 channels via full CONUS satellites. Every channel carried on these satellites is beamed to the homes of all subscribers; however, channels that individual subscribers do not pay to receive are blocked by the use of software in the subscriber's home satellite equipment.

Like cable, satellite service is financed by subscription fees, and it offers better picture quality and more viewing options than broadcast television. Satellite carriers can provide their customers with more national and regional non-broadcast channels than most cable systems; yet before SHVIA was passed, satellite carriers had difficulty competing with cable for urban and suburban customers. The root cause of this difficulty was plain. Cable systems, but not satellite carriers, provided their customers with access to the signals of local broadcast stations. This competitive advantage was rooted not only in technology but also in federal copyright law. Unlike satellite carriers, cable operators have never been required to obtain copyright clearances for the broadcast programming they retransmit to their subscribers. To explain the origins of cable's competitive advantage over satellite, we must briefly review the history that produced the current legal regime governing the relationships among cable, broadcast television, and satellite.

In 1965, long before cable became a major force in the television programming delivery market, the FCC imposed "must-carry" rules on cable systems requiring them to retransmit the signal of any requesting broadcast station that was "significantly viewed" in its local market. *See Quincy Cable TV, Inc. v. FCC,* 768 F.2d 1434, 1438–43 (D.C.Cir.1985) (discussing the early history of cable regulation). The FCC feared that cable might undermine free, local broadcasting unless "local broadcasters were assured access to the whole of their allocated audience." *Id.* at 1441. Specifically, the must-carry rules were designed to aid newer UHF stations, which lacked the signal quality enjoyed by more established VHF stations. The FCC was concerned that in the absence of carriage obligations cable systems would carry only VHF stations and that non-

Seventh Annual Report, CS Docket No. 00–132, 2001 WL 12938 (2001) (FCC Seventh Annual Report). The figures reflect industry data through June 2000. See id. at 106.

The broadcasters contend that satellite service has grown significantly since June 2000 and that satellite market share now exceeds 15 percent of television households.

carried UHF stations would be placed at a competitive disadvantage in the race for advertising dollars. *See id.*

Copyright law had little effect on cable until Congress passed the Copyright Act of 1976, Pub.L. No. 94–553, 90 Stat. 2541, which provides that owners of copyrights in audiovisual works such as television programs have the exclusive right to authorize public performances of those works. 17 U.S.C. § 106(4). Although the Copyright Act of 1909 had granted copyright holders a similar right to control public performances of copyrighted works, cable operators' secondary transmissions of broadcast programs were not regarded as additional performances of those programs under the 1909 Act and thus did not infringe upon the intellectual property rights of the program copyright holders. *See Fortnightly Corp. v. United Artists Television, Inc.,* 392 U.S. 390, 400–01, 88 S.Ct. 2084, 20 L.Ed.2d 1176 (1968). The 1976 Act's legislative history reveals that Congress intended to countermand the result in *Fortnightly* by designating cable's secondary transmissions of broadcast programs as public performances of those programs: "a cable television system is performing when it retransmits the broadcast [of a television program] to its subscribers." H.R.Rep. No. 94–1476, at 63 (1976), *reprinted in* 1976 U.S.C.C.A.N. 5659, 5677. As a result, copyright law now generally requires parties seeking to retransmit the signal of a broadcast television station to obtain authorization from those holding copyrights in each of the programs broadcast by that station. Cable operators, however, have never been subject to this general rule. Congress found "that it would be impractical and unduly burdensome to require every cable system to negotiate with every copyright owner whose work was retransmitted by a cable system." *Id.* at 89, 1976 U.S.C.C.A.N. at 5704. As a result, the 1976 Copyright Act granted cable operators a statutory license that allows them to retransmit broadcast television signals without securing authorization from program copyright holders. *See* 17 U.S.C. § 111(c).

As cable grew in popularity, cable operators and cable programmers began to chafe at the FCC's must-carry rules. Eventually, cable interests challenged the rules as an unconstitutional burden on freedom of speech, and the rules were struck down by the D.C. Circuit in 1985. *See Quincy Cable TV,* 768 F.2d at 1463. The FCC moved quickly to adopt a modified set of carriage rules, but the D.C. Circuit again decided that the rules violated the First Amendment. *See Century Communications Corp. v. FCC,* 835 F.2d 292, 293 (D.C.Cir.1987). After a period of several years during which cable enjoyed the benefits of a statutory copyright license without the burdens of carriage obligations, Congress reimposed must-carry rules by passing the Cable Television and Consumer Protection and Competition Act of 1992 (Cable Act). Pub.L. No. 102–385, 106 Stat. 1460. Like the FCC's original must-carry rules, the Cable Act's must-carry rules were designed to protect broadcast stations that might be refused carriage in the absence of a must-carry requirement.

The Cable Act must-carry rules were also challenged on First Amendment grounds, but were ultimately upheld by the Supreme Court in *Turner Broadcasting System, Inc. v. FCC,* 512 U.S. 622, 114 S.Ct.

2445, 129 L.Ed.2d 497 (1994) (*Turner I*), and *Turner Broadcasting System, Inc. v. FCC,* 520 U.S. 180, 117 S.Ct. 1174, 137 L.Ed.2d 369 (1997) (*Turner II*). In *Turner I* the Supreme Court held that the must-carry rules were content-neutral restrictions on speech, *Turner I,* 512 U.S. at 662, 114 S.Ct. 2445, reviewable under the intermediate First Amendment scrutiny standards established by *United States v. O'Brien,* 391 U.S. 367, 88 S.Ct. 1673, 20 L.Ed.2d 672 (1968). The Court further recognized that the interests served by the must-carry rules—preserving local broadcast television, promoting the "widespread dissemination of information from a multiplicity of sources," and promoting fair competition in the television programming market—were important "in the abstract." *Turner I,* 512 U.S. at 662–63, 114 S.Ct. 2445. However, the Court remanded the case for further factual development on the question of whether these interests were genuinely advanced by the must-carry rules and whether the rules were a narrowly tailored means of promoting these interests. After the remand the Court held in *Turner II* that the cable must-carry rules fully satisfied the *O'Brien* test. As a result, cable operators today enjoy the privileges of a statutory copyright license but are also bound by carriage obligations.

As the above history indicates, the cable industry developed within a context of extensive FCC regulations, but it has been largely unaffected by copyright considerations. Before 1976, cable retransmissions of broadcast programs were not regarded as additional performances of these programs and therefore did not infringe program copyrights. Since 1976, cable has enjoyed a statutory copyright license. In contrast, the satellite industry has until recently enjoyed relative freedom from FCC oversight, but its history has been shaped by a series of changes in federal copyright law. When the 1976 Copyright Act was passed, home satellite service did not exist, and the statutory copyright license created by 17 U.S.C. § 111(c) was granted only to cable systems. Although early satellite carriers lacked the channel capacity to retransmit the signals of local broadcast stations to the local audiences of those stations (called "local-into-local" service), the carriers did have the capacity and the desire to offer their subscribers some distant network signals. In other words, they had enough capacity to carry the signals of network affiliates in a major city (usually New York) throughout the entire country, but not enough capacity to carry local network affiliates in smaller cities. It was unclear, however, whether satellite carriers' secondary transmissions of the signals of network affiliates infringed the copyrights in the various programs broadcast by those stations. Satellite carriers argued that they might be eligible to use the § 111 copyright license as "cable systems," 17 U.S.C. § 111(c), or that their secondary transmissions of broadcast signals were noninfringing under the exemption for passive carriers in 17 U.S.C. § 111(a)(3). Still, they asked Congress to resolve the uncertainties about their copyright liability by passing new legislation.

Congress responded with the Satellite Home Viewer Act of 1988. Pub.L. No. 100–667, 102 Stat. 3949. Recognizing that the high transaction costs involved in clearing the rights to network signals might impede the growth of the fledgling satellite industry, Congress gave carriers a limited copyright license to retransmit the signals of distant network broadcast stations to unserved households that were unable to receive an adequate over-the-air signal through a conventional rooftop antenna. 17 U.S.C. § 119(a)(2)(B) (1994), *amended by* § 119(a)(2)(B) (Supp. V 1999). "Unserved households" were defined in part as those located outside a station's "Grade B contour," as defined by FCC regulations. *Id.* § 119(d)(10) (1994), *amended by* § 119(d)(10) (Supp. V 1999).

Congress limited the copyright license to retransmissions to unserved households in order to respect the terms of network-affiliate contracts, which grant local affiliates the exclusive right to broadcast their networks' programming in their local markets. Congress reasoned that local affiliates would lose the benefits of their bargained-for exclusivity rights if satellite carriers were allowed to import distant network signals into the affiliates' local markets. The limited license created by the 1988 Act spurred the growth of satellite carriers and expanded the viewing options of unserved households, though it did little to help satellite effectively compete with cable in urban and suburban areas where viewers could already receive high quality broadcast signals.

In the late 1990s two problems led Congress to revisit its work in the Satellite Home Viewer Act of 1988. First, cable continued to enjoy a virtual monopoly in subscription television services in metropolitan areas, and as a result cable subscribers were paying too much for those services. *See* S.Rep. No. 106–51, at 1–2 (1999). Second, the 1988 Act failed to deal adequately with the problems of satellite subscribers who lived within the Grade B contours of network television stations. Although these subscribers were ineligible to receive distant network signals under the 1988 Act's limited copyright license, many of them were unable to receive satisfactory over-the-air signals from their local network affiliates and thus remained without any meaningful access to network programming. *See id.* at 3–6. In addition, administrative difficulties in deciding which households were genuinely unserved led to increasingly bitter disputes between satellite carriers and broadcasters, leaving bewildered, angry consumers stuck in the middle. *See, e.g., ABC, Inc. v. PrimeTime 24,* 17 F.Supp.2d 478 (M.D.N.C.1998), *aff'd,* 184 F.3d 348 (4th Cir.1999).

Progress in satellite technology seemed to hold out a solution to both of these problems. Satellite carriers had developed the channel capacity to offer local-into-local service to their subscribers in some markets. Congress recognized that satellite carriers that could offer viewers access to their local broadcast stations could compete effectively with cable and drive down the price of subscription television services. *See* H.R.Rep. No. 106–79, pt. 1, at 14 (1999). In addition, Congress understood that the difficulties in deciding which households were sufficiently unserved to receive distant network signals would be irrelevant if satellite subscribers could watch their local network affiliates. *See id.*

In 1997 and 1998 Congress conducted extensive hearings on the possibility of extending the satellite carriers' statutory copyright license to include local-into-local retransmissions. Representatives from the various industries had ample opportunities to state their views. Satellite industry representatives argued that without a statutory copyright license, the high transaction costs of obtaining the rights to retransmit broadcast programs would effectively prevent satellite carriers from offering local-into-local service. The satellite representatives further explained that their inability to carry local broadcast stations placed them at a competitive disadvantage to cable because viewers want to be able to receive all of the televisions channels they watch from a single source: "most people who walk into a satellite dealer's showroom turn around and walk out because they can't get their local TV channels through DBS." *Reauthorization of the Satellite Home Viewer Act: Hearing Before the Subcommittee on Telecommunications, Trade, and Consumer Protection of the House Committee on Commerce,* 106th Cong. 73 (1999) (1999 House Hearing) (statement of David Moskowitz, an EchoStar executive). The cable representatives stressed the need for regulatory parity, arguing that if satellite carriers were granted a statutory license comparable to that enjoyed by cable, they should also be subject to the must-carry rules and other regulatory constraints imposed on cable. *See The Copyright Office Report on Compulsory Licensing of Broadcast Signals: Hearing Before the Senate Committee on the Judiciary,* 105th Cong. 50 (1997) (statement of Decker Anstrom, President, National Cable Television Association). Finally, representatives of the broadcast industry emphasized that mandatory carriage rules were needed to ensure that satellite local-into-local service would not undermine Congress's interest in preserving a vibrant system of free, local broadcast television. They explained that without carriage rules satellite carriers would choose to retransmit only the signals of major network affiliates in most markets and that competing stations in those markets would suffer from the loss of access to a significant (and growing) part of their potential audiences:

> No rational doubt may exist that a local station denied access to a portion of its inmarket audience is injured. Lack of carriage reduces potential audience and, therefore, actual audience. Reduced audiences translate to reduced revenue. Even where revenue reductions are less than fatal, they still affect a station's ability to provide the best practicable service to the public. At best, a local station which a satellite carrier refuses to carry would be placed at a demonstrable disadvantage vis-a-vis competing broadcast television stations which are carried.

Copyright Licensing Regimes Covering Retransmission of Broadcast Signals (Part II): Hearing Before the Subcommittee on Courts and Intellectual Property of the House Committee on the Judiciary, 105th Cong. 68 n. 38 (1998) (1998 House Hearing) (statement of James J. Popham, Vice

President and General Counsel, Association of Local Television Stations).

Congress sought to balance all of these concerns when it enacted SHVIA on November 29, 1999. The Conference Report explained that the legislation was designed to promote competition between satellite and cable while "preserv[ing] free television for those not served by satellite or cable systems." SHVIA Conf. Rep. at 101. Two interrelated provisions form the heart of SHVIA. The first provision, codified at 17 U.S.C. § 122, amended the Copyright Act to create a statutory copyright license for satellite carriers similar to that enjoyed by cable operators. The license enables satellite carriers to make secondary transmissions of a broadcast station's signal into that station's local market without obtaining the authorization of those holding copyrights in the individual programs broadcast by that station. 17 U.S.C. § 122(a). Satellite carriers that make use of this license pay no royalties to program copyright holders. The second provision, codified at 47 U.S.C. § 338, amended the Communications Act of 1934 by creating mandatory carriage rules, including the carry one, carry all rule that is the focus of this litigation. 47 U.S.C. § 338(a)(1).

Since SHVIA's passage in late 1999 satellite carriers have enjoyed the benefits of the § 122 license without the burdens of the carry one, carry all rule. In order to phase in satellite carriage obligations, Congress decided that the rule would not become effective until January 1, 2002. Id. § 338(a)(3). As of that date the rule will require all satellite carriers who use the § 122 license to make local-into-local retransmissions in a local broadcast market to "carry upon request the signals of all television broadcast stations located within that local market." Id. § 338(a)(1). In other words, the voluntary decision to carry one local station in a market under the statutory copyright license will trigger an obligation to carry all the requesting stations in that market.

Like the cable must-carry rules, SHVIA's carry one, carry all rule was designed to preserve a rich mix of broadcast outlets for consumers who do not (or cannot) pay for subscription television services. SHVIA adopts much of the machinery of the cable rules. For example, broadcast stations may seek carriage from satellite carriers under either § 338's mandatory carriage requirements, 47 U.S.C. 325(b)(1)(C), or under the Act's retransmission consent provision, 47 U.S.C. 325(b)(1)(A), which allows broadcast stations to receive compensation from satellite carriers in exchange for permission to retransmit the broadcast stations' signals. In allowing broadcasters to choose between retransmission consent and mandatory carriage, both SHVIA's carry one, carry all rule and the cable must-carry rules recognize the practical realities of the television marketplace. Major network affiliates have bargaining power and will be carried voluntarily in most instances, so they will normally elect to proceed under the retransmission consent provision. See Turner II, 520 U.S. at 191, 117 S.Ct. 1174 (explaining that the Cable Act's retransmission consent provision reflects the "popularity and strength of some broadcasters"). In contrast, independent stations (affiliates of emerging networks, independent commercial stations, and noncommercial stations) may need the protection of must-carry rules and will normally elect mandatory carriage.

The primary difference between § 338 and the cable must-carry rules is that § 338's obligations are conditioned upon the satellite carrier's voluntary choice to make use of the § 122 license in a particular television market, but the cable must-carry rules are mandatory in all markets. This difference reflects the technological dissimilarities between cable and satellite. Cable systems are local, and nearly all have enough channel capacity to carry all the broadcast stations in their local market and still provide an attractive mix of national and regional nonbroadcast programming. The satellite carriers, in contrast, currently beam the same 450 to 500 channels throughout the continental United States and thus could not comply with a rule requiring them to retransmit the signals of each of the country's roughly 1,600 local broadcast stations. *See* 1999 House Hearing at 95 (statement of David Moskowitz). While Congress recognized that satellite technology continues to improve and that eventually an unconditional must-carry rule might be possible, it still had to decide how to structure the satellite copyright license in the interim.

Although minor variations were possible, Congress had two basic options. It could have decided to give satellite carriers a station-by-station copyright license that could be used free of carriage obligations. Under such a license, satellite carriers could "cherry pick" the stations they wanted in each local market. Congress predicted that in practical terms a station-by-station license would result in satellite carriers using their available local-into-local capacity to carry only the major network affiliates in as many markets as possible, beginning with the largest markets and working toward the smaller ones. The other choice was to impose the carry one, carry all rule in order to create a market-by-market copyright license. This kind of license forces satellite carriers to expand their local-into-local service one market at a time, beginning with the carriage of all requesting local stations in the largest markets and expanding from there. In sum, Congress either could have allowed satellite carriers to cherry pick by retransmitting *some* stations (the major network affiliates) in *many* markets, or it could have allowed satellite carriers to retransmit *all* of the stations in *some* markets. While satellite carriers would have preferred (and now argue for) the first result, Congress chose the second because it feared that cherry picking of major network affiliates within local markets would make it more difficult for non-carried stations in those markets to reach their audiences:

> Although the conferees expect that subscribers who receive no broadcast signals at all from their satellite service may install antennas or subscribe to cable service in addition to satellite service, the Conference Committee is less sanguine that subscribers who receive network signals and hundreds of other programming choices

from their satellite carrier will undertake such trouble and expense to obtain over-the-air signals from independent broadcast stations.

SHVIA Conf. Rep. at 102. Non-carried stations in cherry-picked markets would "face the same loss of viewership Congress previously found with respect to cable noncarriage." *Id.* at 101. Congress therefore concluded that the carry one, carry all rule would protect the ability of all local broadcasters to reach their audiences and thereby "preserve free television for those not served by satellite or cable systems and ... promote widespread dissemination of information from a multiplicity of sources." *Id.*

B.

As directed by Congress, *see* 47 U.S.C. 338(g), the FCC issued a report and order implementing § 338's carriage requirements on November 29, 2000. *In the Matter of: Implementation of the Satellite Home Viewer Improvement Act of 1999: Broadcast Signal Carriage Issues, Retransmission Consent Issues,* CS Docket Nos. 00–96 and 99–363 (2000) (SHVIA Order). The only aspect of the SHVIA Order at issue here is the a la carte rule adopted in paragraph 99 of the order. The FCC concluded in that paragraph that § 338(d) does not require satellite carriers to sell all local television stations in a given market as one package. Instead, the Commission ruled that carriers could offer local stations "as a package or a la carte, at comparable rates." SHVIA Order at ¶ 99. This language would arguably permit satellite carriers to offer their subscribers a package including only the major network affiliates while offering independent broadcast stations only on an a la carte basis. However, in a subsequent order issued while these cases were under consideration, the FCC clarified its a la carte rule by stating that satellite carriers may not offer their subscribers a package including some subset of the local stations in a market (for example, the major network affiliates) while offering other local stations on an individual basis. *See In the Matter of: Implementation of the Satellite Home Viewer Improvement Act of 1999: Broadcast Signal Carriage Issues, Order on Reconsideration,* CS Docket No. 00–96, at ¶ 48 (2001) (Reconsideration Order). In other words, the Commission has now ruled that satellite carriers offering local-into-local service may offer their subscribers only two options: subscribers may buy the local stations of their choice a la carte at comparable prices, or they may buy a package of all the local stations for a price less than or equal to the cost of subscribing to all the stations individually (for example, 12 stations at one dollar each or all 12 for $12 or less). *See id.*

C.

The present SHVIA litigation began on September 20, 2000, when SBCA, DirecTV, EchoStar, and DISH Network filed a complaint in the United States District Court for the Eastern District of Virginia alleging that SHVIA's carry one, carry all rule, 47 U.S.C. § 338(a)(1), exceeds Congress's power under the Copyright Clause and violates the First Amendment and the Due Process and Takings Clauses of the Fifth

Amendment. NAB and PBS intervened on the side of the FCC in order to defend the statute. The satellite carriers moved for summary judgment, but the FCC and its supporting intervenors filed Rule 56(f) motions requesting discovery in order to respond to the satellite carriers' motion. The district court granted their motions, and discovery began. The FCC and its supporting intervenors then filed a Rule 12(b)(6) motion to dismiss and (ultimately) a cross-motion for summary judgment. After the parties had conducted extensive discovery in support of their summary judgment motions, the district court granted the FCC and its intervenors' motion to dismiss on June 19, 2001. *See Satellite Broad. & Communications Ass'n v. FCC,* 146 F.Supp.2d 803, 809 (E.D.Va.2001). The district court treated the carry one, carry all rule as a content-neutral regulation of the satellite carriers' speech and upheld the rule under intermediate First Amendment scrutiny. In addition, the court rejected the satellite carriers' arguments alleging violations of the Copyright Clause and the Fifth Amendment. The satellite carriers appealed. That appeal has been consolidated with three petitions for review of the FCC's SHVIA Order. SBCA filed a petition for review of the SHVIA Order in this circuit, and EchoStar filed a similar petition in the Tenth Circuit. Both petitions advanced constitutional challenges to SHVIA similar to those advanced by the satellite carriers in the Eastern District of Virginia. NAB filed a petition for review in the D.C. Circuit challenging the FCC's a la carte rule as arbitrary, capricious, and not in accordance with law. *See* 5 U.S.C. § 706(2)(A). Paxson Communications intervened in this last petition on the side of NAB. The three petitions for review were consolidated and assigned to this circuit pursuant to 28 U.S.C. § 2112(a)(3).

II.

A.

The parties devote the lion's share of their attention to the satellite carriers' First Amendment challenge to the carry one, carry all rule enacted in 47 U.S.C. § 338. Satellite carriers, like cable operators, function primarily as conduits for the speech of others. They transmit programming from a variety of sources (national and regional non-broadcast channels, superstations, and local broadcast stations) to their subscribers "on a continuous and unedited basis." *Turner I,* 512 U.S. at 629, 114 S.Ct. 2445. Yet both satellite carriers and cable operators engage in speech protected by the First Amendment when they exercise editorial discretion over the menu of channels they offer to their subscribers. *See id.* at 636–37, 114 S.Ct. 2445. Insofar as the carry one, carry all rule seeks to influence the exercise of that discretion, it is open to challenge under the First Amendment. * * *

In considering the satellite carriers' First Amendment challenge, our first task is to determine the appropriate standard of review. * * * A satellite carrier that privately negotiates the required copyright clearances can retransmit the signal of a local broadcast station without incurring any carriage obligations, but a carrier that retransmits the same signal by means of the statutory copyright license must comply with the carry one, carry all rule. Thus, the burdens of the rule do not depend on a satellite carrier's choice of content, but on its decision to transmit that content by using one set of economic arrangements rather than another. Accordingly, we hold that the carry one, carry all rule is content neutral on its face.

Next, we must decide whether the carry one, carry all rule is content-based in its purpose. The satellite carriers claim that the rule has a content-based purpose because it seeks to promote the survival of independent broadcast stations, including affiliates of emerging networks, commercial independent stations, and public broadcasting stations. In support of this claim they cite language from the Conference Report indicating that Congress was concerned that satellite carriers would choose to carry only affiliates of the major networks and that other local broadcasters would be cut off from portions of their potential viewing audiences. *See* SHVIA Conf. Rep. at 102. In addition, the satellite carriers rely on legislative history suggesting that Congress sought to protect local broadcast stations because those stations provide valuable news and public affairs programming to their communities. *See id.* at 92.

Again, we conclude that these points do not distinguish the present case from *Turner I*. Both Congress and the Supreme Court understood perfectly well that the cable must-carry rules primarily benefited independent broadcast stations. *See Turner I*, 512 U.S. at 672–73, 114 S.Ct. 2445 (Stevens, J., concurring in part and concurring in the judgment); *Turner II*, 520 U.S. at 191–92, 117 S.Ct. 1174. * * * In sum, *Turner I* held that the cable must-carry rules were content neutral in purpose even though the rules were meant to protect independent broadcast stations and even though Congress recognized that those stations provided valuable local programming. Here, the satellite carriers do no more than point to legislative history indicating that Congress had the same purpose in enacting SHVIA and that Congress continued to appreciate the distinctive value of local broadcast programming. This is not enough to establish that SHVIA has a content-based purpose.

We conclude, then, that the carry one, carry all rule should not be subject to strict scrutiny. At most, it is a content-neutral measure that imposes incidental burdens on speech and is therefore subject to intermediate First Amendment scrutiny under *United States v. O'Brien*, 391 U.S. 367, 88 S.Ct. 1673, 20 L.Ed.2d 672 (1968). Because, as we explain below, the carry one, carry all rule passes constitutional muster under *O'Brien*, we need not address the FCC and its intervenors' argument that the rule should be evaluated under a more lenient standard. * * *

We agree that the carry one, carry all rule is meant to preserve the ability of independent broadcasters to reach their local audiences, but Congress did not view that goal as an end in itself. Instead, Congress recognized that protecting independent broadcasters from the harmful effects of satellite cherry picking would further two substantial government interests. The first is the government's interest in preserving a multiplicity of local broadcast outlets for over-the-air viewers, those who do not subscribe to satellite or cable service. The second is the government's interest in preventing its grant of a statutory copyright license to satellite carriers from undermining competition in local markets for broadcast television advertising. Though these two interests are closely related because both would be threatened in the same manner without the carry one, carry all rule, they are distinct because the first involves harms to over-the-air viewers while the second involves harms to local advertisers and to independent broadcasters themselves. As we explain next in the first part of our *O'Brien* analysis, we find that both interests are materially advanced by the carry one, carry all rule. We will now address each interest in turn.

1.

Congress enacted the carry one, carry all rule to "preserve free television for those not served by satellite or cable systems and to promote widespread dissemination of information from a multiplicity of sources." SHVIA Conf. Rep. at 101. These interests are clearly substantial and unrelated to the suppression of free expression. *See Turner I,* 512 U.S. at 662–63, 114 S.Ct. 2445 (stating that the government's interests in "preserving the benefits of free, over-the-air local broadcast television" and "promoting the widespread dissemination of information from a multiplicity of sources" were both important and unrelated to the suppression of free expression). In deciding whether § 338 materially advances these two interests, it is useful to characterize them more precisely. We therefore adopt the characterization suggested in *Turner II,* where the Supreme Court treated the two interests as a unified whole: "Congress has an independent interest in preserving a multiplicity of broadcasters to ensure that all households have access to information and entertainment on an equal footing with those who subscribe to cable." *Turner II,* 520 U.S. at 194, 117 S.Ct. 1174; *see also id.* at 193, 117 S.Ct. 1174 (stating that Congress's interest in "preserving the existing structure of the broadcast industry discloses a purpose to prevent any significant reduction in the multiplicity of broadcast programming sources available to noncable households" (internal quotation marks and citation omitted)); *id.* at 226, 117 S.Ct. 1174 (Breyer, J., concurring in part) (describing the Cable Act's purpose as "provid[ing] over-the-air viewers who lack cable with a rich mix of over-the-air programming" and "assur[ing] the over-the-air public access to a multiplicity of information sources" (internal quotation marks and citation omitted)). In short, the government interests served by the carry one, carry all rule are best characterized as a single interest in preserving a multiplicity of broadcast outlets for over-the-air viewers. * * *

When Congress passed the Cable Act of 1992, cable television was the sole threat to the government's interest in preserving a multiplicity of broadcast outlets for over-the-air viewers. The substantial deterioration standard employed in *Turner II* assumes the existence of a unitary threat by insisting that the government show that denial of carriage on an individual medium would threaten the viability of independent broadcasters. *See Turner II,* 520 U.S. at 195, 117 S.Ct. 1174. But the substantial deterioration standard was not meant to address situations in which the threat to broadcasters comes from competitors in multiple mediums, and it yields implausible results when applied outside its intended context. Suppose, for example, that five different television delivery mediums each served 15 percent of television households, together serving 75 percent of those households. If the standard applied in these circumstances, it would mean that Congress could not impose must-carry rules on any of the mediums because stations denied carriage on any one medium would lose access to only 15 percent of their audiences and therefore would not suffer substantial deterioration. That cannot be the law.

In enacting SHVIA, Congress properly considered the effects of satellite and cable together in deciding to protect over-the-air viewers from any significant reduction in their viewing options. Cable and satellite together currently serve around 80 percent of America's television households, with cable accounting for about 65 percent and satellite about 15 percent. We have already explained that both services pose the same kind of threat to broadcast stations because both—by making selective carriage decisions—threaten to cut off independent broadcast stations from parts of their audiences. Together, cable and satellite would pose an overwhelming threat to independent broadcasters if neither were bound by carriage rules. Congress evidently reasoned that with increasing competition from satellite carriers, the threat to independent broadcasters posed by cable would become a threat jointly posed by cable and satellite. It therefore concluded that it could regulate both contributors to that common threat: "The [Conference Committee] expect[s] that, by January 1, 2002, satellite carriers' market share will have increased and that the Congress'[s] interest in maintaining free over-the-air television will be undermined if local broadcasters are prevented from reaching their viewers *by either cable or satellite distribution systems.*" SHVIA Conf. Rep. at 101 (emphasis added).

The satellite carriers contend that the carry one, carry all rule needlessly restricts their speech because it is not necessary to protect the interests of over-the-air viewers. Again, they claim that those interests are not threatened because broadcasters denied satellite carriage will not lose access to enough of their audiences to suffer substantial deterioration. But if over-the-air viewers are currently safe, that only reflects the fact that cable is *already* bound by must-carry rules. In other words, the satellite carriers' arguments boil down to the claim that even if both cable and satellite jointly contribute to a common threat to the government's interest in protecting a multiplicity of broadcast outlets for over-the-air viewers, Congress may not impose carriage rules on satellite carriers because their contribution to that common threat is smaller and because cable is already regulated. The First Amendment does not require this result. It is more sensible to allow Congress the latitude to view the regulatory landscape as a whole by considering the cumulative effects of cable and satellite without making fine distinctions regarding their relative contributions in creating those effects. Where multiple competitors jointly pose a common threat with a common structure, the First Amendment permits Congress to protect important government interests from that threat by imposing reasonable content-neutral restrictions on every competitor who significantly contributes to that threat.

Under this standard, Congress's factual predictions easily justify the imposition of the carry one, carry all rule. Even if it is debatable whether satellite's *current* market share is sufficient to count as a significant contribution to the common threat posed by cable and satellite, Congress surely had a substantial basis for concluding that satellite would soon become a significant challenger to cable in the television programming delivery market. Accordingly, we hold that Congress reasonably concluded that the carry one, carry all rule addressed a real threat to the government's interest in preserving a multiplicity of broadcast outlets for over-the-air viewers. That interest therefore survives the first part of the *O'Brien* inquiry: it is substantial, and it is genuinely advanced by the carry one, carry all rule.

2.

The FCC argues that the carry one, carry all rule also materially advances a second substantial government interest: the interest in preventing SHVIA's grant of a statutory copyright license to satellite carriers from undermining competition in local markets for broadcast television advertising. This interest is, as we have said, closely related to the interest in preserving a multiplicity of broadcast stations for over-the-air viewers. Both interests are threatened when independent broadcasters lose access to parts of their local audiences as a result of cherry picking by satellite carriers. But although cherry picking threatens both interests in the same way, the interests are nonetheless distinct. The first interest is ultimately an interest in protecting over-the-air television viewers. The second is an interest in protecting the broadcasters themselves, as well as the advertisers who benefit from vigorous competition among the broadcast stations in their local markets. * * *

This interest in preserving a level playing field in local broadcast advertising markets seems to us at least as significant as many interests which the Supreme Court has found to be important or substantial. *See, e.g., Clark v. Community for Creative Non Violence,* 468 U.S. 288, 296, 104 S.Ct. 3065, 82 L.Ed.2d 221 (1984) (holding that government had a substantial interest in maintaining parks in Washington, D.C., in "an attractive and intact condition"); *Members of City Council v. Taxpayers for Vincent,* 466 U.S. 789, 807, 104 S.Ct. 2118, 80 L.Ed.2d 772 (1984) (holding that city had a substantial interest in preventing "the visual assault on the citizens of Los Angeles presented by an accumulation of signs posted on public property"). We therefore conclude that Congress's interest in minimizing the unintended adverse effects of its legislation on local broadcast advertising markets is substantial enough to justify incidental, content-neutral restrictions on speech. The carry one, carry all rule advances this interest in a material way because it preserves a level playing field on which local broadcasters can compete for advertising revenue by preventing satellite carriers from making selective carriage decisions within local television markets. Accordingly, we hold that this interest also satisfies the first part of the *O'Brien* analysis.

3.

We have identified two interests that pass scrutiny under the first part of the *O'Brien* analysis. The second part of the *O'Brien* analysis employed in *Turner II* requires us to ask whether the carry one, carry all rule is a narrowly tailored means of advancing these interests. The government has considerable latitude under this test. It may "employ the means of its choosing so long as the ... regulation promotes a substantial governmental interest that would be achieved less effectively absent the regulation and does not burden substantially more speech than is necessary to further that interest." *Turner II*, 520 U.S. at 213–14, 117 S.Ct. 1174 (internal quotation marks and citation omitted). The parties have devoted relatively little attention to this aspect of the *O'Brien* analysis, and with good reason. Congress enacted the carry one, carry all rule to protect independent broadcast stations from the harm they would suffer if satellite carriers denied them carriage while retransmitting the signals of the major network affiliates in their markets. As we have explained, the rule genuinely advances two important interests: the interest in preserving a multiplicity of local broadcast outlets for those who do not subscribe to cable or satellite and the interest in minimizing the unintended effects of SHVIA's statutory copyright license on local broadcast advertising markets. The satellite carriers concede that without the carry one, carry all rule, they would have chosen to carry only major network affiliates in many local markets and would therefore have threatened independent broadcasters with the very harms that Congress sought to prevent. Accordingly, any legislation that created a statutory copyright license without imposing some form of mandatory carriage requirement would have been significantly less effective—indeed, it would have been completely ineffective—in advancing the government's interests. That is sufficient to satisfy *O'Brien*'s narrow tailoring requirement. Further, the particular form of carriage requirement imposed by SHVIA is not an excessive burden on satellite carriers because it leaves them with the choice of when and where they will become subject to the carry one, carry all rule. As a result, we hold that the rule is a narrowly tailored means of promoting the government's important ends of preserving a vibrant mix of local broadcast outlets for over-the-air viewers and minimizing the unintended side effects of SHVIA's statutory copyright license on local broadcast advertising markets. The carry one, carry all rule is therefore consistent with the First Amendment. * * *

V.

For the foregoing reasons, we hold that the carry one, carry all rule does not violate the Constitution and that the a la carte rule is not arbitrary and capricious or contrary to law. Accordingly, the order of the district court is affirmed, and the petitions for review of the FCC's SHVIA Order are denied.

Note

1.   In 1999, Congress amended the *Satellite Home Viewer Improvement Act (SHVIA)* Communications Act of 1934, § 338(a)(1)(2), as amended, 47 U.S.C.A. § 338(a)(1), which provides in part:

> Subject to the limitations of paragraph (2), each satellite carrier providing, under section 122 of Title 17, secondary transmissions to subscribers located within the local market of a television broadcast station of a primary transmission made by that station shall carry upon request the signals of all television broadcast stations located within that local market, subject to section 325(b) of this title. . . . The remedies for any failure to meet the obligations under this subsection shall be available exclusively under section 501(f) of Title 17. *Id.*

*

Part III

MUSIC LAW

Chapter 14

MUSIC BUSINESS RELATIONSHIPS

———

Music, like the other entertainment genre, is a relationship business. A great team is an asset to any star in the music business. In addition to supportive band mates, an artist needs a good agent, lawyer, personal manager, and business manager.

The Making of the Band, American Idol, and *Star Search* have demystified the talent search process for most television viewers. The shows have taken the search out of the dingy clubs and bars and put it on a soundstage in front of television cameras. While the shows have sensationalized the process, they are fairly reflective of reality in their selection and evaluation criteria. Simon Cowell on *American Idol* accurately represents the cruel process of evaluation of talent that occurs everyday in record company offices around the world. Artist and Repertoire (A & R) executives scour the earth for the next great million seller. A & R people listen to demos and go to clubs to find talent. For more on what they are listening for, see Henslee's article on *The Evolving Role of the Lawyer in the Representation of Talent in the Music Business* in Section D below.

A band trying to get discovered needs to play live gigs to develop a following, show some personnel stability, and have a solid demo. A & R people travel to clubs and bars to find new talent. In addition, they listen to demo tapes or compact discs. If a demo tape doesn't catch their attention in the first few seconds, they will move on to the next one. A demo tape should begin with the strongest material from the group. Record companies will listen to material received from a reputable manager, agent, or lawyer long before they will listen to unsolicited material submitted by the band. In addition, they will listen to more of the music submitted if it comes from a reputable source.

Typically, an A&R person will have to present the group to the president of the record company before making the final decision on signing. Before the act is presented to the president, the group may have to be filtered through one or two A&R vice-presidents. The decision makers will usually want to see the group perform live. In most record companies, the president has the final say on all artist signings because of the large amount of money that will have to be spent in order to develop the artist's career.

After signing a record contract, the group will be given a budget to produce an album. The budget typically includes an artist advance for living expenses. The budget must pay for the producers, the studio time, the engineer, the guest musicians, vocalists, arrangers, instrument rentals, transportation, and studio food and drinks (and sometimes drugs). The producer of a record is like the director of a movie. The producer is a creative person who makes songs into hits. The engineer is like the cinematographer (camera operator). The engineer sets up the microphones in the studio, adjusts the recording levels on the soundboard, and records the tracks on a 2–inch, multi-track tape. Every studio has an in-house engineer who is familiar with the soundboard. If a producer wants his or her own engineer, the artist will have to pay for two engineers, the in-house engineer and the producer's engineer. To begin the recording process, the entire group may play the song together. The engineer will record the various instruments to use as a reference for the rerecording of the tracks. The vocalist will sing the song so that the musicians can hear the vocals as they lay down the final tracks. The vocals recorded with the group are called "scratch vocals." The reason that the group recording is not used on the final mix is that in the small sound studio, one instrument will bleed into another instrument's track, making it impossible to fix a mistake. Songs are recorded one instrument at a time, with the final vocals added last. By recording each instrument separately, any missed note can be fixed by rerecording the single missed note. A good engineer can "punch" in the correct note to make the group sound perfect on their recording. With enough time, anyone can sound perfect on a track recorded in the studio. It can take days to record the instruments and vocals for one song.

After the songs are recorded on the 2–inch tape, the various tracks are mixed down onto a two-track, quarter-inch or half-inch tape. The mixed tape is the version submitted to the record company for use in the manufacturing process. While the compact discs are being pressed, the artwork and liner notes are prepared. The entire process, from signing, to recording, to pressing, to delivery and sales, can take six months to two years.

Before the money starts coming in, a group needs an organizational agreement to delineate how the money will be split, how to remove an original member from the group, how to add new members, who gets the name when the members of the group leave, and how to handle songwriting credits and income. Band partnership agreements are covered in Section A.

A well-connected personal manager can help a group find a lawyer, an agent, and a record deal. Managers spend the majority of their time working with the artist to develop the artist's career. Managers shield the artist from his or her new best friends who suddenly appear once a record deal has been signed. The manager, in consultation with the artist, develops and controls the artist's image through publicity and live appearances. Managers are covered in Section B.

What a band really needs is a good booking agent. It is nearly impossible to get discovered if no one ever sees the band play live. Live appearances help build a following for the band that helps attract record companies. Bands with large followings have an easier time getting signed by a label because the labels believe that the band's fans will buy albums and encourage their friends to buy albums. A good booking agent is critical for a band to tour and play at good venues. Booking agents are covered in Section C.

A band needs a music lawyer to help them get started. Most bands can't afford a lawyer when they are starting out. Section D covers band/lawyer relationships below.

The chapter concludes with a Section E on songwriters and producers. Both are critical to the success of any musical success story.

A. BAND PARTNERSHIP AGREEMENTS

The most important document that a lawyer can prepare for a group is the band organization agreement. There are a number of important issues to cover in a band partnership agreement. The first issue is to determine the organizational structure of the band and the type of business entity to form (i.e. a corporation, an LLC, or a partnership). Other organizational issues that need to be discussed are the governance issues and the splits of the profits and losses. Songwriting credits, publishing ownership, and income splits are issues that can destroy a group if they are not fully understood and agreed upon before the songs start making money. While the band members are still friends, and before the money starts coming in, the inevitable breakup of the band needs to be discussed. The group needs to decide how to remove members, how to add members, and as the cases below will show, who gets to use the name of the band when some or all of the original members are no longer playing in the group. Each member of the band should be represented by separate counsel. Part A concludes with a segment discussing the legal issues involved with symphony orchestras.

KASSBAUM v. STEPPENWOLF PRODUCTIONS, INC.

United States Court of Appeals, Ninth Circuit, 2000.
236 F.3d 487.

GOULD, Circuit Judge.

This case raises the issue of whether a contract between the parties or section 32(1)(a) of the Lanham Trade–Mark Act, 15 U.S.C. § 1114(1)(a) ("Lanham Act"), bars Nicholas Kassbaum ("Kassbaum"), a former member of the rock band "Steppenwolf," from referring to himself in promotional materials for a new band as "formerly of Steppenwolf," an "original member of Steppenwolf," or an "original founding member of Steppenwolf." * * *

FACTS AND PROCEDURAL HISTORY

In 1967, John Kay, Jerry Edmonton, Michael Monarch and Goldie McJohn formed a musical band called "Steppenwolf." In 1968, Nicholas Kassbaum, who is professionally known as "Nick St. Nicholas," joined Steppenwolf as a bass player. That year, the band members entered into a partnership agreement whereby the members became co-equal partners and owners in Steppenwolf, and agreed to share equally the band's expenses and income. Also in 1968, the band members signed a recording agreement with Dunhill Records both as partners and as Steppenwolf band members.

From late 1968 until late April 1970, Steppenwolf, with Kassbaum as its bass player, toured the world in concerts and recorded Steppenwolf's well-received music. Kassbaum appeared prominently on Steppenwolf record album covers and authored Steppenwolf compositions. In 1971, John Kay, who had asserted control over Steppenwolf, excluded Kassbaum from the band. In 1975, after Kassbaum and Michael Monarch had been excluded, and John Kay had stopped performing as Steppenwolf, Kassbaum and Goldie McJohn began to perform as "The New Steppenwolf." This began a series of legal disputes over the different band members' use of the name Steppenwolf.

In 1976, Kassbaum filed a complaint against SI [Steppenwolf, Inc.] and SPI [Steppenwolf Productions, Inc.] to obtain an order prohibiting SPI from interfering with Kassbaum's performances as The New Steppenwolf. In 1977, Kassbaum paid $17,500.00 to John Kay and SPI in exchange for their agreement to grant Goldie McJohn and Kassbaum the exclusive right to the use of the name Steppenwolf for the purposes of live performances and recordings.

In 1979, Kassbaum entered into a second agreement whereby SI and SPI granted The New Steppenwolf, Inc. the exclusive right to use the name Steppenwolf until 1981 in connection with recording, production, manufacture, sale and distribution of records and tapes containing performances of a musical group. Kassbaum performed as Steppenwolf from 1977 through 1980.

On May 27, 1980, Kassbaum, The New Steppenwolf, Inc., SI and SPI entered into a third contract ("the 1980 contract") which states, in relevant part:

ACKNOWLEDGEMENT [sic] AND WAIVER. [KASSBAUM], THE NEW STEPPENWOLF, INC. and GEOFFREY EMORY hereby acknowledge and agree that [SI] and [SPI] own all right, title and interest in the name "STEPPENWOLF". [KASSBAUM], THE NEW STEPPENWOLF, INC., and GEOFFREY EMORY hereby acknowledge and agree that [SI] and [SPI] have the sole and exclusive right to use the name "STEPPENWOLF" in connection with the production, manufacture and distribution of phonograph records, in live, in-concert performances of a musical group, and all other uses of the name "STEPPENWOLF" in the entertainment industry. [KASSBAUM], THE NEW STEPPENWOLF, INC. and GEOFFREY EMORY now and forever, waive, relinquish and release any and all of their individual or collective rights in the name "STEPPENWOLF" or any other word or phrase incorporating the name "STEPPEN-WOLF" for any purpose whatsoever. [KASSBAUM], THE NEW STEPPENWOLF, INC. and GEOFFREY EMORY hereby agree to waive, relinquish and release any trademark, trade name, service mark, or service name rights any or all of them may have in the name "STEPPENWOLF." [KASSBAUM], THE NEW STEPPEN-WOLF, INC. and GEOFFREY EMORY further agree to transfer or assign all such trademark, trade name, service mark or service name rights they may have in the name "STEPPENWOLF" to [SI] and [SPI]. Notwithstanding anything to the contrary in the foregoing, nothing contained herein shall be deemed an acknowledgment on the part of [SI] and [SPI] that [KASSBAUM], THE NEW STEP-PENWOLF, INC., and/or GEOFFREY EMORY, ever acquired or held any such trademark, trade name, service mark or service name right in the name "STEPPENWOLF."

The contract also provided that, in exchange for this acknowledgment and waiver,

"[SI] and [SPI] agree to pay [KASSBAUM], THE NEW STEPPEN-WOLF, INC. and GEOFFREY EMORY the sum of THREE THOU-SAND DOLLARS ($3,000.00)."

From 1980, when the contract was executed, until 1996, Kassbaum performed as "Lone Wolf." During that time, without objection from the parties to the 1980 contract, Kassbaum referred to his historical association with Steppenwolf, describing himself as a "former member of" or "previous member of" Steppenwolf.

From 1996 until the present, Kassbaum has performed in a group called World Classic Rockers. The group is comprised of former members of various musical groups well known to rock music fans including: Randy Meiser, a former member of "Wings;" Spencer Davis, a former member of the "Spencer Davis Group;" Bruce Gary, a former member of "Knack;" and Michael Monarch and Kassbaum, former members of Steppenwolf. While performing as the World Classic Rockers, Kassbaum and the other band members often identified themselves by referring to their former musical associations. For example, one advertisement iden-tifies Kassbaum as "NICK ST. NICHOLAS former member of Steppen-wolf." Kassbaum also promoted himself as being a "Former Original Member of Steppenwolf," "Original Founding Member of Steppenwolf," and "Formerly of Steppenwolf."

In response to these promotional claims, SPI and SI sent Kassbaum cease and desist letters asserting that Kassbaum's historical references to Steppenwolf violated federal trademark law and the 1980 contract. Kassbaum then filed a complaint in federal district court seeking a declaration that he is entitled to refer to himself as "Formerly of Steppenwolf," an "Original Member of Steppenwolf," and an "Original Founding Member of Steppenwolf." SPI answered and filed a counterclaim alleging trademark infringement, unfair competition and breach of contract. Thereafter, SPI and SI moved for summary judgment on Kassbaum's complaint for declaratory relief and SPI's counterclaim for breach of contract. SPI and SI also sought permanently to enjoin Kassbaum and his agents from using the name Steppenwolf.

The district court granted SPI and SI's motion for summary judgment on Kassbaum's complaint for declaratory relief, granted SPI's counterclaim for breach of contract, dismissed Kassbaum's complaint for declaratory relief, and granted SPI and SI's request for a permanent injunction forbidding Kassbaum from using the designations "Formerly of Steppenwolf," "Original Member of Steppenwolf" and "Original Founding Member of Steppenwolf," in promotional materials. Kassbaum appeals, contending that the district court erred. We agree, and we reverse and remand.

DISCUSSION

I. Summary Judgment and Dismissal of Declaratory Judgment Complaint

We must decide whether either the 1980 contract or the Lanham Act bars Kassbaum from referring to himself as a former member of Steppenwolf.

A. The Contract

As described above, the parties entered into the 1980 contract on May 28, 1980. We must decide whether, by the terms of the contract, Kassbaum agreed that he would not identify himself, for promotional purposes or otherwise, with a true statement that he is a former member of the band Steppenwolf. * * *

As Kassbaum concedes, there is no doubt that the 1980 contract "absolutely precludes" Kassbaum from "performing, sponsoring, or endorsing a band entitled Steppenwolf." The question is whether the contracting parties intended that broad language such as "waive, relinquish and release any and all ... rights in the name 'STEPPENWOLF' or any other word or phrase incorporating the name 'STEPPENWOLF' for any purpose whatsoever" would bar Kassbaum from such things as truthfully answering a question about his past (for example) on a talk show, distributing a resume, or truthfully describing his past musical affiliations in promotional materials connected with the World Classic Rockers.

Taken out of context, the language "name 'STEPPENWOLF' "and "for any purposes whatsoever," might be read so broadly as to preclude Kassbaum from writing "Steppenwolf" on the sidewalk in chalk. While SPI and SI do not advocate a restriction that broad, they do appear to contend that the contract language prohibits virtually any reference by Kassbaum to the name Steppenwolf in the context of the "entertainment industry." Thus, SPI and SI contend that Kassbaum contracted away his ability to refer to his past association with Steppenwolf in a resume sent to a recording company, or in a music industry interview touching upon his background, or, at the center of this case, in his promotional references relating to his performance with World Classic Rockers.

We must read the words of the 1980 contract in context. Cal. Civ. Code § 1641. ("The whole of a contract is to be taken together, so as to give effect to every part, if reasonably practicable, each clause helping to interpret the other."); *Id.* § 1650 ("Particular clauses of a contract are subordinate to its general intent."). We may not read the contract in a manner that leads to an absurd result. *Id.* § 1638 (courts must look at contract language to discern parties' intent so long as the result "does not involve an absurdity"); *Id.* § 1639. Rather, when we encounter broad language such as "for any purposes whatsoever," we must extend the meaning of such language to cover only those things which it appears the parties intended to contract. *Id.* § 1648 ("However broad may be the terms of a contract, it extends only to those things concerning which it appears that the parties intended to contract."). When broad language is at issue, we must look to the circumstances under which the parties contracted to determine their intentions at the time of contracting. *Id.* § 1647.

Here, those circumstances are a continuing dispute between the parties about ownership and control over the trade name Steppenwolf. Over the years, such ownership and control was transferred from party to party through a series of contracts. First, all of the original band members owned the trade name Steppenwolf. Then, in 1977, after Kassbaum was asked to leave Steppenwolf and began to perform as The New Steppenwolf, the parties resolved a dispute over the right to the trade name Steppenwolf by having Kassbaum pay $17,500.00 to SPI in exchange for the exclusive right to perform as Steppenwolf for the purpose of live performances and recordings. The parties entered into a second agreement in 1979, whereby SI and SPI granted Kassbaum and The New Steppenwolf, Inc. the exclusive right to use the name Steppenwolf in connection with recording, production, manufacture, sale and distribution of records and tapes embodying performance of a musical group until 1981. At the time the parties entered into the 1980 contract, Kassbaum owned the trade name Steppenwolf to the extent specified by the 1979 contract, and had been performing as The New Steppenwolf. The 1980 contract effected the transfer of the trade name Steppenwolf from Kassbaum and The New Steppenwolf to SPI and SI. Thereafter, Kassbaum discontinued his performances as The New Steppenwolf, and began to perform as Lone Wolf and later as a part of the World Classic Rockers.

Under these circumstances, it is clear that the contract's broad language "for any purposes whatsoever," and "all other uses of the name 'STEPPENWOLF' in the entertainment industry" refers to use of the *trade name* Steppenwolf, and not to the simple use of the name to provide accurate historical information that would not lead reasonable people to think Kassbaum's new band was Steppenwolf. The terms of the contract do not bar Kassbaum from referring to his former membership in Steppenwolf in the entertainment industry or otherwise. We therefore hold that the district court erred by granting summary judgment to SPI and SI on the contract counterclaim and by dismissing Kassbaum's complaint for declaratory relief on contract grounds.

C. The Lanham Act

Kassbaum's complaint requests, inter alia, a declaratory judgment that section 32(1)(a) of the Lanham Act, 15 U.S.C. § 1114(1)(a), does not bar him from stating, particularly in promotional materials, that he was "Formerly of Steppenwolf," an "Original Member of Steppenwolf," or an "Original Founding Member of Steppenwolf." The district court dismissed Kassbaum's complaint and granted SPI and SI's motion for summary judgment. We reverse. * * *

First, we believe the phrases "Formerly of," "Original Member of" and "Original Founding Member of," immediately preceding the name "Steppenwolf" in the promotional materials for World Classic Rockers greatly reduce the likelihood of confusion about the source of the band's music.

Additionally, the context of the historical references to Kassbaum's affiliation with Steppenwolf in World Classic Rockers' promotional materials further reduces any likelihood of confusion between these two bands. In all promotional materials presented to the district court, references to World Classic Rockers are more prominent than are references to Steppenwolf. The materials display the title "World Classic Rockers" on the top or at the center of the page, while references to the band members' former groups, including Steppenwolf, are displayed on the bottom or around the edges of the page. Also, the title "World Classic Rockers" appears in large and bold lettering, while smaller and plainer lettering is used for the titles of the former groups, including Steppenwolf. Finally, while the materials mention multiple former groups, the materials promote only World Classic Rockers, not Steppenwolf, or any other former band. * * *

Finally, we wholeheartedly agree with Justice Holmes's statement about the limits of trademark protection in *Prestonettes, Inc. v. Coty*, 264 U.S. 359, 368 (1924): "When the mark is used in a way that does not deceive the public we see no such sanctity in the word as to prevent its being used to tell the truth. It is not taboo." We reverse the district court's order granting summary judgment to SPI and SI and dismissing Kassbaum's complaint for declaratory judgment as to the Lanham Act issue.

II. Permanent Injunction

The district court granted SPI and SI's request for a permanent injunction precluding Kassbaum and his agents from using the designations "Formerly of Steppenwolf," "Original Member of Steppenwolf," and "Original Founding Member of Steppenwolf" in promotional materials. Because we hold that Kassbaum is not barred by contract or by the Lanham Act from using these designations, we reverse. * * *

CONCLUSION

We reverse the district court's order (1) granting summary judgment to SPI and SI on the complaint for declaratory judgment and on the contract counterclaim; (2) dismissing Kassbaum's complaint for declaratory judgment; and (3) granting SPI and SI's request for a permanent injunction. We remand to the district court with instructions to reinstate Kassbaum's complaint for declaratory relief and for further proceedings consistent with this opinion.

REVERSED and REMANDED.

FAR OUT PRODUCTIONS, INC. v. OSKAR

United States Court of Appeals, Ninth Circuit, 2001.
247 F.3d 986.

BREYER, District Judge.

Far Out Productions, Inc., filed suit against Howard Scott, an original member of the musical group "WAR," and other artists with whom Scott was performing, alleging infringement of the federally-registered trademark "WAR." Scott responded by filing a counterclaim alleging, *inter alia,* fraud, conversion, and trademark infringement. Harold Brown, another original member of the group, filed a direct action against Far Out Productions and its president Jerry Goldstein (collectively, "the appellees"), alleging that the appellees had obtained the trademark fraudulently. The cases were consolidated, and Scott and Brown ("the appellants") appeal the district court's orders: (1) denying the appellants' motion for summary judgment; (2) granting the appellees' motion for summary judgment; and (3) denying the appellants' motion for a new trial. We have jurisdiction pursuant to 28 U.S.C. § 1291, and we affirm.

I. BACKGROUND

A. *Factual Background*

In the late 1960s, the appellee Jerry Goldstein, Steven Gold, and Eric Burdon, the former lead singer of a British band known as The Animals, formed Far Out Productions, Inc., Far Out Music, Inc., and Far Out Management, Ltd. (collectively, "the Far Out entities"). In January 1969, Goldstein, Gold, and Burdon met with members of a band known as "The Night Shift," whose members included the appellants, to discuss forming a band. The parties agreed to form a band known as "Eric Burdon and WAR."

On June 8, 1969, the group performed commercially for the first time at a nightclub known as Mother Lizard's Ball in San Bernardino, California. The band began production of its first album, entitled "Eric Burdon Declares WAR," soon afterward, and the album was released in March 1970. The album became very successful, and the original members of the band eventually signed exclusive recording and publishing agreements with the Far Out entities.

Burdon eventually lost interest in the group. Goldstein then decided to produce a second album with the musicians who had previously been Burdon's back-up band. According to Goldstein, he decided to permit the group to use the name "WAR" on the album.

A long series of lawsuits and settlements soon followed. In 1979, the members individually signed a set of contracts with the Far Out entities, including an agreement that transferred ownership of the trademark "WAR" to Far Out Productions. On July 2, 1979, soon after executing those contracts, Far Out Productions filed an application for the service mark "WAR" with the United States Patent and Trademark Office ("PTO"). The PTO issued Trademark Registration No. 1,169,651 to Far Out Productions on September 15, 1981.

B.   The Florida Judgment

In November 1982, four of the five remaining original members of the band, including Brown and Scott, sued the Far Out entities, Gold, and Goldstein in Florida state court. The appellants alleged that the Far Out entities had breached the 1979 contracts and that the Far Out entities had fraudulently secured the 1979 agreements by promising the appellants that the appellants would retain ownership of the trademark. Brown later voluntarily dismissed himself from the action. In an affidavit allegedly filed with the Florida court, Brown indicated that the suit was without merit and was filed fraudulently in order to terminate the 1979 agreements. Meanwhile, the Far Out entities were in deep financial trouble. Far Out Productions and Goldstein filed for bankruptcy under Chapter 11 on June 19, 1984.

On October 11, 1984, the Florida trial court entered an order and a partial final judgment in favor of the appellant Scott and the band members. The court deemed as established the material allegations of the complaint, including that the trademark "WAR" was procured by fraud. However, the court noted that its orders did not impact upon Far Out Productions in a manner inconsistent with the Federal Bankruptcy Code. In a final judgment entered on January 10, 1986, the court also noted that the claims against Goldstein and Far Out Productions were severed by virtue of the appellees' pending bankruptcies.

C.   Proceedings After the Florida Judgment and Before the Present Suits

In 1985, the appellant Scott and other band members filed a petition for cancellation of Far Out Productions' mark "WAR" with the PTO. That proceeding was halted due to the bankruptcy stay. Meanwhile, in 1986, the appellees licensed Brown to perform publicly as WAR. When the appellees learned that Scott and some of the other band members were also performing as WAR, the appellees applied to the bankruptcy court for permission to bring suit to enforce the trademark. After receiving permission to bring suit, Far Out Productions filed an action for trademark infringement that was nearly identical to its present complaint.

Shortly after the suit was filed, Far Out Productions entered into a global settlement with the appellants and the other band members. On April 1, 1987, each of the band members signed written agreements that agreed to dismiss with prejudice any and all lawsuits, even if the lawsuit had been reduced to a final judgment. The contracts also reaffirmed Far Out Productions' exclusive ownership in the name "WAR." Scott also eventually executed joint stipulations to dismiss with prejudice and vacate the Florida judgment.

On August 24, 1987, Goldstein filed an incontestability affidavit with the PTO on behalf of Far Out Productions. The affidavit declared that Far Out Productions was the owner of the mark and that the mark had been in continuous use for five consecutive years. The declaration also indicated that there had been no final decision adverse to the registrant's claim to ownership of the mark and that there were no proceedings pending in any court.

[Procedural History and Part II omitted]

III. DISCUSSION

A. The Preclusive Effect of the Florida State Court Judgment

The appellants assert that the district court erred in declining to give preclusive effect to the Florida judgment. Because the Florida judgment determined that the Far Out entities obtained the trademark fraudulently, the appellants argue, the appellees have no right to the trademark. Moreover, the appellants claim that since the Florida judgment was an adverse decision against the appellees, the appellees' incontestability affidavit was false. Because deciding whether to apply issue preclusion (also referred to as collateral estoppel) is a question of law, we review de novo a district court's refusal to give a state court judgment preclusive effect. *See Zamarripa v. City of Mesa,* 125 F.3d 792, 793 (9th Cir.1997). * * *

[2.] The Preclusive Effect of the Florida Judgment

The appellants contend that the Florida judgment involved the same parties and the same issues and resulted in a final judgment on the merits. Even though the final judgment was only issued against Far Out Music, Far Out Management, and Gold, the appellants argue that Far Out Productions and Goldstein controlled the Florida litigation and had filed for bankruptcy merely to avoid being subject to the Florida suit. While the Florida judgment did resolve some of the same issues as the present suit, it did not involve the same parties.

a. Whether the Florida Judgment Decided the Identical Issue

The parties do not seriously dispute whether the Florida judgment decided at least some of the same issues present in this litigation. The Florida court's partial final judgment found that Gold and Goldstein had fraudulently induced the band members into assigning the trademark to the Far Out entities in the 1979 contracts. While the court did not assign the trademark to the band members or enjoin the Far Out entities from asserting the trademark in the future, it did actually and necessarily resolve whether the Far Out entities legitimately obtained ownership in the trademark through the 1979 contracts. If the Florida judgment were to otherwise satisfy the requirements for collateral estoppel, the appellees would be precluded from asserting that they own the trademark as a result of the 1979 contracts.

b. *Whether the Florida Judgment Involved the Same Parties*

Whether the Florida judgment involved the same parties is a somewhat more difficult question. On its face, the Florida judgment did not apply to Goldstein and Far Out Productions. The trial court specifically noted in its default order, partial final judgment, and final judgment that its orders did not affect Far Out Productions or Goldstein in a manner inconsistent with the Bankruptcy Code and that the claims against Goldstein and Far Out Productions were severed by virtue of the appellees' pending bankruptcies. On the surface, then, the Florida judgment did not involve the same parties as the present suit and therefore should not collaterally estop the appellees from relitigating whether they legitimately own the trademark.

The appellants contend, however, that the appellees should be estopped from arguing that they did not participate in the Florida litigation since they were in privity with the other Far Out entities. The appellants assert that all three of the Far Out entities were essentially a single enterprise and that the appellees declared bankruptcy merely to avoid being bound by the Florida judgment.

The appellants' argument is unavailing. For a third party to be considered in privity with a party involved in litigation under Florida law, the third party "must have an interest in the action such that she will be bound by the final judgment as if she were a party" or must be "virtually represented by one who is a party ..." *Stogniew v. McQueen*, 656 So.2d 917, 920 (Fla.1995). There is nothing in the record to indicate that Far Out Productions and Goldstein were virtually represented by the other Far Out entities and Gold at the time of the Florida judgment.

More importantly, the Florida judgment cannot be binding on the appellees as a matter of federal bankruptcy law. When a debtor files for bankruptcy, subject to certain exceptions not present here, section 362(a) of the Bankruptcy Code automatically stays any other judicial proceeding involving the debtor. *See* 11 U.S.C. § 362(a)(1). The automatic stay provision of the Bankruptcy Code "plays a vital role in bankruptcy. It is designed to protect debtors from all collection efforts while they attempt to regain their financial footing." *In re Schwartz*, 954 F.2d 569, 571 (9th Cir.1992) (describing the automatic stay as "one of the fundamental debtor protections provided by the bankruptcy laws"). The provision provides stability and certainty to both the debtor and creditors who might otherwise be tempted to bring independent actions to obtain default judgments. *See id.* at 571–72.

In fact, the automatic stay provision is so central to the functioning of the bankruptcy system that this circuit regards judgments obtained in violation of the provision as void rather than merely voidable on the motion of the debtor. *See id.* at 571. Courts regularly void state court default judgments against debtors when the judgments are obtained in violation of the automatic stay provision, even where the debtor filed for bankruptcy in the midst of the state court proceedings. * * *

On occasion, courts have recognized a narrow equitable exception to the strict enforcement of the automatic stay provision, such as when the debtor has participated extensively in a suit leading to a default judgment before declaring bankruptcy. * * * Although the Florida suit was initially filed in November 1982 and Goldstein and Far Out Productions did not file for bankruptcy until June 1984, the record here does not reflect that Goldstein or Far Out Productions participated in the Florida litigation in a meaningful way before declaring bankruptcy, that the appellees declared bankruptcy merely to avoid being subject to the Florida judgment, or that the appellees failed to notify the Florida plaintiffs of the bankruptcy applications.

In fact, the equities here may very well favor the appellees. The appellant Brown admitted in an affidavit that the Florida suit was fraudulent in several respects (including jurisdictionally), the appellants signed contracts explicitly releasing the appellees from the Florida judgment, and the appellants even moved to vacate the judgment in accordance with those agreements. Permitting the appellants to assert the Florida judgment as preclusive in spite of the bankruptcy stay provision under those circumstances would not be a very compelling exercise of equitable discretion. Given the facial inapplicability of the Florida judgment to the appellees, the importance of the automatic stay provision, and the equitable considerations, the Florida judgment did not involve the same parties, and the district court did not err in declining to give the Florida judgment preclusive effect.

c.   Whether the Florida Judgment was Final

Because the Florida judgment did not involve the same parties, this Court need not consider whether the judgment was final under Florida law.

3.   Whether the Incontestability Affidavit was False

The appellants also argue that the incontestability affidavit Goldstein submitted to the PTO in 1987 was false. In filing an incontestability affidavit, a trademark owner must swear that there has been no final decision adverse to the registrant's claim of ownership or right to register the mark. *See* 15 U.S.C. § 1065.

For the same reasons that the Florida judgment does not have a preclusive effect in this litigation, Goldstein was not required to disclose the judgment. He was not a party to the Florida suit, and the 1987 agreements with the appellants vacated the Florida judgment. His incontestability affidavit was therefore not false.

Even if the Florida judgment were a final adverse decision, Goldstein can only be adjudicated to have filed a fraudulent oath if he acted with scienter. If Goldstein had a good faith belief that the Florida judgment was irrelevant, he cannot be found to have submitted a false affidavit. *See* J. Thomas McCarthy, *McCarthy on Trademarks and Unfair Competition,* § 31.79, at 31–136.1. The appellants did not present any evidence, either on appeal or, apparently, in the district court, that Goldstein acted in bad faith or with knowledge that he should have disclosed the Florida judgment. Since the appellants did not present any evidence of Goldstein's state of mind, they did not even meet their initial burden in moving for summary judgment. * * *

Moreover, even if Goldstein knowingly submitted a false declaration such that the appellees' federal registration should be canceled, the appellees could (and did) still bring suit alleging common law trademark infringement. *See McCarthy on Trademarks,* § 31:60, at 31–109 (noting that "[i]t has been held several times that even if defendant succeeds in proving that the plaintiff's registration was fraudulently obtained, plaintiff's common law rights in the mark continue unabated" even if the registration is canceled). The district court therefore did not err in denying the appellants' motion for summary judgment as to the appellees' incontestability affidavit. * * * [Part B omitted.]

C. The Appellants' Motion for a New Trial or to Amend the Judgment

The appellants contend that the district court erred in denying their motion for a new trial or to amend the judgment. The appellants raised several grounds before the district court for revising the judgment, including the discovery of allegedly new evidence regarding the initial use of the trademark and an assertion that the appellees' attorney had committed misconduct and submitted false testimony. To establish that the district court abused its discretion in denying their motion for a new trial based on the newly discovered evidence, the appellants must show that they discovered the evidence after trial, that they could not have discovered the evidence sooner through the exercise of reasonable diligence, and that the new evidence is of such magnitude that it would likely have changed the outcome of the case. *See Defenders of Wildlife,* 204 F.3d at 929.

On appeal, the appellants identify two pieces of "new" evidence as sufficient to justify amending the judgment or permitting a new trial. First, the appellants presented evidence to the district court that Far Out Productions was not incorporated until October 1969. The district court properly rejected that argument, both procedurally, since the appellants could have obtained that evidence sooner, and substantively, because the precise date of Far Out Productions' incorporation is immaterial given that Goldstein could have owned the mark through his personal efforts or through the 1987 settlement contracts. * * *

The other piece of new evidence is an article, apparently not presented to the district court, describing WAR's first commercial performance in June 1969. In the appellants' view, the article is "documentary" proof that the group made first commercial use of the mark before Far Out Productions was incorporated, thereby vesting the members of the band, not the appellees, with ownership of the mark. * * *

Like the appellants' "new" evidence of Far Out Productions' incorporation date, the article is insufficient to establish that the district court abused its discretion in denying the appellants' motion for a new trial. As a procedural matter, it is not clear that the appellants may properly raise the article as new evidence. They have not shown that they discovered the evidence after trial or that they could not have discovered the evidence sooner through the exercise of reasonable diligence. Indeed, the appellants could have submitted declarations of their own describing the group's first commercial use of the name "WAR" to support their claim to first use.

Moreover, the article is simply immaterial. The article, which labels the group as "Eric Burdon's War," merely describes the group's performance. The article is consistent with Goldstein's declaration regarding the early formation and management of the group and does not call into question the appellees' claim that the band members were hired as employees to serve as back-up for Burdon. The article might be pertinent if there were two competing groups claiming that they were the real WAR and the article identified which group first made commercial use of the mark. However, since this dispute is between individuals who used the name together, the article is of little significance in resolving which party owns the trademark, let alone of such magnitude that its production would have changed the outcome of the case. Moreover, the article does not (and could not) say anything about the subsequent contracts in which the band members assigned their interests in the trademark to Far Out Productions.

The district court therefore did not err in denying the appellants' motion for a new trial. The appellants' other asserted bases for a new trial—attorney misconduct and false testimony—have no support in the record submitted on appeal.

IV. Conclusion

Because the district court did not err in declining to give the Florida judgment preclusive effect, the court did not err in denying the appellants' motion for summary judgment. The district court also did not err in granting the appellees' motion for summary judgment and denying the appellants' motion for a new trial. Accordingly, the district court's orders are

AFFIRMED.

Notes

1. Compare the outcomes between the WAR and the Steppenwolf cases. Can the two cases be reconciled? For policy reasons, should an individual be able to sign away his ability to reference his past?

2.   In *Boogie Kings v. Guillory*, the issue was whether an unincorporated association (the band) could continue to use the name "Boogie Kings" after the majority elected leader left the band. The trial judge concluded that the former leader and defendant in the case never acquired a proprietary interest in the name, therefore the name belonged to the association as a whole. The appellate court affirmed the lower court's decision, reasoning that the band as a whole began using the name and continued to do so since that time. Therefore, the name belonged to the band as a whole. The defendant claimed that the previous leader of the band had given him (Guillory) exclusive rights to the name. However, the court rejected the reasoning that the previous leader could not give rights to that which he did not own. *See* Boogie Kings v. Guillory, 188 So.2d 445 (La. Ct. App. 1966).

3.   In *Grondin v. Rossington*, the widow of a deceased band member of the group "Lynyrd Skynyrd" sued the band for breach of contract to cease use of the name. After the tragic plane crash and resulting death of two members of the original group, a non-use agreement was enacted whereby the remaining members would no longer use the name "Lynyrd Skynyrd." The non-use agreement was observed by all concerned for the next ten years. In 1987, the surviving members elected to do a "tribute" tour. Grondin agreed to allow the use of the name for the 1987 "Tribute Tour." During the tour, a live recording was produced entitled "Lynyrd Skynyrd Live." Another tour was planned in 1988 by the band. Grondin, the plaintiff, had objected to the 1988 tour and the use of the name "Lynyrd Skynyrd" being used on the album cover. After failing to reach an agreement, Grondin sued the remaining band members. The Court concluded that since the airplane crash was well publicized, it was unlikely that confusion would arise that the "Tribute" recording was the original band. Further, with respect to the tour, the Court balanced the hardships, and concluded to enjoin the defendants would create an undue expense since the tour was already underway. *See Grondin v. Rossington*, 690 F.Supp. 200 (S.D.N.Y. 1988).

4.   The wrongful suggestion of sponsorship by the original band is a violation of the Lanham Act. In *Brother Records, Inc. v. Jardine*, the court found that a former member of the band, the Beach Boys, touring under the name "Beach Boys Family and Friends" infringed upon the trademark. The name "Beach Boys" was displayed in advertisements more prominently than "Family and Friends," thus creating confusion as to who was really performing. The defendant admitted including the trademark to create or enhance marketing value. *See Brother Records, Inc. v. Jardine*, 318 F.3d 900 (9th Cir. 2003).

5.   In *Greene v. Sha–Na–Na*, 637 F.Supp. 591 (D. Conn. 1986). Frederick Dennis Greene, an original member of the group, Sha–Na–Na, sued his former bandmates, and the partnerships under which the band operated, asserting trademark infringement. Greene refused to perform with the group in Las Vegas because he stated that the Las Vegas gig was for an amount that was below the minimum amount the group had agreed to accept for any live performances. The other band members voted Greene out of the band and the partnership, dissolved the partnership, and created a new partnership without Greene. Greene sued in federal court in Connecticut. None of the other members of the band lived in Connecticut. Defendants moved to dismiss for lack of personal jurisdiction and improper venue. The court held

that: (1) events occurring subsequent to service of complaint could not form a basis for the court to exercise personal jurisdiction over defendants. (2) The loss of income and damage to the reputation of plaintiff in Connecticut was too remote and speculative to support a finding of jurisdiction under the Connecticut long-arm statute provision. And (3) the events occurring subsequent to filing of complaint could not be considered in determining proper venue. Was this a fair result given that Greene was merely trying to enforce the partnership agreement he had with his bandmates and it ended up getting him removed from the group?

Sherri Burr
Classical Music: Striving for 'Undemocratic Oneness': Author Interviews with Conductors Guillermo Figueroa and Samuel Wong

Copyright © 2004 by Sherri Burr.

collective bargaining rights

Symphony orchestras are a unique form of musical organization. While they loosely resemble bands in that two or more musicians come together to make music, they are not legally formed around partnerships. Rather, orchestras are structured as a corporation or 501(c)(3) charitable organization that may endure for centuries as musicians and their conductors come and go. Orchestras also operate under a collective bargaining agreement that management negotiates with the musicians' union representatives.

Samuel Wong, the conductor of the Honolulu Symphony who previously trained as a doctor at the Harvard Medical School, describes orchestras as striving for an "undemocratic oneness." In a September 1999 interview on the Honolulu cable television show *Arts Talk*,[1] he said, "You have a hundred people who have different backgrounds, different passions, different upbringings, different styles, and you have to unify in a very undemocratic way. A unity has to be achieved that is not questioned. Nobody can stray one millisecond from the interpretation."

Wong depicts the conductor as "part high priest, part psychologist, part therapist, part military commander, part teacher, and part student, all at the same time. All those roles are necessary because of the nature of what we do." Wong says conductors must be "a fire to warm the whole room. You have to put things in order. You want to make sure the engine is playing at the same time, the same thing, the same way, the same dynamic, and the same spirit."

The power of conductors has changed over time. New York Philharmonic conductor Leonard Bernstein was known to fire musicians on the spot if they played off key one too many times. Wong says that Artur Rodzinski, a former conductor of the New York Philharmonic, which was

---

1. *Arts Talk* is a cable television show that Sherri Burr created in 1998. It ran on Honolulu's Olelo station from 1998–2002 and continues to run on Channel 27 in Albuquerque, New Mexico. In addition to Wong, Burr has interviewed New Mexico Symphony Orchestra conductor Guillermo Figueroa, Honolulu Pops conductor Matt Catingub and other musicians.

founded in 1842, was "reported to have carried a loaded gun when he rehearsed. And, of course, people didn't cross his path."

Wong says the best style for modern conductors is to be "collegial and congenial. No one takes too well to being browbeaten." Wong, who made his debut with the New York Philharmonic by substituting for Leonard Bernstein, speaks from a wealth of experience. He has since conducted orchestras in Tokyo, Mexico, Toronto, Rome, Seattle, and Seoul.

Unions

Unions have impacted the conductor's authority. The American Federation of Musicians (AFM) was founded in 1896 to improve the professional lives of musicians. The union considers any individual who receives pay for his musical services as a professional musician. Within its first ten years, the AFM represented 45,000 musicians throughout North America. It currently has approximately 251 local chapters, representing over 100,000 members. The local chapters negotiate with management on behalf of the musicians.

"Our basic reason for existing is to protect the interest of musicians in the working field," says Larry Wheeler, president of the New Mexico branch of the AFM, Local #618. The cost to join AFM depends on where the musician is located. The New Mexico local charges musicians $60 to join the federal union, $20 to join the local union and $95 for yearly dues. Wheeler says, "The main benefit is that musicians have local representation if they believe they are unduly let go." He also says that the union makes available individual contracts and represents union members to produce collective bargaining agreements with management.

Guillermo Figueroa, a concert violinist, has sat on both sides of the union fence. Figueroa became the first Puerto Rican born conductor to lead an important orchestra in the United States when he was chosen to lead the New Mexico Symphony Orchestra in 2001. On February 25, 2004, he said in a phone interview from his Albuquerque home, "I am of two minds about it. All my life I have been an orchestra player. It was true that for a very long time that management was not favorable to players. With the advent of the unions, musicians have done much better. We came much later to the union process than other industries."

As a conductor, Figueroa says that working with the unions is one of his biggest jobs, as "everything is ruled by a master agreement that is negotiated for a term of years. There are rules that govern how people interact with each other. It's hard to change things once the agreement is done, even when common sense tells you that you can break something if it is in everyone's best interest. However, both sides feel that if they open up a certain point that is not in the contract, the other side will want something in return. It makes it hard to use common sense. If a rehearsal is supposed to end at 9:00 p.m., you can't go 1 minute over or you have to pay an hour's overtime, even when you didn't start on time."

In his final assessment, Figueroa concludes, "There are great people on both sides. There are also intransigent people on both sides."

As a world-renowned violinist who has recorded two violin-concerto CDs, Figueroa also has experience with the classical music recording industry. He produced his CDs with his own money and then obtained a distributing company, Eroica Classical Recording label, to disseminate his recordings. He hired the engineer and the studio, and negotiated with the distributing company for a cut of the sales. He says, "In classical music, unless you're an Itzak Pearlman or Yo–Yo Ma, very few people will pay you to put out a record. Once your records sell, you get more clout."

The classical music industry also struggles with an aging audience. Sam Wong says that media and advertising are hostile to classical music. He cites as an example ads that portray "opera as stuffy and boring, the fat lady singing, people falling asleep. There's a misconception that it's for the powerful, the elite, the stuffy, and the nearly dead. Classical music is vibrant, relevant, energizing and life-giving in every sense."

Note

1. The AFM and its locals file grievances and/or lawsuits against symphonies on behalf of their members. In *American Federation of Musicians v. St. Louis Symphony*, 203 F.3d 1079 (8th Cir. 2000), the union brought an action in the district court to compel the symphony to arbitrate a grievance pursuant to the parties' collective bargaining agreement. The union was granted its motion for summary judgment but was denied its motion for attorneys' fees; the Eight Circuit affirmed. The dispute arose after violist Louis Kampouis, who had initially been hired to perform in 1949, was informed on September 2, 1997, when he reported to work that he could no longer rehearse or perform with the orchestra. Kampouris, who was 68 at the time, sued the symphony for age discrimination and intentional infliction of emotional distress after it discontinued his salary and benefits. The Eight Circuit affirmed the denial of attorneys' fees because the union's proposed arbitration panel included arbitrators from outside the St. Louis metropolitan area. In a different arbitration, the union and symphony had agreed to limit themselves to local arbiters. The court found that the symphony's reliance on the previous agreement was not unreasonable.

MICHIGAN EMPLOYMENT RELATIONS COMMISSION v. DETROIT SYMPHONY ORCHESTRA

Supreme Court of Michigan, 1974.
393 Mich. 116, 223 N.W.2d 283.

FITZGERALD, Justice.

The principal question before us is whether the Court of Appeals erred in reversing a determination of the Michigan Employment Relations Commission Board in favor of plaintiff-appellant Chase on the ground that the findings of fact of the Board were not supported by substantial evidence. We conclude that the Court of Appeals correctly applied the 'substantial evidence' standard and affirm.

I

It is the position of plaintiff Allen Chase that he lost his employment with the Detroit Symphony Orchestra because of his continued participation in union organizational activities contrary to M.C.L.A. § 423.16; M.S.A. § 17.454(17). Undisputed evidence introduced at an evidentiary hearing held before a trial examiner of the Labor Mediation Board indicates that plaintiff's 'discharge'[1] by the Symphony is traceable to events occurring on February 27, 1968 and shortly thereafter.

The master contract governing relations between the Detroit Symphony Orchestra and the Detroit Federation of Musicians, plaintiff Chase's union, provided that employment contracts should be signed and in by March 1, 1968. Past practice indicated, however, that the Symphony had not always strictly adhered to this cutoff date. Early in February 1968, Chase, a trombonist for many years with the Symphony, was offered a one-year contract of employment. On February 27, Chase approached Bistritzky, personnel manager of the Symphony and a union-management agent, and Harrington, general manager of the Symphony, to 'negotiate' his contract. He was offered a $10 per week raise and rejected it out of hand, stating, 'Get yourself another boy. I do not accept.' When contacted shortly thereafter by Bistritzky, Chase indicated that he had not changed his mind. On March 1, 1968, Bistritzky informed the union that Chase's position was vacant.

Chase later contacted Bistritzky on March 2, 1968 and at that point was informed that the Symphony was auditioning another trombonist for his position. He then stated that he accepted the offer only to learn from Bistritzky that in the Symphony's view the offer had been withdrawn. A series of events ensued which entailed Chase's reapplication for employment with the Symphony and the eventual hiring of another trombonist. Chase introduced evidence in an effort to show that the Symphony's actions in failing to hire him were discriminatory and attributable to anti-union animus.

Joseph Bixler, the trial examiner presiding at the evidentiary hearing, concluded after a lengthy recitation and discussion of the facts:

> 'There is not sufficient evidence in this record to establish that the orchestra discriminated against Chase in violation of the Act. * * * Chase quit the Orchestra when he rejected the contract and the offered raise with the abrupt "get yourself another boy."

He therefore recommended that the charges be dismissed. The MERC Board disagreed with the findings of its examiner, concluding:

> ' * * * the Symphony applied the March 1 cut-off discriminatorily with respect to Chase.'; and '(T)he only plausible reason for the Symphony's discriminatory treatment of Chase is his union activity.'

---

1. The term 'discharge' is used advisedly because there is dispute as to whether   plaintiff Chase quit or was fired.

The Court of Appeals initially refused to enforce the order of the MERC Board in favor of Chase, concluding in an order of that Court that the Board's findings of fact were not supported by substantial evidence. Upon further review, this Court (387 Mich. 424, 196 N.W.2d 763 (1972)) determined that the decisional process employed by the Court of Appeals had been 'unsound' and remanded for further consideration and preparation of a full opinion. Upon remand the Court of Appeals again denied enforcement to the order of the MERC Board, reiterating, in an unpublished per curiam opinion containing discussion of the facts, that Court's view that the Board's finding of facts were not supported by substantial evidence. The case is before us on leave granted.

II

The standard of appellate review of MERC Board findings of fact is set forth in the labor mediation act as follows:

' * * * The findings of the board with respect to questions of fact if supported by competent, material and substantial evidence on the record considered as a whole shall be conclusive. * * *' M.C.L.A. § 423.23(e); M.S.A. § 17.454(25)(e). * * *

III

We turn now to apply the foregoing principles to the record before us. In so doing, our focus is upon what we perceive to be the critical issue: is the MERC Board's conclusion that the Symphony's failure to rehire plaintiff Chase was motivated by anti-union animus supported by substantial evidence?

The trial examiner, in reaching a conclusion contrary to that of the MERC Board, stated:

'(T)he only question in this case is whether the refusal of the contract to Chase on March 2, was motivated by animosity arising out of the activities of Chase on behalf of the Federation of Musicians. The record is devoid of any evidence of animosity toward Chase prior to March 2, 1968. As far as this record reveals, on February 29, the Symphony Orchestra was anxious to have the services of Chase as first trombonist. He was offered a contract, as were all the musicians, and upon his protest that he had been offered less than he deserved, the general manager agreed and offered Chase a $10.00 a week increase over the contract offer. The record reveals that such an increase was granted to only nine other employees in the Orchestra.

'It is the absence of evidence of animosity toward Chase for any reason and the apparent willingness and anxiousness of the Symphony Orchestra to employ Chase on February 29, that militates most heavily against the contention that the March 2 refusal to allow Chase to sign the contract was discriminatorily motivated.' In disputing these conclusions the Board stated in part:

'The fact that Chase was offered a raise does not, Per se, indicate that the Symphony was anxious to hire Chase. On the contrary, when it is remembered that other members of the orchestra had engaged in extensive individual negotiations in previous years and that Chase had not, the Symphony may have believed that the increase it offered to Chase would be rejected. Indeed, the Symphony's offer may have been calculated to generate a prompt rejection from Chase.'

While the hearing examiner's analysis is based upon permissible inference from record evidence, the above statements of the Board are nothing but convoluted conjecture tantamount to speculation. As such, they do not support a finding of anti-union animus.

Beyond this, the Appeal Board finding of anti-union animus rests solely upon the Board's interpretation of certain conversations between plaintiff Chase and Sixten Ehrling, the conductor of the orchestra, who was instrumental in the Symphony's ultimate decision to employ another trombonist. The trial examiner and Board's differing views as to the 'credibility' of these witnesses explain the divergence in their ultimate conclusions.[9]

Our reading of the cold record indicates that the finding of the trial examiner is more plausible than the finding of the Board. Given this reading, are we to ignore the determination as to credibility of the only decision-maker to hear testimony firsthand and, in effect, credit the contrary determination of the Board? We think not. The findings of the trial examiner are a part of the record we are entitled to consider in exercising our review power. In *Universal Camera Corp. v. National Labor Relations Board*, 340 U.S. 474, 71 S.Ct. 456, 95 L.Ed.2d 456 (1951), the United States Supreme Court, applying the Federal 'substantial evidence' test under the National Labor Relations Act, similarly concluded that a reviewing court was entitled to consider examiner findings. We adopt as our own the following comments of that Court:

> We do not require that the examiner's findings be given more weight than in reason and in the light of judicial experience they deserve. The 'substantial evidence' standard is not modified in any way when the Board and its examiner disagree. We intend only to recognize that evidence supporting a conclusion may be less substantial when an impartial, experienced examiner who has observed the witnesses and lived with the case has drawn conclusions different from the Board's than when he has reached the same conclusion. The findings of the examiner are to be considered along with

9. Plaintiff Chase recounted conversations with Ehrling from which it might be inferred that dismissal flowed from anti-union animus on the part of the Symphony. Ehrling's recollection of these conversations differed from that of Chase and Ehrling expressly commented that the decision not to rehire Chase was made for artistic reasons, having nothing to do with Chase's union activities. The crucial decision as to 'credibility' of which we speak is that prerogative which permits the decision-maker confronted with conflicting testimony of a subjective nature to assign weight to, or find more inherently reliable, the testimony of a particular witness.

the consistency and inherent probability of testimony. The significance of his report, of course, depends largely on the importance of credibility in the particular case. To give it this significance does not seem to us materially more difficult than to heed the other factors which in sum determine whether evidence is 'substantial.' * * * 340 U.S. 474, 496–497, 71 S.Ct. 456, 469.

Ascribing due weight to the unique opportunity of the trial examiner to weigh the testimony of witnesses, our reading of the cold record is confirmed. We conclude that the critical finding of the MERC Board is not supported by 'substantial evidence'. Affirmed.

Note

1.   Trombonist Allen Chase's case was heard initially by a trial examiner and then by the Michigan Employment Relations Commission (MERC) board before being appealed to the Michigan Court of Appeals and Supreme Court. An attorney who is interested in representing either symphony management or musicians should obtain specialized knowledge and experience in both labor law and administrative law.

B.   BAND/MANAGEMENT AGREEMENTS

The right manager can help a band move from a popular group playing the local club scene to a major recording and touring act. Managers with a history of success can introduce the band to labels, lawyers, agents, and producers who can help manipulate the band to the top.

More often than not, a beginning band's first manager is the best friend who couldn't sing or play an instrument. There are no formal qualifications for being a manager in the entertainment business. Anyone can be a manager. Unlike talent agents, managers are not regulated by the states. You are a manager if you say you are a manager. Because of the lack of qualifications and the huge responsibility the manager of a major label recording act will have, the major record labels will try to force an up-and-coming act to fire its old manager and hire a well-known manager who the label feels can help the band focus on success and leave behind its old carefree ways.

The easiest way for a band to shed itself of its old management is to look for a violation of a state talent act. To protect talent agents from competition, it is a violation of the act for a non-registered agent to procure employment for a client. The penalties for violating an act can be quite severe. Most statutes include penalties that allow the management contract to be voided and require the manager to pay back the commissions earned over the past twelve months. Because a new group cannot find a registered booking agent to work with until the group signs a record contract, the manager is usually the person who ends up doing the booking. The manager's reward for taking a band from the garage to the record label is to be fired for violating the talent act. "Money can't buy you love."

A good personal manager is someone who has contacts at the record labels and who knows the A-list lawyers, agents, and producers. The manager must be adroit at handling the individual egos of the band members, organizing the band member's personal and professional lives, and protecting the band from the fake friends who want to latch onto the band members who have newly acquired fame and fortune.

The agreement between the band and the manager is another very important document that should be negotiated to protect the band and the manager. Issues that are important to the band include the manager's percentage of the income and the sources of the income. Both parties need to know how to get out of the agreement and what they get when the relationship is terminated. Both parties need separate counsel.

AHERN v. SCHOLZ

United States Court of Appeals, First Circuit, 1996.
85 F.3d 774.

TORRUELLA, Chief Judge.

The parties in this breach of contract case, a successful musician and his former manager, dispute whether royalties from record albums have been accounted for and paid to each other. The appeal is from a final judgment by the district court after a jury trial, disposing of all claims in respect to all parties.

Background: A Band Out of Boston

In this case, the parties dispute many of the facts and the inferences to be drawn from them. Thus we start with a sketch of the basic facts, and address the individual issues in more detail below. Appellant and cross-appellee Donald Thomas Scholz ("Scholz") is a musician, composer, and record producer who was, and is, a member of the musical group BOSTON ("BOSTON"). In late 1975, Scholz entered into three agreements with appellee and cross-appellant Paul F. Ahern ("Ahern"), who was engaged in the business of promoting and managing music groups, and his then partner, Charles McKenzie ("McKenzie") (collectively, the "1975 Agreements"). First, Scholz made a recording agreement (the "Recording Agreement") with Ahern and McKenzie d/b/a P.C. Productions, to which Bradley Delp, the lead singer of BOSTON, was also a party. Second was a management agreement (the "Management Agreement"), also between Scholz and P.C. Productions, under which Ahern and McKenzie were appointed Scholz' exclusive personal managers worldwide. The third agreement was a songwriter agreement made between Scholz and Ahern, under which Scholz was obligated to furnish Ahern his exclusive songwriting services for a period of five years.

In early 1976, CBS Records ("CBS") and Ahern Associates, a business name of Ahern and McKenzie, entered into a recording agreement for the exclusive recording services of BOSTON. The group's first album (the "first album") was released in 1976, and sold approximately 11 million copies—one of the highest-selling debut albums ever. Its second album (the "second album") was released in August 1978, and sold approximately 6 million copies.

In 1978, Scholz and the other members of BOSTON entered into a modification agreement with Ahern and P.C. Productions, dated April 24, 1978. Among other things, the First Modification Agreement modified the 1975 Agreements and changed the financial relationship between Scholz and his managers. Ahern and McKenzie dissolved their partnership. A few years later, in May of 1981, Ahern and Scholz, individually and under various business names, entered into a further modification agreement (the "Further Modification Agreement" or "FMA"), which is at the heart of this dispute. Ahern ceased to be Scholz' manager.

In 1982, with the third album not yet released, CBS cut off the payment of royalties generated from the first and second albums. In 1983, CBS brought suit against Scholz, Ahern, and the members of BOSTON for failure to timely deliver record albums. Scholz' counsel in that action was Donald S. Engel ("Engel"); Ahern had his own counsel. While that litigation was pending, the third album was released by MCA Records ("MCA") in 1986 and sold well over 4 million copies. At the close of trial—seven years after the CBS litigation began—the jury found that Scholz was not in breach of contract. Scholz incurred legal fees of about $3.4 million dollars.

In February 1991, Ahern commenced this action against Scholz for breach of the FMA claiming a failure to pay royalties due under the third album. Scholz asserted various affirmative defenses and counterclaims against Ahern, including breach of the FMA. During trial, Engel, Scholz' lead trial counsel, was twice called as a witness. At the close of the evidence, the court granted Scholz' directed verdict dismissing Ahern's Count III for fraud and IV for breach of implied covenant of good faith and fair dealing. The court also granted Ahern's motion for directed verdict dismissing Scholz' First, Second, and Third Counterclaims and his, Third, Fourth, and Fifth affirmative defenses. Only the parties' respective breach of contract claims went to the jury. The jury found that Scholz breached section 5.2.1 of the FMA to pay Ahern royalties from the third album, and found that Ahern had not breached the FMA to account for and pay Scholz royalties due from the first and second albums. It awarded Ahern $547,007 in damages.

The trial court sitting without a jury also found Scholz had breached the FMA, and heard Ahern's Count II for declaratory relief and Count V for violation of Mass. Gen. L. ch. 93A and Scholz' Fifth Counterclaim for rescission of contract for failure to obtain a license. The court denied the declaratory relief Ahern sought in Count I, and awarded him costs, interest and attorney's fees pursuant to Count V for violation of Mass. Gen. L. ch. 93A §§ 2 & 11. The court denied the relief sought by Scholz in his Fifth Counterclaim and held that he waived his Counts VI and VII at oral argument. After a hearing on Ahern's bill of costs and application for reasonable attorney's fees and interest, the court awarded Ahern $265,000 in attorney's fees and $135,000 in costs.

The district court denied, without a hearing, Scholz' motion for a new trial, motion to amend the court's memorandum and order and judgment entered thereon, motion to admit new evidence, and motion to amend the court's memorandum and order and the judgment entered thereon regarding Scholz' Sixth Counterclaim. This appeal followed.

Motion for a New Trial

Appellant first argues that the district court erred in denying his motion for a new trial. In reviewing the record of the 16–day trial, we note that both parties presented extensive evidence. The jury heard testimony regarding a history that spans two decades, involves at least seven contracts, includes detailed numerical accounting, and references more than half a dozen other legal battles. The parties called a total of fifteen witnesses, seven of whom, including Ahern, Scholz, and Engel, Scholz' counsel, testified twice. In short, the jury faced a complex and sometimes conflicting set of facts in making its decision as to whether either, neither, or both parties breached the 1981 Further Modification Agreement. Ultimately, we find that the jury's verdict was not against the clear weight of the evidence, and the district court did not abuse its discretion in so finding.

[Section A. omitted]

B.   Did Ahern Breach the FMA?

Scholz argues that Ahern breached his obligations under the 1981 FMA to both account for and pay to Scholz, every six months, his share of the royalties from the compositions on the first and second albums: indeed, Ahern admitted at trial that he had failed to make some payments he owed Scholz under the FMA. The jury and the trial court disagreed with Scholz, however, and found that Ahern's breach of the FMA was not material. The question facing us, then, is whether the district court abused its discretion in finding that the jury's decision was not against the weight of the evidence. After careful review of the record, we find no abuse of discretion in the lower court's decision not to disturb the jury's finding.

Scholz argues at some length on appeal that Ahern's breach was by definition material, both for his failure to account and his failure to pay. As for the first contention, we note that while Scholz' reading of the FMA as requiring that Ahern render Scholz direct accountings every six months is a convincing one, it is not the only plausible one. Indeed, Ahern contends that the FMA only required him to send irrevocable letters of direction to various entities involved directing them to send Scholz his share of the royalties when collected. In the end, it would not be against the clear weight of the evidence to find that letters of directions would satisfy Ahern's accounting obligations under the FMA, and that such letters were sent. Therefore, Ahern's failure to account every six months was not a material breach.

As for the second contention, Scholz [contends that Ahern's failure to pay an amount totaling $459,000 is clearly substantial]. * * *

We are not convinced. * * * While we note that Ames' final estimate was $277,000, for a total of $459,000 with interest, we cannot assume that the jury accepted this figure as gospel. Given that Ahern sought over a million dollars in principal and interest from Scholz, the jury may reasonably have found that the Ames figure was not a substantial breach in the particular context of this case. It may have determined that the amount of money Ahern owed, taken in the perspective of the contract, Ahern's obligations, and the total amounts of money concerned, was not so significant a breach as to violate "an essential and inducing feature of the contract." * * * Ultimately, examining the record in full, the evidence clearly provides the jury and trial court with a basis for finding that Ahern did not substantially breach the FMA. * * *

C. Did Scholz Breach the FMA?

Ahern claimed below that Scholz breached his obligation under section 5.2.1 of the FMA to pay Ahern his share of the royalties due from the third album. The evidence presented at trial centered on a document entitled "Artist Royalty Statement" ("the Scholz Statement"), which Scholz presented to Ahern. That statement listed over $6 million in gross royalties reported by MCA prior to December 31, 1993, but reduced that figure by deducting, among other things, a producer share and artist costs, so that the net artist royalties fell to below zero—and Ahern was not entitled to any money. Scholz argued at trial that he did not breach the FMA, but the jury and the trial court disagreed. * * *

On appeal, Scholz contends [that the jury] finding is against the weight of the evidence, because Ahern's prior material breaches excused Scholz' performance under the Further Modification Agreement. * * * Scholz shapes his argument on appeal as follows: Since Ahern's only agreement of substance was his agreement to account for and pay royalties to Scholz for prior BOSTON albums, Ahern's breach of his commitment excused Scholz' performance. * * *

Considering this, Scholz points out that his first royalty statement regarding the third album was rendered by MCA on April 1, 1987. Thus the earliest he could have owed money to Ahern under the FMA was August 15, 1987—and by that date, he argues, Ahern had already failed to account to Scholz or pay him royalties with respect to the first two albums for over five years. Therefore, Scholz maintains he was excused, at least until Ahern tendered payment, from rendering an accounting or paying royalties to Ahern from the third album. At the very least, Scholz argues, he could have withheld payment of the $459,000 admittedly owed him as a set-off against any amount he owed Ahern. *See Record Club of*

America v. United Artists Records, Inc., 80 B.R. 271, 276 (S.D.N.Y.1987), *vacated on other grounds,* 890 F.2d 1264 (2d Cir.1989).

In so arguing, Scholz does not contend that he did not in fact breach the FMA: he simply maintains that Ahern did so first. Since Scholz does not revisit the merits of the evidence presented at trial regarding his breach, we will not do so here. However, since we have already found that the verdict that Ahern did not substantially breach the FMA was not against the clear weight of the evidence, Scholz' argument here must fail. Clearly, it would be inconsistent with our acceptance of the verdict that Ahern did not substantially breach the FMA to find that Scholz' performance was excused by Ahern's material breach. Accordingly, we affirm the district court's decision to refuse the motion for a new trial on this issue. * * *

COUNTERCLAIM FOR FRAUD AND DECEIT AND AFFIRMATIVE DEFENSES

The Further Modification Agreement provided that Ahern was entitled to a share of the royalties of any album completed before October 24, 1984. Had the parties adhered to this provision, Ahern would not be entitled to any moneys from the third album, as it was completed after that date. Instead, Scholz waived the deadline, conveying his waiver through communications between the parties' attorneys in May of 1984. In this action, Scholz drew on his waiver of the deadline in his third counterclaim and several of his affirmative defenses to argue for rescission of the waiver agreement on the grounds of fraud and deceit and, alternatively, its invalidation. On appeal before us, he appeals the district court's directed verdict against him on these claims. * * *

A. *Rescission*

* * * Scholz sought rescission [in counterclaim] of the waiver agreement on the grounds that Ahern fraudulently induced him to enter into the agreement by not disclosing that he had neither accounted for nor paid, since at least 1981, the royalties he owed Scholz under the FMA. Under New York law, applied here pursuant to the FMA choice of law provision, a party seeking to prove common law fraud must show that: (1) the [cross-] defendant made a material false representation, (2) the [cross-] defendant intended to defraud the [cross-] plaintiff thereby, (3) the [cross-] plaintiff reasonably relied upon the representation, and (4) the [cross-]plaintiff suffered damage as a result of such reliance. *Banque Arabe et Internationale D'Investissement v. Maryland Nat'l Bank,* 57 F.3d 146, 153 (2d Cir. 1995) (analyzing elements in context of claim for rescission based on fraud). * * * The first element may be met by demonstrating not only a misrepresentation, but also a concealment or nondisclosure of a material fact. *See Allen v. WestPoint–Pepperell, Inc.,* 945 F.2d 40, 44 (2d Cir. 1991). In addition, the party claiming fraudulent concealment must demonstrate that the opposing party had a duty to disclose the material information in question and demonstrate each element of the claim by clear and convincing evidence. *See Banque Arabe et Internationale D'Investissement,* 57 F.3d at 153. We begin our analysis

by weighing what duty Ahern owed Scholz, and then turn to the elements listed above, ultimately concluding that the district court erred in directing a verdict.

In the instant case, Scholz argues that Ahern owed Scholz a duty to disclose because he was a fiduciary. *See Brass v. American Film Techs.*, 987 F.2d 142, 150 (2d Cir.1993). Ahern contests that at the time the waiver was given in May 1984, the Management Agreement had terminated and so there was no fiduciary duty and, thus, no duty to disclose. "Under New York law, a fiduciary relationship includes 'both technical fiduciary relations and those informal relations which exist whenever one [person] trusts in, and relies upon, another.' " *Allen,* 945 F.2d at 45. * * * "New York courts typically focus on whether one person has reposed trust or confidence in another who thereby gains a resulting superiority or influence over the first." *Litton Inds., Inc. v. Lehman Bros. Kuhn Loeb Inc.,* 767 F.Supp. 1220, 1231 (S.D.N.Y. 1991), *rev'd on other grounds,* 967 F.2d 742 (2d Cir. 1992). * * *

[At] the time of the waiver in 1984 Ahern and Scholz had a long history of business dealings, marked by a series of agreements and modification agreements. Also the relationship between the parties here was a profitable one for Ahern. However, * * * Ahern no longer, as of several years previously, was Scholz' manager. Indeed, Scholz testified that in 1978, when he first started the process that culminated in the FMA, he was no longer on speaking terms with Ahern. While we do not doubt—and Ahern admitted at trial—that Ahern had a fiduciary duty to Scholz until 1981, the question remains whether there was such a special relationship of trust and confidence between the parties at the time of the waiver that a fiduciary relationship, at least as regards Ahern's duty to pay Scholz' share of the royalties from the first and second albums, remained. Since a reasonable juror could find that it did, however, a directed verdict is inappropriate on the question of whether Ahern owed Scholz a fiduciary duty. Therefore, we continue our analysis and turn to the evidence presented on the elements listed above. * * *

As for whether Scholz reasonably relied on Ahern's nondisclosure, his case is damaged by the fact that the evidence is undisputed that Ahern did not actually solicit the waiver. Scholz' attorney contacted his counsel and offered it to him. * * * However, Scholz points to his testimony at trial that he "obviously" would not have agreed to the waiver had he known of Ahern's failure to pay him publishing royalties as evidence of his reliance. Giving Scholz the benefit of all the inferences, a reasonable juror could find under these circumstances that Ahern sought to induce Scholz into a fraudulent agreement, once it had been offered to him, through nondisclosure of his failure to pay. * * * Given all of the above, we find that Scholz has mustered sufficient evidence for the issue to go to the jury. * * *

MASSACHUSETTS LAW CLAIMS

We next turn to Ahern's claim against Scholz under Massachusetts General Law Chapter 93A, sections 2 and 11 ("Chapter 93A"). The district court found that Scholz' failure to pay royalties as provided in the FMA violated Chapter 93A. More specifically, it held that the Scholz Statement regarding the royalties on the third album constituted an unfair and deceptive business practice, and that it was a "deliberate and blatant attempt to deprive Plaintiff Ahern of moneys rightfully due and owing to him." * * * [Part A. omitted].

B.   The District Court's Findings

The district court determined that Scholz had violated sections 2 and 11 through his failure to pay Ahern royalties from the third album, and made the following findings in its Memorandum and Order. First, it found that Scholz agreed to pay Ahern royalties after deduction of only a producer's royalty and all commercially reasonable recording expenses. Second, the court held that the Scholz Statement constituted an unfair and deceptive business practice. More specifically, it found that the deductions taken for legal fees, payment to Jeff Dorenfeld, time spent in the studio, and the resulting recording costs were all not commercially reasonable recording expenses. Rather, the court stated, $500,000 in recording expenses would be commercially reasonable. It next found that Scholz' Statement was a deliberate and blatant attempt to deprive the Plaintiff Ahern of monies rightfully due and owing to him as royalties from the sales of the third BOSTON album. Such egregious conduct ... is patently an unfair and deceptive practice. The submission of [the Scholz Statement] as an accounting by Scholz to Ahern is a shocking display of arrogant disdain for Ahern's contractual rights and was rendered in obvious bad faith. * * *

Here, the district court found that Scholz breached the FMA, that four of his deductions were commercially unreasonable, while a figure of $0.5 million would be reasonable; and that the Scholz Statement was "a deliberate and blatant attempt to deprive" Ahern of moneys owed him. It is a question of law whether this attempt to deprive Ahern rises to the level of a violation of Chapter 93A, as the lower court held, and we believe the decision includes enough of a basis for the Chapter 93A finding to save the decision from remand. The district court has provided us with more than mere conclusions. We note, however, that our task would have been much simpler in this and other issues had the district court seen fit to explicate more of its decision-making on paper. There is a gap between finding that deductions are commercially unreasonable and finding that the Scholz Statement as a whole is an attempt to deprive Ahern deserving of the modifiers "unfair" and "deceptive": while we are willing to follow the lower court across the distance between them, a bridge would have been more than welcome.

C.   Scholz' Challenge to the Chapter 93A Findings

Having set forth our standard of review and the findings of the district court, we turn to the heart of Scholz' challenge to the Chapter 93A award. As noted above, whether an act was unfair and/or deceptive is a question of fact. Based on our review of the evidence, we do not hesitate to find that the district court's findings of fact are not clearly erroneous, and we will not disturb them. * * *

There is no clear definition of what conduct constitutes an "unfair or deceptive" act. * * * In evaluating whether an act or practice is unfair, we assess "the equities between the parties," including what both parties knew or should have known. *Swanson v. Bankers Life Co.,* 450 N.E.2d 577, 580 (1983).

It is well established that breach of a contract can lead to a violation of Chapter 93A. *See, e.g., Anthony's Pier Four, Inc. v. HBC Assocs.,* 583 N.E.2d 806, 821 (1991). The simple fact that a party knowingly breached a contract does not raise the breach to the level of a Chapter 93A violation, however. * * * In the breach of contract context, the Massachusetts Supreme Judicial Court has "said that conduct 'in disregard of known contractual arrangements' and intended to secure benefits for the breaching party constitutes an unfair act or practice for [Chapter] 93A purposes." *Anthony's Pier Four,* 583 N.E.2d at 821. * * *

Here, the court found that Scholz knowingly breached the contract in order to gain a benefit—Ahern's share of the royalties. But that would be true of any knowing breach of a contract. The question, then, is whether the level of "rascality" is sufficient to rise to the level of a violation of Chapter 93A. We find it is not. First, while the deductions that the court deemed commercially unreasonable ate up more than half of the royalties reported, we note that Scholz did not seek to conceal the nature of the deductions: he laid them out on the Scholz Statement in varying levels of detail. Next, while Scholz has an extensive degree of control over the moneys from the third album, there has been no allegation that he did not report all of the royalties from MCA on the Scholz Statement. Evidence was presented that the number of hours spent on the album was reconstructed after the fact, but the district court did not find that the figures given were inaccurate, just that they were not deductible. Scholz' breach amounted to more than a dispute over the commercial reasonableness of certain deductions, as he would have us believe. Nonetheless, his acts did not rise to the level of rascality required for Chapter 93A liability. Ultimately, therefore, we conclude that the district court erred as a matter of law in finding Scholz violated Chapter 93A, and reverse that holding. * * *

CONCLUSION

For the reasons stated above, we *reverse* the lower court's decision regarding Chapter 93A violations, *affirm* its other holdings except on rescission, and *remand* for trial on the issue of rescission.

Notes

1. The "power of attorney" clause is standard in both management and record contracts. How would you limit the scope of the clause to protect your clients?

2. Simon Fuller [manager for Spice Girls], nicknamed "Svengali Spice," got the axe in 1997. Fuller's management had taken the group to

mega stardom. Reportedly, Fuller gave the group little time off and took a whopping 20% of the group's earnings. That amount translated into Fuller making more than any one member of the group. Fuller's settlement was estimated at $17 to $25 million. David Gritten, *The Life of Spice Amid the Beatle-esque frenzy, managerial turmoil and slow sales of their new album, the Girls just want to have fun. Next: the movie,* L.A. TIMES, Dec. 7, 1997, at 8.

3.   In *Far Out Prod. v. Oskar* above, the band lost their name to their manager. How would you prevent that from happening in the future? Would you add a paragraph in your management agreement that states that management is not a member of the band and that management has no claim to the name or any of the band's tradenames and trademarks?

C.   BAND/AGENT AGREEMENTS

What every band needs to get started is a booking agent. A band needs to try out its material on a live audience and establish a following before a record label is going to take a chance on signing the group. Getting into the good venues requires the services of a booking agent. Before a band gets a record deal, no booking agent is going to want to work with the band. It is a Catch–22 situation for the band.

California statutes prohibit anyone but a registered booking agent from procuring employment for a band. Because a booking agent will not work with an unsigned band, one of the band members must secure the bookings until the group is able to attract a registered booking agent. If the manager or lawyer performs the booking function for the group, the band can file a claim with the Labor Commission to have the manager or lawyer fired and for the return of the money the group paid to the manager or lawyer in the past twelve months. Violation of the statute is the most common and easiest way for a new band to get out of its contract with its original manager. A number of states have similar statutes.

WIL-HELM AGENCY v. LYNN

Tennessee Court of Appeals, 1981.
618 S.W.2d 748.

MATHERNE, Judge.

The Wil–Helm Agency sues for damages due to the breach of a theatrical agency contract entered into between the agency and Loretta Lynn, an artist. Loretta Lynn filed a counterclaim wherein she avers that the agency breached the contract and, therefore, owes her damages and she further alleges that the agency released her from the contract. The chancellor found that the agency had breached the contract and, in addition, had released Loretta Lynn from the contract. The chancellor further held that the amounts due each party offset each other and allowed no monetary award to either party.

The agency appeals insisting that the chancellor erred in finding: (1) that the agency breached the contract; (2) that the agency released

Loretta Lynn from the contract; and (3) that the damages due the parties offset each other.

I. Court Proceedings to Date

This lawsuit was originally heard by Chancellor Ned Lentz, who by Judgment entered on December 1, 1971, held that certain written communications between the attorneys for the parties constituted a release of the contract by the agency as of May 8, 1971. The agency appealed that decision, and this court reversed the chancellor and remanded for a trial. The Supreme Court of Tennessee granted certiorari and by Memorandum and Order, filed October 19, 1973, set aside the Judgments of both lower courts, and remanded the lawsuit to the trial court for "a hearing on all of the issues raised in the pleadings." The basis for the remand was that under the record complete justice could not be done the parties, and it appeared that more satisfactory evidence was available upon the primary issues raised, which when presented, would enable a court to reach the proper conclusion.

On remand the lawsuit was tried by Chancellor Ben H. Cantrell, who held that the agency had released Loretta Lynn from the contract and that the agency had breached the contract. The matter was referred to the clerk and master "for a hearing as to damages and as to accounting." The clerk and master reported that, after the filing of numerous depositions, he could not ascertain the amount of damages due either party without a ruling on the law applicable to the measure of damages. The chancellor, thereupon, proceeded to consider the entire matter of damages and ruled that the damages due each party was offset by the damages each party owed the other. This appeal is from Chancellor Cantrell's rulings in the lawsuit.

II. The Contract and Facts Surrounding the Alleged Breach Thereof

Loretta Lynn was born in the area of Van Leer, Kentucky, and at the age of fourteen years married O. V. Lynn of that same area. A few months after the marriage, O. V. Lynn went to the state of Washington and obtained employment as an agricultural laborer. Later Loretta joined him at Custer, Washington. Loretta began singing at local gatherings and formed a band which soon became fully booked in the area at various local places of entertainment. She appeared on the Buck Owens show and entered into a recording contract under the Zero label. Loretta wrote and recorded the song "I'm a Honky Tonk Girl," appeared on various radio shows, appeared as a guest performer on the Grand Ole Opry, and was becoming recognized as a budding young artist.

In 1961 she and her husband moved to Nashville, Tennessee. In that year she entered into her first two-year contract with the Wil–Helm Agency. Thereafter, she entered into another five-year contract with that agency. On April 12, 1966, she and the agency entered into the contract now under consideration. This contract provides in pertinent part as follows:

WITNESSETH

1. The Artist hereby engages the Agent as his sole and exclusive personal representative and adviser in the radio, television, recording and personal appearances field of entertainment throughout the world and in outer space for a period of Twenty years (20 years). *20yrs*

2. The Agent's duties hereunder shall be as follows: To us all reasonable efforts to procure employment for the artist in any branch of the field of entertainment in which the Artist notifies the Agent that his services are or will be available. In addition, at the Artist's request to:

(a) Assist the Artist in negotiating with respect to all forms of advertising and commercial tie-ups in all fields, wherever the Artist's name, business likeness or voice may be used, including but not limited to the radio, television, recording and personal appearances field of entertainment.

(b) Counsel and advise the Artist in matters which concern his professional interest in the radio, television, recording and personal appearances field of entertainment.

3. The Agent hereby accepts this engagement and agrees to perform the services specified herein. The Agent shall have the right to render his services to other persons, either in a capacity in which he is hereby engaged or otherwise. However, the Artist agrees not to engage any other person to act for him in the capacity for which the Agent has been engaged. The Artist hereby represents and warrants that he is wholly free to enter into this agreement and has no contract or obligations which will conflict with it.

An Amendment of the same date was attached to the contract which provides in part as follows:

(3) This Amendment and the Agreement shall be null and void in the event there is a change of ownership in the Agency. It being the Artist (demands) that she be associated only with current management.

The contract and the amendment were signed by Smiley Wilson for the agency and by Loretta Lynn. The Wil–Helm Agency apparently was a partnership composed of the four Wilburn brothers: Doyle, Teddy, Leslie and Lester. As we view the lawsuit, it is immaterial whether there was a change in the ownership of the agency, and the amendment to the contract will not be further considered.

The parties enjoyed several years of successful association. Loretta's popularity grew, and she is now recognized as an outstanding star in the field of country music. From 1961 through the latter part of the 1960's, the agency assisted Loretta and played an important part in her rise to stardom. Teddy Wilburn worked closely with Loretta. When the 1966 contract was signed, he was spending several hours almost daily with Loretta. He assisted her in rewriting her songs and advised her on costumes, mannerisms, and lines. Loretta was very fond of Teddy Wilburn; she sought his counsel and followed his advice. She appeared as the only female artist on the Wilburn Brothers Show. The agency obtained a recording contract for Loretta with Decca Records. She made appearances on national television and followed a hard-working road show schedule.

In about 1967, Doyle Wilburn began to drink alcohol in excessive amounts. When drinking or drunk, he was extremely abusive and boorish. This conduct by Doyle resulted in Teddy Wilburn leaving the show in 1968. Teddy moved to California and returned to Nashville only to do certain television work. It appears that Smiley Wilson then became the member of the agency upon whom Loretta depended. Wilson did his job and aided the artist; however, she missed the expertise and experience of Teddy Wilburn. It seems that Teddy did relent and return to the show, only to leave again in 1971 for the same reason as previously stated.

With Teddy gone, it appears that Doyle Wilburn took it upon himself to be more closely identified with Loretta and her work. The record is replete with instances which reveal almost constant misconduct on the part of Doyle Wilburn acting as the agent of Loretta. Some of the more glaring instances of misconduct are: (1) insulting the producer of the Johnny Carson Show while there to close a deal for Loretta to appear on that show; (2) drunkenness on the part of Doyle Wilburn while on the stage acting as master of ceremonies; (3) actually disturbing Loretta during performances; (4) the telling of sacrilegious jokes on Loretta's show in Boston, Massachusetts; (5) drunken vomiting on the dinner table at a post-performance party given for patrons, promoters, disc jockeys and their wives; (6) drunkenness throughout most of a tour in England; (7) drunkenness during the time Loretta was preparing jingles for the Coca Cola ads; (8) getting drunk and passing out during the signing of the Glo-coat contract; (9) being so drunk while emceeing Loretta's performance at a rodeo that he fell off the stage; (10) drunkenness when taping Loretta on the Ed Sullivan Show; (11) insulting the black musicians while on the David Frost Show; (12) being drunk on practically every road trip, interfering with Loretta's need for rest on the bus, ignoring instructions of airline personnel while on flights, and generally being an obnoxious drunk in the presence of people upon whom the success of the artist depended. This conduct was carried on while Doyle Wilburn was acting as the representative of the agency with whom Loretta had contracted. This conduct was known to all members of the agency; some effort was made to reason with Doyle, but to no avail.

In about October 1970 Smiley Wilson left the agency. He was replaced by Mr. Brumley who was then replaced by Leslie Hart. Hart advised Loretta that she was being woefully mismanaged and recommended that she see an attorney. Up to this time Loretta had not received independent advice on anything. The agency kept her books, handled her financing, and referred her to the agency's lawyer for any personal legal advice. Upon the advice of Hart, Loretta employed an attorney. Upon investigating the situation, the attorney wrote a letter dated April 1, 1971, to the agency saying the agency had breached the contract, and Loretta would not further abide by it. Further negotiations between the lawyers resulted in certain letters which the chancellor found constitute a release of the contract by the agency. As we view the situation, it is of no import whether the agency released Loretta from the contract; we hold that the contract was breached by the agency.

We agree with the chancellor that the conduct of Doyle Wilburn as the representative of the agency was entirely inconsistent with the duty owed the artist under the contract. The agreement is a bilateral contract wherein each party was obligated to the other to render certain performances, the carrying out of which by each party was essential to the realization of benefits under the contract. Each party to the contract was under an implied obligation to restrain from doing any act that would delay or prevent the other party's performance of the contract. *Fritz-Rumer–Cooke Co. v. United States,* 279 F.2d 200 *(6th Cir. 1960).* Each party had the right to proceed free of hindrance by the other party, and if such other party interfered, hindered, or prevented the performance to such an extent as to render the performance difficult and diminish the benefits to be received, the first party could treat the contract as broken and was not bound to proceed under the added burdens. *See, Anvil Mining Co. v. Humble,* 153 U.S. 540 (1894). * * *

There is ample material evidence that the agency, by the conduct of its representative, committed a substantial breach of its contract with Loretta Lynn. The chancellor is affirmed in this respect.

III. DAMAGES

The chancellor referred the question of damages to the clerk and master, but, after the taking of considerable proof, that official passed the issue back to the chancellor without making a finding of any kind. Thereupon, the chancellor found as follows:

> After sifting through the proof and after reviewing the previous Memorandum and the orders based on it, the Court concludes that the claims of the parties off-set each other and should be dismissed. The plaintiff Agency claims $178,556.72 due on the contract up until the date of termination with allowances for dates already booked to November of 1971. The defendant counter-claimed for damages for breach of the management agreement. The proof shows that the defendant was being booked at a fee of $2,500.00 to $4,000.00 per appearance up until the date of termination of the agreement while an artist of her stature should have commanded a much higher figure. A simple calculation based on the number of dates she worked in a few years prior to 1971 shows how much of a loss that was. In addition, the failure to expose her to national television and the stress of the conditions under which she worked result in

damages that are reasonably certain and should off-set the plaintiff's claim.

The Court declines to speculate on the amount of damages the plaintiff would be entitled to if the decision had been otherwise. We accept the figure of $178,556.72 as the amount due the agency under the contract up until the date of termination with allowances for dates already booked to November 1971. The artist claims that this amount can not be awarded to the plaintiff agency because the plaintiff breached the contract and is not entitled to any amount thereunder. We disagree with the artist in this respect.

The record reveals that the plaintiff agency committed a substantial breach of the contract. The defendant artist did not commit any breach of the contract. Therefore, if the plaintiff is to recover at all, it must do so upon the theory that it has rendered a part performance of value, that it has done more good than harm to the artist, and that the artist will be unjustly enriched and the plaintiff unjustly penalized if the artist is allowed to retain the beneficial part performance without paying anything in return. 5A Corbin on Contracts § 1124 (1964). By the same token, the plaintiff is the wrongdoer, and it must not be allowed to profit from its own wrong. Therefore, allowance must be made to the defendant artist in damages for the full extent of the injury that the plaintiff's breach has caused her. Corbin, supra. Under the facts of this bilateral contract, whereby each party agreed to carry out certain performances in return for performances by the other party, we conclude that the plaintiff agency is entitled to its commissions based upon its part performance less the amount of the injury to the artist caused by the breach. Having accepted the figure of $178,556.72 as the amount due the agency for its part performance, it must now be determined in what amount, if any, the artist was damaged by the breach.

The defendant artist averred by counterclaim that due to the conduct of Doyle Wilburn, she had been deprived of engagements as an artist, that she had suffered physical and emotional distress and had been rendered unable to perform to her capacity, and that subsequent to the breach and the termination of the contract, the agency had held itself out as the sole and exclusive agent of the artist thereby depriving her of engagements and the resulting revenues therefrom. By amendment to the counterclaim, the artist averred that over the years the agency had booked her for engagements at a price below that to which she was entitled and had entered into a recording contract for her at a rate substantially less than her professional ability demanded, all to her financial detriment and in breach of the agency's duties under the contract.

As noted, the chancellor found (1) that the artist was booked at a fee below that which an artist of her stature should have commanded, and (2) that the stress of the conditions under which she was forced to work resulted in damages that are reasonably certain.

There is competent and material evidence that Loretta Lynn won more awards, had a larger following, and was more sought after than any other artist in her field of entertainment. There is competent and material evidence that artists of less ability, following, and demand were drawing from $5,000 to $7,500 for a performance during the late 1960's and up to 1971. There is ample proof that Loretta Lynn should have been drawing those amounts instead of the $2,500 to $4,000 range in which she was booked. The plaintiff agency presented proof which purported to list every performance of Loretta Lynn for which the agency claimed a commission. From a review of the number of those performances and an application of a reasonable average fee at which the artist should have been booked, the chancellor concluded that the damage she suffered from having been "underbooked" for several years more than offset the amount proved by the agency as owing to it.

The chancellor properly held that strain and stress unnecessarily suffered by the actress due to the conduct of the agency representatives resulted in damages for which the artist could recover. There is ample material evidence to sustain the finding that the conditions under which she had to work, rendered the artist nervous, uncertain, dismayed, and embarrassed, all to her professional detriment through no fault of her own.

Although not ruled on by the chancellor, we find another element of damage to the artist based upon the recording contract it entered into for the artist with Decca Records. It seems that in the early years of the recording industry a recording company suffered substantial losses due to records being broken while in transit to the buyers. As a result, a custom built up that when contracting with an artist the recording company would deduct 10% from the sales figures to take care of this breakage, and the artist was paid a royalty based upon 90% of the sales figure. Later records were made of plastic or some other material not subject to the breakage previously sustained. The proof establishes that as of 1966, when Decca contracted to record Loretta, all recording contracts being renewed and all new contracts being entered into provided for a royalty based upon the 100% figure. This was done at the mere request of the artist or agent. However, the plaintiff agency booked Loretta at a royalty based upon the 90% figure. In 1972, after the parties had gone their separate ways, Decca voluntarily changed the contract so as to pay royalties on the 100% figure. There is material evidence that the loss suffered by the artist because of this breach of duty on the part of the agency amounted to approximately $200,000 during the period from 1966 to 1971.

We, therefore, agree with the chancellor that the damages suffered by the artist more than offset those amounts claimed by the agency for its part performance of the contract. Admittedly, neither the chancellor nor this court fix the actual amount of damages to which the artist is entitled due to the breach of the contract by the agency. We have, however, fully satisfied ourselves that the damages thus suffered exceed the amount due the plaintiff agency. The artist did not appeal. We conclude that under all the circumstances of this lawsuit, the chancellor's decree is supported by a preponderance of the evidence, and that decree is affirmed.

The cost in this court is adjudged against the appellant, Wil–Helm Agency, for which execution may issue, if necessary.

Notes

1. California's regulation of licensing talent agencies is set forth in section 1700 of the California Labor Code, also known as the Talent Agencies Act. California Labor Code, section 1700.4, defines the meaning of "talent agency." It is reprinted in Chapter 3, Agents, Managers, Lawyers and Unions. For information on other jurisdiction's regulation of agents, see: Fla. Stat. Ann. § 468.401 (West 2004); N.Y. Arts and Cultural Affairs Law § 37.07 (McKinney 2003); 23 P.R. Laws Ann. § 691b (2003); Tex. Occ. Code Ann. § 2105.103 (Vernon 2004); and Wis. Stat. Ann. § 645 (West 2003).

2. In *Park v. Deftones,* 71 Cal.App.4th 1465 (Ct. App. 1999). Plaintiff Park filed suit against the group for breach of management agreement. Plaintiff also filed suit against Maverick records and one of its agents for interference with contractual agreements. Park claimed that Maverick interfered with agreements between Park and the "Deftones." The "Deftones" followed by filing a petition to void the management agreements with Park. They argued that the agreements were void because Park was not a licensed talent agency. Park argued that he only procured employment for the group to secure a recording contract and was not paid to procure the performances. Unlike talent agents, managers are not regulated by the Talent Agencies Act. "Personal managers primarily advise, counsel, direct, and coordinate the development of the artist's career." *Id.* at 1470. However, the casual booking exception for managers was rejected in *Waisbren v. Peppercorn Prod., Inc.,* 41 Cal.App.4th 246, 252–53, 48 Cal.Rptr.2d 437 (Ct. App. 1995). The court found that Park's contract did provide for compensation, therefore was subject to the Act, even though the procurement of employment was incidental to securing a recording contract. *Id.* at 1465–72, 48 Cal.Rptr.2d 437.

D. BAND/ATTORNEY AGREEMENTS

Every band needs a music lawyer to help the band get the best record and music publishing deals possible. The best music lawyers are as selective as the record labels when it comes to representing a new act. Record labels research the band's lawyer to determine who they are dealing with and how much to try to get away with.

A-list lawyers have access to and clout with the record labels. The major music law firms have pre-negotiated forms with each label so that they do not have to waste time negotiating points that they have negotiated for previous clients. If the label is unfamiliar with the artist's lawyer, the label will send a very one-sided form to begin the negotiations. The starting point often influences where the negotiations will end. Each new contract an artist receives during his or her career should be a little more artist-friendly than the previous contract. Recording contracts are discussed in Chapter 16 Record Companies and Recording Agreements.

Ethical conflicts are ever-present in the music business. Lawyers and clients should be aware of the potential conflicts that may arise through representation. Clarification of the relationships and potential conflicts at the beginning of the relationship can prevent ill will and litigation at the end of the relationship. A band's selection of a lawyer is critical to the long-term financial success of the band. As with the other relationships, each side should be represented by separate counsel.

CROCE v. KURNIT

United States District Court, New York, 1982.
565 F.Supp. 884.

SWEET, District Judge.

This diversity action, a portion of which was tried to the court, presented facts which evoked memories of "A Star Is Born," except that the star in this case, James Croce, died all too soon after his ascendancy. The complaint filed by Ingrid Croce, his widow and heir ("Mrs. Croce"), a California resident, sought to obtain certain damages from the defendants, citizens of states other than California, arising out of an alleged breach of certain contracts as well as rescission of the contracts on the ground of fraud, and breach of fiduciary duty. On the findings and conclusions set forth below, judgment will be granted to the defendants dismissing the claims of unconscionability and breach of fiduciary duty against Cashman and West and granting Croce's breach of fiduciary claim against Kurnit. The defendants' motion for judgment notwithstanding the verdict is denied. * * *

FINDINGS OF FACT

James Joseph Croce ("Jim Croce") was born in 1943 and in the course of his schooling attended Villanova University. There he met Ingrid, who subsequently became his wife, and also Tommy West, who became both his friend and, as it developed, a business associate. During the college years Jim Croce sang, played guitar and wrote songs, as did West.

After graduation from college, Jim Croce sought to shape a career out of his interest in music, played and sang in coffee houses, and developed both his own style and his own music. He managed to produce a record album entitled *Facets* containing certain of his songs which he performed. He sent the album to Tommy and sought to interest the latter in his work.

West in the meantime also developed a career in music, producing, singing and playing for commercials. He had met Cashman with whom he collaborated as well as Kurnit, an attorney who had been working at

ABC Records, Inc. By 1968 all three, West, Cashman and Kurnit were at CBS, Cashman and West in the music department and Kurnit serving in the legal department. The two musicians together with Eugene Pistilli ("Pistilli") decided to enter the record business on their own and set up CP & W for that purpose. Kurnit was also a participant in the enterprise.

In the summer of 1968, while Kurnit was still at CBS, Jim and Ingrid Croce arrived in New York, stayed with West, and met Kurnit, who was introduced to them as "the lawyer." West and the Croces discussed the possibility of CP & W producing a record by Jim Croce. The outlines of the contractual arrangements were discussed, the Croces returned to Pennsylvania and according to West, proposed contracts were taken to them after their trip to New York and before their return to New York on September 17, 1968. Whether or not that occurred (Mrs. Croce maintains it did not), the Croces did not conduct any meaningful review of the contract until September 17, 1968.

On that date the Croces were in New York again, staying with the Wests. They met Kurnit for the second time. He outlined the contract terms to them in a two to three hour meeting. According to Kurnit, there was no negotiation although a minor change in the proposed contract was made. The Croces signed three agreements, a recording contract with CP & W, a publishing contract with Blendingwell and a personal management contract also with Blendingwell ("the contracts"). The Croces were unrepresented, and they were not advised to obtain counsel by Kurnit who signed the contracts on behalf of the corporate entities. Kurnit was known to the Croces to be a participant with Cashman, Pistilli and West in their enterprises. The Croces did not enter into any retainer agreement with Kurnit, were never billed by him in connection with the contracts, and aside from the meeting of September 17, received no advice from him concerning the contracts.

The contracts that were executed on September 17, 1968 provided that Croce would perform and record exclusively for CP & W, as well as the terms under which all the Croce's songs would be published and managerial services would be provided for the Croces. The contracts placed no affirmative requirements on the defendants other than to pay each of the Croces approximately $600 a year and to make certain royalty payments in the event that music or records were sold. The duration of the contracts was seven years if options to extend were exercised by the defendants. All rights to the Croces' musical performances and writings were granted to the defendants. The management contract was assignable.

The expert testimony offered by Mrs. Croce focused on the effect of the assignability of the management contract, the lack of any objective threshold to be achieved before the exercise of options, and the interrelationship of the three contracts. In addition other significant provisions were cited as being unfavorable to the Croces which would have been the subject of negotiation had the Croces in September, 1968 been represented by the expert retained in 1982. These included the term of the contracts, the royalty rate and its escalation, a revision of the copyrights, a minimum recording sides obligation, and the time for making objections to royalty statements.

However, certain of the provisions which were under attack were also contained in the forms published by various organizations involved in the entertainment industry, and there was no evidence presented in this action, meticulously prepared by able counsel on both sides, which established that the terms of these contracts differed significantly from others prepared by Kurnit on behalf of the defendants. These contracts include many terms of art and are customarily the subject of hard bargaining in the event that the artist and the producer both have established economic power. Here, however, no significant changes were made in the contracts as initially proposed by Kurnit on behalf of the other defendants.

After the contracts were executed, the parties undertook their performance. In the summer of 1969 the recording contract was assigned to Interrobang Productions, Inc. ("Interrobang"), as was the management contract a year later. Cashwest is the successor in interest to Interrobang. The management contract was assigned to Showcase Management, a company in which CP & W had an interest, a demonstration record was prepared (a "demo") and thereafter Capital Records undertook to produce a Croce recording under the direction of Nick Vanet. This recording was published in the spring of 1969 and after its publication, Jim Croce worked hard to promote it. By the winter of 1969–70 it was apparent the album was a failure, and Jim turned to other pursuits.

In the fall of 1968 Kurnit represented the Croces in connection with a lease. In April 1969, Kurnit listed his firm as the party to whom all ASCAP correspondence for Croce should be sent. In January, 1970 Kurnit executed a document as attorney in fact for the Croces and also was involved in the dispute between the Croces and their then manager.

Notwithstanding, on March 19, 1970, Jim and Ingrid, unhappy with the management with which they had been provided, sought legal advice with respect to breaking the contracts. They retained Robert Cushman ("Cushman") of Pepper, Hamilton & Schatz in Philadelphia. On June 9, 1970, Croce wrote to Kurnit seeking to terminate the contracts and advising him that "Ingrid and I are getting out of music." In the summer of 1970, Cushman met with Kurnit and discussed the grievances which the Croces had expressed to him, supported at one point by a statement of Pistilli which, according to Cushman, established that the Croces had been defrauded. Some revisions and amendments to the contracts were discussed.

In December 1970 Ingrid became pregnant, and Jim returned to songwriting and performing. Thereafter, he sent material to West who expressed interest and delight. Cushman requested a further retainer to pursue the revision or cancellation of the contracts and never heard again from either of the Croces.

In the early part of 1971 West and Cashman worked with Croce and prepared a demo. With Kurnit's help, they sold the idea of its production to ABC, interested an established management agency in Croce with the result that Interrobang delegated its management contract for Croce to BNB Associates, Ltd. ("BNB") in September 1971. Once the relationship with the defendants resumed in 1971, Kurnit represented the Croces on various matters. After the summer of 1971 and the birth of his son in September, Jim's career began to move. His work was well received and in April 1972, ABC records contracted to manufacture, distribute and sell Croce records. Jim was on the road late in 1971 and 1972 promoting and performing. His career skyrocketed and until September 20, 1973 the future appeared halcyon for all concerned. During 1972 Kurnit represented Croce on matters other than the contracts.

On September 20, 1973, after a concert in Louisiana, Croce took off in a private plane. The plane crashed in a thunderstorm, and Croce was killed. Very shortly thereafter Kurnit visited Mrs. Croce and offered to represent the estate and to take care of the wrongful death action arising from the crash. On September 26, 1973, Kurnit became the attorney for the Estate and Mrs. Croce. In connection with the wrongful death action, Kurnit later stated on the form filed with the Appellate Division on October 4, 1973: "Ingrid Croce, and her deceased husband, James J. Croce, have been my clients since 1968. I have been their personal attorney in a majority of their legal matters." Kurnit served as counsel to the estate from September 26, 1973, until June 24, 1976. During the spring of 1976 Kurnit, on behalf of the defendants, had consulted Donnenfeld and Brent, a Los Angeles law firm, with respect to a movie proposal. Thereafter, at his request on June 24, 1976 that firm was substituted for him as counsel for the estate.

In 1975, Mrs. Croce remarried and in the company of her husband discussed with Kurnit the use of certain material which had not been the subject of the contracts. These discussions, involving what the parties have termed "the estate sides," were the subject of the contract issues concerning the publication of "The Faces I Have Been" album resolved by the jury's Special Verdict. During these discussions Kurnit represented CP & W and after the initial discussion, Mrs. Croce retained Ivan Hoffman, an attorney, to represent her. Hoffman and Kurnit exchanged correspondence, drafts and telephone calls. There is no evidence that Hoffman was consulted about the contracts or Mrs. Croce's rights which resulted from the contracts.

However, in November 1975, Mrs. Croce retained Howard Thaler to represent her on a number of matters unrelated to the contracts. At his deposition, Thaler invoked the attorney/client privilege when questioned about his discussions with Mrs. Croce about the contracts. Thaler's invocation of the privilege may imply that Thaler has information against Mrs. Croce's interests in this action. However, even assuming that this inference is permitted, Kurnit has failed to establish the date on which Mrs. Croce conferred with Thaler concerning the contracts prior to June 10, 1976.

On that day Thaler met with Donnenfeld and some discussion was had concerning Mrs. Croce's rights under the contracts. Mrs. Croce was advised that since the Estate had been referred to them by Kurnit, a conflict of interest existed which precluded their initiating any claim against Kurnit. It was pointed out, however, that since the Estate was shortly to be terminated, Mrs. Croce would thereafter initiate any action she felt appropriate. Obviously these issues had been discussed between Mrs. Croce and Thaler prior to June 10, 1976, but Kurnit has not sustained his burden of proof to establish an earlier date to end the toll of the statute of limitations. * * * The Estate was closed on September 27, 1977 and this action was initiated on July 21, 1978.

During the period from 1968 to date the defendants received approximately $6.9 million as a consequence of the performance of the contracts. The recording and entertainment career of Croce is not atypical, representing as it does, initially a famine, and ultimately a feast. No expert who testified claimed the prescience to determine in advance what records the public will buy or in what amount. Though the returns on a successful record are unbelievably high, the risk of initial failure is also high. Judgment, taste, skill and luck far outweigh the time spent or the capital expended on any particular recording.

It is on these facts that Mrs. Croce's claims of unconscionability and breach of fiduciary duty, must be resolved. * * * The claim of fraud has not been pressed by Mrs. Croce, and indeed there is no proof of misrepresentation, falsity or reliance except in connection with the fiduciary duty claims.

1. Representation by Kurnit

The claims of breach of fiduciary duty and procedural unconscionability are based on the role and actions of Kurnit at the signing and during the performance of the contracts. Indeed, the nature of Kurnit's relationship with the Croces determines whether this action is barred by the statute of limitations. Therefore, this court will assess the September 17, 1968, transaction before proceeding to the merits of each claim.

Mrs. Croce asserts that after Kurnit had been introduced to the Croces on a prior occasion as "the lawyer," Kurnit acted as the Croces' attorney at the signing of the contracts or in such a manner as to lead the Croces to reasonably believe that they could rely on his advice. The Croces were aware of the fact that Kurnit was an officer, director and shareholder of Blendingwell and Cashwest on whose behalf Kurnit signed the contracts.

In light of the facts set forth above, Kurnit did not act as the Croces' attorney at the signing of the contracts. Even in the absence of an express attorney-client relationship, however, a lawyer may owe a fiduciary obligation to persons with whom he deals. *Westinghouse Electric Corp. v. Kerr–McGee Corp.*, 580 F.2d 1311, 1319 (7th Cir. 1978). * * * In particular, a fiduciary duty arises when a lawyer deals with persons who, although not strictly his clients, he has or should have reason to believe rely on him. *In re Goldberg,* 12 B.R. 180, 183 (Bkrtcy.D.N.J. 1981). * * * Kurnit's introduction as "the lawyer," his explanation to the Croces of the "legal ramifications" of the contracts which contained a number of legal terms and concepts, his interest as a principal in the transactions, his failure to advise the Croces to obtain outside counsel, and the Croces lack of independent representation taken together establish both a fiduciary duty on the part of Kurnit and a breach of that duty.

In *Howard v. Murray,* 43 N.Y.2d 417, 372 N.E.2d 568, 401 N.Y.S.2d 781 (1977), an action to rescind a mortgage, bond and option arrangement, an attorney-client relationship had existed between the parties before the attorney became a principal in the transaction. The court concluded that any doubt as to whether an attorney-client relationship existed at the time of the transaction "should readily have been resolved against the defendant, absent proof of a clear and forthright statement to his clients that he was no longer their attorney and that they should obtain outside counsel before continuing any negotiations." *Id.* at 422, 372 N.E.2d at 570, 401 N.Y.S.2d at 784. Although I conclude that Kurnit did not act as counsel to the Croces before September, 1968, the events surrounding the execution of the contracts, in particular his failure to advise the Croces to obtain counsel, establish the applicability of *Howard v. Murray* in determining the obligations of Kurnit.

Moreover, the limits of the fiduciary relationship as defined in *Penato v. George,* 52 A.D.2d 939, 383 N.Y.S.2d 900 (2d Dep't 1976) apply. The court there realized that the exact limits of such a relationship are impossible of statement (see Bogert, Trusts & Trustees [2d ed.], § 481). Broadly stated, a fiduciary relationship is one founded upon trust or confidence reposed by one person in the integrity and fidelity of another. It is said that the relationship exists in all cases in which influence has been acquired and abused, in which confidence has been reposed and betrayed. The rule embraces both technical fiduciary relations and those informal relations which exist whenever one man trusts in, and relies upon, another.

This definition of a fiduciary duty applies not only to Kurnit's relationship but also on the facts of this case to West and Cashman, in whom the Croces placed their trust. Before further addressing Mrs. Croce's breach of fiduciary duty allegations, however, the defendants' statute of limitations defense warrants examination. For these purposes, Kurnit's relationship with the Croces controls.

[Part 2 omitted].

3. *Unconscionability and Breach of Fiduciary Duty*

Mrs. Croce contends that the contracts were unconscionable. An unconscionable contract "affronts the sense of decency," *Gimbel Bros., Inc. v. Swift,* 62 Misc.2d 156, 307 N.Y.S.2d 952 (Civ.Ct.1970), and usually involves gross onesidedness, lack of meaningful choice and susceptible clientele. J. Calamari & J. Perillo, *Contracts* § 9–40 (2d ed. 1977). A claim of unconscionability "requires some showing of 'an absence of meaningful choice on the part of one of the parties together with contract terms which are unreasonably favorable to the other party.' " *State v. Avco Financial Serv.*, 50 N.Y.2d 383, 406 N.E.2d 1075, 429 N.Y.S.2d 181, 185 (1980).

Additionally, Mrs. Croce alleges that defendants breached their fiduciary duty to the Croces. A fiduciary relationship is bound by a standard of fairness, good faith and loyalty. *Newburger, Loeb & Co. v. Gross*, 563 F.2d 1057, 1078 (2d Cir.1977).

Substantial testimony was adduced on the subject of the inherent conflict presented by the control of the management contract by the publisher. The management contract, of course, served only the interest of the artist, although obviously the interest of the artist and his career were inextricably interwoven with the publication and promotion of his product. For example, BWB, when undertaking the assignment to manage Croce, immediately obtained a royalty rate increase, of course, thus affecting its own compensation.

The significance of management contracts depends on the needs of artists, some of whom are entirely capable of performing all the business and promotion duties while others seek to concentrate solely on their artistic efforts. As the relationship developed, Croce depended on his manager significantly, but the conflict between the artist and the producer does not so completely overbalance the mutuality of their interest as to make management and recording contracts held or controlled by the same interests, as occurred here, in and of itself, determinative of the issues of unfairness and unconscionability. Indeed, it was Kurnit who ultimately arranged for a separate management contract, albeit that the contract with BWB barred the manager from urging the artist to terminate the contracts.

As the facts stated above indicate, the contracts were hard bargains, signed by an artist without bargaining power, and favored the publishers, but as a matter of fact did not contain terms which shock the conscience or differed so grossly from industry norms as to be unconscionable by their terms. The contracts were free from fraud and although complex in nature, the provisions were not formulated so as to obfuscate or confuse the terms. Although Jim Croce might have thought that he retained the right to choose whether to exercise renewal options, this misconception does not establish that the contracts were unfair. Because of the uncertainty involved in the music business and the high risk of failure of new performers, the contracts, though favoring the defendants, were not unfair. *See Wilson Trading Corp. v. David Ferguson, Ltd.*, 23 N.Y.2d 398, 403–04, 244 N.E.2d 685, 688, 297 N.Y.S.2d 108, 112 (1968) ("Whether a contract or any clause of the contract is unconscionable is a matter for the court to decide against the background of the contract's commercial setting, purpose, and effect."). Therefore, I conclude that the terms of the contracts were neither unconscionable nor unfair and that Cashman and West did not breach a fiduciary duty.

In considering procedural unconscionability this court notes that the instant situation lacks the elements of haste and high pressure tactics, *Industralease Automated & Scientific Equipment Corp. v. R.M.E. Enter., Inc.,* 58 A.D.2d 482, 396 N.Y.S.2d 427, 431 n. 4 (2d Dep't 1977), and that the contracts did not provide for the sole benefit of the defendants, *Miner v. Walden,* 101 Misc. 2d 814, 422 N.Y.S.2d 335, 338 (Sup. Ct. 1979). Indeed, they benefited the Croces by millions of dollars. Thus Kurnit's actions do not rise to the level of procedural unconscionability. Kurnit, however, as a lawyer and principal, failed to advise the Croces to retain independent counsel and proceeded to give legal advice to the Croces in explaining the contracts to them. These actions, as discussed above, constitute a breach of the fiduciary duty Kurnit owed the Croces. *See Howard v. Murray,* 43 N.Y.2d 417, 372 N.E.2d 568, 401 N.Y.S.2d 781, 784 (1977).

3. [sic] *Remedy*

Mrs. Croce seeks rescission of the contracts or more specifically termination of the contracts on the date of judgment. Since Mrs. Croce sued for breach of contract in Counts 4, 5 and 6, defendants assert that she is barred from seeking rescission because of the doctrine of election of remedies, which prevents a party who pursued two inconsistent theories from obtaining duplicative relief. * * *

Although the doctrine of election of remedies does not preclude rescission, I find that rescission is inappropriate on the facts of this case. The Second Circuit has recognized that rescission is an extraordinary remedy, *Canfield v. Reynolds,* 631 F.2d 169, 178 (2d Cir.1980), which is granted only where the breach is found to be "material and willful, or, if not willful, so substantial and fundamental as to strongly tend to defeat the object of the parties in making the contract." *Callanan v. Powers,* 199 N.Y. 268, 284, 92 N.E. 747, 752 (1910). * * * The breach of fiduciary duty by Kurnit is not so fundamental as to defeat the intent or purpose of the contract.

Moreover, the contracts have been performed. In attempting to return to the status quo Mrs. Croce would have the defendants retain the money they received under the contracts as compensation for their services and return the master tapes and copyrights to her. Defendants oppose this remedy as unjust enrichment. Although this court has difficulty perceiving how the status quo ante could ever be determined, achieving this possibility does not make rescission appropriate when, as in the instant case, the breach of fiduciary duty is not a breach going to the root of the contract.

Mrs. Croce is, however, entitled to damages resulting from Kurnit's breach of fiduciary duty in failing to advise the Croces to seek independent counsel. *See supra,* text at n. 3. Given the bifurcated nature of this lawsuit, and the fact that, but for Kurnit's breach, the second branch of Mrs. Croce's complaint, claiming fraud, unconscionability, and breach of fiduciary duty, would in all likelihood not have arisen, this court assesses Mrs. Croce's damages to be the costs and attorneys' fees expended in prosecuting those claims, and determines that Kurnit is liable for this amount.

Finally, with regard to the contract claims, defendants move for judgment notwithstanding the verdict or reconsideration of this court's directed verdict in favor of Mrs. Croce on Blendingwell's counterclaim and Mrs. Croce's claim concerning songwriter's royalties with regard to ABC/Blendingwell. Neither party disputes the propriety of directing a verdict with respect to these particular contested claims, though obviously defendants argue that the court's conclusions previously expressed were in error. Notwithstanding, defendants' motions are denied. * * *

Notes

1. Can an entertainment attorney adequately represent the artist and the recording company at the same time? In 1992, singer Billy Joel filed a $90 million law suit against his lawyer claiming the lawyer had a conflict of interest. Besides representing Joel, the Defendant Grubman also represented Joel's record company [Sony's CBS Records] and Joel's manager. Joel claimed he was not informed that Grubman represented either the record company or his manager. Chuck Philips, *Joel Lawsuit an 'Alarm Bell' for Music Industry Pop: The suit against attorney Allen Grubman highlights an ethical dilemma: Can a lawyer represent a pop client as well as the firm that markets his music?*, L.A. TIMES, Oct. 14, 1992, at 1. Sony records [not named as a party to the suit], finally settled with Billy Joel to drop his suit against Grubman. In 1993, Joel received $3 million. Chuck Philips, *Company Town Attorney to the Superstars Lawyer Plays to Both Sides of Record Industry*, L.A. TIMES, Aug. 22, 1997, at D4. Why do you think the company would get involved and settle the claim?

2. What are the advantages and disadvantages of a lawyer representing both the artist and his or her record company? How do you avoid the inherent ethical problems of representing both parties to an agreement?

3. In addition to being knowledgeable about music law, record companies expect more from the artist's lawyers they deal with. The following article discusses some of the additional skills needed to be a successful music lawyer.

Willian Henslee
Evolving Role of the Lawyer in the Representation of Talent in the Music Business

Evolution in the music business has created a number of opportunities for lawyers. On the record company and music publishing company sides, lawyers work as in-house company lawyers and in non-legal roles as business people. As with any corporate legal position, the companies prefer that a lawyer get some training at a law firm that handles the same kind of work the lawyer will perform once he or she moves in-house. Two years of work following law school is usually a minimum prerequisite.

For lawyers who prefer to work with talent, or who are too impatient to work for a firm for two or more years until a lateral position opens up, artist representation is the easiest way to get into the business. There are an unlimited number of unsigned bands that need representation and that would love to be able to say that they have a lawyer. The problem is that most of the unsigned bands that want your help will take up a lot of time and not provide any return. Most beginning bands don't know what they need from a lawyer, and as a new lawyer in the music business, you may not know what they need either.

A lawyer representing clients in the music business needs to be familiar with the business and legal needs of the client. Organizing the group as a partnership or a corporation is one of the first services the music lawyer should perform for the group. Figuring out how to split the money, songwriter's credits, how to replace an original member, and who gets the name in the inevitable divorce are critical issues that should be discussed and agreed to by the group while they are still friends, before the money starts rolling in. Copyright and trademark ownership issues should be explained and, again, the ownership of the intellectual property after the inevitable divorce must be delineated. In order to adequately represent the group in their first record contract, you need to know about all of the negotiable terms and the industry standards in the recording contract presented by the record company. Music publishing contracts need to be negotiated, managers and agents need to be hired, and the group needs to be able to rely on you for competent advice as they evolve from friends playing music for the love of the music into a money-making music business entity. You need to be comfortable advising the clients on the various aspects of the music business. While legal representation of an artist can involve complicated contracts with protracted negotiations, that is a different article.

The Lawyer as an A&R Person

Artist and Repertoire (A&R) people are music scouts. A&R people are usually eighteen-to twenty-five-year-olds who go to clubs and listen to demo submissions to find the next great group. They scour the clubs for talent and listen to hundreds of tapes (CDs) from hopeful musicians in an effort to discover the next chart-topping act. An A&R person listens to bands in clubs with poor sound systems and evaluates demo tapes and CDs to find the next diamond in the rough. Often times, the initial determination on the next star-to-be is based on hearing the group under less than perfect conditions.

When an A&R person decides to recommend a group to be signed by a major label, he or she typically makes a presentation to the president of the company. The record company president will ask the A&R person if he or she is willing to risk his or her job on the success of the band. If the answer is an unequivocal yes, the band will be signed. If there is any hesitation in the recommendation, the A&R person will be sent back out to find a different group. When a record label must commit $500,000 to $1,000,000 to sign and release the first album for a new group, the label wants to be sure that they have made the right choice in selecting the group. A record label can't afford to make many mistakes. Selecting talent to be signed to a label is a gamble. The record company must project the listening and music buying tastes of the public one year to eighteen months in the future, which is the usual timetable for a group who signs a contact, records the masters, and turns the material over to the record company for marketing and distribution. The initial release of the first single is months after the initial decision is made to take a risk on a particular group.

Music lawyers are now being asked to screen talent before they present a group to a record company. Your reputation at the labels as a lawyer will, in part, depend on your ability to work with groups that have the talent the record company is looking for. If you are going to risk your music business reputation as a lawyer on an act, you need to make sure that you understand what the record company is looking for and whether your group has a chance at being accepted by the company. Lawyers who are good at finding new talent have access to the decision makers at the record companies. While that access is earned over time, it can easily be lost by a few frivolous submissions. In order to avoid losing your goodwill with the record company, you need to know how to screen talent for the record company. You need to know how to perform the function of the label A&R representative.

What Is an A&R Person Listening For?

There are thousands of talented singers and musicians who will never be famous. Some of the best voices can be found in church choirs and chorales. Some of the best musicians can be found in small clubs playing with bands that are going nowhere. Professional studio musicians are often better at their craft than most players in successful bands. If there is so much talent out there, what does it take to separate a star from a lounge singer? What are you really listening for when you are making decisions on talent?

Unique Vocal Quality! That's all there is to it. The vocalist is the band. Now that everyone who plays an instrument has been insulted, think about these examples. In 1985, Michael Jackson and Lionel Richie wrote a song that has endured since that time as the perfect example of what an A&R person is looking for. In alphabetical order: Dan Aykroyd, Harry Belafonte, Lindsey Buckingham, Kim Carnes, Ray Charles, Bob Dylan, Sheila E., Bob Geldof, "Hall & Oates," James Ingram, Jackie Jackson, LaToya Jackson, Marlon Jackson, Michael Jackson, Randy Jackson, Tito Jackson, Al Jarreau, Waylon Jennings, Billy Joel, Cyndi Lauper, "Huey Lewis & The News," Kenny Loggins, Bette Midler, Willie Nelson, Jeffrey Osbourne, Steve Perry, "The Pointer Sisters," Lionel Richie, Smokey Robinson, Kenny Rogers, Diana Ross, Paul Simon, Bruce Springsteen, Tina Turner, Dione Warwick, and Stevie Wonder sang parts of the song entitled "We Are The World." Each time one of them opened his or her mouth to sing, music fans could name the person singing. That unique vocal quality that distinguishes one vocalist from the others is what an A&R person is looking for.

A more modern example was recorded in 2001 when Artists Against AIDS Worldwide recorded the 1970 song written by Renaldo Benson, Alfred Cleveland, and Marvin Gaye entitled "What's Going On." The Dupri Original Mix was rapped and sung by (in order of appearance): P. Diddy, Jermaine Dupri, Bono, Gwen Stefani, Aaron Lewis, Nona Gaye, "Backstreet Boys," Christina Aguilara, Britney Spears, J–Lo, "Destiny's Child," Ja Rule, Nelly Furtado, Michal Stipe, Alicia Keyes, " *NSYNC," Mary J. Blige, Darren Hayes, Nelly, Nas, Eve, and Fred Durst. Again, each time one of them begins to sing, his or her distinct vocal quality allows you to identify the vocalist. It is that unique vocal quality that separates the lounge singers from the stars. There are exceptions to every rule, but it is that unique vocal quality that the A&R people are looking for when they are scouting for new talent.

THE MAGIC QUESTION

Every time you hear a new artist, ask yourself this question, "Who does the vocalist sound like?" If you can't answer the question, the vocalist may have the magic it takes to become a star. If you can answer the question, that vocalist will most likely never be famous as an individual recording artist. There is no magic, unique vocal quality if the question can be answered. The vocalist may sing in a tribute band or back-up for the original, but if the vocalist doesn't have a unique voice, he or she is not going to get signed to a record deal. The original already exists and there is no need for a copy. It is a harsh business, but that is the reality of the situation. All of those people with fantastic voices are destined to entertain their friends and family, but they are not going to be recording platinum records. Among others, Bob Dylan, Janis Joplin, Jimi Hendrix, Bruce Springsteen, Axl Rose, Tom Waits, Rod Stewart, Scott Stapp, Fred Durst, Jack White, Kidd Rock, Snoop Dogg, and 50 Cent probably never sang in a church choir. One could debate the aesthetic quality of their voices, but they don't have to please everyone, they just have to be uniquely recognizable. The world needs lounge singers, back-up singers, chorus members, and tribute bands, but the world doesn't need two (fill in your favorite artist's name).

OTHER CONSIDERATIONS

After you have found someone with a magic voice, you need to determine if they have the stage presence that is needed to become a star. A star draws the attention of everyone in a room when he or she enters. That charismatic aura that surrounds a star is a critical component for the success of a pop star. In other genre, the vocal quality can make up for a lack of "star quality." If the vocalist has that "star quality," you may have found the next platinum recording artist.

You can buy songs and hire producers to make hit songs. The vocalist will make more money if he or she can write the songs, but songwriting ability is not required for a singer to become a star. If you have found someone with a magic voice, you can hire everyone else you need to make the singer's dream come true.

If you think that by listening to a song on the radio that you can determine whether or not it will be a hit, you have missed the point. In order to be a successful lawyer/A&R screener, you have to be able to go into a bar or listen to a demo tape and then make the decision on the singer's unique vocal quality based on what you hear in the less than perfect circumstances. By the time a song gets on the radio, it has already gone through several layers of screening. It better be a hit and the artist better have a unique voice by the time you hear it on the radio or the screening system has broken down and some record company is wasting a lot of money on a pet project.

The Bottom Line

Knowing the law isn't enough. In order to be a competent lawyer, you must understand the music business and what the record companies are looking for in order to effectively represent music industry clients. You must study the contract forms and know what you can and can't negotiate. You need to understand the music business and the current industry standards.

In addition, you have to be familiar with the past and present recording artists so that you can ask the magic question after you listen to a vocalist. You have to be able to give your client honest feedback on his or her prospects of getting a record deal. The only way to be able to do that is to listen to music and be familiar with the vocalists who already have record deals.

To be a successful music lawyer, you have to evolve your skills to include music screening. Now that you know how to listen to music like an A&R person, you should be able to realize your dream of being a successful lawyer in the music business.

E. SONGWRITERS AND PRODUCERS

Producers turn good songs into hits. Producers work the magic that makes a song memorable. Music producers are the equivalent of film directors; they bring creative vision to the project and mold raw material into works of art. Music producers typically charge a flat fee plus a percentage of the album's profits. In addition, producers often claim a portion of the copyright in the underlying musical composition.

The practice of claiming songwriter's credit has long been a tradition among producers who add their names to the copyright forms for creative credit and profit. Songwriters receive mechanical and performance royalties while producers do not. By adding the producer's name to the list of songwriters, the producer is staking a claim to future income to which he or she may not be entitled.

While every creative songwriter deserves songwriter's credit, those who only participated in a tangential way, like producing, arranging, or engineering the song, should not receive songwriter's credit. Arrangements are separately copyrightable, but an arranger does not typically receive credit or royalties as a songwriter. To be a co-author, 17 U.S.C. § 101 of the Copyright Act states, "A 'joint work' is a work prepared by two or more authors with the intention that their contributions be merged into inseparable or interdependent parts of a unitary whole." In addition, "(a) Initial Ownership.—Copyright in a work protected under this title vests initially in the author or authors of the work. The authors of a joint work are co-owners of copyright in the work." 17 U.S.C. § 201.

As the cases below illustrate, authorship of a popular song can provide lifelong income. Dilution of the songwriters' shares is worth fighting over.

GOODMAN v. LEE

United States Court of Appeals, Fifth Circuit, 1987.
815 F.2d 1030.

WILLIAMS, Circuit Judge.

Shirley Goodman brought this action against Audrey and Nikki Lee in the United States District Court for the Eastern District of Louisiana under the Declaratory Judgment Act, 28 U.S.C. § 2201 *et seq.*, and the Copyright Act, 17 U.S.C. § 101 *et seq.* Goodman claimed to have written the song "Let The Good Times Roll" in conjunction with Leonard Lee, the deceased husband and father of appellees. She sought to have the copyright registration changed to reflect her co-authorship. The Lees moved for summary judgment, which the district court granted for lack of subject matter jurisdiction. Because we determine that federal jurisdiction does exist in an action for a declaratory judgment to establish co-authorship under copyright legislation, we reverse and remand for trial on the merits.

I. FACTS

Appellant Shirley Goodman and Leonard Lee grew up in the same neighborhood in New Orleans and had been good friends since early childhood. Both Goodman and Lee were very interested in music and, in 1952, began composing songs together. They also recorded their songs under the professional name of "Shirley and Lee." Their biggest hit, "Let The Good Times Roll," has also been recorded by such musical luminaries as Barbra Streisand, Ray Charles, Roy Orbison, and Jerry Lee Lewis.

Leonard Lee was responsible for managing the business affairs of "Shirley and Lee," including copyright registration of the jointly composed songs. The first copyrights obtained by Lee listed Goodman and Lee as co-authors. Later songs, including "Let The Good Times Roll," were registered only in the name of Leonard Lee. Goodman did not receive any publishing royalties from the songs registered solely under Lee's name.

Goodman claims that she did not learn that the songs were registered only in Lee's name until the original copyrights were up for renewal in 1984. After acquiring this knowledge, she filed an application to have the registration renewed in the names of Shirley Goodman and Leonard Lee as co-authors. Copyright Office regulations provide that the registration could be changed only by the proprietor of the copyright. Goodman then filed suit in district court against Audrey Lee, Leonard Lee's widow, and Nikki Lee, his minor child. She sought a declaratory judgment to the effect that the song "Let The Good Times Roll" was a joint work within the meaning of § 101 of the Copyright Act. She also requested the court to include her name as a co-author with Lee and to order an accounting of all royalty income to which she was otherwise entitled.

The district court granted the Lees' motion for summary judgment dismissing the cause of action for lack of subject matter jurisdiction. Goodman filed the timely notice of appeal.

II.   SUBJECT MATTER JURISDICTION

A federal district court has exclusive original jurisdiction over civil actions which arise under congressional acts relating to copyrights. *See* 28 U.S.C. § 1338(a). "[A]n action 'arises under' the Copyright Act if and only if the complaint is for a remedy expressly granted by the Act ... or asserts a claim requiring constructing of the Act, ... or, at the very least and perhaps more doubtfully, presents a case where a distinctive policy of the Act requires that federal principles control the disposition of the claim." *T.B. Harms Co. v. Eliscu,* 339 F.2d 823, 828 (2d Cir.1964), *cert. denied,* 381 U.S. 915 (1965). Goodman's complaint alleges that she is an actual joint co-author of "Let The Good Times Roll." She also claims that she is entitled to receive one-half of all proceeds from the use and exploitation of that song, which could involve state law issues within our pendent jurisdiction. In any event, the case clearly involves the application and interpretation of the copyright ownership provisions of 17 U.S.C. § 201(a). Therefore, federal jurisdiction over this case was proper, and the district court erred in dismissing Goodman's cause of action.

We reach this conclusion based upon the clear wording of the statute. This view is also confirmed in litigation and by scholarly inquiry. An acknowledged leading case in this area is *Lieberman v. Estate of Chayefsky,* 535 F. Supp. 90 (S.D.N.Y. 1982). *Lieberman* involved a dispute over the ownership of the copyright to the novel and screenplay, "Altered States." As in the case now before us, the plaintiff claimed that he was a co-author of the copyrighted material and that it was a joint work under the definition contained in 17 U.S.C. § 101. The defendant moved to dismiss for lack of subject matter jurisdiction, but the court denied the motion. It determined that federal jurisdiction existed because "the claimed right upon which plaintiff bases his claim arises directly from the statute" and "[r]esolution of the central issue in this case depends upon the application of [the] statutory definition [of 17 U.S.C. § 101]." *Id.* at 91.

The district court, in granting the Lees' motion for summary judgment, relied upon a "line of Southern district in New York cases" which it considered to be "correct in their appraisal of the jurisdiction question." These cases held generally that an action to establish title is not one which "arises under" the Copyright Act and that, therefore, no federal jurisdiction exists. *See, e.g., Rotardier v. Entm't Co. Music Group,* 518 F.Supp. 919 (S.D.N.Y. 1981); *Keith v. Scruggs,* 507 F.Supp. 968 (S.D.N.Y. 1981); *Harrington v. Mure,* 186 F.Supp. 655 (S.D.N.Y. 1960). *Lieberman,* however, has been recognized as presenting the "better view" of the jurisdiction question. *See* 3 *Nimmer on Copyright* § 12.01[A], at 12–7 (1986). Further, Goodman's claim is thoroughly distinguishable from the cases relied upon by the district court. The *Rotardier, Keith,* and *Harrington* cases concerned ownership disputes arising from contractual agreements between the parties. In *Rotardier,* for example, the plaintiff assigned the copyrights for a musical score to the defendant with the understanding that if certain conditions were not met, the copyrights would be reassigned back to the plaintiff. A dispute arose, and Rotardier filed suit in federal district court. The court dismissed the complaint, stating that "[t]he controlling issue involves a dispute over title to a copyright arising from an alleged breach of contract. The determination of this issue is dependent upon principles of common law and equity, not the federal copyright laws." 518 F. Supp. at 921. Thus, the issue involved a contract, the subject of which was a copyright. Goodman's claim, in clear contrast, involves the validity of the copyright itself under the Copyright Act.

III. CONCLUSION

Because we find that exclusive federal district court jurisdiction exists in an action for a declaratory judgment to establish joint authorship of a copyrighted work, the summary judgment of the district court dismissing Shirley Goodman's cause of action against Audrey and Nikki Lee must be reversed.

REVERSED.

C & C ENTERTAINMENT, INC. v. RIOS–SANCHEZ

District Court of Puerto Rico, 2002.
208 F.Supp.2d 139.

CEREZO, District Judge.

This is an action for violation of the Copyright Act of 1976. 17 U.S.C. §§ 101, et. sec. Plaintiff Angel Luis Rivera alleges that he is the composer of a song entitled "Nuestro Amor es Veneno" ["Veneno"]. He sold the copyright to plaintiff Carlos Donato d/b/a/Yagrumo Music which is now incorporated as C & C Entertainment. [The plaintiffs will all be referred to as Rivera].

Rivera alleges that defendant Pascual Castillo Paredes falsely claimed authorship of "Veneno" and, along with codefendant Lamrica Agency, Inc., obtained a false copyright shortly after plaintiff's own copyright was filed. Plaintiffs' copyright was registered on May 28, 1998. Castillo Paredes' copyright over the same song, listing himself as the composer, is dated June 28, 1998. GRS Records published the song in an album which they produced. Defendant Disco Hit was contracted by its co-defendants to manufacture the compact discs and distribute them. Prior to the dispute and the removal of the album from the market, the disc jacket listed Rivera as the sole author of the song.

Plaintiffs allege that defendants have acted in concert to avoid paying royalties to which he is entitled, thus violating his copyright

This action is before us on three separate Motions for Summary Judgment; Disco Hit, Lamrica Agency, and GRS Records and Castillo. Plaintiffs filed an opposition to the first two motions; the third motion is unopposed. Disco Hit replied to the opposition.

Disco Hit, in its Motion to Dismiss alleges that it merely manufactured and distributed the album, of which "Veneno" was one song. All the material and composer credits were supplied by the record company. The dispute engendering this action began after the album was distributed and Disco Hit alleges that Rivera did not register his copyright until the dispute over royalties arose. It further points out that Rivera was listed as the composer of the song on the disc cover. Disco Hit states that song was removed from the album as soon as it learned of the dispute.

Lamrica alleges that it obtained the rights to "Veneno" from Castillo Paredes who claimed to be the composer and owner of the rights to the song. It further alleges that this action is a contract suit between Rivera and Castillo Paredes. Lamrica argues that there is joint ownership of the song between Rivera and Castillo *or,* in the alternative, that no effort to copyright the song was made until after it was already in the public domain.

Plaintiff's factual and legal theory includes the fact that Rivera "granted a nonexclusive license to defendants to reproduce [Veneno] rearranged as a 'bachata' by Pascual Castillo Paredes, who himself and with the other co-defendants incorporated such song . . . recognizing the author . . . to be Rivera, for which song Rivera expected to be paid royalties."

GRS Records and Pascual Castillo–Paredes' Motion for Summary Judgment relies heavily on Rivera's admission in his deposition testimony that he gave Castillo-Paredes the lyrics with the intention that they be arranged as a bachata, that Rivera approved the music over the telephone, approved the change of title, and all albums produced gave him the credit for the song. They contend that Rivera gave defendants' an implied license to use the lyrics, and compose the music for them and, therefore, the song is a "joint work" as defined by Copyright Act 17 U.S.C. § 101.

Plaintiff has acknowledged in his deposition that he gave Castillo–Paredes the lyrics for the express purpose of composing bachata music for it and including it in his album. * * * In his opposition to the motions for summary judgment there is no allegation that the defendants exploited the song beyond the scope of the non-exclusive license that the plaintiff admittedly gave Castillo–Paredes. As to the concept of joint authorship raised by defendants, plaintiff has acknowledged in his deposition that he gave Castillo–Paredes the lyrics for the express purpose of composing "bachata" music for it and including it in his album. * * *

A co-authorship claimant bears the burden of establishing that each of the putative coauthors (1) made independently copyrightable contributions to the work; and (2) fully intended to be co-authors. *Thomson v. Larson* 147 F.3d 195 (2nd Cir.1998) citing *Childress v. Taylor* 945 F.2d 500 (2nd Cir.1991) which establishes "the test." *Childress* recognizes, however, that the issue of co-authorship intent "requires less exacting consideration in the context of traditional forms of collaboration", such as between the creators of the lyrics and music of a song and that "parts of a unitary whole are 'interdependent' when they have some meaning standing alone but achieve their primary significance because of their combined effect *as in the case of the words and music of a song.*" *Id.*, at 505, 503. Before that, in *Edward B. Marks Music Corp. v. Jerry Vogel Music Co.,* 140 F.2d 268 (2nd Cir.1944) Judge Learned Hand endorsed the formulation of a "joint work" or "joint authorship." There, a lyricist and composer were found to be co-authors where the lyricist wrote the words for the song ('December and May'), intending that someone else would eventually compose the music for those particular words. Judge Hand masterfully explains the concept of "joint work" in this case, at page 267: [I]f one of several authors took out the copyright in his own name upon a joint work, the copyright was valid, but the copyright owner held it upon a constructive trust for the other authors....

[I]t makes no difference whether the authors work in concert, or even whether they know each other; it is enough that they mean their contributions to be complementary in the sense that they are to be embodied in a single work to be performed as such. That was the case here: Marks wrote the words for a song; Loraine composed the music as music for that song. It is true that each knew that his part could be used separately; the words, as a 'lyric;' the melody as music. But that was not their purpose; the words and the music were to be enjoyed and performed together; unlike the parts of a 'composite work,' each of which is intended to be used separately, and whose only unity is that they are bound together.... The popularity of a song turns upon both the words and the music; the share of each in its success cannot be appraised; they interpenetrate each other as much as the notes of the melody, or separate words of the 'lyric.' The value of the privilege of renewal is measured by the survival of their combined power to please the public taste. To allow the author to prevent the composer, or the composer to prevent the author, from exploiting the power to please, would be to allow him to deprive his fellow of the most valuable part of his contribution; to take away the kernel and leave him only the husk.

The undisputed facts of this case bring it within these parameters: Rivera gave Castillo–Paredes the words to the song, intending that the latter write the music ("bachata") and include it in his album. The evidence shows that when plaintiff chose Castillo–Paredes to compose the music for "Veneno" he intended that the words and the music be enjoyed and performed together. We, therefore, find that the song "Veneno" was the joint work of plaintiff and Castillo–Paredes and defendants did not infringe on Rivera's copyright.

With regard to the allegation of infringement by Castillo–Paredes for having registered a copyright over the same material under his name, one month after plaintiff did so, we find this is not material to the infringement issue: 17 U.S.C. § 201(a) states in pertinent part, ". . . copyright in a work protected under this title vests initially in the author or authors of the work. The authors of a joint work are co-owners of the copyright in the work." As composer of the music, Castillo–Paredes would have an ownership interest in the copyright, too.

Rivera further contends that his copyright has been infringed by defendants failure to pay him royalties. Rivera cites the answers to his interrogatories #5 and #6 as evidence of the agreement for royalties: 5. [After] *noticing that the royalties were forthcoming,* . . . Rivera visited Mr. Richard Viera. . . . 6. [O]n many times after that, both plaintiff Mr. Rivera and Mr. Castillo ratified *their unspoken agreement that he would receive royalties for the song.* [court's emphasis.] The statement reveals any terms of the alleged agreement. The quotes chosen by Rivera demonstrates that there was no concrete agreement on the amount of royalties, or even if royalties were to be paid for the lyrics.

Plaintiffs' sole remedy for a breach of a royalty agreement, however, would be an action for monetary damages—the Copyright Act need not be construed. *Royal v. Leading Edge Products, Inc.* 833 F.2d 1, 3 (1st Cir. 1987). The issue is, therefore, a contractual one and, even though the contract concerns a copyright, it does not grant the federal courts jurisdiction over what is essentially a garden variety contract dispute. *Id.,* at p. 5. This is simply a state law claim which was not even asserted in the complaint.

For the above-stated reasons, we conclude that Castillo–Paredes had a non-exclusive license to compose music to, and to record and distribute plaintiffs' song, "Veneno" in the album, *Que me las pegues, pero que no me dejes,* that the song was the joint work of plaintiff and Castillo–Paredes as co-authors, and that therefore, defendants have not infringed on plaintiffs' copyright. Accordingly, the Motions for Summary Judgment are GRANTED. * * *

Notes

1. The problem of each author's contribution is discussed in the *Childress* case mentioned above. A more substantial issue arising under the statutory definition of "joint work" is whether the contribution of each joint author must be copyrightable or only the combined result of their joint efforts must be copyrightable. The *Nimmer* treatise argues against a requirement of copyrightability of each author's contribution. 1 NIMMER ON COPYRIGHT § 6.07. Professor Goldstein takes the contrary view. *See* 1 PAUL GOLDSTEIN, COPYRIGHT: PRINCIPLES, LAW AND PRACTICE § 4.2.1.2 (1989); *see also* WILLIAM F. PATRY, LATMAN'S THE COPYRIGHT LAW 116 (6th ed. 1986) (hereinafter "*Latman*"). The case law supports a requirement of copyrightability of each contribution. *See* M.G.B. Homes, Inc. v. Ameron Homes, Inc., 903 F.2d 1486, 1493 (11th Cir.1990). The Register of Copyrights strongly supports this view, arguing that it is required by the statutory standard of "authorship" and perhaps by the Constitution. *See Moral Rights in Our Copyright Laws: Hearings on S. 1198 and S. 1253 Before the Subcomm. on Patents, Copyrights and Trademarks of the Senate Comm. on the Judiciary,* 101st Cong., 1st Sess. 210–11 (1989) (statement of Ralph Oman); Childress v. Taylor, 945 F.2d 500, 506 (2d Cir. 1991).

2. In *Lamothe v. Atlantic Recording Corp.*, the issue was whether there was sufficient evidence of violation of one type of unfair competition under the Lanham Act known as "passing off." This involves selling a good of one person's creation under the name of another. In *Lamothe*, two songs entitled "Scene of the Crime" and "I'm Insane" were authored by members of the band Mac Meda. The group broke up and one member (Crosby) joined another group called "RATT." The songs were later released by "RATT" on one of their albums. Authorship of the songs was attributed only to Crosby and one other member who licensed the songs. Lamothe (plaintiff) and another songwriter did not receive any recognition. The court rejected the defense that the producer was not liable because the songs were licensed. The court held that the defendant is liable if the license affixed incomplete authorship regardless of knowledge. Lamothe v. Atlantic Recording Corp., 847 F.2d 1403 (9th Cir. 1988).

Chapter 15

COPYRIGHT PROTECTION OF MUSIC

Copyright protection of music includes the protection of musical compositions and sound recordings. The musical composition may have been created as a song from its inception or it may be a joint work where the lyrics and music are written by one or more authors. In order for the musical composition to be a joint work, the authors had to have intended to contribute their lyrics or music to create the new, copyrightable, musical composition. All musical compositions are protected from the moment they are fixed in a tangible medium of expression. The songwriters are usually the original owners of the musical compositions. Music publishing companies typically administer songwriters' copyrights.

Sound recordings are usually created in the studio and are originally fixed on multi-track tape. The sound recording is protected as soon as it is fixed in a tangible medium of expression. By definition, it is protected when made.

Registration with the Library of Congress is required before certain rights attach to the protected sound recordings and musical compositions. Basically, registration is required before the copyright owner can sue in federal court for an act of infringement. A full discussion of the importance of formal registration is beyond the scope of this book and best left to a course on copyright law.

A. ORIGINALITY IN DERIVATIVE WORKS

Originality is one of the basic requirements of a work in determining whether it is copyrightable. Because the notes on the musical scale are known, all songwriters must use the same set or sub-set of notes when writing a song. The originality standard is judged on the selection and order of arrangement of the notes. The choice of notes, scales, duration, and instrumentation, and the choice of words (lyrics) and their sequence, duration, and emphasis all contribute to the individual creativity of a particular musical composition and sound recording.

Sampling has become a widely used method of taking from previously copyrighted material, either the lyrics or music or both, from a sound

703

recording, and using it to create a new derivative work. This technique has become widespread in the genre of rap music.

NEWTON v. DIAMOND

United States District Court, California, 2002.
204 F.Supp.2d 1244.

MANELLA, District Judge.

I. INTRODUCTION

The Beastie Boys, an alternative rock and hip-hop band, and their business associates ("Defendants") sampled a six-second, three-note sequence of a flute composition composed and performed by James W. Newton, Jr. ("Plaintiff"). Plaintiff concedes that Defendants licensed the sound recording of his work, but alleges that Defendants' use of the sample infringed upon the underlying musical composition. * * *

II. FACTS

* * * "The practice of sampling portions of pre-existing recordings and compositions into new songs is apparently common among performers of the genre known as rap. Musicians sample pre-existing works either digitally, by lifting part of a song from a pre-existing master recording and feeding it through a digital sampler, or by hiring musicians who replay or re-sing portions of the pre-existing composition." *Williams v. Broadus*, 60 U.S.P.Q. 2d 1051 (S.D.N.Y. 2001).

Plaintiff, a flautist and composer, is the sole author of the musical composition *Choir*, which was registered with the Copyright Office in 1978. * * * Plaintiff asserts that *Choir* is one of multiple songs permissibly covered by a single copyright registration. It is undisputed that Plaintiff holds a valid copyright to the musical composition at issue in this case. It is also undisputed that Plaintiff has no rights to the sound recording of his performance of *Choir,* having licensed it to ECM Records in 1981.

* * * [T]he Beastie Boys, an alternative rock and hip-hop band, obtained a license from ECM Records to sample the copyrighted sound recording of Plaintiff's performance of *Choir.* Pursuant to their license, Defendants copied a three-note sequence with one background note, approximately six seconds long, from *Choir* and looped the passage throughout their song, *Pass the Mic.* * * * It is undisputed that *Choir* and *Pass the Mic* "are substantially dissimilar in concept and feel, that is, in there [sic] overall thrust and meaning." * * *

IV DISCUSSION

A. Copyright Act Claim * * *

Sound recordings and their underlying musical compositions are separate works with their own distinct copyrights. See 17 U.S.C. § 102 (a)(2), (7). "When a copyrighted song is recorded on a phonorecord, there are two separate copyrights: one in the musical composition and the other in the sound recording." T.B. Harms Co. v. Jem Records, Inc., 655 F.Supp. 1575, 1576 (D.N.J. 1987). * * *

It is undisputed that Plaintiff has no rights to the *sound recording* of *his* performance of *Choir,* having licensed it for a fee to ECM Records, who, in turn, granted Defendants a license to sample it. However, Plaintiff contends that Defendants' sampling infringed upon his underlying musical composition. * * *

Plaintiff largely ignores the distinction between musical compositions and sound recordings. Plaintiff argues only that his own techniques render his musical composition unique, as they contribute "something more than a merely trivial variation, something recognizably [his] own" to a prior expression. *ZZ Top v. Chrysler Corp.*, 54 F.Supp.2d 983 (W.D. Wa. 1999). * * * While Plaintiff concedes that he did not invent generic vocalization, simultaneously singing and playing the flute, he argues that his unique approach to vocalization, in particular using breath control to emphasize certain notes, * * * renders *Choir* original. Plaintiff also identifies his technique of overblowing the "C" note to produce multiple pitches ("multiphonics") as the source of his work's originality. * * *

In assessing originality, courts must be "mindful of the limited number of notes and chords available to composers and the resulting fact that common themes frequently appear in various compositions, especially in popular music." *Gaste v. Kaiserman*, 863 F.2d 1061, 1068 (2d Cir. 1988). * * * In the instant case, Plaintiff's three-note sequence (C—D-flat—C) with one background note (C), segregated from the entire piece, cannot be protected, as it is not original as a matter of law. Many courts have found that nearly identical or more substantial samples are not susceptible to copyright protection. In *Jean v. Bug Music, Inc.*, 2002 WL 287786 (S.D.N.Y. Feb. 27, 2002), the defendant allegedly copied a three-note sequence consisting of "C," followed by a "B-flat," followed by another "C," accompanied by the lyric "clap your hands." The court held that this excerpt of the song at issue could not be protected by the plaintiff's copyright "because the sequence of the three notes and the lyrics lack the requisite originality." *Id.* at 5. * * *

In *McDonald v. Multimedia Enter., Inc.*, 20 U.S.P.Q. 2d 1372 (S.D.N.Y. 1991), the court found that the three-note sequence the defendant allegedly misappropriated from the plaintiff's jingle could not be protected by copyright. The court noted the "absurdity" of Plaintiff's claim, given that the three-note sequence is a "common and much-used tone in traditional western music." *Id.* at 1375. * * *

Plaintiff identifies cases in which courts have held that short sequences of notes may be protected by copyright. However, those cases involved sequences consisting of more than three notes. * * * Cases finding that sequences of less than six notes could be qualitatively distinctive have involved: 1) sequences with accompanying lyrics; 2) sequences at the heart of the musical compositions; 3) sequences and lyrics that were repetitive; and/or 4) sequences that were based upon analyses of both the written composition and the sound recording. *See, Santrayll v. Burrell,* 39 U.S.P.Q. 2d 1052, 1054 (S.D.N.Y. 1996) (one measure "hook" and repetition of word "uh-oh" may be distinctive). * * *

In sum, Plaintiff identifies nothing distinctive about the three-note sequence taken from his musical composition. Neither the two notes in the three-note sequence, the common vocalization technique, nor the combination thereof imparts qualitative importance or distinctiveness to the six-second excerpt. * * * [Plaintiff's motion for summary judgment is denied.]

B. COPYRIGHT OWNERSHIP AND TRANSFER

Copyright ownership vests in the author of the original work. When an individual creates a work for him or herself, authorship is generally not in question. When an individual creates a work at the behest of a third party, the work is generally considered a "work for hire" and the third party is considered the author. When two or more people contribute to a work, it is generally considered a joint work and all of the contributors are considered co-authors. Transfers of copyright ownership require a writing.

1. JOINT WORKS AND JOINT OWNERSHIP

MORRILL v. THE SMASHING PUMPKINS

United States District Court, California, 2001.
157 F.Supp.2d 1120.

ORDER GRANTING DEFENDANTS' MOTION FOR SUMMARY JUDGMENT

MORENO, District Judge

Presently before the Court are Defendants The Smashing Pumpkins, Billy Corgan, Virgin Records America, and Modi-vational Films' Motion for Summary Judgment. Having considered the moving papers, the opposition, the reply, and oral argument in support thereof, the Court hereby *grants* Defendants' Motion for the following reasons.

I.

Statement of Facts

The allegations in this case arise from events transpiring in St. Petersburg, Florida in 1986. At that time, Plaintiffs Jonathan Morrill and J.M. Productions ("Morrill") completed an "original music video/documentary" entitled "Video Marked," which depicted Defendant Corgan and his then-existing music group, The Marked. "The purpose of this endeavor was to create an assortment of music videos for Corgan and his bandmates in order to help them get started with their musical careers."

Video Marked was created around the time when Corgan and The Marked were staying at Morrill's home in St. Petersburg. Upon completion of the video, Video Marked was played at some clubs where The Marked performed, as a promotional tool for the band. At some point later in 1986, Corgan left St. Petersburg. After Corgan's departure, Morrill noticed that one of the copies of Video Marked was missing, and his "prime suspect" was Corgan. Morrill never mentioned the missing video to Corgan, nor did he pursue any further use of Video Marked until 1996, when he approached Corgan at a Smashing Pumpkins concert and inquired whether Corgan would consider marketing Video Marked. Upon Corgan's refusal, Morrill abandoned any planned use of Video Marked.

Allegedly unbeknownst to Morrill, in 1994 Defendants Corgan, The Smashing Pumpkins, and Virgin Records America released a video entitled "Vieuphoria," which contained short clips of images taken from Video Marked. Vieuphoria, a ninety-minute video, contained about forty-five seconds of material from Video Marked. Although Vieuphoria was released in 1994, it was not until 1998 that Plaintiff purportedly learned of its existence.

On May 22, 2000, Morrill filed suit in the Superior Court of the State of California, County of Los Angeles. Removal to this Court was ordered because of the likelihood that Plaintiffs' claims were at bottom disguised copyright claims subject to preemption under 17 U.S.C. § 301(a). Plaintiffs moved to remand and Defendants moved for judgment on the pleadings pursuant to Federal Rule of Civil Procedure 12(c). This Court dismissed Plaintiffs motion and treated Defendants' motion as a motion for summary judgment, ultimately dismissing Plaintiffs' breach of contract, negligent misrepresentation, and constructive trust claims. Plaintiffs filed a First Amended Complaint, followed by a Second Amended Complaint. On July 19, 2001, Defendants moved for summary judgment on Plaintiffs' remaining claims for copyright infringement, breach of confidence, fraud and deceit, declaratory relief, and injunctive relief. Defendants' Motion is presently before this Court. * * *

III.

Analysis

A. *Copyright Infringement*

Morrill alleges that he is the sole owner of the copyright for Video Marked. He asserts that the certificate of registration he obtained in 1998 from the Register of Copyrights is proof of his sole copyright ownership. Morrill further contends that use, without his authorization, of portions of Video Marked in The Smashing Pumpkins' video, Vieuphoria, is an infringement of his copyright in Video Marked.

Defendants allege that Morrill's copyright infringement claims are invalid for several reasons: (1) Defendant Corgan is a joint author of Video Marked and therefore cannot be held liable for infringing the copyright of a work he co-owns; (2) Morrill's claims are barred by the copyright statute of limitations, which states: "[n]o civil action shall be maintained under the provisions of this title unless it is commenced within three years after the claim accrued," 17 U.S.C. § 507(b); and (3) Morrill's claims are barred by the doctrine of laches. * * *

Section 101 of the Copyright Act of 1976 defines a "joint work": "A 'joint work' is a work prepared by two or more authors with the intention that their contributions be merged into inseparable or interdependent parts of a unitary whole." 17 U.S.C. § 101. As the Ninth Circuit has determined, "for a work to be a 'joint work' there must be (1) a copyrightable work, (2) two or more 'authors,' and (3) the authors must intend their contributions be merged into inseparable or interdependent parts of a unitary whole." *Aalmuhammed v. Lee*, 202 F.3d 1227, 1231 (9th Cir. 2000).

It is undisputed that Video Marked is a copyrightable work and that it was intended to serve as a unitary whole, specifically as a music video created to promote Defendant Corgan and his band, The Marked. It is also undisputed that Morrill directed, produced, and edited the video and that Corgan and The Marked composed and performed the music played in the video. Both contributions, Morrill's filming and editing of the video and Corgan's performance and composition of the songs, satisfy the requisite level of copyrightable expression necessary to support a claim of joint authorship. *See Ashton–Tate Corp. v. Ross*, 916 F.2d 516, 521 (9th Cir. 1990) ("our circuit holds that joint authorship requires each author to make an independently copyrightable contribution").

Merely making a copyrightable contribution is not enough to establish joint authorship, however. *See Aalmuhammed*, 202 F.3d at 1232 ("authorship is not the same thing as making a valuable and copyrightable contribution"). Each contributor must also be deemed an "author" of the work. The Ninth Circuit's *Aalmuhammed* decision lists three criteria for determining, in the absence of a contract, whether a contributor should be considered an "author" for the purpose of joint authorship: (1) whether the purported author controls the work and is " 'the inventive or master mind' who 'creates, or gives effect to the idea,' " *Aalmuhammed*, 202 F.3d at 1234 (quoting *Burrow-Giles Lithographic Co. v. Sarony*, 111 U.S. 53, 61 (1884)); (2) whether the "putative coauthors make objective manifestations of shared intent to be coauthors," *Id.;* and (3) whether "the audience appeal of the work turns on both contributions and 'the share of each in its success cannot be appraised.' " *Id.* (quoting *Edward B. Marks Music Corp. v. Jerry Vogel Music Co.*, 140 F.2d 266, 267 (2d Cir. 1944)).

While these factors are helpful in determining whether a contributor should be considered a joint author of the work, the *Aalmuhammed* court noted that "[t]he factors articulated in this decision ... cannot be reduced to a rigid formula, because the creative relationships to which they apply vary too much." *Aalmuhammed*, 202 F.3d at 1235. In applying these three criteria to the facts involved in *Aalmuhammed*, the

Ninth Circuit found that a consultant on Spike Lee's movie, "Malcolm X," was not a joint author of the film. The court determined that Aalmuhammed's work as an "Islamic Technical Consultant," which included some original script writing, did not rise to the level of control, objective intent, and impact on the film's success necessary to satisfy the requirements for joint authorship.

Morrill's claim that he is the sole author of Video Marked attempts to trace the *Aalmuhammed* factors. First, he asserts that he "exercised total control over the work." Morrill alleges that he shot the videos, chose the locations, directed every individual during shooting, and edited the final product by himself. Second, he contends that the intent of the parties was for Morrill to be the video's sole author. Morrill supports this claim with evidence that he affixed his name as the producer on several segments of Video Marked, and that he retained sole possession of the copies of Video Marked. Morrill does not discuss the third *Aalmuhammed* factor, the source of the audience appeal in the work.

Morrill's attempt to paint himself as the sole force behind Video Marked misses the primary purpose of his work: he was shooting a *music* video. The video's music was therefore the central component of the completed work. While Morrill's filming, editing, and producing may have helped shape and present The Marked's music for its audience, without the music itself Video Marked would not exist. Morrill's discussion of ownership and control omits the fact that it was Corgan and his band who wrote and performed the songs filmed by Morrill. Although Morrill may have directed the production and editing of the video, Corgan and The Marked had sole control over the writing and the performing of the video's music. *See Forward v. Thorogood,* 985 F.2d 604, 605 (1st Cir. 1993) ("The performer of a musical work is the author, as it were, of the performance."). In a music video, the creator of the songs and the creator of the images are both "the inventive or master mind[s]" whose work comes together to produce a unitary whole. *See Aalmuhammed,* 202 F.3d at 1229. Since both parties had creative control over separate and indispensable elements of the completed product, the first *Aalmuhammed* factor favors a finding of joint authorship.

The other two criteria discussed by the court in *Aalmuhammed* also suggest joint authorship of Video Marked. First, the parties' words and behavior evidences an intent to be co-authors of the video. Morrill videotaped The Marked as a promotional tool for the band; he admits that Video Marked was shown to audiences at venues where The Marked was performing. In his Complaint, Morrill described Video Marked as a work "created with Corgan and his band." In his deposition, Morrill referred to Video Marked on multiple occasions as a "collaboration" between himself and Corgan. Further, in 1996 Morrill asked Corgan for his permission to market Video Marked. These statements and actions by Morrill are inconsistent with an intent to be the video's sole author. Instead, Morrill's words and actions appear to be "objective manifestations of a shared intent to be coauthors." *Aalmuhammed,* 202 F.3d at 1234.

Morrill's claim that the parties had agreed that Morrill was to be the sole author of Video Marked is based on, if anything, his own subjective intent. Morrill contends that his affixation of his name as the producer of the video signifies that he was the sole author. However, "producer" does not necessarily mean "author." *See Aalmuhammed,* 202 F.3d at 1232 (noting that an author of a movie might be a director, a star, a producer, a cinematographer, an animator, or a composer).

Morrill also asserts that since he retained possession of all of the copies of Video Marked, he was its sole owner. Mere possession of a videotape does not translate into copyright ownership, however. The case of *Forward v. Thorogood,* 985 F.2d 604 (1st Cir. 1993), is directly on point. The plaintiff in *Forward* had paid for and arranged recording sessions for the band, George Thorogood and the Destroyers. After the sessions were complete, the band had agreed that the plaintiff could keep the tapes for his own enjoyment. Later, the plaintiff claimed that his possession of the tapes made him the sole owner of the copyright to the tapes. The First Circuit upheld the district court's determination that the mere agreement by the band that the plaintiff could have physical possession of its recording tapes did not mean that band had consented to convey its interest in the copyright of those tapes to the plaintiff. *Id.* at 606. Like the plaintiff in *Forward,* Morrill's possession of the copies of Video Marked does not translate into sole copyright ownership of the tapes. Further, Morrill's own failure to trace or recover his missing copy of Video Marked, after he suspected that Corgan had taken it, discredits his claim of sole ownership.

Finally, Morrill's own statements, made during his deposition, reveal the parties' shared intent to create a joint work. In recounting his 1996 conversation with Corgan in which Morrill requested permission to use Video Marked, Morrill stated, "I said, 'Billy, now that you have achieved this superstar status, don't you think that *our early collaborations* have certain marketability?' " When Corgan turned down Morrill's offer, Morrill recalled thinking, "I appreciated an artist not being satisfied with the quality of *his work* and not wanting to have it marketed." Morrill remembered that Corgan "expressed an opinion on not wanting [Video Marked] to be marketed because of the poor audio quality on his end. He loved the video aspects that I took care of." Thus, Morrill's own deposition describes a shared intent to be joint authors; the parties agreed that Morrill would execute "video aspects" and Corgan would supply the music.

Morrill does not discuss the third *Aalmuhammed* factor, the source of the audience appeal of the work. *See Aalmuhammed,* 202 F.3d at 1234. At the time when Video Marked was first displayed, at the clubs where The Marked was playing, the appeal of the work presumably was based on the audience's ability to hear additional performances by the band and to view the band in a different light. After Corgan's new band, The Smashing Pumpkins, gained success, the appeal of "View Marked" was most likely based on the audience's ability to view images of a younger Corgan. This is suggested by the packaging for Vieuphoria, which advertises "super secret, super special extra stuff shot by the band." Since the audience appeal, then, rests both on the video's visual aspects and on the composition and performance of the music, this factor also weighs in favor of finding View Marked to be a joint work.

Notwithstanding the *Aalmuhammed* factors, Morrill additionally asserts that the certificate of registration he obtained from the Register of Copyrights demonstrates that he is the sole author of Video Marked. This registration did not occur until 1998, however, about twelve years after the video's initial publication. Section 410(c) of the Copyright Act states that a certificate of registration is prima facie evidence of the validity of the copyright only if registration occurred "before or within five years after first publication of the work." 17 U.S.C. § 410(c). In cases where registration occurs more than five years after initial publication, "[i]t is within the court's discretion what weight to give the copyright registrations in determining the validity of the copyright interests of those works for which plaintiffs are not entitled to an automatic presumption of validity." *Religious Tech Center v. Netcom On–Line Comm. Serv., Inc.*, 923 F.Supp. 1231, 1242 (N.D. Cal. 1995).

Here, as discussed above, all three factors discussed by the *Aalmuhammed* court point towards a finding of joint authorship for Video Marked. This music video was created by two authors, the video's producer and the band itself, with the intention that their respective contributions be merged into inseparable parts of a unitary whole. In discussing the question, "Who, in the absence of a contract, can be considered an author of a movie?" the Ninth Circuit in *Aalmuhammed* stated that depending on the type of movie, different individuals might be considered its author. Most significantly, the court noted, "[w]here the visual aspect of the movie is especially important, the chief cinematographer might be regarded as the author. And for, say, a Disney animated movie like 'The Jungle Book,' [the author] might perhaps be the animators and the composers of the music." *Aalmuhammed*, 202 F.3d at 1232. Similarly, for a music video, authorship is found in both the band's music and the director's visual animation of the band.

In the case of a sound recording, the law is clear: absent an employment relationship or express assignment of copyright, the copyright for the sound recording "will be either exclusively in the performing artists, or (assuming an original contribution by the sound engineers, editors, etc., as employees of the record producer), a joint ownership between the record producer and the performing artists." M. Nimmer & D. Nimmer, 1 *Nimmer on Copyright* § 2.10[A] [3] (2001). The case of a music video is equally clear: absent a written agreement, the copyright for the music video is a joint ownership between the performing artists and the video's producer (assuming an original contribution by the producer or an employee of the producer). [footnote omitted]. Therefore, this court finds that Corgan is a joint author of View Marked.

As a joint author, Corgan cannot be held liable for copyright infringement based on his use of View Marked in The Smashing Pumpkins' video, Vieuphoria. Each author of a joint work is a tenant in common. *See Picture Music, Inc. v. Bourne, Inc.,* 314 F.Supp. 640, 646 (S.D.N.Y. 1970). "A co-owner of a copyright cannot be liable to another co-owner for infringement of the copyright." *Oddo v. Ries,* 743 F.2d 630, 632–33 (9th Cir. 1984). The fact that Corgan used only visual elements of View Marked in Vieuphoria does not subject him to liability for copyright infringement; since a joint work is created as a unitary whole, a joint author can use or license any portion of the joint work without infringing its copyright. *Id.* at 633. Morrill therefore has no standing to sue Corgan for infringement of the copyright in View Marked.

Finally, Corgan's position as a joint author of View Marked gives him the power to grant a non-exclusive license for the use of this work. *See Effects Assocs., Inc. v. Cohen,* 908 F.2d 555, 558–59 (9th Cir. 1990). Consistent with this right, Corgan granted Defendant Virgin Records America a non-exclusive license to distribute Vieuphoria, which contained scenes from View Marked. A non-exclusive license to use a joint work need not be explicit. *See id.* By conveying a video that used material from his joint work, Corgan impliedly granted a non-exclusive license to Virgin to distribute this material. Virgin, as a non-exclusive licensee of a copyright co-owner, therefore cannot be subject to copyright liability for its use of Video Marked.

Based on the foregoing discussion, Defendants' Motion for Summary Judgment on Plaintiffs' claim of copyright infringement is *granted.* * * *

IV.

Conclusion

For the reasons stated above, Defendants' Motion for Summary Judgment is hereby *granted.*

IT IS SO ORDERED.

2. PRE–1972 SOUND RECORDINGS

The 1909 Copyright Act still has relevance to practitioners in the music business. Whether a work has entered the public domain can mean the difference between winning or losing a copyright infringement suit when the defendant has used a previously written song.

Prior to Congressional action in 1997, the copyright status of thousands of songs recorded prior to January 1, 1978, the effective date of the 1976 Act, was in question. Conflicting rulings from different federal circuit decisions left many pre–1978 songs either in the public domain and free for all to use, or protected by common law copyright. This split of authority also called into question the validity of thousands of licensing agreements and assignments of ownership related to musical works created before 1978.

LONE RANGER TELEVISION, INC.
v. PROGRAM RADIO CORP.

United States Court of Appeals, Ninth Circuit, 1984.
740 F.2d 718.

WALLACE, Circuit Judge.

* * * The Lone Ranger, Incorporated, owned several original scripts for radio plays about the Lone Ranger, a fictitious early Western hero. * * * By 1954 the company held federal copyrights in all fifteen scripts. Meanwhile, it had recorded a production of each episode on magnetic tape. It first broadcast the radio plays in 1953 and 1954. * * * The copyrights in all fifteen scripts remained valid, either in their original term or by renewal. * * *

In 1979, Jim Lewis, a former radio announcer, began unlicensed leasing of Lone Ranger episodes to radio stations. He bought reel-to-reel copies of the tapes from some collectors and re-mixed the recordings onto broadcast cartridges for radio play. The original tapes contained a copyright notice by The Lone Ranger, Incorporated at the end of each episode. Lewis's tapes reproduced this notice, although with disputed clarity. * * * Lone Ranger TV sued Lewis and his two distribution companies (including Program Radio) in federal district court in California, claiming infringement of its federal copyrights in the fifteen scripts and conversion of its intangible property rights in the tapes. * * *

The Copyright Act of 1909 did not permit owners of copyrights in scripts to copyright separately any sound recordings produced from them. When the 1909 Act was repealed by the Copyright Act of 1976, protection of sound recordings of copyrighted scripts was not extended to those "fixed" for playing before 1972. *See Goldstein v. California,* 412 U.S. 546 (1973). Consequently, Lone Ranger TV has never registered any separate federal copyrights in the Lone Ranger tapes. Program Radio argues that, in the absence of such separate copyrights, duplication and distribution of the tapes cannot amount to a federal infringement. * * *

Program Radio admits that Lone Ranger TV's licensed broadcasts, leases, and sales of recordings based on the scripts have not dedicated the scripts to the public domain for purposes of federal copyright protection. * * * It continues to claim, however, that Lone Ranger TV has not properly recorded the transfers of title in the scripts' copyrights, and thus may not sue for their infringement. * * *

Although Lone Ranger TV holds valid copyrights in the scripts. Program Radio correctly refused to consider the tapes produced by the copyright owners as "copies" of the scripts under the 1909 Act. * * * However, the 1909 Act not only restricted to the copyright holder the right to copy an original writing, it also restricted to the holder the sole rights to prepare derivative works from a literary writing. * * * These provisions give the copyright holder an exclusive right to derivative productions from his copyrighted scripts. * * * The Lone Ranger tapes meet this test: the contribution of independent expression by the actors, together with the contribution of independent expression by the special production methods of taping and editing for radio, effectively created a new work for a market different from both the market for printed scripts and the market for live dramas. * * *

In duplicating, remixing, and distributing the Lone Ranger tapes, Lewis in effect sought to manufacture and publish his own derivative work from the underlying scripts or make his own public production of the underlying scripts, just as if he had hired the actors, sound effects crew, and producers originally used for the tapes to do a second interpretation of the scripts for an audience. * * * [I]nterference with Lone Ranger TV's exclusive derivative rights in the scripts constitutes infringement. * * *

[T]he protection of derivative rights extends beyond mere protection against unauthorized copying. * * * It makes no difference that the derivation may not satisfy certain requirements for statutory copyright registration itself. * * * [W]e hold the district court did not abuse its discretion. * * * AFFIRMED.

LA CIENEGA MUSIC v. ZZ TOP

United States Court of Appeals, Ninth Circuit, 1995.
53 F.3d 950.

O'SCANNLAIN, Circuit Judge.

* * * In its copyright infringement suit against the Texas blues-rock band "ZZ Top" and others, La Cienega Music Company ("La Cienega") accuses them of plagiarism in the composition of the song "La Grange," which the band wrote and recorded over twenty years ago. The song, which is ZZ Top's signature song, has had global circulation as a phonorecord, has been recorded by other prominent artists, has been prominently featured in a national television advertising campaign, and has been performed at thousands of ZZ Top concerts.

In 1948, John Lee Hooker and Bernard Besman wrote a musical composition called *Boogie Chillen*. * * * Later, Hooker assigned his rights in the composition to Besman, who now is the sole proprietor of La Cienega. Besman registered *Boogie Chillen* with the Copyright Office in 1967. * * *

Besman states that, upon investigation, he realized that *La Grange* was very similar to the *Boogie Chillen* songs. Besman then notified the publisher of *La Grange*, Hamstein Music Company, that it was infringing upon his copyright. * * *

ZZ Top filed a 12(b)(6) motion asserting that (1) the compositions were within the public domain, and therefore were not protected by copyright, and (2) even if the compositions had been protected at the time that ZZ Top released *La Grange*, La Cienega's action was barred by a statute of limitations. * * *

Under the Copyright Act of 1909, a properly recorded artistic work receives copyright protection for "twenty eight years from the date of first publication," and the author may renew the copyright term for an additional 28–year period. Copyright Act of 1909, ch. 320, § 23, 35 Stat. 1075, 1080. Under the 1909 Act, an unpublished work was protected by state common law copyright from the moment of its creation until it was either published or until it received protection under the federal copyright scheme. *Roy Export Co. Establishment of Vaduz v. CBS, Inc.,* 672 F.2d 1095, 1101 (2d Cir. 1982). * * * When a work was published, it lost state common law protection. The owner could, however, obtain federal protection for the published work by complying with the requirements of the 1909 Act. If the owner failed to satisfy the Act's requirements, the published work was injected irrevocably into the public domain. * * *

The parties dispute when the various versions of *Boogie Chillen* were published within the meaning of the 1909 Act. According to ZZ Top, La Cienega published these recordings when it released them to the general public (*i.e.* 1948, 1950, and 1970). La Cienega counters that publication did not occur until it filed a notice of copyright with the Copyright Office in 1967, 1970, and 1992, respectively. Until that time, it claims, the recordings were "unpublished" and, therefore, retained their state common law copyright protection. Congress declined to define "publication" in the 1909 Act and courts have split over how to define the term for copyright purposes. * * *

The courts in applying the 1909 Act, were in most instances unpersuaded by the argument that no publication occurs by virtue of the sale of a phonorecord because the record is not a "copy" of the work recorded. On the contrary, the relatively few courts which considered the question were almost unanimous in determining that *public sale or other distribution of phonorecords does constitute a publication and hence a divestment of common law rights in the works recorded.* This conclusion is certainly consistent with the common understanding of the term "copy." Moreover, it is in accord with the underlying rationale of the publication doctrine. That is, an author in permitting records of his work to be publicly marketed is certainly engaging in a form of exploitation of his work and should therefore be required to seek protection, if at all, only under the limited monopoly concept of the federal Copyright Act. * * *

We adopt the majority rule and hold that selling recordings constitutes "publication" under the Copyright Act of 1909. Consequently, the compositions were published in 1948, 1950, and 1970, respectively.

III

Given that the compositions were published when recordings were sold to the public, we must next decide when the compositions entered the public domain. The answer turns on whether Besman complied with the copyright requirements of the 1909 Act. Under section 9 of the Act, [a]ny person entitled thereto by [the 1909 Act] may secure copyright for his work by publication thereof with the notice of copyright required by this title; and such notice shall be affixed to each copy thereof published or offered for sale in the United States. Copyright Act of 1909, ch. 320, § 9, 35 Stat. 1075, 1077. * * * If Besman failed to satisfy these requirements, his compositions entered the public domain immediately upon the sale of recordings to the public. * * *

The record fails to reveal whether Besman complied with the copyright requirements of the 1909 Act. This omission is not decisive in the case of the 1948 and 1950 versions of *Boogie Chillen,* however. Failure to renew a copyright after 28 years irrevocably injects the work at issue into the public domain. Copyright Act of 1909, ch. 320, § 23, 35 Stat. 1075, 1080. Thus, even if Besman complied with the requirements of the 1909 Act, his compositions entered the public domain in 1976 and 1978 respectively, when the statutory copyrights expired without renewal.

Besman's compliance or lack thereof affects the resolution of his claim with respect to the 1970 version of *Boogie Chillen,* however. If Besman complied with the statutory requirements, then his composition was copyrighted at the time of publication in 1970. If Besman failed to comply with such requirements, the 1970 version of *Boogie Chillen* was irrevocably injected into the public domain upon publication in 1970, and Besman would not be entitled to recover for the claimed infringements. To resolve this matter, we must remand to the district court for further findings. * * *

Notes

1. The Ninth Circuit decided in *La Cienega* that the distribution of phonorecords constituted a "publication" of the underlying music. This ruling was in direct conflict with decisions reached in similar cases by the Second Circuit. Congress reacted to the conflict by amending the Copyright Act of 1976, essentially overturning the *La Cienega* ruling. In 1997, Congress amended the Copyright Act of 1976 to exempt all songs fixed in a phonorecord and distributed before 1978 from the status of "published" works. The 1997 Copyright Amendment was confirmed in a subsequent Ninth Circuit case. *See* ABKCO Music, Inc. v. LaVere, 217 F.3d 684 (9th Cir. 2000).

2. Sound recordings fixed before 1972 are not protected under federal copyright law. 17 U.S.C. § 104A(h)(6)(ii). However, pre–1972 original recordings are covered by state common law until Feb. 15, 2067. Under New York common law, copyright infringement is considered an unfair competition cause of action. In *Capital Records, Inc. v. Naxos of America, Inc.,* 274 F.Supp.2d 472 (S.D.N.Y. 2003), the court found no infringement when the NAXOS label purchased "shellacs, containing original performances dating back to the 1930's, digitally restored then sold the recordings." Capital Records held copyrights to the shellacs. It was determined that NAXOS worked to create a new product with superior sound and never falsely advertised its recordings as a "duplicate" of the original, nor did NAXOS take advantage of the "commercial qualities" of the original. The Court viewed NAXOS' restorations as a means of insuring that "quality historic

performances are commercially available for the present generation and well-preserved for the next."

3. Ownership of state law rights in pre–1972 sound recordings can be established much more informally than ownership of a federal copyright. A federal copyright is independent of the tangible object in which it is embodied, 17 U.S.C. § 202, and cannot be transferred without a signed writing, 17 U.S.C. § 204.

4. The Federal Copyright Act, which generally preempts state law protection equivalent to copyright, carves out an exception for pre–1972 sound recordings. Under 17 U.S.C. § 301(c), as recently amended by the Sonny Bono Copyright Term Extension Act (P.L. 105–298), the common law copyright in these recordings, and state statutes offering copyright-like protection, will not be preempted by federal law until Feb. 15, 2067. The potentially indefinite term of state law protection for these works will therefore end in 2067, 95 years after the recordings first became eligible for federal copyright in 1972. In California, current law provides for an end to state statutory protection in 2047. Cal. Civ. Code § 980 (a)(2). Well in advance of that date, however, the legislature will probably extend the term to correspond to the additional 20 years of protection now permitted under the Sonny Bono Act.

Despite the general rule precluding federal copyright protection for pre–1972 sound recordings, the 1994 GATT/TRIPS amendments, codified at Section 104A of the Copyright Act, extend protection to such recordings when they: (a) were first published in a country that is a signatory to the Berne Convention, the WIPO Performances and Phonograms Treaty, or is a member of the WTO; and (b) were not subsequently published in the United States during the 30–day period following that initial publication. 17 U.S.C. § 104A(f)(6)(C)-(E).

Consequently, these foreign recordings are protected by federal copyright despite their fixation prior to 1972, and their term of protection is the same as it would have been had they been protected under U.S. federal law ab initio, i.e., 95 years from publication. Virtually all works "restored" under this provision will therefore lapse into the public domain sooner than domestic recordings, which will enjoy state law protection until 2067 regardless of their initial publication date. *See* Robert Clarida, *The Intellectual Property Strategist*, Nov. 13, 2000, *available at* http://www22.brinkster.com/paradio/pages/pre1972.htm.

3. TERMINATION RIGHTS

Termination rights will become significant as copyrights age and the termination rights mature. While there has not been a great deal of litigation under 17 U.S.C § 304, the future will likely bring litigation of copyright ownership and the exercise of termination rights under sections 304 and 203.

MILLS MUSIC, INC. v. SNYDER

United States Supreme Court, 1985.
469 U.S. 153, 105 S.Ct. 638, 83 L.Ed.2d 556.

JUSTICE STEVENS delivered the opinion of the Court.

This is a controversy between a publisher, Mills Music, Inc. (Mills), and the heirs of an author, Ted Snyder (Snyder), over the division of royalty income that the sound recordings of the copyrighted song "Who's Sorry Now" (the Song). The controversy is a direct outgrowth of the general revision of copyright law that Congress enacted in 1976. The 1976 Act gave Snyder's heirs a statutory right to reacquire the copyright that Snyder had previously granted to Mills; however, it also provided that a "derivative work prepared under authority of the grant before its termination may continue to be utilized under the terms of the grant after its termination." * * *

Under the Copyright Act of 1909, 35 Stat. 1075, the copyright in a musical composition lasted for 28 years from the date of its first publication, and the author could renew the copyright for an additional term of 28 years. Although Mills had acquired ownership of the original copyright from the trustee in bankruptcy, it needed the cooperation of Snyder in order to acquire an interest in the 28–year renewal term. Accordingly, in 1940 Mills and Snyder entered into a written agreement defining their respective rights in the renewal of the copyright. In essence, Snyder assigned his entire interest in all renewals of the copyright to Mills in exchange for an advance royalty and Mills' commitment to pay a cash royalty on sheet music and 50 percent of all net royalties that Mills received for mechanical reproductions. * * *

Section 304 of the 1976 Act significantly affected the rights of Mills and the Snyders in three ways. First, § 304(b) provided an automatic extension of the life of the copyright; instead of expiring in 1980 at the end of the second renewal period, the copyright on the Song will endure until 1999. * * * Second, § 304(c) gave the widow and surviving son of Snyder a right to terminate the grant to Mills of rights in the renewal copyright. * * * Third, § 304(c)(6) provided that the termination would cause all rights "covered by the terminated grant" to revert to Snyder's widow and son. That reversion was, however, subject to an exception that permitted a previously prepared derivative work to continue to be utilized after the termination "under the terms of the grant." * * *

We are not persuaded that Congress intended to draw a distinction between authorizations to prepare derivative works that are based on a single direct grant and those that are based on successive grants. Rather, we believe the consequences of a termination that § 304 authorizes simply do not apply to derivative works that are protected by the Exception defined in § 304(c)(6)(A). * * *

The critical subparagraph, § 304(c)(6)(A), carves out an exception from the reversion of rights that takes place when an author exercises his right to termination. A single sentence that uses the word "grant" three times defines the scope of the Exception. It states: "A derivative work prepared under authority of the *grant* before its termination may continue to be utilized under the terms of the *grant* after its termination, but this privilege does not extend to the preparation after the termination of other derivative works based upon the copyrighted work covered by the *terminated grant*." 17 U.S.C. § 304(c)(6)(A) (emphasis supplied). The third reference is to "the terminated grant" which, in this case, must refer to Snyder's grant to Mills in 1940. It is logical to assume that the same word has the same meaning when it is twice used earlier in the same sentence. * * *

It is undisputed that the 1940 grant did not itself specify the terms that would apply to the use of any particular derivative work. The licenses that Mills * * * executed contain those terms. But if the underlying grant from Snyder to Mills in 1940 had not authorized those separate licenses, they would have been nullities. Moreover, if the licenses are examined separately from that earlier grant, they merely require that royalty payments be made to Mills. In terms, they do not provide for any payments at all to the Snyders. The source of the Snyders' entitlement to a 50 percent share in the royalty income is the 1940 grant. Thus, a fair construction of the phrase "under the terms of the grant" as applied to any particular licensee would necessarily encompass both the 1940 grant and the individual license executed pursuant thereto. * * *

The licenses issued to the record companies are the source of their contractual obligation to pay royalties; viewed apart from the 1940 grant, those licenses confer no rights on the Snyders. Moreover, although the termination has caused the ownership of the copyright to revert to the Snyders, nothing in the statute gives them any right to acquire any contractual rights that the Exception preserves. The Snyders' status as owner of the copyright gives them no right to collect royalties by virtue of the Exception from users of previously authorized derivative works. * * *

The principal purpose of the amendments in § 304 was to provide added benefits to authors. The extension of the duration of existing copyrights to 75 years, the provision of a longer term (the author's life plus 50 years) for new copyrights, and the concept of a termination right itself, were all obviously intended to make the rewards for the creativity of authors more substantial. More particularly, the termination right was expressly intended to relieve authors of the consequences of ill-advised and unremunerative grants that had been made before the author had a fair opportunity to appreciate the true value of his work product. * * *

The Exception in § 304(c)(6)(A) was designed, however, to exclude a specific category of grants, even if they were manifestly unfair to the author, from that broad objective. The purpose of the Exception was to "preserve the right of the owner of a derivative work to exploit it, notwithstanding the reversion." Therefore, even if a person acquired the right to exploit an already prepared derivative work by means of an unfavorable bargain with an author, that right was to be excluded from the bundle of rights that would revert to the author when he exercised his termination right. The critical point in determining whether the right to continue utilizing a derivative work survives the termination of a transfer of a copyright is whether it was "prepared" before the termination. * * *

[T]he Exception protects the utilizer of a derivative work from being required to pay an increased royalty to the author. It provides no support, however, for the proposition that Congress expected the author to be able to collect an increased royalty for the use of a derivative work. On the contrary, this history is entirely consistent with the view that the terms of the grant that were applicable to the use of derivative works at the time of termination should remain in effect. * * * Under the terms of the grant in effect at the time of termination, Mills is entitled to a share of the royalty income in dispute.

The judgment of the Court of Appeals is reversed.

JUSTICE WHITE, with whom JUSTICE BRENNAN, JUSTICE MARSHALL, and JUSTICE BLACKMUN join, dissenting.

* * * The right to terminate defined in § 304(c) encompasses not only termination of the grant of copyright itself, but also termination of the grant of "any right under" that copyright. Subsection (6) of this provision reiterates this point, stating that "all of a particular author's rights under this title that were covered by the terminated grant revert, upon the effective date of termination," to the author or his heirs. A straightforward reading of this language is that it allows the author or his heirs to reclaim the copyright he formerly bargained away, as well as any other right granted under the copyright. Surely this termination right extends to recapturing the right previously given to the grantee, in this case Mills, to share in royalties paid by licensees. * * *

It is strange, to say the least, to hold, as the Court does today, that the terms of utilization by the licensee include the agreement between Mills and Snyder to divide royalties, an agreement that is entirely irrelevant to protecting utilization of the derivative work. * * *

The majority claims that it is essential to read the Exception as preserving Mills' rights because the terms under which the derivative works are utilized identify Mills, * * * as the recipient of the royalties. It is surely true that the licenses say this, but that is a surprisingly weak reed on which to rest a judgment of this Court. It can mean only that, if the utilizer of the derivative work wishes to continue to pay royalties, he may do so. * * *

Notes

1. The Copyright Act provides that copyright ownership "vests initially in the author or authors of the work." 17 U.S.C. § 201(a). However, if the work is made for hire, "The employer or other person for whom the work was prepared is considered the author and [without a written agreement stating otherwise] owns all the rights in the copyright." 17 U.S.C. § 201(b). A "work made for hire" is defined by the Copyright Act, Section 101, as: (1) a work prepared by an employee within the scope of his or her employment; (2) a work specially ordered or commissioned for use.

2. In November 1999, Congress passed the Consolidated Appropriations Act 2000, which included an amendment that added "sound recordings" to the list of works that could be a "work made for hire" as a commissioned work under the definition in the Copyright Act. The addition of these two words was considered to have a profound effect on the recording artists who would lose rights to their compositions when contracting with a producer. The reaction within the entertainment industry to this amendment was unexpected by Congress, and the addition of "sound recordings" to Section 101 of the amendment was rescinded in September 2000.

4. WORKS FOR HIRE

Songs that are specially commissioned for use in television shows and commercials are contractually considered "works for hire." In a "work for hire," the commissioning party, typically a production company or producer, is considered the author of the work. When a particular situation is ambiguous, at least in the mind of one of the parties, authorship is worth litigating because of the rights that flow to an author of a musical composition. Performance royalties, mechanical royalties, and the right to authorize derivative works are some of the more valuable rights retained by the author of a musical composition.

MORAN v. LONDON RECORDS, LTD.

United States Court of Appeals, Seventh Circuit, 1987.
827 F.2d 180.

MANION, Circuit Judge.

Larry Moran sued the defendants—record companies, music publishing companies, and musicians—alleging copyright infringement. On defendant MCA Records' motion, the district court dismissed the suit, holding that Moran had no standing to sue for infringement under the Copyright Act of 1976, 17 U.S.C. §§ 101–810. For the reasons set forth below, we affirm.

I.

* * * Moran is a professional commercial announcer who has spent years developing the ability to speak in a wide range of styles, voices, and deliveries. Quaker Oats Company (Quaker) hired Moran to make a sound recording that Quaker used in a commercial for Kibbles 'N Bits

dog food. Quaker subsequently secured and registered a copyright on the commercial. Moran signed an employment agreement (which he attached as an exhibit to his complaint) with Quaker that provided that Moran had no "right, title, or interest of any kind or nature whatsoever in or to the commercial." However, the employment agreement stated that it was "subject to all of the terms and conditions of the [Screen Actors Guild Standard 1982 Commercials Contract]" (Commercials Contract). The Commercials Contract (the relevant part of which Moran also attached as an exhibit to his complaint) provided that before Quaker could use Moran's recording for any purpose other than a television commercial, Quaker had to bargain and agree with Moran concerning that proposed use. Neither the employment agreement nor the Commercials Contract granted Moran the right to sue copyright infringers.

Defendants Larry Steinbacheck, Steve Bronski, and Larry Sommerville (Sommerville's name appears as a defendant in the caption to the complaint, but does not appear in the caption of the district court's opinion or in the caption of Moran's brief) are songwriters and musicians who comprise the musical performing group Bronski Beat. Without Moran's knowledge, Steinbacheck, Bronski, and Sommerville obtained a recording of Moran's performance in the Kibbles 'N Bits commercial and incorporated it into a song they co-authored and recorded, entitled "Junk." Steinbacheck, Bronski, and Sommerville assigned the right to publish "Junk" to defendants Bronski Music Limited (Bronski Music) and William A. Bong Limited (Bong). With Bronski Music's and Bong's permission, defendant London Records (London) manufactured, distributed, and marketed a phonorecord that included Bronski Beat's recording of "Junk". London exclusively authorized defendant, MCA Records, to manufacture, distribute and market the phonorecord in the United States. Moran sued, claiming that the defendants infringed the copyright in the Kibbles 'N Bits commercial by including his recorded performance in "Junk."

II.

17 U.S.C. § 501(b) grants standing to sue for copyright infringement to the "legal or beneficial owner of an exclusive right under a copyright...." Moran does not assert that he is a legal owner of any exclusive right under the copyright. Thus, we need not decide if the Commercials Contract transferred any legal interest in the copyright or any exclusive right under the copyright to Moran. *See* 17 U.S.C. § 106 (listing the exclusive rights in copyrighted works, including the right "to reproduce the copyrighted work in copies or phonorecords"); 17 U.S.C. § 201(d)(2) (providing that any of the exclusive rights, including any subdivision of the rights listed in § 106, may be transferred and owned separately). Moran bases his standing solely on the theory that the rights granted to him under the Commercials Contract (the right to separately bargain concerning, and receive extra compensation for, any use Quaker makes of his performance other than in a television commercial) make him a beneficial owner of the copyright.

The district court rejected Moran's claim of beneficial ownership because Moran was never part of the chain of title to the copyright. *Moran v. London Records, Ltd.,* 642 F.Supp. 1023, 1025 (N.D. Ill. 1986). According to the district court, "[c]ourts applying both § 501(b) and the 1909 Act ... have held consistently that standing to sue as a beneficial owner requires establishment of a proprietary right in a copyright derived through the chain of title." *Id.* To the extent that the district court implies that beneficial ownership necessarily depends on having been part of the copyright's legal chain of title, we do not agree with this statement. The two cases the district court cited to support the chain of title theory, *Motta v. Samuel Weiser, Inc.,* 768 F.2d 481 (1st Cir.1985), *cert. denied,* 474 U.S. 1033 (1985), and *Bell v. Combined Registry Co.,* 397 F.Supp. 1241 (N.D. Ill. 1975), *aff'd,* 536 F.2d 164 (7th Cir.), *cert. denied,* 429 U.S. 1001 (1976), do not stand for the proposition that a beneficial owner must have been part of the legal chain of title. *Bell* concerned only legal ownership, not beneficial ownership. *See* 397 F.Supp. at 1244–45. Similarly, *Motta* stands only for the proposition that a person claiming beneficial ownership must claim his beneficial interest through the legal owner; the legal owner's interest, in turn, must be established through the chain of title. *See* 768 F.2d at 484–87. Here, Moran claims his beneficial interest through Quaker, the copyright's legal owner.

Although beneficial ownership is not restricted to those in a copyright's legal chain of title, we agree with the district court's conclusion that Moran does not have standing to sue as a beneficial owner. Moran concedes that he performed his part in the commercial within the scope of his employment with Quaker. Therefore, Moran's performance was a work made for hire. *See* 17 U.S.C. § 101 (work made by an employee within the scope of his employment is a work made for hire). 17 U.S.C. § 201(b) provides that the employer (here, Quaker) is considered the author of a work made for hire, and owns *all* of the rights comprised in the copyright unless the parties expressly agree otherwise in writing. *See Baltimore Orioles, Inc. v. Major League Baseball Players Ass'n,* 805 F.2d 663, 667 (7th Cir.1986), *cert. denied,* 107 S. Ct. 1593 (1987).

In enacting § 501(b)'s standing provision, Congress "merely codified the case law that had developed [under the 1909 Copyright Act] with respect to the beneficial owner's standing to sue." *Cortner v. Israel,* 732 F.2d 267, 271 (2d Cir.1984). * * * As the district court noted, courts applying the 1909 Act "invoked common law trust principles to hold that when a copyright owner assigned title in exchange for the right to receive royalties from the copyright's exploitation, a fiduciary relationship arose between the parties, and the assignor became a 'beneficial owner' of the copyright with standing to sue infringers should the assignee fail to do so." 642 F.Supp. at 1025; *see* 3 Nimmer § 1202, at 12–27 to 12–28; *Cortner,* 732 F.2d at 271. For examples of this trust relationship arising out of an assignment in exchange for royalties, see *Nat'l Bank of Commerce v. Shaklee Corp.,* 503 F.Supp. 533, 543 (W.D. Tex. 1980). * * * Similarly, a publisher could obtain and hold a copyright in its name in trust for the true author; the author would thus have standing to sue as a beneficial owner. *See, e.g., Bisel v. Ladner,* 1 F.2d 436 (3d Cir. 1924) (Publisher who told author "I will attend to the copyrighting for you" held copyright in trust for author.); *Schellberg v. Empringham,* 36 F.2d 991, 994 (S.D.N.Y. 1929) (express trust). Nothing in § 501(b) indicates that Congress intended to expand the concept of beneficial ownership beyond that found in the prior case law. Moran has cited no cases applying beneficial ownership in a work for hire arrangement, and our research has revealed none.

Section 501(b)'s legislative history does not help Moran. The legislative history states that "a 'beneficial owner' ... would include, for example, an author who had parted with legal title to the copyright in exchange for percentage royalties based on sales or license fees." H.R.Rep. No. 94–1476, 94th Cong., 2d Sess. 159, *reprinted in* 1976 U.S. Code Cong. & Ad. News 5659, 5775. Although the legislative history does not purport to exhaustively list who may be a beneficial owner, it is significant that the example Congress did give was that of an author who assigned his work in exchange for royalties—the classic example of a beneficial owner in the cases deciding standing to sue under the 1909 Act. Given that no case has held an employee in a work made for hire situation to be a beneficial owner, and that Congress merely intended to codify the existing case law, *see Cortner,* 732 F.2d at 271, the fact that Congress did give only the assignment example supports the conclusion that Congress did not intend to extend the concept of beneficial ownership to include an employee in a work made for hire arrangement.

Moran recorded his performance in the scope of his employment with Quaker; his performance was a work made for hire. Quaker is the commercial's author and owns the commercial's copyright, *see* 17 U.S.C. § 201(b), and Moran's employment contract expressly provides that he has no "right, title, or interest of any kind or nature whatsoever in or to the commercial." Transferring economic rights not amounting to legal title in any exclusive right under the copyright (the case here, by Moran's own concession) will not confer beneficial ownership on the employee. Moran could have secured an interest in the copyright by expressly agreeing with Quaker that he would own the copyright or an exclusive right under the copyright. He did not, and we will not allow Moran into federal court under his claim of beneficial ownership when Congress has precluded entry by § 201(b)'s work made for hire provision. Therefore, we affirm the district court.

AFFIRMED.

Note

1. The "work made for hire" doctrine is a narrow exception to the basic rule that the creator is the owner of the copyright. Contract principles assume that people structure consensual transactions to obtain the benefit of any bargains reached. In an employment context, employees and employers are free to bargain over such terms as salary, benefits, and creative control

over the work. Where an employer makes certain promises but fails to fulfill them, should the employee be able to rescind the contract and recapture the copyrights in the works that were the subject matter of the agreement?

C. COPYRIGHT INFRINGEMENT AND REMEDIES

Suits for copyright infringement are expensive and risky. Even when the original copyright holder wins, the damage award may not cover the cost of litigation. Additionally, success depends on the ears of twelve jurors who may be influenced by the celebrity status of the parties and the testimony of experts. Copyright infringement lawsuits are necessary to protect the rights of the copyright owner, but they are as unpredictable as a sophisticated opera.

BRIGHT TUNES MUSIC CORP. v. HARRISONGS MUSIC

United States District Court, New York, 1976.
420 F.Supp. 177.

OWEN, District Judge.

This is an action in which it is claimed that a successful song, My Sweet Lord, listing George Harrison as the composer, is plagiarized from an earlier successful song, He's So Fine, composed by Ronald Mack, recorded by a singing group called the "Chiffons," the copyright of which is owned by plaintiff, Bright Tunes Music Corp.

He's So Fine, recorded in 1962, is a catchy tune consisting essentially of four repetitions of a very short basic musical phrase, "sol-mi-re," (hereinafter motif A) altered as necessary to fit the words, followed by four repetitions of another short basic musical phrase, "sol-la-do-la-do" (hereinafter motif B). While neither motif is novel, the four repetitions of A, followed by four repetitions of B, is a highly unique pattern. In addition, in the second use of the motif B series, there is a grace note inserted making the phrase go "sol-la-do-la-*re*-do."

My Sweet Lord, recorded first in 1970, also uses the same motif A four times, followed by motif B, repeated three times, not four. In place of He's So Fine's fourth repetition of motif B, My Sweet Lord has a transitional passage of musical attractiveness of the same approximate length, with the identical grace note in the identical second repetition. The harmonies of both songs are identical.

George Harrison, a former member of The Beatles, was aware of He's So Fine. * * * According to Harrison, the circumstances of the composition of My Sweet Lord were as follows. Harrison and his group, which include an American black gospel singer named Billy Preston, were in Copenhagen, Denmark, on a singing engagement. There was a press conference involving the group going on backstage. Harrison slipped away from the press conference and went to a room upstairs and began "vamping" some guitar chords, fitting on to the chords he was playing the words, "Hallelujah" and "Hare Krishna" in various ways.

During the course of this vamping, he was alternating between what musicians call a Minor II chord and a Major V chord.

At some point, * * * he went down to meet with others of the group, asking them to listen, which they did, and everyone began to join in, taking first "Hallelujah" and then "Hare Krishna" and putting them into four part harmony. * * *

Approximately one week after the idea first began to germinate, the entire group flew back to London because they had earlier booked time to go to a recording studio with Billy Preston to make an album. In the studio, Preston was the principal musician. Harrison did not play in the session. He had given Preston his basic motif A with the idea that it be turned into a song, and was back and forth from the studio to the engineer's recording booth, supervising the recording "takes." Under circumstances that Harrison was utterly unable to recall, while everybody was working toward a finished song, in the recording studio, somehow or other the essential three notes of motif A reached polished form. * * *

The Billy Preston recording, listing George Harrison as the composer, was thereafter issued by Apple Records. The music was then reduced to paper by someone who prepared a "lead sheet" containing the melody, the words and the harmony for the United States copyright application.

Seeking the wellsprings of musical composition—why a composer chooses the succession of notes and the harmonies he does—whether it be George Harrison or Richard Wagner, is a fascinating inquiry. It is apparent from the extensive colloquy between the Court and Harrison covering forty pages in the transcript that neither Harrison nor Preston were conscious of the fact that they were utilizing the He's So Fine theme. However, they in fact were, for it is perfectly obvious to the listener that in musical terms, the two songs are virtually identical except for one phrase. There is motif A used four times, followed by motif B, four times in one case, and three times in the other, with the same grace note in the second repetition of motif B.

What happened? I conclude that the composer, in seeking musical materials to clothe his thoughts, was working with various possibilities. As he tried this possibility and that, there came to the surface of his mind a particular combination that pleased him as being one he felt would be appealing to a prospective listener; in other words, that this combination of sounds would work. Why? Because his subconscious knew it already had worked in a song his conscious mind did not remember. Having arrived at this pleasing combination of sounds, the recording was made, the lead sheet prepared for copyright and the song became an enormous success. Did Harrison deliberately use the music of He's So Fine? I do not believe he did so deliberately. Nevertheless, it is clear that My Sweet Lord is the very same song as He's So Fine with different words, and Harrison had access to He's So Fine. This is, under the law, infringement of copyright, and is no less so even though subconsciously accomplished. *Sheldon v. Metro–Goldwyn Pictures Corp.*, 81 F.2d 49, 54 (2d Cir. 1936). * * *

Given the foregoing, I find for the plaintiff on the issue of plagiarism, and set the action down for trial * * * on the issue of damages and other relief as to which the plaintiff may be entitled. So Ordered.

BAXTER v. MCA

United States Court of Appeals, Ninth Circuit, 1987.
812 F.2d 421.

TANG, Circuit Judge.

In this copyright infringement action, plaintiff-appellant Leslie T. Baxter appeals the district court's grant of summary judgment to John Williams and the other defendants-appellees. The district court granted defendants' motion based upon its determination that no substantial similarity of expression existed as between Baxter's copyrighted song Joy and the theme from the motion picture "E.T.: The Extra–Terrestrial" [hereinafter cited as Theme from E.T.]. We reverse the grant of summary judgment and remand for trial.

FACTS AND PROCEDURAL HISTORY

In 1953, Leslie Baxter composed a collection of seven songs intended to invoke or represent emotions. These songs were recorded and published by Capitol Records in 1954 on an album entitled The Passions. Joy, one of the compositions on that album, is the subject of this action. Baxter is the sole owner of all right, title and interest in the copyright to Joy.

Baxter and John Williams, a successful composer and conductor of music, have been personally acquainted for several decades. Williams had previously played the piano for Baxter at a number of recording sessions, and had knowledge of Joy. He participated as the pianist in the orchestra for a public performance of Joy in the Hollywood Bowl in the 1960s. In 1982, Williams composed Theme from E.T. for which he received an Academy Award for best original music. The other appellees utilized Theme from E.T. in the motion picture "E.T.: The Extra–Terrestrial," sound recordings and merchandising.

On November 2, 1983, Baxter filed a complaint for copyright infringement and demand for jury trial in district court. He alleged that Theme from E.T. was largely copied from his copyrighted song Joy. On September 17, 1984, defendants moved for summary judgment on the ground that, as a matter of law, Theme from E.T. was not substantially similar to protectible expression in Joy, and therefore did not infringe it. For the limited purpose of the summary judgment motion only, defendants conceded that: (1) Baxter owned a duly registered copyright in Joy; (2) Williams had "access" to Joy before the creation of Theme from E.T.; and (3) the "general ideas" in the subject songs were substantially similar.

Defendants attached to their motion papers the following items: (1) cassette tape recordings of Joy as it appeared on the album The Passions and the movie soundscore of Theme from E.T.; (2) the twenty-three page written instrumental sheet music of Joy that was copyrighted; and (3) the five page piano score of Theme from E.T. Baxter introduced into evidence, expert testimony and five comparison tapes by Professor Harvey Bacal regarding the degree of similarity between the two compositions.

After reviewing the submitted evidence, the district court granted defendants' motion for summary judgment, stating:

> This Court's "ear" is as lay as they come. The Court cannot hear any substantial similarity between defendant's expression of the idea and plaintiff's. Until Professor Bacal's tapes were listened to, the Court could not even tell what the complaint was about. Granted that Professor Bacal's comparison exposes a musical similarity in sequence of notes which would, perhaps, be obvious to experts, the similarity of expression (or impression as a whole) is totally lacking and could not be submitted to a jury.

Baxter timely appealed.

DISCUSSION

After the defendants stipulated to the plaintiff's ownership of the copyright and access to his work, the district court ruled as a matter of law that there was no substantial similarity between the two works. That holding is subject to our *de novo* review. * * *

To establish a successful claim for copyright infringement, the plaintiff must prove (1) ownership of the copyright, and (2) "copying" of protectible expression by the defendant. See *Sid & Marty Krofft Television Prod., Inc., v. McDonald's Corp.*, 562 F.2d 1157, 1162 (9th Cir. 1977) * * * [and] 2 M. Nimmer, Nimmer on Copyright § 141 at 610–611 (1979) [hereinafter cited as "Nimmer"]). Because direct evidence of copying is rarely available, a plaintiff may establish copying by circumstantial evidence of: (1) defendant's access to the copyrighted work prior to the creation of defendant's work, and (2) substantial similarity of both general ideas and expression between the copyrighted work and the defendant's work. * * * Absent evidence of access, a "striking similarity" between the works may give rise to a permissible inference of copying. See *Selle v. Gibb*, 741 F.2d 896, 901 (7th Cir. 1984); *Shultz v. Holmes*, 264 F.2d 942 (9th Cir. 1959); Nimmer § 13.02[B] at 13–14 (1986). Baxter's ownership of the copyright to Joy is undisputed, and defendants conceded access for the purpose of their summary judgment motion. Defendants further assumed for purposes of their motion that there was substantial similarity of ideas as between the two compositions. Therefore, the only question before us is whether the district court's finding, based on its ear, that substantial similarity of expression was "totally lacking and could not be submitted to a jury," can sustain a grant of summary judgment to the defendants. * * *

Determinations of substantial similarity of expression are subtle and complex. The test to be applied has been labeled an "intrinsic" one by this Court in that it depends not upon external criteria, but instead upon the response of the ordinary reasonable person to the works. *Krofft*, 562 F.2d at 1164. "Analytic dissection" and expert testimony are not called for; the gauge of substantial similarity is the response of the ordinary lay hearer. *Id., quoting Arnstein v. Porter*, 154 F.2d 464, 468 (2d Cir. 1946), *cert. denied*, 330 U.S. 851 (1947). Accordingly, in *Krofft*, this Court rejected extrinsic analysis of similarities and differences among characters in plaintiffs' television show and defendants' TV commercials, in favor of asking whether the defendants' works captured the total concept and feel of plaintiffs' works. *Krofft*, 562 F.2d at 1167. * * *

We do not suggest that our ears are any more sophisticated than those of the district court. Nevertheless, based on our review of the record, we are persuaded that reasonable minds could differ as to whether Joy and Theme from E.T. are substantially similar. As in *Twentieth Century-Fox*, we do not suggest that the works are, in fact, substantially similar. We only state that reasonable minds could differ as to the issue and thus that summary judgment was improper. *See Twentieth Century–Fox*, 715 F.2d at 1329.

We finally address defendants' contention that any similarity between the works can be reduced to a six-note sequence which is not protectible expression under the copyright laws. We disagree.

Even were we to accept *arguendo* defendants' argument over Baxter's response that it is not a six-note sequence but the entire work whose similarity is at issue, this argument ignores the fundamental notion that no bright line rule exists as to what quantum of similarity is permitted before crossing into the realm of substantial similarity. *See generally* 3 M. Nimmer, Nimmer on Copyright § 13.03[A][2] (1986). Here, the ear of the court must yield to the ears of jurors. *See Roy Export Co. Establishment v. CBS*, 503 F.Supp. 1137, 1145 (S.D.N.Y. 1980), *aff'd*, 672 F.2d 1095 (2d Cir. 1982), *cert. denied*, 459 U.S. 826 (1982). Even if a copied portion be relatively small in proportion to the entire work, if qualitatively important, the finder of fact may properly find substantial similarity. *See Walt Disney Prod. v. Air Pirates*, 581 F.2d 751 (9th Cir. 1978), *cert. denied*, 439 U.S. 1132 (1978); *Universal Pictures v. Harold Lloyd*, 162 F.2d 354 (9th Cir.1947); *Heim v. Universal Pictures Co.*, 154 F.2d 480, 488 (single brief phrase so idiosyncratic as to preclude coincidence might suffice to show copying) (dictum); *Fred Fisher, Inc. v. Dillingham*, 298 F. 145 (S.D.N.Y. 1924) (L. Hand, J.) (eight note "ostinato" held to infringe copyright in song). *See also Meeropol v. Nizer*, 560 F.2d 1061 (2d Cir. 1977) (words copied amounted to less than one percent of defendant's entire work; fair use), *cert. denied*, 434 U.S. 1013 (1977); *Robertson v. Batten, Barton, Durstine & Osborne, Inc.*, 146 F.Supp. 795, 798 (S.D. Cal. 1956) (portions of song used constituted element upon which popular appeal and hence commercial success depended; fair use). *See generally* Nimmer § 13.03[A][2] at 13–36, and citations therein (notion that copying of three bars from musical work can never constitute infringement is without foundation). Certainly, evidence that the sequence in question is found in other works would be admissible to rebut an inference of copying; such evidence demonstrates that the sequence is so common that the probability of independent, coincidental creation was high. *Granite Music Corp. v. United Artists Corp.*, 532 F.2d 718, 720 (9th Cir. 1976).

But we do not understand Baxter's claim to center solely on one six-note sequence. The jury upon remand may, of course, determine that any similarity is confined to the sequence, and that the similarity is insubstantial.

Conclusion

Based upon our review of the record, we cannot say that Joy and Theme from E.T. are so dissimilar that reasonable minds could not differ as to a lack of substantial similarity between them. Therefore, the district court erred in granting defendants' motion for summary judgment.

Reversed and remanded for proceedings not inconsistent with this opinion.

THREE BOYS MUSIC CORP. v. BOLTON

United States Court of Appeals, Ninth Circuit, 2000.
212 F.3d 477.

NELSON, Circuit Judge.

In 1994, a jury found that Michael Bolton's 1991 pop hit, "Love Is a Wonderful Thing," infringed on the copyright of a 1964 Isley Brothers' song of the same name. The district court denied Bolton's motion for a new trial and affirmed the jury's award of $5.4 million.

Bolton, his co-author, Andrew Goldmark, and their record companies ("Sony Music") appeal, arguing that the district court erred in finding that: (1) sufficient evidence supported the jury's finding that the appellants had access to the Isley Brothers' song; (2) sufficient evidence supported the jury's finding that the songs were substantially similar; (3) subject matter jurisdiction existed based on the Isley Brothers registering a complete copy of the song; * * * We affirm.

I. Background

The Isley Brothers, one of this country's most well-known rhythm and blues groups, have been inducted into the Rock and Roll Hall of Fame. They helped define the soul sound of the 1960s with songs such as "Shout," "Twist and Shout," and "This Old Heart of Mine," and they mastered the funky beats of the 1970s with songs such as "Who's That Lady," "Fight the Power," and "It's Your Thing." In 1964, the Isley Brothers wrote and recorded "Love is a Wonderful Thing" for United Artists. The Isley Brothers received a copyright for "Love is a Wonderful Thing" from the Register of Copyrights on February 6, 1964. The following year, they switched to the famous Motown label and had three top–100 hits including "This Old Heart of Mine."

Hoping to benefit from the Isley Brothers' Motown success, United Artists released "Love is a Wonderful Thing" in 1966. The song was not released on an album, only on a 45–record as a single. Several industry publications predicted that "Love is a Wonderful Thing" would be a hit—"Cash Box" on August 27, 1966, "Gavin Report" on August 26, 1966, and "Billboard" on September 10, 1966. On September 17, 1966, Billboard listed "Love is a Wonderful Thing" at number 110 in a chart titled "Bubbling Under the Hot 100." The song was never listed on any other Top 100 charts. In 1991, the Isley Brothers' "Love is a Wonderful Thing" was released on compact disc. *See* Isley Brothers, *The Isley Brothers—The Complete UA Sessions,* (EMI 1991).

Michael Bolton is a singer/songwriter who gained popularity in the late 1980s and early 1990s by reviving the soul sound of the 1960s. Bolton has orchestrated this soul-music revival in part by covering old songs such as Percy Sledge's "When a Man Love a Woman" and Otis Redding's "(Sittin' on the) Dock of the Bay." Bolton also has written his own hit songs. In early 1990, Bolton and Goldmark wrote a song called "Love Is a Wonderful Thing." Bolton released it as a single in April 1991, and as part of Bolton's album, "Time, Love and Tenderness." Bolton's "Love Is a Wonderful Thing" finished 1991 at number 49 on Billboard's year-end pop chart.

On February 24, 1992, Three Boys Music Corporation filed a copyright infringement action for damages against the appellants under 17 U.S.C. §§ 101 *et seq.* (1988). The parties agreed to a trifurcated trial. On April 25, 1994, in the first phase, the jury determined that the appellants had infringed the Isley Brothers' copyright. At the end of second phase five days later, the jury decided that Bolton's "Love Is a Wonderful Thing" accounted for 28 percent of the profits from "Time, Love and Tenderness." The jury also found that 66 percent of the profits from commercial uses of the song could be attributed to the inclusion of infringing elements. On May 9, 1994, the district court entered judgment in favor of the Isley Brothers based on the first two phases. * * *

On December 5, 1996, the district court adopted the findings of the Special Master's Amended Report about the allocation of damages (third phase). In the final judgment entered against the appellants, the district court ordered Sony Music to pay $4,218,838; Bolton to pay $932,924; Goldmark to pay $220,785; and their music publishing companies to pay $75,900. They timely appealed.

II. Discussion

Proof of copyright infringement is often highly circumstantial, particularly in cases involving music. A copyright plaintiff must prove (1) ownership of the copyright; and (2) infringement—that the defendant copied protected elements of the plaintiff's work. * * * Absent direct evidence of copying, proof of infringement involves fact-based showings that the defendant had "access" to the plaintiff's work and that the two works are "substantially similar." * * *

Given the difficulty of proving access and substantial similarity, appellate courts have been reluctant to reverse jury verdicts in music cases. * * * The guiding principle in deciding whether to overturn a jury verdict for insufficiency of the evidence is whether the evidence is such that, without weighing the credibility of the witnesses or otherwise considering the weight of the evidence, there can be but one conclusion as to the verdict that reasonable men could have reached. * * * In *Arnstein v. Porter,* the seminal case about musical copyright infringement, Judge Jerome Frank wrote: Each of these two issues—copying and improper appropriation—is an issue of fact. If there is a trial, the conclusions on those issues of the trier of the facts—of the judge if he sat without a jury, or of the jury if there was a jury trial—bind this court on appeal, provided the evidence supports those findings, regardless of whether we would ourselves have reached the same conclusions. *Arnstein v. Porter,* 154 F.2d 464, 469 (2d Cir. 1946).

As a general matter, the standard for reviewing jury verdicts is whether they are supported by "substantial evidence"—that is, such relevant evidence as reasonable minds might accept as adequate to support a conclusion. * * * The credibility of witnesses is an issue for the jury and is generally not subject to appellate review. * * *

We affirm the jury's verdict in this case in light of the standard of review and copyright law's "guiding principles." Although we will address each of the appellant's arguments in turn, we focus on access because it is the most difficult issue in this case. Our decision is predicated on judicial deference—finding that the law has been properly applied in this case, viewing the facts most favorably to the appellees, and not substituting our judgment for that of the jury.

A. Access

Proof of access requires "an opportunity to view or to copy plaintiff's work." *Sid and Marty Krofft Television Prod., Inc. v. McDonald's Corp.,* 562 F.2d 1157, 1172 (9th Cir. 1977). This is often described as providing a "reasonable opportunity" or "reasonable possibility" of viewing the plaintiff's work. 4 Melville B. Nimmer & David Nimmer, *Nimmer on Copyright,* § 13.02[A], at 13–19 (1999); *Jason v. Fonda,* 526 F.Supp. 774, 775 (C.D. Cal. 1981), *aff'd,* 698 F.2d 966 (9th Cir. 1982). We have defined reasonable access as "more than a 'bare possibility.' "*Jason,* 698 F.2d at 967. Nimmer has elaborated on our definition: "Of course, reasonable opportunity as here used, does not encompass any bare possibility in the sense that anything is possible. Access may not be inferred through mere speculation or conjecture. There must be a reasonable possibility of viewing the plaintiff's work—not a bare possibility." 4 Nimmer, § 13.02[A], at 13–19. "At times, distinguishing a 'bare' possibility from a 'reasonable' possibility will present a close question." *Id.* at 13–20.

Circumstantial evidence of reasonable access is proven in one of two ways: (1) a particular chain of events is established between the plaintiff's work and the defendant's access to that work (such as through dealings with a publisher or record company), or (2) the plaintiff's work has been widely disseminated. *See* 4 Nimmer, § 13.02[A], at 13–20–13–21; 2 Paul Goldstein, *Copyright: Principles, Law, and Practice* § 8.3.1.1., at 90–91 (1989). Goldstein remarks that in music cases the "typically more successful route to proving access requires the plaintiff to show that its work was widely disseminated through sales of sheet music, records, and radio performances." 2 Goldstein, § 8.3.1.1, at 91. Nimmer, however, cautioned that "[c]oncrete cases will pose difficult judgments as to where along the access spectrum a given exploitation falls." 4 Nimmer, § 13.02[A], at 13–22.

Proof of widespread dissemination is sometimes accompanied by a theory that copyright infringement of a popular song was subconscious. Subconscious copying has been accepted since Learned Hand embraced it in a 1924 music infringement case: "Everything registers somewhere in our memories, and no one can tell what may evoke it.... Once it appears that another has in fact used the copyright as the source of this production, he has invaded the author's rights. It is no excuse that in so doing his memory has played him a trick." *Fred Fisher, Inc. v. Dillingham,* 298 F. 145, 147–48 (S.D.N.Y. 1924). In *Fred Fisher,* Judge Hand found that the similarities between the songs "amount[ed] to identity" and that the infringement had occurred "probably unconsciously, what he had certainly often heard only a short time before." *Id.* at 147.

In modern cases, however, the theory of subconscious copying has been applied to songs that are more remote in time. *ABKCO Music, Inc. v. Harrisongs Music, Ltd.,* 722 F.2d 988 (2d Cir. 1983) is the most prominent example. In *ABKCO,* the Second Circuit affirmed a jury's verdict that former Beatle George Harrison, in writing the song "My Sweet Lord," subconsciously copied The Chiffons' "He's So Fine," which was released six years earlier. *See id.* at 997, 999. Harrison admitted hearing "He's So Fine" in 1963, when it was number one on the Billboard charts in the United States for five weeks and one of the top 30 hits in England for seven weeks. *See id.* at 998. The court found: "the evidence, standing alone, 'by no means compels the conclusion that there was access ... it does not compel the conclusion that there was not.' "*Id.* (quoting *Heim v. Universal Pictures Co.,* 154 F.2d 480, 487 (2d Cir. 1946)). In *ABKCO,* however, the court found that "the similarity was so striking and where access was found, the remoteness of that access provides no basis for reversal." *Id.* Furthermore, "the mere lapse of a considerable period of time between the moment of access and the creation of defendant's work does not preclude a finding of copying." 4 Nimmer, § 13.02[A], at 13–20 (citing *ABKCO,* 722 F.2d at 997–98).

The Isley Brothers' access argument was based on a theory of widespread dissemination and subconscious copying. They presented evidence supporting four principal ways that Bolton and Goldmark could have had access to the Isley Brothers' "Love is a Wonderful Thing":

(1) Bolton grew up listening to groups such as the Isley Brothers and singing their songs. In 1966, Bolton and Goldmark were 13 and 15, respectively, growing up in Connecticut. Bolton testified that he had been listening to rhythm and blues music by black singers since he was 10 or 11, "appreciated a lot of Black singers," and as a youth was the lead singer in a band that performed "covers" of popular songs by black singers. Bolton also testified that his brother had a "pretty good record collection."

(2) Three disk jockeys testified that the Isley Brothers' song was widely disseminated on radio and television stations where Bolton and Goldmark grew up. First, Jerry Blavitt testified that the Isley Brothers' "Love is a Wonderful Thing" was played five or six times during a 13–week period on the television show, "The Discophonic Scene," which he said aired in Philadelphia, New York, and Hartford–New Haven. Blavitt also testified that he played the song two to three times a week as a disk jockey in Philadelphia and that the station is still playing the song today. Second, Earl Rodney Jones testified that he played the song a minimum of four times a day during an eight to 14 to 24 week period on WVON radio in Chicago, and that the station is still playing the song today. Finally, Jerry Bledsoe testified that he played the song on WUFO radio in Buffalo, and WWRL radio in New York was playing the song in New York in 1967 when he went there. Bledsoe also testified that he played the song twice on a television show, "Soul," which aired in New York and probably in New Haven, Connecticut, where Bolton lived.

(3) Bolton confessed to being a huge fan of the Isley Brothers and a collector of their music. Ronald Isley testified that when Bolton saw Isley at the Lou Rawls United Negro College Fund Benefit concert in 1988, Bolton said, "I know this guy. I go back with him. I have all his stuff." Angela Winbush, Isley's wife, testified about that meeting that Bolton said, "This man needs no introduction. I know everything he's done." (4) Bolton wondered if he and Goldmark were copying a song by another famous soul singer. Bolton produced a work tape attempting to show that he and Goldmark independently created their version of "Love Is a Wonderful Thing." On that tape of their recording session, Bolton asked Goldmark if the song they were composing was Marvin Gaye's "Some Kind of Wonderful."

The district court, in affirming the jury's verdict, wrote about Bolton's Marvin Gaye remark: This statement suggests that Bolton was contemplating the possibility that the work he and Goldmark were creating, or at least a portion of it, belonged to someone else, but that Bolton wasn't sure who it belonged to. A reasonable jury can infer that Bolton mistakenly attributed the work to Marvin Gaye, when in reality Bolton was subconsciously drawing on Plaintiff's song.

The appellants contend that the Isley Brothers' theory of access amounts to a "twenty-five-years-after-the-fact-subconscious copying claim." Indeed, this is a more attenuated case of reasonable access and subconscious copying than *ABKCO*. In this case, the appellants never admitted hearing the Isley Brothers' "Love is a Wonderful Thing." That song never topped the Billboard charts or even made the top 100 for a single week. The song was not released on an album or compact disc until 1991, a year after Bolton and Goldmark wrote their song. Nor did the Isley Brothers ever claim that Bolton's and Goldmark's song is so "strikingly similar" to the Isley Brothers' that proof of access is presumed and need not be proven.

Despite the weaknesses of the Isley Brothers' theory of reasonable access, the appellants had a full opportunity to present their case to the jury. Three rhythm and blues experts (including legendary Motown songwriter Lamont Dozier of Holland–Dozier–Holland fame) testified that they never heard of the Isley Brothers' "Love is a Wonderful Thing."

Furthermore, Bolton produced copies of "TV Guide" from 1966 suggesting that the television shows playing the song never aired in Connecticut. Bolton also pointed out that 129 songs called "Love is a Wonderful Thing" are registered with the Copyright Office, 85 of them before 1964.

The Isley Brothers' reasonable access arguments are not without merit. Teenagers are generally avid music listeners. It is entirely plausible that two Connecticut teenagers obsessed with rhythm and blues music could remember an Isley Brothers' song that was played on the radio and television for a few weeks, and subconsciously copy it twenty years later. Furthermore, Ronald Isley testified that when they met, Bolton said, "I have all his stuff." Finally, as the district court pointed out, Bolton's remark about Marvin Gaye and "Some Kind of Wonderful" indicates that Bolton believed he may have been copying someone else's song.

Finally, with regard to access, we are mindful of Judge Frank's words of caution in *Arnstein v. Porter:* "The judge characterized plaintiff's story as 'fantastic'; and in the light of the references in his opinion to defendant's deposition, the judge obviously accepted the defendant's denial of access and copying.... [Y]et plaintiff's credibility, even as to those improbabilities, should be left to the jury." *Arnstein,* 154 F.2d at 469. In this case, Judge Baird heeded Judge Frank's admonition: [T]his Court is not in a position to find that the only conclusion that a reasonable jury could have reached is that Defendants did not have access to Plaintiff's song. One must remember that the issue this Court must address is not whether Plaintiff has proven access by a preponderance of evidence, but whether *reasonable minds* could find that Defendants had a *reasonable opportunity* to have heard Plaintiff's song before they created their own song.

Although we might not reach the same conclusion as the jury regarding access, we find that the jury's conclusion about access is supported by substantial evidence. We are not establishing a new standard for access in copyright cases; we are merely saying that we will not disturb the jury's factual and credibility determinations on this issue.

B. Substantial Similarity

Under our case law, substantial similarity is inextricably linked to the issue of access. In what is known as the "inverse ratio rule," we "require a lower standard of proof of substantial similarity when a high degree of access is shown." *Smith*, 84 F.3d at 1218 (citing *Shaw v. Lindheim*, 919 F.2d 1353, 1361–62 (9th Cir. 1990); *Krofft*, 562 F.2d at 1172). Furthermore, in the absence of any proof of access, a copyright plaintiff can still make out a case of infringement by showing that the songs were "strikingly similar." *See Smith*, 84 F.3d at 1220; *Baxter v. MCA, Inc.*, 812 F.2d 421, 423, 424 n. 2 (9th Cir. 1987).

Proof of the substantial similarity is satisfied by a two-part test of extrinsic similarity and intrinsic similarity. *See Krofft*, 562 F.2d at 1164. Initially, the extrinsic test requires that the plaintiff identify concrete elements based on objective criteria. *See Smith*, 84 F.3d at 1218; *Shaw*, 919 F.2d at 1356. The extrinsic test often requires analytical dissection of a work and expert testimony. *See Apple Computer, Inc. v. Microsoft Corp.*, 35 F.3d 1435, 1442 (9th Cir. 1994). Once the extrinsic test is satisfied, the fact finder applies the intrinsic test. The intrinsic test is subjective and asks "whether the ordinary, reasonable person would find the total concept and feel of the works to be substantially similar." *Pasillas v. McDonald's Corp.*, 927 F.2d 440, 442 (9th Cir. 1991) (internal quotations omitted).

We will not second-guess the jury's application of the intrinsic test. *See Krofft* 562 F.2d at 1166 ("Since the intrinsic test for expression is uniquely suited for determination by the trier of fact, this court must be reluctant to reverse it.") (citations omitted). Furthermore, we will not reverse factual determinations regarding the extrinsic test absent a clearly erroneous application of the law. *See id.* It is well settled that a jury may find a combination of unpredictable elements to be protectible under the extrinsic test because " 'the over-all impact and effect indicate substantial appropriation.' " *Id.* at 1169 (quoting *Malkin v. Dubinsky*, 146 F. Supp. 111, 114 (S.D.N.Y. 1956)).

1. Evidence of Substantial Similarity

Bolton and Goldmark argue that there was insufficient evidence of substantial similarity because the Isley Brothers' expert musicologist, Dr. Gerald Eskelin, failed to show that there was copying of a *combination* of unpredictable elements. On the contrary, Eskelin testified that the two songs shared a combination of five unpredictable elements: (1) the title hook phrase (including the lyric, rhythm, and pitch); (2) the shifted cadence; (3) the instrumental figures; (4) the verse/chorus relationship; and (5) the fade ending. Although the appellants presented testimony from their own expert musicologist, Anthony Ricigliano, he conceded that there were similarities between the two songs and that he had not found the combination of unpredictable elements in the Isley

Brothers' song "anywhere in the prior art." The jury heard testimony from both of these experts and "found infringement based on a unique compilation of those elements." We refuse to interfere with the jury's credibility determination, nor do we find that the jury's finding of substantial similarity was clearly erroneous.

2. Independent Creation

Bolton and Goldmark also contend that their witnesses rebutted the Isley Brothers' prima facie case of copyright infringement with evidence of independent creation. By establishing reasonable access and substantial similarity, a copyright plaintiff creates a presumption of copying. The burden shifts to the defendant to rebut that presumption through proof of independent creation. *See Granite Music Corp. v. United Artists Corp.*, 532 F.2d 718, 721 (9th Cir. 1976).

The appellants' case of independent creation hinges on three factors: the work tape demonstrating how Bolton and Goldmark created their song, Bolton and Goldmark's history of songwriting, and testimony that their arranger, Walter Afanasieff, contributed two of five unpredictable elements that they allegedly copied. The jury, however, heard the testimony of Bolton, Goldmark, Afanasieff, and Ricigliano about independent creation. The work tape revealed evidence that Bolton may have subconsciously copied a song that he believed to be written by Marvin Gaye. Bolton and Goldmark's history of songwriting presents no direct evidence about this case. And Afanasieff's contributions to Bolton and Goldmark's song were described by the appellants' own expert as "very common." Once again, we refuse to disturb the jury's determination about independent creation. The substantial evidence of copying based on access and substantial similarity was such that a reasonable juror could reject this defense. * * *

The district court heard all of the evidence in this case, instructed the jury on the applicable law, yet refused to reverse the jury's verdict pursuant to motion for a judgment as a matter of law. Having found that the law was properly applied in this case, we leave the district court's decisions and the jury's credibility determinations undisturbed. AFFIRMED.

Note

1.   In *Selle v. Gibb,* 741 F.2d 896 (7th Cir. 1984), the plaintiff, Ronald H. Selle, brought a suit against three brothers, Maurice, Robin and Barry Gibb, known collectively as the "Bee Gees," alleging that the Bee Gees, in their hit tune "How Deep Is Your Love," had infringed the copyright of his song, "Let It End." Selle composed his song, "Let It End," in one day in the fall of 1975 and obtained a copyright for it on Nov. 17, 1975. He played his song with his small band two or three times in the Chicago area and sent a tape and lead sheet of the music to eleven music recording and publishing companies. Eight of the companies returned the materials to Selle; three did not respond. This was the extent of the public dissemination of Selle's song.

The jury returned a verdict in plaintiff's favor on the issue of liability in a bifurcated trial. District court judge George N. Leighton granted the defendants' motion for judgment notwithstanding the verdict and, in the alternative, for a new trial. The judge stated that the plaintiff had failed to prove access. *Selle v. Gibb,* 567 F.Supp. 1173 (N.D. Ill. 1983). The court of appeals affirmed the grant of the motion for judgment notwithstanding the verdict.

D. FAIR USE

The fair use doctrine is a body of law and court decisions that provide limitations and exceptions to copyright. Fair use attempts to balance the interests of copyright holders with the public interest in the wider distribution and use of creative works by allowing certain limited uses that might otherwise be considered infringement.

CAMPBELL v. ACUFF–ROSE MUSIC, INC.

United States Supreme Court, 1994.
510 U.S. 569, 114 S.Ct. 1164, 127 L.Ed.2d 500.

Justice SOUTER delivered the opinion of the Court.

We are called upon to decide whether 2 Live Crew's commercial parody of Roy Orbison's song, "Oh, Pretty Woman," may be a fair use within the meaning of the Copyright Act of 1976, 17 U.S.C. § 107 (1988 ed. and Supp. IV). Although the District Court granted summary judgment for 2 Live Crew, the Court of Appeals reversed, holding the defense of fair use barred by the song's commercial character and excessive borrowing. Because we hold that a parody's commercial character is only one element to be weighed in a fair use enquiry, and that insufficient consideration was given to the nature of parody in weighing the degree of copying, we reverse and remand.

I

In 1964, Roy Orbison and William Dees wrote a rock ballad called "Oh, Pretty Woman" and assigned their rights in it to respondent Acuff–Rose Music, Inc. Acuff–Rose registered the song for copyright protection. Petitioners Luther R. Campbell, Christopher Wongwon, Mark Ross, and David Hobbs are collectively known as 2 Live Crew, a popular rap music group. In 1989, Campbell wrote a song entitled "Pretty Woman," which he later described in an affidavit as intended, "through comical lyrics, to satirize the original work. . . ." On July 5, 1989, 2 Live Crew's manager informed Acuff–Rose that 2 Live Crew had written a parody of "Oh, Pretty Woman," that they would afford all credit for ownership and authorship of the original song to Acuff–Rose, Dees, and Orbison, and that they were willing to pay a fee for the use they wished to make of it. Enclosed with the letter were a copy of the lyrics and a recording of 2 Live Crew's song. Acuff–Rose's agent refused permission, stating that "I am aware of the success enjoyed by 'The 2 Live Crews', but I must inform you that we cannot permit the use of a parody of 'Oh, Pretty

Woman.'" Nonetheless, in June or July 1989, 2 Live Crew released records, cassette tapes, and compact discs of "Pretty Woman" in a collection of songs entitled "As Clean As They Wanna Be." The albums and compact discs identify the authors of "Pretty Woman" as Orbison and Dees and its publisher as Acuff–Rose.

Almost a year later, after nearly a quarter of a million copies of the recording had been sold, Acuff–Rose sued 2 Live Crew and its record company, Luke Skyywalker Records, for copyright infringement. The District Court granted summary judgment for 2 Live Crew, reasoning that the commercial purpose of 2 Live Crew's song was no bar to fair use; that 2 Live Crew's version was a parody, which "quickly degenerates into a play on words, substituting predictable lyrics with shocking ones" to show "how bland and banal the Orbison song" is; that 2 Live Crew had taken no more than was necessary to "conjure up" the original in order to parody it; and that it was "extremely unlikely that 2 Live Crew's song could adversely affect the market for the original." The District Court weighed these factors and held that 2 Live Crew's song made fair use of Orbison's original. * * *

The Court of Appeals for the Sixth Circuit reversed and remanded. 972 F.2d 1429, 1439 (1992). Although it assumed for the purpose of its opinion that 2 Live Crew's song was a parody of the Orbison original, the Court of Appeals thought the District Court had put too little emphasis on the fact that "every commercial use ... is presumptively ... unfair," *Sony Corp. of America v. Universal City Studios, Inc.,* 464 U.S. 417, 451 (1984), and it held that "the admittedly commercial nature" of the parody "requires the conclusion" that the first of four factors relevant under the statute weighs against a finding of fair use. 972 F.2d, at 1435, 1437. Next, the Court of Appeals determined that, by "taking the heart of the original and making it the heart of a new work," 2 Live Crew had, qualitatively, taken too much. *Id.,* at 1438. Finally, after noting that the effect on the potential market for the original (and the market for derivative works) is "undoubtedly the single most important element of fair use," *Harper & Row, Publishers, Inc. v. Nation Enter.,* 471 U.S. 539, 566 (1985), the Court of Appeals faulted the District Court for "refus[ing] to indulge the presumption" that "harm for purposes of the fair use analysis has been established by the presumption attaching to commercial uses." 972 F.2d, at 1438–39. In sum, the court concluded that its "blatantly commercial purpose ... prevents this parody from being a fair use." *Id.,* at 1439.

We granted certiorari, 507 U.S. 1003 (1993), to determine whether 2 Live Crew's commercial parody could be a fair use.

II

It is uncontested here that 2 Live Crew's song would be an infringement of Acuff–Rose's rights in "Oh, Pretty Woman," under the Copyright Act of 1976, 17 U.S.C. § 106 (1988 ed. and Supp. IV), but for a finding of fair use through parody. From the infancy of copyright protection, some opportunity for fair use of copyrighted materials has been thought necessary to fulfill copyright's very purpose, "[t]o promote the Progress of Science and useful Arts...." U.S. Const., Art. I, § 8, cl. 8. For as Justice Story explained, "[i]n truth, in literature, in science and in art, there are, and can be, few, if any, things, which in an abstract sense, are strictly new and original throughout. Every book in literature, science and art, borrows, and must necessarily borrow, and use much which was well known and used before." *Emerson v. Davies,* 8 F. Cas. 615, 619 (No. 4,436) (C.C.D. Mass. 1845). * * * [F]air use remained exclusively judge-made doctrine until the passage of the 1976 Copyright Act. * * *

Congress meant § 107 "to restate the present judicial doctrine of fair use, not to change, narrow, or enlarge it in any way" and intended that courts continue the common-law tradition of fair use adjudication. H.R. Rep. No. 94–1476, p. 66 (1976) (hereinafter House Report); S. Rep. No. 94–473, p. 62 (1975) U.S. Code Cong. & Admin. News 1976, pp. 5659, 5679 (hereinafter Senate Report). The fair use doctrine thus "permits [and requires] courts to avoid rigid application of the copyright statute when, on occasion, it would stifle the very creativity which that law is designed to foster." *Stewart v. Abend,* 495 U.S. 207, 236 (1990). * * *

The text employs the terms "including" and "such as" in the preamble paragraph to indicate the "illustrative and not limitative" function of the examples given, § 101; see *Harper & Row, supra,* 471 U.S., at 561, which thus provide only general guidance about the sorts of copying that courts and Congress most commonly had found to be fair uses. Nor may the four statutory factors be treated in isolation, one from another. All are to be explored, and the results weighed together, in light of the purposes of copyright. * * *

A

The first factor in a fair use enquiry is "the purpose and character of the use, including whether such use is of a commercial nature or is for nonprofit educational purposes." § 107(1). This factor draws on Justice Story's formulation, "the nature and objects of the selections made." *Folsom v. Marsh, supra,* at 348. The enquiry here may be guided by the examples given in the preamble to § 107, looking to whether the use is for criticism, or comment, or news reporting, and the like, see § 107. The central purpose of this investigation is to see, in Justice Story's words, whether the new work merely "supersede[s] the objects" of the original creation, *Folsom v. Marsh, supra,* at 348; accord, *Harper & Row, supra,* 471 U.S., at 562 ("supplanting" the original), or instead adds something new, with a further purpose or different character, altering the first with new expression, meaning, or message; it asks, in other words, whether and to what extent the new work is "transformative." Although such transformative use is not absolutely necessary for a finding of fair use, *Sony, supra,* 464 U.S., at 455, n. 40, * * * the goal of copyright, to promote science and the arts, is generally furthered by the creation of transformative works. Such works thus lie at the heart of the fair use doctrine's guarantee of breathing space within the confines of copyright, see, *e.g., Sony, supra,* at 478–480 (BLACKMUN, J., dissenting), and the more transformative the new work, the less will be the significance of other factors, like commercialism, that may weigh against a finding of fair use.

This Court has only once before even considered whether parody may be fair use, and that time issued no opinion because of the Court's equal division. *Benny v. Loew's Inc.,* 239 F.2d 532 (9th Cir. 1956), aff'd *sub nom. Columbia Broad. Sys., Inc. v. Loew's Inc.,* 356 U.S. 43 (1958). Suffice it to say now that parody has an obvious claim to transformative value, as Acuff–Rose itself does not deny. Like less ostensibly humorous forms of criticism, it can provide social benefit, by shedding light on an earlier work, and, in the process, creating a new one. We thus line up with the courts that have held that parody, like other comment or criticism, may claim fair use under § 107. See, *e.g., Fisher v. Dees,* 794 F.2d 432 (9th Cir. 1986) ("When Sonny Sniffs Glue," a parody of "When Sunny Gets Blue," is fair use); *Elsmere Music, Inc. v. Nat'l Broad. Co.,* 482 F.Supp. 741 (S.D.N.Y.), aff'd, 623 F.2d 252 (2d Cir. 1980) ("I Love Sodom," a "Saturday Night Live" television parody of "I Love New York," is fair use); see also House Report, p. 65; Senate Report, p. 61, U.S. Code Cong. & Admin. News 1976, pp. 5659, 5678 ("[U]se in a parody of some of the content of the work parodied" may be fair use).

The germ of parody lies in the definition of the Greek *parodeia,* quoted in Judge Nelson's Court of Appeals dissent, as "a song sung alongside another." 972 F.2d, at 1440, quoting 7 Encyclopedia Britannica 768 (15th ed. 1975). Modern dictionaries accordingly describe a parody as a "literary or artistic work that imitates the characteristic style of an author or a work for comic effect or ridicule," or as a "composition in prose or verse in which the characteristic turns of thought and phrase in an author or class of authors are imitated in such a way as to make them appear ridiculous." For the purposes of copyright law, the nub of the definitions, and the heart of any parodist's claim to quote from existing material, is the use of some elements of a prior author's composition to create a new one that, at least in part, comments on that author's works. If, on the contrary, the commentary has no critical bearing on the substance or style of the original composition, which the alleged infringer merely uses to get attention or to avoid the drudgery in working up something fresh, the claim to fairness in borrowing from another's work diminishes accordingly (if it does not vanish), and other factors, like the extent of its commerciality, loom larger. Parody needs to mimic an original to make its point, and so has some claim to use the creation of its victim's (or collective victims') imagination, whereas satire can stand on its own two feet and so requires justification for the very act of borrowing. * * *

The Act has no hint of an evidentiary preference for parodists over their victims, and no workable presumption for parody could take account of the fact that parody often shades into satire when society is lampooned through its creative artifacts, or that a work may contain both parodic and nonparodic elements. Accordingly, parody, like any other use, has to work its way through the relevant factors, and be judged case by case, in light of the ends of the copyright law.

Here, the District Court held, and the Court of Appeals assumed, that 2 Live Crew's "Pretty Woman" contains parody, commenting on and criticizing the original work, whatever it may have to say about society at large. As the District Court remarked, the words of 2 Live Crew's song copy the original's first line, but then "quickly degenerat[e] into a play on words, substituting predictable lyrics with shocking ones ... [that] derisively demonstrat[e] how bland and banal the Orbison song seems to them." 754 F.Supp., at 1155 (footnote omitted). Judge Nelson, dissenting below, came to the same conclusion, that the 2 Live Crew song "was clearly intended to ridicule the white-bread original" and "reminds us that sexual congress with nameless streetwalkers is not necessarily the stuff of romance and is not necessarily without its consequences. The singers (there are several) have the same thing on their minds as did the lonely man with the nasal voice, but here there is no hint of wine and roses." 972 F.2d, at 1442. Although the majority below had difficulty discerning any criticism of the original in 2 Live Crew's song, it assumed for purposes of its opinion that there was some.
* * *

We have less difficulty in finding that critical element in 2 Live Crew's song than the Court of Appeals did, although having found it we will not take the further step of evaluating its quality. The threshold question when fair use is raised in defense of parody is whether a parodic character may reasonably be perceived. Whether, going beyond that, parody is in good taste or bad does not and should not matter to fair use. As Justice Holmes explained, "[i]t would be a dangerous undertaking for persons trained only to the law to constitute themselves final judges of the worth of [a work], outside of the narrowest and most obvious limits. At the one extreme some works of genius would be sure to miss appreciation. Their very novelty would make them repulsive until the public had learned the new language in which their author spoke." *Bleistein v. Donaldson Lithographing Co.*, 188 U.S. 239, 251 (1903) (circus posters have copyright protection); cf. *Yankee Publ'g Inc. v. News America Publ'g, Inc.*, 809 F.Supp. 267, 280 (S.D.N.Y. 1992) (Leval, J.) ("First Amendment protections do not apply only to those who speak clearly, whose jokes are funny, and whose parodies succeed") (trademark case).

While we might not assign a high rank to the parodic element here, we think it fair to say that 2 Live Crew's song reasonably could be perceived as commenting on the original or criticizing it, to some degree. 2 Live Crew juxtaposes the romantic musings of a man whose fantasy comes true, with degrading taunts, a bawdy demand for sex, and a sigh of relief from paternal responsibility. The later words can be taken as a comment on the naiveté of the original of an earlier day, as a rejection of its sentiment that ignores the ugliness of street life and the debasement that it signifies. It is this joinder of reference and ridicule that marks off the author's choice of parody from the other types of comment and criticism that traditionally have had a claim to fair use protection as transformative works.

The Court of Appeals, however, immediately cut short the enquiry into 2 Live Crew's fair use claim by confining its treatment of the first factor essentially to one relevant fact, the commercial nature of the use. The court then inflated the significance of this fact by applying a presumption ostensibly culled from *Sony*, that "every commercial use of copyrighted material is presumptively ... unfair...." *Sony*, 464 U.S., at 451. In giving virtually dispositive weight to the commercial nature of the parody, the Court of Appeals erred.

The language of the statute makes clear that the commercial or nonprofit educational purpose of a work is only one element of the first factor enquiry into its purpose and character. Section 107(1) uses the term "including" to begin the dependent clause referring to commercial use, and the main clause speaks of a broader investigation into "purpose and character." As we explained in *Harper & Row,* Congress resisted attempts to narrow the ambit of this traditional enquiry by adopting categories of presumptively fair use, and it urged courts to preserve the breadth of their traditionally ample view of the universe of relevant evidence. 471 U.S., at 561; House Report, p. 66, U.S. Code Cong. & Admin. News 1976, pp. 5659, 5679. Accordingly, the mere fact that a use is educational and not for profit does not insulate it from a finding of infringement, any more than the commercial character of a use bars a finding of fairness. If, indeed, commerciality carried presumptive force against a finding of fairness, the presumption would swallow nearly all of the illustrative uses listed in the preamble paragraph of § 107, including news reporting, comment, criticism, teaching, scholarship, and research, since these activities "are generally conducted for profit in this country." *Harper & Row, supra,* at 592 (Brennan, J., dissenting). Congress could not have intended such a rule, which certainly is not inferable from the common-law cases, arising as they did from the world of letters in which Samuel Johnson could pronounce that "[n]o man but a blockhead ever wrote, except for money." 3 Boswell's Life of Johnson 19 (G. Hill ed. 1934).

Sony itself called for no hard evidentiary presumption. There, we emphasized the need for a "sensitive balancing of interests," 464 U.S., at 455, n. 40, noted that Congress had "eschewed a rigid, bright-line approach to fair use," *id.,* at 449, n. 31, and stated that the commercial or nonprofit educational character of a work is "not conclusive," *id.,* at 448–449, but rather a fact to be "weighed along with other[s] in fair use decisions," *id.,* at 449, n. 32, (quoting House Report, p. 66) U.S. Code Cong. & Admin. News 1976, pp. 5659, 5679. The Court of Appeals' elevation of one sentence from *Sony* to a *per se* rule thus runs as much counter to *Sony* itself as to the long common-law tradition of fair use adjudication. Rather, as we explained in *Harper & Row, Sony* stands for the proposition that the "fact that a publication was commercial as opposed to nonprofit is a separate factor that tends to weigh against a finding of fair use." 471 U.S., at 562. But that is all, and the fact that even the force of that tendency will vary with the context is a further reason against elevating commerciality to hard presumptive significance. The use, for example, of a copyrighted work to advertise a product, even in a parody, will be entitled to less indulgence under the first factor of the fair use enquiry than the sale of a parody for its own sake, let alone one performed a single time by students in school. * * *

B

The second statutory factor, "the nature of the copyrighted work," § 107(2), draws on Justice Story's expression, the "value of the materials used." *Folsom v. Marsh*, 9 F. Cas., at 348. This factor calls for recognition that some works are closer to the core of intended copyright protection than others, with the consequence that fair use is more difficult to establish when the former works are copied. See, *e.g., Stewart v. Abend*, 495 U.S., at 237–38 (contrasting fictional short story with factual works); *Harper & Row*, 471 U.S., at 563–64 (contrasting soon-to-be-published memoir with published speech); *Sony*, 464 U.S., at 455, n. 40 (contrasting motion pictures with news broadcasts); *Feist*, 499 U.S., at 348–51 (contrasting creative works with bare factual compilations); 3 M. Nimmer & D. Nimmer, Nimmer on Copyright § 13.05[A][2] (1993) (hereinafter Nimmer); Leval 1116. We agree with both the District Court and the Court of Appeals that the Orbison original's creative expression for public dissemination falls within the core of the copyright's protective purposes. 754 F.Supp., at 1155–56; 972 F.2d, at 1437. This fact, however, is not much help in this case, or ever likely to help much in separating the fair use sheep from the infringing goats in a parody case, since parodies almost invariably copy publicly known, expressive works.

C

The third factor asks whether "the amount and substantiality of the portion used in relation to the copyrighted work as a whole," § 107(3) (or, in Justice Story's words, "the quantity and value of the materials used," *Folsom v. Marsh, supra*, at 348) are reasonable in relation to the purpose of the copying. Here, attention turns to the persuasiveness of a parodist's justification for the particular copying done, and the enquiry will harken back to the first of the statutory factors, for, as in prior cases, we recognize that the extent of permissible copying varies with the purpose and character of the use. * * * The facts bearing on this factor will also tend to address the fourth, by revealing the degree to which the parody may serve as a market substitute for the original or potentially licensed derivatives. * * *

The District Court considered the song's parodic purpose in finding that 2 Live Crew had not helped themselves overmuch. 754 F.Supp., at 1156–57. The Court of Appeals disagreed, stating that "[w]hile it may not be inappropriate to find that no more was taken than necessary, the copying was qualitatively substantial.... We conclude that taking the heart of the original and making it the heart of a new work was to purloin a substantial portion of the essence of the original." 972 F.2d, at 1438.

The Court of Appeals is of course correct that this factor calls for thought not only about the quantity of the materials used, but about their quality and importance, too. In *Harper & Row,* for example, the Nation had taken only some 300 words out of President Ford's memoirs, but we signaled the significance of the quotations in finding them to amount to "the heart of the book," the part most likely to be newsworthy and important in licensing serialization. 471 U.S., at 564–66 (internal quotation marks omitted). We also agree with the Court of Appeals that whether "a substantial portion of the infringing work was copied verbatim" from the copyrighted work is a relevant question, for it may reveal a dearth of transformative character or purpose under the first factor, or a greater likelihood of market harm under the fourth; a work composed primarily of an original, particularly its heart, with little added or changed, is more likely to be a merely superseding use, fulfilling demand for the original.

Where we part company with the court below is in applying these guides to parody, and in particular to parody in the song before us. Parody presents a difficult case. Parody's humor, or in any event its comment, necessarily springs from recognizable allusion to its object through distorted imitation. Its art lies in the tension between a known original and its parodic twin. When parody takes aim at a particular original work, the parody must be able to "conjure up" at least enough of that original to make the object of its critical wit recognizable. * * *

What makes for this recognition is quotation of the original's most distinctive or memorable features, which the parodist can be sure the audience will know. Once enough has been taken to assure identification, how much more is reasonable will depend, say, on the extent to which the song's overriding purpose and character is to parody the original or, in contrast, the likelihood that the parody may serve as a market substitute for the original. But using some characteristic features cannot be avoided.

We think the Court of Appeals was insufficiently appreciative of parody's need for the recognizable sight or sound when it ruled 2 Live Crew's use unreasonable as a matter of law. It is true, of course, that 2 Live Crew copied the characteristic opening bass riff (or musical phrase) of the original, and true that the words of the first line copy the Orbison lyrics. But if quotation of the opening riff and the first line may be said to go to the "heart" of the original, the heart is also what most readily conjures up the song for parody, and it is the heart at which parody takes aim. Copying does not become excessive in relation to parodic purpose merely because the portion taken was the original's heart. If 2 Live Crew had copied a significantly less memorable part of the original, it is difficult to see how its parodic character would have come through. * * *

This is not, of course, to say that anyone who calls himself a parodist can skim the cream and get away scot free. In parody, as in news reporting, * * * context is everything, and the question of fairness asks what else the parodist did besides go to the heart of the original. It is significant that 2 Live Crew not only copied the first line of the original, but thereafter departed markedly from the Orbison lyrics for its own ends. 2 Live Crew not only copied the bass riff and repeated it, but also produced otherwise distinctive sounds, interposing "scraper" noise, overlaying the music with solos in different keys, and altering the drum beat. * * * This is not a case, then, where "a substantial portion" of the parody itself is composed of a "verbatim" copying of the original. It is not, that is, a case where the parody is so insubstantial, as compared to the copying, that the third factor must be resolved as a matter of law against the parodists.

Suffice it to say here that, as to the lyrics, we think the Court of Appeals correctly suggested that "no more was taken than necessary," * * * but just for that reason, we fail to see how the copying can be excessive in relation to its parodic purpose, even if the portion taken is the original's "heart." As to the music, we express no opinion whether repetition of the bass riff is excessive copying, and we remand to permit evaluation of the amount taken, in light of the song's parodic purpose and character, its transformative elements, and considerations of the potential for market substitution sketched more fully below.

D

The fourth fair use factor is "the effect of the use upon the potential market for or value of the copyrighted work." § 107(4). It requires courts to consider not only the extent of market harm caused by the particular actions of the alleged infringer, but also "whether unrestricted and widespread conduct of the sort engaged in by the defendant . . . would result in a substantially adverse impact on the potential market" for the original. * * * The enquiry "must take account not only of harm to the original but also of harm to the market for derivative works." * * *

Since fair use is an affirmative defense, its proponent would have difficulty carrying the burden of demonstrating fair use without favorable evidence about relevant markets. In moving for summary judgment, 2 Live Crew left themselves at just such a disadvantage when they failed to address the effect on the market for rap derivatives, and confined themselves to uncontroverted submissions that there was no likely effect on the market for the original. They did not, however, thereby subject themselves to the evidentiary presumption applied by the Court of Appeals. In assessing the likelihood of significant market harm, the Court of Appeals quoted from language in *Sony* that " '[i]f the intended use is for commercial gain, that likelihood may be presumed. But if it is for a noncommercial purpose, the likelihood must be demonstrated.' " 972 F.2d, at 1438, quoting *Sony,* 464 U.S., at 451. The court reasoned that because "the use of the copyrighted work is wholly commercial, . . .

we presume that a likelihood of future harm to Acuff–Rose exists." * * *
In so doing, the court resolved the fourth factor against 2 Live Crew, just
as it had the first, by applying a presumption about the effect of
commercial use, a presumption which as applied here we hold to be
error.

No "presumption" or inference of market harm that might find
support in *Sony* is applicable to a case involving something beyond mere
duplication for commercial purposes. *Sony*'s discussion of a presumption
contrasts a context of verbatim copying of the original in its entirety for
commercial purposes, with the noncommercial context of *Sony* itself
(home copying of television programming). In the former circumstances,
what *Sony* said simply makes common sense: when a commercial use
amounts to mere duplication of the entirety of an original, it clearly
"supersede[s] the objects," * * * of the original and serves as a market
replacement for it, making it likely that cognizable market harm to the
original will occur. * * * But when, on the contrary, the second use is
transformative, market substitution is at least less certain, and market
harm may not be so readily inferred. Indeed, as to parody pure and
simple, it is more likely that the new work will not affect the market for
the original in a way cognizable under this factor, that is, by acting as a
substitute for it ("supersed[ing] [its] objects"). * * * This is so because
the parody and the original usually serve different market functions.
* * *

We do not, of course, suggest that a parody may not harm the
market at all, but when a lethal parody, like a scathing theater review,
kills demand for the original, it does not produce a harm cognizable
under the Copyright Act. Because "parody may quite legitimately aim at
garroting the original, destroying it commercially as well as artistically,"
the role of the courts is to distinguish between "[b]iting criticism [that
merely] suppresses demand [and] copyright infringement[, which] usurps
it." * * *

This distinction between potentially remediable displacement and
unremediable disparagement is reflected in the rule that there is no
protectible derivative market for criticism. The market for potential
derivative uses includes only those that creators of original works would
in general develop or license others to develop. Yet the unlikelihood that
creators of imaginative works will license critical reviews or lampoons of
their own productions removes such uses from the very notion of a
potential licensing market. "People ask ... for criticism, but they only
want praise." S. Maugham, Of Human Bondage 241 (Penguine ed. 1992).
Thus, to the extent that the opinion below may be read to have
considered harm to the market for parodies of "Oh, Pretty Woman,"
* * * the court erred. * * *

In explaining why the law recognizes no derivative market for
critical works, including parody, we have, of course, been speaking of the
later work as if it had nothing but a critical aspect (*i.e.,* "parody pure
and simple,"). But the later work may have a more complex character,
with effects not only in the arena of criticism but also in protectible

markets for derivative works, too. In that sort of case, the law looks beyond the criticism to the other elements of the work, as it does here. 2 Live Crew's song comprises not only parody but also rap music, and the derivative market for rap music is a proper focus of enquiry. * * * Evidence of substantial harm to it would weigh against a finding of fair use, because the licensing of derivatives is an important economic incentive to the creation of originals. See 17 U.S.C. § 106(2) (copyright owner has rights to derivative works). Of course, the only harm to derivatives that need concern us, as discussed above, is the harm of market substitution. The fact that a parody may impair the market for derivative uses by the very effectiveness of its critical commentary is no more relevant under copyright than the like threat to the original market.

Although 2 Live Crew submitted uncontroverted affidavits on the question of market harm to the original, neither they, nor Acuff–Rose, introduced evidence or affidavits addressing the likely effect of 2 Live Crew's parodic rap song on the market for a nonparody, rap version of "Oh, Pretty Woman." And while Acuff–Rose would have us find evidence of a rap market in the very facts that 2 Live Crew recorded a rap parody of "Oh, Pretty Woman" and another rap group sought a license to record a rap derivative, there was no evidence that a potential rap market was harmed in any way by 2 Live Crew's parody, rap version. The fact that 2 Live Crew's parody sold as part of a collection of rap songs says very little about the parody's effect on a market for a rap version of the original, either of the music alone or of the music with its lyrics. The District Court essentially passed on this issue, observing that Acuff–Rose is free to record "whatever version of the original it desires," * * * the Court of Appeals went the other way by erroneous presumption. Contrary to each treatment, it is impossible to deal with the fourth factor except by recognizing that a silent record on an important factor bearing on fair use disentitled the proponent of the defense, 2 Live Crew, to summary judgment. The evidentiary hole will doubtless be plugged on remand.

III

It was error for the Court of Appeals to conclude that the commercial nature of 2 Live Crew's parody of "Oh, Pretty Woman" rendered it presumptively unfair. No such evidentiary presumption is available to address either the first factor, the character and purpose of the use, or the fourth, market harm, in determining whether a transformative use, such as parody, is a fair one. The court also erred in holding that 2 Live Crew had necessarily copied excessively from the Orbison original, considering the parodic purpose of the use. We therefore reverse the judgment of the Court of Appeals and remand the case for further proceedings consistent with this opinion.

It is so ordered.

APPENDIX A TO OPINION OF THE COURT

"Oh, Pretty Woman" by Roy Orbison and William Dees

Pretty Woman, walking down the street,

Pretty Woman, the kind I like to meet,

Pretty Woman, I don't believe you, you're not the truth,

No one could look as good as you

Mercy

Pretty Woman, won't you pardon me,

Pretty Woman, I couldn't help but see,

Pretty Woman, that you look lovely as can be

Are you lonely just like me?

Pretty Woman, stop a while,

Pretty Woman, talk a while,

Pretty Woman give your smile to me

Pretty Woman, yeah, yeah, yeah

Pretty Woman, look my way,

Pretty Woman, say you'll stay with me

'Cause I need you, I'll treat you right

Come to me baby, Be mine tonight

Pretty Woman, don't walk on by,

Pretty Woman, don't make me cry,

Pretty Woman, don't walk away,

Hey, O.K.

If that's the way it must be, O.K.

I guess I'll go on home, it's late

There'll be tomorrow night, but wait!

What do I see

Is she walking back to me?

Yeah, she's walking back to me!

Oh, Pretty Woman.

APPENDIX B TO OPINION OF THE COURT

"Pretty Woman" as Recorded by 2 Live Crew

Pretty woman walkin' down the street

Pretty woman girl you look so sweet

Pretty woman you bring me down to that knee

Pretty woman you make me wanna beg please

Oh, pretty woman

Big hairy woman you need to shave that stuff

Big hairy woman you know I bet it's tough

Big hairy woman all that hair it ain't legit

'Cause you look like 'Cousin It'

Big hairy woman

Bald headed woman girl your hair won't grow

Bald headed woman you got a teeny weeny afro

Bald headed woman you know your hair could look nice

Bald headed woman first you got to roll it with rice

Bald headed woman here, let me get this hunk of biz for ya

Ya know what I'm saying you look better than rice a roni

Oh bald headed woman

Big hairy woman come on in

And don't forget your bald headed friend

Hey pretty woman let the boys

Jump in

Two timin' woman girl you know you ain't right

Two timin' woman you's out with my boy last night

Two timin' woman that takes a load off my mind

Two timin' woman now I know the baby ain't mine

Oh, two timin' woman

Oh pretty woman

[Concurring opinion omitted]

Notes

1. Fair use and parody: Producers or creators of work that is a satire or parody of a copyrighted work have been sued for infringement by the targets of their satire, even though such use may be protected as fair use. According to Jay Levy, Weird Al Yankovich's manager, "Al believes that getting permission to use the songs is the ethical thing to do. It's not a legal issue to him; it's the right thing to do. The main reason Al gets permission from the artist is because he wants the artist to be in on the joke." Bill Henslee Telephone Interview with Jay Levy, Al Yankovich's Manager (July 3, 2003).

2. In *MCA, Inc. v. Wilson*, 425 F.Supp. 443 (S.D.N.Y. 1976), the court was presented with the question of whether the song "Cunnilingus Champion of Company C" as used in the play "Let My People Come: A Sexual Musical" infringed upon the copyright of the song "Boogie Woogie Bugle Boy of Company B." Finding that the defendant's song, although it "may have

sought to parody life, or more particularly sexual mores and taboos," did not attempt to parody or "comment ludicrously upon Bugle Boy" itself, the court held that there had been no fair use, and that as a result the plaintiff's copyright had been infringed.

3. In *Walt Disney Prod. v. Mature Pictures Corp.,* 389 F.Supp. 1397 (S.D.N.Y. 1975), the court held that, while the defendants may have been seeking in their display of bestiality to parody life, they did not parody the Mickey Mouse March but sought only to improperly use the copyrighted material.

4. In *Elsmere Music, Inc. v. NBC,* 482 F.Supp. 741 (S.D.N.Y. 1980), a Saturday Night Live skit called "I love Sodom" was held to be a parody of "I Love New York." The defendant argued that the use it made was insufficient to constitute copyright infringement. The Court disagreed, finding the taking was relatively slight, but was the heart of the composition.

A&M RECORDS, INC. v. NAPSTER, INC.

United States Court of Appeals, Ninth Circuit, 2001.
239 F.3d 1004.

BEEZER, Circuit Judge.

Plaintiffs are engaged in the commercial recording, distribution and sale of copyrighted musical compositions and sound recordings. The complaint alleges that Napster, Inc. ("Napster") is a contributory and vicarious copyright infringer. On July 26, 2000, the district court granted plaintiffs' motion for a preliminary injunction. The injunction was slightly modified by written opinion on August 10, 2000. *A & M Records, Inc. v. Napster, Inc.,* 114 F. Supp. 2d 896 (N.D. Cal. 2000). The district court preliminarily enjoined Napster "from engaging in, or facilitating others in copying, downloading, uploading, transmitting, or distributing plaintiffs' copyrighted musical compositions and sound recordings, protected by either federal or state law, without express permission of the rights owner." *Id.* at 927. Federal Rule of Civil Procedure 65(c) requires successful plaintiffs to post a bond for damages incurred by the enjoined party in the event that the injunction was wrongfully issued. The district court set bond in this case at $5 million.

We entered a temporary stay of the preliminary injunction pending resolution of this appeal. We have jurisdiction pursuant to 28 U.S.C. § 1292(a)(1). We affirm in part, reverse in part and remand.

I

We have examined the papers submitted in support of and in response to the injunction application and it appears that Napster has designed and operates a system which permits the transmission and retention of sound recordings employing digital technology.

In 1987, the Moving Picture Experts Group set a standard file format for the storage of audio recordings in a digital format called MPEG–3, abbreviated as "MP3." Digital MP3 files are created through a process colloquially called "ripping." Ripping software allows a computer owner to copy an audio compact disk ("audio CD") directly onto a computer's hard drive by compressing the audio information on the CD into the MP3 format. The MP3's compressed format allows for rapid transmission of digital audio files from one computer to another by electronic mail or any other file transfer protocol.

Napster facilitates the transmission of MP3 files between and among its users. Through a process commonly called "peer-to-peer" file sharing, Napster allows its users to: (1) make MP3 music files stored on individual computer hard drives available for copying by other Napster users; (2) search for MP3 music files stored on other users' computers; and (3) transfer exact copies of the contents of other users' MP3 files from one computer to another via the Internet. These functions are made possible by Napster's MusicShare software, available free of charge from Napster's Internet site, and Napster's network servers and server-side software. Napster provides technical support for the indexing and searching of MP3 files, as well as for its other functions, including a "chat room," where users can meet to discuss music, and a directory where participating artists can provide information about their music.

A. ACCESSING THE SYSTEM

In order to copy MP3 files through the Napster system, a user must first access Napster's Internet site and download the MusicShare software to his individual computer. *See http://www.Napster.com.* Once the software is installed, the user can access the Napster system. A first-time user is required to register with the Napster system by creating a "user name" and password.

B. LISTING AVAILABLE FILES

If a registered user wants to list available files stored in his computer's hard drive on Napster for others to access, he must first create a "user library" directory on his computer's hard drive. The user then saves his MP3 files in the library directory, using self-designated file names. He next must log into the Napster system using his user name and password. His MusicShare software then searches his user library and verifies that the available files are properly formatted. If in the correct MP3 format, the names of the MP3 files will be uploaded from the user's computer to the Napster servers. The content of the MP3 files remains stored in the user's computer.

Once uploaded to the Napster servers, the user's MP3 file names are stored in a server-side "library" under the user's name and become part of a "collective directory" of files available for transfer during the time the user is logged onto the Napster system. The collective directory is fluid; it tracks users who are connected in real time, displaying only file names that are immediately accessible.

C. Searching For Available Files

Napster allows a user to locate other users' MP3 files in two ways: through Napster's search function and through its "hotlist" function.

Software located on the Napster servers maintains a "search index" of Napster's collective directory. To search the files available from Napster users currently connected to the network servers, the individual user accesses a form in the MusicShare software stored in his computer and enters either the name of a song or an artist as the object of the search. The form is then transmitted to a Napster server and automatically compared to the MP3 file names listed in the server's search index. Napster's server compiles a list of all MP3 file names pulled from the search index which include the same search terms entered on the search form and transmits the list to the searching user. The Napster server does not search the contents of any MP3 file; rather, the search is limited to "a text search of the file names indexed in a particular cluster. Those file names may contain typographical errors or otherwise inaccurate descriptions of the content of the files since they are designated by other users." *Napster*, 114 F.Supp.2d at 906.

To use the "hotlist" function, the Napster user creates a list of other users' names from whom he has obtained MP3 files in the past. When logged onto Napster's servers, the system alerts the user if any user on his list (a "hotlisted user") is also logged onto the system. If so, the user can access an index of all MP3 file names in a particular hotlisted user's library and request a file in the library by selecting the file name. The contents of the hotlisted user's MP3 file are not stored on the Napster system.

D. Transferring Copies of an MP3 file

To transfer a copy of the contents of a requested MP3 file, the Napster server software obtains the Internet address of the requesting user and the Internet address of the "host user" (the user with the available files). *See generally, Brookfield Communications, Inc. v. West Coast Entm't Corp.*, 174 F.3d 1036, 1044 (9th Cir. 1999) (describing, in detail, the structure of the Internet). The Napster servers then communicate the host user's Internet address to the requesting user. The requesting user's computer uses this information to establish a connection with the host user and downloads a copy of the contents of the MP3 file from one computer to the other over the Internet, "peer-to-peer." A downloaded MP3 file can be played directly from the user's hard drive using Napster's MusicShare program or other software. The file may also be transferred back onto an audio CD if the user has access to equipment designed for that purpose. In both cases, the quality of the original sound recording is slightly diminished by transfer to the MP3 format.

This architecture is described in some detail to promote an understanding of transmission mechanics as opposed to the content of the transmissions. The content is the subject of our copyright infringement analysis. * * *

III

Plaintiffs claim Napster users are engaged in the wholesale reproduction and distribution of copyrighted works, all constituting direct infringement. The district court agreed. We note that the district court's conclusion that plaintiffs have presented a prima facie case of direct infringement by Napster users is not presently appealed by Napster. We only need briefly address the threshold requirements.

A. Infringement

Plaintiffs must satisfy two requirements to present a prima facie case of direct infringement: (1) they must show ownership of the allegedly infringed material and (2) they must demonstrate that the alleged infringers violate at least one exclusive right granted to copyright holders under 17 U.S.C. § 106. *See* 17 U.S.C. § 501(a) (infringement occurs when alleged infringer engages in activity listed in § 106); *see also Baxter v. MCA, Inc.,* 812 F.2d 421, 423 (9th Cir. 1987); *see, e.g., S.O.S., Inc. v. Payday, Inc.,* 886 F.2d 1081, 1085 n. 3 (9th Cir. 1989) ("The word 'copying' is shorthand for the infringing of any of the copyright owner's five exclusive rights. . . ."). Plaintiffs have sufficiently demonstrated ownership. The record supports the district court's determination that "as much as eighty-seven percent of the files available on Napster may be copyrighted and more than seventy percent may be owned or administered by plaintiffs." *Napster,* 114 F.Supp.2d at 911.

The district court further determined that plaintiffs' exclusive rights under § 106 were violated: "here the evidence establishes that a majority of Napster users use the service to download and upload copyrighted music. . . . And by doing that, it constitutes—the uses constitute direct infringement of plaintiffs' musical compositions, recordings." *A & M Records, Inc. v. Napster, Inc.,* Nos. 99–5183, 00–0074, 2000 WL 1009483, at *1 (N.D. Cal. July 26, 2000) (transcript of proceedings). The district court also noted that "it is pretty much acknowledged . . . by Napster that this is infringement." We agree that plaintiffs have shown that Napster users infringe at least two of the copyright holders' exclusive rights: the rights of reproduction, § 106(1); and distribution, § 106(3). Napster users who upload file names to the search index for others to copy violate plaintiffs' distribution rights. Napster users who download files containing copyrighted music violate plaintiffs' reproduction rights.

Napster asserts an affirmative defense to the charge that its users directly infringe plaintiffs' copyrighted musical compositions and sound recordings.

B. Fair Use

Napster contends that its users do not directly infringe plaintiffs' copyrights because the users are engaged in fair use of the material. *See*

17 U.S.C. § 107 ("[T]he fair use of a copyrighted work ... is not an infringement of copyright."). Napster identifies three specific alleged fair uses: sampling, where users make temporary copies of a work before purchasing; space-shifting, where users access a sound recording through the Napster system that they already own in audio CD format; and permissive distribution of recordings by both new and established artists.

The district court considered factors listed in 17 U.S.C. § 107, which guide a court's fair use determination. Those factors are: (1) the purpose and character of the use; (2) the nature of the copyrighted work; (3) the "amount and substantiality of the portion used" in relation to the work as a whole; and (4) the effect of the use upon the potential market for the work or the value of the work. See 17 U.S.C. § 107. The district court first conducted a general analysis of Napster system uses under § 107, and then applied its reasoning to the alleged fair uses identified by Napster. The district court concluded that the Napster users are not fair users. We agree. We first address the overall fair use analysis.

1. Purpose and Character of the Use

This factor focuses on whether the new work merely replaces the object of the original creation or instead adds a further purpose or different character. In other words, this factor asks "whether and to what extent the new work is 'transformative.'" See Campbell v. Acuff-Rose Music, Inc., 510 U.S. 569, 579 (1994).

The district court first concluded that downloading MP3 files does not transform the copyrighted work. Napster, 114 F.Supp.2d at 912. This conclusion is supportable. Courts have been reluctant to find fair use when an original work is merely retransmitted in a different medium. See, e.g., Infinity Broadcast Corp. v. Kirkwood, 150 F.3d 104, 108 (2d Cir. 1998) (concluding that retransmission of radio broadcast over telephone lines is not transformative); UMG Recordings, Inc. v. MP3.com, Inc., 92 F.Supp.2d 349, 351 (S.D.N.Y.) (finding that reproduction of audio CD into MP3 format does not "transform" the work), certification denied, 2000 WL 710056 (S.D.N.Y. June 1, 2000) ("Defendant's copyright infringement was clear, and the mere fact that it was clothed in the exotic webbing of the Internet does not disguise its illegality.").

This "purpose and character" element also requires the district court to determine whether the allegedly infringing use is commercial or noncommercial. See Campbell, 510 U.S. at 584–85. A commercial use weighs against a finding of fair use but is not conclusive on the issue. The district court determined that Napster users engage in commercial use of the copyrighted materials largely because (1) "a host user sending a file cannot be said to engage in a personal use when distributing that file to an anonymous requester" and (2) "Napster users get for free something they would ordinarily have to buy." Napster, 114 F.Supp.2d at 912. The district court's findings are not clearly erroneous.

Direct economic benefit is not required to demonstrate a commercial use. Rather, repeated and exploitative copying of copyrighted works, even if the copies are not offered for sale, may constitute a commercial use. *See Worldwide Church of God v. Philadelphia Church of God,* 227 F.3d 1110, 1118 (9th Cir. 2000) (stating that church that copied religious text for its members "unquestionably profit[ed]" from the unauthorized "distribution and use of [the text] without having to account to the copyright holder"); *American Geophysical Union v. Texaco, Inc.,* 60 F.3d 913, 922 (2d Cir. 1994) (finding that researchers at for-profit laboratory gained indirect economic advantage by photocopying copyrighted scholarly articles). In the record before us, commercial use is demonstrated by a showing that repeated and exploitative unauthorized copies of copyrighted works were made to save the expense of purchasing authorized copies. *See Worldwide Church,* 227 F.3d at 1117–18; *Sega Enters. Ltd. v. MAPHIA,* 857 F.Supp. 679, 687 (N.D. Cal. 1994) (finding commercial use when individuals downloaded copies of video games "to avoid having to buy video game cartridges"); *see also American Geophysical,* 60 F.3d at 922. Plaintiffs made such a showing before the district court.

We also note that the definition of a financially motivated transaction for the purposes of criminal copyright actions includes trading infringing copies of a work for other items, "including the receipt of other copyrighted works." *See* No Electronic Theft Act ("NET Act"), Pub. L. No. 105–147, 18 U.S.C. § 101 (defining "Financial Gain").

2. The Nature of the Use

Works that are creative in nature are "closer to the core of intended copyright protection" than are more fact-based works. *See Campbell,* 510 U.S. at 586. The district court determined that plaintiffs' "copyrighted musical compositions and sound recordings are creative in nature ... which cuts against a finding of fair use under the second factor." *Napster,* 114 F.Supp.2d at 913. We find no error in the district court's conclusion.

3. The Portion Used

"While 'wholesale copying does not preclude fair use per se,' copying an entire work 'militates against a finding of fair use.' "*Worldwide Church,* 227 F.3d at 1118 (quoting *Hustler Magazine, Inc. v. Moral Majority, Inc.,* 796 F.2d 1148, 1155 (9th Cir. 1986)). The district court determined that Napster users engage in "wholesale copying" of copyrighted work because file transfer necessarily "involves copying the entirety of the copyrighted work." *Napster,* 114 F.Supp.2d at 913. We agree. We note, however, that under certain circumstances, a court will conclude that a use is fair even when the protected work is copied in its entirety. *See, e.g., Sony Corp. v. Universal City Studios, Inc.,* 464 U.S. 417, 449–50 (1984) (acknowledging that fair use of time-shifting necessarily involved making a full copy of a protected work).

4. Effect of Use on Market

"Fair use, when properly applied, is limited to copying by others which does not materially impair the marketability of the work which is copied." *Harper & Row Publishers, Inc. v. Nation Enters.*, 471 U.S. 539, 566–67 (1985). "[T]he importance of this [fourth] factor will vary, not only with the amount of harm, but also with the relative strength of the showing on the other factors." *Campbell*, 510 U.S. at 591 n. 21. The proof required to demonstrate present or future market harm varies with the purpose and character of the use: A challenge to a noncommercial use of a copyrighted work requires proof either that the particular use is harmful, or that if it should become widespread, it would adversely affect the potential market for the copyrighted work.... *If the intended use is for commercial gain, that likelihood [of market harm] may be presumed. But if it is for a noncommercial purpose, the likelihood must be demonstrated. Sony,* 464 U.S. at 451 (emphasis added).

Addressing this factor, the district court concluded that Napster harms the market in "at least" two ways: it reduces audio CD sales among college students and it "raises barriers to plaintiffs' entry into the market for the digital downloading of music." *Napster,* 114 F.Supp.2d at 913. The district court relied on evidence plaintiffs submitted to show that Napster use harms the market for their copyrighted musical compositions and sound recordings. In a separate memorandum and order regarding the parties' objections to the expert reports, the district court examined each report, finding some more appropriate and probative than others. *A & M Records, Inc. v. Napster, Inc.*, Nos. 99–5183 & 00–0074, 2000 WL 1170106 (N.D. Cal. August 10, 2000). Notably, plaintiffs' expert, Dr. E. Deborah Jay, conducted a survey (the "Jay Report") using a random sample of college and university students to track their reasons for using Napster and the impact Napster had on their music purchases. *Id.* at *2. The court recognized that the Jay Report focused on just one segment of the Napster user population and found "evidence of lost sales attributable to college use to be probative of irreparable harm for purposes of the preliminary injunction motion." *Id.* at *3.

Plaintiffs also offered a study conducted by Michael Fine, Chief Executive Officer of Soundscan, (the "Fine Report") to determine the effect of online sharing of MP3 files in order to show irreparable harm. Fine found that online file sharing had resulted in a loss of "album" sales within college markets. After reviewing defendant's objections to the Fine Report and expressing some concerns regarding the methodology and findings, the district court refused to exclude the Fine Report insofar as plaintiffs offered it to show irreparable harm. *Id.* at *6.

Plaintiffs' expert Dr. David J. Teece studied several issues ("Teece Report"), including whether plaintiffs had suffered or were likely to suffer harm in their existing and planned businesses due to Napster use. *Id.* Napster objected that the report had not undergone peer review. The district court noted that such reports generally are not subject to such scrutiny and overruled defendant's objections. *Id.*

As for defendant's experts, plaintiffs objected to the report of Dr. Peter S. Fader, in which the expert concluded that Napster is *beneficial* to the music industry because MP3 music file-sharing stimulates more audio CD sales than it displaces. *Id.* at *7. The district court found problems in Dr. Fader's minimal role in overseeing the administration of the survey and the lack of objective data in his report. The court decided the generality of the report rendered it "of dubious reliability and value." The court did not exclude the report, however, but chose "not to rely on Fader's findings in determining the issues of fair use and irreparable harm." *Id.* at *8.

The district court cited both the Jay and Fine Reports in support of its finding that Napster use harms the market for plaintiffs' copyrighted musical compositions and sound recordings by reducing CD sales among college students. The district court cited the Teece Report to show the harm Napster use caused in raising barriers to plaintiffs' entry into the market for digital downloading of music. *Napster,* 114 F.Supp.2d at 910. The district court's careful consideration of defendant's objections to these reports and decision to rely on the reports for specific issues demonstrates a proper exercise of discretion in addition to a correct application of the fair use doctrine. Defendant has failed to show any basis for disturbing the district court's findings. * * *

Moreover, lack of harm to an established market cannot deprive the copyright holder of the right to develop alternative markets for the works. *See L.A. Times v. Free Republic,* 54 U.S.P.Q.2d 1453, 1469–71 (C.D. Cal. 2000) (stating that online market for plaintiff newspapers' articles was harmed because plaintiffs demonstrated that "[defendants] are attempting to exploit the market for viewing their articles online"); *see also UMG Recordings,* 92 F.Supp.2d at 352 ("Any allegedly positive impact of defendant's activities on plaintiffs' prior market in no way frees defendant to usurp a further market that directly derives from reproduction of the plaintiffs' copyrighted works."). Here, similar to *L.A. Times* and *UMG Recordings,* the record supports the district court's finding that the "record company plaintiffs have already expended considerable funds and effort to commence Internet sales and licensing for digital downloads." 114 F.Supp.2d at 915. Having digital downloads available for free on the Napster system necessarily harms the copyright holders' attempts to charge for the same downloads. * * *

5. *Identified Uses*

Napster maintains that its identified uses of sampling and space-shifting were wrongly excluded as fair uses by the district court.

a. *Sampling*

Napster contends that its users download MP3 files to "sample" the music in order to decide whether to purchase the recording. Napster argues that the district court: (1) erred in concluding that sampling is a commercial use because it conflated a noncommercial use with a personal use; (2) erred in determining that sampling adversely affects the market for plaintiffs' copyrighted music, a requirement if the use is noncommercial; and (3) erroneously concluded that sampling is not a fair use because it determined that samplers may also engage in other infringing activity.

The district court determined that sampling remains a commercial use even if some users eventually purchase the music. We find no error in the district court's determination. Plaintiffs have established that they are likely to succeed in proving that even authorized temporary downloading of individual songs for sampling purposes is commercial in nature. *See Napster,* 114 F. Supp. 2d at 913. The record supports a finding that free promotional downloads are highly regulated by the record company plaintiffs and that the companies collect royalties for song samples available on retail Internet sites. *Id.* Evidence relied on by the district court demonstrates that the free downloads provided by the record companies consist of thirty-to-sixty second samples or are full songs programmed to "time out," that is, exist only for a short time on the downloader's computer. *Id.* at 913–14. In comparison, Napster users download a full, free and permanent copy of the recording. *Id.* at 914–15. The determination by the district court as to the commercial purpose and character of sampling is not clearly erroneous.

The district court further found that both the market for audio CDs and market for online distribution are adversely affected by Napster's service. As stated in our discussion of the district court's general fair use analysis: the court did not abuse its discretion when it found that, overall, Napster has an adverse impact on the audio CD and digital download markets. Contrary to Napster's assertion that the district court failed to specifically address the market impact of sampling, the district court determined that "[e]ven if the type of sampling supposedly done on Napster were a non-commercial use, plaintiffs have demonstrated a substantial likelihood that it would adversely affect the potential market for their copyrighted works if it became widespread." *Napster,* 114 F.Supp.2d at 914. The record supports the district court's preliminary determinations that: (1) the more music that sampling users download, the less likely they are to eventually purchase the recordings on audio CD; and (2) even if the audio CD market is not harmed, Napster has adverse effects on the developing digital download market.

Napster further argues that the district court erred in rejecting its evidence that the users' downloading of "samples" increases or tends to increase audio CD sales. The district court, however, correctly noted that "any potential enhancement of plaintiffs' sales ... would not tip the fair use analysis conclusively in favor of defendant." *Id.* at 914. We agree that increased sales of copyrighted material attributable to unauthorized use should not deprive the copyright holder of the right to license the material. *See Campbell,* 510 U.S. at 591 n. 21 ("Even favorable evidence, without more, is no guarantee of fairness. Judge Leval gives the example of the film producer's appropriation of a composer's previously unknown song that turns the song into a commercial success; the boon to the song does not make the film's simple copying fair."); *see also L.A. Times,* 54 U.S.P.Q.2d at 1471–72. Nor does positive impact in one market, here the audio CD market, deprive the copyright holder of the right to develop identified alternative markets, here the digital download market. *See id.* at 1469–71. * * *

b. Space–Shifting

Napster also maintains that space-shifting is a fair use. Space-shifting occurs when a Napster user downloads MP3 music files in order to listen to music he already owns on audio CD. *See id.* at 915–16. Napster asserts that we have already held that space-shifting of musical compositions and sound recordings is a fair use. *See Recording Indus. Ass'n of Am. v. Diamond Multimedia Sys., Inc.,* 180 F.3d 1072, 1079 (9th Cir. 1999) ("Rio [a portable MP3 player] merely makes copies in order to render portable, or 'space-shift,' those files that already reside on a user's hard drive.... Such copying is a paradigmatic noncommercial personal use."). *See also generally Sony,* 464 U.S. at 423 (holding that "time-shifting," where a video tape recorder owner records a television show for later viewing, is a fair use).

We conclude that the district court did not err when it refused to apply the "shifting" analyses of *Sony* and *Diamond.* Both *Diamond* and *Sony* are inapposite because the methods of shifting in these cases did not also simultaneously involve distribution of the copyrighted material to the general public; the time or space-shifting of copyrighted material exposed the material only to the original user. In *Diamond,* for example, the copyrighted music was transferred from the user's computer hard drive to the user's portable MP3 player. So too *Sony,* where "the majority of VCR purchasers ... did not distribute taped television broadcasts, but merely enjoyed them at home." *Napster,* 114 F.Supp.2d at 913. Conversely, it is obvious that once a user lists a copy of music he already owns on the Napster system in order to access the music from another location, the song becomes "available to millions of other individuals," not just the original CD owner. *See UMG Recordings,* 92 F.Supp.2d at 351–52 (finding space-shifting of MP3 files not a fair use even when previous ownership is demonstrated before a download is allowed); *cf. Religious Tech. Ctr. v. Lerma,* No. 95–1107A, 1996 WL 633131, at *6 (E.D. Va. Oct.4, 1996) (suggesting that storing copyrighted material on computer disk for later review is not a fair use).

c. Other Uses

Permissive reproduction by either independent or established artists is the final fair use claim made by Napster. The district court noted that plaintiffs did not seek to enjoin this and any other noninfringing use of the Napster system, including: chat rooms, message boards and Napster's New Artist Program. *Napster,* 114 F.Supp.2d at 917. Plaintiffs do not challenge these uses on appeal.

We find no error in the district court's determination that plaintiffs will likely succeed in establishing that Napster users do not have a fair use defense. Accordingly, we next address whether Napster is secondarily liable for the direct infringement under two doctrines of copyright law: contributory copyright infringement and vicarious copyright infringement.

IV

We first address plaintiffs' claim that Napster is liable for contributory copyright infringement. Traditionally, "one who, with knowledge of the infringing activity, induces, causes or materially contributes to the infringing conduct of another, may be held liable as a 'contributory' infringer." *Gershwin Publ'g Corp. v. Columbia Artists Mgmt., Inc.*, 443 F.2d 1159, 1162 (2d Cir. 1971); *see also Fonovisa, Inc. v. Cherry Auction, Inc.*, 76 F.3d 259, 264 (9th Cir. 1996). Put differently, liability exists if the defendant engages in "personal conduct that encourages or assists the infringement." *Matthew Bender & Co. v. West Publ'g Co.*, 158 F.3d 693, 706 (2d Cir. 1998).

The district court determined that plaintiffs in all likelihood would establish Napster's liability as a contributory infringer. The district court did not err; Napster, by its conduct, knowingly encourages and assists the infringement of plaintiffs' copyrights.

A.   KNOWLEDGE

Contributory liability requires that the secondary infringer "know or have reason to know" of direct infringement. *Cable/Home Communication Corp. v. Network Prods., Inc.*, 902 F.2d 829, 845 & 846 n. 29 (11th Cir. 1990); *Religious Tech. Ctr. v. Netcom On–Line Communication Servs., Inc.*, 907 F. Supp. 1361, 1373–74 (N.D. Cal.1995) (framing issue as "whether Netcom knew or should have known of" the infringing activities). The district court found that Napster had both actual and constructive knowledge that its users exchanged copyrighted music. The district court also concluded that the law does not require knowledge of "specific acts of infringement" and rejected Napster's contention that because the company cannot distinguish infringing from noninfringing files, it does not "know" of the direct infringement. 114 F.Supp.2d at 917.

It is apparent from the record that Napster has knowledge, both actual and constructive, of direct infringement. Napster claims that it is nevertheless protected from contributory liability by the teaching of *Sony Corp. v. Universal City Studios, Inc.*, 464 U.S. 417 (1984). We disagree. We observe that Napster's actual, specific knowledge of direct infringement renders *Sony*'s holding of limited assistance to Napster. We are compelled to make a clear distinction between the architecture of the Napster system and Napster's conduct in relation to the operational capacity of the system.

The *Sony* Court refused to hold the manufacturer and retailers of video tape recorders liable for contributory infringement despite evidence that such machines could be and were used to infringe plaintiffs' copyrighted television shows. *Sony* stated that if liability "is to be imposed on petitioners in this case, it must rest on the fact that *they have sold equipment with constructive knowledge of the fact that their customers may use that equipment to make unauthorized copies* of copyrighted material." *Id.* at 439 (emphasis added). The *Sony* Court declined to impute the requisite level of knowledge where the defendants made and sold equipment capable of both infringing and "substantial noninfringing uses." *Id.* at 442 (adopting a modified "staple article of commerce" doctrine from patent law). *See also Universal City Studios, Inc. v. Sony Corp.,* 480 F.Supp. 429, 459 (C.D. Cal. 1979) ("This court agrees with defendants that their knowledge was insufficient to make them contributory infringers."), *rev'd,* 659 F.2d 963 (9th Cir. 1981), *rev'd,* 464 U.S. 417 (1984); Alfred C. Yen, *Internet Service Provider Liability for Subscriber Copyright Infringement, Enterprise Liability, and the First Amendment,* 88 Geo. L.J. 1833, 1874 & 1893 n.210 (2000) (suggesting that, after *Sony,* most Internet service providers lack "the requisite level of knowledge" for the imposition of contributory liability).

We are bound to follow *Sony,* and will not impute the requisite level of knowledge to Napster merely because peer-to-peer file sharing technology may be used to infringe plaintiffs' copyrights. *See* 464 U.S. at 436 (rejecting argument that merely supplying the " 'means' to accomplish an infringing activity" leads to imposition of liability). We depart from the reasoning of the district court that Napster failed to demonstrate that its system is capable of commercially significant noninfringing uses. *See Napster,* 114 F.Supp.2d at 916, 917–18. The district court improperly confined the use analysis to current uses, ignoring the system's capabilities. *See generally Sony,* 464 U.S. at 442–43 (framing inquiry as whether the video tape recorder is "*capable* of commercially significant noninfringing uses") (emphasis added). Consequently, the district court placed undue weight on the proportion of current infringing use as compared to current and future noninfringing use. *See generally Vault Corp. v. Quaid Software Ltd.,* 847 F.2d 255, 264–67 (5th Cir. 1988) (single noninfringing use implicated *Sony*). Nonetheless, whether we might arrive at a different result is not the issue here. The instant appeal occurs at an early point in the proceedings and "the fully developed factual record may be materially different from that initially before the district court...." Regardless of the number of Napster's infringing versus noninfringing uses, the evidentiary record here supported the district court's finding that plaintiffs would likely prevail in establishing that Napster knew or had reason to know of its users' infringement of plaintiffs' copyrights.
* * *

We agree that if a computer system operator learns of specific infringing material available on his system and fails to purge such material from the system, the operator knows of and contributes to direct infringement. *See Netcom,* 907 F.Supp. at 1374. Conversely, absent any specific information which identifies infringing activity, a computer system operator cannot be liable for contributory infringement merely because the structure of the system allows for the exchange of copyrighted material. *See Sony,* 464 U.S. at 436, 442–43. To enjoin simply because a computer network allows for infringing use would, in our opinion, violate *Sony* and potentially restrict activity unrelated to infringing use.

We nevertheless conclude that sufficient knowledge exists to impose contributory liability when linked to demonstrated infringing use of the Napster system. *See Napster,* 114 F.Supp.2d at 919 (*"Religious Technology Center* would not mandate a determination that Napster, Inc. lacks the knowledge requisite to contributory infringement."). The record supports the district court's finding that Napster has *actual* knowledge that *specific* infringing material is available using its system, that it could block access to the system by suppliers of the infringing material, and that it failed to remove the material. *See Napster,* 114 F.Supp.2d at 918, 920–21.

B.   MATERIAL CONTRIBUTION

Under the facts as found by the district court, Napster materially contributes to the infringing activity. Relying on *Fonovisa,* the district court concluded that "[w]ithout the support services defendant provides, Napster users could not find and download the music they want with the ease of which defendant boasts." *Napster,* 114 F.Supp.2d at 919–20 ("Napster is an integrated service designed to enable users to locate and download MP3 music files."). We agree that Napster provides "the site and facilities" for direct infringement. *See Fonovisa,* 76 F.3d at 264; *cf. Netcom,* 907 F.Supp. at 1372 ("Netcom will be liable for contributory infringement since its failure to cancel [a user's] infringing message and thereby stop an infringing copy from being distributed worldwide constitutes substantial participation."). The district court correctly applied the reasoning in *Fonovisa,* and properly found that Napster materially contributes to direct infringement.

We affirm the district court's conclusion that plaintiffs have demonstrated a likelihood of success on the merits of the contributory copyright infringement claim. We will address the scope of the injunction in part VIII of this opinion.

[Parts V–VII omitted.] * * *

VIII

The district court correctly recognized that a preliminary injunction against Napster's participation in copyright infringement is not only warranted but required. We believe, however, that the scope of the injunction needs modification in light of our opinion. Specifically, we reiterate that contributory liability may potentially be imposed only to the extent that Napster: (1) receives reasonable knowledge of specific infringing files with copyrighted musical compositions and sound recordings; (2) knows or should know that such files are available on the Napster system; and (3) fails to act to prevent viral distribution of the works. * * * The mere existence of the Napster system, absent actual notice and Napster's demonstrated failure to remove the offending material, is insufficient to impose contributory liability. * * *

Conversely, Napster may be vicariously liable when it fails to affirmatively use its ability to patrol its system and preclude access to potentially infringing files listed in its search index. Napster has both the ability to use its search function to identify infringing musical recordings and the right to bar participation of users who engage in the transmission of infringing files.

The preliminary injunction which we stayed is overbroad because it places on Napster the entire burden of ensuring that no "copying, downloading, uploading, transmitting, or distributing" of plaintiffs' works occur on the system. As stated, we place the burden on plaintiffs to provide notice to Napster of copyrighted works and files containing such works available on the Napster system before Napster has the duty to disable access to the offending content. Napster, however, also bears the burden of policing the system within the limits of the system. Here, we recognize that this is not an exact science in that the files are user named. In crafting the injunction on remand, the district court should recognize that Napster's system does not currently appear to allow Napster access to users' MP3 files.

Based on our decision to remand, Napster's additional arguments on appeal going to the scope of the injunction need not be addressed. We, however, briefly address Napster's First Amendment argument so that it is not reasserted on remand. Napster contends that the present injunction violates the First Amendment because it is broader than necessary. The company asserts two distinct free speech rights: (1) its right to publish a "directory" (here, the search index) and (2) its users' right to exchange information. We note that First Amendment concerns in copyright are allayed by the presence of the fair use doctrine. * * * There was a preliminary determination here that Napster users are not fair users. Uses of copyrighted material that are not fair uses are rightfully enjoined. *See Dr. Seuss Enters. v. Penguin Books USA, Inc.,* 109 F.3d 1394, 1403 (9th Cir. 1997) (rejecting defendants' claim that injunction would constitute a prior restraint in violation of the First Amendment). * * * We affirm in part, reverse in part and remand. * * *

Notes

1. The music business hasn't been the same since Napster went online. The Internet hasn't been the same since Napster ceased operations. A number of peer-to-peer music file sharing websites have appeared since the demise of Napster. CD sales are depressed and despite the RIAA's attempt to stop unauthorized downloading by filing suits against illegal downloaders, filesharing on the Internet continues. What is your solution to the tough position the record companies find themselves in? Can the record companies continue to operate as they have in the past with "free" music available on the Internet?

2. In January 2004, the Recording Industry Association of America (RIAA) launched copyright infringement suits against 532 individual file

sharers who illegally download music on behalf of its member companies. The suits were filed in federal court in Atlanta, Orlando, Philadelphia, and Trenton, New Jersey. Cary Sherman, President of the RIAA, said, "[the legal online music services] shouldn't have to compete with businesses based on illegal downloading. That's why we are sending a clear message that downloading or 'sharing' music from a peer-to-peer network without authorization is illegal, it can have consequences and it undermines the creative future of music itself." http://www.riaa.com/news/ newsletter/021704.asp

Chapter 16

RECORD COMPANIES AND RECORDING AGREEMENTS

Record companies regularly risk large sums of money on unknown artists in an attempt to find the next popular act. They employ Artist and Repertoire (A&R) people to search bars and clubs for new talent. The A&R people listen to demo disks and try to predict what new sounds and new groups the listening public will want to hear in twelve to eighteen months. It is an inexact science.

Risking $500,000 to $1,000,000 to record and market a new group that may or may not strike a cord with the listening public makes the record companies zealously fight for as much control and the best deal that they can possibly get. Record companies are not known for their benevolence to their signed recording artists. Record company contracts often contain harsh terms that make it nearly impossible for an artist to recoup the recording advance and make money on record sales. Only top-selling albums make money for the recording artists. Most recording artists are surprised to learn that they will not be "living like a rock star" unless they write the songs and/or the record goes platinum. Most artists begin to complain about the terms of their recording contracts after they discover that they will not be making as much money as they had originally dreamed.

Many artists have sued their record company over one term or another in the record contract. When the lawsuits have not produced the changes that they had hoped for, some artists have taken their plight to their state legislatures and Congress. The following cases illustrate some of the complaints that artists have with their record companies.

A. RECORD COMPANY CONTRACTS

ISLEY v. MOTOWN RECORD CORP.

United States District Court, Southern District of New York, 1975.
69 F.R.D. 12.

OWEN, District Judge.

Plaintiffs, three brothers, are 'pop' singers and recording artists. A jury found facts in their favor establishing their right to the income from a 'hit' song they recorded with instruments and voices called 'It's Your Thing'. This favorable verdict was based solely upon their own testimony in the course of which they repudiated their own earlier sworn testimony which clearly supported a contrary conclusion, characterizing such earlier conflicting testimony variously as a lie and false. Given this basis for the verdict, and there being persuasive documentary and testimonial evidence to the contrary, the plaintiffs' favorable verdict cannot stand. It is set aside and a new trial is ordered.

In the mercurial field of popular music, the plaintiffs, brothers Ronald, Rudolph and O'Kelly Isley, singers and recording artists under the name Isley Brothers, had had their ups and downs. In 1968 they had been under contract to defendant Motown Record Corporation for several years and were not doing well. Under that contract from time-to-time they would record new songs, sometimes composed by themselves, sometimes by others. The tapes of those recording sessions were then delivered to Motown to press into records and distribute and the Isleys were paid royalties thereon. In December 1968, the Isleys applied for and obtained a release from the Motown contract. Thereafter, using two wholly-owned companies, Triple Three for the sheet music and T–Neck for the records, the Isleys published and pressed records of 'It's Your Thing' using defendant Buddha Records, an independent firm, merely as a distributor. There is no question that the Isleys' income was greatly enhanced by marketing 'It's Your Thing' under their own label rather than on the Motown label, for 'It's Your Thing' was a hit and sold 1,750,000 copies.

The basic issue on the trial was the date on which 'It's Your Thing' was first recorded. Motown offered substantial documentary and testimonial proof to the effect that 'It's Your Thing' was first recorded at the A & R Studios in New York on November 6, 1968 at a session for which Motown had advanced the money on condition the Isleys record original tunes; that at that time the Isleys were under contract to it, and that it was therefore entitled to the income from 'It's Your Thing' less the Isleys' royalties. The Isleys, to the contrary, testified that 'It's Your Thing' was composed in late December 1968, shortly after they got the release from their Motown contract, was first recorded on January 3, 1969, and that Motown had no rights in it at all.

The jury answered three written questions as follows:

1. Have Motown and Jobete proved by a preponderance of the evidence that O'Kelly Isley on behalf of the Isley Brothers agreed on or about November 1, 1968 with Ralph Seltzer of Motown to obtain and furnish him with songwriter agreements on the forthcoming recording session as part of Seltzer's agreement to advance the money for the session? 'No.'

2. Do you find that Motown and Jobete had proved by a preponderance of the evidence that 'It's Your Thing' and 'Turn On, Tune In, Drop Out' were recorded on November 6, 1968 at the A & R Studios in New York? * * * 'No.'

3. Do you find that the Isleys have proved by a preponderance of the evidence that 'It's Your Thing' and 'Turn On, Tune In, Drop Out' were recorded for the first time on January 3, 1969 at the Town Sound Studios in Englewood, New Jersey? 'Yes.'

The infirmity in the Isleys' collective testimony, which was the sole support for the jury's several conclusions, is clearly demonstrated by a comparison of their 1969–70 testimony in depositions or before Judge Lasker with their 1975 testimony given on the trial.

The 1969–70 testimony was to the effect that after actually having auditioned another band, they engaged a band called the Midnight Movers as a second choice to do a couple of 'ideas' they (the Isleys) had; that they thereafter wrote Motown on November 1 that they were going to do a session with the Midnight Movers and asked for money for the session and agreed to deliver the tape after the session; that they received from Motown songwriters agreements to be executed for original tunes; that in preparation for the recording session they had a 3–4 hour rehearsal on the night of November 5; that Ronald and O'Kelly Isley composed the music the Midnight Movers rehearsed; that O'Kelly Isley arranged for the recording studio for November 6, and told A & R how to set it up; that the Midnight Movers were paid $850 for the recording session; that although the Isleys were supposed to send the tape of the session to Motown, they did not, and the tape was still [as of 1969–70] somewhere at O'Kelly's home.

Thus, in 1969–70, while the Isleys maintained that they had not recorded 'It's Your Thing' at the November 6 session, they clearly acknowledged that on that date they had made the various customary arrangements for a substantial recording session of *music of their own*, and absent the production of the tape, a trier of the fact could well conclude, given other evidence, that what they recorded was in fact 'It's Your Thing'.

However, on the trial in 1975 they presented a new story as follows: In the fall of 1968, they were broke and needed money for household expenses and Christmas presents; in order to get Motown to advance them some money, they decided to make up a story about doing a session; they told Motown of this stratagem to which Motown agreed, and wrote the November 1 letter to Motown about the 'session' at Motown's suggestion so that there would be a basis for sending the money; that the name of the Midnight Movers was inserted in the letter just to have the name of a band, not having any real awareness of whether that band was available or not; that they had but a 45–60 minutes rehearsal; that they did no 'ideas' of the Isleys, and no music composed by the Isleys was performed at either the rehearsal or the session at A & R the next night and in fact there was no vocal music at all; that the Midnight Movers were only paid $400 or $450 and the Isleys, pursuant to plan, pocketed the balance of the $850 they got from Motown for the band; and finally, that the tape from the session was thrown out by the Isleys' mother in cleaning O'Kelly's basement in December 1968, the month following the session.

Motown's proof consisted first of contemporaneous writings of both parties which were strong circumstantial if not direct evidence that the Isleys intended to and did record new vocal music in the November 6 session. These writings included 1) the Isleys' letter of November 1, written five days before the session, 2) the records of the A & R Studios for the studio on November 6, showing two things, first that the studio had been set up for a solo vocal with a group vocal to be 'overdubbed', * * * and second, that during the recording session itself, a change was made as to which microphone was assigned to the 'vocal'; 3) the Motown letter sent prior to the session after discussion with the Isleys enclosing songwriters agreements to be executed for the original tunes to be recorded, and 4) the letters exchanged a few weeks later when the Isleys demanded releases, at which time Motown wrote insisting on repayment of the entire cost of the session since the Isleys had sent no tapes, to which the Isleys agreed, and repayment was made.

Motown's second area of proof was the testimony of one of the Midnight Movers, George Chillious, a trombone player who played at the November 6, 1968 but not at the January 3, 1969 session. He testified that he played the music for 'It's Your Thing' in the November 6 session from a written trombone part bearing the title 'It's Your Thing', and after the end of the instrumental session heard Ronald Isley record the vocal part.

While I would not on this record, permit this verdict to stand in any event, this is an especially appropriate case for the granting of a new trial since much direct proof is available on a new trial that was not heretofore presented. Frequently, in directing a new trial, a court is faced with the fact that a second jury can do no more than reappraise the same evidence heard on the first trial. Here, however, there are perhaps as many as ten other 'Midnight Movers' available who could give testimony as to what was recorded on November 6, 1968, as could the sound engineer of the A&R Studio that night.

On such disinterested testimony, a second jury could obviously *better* determine the issues.

The law is well established that it is the duty of the trial judge to set aside a verdict and grant a new trial if, in his opinion, the verdict is based upon evidence which is false or the verdict results in a miscarriage of justice. The trial court is empowered to do this even though there may

set
aside
verdict
if

be substantial evidence which would prevent the direction of a verdict. *Aetna Cas. & Surety Co. v. Yeatts*, 122 F.2d 350 (4th Cir. 1941); *Reyes v. Grace Line, Inc.*, 334 F.Supp. 1104 (S.D.N.Y.1971). In my judgment, this verdict, on this record, results in a miscarriage of justice and was in part, if not in whole, based upon evidence which was false. I deem it fundamental that a party may not do a testimonial about-face, concede prior testimony to be false or a lie and then prevail solely upon the basis of that altered self-serving testimony.

For the foregoing reasons * * * the conclusions of the jury as to all issues raised by the three questions submitted to it are set aside and a new trial is ordered. * * *

BELL v. STREETWISE RECORDS

United States District Court, Massachusetts, 1986.
640 F.Supp. 575.

ZOBEL, District Judge.

Plaintiffs Bell, Bivins, Brown, DeVoe and Tresvant, members of a singing group, are known to teenagers across the nation and around the world by the name "New Edition." Together with their present recording company, MCA Records, Inc. ("MCA"), they seek to establish their exclusive right to appear, perform and record under that mark. Defendants and counterclaimants (hereinafter "defendants"), Boston International Music, Inc. ("BIM"), and Streetwise Records, Ltd. ("Streetwise") produced, recorded and marketed the first New Edition long-playing album, "Candy Girl," as well as the singles from that album. Defendants claim that they employed the five individual plaintiffs to serve as a public front for a "concept" which they developed, and to promote musical recordings embodying that "concept." Because the mark New Edition allegedly identifies those recordings, and not the group members, defendants assert that they are its rightful owners. Each side has asked that this court enjoin the other from using the mark. * * *

FINDINGS OF FACT AND RULINGS OF LAW

Background

The five plaintiffs, calling themselves New Edition, form one of the hottest song-and-dance acts on the entertainment scene today. They have released four albums, numerous singles and several videos. They have performed throughout this country, filling major concert halls. They have toured Britain and Germany, and have plans for an upcoming trip to Japan. They have appeared on television shows, at charity events, and—the crowning sign of success—they have even been featured in a COKE commercial.

The group got its start in 1981 when four of the five current members performed in a talent show at Roscoe's Lounge, in Boston. They were each about thirteen years old at the time and they called themselves New Edition. Travis Gresham, who knew Bell and Tresvant from the marching band he directed, saw the show and thought they had potential. Within a week or two he became their manager and Brook Payne, who had collaborated with Bell, Bivins and Brown on an earlier endeavor, became their choreographer.

Greshman booked a series of performances for the group. Their sixth engagement, on November 15, 1981, was the "Hollywood Talent Night" at the Strand Theatre, where the group performed a medley of songs made famous by the Jackson Five. First prize and plaintiffs' goal for the night was a recording contract with Maurice Starr, president of defendant BIM, who originated and organized the event. New Edition came in second but Starr, who had an agenda of his own, decided to work with them anyway.

Maurice Starr, who partly from his "Hollywood Talent Nights" had become something of a local celebrity, had been in the music business for a long time. Starr—originally Larry Johnson—performed with his five brothers in a rock band in the early seventies. Modeled after the Jackson Five, whom they sought to emulate, Starr and his brothers called themselves the Johnson Six. They achieved moderate success but broke up in the mid-seventies when they became too mature for the image.

It was around this time that Starr began developing the "concept," which, in its final form, he dubbed "black bubble gum music of the eighties." The concept is essentially the Jackson Five updated by the addition of modern elements like synthesizers (electronic instrumentation) and rap (speaking parts). As early as 1972 Starr began to search for the right kids to act out his concept. In November 1981, when he first encountered Bell, Bivins, Brown and Tresvant, he was still looking.

Although he decided to work with them, Starr believed plaintiffs were short on talent. They had no training to speak of; none could read or write music. Nevertheless, he used the four boys to create a demonstration tape of a song he had composed earlier, entitled Candy Girl. Starr played all the instruments, sang background vocals and did the arranging and mixing. He had to teach the thirteen-year-old group members everything, and while it is disputed whether lead singer Ralph Tresvant had to record his part bar-by-bar or note-by-note, it is clear Starr ran the show in the sound studio.

The tape was completed in the winter of 1982, and Starr expended considerable effort attempting to sell it to a recording company. He finally connected with Streetwise in the following fall. In the meantime, under the supervision of Gresham and Payne, plaintiffs continued to rehearse their dance routines and to perform locally. Starr played little if any role in these activities.

During this period Starr and the group members had three disagreements, all stemming from Starr's desire to make the group more like the Jackson Five. First, Starr insisted they acquire a fifth member. The boys resisted, but Starr prevailed. Plaintiffs selected Ronnie DeVoe, a nephew of Brook Payne, whom Starr approved. Second, he wanted the group to grow "afros." They refused. Third, and perhaps most significant, he wanted the newly expanded group to change its name to the MaJic Five [sic]; the upper case "J," not surprisingly, to evoke "Jackson." Plaintiffs were adamantly opposed and remained New Edition.

In November and December of 1982, Streetwise entered into separate recording contracts with each of the five plaintiffs, who were at the time approximately age fourteen. Each contract granted to Streetwise the exclusive right to use the name. Each, except Tresvant's, confirmed that the name "The New Edition" was wholly owned by BIM.

Streetwise released the "Candy Girl" single in February 1983. The long-playing album—containing ten songs selected, produced, and for the most part written by Starr—came out the following June. Streetwise launched an unusually extensive and elaborate promotional campaign, placing advertisements in print and on radio, and producing three videos. After the single was released, plaintiffs—high school students at the time—performed every weekend night, in Massachusetts and beyond. At first they "lip-synched" to a recorded track; later they sang to a live band. For a period of time Starr accompanied them on these tours, announcing the group, playing instruments * * * and performing background vocals. The records and the group were smash hits.

Sometime in the summer of 1983 plaintiffs began to perform without Starr. In August, they fired Gresham and Payne. That same month they performed in Britain and Germany. In September they acquired new management and in November they disaffirmed their contracts with Streetwise. After defendants revealed plans to issue New Edition records featuring five different young singers, and after they sought federal registration of the New Edition mark, plaintiffs commenced this lawsuit.

One postscript completes the evidentiary picture before the court. In January of 1984, Jheryl Busby, a senior vice president at MCA, was dragged by his fourteen-year-old son to see a performance of New Edition. None too impressed, he left to meet a friend at a nearby hotel. Young girls had swarmed the place. When he asked his friend what was going on he was told, "that group, New Edition, is staying here and those little girls have been looking for them all night." Busby signed the group.

Discussion

* * * It is settled law that ownership of a mark is established by priority of appropriation. *Blanchard Importing & Distributing Co. v. Charles Gelman*, 353 F.2d 400, 401 (1st Cir. 1965). Priority is established not by conception but by bona fide usage. The claimant "must demonstrate that his use of the mark has been deliberate and continuous, not sporadic, casual or transitory." *La Societe Anonyme des Parfums LeGalion v. Jean Patou, Inc.*, 495 F.2d 1265, 1272 (2d Cir. 1974). While it is not required that a product be an instant success the moment it hits the market, its usage must be consistent with a "present plan of commercial exploitation." *Id.* at 1273. Finally, while the Lanham Act is invoked only

through use in interstate commerce, common law rights can be acquired through interstate *or* intrastate usage. *Noah's Inc. v. Nark, Inc.*, 560 F.Supp. 1253, 1258 (E.D. Mo. 1983), *aff'd*, 728 F.2d 410 (8th Cir. 1984) (citing *Weiner King, Inc. v. Weiner King Corp.*, 201 U.S.P.Q. 894, 908 (TTAB 1979)).

With these principles in mind, I make the following findings of fact. First, on the basis of testimony by Mr. Busby and by defendants' expert, Thomas Silverman, I find that there is only one relevant market at issue here: the entertainment market. Second, I find that as of the release of "Candy Girl" in February 1983—the first use in commerce—plaintiffs, calling themselves New Edition, had publicly performed in the local entertainment market on at least twenty occasions. Those performances (for which they frequently received compensation; albeit in nominal amounts), the promotional efforts by Travis Gresham on their behalf, their regular rehearsals with Gresham and Payne, their attempt to win a recording contract, and their hard work with Maurice Starr to further their career, all evidence a "present plan of commercial exploitation."

I accordingly conclude that plaintiffs have acquired legal rights to the mark New Edition through their prior use in intrastate commerce. Even if defendants' use had been the first in interstate commerce, they used the name simultaneously in Massachusetts, where plaintiffs had already appropriated it. And while it is well recognized that a junior user may occasionally acquire superior rights to a mark it used in good faith and in a different market, *see* 2 J. McCarthy, § 26:3 at 289–292 (2d ed. 1984), and cases cited therein, that was obviously not the case here. On this basis alone, plaintiffs own the mark.

prior appropriation

II.

Even assuming there was no prior appropriation by the plaintiffs, however, they nonetheless own the mark under the controlling standard of law. Defendants correctly state that in the case of joint endeavors, where prior ownership by one of several claimants cannot be established, the legal task is to determine which party "controls or determines the nature and quality of the goods which have been marketed under the mark in question." *See In re Polar Music International AB*, 714 F.2d 1567 (Fed. Cir. 1983). The difficulty in performing that task in this case, however, is in deciding what the "goods" are. The parties have given the court little guidance in how to go about making that determination. Rather, each side baldly asserts the result that leads most logically to a decision in its favor. Defendants claim the goods are the recordings; plaintiffs claim they are the entertainment services of Bell, Bivins, Brown, DeVoe and Tresvant.

The role of "public association" in determining ownership has been much disputed in this case. Defendants have argued, and the Court of Appeals has confirmed, that the "finding that the public associate[s] the name NEW EDITION with the plaintiffs [does not compel] the conclusion that the name belong[s] to the plaintiffs." *Bell, supra*, 761 F.2d at 76. *See, e.g., Wallpaper Mfgrs. Ltd. v. Crown Wallcovering Corp.*, 680

F.2d 755, 762 (C.C.P.A. 1982) ("Trademark rights are neither acquired or lost on the basis of comparative popularity. . . .") But defendants are wrong when they say that public association plays no part in determining ownership. It is crucial in establishing just what the mark has come to identify, i.e., what the "goods" are. * * *

In order to determine ownership in a case of this kind, a court must first identify that quality or characteristic for which the group is known by the public. It then may proceed to the second step of the ownership inquiry, namely, who controls that quality or characteristic. * * *

As a preliminary matter, I find that the norm in the music industry is that an artist or group generally owns its own name. This case does not fit into one of the clearer exceptions to this rule. The name New Edition has not been assigned, transferred, or sold. * * * Nor is New Edition a "concept group," whose name belongs to the person or entity that conceived both concept and name. *Compare O & L Associates v. Del Conte,* No. 83–7939, slip op. (S.D.N.Y. Dec. 3, 1984). * * *

With respect to defendants, although Maurice Starr's contribution to the "Candy Girl" records was substantial, I find that all the functions he performed were consistent with the duties of a producer. He was credited and compensated separately for each role. Similarly, while Streetwise's promotional work was unusually extensive, and though it proceeded at considerable risk, marketing—or "educating your label," as one witness put it—is a normal function of a recording company.

With respect to the plaintiffs themselves, as noted elsewhere in this opinion, they existed and performed as New Edition long before defendants released "Candy Girl." They had already used songs of the Jackson Five. Their membership has been essentially constant; they were not, as defendants contend, replaceable actors in a play written by Maurice Starr. (*Compare Rick v. Buchansky, supra,* where the four-person "Vito and the Salutations" had had twenty-two different members, including ten different "Vitos," to its one manager, Rick—who was found to own the name.) They were individual persons that the public came to know as such. While defendants would have us believe this is only the result of their successful promoting, I find that it was personality, not marketing, that led to the public's intimacy with plaintiffs. The "magic" that sold New Edition, and which "New Edition" has come to signify, is these five young men.

Based on the totality of the evidence, I conclude that the quality which the mark New Edition identified was first and foremost the five plaintiffs with their distinctive personalities and style as performers. The "goods" therefore are the entertainment services they provide. They and no one else controlled the quality of those services. They own the mark.

CONCLUSION

I accordingly conclude that plaintiffs have demonstrated a likelihood of success on the merits, and that defendants have failed to do so. I am also persuaded by the testimony of Jheryl Busby, that failure to enjoin defendants would irreparably injure plaintiffs by weakening the mark—far in excess of the minor injury this injunction will cause defendants.

Finally, as the Court of Appeals has made plain, the public interest will best be served by an exclusive award of the name.

For all these reasons, plaintiffs' motion requesting a preliminary injunction is allowed. * * *

Notes

1. For more cases and information dealing with the ownership of a band's name, see Chapter 14, Music Business Relationships.

2. The band "Hole" filed suit against the recording company giant Universal Music Group claiming unjust enrichment and withholding accounting records, among other things. According to Los Angeles Times Article, when several major record companies merged, the band was shuffled to Interscope Records and the band's album was ignored. After negotiations failed to resolve their differences, the band's leader, Courtney Love, informed the record company that she would no longer record under the Interscope label. Universal then sued Love claiming she breached its contract. Several lawyers "in the business" advised Love to settle, saying "it's always been like that." Love refused to give in, and finally "stepped outside the tight circle of entertainment lawyers" and found Barry Cappello to represent the band. Cappello filed a $30 million suit against Universal on behalf of Hole. What was UMG's response to the suit? The recording giant characterized Love as a "37 year old has-been" who didn't have time to fulfill her contract. Kathleen Sharp, *The Big–Game Hunter's Big Gamble Santa Barbara Attorney A. Barry Cappello and His Client, Courtney Love, Are After Some Very Big Prey-the Universal Music Group. They Could Really Score. Or They Could Be Eaten Alive*, L. A.TIMES, July 29, 2001, at 16.

Rather than try their luck in court, Universal and Love settled their differences by Universal agreeing to increase Love's royalty rate and Love agreeing to drop the lawsuit and continue to record for Universal.

3. In *Polygram Records, Inc. v. Buddy Buie Productions, Inc.,* the group "The Atlanta Rhythm Section" was sued by their former label for breach of an option contract. The group had a contract with Polygram to do four albums with an option to renew. The group signed with CBS records, and Polygram claimed time had not expired to renew their contract. The Court found that Polygram had not timely exercised their option and dismissed the case. *See Polygram Records, Inc. v. Buddy Buie Productions, Inc.,* 520 F.Supp. 248 (S.D.N.Y. 1981).

4. All California based recording contracts must contain a minimum compensation clause in order for the label to enforce the contract in equity. The minimum compensation clause requires the label to guarantee that the artist will make a minimum of $9,000.00 in the first year of the contract, $12,000 in the second year, and $15,000 for years three through seven.

Personal service contracts in California have a seven year maximum. The minimum amount escalates for each year of the contract. *See* Cal. Civ. Code § 3423.

William Henslee
Making the Band:
Author Interview with Lou Pearlman.
Copyright © 2003, William Henslee.

[Lou Pearlman, the CEO of Trans Continental Companies, created or discovered the Backstreet Boys, *NSYNC, and O–Town.]

Q. Is there a formula for creating a successful band?

A. Growing up, I watched my cousin, Art Garfunkel, become successful singing tight harmonies. I took that formula and applied it when we started the Backstreet Boys. Again, we were looking for tight harmonies when we put together *NSYNC. All of the artists we have signed have been strong vocally. I have followed that formula with LFO, O–Town, and Natural and with the new talent we are working with: Brooke Hogan and an upcoming guy Sean Van Der Wilt. We have been working with a few groups over the years that have really been very promising and I think that as you develop talent and you understand what a group needs to succeed. You weed out those that don't stand out of the crowd and you go with your instincts. When you are putting a band together, you need to find people who fulfill a need for the group. You may need people who can sing, dance, or play instruments. Each situation is different depending on what type of group you are trying to create.

Q. What are you looking for initially when you're searching for talent?

A. Initially we are looking for talent depending upon what our marketing approach is going to be. If we are looking for a band that plays its own instruments, then naturally we look for individuals as well as existing bands. If we want to have an edge where they can sing and dance and play instruments we hone in on those skills. We hire great choreographers and vocal coaches to make sure everybody has the proper potential and the proper guidance. If we are going to be looking for a group that just sings, then we are going to look primarily for vocal coaching. It depends on what the mission is.

Q. Why did Backstreet Boys and *NSYNC work and then why did O–Town not work?

A. O–Town actually sold seven million albums so they did pretty good considering they were a made for television band. Backstreet Boys and *NSYNC were made for being a band. Neither the Backstreet Boys nor *NSYNC was made through a TV show. The television show was an idea that I had to see if we could do a talent search and make a band out of it. It worked! O–Town did not work like the Backstreet Boys in this country; their album hit number 69 in the Billboard charts in the United States and then they went over to Europe. In Europe, O–Town's album hit the top five. They exploded in Europe and Asia and then came back around to the United States. In the United States, they seemed to work slowly. It wasn't until we had the Disney Channel help us with promotion and marketing that they worked. So every group has their own path to success but they made it work because the talent was great.

O–Town had great talent; however one of the guys decided to get married and he lost his potential for being a teeny bopper solo artist or being a band member. These things happen, but O–Town successfully captured an audience that was the first ever band made from a television show. It was reality based television before there was a reality television show on network TV. "Making the Band" was a very successful reality based television show because we used music as the generator to turn on a large popular audience. The show is still running. It is in its fifth season right now on television. It started on ABC network where it ran for a few years and then it moved over to MTV which has the primary demographic. When VIACOM bought CBS in the interim, they weren't going to renew an ABC competitor.

As time progressed we found that O–Town did quite well. A lot of guys were very well liked and they did a lot of successful touring. They had some big top ten hits so it was great.

Q.   What have you learned from the Backstreet Boys, *NSYNC, and O–Town that you expect to translate into success for Natural?

A.   We prefer that they all want to stay together as a band unit. That is the most important thing. Natural is a band that plays together. They all met in advance. They came to me as a unit. They were not a band that we put together. I think that says a lot, too, because then naturally, no pun intended, they got together and performed. That's a positive statement when people get together and they work to develop their own potential.

Q.   Do you like bands that can create their own material or do you go out and find material for them?

A.   Only if the band has great writing potential like LFO. Their first single, "Summer Girls", was written by Rich Cronin, a band member. We also have a scenario where we may use a song written by someone who is a famous writer. That helps get you credibility in the marketplace, especially radio. Radio program directors may listen to somebody sing a song written by a very famous songwriter rather than by an unknown writer. It's not always about the origin of the song; it's about the hit.

It helps if the group can write songs. We like that a lot. But if they can't write, it's not a detriment. A rock and roll band should definitely be able to write a lot of their own stuff. But if you're a boy band, it's okay not to write the songs. It's really about when they are out there performing. The performance is key.

Q.   Do you think part of your success has been that you stuck primarily to a single genre? I know you're branching out now and you've got some hip hop acts. Have you been as successful with groups in other genre?

A. Hip hop is number one on MTV. Hip hop artists have sold millions of albums and are doing quite well; but there is nothing more spectacular than the pop market. The pop market is the most mainstream and that's where you sell the most records. That is why we like to stick with the pop market. We stick primarily with boy bands because guys are naturally attracted to girls and vise-a-versa and girls become fanatics and fanatics are what we want. We want people who will buy albums, merchandise, toys, and so on. When I got in this business I learned that New Kids on the Block had two hundred million dollars in record sales and eight hundred million dollars in toys and merchandise sales. I knew which was better. Record sales are great, but with downloading today and all of the other ways to get music, record sales are slowing down. To us it's not that big a deal because we sell a lot of toys and merchandising. Our bands have endorsement deals. For what we see in the marketplace now, the pop market boys are going to shine and be bigger. Sometimes country becomes pop; sometimes R&B becomes pop; sometimes rock becomes pop; but pop is worth lots of money.

Q. Do you try to go for crossover or do you try to stick with groups that go or fit in a certain pigeon hole?

A. We stick to pop, R&B pop, or hip hop pop. Smilez and Southstar are a hip hop pop duo and Natural is more of a pop rock group. It works. Those are the times.

Q. Do you have a marketing secret that you've used to get your bands out there and make them well known?

A. The marketing secret is having something for everybody. Having a solo artist is more difficult because he or she is up there and you either like the person or you don't. But with a band, some people will have their favorite individual members. An individual member can attract fans for the band, that's why bands are easier to market and are more successful. Guys are going to go out there and listen to a band that's more rock and roll and where they play their own instruments. They don't really go for the dancing that much. They don't watch guys dancing that much, but they will listen to the music. Girls they like it all. Girls like everything and you put it all together and you have a winning formula. That's what we try to do.

Q. How has the consolidation of the radio stations affected your approach to the market?

A. It makes it simpler. You go to Clear Channel, you go to Cox, and you go to certain ones that you work with. Clear Channel, being the biggest, is perfect because if one station likes it they all talk to each other in the same company and spread the word. It's good and bad; when they don't like something they spread the word too.

Q. Is it more difficult to break a new act now that there is consolidation?

A. It's a different time right now. When we did Backstreet Boys, we didn't use television. Today, if you don't have a television show or something major like that it is very difficult to break in. You need TV behind you, not just radio MTV or preferably a major network like FOX or Warner Brothers. Those channels deliver the target demographic.

Q. How have you been using television to play their music or to place their music on television shows?

A. For example, American Idol is a perfect example of that. They copied "Making the Band" and the show is doing very well. Other TV shows like that have been running on the air and people get on the shows. We get our music on sitcoms and we try to get our people to appear on the shows. Concert specials and other appearances on talk shows or anything else that people watch is helpful to let people see our artists. We need people to see and hear our artist because that's how the pop business works.

Q. Is it important to have good looks too?

A. If you want to be in the pop market it does. Teeny boppers love the good looking guys. Good looks help a lot in the pop market.

Q. How has touring been affected by the new consolidation in venue ownership?

A. Tours are unaffected. Ticket costs are higher, but true fans are unaffected. Fans are going to buy the tickets to see the artists they love. It doesn't matter if you are a rich family or a poor family; you're not going to deprive your daughter or young son of a show that they really want to see. That's why we like the fanatical fans; they won't be deprived of their merchandise and shows.

Q. How does the European market affect the way you develop your bands?

A. Actually, a lot of people don't realize that the Backstreet Boys and *NSYNC had their first gold records in Germany. Natural got its first gold record here in the United States, but we blew them up bigger in Germany as well because if the formula is not broke, don't fix it. That formula is nothing more than the same formula used by the Beatles. We repeated the Beatles formula. The Beatles did not get big in England; they got big in Hamburg, Germany. We followed that success and we developed Backstreet Boys, *NSYNC, and LFO the same way. Natural is following the same formula. Smilez and Southstar broke in the United States because the hip hop market is bigger here. O–Town broke in the United States because of the TV show.

Before we could launch our girl's group, Innocence, the youngest would-be member decided to go solo. Our attorney at the time brought her over to Jive Records, the same folks that were doing Backstreet for us, and she ended up coming out as a solo artist. That was Britney Spears and we are so proud of her. She's doing great! You can keep going on and on because the market just keeps going. People ask me when this boy band business is going to be over? I know exactly when it's going to be over. It's going to be over when God stops making little girls.

Q. Do you think that that being located in Orlando has affected your ability to attract groups?

A. Yes. We came down here in 1991–92. A young lady friend and I got together and created the Backstreet Boys. One of the guys, Kevin Richardson, was Aladdin at Disney's Magic Kingdom. Being in Orlando certainly helped us find talent. With *NSYNC, Justin and J.C. were both with the Mickey Mouse Club. Needless to say, it's a good place to be. There is a very large talent pool here. We are the big fish in a small pond and it's very nice. With cheaper land costs, we built a studio complex here for the kids to practice in and we have a recording studio that is used by a lot of groups.

Q. Do your people have a traditional A&R people?

A. Yes, we do have an A&R department. We have all the traditional departments you need from A&R to marketing to legal. Our head of A&R figures out what artists are good for, whether it be a group or as a solo act. We do have a typical record company but we traditionally release our albums through a major label that has distribution, marketing, radio representatives, and so forth. That has been our modus operandi.

We have A&R people who go out to scout for talent as well as people who work to create new groups. We spotted Natural in our studio. They came in while we were doing the show "Making the Band." The day before Creed was in our studio. We couldn't ask for Creed to let our artists use the studio, so when they finished, I went to the studio to hear our guys. I walked in and saw Natural recording in one of our studios. I said, "Who are you guys?".... "We're Natural.".... "So what are you doing here?".... "Waiting for you to walk through the door." They actually spent money and rented studio space hoping they'd get discovered. It worked for them. We do scout our studios. So that's one way we find talent. Another way is to be out and about in the clubs or in the malls.

Q. So what do you think the prospects for the music business are now with the internet downloading?

A. I think that it's really a shame that we didn't think this out because kids understand its stealing. They're not stupid and they'd love not to steal but they don't have credit cards. You don't give someone a gun with bullets and tell them not to use it. It's the same with a computer. Now you can't get a computer without a CD burner and

Internet access so a kid is either going to download a song or burn a CD. It is not a good situation.

To continue to create a need to buy the CD, the record business has to change what it is selling. In our case, what we do is we use reverse psychology. We are selling a hardbound book, glossy color photos, beautiful pictures, baby photos, live concert photos, and song lyrics and so on on a really nice non-bleed paper. You get the book and we give you the album for free. Because the album is free with the book, they won't have to download the music. Instead of selling albums, we are selling the book and the album comes for free. As long as you keep doing it that way, sales will continue. It makes for a very tough market. It is a very bad thing to have downloading and CD burning and it's only going to get worse. But again, like I said, album sales are a small part of the business when you consider the toys and merchandising. You are fully protected by copyright laws, trademarks, and so on so there is no way you can lose those. One day there will be control on the web. Everybody says the web can't be controlled, but that's impossible. There will be controls so that the computers can be used as television sets. They will have multiple television channels for free on the web and broadcasters will have to pay license fees for the use of the programs. For that to happen, they are going to have to figure out how to collect the license fees. There will be regulations and control of the web in the near future. I think we're going to have to build a firewall around the United States to block anything from coming in that's not regulated. Other countries will do the same. Just like television stations are broadcast on regulated frequencies, the Internet will have to be regulated.

Q. Do you think that the Internet will change the industry paradigm of the twelve song album when people can download their favorite song without having to buy the other eleven songs that they really didn't want?

A. If you're a fan, you'll get the whole album. If you just want one or two songs, you download those two songs but you still may go to the concert. When you're at the concert and you hear the two songs that you like, that's great. After the concert, maybe you'll like the rest of the songs and buy the album. There will always be a market for good music.

B. FILM AND TELEVISION USE OF MUSIC

Music sets the mood for a scene. Music, both background and featured, can be either prerecorded or written specially for the film or show. Background music is music that is played behind the scene for mood. Featured music is a part of the scene. Music written specially for the production company is considered a work for hire and covered in Chapter 15, Protecting Music Through Copyrights. Prerecorded music, owned by a record company, must be licensed.

A record company will issue a master use license to the production company for the use of some or all of the soundrecording. The master use allows the production company to add the recorded music to the soundtrack of the audiovisual work. The production company must secure a synchronization license from the music publishing company in addition to the master use license.

synchro license

AGEE v. PARAMOUNT COMMUNICATIONS, INC.

United States Court of Appeals, Second Circuit, 1995.
59 F.3d 317.

NEWMAN, Chief Judge.

ISSUE

The primary issue presented by this appeal is whether incorporating a copyrighted sound recording into the soundtrack of a taped commercial television production infringes the copyright owner's exclusive right of reproduction under the Copyright Act of 1976, 17 U.S.C. §§ 106 and 114(b) (1993). We hold that it does.

Plaintiff-appellant Michael L. Agee appeals from the June 3, 1994, judgment of the District Court for the Southern District of New York (Constance Baker Motley, Judge) granting summary judgment against him on his copyright claim against defendants-appellees Paramount Communications, Inc., Paramount Pictures, and Paramount Television Group ("Paramount") and the owners of 129 television stations ("TV stations"), and dismissing his Lanham Act and unfair competition claims for failure to state a cause of action. *See Agee v. Paramount Communications, Inc.*, 853 F.Supp. 778 (S.D.N.Y.1994). Paramount copied portions of Agee's sound recording to make the audio track of a segment of a television program, and transmitted the program to the TV stations, which in turn made their own copies for transmission to the viewing public.

ephemeral recording exemption

We conclude that Paramount violated Agee's exclusive right of reproduction when it copied his sound recording on tape as part of the television program's soundtrack. However, we find that the copies of the program, including the duplicated portions of Agee's work, made by the TV stations are protected by the statute's "ephemeral recording" exemption, *see* 17 U.S.C. § 112. We agree with the dismissal of Agee's Lanham Act and unfair competition claims. We therefore affirm in part, reverse in part, and remand.

BACKGROUND

Plaintiff-appellant Michael L. Agee, a California resident, is proprietor of L & H Records, a music recording studio located in California. Through L & H Records, Agee owns copyrights in two sound recordings, "Laurel and Hardy's Music Box" ("Music Box") and "Laurel and Hardy's Music Box: Volume II" ("Music Box–Two"). Agee does not own the copyright in the musical compositions embodied in these sound recordings.

Defendant-appellee Paramount Communications, Inc. is a Delaware corporation whose principal place of business is California. Defendants-appellees Paramount Pictures and Paramount Television Group are divisions of Paramount. Paramount Pictures produces the daily, half-hour news magazine television program *Hard Copy* and transmits it to independently owned and operated television stations for broadcast nationwide.

Paramount copied portions of three songs from Agee's "Music Box–Two," entitled "Ku–Ku," "Cops," and "The Donkey's Ears," to make the audio track of a four-minute segment of its *Hard Copy* feature called "Caught on Tape." After duplicating parts of the recording, Paramount created an audiovisual work that timed or "synchronized" portions of the duplicated recording to visual images showing two young men engaged in an unsuccessful burglary attempt.

Paramount recorded the "Caught on Tape" feature on February 15, 1993, and integrated it into the *Hard Copy* program for satellite transmission to the TV stations for airing the next day. Portions of the feature, including Agee's recording, were also included in the opening and closing credits of the program. In addition, Paramount produced and transmitted to the TV stations a promotional commercial excerpted from the program, again including Agee's copyrighted work. The TV stations made their own copies of the program and the commercial and broadcast them to the public. Paramount neither sought nor obtained a license from Agee for the use of his recording, nor did it refer to him in the program's credits.

[handwritten margin note: no license from Agee for the use of his recording]

On September 10, 1993, Agee brought a copyright infringement action against Paramount and the TV stations for the unauthorized copying and synchronization of the songs from his sound recording, creation of a derivative work, and distribution or publication of that work to the public. Agee also alleged that defendants had engaged in unfair competition and that Paramount's use of his recording violated section 43(a) of the Lanham Act.

[handwritten margin note: 43(a) Lanham Act]

Agee moved by order to show cause for a temporary restraining order on November 19, 1993, seeking a preliminary injunction prohibiting the TV stations from rebroadcasting and Paramount from retransmitting the tape. The temporary restraining order was granted and then dissolved on the same day upon defense counsel's oral representation that the program would not be broadcast again. Thereafter, and prior to any discovery, Paramount and the TV stations moved for dismissal of the complaint and, alternatively, for summary judgment.

The District Court granted defendants' motion, dismissing Agee's state law and Lanham Act claims, and granting summary judgment on the copyright infringement claim after concluding that defendants had not infringed any of Agee's exclusive rights under the Copyright Act, which include the right to (1) reproduce the sound recording, (2) prepare a derivative work based upon the sound recording, and (3) distribute copies of the sound recording to the public. *See* 17 U.S.C. §§ 106, 114(b) (1993).

With respect to the exclusive right to reproduce a copyrighted sound recording, the District Court held that although the synchronization or "synch" right (*i.e.*, the right to use recorded music in synchronization with visual images on the soundtrack of a television program or motion picture) had been held to be a subset of a music publisher's right to reproduce his work, *see, e.g., Angel Music, Inc. v. ABC Sports, Inc.*, 631 F.Supp. 429, 433 n. 4 (S.D.N.Y.1986), such a synch right was not part of the sound recording copyright owner's exclusive reproduction right, which was more limited. *See* 853 F.Supp. at 786–87. Rather, the Copyright Act proscribed only the "unauthorized sale or public distribution" of phonorecords or audiovisual works containing Agee's sound recordings, "which did not happen in this case." *Id.* at 787.

In addition, the District Court concluded that Paramount had not violated Agee's exclusive right to prepare derivative works from his recording because there was "no evidence that the sounds in [Agee's] recording were remixed, or that additional lyrics or musical variations were added, or that defendant took his recording and transformed it into a new original work." *Id.* at 788–89.

The District Court also held that Paramount's "transmission" of *Hard Copy*, together with Agee's sound recording, to the TV stations and the TV stations' transmission of the program to the public did not amount to "distributions" of copies of Agee's recording to the public, but were simply public "performances" of that recording. Because sound recording copyright owners do not have exclusive performance rights, *see* 17 U.S.C. § 114(a), these transmissions did not infringe Agee's rights. 853 F.Supp. at 789.

Additionally, the District Court noted that the TV stations' copies of the program were protected under the "ephemeral recording" exemption, 17 U.S.C. § 112, which permits "transmitting organization[s]" with the right to transmit any work to make a single copy of a particular program embodying the work if certain prerequisites are satisfied. 853 F.Supp. at 789–90.

Finally, the District Court found that Agee had failed to state a cause of action under either the Lanham Act or unfair competition law. Agee's complaint did not allege that Paramount had misrepresented the source of the music used in the "Caught On Tape" segment or that it possessed a copyright in Agee's sound recordings. Rather, Agee's Lanham Act claim arose "from the same basic facts which support his failed copyright claim—defendants' alleged unauthorized use of his sound recording in their television program without paying him a royalty or recognizing him in the credits to the program." *Id.* at 791. As to the unfair competition claim, the District Court found that Agee had failed to plead facts or introduce evidence that his record sales or licensing revenues had been affected by defendants' use of his sound recording. *Id.*

This appeal followed.

Discussion

Paramount's duplication and transmission of Agee's sound recording as part of the soundtrack of *Hard Copy,* and the TV stations' subsequent duplication and transmission of that program to the viewing public, are far removed from the record piracy that prompted Congress to enact legislation protecting sound recording copyright owners. That legislation is in some respects quite limited, denying owners of copyrights in sound recordings certain exclusive rights that are available to music publishers or to owners of copyrights in the underlying musical compositions. Nevertheless, applying *de novo* review, *see Longo v. Shore & Reich, Ltd.,* 25 F.3d 94, 96 (2d Cir. 1994), we conclude that Paramount's use of Agee's sound recording infringed his exclusive right to reproduce his work, notwithstanding the fact that the *Hard Copy* program containing his recording was broadcast only once and was not distributed to the public for sale or rental. However, we find no violation of Agee's exclusive right to distribute copies of his sound recording to the public. Moreover, although Paramount might have infringed Agee's exclusive right to prepare derivative works, we need not resolve that question because such an infringement would not expand Paramount's liability or alter our conclusion that the TV stations' duplication and broadcast of Agee's work was protected by the ephemeral recording exemption.

A. Copyright Claim

Statutory Background. Section 106 of the Copyright Act of 1976 gives owners of copyrights in most works the exclusive right to reproduce the copyrighted work in copies or phonorecords, to prepare derivative works based upon the copyrighted work, to distribute copies or phonorecords of the copyrighted work to the public by sale or other transfer of ownership, or by rental, lease, or lending, to perform the work publicly, and to display the work publicly. 17 U.S.C. § 106. However, with respect to copyrights in sound recordings, which the Act defines as "works that result from the fixation of a series of musical, spoken, or other sounds," *id.* § 101, the Act confers more limited rights. Only the rights of reproduction, preparation of derivative works, and distribution of copies are conferred, and a performance right is explicitly not conferred. *Id.* § 114(a). Moreover, the rights that are conferred are more limited than in the case of other works.

The reproduction right is limited to the right "*to duplicate the sound recording in the form of phonorecords, or of copies of motion pictures and other audiovisual works, that directly or indirectly recapture the actual sounds fixed in the recording.*" *Id.* § 114(b) (emphasis added). The derivative work right is limited to the right "to prepare a derivative work in which the actual sounds fixed in the sound recording are rearranged, remixed, or otherwise altered in sequence or quality." *Id.*

Also pertinent to our inquiry in this case is the exemption that section 114 extends to broadcasters for "ephemeral recordings." Specifically, it is not an infringement for a "transmitting organization entitled to transmit to the public a performance or display of a work, under a license or transfer of the copyright or under the limitations on exclusive rights in sound recordings specified by section 114(a), to make no more than one copy or phonorecord of a particular transmission program embodying the performance or display." *Id.* § 112(a).

Exemption

To be eligible for this exemption, a "transmitting organization" must satisfy three conditions: (1) the copy must be used solely by the transmitting organization that made it, and no further copies can be reproduced from it; (2) the copy must be used "solely for the transmitting organization's own transmissions within its local service area, or for purposes of archival preservation or security"; and (3) unless preserved exclusively for archival purposes, the copy must be destroyed within six months from the date the program was first transmitted to the public.

1. *Reproduction Right.* Congress's primary intention in granting sound recording copyright owners the exclusive right of reproduction was to prevent the unauthorized duplication of sound recordings that was causing substantial losses in the recording industry. *See United States v. Taxe,* 380 F.Supp. 1010, 1014 (C.D. Cal. 1974) ("The legislative history of the [Sound Recording Amendment of 1971] indicates that its intent was to put record 'pirates' out of business."), *aff'd,* 540 F.2d 961 (9th Cir. 1976), *cert. denied,* 429 U.S. 1040 (1977). Indeed, the impetus behind the Sound Recording Amendment, which was largely incorporated into the Copyright Act, was the perceived need to prevent "widespread unauthorized reproduction of phonograph records and tapes." H.R. Rep. No. 487, 92nd Cong., 1st Sess. at 1 (1971) ("House Report").

synch right

Nevertheless, as *amicus* Register of Copyrights observes, the statutory language pertaining to the sound recording reproduction right is broad enough to include a synch right, which would require a producer to obtain authorization from the owner of a sound recording before reproducing that recording in the soundtrack of an audiovisual work. *See* 17 U.S.C. § 114(b).

In addition, the legislative history indicates that Congress intended to proscribe the unauthorized duplication of sound recordings in the soundtrack of audiovisual works. *See* House Report at 106 (infringement of copyright owner's reproduction right takes place "whenever all or any substantial portion of the actual sounds that go to make up a copyrighted sound recording are reproduced in phonorecords ... by reproducing them in the soundtrack or audio portion of a motion picture or other audiovisual work"). It thus appears that although the sound recording legislation was enacted primarily to combat piracy, that legislation, in its terms and its intent, is broad enough to cover some forms of reproduction even in situations where copies are not distributed to the public. The District Court considered a synch right to be an extension of the reproduction right defined by section 114(b). 853 F.Supp. at 787. We disagree. A synchronization of previously recorded sounds onto the soundtrack of an audiovisual work is simply an example of the reproduction right explicitly granted by section 114(b) to the owner of rights in a sound recording.

Moreover, the Copyright Act specifically permits certain entities to reproduce sound recordings in soundtracks, provided that copies of the programs containing those recordings are not distributed to the public. For example, Congress provided in section 114(b) that noncommercial broadcasting entities have the right to include sound recordings in educational radio and television broadcasts, and may distribute and transmit copies or phonorecords as long as "copies or phonorecords of said programs are not commercially distributed by or through public broadcasting entities to the general public." 17 U.S.C. § 114(b). The plain implication of section 114(b) is that commercial entities like Paramount may not reproduce sound recordings on soundtracks of audiovisual works, whether or not the reproduction involves synchronization.

Paramount acknowledges that its use of Agee's sound recordings in conjunction with visual images was technically a "reproduction," but argues that the pre-recording of the *Hard Copy* soundtrack with Agee's recorded sounds was purely "incidental" to a single, tape-delayed television performance—the technological equivalent of a live broadcast. Paramount observes that it could have played Agee's recording, in synchronization with the video tape, as part of a live performance of *Hard Copy* without infringing Agee's reproduction right. Just as recording a television program for later viewing permits a home viewer to shift the effective time of the performance, *see Sony Corp. v. Universal City Studios*, 464 U.S. 417, 429 (1984), duplicating Agee's recording onto the soundtrack of an audiovisual work merely permitted Paramount to shift the time of the recording's broadcast to viewers. Paramount asserts that no copies of the program containing Agee's recording were made for distribution or sale.

In *Sony*, the Supreme Court held that consumers were not infringing copyrights in broadcast programs when taping television shows for later viewing. *Id.* at 447–55. In concluding that this recording was a fair use of the copyright, the Court noted that the work was transmitted free of charge over the broadcast airwaves, and the copy was a "time-shifting" one. *Id.* at 449. No evidence indicated that a consumer had published or otherwise attempted to profit from a time-shifting copy. *Id.* The nature of a televised copyrighted audiovisual work and the fact that time-shifting merely enabled viewers to view at a later time works that they had previously been invited to watch rebutted the presumption that reproducing a copyrighted work in its entirety was unfair. *Id.* at 449–50. In addition, the Court held that time-shifting reproductions had no demonstrable effect upon the potential market for, or the value of, a copyrighted work, and that time-shifting yielded societal benefits by expanding public access to broadcast television programs. *Id.* at 454.

We need not decide in this case whether all copying of sound recordings, including commercial copying solely for time-shifting purposes, infringes the copyright owner's exclusive right of reproduction, because Paramount's duplication and synchronization of Agee's sound recording were designed to achieve more than a time-shifted performance of that recording. Paramount derived independent commercial value from copying Agee's sound recording because that reproduction not only shifted the timing of performance but actually enhanced the performance by ensuring that there would be no mistakes in the synchronized program broadcast to viewers. Reproducing Agee's recording in the soundtrack of *Hard Copy* also enabled Paramount to preserve the program intact for possible distribution or re-broadcast at a later date.

Indeed, Paramount's characterization of its reproduction as merely a time-shifted performance is belied by the additional copies and uses Paramount made of the taped synchronization. In addition to copying Agee's sound recording as part of its synchronization of the recording with the "Caught On Tape" segment, Paramount incorporated a portion of the "Caught On Tape" segment, including Agee's copyrighted work, into a promotion of the next day's program and also prepared a commercial that contained a portion of the segment along with Agee's recording. Although Paramount has not distributed copies of *Hard Copy* to the public or impaired the market for Agee's sound recording in any obvious sense, its uses of its taped program suggest the value to Paramount, apart from time-shifting, of reproducing Agee's work.

In short, Paramount purchased Agee's sound recording but made no attempt to obtain a license for its reproduction in the soundtrack of its program. It therefore infringed Agee's sound recording at the moment it put portions of his recording on tape to make a segment of *Hard Copy*. Its incorporation of the sound recording without permission violated Agee's reproduction right.[5]

2. *Derivative Works.* Agee contends that Paramount also infringed his exclusive right to prepare derivative works based upon his sound recording. Under the Copyright Act, a "derivative work" is defined as a work based upon one or more preexisting works, such as a translation, musical arrangement, dramatization, fictionalization, motion picture version, sound recording, art reproduction, abridgement, condensation, or any other form in which a work may be recast, transformed, or adapted. *See* 17 U.S.C. § 101.

In the case of sound recordings, the Copyright Act imposes additional requirements before such a "transformation" of a preexisting work is sufficient to create a derivative work. *See id.* § 114(b); House Report at 106. Under section 114(b), the use of a sound recording qualifies as a

---

5. As *amicus* Recording Industry Association of America, Inc. observes, producers of movies, television shows, and commercials often obtain master use licenses from sound recording copyright owners that allow them to synchronize sound recordings with visual images, as well as to copy and distribute the audiovisual work. *See Platinum Record Co. v. Lucasfilm, Ltd.,* 566 F.Supp. 226, 226–27 (D.N.J. 1983) (referring to synchronization or master use license for use of sound recordings in movie, "American Graffiti"); Nimmer, § 24.04[C][2] (referring to need for motion picture companies to obtain master use license before incorporating copyrighted sound recordings in motion pictures).

derivative work only if "the actual sounds fixed in the sound recording are rearranged, remixed, or otherwise altered in sequence or quality." 17 U.S.C. § 114(b). Thus, before the *Hard Copy* episode could be considered a derivative work of Agee's sound recording, it must be found that Paramount altered Agee's recording in a manner that "rearranged, remixed or altered in sequence or quality" the actual sounds in the recording. To the extent Agee contends that the mere synchronization of his sound recording with visual images created an infringing derivative work, we disagree. Although a few cases may exist where a motion picture or television program is "based upon" a preexisting musical composition or sound recording, sound recordings are most often used in audiovisual works for background or performance, as in this case. Moreover, even if the mere transfer of Agee's recording to the sound-track of an audiovisual work in itself amounted to a "transformation," such synchronization would not rearrange, remix or alter the actual sounds of the recording.

[handwritten: synch is not an infringement]

However, Agee also alleges that Paramount edited his recordings, incorporating sound effects and narration with Agee's recordings in the soundtrack. Agee claims that "defendants altered the expression embodied in Agee's recording by abridging and condensing it, reordering it, [and] adding various sound effects." At oral argument, appellant contended that Paramount reordered and interspersed the actual sounds of the songs on his recording. The District Court concluded that although the soundtrack of *Hard Copy* added sound effects to Agee's recording, these additions did not alter the recording itself, but were designed only to "highlight" the visual images on the program. *See* 853 F.Supp. at 788.

Although the interspersing and abridgement of a sound recording may not, strictly speaking, involve sampling or amount to the traditional creation of a derivative work, such use of a recording appears to fall within the language of section 114(b), perhaps constituting a rearrangement or alteration in sequence. We need not determine the extent to which the recording was altered, however, because the finding that Paramount created a derivative work is unnecessary to a finding of infringement in light of Paramount's reproduction of Agee's recording, *see Twin Peaks Productions, Inc. v. Publications International, Ltd.*, 996 F.2d 1366, 1373 (2d Cir. 1993), and, as discussed below, would not affect our analysis with respect to the TV stations.

3. *Distribution Right.* Agee contends that Paramount infringed his exclusive right to distribute his sound recording when it transmitted *Hard Copy*, including his work, by satellite to the TV stations because such a transmission constituted a distribution of one or more copies of his recording "to the public" under 17 U.S.C. § 106(3). His contention is meritless.

The Copyright Act provides no definition of "distribution." As Agee observes, however, at least one court has concluded that the distribution right is essentially synonymous with the exclusive right of "publication" referred to in the 1909 Copyright Act. * * * The 1976 Act defines "publication" as "the distribution of copies or phonorecords of a work to the public by sale or other transfer of ownership, or by rental, lease, or lending." 17 U.S.C. § 101. In addition, "[t]he offering to distribute copies or phonorecords to a group of persons for purposes of further distribution, public performance, or public display, constitutes "publication." * * *

We find no basis for concluding that Paramount's transmission of Agee's recording to viewers via the TV stations, rather than directly, was a "distribution." In a slightly different context, a number of courts have held that "[t]ransmissions by a cable network or service to local cable companies who in turn transmit to individual cable subscribers constitute 'public performances' by the network under [the Copyright Act]." *Coleman v. ESPN, Inc.,* 764 F.Supp. 290, 294 (S.D.N.Y. 1991); *see also David v. Showtime/The Movie Channel, Inc.,* 697 F.Supp. 752, 759 n. 3 (S.D.N.Y. 1988) (transmission to cable operator by cable programmer is public performance under Copyright Act); *WGN Continental Broadcasting Co. v. United Video, Inc.,* 693 F.2d 622, 625 (7th Cir. 1982).

Treating such satellite transmissions as public performances protects music publishers and owners of copyrights in musical compositions, who have exclusive performance rights under the Copyright Act; otherwise, producers and networks could avoid liability by relying on local stations to perform a copyrighted work. *See David v. Showtime/The Movie Channel, Inc.,* 697 F. Supp. at 759 ("Congress apparently did not anticipate the eventual proliferation of organizations such as SMC who 'broadcast' their programs to the public indirectly, through local cable companies who pass the signal along to their individual customers.").

By contrast, in transmitting *Hard Copy,* along with Agee's recording, to the TV stations for transmission to the public, Paramount was not attempting to evade liability for performing Agee's copyrighted work because Paramount itself had the right to perform that work.

It is clear that merely transmitting a sound recording to the public on the airwaves does not constitute a "distribution"; otherwise, sound recording copyright owners would have the performance rights expressly denied to them under the statute. For this reason, distribution is generally thought to require transmission of a "material object" in which the sound recording is fixed: a work that is of "more than transitory duration." *See* 17 U.S.C. § 101 (defining "copy"). * * *

Although we are unwilling to say that disseminations must always be in physical form to constitute "distributions," *see, e.g., Playboy Enterprises, Inc. v. Frena,* 839 F.Supp. 1552 (M.D. Fla. 1993) (unauthorized uploading of copyrighted images onto computer bulletin board with knowledge that images would be downloaded by other bulletin board subscribers), in the broadcasting context, the distinction between material and non-material embodiments, and the fact that Paramount, like most television and radio broadcasting networks, transmitted its program for broadcast to the public, are relevant factors in determining whether Paramount engaged in broadcasting rather than distribution.

performance v. distribution

We conclude that Paramount's transmission of Agee's recording constituted a performance of that recording and not a distribution.

4. *Ephemeral Recording Exemption.* The District Court found the ephemeral recording exemption, *see* 17 U.S.C. § 112(a), applicable to both Paramount and the TV stations. This exemption permits "transmitting organizations," defined as broadcasting networks or local broadcasters, *see* House Report at 102, to make a single copy of a copyrighted work to facilitate their broadcast, provided certain prerequisites are met. Paramount now concedes that it is ineligible for this exemption because it is a program supplier rather than a broadcaster, and thus is not a "transmitting organization" under the statute. However, appellees contend that the exemption applies to the TV stations and thus protects the TV stations' copying and broadcast of Agee's recording.

There is no dispute that the TV stations are "transmitting organizations" for purposes of section 112(a). The TV stations also appear to have complied with the preconditions for invoking the ephemeral recording exemption, *see* 17 U.S.C. § 112(a), because they made a single copy of the program containing Agee's sound recording, used this copy solely for their own transmission in their service area, and, pursuant to their contract with Paramount, had to destroy their tape or return it to Paramount.

Agee contends, however, that the TV stations are not entitled to the ephemeral recording exemption because they copied and broadcast an unauthorized reproduction or derivative work containing Agee's sound recording. This contention is arguably supported by the language of section 112(a), which allows transmitting organizations to make a copy of a copyrighted work only if they are "entitled to transmit to the public a performance or display of a work, under a license or transfer of the copyright or under the limitations on exclusive rights in sound recordings specified by section 114(a)." *Id.* § 112(a). According to Agee, because the *Hard Copy* program was "tainted" by Paramount's unauthorized use of his work, the TV stations could not copy or perform the program without first obtaining Agee's permission. *See* House Report at 102 ("unless all [limitations on the scope of the ephemeral recording privilege] are met the making of an 'ephemeral recording' becomes fully actionable as an infringement").

We reject this argument, despite its surface plausibility and despite the fact that Paramount reproduced, and perhaps also prepared a derivative work based upon, Agee's recording. Because Agee has no exclusive performance rights, *see* 17 U.S.C. § 114(a), the TV stations were entitled to broadcast his recording without his consent. Nothing in the statute would prohibit the TV stations from also broadcasting a *reproduction* of Agee's sound recording since, like Paramount's transmission of its program to the TV stations, such a broadcast would still constitute a "performance." Had the TV stations themselves purchased Agee's sound recording, copied it, and then broadcast the recording to the public using the copy, they would have been at most liable for the duplication and not for the broadcast. The fact that Paramount, rather than the TV stations, reproduced Agee's recording does not alter the result.

The TV stations also would have been entitled to perform a *derivative work* that Paramount had created using Agee's sound recording. The statute states only that sound recording copyright owners have the exclusive right to "prepare" derivative works, *see* 17 U.S.C. § 114(b); it says nothing about the right to *perform* such works. Although some performances might create a derivative work (e.g., an improvised performance that recasts or remixes a sound recording), in this case, it was Paramount who prepared the work, with the TV stations merely broadcasting that work to the public.

Because the TV stations had the right to broadcast Agee's reproduced or altered sound recording "under the limitations on exclusive rights in sound recordings specified by section 114(a)," the stations are protected by the ephemeral recording exemption. * * *

CONCLUSION

For the reasons set forth above, we affirm the dismissal of Agee's Lanham Act and state law claims as well as the grant of summary judgment in favor of the TV stations. With respect to Agee's claim of copyright infringement, we reverse the grant of summary judgment in favor of Paramount, and, because no genuine issues of material fact exist with respect to that claim, direct the entry of summary judgment for the plaintiff on the issue of Paramount's liability for copyright infringement, and we remand for determination of appropriate relief.

PLATINUM RECORD CO., INC. v. LUCASFILM, LTD.

United States District Court, New Jersey, 1983.
566 F.Supp. 226.

FISHER, Chief Judge.

Plaintiff, Platinum Record Company, Inc., has brought suit against defendants Universal City Studios, Inc. and MCA, Inc. for breach of contract, misappropriation, unjust enrichment, and tortious interference with business opportunities. Defendants have moved for summary judgment on the merits. For the reasons outlined herein, the motion is granted.

In January 1973 Lucasfilm, Ltd. entered into an agreement (Agreement) with Chess Janus Records, plaintiff's predecessor-in-interest. Under this Agreement Chess Janus gave Lucasfilm the right to use the "master recordings" or "matrixes" of four popular songs for use on the soundtrack of the motion picture *American Graffiti*.[1] The conditions for the use of the recordings were set out in paragraph 2 of the Agreement:

1. The songs covered under the contract were "Almost Grown" and "Johnnie B. Goode," both recorded by Chuck Berry; "Book of Love," recorded by the Monotones; and "Goodnight Sweetheart," recorded by the Spaniels.

(f) Subject to our performance of the terms and conditions herein contained, you agree that we have the right to record, dub and synchronize the above mentioned master recordings, or portions thereof, into and with our motion picture and trailers therefore, and to exhibit, distribute, exploit, market and perform said motion picture, its air, screen and television trailers, perpetually throughout the world by any means or methods now or hereafter known.

Lucasfilm produced *American Graffiti* under a contract with Universal, and the film was released by a Universal subsidiary for national theatrical exhibition in August 1973. *American Graffiti* proved to be a major commercial success in its theatrical release and has subsequently been shown on cable television and on network and local television. In 1980 MCA Distributing Corp., a Universal affiliate, released the film for sale and rental to the public on video cassettes and video discs. This last distribution of the picture forms the basis of plaintiff's action before this court.

Plaintiff contends that its predecessor's Agreement with Lucasfilm, Ltd. (to whose rights defendants have succeeded) does not grant defendants the right to distribute *American Graffiti* on video discs and video cassettes. It asserts that the Agreement does not "speak for itself" in providing defendants with these rights. In any event, plaintiff believes it necessary to look beyond the actual terms of the Agreement to determine the parties' intent at the time of contracting. Plaintiff argues that the contracting parties' state of mind (as to whether or not video discs and video cassettes were to be included under the Agreement) remains to be determined, and that this presents a material issue of fact which precludes summary judgment at this point.

Paragraph 2 of the Agreement specifically gives defendants the right "to exhibit, exploit, market and perform [*American Graffiti*] perpetually throughout the world *by any means or methods now or hereafter known*" (emphasis added). This language is extremely broad and completely unambiguous, and precludes any need in the Agreement for an exhaustive list of specific potential uses of the film. As a previous motion-picture-related case cited by plaintiff itself has held, "[i]f the words are broad enough to cover the new use, it seems fairer that the burden of framing and negotiating an exception should fall on the grantor." *Bartsch v. Metro–Goldwyn–Mayer, Inc.*, 391 F.2d 150, 155 (2d Cir. 1968). Similarly, in the recent case of *Rooney v. Columbia Pictures Industries*, 538 F.Supp. 211 (S.D.N.Y. 1982), a district court found that "[w]here ... a party has acquired a contractual right which may fairly be read as extending to media developed thereafter," the other party may not escape that part of the agreement by showing that the specific nature of the new development was not foreseen at the time. *Id.* at 229. It is obvious that the contract in question may "fairly be read" as including newly developed media, and the absence of any specific mention in the Agreement of videotapes and video cassettes is thus insignificant.

Plaintiff places great emphasis on its argument that the showing of *American Graffiti* on video discs and video cassettes is not an exhibition of the film as covered by the Agreement. It presents no clear-cut definition, however, which would set out exactly what does or does not qualify as exhibition of a motion picture. Plaintiff apparently does not feel that the term encompasses only theatrical showings, as it has registered no objections in the past to the repeated showing of *American Graffiti* on cable and over-the-air television. I am persuaded by the rationale adopted by the *Rooney* court when it found that "whether the exhibition apparatus is a home videocassette player or a television station's broadcast transmitter, the films are 'exhibited' as images on home television screens." *Rooney v. Columbia Pictures Industries,* 538 F.Supp. at 228. A motion picture is exhibited when it is presented for viewing by an audience on a theater or television screen; the video cassette and video disc operate as a means of exhibition, not as something of an altogether different nature from exhibition.

Finally, plaintiff insists that, even if the terms of the Agreement clearly give defendants rights to the music in question for home video presentation, we should look behind the written contract to determine whether the parties actually intended it to encompass this area. It has already been established that it is immaterial whether plaintiff anticipated all potential future developments in the manner of exhibiting motion pictures. There was no mistake as to the terms of the contract, as plaintiff alleges. Thus, there are no material facts remaining to be determined in this case.

Defendants' motion for summary judgment is granted. An order accompanies this opinion. No costs.

C. BANKRUPTCY AND TAX TREATMENTS OF MUSIC CONTRACTS

High profile entertainers have been the target of Internal Revenue audits because of the high income and the large expenses deducted. Most audits end in a settlement rather than a court case. In the following case, Willie Nelson did not get the outcome he was hoping for.

United States Tax Court, 1985.
85 T.C. 914.

CANTREL, Special Trial Judge.

These cases are before the Court on petitioners' Motions to Seal filed in each case on May 16, 1985. They were called for hearing at Washington, D.C. on June 5, 1985, at which time counsel for the parties appeared and presented argument. At the conclusion of the hearing the Court took the motions under advisement. * * *

Respondent, in his notice of deficiency issued on October 15, 1984 to petitioners Willie H. Nelson and Connie Nelson, petitioners in docket number 1193–85, determined the following deficiencies and additions to tax:

Additions to tax, I.R.C. 1954

Years	Income tax	Sec. 6653(b)	Sec. 6653(a)
1975	$259,775	$141,995	0
1976	405,180	283,312	0
1977	384,389	305,290	0
1978	465,408	0	$23,270.40
	1,514,752	730,597	23,270.40

* * * In their motions to seal, petitioners seek a protective order sealing the entire record of both cases (including but not limited to all pleadings, depositions, exhibits, papers and filings) to be opened only by order of the Court and directing that the parties and their counsel in these cases be prohibited from disclosing to the media or public the contents of the sealed records. At the hearing petitioners' counsel modified his motions in requesting that the records be sealed only up to the time of trial.

In support of their motions petitioners argue that Willie H. and Connie Nelson as nationally known personalities are subject to 'intense and continual' scrutiny by the media. The Willie Nelson Music Company (hereinafter referred to as the Company) is wholly owned and controlled by Willie H. and Connie Nelson and as a result, the company is also subject to 'intense and continual' scrutiny by the media. Petitioners contend that the media coverage has attached undue creditability to respondent's allegations and has resulted in wide publicity and sensationalization. Thus, petitioners assert that they have been seriously and irreparably damaged by the public's impressions. Petitioners maintain that the damage is caused in part by newspaper headlines which indicate that petitioners are subject to criminal prosecution thus causing petitioners undue embarrassment and considerable emotional distress. Additionally, petitioners urge that as a result of the publicity they have been financially injured in that now they are unable to negotiate large up front payments in long term endorsement contracts.

Respondent opposes petitioners' motions and argues that common law, statutory law, and the Constitution require that the motions be denied. Our research has failed to disclose any reported Tax Court case where the fraud additions to tax have been determined and the record was sealed, nor has any such case been advanced by the parties. * * *

As a general rule, common law, statutory law and the United States Constitution support the proposition that official records of all courts, including this Court, shall be open and available to the public for inspection and copying. *Nixon v. Warner Communications, Inc.*, 435 U.S.

589, 597 (1978) (where a transcript of some 22 hours of tape recordings was furnished to reporters, but, release of Watergate tapes used as evidence in criminal trial to copy, broadcast and sell denied). * * *

In these cases members of the public have an interest in free access to the facts and in understanding disputes that are presented to this forum for resolution. * * * Nevertheless, the presumptive right to access may be rebutted by a showing that there are countervailing interests sufficient to outweigh the public interest in access. * * *

Historically, good cause has been demonstrated and records sealed where patents, trade secrets or confidential information is involved. However, a showing that the information would harm a party's reputation is generally not sufficient to overcome the strong common law presumption in favor of access to court records. 'Indeed, common sense tells us that the greater the motivation a corporation has to shield its operations the greater the public's need to know.' *Brown & Williamson Tobacco Corp. v. F.T.C., supra* at 1179–1180. * * *

Courts have not only accorded business entities' 'confidential' information protection but have also issued protective orders to protect an individual's confidentiality and right to privacy. *Sendi v. Prudential–Bache Securities,* 100 F.R.D. 21 (D.D.C. 1983); *In Re Smith,* 656 F.2d 1101 (5th Cir. 1981); *In Re Caswell,* 18 R.I. 835, 29 A. 259 (1893), (where the Court in holding that no one has a right to examine or obtain copies of public records from mere curiosity, or for the purpose of creating public scandal, refused to turn over judicial records respecting a divorce). However, these cases bear no resemblance to the instant cases. * * *

[P]etitioners have not demonstrated any harm (financial or otherwise) that they have suffered or will suffer if their motions are denied; their contentions are wholly unsupported by the record. Petitioners are correct when they argue [the Court may], in its discretion, to seal its records including pleadings to protect a party from embarrassment or harassment. Nevertheless, merely asserting annoyance and embarrassment is wholly insufficient to demonstrate good cause.

We have carefully studied the 37 newspaper articles submitted on petitioners' behalf at the hearing. All of them were published in Texas newspapers in February 1985: twelve of the articles were published on February 6, twenty-two on February 7, two on February 8 and one on February 9.None of them, in our opinion, even remotely suggest that petitioners are subject to criminal prosecution, albeit thirty-one of the articles report that Willie Nelson has been accused of CIVIL TAX FRAUD. Twenty-six articles report that petitioners' counsel, who is one of petitioners' counsel in these cases, was contacted and his replies were to the effect that it is believed the IRS position is grossly exaggerated, petitioner is certainly not guilty of any fraud, we expect to prevail in the litigation, or since the matter is in the courts we'll let it be resolved there. On the whole, we think the articles gave a factual report on petitioners' tax situation and, in fact, emphasized petitioners' claims that all of the deficiencies and additions to tax are in controversy and that no part of any underpayment is due to fraud.

Petitioners further claim that the publications they submitted have caused the public to question Willie Nelson's availability for performances in light of 'potential criminal prosecution'. Petitioners did not show one instance where this happened. In fact since the filing of the petitions Willie Nelson has performed at the Merriweather Post Pavillion in Maryland, appeared in Plains, Georgia to help former President and Mrs. Carter celebrate Plains' 100th Birthday, performed at his annual July 4 picnic in Austin, Texas, and performed five nights at New York City's Radio City Music Hall. On May 6, 1985 Willie Nelson won the Academy of Country Music's single record of the year award for 'To All The Girls I Loved Before,' which he sang with Julio Iglesias. If anything, in our view, Willie Nelson's popularity and desirability as a performer has remained intact, if not, increased.

We think a few final observations are in order. Attached to each petition is a full copy of the statutory notice of deficiency, which lists all of respondent's determinations. The petitions on file contest all of those determinations and in the appropriate portions thereof 'facts' are alleged. Respondent, IN HIS YET TO BE FILED ANSWERS, must set forth facts to sustain his determinations under section 6653(b), the burden of proof for which is placed upon him. * * * Thereafter, petitioners may file replies controverting respondent's answers wherein they shall set forth 'a clear and concise statement of every ground, together with the facts in support thereof, on which the petitioner relies affirmatively or in avoidance of any matter in the answer on which the Commissioner has the burden of proof.' * * *

On these records, after exhaustive analysis and research, we find and hold that petitioners have demonstrated no probative evidence of good cause sufficient to outweigh the public interests. The possibility that petitioners' status as nationally known entertainers may cause these cases to gain some notoriety is not a compelling enough reason to seal these records up to the time of trial. *See U.S. v. Hooker Chemicals & Plastics Corp.*, 90 F.R.D. 421, 426 (W.D.N.Y. 1981). Since good cause has not been demonstrated, petitioners' motions will be denied.

To reflect the foregoing [a]ppropriate orders will be issued.

Notes

1. In 2003 and 2004, Willie Nelson used the notoriety from his tax problems to his benefit. He made several humorous commercials for H & R Block for use during the tax season.

2. Several artists have attempted to use the Bankruptcy Court to get out of bad contracts. It is a risky strategy that has only been successful when the artist was truly in dire financial straits.

IN RE TAYLOR

United States Bankruptcy Court, District of New Jersey, 1989.
103 B.R. 511.

POLITAN, District Judge.

This matter comes before the Court as an appeal pursuant to 28 U.S.C. § 158(a) from the Final Order of the Honorable William F. Tuohey, Judge of the United States Bankruptcy Court for the District of New Jersey, entered on September 14, 1988. In that Order, Judge Tuohey granted the debtor James Taylor's motion to reject certain executory contracts, including contracts with appellants PolyGram Records, Inc., PolyGram Songs, Inc., and Delightful Music, Ltd. The Order also denied appellants' cross-motions to dismiss Taylor's bankruptcy petition on the grounds that it was filed in bad faith or in the alternative, for abstention from hearing Taylor's motion to reject. * * *

From 1979 until February 1988, James Taylor ("debtor") was the lead singer in a group known professionally as "Kool and the Gang". Through 1988, all contracts and legal relationships for the group were arranged through "furnishing companies". These furnishing companies were the actual contracting entities for the performers. The furnishing companies used by the group most frequently included: Quintet Associates, Inc., a corporation formed by the group's members as the primary vehicle to arrange recording and other performance related contracts; Fresh Start Music, Inc., a corporation through which song publishing was conducted; and a third corporation, variously called Road Gang Enterprises, Inc. and/or Road Gang Associates Ltd., that furnished services of the group in connection with concerts and tours.

Until 1985, the group was contractually obligated to furnish recording and publishing services to De–Lite Recorded Sound Corporation ("De–Lite"). In November 1985, De–Lite assigned its rights under the recording agreement to PolyGram Records, Inc. ("PolyGram"). At that time, the assigned contract was voluntarily terminated and a new agreement for the exclusive recording services of the group was executed between PolyGram and Quintet. In exchange for the group's services, PolyGram agreed to pay certain royalties to Quintet based on sales of the group's recordings. In addition, PolyGram agreed to advance funds to the group to cover living and recording expenses with the expectation that these funds would be recouped from future royalties.

At about the same time, Quintet executed a music-publishing agreement with De-Lite's affiliate, Delightful Music Ltd. ("Delightful"). Under this agreement, Delightful was given an exclusive grant of worldwide copyrights in all of the musical compositions written and recorded by the group for up to an eight album term. In return, Delightful was obligated to provide various services, including collecting performance fees and accounting for all monies received.

A third agreement was executed in November 1986 between Fresh Start and PolyGram Songs, Inc. Under the terms of this agreement,

Fresh Start would furnish the services of group members as songwriters. For this service PolyGram Songs agreed to pay royalties for songs written by a group member but not recorded by the group.

Each of these three contracts contained a "leaving member clause" binding each individual member of the group to perform as a solo artist under the terms of the respective contracts in the event of his departure from the group. In addition, the individual members of the group, including the debtor, were required to sign "inducement letters" in connection with the PolyGram recording contracts. Under the terms of the inducement letters, a member departing from the group was obligated to furnish his services directly to PolyGram, in the event that Quintet was unable to provide the services of the leaving member.

Taylor last performed as an artist with Kool and the Gang in early February 1988. At about the same time the debtor opened discussions with PolyGram concerning his future as a solo performer. On February 8, 1988, PolyGram wrote to Quintet and advised Quintet that it was exercising its rights to continue as the recording company for Taylor pursuant to the inducement letter and "leaving member" provisions of the Quintet recording contract. The debtor was also obligated to perform under the other contracts with Delightful and PolyGram Songs. On February 16, 1988, the debtor wrote to the manager of the group and revoked a general power of attorney held by the manager.

The financial events which ultimately lead the debtor to seek relief under Chapter 11 of the Bankruptcy Code arose out of cash flow problems experienced by Kool and the Gang starting in 1986. By October of that year Kool and the Gang entities had accumulated debts in excess of $1,719,000, exclusive of any advances on royalties from PolyGram. The groups' financial problems continued into 1987 when they entered into a loan and security agreement with PolyGram by which PolyGram advanced an additional $500,000 to Quintet. At a meeting held in December 1987 the group was presented with a report listing currently outstanding bills. This list reflected outstanding loans and accounts payable owed by the group of $3,352,109. The report noted that this sum did not include PolyGram advances which, at the time, were approximately $950,000. Of the debts owed by the various Kool and the Gang entities, certain debts had been personally guaranteed by members of the group, including the debtor. Three of these loans are at issue in this case: a loan from First InterCounty Bank in the amount of $515,000; a second loan from First City National Bank in the amount of $265,000; and several advances from Norby Walters totaling $514,000.

On May 24, 1988 James Taylor filed a petition for relief pursuant to Chapter 11 of the Bankruptcy Code in the United States Bankruptcy Court for the District of New Jersey. On June 13, 1988 Taylor filed a Motion for Authority to Reject certain executory contracts, including the PolyGram Recording Agreement, the PolyGram Co-Publishing Agreement, the Delightful Publishing Agreement, and any other written or oral executory agreements between Taylor and the Kool and the Gang entities. In response to this motion, appellants Delightful and PolyGram filed a cross-motion seeking dismissal of the debtor's Chapter 11 petition as having been filed in bad faith or, in the alternative, abstention by the Bankruptcy Court from hearing the debtor's motion to reject in accordance with § 305 of the Bankruptcy Code. The Bankruptcy Court issued its Opinion and Order on September 14, 1988, granting the debtor's motion to reject the executory contracts and denying appellants' motion to dismiss and for abstention. PolyGram filed a Notice of Appeal on September 20, 1988 and Delightful filed its Notice of Appeal on September 26, 1988. Although not formally consolidated, these two appeals raise similar issues regarding the rejection of personal service contracts and the filing of the Chapter 11 petition in bad faith. Because of the similarity of issues presented, this Court's Opinion applies with equal force to the appeal of PolyGram as well as Delightful.

I. REJECTION OF EXECUTORY CONTRACTS

The primary issue before the Court on this appeal is whether a debtor's executory personal service contracts may be rejected in a bankruptcy proceeding. Appellants PolyGram and Delightful argue that the Bankruptcy Court erred in permitting rejection of the executory personal service contracts because such contracts are not part of the debtor's estate under § 541 of the Code and therefore the trustee has no power to act on these contracts. Moreover, appellants argue that under § 365(c)(1)(A) of the Bankruptcy Code, the trustee is precluded from rejecting a personal service contract because that section speaks only to assignment or assumption of such contracts. Because the provision does not specifically address rejection of such contracts, appellants argue that the trustee has no authority to take such action.

The debtor, on the other hand, argues that executory contracts for personal services must be rejected upon the filing of a petition in bankruptcy because, under principles of nonbankruptcy law, such contracts cannot be assumed by the trustee. The debtor argues that to hold otherwise would frustrate an important purpose of the Bankruptcy Code: to ensure the debtor a "fresh start" after filing a petition for relief.

The issue before this Court is one of first impression and there is no case law on point in this Circuit or any other circuit for the Court to consider. This Court concludes that executory personal service contracts can be rejected in any bankruptcy proceeding filed in good faith.

Section 541 of the Bankruptcy Code defines property of the bankrupt estate as "all legal or equitable interests of the debtor in property as of the commencement of the case." 11 U.S.C. § 541(a)(1) (1982 and Supp. V 1987). An exception to the broad sweep of this provision is established for "earnings from services performed by an individual debtor after the commencement of the case." 11 U.S.C. § 541(a)(6) (Supp. V 1987). Under this exception, the debtor's post-petition earnings for performance under his personal service contracts are not considered property of the estate. It is unclear at this stage whether personal service contracts themselves are to be included in the bankrupt's estate at the commencement of the case. However, it is logical to conclude that if the debtor's earnings under these contracts are not part of the estate, the contracts also should not be considered part of the estate at the commencement of the case.

Pursuant to 11 U.S.C. § 365(a), the trustee "subject to the court's approval, may assume or reject any executory contract or unexpired lease of the debtor." 11 U.S.C. § 365(a) (Supp. V 1987). This language, by its express terms, permits the assumption or rejection of all executory contracts; no distinction is made between contracts which are part of the debtor's estate and those which are not so included at the time of commencement of the case. The trustee's general power to assume or reject any executory contract is limited only when additional restrictions or limitations have been established in the Bankruptcy Code. * * *

In the instant case, the debtor is obligated to work as an individual performer under three recording contracts pursuant to the "leaving member" and "inducement letter" clauses in the respective agreements. The debtor also remains personally liable for all advances made to the group over the past few years. As a result, any royalties earned from the debtor's individual performances can be used to offset the more than $900,000 advanced to the group by the recording companies prior to the debtor's terminating his relationship with Kool and the Gang. Allowing the debtor to remain liable for these advances is inconsistent with the principle of allowing the debtor a "fresh start". In addition, the Court recognizes that enforcing the performance obligations under the recording contracts would force the debtor into involuntary servitude under the personal service contracts. Therefore, this Court concludes that it is in the best interests of the debtor to allow rejection of his executory personal service contracts. * * *

II. LIABILITY FOR CONTINGENT OBLIGATIONS

Appellants also maintain in their appeal that the Bankruptcy Court's Opinion and Order was in error because the Court made findings based on evidence not in the record and ignored or improperly applied relevant law when reviewing and analyzing the three principal contingent liabilities of the debtor—the First InterCounty Bank of New York loan, the First City National Bank & Trust Co. loan, and the loan from Norby Walters.

Addressing the First InterCounty obligation, the Bankruptcy Court concluded that this obligation qualified as a legitimate contingent liability owed by the debtor. *See In re Taylor*, 91 B.R. 302, 308 (Bankr.D.N.J. 1988). The Court based its conclusion on the fact that the entire sum was backed by a loan guaranty personally signed by the individual members of the group Kool and the Gang, including the debtor.

Under the terms of the First InterCounty Bank guaranty signed by the debtor, the bank is expressly given the right to modify, renew or alter in any way the terms of the underlying indebtedness. Subsequent to the debtor signing this guaranty, the repayment terms of the original obligation in fact were modified by a settlement agreement between the parties to extend the time for repayment. Where a guarantor has given prior consent to changes, modifications, extensions or renewals of the underlying obligation, he is not released by a subsequent agreement which simply modifies the terms for repayment of the underlying note. *See National Bank of North America v. Sobel,* 31 A.D.2d 750, 297 N.Y.S.2d 476, 477–78 (App.Div.1969); *see also* Restatement of Security, § 129(1) comment b (1941).

Appellants argue that the Bankruptcy Court failed to consider Paragraph 10 of the subsequent settlement which provides that the "agreement constitutes the entire understanding between the parties, and merges and supersedes any prior agreements, negotiations or discussions concerning the parties...." Appellants argue that this language creates a novation discharging the debtor's prior guaranty, including its consent language. Because the debtor's prior guaranty has been discharged, the debtor's liability has also been discharged.

Appellants' argument suffers a fatal flaw. An essential element of any novation is that the substituted contract include as a party one who was neither the obligor nor the obligee of the original duty. *See* Restatement (2d) Contracts, § 280 (1979); *The Law of Contracts,* § 21–8 at 873. The settlement agreement, executed in April 1988, provided for repayment of the First InterCounty debt by the Kool and the Gang group and was signed by each individual member, except the debtor. Because no new additional party was made part of the substituted agreement, the doctrine of novation does not apply and the debtor remains obligated under the prior guaranty.

The second obligation attacked by the appellants arises out of a $250,000 loan undertaken by the Kool and the Gang group from First City National. In its Opinion, the Bankruptcy Court included a brief description of the facts giving rise to this obligation and then stated that this debt is among the obligations of the "debtor's tangled web of finances" due to "promissory notes and guarantees signed by the debtor." 91 B.R. at 309. The Bankruptcy Court made no analysis of the debtor's personal liability for this loan in its September 14th Opinion.

In his deposition, the group's manager, Gerard Delet testified that the First City National Bank loan represented a refinancing of a portion of the debt originally owed to the First InterCounty Bank. *See* Deposition Transcript, July 18, 1988, p. 268, 1.1–16. Acting under a general power of attorney, Delet signed the debtor's name to a personal guaranty of this debt to First City National Bank. *See id.* at p. 270, 1.6–14. When the loan was in default, a stipulation of settlement with First City was entered into by the debtor's former manager, Mr. Delet. This stipulation of settlement extended the time for payment of the bank's obligation.

Appellants raise the same arguments as made above for the First InterCounty Bank loan, stating that the stipulation of settlement operates to discharge the debtor's liability as a guarantor because it extends time for payment of the underlying obligation. For reasons previously discussed, this Court concludes that the debtor remains obligated pursuant to a valid personal guaranty on the underlying obligation with First City National Bank.

The third ruling challenged by appellants on this appeal concerns money owed to Norby Walters. Regarding this debt, the Bankruptcy Court found that Walters loaned money to the group through a series of promissory notes on which the individual group members were personally liable. On February 15, 1988, the individual members of the group, excluding Taylor, executed a new promissory note in the sum of $425,000 representing the outstanding balance due Norby Walters. The Bankruptcy Court stated "the record is not clear as to whether Norby Walters has waived any of his rights on the aforesaid promissory notes executed by the debtor, James Taylor, and whether by accepting the promissory note of February 15, 1988, in the sum of $425,000, as a matter of law, Walters, has, in fact, waived his rights against Taylor." 91 B.R. at 308.

The execution of a renewal note does not discharge the obligations created under a prior note unless the parties express a contrary intention at the time of execution of the renewal note. *See Bank of New York v. Cerasaro,* 98 A.D.2d 902, 470 N.Y.S.2d 894, 896 (3d Dept.1983); *see also Peterson v. Crown Financial Corp.,* 661 F.2d 287, 291 (3d Cir.1981). In *Bank of New York,* the Appellate Division of the New York Supreme Court stated "[i]t is well established that a subsequent note does not discharge the original indebtedness secured unless there is an express agreement between the parties." 470 N.Y.S.2d at 896 (citations omitted). In addition, "there is a strong presumption against an intent that the subsequent note was for payment." *Id.* at 896 (citations omitted). The record before the Court does not indicate that there was ever an express agreement to release Taylor from liability on the original note when the February 1988 note was executed. In addition, appellants offer no evidence sufficient to overcome the strong presumption that the subsequent note was not intended as payment for the original debt.

Appellants' argue on appeal that the debtor signed the original note in the capacity of an accommodation maker for the purpose of lending his name to the principal borrower, Road Gang Enterprises, Inc. *See N.Y.U.C.C.Law,* § 3–415(1) (McKinney 1978). Because the debtor did not sign the renewal note, appellants argue he is relieved of liability unless the lender knew of the prior suretyship status of the debtor and expressly reserved the right to recover against him. *See N.Y.U.C.C.Law,* § 3–606(1)(a) (McKinney 1978).

A review of the original notes signed by the debtor and other members of the group indicates that their role in signing the notes was not limited to accommodation makers. While the advances were technically made to Road Gang Enterprises, Inc., the promissory notes expressly made each member of the group jointly and severally liable for the entire amount of funds loaned. In addition, the status of Road Gang as a "furnishing company" under the direct control of the group indicates that the individual group members were the actual beneficiaries of the funds loaned by Walters. Therefore, the Bankruptcy Court was correct in concluding that the debtor remains personally obligated for money advanced by Norby Walters pursuant to original promissory notes.

III. BAD FAITH

* * * The existence of bad faith depends not on the presence of any one specific factor but on a combination of factors after careful examination of the facts of the debtor's case.

This Court concludes, after a thorough review of the debtor's petition and the surrounding circumstances, that the debtor's current financial condition justifies the filing of a voluntary petition in bankruptcy. Specifically, the petition lists liabilities totaling $4,518,701.50 ($2,530,732—secured claims; $1,987,969.50—unsecured claims), and assets totaling only $734,215.00. As discussed above, many of the listed liabilities are obligations for which the debtor may be personally liable. In fact, the three contingent liabilities already discussed total over $1.2 million, and alone establish sufficient debt to justify bankruptcy. The "other indicia of bad faith" to which appellants refer are of peripheral importance and, in any event, either collectively or individually, do not compel a contrary conclusion.

For the foregoing reasons, the decision of the Bankruptcy Court is AFFIRMED.

Notes

1. In *In re Watkins*, members of the singing group TLC filed for Chapter 11 protection under the Bankruptcy Code in an attempt to reject their existing management agreements. The court ruled in their favor. Creditors, including LaFace & Pebbitone Records, moved to dismiss the recording artists' Chapter 11 cases as bad faith filings. The Bankruptcy Court held that the Chapter 11 cases filed by the recording artists when their negotiations with their managers/advisors broke down were not filed solely in an attempt to reject their existing management agreements and did not have to be dismissed as bad faith filings. The negative royalty balance due Pebbitone is payable only from royalties. LaFace & Pebbitone contended that debtors' cases were filed solely to reject certain contracts between the parties. The court agreed that where the *sole* objective of a solvent debtor is to reject a contract in favor of a better one, the petition is in bad faith as it serves no useful reorganization purpose. However, the evidence did not support LaFace & Pebbitone's position. While the debtors did move to reject LaFace & Pebbitone's contracts shortly after filing, this fact alone did not establish bad faith. The real question was whether debtors were experiencing *bona fide* financial problems that warranted bankruptcy relief. T]he Court concluded that they were. *See* In re Watkins, 210 B.R. 394 (Bankr. N.D. Ga. 1997).

2. In *Seals v. Compendia Media Group, Inc.*, the plaintiff sued the defendants alleging copyright infringement. Defendants filed bankruptcy. The court concluded that the bankruptcy order did not unequivocally discharge all claims of infringement. Plaintiff had authorized the defendant's predecessor, Platinum Entertainment, to use his musical works. Instead, Platinum Entertainment made unauthorized duplications of the plaintiff's work and provided it to a third party in the Philippines. In 1997, Platinum acquired Intersound, including the rights and obligations of the license agreement with the plaintiff. On July 26, 2000, Platinum file for relief under Chapter 11 of the Bankruptcy Code, and an amended plan of reorganization. Thereafter, Platinum changed its name to Compendia Media Group. Because the court finds that reproduction within the United States is sufficient to state a claim under the Copyright Act, the Court need not address plaintiff's allegations of infringement related to [unauthorized] distribution within the United States. On its face, Section (D) appears to allow plaintiff to assert the very rights at issue in the instant dispute. Compelled to draw all reasonable inferences in plaintiff's favor, and staying within the four corners of the complaint, the court concludes that the bankruptcy order did not unequivocally discharge all claims of infringement predating. *See* Seals v. Compendia Media Group, Inc., 290 F.Supp.2d 947 (N.D. Ill. 2003).

Chapter 17

MERCHANDISING AND TOURING

Merchandising and touring can be lucrative for popular acts. Merchandising T-shirts, posters, concert programs, buttons, hats, and other memorabilia can provide mega-acts with a significant source of ancillary income. For less popular bands, merchandising can be a way to supplement the tour budget. Unauthorized or bootleg merchandise is a problem for the mega-acts and policing the sale of unauthorized merchandise can be a daunting task.

A. MERCHANDISING CONTRACTS AND ILLEGAL USE OF TRADEMARK

In order to preserve rights in a trademark, the owner must sue to prevent the unauthorized use of the mark. Self-policing is necessary so that the rights in the mark are not lost to competitors.

ELVIS PRESLEY ENTERPRISES, INC. v. BARRY CAPESE

United States Court of Appeal, Fifth Circuit, 1998.
141 F.3d 188.

KING, Circuit Judge.

Plaintiff-appellant Elvis Presley Enterprises, Inc. appeals the district court's judgment that defendants-appellees' service mark, "The Velvet Elvis," does not infringe or dilute its federal and common-law trademarks and does not violate its right of publicity in Elvis Presley's name. Because the district court failed to consider the impact of defendants-appellees' advertising practices on their use of the service mark and misapplied the doctrine of parody in its determination that "The Velvet Elvis" mark did not infringe Elvis Presley Enterprises, Inc.'s marks, we reverse the district court's judgment on the trademark infringement claims and remand the case for entry of an injunction enjoining the use of the infringing mark.

BACKGROUND

Plaintiff-appellant Elvis Presley Enterprises, Inc. (EPE) is the assignee and registrant of all trademarks, copyrights, and publicity rights belonging to the Elvis Presley estate. EPE has at least seventeen federal trademark registrations, as well as common-law trademarks, for "Elvis Presley" or "Elvis" and other registrations for his likeness. However, none of these marks is registered for use in the restaurant and tavern business. Prior to trial, EPE announced plans to open a Memphis nightclub as part of a possible worldwide chain. The Memphis nightclub opened subsequent to trial. EPE licenses a wide variety of products and operates Graceland, Elvis's home, as a tourist attraction with adjacent retail stores and restaurants. Over 700,000 visitors per year come from all fifty states and from around the world to visit Graceland. Merchandise sales have brought in over $20 million in revenue over a five-year period and account for the largest portion of EPE's revenue.

In April 1991, defendant-appellee Barry Capece, operating through the limited partnership Beers 'R' Us, opened a nightclub on Kipling Street in Houston, Texas called "The Velvet Elvis." On August 28, 1991, Capece filed a federal service mark application for "The Velvet Elvis" for restaurant and tavern services with the United States Patent and Trademark Office (PTO). In December 1992, the service mark was published in the *Official Gazette of the United States Patent and Trademark Office* as required by 15 U.S.C. § 1062(a). EPE was aware of this publication, but did not file an opposition to the mark's registration within thirty days under 15 U.S.C. § 1063. Accordingly, the PTO issued a service mark registration to Capece for use of "The Velvet Elvis" mark on March 9, 1993. The Kipling Street nightclub closed in July 1993 for business reasons.

After the Kipling Street location's closing, Capece began soliciting investors to reopen the nightclub at a new location. The new nightclub, to be located on Richmond Avenue, would have the same name, "The Velvet Elvis," but it would be run by a new limited partnership, Velvet, Ltd. Audley, Inc. is the general partner of Velvet, Ltd., and Capece is the sole shareholder of Audley, Inc. Capece began renovating the new location in January 1994. In July 1994, EPE contacted Capece by letter, threatening him with legal action if the bar opened with "Elvis" in its name. The Richmond Avenue location opened in August 1994 under the name "The Velvet Elvis."

The Defendants' bar serves a wide variety of food and liquor, including premium scotches and bourbons. The menu items range from appetizers to full entrees. Live music is regularly featured at the bar, and the bar claims to be the first cigar bar in Houston. Its decor includes velvet paintings of celebrities and female nudes, including ones of Elvis and a bare-chested Mona Lisa. Other "eclectic" decorations include lava lamps, cheap ceramic sculptures, beaded curtains, and vinyl furniture. Playboy centerfolds cover the men's room walls.

In addition to the velvet painting of Elvis, the bar's menu and decor include other Elvis references. The menu includes "Love Me Blenders," a type of frozen drink; peanut butter and banana sandwiches, a favorite of Elvis's; and "Your Football Hound Dog," a hotdog. The menu bears the caption "The King of Dive Bars," and one menu publicized "Oscar at The Elvis," an Academy Awards charity benefit to be held at the bar. Numerous magazine photographs of Elvis, a statuette of Elvis playing the guitar, and a bust of Elvis were also among the decorations. By the time of trial, many of these decorations had been removed from the Defendants' bar and replaced with non-Elvis items.

Pictures and references to Elvis Presley appeared in advertising both for the Kipling Street location and for the Richmond Avenue location from the date it opened through early 1995, and some ads emphasized the "Elvis" portion of the name by "boldly display[ing] the 'Elvis' portion of 'The Velvet Elvis' insignia with an almost unnoticeable 'Velvet' appearing alongside in smaller script. *Elvis Presley Enters. v. Capece,* 950 F. Supp. 783, 789 (S.D. Tex.1996). The Defendants made direct references to Elvis and Graceland in advertisements with phrases such as "The King Lives," "Viva la Elvis," "Hunka–Hunka Happy Hour," and "Elvis has not left the building." Advertisements also included a crown logo above the "V" in "The Velvet Elvis" mark. Advertised promotional events at the Defendants' bar have included parties commemorating Elvis's birth and death and appearances by Elvis impersonators and Elvis Presley's drummer. Some advertisements publicizing the opening of the Richmond Avenue location included direct references to Elvis and used the tag-line "the legend continues" without using "The Velvet Elvis" mark.

In April 1995, EPE filed suit against the Defendants, alleging claims for federal and common-law unfair competition and trademark infringement, federal trademark dilution, and violation of its state-law rights of publicity in Elvis Presley's name and likeness. EPE sought injunctive relief, costs, attorneys' fees, and an order to the Commissioner of Patents and Trademarks to cancel Capece's registration for "The Velvet Elvis." The case was tried to the district court, which ruled in favor of EPE on its claims of trademark infringement and unfair competition relating to the Defendants' advertising practices, but not those claims relating to their use of "The Velvet Elvis" service mark. *Id.* at 796–97. In addition, the court ruled in favor of EPE on its right of publicity claim in relation to the use of Elvis's name and likeness, but again not in relation to the use of "The Velvet Elvis" service mark. *Id.* at 801–02. As to the claims upon which EPE succeeded, the district court granted injunctive relief barring the use, in connection with the promotion or advertising of the bar, of "the image or likeness of Elvis Presley, phrases that are inextricably linked to the identity of Elvis, or from displaying the 'Elvis' portion of their service mark in print larger than that used for its counterpart 'Velvet.'" Upon all other claims, the district court ruled in favor of the Defendants and denied all other relief. EPE now appeals.

II. Discussion

EPE has appealed that portion of the district court's judgment denying relief on its trademark infringement claims, its federal dilution claim, and its right of publicity claim based only upon the Defendants' use of "The Velvet Elvis" mark and the district court's denial of an accounting of profits and attorneys' fees. Because it ruled in favor of the Defendants, the district court did not reach their defenses of laches or acquiescence. The Defendants reassert these defenses on appeal as alternative bases for affirming the district court's judgment. We consider each issue in turn.

A. Trademark Infringement

The district court clearly stated EPE's claim:

> [EPE] claims the inclusion of its "Elvis" trademark in the service mark "The Velvet Elvis" coupled with Defendants' use of the image and likeness of Elvis Presley in advertising, promoting, and rendering bar services creates confusion as to whether EPE licensed, approved, sponsored, endorsed or is otherwise affiliated with "The Velvet Elvis," constituting unfair competition and trademark infringement under the common law and Lanham Act.

* * * The district court also correctly stated the generally applicable law in this circuit to a trademark infringement claim. * * *

[margin note: TM infringement claim]

In this case, we are dealing with a service mark, "The Velvet Elvis," which the Defendants have used at their business location and extensively in advertising. To consider only the Defendants' use of the mark at their business location would ignore highly probative evidence of the meaning of the mark as the public encounters it in commerce and of the Defendants' intent in using the mark. By placing the mark in an Elvis context and in configuring the mark to highlight the "Elvis" portion of the mark, the Defendants have placed the mark in a context that does not alone connote tacky, cheesy art as the district court found. This contrary context of the mark has the ability to alter the psychological impact of the mark and must be considered in determining whether the Defendants' mark creates a likelihood of confusion in relation to EPE's marks. In failing to consider the Defendants' presentation of "The Velvet Elvis" mark to the public in advertising in determining whether the Defendants' use of their mark created a likelihood of confusion, the district court failed to consider the mark as perceived by the public. In addition, by isolating the advertising, the district court failed to consider how the Defendants configured the mark in emphasizing the "Elvis" portion of the name, which is highly probative of the impression they intended to convey.

The fact that the Defendants ceased many of the problematic advertising practices after receiving the cease and desist letter and shortly before EPE filed suit does not make the advertising any less relevant to the question of whether the Defendants' use of the "The Velvet Elvis" mark infringes EPE's marks. The cessation of infringing activity does not affect the determination of liability, but it may make an injunction unnecessary. In this case, the district court found "a definite possibility." *Elvis Presley Enters.*, 950 F.Supp. at 803, that the Defendants would resume their infringing advertising practices and therefore granted injunctive relief in spite of the Defendants professed intent to discontinue infringing activities. Ceasing the infringing activity does not allow an infringing party to escape liability. *See Spring Mills, Inc. v. Ultracashmere House, Ltd.*, 689 F.2d 1127, 1133 (2d Cir.1982).

* * * Parody

As noted earlier, parody is not a defense to trademark infringement, but rather another factor to be considered, which weighs against a finding of a likelihood of confusion. As a leading treatise has stated,

> some parodies will constitute an infringement, some will not. But the cry of "parody!" does not magically fend off otherwise legitimate claims of trademark infringement or dilution. There are confusing parodies and non-confusing parodies. All they have in common is an attempt at humor through the use of someone else's trademark.

Therefore, while not a defense, parody is relevant to a determination of a likelihood of confusion and can even weigh heavily enough to overcome a majority of the digits of confusion weighing in favor of a likelihood of confusion. * * *

In this case, the district court found that "The Velvet Elvis" mark, when combined with the bar's gaudy decor, was "an integral part of Defendants' parody of the faddish, eclectic bars of the sixties." *Elvis Presley Enters.*, 950 F.Supp. at 792. The intent was to parody "a time or concept from the sixties—the Las Vegas lounge scene, the velvet painting craze and *perhaps* indirectly, the country's fascination with Elvis." *Id.* at 795 In his testimony, Capece stated that the Defendants "were trying to make fun of the Hardrock Cafes, the Planet Hollywoods, or some of the places that were more pretentious" and that the Defendants could successfully perform their parody without using Elvis Presley's name. This testimony and the district court's analysis both indicate that neither Elvis Presley nor EPE's marks were a target of the Defendants' parody. * * *

The Defendants' parody of the faddish bars of the sixties does not require the use of EPE's marks because it does not target Elvis Presley; therefore, the necessity to use the marks significantly decreases and does not justify the use. Capece himself conceded that the Defendants could have performed their parody without using Elvis's name. Without the necessity to use Elvis's name, parody does not weigh against a likelihood of confusion in relation to EPE's marks. It is simply irrelevant. As an irrelevant factor, parody does not weigh against or in favor of a likelihood of confusion, and the district court erred in relying upon parody in its determination of the likelihood of confusion. * * *

Type of trademark

* * * The Defendants conceded that EPE's marks have "worldwide fame and almost instantaneous recognition," leading the district court to find that EPE's marks are strong. *Elvis Presley Enters.*, 950 F.Supp. at 792. The Defendants do not dispute this on appeal. Rather, the Defendants argue that "The Velvet Elvis" has a different meaning than EPE's marks and that EPE has not shown distinctiveness outside the entertainment industry. However, these issues are more appropriately considered in relation to other digits of confusion. EPE's marks are very strong and therefore strongly weigh in favor of a likelihood of confusion.

* * * *Similarity of marks*

The similarity of the marks in question is determined by comparing the marks' appearance, sound, and meaning. *See Jordache Enters.*, 828 F.2d at 1484; RESTATEMENT, *supra*, § 21(a); 3 MCCARTHY, *supra*, § 23:21. "Even if prospective purchasers recognize that the two designations are distinct, confusion may result if purchasers are likely to assume that the similarities in the designations indicate a connection between the two users. The relevant inquiry is whether, under the circumstances of the use," the marks are sufficiently similar that prospective purchasers are likely to believe that the two users are somehow associated. RESTATEMENT, *supra*, § 21 cmt. c. * * *

The district court found that "The Velvet Elvis" mark is "symbolic of a faddish art style that belongs to the culture that created it" and that the mark "has no specific connection with [Elvis] other than the coincidence of its use to portray him." *Elvis Presley Enters.*, 950 F.Supp. at 793. The district court made this finding without considering the context into which the Defendants placed their mark. The Defendants used "The Velvet Elvis" mark in advertising that included (1) the image of Elvis Presley; (2) direct references to Graceland and Elvis Presley with phrases such as "The King Lives," "Viva la Elvis," and "Elvis has not left the building"; and (3) the "Elvis" portion of the mark boldly displayed with "an almost unnoticeable 'Velvet' appearing alongside in smaller script." *Id.* at 789. On one of their menus, the Defendants also advertised "Oscar at The Elvis," an Academy Awards charity benefit to be held at the bar. The context of the Defendants' advertising for the first nine months of operation of the Richmond Avenue location has imbued "The Velvet Elvis" mark with a meaning that directly evokes Elvis Presley, despite any independent meaning the mark might have. *Cf. id.* at 797 (noting that the Defendants' advertisements in which "Elvis" is emphasized "creat[e] a definite risk that consumers will identify the bar with Presley or EPE" and that advertisements using Elvis's image cause confusion). The Defendants' mark's connection to Elvis is enhanced by the inclusion of "Elvis" in the mark and the Defendants' decision to emphasize the "Elvis" portion of the mark, leaving the "Velvet" portion almost unnoticeable. *See Lone Star Steakhouse & Saloon, Inc. v. Alpha of Va., Inc.*, 43 F.3d 922, 936 (4th Cir.1995). * * *

The Defendants' use of the mark outside this suggestive context where the faddish art style connotation might predominate does not counteract the Defendants' deliberate association with Elvis in their advertising. The connotation of the marks are similar, and this digit of confusion therefore weighs in favor of a likelihood of confusion.

Similarity of products and services

"The greater the similarity between products and services, the greater the likelihood of confusion." *Exxon Corp. v. Texas Motor Exch. of Houston, Inc.,* 628 F.2d 500, 505 (5th Cir.1980). Direct competition between the parties' services or products is not required in order to find a likelihood of confusion. *Professional Golfers Ass'n of Am. v. Bankers Life & Cas. Co.,* 514 F.2d 665, 669–70 (5th Cir.1975); *see also* 3 MCCARTHY, *supra,* §§ 24:13–: 14. * * *

While we recognize that EPE has plans to open a worldwide chain of Elvis Presley restaurants and has opened its Memphis restaurant since the district court's decision, our proper focus is on (1) whether the products and services of EPE and the Defendants are similar enough to cause confusion as to source or affiliation or (2) whether the Defendants' bar is in a market into which EPE would naturally be perceived to expand. The Velvet Elvis serves food, cigars, and alcohol; provides live music; and sells t-shirts and hats. EPE licenses its marks on a wide variety of products, including t-shirts and hats, and the Defendants concede that EPE's marks are particularly strong in the music, television, and movie industries. EPE also operates family-oriented restaurants and an ice cream parlor at Graceland. Despite the breadth of EPE's licensed products, these products and services may not be similar enough to weigh in favor of a likelihood of confusion, but it is a question that we need not reach.

The pervasiveness of EPE's marks across the spectrum of products and the success and proliferation of entertainment and music-themed restaurants like Planet Hollywood and Hard Rock Cafe—which Capece testified inspired their parody—support a likelihood of confusion. *Cf. Armco,* 693 F.2d at 1161 ("Diversification makes it more likely that a potential customer would associate the nondiversified company's services with the diversified company, even though the two companies do not actually compete."). These restaurants have led the way, and an Elvis Presley restaurant would be a natural next step due to the public's strong familiarity with such restaurants and with Elvis. Given that EPE licenses so many products and is a strong presence in the entertainment business and that Planet Hollywood and Hard Rock Cafe have shown the success and popularity of entertainment and music-themed restaurants, the restaurant and bar business with live music is a natural area of expansion for EPE, and this digit of confusion weighs in favor of a likelihood of confusion.

* * * The Defendants' intent

Proof of an intent to confuse the public is not necessary to a finding of a likelihood of confusion. If a mark was adopted with the intent to confuse the public, that alone may be sufficient to justify an inference of a likelihood of confusion. If the defendant acted in good faith, then this digit of confusion becomes a nonfactor in the likelihood-of-confusion analysis, rather than weighing in favor of a likelihood of confusion. *See Fuji Photo*, 754 F.2d at 597–98. However, an innocent intent in adopting a mark does not immunize an intent to confuse in the actual use of the mark. * * *

The district court found that the Defendants' subjective intent was an intent to parody, rather than an intent to confuse. Based upon this finding, the Defendants' intent would not support a finding of a likelihood of confusion. However, the Defendants' advertisements using the image of Elvis, referencing Elvis, and emphasizing the word "Elvis" in the mark are other circumstances that support an intent to confuse. *See Elvis Presley Enters.*, 950 F.Supp. at 797 (noting that "use of this type of advertisement *can only indicate* a marketing scheme based on the tremendous drawing power of the Presley name and its ability to attract consumer interest and attention" (emphasis added)). These circumstances increase the risk of confusion and are more than just "a failure to take reasonable steps to minimize the risk of confusion." * * *

The district court found that Capece's subjective intent in adopting the mark was an intent to parody, but in determining a defendant's intent, evidence of the defendant's actions is highly probative and should be considered. *See Oreck Corp.*, 803 F.2d at 173 ("[The defendant's] actions speak louder than its words...."). The Defendants' use of "The Velvet Elvis" mark in their advertising evidences an intent to market the bar by relying upon the drawing power of Elvis, as found by the district court. *See Elvis Presley Enters.*, 950 F.Supp. at 797. Therefore, the facts under this digit of confusion weigh in favor of a likelihood of confusion.

* * * *Actual confusion*

Evidence of actual confusion is not necessary to a finding of a likelihood of confusion, but "it is nevertheless the best evidence of a likelihood of confusion." *Amstar Corp.*, 615 F.2d at 263. Actual confusion that is later dissipated by further inspection of the goods, services, or premises, as well as post-sale confusion, is relevant to a determination of a likelihood of confusion. *See* 3 MCCARTHY, *supra*, §§ 23:6–: 7. "Infringement can be based upon confusion that creates initial consumer interest, even though no actual sale is finally completed as a result of the confusion." *Id.* at § 23:6. * * *

EPE presented witnesses who testified that they initially thought the Defendants' bar was a place that was associated with Elvis Presley and that it might have Elvis merchandise for sale. The witnesses all testified that, upon entering and looking around the bar, they had no doubt that EPE was not affiliated with it in any way. Despite the confusion being dissipated, this initial-interest confusion is beneficial to the Defendants because it brings patrons in the door; indeed, it brought

INITIAL CONFUSION

at least one of EPE's witnesses into the bar. Once in the door, the confusion has succeeded because some patrons may stay, despite realizing that the bar has no relationship with EPE. This initial-interest confusion is even more significant because the Defendants' bar sometimes charges a cover charge for entry, which allows the Defendants to benefit from initial-interest confusion before it can be dissipated by entry into the bar. Additionally, the finding by the district court that the Defendants' advertising practices caused actual confusion shows that actual confusion occurred when consumers first observed the mark in commerce. * * *

ACTUAL CONFUSION

An absence of, or minimal, actual confusion, however, over an extended period of time of concurrent sales weighs against a likelihood of confusion. In this case, the lack of complaints is relevant but should have less weight than the district court gave it. Approximately one year after the Richmond location opened, EPE's suit against the Defendants was reported in the press, and this lessens the weight of the lack of complaints because there would be no reason to complain to EPE if one knows EPE is aware of the possible infringer and has begun legal action. * * *

Based upon the above facts, this digit of confusion weighs in favor of a likelihood of confusion, and this finding is supported by the district court's finding of actual confusion in relation to the Defendants' advertising practices.

Weighing the digits of confusion

After considering the Defendants' advertising practices and dropping parody from the analysis, all five digits of confusion that we considered de novo weigh in favor of a likelihood of confusion, and only the identity of retail outlets and purchasers weighs against a likelihood of confusion. Giving each digit of confusion its due weight, we find that a likelihood of confusion exists between EPE's marks and the Defendants' use of "The Velvet Elvis" mark. Therefore, the Defendants have infringed EPE's marks with the use of their service mark, "The Velvet Elvis." * * *

CONCLUSION

For the foregoing reasons, we REVERSE the district court's judgment and REMAND this case to the district court to enter judgment for EPE and for further proceedings consistent with this opinion. EPE's motion for this court to take judicial notice of an action of the PTO, which was carried with the appeal, is dismissed as moot.

NEW KIDS ON THE BLOCK v. NEWS AMERICA PUBLICATIONS, INC.

United States Court of Appeals, Ninth Circuit, 1992.
971 F.2d 302.

KOZINSKI, Judge.

The individual plaintiffs perform professionally as The New Kids on the Block, reputedly one of today's hottest musical acts. This case

FAIRUSE-A
uses 91's mark
to
describe
91 product

requires us to weigh their rights in that name against the rights of others to use it in identifying the New Kids as the subjects of public opinion polls. * * *

No longer are entertainers limited to their craft in marketing themselves to the public. This is the age of the multi-media publicity blitzkrieg: Trading on their popularity, many entertainers hawk posters, T-shirts, badges, coffee mugs and the like—handsomely supplementing their incomes while boosting their public images. The New Kids are no exception; the record in this case indicates there are more than 500 products or services bearing the New Kids trademark. Among these are services taking advantage of a recent development in telecommunications: 900 area code numbers, where the caller is charged a fee, a portion of which is paid to the call recipient. Fans can call various New Kids 900 numbers to listen to the New Kids talk about themselves, to listen to other fans talk about the New Kids, or to leave messages for the New Kids and other fans.

The defendants, two newspapers of national circulation, conducted separate polls of their readers seeking an answer to a pressing question: Which one of the New Kids is the most popular? * * * Fearing that the two newspapers were undermining their hegemony over their fans, the New Kids filed a shotgun complaint in federal court. * * * The two papers raised the First Amendment as a defense, on the theory that the polls were part and parcel of their "news-gathering activities." * * *

Δ's
newspapers
↓
1A as
defense
polls part
of
newsgathering

To be sure, this is not the classic fair use case where the defendant has used the plaintiff's mark to describe the defendant's *own* product. Here, the New Kids trademark is used to refer to the New Kids themselves. We therefore do not purport to alter the test applicable in the paradigmatic fair use case. If the defendant's use of the plaintiff's trademark refers to something other than the plaintiff's product, the traditional fair use inquiry will continue to govern. But, where the defendant uses a trademark to describe the plaintiff's product, rather than its own, we hold that a commercial user is entitled to a nominative fair use defense provided he meets the following three requirements: First, the product or service in question must be one not readily identifiable without use of the trademark; second, only so much of the mark or marks may be used as is reasonably necessary to identify the product or service; and third, the user must do nothing that would, in conjunction with the mark, suggest sponsorship or endorsement by the trademark holder. * * *

① ②

The New Kids do not claim there was anything false or misleading about the newspapers' use of their mark. Rather, the first seven causes of action, while purporting to state different claims, all hinge on one key factual allegation: that the newspapers' use of the New Kids name in conducting the unauthorized polls somehow implied that the New Kids were sponsoring the polls. It is no more reasonably possible, however, to refer to the New Kids as an entity than it is to refer to the Chicago Bulls, Volkswagens or the Boston Marathon without using the trademark. Indeed, how could someone not conversant with the proper names of the individual New Kids talk about the group at all? While plaintiffs' trademark certainly deserves protection against copycats and those who falsely claim that the New Kids have endorsed or sponsored them, such protection does not extend to rendering newspaper articles, conversations, polls and comparative advertising impossible. The first nominative use requirement is therefore met.

Also met are the second and third requirements. Both *The Star* and *USA Today* reference the New Kids only to the extent necessary to identify them as the subject of the polls; they do not use the New Kids' distinctive logo or anything else that isn't needed to make the announcements intelligible to readers. Finally, nothing in the announcements suggests joint sponsorship or endorsement by the New Kids. The *USA Today* announcement implies quite the contrary by asking whether the New Kids might be "a turn off." *The Star*'s poll is more effusive but says nothing that expressly or by fair implication connotes endorsement or joint sponsorship on the part of the New Kids.

The New Kids argue that, even if the newspapers are entitled to a nominative fair use defense for the announcements, they are not entitled to it for the polls themselves, which were money-making enterprises separate and apart from the newspapers' reporting businesses. According to plaintiffs, defendants could have minimized the intrusion into their rights by using an 800 number or asking readers to call in on normal telephone lines which would not have resulted in a profit to the newspapers based on the conduct of the polls themselves. * * *

While the New Kids have a limited property right in their name, that right does not entitle them to control their fans' use of their own money. Where, as here, the use does not imply sponsorship or endorsement, the fact that it is carried on for profit and in competition with the trademark holder's business is beside the point. * * * Voting for their favorite New Kid may be, as plaintiffs point out, a way for fans to articulate their loyalty to the group, and this may diminish the resources available for products and services they sponsor. But the trademark laws do not give the New Kids the right to channel their fans' enthusiasm (and dollars) only into items licensed or authorized by them. * * * The New Kids could not use the trademark laws to prevent the publication of an unauthorized group biography or to censor all parodies or satires which use their name. * * * The district court's judgment is AFFIRMED.

Rex Heinke*
NEW KIDS v. NEWS AMERICA PUBLISHING

Important legal rules are sometimes established by cases over seemingly unimportant situations. *The New Kids On The Block v. News America Publishing*, 971 F.2d 302 (9th Cir. 1992), is one of those cases. The New Kids were a teenage rock band that burst on the pop scene, soared to incredible heights and then disappeared. But while the New Kids were popular, many others tried to use their name to sell everything from coffee mugs to key chains. The New Kids brought several lawsuits to prevent what they felt was improper exploitation of their name including this case. They probably did not imagine that one of their cases would establish an important precedent about the use of celebrities' and public figures' names and likenesses.

The two newspaper defendants conducted polls of their readers to determine which one of the New Kids was the most popular. Callers were charged 50 or 95 cents per minute for such calls. The newspapers then reported or were about to report the results when litigation was threatened.

The New Kids asserted they were entitled to any profits that defendants made because they had created the value in their name. The New Kids asserted ten different claims for relief, although their case essentially made two claims. First, they claimed use of their name, which was trademarked, was likely to confuse consumers as to the source of the polls. Second, they claimed that even if there was no confusion, the use of their name violated their rights of publicity. Thus, the case involved an issue important to all celebrities and public figures, and those who comment about them: when can celebrities and other public figures stop others from using their names, likenesses, etc. to make money?

Defendants contended that their use of "The New Kids On The Block" did not violate any of plaintiffs' rights and that even if it did, it was constitutionally protected speech. The District Court agreed on First Amendment grounds. It accepted our argument that if plaintiffs prevailed, no one would be able to talk about celebrities and public figures without their permission. For example, all polling companies would be out of business because they also use the names of celebrities and public figures without permission or payment of a licensing fee when they conduct their polls.

The Ninth Circuit, however, did not reach the First Amendment issue. Instead, it found plaintiffs had no viable claims for relief.

As to the trademark infringement claim, the Ninth Circuit recognized that while trademarks are property, they are a limited property

---

* Mr. Heinke represented Defendant News America Publishing. He is a partner in Akin Gump Strauss Hauer & Feld LLP in Los Angeles, California.

[handwritten margin note: TM can only prevent use of its mark when it will cause confusion as to the source]

right. A trademark owner can only prevent use of its mark by another if that use is likely to confuse consumers as to the source of a good or service. The Ninth Circuit went on to create a new nominative fair use defense, recognizing that often the use of a trademark is necessary to refer to a person or a group. It, therefore, held that this defense was available if: (1) The product or service was one that is not readily identifiable without the use of the mark; (2) Only so much of the mark is used as is reasonably necessary to identify the product or service, and (3) The user did nothing that suggests sponsorship or endorsement by the trademark owner.

[handwritten margin note: FAIR USE IF (1) (2) (3)]

The Ninth Circuit found each of these elements was met here. There was no other way to refer to The New Kids; only their names were used; and there was no suggestion they had approved the poll.

The Ninth Circuit also rejected plaintiffs' right of publicity. Use of plaintiffs' name was not actionable because it was used in connection with a news or public affairs account. Any other ruling would have made the media liable for every use of a person's name in any article or broadcast.

[handwritten margin note: right of publicity used in connection w/ a news account]

Not everyone thought the Ninth Circuit's ruling was proper. Many people who represent celebrities felt their clients had been deprived of the value of something they had created by their hard work. They argued that others were making money off of their clients' hard work. However, any other result would have severely constrained all commentary about celebrities or public figures. No one would have consented to use of their name if the comment was going to be adverse no matter how much the speaker was willing to pay.

GREAT ENTERTAINMENT MERCHANDISING, INC. v. VN MERCHANDISING

United States District Court, Southern District of New York, 1996.
1996 WL 355377.

SAND, District Judge.

Plaintiff Great Entertainment Merchandise brings this breach of contract action against performing artist Vince Neil and his loan-out corporation, VN Merchandising, after Neil failed to perform before a guaranteed number of paid attendees at his concerts. Plaintiff alleges that this failure violates the terms of their legal commitments and obligates both Vince Neil and his loan-out corporation to repay the unearned portion of a $1,000,000 advance. Defendant VN Merchandising does not oppose plaintiff's motion for summary judgment. Defendant Vince Neil, however, contests liability, asserting that the language of the contract does not bind him as he is not a guarantor for the debts of his loan-out corporation. In response, plaintiff Great Entertainment Merchandise has moved for summary judgment. Summary judgment is granted as to defendant VN Merchandising, and is denied with respect to Vince Neil.

BACKGROUND

Plaintiff Great Entertainment Merchandise ("GEM") engages in the acquisition and exploitation of merchandising rights to the names and likenesses of performing artists. Defendant Vince Neil ("Neil") is a heavy metal performing artist. In May 1993, plaintiff GEM entered into negotiations with Neil in order to secure a license of Neil's trademark and merchandising rights to manufacture T-shirts for his upcoming concert tour. In anticipation of the agreement with GEM, Neil arranged for the incorporation of a loan-out company. Established for the sole purpose of holding Neil's rights and licensing them to GEM, VN Merchandising ("VN") was incorporated on June 22, 1993. One day later, VN licensed its sole asset, Neil's trademark and merchandising rights, to GEM. The terms of the license are embodied in a contract known to the parties as the "Agreement".

Once the Agreement was executed, GEM paid VN $1,000,000. According to the contract, this sum was an advance on the royalties VN expected to accrue from GEM's exploitation of VN's merchandising rights. In exchange for the one million dollar outlay, the Agreement provided that VN "agrees to cause [Neil] to undertake a concert tour (the 'Tour') . . . before an aggregate of eight hundred thousand (800,000) paid attendees."

Apparently, GEM provided the advance with the expectation that Neil's performances for 800,000 paid attendees would generate sufficient merchandise demand such that GEM could have a realistic opportunity to earn back the advance it paid to VN and make a profit.

In addition to the advance terms, the Agreement provided: "In the event Grantor fails to perform . . . before an aggregate of Eight Hundred Thousand (800,000) paid attendees . . . [then] GEM may, by written notice to Grantor, demand that Grantor repay to GEM the full amount of the unrecouped Advances theretofore paid to Grantor by GEM, in which event Grantor shall immediately repay such amount to GEM. . . ."

The rights and duties of both GEM and VN having been established in the Agreement, the parties turned their attention to documenting the obligations of Neil individually. Therefore, concurrent with the execution of the Agreement, GEM and Neil signed an Inducement Letter. A routine practice in the entertainment industry, the function of an inducement letter is to ensure that the performing artist subscribes to the underlying obligations of the loan-out company's contract. Since the purchaser of the service enters into a contract with an often undercapitalized company, whose only asset is the underlying right which is to be purchased, the purchaser needs some assurance that the performer is willing to honor the contract of his furnishing company; lest its only recourse being against a shell corporation. Inducement letters, in effect, allow the loan out company to guarantee the personal services of the individual artist. Therefore, at the same time as GEM entered into the Agreement with VN, Neil signed an Inducement Letter, stipulating his direct commitment to honor the underlying contract.

Incorporated as part of the Agreement, the Inducement Letter provides:

"I [Neil] have been advised that Grantor [VN] is entering into a written agreement with you [GEM] of even date herewith (the 'Agreement'), pursuant to which [VN] is agreeing to furnish such rights to you. I am familiar with each provision of the Agreement relating to my obligations, which include certain obligations with regard to my performance of live concert tours, and I approve all of such provisions of the Agreement. . . .

In consideration of your executing the Agreement and as further inducement for you to do so (it being to my benefit that you execute the same), I hereby agree as follows:

1.   I confirm, warrant, guarantee and agree that I will duly and to the best of my ability, perform and discharge all of the obligations undertaken by me pursuant to the terms and conditions of my agreement with Grantor so as to fulfill all of the commitments, warranties, and representations contained in the Agreement and in all of the provisions as the same apply to me."

The issue in this case concerns the interpretation of the above language. Plaintiff contends that this paragraph obligates Neil to serve as guarantor for all VN's duties, including VN's financial obligations to repay the unearned portion of the $1,000,000 advance. Defendant contends that the language does not cause him to be the financial guarantor of his loan out company; rather, it merely binds him to use his best efforts to fulfill his personal obligation to perform in front of audiences aggregating 800,000 people.

The controversy arises because by the time Neil's concert tour was completed, he had performed before an aggregate number of 533,032 paid attendees, far short of the 800,000 guaranteed number. By letter dated September 22, 1995, GEM demanded that VN and Neil repay the full amount of the unrecouped $1,000,000 advance paid to VN. Responding that Neil was not liable for the debts of VN, Neil refused to tender payment. As of this date, neither VN nor Neil have paid to GEM the unrecouped advances. GEM, therefore, moves for summary judgment on its breach of contract claims against both VN and Neil.

Discussion

* * * Defendant VN concedes liability on the breach of contract claim and therefore does not oppose the motion [for summary judgment]. Accordingly, summary judgment is granted as to defendant VN. Defendant Neil, however, contests plaintiff's assertion that he is liable for the payment of the unrecouped $1,000,000 advance. Rather, he argues that neither the language of the Agreement nor the Inducement Letter creates such an obligation.

It is important to note what is not at issue in this present motion. Plaintiff has not asked this Court to assess the validity of its alter ego claim for relief. Accordingly, this Court leaves the highly relevant issue of piercing the corporate veil for a later day. * * * Focusing our attention on the breach of contract claim before the Court, both parties have stipulated that New York law governs the contract. It is well settled that New York law requires that the guarantee of an undertaking be in writing. *See* New York General Obligations Law § 5–701(a)(2); *Fort Howard Paper Co. v. William D. Witter, Inc.,* 787 F.2d 784, 795 (2d Cir. 1986). * * *

Turning to the language of the Inducement Letter, Neil agreed "to perform and discharge all of the obligations undertaken by me pursuant to the terms and conditions of my agreement with Grantor [VN] so as to fulfill all of the commitments, warranties, and representations contained in the Agreement and in all of the provisions as the same apply to me." * * *

Defendant Neil urges that the paragraph be read according to its plain meaning. Arguing that Neil merely promised to use his best efforts to perform his own obligations, i.e. perform for 800,000 attendees, rather than those of his loan out corporation, defendant raises a convincing argument. Nowhere in the Inducement Letter does Neil appear to unequivocally guaranty VN's financial obligations. Rather, the bold-faced words suggest that Neil is merely guarantying his own musical performance.

Plaintiff argues that the bold-faced language was meant to be more inclusive, embodying not only the obligations of Neil, the individual, but also that of his loan out company. Seeing the obligation to perform and the obligation to repay as a single bundle of rights and obligations, plaintiff urges a broader reading, relying on both the interplay of various contractual paragraphs and the objective intent of the parties when the Agreement was executed.

Assessing the plain language in light of the entire contractual sequence, we are troubled by the apparent lack of wording specifying a financial guarantee. It seems only logical that when GEM entered into contract negotiations with VN, it bargained for some assurance that the $1,000,000 advance could be recoupable against a financially viable party. Indeed GEM repeatedly asserts, and we find it quite believable, that it would never have entered into a contract with a single asset company, incorporated the day before the contract was signed, without the protection of a financially responsible guarantor. GEM's intent is plainly manifest; it intended to enter into a contract that would provide it with a viable recourse if defendant Neil was not able to honor the 800,000 attendee agreement.

In contrast, defendant Neil's intent is not as clear. In his deposition on May 29, 1996, it is evident that Neil delegated to his advisors control over his finances and businesses. As he succinctly states, "I'm a performer ... I'm not an attorney or anything ... I need to get T-shirts out for fans and my attorneys and managers took care of it." Neil states that he does not know what a loan out or furnishing corporation is. Similarly, he testifies to being unsure as to what an Inducement Letter is. It is apparent that at the time of contract, Neil did not know that he undertook a commitment to perform in front of a certain fixed number of paid attendees, or for that matter where the advance money was to be paid. When asked if he agreed to personally indemnify GEM for any liability arising out of the breach of the Agreement, Neil responded, "As far as I know, no."

Unlike Neil, his attorneys have a clear view of what Neil's intent was at the time of signing the Inducement Letter. In defendant Neil's affidavit of April 1, 1996, he unequivocally denies undertaking the financial obligations of his loan out company. Neil asserts, "I never intended to be personally responsible for repaying any money owed by my loan-out company to the plaintiff."

This Court is concerned over the discrepancy between Neil's affidavit and deposition testimony. Equally of concern is the dissonance between the language of the Inducement Letter, containing no explicit financial guarantee, and the intent of GEM to assure Neil's personal liability. In light of the New York law that a guarantee must be strictly construed, the Court concludes that summary judgment is not appropriate on the breach of contract issue. Accordingly, summary judgment as to Neil is denied.

Notes

1. In *Nice Man Merchandising,* the court enjoined the defendant Logocraft from promoting all novelty merchandise bearing the images, names, trademarks, logos, or likenesses of artists under contract with the plaintiff, Nice Man Merchandising. Logocraft, a British corporation, with its principle place of business in Pennsylvania, was in the business of bootlegging rock and roll merchandise, primarily posters. Logocraft obtained the posters from two British manufacturers. Logocraft claimed the posters were unused European concert tour posters. The court concluded while there is no merchandise licensing in Europe, if the promotional items were sold in the United States as unauthorized merchandise bearing the likeness, name, trademark, or logo, that sale would be a violation of the Lanham Act. *See* Nice Man Merchandising, Inc. v. Logocraft Ltd., 1992 WL 59133 (E.D. Pa.).

2. In *Winterland Concessions Co. v. MacIntosh,* the Plaintiff Winterland, was the licensee of exclusive merchandising rights of several musical artists. The defendant MacIntosh was producing and distributing unauthorized merchandise of which the defendant had a license. The Court ordered a permanent injunction against Defendant. *See* Winterland Concessions Co. v. MacIntosh, 1992 WL 170897 (E.D. Pa.).

3. In *Pearl Music Co., Inc. v. Recording Industry Ass'n of America,* an illegal distributor of duplicated cassettes brought an anti-trust suit against the Defendant recording industry, RIAA, which had warned the Plaintiff to cease making and distributing unauthorized copies and Pearl Music responded by filing an anti-trust suit. The Court ruled that an illegal distributor had

no standing to file suit. *See* Pearl Music Co., Inc. v. Recording Industry Ass'n of America, 460 F.Supp. 1060 (Cal. Dist. Ct. 1978).

B. TOURS

Touring is an important part of the music business. It is a way for a band to expand its fan base and keep its existing fans interested. Tours sell albums and merchandise and help generate local airplay.

Bands, at every stage of their careers, tour. In the beginning of a career, the band tours to establish a following and to get discovered by an A & R person who hears about the buzz the band's tour is generating. Following the release of each album, the band needs to tour to support the album. Record companies build in a time gap between albums to encourage the band to tour. In the twilight of a career, bands go on nostalgia tours to earn money and to continue their rock-and-roll lifestyles.

Tours can be very expensive depending on the method of travel, the number of people traveling, and the amount of equipment that must be transported. Beginning bands have a difficult time making money on tour. Breaking even is the goal for most bands, although tours by Bruce Springsteen, the Eagles, the Rolling Stones, and other major recording acts can make huge sums of money.

1. FAILURE TO PERFORM TOURING AGREEMENTS

Personal service contracts cannot be specifically enforced. If a performer does not feel like performing, there is no way to force him or her on stage. Once on stage, the question of whether the performance satisfied the artist's commitment is difficult to answer. The quality of the performance depends on the reviewer.

KASS v. YOUNG

California Court of Appeals, 1977.
67 Cal.App.3d 100, 136 Cal.Rptr. 469.

DEVINE, Associate Justice.

Plaintiff Kass appeals from an order vacating a default judgment in a class action and vacating the default of defendant Neil Young insofar as it relates to a class action, but allowing the default to remain against appellant Young to the extent that defendant as an individual is concerned (judgment to be subject to proof of damages as to plaintiff's individual rights). Appellant Young cross-appeals from the order allowing the limited default to remain. Both sides agree that the case appears to be one of first impression as to the effect of default in an alleged class action.

The complaint alleges that Kass was one of about 14,000 patrons at a 'rock' concert on March 31, 1973 at the Oakland Coliseum. Defendant Young was the star performer. He terminated the concert by abruptly walking off the stage. The purchasers of tickets 'did not receive the consideration of a full concert performance for which they had paid.' Damages are alleged to be about $98,000, including ticket prices, transportation and parking expenses. It is alleged that the entire class of patrons is affected exactly as is plaintiff.

Summons and complaint were served personally on Young on September 30, 1973. His default was entered on November 12, 1973.

At the hearing, Kass testified that about 14,000 were present; that Young walked out in the middle of a song; that everyone stood for a long time clapping and yelling, but Young did not return. Counsel for Kass presented three ticket stubs, one of which was Kass's; he proposed $91,000 as the amount of damages, calculated by multiplying 14,000 by the median price of $6.50 (tickets were $7.50, $6.50 and $5.50, but there was no evidence of the number sold of each category); he waived (for the whole class presumably) the parking fee item; by silence, he waived (for the class) punitive damages which had been prayed for, based on alleged malice. Read into the record were newspaper accounts which reported that the 'jarring' walk-off, a 'rip off,' a 'temper tantrum' occurred about an hour after the concert started, and reported that Young had said he couldn't go on because of repressive action of the security guards. Although at the hearing nothing was made definite about the subject of proof of membership in the class, there was a suggestion by counsel that refunds would be made to those who had retained ticket stubs.

The judge (not the judge from whose order the present appeals are taken) rendered judgment on June 26, 1974, awarding to plaintiff Kass, on behalf of himself and of all others who purchased tickets for the concert, the sum of $91,000; 40 per cent of the recovery was awarded to plaintiff's attorney; the whole amount collected was to be deposited in the attorney's trust account; payment was to be made to those who proved to the satisfaction of Counsel that they were members of the class (no method of determining the amount to be paid to each is stated; presumably each would be reimbursed his or her actual outlay); the balance unclaimed, after a reasonable time (which was not defined), would be disposed of by the court. There was no provision for notice even by publication.

On October 10, 1974, Young moved to vacate the default and the default judgment. One of the grounds was that the default and the judgment were jurisdictionally defective in that no notice had been given to the alleged class and that no class had been certified. On this ground the vacating order was made and the proposed answer of Young was permitted to be filed. (The answer alleges that Young had substantially completed his performance when he was forced to leave the stage by unnerving disturbance among the audience.)

I. Vacating of the Default Judgment

It was proper to set aside the default judgment because of a jurisdictional deficiency, namely, that there had been no certification of the asserted class and no provision for notice to the asserted class. A default judgment which is in excess of jurisdiction may be set aside at any time either by motion or an independent action in equity. *Sullivan v. Sullivan,* 64 Cal. Rptr. 82. Although, as was said at the outset, a case involving default judgment in a class action has not been found, it is to be inferred from the cases relating to the necessity for certification and for notice in class actions that the procedures which have been decreed to be mandatory establish these procedures as jurisdictional; wherefore, default judgment rendered without compliance with them is subject to vacation. In *Home Savings and Loan Association v. Superior Court,* 117 Cal. Rptr. 485, a peremptory writ of prohibition was issued restraining the trial court from proceeding to trial on the substantive merits of the cause without prior adjudication of the suitability of the lawsuit as a class action, determination of the composition of the class, and appropriate notification to its members. Although the court in that case did not refer to the failure to meet the prescribed procedures as a jurisdictional defect in so many words, nevertheless the facts that it issued a writ which normally at least is employed only to restrain a lower tribunal from exceeding its jurisdiction, *Abelleira v. District Court of Appeal,* 109 P.2d 942; 5 Witkin, Cal. Procedure (2d ed. 1971) Extraordinary Writs, s 39, p. 3813), and that the court in Home Savings and Loan Association based its decision in part on the constitutional requirement of due process of law, 42 Cal. App. 3d at pp. 1012, 1014, 117 Cal. Rptr. 485, give evidence that the court did not regard the trial court's failure as mere procedural error.

But if *Home Savings and Loan Association* be not authority for the proposition that the mandatory procedures are truly jurisdictional, we do not hesitate to declare them so. The strong language about the necessity of these procedures and the careful explanations of the reasons for that necessity appearing not only in *Home Savings and Loan Association* but also in the *City of San Jose v. Superior Court,* 525 P.2d 701; *Vasquez v. Superior Court,* 484 P.2d 964; *Blue Chip Stamps v. Superior Court,* 556 P.2d 755, are persuasive of the jurisdictional nature of prejudgment adjudication of the suitability of the action as a class action, determination of the composition, and appropriate notification. The elaborate and scholarly reasoning exhibited in those decisions need not be repeated here, but a few words may be said about the application of the principles established by those authorities to the present case. First, as to the parties: without determination of the proper class and of appropriate notice, the defendant would be subject not only to judgment in the purported class action but also to suits by individuals acting alone or in other asserted classes. *Home Sav. & Loan Assn. v. Superior Court,* 117 Cal. Rptr. 485. To be sure, defendant Young chose not to answer the complaint; but a party in default is not made subject to unlimited effects of his default. Relief may not be given beyond that prayed for (Code Civ. Proc., § 580); damages except when fixed by contract must be proved (Code Civ. Proc., § 585). * * *

In a purported class action, the defaulting defendant should be entitled to have the court either on motion of plaintiff's counsel or on its own motion decide the appropriateness of the class action so that if it truly be suitable and if the necessary notice be given to potential plaintiffs, there will be but a single binding judgment against him. As to potential plaintiffs, the prejudgment procedures are so connected with due process as to be jurisdictional. These persons are entitled to the best practical notice under the circumstances, advising them that they may be excluded from the class if they so request and that they will be bound by the judgment, whether favorable or not, if they do not request exclusion. *Home Sav. & Loan Assn. v. Superior Court,* 117 Cal. Rptr. 485. * * *

Then there is a consideration of damages in this particular case relating to the potential plaintiffs which is rather unique. The representative plaintiff has simply assumed that all 14,000 patrons of the concert were equally damaged and that their damages amounted to the price of the average ticket. It may be that many of the patrons or 'fans' of the performer who had entertained them for an hour did not regard themselves cheated or that some may have sympathized with his antagonism toward a number of the security guards. In the absence of notice, the single plaintiff has been able to enlist 14,000 persons, willing or not, and wherever they may be, to join his cause. In *Weaver v. Pasadena Tournament of Roses,* 198 P.2d 514, 515, four appellants "on behalf of themselves and all others similarly situated" brought an action for damages, seeking $100 for each person (it was estimated there were 1,850) who had been promised that upon standing in line at the box office, he could purchase two tickets to the Rose Bowl. The box office was closed early and tickets were withdrawn from sale and distributed to favored parties. The trial court held that this was not a proper representative action; there was but a large number of individuals, each of whom may or may not have, or care to assert, a claim against defendants. Appellants' complaint, said the court, as we do now, can be regarded as no more than an invitation to such persons as may be interested in joining with them in their action.

Nor are the interests of the litigants the only ones to be considered in the prejudgment determination. The representative plaintiff must show that substantial benefit will result both to the litigants and to the court. *Blue Chip Stamp v. Superior Court,* 556 P.2d 755. * * * The resources of the judicial system may be called upon by one or more persons, under Code of Civil Procedure, section 382, when the parties are numerous and it is impracticable to bring them all before the court, for the *benefit of all*.

Plaintiff-appellant contends that, although ordinarily class action issues should be resolved before trial, the defendant has admitted the allegations relating to class by failing to answer. In support of this proposition, plaintiff cites *Hypolite v. Carleson,* 125 Cal. Rptr. 221. *Hypolite* was described by its author as 'not a typical case.' The defendant expressly admitted the pertinent class action allegations in his answer. Although the class action issues of the case were not decided until after trial, appeal, reversal and remand, the facts were such that by reason of uncomplicated identification of the parties from existing records, the class action issues were as readily resolved as they could have been at the earlier and proper time. Plaintiff-appellant also argues that notice to the class was provided by the judgment itself by the mandate 'that any unclaimed monies remaining in the trust account of counsel is to be disposed of by proper application to this Court for further orders.' This is by no means provision for notice. Besides, there was no certification of the class. Certification is essential and in this case it is completely lacking.

Finally, there is the matter of necessary showing that the jurisdictional amount required for suit in the superior court be made if the action be not sustained in its representative grade. The order setting aside the default judgment must be affirmed.

II. Vacating the Default

Plaintiff-appellant contends that it was error to set aside the default, which is a ministerial act, simply because this is a class action and that the plaintiff asserting his representative status need not give the defaulting defendant additional time to answer by withholding default until a class is ascertained. Defendant-appellant Young contends that the default as to the class was properly vacated but it was error to allow the default to stand as to the individual plaintiff because there can be but one judgment, and that if plaintiff were to proceed as an individual, his claim would fall within the jurisdiction of the municipal court. We agree with plaintiff-appellant that the default should not have been set aside at all. Although service of summons was the subject of controversy, the judge, after hearing the motion to vacate, concluded that defendant had flouted the process of the court. (There was evidence that Young tore up the summons and complaint.) The default, in our opinion, is an indivisible thing. The defendant has chosen not to reply. To set the default aside would, as plaintiff-appellant says, give to the defendant time in addition to that specified in the summons. Courts, out of respect to their own dignity, cannot permit parties to choose, without peril to themselves, to ignore the court's own process. It has been held that an action which is described in the pleadings as a class action remains such an action unless and until the court decides that it is one which is unsuitable for prosecution as a class action. * * *

Ordinarily, if a default were allowed to remain, the vacating of a default judgment would be meaningless, because the plaintiff would be entitled at once to a renewed judgment. But in the case of an asserted class action, there still must be decided, following default, as a jurisdictional matter, the suitability of the lawsuit as a class action as set forth under heading I. This is so because the rights of other persons, potential plaintiffs, must be canvassed, which is not so in the ordinary action; because the defendant, although deprived of his right to respond on the merits to the cause of action as stated in the complaint, is entitled to protection against two or more judgments of which but one would be rendered in the instant case; and because the courts must, for the benefit of all litigants, protect themselves from the unnecessary multiplication of lawsuits on the one hand and from being used almost purposelessly save for the compensation of counsel. The order vacating the default is reversed. The default will remain. The order allowing the filing of the purported answer by defendant is reversed.

III. FURTHER PROCEEDINGS

So far as the individual plaintiff is concerned, his case may proceed following determination of the propriety of the class action. Perhaps it will have to be removed to the municipal court. If the cause proceeds as a class action, there will, of course, be but one judgment.

As was said at the outset, case law on the subject of defaults in class actions seems to be nonexistent. In our opinion, the defendant has lost his rights to defend on the merits of the action if the condition for class action be fulfilled. But the trial court, by reason of its authorities cited under heading I, must decide upon the suitability of the cause as a class action: whether it is manageable as such, whether the true purpose of a class action will be served, who the members of the class shall be, and if a class be certified, what notice shall be given. To be sure, in making inquiry into these matters, the court's scrutiny necessarily will come close into taking into account the merits of the case itself. But the court will observe a distinction, narrow though it may be, between the two subjects. The court will be concerned with such questions as: potential recovery to the individuals making up the asserted class; whether this recovery would be small in comparison with the time and expense consumed in distribution * * * whether the court's resources would really be employed for the benefit of the 14,000 or mainly for the class action attorney; * * * whether the action would have a beneficial deterrent effect; what likelihood there is that individual patrons would be able to prove or would care to assert their participation at the concert and any resulting damages. These and other questions the court must answer in order to decide whether the lawsuit is to proceed as a class action.

The order vacating the default judgment is affirmed. The order setting aside the default and permitting the filing of defendant's answer is reversed. The cause is remanded for further proceedings in accordance with the views expressed herein. Costs on appeal to be borne one-half by each party.

MICHAEL COPPEL PROMOTIONS PTY. LTD. v. BOLTON

United States District Court, Southern District of New York, 1997.
982 F.Supp. 950.

CHIN, District Judge.

This is a breach of contract action filed by Michael Coppel Promotions Pty. Limited ("MCP"), an Australian corporation engaged in

the business of marketing and promoting concerts, against Michael
Bolton ("Bolton"), the pop singer, and MBO Tours, a corporation used
by Bolton to arrange concert tours. In essence, MCP claims that defendants "unjustifiabl[y] repudiat[ed]" a 1996 concert agreement when
Bolton abruptly cancelled an eight-concert tour of Australian cities just
two weeks before the tour was scheduled to begin.

Defendants move to dismiss the complaint. They contend that
plaintiff has failed to state a claim for the following reasons: (1) MCP's
telefax of April 22, 1996 constitutes a counteroffer extinguishing its prior
offer; (2) defendants expressly made written acceptance and payment of
an advance the preconditions for an enforceable contract; and (3) the
complaint fails to sufficiently allege the existence of an oral contract.
* * * For the reasons set forth below, defendants' motion is denied.

Background

Plaintiff's Amended Complaint alleges that in early March of 1996
representatives of the parties "orally agreed [to] the material terms" of a
concert agreement. Under the terms of this alleged contract, Bolton
promised to perform eight concerts in various Australian cities between
May 14–28, 1996 (the "Australian Tour"). In return, Bolton would be
paid "the greater of $1,200,000 or 85% of the net door receipts of ticket
sales." With the apparent consent of defendants' booking agent and in
accordance with the "prevailing custom and usage in the concert promotion and touring business," MCP immediately commenced ticket sales
for six of the eight tour dates and engaged in extensive promotional
activities.

The parties continued to exchange telefaxes and telephone calls
regarding various issues relating to the tour. In separate telephone
conversations in March of 1996, Podell of ICM allegedly requested that
MCP delay ticket sales for one week due to problems with the Korean
tour, and then assured MCP that ticket sales could begin on March 29,
1996.

On or about April 16, 1997 ICM sent MCP a short form of the
alleged concert agreement (the "Short Form"). Approximately one week
later, MCP received from ICM a contract rider (the "Rider"). Plaintiff
alleges that the Short Form and Rider "fairly and accurately reflected
the material terms" of the previous oral agreement, but also contained
conflicting new terms, such as those concerning to which institution
Bolton's advance should be paid.

During the week of April 22, 1996, plaintiff learned that the Korean
tour had been cancelled. Shortly thereafter, Podell called Coppel to
suggest that MCP cancel the Australian Tour. Coppel refused, citing the
expenses already incurred and the likelihood of a last-minute surge in
ticket sales.

On or about April 26, 1996 Podell cancelled the Australian Tour on
behalf of Bolton and MBO, citing poor ticket sales. Plaintiff alleges that
defendants backed out of the agreement "either because Bolton did not

wish to endure the embarrassment of playing to less than capacity crowds if ticket sales did not improve at the Australian venues, or because the cancellation of the Korean tour dates had decreased the potential profitability of his Southeast Asian tour plans, or both.''

Discussion

[Part A. omitted].

B. Defendants' Motion to Dismiss

Accepting as true the factual allegations set forth in the complaint and drawing all reasonable inferences in plaintiff's favor, I hold that plaintiff has stated a claim upon which relief may be granted.

1. The April 22, 1996 Telefax

Defendants insist that no agreement, oral or written, was ever reached, and that continued negotiations reflect the unresolved state of affairs. Defendants argue that Coppel's April 22, 1996 telefax to Nash represents a ''counteroffer'' that ''extinguished'' defendants' initial ''offer.''

In the fax, Coppel states:

I've received three different sets of instructions for the transfer of the deposit, nominating variously: Chase Manhattan (fax dated 16 April), Barclays' Bank PLS, London (in all versions of the contract received to date), Chemical Bank, New York (fax dated 19 April). Even if I assume that the most recent instruction is the routing information actually required I cannot comply with your instruction to transfer funds directly to the artist's account—these funds should be held by I.C.M. pending the performance of the contract, which is the way I have always operated.

Clause 4. A. My offer specified that I would be responsible for ''hotel accommodation'' (room rate only)—please delete the words ''inclusive of breakfast.'' B. Peter—frankly I have a problem with the tour party increasing to 42 persons—for the previous Australian tour the touring party was 29 persons.

Clause 13. Noted that sponsorship arrangements have been approved and agreed, and in this regard it is requested that the sponsorship terms agreed be attached as an addendum to the contract.

This document constitutes a counteroffer only if no enforceable oral agreement previously had been reached in March of 1996. At this early stage in the proceeding, I cannot conclude as a matter of law that no oral agreement was reached in March or that MCP's April 22, 1996 fax constituted a counteroffer. The fax is consistent with either plaintiff's or defendant's theory of the case. It can be construed either as a counteroffer or merely as evidence of ongoing negotiations as to ancillary details, representing only Coppel's request for clarification of the wire transfer procedure and his objection to the enlargement of Bolton's entourage. The fax may tend to show, as defendants claim, that agreement as to material terms had not yet been reached; on the other hand, the document does not undermine plaintiff's principal argument that agreement had been reached as to the major terms and that only secondary issues remained.

Moreover, whether this document constitutes a counteroffer cannot be resolved on a motion to dismiss where, as here, the issue is bound inextricably with the fact question of whether an oral agreement has been reached. As the Second Circuit has made clear, "the issue of whether (and when) the parties intended to be bound is a factual issue that should [be] submitted to the jury." *International Minerals & Resources, S.A. v. Pappas*, 96 F.3d 586, 593 (2d Cir.1996). Thus, the April 22, 1996 fax does not bar plaintiff's suit.

2. Conditions Precedent to an Enforceable Contract

Defendants also insist that plaintiff failed to comply with two conditions precedent to the formation of the concert agreement: written acceptance of the contract and payment of an advance. They point to the Rider as evidence that both conditions were "explicitly made prerequisite to formation" of a binding contract.

Under New York law, where parties unequivocally indicate a desire not to be bound by an agreement "until it is reduced to writing and signed by both of them, they are not so bound ... until it has been written out and signed." *Scheck v. Francis*, 260 N.E.2d 493, 494 (1970). * * *

In this case, however, the Rider does not constitute unambiguous evidence of the parties' intent not to be bound by an oral agreement. Assuming, as I must, that an oral contract was reached in March 1996, the unsigned Rider received one month later does not conclusively prove that the conditions set forth therein were raised during formation of the alleged oral contract. Furthermore, because the Rider was unilaterally issued by defendants and was never signed by either party, this Court cannot conclude that the parties ever *agreed* to payment of an advance and written codification of the terms of the agreement as conditions precedent. At this point, defendants have failed to show that these conditions were clearly established "at the time of contracting." *Consarc Corp. v. Marine Midland Bank*, 996 F.2d 568, 576 (2d Cir.1993); *see Oppenheimer & Co. v. Oppenheim, Appel, Dixon & Co.*, 660 N.E.2d 415, 416 (1995) (parties' expression not to be bound orally unequivocal where they had executed letter agreement indicating there would be no valid sublease unless certain conditions were met).

Plaintiff's claim of partial performance of the alleged oral contract further militates against dismissal of the complaint. MCP alleges that it relied on defendants' repeated representations and assurances for a full month, expending considerable time and money performing its contractual obligations. As the Second Circuit has noted, "partial performance is an unmistakable signal that one party believes there is a contract; and the party who accepts performance signals, by that act, that it also understands a contract to be in effect." *R.G. Group, Inc., v. Horn &*

Hardart Co., 751 F.2d 69, 75 (2d Cir.1984). In light of defendants' failure to show that either party signaled its desire not to be bound by an oral contract alone, this Court may not ignore plaintiffs' allegations of partial performance.

In short, "[s]imply because the parties contemplate memorializing their agreement in a formal document does not prevent [an] agreement from coming into effect before written documents are drawn up." *International Minerals,* 96 F.3d at 593. Because the Rider does not clearly demonstrate "whether or not the parties intended to be bound prior to the formal execution of the suggested ... agreement," defendants' motion to dismiss on the basis of the Rider is denied. *Buschman v. Diamond Shamrock Corp.,* 35 A.D.2d 926 (1st Dep't 1970).

3. The Sufficiency of MCP's Allegations

Finally, defendants contend that plaintiff has failed to particularize the terms of the alleged oral agreement. Under New York law, an agreement is enforceable if a meeting of the minds has occurred as to the contract's "material terms." *Four Seasons Hotels Ltd. v. Vinnik,* 127 A.D.2d 310, 317 (1st Dep't 1987). So long as such agreement has been achieved, subsequent discussions thereafter over related or tangential matters does not render the contract inchoate or invalid. See *id.; see also Teachers Ins. & Annuity Assoc. of Am. v. Tribune Co.,* 670 F.Supp. 491, 498 (S.D.N.Y.1987) (describing two varieties of enforceable contracts— the first where complete agreement as to "major terms" has been reached, and the second where the parties have expressed a "binding preliminary commitment" to negotiate in good faith).

Plaintiff has more than adequately stated a claim for breach of contract. MCP alleges that the parties reached a binding oral concert agreement in March of 1996. And although defendants contend that plaintiff fails to specify the terms of the oral contract in the complaint, plaintiff has in fact specifically described such terms—Bolton would perform eight concerts at various Australian venues, and was in turn promised specific compensation: the greater of $1,200,000 or 85% of net proceeds from ticket sales. MCP further alleges that industry practice permits the promotion of concerts once initial agreement has been achieved as to material terms, even though additional details remain to be finalized. While defendants assert that concert agreements customarily require a meeting of the minds on "many significant particulars", they fail to specify any other material terms required of a binding contract as a matter of industry practice, but as to which no agreement was had in this case.

In sum, MCP has pled a viable claim for breach of contract. Accordingly, plaintiff is entitled to offer evidence in support of its action.

Conclusion

Defendants' motion to dismiss is denied.

[handwritten margin note:] industry custom permits promotion of concerts once initial agmt has been achieved even though details remain to be finalized

Notes

1. In 2003, pop singer Michael Jackson lost a multimillion dollar lawsuit filed by a concert promoter for canceling two concerts. The concert promoter filed suit against Jackson for breach of contract and fraud. Jackson had agreed to perform two concerts on New Year's Eve 1999. The concert promoter sought $25 million in damages. Jackson claimed that the promoter canceled the contract, not him. A jury found for the plaintiff promoter and awarded him $5.3 million in damages. http://www.cnn.com/2003/LAW/03/13/jackson.lawsuit.

2. In *Finley v. River North Records, Inc.,* promoters brought action of fraud against River North Records for misrepresenting who would appear in concert. The court found that the misrepresentation had caused damage to the promoters' reputations and awarded punitive damages. *See* Finley v. River North Records, Inc., 148 F.3d 913 (8th Cir. 1998).

2.   ON TOUR: CONCERT VIOLENCE AND TORT LIABILITY

Violence and concerts have a long history together. Regardless of who is responsible for the violence, the band onstage is usually sued. Lawsuits filed against bands on tour is one of the hazards of the road. Insurance and an indemnity from the venue are the only protection a band has from injured fans.

BOWES v. CINCINNATI RIVERFRONT COLISEUM, INC.

Ohio State Court of Appeals, 1983.
12 Ohio App.3d 12, 465 N.E.2d 904.

PER CURIAM. * * *

On December 3, 1979, The Who rock group performed at a concert at Cincinnati Riverfront Coliseum. Patrons and would-be patrons died while entering the Coliseum. These cases seek damages for the alleged wrongful deaths and personal injuries. [Eleven deaths occurred. Actions were brought on behalf of ten.]. The caption herein delineates the defendants, but we shall nevertheless additionally identify them. The defendants are: the Cincinnati Riverfront Coliseum, Inc. ("Coliseum"), locale of the rock performance; Brian E. Heekin, who was on December 3, 1979, a shareholder, director, the President and chief operating officer of the Coliseum, taking an active part in its day-to-day operations; the city of Cincinnati; The Who, and its four partners individually, as well as William George Curbishley, the group's personal manager who was present at the Coliseum on the evening of the instant incident; Electric Factory Concerts, local promoter of The Who on December 3, 1979; Tidal Wave Promotions, Inc., which was responsible for providing the touring facilities for The Who; nine directors of the Coliseum and Dalpepper Enterprises, Ltd., technical employer of The Who for performances outside the United Kingdom. * * *

[Part I omitted].

II

* * * Plaintiffs contend that the city of Cincinnati was negligent and that it is not protected by the doctrine of municipal immunity (sometimes referred to as sovereign or governmental immunity) as held below, that the city violated R.C. 723.01 in permitting the accumulation of such a crowd on December 3, 1979, as amounted to a nuisance; and that the city is liable under Section 1983, Title 42, U.S.Code, for a violation of the civil rights of the patrons on December 3, in that the city failed legislatively or administratively to prohibit festival seating at the Coliseum or to take affirmative steps adequately and effectively to obviate certain hazards.

We agree that the trial court did err in granting summary judgment in favor of the city vis-a-vis the claimed negligence or wrongful acts or omissions of its agents or employees. Plaintiffs argue that this result is mandated by *Haverlack v. Portage Homes, Inc.* (1982), 442 N.E.2d 749, and *King v. Williams* (1983), 449 N.E.2d 452. We reverse this portion of the summary judgment in favor of the city upon the authority of *Haverlack* and *King, supra,* but particularly upon *Enghauser Mfg. Co. v. Eriksson Engineering Ltd.* (1983), 451 N.E.2d 228, the syllabus of which holds:

"1. The judicially created doctrine of municipal immunity is, within certain limits, abolished, thereby rendering municipal corporations subject to suit for damages by individuals injured by the negligence or wrongful acts or omissions of their agents or employees whether such agents and employees are engaged in proprietary or governmental functions. (*Dayton v. Pease,* 4 Ohio St. 80, and its progeny overruled;

"2. Under this decision abolishing municipal immunity, no tort action will lie against a municipal corporation for those acts or omissions involving the exercise of a legislative or judicial function or the exercise of an executive or planning function involving the making of a basic policy decision which is characterized by the exercise of a high degree of official judgment or discretion. However, once the decision has been made to engage in a certain activity or function, municipalities will be held liable, the same as private corporations and persons, for the negligence of their employees and agents in the performance of the activities."

In *Enghauser* the Supreme Court emphasized that so far as municipal government is concerned, the rule is liability—the exception is immunity. None of the exceptions to municipal liability delineated in *Enghauser* exists here.

We agree with the trial court in its holding that there is no genuine issue as to any material fact raised in the plaintiffs' complaint on either the nuisance theory or the contention that the city violated the civil rights of plaintiffs or plaintiffs' decedents contrary to Section 1983, Title 42, U.S. Code. Thus, assignment of error three is reversed in part and affirmed in part as indicated. * * *

[Plaintiffs also assert] "The trial court erred in rendering summary judgment in favor of the board of directors of Riverfront Coliseum." Presented thereby for appellate review is whether the actions of the Coliseum directors *as directors,* with particular respect to the December 3, 1979 incident, constitute triable issues of fact. The summary judgment in their favor, if it stands, of course removes them from this Coliseum litigation. * * *

Unquestionably, the directors delegated to Brian Heekin and other members of an operating team for the Coliseum many responsibilities, which, under law, they were justified in doing. There is evidence that Brian Heekin and his "team" were experienced. On the other hand, as plaintiffs argue, the directors as a board did not make or participate in any decisions or undertake any assignments pertinent to concerts generally, or crowd control, seating policies, or security measures specifically. The directors' own brief acknowledges this abdication. We are confronted with the question of whether under all the circumstances the directors were lawfully justified in delegating to others to the extent that they did. * * *

The directors were fully aware of the public nature of the Coliseum's business. * * * This complete awareness of the public nature of the Coliseum's actual and intended operation was typical of all six directors deposed.

On and prior to December 3, 1979, the directors of the Coliseum also knew of the festival seating and crowd control problems. For instance, immediately following the Elton John concert on August 3, 1976, then City Manager William V. Donaldson commissioned a "Public Safety Study Team—Riverfront Coliseum" (hereinafter "PSST") whose chairperson was James D. Jester, Superintendent of the Highway Maintenance Division of the city of Cincinnati. The purpose of PSST was to have representatives of the different city agencies meet with Coliseum officials in an attempt to address and correct crowd problems at Coliseum events which had at that time—in 1976—already occurred a number of times. The directors of the Coliseum were aware of the festival seating problems and the formation of PSST and the reason why the city manager established PSST.

It is emphasized that the record *sub judice* shows that the directors were aware of patron safety problems at the Coliseum. In view of this knowledge, the direct question confronting this court then is whether the trial court ruled correctly in holding as a matter of law that there is no genuine issue of material fact as to whether the directors acted with legal responsibility or whether they did absolutely nothing, or not enough. To affirm what was decided below we would have to be convinced that reasonable minds could come to but one conclusion and that conclusion would be adverse to the plaintiffs. We are unable so to conclude. Ultimate personal liability of the directors is not presently before us; rather, we find that * * * the directors of the Coliseum should not have been dismissed from the Coliseum litigation. Therefore, the fourth assignment is well-taken. * * *

[Plaintiff also asserts that] the trial court erred in rendering summary judgment in favor of Brian Heekin and dismissing him. * * * The appellants' interpretation of the issue thus presented for review and arguments follows: "The record in this case presents factual issues concerning the personal liability of Brian Heekin, as a Coliseum officer and director, for The Who concert tragedy."

Not surprisingly, the plaintiffs assert that if the decision of the trial court that the directors were entitled to summary judgment and dismissal is reversed, "then the reversal of the summary judgment for Brian Heekin must automatically follow." In a word, the plaintiffs are correct in this contention. Brian Heekin was a director himself, shareholder, and the President of the Cincinnati Riverfront Coliseum. As the chief operating officer he was manifestly *the* Coliseum's headman with untrammeled sanction from the board; the power was concentrated in him and he exercised it authoritatively.

Under Ohio law, corporate officers may be held personally liable in tort. In *Schaefer v. D. & J. Produce* (1978), 403 N.E.2d 1015, motion to certify overruled (Nov. 3, 1978), the Court of Appeals for Erie County was confronted with a case involving personal injuries and ensuing death as a result of a vehicle accident which occurred when a truck owned by defendant D & J Produce, Inc. failed to stop at a stop sign and collided with the vehicle driven by plaintiff's decedent. Plaintiff contended that the offending vehicle had a defective braking system, no operative hand brake, and no operative horn or other audible signal. Plaintiff also contended that it was the duty of two officers of D & J Produce to inspect and maintain the vehicle in a safe operating condition and further contended that the two officers dispatched the truck driver in a vehicle they knew or should have known was not in a safe operating condition. The trial court dismissed the two officers * * *, but the court of appeals reversed, holding that the summary judgment was improperly granted in favor of the two officers who therefore remained as defendants. In the third paragraph of the syllabus, which is faithful to the law of the case, it is stated: "A corporate officer is individually liable for injuries to a third party when the corporation owes a duty of care to the third person, the corporation delegates that duty to the officer, the officer breaches that duty through personal fault (whether by malfeasance, misfeasance, or nonfeasance), and the third person is injured as a proximate result of the officer's breach of that duty."

We find assignment of error five well-taken.

III

We return to consider the second assignment of error. It alleges that: "The trial court erred in rendering partial summary judgment in favor of all defendants on the plaintiffs' claim for wanton and reckless misconduct." * * *

Following this state's law on punitive damages, * * * [w]e reverse the decisions below granting those partial summary judgments which dismissed punitive damage claims against the Coliseum, The Who and its four general partners, William Curbishley and Electric Factory Concerts. Initially we dispose of the punitive damage issue as to Tidal Wave Promotions, Inc. and Dalpepper Enterprises, Ltd.

Regarding Tidal Wave Promotions, Inc. ("Tidal Wave"), it negotiated a contract dated October 17, 1979, with the local promoter of The Who concert on December 3, 1979. One of the contract's provisions established a sound check for "approximately 6:00 p.m." on the night of the incident. On the face of it, there is nothing improper with scheduling a sound check for 6:00 p.m. What is material in the sequence of events is whether The Who's tardy arrival, a fact demonstrated in the record, was causally related to the tragedy. There is no indication that Tidal Wave's involvement extended beyond the contract referenced above. For example, there is no evidence that a Tidal Wave employee or agent was present on the scene. Finding no genuine issue of material fact as to Tidal Wave's participation which would amount to reckless, willful or wanton behavior, we affirm the trial court's dismissal of Tidal Wave as to punitive damage liability.

We affirm also as to Dalpepper Enterprises, Ltd. because we find nothing in the record which would amount to a genuine issue of material fact of any such involvement in The Who concert as would amount to reckless, willful or wanton behavior. It was properly dismissed below as to punitive damage liability.

So far as the Coliseum's liability for punitive damages is concerned, the record is replete with an awareness by its officers and employees of the safety problems presented by large and uncontrolled crowds at rock concerts at the Coliseum prior to December 3, 1979. See depositions of Richard D. Morgan, Director of Operations at the Coliseum, Cincinnati Police Lt. Dale Menkhaus, and Brian Heekin. Moreover, the record contains communications sent by past rock concert patrons to Coliseum officials sounding danger signals for similar future events if solutions to the problems were not implemented. The letters were answered by the Coliseum's Director of Public Relations, John Patrick Tafaro. This correspondence is included as exhibits attached to his deposition. Therefore, a jury question of punitive damages is raised, and the dismissal of the Coliseum as to such damages was erroneous.

awareness of officers of safety problems

What about the possibility of punitive damage recoverability from The Who, including the general partners Daltrey, Townshend, Entwistle and Jones? The group arrived late for a sound check. See deposition of Lt. Dale Menkhaus. There is a genuine issue of material fact as to whether there is a causal connection between that development and the tardy opening of the Coliseum doors and the ensuing deaths and injuries. Thus, the trial court erred by dismissing claims for punitive damages against The Who.

As personal manager for The Who, William Curbishley was on the scene on December 3, 1979, and had the responsibility for contacts between The Who and others implicated in the concert. According to one of The Who partners, Roger Daltrey, Curbishley had the authority, so far as The Who was concerned, to approve festival seating. In his deposed testimony Daltrey also recognized the possibility that Curbishley might have had authority on December 3, 1979 to decide how many entrance doors would be open and when. A jury question as to punitive damages exists for Curbishley.

Lastly, the motion of defendant Electric Factory Concerts ("EFC") for partial summary judgment on punitive damages was erroneously granted. EFC, a partnership, is a promoter of various events, maintains an office in the Coliseum, and was the promoter of the concert at the Coliseum on December 3, 1979. On October 17, 1979, EFC and the Coliseum executed a written instrument termed "Permit" by which the Coliseum granted permission to EFC to use and occupy its arena on December 3, 1979, from 8:00 p.m. until 11:00 p.m. Under the provisions of the "Permit," the Coliseum reserved many prerogatives to itself, but also awarded certain functions to EFC—and some authority they shared. For instance, provision 4(d) of the "Permit" provided:

> "Permittee [EFC] shall have in attendance, at Permittee's cost, a prescribed number of security and safety personnel, the exact number and suitability to be determined by the Coliseum and, if necessary, such determination shall be made after Coliseum's consultation with the City Police and Fire Department.

> "The 'Permit' strikingly evidences the meaningful promotional role of EFC in The Who show on the subject date."

Charles A. Levy, who went by the name of "Cal" Levy, was general manager and office manager for EFC at the time of the 1979 disaster. Levy was present at the Coliseum on December 3 at the concert in his capacity of general manager and actively oversaw the entire panorama for his employer EFC. The deposition in the matter *sub judice* tends to demonstrate that Levy was a key person in the determination of when the doors would open on the night of the concert. * * *

As heretofore expressed, there remain genuine issues of material fact as to whether the claims against EFC for punitive damages are meritorious. [T]he summary adjudication below in favor of Tidal Wave and Dalpepper Enterprises was proper; the other summary adjudications were not.

[Part IV omitted].

V

In summary, our holdings with respect to the liability of the various parties follow. These recapitulations below are to be credited only as they correspond to elucidative subject matter in this decision proper.

1. We reverse the order of the trial court dismissing punitive damage claims against the Cincinnati Riverfront Coliseum, Inc.

2. We reverse a similar order dismissing punitive damage claims against The Who, Daltrey, Jones, Entwhistle, Townshend and Curbishley.

3. We affirm the order below dismissing punitive damage claims against Tidal Wave Promotions, Inc. and Dalpepper Enterprises, Ltd.

4. We reverse the order below dismissing punitive damage claims against Electric Factory Concerts.

5. We reverse the order of the trial court dismissing all claims against members of the board of directors of the Coliseum and its President, Brian Heekin.

6. We reverse the dismissal of all claims by plaintiffs against the city of Cincinnati insofar as they sound in negligence.

7. We affirm the dismissal of all claims by plaintiffs against the city insofar as they sound in nuisance or a violation of civil rights.

8. We reverse the trial court's dismissal of all cross-claims against the city except as in 9, *infra*.

9. We affirm that portion of the trial court's order which preserves the claim of the Coliseum against the city.

10. The city's cross-claims for possible indemnification and/or contribution against the board of directors individually and Brian Heekin remain viable.

Judgment accordingly.

CROWN v. KIEDAS

Virginia Circuit Court, 1992.
1992 WL 884644.

FORTKORT, Judge.

The events giving rise to this litigation are given in the plaintiff's Motion for Judgment and in the parties' memoranda. The defendants Anthony Kiedas, John Fruscianti, Chad Smith, and Michael Balzary, appearing as "Red Hot Chili Peppers," held a concert on the campus of George Mason University on April 21, 1989. The defendant Lindy Goetz/L.G. Management negotiated the contract between Red Hot Chili Peppers and GMU. The plaintiff claims in the Motion for Judgment that after the April 21st concert, as part of her duties as a member of the Program Board, she waited in the hallway of the Student Union Building opposite the room in which the band members were taken after their performance. While she and another female member of the Program Board sat waiting outside the room, Kiedas, Fruscianti, Smith, and Balzary came out of the room and approached them in the hallway. At that time, Kiedas asked if they [would engage in oral sex]. Fruscianti and Smith stood on either side, and Balzary stood behind Kiedas. When the two women protested, Kiedas approached the plaintiff as the other woman moved away. Kiedas then pulled down his pants and thrust his penis into the plaintiff's face, poking her in the cheek. The plaintiff claims that Kiedas assaulted and battered her intentionally, unlawfully, violently, and without her consent; and that Fruscianti, Smith, and Balzary aided and abetted in the assault and battery. Count I of the Motion for Judgment also claims that the four band members went to the plaintiff's car, knocked her to the ground, took her keys, and entered her car to leave without her permission or consent to take the car. The plaintiff seeks consequential damages of $1,000,000 in Count I from defendants Kiedas, Fruscianti, Smith, and Balzary.

Count II claims $1,000,000 in consequential damages from the defendants Lindy Goetz/L.G. Management and Variety Artists International. The plaintiff contends that these defendants knew or should have known that the band members had acted in a violent and sexually abusive manner before and after previous concerts, and that the assault and battery as described in Count I of the Motion for Judgment were likely to occur. The plaintiff claims that these defendants owed a duty to the plaintiff not to expose her to the likelihood of such assaults, and that as a result of the breach of that duty, the band members injured the plaintiff.

Count III of the Motion for Judgment contends that the defendants Commonwealth of Virginia and George Mason University owed a duty to the students in public universities in Virginia to protect them from the acts of persons brought onto campus and to ensure that the activities of campus-sponsored organizations do not expose the student body to unnecessary and foreseeable risks. The plaintiff claims that the Commonwealth and GMU knew or should have known that the band members had acted in a violent and sexually abusive manner before and after previous concerts. She also claims that as a direct result of the breach of duty by the Commonwealth and GMU, the plaintiff sustained injuries from the band members. In this Count, the plaintiff seeks consequential damages of $1,000,000. The plaintiff also asks for $1,000,000 in punitive damages from all defendants.

The Court has before it today the Demurrer of defendant Lindy Goetz/L.G. Management. As grounds for the Demurrer, the defendant claims that he did not owe any duty of care to the plaintiff to protect her from the harm caused by the band members. In their Memoranda on the Demurrer, both parties cite Marshall v. Winston, 389 S.E.2d 902 (1990), in providing Virginia law as to the duty to protect another from the criminal acts or intentional torts of third parties: Generally, a person owes no duty to control the conduct of third persons in order to prevent harm to another.... This is especially the case when the third person commits acts of assaultive criminal behavior because such conduct cannot reasonably be foreseen....

The general rule applies unless "(a) special relationship exists between the actor and the third person which imposes a duty upon the actor to control the third person's conduct, or (b) a special relation exists between the actor and the other which gives to the other a right to protection." Restatement (Second) of Torts § 315 (1965). * * *

The plaintiff contends that the duty of Lindy Goetz/L.G. Management is based upon both sections of this exception to the general rule. Under subsection (a), she claims that Lindy Goetz had special relationship with the band members that imposed on him a duty to control their conduct. The plaintiff bases this claim on Goetz's contractual relationship with the band members, his negotiation of their contract with GMU, and his knowledge of their violent and sexually abusive conduct toward women. She also claims under subsection (b) that a special relationship existed between her and Lindy Goetz that imposed on him a duty to protect the her from the injury.

The first question before the Court in ruling on the Demurrer is whether a special relationship existed between Lindy Goetz and the band members such that Goetz, who was acting as agent for the Red Hot Chili Peppers Band, is responsible from their intentional torts. The Restatement offers as examples of this special relationship that of a parent controlling the conduct of his child, a master controlling the conduct of his servant, a possessor of land or chattels controlling the conduct of a licensee, and a person taking charge of dangerous person controlling the conduct of that dangerous person. RESTATEMENT (SECOND) OF TORTS §§ 316–319. The parent-child, master-servant, and licensor-licensee examples given in Restatement §§ 316 to 318 are clearly inapplicable to Goetz's relationship with the band members.

The master-servant relationship, however, is worthy of some discussion here because this relationship exists between Red Hot Chili Peppers and Lindy Goetz, and confusion may arise as to which party is responsible for the acts of the other. Restatement § 317 states the duty of a master to control the conduct of the servant:

> A master is under a duty to exercise reasonable care so to control his servant while acting outside the scope of his employment as to prevent him from intentionally harming others or from so conducting himself as to create an unreasonable risk of bodily harm to them, if (a) the servant (i) is upon the premises in possession of the master or upon which the servant is privileged to enter only as his servant, or (ii) is using a chattel of the master, and (b) the master (i) knows or has reason to know that he has the ability to control his servant, and (ii) knows or should know of the necessity and opportunity for exercising such control.

[handwritten margin note: duty of master is to control servant]

This Restatement section is applicable when the servant is acting outside the scope of his employment; if the servant is acting within the scope of his employment, the master may be vicariously liable for his conduct under the agency principle of respondeat superior. In the case presently before the Court, however, it is the servant who is charged with liability for the conduct of the master. A servant cannot be held liable for the intentional acts of the master under basic principles of tort

[handwritten margin note top: foreseeability of the master's conduct is in no way available to the servant.]

law; foreseeability of the master's conduct, for example, is in no way available to the servant. Although Red Hot Chili Peppers and Goetz stand in a master-servant relationship to one another, the relationship is inapplicable in determining Goetz's liability.

The Restatement offers one final example of the special relationship mentioned in § 315(a) which merits consideration in ruling on the Demurrer presently before the Court. Restatement § 319 describes the duty of one in charge of a person having dangerous propensities: "One who takes charge of a third person whom he knows or should know to be likely to cause bodily harm to others if not controlled is under a duty to exercise reasonable care to control the third person to prevent him from doing such harm." RESTATEMENT (SECOND) OF TORTS § 319. The Virginia Supreme Court recently addressed this type of special relationship in *Fox v. Custis,* 372 S.E.2d 373 (1988), finding that a probation officer and a parole officer did not have a special relationship with a parolee who committed numerous torts in violation of his parole. The Court determined that the officers in Fox did not "assert custody in the sense that the parolee is in the personal care and control of the officer." The Court found that the officers did not take charge or exercise control over the dangerous person within the principles articulated in Restatement §§ 315(a) and 319.

*[handwritten margin note: §319 dangerous propensities *]*

As to the present case, this Court finds no duty on the part of Lindy Goetz to control the conduct of the defendant band members. Although for the purposes of Demurrer the band members may be presumed dangerous, Goetz cannot be considered to have asserted custody over the band members as is required under Fox for a finding of liability. Goetz's contractual relationship with the band members, his negotiation of their contract with GMU, and his knowledge of their violent and sexually abusive conduct toward women do not rise to the level of "taking charge" of these third persons as defined by Restatement [§] 319 and Virginia case law.

[handwritten margin note: no duty of Lindy to control band members — no assertion of custody]

The second question in ruling on the Demurrer is whether a special relationship existed under Restatement § 315 (b) between Lindy Goetz and the plaintiff which would give the plaintiff a right to protection provided by Goetz from the conduct of the band members. Restatement § 314 gives as examples of this special relationship that of carrier-passenger, business invitor-invitee, and innkeeper-guest. The Virginia Supreme Court has addressed this special relationship as well in cases in which a tenant seeks to recover damages from his landlord for injuries inflicted on the tenant by a third person. In Klingbeil Management Group Co. v. Vito, 357 S.E. 200 (1987), for example, the Court found that no special relationship exists between the landlord and tenant which would give rise to the landlord's duty to protect the tenant from the intentional torts of third parties.

The plaintiff argues * * * that Lindy Goetz "did owe a duty to Plaintiff or the class of persons (namely female students at Defendant George Mason University) of which Plaintiff was but one." The plaintiff has not alleged, however, that a special relationship or that any relationship existed between her and Lindy Goetz which would give her a right to his protection from the conduct of the band members. She has alleged only that the band members had a reputation for acting in a violent and sexually abusive manner toward women, that such activity was their trademark, and that Goetz knew of their conduct. In view of the examples of the special relationship offered in Restatement § 314 and the Virginia Supreme Court's decision in Klingbeil Management, this Court finds that the relationship as alleged between the plaintiff and Lindy Goetz does not rise to the level required by Virginia law to impose liability.

[handwritten margin note: no relationship to rise to level of liability]

The Court therefore sustains the Demurrer because the plaintiff has not properly alleged a special relationship between Lindy Goetz and the members of Red Hot Chili Peppers which would give rise to Goetz's duty to control the conduct of the band members, or between Lindy Goetz and the plaintiff which would establish Goetz's duty to protect the plaintiff from the band members' actions. However, the plaintiff may amend the cause of action against Lindy Goetz/L.G. Management, if she is able and wishes to do so, within 21 days of this letter date. * * *

Notes

1. Two tragic incidents at Metallica concerts in Ohio involving fans resulted in serious injury. The intoxicated fan was rendered paraplegic after he volunteered to be "launched" in the air by other fans. At another concert venue in Indiana, a fan was injured when he participated in a "mosh pit". He allegedly suffered chest trauma inflicted by fans slamming against his body. The defendant claimed that the fan suffered a heart attack (caused by the loud music) from a congenital heart defect. Adams v. Metallica, Inc., 143 Ohio App.3d 482, 758 N.E.2d 286 (2001).

2. Incidents at rock and rap concerts often result in lawsuits stemming from violence during or after the show. Violence erupted in Detroit at an Everlast concert when Everlast made disparaging remarks about Detroit rapper, Eminem. Fans at the concert, who were also fans of Eminem, charged the stage resulting in various fights. Several people were injured including security staff. http://www.livedaily.citysearch.com/news/printable.html?id=2574

3. At a concert by R & B artist R. Kelly, a fight near a concession stand ended with eight men being stabbed. A total of more than 50 people were injured. The concert went on as scheduled. http://www.newstribune.com/stories/063099/ent_0630990928.asp.

4. About 30 fans attending a concert performed by rapper Eminem were injured during the show. "Excited fans" in the "mosh pit" stormed the stage at Washington D.C. RFK Stadium. The jam-packed crowd went out of control and concert attendees trampled one another. There were several injuries, including to a fan who suffered a heart attack. http://www.eonline.com/News/Items/Pf/0,1527,10013,00.html. At another Eminem concert in Glasgow, Scotland 45 people were injured in a mosh pit incident.

http://www.cbsnews.com/stories/20001/08/26/entertainment/prin-
table308187.shtml.

5. An injury at a U2 concert, however, involved negligence by the
venue rather than violence. At Soldier Field in Chicago, during a concert
performed by the Irish rock group U2, a fan slipped in a puddle of urine
while going for a bathroom break. The incident resulted in a judgment
award of $2.6 million against the venue for knee injuries sustained.
http://www.elevation-tour.com/article340.html.

Chapter 18

MUSIC CENSORSHIP

COMMUNITY STANDARDS v. THE FIRST AMENDMENT

The tension between the First Amendment and community standards is likely one of the reasons the rights were included initially in the Bill of Rights. The right to take an unpopular political stand and speak your mind is at the heart of the First Amendment. State's rights and local standards of decency are at the heart of the advocates for self-rule and the establishment of localized community standards. If the First Amendment did not trump the state and local government's rights to regulate speech, the uncertainty of the applicable standards would likely be as stifling as the actual regulations.

REDGRAVE v. BOSTON SYMPHONY ORCHESTRA

United States Court of Appeals, First Circuit, 1988.
855 F.2d 888.

COFFIN, Circuit Judge.

* * * The plaintiffs, actress Vanessa Redgrave and Vanessa Redgrave Enterprises, Ltd. (Redgrave), brought suit against the Boston Symphony Orchestra (the BSO) for canceling a contract for Redgrave's appearance as narrator in a performance of Stravinsky's "Oedipus Rex." The cancellation occurred in the wake of protests over Redgrave's participation because of her support of the Palestine Liberation Organization. She sought recovery both for breach of contract and for violation of her civil rights under the MCRA [Mass. Civil Rights Act].

A jury awarded Redgrave $100,000 in consequential damages caused by the BSO's breach of contract; sitting in an advisory capacity on Redgrave's MCRA claim, the jury found for the BSO. On the BSO's motion for judgment notwithstanding the verdict on the consequential damages issue, the district court held that the evidence of consequential damages was sufficient but that Redgrave could not recover these damages because of First Amendment limitations. The court also held that the MCRA does not impose liability on a party for acquiescence to third party pressure. Redgrave appealed from these rulings, and the BSO cross-appealed, arguing that the evidence of consequential damages was insufficient.

We conclude * * * that the district court erred in reversing the jury's award of consequential damages, but that Redgrave has presented sufficient evidence to prove only $12,000 in consequential damages, minus certain expenses. * * * [We conclude] the BSO is not subject to MCRA liability in these circumstances. We therefore affirm the judgment for the BSO on the MCRA claim and remand for entry of a reduced judgment for consequential damages on the contract claim.

I. Procedural History

In March 1982, the Boston Symphony Orchestra (BSO) engaged Vanessa Redgrave to narrate Stravinsky's "Oedipus Rex" in a series of concerts in Boston and New York. Following announcement of the engagement, the BSO received calls from its subscribers and from community members protesting the engagement because of Redgrave's political support for the Palestine Liberation Organization and because of her views regarding the state of Israel. On or about April 1, 1982, the BSO cancelled its contract with Redgrave and its performances of "Oedipus Rex."

Redgrave sued the BSO for breach of contract and for violation of the MCRA. The BSO argued at trial that the contract rightfully was cancelled because the cancellation was the result of "a cause or causes beyond the reasonable control" of the BSO. In response to the civil rights claim, BSO agents testified that they had not cancelled the performances in order to punish Redgrave for her past speech or repress her future speech, but because it was felt that potential disruptions, given the community reaction, would implicate the physical safety of the audience and players and would detract from the artistic qualities of the production.

[The] jury found that the BSO wrongfully had breached its contract with Redgrave. On that basis, the district court awarded Redgrave her stipulated performance fee of $27,500. The jury also found that the BSO's cancellation had damaged Redgrave's career by causing loss of future professional opportunities, and awarded Redgrave $100,000 in consequential damages. The district court found that the question whether there was sufficient evidence to support a finding of $100,000 in consequential damages was a "close and debatable" one, but concluded that there was sufficient evidence to support the award. Nevertheless, the district court overturned the grant of consequential damages, finding that a First Amendment right of freedom of speech was implicated by the theory of consequential damages advanced by Redgrave and that Redgrave had not met the strict standards required by the First Amendment for recovery of damages. *Redgrave v. Boston Symphony Orchestra, Inc.,* 602 F.Supp. 1189, 1193–1203 (D.Mass.1985).

Redgrave's MCRA claim was premised on the allegation that the BSO had interfered, "by threats, intimidation, or coercion," with Redgrave's exercise of free speech rights. Mass.Gen.L. ch. 12, §§ 11H—I. The district court utilized the jury in an advisory capacity on this claim. [The] jury found that the BSO did not cancel the contract because of the disagreements of BSO agents with Redgrave's political views. The district court stated that this finding eliminated an "essential factual premise" of Redgrave's primary claim based on the MCRA. 602 F.Supp. at 1192.

But Redgrave also argued that, even if BSO agents had not themselves disagreed with Redgrave's political views and did not cancel the contract because they wished to punish her for past speech or to repress her future speech, the BSO did cancel the contract in response to pressure from third parties who disagreed with and wished to repress Redgrave's speech. Redgrave contended that such acquiescence to third parties on the part of the BSO made it liable under the MCRA. The district court concluded that acquiescence unaccompanied by express personal disagreement with Redgrave's views could not amount to the "threats, intimidation, or coercion" needed to establish a claim under the MCRA. 602 F.Supp. at 1192. The district court, therefore, rejected Redgrave's acquiescence theory and entered judgment for the BSO on Redgrave's MCRA claim.

Redgrave appealed from the district court's entry of judgment notwithstanding the verdict on the consequential damages claim and from the judgment against her on the MCRA claim. The BSO cross-appealed, arguing that even if the First Amendment should be found inapplicable to the consequential damages claim, the evidence of those damages was insufficient to support the verdict.

II. THE CONSEQUENTIAL DAMAGES CLAIM

A. Consequential Damages for Loss of Professional Opportunities

[The] jury found that the BSO's cancellation of the "Oedipus Rex" concerts caused consequential harm to Redgrave's professional career and that this harm was a foreseeable consequence within the contemplation of the parties at the time they entered the contract. A threshold question is whether Massachusetts contract law allows the award of such consequential damages for harm to a claimant's professional career. * * *

The jury was given appropriate instructions to help it determine whether Redgrave had suffered consequential damages through loss of future professional opportunities. They were told to find that the BSO's cancellation was a proximate cause of harm to Redgrave's professional career only if they determined that "harm would not have occurred but for the cancellation and that the harm was a natural and probable consequence of the cancellation." *Redgrave v. BSO,* 602 F.Supp. at 1211. In addition, they were told that damages should be allowed for consequential harm "only if the harm was a foreseeable consequence within the contemplation of the parties to the contract when it was made." *Id.* at 1212. [The] jury found that the BSO's cancellation caused consequential harm to Redgrave's career and that the harm was a foreseeable consequence within the contemplation of the parties.

Although we find that Redgrave did not present sufficient evidence to establish that the BSO's cancellation caused consequential harm to her professional career in the amount of $100,000, we hold that, as a matter of Massachusetts contract law, a plaintiff may receive consequential damages if the plaintiff proves with sufficient evidence that a breach of contract proximately caused the loss of identifiable professional opportunities. This type of claim is sufficiently different from a nonspecific allegation of damage to reputation that it appropriately falls outside the general rule that reputation damages are not an acceptable form of contract damage.

B.   First Amendment Restrictions

* * * The BSO's cancellation of its contract with Redgrave was not * * * an act intended to be a form of symbolic speech or a "statement" by the BSO. As BSO agents testified, the press release announcing the BSO's cancellation went through a number of drafts in order to remove any statement or implication that Redgrave was too controversial or dangerous to hire. In fact, the press release did not even refer to Redgrave by name. Indeed, ... the jury found that the BSO's cancellation and press release did not "impliedly state to others that BSO's managerial agents held the opinion that Vanessa Redgrave was so controversial because of her publicly expressed political views that the risks associated with the series of performances in Boston and New York, in which she was to appear as narrator, were too great to be acceptable to a prudently managed symphony orchestra." 602 F.Supp. at 1205. Thus, the evidence does not support an inference that the BSO intended its cancellation to act as a symbolic message to others.

An act not intended to be communicative does not acquire the stature of First–Amendment-protected expression merely because someone, upon learning of the act, might derive some message from it. Nor is such an act entitled to special protection merely because others speak about it. Accordingly, we believe the district court erred in reasoning that the causal link between the BSO's contract cancellation and Redgrave's harm necessarily involved protected expression by the BSO.

Redgrave's counsel presented two distinct avenues of causation through which the jury could find that the BSO's cancellation caused Redgrave consequential harm and the jury was instructed on both grounds. Besides contending that the BSO's cancellation and press release impliedly stated to others that Redgrave was too controversial to be acceptable to a prudently managed symphony orchestra, Redgrave also contended that "since BSO was a prestigious cultural organization, the very fact that it decided to cancel rather than proceed with performances in which Vanessa Redgrave was to appear would tend to influence others not to offer her future professional opportunities." *Redgrave v. BSO,* 602 F.Supp. at 1212. The jury was instructed to "determine whether the evidence supports either, both, or neither of these contentions" in deciding whether the BSO's cancellation caused Redgrave consequential harm. *Id.*

The jury rejected the "implied message" theory yet still found that the BSO's contract cancellation caused Redgrave to lose future professional opportunities. Apparently, the jury felt that the BSO's cancellation had caused harm to Redgrave's career, despite its conclusion that the BSO had not intentionally sent any implied message regarding Redgrave. Theodore Mann, a director, testified that he chose not to offer Redgrave a job in a theater performance because [t]he Boston Symphony Orchestra had cancelled, terminated Ms. Redgrave's contract. [Because Mann's organization also seeks support from foundations and subscribers], I was afraid . . . and those in my organization were afraid that this termination would have a negative effect on us if we hired her.

Thus, the jury could appropriately have found that even though the BSO did not intend its contract cancellation to be a purposeful symbolic communication, other performing companies may have derived, or feared that their supporters might derive, some message from the cancellation, causing them concern about hiring Redgrave. Under this theory, the jury could have found that the act of cancellation, unprotected by the First Amendment, was the proximate cause of Redgrave's harm.

The district court correctly stated that "plaintiffs must prove that in some way information about BSO's action was communicated to others." 602 F.Supp. at 1197. However, as amici correctly point out, the trial court erred in confusing communication *about* the BSO's contract cancellation with the notion of an implied communication of a particular message *by* the BSO regarding Redgrave. Absent unusual circumstances suggesting primary interest in communicating an idea transcending the immediate act, a contract cancellation would not trigger the concerns ordinarily protected by the First Amendment. * * *

C. *Sufficiency of the Evidence*

The requirements for awarding consequential damages for breach of contract are designed to ensure that a breaching party pays only those damages that have resulted from its breach. Thus, to receive consequential damages, the plaintiff must establish a "basis for an inference of fact" that the plaintiff has actually been damaged, Williston, *Contracts,* § 1345 at 231, and the factfinder must be able to compute the compensation "by rational methods upon a firm basis of facts." *John Hetherington & Sons,* 95 N.E. at 964. * * *

In order for Redgrave to prove that the BSO's cancellation resulted in the loss of other professional opportunities, she must present sufficient facts for a jury reasonably to infer that Redgrave lost wages and professional opportunities subsequent to April 1982, that such losses were the result of the BSO's cancellation rather than the result of other, independent factors, and that damages for such losses are capable of being ascertained "by reference to some definite standard, either market value, established experience or direct inference from known circumstances." *John Hetherington & Sons,* 95 N.E. at 964. During trial, evidence was presented regarding losses Redgrave allegedly suffered in film offers and American theater offers. Based on this testimony, the jury found that the BSO's cancellation of its contract with Redgrave caused Redgrave $100,000 in consequential damages. We find that the evidence presented by Redgrave was not sufficient to support a finding of damages greater than $12,000, less expenses.

Most of Redgrave's annual earnings prior to April 1982 were derived from appearances in films and the English theater. Redgrave presented evidence at trial that she earned more than $200,000 on the average since her company's fiscal year 1976, and she testified that she had a constant stream of offers from which she could choose films that had secure financial backing. After the BSO's cancellation in April 1982, Redgrave contended, her career underwent a "startling turnabout." Redgrave testified that she did not work at all for the fourteen months following the cancellation and that the only offers she received during that time were for films with insufficient financial backing.

The evidence demonstrates that Redgrave accepted three firm film offers in the fourteen months following the BSO cancellation. If these three films had been produced, Redgrave would have earned $850,000 during that period. [The films were not produced because of financial difficulties]. * * * There was no allegation that the financial failures * * * were directly related to the BSO cancellation.

Although there is no doubt that Redgrave did not have a successful financial year following the BSO cancellation, we cannot say that she presented sufficient evidence to prove that her financial difficulties were caused by the BSO cancellation. * * * If [the first film] had been produced, Redgrave would have earned $250,000 in the year following the BSO cancellation—an amount equal to Redgrave's average earnings before April 1982.

Redgrave contends, however, that the film offers she received following the BSO cancellation lacked secure financial backing and were thus significantly different from offers she had received prior to the cancellation. * * * [She] argues that the fact that she had to accept two films that ultimately were not produced was itself a result of the BSO cancellation.

We have some doubt as to whether Redgrave presented sufficient evidence to prove that the type of film offers she received in the year following the BSO cancellation were radically different from the film offers received before the cancellation. * * * Thus, the evidence does not present an effective comparison between the type of film offers received before and after the BSO cancellation and we are left primarily with Redgrave's allegation that the film offers received in the two time periods were significantly different.

Even if we accept, however, that Redgrave proved she had experienced a drop in the quality of film offers following the BSO cancellation, Redgrave must also prove that the drop was proximately caused by the BSO cancellation and not by other, independent factors. Redgrave failed to carry her burden of presenting evidence sufficient to allow a jury reasonably to infer this causal connection.

The defense introduced evidence that Redgrave's political activities and statements had generated much media attention prior to the incident with the BSO. Redgrave conceded that her agents had informed her, prior to April 1982, that certain producers were hesitant to hire her because of the controversy she generated. And, in a newspaper interview in February 1982, Redgrave stated that she "had lost a lot of work because of her political beliefs" but that every time there had been a move to stop her working, "an equally terrific response [came] forward condemning any witch hunts."

To the extent that Redgrave may have experienced a decline in the quality of film offers received subsequent to April 1982, that decline could have been the result of Redgrave's political views and not the result of the BSO's cancellation. Even if the cancellation highlighted for producers the potential problems in hiring Redgrave, it was Redgrave's burden to establish that, in some way, the cancellation itself caused the difference in film offers rather than the problems as highlighted by the cancellation. Redgrave produced no direct evidence from film producers who were influenced by the cancellation. Thus, the jury's inference that the BSO cancellation had caused Redgrave consequential damages was one based more on "conjecture and speculation," *Carlson v. American Safety Equipment Corp.*, 528 F.2d at 386, than on a sufficient factual basis.

Redgrave also claims that the BSO's cancellation caused a drop in her offers to perform on Broadway. Bruce Savan, Redgrave's agent, testified regarding all offers to perform in American theater that had been made to Redgrave prior to April 1982. The offers averaged from two to four plays in the years 1976–1980. There was no evidence of any offers to perform on Broadway made to Redgrave in 1981, the year immediately preceding the BSO cancellation. * * *

Theodore Mann was the one producer who testified regarding his decision not to employ Redgrave in a Broadway production. He explained that the Boston Symphony Orchestra had cancelled, terminated Ms. Redgrave's contract. * * * [We] had conferences about this. We were also concerned about if there would be any physical disturbances to the performance.... And it was finally decided ... that we would not hire [Redgrave] because of all the events that had happened, the cancellation by the Boston Symphony and the effects that we felt it would have on us by hiring her.

The evidence presented by Redgrave concerning her drop in Broadway offers after April 1982, apart from Mann's testimony, is not sufficient to support a finding of consequential damages. We do not, of course, question Redgrave's credibility in any way. Our concern is with the meager factual evidence. Redgrave had to introduce enough facts for a jury reasonably to infer that any drop in Broadway offers was proximately caused by the BSO cancellation and not by the fact that producers independently were concerned with the same factors that had motivated the BSO. Mann's testimony itself reflects the fact that many producers in New York may have been hesitant about hiring Redgrave because of a feared drop in subscription support or problems of physical disturbances. Apart from Mann's testimony, Redgrave presented nothing other than the fact that three expected offers or productions did not materialize. This type of circumstantial evidence is not sufficient to support a finding of consequential damages.

* * * A jury reasonably could infer that the BSO's cancellation did more than just highlight for Mann the potential problems that hiring Redgrave would cause but was actually a cause of Mann's decision, perhaps because Mann's theater support was similar to that of the BSO or because Mann felt influenced to follow the example of a "premier arts organization." Because this is a possible inference that a jury could draw from Mann's testimony, we defer to that inference. We therefore find that Redgrave presented sufficient evidence to prove consequential damages of $12,000, the fee arrangement contemplated by Mann for Redgrave's appearance in *Heartbreak House*, minus expenses she personally would have incurred had she appeared in the play.

III. THE MASSACHUSETTS CIVIL RIGHTS CLAIM AND THE DEFENSE OF ACQUIESCENCE TO THIRD-PARTY PRESSURE

* * * A. *The Nature of the Claim*

The MCRA creates a private cause of action for injunctive and other equitable relief, including damages, against "any person or persons, whether or not acting under color of law, [who] interfere by threats, intimidation or coercion, or attempt to interfere by threats, intimidation or coercion, with the exercise or enjoyment by any other person or persons of rights secured by the constitution or laws of the United States, or of rights secured by the constitution or laws of the commonwealth." Mass.Gen.L. ch. 12, §§ 11H—I (1986). A right is "secured" against private parties under the MCRA even though the constitutional provision from which it emanates applies only to government action. *See Bell v. Mazza*, 474 N.E.2d 1111 (1985). In this fashion the MCRA dispenses with the state action requirement of ordinary civil rights claims, by permitting a plaintiff to sue a private party for action that would be, absent the MCRA, forbidden only to state actors.

Redgrave alleged that the BSO interfered with her "secured" rights of free speech and free association under the First Amendment and the Massachusetts Constitution. Redgrave asserted that her secured rights were violated whether the BSO cancelled the contract because its own agents disagreed with her political views and intended to punish her for past speech or repress her future speech, or whether the BSO cancelled the contract because it acquiesced to pressure from third parties who disagreed with her views and intended to punish her or chill her expression. * * *

[Part B and C omitted].

IV.   THE MASSACHUSETTS CIVIL RIGHTS ACT CLAIM: THE TEACHINGS OF THE SUPREME JUDICIAL COURT

* * * A.   *A Conflict of Rights*

* * * In the present case, this application of the statute is made doubly unusual because, unlike in the typical discrimination case, there are free speech interests on the defendant's side of the balance as well. The plaintiff's statutory "free speech" right against the defendant is to be measured against the defendant's constitutional right against the state. If it were to enforce the statute, the state would be entering the marketplace of ideas in order to restrict speech that may have the effect of "coercing" other speech. * * *

[The Supreme Judicial Court explained] We have no reason to think that the Massachusetts Legislature enacted the MCRA in an attempt to have its courts, at the insistence of private plaintiffs, oversee the editorial judgments of newspapers, the speech-related activities of private universities, or the aesthetic judgments of artists. To be more specific, our examination of these difficulties helps us understand why at least four, and perhaps as many as seven, members of the Supreme Judicial Court wrote opinions indicating that the statute does not impose liability upon the BSO in the circumstances of this case. * * *

[Parts B, C, and D omitted]

E.   *Conclusion*

In these circumstances, and especially in view of our obligation to avoid the unnecessary decision of federal constitutional questions, we see no need to discuss the existence or content of a First Amendment right not to perform an artistic endeavor.

In sum, we decline to reach the federal constitutional issues not only to avoid the unnecessary resolution of very difficult and novel questions of constitutional law, but also to avoid an unnecessary disputation with a state court over the reach and intendment of a state statute.... Accordingly, we hold, in light of our understanding of state law, that the district court correctly entered judgment for the BSO on Redgrave's MCRA claim. The judgment on the MCRA claim is AFFIRMED and the judgment on the contract claim is VACATED and REMANDED for entry of judgment for consequential damages to the extent approved herein. No costs.

Note

1.   In 1990, the district court for Broward County in Ft. Lauderdale, Florida declared 2 Live Crew's "As Nasty As They Wanna Be" obscene, and

not protected by the First Amendment. The case arose from the Broward County Sheriff responding to complaints by residents about the lyrical content of the album. The circuit court judge issued an order stating there was probable cause to believe that he the album was obscene. The sheriff then contacted stores selling the album, and advised them to stop selling the recording. 2 Live Crew's record company, Skywalker Records filed suit to seek legal determination whether the recording was obscene.

The district court applied the Miller obscenity test consisting of three elements "1) that the content appeals to the prurient interest; 2) by community standards describes sexual conduct in a patently offensive way; and 3) the work as a whole lacks artistic value. The district court found that "Nasty As They Wanna Be" failed all elements of the test and declared the recording to be obscene. *See Skyywalker Records v. Navarro*, 739 F.Supp. 578 (S.D.Fla. 1990).

LUKE RECORDS, INC. v. NAVARRO

United States Court of Appeals, Eleventh Circuit, 1992.
960 F.2d 134.

PER CURIAM.

In this appeal, appellants Luke Records, Inc., Luther Campbell, Mark Ross, David Hobbs, and Charles Wongwon seek reversal of the district court's declaratory judgment that the musical recording "As Nasty As They Wanna Be" is obscene under Fla. Stat. § 847.011 and the United States Constitution, contending that the district court misapplied the test for determining obscenity. We reverse.

Appellants Luther Campbell, David Hobbs, Mark Ross, and Charles Wongwon comprise the musical group "2 Live Crew," which recorded "As Nasty As They Wanna Be." In response to actions taken by the Broward County, Florida Sheriff's Office to discourage record stores from selling "As Nasty As They Wanna Be," appellants filed this action in federal district court to enjoin the Sheriff from interfering further with the sale of the recording. The district court granted the injunction, finding that the actions of the Sheriff's office were an unconstitutional prior restraint on free speech. The Sheriff does not appeal this determination.

In addition to injunctive relief, however, appellants sought a declaratory judgment pursuant to 28 U.S.C.A. § 2201 that the recording was not obscene. The district court found that "As Nasty As They Wanna Be" is obscene under *Miller v. California,* [413 U.S. 15 (1973)].

This case is apparently the first time that a court of appeals has been asked to apply the *Miller* test to a musical composition, which contains both instrumental music and lyrics. Although we tend to agree with appellants' contention that because music possesses inherent artistic value, no work of music alone may be declared obscene, that issue is not presented in this case. The Sheriff's contention that the work is not protected by the First Amendment is based on the lyrics, not the music. The Sheriff's brief denies any intention to put rap music to the test, but states "it is abundantly obvious that it is only the 'lyrical' content which makes "As Nasty As They Wanna Be" obscene. Assuming that music is not simply a sham attempt to protect obscene material, the *Miller* test should be applied to the lyrics and the music of "As Nasty As They Wanna Be" as a whole. The basic guidelines for the trier of fact must be: (a) whether "the average person, applying contemporary community standards" would find that the work, taken as a whole, appeals to the prurient interest; (b) whether the work depicts or describes, in a patently offensive way, sexual conduct specifically defined by the applicable state law; and (c) whether the work, taken as a whole, lacks serious literary, artistic, political, or scientific value. 413 U.S. at 24. This test is conjunctive. *Penthouse Intern., Ltd. v. McAuliffe,* 610 F.2d 1353, 1363 (5th Cir.1980). A work cannot be held obscene unless each element of the test has been evaluated independently and all three have been met. *Id.*

Appellants contend that because the central issue in this case is whether "As Nasty As They Wanna Be" meets the definition of obscenity contained in a Florida criminal statute, the thrust of this case is criminal and the Sheriff should be required to prove the work's obscenity beyond a reasonable doubt. In the alternative, appellants assert that at minimum, the importance of the First Amendment requires that the burden of proof in the district court should have been by "clear and convincing evidence," rather than by "a preponderance of the evidence." Assuming, arguendo, that the proper standard is the preponderance of the evidence, we conclude that the Sheriff has failed to carry his burden of proof that the material is obscene by the *Miller* standards under that less stringent standard. Thus, to reverse the declaratory judgment that the work is obscene, we need not decide which of the standards applies.

There are two problems with this case which make it unusually difficult to review. First, the Sheriff put in no evidence but the tape recording itself. The only evidence concerning the three-part *Miller* test was put in evidence by the plaintiffs. Second, the case was tried by a judge without a jury, and he relied on his own expertise as to the prurient interest community standard and artistic value prongs of the *Miller* test.

First, the Sheriff put in no evidence other than the cassette tape. He called no expert witnesses concerning contemporary community standards, prurient interest, or serious artistic value. His evidence was the tape recording itself.

The appellants called psychologist Mary Haber, music critics Gregory Baker, John Leland and Rhodes Scholar Carlton Long. Dr. Haber testified that the tape did not appeal to the average person's prurient interest. Gregory Baker is a staff writer for *New Times Newspaper,* a weekly arts and news publication supported by advertising revenue and distributed free of charge throughout South Florida. Baker testified that he authored "hundreds" of articles about popular music over the previous six or seven years. After reviewing the origins of hip hop and rap music, Baker discussed the process through which rap music is created. He then outlined the ways in which 2 Live Crew had innovated past musical conventions within the genre and concluded that the music in "As Nasty As They Wanna Be" possesses serious musical value.

John Leland is a pop music critic for *Newsday* magazine, which has a daily circulation in New York, New York of approximately six hundred thousand copies, one of the top ten daily newspaper circulations in the country. Leland discussed in detail the evolution of hip hop and rap music, including the development of sampling technique by street disc jockeys over the previous fifteen years and the origins of rap in more established genres of music such as jazz, blues, and reggae. He emphasized that a Grammy Award for rap music was recently introduced, indicating that the recording industry recognizes rap as valid artistic achievement, and ultimately gave his expert opinion that 2 Live Crew's music in "As Nasty As They Wanna Be" does possess serious artistic value.

Of appellants' expert witnesses, Carlton Long testified most about the lyrics. Long is a Rhodes scholar with a Ph.D. in Political Science and was to begin an assistant professorship in that field at Columbia University in New York City shortly after the trial. Long testified that "As Nasty As They Wanna Be" contains three oral traditions, or musical conventions, known as call and response, doing the dozens, and boasting. Long testified that these oral traditions derive their roots from certain segments of Afro-American culture. Long described each of these conventions and cited examples of each one from "As Nasty As They Wanna Be." He concluded that the album reflects many aspects of the cultural heritage of poor, inner city blacks as well as the cultural experiences of 2 Live Crew. Long suggested that certain excerpts from "As Nasty As They Wanna Be" contained statements of political significance or exemplified numerous literary conventions, such as alliteration, allusion, metaphor, rhyme, and personification.

The Sheriff introduced no evidence to the contrary, except the tape. *Second,* the case was tried by a judge without a jury, and he relied on his own expertise as to the community standard and artistic prongs of the *Miller* test.

The district court found that the relevant community was Broward, Dade, and Palm Beach Counties. He further stated:

> This court finds that the relevant community standard reflects a *more* tolerant view of obscene speech than would other communities within the state. This finding of fact is based upon this court's personal knowledge of the community. The undersigned judge has resided in Broward County since 1958. As a practicing attorney, state prosecutor, state circuit judge, and currently, a federal district judge, the undersigned has traveled and worked in Dade, Broward, and Palm Beach. As a member of the community, he has personal knowledge of this area's demographics, culture, economics, and politics. He has attended public functions and events in all three

counties and is aware of the community's concerns as reported in the media and by word of mouth.

In almost fourteen years as a state circuit judge, the undersigned gained personal knowledge of the nature of obscenity in the community while viewing dozens, if not hundreds of allegedly obscene films and other publications seized by law enforcement.

The plaintiffs' claim that this court cannot decide this case without expert testimony and the introduction of specific evidence on community standards is also without merit. The law does not require expert testimony in an obscenity case. The defendant introduced the *Nasty* recording into evidence. As noted by the Supreme Court in *Paris Adult Theatre I* [*v. Slaton,* 413 U.S. 49 (1973)], when the material in question is not directed to a 'bizarre, deviant group' not within the experience of the average person, the best evidence is the material, which 'can and does speak for itself.' *Paris Adult Theatre I,* 413 U.S. at 56 & n. 6.

In deciding this case, the court's decision is not based upon the undersigned judge's personal opinion as to the obscenity of the work, but is an application of the law to the facts based upon the trier of fact's personal knowledge of community standards. In other words, even if the undersigned judge would not find *As Nasty As They Wanna Be* obscene, he would be compelled to do so if the community's standards so required.

It is difficult for an appellate court to review value judgments. Although, generally, these determinations are made in the first instance by a jury, in this case the district judge served as the fact finder, which is permissible in civil cases. Because a judge served as a fact finder, however, and relied only on his own expertise, the difficulty of appellate review is enhanced. A fact finder, whether a judge or jury, is limited in discretion. "Our standard of review must be faithful to both Rule 52(a) and the rule of independent review." "The rule of independent review assigns to appellate judges a constitutional responsibility that cannot be delegated to the trier of fact," even where that fact finder is a judge.

In this case, it can be conceded without deciding that the judge's familiarity with contemporary community standards is sufficient to carry the case as to the first two prongs of the *Miller* test: prurient interest applying community standards and patent offensiveness as defined by Florida law. The record is insufficient, however, for this Court to assume the fact finder's artistic or literary knowledge or skills to satisfy the last prong of the *Miller* analysis, which requires determination of whether a work "lacks serious artistic, scientific, literary or political value."

In *Pope v. Illinois,* 107 S. Ct. 1918 (1987), the Court clarified that whether a work possesses serious value was not a question to be decided by contemporary community standards. The Court reasoned that the fundamental principles of the First Amendment prevent the value of a work from being judged solely by the amount of acceptance it has won within a given community: Just as the ideas a work represents need not obtain majority approval to merit protection, neither, insofar as the First

Amendment is concerned, does the value of the work vary from community to community based on the degree of local acceptance it has won.

The Sheriff concedes that he has the burden of proof to show that the recording *is* obscene. Yet, he submitted no evidence to contradict the testimony that the work had artistic value. A work cannot be held obscene unless each element of the *Miller* test has been met. We reject the argument that simply by listening to this musical work, the judge could determine that it had no serious artistic value.

REVERSED.

Notes

1. The album in this case, "Nasty As They Wanna Be" was released in 1989. That year the group also released a version called "As Clean As They Wanna Be." The "Nasty" album was their third album. The group capitalized on the controversy of the "Nasty" album and entitled a 1990 album "Banned In The U.S.A." The group has released six albums since "Banned" in 1990, two of which were greatest hits albums. The group has not released an album since 1999. www.lyred.com/lyrics/2+live+crew/.

2. Prior to the sheriff's actions that triggered this case, "Nasty As They Wanna Be" had languished on the record store shelves. Following the publicity of the arrest and prosecution, the 2 Live Crew sold over 2 million units. Record stores had difficulty keeping up with demand. Had this action not been filed, very few people would have been aware of the album and the group. The publicity was a tremendous boost to the career of the 2 Live Crew.

http://en.wikipedia.org/wiki/2_Live_Crew.

MARILYN MANSON, INC. v. N.J. SPORTS & EXPOSITION AUTH.

United States District Court, New Jersey, 1997.
971 F.Supp. 875.

WOLIN, District Judge.

Currently before the Court is an application to enjoin the New Jersey Sports Exposition Authority ("NJSEA") from preventing the "OzzFest '97" concert, which includes performer "Marilyn Manson," from being held on June 15, 1997 at Giants Stadium. Marilyn Manson is a heavy metal band that the NJSEA has deemed objectionable. Marilyn Manson's right of passage to perform at Giants Stadium is now impeded by roadblocks created by the collision between well established constitutional and contractual principles. * * * For the reasons stated herein, the Court will grant plaintiffs' request for a preliminary injunction.

BACKGROUND

The parties here dispute whether the plaintiffs have a right, through the Constitution or through contract, to perform their previously scheduled June 15, 1997 OzzFest '97 concert event at Giants Stadium. The Giants Stadium performance of OzzFest '97 would include a performance by the rock band Marilyn Manson.

OzzFest '97 is a "rock-music and lifestyle festival" that will tour twenty-one cities over five weeks in late May and June 1997. The tour is to begin on May 24, 1997 in Washington, D.C. and to conclude on June 29, 1997 in San Bernardino, California. The tour encompasses approximately one dozen bands and many vendors. Marilyn Manson is scheduled to perform at many of the OzzFest '97 tour stops, including Giants Stadium.

Plaintiff Marilyn Manson sells record albums nationally. Its sales statistics rank high on the Billboard charts. Indeed, in its January 23, 1997 issue, Rolling Stone Magazine named Marilyn Manson the best new artist. The band also has performed nationally on Music Television ("MTV"). Currently engaged in a live national concert tour, Marilyn Manson has performed without illegal incident on the part of the band members.

Mitch Slater is the President of Ardee and Co–President and Co–Chief Executive Officer of Delsener/Slater. Howard J. Tytel is the Executive Vice President and General Counsel for S–F–X Broadcasting, Inc. (The parent company of Delsener/Slater and Ardee).

The Giants Stadium is a public outdoor facility located in the Meadowlands Sports Complex, East Rutherford, New Jersey. Giants Stadium has a seating capacity of 77,716. Robert Castronovo is the Executive Vice President and General Manger of Giants Stadium. In consultation with Robert E. Mulcahy III, President and Chief Executive Officer of the NJSEA, and with the NJSEA Commissioners, Castronovo negotiates the events to be held at Giants Stadium.

In late January or early February of 1997, PACE Touring Inc. ("PACE"), the national producer of OzzFest '97, and Creative Artists Agency ("CAA"), as agent for PACE, began discussions with the NJSEA regarding the use of Giants Stadium as a venue for OzzFest '97 in June of 1997. PACE and CAA chose Delsener/Slater to promote the event. Slater contacted Castronovo to discuss the staging of OzzFest in June of 1997 at Giants Stadium. Castronovo discussed the request with Mulcahy, who initially rejected holding the concert at Giants Stadium "because of what he perceived to be safety problems, and because we did not know what acts would be appearing at the concert with Ozzy Osbourne." Castronovo asserts that the promoters, after several conversations with Mulcahy, convinced Mulcahy to approve the concert.

Castronovo and Mulcahy recount that the promoters had agreed to a condition that would allow the NJSEA to remove any acts that it deemed not to be in the best interests of the NJSEA. Plaintiffs allow that on March 14, 1997, Robert Light, a talent agent employed by Creative Artists Agency—representing Ozzy Osbourne and Ozzfest '97, wrote to Mulcahy advising him that he and the promoters "were prepared to listen" to any conditions that the Meadowlands Complex might reasonably require.

Castronovo indicates that he had several conversations, which resulted in his sending Slater his letter of March 20, 1997, which proposed certain conditions for the OzzFest '97 performance. The proposed conditions included: (1) the show would be limited to six hours and end no later than 9:00 p.m., (2) the capacity would be limited to 40,000, (3) the time between sets would be extremely limited and "if possible, Pantera and Marilyn Manson should be eliminated from the bill," (4) the second stage must be kept inside the Stadium or eliminated, (5) the concourse attractions should be within the perimeter fence and none should be on the concourse, (6) the NJSEA would provide fifty State Police and Delsener/Slater would have to hire extra T–Shirt security, and (7) rent would be $175,000 plus expenses.

Castronovo maintains that he requested that "if possible, [Marilyn Manson and Pantera] be removed from the concert because of what we might have perceived as problems with their performances and, in particular, reactions from fans." According to Castronovo, it was his "expectation that if the conditions were accepted and agreed upon, the parties would enter into the form contract incorporating the special terms and conditions of [his] March 20th letter, as has been [NJSEA] practice in the past."

Plaintiffs allege that Slater called Castronovo on March 20, 1997, after receiving the letter, and agreed to the terms of the letter with the specific exception of Castronovo's request that Marilyn Manson not perform. Plaintiffs contend that Slater informed Castronovo that Marilyn Manson was integral to OzzFest '97 and that the headlining performers Ozzy Osbourne and Black Sabbath would appear only if Marilyn Manson was permitted to perform. According to plaintiffs, Castronovo agreed that Marilyn Manson would perform in the event.

Slater understood from this conversation that he had reached a binding agreement with the NJSEA through his conversation with Castronovo and that pursuant to industry custom and practice the agreement would be reduced to writing on or immediately prior to June 15, 1997. According to Castronovo, in contrast, "contracts are always signed prior to the date of performance and, on many occasions, substantially before the date of the performance, as evidence by the contract for the Iglesias concert which was signed on March 14, 1997 for a June 6, 1997 concert."

Castronovo recalls that after March 21, he discussed with Slater the conditions in the March 20 letter, and specifically the seating arrangements. Castronovo states that Slater told him that he would have to discuss the conditions with Light to determine which conditions were acceptable. Castronovo recalls no discussions concerning the inclusion of Marilyn Manson and Pantera in the program.

Castronovo confirms receiving on April 14, 1997 a copy of a proposed advertisement of OzzFest '97. The proposed advertisement stated that

Marilyn Manson would perform at the OzzFest '97 concert and that tickets for the event would go on sale at 9:00 a.m. on Saturday, April 19, 1997. Castronovo remembers receiving the advertisement and that the Marilyn Manson and Pantera bands were listed in the program. After Castronovo reviewed the ad and discussed some matters with a Delsener/Slater representative, Castronovo approved the advertisement.

The approved advertisement appeared in the Village Voice and Aquarian newspapers on Wednesday, April 16, 1997 and in the Bergen Record newspaper on April 18, 1997. In addition, Delsener/Slater contracted for advertisements of the concert to be broadcast from April 16th to April 20th on radio stations in the New York City metropolitan area and on the national cable television network MTV.

According to Castronovo, on April 16, 1997, after he had heard of "additional problems with the Manson band in other venues concerning protest groups and antics that are performed on stage," he reviewed these matters with Mulcahy. Castronovo claims that Mulcahy discussed the concert with the commissioners and on April 17, 1997 advised Castronovo to inform the promoters that the NJSEA did not want Marilyn Manson to be included in the program. Castronovo relayed the information to Slater who objected to the removal of Marilyn Manson.

Castronovo explains that it is not uncommon for acts to be removed from a program after advertisements or even ticket sales. According to Castronovo "[a]cts are removed for various reasons and sometimes announcements are made as late as the day of the performance."

On April 18, 1997, the NJSEA issued a news release entitled "STATEMENT OF THE NEW JERSEY SPORTS AUTHORITY MANAGEMENT REGARDING MARILYN MANSON AND THE OZZFEST CONCERT." The announcement indicated that Marilyn Manson would be prohibited from performing at Giants Stadium and canceled the OzzFest event due to the inclusion of Marilyn Manson: "the promoters have informed us that Marilyn Manson must remain in the show, therefore based upon our stated position we will not allow tickets to go on sale tomorrow."

On April 23, the NJSEA offered to Ardee a contract containing the specific limitations contained in Castronovo's letter of March 20, 1997. The contract was "a standard form contract which is used by the Authority to book events within its facilities." The contract included a clause affording the NJSEA the opportunity to omit any performer from the bill under certain circumstances:

> [The contract provided that] LICENSOR retains approval right of performance, exhibition, or entertainment to be offered under this Agreement and LICENSEE agrees that no such activity or part thereof shall be given or held if LICENSOR files written objection on the grounds of character offensive to public morals, failure to uphold event advertising claims or violation of event content restrictions agreed to by both parties at the time of completion of this

agreement. The contract also specifically excluded both Marilyn Manson and Pantera.

According to Castronovo, Paragraph 8, which refers to the right of the NJSEA to approve the activity or part thereof, has been a standard clause in the NJSEA contract for a "substantial period of time" and has been included in contracts previously signed by Ardee and Delsener/Slater for events that they have staged at the NJSEA.

On April 24, 1997, Tytel rejected the April 23 proposed License Agreement by letter. In this letter, Tytel dismissed the proposed conditions of the March 20, 1997 Castronovo letter as ambiguous and superseded by subsequent discussion. Tytel denounced "the sudden reappearance of an objection to Pantera in [the] letter" as a "transparent attempt to rehabilitate the March 20th letter which had, in all respects, been disregarded by both parties."

DISCUSSION * * *

A.   *The Violation of Plaintiffs' First Amendment Rights* * * *

    1.   *Plaintiffs Have Established a Likelihood of Success on the Merits Even if Giants Stadium Is a Non–Public Forum and the Lowest Level of Scrutiny Were to Apply*

* * * In this case, there is a substantial likelihood that plaintiffs will establish either that NJSEA's restrictions on the ability of Marilyn Manson to perform are unreasonable or content based. The NJSEA has indicated that it excluded Marilyn Manson from the concert because of the band's "antics." According to the NJSEA, these anticipated "antics" may have created security risks and may have tarnished the NJSEA's reputation and ability to remain a lucrative forum for concert events.

Thus, this does not appear to be a case when the government denies access to a forum because of the identity of the speaker; the NJSEA has not endeavored to make that claim. Nor does this appear to be a case in which the government denies access of an individual to a forum because of a subject matter limitation; indeed, the NJSEA would allow the remaining bands in the show and all of these bands are of the same musical genre—heavy metal. Rather, it appears that the NJSEA would deny Marilyn Manson access to Giants Stadium because of anticipated antics, *i.e.,* because of the anticipated content of Marilyn Manson's performance. The NJSEA's motivation, thus, appears to be content based rather than viewpoint neutral.

The clause on which the NJSEA relies for its authority to exclude Marilyn Manson from the show confirms the motivation of the NJSEA. Under the NJSEA's proposed contract, it may exclude a performer for: "grounds of character offensive to public morals, failure to uphold event advertising claims or violation of event content restrictions agreed to by both parties at the time of completion of this agreement." The only aspect of this clause that the NJSEA relies upon is that Marilyn Manson's performance is anticipated to be "offensive to public morals."

This appears to be the quintessential essence of content based regulation.

The NJSEA has argued that safety concerns prompted its refusal to allow Marilyn Manson to play at Giants Stadium. But the NJSEA has put forth no evidence that its proffered safety concerns are legitimate rather than pretextual. To the contrary, no unlawful or violent activity has occurred on Marilyn Manson's current tour. And it appears that the plaintiffs have complied with NJSEA's requests for concessions intended to bolster security. Plaintiffs, for example, agreed to provide additional security and to address other safety measures. Thus, the proffered security concerns have been addressed and are no longer an impediment to the performance.

The NJSEA also argued that the inclusion of Marilyn Manson would tarnish NJSEA's reputation and ability to earn revenue. But, the NJSEA conceded at oral argument that the decision to exclude Marilyn Manson was not based on the economics of the show in question; the show was anticipated to earn substantial revenue. Rather, NJSEA argued that the inclusion of Marilyn Manson would somehow affect NJSEA's future ability to use the stadium. The NJSEA's argument is insufficiently concrete to be persuasive and there are no written guidelines defining what might endanger NJSEA's reputation. Consequently, the Court is not persuaded.

Additionally, it appears that the NJSEA's requirement that all performers sign a contract allowing the NJSEA to regulate the morality of concert programs may be an unreasonable restriction on access to even a non-public forum. Plaintiffs argue that the NJSEA's authority to reject any performer based on inadequately defined guidelines is an unconstitutional prior restraint on speech. The Court finds that there is a substantial likelihood that plaintiffs will prevail on this claim. Although the NJSEA may require that performers satisfy reasonable requirements in order to perform at Giants Stadium, it is not clear that all of the conditions that Giants Stadium imposes are reasonable—especially insofar as a required agreement that allows the NJSEA unfettered discretion in rejecting the content of a proposed performance on the basis of its morality. * * *

The lack of any identifiable guidelines in restricting the content of programs appears clearly unreasonable. And the contractual provision allowing the NJSEA to reflect a performance because it does not comport with public morality appears equally problematic. Without proof of at least reasonable guidelines, the NJSEA system of choosing concert performances probably cannot pass constitutional muster. * * *

[2. omitted].

B.   Contract Formation and Terms

* * * Plaintiffs allege that on March 20, 1997 Delsener/Slater and the NJSEA entered into an oral agreement under which Delsener/Slater leased Giants Stadium to OzzFest '97 including Marilyn Manson for

June 15, 1997. The NJSEA disagrees. There is no dispute that the parties had agreed on the price, the time, and other essential terms. The NJSEA argues that it did not intend to be bound until a final written contract was signed. Plaintiffs counter that they thought there was a done deal, with a written contract to be signed as a mere memorialization.

The Court is persuaded by plaintiffs' explanation that contracts in the concert music industry are not reduced to writing until a late date. Additionally, the Court observes that the NJSEA appeared to express continued assent to OzzFest '97 and Marilyn Manson playing at Giants Stadium on June 15, 1997 when the NJSEA approved an advertisement displaying all of the relevant details about the concert including Marilyn Manson's performance. Thus, notwithstanding the NJSEA's apparent policy of not becoming bound until a formal contract is signed, plaintiffs have a reasonable likelihood of success on the merits. Moreover, were a jury to find that no contract was formed, plaintiffs would have a reasonable likelihood of success on a promissory estoppel theory. * * *

[C. omitted].

III. Plaintiffs Have Demonstrated that They Will Suffer Irreparable Harm if the Preliminary Injunction Is Not Granted

Plaintiffs contend that if the injunctive relief is not granted, plaintiffs will have missed their only opportunity for "exposure to the national media and music industry representatives headquartered in New York City." Delsener/Slater charges that if the NJSEA is permitted to repudiate its agreement with Delsener/Slater, "NJSEA will have injured Delsener/Slater's business and reputation in the concert industry as a promoter that can be relied upon to provide a suitable New York area venue." Additionally, plaintiffs argue that a refusal to allow them to perform would be a deprivation of their First Amendment rights.

The NJSEA claims that there will be no irreparable harm for several reasons, including: (1) plaintiffs have no right to play at Giants Stadium because they did not sign a contract, (2) plaintiffs have waived their First Amendment rights, (3) plaintiffs' interest in the concert is merely financial, (4) Marilyn Manson could perform at other venues, and (5) OzzFest '97 could be held at another forum.

The Court disagrees with the NJSEA. The plaintiffs' potential First Amendment deprivation is undoubtedly an irreparable injury. And the plaintiffs will suffer other irreparable injuries, as well, including loss to reputation in the case of the promoters, and reduced public exposure in the case of the artists. Thus, the plaintiffs have established the prospect of irreparable injury sufficient to meet the requirement for a preliminary injunction.

[Part IV. omitted].

[V.] The Public Interest Will Best Be Served Through Granting Plaintiffs' Requested Injunctive Relief

The NJSEA argues that the public interest will suffer if the preliminary injunction is granted because the NJSEA will no longer be able to act in a manner that will guarantee that the public interest will be promoted. The NJSEA has demonstrated no concrete need (in keeping with its public mandate) to exclude Marilyn Manson while allowing the other heavy metal bands to perform. And the NJSEA has indicated that the show will likely be a profitable economic endeavor, a strong indicator that a substantial number of community citizens would like to attend Marilyn Manson's performance. For these reasons, the Court finds that to promote the free expression of ideas, uncensored by a state actor who exercises unfettered discretion, warrants the grant of this preliminary injunction.

Conclusion

For the reasons discussed above, plaintiffs' motion for a preliminary injunction will be granted.

Notes

1. Should music for adults be censored? In *Betts v. McCaughtry*, Betts, a prisoner, brought suit against prison Warden McCaughtry. Betts alleged that his constitutional rights were violated by the prison's rules against musical cassettes with parental advisory labels. The district court held that for security reasons it was reasonable for prison officials to impose censorship regulations of music that encouraged violence. Therefore, it was not a violation of First Amendment rights. *See* Betts v. McCaughtry, 827 F.Supp. 1400 (W.D. Wis. 1993).

2. In 1985, the Parents Music Resource Center (PMRC) was founded with the purpose of informing parents of explicitly sexual or violent music lyrics. Tipper Gore was instrumental in founding the group and pushing for the RIAA to affix parental advisory labels. The recording industry resisted implementing a ratings system similar to the film industry, but did voluntarily place advisory labels on explicit recordings. In response to PMRC efforts, the U.S. Senate held hearings on record labeling in September 1985. The purpose of the hearings was not to promote legislation, but to provide a public forum for the issue and bring it to the attention of the public. Mathieu Deflem, *Rap, Rock and Censorship: Popular Culture and the Technologies of Justice,* http:// www.cla.sc.edu/socy/faculty/deflem/zzcens97.htm

3. Wal–Mart has been willing to draw the line where the Supreme Court has not when it comes to offensive lyrics in music. The nation's largest retailer has refused to sell music recordings that have a parental advisory label. They also do not sell CDs with objectionable covers. What effect has this had? Musicians that choose to sell more copies of their music by reaching Wal–Mart's customers must present a "clean" version. The result is that the artist must decide between profit and "artistic freedom." http://www.massmic.com/walmart.html.

4. To view a website that chronicles the last decade of censorship incidents, see http://ericnuzum.com/banned/incidents/90s.html. For more in-

formation on music censorship, see "The Devil Music Made Me Do It" in the last chapter of this book.

Part IV

GLOBALIZATION & THE DEVIL
MEDIA MADE ME DO IT

Chapter 19

GLOBALIZATION OF THE FILM, TELEVISION, AND MUSIC INDUSTRIES

This chapter confronts the ongoing internationalization of the entertainment business and the legal consequences that flow therefrom. Nations in the early stages of economic development have an incentive to encourage the pilfering of intellectual property creations like film, television and music, as their citizens are enlightened without having to pay the full price.

Prior to World War II, the United States was a net importer of intellectual property and one of the world's biggest pirates. After World War II, the United States became a net exporter of intellectual property creations and strengthened its laws. It also campaigned to have more recent developing countries curtail theft as the U.S. economy became dependent on protecting intellectual property rights for its continued growth. In the following excerpt, the Los Angeles Times reports:

* * * Thailand has made some progress on patent protection for pharmaceuticals, has implemented a stronger trademark law and has promised to extend copyright protection to computer software. But the U.S. entertainment industry says Thailand is renowned for pirating movies and music, and the industry is pressing American officials to retaliate immediately.

Pirates control 90% of the video market here and reportedly cost the U.S. film industry about $30 million last year. To many in Hollywood, the time for talking has passed. Total U.S. losses due to piracy in Thailand were about $123 million in 1992, including $49 million on computer programs and $20 million on books, according to industry officials.

"There is no point in engaging in the charade that to date has characterized copyright enforcement in Thailand," the Motion Picture Assn. of America said last week in an angry letter to U.S. trade officials.

The International Intellectual Property Alliance, an umbrella organization founded in 1984 that represents the American recording, publishing, computer software and motion picture industries, is also urging Washington to impose sanctions immediately. Last year, U.S. industry sustained losses of $4.6 billion worldwide due to copyright violations, the IIPA said. * * *

International Trade Thai Piracy Likely to Top U.S. Hit List Property rights: The entertainment industry, among others, is pressing for sanctions to protect copyrights and patents, L.A. TIMES, Apr. 26, 1993, at D2.

More than a decade later the problem with international theft of films, television, and music produced in the United States has expanded rather than contracted, as technology has made it easier to steal with impunity. Films appear on the Internet the day of their release, sometimes with a laughter track that indicates they were surreptitiously taped in front of a theater audience. Sometimes, movies even appear on the Internet or bootleg copies become available for purchase before they are released at the theater. Further, computers permit individuals to file-swap their collections, thus enabling the avoidance of trips to the store to purchase copies. On the horizon are computers so sophisticated that individuals will be able to download theater-quality films onto their personal systems for playback on home screens.

With this level of theft occurring, the entertainment industry may be battling a beast that cannot be slain. The following article excerpt reveals the historical efforts of two pioneers to stop the international pilfering of their work.

Sherri Burr
The Piracy Gap: Protecting Intellectual Property in an Era of Artistic Creativity and Technological Change

33 WILLAMETTE L.R. 245, 248–250 (1997) (footnotes omitted).

During his seventy-five years, Mark Twain became an advocate of copyright protection for authors. Twain wrote during a time when the United States, as a developing country, tolerated piracy of intellectual property. This may seem surprising for United States citizens familiar with the current efforts by the U.S. Trade Representative to encourage China, Korea, and Taiwan to strengthen their intellectual property laws. Throughout history, however, developing countries have permitted the piracy of intellectual property while developed countries have sought to protect it.

Charles Dickens also became an avid promoter of copyright laws in the United States. On his tour of the United States in 1840s, Dickens was greeted as a hero of the common man until he complained about American booksellers routinely printing and selling his books without paying him royalties. On hearing Dickens' complaints, the press openly criticized him. He exacted revenge, however, with his unflattering portrait of the United States in *American Notes* and *Martin Chuzzlewit*. Thus, Dickens proved the old admonition to never pick a fight with someone who has more ink than you do. Or, never pick a fight with someone who can use the ink with more talent.

Twain encountered a mirror image of Dickens' problems. English and Canadian publishers printed his books and not only refused to pay for copies sold in England and Canada, but also shipped these pirated copies into the United States for resale at discount prices without paying Twain royalties. This theft incensed Twain. He commented with his trademark humor, "a generation of this sort of [piracy] ought to make this the most intelligent and the best-read nation in the world."

Because copyrights are territorial property rights, he could not protect his works in England or Canada without a separate registration process, which was limited to native citizens. Twain responded by battling against copyright infringement in his letters and in court, even against a boy who tried to sell him a pirated version of *The Adventures of Tom Sawyer*. Twain became an aficionado of British, Canadian, and American copyright law.

When one of his several lawsuits failed, Twain wrote:

A Massachusetts judge has just decided in open court that a Boston publisher may sell not only his own property in a free and unfettered way, but also may as freely sell property which does not belong to him but to me—property which he has not bought and which I have not sold. Under this ruling, I am now advertising that the judge's homestead is for sale and if I make as good a sum out of it as I expect, I shall go out and sell the rest of his property.

The record does not reflect that Twain ever carried out his threat.

Twain associated copyright protection with the right of economic exploitation (to sell, lease, or lend his protected work). He connected copyright protection to right to earn a living. To the extent that he could not protect his copyrights, he suffered economic losses.

As a victim of an international piracy gap, Twain campaigned actively for international copyright protection, seeking reciprocal recognition of protected works. He consulted with several United States presidents in his eventually successful quest for the enactment of an international copyright convention. Twain suggested to President Grover Cleveland that he make international copyright the child of his administration. In addition, Twain dined with Mrs. Cleveland and became an active participant in her circle of friends, perhaps to influence their beliefs on copyright matters.

The humorist was rewarded for his efforts in 1886, when several nations adopted the Berne Convention for the Protection of Literary and Artistic Works. The most important component of the Berne Convention is the rule of national treatment, which provides that authors enjoy the same protection for their works in other countries as those countries' own citizens enjoy. The Berne Convention's goals include: (1) elimination of discrimination against non-native works in all nations, and (2) promotion of uniform international legislation for the protection of literary and artistic works.

The Berne convention thus permitted Twain to protect his work in other countries. He could worry less about booksellers printing his books in England and Canada while importing them into the United States. If they did this, he could sue them in England and Canada for violating his copyrights. For Twain, Berne was a welcome response to the international piracy gap.

Unfortunately the international piracy gap in his native country would continue for over a century until the United States joined the Berne Convention in 1988. To its credit, however, the United States was a founding member of the Universal Copyright convention, adopted in 1952 under the auspices of the United Nations Educational, Scientific, and Cultural Organization (UNESCO.

Notes

1.   Are current efforts to fight international piracy of films, television, and music, an indication of the French phrase *la plus ça change, la plus c'est la meme chose*, the more things change, the more they stay the same? Dickens and Twain fought the good fight for protection of literary works in the 1800s, now the Motion Picture Association of America is carrying the banner to protect films in the 2000s.

2.   As you read the following cases and materials, note the difficulties that arise in trying to protect films, television, and music from being stolen. Even when a company has sufficient evidence of theft, they may have trouble finding an appropriate forum to try the case.

A.   GLOBALIZATION OF THE FILM INDUSTRY

LONDON FILMS v. INTERCONTINTENTAL COMMUNICATIONS

U.S. District Court, Southern District of New York, 1984.
580 F.Supp. 47.

CARTER, District Judge.

This case presents a novel question of law. Plaintiff, London Film Productions, Ltd. ("London"), a British corporation, has sued Intercontinental Communications, Inc. ("ICI"), a New York corporation based in New York City, for infringements of plaintiff's British copyright. The alleged infringements occurred in Chile and other South American countries. In bringing the case before this Court, plaintiff has invoked the Court's diversity jurisdiction. 28 U.S.C. § 1332(a)(2). Defendant has moved to dismiss plaintiff's complaint, arguing that the Court should abstain from exercising jurisdiction over this action.

BACKGROUND

London produces feature motion pictures in Great Britain, which it then distributes throughout the world.[1] ICI specializes in the licensing of motion pictures, produced by others, that it believes are in the public domain. London's copyright infringement claim is based mainly on license agreements between ICI and Dilatsa S.A., a buying agent for Chilean television stations. The agreements apparently granted the latter the right to distribute and exhibit certain of plaintiff's motion pictures on television in Chile. London also alleges that ICI has marketed several of its motion pictures in Venezuela, Peru, Equador, Costa Rica and Panama, as well as in Chile.

Plaintiff alleges that the films that are the subjects of the arrangements between Dilatsa S.A. and defendant are protected by copyright in Great Britain as well as in Chile and most other countries (but not in the United States) by virtue of the terms and provisions of the Berne Convention.[2] The license agreements, it maintains, have unjustly enriched defendants and deprived plaintiff of the opportunity to market its motion pictures for television use.

Defendant questions this Court's jurisdiction because plaintiff has not alleged any acts of wrongdoing on defendant's part that constitute violations of United States law, and, therefore, defendant claims that this Court lacks a vital interest in the suit. In addition, assuming jurisdiction, defendant argues that because the Court would have to construe "alien treaty rights," with which it has no familiarity, the suit would violate, in principle, the doctrine of *forum non conveniens*. In further support of this contention, defendant maintains that the law would not only be foreign, but complex, since plaintiff's claims would have to be determined with reference to each of the South American states in which the alleged copyright infringements occurred.

DETERMINATION

There seems to be no dispute that plaintiff has stated a valid cause of action under the copyright laws of a foreign country. Also clear is the fact that this Court has personal jurisdiction over defendant; in fact, there is no showing that defendant may be subject to personal jurisdiction in another forum. Under these circumstances, one authority on copyright law has presented an argument pursuant to which this Court has jurisdiction to hear the matter before it. M. Nimmer, 3 *Nimmer on Copyright*, (1982). It is based on the theory that copyright infringement constitutes a transitory cause of action, and hence may be adjudicated in the courts of a sovereign other than the one in which the cause of action arose. *Id.* at § 1703. That theory appears sound in the absence of convincing objections by defendant to the contrary.

1. These include: "The Private Life of Henry VIII", "Things To Come", and "Jungle Book", all of which are subjects of this suit.

2. The Berne Convention is a shorthand designation for the "International Union for the Protection of Literary and Artistic Works", signed in Berne, Switzerland on September 9, 1886, as amended. The text of the Convention as most recently revised in Paris in 1971, is reproduced in 4 Nimmer on Copyright, Appendix 27 (1983). Chile adhered to the Convention on June 5, 1970. * * *

Although plaintiff has not alleged the violation of any laws of this country by defendant, this Court is not bereft of interest in this case. The Court has an obvious interest in securing compliance with this nation's laws by citizens of foreign nations who have dealings within this jurisdiction. A concern with the conduct of American citizens in foreign countries is merely the reciprocal of that interest. An unwillingness by this Court to hear a complaint against its own citizens with regard to a violation of foreign law will engender, it would seem, a similar unwillingness on the part of a foreign jurisdiction when the question arises concerning a violation of our laws by one of its citizens who has since left our jurisdiction. This Court's interest in adjudicating the controversy in this case may be indirect, but its importance is not thereby diminished.

Of course, not every violation of foreign law by a citizen of this country must be afforded a local tribunal, and defendants cite several cases in which, basically under general principles of comity, it would be inappropriate for this Court to exercise its jurisdiction. Cf. *Kalmich v. Bruno,* 404 F. Supp. 57, 61 (N.D.Ill. 1975), *rev'd on other grounds,* 553 F.2d 549 (7th Cir. 1977), *cert. denied,* 434 U.S. 940, 98 S.Ct. 432, 54 L.Ed.2d 300 (1977). This is not one of those. The line of cases on which defendants rely can be distinguished on significant points. The Court in *Vanity Fair Mills, Inc. v. T. Eaton, Ltd.,* 234 F.2d 633 (2d Cir.) *cert. denied,* 352 U.S. 871, 77 S.Ct. 96, 1 L.Ed.2d 76 (1956), the principal case of those cited, found that the district court had not abused its discretion in declining to assume jurisdiction over a claim for acts of alleged trademark infringement and unfair competition arising in Canada under Canadian law. As defendant here has acknowledged, the complaint raised a "crucial issue" as to the validity of Canadian trademark law. This factor weighed heavily in the Court's decision.

We do not think it the province of United States district courts to determine the validity of trademarks which officials of foreign countries have seen fit to grant. To do so would be to welcome conflicts with the administrative and judicial officers of the Dominion Canada. *Id.* at 647. But as Nimmer has noted, "[i]n adjudicating an infringement action under a foreign copyright law there is ... no need to pass upon the validity of acts of foreign government officials," 3 Nimmer, *supra,* at § 1703, since foreign copyright laws, by and large, do not incorporate administrative formalities which must be satisfied to create or perfect a copyright. *Id.*

The facts in this case confirm the logic of Nimmer's observation. The British films at issue here received copyright protection in Great Britain simply by virtue of publication there. Copinger, *Law of Copyright,* (9th ed. 1958), 21 *et seq.* Chile's adherence to the Berne Convention in 1970 automatically conferred copyright protection on these films in Chile. Therefore, no "act of state" is called into question here. Moreover, there is no danger that foreign courts will be forced to accept the inexpert determination of this Court, nor that this Court will create "an unseemly conflict with the judgment of another country." *See*

Packard Instrument Co. v. Beckman Instruments, Inc., 346 F.Supp. 408, 410 (N.D.Ill. 1972). The litigation will determine only whether an American corporation has acted in violation of a foreign copyright, not whether such copyright exists, nor whether such copyright is valid.

With respect to defendant's *forum non conveniens* argument, it is true that this case will likely involve the construction of at least one, if not several foreign laws.[6] However, the need to apply foreign law is not in itself reason to dismiss or transfer the case. *Manu Int'l S.A. v. Avon Products, Inc.,* 641 F.2d 62, 67–68 (2d Cir. 1981). Moreover, there is no foreign forum in which defendant is the subject of personal jurisdiction, and an available forum is necessary to validate dismissal of an action on the ground of *forum non conveniens,* for if there is no alternative forum "the plaintiff might find himself with a valid claim but nowhere to assert it." Farmanfarmaian v. Gulf Oil Corp., 437 F.Supp. 910, 915 (S.D.N.Y. 1977) (Carter, J.), *aff'd,* 588 F.2d 880 (2d Cir. 1978).

While this Court might dismiss this action subject to conditions that would assure the plaintiff of a fair hearing, *Mizokami Bros. of Ariz v. Mobay Chem. Corp.,* 660 F.2d 712, 719 (8th Cir. 1981), neither plaintiff nor defendant has demonstrated the relative advantage in convenience that another forum, compared to this one, would provide. *Overseas Programming Companies v. Cinematographische Commerz–Anstalt,* 684 F.2d 232, 235 (2d Cir. 1982). The selection of a South American country as an alternative forum, although it would afford greater expertise in applying relevant legal principles, would seem to involve considerable hardship and inconvenience for both parties. A British forum might similarly provide some advantages in the construction of relevant law, however, it would impose additional hardships upon defendant, and would raise questions, as would the South American forum, regarding enforceability of a resulting judgment. *See American Rice, Inc. v. Arkansas Rice Growers Co-op. Ass'n.,* 701 F.2d 408, 417 (5th Cir. 1983). Where the balance does not tip strongly in favor of an alternative forum it is well-established that the plaintiff's choice of forum should not be disturbed.

For all of the above reasons, the Court finds it has jurisdiction over the instant case and defendant's motion to dismiss is denied, as is its motion to have the Court abstain from exercising its jurisdiction here.
* * *

Note

1. How should a court balance the private and public interest in deciding whether a plaintiff's choice of forum should be rejected on grounds of forum non conveniens? In *Overseas Programming Companies, Ltd. v.*

6. Plaintiff has alleged infringements in Chile, Venezuela, Peru, Equador, Costa Rica and Panama. Since, under the Berne Convention, the applicable law is the copyright law of the state in which the infringement occurred, defendant seems correct in its assumption that the laws of several countries will be involved in the case. 3 Nimmer, *supra* at § 17.05.

Cinematographische Commerz–Anstalt, 684 F.2d 232 (2d Cir. 1982), Judge Newman wrote, "Among a litigant's private interests to be considered are the 'relative ease of access to sources of proof,' the 'availability of compulsory process for attendance of unwilling, and the cost of obtaining willing, witnesses,' and other matters affecting the cost, speed, and ease of litigating a suit in a particular forum. Furthermore, a court must evaluate the enforceability of a judgment rendered by it, 'weigh relative advantages and obstacles to fair trial,' and determine whether the plaintiff has instituted suit in a particular forum with the intent to vex or harass the defendant." *Id.* (Citing Gulf Oil Corp. v. Gilbert, 330 U.S. 501, 508, 67 S.Ct. 839, 91 L.Ed. 1055). The public interests to be considered include the administrative burdens imposed on already congested courts by suits that are properly centered elsewhere and the burden of jury duty on members of a community with no real relation to the dispute. The Court stated that a community has an interest in having "localized controversies decided at home." *Id.* at 509. Finally, the Court noted that "[t]here is an appropriateness ... in having the trial of a diversity case in a forum that is at home with the state law that must govern the case, rather than having a court in some other forum untangle problems in conflict of laws, and in law foreign to itself." *Id.* * * * The Supreme Court has cautioned that "unless the balance (of factors) is strongly in favor of the defendant, the plaintiff's choice of forum should rarely be disturbed." Gulf Oil Co., 333 U.S. at 508.

SUBAFILMS, LTD. v. MGM–PATHE COMMUNICATIONS CO.

United States Court of Appeals, Ninth Circuit, 1994.
24 F.3d 1088

NELSON, Circuit Judge.

In this case, we consider the "vexing question" of whether a claim for infringement can be brought under the Copyright Act, 17 U.S.C. § 101 *et seq.* (1988), when the assertedly infringing conduct consists solely of the authorization within the territorial boundaries of the United States of acts that occur entirely abroad. We hold that such allegations do not state a claim for relief under the copyright laws of the United States.

Factual and Procedural Background

In 1966, the musical group The Beatles, through Subafilms, Ltd., entered into a joint venture with the Hearst Corporation to produce the animated motion picture entitled "Yellow Submarine" (the "Picture"). Over the next year, Hearst, acting on behalf of the joint venture (the "Producer"), negotiated an agreement with United Artists Corporation ("UA") to distribute and finance the film. Separate distribution and financing agreements were entered into in May, 1967. Pursuant to these agreements, UA distributed the Picture in theaters beginning in 1968 and later on television.

In the early 1980s, with the advent of the home video market, UA entered into several licensing agreements to distribute a number of its films on videocassette. Although one company expressed interest in the Picture, UA refused to license "Yellow Submarine" because of uncertainty over whether home video rights had been granted by the 1967 agreements. Subsequently, in 1987, UA's successor company, MGM/UA Communications Co. ("MGM/UA"), over the Producer's objections, authorized its subsidiary MGM/UA Home Video, Inc. to distribute the Picture for the domestic home video market, and, pursuant to an earlier licensing agreement, notified Warner Bros., Inc. ("Warner") that the Picture had been cleared for international videocassette distribution. Warner, through its wholly owned subsidiary, Warner Home Video, Inc., in turn entered into agreements with third parties for distribution of the Picture on videocassette around the world.

In 1988, Subafilms and Hearst ("Appellees") brought suit against MGM/UA, Warner, and their respective subsidiaries (collectively the "Distributors" or "Appellants"), contending that the videocassette distribution of the Picture, both foreign and domestic, constituted copyright infringement and a breach of the 1967 agreements. The case was tried before a retired California Superior Court Judge acting as a special master. The special master found for Appellees on both claims, and against the Distributors on their counterclaim for fraud and reformation. Except for the award of prejudgment interest, which it reversed, the district court adopted all of the special master's factual findings and legal conclusions. Appellees were awarded $2,228,000.00 in compensatory damages, split evenly between the foreign and domestic home video distributions. In addition, Appellees received attorneys' fees and a permanent injunction that prohibited the Distributors from engaging in, or authorizing, any home video use of the Picture.

A panel of this circuit, in an unpublished disposition, affirmed the district court's judgment on the ground that both the domestic and foreign distribution of the Picture constituted infringement under the Copyright Act. *See Subafilms, Ltd. v. MGM–Pathe Communications Co.,* Nos. 91–56248, 91–56379, 91–56289, 1993 WL 39269 (9th Cir. Feb. 17, 1993). With respect to the foreign distribution of the Picture, the panel concluded that it was bound by this court's prior decision in *Peter Starr Prod. Co. v. Twin Continental Films, Inc.,* 783 F.2d 1440 (9th Cir. 1986), which it held to stand for the proposition that, although " 'infringing actions that take place entirely outside the United States are not actionable' [under the Copyright Act, an] 'act of infringement within the United States' [properly is] alleged where the illegal *authorization* of international exhibitions t[akes] place in the United States," *Subafilms,* slip op. at 4917–18 (quoting *Peter Starr,* 783 F.2d at 1442, 1443 (emphasis in original) (alterations added)). Because the Distributors had admitted that the initial authorization to distribute the Picture internationally occurred within the United States, the panel affirmed the district court's holding with respect to liability for extraterritorial home video distribution of the Picture.[3]

---

3. At oral argument before this court Appellants' counsel conceded that the relevant authorization occurred within the United States. Counsel for Appellees, ac-

We granted Appellants' petition for rehearing en banc to consider whether the panel's interpretation of *Peter Starr* conflicted with our subsequent decision in *Lewis Galoob Toys, Inc. v. Nintendo of Am., Inc.*, 964 F.2d 965 (9th Cir. 1992), *cert. denied*, 507 U.S. 985, 113 S.Ct. 1582, 123 L.Ed.2d 149 (1993), which held that there could be no liability for authorizing a party to engage in an infringing act when the authorized "party's use of the work would not violate the Copyright Act," *id.* at 970. * * * Because we conclude that there can be no liability under the United States copyright laws for authorizing an act that *itself* could not constitute infringement of rights secured by those laws, and that wholly extraterritorial acts of infringement are not cognizable under the Copyright Act, we overrule *Peter Starr* insofar as it held that allegations of an authorization within the United States of infringing acts that take place entirely abroad state a claim for infringement under the Act. Accordingly, we vacate the panel's decision in part and return the case to the panel for further proceedings.

DISCUSSION

I.   The Mere Authorization of Extraterritorial Acts of Infringement does not State a Claim under the Copyright Act

As the panel in this case correctly concluded, *Peter Starr* held that the authorization within the United States of entirely extraterritorial acts stated a cause of action under the "plain language" of the Copyright Act. *Peter Starr*, 783 F.2d at 1442–43. Observing that the Copyright Act grants a copyright owner "the *exclusive rights* to do and *to authorize*" any of the activities listed in 17 U.S.C. § 106(1)-(5), *id.* at 1442 (emphasis in original), and that a violation of the "authorization" right constitutes infringement under section 501 of the Act, the *Peter Starr* court reasoned that allegations of an authorization within the United States of extraterritorial conduct that corresponded to the activities listed in section 106 "allege[d] an act of infringement within the United States," *id.* at 1442–43. Accordingly, the court determined that the district court erred "in concluding that 'Plaintiff allege[d] only infringing acts which took place outside of the United States,' "and reversed the district court's dismissal for lack of subject matter jurisdiction. *Id.* at 1443.

The *Peter Starr* court accepted, as does this court,[6] that the acts *authorized* from within the United States themselves could not have constituted infringement under the Copyright Act because "[i]n general, United States copyright laws do not have extraterritorial effect," and

cepting this concession, additionally insisted that the authorization necessarily included the making of a copy of the negative of the Picture within the United States. Appellants' counsel responded that this contention was made before neither the special master nor the panel, and was not supported by the record. For the purposes of this decision, we assume, as apparently

the panel did, that each of the defendants made a relevant "authorization" within the United States, and that the acts of authorization consisted solely of entering into licensing agreements.

6. We reaffirm below that the Copyright Act does not extend to acts of infringement that take place entirely abroad. See infra Part II.

therefore, "infringing actions that take place entirely outside the United States are not actionable." *Peter Starr,* 783 F.2d at 1442 (citing *Robert Stigwood Group, Ltd. v. O'Reilly,* 530 F.2d 1096, 1101 (2d Cir.), *cert. denied,* 429 U.S. 848, 97 S.Ct. 135, 50 L.Ed.2d 121 (1976)). The central premise of the *Peter Starr* court, then, was that a party could be held liable as an "infringer" under section 501 of the Act merely for authorizing a third party to engage in acts that, had they been committed *within* the United States, would have violated the exclusive rights granted to a copyright holder by section 106.

Since *Peter Starr,* however, we have recognized that, when a party authorizes an activity *not* proscribed by one of the five section 106 clauses, the authorizing party cannot be held liable as an infringer. In *Lewis Galoob,* we rejected the argument that "a party can unlawfully authorize another party to use a copyrighted work even if that party's use of the work would not violate the Copyright Act," *Lewis Galoob,* 964 F.2d at 970, and approved of Professor Nimmer's statement that " 'to the extent that an activity does not violate one of th[e] five enumerated rights [found in 17 U.S.C. § 106], authorizing such activity does not constitute copyright infringement,' " *id.* (quoting 3 David Nimmer & Melville B. Nimmer, Nimmer on Copyright § 12.04[A][3][a], at 12–80 n. 82 (1991)). Similarly, in *Columbia Pictures,* we held that no liability attached under the Copyright Act for providing videodisc players to hotel guests when the use of that equipment did not constitute a "public" performance within the meaning of section 106 of the Act, *see Columbia Pictures,* 866 F.2d at 279–81.

The apparent premise of *Lewis Galoob* was that the addition of the words "to authorize" in the Copyright Act was not meant to create a new form of liability for "authorization" that was divorced completely from the legal consequences of authorized conduct, but was intended to invoke the preexisting doctrine of contributory infringement. *See Lewis Galoob,* 964 F.2d at 970 ("Although infringement by authorization is a form of direct infringement [under the Act], this does not change the proper focus of our inquiry; a party cannot authorize another party to infringe a copyright unless the authorized conduct would itself be unlawful."). We agree. * * *

As the Supreme Court noted in *Sony,* and this circuit acknowledged in *Peter Starr,* under the 1909 Act courts differed over the *degree* of involvement required to render a party liable as a contributory infringer. *See Sony,* 464 U.S. at 437–38 & n. 18, 104 S.Ct. at 786–87 & n. 18; *Peter Starr,* 783 F.2d at 1443. Viewed with this background in mind, the addition of the words "to authorize" in the 1976 Act appears best understood as merely clarifying that the Act contemplates liability for contributory infringement, and that the bare act of "authorization" can suffice. This view is supported by the legislative history of the Act:

> The exclusive rights accorded to a copyright owner under section 106 are "to do and to authorize" any of the activities specified in the five numbered clauses. *Use of the phrase "to authorize" is intended*

to avoid any questions as to the liability of contributory infringers. For example, a person who lawfully acquires an authorized copy of a motion picture would be an infringer if he or she engages in the business of renting it to others for purposes of unauthorized public performance.

H.R.Rep. No. 1476, 94th Cong., 2d Sess. 61, *reprinted in* 1976 U.S.C.C.A.N. 5659, 5674 (emphasis added).

Consequently, we believe that " 'to authorize' [wa]s simply a convenient peg on which Congress chose to hang the antecedent jurisprudence of third party liability." 3 Nimmer, *supra*, § 12.04[A][3][a], at 12–84 n. 81. * * *

Appellees resist the force of this logic, and argue that liability in this case is appropriate because, unlike in *Lewis Galoob* and *Columbia Pictures,* in which the alleged primary infringement consisted of acts that were entirely outside the purview of 17 U.S.C. § 106(1)-(5) (and presumably lawful), the conduct authorized in this case was precisely that prohibited by section 106, and is only uncognizable because it occurred outside the United States. Moreover, they contend that the conduct authorized in this case would have been prohibited under the copyright laws of virtually every nation. *See also* 1 Goldstein, *supra*, § 6.1, at 706 n. 4 (suggesting that *"Peter Starr*'s interpretation of section 106's authorization right would appear to be at least literally correct since the statute nowhere requires that the direct infringement occur within the United States."); *ITSI T.V. Prods., Inc. v. California Auth. of Racing Fairs,* 785 F.Supp. 854, 863 (E.D.Cal. 1992) (asserting that "because 'authorization' is itself actionable as a 'direct' act of copyright infringement, the fact that the act 'authorized' occurs abroad is irrelevant"), *rev'd on other grounds,* 3 F.3d 1289 (9th Cir. 1993).

Even assuming *arguendo* that the acts authorized in this case would have been illegal abroad, we do not believe the distinction offered by Appellees is a relevant one. Because the copyright laws do not apply extraterritorially, each of the rights conferred under the five section 106 categories must be read as extending "no farther than the [United States'] borders." 2 Goldstein, *supra*, § 16.0, at 675. *See, e.g., Robert Stigwood,* 530 F.2d at 1101 (holding that no damages could be obtained under the Copyright Act for public performances in Canada when preliminary steps were taken within the United States and stating that "[t]he Canadian performances, while they may have been torts in Canada, were not torts here"); *see also Filmvideo Releasing Corp. v. Hastings,* 668 F.2d 91, 93 (2d Cir. 1981) (reversing an order of the district court that required the defendant to surrender prints of a film because the prints could be used to further conduct abroad that was not proscribed by United States copyright laws). In light of our above conclusion that the "authorization" right refers to the doctrine of contributory infringement, which requires that the authorized act *itself* could violate one of the exclusive rights listed in section 106(1)-(5), we believe that "[i]t is simply not possible to draw a principled distinction" between an act that does not violate a copyright because it is not the type of conduct proscribed by section 106, and one that does not violate section 106 because the illicit act occurs overseas. *Danjaq, S.A. v. MGM/UA Communications, Co.*, 773 F.Supp. 194, 203 (C.D.Cal. 1991), *aff'd on other grounds*, 979 F.2d 772 (9th Cir. 1992). In both cases, the authorized conduct could not violate the exclusive rights guaranteed by section 106. In both cases, therefore, there can be no liability for "authorizing" such conduct. *See also* 3 Nimmer, *supra*, § 12.04[A][3][b], at 12–87 to 12–88.

To hold otherwise would produce the untenable anomaly, inconsistent with the general principles of third party liability, that a party could be held liable as an infringer for violating the "authorization" right when the party that it authorized could not be considered an infringer under the Copyright Act. Put otherwise, we do not think Congress intended to hold a party liable for *merely* "authorizing" conduct that, had the *authorizing* party chosen to engage in itself, would have resulted in no liability under the Act. *Cf. Robert Stigwood*, 530 F.2d at 1101.

Appellees rely heavily on the Second Circuit's doctrine that extraterritorial application of the copyright laws is permissible "when the type of infringement permits further reproduction abroad." *Update Art, Inc. v. Modiin Publ'g, Ltd.*, 843 F.2d 67, 73 (2d Cir. 1988). Whatever the merits of the Second Circuit's rule, and we express no opinion on its validity in this circuit, it is premised on the theory that the copyright holder may recover damages that stem from a direct infringement of its exclusive rights that occurs *within* the United States. *See Robert Stigwood*, 530 F.2d at 1101; *Sheldon v. Metro–Goldwyn Pictures Corp.*, 106 F.2d 45, 52 (2d Cir. 1939) (L. Hand, J.) ("The negatives were 'records' from which the work could be 'reproduced', and it was a tort to make them in this country. The plaintiffs acquired an equitable interest in them as soon as they were made, which attached to any profits from their exploitation. . . ."), *aff'd*, 309 U.S. 390, 60 S.Ct. 681, 84 L.Ed. 825 (1940); *see also Ahbez v. Edwin H. Morris & Co., Inc.*, 548 F.Supp. 664, 667 (S.D.N.Y. 1982); *Famous Music Corp. v. Seeco Records, Inc.*, 201 F.Supp. 560, 568–69 (S.D.N.Y.1961). * * * In these cases, liability is not based on contributory infringement, but on the theory that the infringing use would have been actionable *even if* the subsequent foreign distribution that stemmed from that use never took place. *See, e.g., Famous Music*, 201 F.Supp. at 569 ("[T]hat a copyright has no extra-territorial effect[ ] does not solve th[e] problem of [whether liability should attach for preparing within the United States tapes that were part of a] manufacture [completed abroad] since plaintiffs seek to hold defendant for what it did *here* rather than what it did abroad." (emphasis in original)). These cases, therefore, simply are inapplicable to a theory of liability based merely on the authorization of noninfringing acts.

Accordingly, accepting that wholly extraterritorial acts of infringement cannot support a claim under the Copyright Act, we believe that the *Peter Starr* court, and thus the panel in this case, erred in concluding that the mere authorization of such acts supports a claim for infringement under the Act.

II. The Extraterritoriality of the Copyright Act

Appellees additionally contend that, if liability for "authorizing" acts of infringement depends on finding that the authorized acts themselves are cognizable under the Copyright Act, this court should find that the United States copyright laws *do extend* to extraterritorial acts of infringement when such acts "result in adverse effects within the United States." Appellees buttress this argument with the contention that failure to apply the copyright laws extraterritorially in this case will have a disastrous effect on the American film industry, and that other remedies, such as suits in foreign jurisdictions or the application of foreign copyright laws by American courts, are not realistic alternatives.

We are not persuaded by Appellees' parade of horribles. More fundamentally, however, we are unwilling to overturn over eighty years of consistent jurisprudence on the extraterritorial reach of the copyright laws without further guidance from Congress.

The Supreme Court recently reminded us that "[i]t is a longstanding principle of American law 'that legislation of Congress, unless a contrary intent appears, is meant to apply only within the territorial jurisdiction of the United States.' " *EEOC v. Arabian American Oil Co. (Aramco)*, 499 U.S. 244, 248, 111 S.Ct. 1227, 1230, 113 L.Ed.2d 274 (1991) (quoting *Foley Bros., Inc. v. Filardo*, 336 U.S. 281, 285, 69 S.Ct. 575, 577, 93 L.Ed. 680 (1949)). Because courts must "assume that Congress legislates against the backdrop of the presumption against extraterritoriality," unless "there is 'the affirmative intention of the Congress clearly expressed' "congressional enactments must be presumed to be " 'primarily concerned with domestic conditions.' " *Id.* 499 U.S. at 248, 111 S.Ct. at 1230 (quoting *Foley Bros.*, 336 U.S. at 285, 69 S.Ct. at 577 and *Benz v. Compania Naviera Hidalgo, S.A.*, 353 U.S. 138, 147, 77 S.Ct. 699, 704, 1 L.Ed.2d 709 (1957)).

The "undisputed axiom," 3 Nimmer, *supra*, § 12.04[A][3][b], at 12–86, that the United States' copyright laws have no application to extraterritorial infringement predates the 1909 Act, *see, e.g., United Dictionary Co. v. G. & C. Merriam Co.*, 208 U.S. 260, 264–66, 28 S.Ct. 290, 290–91, 52 L.Ed. 478 (1908) (Holmes, J.), and, as discussed above, the principle of territoriality consistently has been reaffirmed, *see, e.g., Capitol Records, Inc. v. Mercury Records Corp.*, 221 F.2d 657, 662 (2d Cir. 1955). * * * There is no clear expression of congressional intent in either the 1976 Act or other relevant enactments to alter the preexisting extraterritoriality doctrine. Indeed, the *Peter Starr* court itself recognized the continuing application of the principle that "infringing actions that take place entirely outside the United States are not actionable in United States federal courts." *Peter Starr*, 783 F.2d at 1442 (citing *Robert Stigwood*, 530 F.2d at 1101).

Furthermore, we note that Congress chose in 1976 to expand one specific "extraterritorial" application of the Act by declaring that the unauthorized importation of copyrighted works constitutes infringement even when the copies lawfully were made abroad. *See* 17 U.S.C.A. § 602(a) (West Supp.1992). Had Congress been inclined to overturn the preexisting doctrine that infringing acts that take place wholly outside the United States are not actionable under the Copyright Act, it knew how to do so. * * * Accordingly, the presumption against extraterritoriality, "far from being overcome here, is doubly fortified by the language of [the] statute," *Smith v. United States*, 507 U.S. 197, ___, 113 S.Ct. 1178, 1183, 122 L.Ed.2d 548 (1993) (quoting *United States v. Spelar*, 338 U.S. 217, 222, 70 S.Ct. 10, 13, 94 L.Ed. 3 (1949)), as set against its consistent historical interpretation.

Appellees, however, rely on dicta in a recent decision of the District of Columbia Circuit for the proposition that the presumption against extraterritorial application of U.S. laws may be "overcome" when denying such application would "result in adverse effects within the United States." *Environmental Defense Fund, Inc. v. Massey*, 986 F.2d 528, 531 (D.C.Cir. 1993) (noting that the Sherman Act, Lanham Act, and securities laws have been applied to extraterritorial conduct). However, the *Massey* court did not state that extraterritoriality would be *demanded* in such circumstances, but that "the *presumption* is *generally* not *applied* where the failure to extend the scope of the statute to a foreign setting will result in adverse [domestic] effects." *Id.* at 531 (emphasis added). In each of the statutory schemes discussed by the *Massey* court, the ultimate touchstone of extraterritoriality consisted of an ascertainment of congressional intent; courts did not rest *solely* on the consequences of a failure to give a statutory scheme extraterritorial application. More importantly, as the *Massey* court conceded, *see id.* at 532–33, application of the presumption is particularly appropriate when "[i]t serves to protect against unintended clashes between our laws and those of other nations which could result in international discord," *Aramco*, 499 U.S. at 248, 111 S.Ct. at 1230. * * *

We believe this latter factor is decisive in the case of the Copyright Act, and fully justifies application of the *Aramco* presumption even assuming *arguendo* that "adverse effects" within the United States "generally" would require a plenary inquiry into congressional intent. At the time that the international distribution of the videocassettes in this case took place, the United States was a member of the Universal Copyright Convention ("UCC"), and, in 1988, the United States acceded to the Berne Convention for the Protection of Literary and Artistic Works ("Berne Conv."). The central thrust of these multilateral treaties is the principle of "national treatment." A work of an American national first generated in America will receive the same protection in a foreign nation as that country accords to the works of its own nationals. *See* UCC Art. II; Berne Conv. Art. V. * * *[15] it is commonly acknowledged

15. The Berne Convention specifies that domestic law governs a work's protection in V(3). For acts of infringement that occur in its country of origin. See Berne Conv. Art.

that the national treatment principle implicates a rule of territoriality. *See London Film Prods. Ltd. v. Intercontinental Communications, Inc.,* 580 F.Supp. 47, 50 n. 6 (S.D.N.Y.1984). * * * Indeed, a recognition of this principle appears implicit in Congress's statements in acceding to Berne that "[t]he primary mechanism for discouraging discriminatory treatment of foreign copyright claimants is the principle of national treatment," H.R.Rep. No. 609, 100th Cong., 2d Sess. 43 [hereinafter House Report], and that adherence to Berne will require "careful due regard for the[ ] values" of other member nations, *id.* at 20.

In light of the *Aramco* Court's concern with preventing international discord, we think it inappropriate for the courts to act in a manner that might disrupt Congress's efforts to secure a more stable international intellectual property regime unless Congress otherwise clearly has expressed its intent. The application of American copyright law to acts of infringement that occur entirely overseas clearly could have this effect. Extraterritorial application of American law would be contrary to the spirit of the Berne Convention, and might offend other member nations by effectively displacing their law in circumstances in which previously it was assumed to govern. Consequently, an extension of extraterritoriality might undermine Congress's objective of achieving " 'effective and harmonious' copyright laws among all nations." House Report, *supra,* at 20. Indeed, it might well send the signal that the United States does not believe that the protection accorded by the laws of other member nations is adequate, which would undermine two other objectives of Congress in joining the convention: "strengthen[ing] the credibility of the U.S. position in trade negotiations with countries where piracy is not uncommon" and "rais[ing] the like[li]hood that other nations will enter the Convention." S.Rep. 352, 100th Cong., 2d Sess. 4–5, *reprinted in* 1988 U.S.C.C.A.N., 3706, 3709–10.

Moreover, although Appellees contend otherwise, we note that their theory might permit the application of American law to the distribution of protected materials in a foreign country conducted exclusively by citizens of that nation. A similar possibility was deemed sufficient in *Aramco* to find a provision that, on its face, appeared to contemplate that Title VII would be applied overseas, insufficient to rebut the presumption against extraterritoriality. *See Aramco,* 499 U.S. at 254, 111 S.Ct. at 1234. Of course, under the Berne Convention, all states must guarantee minimum rights, *see* Berne Conv. Art. IV; Stewart, *supra,* at 39–40, and it is plausible that the application of American law would yield outcomes roughly equivalent to those called for by the application of foreign law in a number of instances. Nonetheless, extending the reach of American copyright law likely would produce difficult choice-of-law problems, *cf.* House Report, *supra,* at 43 ("'[Berne] does not, howev-

other nations, however, the treaty uses the ambiguous concept of the "law of the country where protection is claimed." Id. Art. V(2). See generally Eugen Ulmer, Intellec-

tual Property Rights and the Conflict of Laws 11–12 (1978); World Intellectual Property Organization, Guide to the Berne Convention 32–34 (1978).

er, require all countries to have identical legal systems and procedural norms."), dilemmas that the federal courts' general adherence to the territoriality principle largely has obviated. *See* 3 Nimmer, *supra,* § 17.05, at 17–39 (noting that the "national treatment" principle has resulted in the absence of "[c]onflicts of law problems ... in the law of copyright"); *see also* 2 Goldstein, *supra,* § 16.2, at 681–82, § 16.3, at 683. Even if courts, as a matter of comity, would assert extraterritorial jurisdiction only when the effects in the United States and the contacts of the offending party with this country are particularly strong, *cf. Timberlane Lumber Co. v. Bank of Am., N.T. & S.A.,* 549 F.2d 597, 615 (9th Cir. 1976), *cert. denied,* 472 U.S. 1032, 105 S.Ct. 3514, 87 L.Ed.2d 643 (1985), that the assertion of such jurisdiction would engender new and troublesome choice-of-law questions provides a compelling reason for applying the *Aramco* presumption. *Cf. Massey,* 986 F.2d at 533 (noting that the *absence* of " 'choice of law' dilemmas" in applying the National Environmental Policy Act to projects in Antarctica provided a reason for *not* applying the presumption).

Accordingly, because an extension of the extraterritorial reach of the Copyright Act by the courts would in all likelihood disrupt the international regime for protecting intellectual property that Congress so recently described as essential to furthering the goal of protecting the works of American authors abroad, *see supra* note 10, we conclude that the *Aramco* presumption must be applied. * * * Because the presumption has not been overcome, we reaffirm that the United States copyright laws do not reach acts of infringement that take place entirely abroad. It is for Congress, and not the courts, to take the initiative in this field. * * *

Conclusion

We hold that the mere authorization of acts of infringement that are not cognizable under the United States copyright laws because they occur entirely outside of the United States does not state a claim for infringement under the Copyright Act. *Peter Starr* is overruled insofar as it held to the contrary. Accordingly, we vacate Part III of the panel's disposition, in which it concluded that the international distribution of the film constituted a violation of the United States copyright laws. We also vacate that portion of the disposition that affirmed the damage award based on foreign distribution of the film and the panel's affirmance of the award of attorneys' fees. Finally, we vacate the district court's grant of injunctive relief insofar as it was based on the premise that the Distributors had violated the United States copyright laws through authorization of the foreign distribution of the Picture on videocassettes. *Cf. Filmvideo,* 668 F.2d at 93–94.

The cause is remanded to the panel for further proceedings consistent with the mandate of this court.

Notes

1. The *Subafilms* case was reported on in the trade press in *U.S. District Courts Do Not Have Jurisdictions to Hear Cases Alleging Copyright Infringements Committed Abroad*, 16 NO. 5 Ent. L. Rep. 10 (Oct. 1994).

2. One of the most difficult problems that studios face is the pirating of their technology abroad by the posting items on the Internet. The Los Angeles Times reported, for example, that scores of people "are flooding the Internet with pirated copies of new films. "The Blair Witch Project" was online months before it hit theaters. Days before studios released blockbusters "The Matrix" and "American Pie," consumers could grab the movies off the Net. All free for the taking, for people with a computer and a fast connection." *Studios Fume as Pirates Flood Internet With Films Technology: 'z' and other bootleggers are making first-run movies freely available via computer*, L.A. TIMES, Aug. 14, 1999 at A1.

It further reported, "Unless the film industry curbs such Internet bootlegging now, possibly by the studios selling film online, it may well follow the path of the $40–billion recording industry. The music business so far is losing the fight against rampant online music piracy brought about by the popularity of MP3 technology." *Id.*

3. What can the film industry do to keep people from surreptitiously taping their films in studios and posting them for free on the web? The day *Star Wars: Phantom Menace* was released in the studios, for example, someone posted a copy, complete with the audience's laughter track, on the web. Should studios retain Internet police to patrol the web for bootleg copies of their work? In response to the bootlegging of *Phantom Menace*, Lucasfilm attorneys sent cease-and-desist letters to several suspected pirates and Lucas' staff worked with the FBI on the issue. *Studios Fume as Pirates Flood Internet With Films Technology: 'z' and other bootleggers are making first-run movies freely available via computer*, LA. TIMES, Aug. 14, 1999, at A1.

4. Should Microsoft and other companies who make the software that make Internet bootlegging be held responsible as contributory infringers? According to the L.A. Times, "Microsoft officials insist they cannot be held responsible for such film piracy. 'We make technology, and people use it in different ways,' said David Britton, lead product manager of Microsoft's Windows Media division. 'We can't control what everyone does with our software.'" *Studios Fume as Pirates Flood Internet With Films Technology: 'z' and other bootleggers are making first-run movies freely available via computer*, LA. TIMES, Aug. 14, 1999, at A1. After the *Sony* betamax case, discussed in Chapter 15 "Copyright Protection of Music," it's likely that Microsoft would win any case charging them with contributory infringement.

5. Globalization has also brought foreign firms to the United States seeking to purchase Hollywood studios. Sometimes these firms have been in for a rude awaking. Given that Hollywood is in the fantasy business, can these firms count on such studios to continue year after year to produce the same quality hits? Does investing in a Hollywood studio require the buyer to acknowledge the Latin principal *caveat emptor*, buyer beware? The L.A.

Times, *Universal Sued by Kirch Over Film Quantity, Quality*, Dec. 16, 1999, reported:

> Kirch Group, the German television giant that threw huge sums of money at Hollywood three years ago to lock up film and TV rights for its fledgling digital pay-TV systems, on Wednesday sued Universal Studios Inc. for more than $2 billion, saying that it isn't happy with what the studio is producing.
>
> The lawsuit argues that Kirch was effectively duped because Universal isn't the studio now that it was then. Kirch argues that it was led to believe Universal would continue making movies and TV shows "of the same quality and quantity" that it had been producing.
>
> Instead, Kirch argues, Universal breached the deal by slashing its film output roughly in half, hasn't produced the kind of entertainment with international appeal that it promised, negotiated a deal to turn over its TV business to mogul Barry Diller and shifted away from film and TV production toward the music business. * * *
>
> Universal's film division has been erratic since the Kirch deal was made, releasing such duds as "Babe: Pig in the City" and "Meet Joe Black" last year. This year, the studio released such hits as "Notting Hill," "American Pie" and "The Mummy," but also had such disappointments as "Mystery Men" and "EdTv." Like other studios trying to contain spiraling costs, Universal has been releasing fewer films. * * *
>
> In the lawsuit, Kirch said that it believed that Universal would make available about 20 to 30 films a year, but instead is providing only a fraction of that.

Universal Sued by Kirch Over Film Quantity, Quality, L.A. TIMES, Dec. 16, 1999, at C1.

6.   Hollywood is not the only film industry where financial success may be an illusory proposition. Variety reported,

> "At first glance, the bottom line on Australia's film industry is simple. While sales agents and other investors might turn small profits, fewer than 10% of films ever fully recoup their entire production budgets and go into overall profit. Indeed, a crop of dark, edgy Oz films (and some comedies and kidpics) commanded just 4% of Oz b.o. in 1998. * * *

Of the 110 or so films that the FFC [Film Finance Corp.] invested in through June 1997, about seven have gone into profit, including "Sirens," "Green Card," "Shine," "Strictly Ballroom," "Priscilla," and "Muriel's Wedding," with "Kiss or Kill" set to do so. While Beyond marketing topper John Thornhill believes that "that's not a bad hit rate," Southern Star sales chief Robyn Watts says, "It's tough andour TV business is the area that makes the most money, but our small, yet focused, film sales business turns a profit. We're operating on tougher parameters than Canada, with whom our films' (profiles are) on a par.

Oz Bottom Line Shaky (Australian Film Industry), VARIETY, Feb. 22, 1999.

B. GLOBALIZATION OF THE TELEVISION MARKET

BYRNE v. BRITISH BROADCASTING CORP.

U.S. District Court, Southern District of New York, 2001.
132 F.Supp.2d 229.

STEIN, District Judge.

Christopher Byrne brought this action against the British Broadcasting Corporation alleging that the BBC infringed his copyright in a song entitled "Fenians" (the "Song") in both the United States and the United Kingdom. The BBC now moves for: (1) partial summary judgment declaring that it did not infringe Byrne's United States copyright; and (2) dismissal of the action on the grounds of *forum non conveniens*. The motion for a declaration of non-infringement is denied because disputed issues of material fact exist on the question of whether the BBC's use of "Fenians" was a "fair use" pursuant to the Copyright Act. Its motion to dismiss the action on the grounds of *forum non conveniens* is denied because the BBC has not shown that the public and private interest factors set forth in *Gulf Oil Corp. v. Gilbert*, 330 U.S. 501, 67 S.Ct. 839, 91 L.Ed. 1055 (1947), weigh "strongly in favor" of litigating in the United Kingdom.

I. BACKGROUND

The following facts are undisputed, unless otherwise noted.

Byrne is a musician and political activist outspoken in his opposition to British involvement in the affairs of Northern Ireland. He and a co-author wrote "Fenians" in 1997, and he subsequently recorded it with his group, Seanchai. Since its publication, Byrne and his coauthor have been the sole proprietors of all rights, title and interest to the copyrights in the Song.

In 1999, the BBC decided to investigate and produce a story on an FBI investigation and subsequent arrest of four individuals in Florida on charges of smuggling guns into Northern Ireland for its newsmagazine program "Spotlight." While planning the story, BBC producer Justin O'Brien decided to explore Irish–American media reaction to the investigation. To that end, O'Brien placed a call from his office in Belfast to John McDonagh, producer and host of a radio program called Radio Free Eireann, broadcast from the New York City studios of radio station WBAI. During that call, O'Brien obtained permission for a BBC crew to film a live broadcast of the radio show during which the Florida arrests would be discussed.

This telephone call was not O'Brien's first experience with Radio Free Eireann. O'Brien had been to the WBAI studio earlier in the summer during an airing of the program, and he periodically visits the program's Internet website at www.wbaifree.org/radiofreeeireann/.

WBAI uses, with permission, a portion of the Song as the musical introduction to Radio Free Eireann. O'Brien was aware from his experience as a television producer that WBAI used the Song; he was interested enough in the Song to ask McDonagh about it; McDonagh told him that "Fenians" was the theme music for Radio Free Eireann and had been so for some time.

The BBC crew, including O'Brien, traveled from Northern Ireland to the United States to obtain raw film footage for the story in early September 1999. After spending approximately two weeks in Florida, the crew traveled to New York, where they planned to attend and record the September 11, 1999 broadcast of Radio Free Eireann. During that broadcast, the BBC camera was plugged into the mixing desk of the radio station to record the broadcast audio while the BBC simultaneously filmed the interior of the studio. The BBC crew recorded "substantially all" of the September 11, 1999, broadcast, including the portion of the Song used to open the program.

After spending five days in New York obtaining footage, the BBC crew traveled to San Francisco and Miami to do further research. By the end of September, they had left the United States and returned to Belfast, where they transformed the raw footage into a story suitable for television broadcast.

The producers of the story used a technique called a "clean fade" three times in the story. A "clean fade" involves synchronizing visual images of a setting with sounds, in order to ease the viewer into a new segment of the story. The first clean fade consists of images of the Florida coast synchronized with the sound of portions of local weather reports. The second clean fade consists of images of the Miami skyline synchronized with a portion of Jimi Hendrix's "Sweet Angel." The third clean fade consists of images of the New York skyline synchronized with three seconds of drum beats and that portion of the Song that is used by WBAI as the opening music to Radio Free Eireann. This fade ends with a visual segue into the WBAI studio, where the broadcast audio portion of Radio Free Eireann is synchronized with the visual images captured by the BBC crew during the September 11, 2000, broadcast. The BBC never sought or obtained permission from Byrne or his co-author for the use of the Song in its broadcast.

The story was ultimately broadcast on television twice: once on BBC NI at 9:30 p.m. on October 5, 1999, and again on BBC Choice NI five days later. The story has never been sold or licensed for broadcast or use anywhere else in the world.

On April 25, 2000, Byrne brought this action alleging claims for copyright infringement pursuant to both United States and United Kingdom law. The BBC now moves for partial summary judgment of non-infringement under United States law and dismissal of the action on the grounds of *forum non conveniens.*

II.   PARTIAL SUMMARY JUDGMENT OF NON-INFRINGEMENT

Summary judgment will be granted "only when the moving party demonstrates that 'there is no genuine issue as to any material fact and that the moving party is entitled to judgment as a matter of law.'" *Allen v. Coughlin,* 64 F.3d 77, 79 (2d Cir. 1995) (quoting Fed. R. Civ. P. 56(c)). In determining whether a genuine dispute remains as to a material fact, the court must resolve all ambiguities, and draw all reasonable inferences, against the moving party. *See Matsushita Electrical Industrial Co. v. Zenith Radio Corp.,* 475 U.S. 574, 587–88, 106 S.Ct. 1348, 89 L.Ed.2d 538 (1986).

A.   The Recording of the Song is a Prima Facie Violation of the Copyright Act

To establish a claim of copyright infringement, a plaintiff must establish (1) ownership of a valid copyright and (2) unauthorized copying or a violation of one of the other exclusive rights afforded copyright owners pursuant to the Copyright Act. *Twin Peaks Productions v. Publications Int'l. Ltd.,* 996 F.2d 1366, 1372 (2d Cir. 1993). Among these rights are the rights to reproduce and publicly perform the copyrighted work. *See* 17 U.S.C. § 106(1), (5). It is undisputed that Byrne owns a valid copyright in "Fenians" and that the BBC's recording of it in the United States and subsequent broadcast in Northern Ireland were unauthorized. The BBC contends, however, that the "act of filming" copyrighted material, even if unauthorized, does not constitute infringement when the film is to be used for "a program or movie," and that the only possible infringement was the broadcast in Northern Ireland, which is governed by U.K. law. Byrne agrees that U.K. law governs the broadcast.

The BBC's argument is belied by the words of the Copyright Act, which provide that among a copyright owner's "exclusive rights" is the right "to do and to authorize ... reproduc[tion of] the copyrighted work in copies." 17 U.S.C. § 106. Thus, unauthorized copying is a *prima facie* infringement of a copyright owner's rights. *See, e.g., UMG Recordings, Inc. v. MP3.Com,* 92 F.Supp.2d 349, 350 & n. 1 (S.D.N.Y.2000); *A & M Records, Inc. v. Napster, Inc.,* 114 F.Supp.2d 896, 912 (N.D.Cal.2000). Moreover, the fact that the BBC later broadcast the Song without authorization does not transform the recording and broadcast into a unitary act of infringement. An unauthorized copying of a copyrighted work constitutes a completed act of infringement, even when the copy is made for the purpose of transmission or broadcast abroad. *See Los Angeles News Serv. v. Reuters Television Int'l, Ltd.,* 149 F.3d 987, 991 (9th Cir. 1998).

B.   Was the Recording of the Song a "Fair Use"?

The BBC also contends that both the unauthorized recording and the unauthorized broadcast were "fair uses" of the Song within the intendment of 17 U.S.C. § 107. Because the parties agree that U.K. law applies to the BBC broadcast in the United Kingdom—as distinct from the recording of the Song in the United States—the "fair use" analysis pursuant to section 107 that follows is confined to the BBC's recording of the Song in the United States.

The doctrine of fair use has been used since "the infancy of copyright protection" to insure that copyright promotes, rather than hinders, "the Progress of Science and useful Arts." *Campbell v. Acuff-Rose Music, Inc.*, 510 U.S. 569, 575, 114 S.Ct. 1164, 127 L.Ed.2d 500 (1994) (quoting U.S. Const., art, I, § 8, cl. 8). The doctrine was codified in section 107 of the Copyright Act of 1976, which lists several examples of uses protected by the doctrine, including "news reporting," and mandates that courts consider four factors in determining whether a particular use is "fair": "(1) the purpose and character of the use, including whether such use is of a commercial nature * * *) the nature of the copyrighted work; (3) the amount and substantiality of the portion used in relation to the copyrighted work as a whole; and (4) the effect of the use upon the potential market for or value of the copyrighted work." 17 U.S.C. § 107. These four factors "guide but do not control [the] fair use analysis and 'are to be explored, and the results weighed together, in light of the purposes of copyright.'" *Castle Rock Entm't, Inc. v. Carol Publ'g Group, Inc.*, 150 F.3d 132, 141 (2d Cir. 1998) (quoting *Campbell*, 510 U.S. at 577–78), 114 S.Ct. 1164. The burden of proving "fair use" rests squarely on the alleged infringer. *See Infinity Broadcast Corp. v. Kirkwood*, 150 F.3d 104, 107 (2nd Cir. 1998).

In the summary judgment context, courts have often noted that as a mixed question of law and fact, the issue of whether an alleged infringement constitutes fair use is usually unsuited to summary disposition. * * * Where there are no disputed issues of material fact, however, summary judgment based on the defense of fair use may be appropriate. *See, e.g., Castle Rock Entm't,* 150 F.3d at 137. * * *

In this case, disputed issues of material fact exist, rendering summary judgment on the BBC's fair use defense inappropriate. Each of the statutory fair use factors will be examined in turn.

1. Purpose and character of the use

The first factor set forth in the statute to consider is "the purpose and character of the [allegedly infringing] use, including whether such use is of a commercial nature or is for nonprofit educational purposes." 17 U.S.C. § 107(1). The two most common inquiries in analyses of this factor are whether the use was for a commercial purpose and the extent to which the use was "transformative," *i.e.*, "whether the allegedly infringing work 'merely supersedes' the original work 'or instead adds something new, with a further purpose or different character, altering the first with new ... meaning [ ] or message.'" *Castle Rock Entm't,* 150 F.3d at 142 (quoting *Campbell*, 510 U.S. at 595, 114 S.Ct. 1164). The extent to which the use is transformative is "the more critical inquiry." *Id.*

The BBC contends that because it is a not-for-profit corporation, its use of the Song was necessarily "non-commercial," and was instead "for nonprofit educational purposes." However, "non-profit organizations enjoy no special immunity from determinations of copyright violation. The question under factor one is the purpose and character of the use, not of the alleged infringer." *Lish v. Harper's Magazine Found.*, 807 F.Supp. 1090, 1100–01 (S.D.N.Y.1992). The BBC also contends that because it recorded "Fenians" for use in a news program, its use constitutes "news reporting" within the meaning of 17 U.S.C. § 107—a "transformative" use—and, thus, it contends, the first fair use factor weighs in its favor.

Not all unlicensed uses of copyrighted material for inclusion in broadcasts that present material of interest to the public are protected by the fair use doctrine, even if they are labeled "news reporting" by defendants. If the purpose of the use was to entertain, rather than inform, *see Schumann v. Albuquerque Corp.*, 664 F.Supp. 473, 477 (D.N.M.1987), or if equally informative non-infringing alternatives were available, *see Roy Export Co. v. Columbia Broad. Sys., Inc.*, 503 F.Supp. 1137, 1144 (S.D.N.Y.1980), then the first fair use factor tips in favor of the plaintiff. *Cf. Los Angeles News Serv.*, 149 F.3d at 994 (copying of news footage for redistribution to overseas news organizations was not fair use).

As discussed above, the overall topic of the television news story was the investigation and arrest of four Irish nationals on charges of gun running. The purpose of recording the WBAI radio program, according to O'Brien, was "to explore how the Irish–American media was reacting" to the criminal investigation. It is unclear, however, how recording the Song, as opposed to recording the on-air statements of the radio show's hosts and guests, served the BBC's stated purpose. Indeed, a reasonable jury could find, on the record as it exists so far, that recording the Song was wholly unnecessary to reporting on "how the Irish–American media was reacting" to the FBI investigation.

Moreover, there is ample evidence from which a reasonable jury could infer that the BBC's intent in recording the Song was not to gather facts on Irish–American media reaction, but to obtain music that would make the story more entertaining to viewers. As discussed above, the "clean fade" technique was used three times in the 20–minute story. These sequences involved both images and sounds that did not directly pertain to the topic of the story—the criminal investigation—but that were arguably used to make the story more appealing and entertaining to viewers. In each of the sequences, the sounds used were not the ambient sounds that accompanied the visual images as they were being filmed, but rather the work of third parties unrelated to the moment of filming, *i.e.*, the Song, Jimi Hendrix's "Sweet Angel," and weather reports from Florida broadcasters, obtained during the crew's stay in the United States. Accordingly, a reasonable jury could infer that the crew sought to record not only footage necessary to its news reporting, but also footage, including the Song, that would entertain, rather than inform, as its primary purpose.

The BBC's reliance on the decision in *Italian Book Corp. v. American Broadcasting Cos.*, 458 F.Supp. 65 (S.D.N.Y.1978), is misplaced. In *Italian Book Corp.*, a television news crew had recorded images of a New York street fair, the San Gennaro festival, including a portion of a parade consisting of a band on a float playing music—copyrighted by the plaintiff—for use in a news report about the festival. 458 F.Supp. at 67. That court found that the parade was "one of the most significant aspects of the festival," and that "ABC's employees had no advance knowledge that a band would come along on a float playing this particular song." *Id.* at 67–68. Thus, ABC's recording and subsequent broadcast of portions of the song was "wholly fortuitous." *Id.* at 68. In this case, in contrast, O'Brien had visited the WBAI studios before and "was ... aware ... that the music was closely associated with the station" before recording. Moreover, there is evidence to suggest that the BBC crew sought to record footage for entertainment, rather than news reporting, purposes. On this record, a reasonable jury could find that the BBC's recording of the Song was not "fortuitous," but a calculated attempt to obtain entertaining footage only tenuously related to its news reporting purpose.

In addition, a reasonable jury could find that even if the Song were recorded as part of an effort "to explore how the Irish–American media was reacting" to the reported investigation, there were equally informative non-infringing alternatives available. As discussed above, the on-air statements of the radio show's hosts and guests are an obvious alternative. The BBC crew presumably could also have interviewed other Irish–American media figures, or sought permission to use the work of other Irish–American artists.

In sum, the purpose and character of the use is a disputed issue of fact. At the summary judgment stage, therefore, this factor favors Byrne, the non-moving party.

2. The nature of the copyrighted work

The second factor set forth in section 107 of the Copyright Act to employ in determining whether an alleged infringement is a permissible fair use is "the nature of the copyrighted work." It is undisputed that "Fenians" is a creative work, and, thus, the type of work at "the core" of copyright law's protection. *See Campbell*, 510 U.S. at 586, 114 S.Ct. 1164. The BBC, relying on Judge John S. Martin's opinion in *Baraban v. Time Warner*, 54 U.S.P.Q.2d 1759 (S.D.N.Y.2000), contends, however that because the Song has been widely disseminated, the nature of the work favors it or is neutral.

Unpublished works are the "favorite sons" of the second fair use factor, and where a plaintiff proves unauthorized publication of an unpublished work, this factor weighs heavily against a finding of fair use. *See Wright v. Warner Books*, 953 F.2d 731, 737 (2d Cir. 1991). Previously published works, on the other hand, qualify for "far less protection" against fair use, and, therefore, even where the work is "creative," the second factor may not weigh as "decisively" in the copyright holder's favor where the work has been previously distributed. *See Baraban,* 54 U.S.P.Q.2d at 1762–63.

Baraban does not hold, however, as the BBC contends, that the wide dissemination of a work tips this factor in the alleged infringer's favor. Rather, *Baraban* stands for the straightforward proposition that the second fair use factor may have little significance in the context of a transformative use. *See Baraban,* 54 U.S.P.Q.2d at 1763; *see also, e.g., Castle Rock Entm't,* 150 F.3d at 143–44. Where the allegedly infringing use is minimally transformative, however, the creative nature of a copyrighted work remains significant. *Castle Rock Entm't,* 150 F.3d at 144.

As noted above, whether the Song was recorded for a transformative purpose is a disputed issue of fact. Accordingly, the creative nature of work weighs in favor of Byrne on a motion for summary judgment.

3. *The amount and substantiality of the portion used*

Courts must examine the third fair use factor—"the amount and substantiality of the portion [of the copyrighted work] used in relation to the copyrighted work as a whole"—in context. *Castle Rock Entm't,* 150 F.3d at 144. "The inquiry must focus upon whether '[t]he extent of . . . copying' is consistent with or more than necessary to further 'the purpose and character of the use.' " *Id.* (quoting *Campbell,* 510 U.S. at 587–87, 114 S.Ct. 1164).

The BBC recorded the entire 50–second portion of the Song used by WBAI.[2] The BBC contends that because this was no more of the Song than was necessary to reproduce the radio program in its entirety, the third fair use factor weighs in its favor. This argument assumes, however, that reproduction of the radio program in its entirety was necessary to a transformative purpose, which, as discussed above, is in dispute.

At the summary judgment stage, the Court draws the inference that no part of the recording of the Song was necessary to the BBC's asserted news reporting purpose. The third fair use factor, therefore, favors Byrne.

4. *Effect of the use on the market for or value of the original*

The fourth factor to be employed in determining whether the use of the copyrighted work was a fair use is "the effect of the use on the potential market for or value of the copyrighted work." The BBC asserts that its "mere recordation . . . cannot possibly have any effect on the actual or potential market" for the Song. When evaluating this fourth factor, however, the court must "consider not only the extent of market harm caused by the particular actions of the alleged infringer, but also whether unrestricted and widespread conduct of the sort engaged in by the defendant . . . would result in a substantially adverse impact on the

---

2. The BBC concedes that its recording of the Song constitutes more than a "de minimis" use. See Def.'s Mem. at 7. See generally Sandoval v. New Line Cinema, 147 F.3d 215, 217 (2d Cir.1998).

potential market" for the original or derivative works. *Campbell,* 510 U.S. at 590, 114 S.Ct. 1164.

As set forth above, a reasonable jury could infer that the BBC intentionally recorded the Song for the purpose of providing an audio component of a "clean fade." When a broadcaster makes an unauthorized copy of a song for such use, it has no need to purchase a copy from the copyright holder or his licensees, thus lessening the market for the song. *Cf. Los Angeles News Serv. v. Reuters Television Int'l Ltd.,* 149 F.3d 987, 994 (9th Cir. 1998). Accordingly, this factor favors Byrne.

5. *Other factors*

Although the four statutory fair use factors are not exclusive, and courts may consider other factors, *see Castle Rock Entm't,* 150 F.3d at 146, the parties have not addressed any additional factors and the Court limits its analysis to the four statutory factors.

Considering the four statutory factors, the BBC's motion for summary judgment based on the fair use defense should be denied. The purpose and character of the BBC's use of the Song is a disputed issue of fact implicating each of the fair use factors and summary disposition is therefore inappropriate.

III. FORUM NON CONVENIENS

The doctrine of *forum non conveniens* was developed to thwart "a strategy of forcing the trial at a most inconvenient place for an adversary." *Gulf Oil Corp. v. Gilbert,* 330 U.S. 501, 507, 67 S.Ct. 839, 91 L.Ed. 1055 (1947). The doctrine permits a court to dismiss an action to enable it to be re-filed in a more convenient foreign forum. *See DiRienzo v. Philip Servs. Corp.,* 232 F.3d 49, 56 (2d Cir.2000). * * *

Whether an action should be dismissed based upon *forum non conveniens* is a discretionary determination, *see Piper Aircraft Co.,* 454 U.S. at 247, 102 S.Ct. 252; *Alfadda v. Fenn,* 159 F.3d 41, 45 (2d Cir. 1998), and involves two steps: (1) determining whether there is an adequate alternate forum for the dispute; and (2) balancing the public and private interests factors set forth by the United States Supreme Court in *Gilbert* to determine "whether the convenience of the parties and the ends of justice would best be served by dismissing the action." *Murray v. British Broadcasting Corp.,* 81 F.3d 287, 292–93 (2d Cir. 1996); *Alfadda,* 159 F.3d at 45.

A. *An Adequate Alternative Forum Exists*

Dismissal of an action on the grounds of *forum non conveniens* is inappropriate in the absence of an adequate alternative forum "because application of the doctrine 'presupposes at least two forums in which the defendant is amenable to process.'" *Murray,* 81 F.3d at 292 (2d Cir. 1996) (quoting *Gilbert,* 330 U.S. at 507, 67 S.Ct. 839); *see also Bybee v. Oper der Standt Bonn,* 899 F.Supp. 1217, 1222 (S.D.N.Y.1995). This requirement "is ordinarily satisfied if the defendant is amenable to process in another jurisdiction, except in 'rare circumstances' when 'the remedy offered by the other forum is clearly unsatisfactory.' " *Murray,* 81 F.3d at 292 (quoting *Piper Aircraft Co.,* 454 U.S. at 254 n. 22, 102 S.Ct. 252).

Byrne does not dispute that the BBC is amenable to suit in the United Kingdom, or that his remedies in the United Kingdom are both substantively and procedurally adequate. Rather, Byrne claims that the financial barriers he would face in bringing this action in either Northern Ireland or England, including the lack of a contingency-fee system in Northern Ireland, "effectively mean that the United Kingdom would be no forum at all."

The United States Court of Appeals for the Second Circuit, however, has explicitly held that a plaintiff's financial burdens, including hardships resulting from the absence of contingent fee arrangements, should be considered as one of the *Gilbert* factors only after a court determines that an alternative forum is available. *See Murray,* 81 F.3d at 292–93. Accordingly, this Court finds that the United Kingdom is an adequate alternative forum for this dispute.

B. *Application of the Gilbert Factors*

In applying the public and private interest factors of *Gilbert,* the plaintiff's choice of forum is ordinarily given great deference, especially where the plaintiff has chosen its "home forum." *Piper Aircraft Co.,* 454 U.S. at 255, 102 S.Ct. 252; *Murray,* 81 F.3d at 290; *see also Bybee,* 899 F.Supp. at 1222. A foreign plaintiff's choice of forum, however, is given less deference than that of a domestic plaintiff. *See Piper Aircraft Co.,* 454 U.S. at 256, 102 S.Ct. 252; *Murray,* 81 F.3d at 290. Byrne is a United States citizen living in the United States. The BBC contends, however, that the deference ordinarily given to Byrne's choice of forum should be diminished by his dual citizenship—he is also a citizen of the Republic of Ireland—and his regular travel to, and contacts with, Northern Ireland.

The Second Circuit, however, has recently held that courts should accord the choice of forum of foreign citizens who are legal residents of the United States the same deference as the choice of forum of United States citizens. *See Wiwa v. Royal Dutch Petroleum Co.,* 226 F.3d 88, 103. Certainly, then, Byrne's dual citizenship cannot diminish the deference his choice of forum will be given by this Court. Similarly, regular travel to the alternative forum does not diminish the deference given to plaintiff's choice, although it may be considered in the evaluation of the "private interests" of the parties. *See, e.g., Massaquoi v. Virgin Atlantic Airways,* 945 F.Supp. 58, 62–63 (S.D.N.Y.1996); *Sablic v. Armada Shipping Aps,* 973 F.Supp. 745, 748 (S.D.Tex.1997). Thus, in order to prevail on its motion to dismiss, the BBC must show that the balance of public and private interests is "strongly" in favor of litigating in the United Kingdom "in order to overcome the substantial weight accorded [Byrne's] choice of forum." *Bybee,* 899 F. Supp. at 1222; *see also DiRienzo,* 232 F.3d at 56 (quoting *Gilbert,* 330 U.S. at 508, 67 S.Ct. 839).

The public interest factors include: (1) "the administrative difficulties flowing from court congestion"; (2) "the local interest in having controversies decided at home"; (3) "the interest in having the trial in a forum that is familiar with the law governing the action"; (4) "the avoidance of unnecessary problems in conflict of laws or in the application of foreign law"; and (5) "the unfairness of burdening citizens in an unrelated forum with jury duty." *Murray*, 81 F.3d at 293. None of these factors weighs heavily in favor of dismissal.

Each of the public interest factors are neutral. The parties have not demonstrated that the courts of the United Kingdom are any more or less congested than is the Southern District of New York. Moreover, both localities have an interest in having this dispute decided at home—the action involves alleged violations of the laws of both the United States and the United Kingdom based on acts that took place in each country. Courts in either country would have to apply the law of the other, and the application of the law of another English common law jurisdiction "does not impose a significant burden on this Court." *Gordon v. Long Bay (1980) Ltd.*, 94 Civ. 2141, 1995 WL 489474, at * 4 (S.D.N.Y. Aug. 16, 1995). Finally, neither the United States nor the United Kingdom is an "unrelated forum," and, in addition, there is no right to a jury in this action in the United Kingdom.

The private interest factors include: (1) "the relative ease of access to sources of proof"; (2) "the availability of compulsory process for attendance of unwilling witnesses"; (3) "the cost of obtaining attendance of willing witnesses"; (4) "[i]ssues concerning the enforceability of a judgment"; and (5) "all other practical problems that make trial of a case easy, expeditious, and inexpensive—or the opposite." *Murray*, 81 F.3d at 294. As with the public interest factors, none of the public interest factors weigh heavily in favor of dismissal.

The first four factors are neutral. Documentary evidence and witnesses exist on both sides of the Atlantic. For example, while the BBC's raw footage is currently located in Northern Ireland, the records of Irish–American media outlets are in the United States. Similarly, while members of the BBC crew live or work in the United Kingdom and are presumably subject to compulsory process in United Kingdom courts, plaintiff, WBAI personnel, and plaintiff's experts all live or work within the subpoena power of this Court. There has been no showing that the cost of obtaining the attendance of willing witnesses would be significantly greater for either side in either forum, and the parties have not identified any issues relating to the enforceability of a judgment obtained in either the United Kingdom or the United States.

Although Byrne has submitted evidence that a trial in New York would be easier for him to finance because he has already obtained counsel on a contingency basis and he already maintains a home here, the BBC has submitted evidence that Byrne regularly visits the United Kingdom. Accordingly, the fifth factor is largely neutral, or, at most, weighs slightly in favor of denying the motion to dismiss.

Waxing creative, the BBC claims that "all roads lead to Britannia," Def.'s Mem. at 34, and Byrne asserts that "there's no place like home," Pl.'s Mem. at 33. Home is where Byrne is entitled to stay absent a showing that the *Gilbert* factors weigh "strongly in favor" of dismissal. *See Bybee,* 899 F.Supp. at 1222. The BBC has failed to make such a showing. Accordingly, the BBC's motion to dismiss the complaint on the grounds of *forum non conveniens* is denied.

IV. CONCLUSION

For the reasons set forth above, the BBC's motions for partial summary judgment of non-infringement under United States law and dismissal of the action on the grounds of *forum non conveniens* are denied.

MURRAY v. BRITISH BROADCASTING CORP.

United States Court of Appeals, Second Circuit, 1996.
81 F.3d 287.

WINTER, Circuit Judge.

Dominic Murray, a British national, appeals from Judge Stanton's dismissal of his complaint based on the doctrine of *forum non conveniens*. The action was brought against the British Broadcasting Corporation ("the BBC"), a corporation organized under the laws of the United Kingdom, and BBC Lionheart Television International ("Lionheart"), a Delaware corporation and wholly-owned subsidiary of the BBC. It asserted claims based on copyright infringement under both United States and English law, false designation of origin, and unfair competition. Murray's principal arguments on appeal are that *forum non conveniens* was misapplied either because the district court should have granted greater deference to his choice of forum or because a contingent fee arrangement is not available in the United Kingdom for this kind of litigation. Alternatively, Murray contends that the district court abused its discretion in weighing the various factors applicable under *forum non conveniens* doctrine. We affirm.

BACKGROUND

Murray is a self-employed designer and manufacturer of costumes and props in London, England. In July 1992, the BBC engaged Murray to produce a disguise costume for Noel Edmonds, the host of a BBC television program styled "Noel's House Party." The costume, named Mr. Blobby, was to be worn by Edmonds in order to surprise celebrity guests on the program. The British public began identifying Mr. Blobby as a character rather than a costume. As a consequence, the Mr. Blobby costume, now worn by an actor instead of Mr. Edmonds, has become an unexpected success and has been put to a wider use. In 1993, the BBC began authorizing and licensing products bearing the likeness of Mr. Blobby in the United Kingdom. According to Murray, he consulted with English counsel at that time concerning an action for infringement of his copyright in the Mr. Blobby costume. He allegedly declined to pursue his claim because he could neither pay the 100,000 to 200,000 pounds necessary to bring his case to trial nor post the security necessary to obtain a loan for that amount. In June 1994, the defendants brought Mr. Blobby to New York for his American debut at the International Licensing and Merchandising Conference and Exposition and began actively marketing Mr. Blobby in the United States. Shortly thereafter, Murray obtained American counsel under a contingent fee arrangement. This action ensued. Although it appears that no Mr. Blobby products have yet been produced for the American market, Murray has also filed suit against several alleged licensees, *Murray v. The Beanstalk Group, et al.*, 95–Civ–5358 (S.D.N.Y. filed July 18, 1995), which is still pending in the Southern District. As noted, Judge Stanton dismissed the action against the BBC and Lionheart on the ground of *forum non conveniens, Murray v. British Broadcasting Corp.*, 906 F.Supp. 858 (1995), and Murray brought this appeal.

DISCUSSION

1. Deference to Murray's Choice of Forum

The doctrine of *forum non conveniens* permits a court to "resist imposition upon its jurisdiction even when jurisdiction is authorized by the letter of a general venue statute," *Gulf Oil Corp. v. Gilbert*, 330 U.S. 501, 507, 67 S.Ct. 839, 842, 91 L.Ed. 1055 (1947), if dismissal would "best serve the convenience of the parties and the ends of justice." *Koster v. (American) Lumbermens Mut. Casualty Co.*, 330 U.S. 518, 527, 67 S.Ct. 828, 833, 91 L.Ed. 1067 (1947). There is ordinarily a strong presumption in favor of the plaintiff's choice of forum, *Piper Aircraft Co. v. Reyno*, 454 U.S. 235, 255, 102 S.Ct. 252, 265, 70 L.Ed.2d 419 (1981); *Gilbert,* 330 U.S. at 508, 67 S.Ct. at 843 ("the plaintiff's choice of forum should rarely be disturbed"). Where a foreign plaintiff is concerned, however, its choice of forum is entitled to less deference, *Piper Aircraft,* 454 U.S. at 256, 102 S.Ct. at 266. The Supreme Court has emphasized that this rule is not based on a desire to disadvantage foreign plaintiffs but rather on a realistic prediction concerning the ultimate convenience of the forum:

> [w]hen the home forum has been chosen, it is reasonable to assume that this choice is convenient. When the plaintiff is foreign, however, this assumption is much less reasonable. Because the central purpose of any *forum non conveniens* inquiry is to ensure that the trial is convenient, a foreign plaintiff's choice deserves less deference.

Id. at 255–56, 102 S.Ct. at 266 (footnote omitted). Nevertheless, some weight must still be given to a foreign plaintiff's choice of forum. *R. Maganlal & Co. v. M.G. Chem. Co.*, 942 F.2d 164, 168 (2d Cir. 1991). Indeed, we have cautioned that "this reduced weight is not an invitation to accord a foreign plaintiff's selection of an American forum *no* deference since dismissal for *forum non conveniens* is the exception rather than the rule." *Id.* (citations and internal quotation marks omitted and emphasis added)

Murray quarrels with neither the rule concerning foreign plaintiffs nor the reason underlying it. Instead, he argues that his choice of an American forum must, as a matter of law, be accorded the deference given domestic plaintiffs because of the Berne Convention for the Protection of Literary and Artistic Works, to which both the United States and the United Kingdom are signatories. This is a matter of law that we review *de novo.*

The Convention provides in pertinent part that "the extent of protection, *as well as the means of redress afforded to the author to protect his rights,* shall be governed exclusively by the laws of the country where protection is claimed." Berne Convention for the Protection of Literary and Artistic Works, Paris Text, July 24, 1971, Art. V ¶ 2, S. TREATY DOC. NO. 27, 99th Cong., 2d Sess. 40 (1986), *reprinted in* 6 David Nimmer & Melville B. Nimmer, *Nimmer on Copyright,* Appendix 27–5 (1995) (emphasis added). Under the Berne Convention, Murray argues, he is deemed to be in the shoes of an American plaintiff and entitled to greater deference in his choice of forum than the district court believed. The principle set out in Article V, paragraph 2 of the Berne Convention is one of "national treatment," *see Creative Technology, Ltd. v. Aztech Sys. Pte,* 61 F.3d 696, 700 (9th Cir. 1995), a choice-of-law rule mandating that the applicable law be the copyright law of the country in which the infringement occurred, not that of the country of which the author is a citizen or in which the work was first published. 3 *Nimmer on Copyright* § 17.05. Murray argues, in essence, that the principle of national treatment contained in the Berne Convention mandates procedural opportunities identical to those accorded American plaintiffs alleging copyright infringement. We disagree.

Murray relies on *Irish Nat'l Ins. Co. v. Aer Lingus Teoranta,* 739 F.2d 90 (2d Cir. 1984), in which we held that the Treaty of Friendship, Commerce and Navigation between the United States and Ireland required the application of the same *forum non conveniens* standards to the Irish plaintiff as a court would have applied to a United States citizen. *Id.* at 91–92. However, we do not agree that *Aer Lingus* applies in the instant matter. The Treaty of Friendship, Commerce and Navigation between the United States and Ireland provided for "national treatment with respect to ... having access to the courts of justice." *Id.* at 91 (internal quotation marks and citation omitted). In contrast, the national treatment provision of the Berne Convention contains no such language. We are confident that the inclusion of the quoted language in the Treaty with Ireland was not superfluous, and its omission in the Berne Convention was no oversight. When drafters of international agreements seek to provide equal access to national courts, the long-established practice is to do so explicitly. The United States first concluded a treaty with such a provision in 1775, Robert R. Wilson, *Access-to-Courts Provisions in United States Commercial Treaties,* 47 Am. J. Int'l L. 20, 33 (1953), and explicit "access to courts" clauses appear regularly in treaties to which the United States is a signatory. Indeed, over a dozen treaties have included such language since 1990. * * *

History and practice thus teach that a principle of equal access must be explicitly adopted. In the absence of such an explicit provision in the Berne Convention, we cannot construe a simple declaration of "national treatment" to imply such a principle and to extend *Aer Lingus* and cases following it to this case. * * *

Murray seeks to bolster his argument by resort to the legislative history of the Berne Convention Implementation Act of 1988. He relies chiefly on House Report Number 609, 100th Cong., 2d Sess. (1988), *reprinted in* 6 *Nimmer on Copyright,* Appendix 32, which states that "[w]hatever restrictions or procedures are imposed on foreign nationals must also be imposed on the citizens of the country where protection is claimed." *Id.* at App. 32–43. However, the House report cannot bear the weight Murray places on it. The discussion in question concerns only the issue of whether the Convention invalidates the procedural registration requirements of the pre-Berne Convention Copyright Act, in particular the 17 U.S.C. § 411(a) requirement that a copyright owner must seek registration of a copyright as a prerequisite to an action for infringement. The discussion has no bearing on the application of the doctrine of *forum non conveniens.*

There is, therefore, little support for Murray's position in the legislative history relied upon, and we conclude that the district court correctly accorded Murray's choice of forum less deference than that given to domestic plaintiffs.

2. *Existence of an Alternative Forum*

When addressing a motion to dismiss for *forum non conveniens,* a court must determine whether an alternative forum is available, because application of the doctrine "presupposes at least two forums in which the defendant is amenable to process." *Gilbert,* 330 U.S. at 506–07, 67 S.Ct. at 842. The requirement of an alternative forum is ordinarily satisfied if the defendant is amenable to process in another jurisdiction, except in "rare circumstances" when "the remedy offered by the other forum is clearly unsatisfactory." *Piper Aircraft,* 454 U.S. at 254 n. 22, 102 S.Ct. at 265 n. 22 (dismissal would not be appropriate where the alternative forum does not recognize the cause of action). The BBC can obviously be sued in the United Kingdom. Murray argues, however, that he is financially unable to litigate this dispute in England because a contingent-fee arrangement is not permitted in this kind of case. In his view, this professed inability to bring suit renders the English forum unavailable as a matter of law. We review this legal issue *de novo* but disagree with Murray.

There is a division of authority on whether financial hardships facing a plaintiff in an alternative forum as a result of the absence of contingent fee arrangements may cause a forum to be deemed unavailable. *Compare Rudetsky v. O'Dowd,* 660 F.Supp. 341, 346 (E.D.N.Y.1987) ("[t]he lack of a contingency fee system ... does not constitute one of those [rare] circumstances") *with McKrell v. Penta Hotels*, 703 F.Supp. 13, 14 (S.D.N.Y.1989) (denying motion to reject magistrate's report which concluded that alternative forum was not available in part because it had no contingent-fee system). The majority of courts deem a plaintiff's financial hardships resulting from the absence of contingent fee arrangements to be only one factor to be weighed in determining the balance of convenience *after* the court determines that an alternative forum is available. *See Coakes v. Arabian American Oil Co.*, 831 F.2d 572, 575 (5th Cir. 1987) (plaintiff pointing to absence of contingent fee system "cannot actually argue that England is not an available, alternate forum" because defendant is amenable to process there); *Kryvicky v. Scandinavian Airlines Sys.*, 807 F.2d 514, 517 (6th Cir. 1986) (holding that financial burden on plaintiff "is only one factor used in the balancing process, and it alone would not bar dismissal based on *forum non conveniens*"); *Reid-Walen v. Hansen*, 933 F.2d 1390, 1393 n. 2 & 1398 (8th Cir. 1991) (as part of analysis of private interests favoring or counseling against dismissal, court must consider practical problems, financial and otherwise, encountered by plaintiffs) (citing *Rudetsky*, 660 F.Supp. at 346).

We agree with the majority rule. Balancing the plaintiff's financial burdens as one of several relevant factors serves the "repeatedly emphasized ... need to retain flexibility" in the application of the *forum non conveniens* doctrine. *Piper Aircraft*, 454 U.S. at 249, 102 S.Ct. at 262. Indeed, to do otherwise would render the financial burden on a plaintiff the "determinative factor," *Coakes*, 831 F.2d at 575, notwithstanding overwhelming public and private interests weighing in favor of dismissal of the American action. Such a result would ignore the Supreme Court's admonition that "[i]f central emphasis [is] placed on any one factor, the *forum non conveniens* doctrine would lose much of the very flexibility that makes it so valuable." *Piper Aircraft*, 454 U.S. at 249–50, 102 S.Ct. at 263. As the Fifth Circuit has noted, "[i]f the lack of a contingent-fee system were held determinative, then a case could almost never be dismissed because contingency fees are not allowed in most foreign forums." *Coakes*, 831 F.2d at 576.* * * We therefore conclude that Murray's claim of financial hardship may not be considered in determining the *availability* of an alternative forum but must be deferred to the balancing of interests relating to the forum's convenience.

3. *The Balancing of Interests*

Once the court has identified an alternative forum, it must proceed to balance public and private interests to determine whether the convenience of the parties and the ends of justice would best be served by dismissing the action. *See Gilbert*, 330 U.S. at 508–09, 67 S.Ct. at 843. We review the district court's balancing of interests for abuse of discretion. *See Piper Aircraft*, 454 U.S. at 257, 102 S.Ct. at 266.

The public interest factors enumerated in *Gilbert* and summarized in *Piper Aircraft* include: the administrative difficulties flowing from court congestion; the local interest in having controversies decided at home; the interest in having the trial in a forum that is familiar with the law governing the action; the avoidance of unnecessary problems in conflict of laws or in the application of foreign law; and the unfairness of burdening citizens in an unrelated forum with jury duty. *Piper Aircraft,* 454 U.S. at 241 n. 6, 102 S.Ct. at 258 n. 6 (citing *Gilbert,* 330 U.S. at 509, 67 S.Ct. at 843).

Murray argues that two public interest factors weigh strongly in favor of permitting his American action to go forward. First, he argues that American copyright law will apply to his copyright infringement claims arising in the United States, militating in favor of an American forum. Murray argues second that the district court erroneously failed to acknowledge that the United States has localized interests in this controversy: the "obvious interest in securing compliance with this nation's laws by citizens of foreign nations who have dealings within this jurisdiction," *London Film Productions Ltd. v. Intercontinental Communications, Inc.,* 580 F.Supp. 47, 49 (S.D.N.Y.1984), and an interest in whether Mr. Blobby merchandise will be available for sale in the United States. Once again, we disagree.

We are, quite frankly, at a loss to see how this lawsuit has any but the most attenuated American connection. The central issue in dispute concerns the circumstances surrounding the creation of Mr. Blobby. Once that dispute is resolved, the right to exploit the character will be quickly resolved. The crux of the matter, therefore, involves a dispute between British citizens over events that took place exclusively in the United Kingdom. Moreover, it appears that much of the dispute over the creation of Mr. Blobby implicates contract law. British law governs those issues. The United States thus has virtually no interest in resolving the truly disputed issues.

The Berne Convention's national treatment principle insures that no matter where Murray brings his claim, United States copyright law would apply to exploitation of the character in this country. *See supra.* We therefore see little chance that the United States' interest in the application of its laws would be ill-served by a lawsuit in an English forum. Murray makes a great deal of the need to bring additional litigation in the United States to enforce his copyright if this matter is dismissed in favor of an English forum. However, he has offered no reason why his action against the American licensees of Mr. Blobby, currently pending in the Southern District of New York, *see supra,* may not be placed on the suspense calendar pending a resolution of the truly disputed issues in the English courts. Again, once those issues are resolved, everything else will fall into place. * * *

Finally, we note that the forum in which actual infringement of Murray's putative copyright has occurred is not the United States but England. It appears that no Mr. Blobby products have yet been produced for the American market. In virtually all respects, the connection of this case to the United States is as tenuous as its connection to the United

Kingdom is strong. We therefore hold that the district court did not abuse its discretion in finding that the public interest factors militated in favor of dismissal.

We turn now to the balancing of private interests. The relevant private interests set forth in *Gilbert* include the relative ease of access to sources of proof; the availability of compulsory process for attendance of unwilling witnesses; the cost of obtaining attendance of willing witnesses; and all other practical problems that make trial of a case easy, expeditious, and inexpensive—or the opposite. Issues concerning the enforceability of a judgment should also be considered. 330 U.S. at 508, 67 S.Ct. at 843.

Murray's challenge to the district court's balancing of private interest factors is largely directed at Judge Stanton's conclusion that the financial "difficulties Murray may encounter in litigating in England are not sufficiently severe" to tip the private interest inquiry in Murray's favor. *Murray,* 906 F.Supp. at 865. We note first that the unavailability of contingent fee arrangements in England is of little weight in the present matter. The availability of such arrangements in the United States is based on a policy decision regarding the assertion of rights in American courts where the parties or the claims have some tangible connection with this country. The decision to permit contingent fee arrangements was not designed to suck foreign parties disputing foreign claims over foreign events into American courts. There is, therefore, no American policy regarding contingent fees that weighs in favor of resolving the underlying dispute over the rights to Mr. Blobby in an American court.

In any event, we agree with Judge Stanton's conclusion that Murray's financial condition is less severe than those that have previously justified retention of litigation in an otherwise inconvenient forum. *Id.,* 906 F.Supp. at 864. Murray mischaracterizes that conclusion by arguing that the district court implicitly and erroneously held that a plaintiff must be "destitute" before losing the ability to litigate in a foreign forum. Judge Stanton merely surveyed the caselaw and sensibly observed that plaintiffs found to be unable to litigate in a foreign forum "generally ha[ve] a much lower income and fewer assets than Murray." *Id.*

We are also unpersuaded by Murray's argument that his financial condition poses insurmountable barriers to litigation in England. For the calendar year ending October 31, 1992, Murray had total pre-tax personal income, after business expenses, of 46,066 pounds sterling and 57,515 pounds sterling for the year ending October 31, 1993, with an estimated 1994 pre-tax income of approximately 45,000 pounds sterling. *Id.* Moreover, we cannot disturb the district court's factual finding that Murray is "credit-worthy." *Id.* Murray has referred us to no case holding that a plaintiff in a similar financial position was financially unable to litigate. In the absence of such authority, we are not prepared to hold that the district court was in error in concluding that Murray is "not of such limited means that the English prohibition on contingent-fee arrangements would prevent him from pursuing his claim." *Id.*

There is no merit in Murray's objections to the district court's balancing of the remaining private interest factors. Murray suggests that the defendants have strained to "pad" their list of English witnesses, raising false issues and naming witnesses who are irrelevant or peripheral to whether he possesses a copyright in Mr. Blobby. This characterization is in fact a caricature that vastly oversimplifies the issues in this case, which entail all the details of his relationship with the BBC and of the creative efforts and contribution of ideas by him and others. Indeed, it appears that Murray himself discarded design drawings prepared during the construction of the Mr. Blobby costume. As the district court found, therefore, the testimony of "Noel's House Party" personnel and the assistants in Murray's studio will be crucial in determining the relative contributions of Murray and the BBC staff. *Id.* Nor can we agree with Murray that numerous witnesses on the appellees' witness list, claimed by appellees to be relevant to the existence of equitable ownership or an implied license to use Mr. Blobby, are in fact unnecessary. Murray has failed to convince us that appellees' equitable ownership claim is frivolous, and trial of this claim will require the testimony of English witnesses. In addition, a major issue in this action concerns the terms of the contract between Murray and the BBC. To the extent that this inquiry necessarily includes within its ambit the scope of any implied license to exploit Mr. Blobby, these issues also require testimony from English witnesses concerning the parties' contractual intent. In short, the district court in no way abused its discretion in finding that the location of witnesses weighed heavily in favor of appellees.

With respect to the location of documentary and physical evidence, Judge Stanton concluded that virtually all of it is located in England. *Id.* at 863. Murray disputes this, arguing that the burden on the appellees of trying the case in the United States was "greatly overstated" by the district court. We do not agree. First, as Judge Stanton found, appellees might be unable to compel third parties in England to produce documents—specifically, telephone records and documents evidencing Murray's course of dealings with customers other than the BBC—for a trial in the United States. In addition, we note that Judge Stanton conceded that "it would not be overly burdensome for the defendants to transport that [documentary] evidence, which consists of a moderate number of documents, notebooks, drawings, costumes, and props, to the United States." *Id.* He found, however, that the possibility that appellees might not be able to compel third parties located in England to produce documents tipped in favor of appellees. *Id.* We do not think that Judge Stanton overstated the burden on appellees. We therefore hold that he did not abuse his discretion in finding that the location of proof preponderated in favor of the BBC. Thus, all of the relevant private interest factors favor appellees.* * *

We therefore affirm.

Note

1. Reality television has been exported and shared abroad. See, for example, Patsy Crawford, *Box Office: Behind The Scenes—Movie Gossip: What Goes On When The Cameras Stop Rolling,* Independent on Sunday (London) March 9, 2003, who writes:

As the contestants of any reality TV show will tell you, there is no limit to what some people will do for their 15 minutes of fame. And no one knows this better than Johnny Knoxville * * *, the man who shocked America with stunts ranging from the ridiculous to the extremely dangerous in *Jackass: The Movie.* Disaster is never far off when Knoxville is around—he was hospitalized twice during filming when stunts went wrong. Needless to say, members of the film's crew were regularly picked up by the police for doing things like stapling their scrotum to their thighs and pretending to hold up banks, while guns were pulled on Knoxville himself when he was spotted dressed in an orange prison jumpsuit, pretending to saw off his handcuffs. Strangely, it's not their tasteless pranks that have landed the film's owners in hot water: a man named Jack Ass has filed a law suit against Viacom Inc. Mr. Ass changed his name from Bob Craft in late 1997 and is now suing for "defamation of character". Meanwhile, Jet Li is back with some serious stunt action in Cradle 2 The Grave. Unlike Knoxville, Li secured his 15 minutes of fame a long time ago and had a professional stunt man on set to help him with his butt-kicking moves. *Id.*

C. GLOBALIZATION OF THE MUSIC INDUSTRY

RICHARD FEINER AND CO., INC.
v. BMG MUSIC SPAIN, S.A.

United States District Court, Southern District of New York, 2003.
2003 WL 740605.

RAKOFF, U.S. District Judge.

* * * The works here in question consist of a compact disc recording of the soundtrack from the movie Marjorie Morningstar, along with accompanying cover art from the film. As the Court stated at the February 15, 2002 hearing, the undisputed facts of record establish beyond genuine dispute that the defendants' predecessor-in-interest, Radio Corporation of America ("RCA"), produced all the sound recordings here in issue except for the recording of the song "A Very Precious Love." While plaintiff contends that Warner Brothers (plaintiff's predecessor-in-interest) acquired the copyrights, under the work-for-hire doctrine, because the recording producer, Ray Heindorf, was an employee of Warner Brothers, the recording contract, dated March 18, 1958, between Ray Heindorf and RCA, unequivocally provides that the recordings are being made for RCA, not Warner.

Accordingly, defendants are entitled to summary judgment as to all sound recordings except the recording of "A Very Precious Love." As to the latter, however, triable issues still remain precluding summary judgment for either side. * * *

Turning, finally, to the musical compositions, defendants acknowledge that they do not possess an ownership interest in these compositions, but instead contend that this Court lacks subject matter jurisdiction to consider any infringement of plaintiff's rights that may have occurred. Specifically, defendants argue that even assuming, arguendo, that their production of compact discs containing the Marjorie Morningstar soundtrack was a copyright infringement, the fact that all of the discs at issue were produced in compliance with Spanish licensing laws for sale in Europe means that only Spanish law governs and that United States copyright law should not be here extended extraterritorially to govern as well. * * *

However, while the United States copyright regime does not generally have extraterritorial application, *see id.*, an exception exists where the defendant commits a predicate act of infringement within the U.S. *See id.* at 73. Here, it cannot be determined at this stage whether or not that exception applies. While defendant BMG Spain produced the allegedly infringing discs in Spain and sold the entirety to a Spanish corporation for European distribution, it is alleged that BMG Spain was able to produce discs only by first copying a master copy of the recordings from the New York offices of co-defendant Berteslsmann Music Group, Inc., which was then utilized in the Spanish production. In addition, disputed issues of fact remain as to what portion of the Spanish production, if any, found their way to the U.S. market, and, more generally, as to the extent if any, of plaintiff's damages.

For the foregoing reasons, while plaintiff's summary judgment motion is denied in its entirety, defendants' cross motion is granted except as to the alleged infringement of (a) the musical composition copyrights in the sound track songs and (b) the sound recording copyright of "A Very Precious Love."

ARMSTRONG v. VIRGIN RECORDS, LTD.

United States District Court, Southern District of New York, 2000.
91 F.Supp.2d 628.

SWEET, District Judge.

* * * Armstrong is a professional entertainer and well-regarded jazz musician, as well as a college music professor. In the 1970's, he made various recordings with an ensemble known as the Mahavishnu Orchestra.

Massive Attack is a musical group whose members are British citizens residing in the United Kingdom. In 1990, Massive Attack recorded an album entitled "Blue Lines" ("the album" or "Blue Lines") in England pursuant to a recording agreement with Virgin UK, a corporation organized under the laws of the United Kingdom. Virgin UK's principal offices are located in London.

One of the tracks on "Blue Lines" was a recording of a musical composition entitled "Unfinished Sympathy" ("Unfinished Sympathy" or "the song"). That composition was credited as being written by the members of Massive Attack, as well as two other individuals, J. Sharp ("Sharp") and S. Nelson ("Nelson"). Neither Sharp nor Nelson is a party to this action. Island, a United Kingdom corporation with its principal offices in London, obtained worldwide copyrights for Massive Attack's compositions, including "Unfinished Sympathy."

The "Blue Lines" album was released in 1991 by Virgin UK in England and Ireland. Under an agreement between Virgin UK and EMI Services, which is not a party to this action, the master recordings embodied on "Blue Lines" were in turn licensed by EMI Services to other companies around the world for manufacturing and distribution. EMI Services ultimately licensed defendant Virgin America to manufacture and distribute the album in the United States.

In addition to the licenses concerning master recordings of the album, mechanical licenses were also obtained to enable exploitation of the compositions contained on "Blue Lines." Virgin UK obtained a mechanical license for "Unfinished Sympathy" from the Mechanical Copyright Protection Society ("MCPS"), which acted on behalf of Island. Virgin America obtained a mechanical license from The Harry Fox Agency ("Fox") on behalf of Songs of Polygram International, Inc. ("Songs of Polygram") and WB Music Co. ("WB"), two of the subpublishers of the composition in the United States. Virgin America's right to manufacture and distribute "Blue Lines" was to be limited to the United States and its territories and possessions.

Subsequent to its release on "Blue Lines," "Unfinished Sympathy" enjoyed significant success. In 1993, "Unfinished Sympathy" was included in the motion picture "Sliver," which featured actress Sharon Stone, as well as on the soundtrack album of that film. The "Sliver" soundtrack album subsequently achieved "gold" record status, due to its brisk sales in the United States.

As with "Blue Lines," the "Sliver" soundtrack album was released in the United Kingdom and Ireland by Virgin UK, and in the United States by Virgin America. Mechanical licenses were issued in the United Kingdom and Ireland by MCPS, on behalf of Island, and in the United States by Fox, on behalf of the United States publishers of the composition.

Additionally, in 1996, defendant Leagas Delaney ("Delaney") licensed "Unfinished Sympathy" for use in a television commercial it ultimately produced for defendant adidas America ("adidas").

On July 1, 1998, Armstrong filed his complaint in this action, alleging three causes of action: (1) a claim for copyright infringement under the Copyright Act; (2) a claim for infringement under unspecified "international" copyrights; and (3) a Lanham Act claim against all defendants other than adidas and Leagas Delaney. More specifically, Armstrong alleged that Massive Attack's recording of "Unfinished Sympathy" contains an infringing sample from a composition recorded by the Mahavishnu Orchestra on its 1978 album "Inner Worlds." According to Armstrong, that composition, entitled "Planetary Citizen," was created and written by Armstrong prior to 1975. * * *

The principal questions presented are (1) whether subject matter jurisdiction could exist over Armstrong's copyright claims, both foreign and domestic; (2) whether this Court could possess personal jurisdiction over defendants Island and Virgin UK; (3) whether any or all of Armstrong's claims under domestic copyright law are necessarily barred by the relevant statute of limitations; (4) whether Armstrong's claims could be barred by the equitable defenses of laches, waiver, or estoppel; and (5) whether Armstrong's Lanham Act claim can withstand challenge. * * *

It is worth noting at the outset that both Armstrong and the defendants have, at points, noted that formal discovery has yet to commence in this action, and that this failure to obtain discovery prevents resolution of certain of the matters presently before the Court. Predictably, the parties make this point at certain junctures but not others, depending upon the claim being made.

As discussed below, this failure to obtain discovery prior to engaging in motion practice has rendered the moving parties' respective motions of questionable utility. Other than granting the Virgin/Island and EMI Group Defendants' request to dismiss Armstrong's Lanham Act claim, the Court denies the motions in all respects. * * *

More difficult to untangle are the parties' contentions concerning this Court's subject matter jurisdiction over Armstrong's copyright claims.

The parties in this action have made a variety of arguments concerning the applicability of United States copyright law to defendants and/or acts of infringement located abroad, as well as concerning the applicability of foreign copyright law to infringements committed abroad, some of which have tended to confuse the issues at play with respect to subject matter jurisdiction. Armstrong's complaint asserts causes of action under both domestic and foreign copyright law. These claims are governed by distinct legal regimes.

I.   Subject Matter Jurisdiction Over Claims Asserted Under the Copyright Act

As a general principle, it is not seriously disputed that United States copyright laws do not have extraterritorial effect, and that infringing acts that take place entirely outside of the United States are not actionable under our copyright laws. *See Richard Feiner & Co. v. Turner Entertainment Co.*, 1998 U.S. Dist. LEXIS 1947, No. 96 Civ. 1472(RO), 1998 WL 78180, at *1 (S.D.N.Y. Feb. 24, 1998). * * *

As with all general principles and broad pronouncements, however, there are exceptions. Under established precedent, for example, a claim under United States law may arise for acts of infringement committed abroad where those acts are permitted or initiated by predicate acts of infringement within the United States. *See Update Art, Inc. v. Modiin Pub., Ltd.*, 843 F.2d 67, 73 (2d Cir. 1988). * * * For example, the unauthorized manufacture of infringing goods within the United States for subsequent sale abroad may give rise to a cause of action under the Copyright Act, even where the actual sale and distribution of infringing goods occurs outside of the United States proper. *See Update Art*, 843 F.2d at 72.

Moreover, while no longer authoritative, a number of older cases held that a United States court has subject matter jurisdiction under our nation's copyright laws when a defendant "authorizes" another to commit infringing acts, notwithstanding the fact that such acts are committed abroad. *See Peter Starr Prod. Co. v. Twin Continental Films, Inc.*, 783 F.2d 1440, 1443 (9th Cir. 1986); *ITSI T.V. Prods., Inc. v. California Auth. of Racing Fairs*, 785 F. Supp. 854, 862 (E.D. Cal. 1992), aff'd in part, rev'd in part, 3 F.3d 1289 (9th Cir. 1993). This line of cases has been subsequently repudiated, and it is now generally accepted that there can be no liability under the Copyright Act for authorizing an act that itself could not constitute infringement of rights secured by United States law. *See Subafilms, Ltd. v. MGM–Pathe Communications Co.*, 24 F.3d 1088, 1093–94 (9th Cir. 1994); *see also Fun–Damental Too*, 1996 WL 724734, at *6 (holding that "mere authorization and approval of copyright infringements taking place outside the United States is not a copyright violation and does not create jurisdiction over those extraterritorial acts").

However, as the Virgin/Island Defendants have correctly observed in their papers, the flow of events in this case does not parallel that of Update Art and its progeny. See Update Art, 843 F.2d at 73 ("As the applicability of American copyright laws over the Israeli newspapers depends on the occurrence of a predicate act in the United States, the geographic location of the illegal reproduction is crucial. If the illegal reproduction of the poster occurred in the United States and then was exported to Israel, the magistrate properly could include damages accruing from the Israeli newspapers. If * * * this predicate act occurred in Israel, American copyright laws would have no application. . . ."). * * * Given the record presented and Armstrong's allegations, no predicate acts of infringement would appear to have occurred within the United States that could justify application of United States copyright law to subsequent acts of infringement undertaken in the United Kingdom or beyond. Rather, even when crediting Armstrong's claims of infringement, it would seem that our unfolding story of infringement begins abroad, with the composition, distribution, and licensing of "Blue Lines" in Great Britain. Insofar as subject matter jurisdiction is concerned, however, United States copyright law cannot be applied to wholly foreign acts of infringement merely because foreign infringement will have adverse effects within the United States. Consequently, to the extent that Armstrong seeks to recover for alleged acts of infringement solely committed abroad, such as the distribution and sale of "Blue Lines" albums in the United Kingdom, he could not obtain such recovery under our copyright laws.

This is not the end of the story, however.

A defendant in an infringement action may be held liable for acts of infringement if that defendant is either contributorily or vicariously liable for another's direct act of infringement. Where those acts of infringement occur within the United States and a plaintiff seeks to hold a foreign defendant contributorily or vicariously liable for those acts, it has been held that subject matter jurisdiction may exist, and that the exercise thereof does not conflict with the doctrine of nonextraterritoriality. See *Blue Ribbon Pet Prods., Inc. v. Rolf C. Hagen (USA) Corp.*, 66 F.Supp.2d 454, 461–63 (E.D.N.Y. 1999); *Stewart v. Adidas A.G.*, 1997 U.S. Dist. LEXIS 5778, No. 96 Civ. 6670(DLC), 1997 WL 218431, at *3 (S.D.N.Y. Apr. 30, 1997); *GB Marketing USA Inc. v. Gerolsteiner Brunnen GmbH & Co.*, 782 F.Supp. 763, 773 (W.D.N.Y. 1991); *c.f. Metzke*, 878 F.Supp. at 760 (holding, despite defendant's claim that it could not be held liable for infringing acts of third-parties, that defendant could be held liable for foreign third party's infringement "if it knew or should have known that [third party] Maru Fung's copies of Ms. Metzke's designs would be distributed by non-May retailers in the United States."). As the Honorable Lawrence K. Karlton held in ITSI T.V. Productions, "to satisfy the jurisdictional requirement that the defendant commit an act of infringement in the United States, the plaintiff must show only that the direct act of infringement for which defendant is contributorily or vicariously liable occurred in the United States." 785 F.Supp. at 864. As Judge Karlton noted, merely because the situs of a particular defendant's activities is located abroad does not prevent the court from exercising subject matter jurisdiction over claims brought under United States law:

> Plaintiff need not show that defendant's acts which give rise to contributory or vicarious liability occurred in the United States. Such a requirement is not mandated by the doctrine of nonextraterritoriality and would confound the questions of subject matter and personal jurisdiction. Subject matter jurisdiction requires the court to determine whether a claim actionable in this court has been stated; personal jurisdiction requires the court to determine whether a particular defendant has sufficient contacts with the forum state to permit the court to exercise power over that defendant. Put another way, it is possible for a defendant to commit acts outside the United States sufficient to find it contributorily or vicariously liable for acts of infringement committed by others within the United States, but the defendant's conduct might not be sufficient to permit the court to exercise personal jurisdiction over the defendants.

Thus, to the extent that any of the foreign defendants in this action could be found contributorily or vicariously liable for acts of subsequent infringement within the United States, this Court would possess subject matter jurisdiction over Armstrong's Copyright Act claims against those defendants.

As the Second Circuit has held, "one who, with knowledge of the infringing activity, induces, causes or materially contributes to the infringing conduct of another, may be held liable as a 'contributory' infringer." *Gershwin Publ'g Corp. v. Columbia Artists Management, Inc.*, 443 F.2d 1159, 1162 (2d Cir. 1971); *see Cable/Home Communication Corp. v. Network Prods.*, 902 F.2d 829, 845 (11th Cir. 1990). It is, of course, an open question whether Armstrong could make such a showing concerning those defendants located in the United Kingdom. In evaluating claims of contributory infringement under analogous circumstances, for example, courts have often looked to the relationship between the defendants, as well as to the alleged contributory infringer's level of awareness concerning the infringing nature of the protected materials distributed or sold within the United States. *See ITSI T.V. Prods.*, 785 F.Supp. at 866. * * *

II.   SUBJECT MATTER JURISDICTION OVER CLAIMS ASSERTED UNDER FOREIGN COPYRIGHT LAW(S)

The parties have also jousted over Armstrong's ability to recover from the defendants based upon "international" copyright law. At times, it has appeared unclear whether Armstrong premises his claims upon violations of copyrights he claims to possesses in other fora, or whether his claims are premised upon the infringement, under the laws of other nations, of his alleged United States copyright.

To be sure, Armstrong's second cause of action is not a model of clarity. Nevertheless, to the extent that Armstrong alleges that some or all of the defendants in this action committed violations of foreign copyright laws, summary judgment would not be appropriate in favor of either Armstrong or the Virgin/Island Defendants.

The question presented is whether, if any of the defendants committed acts of infringement abroad actionable under the laws of foreign nations, this Court may exercise subject matter jurisdiction over such claims, not whether it is advisable, convenient, or wise to hear such claims. Moreover, whether or not various foreign defendants are amenable to suit within this district does not affect the Court's inquiry with respect to subject matter jurisdiction. It is, after all, possible for a court to have subject matter jurisdiction over a particular set of claims, but not personal jurisdiction over a particular defendant.

While certain courts have, at times, demonstrated their reluctance to "enter the bramble bush of ascertaining and applying foreign law without an urgent reason to do so," *see ITSI T.V. Prods.*, 785 F.Supp. at 866, there is no principled reason to bar, in absolute fashion, copyright claims brought under foreign law for lack of subject matter jurisdiction. Not only is this Court called upon to enter bramble bushes, briar patches, and other thorny legal thickets on a routine basis, *see, e.g., Briarpatch Ltd. v. Pate*, 81 F.Supp. 2d 509, 511 (S.D.N.Y. 2000), but a number of persuasive authorities and commentators have also indicated that the exercise of subject matter jurisdiction is appropriate in cases of transnational copyright infringement. *See London Film Prods. Ltd. v. Intercontinental Communic.*, 580 F.Supp. 47, 48–50 (S.D.N.Y. 1984). As Professor Nimmer has explained: Even if the United State Copyright Act is clearly inoperative with respect to acts occurring outside of its jurisdiction, it does not necessarily follow that American courts are without [subject matter] jurisdiction in such a case. If the plaintiff has a valid cause of action under the copyright laws of a foreign country, and if personal jurisdiction of the defendant can be obtained in an American court, it is arguable that an action may be brought in such court for infringement of a foreign copyright law. This would be on a theory that copyright infringement constitutes a transitory cause of action, and hence, may be adjudicated in the courts of a sovereign other than the one in which the cause of action arose. 3 Nimmer § 17.03. * * *

In the present case, this Court would unquestionably have subject matter jurisdiction over any claims properly arising under United States copyright law, potentially allowing the Court to exercise pendent jurisdiction over claims arising under foreign law. Moreover, there would appeal to be complete diversity as among the parties to this action.

There is therefore no reason to believe, at this point, that this Court would be absolutely foreclosed from applying foreign law to Armstrong's claims of infringement. Whether a court has personal jurisdiction over a particular foreign defendant is, of course, a different matter, as is whether or not a United States court is the appropriate forum for asserting copyright claims under foreign law. * * **

III. PERSONAL JURISDICTION OVER DEFENDANTS ISLAND AND VIRGIN UK

In their papers, the Virgin/Island Defendants suggest that this Court lacks personal jurisdiction over Island and Virgin UK because it is undisputed that both are United Kingdom companies that neither solicit business nor maintain bank accounts, offices, or employees in the United States. These defendants also claim that Virgin UK and Island have not transacted business in the United States, and would not be subject to New York's "long-arm" statute.

However, it is not altogether clear that these defendants' status as United Kingdom corporations, or the fact that they did not maintain a formal presence in New York, necessarily shields them from suit in the United States. Jurisdiction over these foreign defendants may well depend on the nature of their licensing activities, as well as their business relationship(s) with domestic entities accused of infringement. *See Mattel, Inc. v. MCA Records, Inc.*, 28 F.Supp.2d 1120, 1127–28 (C.D. Cal. 1998). * * *

Furthermore, at least one court within this district has held that a foreign defendant's vicarious or contributory liability for the infringing acts of another within the United States may give rise to long-arm jurisdiction under New York law. To be sure, not every licensing agreement concerning allegedly infringing material will automatically subject a foreign licensor to jurisdiction in the New York courts. However, courts have found foreign corporations accused of copyright violations to be within the personal jurisdiction of United States courts, even where those entities did not themselves commit acts of infringement within the United States. *See Larball*, 664 F.Supp. at 708.

As Armstrong has noted in opposing the Virgin/Island Defendants' motion, discovery has yet to be obtained from the defendants in this action. Moreover, as with many of the issues presented by the parties' motions, the showing required of Armstrong is highly dependant upon facts concerning the corporate structure, distribution practices, and business dealings of the defendants. These are facts that Armstrong is entitled to make efforts to obtain, and it would be improper to dismiss this action without affording him the opportunity to do so. Consequently, the Virgin/Island Defendants' motion for summary judgment is denied to the extent that it seeks a ruling that Island or Virgin UK are unamenable to suit in the United States. Leave is granted to renew that motion at the close of discovery in this action.

IV.   APPLICATION OF THE STATUTE OF LIMITATIONS

The statute of limitations applicable to copyright infringement actions is contained in 17 U.S.C. § 507(b) ("Section 507(b)"), which provides that "no civil action shall be maintained under the provisions of this title unless it is commenced within three years after the claim accrued." 17 U.S.C. § 507(b).

In his papers, Armstrong contends that he is entitled to summary judgment dismissing the defendants' statute of limitations defenses, asserting that his claims for infringement only "accrued" once he "learned that Unfinished Sympathy included a wrongful use of his musical work." According to Armstrong, he only became aware of the use of his copyrighted material in April of 1996, when he had occasion to see an adidas commercial during a baseball game. According to Armstrong, the commercial contained an unauthorized sampling of his copyrighted musical work, and he promptly engaged an attorney to protect his intellectual property rights. Because his Complaint was filed less than three years thereafter, Armstrong asserts that he is entitled to recover for infringement claims that would otherwise be time-barred.

Not unexpectedly, this position has not remained unchallenged by a number of defendants, who have claimed that (1) Armstrong's claim accrued earlier than he asserts, either at the initiation of allegedly infringing activity or at various points prior to 1996; and/or (2) notwithstanding the accrual date of Armstrong's claims, he is only entitled to recover damages for those infringing acts committed within three years of suit.

For the purposes of copyright law, a claim accrues when the plaintiff knew or should have known of the infringement. *See Stone v. Williams*, 970 F.2d 1043, 1048 (2d Cir. 1992). * * * Ordinarily the statute of limitations begins to run when the plaintiff has knowledge of, or with reasonable diligence should have discovered, the critical facts of infringement. * * * However, if it is assumed for the sake of argument that the accrual date of Armstrong's claims was, in fact, April of 1996, then the differences between a statute of limitations and an absolute limitation of liability are apparent. Unlike the standard case where infringing acts straddle the limitations period and the earlier acts are time-barred, with Section 507(b) applied to allow suit only over those acts of infringement occurring within three years of suit, accepting Armstrong's position with respect to the initial accrual date of his copyright claims would mean that even the earlier acts of infringement could form the basis for valid infringement claims. Indeed, counting back from the date of suit would therefore be unnecessary and unwarranted, because recovery could be predicated upon events occurring between 1991 and July of 1995—notwithstanding the fact that such events occurred more than three years prior to Armstrong's initiation of this action.

Thus, to the extent that the defendants request that this Court impose an interpretive gloss on Section 507(b) delimiting a plaintiff's recovery of damages to those damages occurring within three years of suit for copyright infringement, notwithstanding the initial accrual date of a plaintiff's claims or any other tolling of the limitations period, the Court declines the invitation.

Because the Court finds that the defendants' statute of limitations defenses do not lend themselves to summary disposition, the Court therefore denies Armstrong's motion for summary judgment dismissing the defendants' statute of limitations-based defenses, as well as the moving defendants' reciprocal motions. * * **

CONCLUSION

For the reasons set forth above, the motions presently under consideration are granted in part and denied in part, and Armstrong's Lanham Act claim is dismissed. It is so ordered.

Notes

1.   Can reissuing musical works that are in the public domain in one country create problems for a foreign company? *See* Howard C. Anawalt, *International Distribution of Intellectual Property Protected Works in the United states, In Japan, and in the Future*, 18 SANTA CLARA COMP. & HIGH TECH. L. J. 207 (2003) (discussing Bridgeman Art Library, Ltd. v. Corel Corp., 25 F.Supp.2d 421 (S.D.N.Y. 1998) ("the plaintiff was an English company that marketed faithful reproductions of public domain works through the media of transparencies and CD ROMs. The trial court granted the defendant's motion to dismiss, and in a second proceeding reaffirmed that order. * * * The basis of the dismissal was that under United States law, a mere reproduction of a public domain work does not have sufficient originality to qualify for protection.")).

2.   The International Federal Phonographic Industry (IFPI) is a global watchdog organization with over 1500 members in 76 countries. In a speech

before the House Committee on International Relations on July 16, 2003, IFPI's Head of Enforcement, Iain Grant, called music piracy a type of terrorism backed by organized crime. Grant estimated the global music piracy market to be worth between four and five billion U.S. dollars each year, and that organized crime is "firmly entrenched" in this area of criminality. "The majority of music piracy is not down to 'mom and pop' operations working out of the family garage. * * * I believe organized criminal elements to be involved in the greater percentage of physical music piracy either at the manufacture or distribution stages. The advent of the compact disc clearly accelerated this phenomenon as it provided the pirate with the ability to produce near perfect illegal recordings in their millions and the recent developmental of cheap recordable optical discs has created another means of mass illegal duplication. The situation is exacerbated by the global optical disc manufacturing capacity massively exceeding legitimate demand, creating an international business environment ripe for exploitation by criminal syndicates." *See* wwwa.house.gov/INTERNATIONAL–RELATIONS/108/Grant.pdf.

3.   The global epidemic in music piracy has hit countries as diverse as Italy and Egypt. In 2001, the pirate music market in Italy was reportedly valued at $121 million, placing Italy in sixth place worldwide in terms of piracy. Jay Berman, chairman and CEO of IFPI said: "Italy has a rich and vibrant musical culture, but the value of this music is being undermined by piracy on a massive scale. Despite increased efforts by the Italian police to tackle this problem, the fact remains that pirate CD's are still sold everywhere in the streets. Even when prosecutions do reach the courts, pirates often get off much too lightly." *See* www.ifpi.org/site-content/press/20021008a.html.

Meanwhile in Egypt, police from the Giza Security Department seized nearly two million counterfeit Arab language music cassettes owned by various Egyptian record production companies in the largest ever music piracy seizure in the Middle East on July 7, 2003. Next to Lebanon, where the piracy rate is almost 70%, Egypt has one of the highest piracy rates in the Middle East region at about 50%. *See* www.ifpi.org/site-content/press/20030707.html.

4.   How much would you estimate that U.S. copyright holders lose every year from the global sales of pirated CDs? According to a report published by the international recording industry on July 10, 2003, such sales have more than doubled in the last three years and now generate an illegal international business of more than U.S. $4.6 billion. Sales of pirated CDs are estimated to have risen by 14%, exceeding 1 billion units for the first time last year—meaning that one in three of all CDs sold worldwide is a fake—while the total value of the pirate music market, including cassettes, was U.S. $4.6 billion, up 7% on the previous year. The figures mean that the global pirate music market, at U.S. $4.6 billion, is of greater value than the legitimate music market of every country in the world, except the USA and Japan.   http://www.ifpi.org/site-content/antipiracy/piracy2003-piracy-statistics.html.

Chapter 20

THE DEVIL MEDIA MADE ME DO IT

Over the years, there have been lawsuits filed by crime victims against media companies seeking to recover damages for the criminal or tortious acts of a third party who blames his or her violent conduct on a particular film, television program, or song. As you will see from the cases below, the courts have not been very receptive to the plaintiff's claims. While the claims demonstrate creativity on the part of the plaintiff and the plaintiff's counsel, they typically do not exhibit enough creativity to sway a decision in the plaintiff's favor.

Rice v. Paladin is the only case where the media defendant was held liable for the criminal acts of a third party.

RICE v. PALADIN ENTERPRISES, INC.

United States Court of Appeals, Fourth Circuit, 1997.
128 F.3d 233.

LUTTIG, Circuit Judge.

* * * I.

On the night of March 3, 1993, readied by these instructions and steeled by these seductive adjurations from *Hit Man: A Technical Manual for Independent Contractors*, a copy of which was subsequently found in his apartment, James Perry brutally murdered Mildred Horn, her eight-year-old quadriplegic son Trevor, and Trevor's nurse, Janice Saunders, by shooting Mildred Horn and Saunders through the eyes and by strangling Trevor Horn. Perry's despicable crime was not one of vengeance; he did not know any of his victims. Nor did he commit the murders in the course of another offense. Perry acted instead as a contract killer, a "hit man," hired by Mildred Horn's ex-husband, Lawrence Horn, to murder Horn's family so that Horn would receive the $2 million that his eight-year-old son had received in settlement for injuries that had previously left him paralyzed for life. At the time of the murders, this money was held in trust for the benefit of Trevor, and, under the terms of the trust instrument, the trust money was to be distributed tax-free to Lawrence in the event of Mildred's and Trevor's deaths.

In soliciting, preparing for, and committing these murders, Perry meticulously followed countless of *Hit Man*'s 130 pages of detailed factual instructions on how to murder and to become a professional killer.

Perry, for example, followed many of the book's instructions on soliciting a client and arranging for a contract murder in his solicitation of and negotiation with Lawrence Horn. Cautioning against the placement of advertisements in military or gun magazines, as this might prompt "a personal visit from the FBI," *Hit Man* instructs that "as a beginner" one should solicit business "through a personal acquaintance whom you trust." *Hit Man* at 87. James Perry offered his services as a professional killer to Lawrence Horn through Thomas Turner, a "good friend" of Perry's, and Lawrence Horn's first cousin. *Perry v. State*, 686 A.2d 274, 278 (1996), *cert. denied*, 520 U.S. 1146, 117 S. Ct. 1318, 137 L.Ed.2d 480 (1997).

Hit Man instructs to request "expense money" from the employer prior to committing the crime, advising the contract killer to get "*all expense money up front.*" *Hit Man* at 92 (emphasis added). The manual goes on to explain that this amount should generally range from five hundred to five thousand dollars, "depending on the type of job and the job location," and that the advance should be paid in cash. *Id.* Prior to commission of the murders, Lawrence Horn paid James Perry three thousand five hundred dollars through a series of wire transfers using phony names. *Perry*, 686 A.2d at 280.

Hit Man instructs that the victim's personal residence is the "initial choice" location for a murder and "an ideal place to make a hit," depending on its "layout" and "position." *Hit Man* at 81–82. James Perry murdered the Horns at their place of residence. *Perry*, 686 A.2d at 277.

Hit Man instructs its readers to use a rental car to reach the victim's location, *Hit Man* at 98, and to "steal an out-of-state tag" and use it to "replace the rental tag" on the car, explaining that "[s]tolen tags only show up on the police computer of the state in which they are stolen." *Id.* James Perry stole out-of-state tags and affixed them to his rental car before driving it to the Horns' residence on the night of the murders. *Perry*, 686 A.2d at 276.

Hit Man instructs the reader to establish a base at a motel in close proximity to the "jobsite" before committing the murders. *Hit Man* at 101. On the night that he killed Mildred and Trevor Horn and Janice Saunders, James Perry took a room at a Days Inn motel in Rockville, Maryland, a short drive from the Horns' residence. *Perry*, 686 A.2d at 276.

Hit Man instructs that one should "use a made-up [license] tag number" when registering at the motel or hotel. *Hit Man* at 102. James

Perry gave a false license tag number when he registered at the Days Inn on the night of the murders. *Perry,* 686 A.2d at 276.

Hit Man instructs that a "beginner" should use an AR–7 rifle to kill his victims. *Hit Man* at 21. James Perry used an AR–7 rifle to slay Mildred Horn and Janice Saunders. *Perry,* 686 A.2d at 279.

Hit Man instructs its readers where to find the serial numbers on an AR–7 rifle, and instructs them that, prior to using the weapon, they should "completely drill[ ] out" these serial numbers so that the weapon cannot be traced. *Hit Man* at 23. James Perry drilled out the serial numbers of his weapon exactly as the book instructs. *Perry,* 686 A.2d at 280.

Hit Man instructs in "explicit detail" (replete with photographs) how to construct, "without [the] need of special engineering ability or machine shop tools," a homemade, "whisper-quiet" silencer from material available in any hardware store. *Hit Man* at 39–51. James Perry constructed such a homemade silencer and used it on the night that he murdered Mildred and Trevor Horn and Janice Saunders.

Perry also followed any number of *Hit Man's* instructions on how to commit the murder itself. The manual, for example, instructs its readers to kill their "mark" at close range, so that they will "know beyond any doubt that the desired result has been achieved." *Hit Man* at 24. The book also cautions, however, that the killer should not shoot the victim at point blank range, because "the victim's blood [will] splatter [the killer] or [his] clothing." *Id.* Ultimately, the book recommends that its readers "shoot [their victims] from a distance of three to six feet." *Id.* James Perry shot Mildred Horn and Janice Saunders from a distance of three feet. *Hit Man* specifically instructs its audience of killers to shoot the victim through the eyes if possible: At least three shots should be fired to insure quick and sure death. . . . [A]im for the head—preferably the eye sockets if you are a sharpshooter. *Hit Man* at 24. James Perry shot Mildred Horn and Janice Saunders two or three times and through the eyes. *Perry,* 686 A.2d at 277.

Finally, Perry followed many of *Hit Man's* instructions for concealing his murders. *Hit Man* instructs the killer to "[p]ick up those empty cartridges that were ejected when you fired your gun." *Hit Man* at 104. Although Perry fired his rifle numerous times during the murders, no spent cartridges were found in the area. *Cf. Perry,* 686 A.2d at 277, *with id.* at 280.

Hit Man instructs the killer to disguise the contract murder as burglary by "mess[ing] the place up a bit and tak[ing] anything of value that you can carry concealed." *Hit Man* at 104. After killing Mildred and Trevor Horn and Janice Saunders, James Perry took a Gucci watch, as well as some credit cards and bank cards from Mildred Horn's wallet. *Perry,* 686 A.2d at 278. According to the police report, a few areas of the Horns' residence appeared "disturbed" or "slightly tossed," and "a rug and cocktail table in the living room had been moved." *Id.* at 277.

Hit Man instructs that, after murdering the victims, the killer should break down the AR–7 in order to make the weapon easier to conceal. *Hit Man* at 105. James Perry disassembled his weapon after the murders, in accordance with the instructions in *Hit Man. Perry,* 686 A.2d at 280.

Hit Man instructs killers to use specified tools to alter specified parts of the rifle. *Hit Man* at 25. The author explains that the described alterations will prevent the police laboratory from matching the bullets recovered from the victims' bodies to the murder weapon. James Perry altered his AR–7 in accordance with these instructions. *Perry,* 686 A.2d at 280.

Hit Man also instructs the killer to dispose of the murder weapon by scattering the disassembled pieces of the weapon along the road as he leaves the crime scene. *Hit Man* at 105. And, after killing Mildred and Trevor Horn and Janice Saunders, Perry scattered the pieces of his disassembled AR–7 rifle along Route 28 in Montgomery County. *Perry,* 686 A.2d at 280.

In this civil, state-law wrongful death action against defendant Paladin Enterprises—the publisher of *Hit Man*—the relatives and representatives of Mildred and Trevor Horn and Janice Saunders allege that Paladin aided and abetted Perry in the commission of his murders through its publication of *Hit Man*'s killing instructions. For reasons that are here of no concern to the court, Paladin has *stipulated* to a set of facts which establish as a matter of law that the publisher is civilly liable for aiding and abetting James Perry in his triple murder, unless the First Amendment absolutely bars the imposition of liability upon a publisher for assisting in the commission of criminal acts. As the parties stipulate: "The parties agree that the sole issue to be decided by the Court . . . is whether the First Amendment is a complete defense, as a matter of law, to the civil action set forth in the plaintiffs' Complaint. * * *

Paladin, for example, has stipulated for purposes of summary judgment that Perry followed the above-enumerated instructions from *Hit Man,* as well as instructions from another Paladin publication, *How to Make a Disposable Silencer, Vol. II,* in planning, executing, and attempting to cover up the murders of Mildred and Trevor Horn and Janice Saunders. Paladin has stipulated not only that, in marketing *Hit Man,* Paladin "intended to attract and assist criminals and would-be criminals who desire information and instructions on how to commit crimes,", but also that it "intended *and* had knowledge" that *Hit Man* actually "would be used, *upon receipt,* by criminals and would-be criminals to plan and execute the crime of murder for hire." Indeed, the publisher has even stipulated that, through publishing and selling *Hit Man,* it assisted Perry in particular in the perpetration of the very murders for which the victims' families now attempt to hold Paladin civilly liable. * * *

Notwithstanding Paladin's extraordinary stipulations that it not only knew that its instructions might be used by murderers, but that it actually *intended* to provide assistance to murderers and would-be murderers which would be used by them "upon receipt," and that it in fact assisted Perry in particular in the commission of the murders of Mildred and Trevor Horn and Janice Saunders, the district court granted Paladin's motion for summary judgment and dismissed plaintiffs' claims that Paladin aided and abetted Perry, holding that these claims were barred by the First Amendment as a matter of law.

Because long-established caselaw provides that speech—even speech by the press—that constitutes criminal aiding and abetting does not enjoy the protection of the First Amendment, and because we are convinced that such caselaw is both correct and equally applicable to speech that constitutes civil aiding and abetting of criminal conduct (at least where, as here, the defendant has the specific purpose of assisting and encouraging commission of such conduct and the alleged assistance and encouragement takes a form other than abstract advocacy), we hold ... that the First Amendment does not pose a bar to a finding that Paladin is civilly liable as an aider and abetter of Perry's triple contract murder. We also hold that the plaintiffs have stated against Paladin a civil aiding and abetting claim under Maryland law sufficient to withstand Paladin's motion for summary judgment. For these reasons, which we fully explain below, the district court's grant of summary judgment in Paladin's favor is reversed and the case is remanded for trial.

* * * Through its stipulation that it intended *Hit Man* to be used by criminals and would-be criminals to commit murder for hire *in accordance with the book's instructions,* Paladin all but concedes that, through those instructions, *Hit Man* prepares and steels its readers to commit the crime of murder for hire. But even absent the publisher's stipulations, it is evident from even a casual examination of the book that the prose of *Hit Man* is at the other end of the continuum from the ideation at the core of the advocacy protected by the First Amendment.

The cover of *Hit Man* states that readers of the book will "[l]earn how a pro makes a living at this craft [of murder] without landing behind bars" and, how he gets hit assignments, creates a false working identity, makes a disposable silencer, leaves the scene without a trace of evidence, watches his mark unobserved, and more ... how to get in, do the job, and get out—without getting caught.

In the first pages of its text, *Hit Man* promises, consistent with its title as "A Technical Manual for Independent Contractors," that the book will prepare the reader, step by step, to commit murder for hire:

> Within the pages of this book you will learn one of the most successful methods of operation used by an independent contractor. You will follow the procedures of a man who works alone, without backing of organized crime or on a personal vendetta. Step by step you will be taken from research to equipment selection to job preparation to successful job completion. You will learn where to find employment, how much to charge, and what you can, and *cannot,* do with the money you earn. * * *

Paladin Press in this case has *stipulated* that it specifically targeted the market of murderers, would-be murderers, and other criminals for sale of its murder manual. Paladin has *stipulated both* that it had knowledge *and* that it intended that *Hit Man* would immediately be used by criminals and would-be criminals in the solicitation, planning, and commission of murder and murder for hire. And Paladin has *stipulated* that, through publishing and selling *Hit Man,* it "assisted" Perry in particular in the perpetration of the brutal triple murders for which plaintiffs now seek to hold the publisher liable. Beyond these startling stipulations, it is alleged, and the record would support, that Paladin assisted Perry through the quintessential speech act of providing Perry with detailed factual instructions on how to prepare for, commit, and cover up his murders, instructions which themselves embody not so much as a hint of the theoretical advocacy of principles divorced from action that is the hallmark of protected speech. And it is alleged, and a jury could find, that Paladin's assistance assumed the form of speech with little, if any, purpose beyond the unlawful one of facilitating murder.

Paladin's astonishing stipulations, coupled with the extraordinary comprehensiveness, detail, and clarity of *Hit Man*'s instructions for criminal activity and murder in particular, the boldness of its palpable exhortation to murder, the alarming power and effectiveness of its peculiar form of instruction, the notable absence from its text of the kind of ideas for the protection of which the First Amendment exists, and the book's evident lack of any even arguably legitimate purpose beyond the promotion and teaching of murder, render this case unique in the law. In at least these circumstances, we are confident that the First Amendment does not erect the absolute bar to the imposition of civil liability for which Paladin Press and *amici* contend. Indeed, to hold that the First Amendment forbids liability in such circumstances as a matter of law would fly in the face of all precedent of which we are aware, not only from the courts of appeals but from the Supreme Court of the United States itself. *Hit Man* is, we are convinced, the speech that even Justice Douglas, with his unrivaled devotion to the First Amendment, counseled without any equivocation "should be beyond the pale" under a Constitution that reserves to the people the ultimate and necessary authority to adjudge some conduct—and even some speech—fundamentally incompatible with the liberties they have secured unto themselves.

The judgment of the district court is hereby reversed, and the case remanded for trial.

Note

1. As you read the following cases keep the *Rice* decision in mind. Think about how the following cases differ from *Rice*. Think about how you may have presented the case differently in order to secure a different outcome.

A. THOSE DEVIL FILMS MADE ME DO IT

Copycat crimes are a problem that filmmakers confront when they decide how to depict a particular violent or devious act in a film. Social responsibility, and the MPAA ratings system, do affect the cuts that are made to a particular film. With the knowledge that life imitates art, where does the filmmaker draw the line with his or her depictions of new ways for people to inflict pain and suffering on a fellow human being? Should the filmmaker censor him or herself because a few sick individuals will use the film as inspiration for a heinous crime? What is the studio's responsibility to the public in the advertising and distribution of a film that may inspire violence? Think about these questions as you read the next few cases.

BYERS v. EDMONDSON

Louisiana Court of Appeals, 2002.
826 So.2d 551.

CARTER, Chief Judge.

This is an appeal of a judgment dismissing the director and producers of the film, *Natural Born Killers,* from a lawsuit filed by plaintiffs, who claimed the film incited the incident wherein one of the plaintiffs was physically injured.

FACTS AND PROCEDURAL HISTORY

On March 8, 1995, Patsy Byers was shot during an armed robbery of a convenience store where she worked in Ponchatoula, Louisiana. As a result of the shooting, Patsy Byers was rendered a paraplegic. The perpetrator of this armed robbery was Sarah Edmondson, who, along with her boyfriend, Benjamin Darrus, set out from Oklahoma originally intending to attend a Grateful Dead concert in Memphis, Tennessee. Tragically, within three days of leaving Oklahoma, Darrus had murdered William Savage during the course of an armed robbery in Mississippi, and Edmondson had shot Byers. *See State v. Edmondson,* 97–2456, p.2 (La.7/8/98), 714 So.2d 1233, 1235. Whether *Natural Born Killers* incited Edmondson and Darrus to commit their horrific and senseless crimes and whether this action seeking damages from the director and producers of the film can proceed is the subject of this appeal.

Edmondson and Darrus did not return to Oklahoma for several weeks following the Byers shooting. There is no indication that they engaged in any other violent crimes. Edmondson and Darrus were eventually implicated in the Byers shooting. Edmondson gave a statement to the authorities wherein she revealed that the night before they left for Memphis, she and Darrus spent the night at a cabin owned by her family in Welling, Oklahoma. It was there that they watched *Natural Born Killers.* In Edmondson's initial statement given to police, she commented that "Ben really loved this movie."

On July 26, 1995, Byers filed suit against Edmondson and Darrus seeking damages for the injuries she sustained as a result of the shooting. Byers amended her petition several times adding additional defendants. Included in the additional defendants are Time Warner Entertainment Company, L.P., Alcor Film & TV, GMBH & Co. Productions KG, Jane and Don Productions, Inc., and Oliver Stone (hereinafter collectively referred to as the Stone/Warner defendants). Byers alleged that Edmondson and Darrus embarked on a crime spree that culminated in the shooting of Pasty Byers as a result of seeing and becoming inspired by the movie *Natural Born Killers,* which was produced, directed, and distributed by the Stone/Warner defendants.

The Stone/Warner defendants previously attempted to dismiss the actions against them by filing a peremptory exception raising the objection of no cause of action on the basis that the film was protected speech under the First Amendment of the United States Constitution. Although the trial court granted this exception, this court overruled that decision and found that Byers had indeed stated a cause of action against these defendants. *Byers v. Edmondson,* 97–0831 (La. App. 1st Cir. 5/15/98), 712 So. 2d 681, 689, *writ denied,* 98–1596 (La. 10/9/98), 726 So. 2d 29, *cert. denied, sub nom Time Warner Entertainment Co., L.P. v. Byers,* 526 U.S. 1005 (*Byers I*).

In the procedural posture of *Byers I,* this court was bound to accept the allegations of Byers' petition as true. Following an examination of Byers' petition, we found that, because Byers had alleged that these defendants produced and released a film containing violent imagery that was intended to cause viewers to imitate the violent imagery, the petition stated a cause of action under Louisiana law and made sufficient allegations to remove the film from First Amendment protection on the basis that it incited imminent lawless activity. The substantive issue of whether *Natural Born Killers* is protected speech under the First Amendment was not addressed in *Byers I.*

The Stone/Warner defendants filed a motion for summary judgment seeking dismissal of this action on the basis that they were entitled to judgment as a matter of law according to Louisiana tort law, Louisiana constitutional law, and United States constitutional law. In our review of the trial court's granting of summary judgment, the central issue is whether *Natural Born Killers* is protected speech under the First Amendment.

DISCUSSION

The First Amendment to the Constitution of the United States provides: Congress shall make no law respecting an establishment of religion, or prohibiting the free exercise thereof; or abridging the freedom of speech, or of the press; or the right of the people peaceably to assemble, and to petition the Government for a redress of grievances.

Motion pictures are a significant medium for the communication of ideas and, like other forms of expression, are protected by the First

Amendment. *Joseph Burstyn, Inc. v. Wilson,* 343 U.S. 495, 501–02 (1952). The fact that a case does not involve government restriction of speech does not prevent the barring of an action that violates the First Amendment. The chilling effect of permitting the imposition of civil liability based on negligence is obvious the fear of damage awards may be markedly more inhibiting than the fear of prosecution under a criminal statute. *New York Times Co. v. Sullivan,* 376 U.S. 254, 277 (1964).

The First Amendment guarantee of freedom of speech is not without some carefully considered limitations. The United States Supreme Court has stated that the "unconditional phrasing of the First Amendment was not intended to protect every utterance." *Roth v. United States,* 354 U.S. 476, 483 (1957). * * * There are four categories of speech that do not receive any constitutional protection: (1) obscene speech, *Miller v. California,* 413 U.S. 15 (1973); (2) defamatory invasions of privacy, *Beauharnais v. Illinios,* 343 U.S. 250 (1952); (3) fighting words, *Chaplinsky v. New Hampshire,* 315 U.S. 568 (1942); and (4) words likely to produce imminent lawless action (incitement), *Brandenburg v. Ohio,* 395 U.S. 444 (1969) (per curiam).

Byers alleges that *Natural Born Killers* is not entitled to First Amendment protection because it is inciteful and obscene. The inquiry into the protected status of speech is one of law, not fact. *Connick v. Myers,* 461 U.S. 138, 148 n. 7 (1983). Accordingly, the central issue of this appeal is whether *Natural Born Killers* loses its First Amendment protection because of its content. A copy of the film is in the record, and Oliver Stone, the director of *Natural Born Killers,* certified through his affidavit that this copy is in the same form in which it was released to the public in 1994 in theaters and later on videocassettes. Because we are bound to determine as a matter of law whether the film is protected speech, this is a proper determination under a motion for summary judgment. * * *

[A.] *Incitement*

To justify a claim that speech should be restrained or punished because it is or was an incitement to lawless action, the court must be satisfied that the speech (1) was directed or intended toward the goal of producing imminent lawless conduct and (2) was likely to produce such imminent conduct. Speech directed to action at some indefinite time in the future will not satisfy this test. Moreover, speech does not lose its First Amendment protection merely because it has a tendency to lead to violence. *Hess v. Indiana,* 414 U.S. 105, 108–09 (1973).

This court is aware that, because of the abundance of imagery used in the film, there is certainly room for a wide variety of interpretations. It is not the prerogative of this court to provide an allegorical interpretation of this movie or to provide an artistic critique. Based on our viewing of the film, we conclude that nothing in it constitutes incitement. *Natural Born Killers* is not just about the killing spree of its main characters, Mickey and Mallory Knox, but also portrays how their exploits are glorified by the media to the point where they become cultural icons. The basic plot of the movie follows Mickey and Mallory as they meet, murder her abusive parents, and then engage in a killing spree. It also chronicles their capture, imprisonment, and Mickey's interview with a tabloid journalist that causes a prison riot facilitating their escape.

Throughout the film, images frequently switch from color to black and white, and even live-action video. Some of the scenes employ facial distortions, sitcom laugh tracks, newspaper and cartoon clips, slow motion and oblique camera angles. Such techniques place this film in the realm of fantasy. *Natural Born Killers* is permeated with violent imagery, which goes to the core of the issue. The violence in the film is presented in the format of imagery and fictionalized violence. Although we acknowledge that such a portrayal of violence can be viewed as a glorification and glamorization of such actions, such a portrayal does not rise to the level of incitement, such that it removes the film from First Amendment protection.

When considering the guidelines that courts have used in determining whether speech is classified as inciteful, we cannot say that *Natural Born Killers* exhorts, urges, entreats, solicits, or overtly advocates or encourages unlawful or violent activity on the part of viewers. *See Yakubowicz*, 536 N.E.2d at 1071. *Natural Born Killers* does not purport to order or command anyone to perform any concrete action immediately or at any specific time. *See McCollum v. CBS, Inc.*, 249 Cal. Rptr. 187 (1988). Nor do we find this film promotes crime in concrete, non-abstract terms. At no point during this film is the viewer directed or urged to commit any type of imminent lawless activity.

As we note, Byers alleges that Edmondson and Darrus became inspired by what was shown in *Natural Born Killers*. The concept of "copycat" actions has been addressed in *Rice v. Paladin Enterprises, Inc.*, 128 F.3d at 266, wherein the United States Fourth Circuit Court of Appeals commented, "[I]n virtually every 'copycat' case, there will be lacking in the speech itself any basis for a permissible inference that the 'speaker' intended to assist and facilitate the criminal conduct described or depicted. Of course, with few, if any, exceptions, the speech which gives rise to the copycat crime will not directly and affirmatively promote the criminal conduct, even if, in some circumstances, it incidentally glamorizes and thereby indirectly promotes such conduct." (Emphasis ours).

After viewing *Natural Born Killers*, we are convinced that the present case presents such a copycat scenario. We are mindful of the United States Supreme Court's guideline that speech does not lose its First Amendment protection merely because it has "a tendency to lead to violence." *Hess v. Indiana*, 414 U.S. at 109. Edmondson and Darrus may very well have been inspired to imitate the actions of Mickey and Mallory Knox, but the film does not direct or encourage them to take such actions. Accordingly, as a matter of law, we find *Natural Born Killers* cannot be considered inciteful speech that would remove it from First Amendment protection.

Although the plaintiffs have gone to great lengths in attempting to demonstrate the particular intent of the defendants, particularly the intent of Oliver Stone in creating *Natural Born Killers,* such a determination is not essential to the disposition of this matter. The allegations in Byers' petition alleged that the Stone/Warner defendants are liable as a result of their misfeasance in that they produced and released a film containing violent imagery which was intended to cause viewers to imitate the violent imagery. We find as a matter of law that *Natural Born Killers* is not inciteful speech. Therefore, the intent of the Stone/Warner defendants is not material, since *Natural Born Killers* is not inciteful speech.

[B.]   *Obscenity*

To constitute obscenity, there must be independent proof of the following factors: (1) the average person, applying contemporary community standards, would find that the work, taken as a whole, appeals to the prurient interest; (2) measured by contemporary community standards, the work depicts or describes, in a patently offensive way, sexual conduct specifically defined by applicable state law; and (3) the work, taken as a whole, lacks serious literary, artistic, political or scientific value. *Miller v. California,* 413 U.S. at 25.

Byers does not allege that *Natural Born Killers* meets the Miller criteria for obscenity; rather Byers argues that "[t]here is no reason why senselessly violent speech like [*Natural Born Killers*] cannot also be labeled as obscene, as it does precisely the same thing." The Louisiana Supreme Court has previously recognized that the First Amendment does not permit a violence-based notion of obscenity. *State v. Johnson,* 343 So. 2d 705, 709–10 (La. 1977). Accordingly, we decline to extend the obscenity exception to the First Amendment to cover the violence of *Natural Born Killers.*

CONCLUSION

It is an unfortunate aspect of our society that certain individuals seek to emulate fictional representations. However, the constitutional protection accorded to the freedom of speech and of the press is not based on the naïve belief that speech can do no harm, but on the confidence that the benefits society reaps from the free flow and exchange of ideas outweigh the costs society endures by receiving reprehensible or dangerous ideas. *Herceg v. Hustler Magazine, Inc.,* 814 F.2d 1017, 1019 (5th Cir.1987). Edmondson's and Darrus' decision to imitate the characters of a film is more a regrettable commentary on their own culpability, than a danger of free expression requiring courts to chill such speech through civil penalties. Because we find as a matter of law that the film *Natural Born Killers* is protected by the First Amendment, an action seeking civil damages based on the effect of the film cannot be sustained. The decision of the trial court granting the summary judgment and dismissing Time Warner Entertainment Company, L.P., Alcor Film & TV, GMBH & Co. Productions KG, Jane and Don Productions, Inc., and Oliver Stone is affirmed. All costs of this appeal are assessed to the plaintiffs, the estate of Pasty Byers, Lonnie Wayne Byers, individually, and as natural tutrix for Jacob Eugene Byers, and Joshua Noah Byers.

AFFIRMED.

SANDERS v. ACCLAIM ENTERTAINMENT, INC.

United States District Court, Colorado, 2002.
188 F.Supp.2d 1264.

BABCOCK, Chief Judge.

* * * Defendants Acclaim Entertainment, Inc., Activision, Inc., Capcom Entertainment, Inc., EIDOS Interactive, ID Software, Inc., Infogrames, Inc., f/k/a GT Interactive Software Corp., Interplay Entertainment, Corp., Midway Home Entertainment, Nintendo of America, Palm Pictures, Sony Computer Entertainment America, and Time Warner, Inc. move * * * to dismiss * * * as to all claims brought against them by Plaintiffs Linda Sanders, Constance Adams and Cynthia Thirouin (collectively, Plaintiffs) the widow and stepchildren of William David Sanders, a teacher killed in the April 20, 1999 attack on Columbine High School. * * * After consideration of the motions, briefs and pertinent case law and for the following reasons, I grant the * * * [motions to dismiss].

I. FACTS

Plaintiffs allege that Columbine High School (Columbine) students Dylan Klebold and/or Eric Harris, both approximately 17 years of age, were co-conspirators in a plot and scheme to assault, terrorize and kill Columbine teachers and students. On April 20, 1999 at approximately 11:20 a.m., Klebold and Harris approached the school armed with multiple guns and other "weapons of destruction" including explosive devices.

After shooting at people outside the school, the pair entered the school building and continued their deadly assault inside Columbine. Twelve students and teacher William Sanders were killed. Dozens of others were injured.

In the aftermath of the massacre the police allegedly learned that Harris and Klebold were avid, fanatical and excessive consumers of violent ... video games ... [and] consumers of movies containing obscenity, obscenity for minors, pornography, sexual violence, and/or violence. One movie the pair viewed was "The Basketball Diaries" in which "a student massacres his classmates with a shotgun."

According to Plaintiffs, "but for the actions of the Video Game Defendants and the Movie Defendants, in conjunction with the acts of the other defendants herein, the multiple killings at Columbine High School would not have occurred." Based on the foregoing, Plaintiffs filed this action on April 19, 2001. * * *

[Parts II–IV omitted.]

V. CLAIMS ANALYSIS

A. Negligence

Plaintiffs allege negligence in Claim One against the Movie Defendants and in Claim Two against the Video Game Defendants. Under Colorado law, to recover for the negligent conduct of another, a plaintiff must establish: 1) the existence of a legal duty owed to the plaintiff by the defendant; 2) breach of that duty; 3) injury to the plaintiff; and 4) actual and proximate causation. *Leake v. Cain,* 720 P.2d 152, 155 (Colo. 1986).

1. Duty

* * * In resolving the threshold legal question whether the Video Game and Movie Defendants have a cognizable duty to the Plaintiffs, I consider: 1) foreseeability of the injury or harm that occurred; 2) the social utility of Defendants' conduct; 3) the magnitude of the burden of guarding against the injury or harm; and 4) the consequences of placing the burden on the Defendants. *See Bailey v. Huggins Diagnostic & Rehabilitation Center,* 952 P.2d 768 (Colo.App.1997). No single factor is controlling. *Whitlock,* 744 P.2d at 57.

The question whether a duty should be imposed in a particular case is "essentially one of fairness under contemporary standards—whether reasonable persons would recognize a duty and agree that it exists." *Taco Bell, Inc. v. Lannon,* 744 P.2d 43, 46 (Colo. 1987). Generally, a person does not have a duty to prevent a third person from harming another absent special circumstances warranting imposition of such a duty. * * *

a. Foreseeability

The Colorado Supreme Court teaches that foreseeability is "based on common sense perceptions of the risks created by various conditions and circumstances and includes whatever is likely enough in the setting of modern life that a reasonably thoughtful person would take account of it in guiding practical conduct." *Perreira,* 768 P.2d at 1209.

Generally, under Colorado law a person has no responsibility to foresee intentional violent acts by others. *See Walcott v. Total Petroleum, Inc.,* 964 P.2d 609, 612 (Colo. App. 1998), *cert. denied,* (Colo. 1999). * * *

In the circumstances alleged here, the Video Game and Movie Defendants likewise had no reason to suppose that Harris and Klebold would decide to murder or injure their fellow classmates and teachers. Plaintiffs do not allege that these Defendants had any knowledge of Harris' and Klebold's identities, let alone their violent proclivities. Nor, for that matter, did the Video Game and Movie Defendants have any reason to believe that a shooting spree was a likely or probable consequence of exposure to their movie or video games. At most, based on Plaintiffs' allegations that children who witness acts of violence and/or who interactively involved with creating violence or violent images often act more violently themselves and sometimes recreate the violence, these Defendants might have speculated that their motion picture or video games had the potential to stimulate an idiosyncratic reaction in the mind of some disturbed individuals. A speculative possibility, however, is not enough to create a legal duty. * * *

Courts around the country have rejected similar claims brought against media or entertainment defendants. In *Zamora v. Columbia Broadcasting System*, 480 F.Supp. 199 (S.D. Fla. 1979), the Court held that it was not foreseeable to three television networks that a teenager would shoot and kill his neighbor after viewing comparable violence on television over a ten year period. Plaintiff alleged also that watching television had desensitized the teenager to violence and caused him to develop a sociopathic personality. In granting the defendants' motion to dismiss, the *Zamora* Court noted that the three major networks are charged with anticipating: 1) the minor's alleged voracious intake of television violence; 2) his parents' apparent acquiescence in his television viewing, presumably without recognition of any problem; and 3) that Zamora would respond with a violent criminal act. *See id.* at 202. Based in part on the lack of foreseeability, the Court declined to "create such a wide expansion in the law of torts." *Id.* at 203. * * *

I find persuasive the reasoning set out in these cases. Consequently, I conclude under similar Colorado tort law, there is no basis for determining that violence would be considered the likely consequence of exposure to video games or movies. This factor weighs heavily against imposing a duty on the Movie and Video Game Defendants.

b. *Social Utility of Defendants' Conduct*

Creating and distributing works of imagination, whether in the form of video games, movies, television, books, visual art, or song, is an integral component of a society dedicated to the principle of free expression. *See* U.S. CONST., amend. 1; COLO. CONST., art. 11, § 10 ("[n]o law shall be passed impairing the freedom of speech [and] that every person shall be free to speak, write or publish whatever he will on any subject"); *see also* U.S. CONST. art. I, § 8. * * *

Plaintiffs' characterization of the Video Game and Movie Defendants' creative works as "violent" does not alter the social utility analysis. In the context of ordering entry of a preliminary injunction against a city ordinance that limited minors' access to violent video games, the Seventh Circuit observed, "[v]iolence has always been and remains a central interest of humankind and a recurrent, even obsessive theme of culture both high and low." *American Amusement Mach. Ass'n v. Kendrick*, 244 F.3d 572, 577 (7th Cir. 2001). Indeed, "[c]lassic literature and art, and not merely today's popular culture, are saturated with graphic scenes of violence, whether narrated or pictorial." *Id.* at 575.

Moreover, the *Kendrick* Court acknowledged that video games that include pictorial representations of violence are "stories" and contain "age-old themes of literature." *Id.* at 577–78. The Court flatly rejected the notion that society is better served by insulating the vulnerable from exposure to such images: To shield children ... from exposure to violent descriptions and images would not only be quixotic, but deforming; it would leave them unequipped to cope with the world as we know it. *Id.* at 577.

Setting aside any personal distaste, as I must, it is manifest that there is social utility in expressive and imaginative forms of entertainment even if they contain violence. *See Kendrick,* 244 F.3d at 577. Hence, the social utility factor weighs heavily against imposing a duty against the Video Game and Movie Defendants.

c. and d. Magnitude of the Burden of Guarding against Injury or Harm and Consequences of Placing the Burden on the Defendant

* * * Colorado courts have repeatedly rejected efforts to impose overly burdensome and impractical obligations on defendants, including the obligation to identify potential dangers. This is especially so where those obligations would interfere with the social utility of a defendant's conduct or other important societal values. * * *

Given the First Amendment values at stake, the magnitude of the burden that Plaintiffs seek to impose on the Video Game and Movie Defendants is daunting. Furthermore, the practical consequences of such liability are unworkable. Plaintiffs would essentially obligate these Defendants, indeed all speakers, to anticipate and prevent the idiosyncratic, violent reactions of unidentified, vulnerable individuals to their creative works. * * *

Because Plaintiffs' legal theory would effectively compel Defendants not to market their works and, thus, refrain from expressing the ideas contained in those works, the burden imposed would be immense and the consequences dire for a free and open society.

In this case, Plaintiffs do not allege that the Video Game and Movie Defendants *illegally* produced or distributed the movie and video games Harris and Klebold allegedly viewed or played. Finding that these Defendants owed Plaintiffs a duty of care would burden these Defendants' First Amendment rights to freedom of expression. These considerations compel the conclusion that makers of works of imagination including video games and movies may not be held liable in tort based merely on the content or ideas expressed in their creative works. Placing a duty of care on Defendants in the circumstances alleged would chill their rights of free expression. Therefore, these factors also weigh heavily against imposing a duty on Defendants. * * *

Consequently, I hold that the Video Game and Movie Defendants owed no duty to Plaintiffs as a matter of law. Thus, the Video Game and Movie Defendants are entitled to ... dismissal of Plaintiffs' negligence claims.

2. Causation

Even assuming a duty, the Video Game and Movie Defendants argue that they were not the legal cause of Plaintiffs' injuries. I agree. To prevail on their negligence claim, Plaintiffs must show that Defendants' tortuous conduct proximately caused Mr. Sanders' death. "[Proximate cause] is the cause without which the claimed injury would not have been sustained." *City of Aurora v. Loveless,* 639 P.2d 1061, 1063 (Colo. 1981). In Colorado, causation is generally a question of fact for a jury. But a court may decide the issue as a matter of law where the alleged chain of causation is too attenuated to impose liability. *See Largo Corp. v. Crespin,* 727 P.2d 1098, 1103 (Colo. 1986); *Smith v. State Compensation Ins. Fund,* 749 P.2d 462, 464 (Colo. App. 1987). Here, proximate cause requires that Defendants' conduct produced Mr. Sanders' death "in the natural and probable sequence of things."

Where the circumstances make it likely that a defendant's negligence will result in injuries to others and where this negligence is a substantial factor in causing the injuries sustained, proximate causation is satisfied. The intervening or superseding act of a third party, in this case Harris and Klebold, including a third-party's intentionally tortuous or criminal conduct does not absolve a defendant from responsibility if the third-party's conduct is reasonably and generally foreseeable. *See Ekberg v. Greene,* 588 P.2d 375, 376–77 (1978).

It is undisputed that Harris and Klebold murdered or injured the Columbine victims including Mr. Sanders. The issue is whether Harris' and Klebold's intentional criminal acts constitute a superseding cause of the harm inflicted by them, thus relieving the Movie and Video Game Defendants' of liability.

A superseding cause exists when: 1) an extraordinary and unforeseeable act intervenes between a defendant's original tortuous act and the injury or harm sustained by plaintiffs and inflicted by a third party; and 2) the original tortuous act is itself capable of bringing about the injury. Just as foreseeability is central to finding that a duty is owed, it is also "the touchstone of proximate cause" and of the superseding cause doctrine. *Walcott,* 964 P.2d 609. Moreover, a superseding cause relieves the original actor of liability when "the harm is intentionally caused by a third person and is not within the scope of the risk created by the actor's conduct." *Webb v. Dessert Seed Co.,* 718 P.2d 1057, 1062–63 (Colo. 1986). * * *

I hold in this case that Harris' and Klebold's intentional violent acts were the superseding cause of Mr. Sanders' death. Moreover, as I have determined, their acts were not foreseeable. Their criminal acts, therefore, were not within the scope of any risk purportedly created by Defendants. * * * [T]he school shooting was not a normal response to the movies or video.

I conclude as a matter of law that no reasonable jury could find that the Video Game and Movie Defendants' conduct resulted in Mr. Sanders' death in "the natural and probable sequence of events." *See Loveless,*

639 P.2d at 1063. Therefore, Defendants were not a proximate cause of Mr. Sanders' injuries. Defendants are entitled to * * * dismissal as to the negligence claims. * * *

Notes

1. In *Delgado v. American Muli–Cinema,* a theater was held not liable for negligence in connection with a shooting death by a 13–year-old patron who had watched an R-rated film before the shooting. The policy of the theater was not to admit anyone under the age of 17 years old. Despite the policy, the theater admitted a 13–year-old patron and his underage friends without adult supervision. The youths became agitated by the violent film and the 13–year-old patron stated he was going to have to kill somebody. Immediately after leaving the theater, he shot someone on the street about a block and a half from the theater.

The court held that the theater could not be held liable for failing to stop the youth from doing something that any adult could have permitted had they accompanied him (watching an R-rated film). Further, the theater had no control over what occurred on the street which was more than a block away from the theater. *Delgado v. American Multi–Cinema, Inc.,* 72 Cal.App.4th 1403, 85 Cal.Rptr.2d 838 (2 Dist. 1999)

2. Are courts indirectly advocating self-censorship by the entertainment industry for fear of multi-million dollar lawsuits? A $25 million dollar award was entered against the *Jenny Jones* show after a guest killed another guest who had revealed a secret homosexual crush on national television. The judgment was later reversed. The lower court's verdict implied the show incited the murder. The entertainment industry has responded by toning down violence. For example, Miramax changed the film title "Killing Mrs. Tingle" to "Teaching Mrs. Tingle". Also, the WB Network refused to air a program depicting a student attack after the Columbine shooting. The fear of lawsuits could render the exercising of First Amendment rights too high for the industry. See Carolina A. Fornos, *Inspiring The Audience To Kill: Should The Entertainment Industry Be Held Liable For Intentional Acts of Violence Committed by Viewers, Listeners, or Readers?,* 46 Loy. L. Rev. 441 (Summer 2000).

3. Early research findings have suggested that viewing violent depictions in films is a precursor to violent behavior. However, at least one study suggests that youths with a history of delinquent behavior and poor social background develop a preference for violent films. The violent films then serve to reinforce the violent behavior of the offenders. The study showed 64% of violent offenders compared with only 25% of non-violent offenders had a preference for violent films. Kevin Browne and Amanda Pennell, *The Effects Of Video Violence On Young Offenders*, Home Office Research And Statistics Directorate Research Findings No. 65 (1998).

4. In January 1998, a 16–year-old boy and his two teenage cousins were arrested for the murder of Gina Castillo, the mother of one of the boys. According to a Los Angeles County spokesperson, "they admitted to homicide investigators that they killed the mother after getting the idea from the [Scream] movies." Michael Krikorian, *Son, Nephew Inspired by 'Scream'*

Movies kill woman, Police Say. L.A. TIMES, Jan. 15, 1998, *available at* http://www.mediascope.org/pubs/ibriefs/cc.htm.

5. Should violence be considered obscene? Can you make an argument that violence is the ultimate obscenity and that it should be regulated as such? How would the inclusion of violence in the definition of obscenity change what we see at the movies and on television?

B. THE DEVIL TELEVISION PROGRAM MADE ME DO IT

Jackass, Jerry Springer, Jenny Jones, television movies, *Beavis and Butthead*, and many other television shows have been blamed for prompting tortuous and/or criminal behavior. Television programs often get their ideas from newsworthy events. The talk shows solicit ideas from their viewers. In television, art imitates life. The problems develop when the art plants a seed where none was meant to be sewn. As the principal cases below show, while it is convenient to blame deviant behavior on the media, the court system has discouraged suits by consistently ruling in favor of the defendant media.

GRAVES v. WARNER BROS.

Michigan Court of Appeals, 2002.
253 Mich.App. 486, 656 N.W.2d 195.

GRIFFIN, Judge.

Defendants appeal as of right from the entry of judgment in the amount of $29,332,686 following the jury's verdict in plaintiffs' favor in this wrongful death action. We reverse the judgment, vacate the court's order, and remand for entry of a judgment and order in favor of defendants, holding that under the circumstances defendants owed no legally cognizable duty to protect plaintiffs' decedent from the homicidal acts of a third party.

I

The instant case has its origins in the tragic murder of plaintiffs' decedent, Scott Amedure, in March of 1995 by Jonathan Schmitz, who was ultimately convicted of second-degree murder. The facts underlying the highly publicized criminal case are set forth in this Court's decision, *People v. Schmitz*, 231 Mich. App. 521, 523, 586 N.W.2d 766 (1998), which addressed Schmitz' original appeal of his murder conviction:

> This case arises from defendant's killing of Scott Amedure with a shotgun on March 9, 1995. Three days before the shooting, defendant appeared with Amedure and Donna Riley in Chicago for a taping of an episode of the Jenny Jones talk show, during which defendant was surprised by Amedure's revelation that he had a secret crush on him. After the taping, defendant told many friends

and acquaintances that he was quite embarrassed and humiliated by the experience and began a drinking binge.

On the morning of the shooting, defendant found a sexually suggestive note from Amedure on his front door. Defendant then drove to a local bank, withdrew money from his savings account, and purchased a 12–gauge pump-action shotgun and some ammunition. Defendant then drove to Amedure's trailer, where he confronted Amedure about the note. When Amedure just smiled at him, defendant walked out of the trailer, stating that he had to shut off his car. Instead, defendant retrieved the shotgun and returned to the trailer. Standing at the front door, defendant fired two shots into Amedure's chest, leaving him with no chance for survival. Defendant left the scene and telephoned 911 to confess to the shooting.

Following a jury trial, Schmitz was found guilty of second-degree murder and possession of a firearm during the commission of a felony. * * * On remand, Schmitz was again found guilty of second-degree murder and felony-firearm and sentenced to twenty-five to fifty years' imprisonment for the murder conviction. * * *

In the wrongful death action now before this Court, plaintiffs Patricia Graves and Frank Amedure, Sr., as personal representatives of the estate of Scott Amedure, deceased, alleged that Schmitz shot and killed Amedure as a direct and proximate result of the actions of the present defendants, the Jenny Jones Show (the show), its owner, Warner Bros., and its producer, Telepictures. Plaintiffs essentially contended that defendants "ambushed" Schmitz when they taped the episode of the show in question, intentionally withholding from Schmitz that the true topic of the show was same-sex crushes and never attempting to determine, before the show, the effect the ambush might have on Schmitz. Plaintiffs alleged that defendants knew or should have known that their actions would incite violence, with the sole purpose of the show being the increase in television ratings, and that defendants had an affirmative duty to prevent or refrain from placing plaintiffs' decedent in a position that would unnecessarily and unreasonably expose him to the risk of harm, albeit the criminal conduct of a third person. Plaintiffs maintained that the show breached its duty and foreseeably subjected plaintiffs' decedent to an unreasonable risk of harm, ultimately resulting in his death.

Defendants' motions for summary disposition and a directed verdict were denied by the trial court, which opined that there were genuine issues of material fact regarding duty and foreseeability, negligence, and causation. Following extensive trial proceedings, a jury returned a verdict in plaintiffs' favor, and a judgment was subsequently entered thereon awarding plaintiffs $29,332,686 in damages. The trial court denied defendants' post trial motion for judgment notwithstanding the verdict or, in the alternative, a new trial or remittitur. Defendants now appeal.

II

In defendants' first issue on appeal, we are confronted with the cornerstone of this case whether defendants owed a duty to plaintiffs' decedent to protect him from harm caused by the criminal acts of a third party, Jonathan Schmitz. Defendants argue that they owed no such duty and that the trial court erred in denying defendants relief as a matter of law where plaintiffs failed to show a duty to prevent Schmitz' violent conduct. We agree. * * *

Briefly reiterated, a negligence action may be maintained only if a legal duty exists that requires the defendant to conform to a particular standard of conduct in order to protect others against unreasonable risks of harm. * * * This analysis requires a determination whether the relationship of the parties is the sort that a legal obligation should be imposed on one for the benefit of another. * * * In determining whether a duty exists, courts examine different variables, including foreseeability of the harm, existence of a relationship between the parties involved, degree of certainty of injury, closeness of connection between the conduct and the injury, moral blame attached to the conduct, policy of preventing future harm, and the burdens and consequences of imposing a duty and the resulting liability for breach.

Of particular import to the present appeal is the principle that, in general, there is no legal duty obligating one person to aid or protect another. * * * Moreover, an individual has no duty to protect another from the criminal acts of a third party in the absence of a special relationship between the defendant and the plaintiff or the defendant and the third party. * * * The rationale underlying this general rule is the fact that "[c]riminal activity, by its deviant nature, is normally unforeseeable." *Papadimas v. Mykonos Lounge*, 176 Mich. App. 40, 46–47, 439 N.W.2d 280 (1989). Our Court in *Papadimas, id.* at 47, 439 N.W.2d 280, quoting Prosser & Keeton, Torts (5th ed.), § 33, p. 201, emphasized that " '[u]nder all ordinary and normal circumstances, in the absence of any reason to expect the contrary, the actor may reasonably proceed upon the assumption that others will obey the criminal law.' " As further explained by our Supreme Court in *Williams v. Cunningham Drug Stores, Inc.*, 429 Mich. 495, 498–499, 418 N.W.2d 381 (1988): In determining standards of conduct in the area of negligence, the courts have made a distinction between misfeasance, or active misconduct causing personal injury, and nonfeasance, which is passive inaction or the failure to actively protect others from harm. The common law has been slow in recognizing liability for nonfeasance because the courts are reluctant to force persons to help one another and because such conduct does not create a new risk of harm to a potential plaintiff.

Thus, as a general rule, there is no duty that obligates one person to aid or protect another.

Social policy, however, has led the courts to recognize an exception to this general rule where a special relationship exists between a plaintiff and a defendant.... The rationale behind imposing a duty to protect in these special relationships is based on control. In each situation one person entrusts himself to the control and protection of another, with a consequent loss of control to protect himself. The duty to protect is imposed upon the person in control because he is best able to provide a place of safety. * * *

A premises owner's duty is limited to responding reasonably to situations occurring on the premises because, as a matter of public policy, we should not expect invitors to assume that others will disobey the law. A merchant can assume that patrons will obey the criminal law. * * * This assumption should continue until a specific situation occurs on the premises that would cause a reasonable person to recognize a risk of imminent harm to an identifiable invitee. It is only a present situation on the premises, not any past incidents, that creates a duty to respond.

Subjecting a merchant to liability solely on the basis of a foreseeability analysis is misbegotten. Because criminal activity is irrational and unpredictable, it is in this sense invariably foreseeable everywhere. However, even police, who are specially trained and equipped to anticipate and deal with crime, are unfortunately unable universally to prevent it. This is a testament to the arbitrary nature of crime. Given these realities, it is unjustifiable to make merchants, who not only have much less experience than the police in dealing with criminal activity but are also without a community deputation to do so, effectively vicariously liable for the criminal acts of third parties. * * *

Logic compels the conclusion that defendants in this case had no duty to anticipate and prevent the act of murder committed by Schmitz three days after leaving defendants' studio and hundreds of miles away. Here, the only special relationship, if any, that ever existed between defendants and plaintiffs' decedent, or between defendants and Schmitz, was that of business invitor to invitee. However, any duty ends when the relationship ends, *MacDonald, supra; Murdock, supra* at 54–55, 559 N.W.2d 639; *Williams, supra;* 2 Restatement of Torts, 2d, § 314A, comment c, p. 119, and in this instance the invitor/invitee relationship ended on March 6, 1995, three days before the murder, when Schmitz and Amedure peacefully left the Chicago studio following the taping of the episode. Because the evidence, even when viewed from a perspective most favorable to plaintiffs, revealed no ongoing special relationship at the time of the murder, defendants owed no duty to protect plaintiffs' decedent from Schmitz' violent attack on March 9, 1995. The present situation simply cannot, under any reasonable interpretation of the circumstances, be construed as involving an existing special relationship that required defendants to respond to a risk of imminent and foreseeable harm to an identifiable invitee on the premises. Consequently, the trial court erred as a matter of law in denying defendants' motions for summary disposition, a directed verdict, and judgment notwithstanding the verdict on the basis of lack of duty, an essential element of any negligence action. * * *

III

Finally, to the extent the torts of misrepresentation and intentional infliction of emotional distress were either pleaded as alternative theories of recovery or incorporated into the cause of action, over defendants' objection, by the trial court's jury instructions, we conclude that such claims must fail as a matter of law. Amedure's estate cannot recover under the separate tort of intentional misrepresentation, based on defendants' alleged statements to Schmitz, a third party. *Hi-Way Motor Co. v. Int'l Harvester Co.,* 398 Mich. 330, 336, 247 N.W.2d 813 (1976). The elements of intentional infliction of emotional distress are similarly lacking. See *Roberts v. Auto–Owners Ins. Co.,* 422 Mich. 594, 602, 374 N.W.2d 905 (1985). The mental distress that is the subject of this case was allegedly inflicted on Schmitz, a nonparty to this appeal, not on plaintiffs' decedent. Therefore, this count could not be sustained as a matter of law.

IV

In sum, we conclude that defendants owed no duty as a matter of law to protect plaintiffs' decedent from the intentional criminal acts of a third party, Jonathan Schmitz, that occurred three days after the taping of the Jenny Jones Show. While defendants' actions in creating and producing this episode of the show may be regarded by many as the epitome of bad taste and sensationalism, such actions are, under the circumstances, insufficient to impute the requisite relationship between the parties that would give rise to a legally cognizable duty. The trial court therefore erred in denying defendants' motions in this regard. Because we find no antecedent duty, we need not address the other issues raised by defendants on appeal. Accordingly, we reverse the judgment, vacate the order, and remand to the trial court with directions that it enter a judgment and order in favor of defendants. Judgment reversed, order vacated, and case remanded. We do not retain jurisdiction.

Notes

1. Schmitz's criminal conviction and sentence were affirmed by the Michigan Court of Appeals in *People v. Schmitz,* an unpublished opinion per curiam of the Court of Appeals, issued January 22, 2002 (Docket No. 222834, 2002 WL 99740). The *Jenny Jones* episode never aired.

2. There is a Web site dedicated to the memory of Scott Amedure. This site contains information about Amedure and other links to news stories about the trial. The site is located at http://talkshows.about.com/gi/dynamic/offsite.htm?site=http®®www.scottamedure.org®

3. Do you think television shows should be responsible for checking the background of every guest for the protection of other guests? Do you think a similar policy would have saved Amedure's life?

OLIVIA N. v. NBC

California Court of Appeals, 1977.
74 Cal.App.3d 383, 141 Cal.Rptr. 511.

CHRISTIAN, Judge.

Olivia N. appeals from a judgment of dismissal which the court rendered before the commencement of a scheduled jury trial in her action against respondents National Broadcasting Co., Inc. and the Chronicle Broadcasting Company.

Appellant's complaint sought damages from respondents for injuries allegedly inflicted upon her by certain juveniles who were acting upon the stimulus of observing a scene of brutality which had been broadcast in a television drama entitled "Born Innocent." The subject matter of the television film was the harmful effect of a state-run home upon an adolescent girl who had become a ward of the state. In one scene of the film, the young girl enters the community bathroom of the facility to take a shower. She is then shown taking off her clothes and stepping into the shower, where she bathes for a few moments. Suddenly, the water stops and a look of fear comes across her face. Four adolescent girls are standing across from her in the shower room. One of the girls is carrying a "plumber's helper," waving it suggestively by her side. The four girls violently attack the younger girl, wrestling her to the floor. The young girl is shown naked from the waist up, struggling as the older girls force her legs apart. Then, the television film shows the girl with the plumber's helper making intense thrusting motions with the handle of the plunger until one of the four says, "That's enough." The young girl is left sobbing and naked on the floor.

It is alleged that appellant, aged nine, was attacked by minors at a beach in San Francisco. It is alleged that the minors attacked appellant and another minor girl, and forcibly and against her will, "artificially raped" appellant with a bottle. The complaint alleges that the assailants had seen the "artificial rape" scene in "Born Innocent" and that the scene "caused them to decide to do a similar act to a minor girl."

When the case came on for jury trial, respondents moved, before empanelment of a jury, that the court first determine for itself the "constitutional fact" of "incitement"—i.e., whether the film, "Born Innocent," was a vehicle for "inciting" violent and depraved conduct such as the crimes of the juveniles in the present case, of which appellant was the victim.

The trial judge viewed the entire film, made a finding that it did not advocate or encourage violent and depraved acts and thus did not constitute an "incitement," and rendered judgment for respondents without impaneling a jury. The present appeal followed.

Analysis of this appeal commences with recognition of the overriding constitutional principle that material communicated by the public media, including fictional material such as the television drama here at issue, is generally to be accorded protection under the First Amendment to the Constitution of the United States. * * *

Specifically, television broadcasting is a medium which is entitled to First Amendment protection. * * * Thus, expression by means of television dramatization is included within the free speech and free press guarantees of the First and Fourteenth Amendments. Where a television broadcast does not involve unprotected speech, the constitutional protection for free speech limits the state's power to award damages in a negligence action based upon the broadcast. *See New York Times Co. v. Sullivan,* 376 U.S. 254, 265, 277–278 (1964). * * *

The freedom of speech guaranteed by the First Amendment is not, of course, absolute. Certain narrowly limited classes of speech may be prevented or punished by the state consistent with the principles of the First Amendment. Speech which is obscene is not protected by the First Amendment. *Miller v. California,* 413 U.S. 15, 23, 34–35 (1973), *rehg. denied,* 414 U.S. 881. "Born Innocent" is not constitutionally obscene. "[L]ibel, slander, misrepresentation, obscenity, perjury, false advertising, solicitation of crime, complicity by encouragement, conspiracy, and the like" are also outside the scope of constitutional protection. *Konigsberg* v. *State Bar,* 366 U.S. 36, 49, fn. 10 (1961). Libel and slander are considered outside the scope of First Amendment protection because "there is no constitutional value in *false* statements of *fact.*" *Gertz v. Robert Welch, Inc.,* 418 U.S. 323, 340 (1974); italics added. However, the free speech guarantee even requires that some protection be given to falsehood, in certain circumstances, "in order to protect speech that matters." *Gertz v. Robert Welch, Inc., supra,* at p. 341. The constitutional freedom for speech and press also does not immunize "speech or writing used as an integral part of conduct in violation of a valid criminal statute." *Giboney v. Empire Storage Co.,* 336 U.S. 490, 498 (1949). Additionally, speech which is directed to inciting or producing imminent lawless action, and which is likely to incite or produce such action, is also outside the scope of First Amendment protection. *See Brandenburg v. Ohio,* 395 U.S. 444, 447–448 (1969). * * *

The question whether the television film, "Born Innocent," falls within any category of unprotected speech may, where the facts are not disputed, constitute a question of law. * * * In the present case, the film itself was available and the court might perhaps have determined from viewing it in connection with a motion for summary judgment, that the film did not advocate or encourage violent and depraved acts and thus, did not constitute an "incitement." *See Paris Adult Theatre I v. Slaton,* 413 U.S. 49, 56 (1973), *rehg. denied,* 414 U.S. 881. * * * But a motion for summary judgment had earlier been denied by another judge. No such motion was pending when the trial judge rendered the decision now under review.

Trial by jury had been demanded by appellant. That demand put into operation her right, under California Constitution, article I, section 7, to have all fact issues in the case determined by a jury. The trial court's action in viewing the film, and thereupon making fact findings and rendering judgment for respondents, was a violation of appellant's constitutional right to trial by jury. It was both reversible error and an act in excess of jurisdiction. * * *

Here, it is appropriate to acknowledge that, if the cause had proceeded properly to trial before a jury and a verdict awarding damages to appellant had been the result, it would have been the responsibility of the trial court, or perhaps of this court on appeal, to determine upon a reevaluation of the evidence whether the jury's fact determination could be sustained against a First Amendment challenge to the jury's determination of a " 'constitutional fact.' " *Rosenbloom v. Metromedia, supra*, 403 U.S. 29, 54. But the case is not presently ripe for such a determination, appellant having been deprived of her constitutional right to present before a jury evidence which she contends will show that, despite First Amendment protections, the showing of the film, "Born Innocent," resulted in actionable injuries. * * * The judgment is reversed with directions to impanel a jury and proceed to trial of the action.

Notes

1. In May 1999, a 7–year-old boy in North Dallas, Texas accidentally killed his 3–year-old brother after imitating a pro wrestling move he saw on television. When interviewed by authorities, the boy demonstrated what had happened by running toward a doll about the same size as his brother and suddenly striking its neck, knocking it backwards. K. Anderson, *7 year old kid kills his 3 year old brother with a wrestling move*, THE DALLAS MORNING NEWS, July 1, 1999, *available at* http://www.media-scope.org/pubs/ibriefs/cc.htm.

2. In January 1999, two Florida teenagers repeatedly raped their 8–year-old half-sister after allegedly watching an episode about incest on The Jerry Springer Show. A detective asked the boys where they learned to abuse their sister and the older boy responded, "I learned it on The Jerry Springer Show." *Morning Report: Alleged Rapists Blame 'Springer,'* L. A. TIMES, Jan. 8, 1999, *available at* http://www.mediascope.org/pubs/ibriefs/cc.htm..

C.   THE DEVIL MUSIC MADE ME DO IT

Music is life. Music creates emotions and generates memories. The music you listened to between the ages of sixteen and twenty-two will most likely be the music you listen to for the rest of your life. The songs that you listened to during significant events in your life will stimulate memories of those events in the future when you hear those songs again. Music is a key component of our lives and can trigger strong emotional reactions. Songs are a part of our personal history. If music can make us laugh or cry, it is not a far stretch to claim that music can make us kill. Music is life; and in these cases, music is death.

MCCOLLUM v. CBS, INC.

California Court of Appeals, 1988.
202 Cal.App.3d 989, 249 Cal.Rptr. 187.

CROSKEY, Associate Justice.

Plaintiffs, Jack McCollum, Geraldine Lugenbuehl, Estate of John Daniel McCollum, Jack McCollum, Administrator (hereinafter "plaintiffs") appeal from an order of dismissal following the sustaining of a demurrer without leave to amend. The defendants John "Ozzy" Osbourne ("Osbourne"), CBS Records and CBS, Incorporated (hereinafter collectively "CBS"), Jet Records, Bob Daisley, Randy Rhoads, Essex Music International, Ltd., and Essex Music International Incorporated, composed, performed, produced and distributed certain recorded music which plaintiffs claim proximately resulted in the suicide of their decedent. As we conclude that plaintiffs' pleading (1) fails to allege any basis for overcoming the bar of the First Amendment's guarantee of free speech and expression and, in any event, (2) fails to allege sufficient facts to show any intentional or negligent invasion of plaintiffs' rights, we affirm.

FACTUAL AND PROCEDURAL BACKGROUND

On October 26, 1984, the plaintiffs' decedent, John Daniel McCollum ("John"), shot and killed himself while lying on his bed listening to Osbourne's recorded music. John was 19 years old at the time, and had a problem with alcohol abuse as well as serious emotional problems. Alleging that Osbourne's music was a proximate cause of John's suicide, plaintiffs filed suit against all of the named defendants. * * *

In the trial court's view, the First Amendment was an absolute bar to plaintiffs' claims. Nonetheless, the court did invite plaintiffs to seek leave to file a further pleading to see if that hurdle could be overcome. A proposed second amended complaint was submitted and the court made its final decision based on those allegations. For that reason, we here treat such proposed pleading as the operative one before us and assume that its states plaintiffs' case in its strongest light. In accordance with well settled principles, we likewise assume those allegations to be true. * * * They reflect the following facts.

On Friday night, October 26, 1984, John listened over and over again to certain music recorded by Osbourne. He listened repeatedly to side one of an album called, "Blizzard of Oz" and side two of an album called, "Diary of a Madman." These albums were found the next morning stacked on the turntable of the family stereo in the living room. John preferred to listen there because the sound was more intense. However, he had gone into his bedroom and was using a set of headphones to listen to the final side of the two record album, "Speak of the Devil" when he placed a .22 caliber handgun next to his right temple and took his own life. When he was found the next morning he was still wearing his headphones and the stereo was still running with the arm and needle riding in the center of the revolving record.

Plaintiffs allege that Osbourne is well known as the "mad man" of rock and roll and has become a cult figure. The words and music of his songs and even the album covers for his records seem to demonstrate a preoccupation with unusual, anti-social and even bizarre attitudes and beliefs often emphasizing such things as satanic worship or emulation, the mocking of religious beliefs and death. The message he has often conveyed is that life is filled with nothing but despair and hopelessness and suicide is not only acceptable, but desirable. Plaintiffs further allege that all of the defendants, through their efforts with the media, press releases and the promotion of Osbourne's records, have sought to cultivate this image and to profit from it.

Osbourne in his music sought to appeal to an audience which included troubled adolescents and young adults who were having a difficult time during this transition period of their life; plaintiffs allege that this specific target group was extremely susceptible to the external influence and directions from a cult figure such as Osbourne who had become a role model and leader for many of them. Osbourne and CBS knew that many of the members of such group were trying to cope with issues involving self-identity, alienation, spiritual confusion and even substance abuse.

Plaintiffs allege that a "special relationship" of kinship existed between Osbourne and his avid fans. This relationship was underscored and characterized by the personal manner in which the lyrics were directed and disseminated to the listeners. He often sings in the first person about himself and about what may be some of the listener's problems, directly addressing the listener as "you." That is, a listener could feel that Osbourne was talking directly to him as he listened to the music.

One of the songs which John had been listening to on the family stereo *before* he went to his bedroom was called "Suicide Solution" which, plaintiffs allege, preaches that "suicide is the only way out." Included in a 28 second instrumental break in the song are some "masked" lyrics (which are not included in the lyrics printed on the album cover): * * * "Where to hide? Suicide is the only way out. * * *

These lyrics are sung at one and one-half times the normal rate of speech and (in the words of plaintiffs' allegations) "are not immediately intelligible. They are perceptible enough to be heard and understood when the listener concentrates on the music and lyrics being played during this 28–second interval." In addition to the lyrics, plaintiffs also allege that Osbourne's music utilizes a strong, pounding and driving rhythm and, in at least one instance, a "hemisync" process of sound waves which impact the listener's mental state.

Following these general allegations, plaintiffs allege that the defendants knew, or should have known, that it was foreseeable that the music, lyrics and hemisync tones of Osbourne's music would influence

Influence emotions/behavior

the emotions and behavior of individual listeners such as John who, because of their emotional instability, were peculiarly susceptible to such music, lyrics and tones and that such individuals might be influenced to act in a manner destructive to their person or body. Plaintiffs further allege that defendants negligently disseminated Osbourne's music to the public and thereby (1) aided, advised or encouraged John to commit suicide (count I) or (2) created "an uncontrollable impulse" in him to commit suicide (count II); and that John, as a proximate result of listening to such music did commit suicide on October 26, 1984.

In the remaining two counts, plaintiffs allege, respectively, that defendants' conduct constituted (1) an incitement of John to commit suicide count III) and (2) an intentional aiding, advising or encouraging of suicide in violation of Penal Code section 401 (count IV). In all four counts plaintiffs allege that defendants acted maliciously and oppressively and thus are liable for punitive damages.

CONTENTIONS OF THE PARTIES

Plaintiffs argue that Osbourne's music and lyrics were the proximate cause of John's suicide and are not entitled to protection under the First Amendment. They seek recovery here on three separate theories. They claim that Osbourne and CBS (1) were negligent in the dissemination of Osbourne's recorded music, (2) intentionally disseminated that music with knowledge that it would produce an uncontrollable impulse to self-destruction in persons like John and (3) intentionally aided, advised or encouraged John's suicide in violation of Penal Code section 401, thus giving plaintiffs, as members of a group intended to be protected by that statute, a right of action for civil damages.

Defendants' initial and primary response is that plaintiffs' entire action, irrespective of the theory of recovery, is barred by the First Amendment's guarantee of free speech. In addition, they argue that the public dissemination of Osbourne's recorded music did not, as a matter of law, negligently or intentionally invade any right of plaintiffs or constitute a violation of Penal Code section 401.

DISCUSSION

1. The First Amendment Bars Plaintiffs' Action

Our consideration of plaintiffs' novel attempt to seek post publication damages for the general public dissemination of recorded music and lyrics must commence "with [the] recognition of the overriding constitutional principle that material communicated by the public media ... [including artistic expressions such as the music and lyrics here involved], is generally to be accorded protection under the First Amendment to the Constitution of the United States. *Joseph Burstyn, Inc. v. Wilson*, 343 U.S. 495, 501 (1952). * * *

First Amendment guarantees of freedom of speech and expression extend to all artistic and literary expression, whether in music, concerts, plays, pictures or books. *Schad v. Mount Ephraim*, 452 U.S. 61, 65

(1981) (non-obscene nude dancing). As the court in *Schad* noted, "Entertainment, as well as political and ideological speech, is protected; motion pictures, programs broadcast by radio and television, and live entertainment, such as musical and dramatic works, fall within the First Amendment guarantee." *Id.* at p. 65. * * *

However, the freedom of speech guaranteed by the First Amendment is not absolute. There are certain limited classes of speech which may be prevented or punished by the state consistent with the principles of the First Amendment: (1) obscene speech is not protected by the First Amendment, *Miller v. California*, 413 U.S. 15, 23, 34–35 (1973); (2) "libel, slander, misrepresentation, obscenity, perjury, false advertising, solicitation of crime, complicity by encouragement, conspiracy, and the like are also outside the scope of constitutional protection." *Konigsberg v. State Bar*, 366 U.S. 36, 49, fn. 10 (1961); (3) the constitutional freedom for speech and press does not immunize "speech or writing used as an integral part of conduct in violation of a valid criminal statute;" *Giboney v. Empire Storage Co.*, 336 U.S. 490, 498 (1949); and finally, (4) speech which is directed to inciting or producing imminent lawless action, and which is likely to incite or produce such action, is outside the scope of First Amendment protection. *Brandenburg v. Ohio*, 395 U.S. 444–448 (1969).

Plaintiffs argue that it is the last of these exceptions, relating to culpable incitement, which removes Osbourne's music from the protection of the First Amendment. * * *

It is settled that "the constitutional guarantees of free speech and free press do not permit a State to forbid or proscribe advocacy of the use of force or law violation except where such advocacy is directed to inciting or producing imminent lawless action and is likely to incite or produce such action." *Brandenburg v. Ohio*, 395 U.S. 444, 447 (1969). Thus, to justify a claim that speech should be restrained or punished because it is (or was) an incitement to lawless action, the court must be satisfied that the speech (1) was directed or intended toward the goal of producing imminent lawless conduct *and* (2) was likely to produce such imminent conduct. Speech directed to action at some indefinite time in the future will not satisfy this test. *Hess v. Indiana*, 414 U.S. 105, 108 (1973).

In the context of this case we must conclude, in order to find a culpable incitement, (1) that Osbourne's music was *directed and intended* toward the goal of bringing about the imminent suicide of listeners *and* (2) that it was *likely* to produce such a result. It is not enough that John's suicide may have been the result of an unreasonable reaction to the music; it must have been a specifically intended consequence.

We can find no such intent or likelihood here. Apart from the "unintelligible" lyrics quoted above from "Suicide Solution," to which John admittedly was not even listening at the time of his death, there is nothing in any of Osbourne's songs which could be characterized as a command to an immediate suicidal act. None of the lyrics relied upon by

plaintiffs, even accepting their literal interpretation of the words, purport to order or command anyone to any concrete action at any specific
time, much less immediately. Moreover, as defendants point out, the
lyrics of the song on which plaintiffs focus their primary objection can as
easily be viewed as a poetic device, such as a play on words, to convey
meanings entirely contrary to those asserted by plaintiffs. We note this
here not to suggest a reliance upon a construction which is contrary to
plaintiffs' allegations, but to illuminate the very serious problems which
can arise when litigants seek to cast judges in the role of censor.

Problem [handwritten margin note]

Merely because art may evoke a mood of depression as it figuratively
depicts the darker side of human nature does not mean that it constitutes a direct "incitement to imminent violence." The lyrics sung by
Osbourne may well express a philosophical view that suicide is an
acceptable alternative to a life that has become unendurable—an idea
which, however unorthodox, has a long intellectual tradition. If that is
the view expressed, as plaintiffs apparently contend, then defendants are
constitutionally free to advocate it. Plaintiffs' argument that speech may
be punished on the ground it has a tendency to lead to suicide or other
violence is precisely the doctrine rejected by the Supreme Court in *Hess
v. Indiana, supra,* 414 U.S. at pp. 108–09 (the words "We'll take the
f——g street again (or later)," shouted to a crowd at an antiwar
demonstration, amounted to "nothing more than advocacy of illegal
action at some indefinite future time"; words could not be punished as
"incitement" on the ground that they had a "tendency to lead to
violence"). * * *

advocacy of an act or a future indefinite time not enough [handwritten margin note]

Reasonable persons understand musical lyrics and poetic conventions as the figurative expressions which they are. No rational person
would or could believe otherwise nor would they mistake musical lyrics
and poetry for literal commands or directives to immediate action. To do
so would indulge a fiction which neither common sense nor the First
Amendment will permit. * * *

Plaintiffs, recognizing the dearth of case authority which would
support their incitement theory, make essentially a procedural argument. They contend that the court can not determine the question of
whether Osbourne's music and lyrics constituted an incitement but
rather the issue should be left to a jury. They rely on *Olivia N. v.
National Broadcasting Co., supra,* 141 Cal. Rptr. 511 ("Olivia I"), where
the court, in the first of two appellate decisions dealing with the film
"Born Innocent", held that the trial judge, on the day assigned for jury
trial and *without any summary judgment motion pending,* should not
have viewed the film himself and made fact findings that the film did not
advocate or encourage violent or depraved acts. The plaintiff had requested a trial by jury and was entitled to one.

However, plaintiffs' reliance on this case is misplaced. We view it as
strictly a procedural decision dealing with the technical rights of a party
after a proper request for a jury trial has been made. The First
Amendment issue was never reached and the appellate opinion itself

acknowledged that the court could have accomplished the same result *if* a properly noticed summary judgment motion had been before it. To the extent that any broader interpretation is given to "*Olivia I*", we respectfully decline to follow it in this case.

In our view, the plaintiffs have fully pleaded the facts which will be presented on the issue of incitement and we conclude that, as a matter of law, they fail to meet the *Brandenburg* standard for incitement and that therefore Osbourne's music is speech protected by the First Amendment.

The scope of such protection is not limited to merely serving as a bar to the prior restraint of such speech, but also prevents the assertion of a claim for civil damages. "[T]he fear of damage awards ... may be markedly more inhibiting than the fear of prosecution under a criminal statute." *New York Times Co. v. Sullivan*, 376 U.S. 254, 277 (1964). Musical composers and performers, as well as record producers and distributors, would become significantly more inhibited in the selection of controversial materials if liability for civil damages were a risk to be endured for publication of protected speech. The deterrent effect of subjecting the music and recording industry to such liability because of their programming choices would lead to a self-censorship which would dampen the vigor and limit the variety of artistic expression. Thus, the imposition here of post publication civil damages, in the absence of an incitement to imminent lawless action, would be just as violative of the First Amendment as a prior restraint.

2. The First Amendment Bar Aside, Plaintiffs Have Alleged No Basis For Recovery of Damages

a. Defendants Cannot Be Liable In Negligence As They Owed No Duty To Plaintiffs

* * * Plaintiffs rely on *Weirum* for the proposition that harm to John from listening to Osbourne's music was foreseeable. In that case, a radio station was held liable for the wrongful death of a motorist killed by two speeding teenagers participating in the station's promotional give away contest. In live periodic announcements the station advised its mobile listeners that one of its disc jockeys, "the Real Don Steele," was traveling from location to location in a conspicuous red automobile and advised the audience of his intended destinations. The first listener to meet Steele at each location would get a prize. While following Steele's car, the two teenagers forced a motorist into the center divider where his car overturned resulting in his death. *Weirum v. RKO General Inc.*, *supra*, 539 P.2d 36.

In our view, plaintiffs' reliance on *Weirum* is not justified. As the court there noted, the issue was "civil accountability for the foreseeable results of a broadcast which created an undue risk of harm to decedent. The First Amendment does not sanction the infliction of physical injury merely because achieved by word, rather than act." *Id.*, at p. 48, 539 P.2d 36. Indeed, it would not be inappropriate to view the reckless importuning in *Weirum* as a specie of incitement to imminent lawless conduct for which no First Amendment protection is justified. What the conduct in *Weirum* and culpable incitement have in common, when viewed from the perspective of a duty analysis, is a very high degree of foreseeability of undue risk of harm to others. Under such circumstances, imposition of negligence liability does not offend the First Amendment. * * *

While it is true that foreseeability is ordinarily a question of fact, * * * it may be decided as a question of law. * * * This is such a case. John's tragic self-destruction, while listening to Osbourne's music, was not a reasonably foreseeable risk or consequence of defendants' remote artistic activities.

Plaintiffs' case is not aided by an examination of the other factors which are a part of the duty analysis. It can not be said that there was a close connection between John's death and defendants' composition, performance, production and distribution years earlier of recorded artistic musical expressions. Likewise, no moral blame for that tragedy may be laid at defendants' door. John's suicide, an admittedly irrational response to Osbourne's music, was not something which any of the defendants intended, planned or had any reason to anticipate. Finally, and perhaps most significantly, it is simply not acceptable to a free and democratic society to impose a duty upon performing artists to limit and restrict their creativity in order to avoid the dissemination of ideas in artistic speech which may adversely affect emotionally troubled individuals. Such a burden would quickly have the effect of reducing and limiting artistic expression to only the broadest standard of taste and acceptance and the lowest level of offense, provocation and controversy. No case has ever gone so far. We find no basis in law or public policy for doing so here.

b. There Are No Allegations That Defendants Intended To Cause John's Suicide

The third and fourth alleged causes of action are essentially identical. They each rely upon the proposition that defendants incur intentional tort liability for John's suicide because of their intentional dissemination of Osbourne's recorded music with the alleged knowledge that it would result in self-destructive reactions among certain individuals. The third count characterizes this as an intentional incitement to suicide. We have already discussed in some detail why Osbourne's music and lyrics cannot be condemned as an incitement to imminent lawless action. It is also clear that plaintiffs have not adequately alleged a culpable intent. For example, there are no allegations that defendants actually intended any harm to John or any other listener.

It is not sufficient simply to allege that defendants intentionally did a particular act. It must also be shown that such act was done with the intent to cause injury. *Tate v. Canonica,* 5 Cal. Rptr. 28 (1960). In other words, plaintiffs would have to allege that defendants intended to cause John's (or some other listener's) suicide and made the subject recorded music available for that purpose. It is clear that no such allegation can be made in this case. What plaintiffs have alleged does not demonstrate the requisite intent. * * *

Conclusion

Absent an incitement, which meets the standards of *Brandenburg v. Ohio, supra,* 395 U.S. 444, 447, the courts have been universally reluctant to impose tort liability upon any public media for self destructive or tortuous acts alleged to have resulted from a publication or broadcast. * * * We share that reluctance and, for all of the reasons discussed above, conclude that the defendants, as a matter of law, have no liability for John's suicide. * * *

Notes

1. Ozzy Osbourne and his family have become mainstream cult television stars with their MTV show: *The Osbournes.* The show uses a reality television format as cameras follow the family members as they perform their "normal" daily routines. The show demonstrates that even dysfunctional families share the common bond of love.

2. Ozzy Osbourne received his star on the Hollywood Walk of Fame on September 30, 2003.

3. MTV's favorite dad, Ozzy Osbourne, has also had his share of controversy. Known as the "Madman of Rock n' Roll," Osbourne bit the head off of a bat during a concert in 1982. The bat "bit back," and Osbourne had to get rabies shots. In 1983, another biting occurred. This time Osbourne bit the head off of a dove during a business meeting with record executives. http://rockonthenet.com/artists-o/ozzyosbourne.htm

4. In *Waller v. Osbourne,* 763 F.Supp. 1144 (M.D. Ga. 1991), *aff'd,* 958 F.2d 1084 (11th Cir. 1992). A wrongful death action was brought against Ozzy Osbourne and CBS records claiming that the song "Suicide Solution" contained subliminal messages and incited the listener to commit suicide. The court held that the Plaintiff failed to show that the song contained subliminal messages. References to suicide were audible, thus are within the conscious awareness and are not subliminal. The court also held that there was "no evidence that the Defendant's music was intended to produce acts of suicide, and likely to cause imminent acts of suicide; nor could one rationally infer such a meaning from the lyrics." Therefore, the lyrics were found to be protected by the First Amendment from any liability for incitement. Summary Judgment was granted in favor of the Defendants, Osbourne and CBS.

5. What does Ozzy Osbourne say about his songs encouraging his listeners to commit suicide? "If I wrote music for people who shot themselves after listening to my music, I wouldn't have much of a following." (Ozzy Osbourne, 1990) http://rockonthenet.com/artists-o/ozzyosbourne.htm

DAVIDSON v. TIME WARNER, INC.

United States District Court, S.D. Texas, 1997.
1997 WL 405907.

RAINEY, Judge.

I. THE PARTIES

* * * Plaintiffs Linda, Trey Wes and Kimberly Dyan Davidson (collectively, the "Davidsons") are Texas residents. Defendant Tupac Amaru Shakur ("Shakur") was a resident of the state of Georgia. Defendant Time Warner, Inc. ("Time Warner") is a Delaware Corporation with its principal place of business in New York. Defendant Atlantic Recording Corporation ("Atlantic Records") is a subsidiary of Warner Communications, Inc., which in turn is wholly owned by Time Warner. Defendant Interscope Records ("Interscope Records") is a partnership formed by a subsidiary of Atlantic Records in partnership with a California corporation.

II. BACKGROUND

The parties do not dispute the essential facts of this case. In April of 1992, Ronald Howard ("Howard") was driving a stolen automobile through Jackson County, Texas. Officer Bill Davidson, a state trooper, stopped Howard for a possible traffic violation unrelated to the theft of the vehicle. During the traffic stop, Howard fatally shot Officer Davidson with a nine millimeter Glock handgun. At the time of the shooting, Howard was listening to an audio cassette of *2Pacalypse Now*, a recording performed by Defendant Tupac Amaru Shakur that was produced, manufactured and distributed by Defendants Interscope Records and Atlantic Records. In an attempt to avoid the death penalty, Howard claimed that listening to *2Pacalypse Now* caused him to shoot Officer Davidson. The jury apparently did not believe this explanation, because it sentenced Howard to death.

The Davidsons then brought this civil action (after taking a non-suit in state court), echoing several of the arguments made by Howard during his criminal trial. First, the Davidsons claim that the album *2Pacalypse Now* does not merit First Amendment protection because it: (1) is obscene, (2) contains "fighting words," (3) defames peace officers like Officer Davidson, and (4) tends to incite imminent illegal conduct on the part of individuals like Howard. Because the recording lacks constitutional protection, the Davidsons argue that Defendants are liable for producing violent music that proximately caused the death of Officer Davidson.

[Part III omitted].

IV. STATE LAW ISSUES

"Where there is no need to decide a constitutional question, it is a venerable principle of this Court's adjudicatory processes not to do so for the Court will not anticipate a question of constitutional law in advance of the necessity of deciding it." *Webster v. Reproductive Health Serv.*, 492 U.S. 490 (1989) (O'Connor, J., concurring) (citations and internal quotation marks omitted). Although prudence requires the Court to review the First Amendment issues surrounding *2Pacalypse Now*, the Court is of the opinion that this action is properly resolved by reviewing Texas negligence law.

Defendants are not Liable on a Negligence Theory

"In Texas, actionable negligence requires the existence of a legal duty owed by one person to another, a breach of that duty, and damages proximately resulting from breach of that duty." *Federal Sav. & Loan Ins. Corp. v. Texas Real Estate Counselors, Inc.*, 955 F.2d 261, 265 (5th Cir.1992). Existence of a duty is a question of law for the Court to decide from the facts surrounding the occurrence in question. *Texas Real Estate Counselors*, 955 F.2d at 265. Texas courts employ a risk-utility balancing test to determine the existence of a legal duty: In determining whether to impose a duty we are to consider the risk, foreseeability, and likelihood of injury weighed against the social utility of the actor's conduct, the magnitude of the burden of guarding against the injury and the consequences of placing that burden on the actor. *Venetoulias v. O'Brien*, 909 S.W.2d 236, 241 (Tex. App.—Houston 1995, *writ dism'd*). * * *

Foreseeability is the most significant factor when using the risk-utility test. *Washington*, 68 F.3d at 938. * * * "[A] danger is foreseeable when 'the actor, as a person of ordinary intelligence, should have anticipated the dangers that his negligent act created for others.'" *Garza*, 809 F.2d at 1172 (quoting *Nixon v. Mr. Property Management*, 690 S.W.2d 546, 550 (Tex.1985)). "Determinations of foreseeability can properly involve more than actual knowledge of particular incidents and cannot necessarily be divorced from common knowledge. Foreseeability should be measured in the light of common or ordinary experience." *Berly v. D & L Security Serv.*, 876 S.W.2d 179, 182 (Tex. App.—Dallas 1994, writ denied) (citations omitted). After reviewing the facts of this case and drawing all inferences in the Davidsons' favor, the Court must conclude that Defendants had no duty prevent the distribution of *2Pacalypse Now*. See *Washington*, 68 F.3d at 938 (citing *Kendrick v. Allright Parking*, 846 S.W.2d 453, 458 (Tex. App.—San Antonio 1992, writ denied)).

Research by the parties and the Court unveils few cases interpreting Texas law that address foreseeability when a widely distributed publication (such as a recording or magazine) causes injuries to another. Unfortunately for the Davidsons, none of these cases imposed a duty upon a publisher to refrain from distributing a published work. Because of these cases and the policies that support them, the Court predicts that Texas Courts would rule in favor of Defendants on their motion for summary judgment. See *Washington v. Resolution Trust Corp.*, 68 F.3d 935, 937 (5th Cir.1995) (federal courts are charged with making *Erie* prediction when Texas courts have not determined whether a duty exists in a particular fact situation); *Herceg v. Hustler Magazine, Inc.,* 565 F.Supp. 802, 803–804 (S.D. Tex. 1983) (McDonald, J.) (collecting cases of other jurisdictions that address negligent publication theory).

In *Eimann v. Soldier of Fortune Magazine,* 880 F.2d 830 (5th Cir.1989), *cert. denied,* 493 U.S. 1024 (1990), Plaintiff sued *Soldier of Fortune* for negligence and gross negligence for publishing a personal services classified advertisement through which the victim's husband hired an assassin. *Id.* at 831. Plaintiff presented evidence of some three dozen classified ads from *Soldier of Fortune* that offered services as a "Mercenary for Hire," or "bounty hunter." Other ads promised to perform "dirty work" or to "do anything, anywhere at the right price." *Id.* at 832. Plaintiff presented evidence that at least seven of these ✗ advertisements were linked to criminal activity. *Id.* Perhaps most importantly, law enforcement officials contacted the magazine's staff during investigations of two crimes linked to *Soldier of Fortune* classifieds. Thus, the editors of *Soldier of Fortune* were aware that certain classified advertisements were connected to criminal activity.

Despite this evidence, the Fifth Circuit held that the magazine "owed no duty to refrain from publishing a facially innocuous classified advertisement when the ad's context—at most—made its message ambiguous." *Id.* at 834. "To reach this result, the Fifth Circuit employed Texas law and its risk-utility balancing test. *Id.* The Fifth Circuit determined that the probability and gravity of the threatened harm was high because of evidence that several classified ads in the magazine had been linked to criminal activity. "The prospect of ad-inspired crime represents a threat of serious harm." *Id.* at 835. * * *

However, the Fifth Circuit recognized that the burden of preventing the harm also was high, given the ambiguous nature of the advertisement at issue and the pervasiveness of advertising in society. Although the ad in question expressed the desire for " 'high risk assignments' . . . its bare terms reveal no identifiable offer to commit crimes." *Id.* at 836. "The ambiguity persists even if we assume that [*Soldier of Fortune*] knew other ads had been tied to criminal plots. No evidence linked the other ads and crimes to Hearn [the hired assassin]." *Id.*

Finally, although the Fifth Circuit decided not to reach *Soldier of Fortune's* First Amendment arguments, the Court noted "the Supreme Court's recognition of limited first amendment protection for commercial speech . . . highlights the important role of such communication for purposes of risk-benefit analysis." *Id.* at 836. Although the plaintiff noted that the advertising of illegal activity is not protected by the First Amendment, the Fifth Circuit countered that "the possibility of illegal results does not necessarily strip an ad of its commercial speech protection." *Id.* At 837 (citing *Dunagin v. City of Oxford,* 718 F.2d 738, 743 (5th Cir.1983).

Although in this case the variables of the risk-utility equation differ from *Eimann,* the calculation yields the same result. There is no question that *2Pacalypse Now* depicts violence, and a reasonable jury could

[handwritten margin note: AMBIGUITY]

[handwritten margin note: the possibility of illegal results. doesn't necessarily strip an ad of its commercial speech protection]

find that the recording entreats others to act on Shakur's violent message. However, playing a musical recording (even tasteless, violent music like *2Pacalypse Now*) is fundamentally different from placing a classified advertisement seeking employment as a mercenary. The probability that a listener of *2Pacalypse Now* would act on Shakur's message is substantially less than the chance that a person responding to a *Soldier of Fortune* advertisement would hire a "hit man" for illegal activity. The evidence illustrates this common-sense difference. In *Eimann,* the plaintiff presented evidence that at least seven of the magazine's classified ads were tied to criminal activity. By contrast, the Davidsons present no evidence that *2Pacalypse Now* has been the source of "music-inspired crime"; after more than 400,000 sales of *2Pacalypse Now,* the case at bar is the only one alleging violence after listening to Shakur's virulent music. Thus, the probability of harm is very low.

In addition, the burden of preventing the harm is very high, both to Defendants and to society at large. To create a duty requiring Defendants to police their recordings would be enormous and would result in the sale of only the most bland, least controversial music. *See McCollum v. Columbia Broadcasting Systems, Inc.,* 249 Cal. Rptr. 187, 197 (1988). ("it is simply not acceptable to a free and democratic society to impose a duty upon performing artists to limit and restrict their creativity in order to avoid the dissemination of ideas in artistic speech which may adversely affect emotionally troubled individuals. Such a burden would quickly have the effect of reducing and limiting artistic expression to only the broadest standard of taste and acceptance and the lowest level of offense, provocation and controversy. No case has ever gone so far. We find no basis in law or public policy in doing so here."). Further, the *Eimann* Court recognized that First Amendment considerations impact the risk-benefit analysis. Unlike *Eimann,* which addressed commercial speech receiving limited First Amendment protection, *2Pacalypse Now,* as music, receives full First Amendment protection.

Further, at least one Texas court has found media-related injuries to be unforeseeable. In *Way v. Boy Scouts of America,* 856 S.W.2d 230 (Tex. App.—Dallas 1993, writ denied), a twelve year old boy was shot and killed after he read a shooting supplement in *Boy's Life.* The youngster, curious about guns after reading the supplement, located an old rifle. The rifle discharged, killing the child. The parents subsequently sued, claiming that *Boy's Life* was negligent in printing the shooting supplement. The Texas Court of Appeals affirmed the trial court's grant of summary judgment, employing the state's risk-utility balancing test: Although experimentation with firearms obviously poses serious risks to children, to merely focus on that risk would be to ignore the context in which the supplement presented the use of firearms.... Of greatest significance, the record does not support a conclusion that Rocky's experimentation with the rifle and cartridge was a reasonably foreseeable consequence of the publication. *Way,* 856 S.W.2d at 236.

The court noted that the supplement emphasized supervision when using firearms. "Similarly, features present the use of firearms not as an experiment, but as a supervised and safety-conscious activity. A number of manufacturer advertisements in the supplement also depict a child's use of firearms as a supervised activity." *Id.* By contrast, the deadly experiment in which the child engaged was unsupervised. The court concluded, "encouragement of safe and responsible use of firearms by minors in conjunction with Boy Scout and other supervised activities is of significant social utility." *Id.*

The record indicates that Defendants could not reasonably foresee that distributing *2Pacalypse Now* would lead to violence. To be sure, Shakur's music is violent and socially offensive. This fact, by itself, does not make violence a foreseeable result of listening to *2Pacalypse Now*. The killing of Officer Davidson was not a random act of violence against a peace officer; it was an attempt to elude justice by an adult gang member driving a stolen automobile. Other courts have found foreseeability lacking in similar situations. *Sakon v. Pepsico., Inc.*, 553 So.2d 163, 166 (Fla. 1989) (no legal liability when child duplicated stunt in commercial); *McCollum v. CBS, Inc.*, 249 Cal. Rptr. at 196 (no liability after juvenile committed suicide after hearing Ozzy Osbourne song "Suicide Solution"). Considering the murder of Officer Davidson was an irrational and illegal act, Defendants are not bound to foresee and plan against such conduct. *See Houston Transp. Co. v. Phillips*, 801 S.W.2d 523 (Tex.1990) (employer of taxi drivers could not be liable for failing to warn drivers not to carry guns because risk of harm was unforeseeable). * * *

Finally, this is the first incident of violence allegedly caused by the playing of Shakur's album. * * *

For these reasons, summary judgment should be GRANTED as to the Davidsons' negligence claim.

The Davidsons could not sue Defendants on a Products Liability Theory

In *Way* the Texas Court of Appeals held that a person allegedly injured by the content of a shooting supplement could not sue the writer or publisher of the supplement on a strict products liability theory. Texas has adopted the theory of strict tort liability under section 402A of the Restatement (Second) of Torts. *McKisson v. Sales Affiliates, Inc.*, 416 S.W.2d 787, 789 (Tex.1967). That section provides: (1) One who sells a product in a defective condition unreasonably dangerous to the user or consumer or to his property is subject to liability for physical harm thereby caused to the ultimate user or consumer, or to his property. * * *

The Davidsons, like the plaintiff in *Way*, were not harmed by any physical properties of the audio tape. The Davidsons argue that the *ideas* contained in the recording encouraged Howard to kill Officer Davidson, thereby making *2Pacalypse Now* a defective "product." * * *

The *Way* court concluded: "the ideas, thoughts, words, and information conveyed by the magazine and the shooting sports supplement are

ideas words are w/in the
not products meaning of Restatement Torts.

not *products* within the meaning of the Restatement (Second) of Torts." *Way,* 856 S.W.2d at 239. Since the case at bar was brought in diversity, the Court must apply the laws of the state of Texas. The record indicates that Howard's pirated copy of *2Pacalypse Now* functioned adequately. Therefore, the products liability claim must fail.

IV. First Amendment Issues

The Court admits that issues of foreseeability often are nebulous, as they must be in order to address the variety of factual scenarios that fall under the negligence rubric. Therefore, even though the Court believes that Texas Courts would not find a duty to prevent the distribution of *2Pacalypse Now,* the Court will still address the parties' First Amendment arguments.

1A concern

Analysis of *2Pacalypse Now* begins with a recognition that "all political and non-political musical expression, like other forms of entertainment, is a matter of First Amendment concern." *Cinevision Corp. v. City of Burbank,* 745 F.2d 560, 569 (5th Cir.1984), *cert. denied,* 471 U.S. 1054 (1985); *Ward v. Rock Against Racism,* 491 U.S. 781, 790 (1989) ("Music, as a form of expression and communication, is protected under the First Amendment."). First Amendment protection extends to rap music. *Betts v. McCaughtry,* 827 F.Supp. 1400, 1406 (W.D.Wis.1993) ("It is undisputed that rap music constitute speech protected by the First Amendment."), *aff'd* 19 F.3d 21 (7th Cir.1994) (unpublished opinion); *Atlantic Beach Casino, Inc. v. Morenzoni,* 749 F.Supp. 38, 41 (D.R.I.1990) (extending First Amendment protection to live performance of 2 Live Crew). In addition, First Amendment protection is not weakened because the music takes an unpopular or even dangerous viewpoint. * * *

The First Amendment guarantee is not absolute, however, as the "unconditional phrasing of the First Amendment was not intended to protect every utterance." *Roth v. United States,* 354 U.S. 476, 483 (1957). Indeed, there are categories of speech that receive no constitutional protection. These unprotected categories include obscene speech, defamatory invasions of privacy, fighting words, and words likely to produce imminent lawless action (incitement). *See generally R.A.V. v. City of St. Paul,* 505 U.S. 377, 381–90 (1992). In an effort to strip *2Pacalypse Now* of its First Amendment Protection, the Davidsons claim Shakur's album falls into *all* of the above-mentioned categories. Whether *2Pacalypse Now* is unprotected speech is a question of law. Therefore, as a threshold question the Court must determine whether *2Pacalypse Now* loses its protection because of its content. *See Connick v. Myers,* 461 U.S. 138, 148 n. 7 (1983) ("The inquiry into the protected status of speech is one of law, not fact."). * * *

obscene speech
defamatory
invasions of
privacy
fighting words
incitement to
imminent
lawless
conduct.

1. The Davidsons' obscenity arguments do not apply to this case.

In deciding whether *2Pacalypse Now* is obscene, the Court must apply the test enunciated by the Supreme Court in *Miller v. California,* 413 U.S. 15 (1973). To be obscene, there must be independent proof of the following factors: (1) the average person, applying contemporary

Obscene

community standards, would find that the work, taken as a whole, appeals to the prurient interest; (2) measured by contemporary community standards, the work depicts or describes, in a patently offensive way, sexual conduct specifically defined by applicable state law, and (3) the work, taken as a whole, lacks serious literary, artistic, political, or scientific value. *Luke Records, Inc. v. Navarro*, 960 F.2d 134, 136 (11th Cir.), *cert. denied*, 506 U.S. 1022 (1992). * * *

Although one circuit indicated that no musical work could ever be declared obscene, this Court can dismiss the Davidsons' obscenity claim without such sweeping declarations. First, the Court doubts, as a matter of law, that *2Pacalypse Now* could ever satisfy *Miller* obscenity test. *2Pacalypse Now* is riddled with expletives and depictions of violence, and overall the album is extremely repulsive. However, it lacks the "patently offensive representations or descriptions of masturbation, excretory functions, and lewd exhibition of the genitals" required by the Supreme Court. *Miller*, 413 U.S. at 25 (also noting that "patently offensive representations of descriptions of ultimate sexual acts, normal or perverted, actual or simulated" were included in obscene speech). In other words, although the Davidsons allege Shakur intended *2Pacalypse Now* to appeal to the violent "gangsta" subculture, they have presented no evidence the recording was made to appeal to the *prurient* interest. Indeed, the only sexual "appeal" that appears on *2Pacalypse Now's* cassette jacket is the vague statement: "Parental Advisory—Explicit Lyrics." Therefore, the "leer of the sensualist" does not "permeate" this work.

More importantly, a conclusion that *2Pacalypse Now* is an obscene recording would be irrelevant to the Davidsons' suit. The Davidsons allege Shakur's album proximately caused the death of a police officer. However, the Davidsons base this claim on the *violent* nature of the album, not on the recording's *sexual* lyrics. Therefore, to remove constitutional protection from *2Pacalypse Now* on the basis of obscenity would commit a nonsequitur. * * *

3.   The lyrics of 2Pacalypse Now are not "fighting words."

The Supreme Court has recognized there exist "certain well-defined and narrowly limited classes of speech, the prevention and punishment of which has never been thought to raise any Constitutional protections. These include ... 'fighting' words—those which by their very utterance inflict injury or tend to incite an immediate breach of the peace." *Chaplinsky*, 315 U.S. at 571–72. The Davidsons contend that *2Pacalypse Now* contains fighting words, and therefore its creators may be subject to this tort action.

immediate breach of peace

The Court disagrees. To be sure, *2Pacalypse Now* is rife with profanity, but "the Supreme Court has long held that, as a general rule, simple profanity or vulgarity—not rising to the level of 'fighting words' or obscenity—is constitutionally protected speech." *United States v. Hicks*, 980 F.2d 963, 970 (5th Cir.) (citations omitted), *cert. denied*, 508 U.S. 941 (1992). The *Hicks* court defined profanity and vulgarity to include "words that, while not obscene, nevertheless are considered generally offensive by contemporary community standards." *Id.* at 970 n. 9. *See Street v. New York,* 394 U.S. 576, 592 (1969) ("It is firmly settled that under our Constitution the public expression of ideas may not be prohibited merely because the ideas are themselves offensive to some of the hearers."). Without question, *2Pacalypse Now* falls into the category of "generally offensive" speech; however, no reasonable jury could conclude that persons would reflexively lash out because of the language of Shakur's recording. Shakur's words are offensive but are not "by their very nature" likely to cause violence. Further, as the Court describes later, Ronald Howard did not reflexively react based on Shakur's offensive speech. Therefore, the fighting words doctrine does not apply.

The "fighting words" doctrine applies when an individual hurls epithets at another, causing the latter to retaliate against the speaker. In *Chaplinsky,* for example, the Supreme Court upheld a conviction of a person who called the marshal arresting him a "damned racketeer" and a "damned fascist." *Chaplinsky,* 315 U.S. 568. The "fighting words" doctrine generally does not apply when one person's epithets causes another to commit violence against a third, nonhearing party. In other words, the doctrine requires the epithets to be of a personal nature not present in this case. In *Cohen v. California,* 403 U.S. 15, 20 (1971), for example, the Court reversed the conviction of a protester who wore a jacket bearing the insignia "F—k the Draft." The Court did not find the phrase rose to the level of fighting words: This Court has also held that the States are free to ban . . . so-called 'fighting words,' those personally abusive epithets which, when addressed to the ordinary citizen, are, as a matter of common knowledge, inherently likely to provoke violent reaction. * * *

Considering the fact-specific analysis demanded by the Supreme Court, this Court must conclude that the lyrics of *2Pacalypse Now,* a recording which fails to direct its invective at any specific person in this case, were not fighting words. * * *

Finally, the Court recognizes that most courts addressing media violence have relied upon *Bradenburg's* "incitement" analysis rather than *Chaplinsky's* "fighting words" doctrine. Unlike "fighting words," which addresses a person's reactions to another's *personal* insults, "incitement" addresses speech that results in attacks on *third* parties. * * *

4. 2Pacalypse Now does not imminently incite violence under Brandenburg.

The Supreme Court has narrowly defined the class of unprotected, "inciting" speech. To restrain *2Pacalypse Now* in this case, the Court must find the recording (1) was directed or intended toward the goal of producing imminent lawless conduct and (2) was likely to produce such imminent illegal conduct. *See Hess v. Indiana,* 414 U.S. 105, 108 (1973). While the Davidsons may have shown that Shakur *intended* to produce imminent lawless conduct, the Davidson's cannot show that Howard's violent conduct was an *imminent* and *likely* result of listening to Shakur's songs.

In support of the first prong, the Davidsons argue that Shakur describes his music as "revolutionary" that has a purpose of angering the listener. This argument may place too much importance on Shakur's rhetoric. Calling ones music revolutionary does not, by itself, mean that Shakur intended his music to produce imminent lawless conduct. At worst, Shakur's intent was to cause violence some time after the listener considered Shakur's message. The First Amendment protects such advocacy. * * *

The mere abstract teaching of the moral propriety or even moral necessity for a resort to force and violence, is not the same as preparing a group for violent action and steeling it to such action. *Brandenburg v. Ohio*, 395 U.S. 444, 447–48. The Supreme Court has recognized that "in public debate our own citizens must tolerate insulting, and even outrageous, speech in order to provide adequate breathing space to the freedoms protected by the First Amendment." *Boos v. Barry*, 485 U.S. 312, 322 (1988). While *2Pacalypse Now* is both insulting and outrageous, it does not appear that Shakur *intended* to incite *imminent* illegal conduct when he recorded *2Pacalypse Now. See Bill v. Superior Court*, 187 Cal. Rptr. 625, 627–28 (Cal.App.1982) (granting summary judgment on claim that movie theater operator negligently showed movie depicting gang violence and failed to provide security when movie attracted people who were prone to violence and likely to carry weapons).

Assuming, as the Davidsons strenuously argue, that Shakur intended his music to incite imminent, lawless conduct, the Court is of the opinion that the mere broadcast of *2Pacalypse Now* is not *likely* to incite or produce illegal or violent action. The Davidsons are the first to claim that *2Pacalypse Now* caused illegal conduct, three years after the recording *2Pacalypse Now* and after more than 400,000 sales of the album. The Davidsons argue that, because Howard shot Officer Davidson while listening to *2Pacalypse Now*, that Davidson was killed *because* Howard was listening to *2Pacalypse Now*. The Court will not engage in the fallacy of *post hoc ergo propter hoc*. Courts addressing similar issues have repeatedly refused to find a musical recording or broadcast incited certain conduct merely because certain acts occurred after the speech. In this case, it is far more likely that Howard, a gang member driving a stolen automobile, feared his arrest and shot officer Davidson to avoid capture. Under the circumstances, the Court cannot conclude that *2Pacalypse Now* was likely to cause imminent illegal conduct. * * *

The Davidsons also fail to show that the illegal conduct Shakur allegedly encourages would *imminently occur* after listening to the album. First, "no rational person would or could believe otherwise nor would they mistake musical lyrics and poetry for literal commands or directives to immediate action." *McCollum v. Columbia Broad. Sys., Inc.*, 249 Cal.Rptr. 187, 194 (1988). The Davidsons face the difficulty of arguing that *2Pacalypse Now* caused imminent violence when Howard lashed out after listening to recorded music, not a live performance. Shakur's music, however, was not overtly directed at Howard. The Davidsons argue that *2Pacalypse Now* is directed to the violent black "gangsta" subculture in general. However, this group is necessarily too large to remove First Amendment protection from the album: to hold otherwise would remove constitutional protection from speech directed to marginalized groups. *See also Hess v. Indiana*, 414 U.S. 105, 109 (1973) ("Since the uncontroverted evidence showed that Hess' statement was not directed to any person or group of persons, it cannot be said that he was advocating, in the normal sense, any action. And since there was no evidence or rational inference from the import of the language, that his words were intended to produce, and likely to produce, imminent disorder, those words could not be punished by the state on the ground that they had 'a tendency to lead to violence.' ").

Finally, the Davidsons' own evidence undermines their claim that Officer Davidson was murdered as a result of some call to imminent, violent action by Shakur. Howard had been listening to *2Pacalypse Now* repeatedly, rewinding and replaying various songs, for some 45 minutes before killing Officer Davidson. Before listening to *2Pacalypse Now*, Howard had listened to numerous other rap recordings, which the Davidsons' expert claims made Howard more likely to commit violence. Considering Howard allegedly was "addicted" to rap music, including *2Pacalypse Now*, and that he had not lashed out against peace officers from the beginning of his "addiction" until his murder of Officer Davidson, the Court cannot conclude that *2Pacalypse Now* was likely to cause *imminent* lawless conduct. At best, the recording reveals that weak-willed individuals may be influenced by Shakur's work. As the Supreme Court explained, swaying the weak-willed does not remove constitutional protection from speech. * * *

Finally, the Court worries that permitting the Davidsons to proceed with this litigation, would "invariably lead to self-censorship by broadcasters in order to remove any matter that may be emulated and lead to a law suit." *DeFilippo*, 446 A.2d at 1041. "The deterrent effect of subjecting [Defendants] to negligence liability because of their programming choices would lead to self-censorship which would dampen the vigor and limit the variety of public debate." *Bill v. Superior Court*, 187 Cal. Rptr. 625, 627 (1983). In such conditions, those who record albums "would be required to take into account the potential for liability to patrons for acts of violence on the part of persons over whom the producers would have no control." *Bill*, 187 Cal. Rptr. at 628. This self-censorship not only would affect broadcasters, who would be chilled into producing only the most mundane, least emotional material. This self-censorship would also prevent listeners from accessing important social commentary, not just the violent and aesthetically questionable *2Pacalypse Now*. The public, like Mr. Shakur, has the right to access "social, aesthetic, moral, and other ideas and experiences." *Columbia Broadcasting System v. Democratic Nat. Comm.*, 412 U.S. 94, 102 (1973). * * *

2Pacalypse Now is both disgusting and offensive. That the album has sold hundreds of thousands of copies is an indication of society's aesthetic and moral decay. However, the First Amendment became part of the Constitution because the Crown sought to suppress the Framers' own rebellious, sometimes violent views. Thus, although the Court cannot recommend *2Pacalypse Now* to anyone, it will not strip Shakur's free speech rights based on the evidence presented by the Davidsons.

V. CONCLUSION

For these reasons, Defendants Time Warner, Inc. and Tupac Amaru Shakur's joint Motion for Summary Judgment should be GRANTED, rendering MOOT Defendants' Motion to Transfer Venue. [The Court also held a lack of personal jurisdiction in this case].

Notes

1. In *United States v. Jefferson*, 974 F.2d 201 (D.C.Cir. 1992), police were given consent by Defendant's mother to search her backyard because she suspected her son was involved "in various drug activities." Police recovered several bags of cocaine and a sawed off shotgun hidden in a lawnmower grass catcher bag. Defendant was convicted, in the United States District Court for the District of Columbia, for possession of cocaine with the intent to distribute and for using a firearm in connection with drug trafficking. One issue the Court addressed was whether there was sufficient evidence that the shotgun was used to "protect" the drugs. On appeal, the court made reference to a Rap Song to justify the lethal potential of a shotgun: "as attested by the virulent rap song 'Cop Killer.' " *See* Ice–T, Cop Killer, on Body Count (Warner Bros. Records 1992) ("I got my twelve gauge sawed off ... I'm 'bout to dust some cops off."). The court concluded that a "jury could reasonably conclude that the gun was appropriate for the protection of the drugs in Jefferson's possession, and that it was so used."

2. Shortly after the "Cop Killer" incident, the Board of Directors of Time Warner voted to sell Interscope Records because it did not want the company to be associated with the negative lyrics associated with the rap label. Universal Music bought Interscope Records. After the merger, Universal Music became the largest record company in the world.

PAHLER v. SLAYER

Superior Court of San Luis Obispo, California, 2001.
2001 WL 1736476.

BURKE, Judge.

The principal question presented by the demurrers to plaintiffs' Third Amended Complaint is whether plaintiffs may maintain on behalf of the general public an unfair competition action against persons who create, produce and market indecent musical products to minors. The court concludes that such an action may not be maintained under Business and Professions Code section 17200 in the absence of legisla-

ISSUE

tion specifically regulating such activities. The court also concludes that principles of free speech, duty and foreseeability of harm bar plaintiffs' wrongful death cause of action against the recording industry.

I

PROCEDURAL HISTORY

In 1995, David and Lisanne Pahler's daughter Elyse, 15, was kidnapped, tortured, raped and murdered by three adolescent males. The Pahlers sued the killers and their parents for wrongful death. They also sued persons who perform as the musical group called "Slayer" and those who record, promote, market and distribute Slayer products (the "music industry defendants."). The Pahlers allege their daughter's murder parallels acts of murder, rape and ritual sacrifice described in Slayer lyrics.

The case was stayed until criminal proceedings against the persons who killed Elyse Pahler were final. When the stay was lifted, demurrers to an earlier version of the complaint were sustained. A Third Amended Complaint was filed ("complaint") to which the defendants again interposed demurrers.

II

FACTS

In reviewing the sufficiency of a complaint to withstand a demurrer, the court assumes the truth of all properly pleaded material allegations. Material which may be judicially noticed also may be considered and regarded as true. The following facts appear in the complaint or in material that can be judicially noticed. They are assumed to be true.

Slayer is a band that composes and performs music in the death metal genre. Slayer lyrics are profane and glorify grisly violence against women. Slayer band members speak to the pleasure they derive from stalking, kidnapping, beating, torture, rape, ritual sacrifice, cannibalism and murder. They also describe sex acts. The compositions occasionally include commentary about an indifferent and passive government, an ineffective criminal justice system and a country that has "lost its grip." The lyrics are set to atonal, dissonant music which does not vary from piece to piece and has few hints of melody.

Slayer products and performances are harmful to children. Young persons are less able than adults to distinguish fantasy from reality and to understand figurative expressions and metaphors. Plaintiffs allege hundreds of studies confirm a link between graphic portrayals of violence and aggression by troubled adolescents. And although the music industry defendants knew Slayer music and lyrics would produce violent behavior in some disaffected teens, they deliberately marketed the products to the persons most likely to act out. The industry's marketing strategies were designed to entice young persons to buy products its own voluntary rating and labeling system deemed inappropriate for children.

Jacob Delashmutt, Joseph Fiorella and Royce Casey were among the persons targeted by the defendants' marketing practices. They were youthful sociopaths who planned to emulate Slayer in a band of their own. They believed that killing Elyse Pahler would advance their careers in death metal music and said their decision to murder her was influenced by Slayer music and lyrics.

III

A.   The Scope of California's Unfair Competition Law

Unfair Competition

* * * California's Unfair Competition Law (UCL) is broadly cast. It defines unfair competition as "... any unlawful, unfair or fraudulent business act or practice and unfair, deceptive, untrue or misleading advertising...." (§ 17200) As explained in *Stop Youth Addiction, Inc. v. Lucky Stores, Inc.*, 950 P.2d 1086 (1998), the scope and purpose of the UCL's remedial provisions were intended by the legislature to reach "'anything that can properly be called a business practice and that at the same time is forbidden by law.'" * * *

Other than false or misleading advertising (§ 17500), the UCL does not declare any specific conduct or business practice to be unlawful or unfair. Instead, section 17200 borrows violations of other laws. To show that a business practice is "unlawful" under the UCL, a plaintiff must show the practice is prohibited by a statute or regulation. * * * In consumer litigation, it is not clear what parameters apply to a plaintiff's claim that a business practice is unfair. It is settled, however, that a business practice is not "unfair" if it is permitted or protected by law. * * *

Unless the products are harmful to children or incite imminent unlawful conduct, no statute or regulation specifically prohibits or restricts the sale or distribution of Slayer albums to children. Similarly, there is no law that disallows or regulates marketing strategies designed to make Slayer products attractive to children.

If the music industry defendants' activities are not unlawful, the content of Slayer compositions is protected by the First Amendment. Marketing unregulated, protected speech can never constitute an unlawful business practice.

C.   Marketing Slayer Products Is Not An Unlawful Business Practice

Plaintiffs contend the marketing practices of the music industry defendants are unlawful and can be enjoined because Slayer lyrics are 1) harmful to minors within the meaning of Penal Code § 313, subdivision(a), 2) incite or solicit criminal activity (Pen. Code § 653f), 3) contribute to the delinquency of minors (Pen. Code § 272) and 4) aid and abet murderous rampages such as the one that took Elyse Pahler's life (Pen. Code § 31).

1. Matter Harmful to Children

Penal Code section 313.1 provides that any "person who, with knowledge that a person is a minor ... knowingly sells, rents, distributes, sends, causes to be sent, exhibits, or offers to distribute or exhibit by any means ... any harmful matter to the minor" is guilty of a crime. Penal Code section 313, subdivision(a) defines material that is harmful to children as "matter, taken as a whole, which to the average person, applying contemporary statewide standards, [1] appeals to the prurient interest, and is matter which, taken as a whole, [2] depicts or describes in a patently offensive way sexual conduct and which, taken as a whole, [3] lacks serious literary, artistic, political, or scientific value for minors."

The statute limits its application to material that describes sexual conduct in a patently offensive way. It does not make unlawful the distribution of media which offensively describes or depicts death, violence, or brutality. The dominant theme of the material, taken as a whole, must appeal to the prurient interest, which is a "shameful or morbid interest" in sex.

Slayer lyrics, taken as a whole, do not meet the test for harmful material found in Penal Code section 313, subdivision (a). First, it is doubtful that a musical composition can constitute harmful matter on the basis of its lyrics alone; they cannot be divorced from the instrumental context in which they appear. *Luke Records, Inc. v. Navarro*, 960 F.2d 134, 136 (11th Cir. 1992). * * * Second, even if the lyrics alone are examined, the individual songs should be examined in the context of the album or CD as a whole. Cal. Pen. Code § 313, subd. (a). Third, even if the Court may isolate the individual compositions, plaintiffs cite only a few stanzas from the songs they assert are harmful. Such a fractured analysis of the lyrics is constitutionally infirm. * * *

But even the individual stanzas cited by plaintiffs do not allege descriptions of sexual conduct that meet the tests prescribed by *Miller*. The dominant theme of Slayer lyrics is not sex. It is death, violence, brutality, and sociopathic behavior. References to sexual conduct appear infrequently. For example, one particularly offensive composition, "Sex. Murder. Art," refers to the speaker's "sexual fascination" and the act of "raping again and again." But the focus of the composition is not sexual conduct; rather, it is violence and the pleasure derived by the performer in repeatedly whipping, beating, and raping a woman. The lyrics are offensive and abhorrent because of the callous violence described, not because of their sexual content.

Taken as a whole, Slayer recordings do not appeal to a morbid interest in sex and do not, taken as a whole, depict or describe sexual conduct in a patently offensive way. The violent content of Slayer materials does not subject them to regulation under Penal Code section 313.1. * * *

2. Slayer Lyrics Do Not Incite Imminent Unlawful Acts

Brandenburg v. Ohio, 395 U.S. 444 (1969) (per curiam) establishes that the First Amendment does not protect speech "directed to inciting or producing imminent lawless action and [which] is likely to incite or produce such action." *Id.* at p. 447. But *Brandenburg* carefully distinguishes between advocacy or abstract teaching of the need for resort to force or violence in a particular social context, and the actual preparation of "a group for violent action and steeling it to such action." *Id.* at pp. 447–448. Under the principles expressed by *Brandenburg,* it must appear that the Slayer lyrics (1) were directed and intended to cause listeners to commit specific criminal acts; and (2) that they were likely to produce the violent acts urged by the speaker. *Hess v. Indiana,* 414 U.S. 105, 108–109 (1973); *McCollum v. CBS, Inc.,* 249 Cal. Rptr. 187(1988).

The Court must distinguish between artistic, figurative descriptions of violence and actual incitement to commit violence against a specific target. In *McCollum v. CBS, Inc.,* Justice Croskey explained that "musical lyrics and poetry cannot be construed to contain the requisite 'call to action' for the elementary reason that they simply are not intended to be and should not be read literally on their face, nor judged by a standard of prose oratory. Reasonable persons understand musical lyrics and poetic conventions as the figurative expressions which they are. No rational person would or could believe otherwise nor would they mistake musical lyrics and poetry for literal commands or directives to immediate action. To do so would indulge a fiction which neither common sense nor the First Amendment will permit." *McCollum, supra,* 249 Cal. Rptr. 187. * * * Slayer lyrics are repulsive and profane. But they do not direct or instruct listeners to commit the acts that resulted in the vicious torture-murder of Elyse Pahler. * * * And because Slayer lyrics cannot be found to have incited Elyse Pahler's murder, the music industry did not unlawfully aid and abet her killers (Pen. Code § 31), solicit their criminal acts (Pen. Code § 653f) or contribute to their delinquency (Pen. Code § 272).

Creating, recording, marketing and distributing Slayer music cannot provide the foundation for an unlawful business practice. The defendants' marketing practices may be shameful, but they are not illegal. *See* Federal Trade Commission, "Marketing Violent Entertainment to Children: A Review of Self-Regulation and Industry Practices in the Motion Picture, Music Recording & Electronic Game Industries" (2000).

D. The Court Cannot Regulate The Accessibility of Slayer Albums to Minors.

Although Slayer compositions are protected speech and even though the marketing practices of the music industry defendants are not restricted by a narrowly tailored statute, plaintiffs contend the practices can be enjoined as unfair because children should not be exposed to the profanity, graphic violence and sexual conduct contained in Slayer products. Plaintiffs argue that the state has a compelling interest in shielding children from such indecent material and urge the court to impose restrictions upon the distribution of Slayer products. But a trial court's ability to address such important and complex social problems is limited.

1. *Judicial, Legislative and Executive Prerogatives*

The province of the courts in administering the civil justice system is to resolve discrete disputes by adjudicating the rights of individuals affected by the conflict. *Marbury v. Madison,* 5 U.S. (1 Cranch) 137, 170 (1803). * * *

Although it has a broad scope, the sweep of the UCL is not unlimited. It cannot invest trial courts with the power to fashion new rules, regulations or orders that restrict speech in the name of protecting minors from harmful or indecent matter. No reported case has subjected non-commercial speech to judicial scrutiny and the UCL remedies of injunctive relief and restitution. But even if it is theoretically possible under the UCL, courts are neither empowered nor equipped to do so in cases where the issues would require them to address and to manage complex areas of social or economic policy. This is a distinctly legislative function. *See Reno v. ACLU,* 521 U.S. 844, 884–885(1997). * * *

The range of conceivable remedies for the social problem presented by the marketing practices of the music industry defendants is as sweeping as the scope of the UCL. For example, a system of rating lyrics that is tied to point of sale restrictions might be adopted. Or new regulations might merely require labeling that specifically describes album lyrics in order to facilitate parental supervision of the material to which their children are exposed. But whatever regulatory scheme is selected, the choice would have to be informed by behavioral science, political science, sociology, linguistics and other academic disciplines. The effectiveness of existing or other attempts at similar regulation would have to be considered. Enforcement mechanisms would have to be designed and funded. And the political and economic implications of the solution would have to be carefully explored. These tasks are best accomplished by the Legislature.

Plaintiffs must await content-based legislation that restricts distribution to children of material such as that created by Slayer. If the legislature enacts such restrictions, the courts then can judge whether the enacted limits on protected speech meet the strict constitutional scrutiny required by the First Amendment. * * *

IV

Second Cause of Action—Wrongful Death

Plaintiffs contend the music industry defendants should be held liable for Elyse Pahler's death because Slayer lyrics and music were a cause of the crimes committed against her. Plaintiffs assert these defendants knew Slayer lyrics and music would influence the most troubled members of their targeted audience to commit the crimes described in Slayer compositions.

Unless Slayer compositions are directed to inciting imminent lawless action, plaintiffs' wrongful death cause of action is barred by the First Amendment. The "guaranties of freedom of speech and expression extend to all artistic and literary expression, whether in music, concerts, plays, pictures or books." * * * As discussed above, the court cannot conclude that Slayer music and lyrics were directed and intended to bring about the imminent ritual sacrifice of a young woman. And "[i]t is not enough that [Elyse Pahler's murder was] the result of an unreasonable reaction to the music; it must have been a specifically intended consequence."

Moreover, courts that have considered the liability of the entertainment industry for the acts of third persons have consistently held that such acts are not a foreseeable consequence of the industry member's speech. * * * Foreseeability is set by balancing the policy reasons in favor of preventing the harm complained of against the social and other costs attending the burden of imposing liability. Here, a very close connection between the harm and the speech is required because potential liability would restrain and punish artistic expression. The close connection between the importuning of dangerous conduct seen in *Weirum v. RKO Gen., Inc.,* 539 P.2d 36 (1975), was not present in the events that led up to heinous crimes committed against Miss Pahler. *McCollum* clearly teaches that under these circumstances, Elyse Pahler's murder was not a foreseeable risk or consequence of the artistic activities of the music industry defendants. *McCollum, supra,* 249 Cal. Rptr. 187.

V

DISPOSITION

The demurrers of the music industry defendants are sustained without leave to amend. [Defendants] are entitled to a judgment of dismissal. * * *

Rex Heinke and Jessica Weisel
Pahler v. Slayer

Copyright © 2003 by Rex S. Heinke, Esq. and Jessica M. Weisel, Esq.[1]

The old legal adage states that bad facts make bad law.

Pahler v. Slayer, 2001 WL 1736476, 29 Media L. Rep. 2627 (Cal. Sup. Ct. Oct. 29, 2001), could have easily proven that adage correct. The case involved a terrible crime. It was filed by the parents of a teenage girl killed by three teenage boys. During police questioning, one of the boys supposedly told detectives that they had been influenced by the heavy metal music of the rock band Slayer. (The boy later denied making the statement.) The parents subsequently sued the band, its individual

1. Rex S. Heinke and Jessica M. Weisel represented defendants American Recordings and Rick Rubin dba American Def Tune. Mr. Heinke is a partner and Ms. Weisel is a counsel at Akin, Gump, Strauss, Hauer & Feld, LLP in Los Angeles, California.

members, its record company, and various other entities involved in distributing Slayer albums and music. They also sued the boys and their parents but they did not appear to have any assets.

By the time the defendants responded to the complaint, media violence was a hot button issue. Shortly before these motions were litigated, a government report condemned the film, television and music industries for targeting minors with advertisements for programming containing too much violence. As a result, the case became a focal point for public debate about violence in the media.

These circumstances presented the defendants with a challenge. The defendants believed that they had a First Amendment defense so that the plaintiffs' claims were barred as a matter of law. The defendants also believed that, as a factual matter, the Slayer music did not cause the three teenage boys to kill their female classmate. If the former argument was successful, the defendants could avoid the great expense, uncertainty and emotions of a highly charged trial before a local jury that would understandably be sympathetic to the deceased girl's parents. However, it would also require a local judge, who probably saw friends and acquaintances of the plaintiffs every day and who was part of a small community understandably shocked by the girl's death, to throw out a case against the defendants who were not from that community.

Against this backdrop, the defendants decided to focus on the legal issues. They demurred, the California equivalent of a Federal Rule of Civil Procedure 12(b)(6) motion, on First Amendment grounds to try to end the case as soon as possible.

The plaintiffs originally pled their lawsuit primarily as a wrongful death case, but the overwhelming authority in California, as in other jurisdictions, has held that the makers and broadcasters of music, television and film could not be held liable for crimes committed by listeners and viewers. In one key case, *McCollum v. CBS, Inc.*, 249 Cal. Rptr. 187 (1988), the California Court of Appeal held that author of the song "Suicide Solution," musician Ozzy Osbourne, could not be held responsible for allegedly encouraging a listener to commit suicide. Among the reasons the court gave was that music lyrics are incapable of inciting imminent lawless violence under the established test of *Brandenburg v. Ohio*, 395 U.S. 444 (1969).

The San Luis Obispo Judge granted the demurrer, but gave the plaintiffs leave to replead. In their opposition to the first demurrer, the plaintiffs had started to change their strategy, and the change crystallized when they amended their complaint. In the new complaint, the plaintiffs relied on California's Unfair Competition Law, Cal. Bus. & Prof. Code §§ 17200, *et seq.* (the "UCL"), arguing that the court should enjoin the defendants' distribution and advertising of Slayer music, because it allegedly was "harmful" to listeners.

The defendants demurred again maintaining that the UCL had nothing to do with allegedly violent speech and that, if a court imposed restrictions, it would overstep its boundaries by engaging in judicial legislation because no California law made the defendants' alleged conduct illegal.

Plaintiff's reliance on California's UCL, a fairly unique law, helped the defendants keep the briefing focused on the law. The UCL prohibits any unlawful, unfair or fraudulent business practice. The plaintiffs argued that the sale of Slayer albums violated the unlawful and unfair prongs of the UCL. (The plaintiffs did not seriously argue that the defendants had done anything that was fraudulent.)

As to alleged unlawfulness, plaintiffs argued primarily that recording, selling and distributing Slayer albums violated California Penal Code sections 311 and 313, which prohibit the dissemination of "obscene" and "harmful" matter, respectively. Section 311 largely tracks the United States Supreme Court's test for obscenity in *Miller v. California*, 413 U.S. 15 (1973), while Section 313 defines "harmful" matter in a slightly different fashion. Under both statutes, however, the work must appeal to a prurient interest (*i.e.*, be sexually explicit) and be patently offensive to the general public.[2]

The defendants maintained that the songs did not satisfy this test, because these statutes require the works to have a sexual content. The defendants argued that the statutes did not apply to Slayer songs because there was nothing in the songs that appealed to the prurient interest or depicted sex in a patently offensive way. The plaintiffs contended that the "harmful" matter statute could be employed to prohibit speech about violence. However, the defendants argued that these statutes only dealt with speech about certain sexual matter, so they could not apply to this claim.

As to the "unfair" prong of the UCL, the defendants argued that the plaintiffs were asking the court to create its own restrictions under the UCL on protected speech and that the UCL could not be used in that fashion. To do so not only would impinge on the role of the Legislature to decide what the law is, it also would violate the vagueness doctrine by imposing liability on the defendants without having given notice of what speech violates the law. *Grayned v. City of Rockford*, 408 U.S. 104 (1972).

Ultimately, the trial court agreed with the defendants' legal arguments. After the second demurrer, the case was dismissed without leave to amend the complaint. For unknown reasons, the plaintiffs never appealed. No discovery was ever conducted, so the factual question of whether the Slayer music had any effect on the boy's behavior was never determined.

2. The only difference between what is "obscene" to a general audience and what is "harmful" to minors is that the statutes differ on the third prong of the *Miller* test—whether the work lacks serious literary, artistic, political or scientific value. To be "obscene", the work must have no merit for an adult audience. Cal. Pen. Code § 311; *Miller*, 413 U.S. at 24. To be "harmful" matter statute, the work need only lack serious literary, artistic, political or scientific value for minors. Cal. Pen. Code § 313. This difference is important, because while a state may restrict speech to protect minors, speech that is only "harmful" is protected by the First Amendment, while "obscene" speech is not.

The *Pahler* case leaves open one key issue that the court was never forced to address. It remains to be seen if a state could craft a statute prohibiting violent speech for similar reasons as prohibitions on obscenity–that it is offensive under a community standards approach. Traditionally, violent speech has been restricted by either the *Brandenberg* likely to incite imminent lawless action test or by the *Chaplinsky v. New Hampshire*, 315 U.S. 568 (1942), "fighting words" doctrine. Whether violent speech can be restricted under standards similar to obscenity is an issue that courts have yet to face, because laws prohibiting such speech have not been adopted.

Notes

1. Rap artist, Mystikal (aka Michael Tyler) pleaded guilty in June 2003 to charges of extortion and sexual battery. The charges stemmed from an incident caught on camera of the artist and two associates assaulting a woman. http://www.muchmusic.com/music/artists/artistnews.asp?artist=229.

2. In 2000, controversial rapper Eminem, was charged with felony possession of a concealed weapon and assault with a deadly weapon. The artist later plead guilty to the weapon charge and the assault charge was dropped. http://www.rockonthenet.com/artists-e/eminem_main.htm.

3. In 1999, Sean Combs, known as Puff Daddy (now P. Diddy) was arrested for possession of a stolen gun found in his vehicle as he left a night club where three people were shot. http://abcnews.go.com/sections/us/Daily-News/puffy991227.html. He was eventually acquitted.

4. Scott Weiland (Stone Temple Pilots) pleaded guilty in 1998 to felony heroin possession. http://www.rockonthenet.com/artists-s/stonetemplepilots_main.htm.

5. Front man for Guns N' Roses, Axl Rose was charged in 1991 with inciting a riot in St. Louis. The incident occurred when Rose leapt off the stage to attack a concertgoer who was videotaping. http://www.rockonthenet.com/artists-g/gunsnroses_main.htm.

Index

References are to Pages

This list of names of individuals, organizations, parties and topics
is not exhaustive. Some names of parties and topics may
have only been mentioned in passing in the text.

ACTORS AND ACTRESSES
Alan, Alda, 137, 222
Affleck, Ben, 276, 278
Arnaz, Desi, 494
Arness James, 309
Autry, Gene, 189–192
Ball, Lucille, 489
Barr, Roseanne, 306
Barrymore, Drew, 137
Basinger, Kim, 141, 169–183, 202–203, 252
Beatty, Warren, 27–32
Booth, Shirley, 529–536
Branagh, Kenneth, 141
Brando, Marlon, 303
Burton, Richard, 3–7
Caine, Michael, 206
Carrey, Jim, 222
Chan, Jackie, 137
Chaplin, Charlie, 16
Chase, Chevy, 141
Close, Glen, 108
Connery, Sean, 80
Cosby, Bill, 373–379
Costner, Kevin, 564
Crawford, Joan, 91
Crowe, Russell, 222
Crudup, Billy, 108
Cruise, Tom, 222
Cruz, Penelope, 108–109
Culkin, Macaulay, 137
Curtis, Tony, 222
Damon, Matt, 276, 278
Davidson, Jaye, 147
Day, Doris, 222
Depp, Johnny, 222
Dern, Laura, 141
DiCaprio, Leonardo, 137, 269
Downey, Jr., Robert, 199
Eastwood, Clint, 222, 510
Ferrell, Will, 222
Fiorientino, Linda, 182
Fonda, Jane, 140, 222, 303

ACTORS AND ACTRESSES—Cont'd
Garland, Judy, 39–46
Gere, Richard, 179
Gibson, Mel, 278–279
Grammer, Kelsey, 109–115
Hackman, Gene, 204
Hall, Arsenio, 126–130
Hanks, Tom, 222
Harrelson, Woody, 19, 108
Harris, Ed, 137, 178
Hawn, Goldie, 140, 222
Hayek, Salma, 278, 414
Heche, Anne, 199
Hudson, Rock, 222
Hurt, William, 178
Huston, Angelica, 66
Kidman, Nichole, 214
Kilmer, Val, 204
Law, Jude, 214
Lewis, Jerry, 222
Lopez, Jennifer, 414
Loren, Sophia, 222–224
MacLaine, Shirley, 31, 204, 253–258
Madonna, 178–180
Maguire, Tobey, 142,
Malkovich, John, 108
McDaniel, Hattie, 105
Moore, Demi, 105
Murphy, Eddie, 8–18
Murray, Bill, 222
Nicholson, Jack, 19, 142, 147, 148
Pacino, Al, 140
Pfeiffer, Michele, 108
Phillips, Lou Diamond, 414
Phoenix, River, 192
Pickens, Slim, 143
Presley, Elvis, 222
Ratzenberger, John, 495–503
Redford, Robert, 239, 303, 414, 564
Redgrave, Vanessa, 845–853
Reynolds, Burt, 222
Rhames, Ving, 182
Roberts, Julia, 108, 222

969

References are to Pages

†

0–314–15395–0

90000

9 780314 153951